# 2008 | WORLD DEVELOPMENT INDICATORS

THE WORLD BANK

# 2008 | WORLD DEVELOPMENT INDICATORS

Photo credits: Front cover, clockwise from top left, Roobon/The Hunger Project, Curt Carnemark/World Bank, Curt
Carnemark/World Bank, and Digital Vision.

If you have questions or comments about this product, please contact:

Development Data Group
The World Bank
1818 H Street NW, Room MC2-812, Washington, D.C. 20433 USA
Hotline: 800 590 1906 or 202 473 7824; fax 202 522 1498
Email: data@worldbank.org
Web site: www.worldbank.org or www.worldbank.org/data

ISBN 978-0-8213-7386-6

ECO-AUDIT
Environmental Benefits Statement
The World Bank is committed to preserving endangered forests and natural resources. The Office of the Publisher
has chosen to print World Development Indicators 2008 on recycled paper with 30 percent post-consumer waste,
in accordance with the recommended standards for paper usage set by the Green Press Initiative, a nonprofit
program supporting publishers in using fiber that is not sourced from endangered forests. For more information,
visit www.greenpressinitiative.org.

Saved:
70 trees
3,290 pounds of solid waste
25,621 gallons of waste water
6,172 pounds of net greenhouse gases
49 million BTUs of total energy

# PREFACE

Release of the final report of the International Comparison Program (ICP) and publication of new estimates of purchasing power parities (PPPs) in *World Development Indicators 2008* are an important statistical milestone. The estimates offer a consistent and comprehensive set of data on the cost of living in developed and developing countries, the first since 1997, when the results of the previous ICP data collection were published in *World Development Indicators*. The 2005 data cover 146 countries and territories, 29 more than the last round in 1993—and many for the first time.

Collecting data on thousands of products sold through a multitude of outlets, the 2005 ICP is the largest international statistical program ever undertaken. New methods were used to describe the products being priced, record the data, and analyze the results. Countries in Africa took the opportunity to review their national accounts and adopt new standards and methods. In all regions regional coordinators worked closely with national statistical offices to collect and validate the data. The result is a genuine global effort, with an extensive capacity building component.

More work will follow from the ICP. First is the revision of the international ($1 a day) poverty line and estimation of the corresponding poverty rates, certain to change our view of the absolute level of poverty in the world. PPPs have many applications in economic analysis. They are used to determine the relative size of countries and their obligations to international institutions. The publication of new estimates will inspire a new wave of academic studies. And as all of this work goes on, planning for the next round of the ICP will be getting under way.

There is much of interest in this year's *World Development Indicators* besides the ICP results. The Millennium Development Goal targets have been expanded to include new ones for reproductive health, protection of biodiversity, access to treatment for HIV/AIDS, and full and productive employment and decent work for all. Measuring the associated indicators consistently and reporting on progress pose new challenges for statisticians. The World Development Indicators database includes as many of these indicators as possible. The introduction to the *People* section looks at the importance of reproductive health for the well-being of women and children. The *Environment* section considers today's great environmental challenge: climate change.

Governance—the performance of public officials and the quality of government institutions—has long been recognized as an important determinant of development success. But to understand how governance, good or bad, affects development, it must be measured. And to provide guidance for improved performance, it must be measured in ways that are sensible to politicians, citizens, and others responsible for improving governance. The *States and Markets* section discusses how to measure governance and the problems frequently encountered in doing so. The tables provide a selection of governance indicators and other measures of the interaction of states and markets.

*World Development Indicators* remains a rich source of information on the world's people, their economies, and the environment. To make it more useful, we have expanded the *Primary data documentation* section. As always, we could not bring it to you without the help of our many partners and the work of hundreds of thousands of statisticians and others in developed and developing countries who gather the primary data on which these statistics are based.

Shaida Badiee
Director
Development Data Group

# ACKNOWLEDGMENTS

This book and its companion volumes, *The Little Data Book* and *The Little Green Data Book,* are prepared by a team led by David Cieslikowski under the supervision of Eric Swanson and comprising Awatif Abuzeid, Mehdi Akhlaghi, Azita Amjadi, Uranbileg Batjargal, Sebastien Dessus, Richard Fix, Masako Hiraga, Kiyomi Horiuchi, Soong Sup Lee, Ibrahim Levent, Raymond Muhula, Kyoko Okamoto, M.H. Saeed Ordoubadi, Sulekha Patel, Beatriz Prieto-Oramas, Changqing Sun, and K.M. Vijayalakshmi, working closely with other teams in the Development Economics Vice Presidency's Development Data Group. The CD-ROM development team included Azita Amjadi, Ramgopal Erabelly, Reza Farivari, Buyant Erdene Khaltarkhuu, and William Prince. The work was carried out under the management of Shaida Badiee.

The choice of indicators and text content was shaped through close consultation with and substantial contributions from staff in the World Bank's four thematic networks—Financial and Private Sector Development, Human Development, Poverty Reduction and Economic Management, and Sustainable Development—and staff of the International Finance Corporation and the Multilateral Investment Guarantee Agency. Most important, the team received substantial help, guidance, and data from external partners. For individual acknowledgments of contributions to the book's content, please see *Credits.* For a listing of key partners, see *Partners.*

Communications Development Incorporated provided overall design direction, editing, and layout, led by Meta de Coquereaumont, Bruce Ross-Larson, and Christopher Trott. Elaine Wilson created the graphics and typeset the book. Amye Kenall and Joseph Caponio provided proofreading and production assistance. Communications Development's London partner, Peter Grundy of Peter Grundy Art & Design, provided art direction and design. Staff from External Affairs oversaw printing and dissemination of the book.

# TABLE OF CONTENTS

## FRONT

## 1. WORLD VIEW

## 2. PEOPLE

# 3. ENVIRONMENT

# TABLE OF CONTENTS

## 4. ECONOMY

## 5. STATES AND MARKETS

# 6. GLOBAL LINKS

# BACK

# PARTNERS

Defining, gathering, and disseminating international statistics is a collective effort of many people and organizations. The indicators presented in *World Development Indicators* are the fruit of decades of work at many levels, from the field workers who administer censuses and household surveys to the committees and working parties of the national and international statistical agencies that develop the nomenclature, classifications, and standards fundamental to an international statistical system. Nongovernmental organizations and the private sector have also made important contributions, both in gathering primary data and in organizing and publishing their results. And academic researchers have played a crucial role in developing statistical methods and carrying on a continuing dialogue about the quality and interpretation of statistical indicators. All these contributors have a strong belief that available, accurate data will improve the quality of public and private decisionmaking.

The organizations listed here have made *World Development Indicators* possible by sharing their data and their expertise with us. More important, their collaboration contributes to the World Bank's efforts, and to those of many others, to improve the quality of life of the world's people. We acknowledge our debt and gratitude to all who have helped to build a base of comprehensive, quantitative information about the world and its people.

For easy reference, Web addresses are included for each listed organization. The addresses shown were active on March 1, 2008. Information about the World Bank is also provided.

## International and government agencies

### Carbon Dioxide Information Analysis Center

The Carbon Dioxide Information Analysis Center (CDIAC) is the primary global climate change data and information analysis center of the U.S. Department of Energy. The CDIAC's scope includes anything that would potentially be of value to those concerned with the greenhouse effect and global climate change, including concentrations of carbon dioxide and other radiatively active gases in the atmosphere; the role of the terrestrial biosphere and the oceans in the biogeochemical cycles of greenhouse gases; emissions of carbon dioxide to the atmosphere; long-term climate trends; the effects of elevated carbon dioxide on vegetation; and the vulnerability of coastal areas to rising sea levels.

For more information, see http://cdiac.esd.ornl.gov/.

### Deutsche Gesellschaft für Technische Zusammenarbeit

The Deutsche Gesellschaft für Technische Zusammenarbeit (GTZ) GmbH is a German government-owned corporation for international cooperation with worldwide operations. GTZ's aim is to positively shape political, economic, ecological, and social development in partner countries, thereby improving people's living conditions and prospects.

For more information, see www.gtz.de/.

### Food and Agriculture Organization

The Food and Agriculture Organization, a specialized agency of the United Nations, was founded in October 1945 with a mandate to raise nutrition levels and living standards, to increase agricultural productivity, and to better the condition of rural populations. The organization provides direct development assistance; collects, analyzes, and disseminates information; offers policy and planning advice to governments; and serves as an international forum for debate on food and agricultural issues.

For more information, see www.fao.org/.

## International Civil Aviation Organization

The International Civil Aviation Organization (ICAO), a specialized agency of the United Nations, is responsible for establishing international standards and recommended practices and procedures for the technical, economic, and legal aspects of international civil aviation operations. ICAO's strategic objectives include enhancing global aviation safety and security and the efficiency of aviation operations, minimizing the adverse effect of global civil aviation on the environment, maintaining the continuity of aviation operations, and strengthening laws governing international civil aviation.

For more information, see www.icao.int/.

## International Labour Organization

The International Labour Organization (ILO), a specialized agency of the United Nations, seeks the promotion of social justice and internationally recognized human and labor rights. As part of its mandate, the ILO maintains an extensive statistical publication program.

For more information, see www.ilo.org/.

## International Monetary Fund

The International Monetary Fund (IMF) is the world's central organization for international monetary cooperation. Its 184 member countries work together to promote sustainable economic growth and rising living standards by ensuring the stability of the international monetary system—the system of exchange rates and international payments that enables countries (and their citizens) to buy goods and services from each other. The IMF reviews national, regional, and global economic and financial developments, provides financial advice to member countries, and serves as a forum where they can discuss the national, regional, and global consequences of their policies.

The IMF also makes financing temporarily available to member countries to help them address balance of payments problems and provides technical assistance and training to help countries build the expertise and institutions they need for economic stability and growth.

For more information, see www.imf.org/.

## International Telecommunication Union

The International Telecommunication Union (ITU) is the leading UN agency for information and communication technologies. ITU's mission is to enable the growth and sustained development of telecommunications and information networks and to facilitate universal access so that people everywhere can participate in, and benefit from, the emerging information society and global economy. A key priority lies in bridging the so-called Digital Divide by building information and communication infrastructure, promoting adequate capacity building, and developing confidence in the use of cyberspace through enhanced online security. ITU also concentrates on strengthening emergency communications for disaster prevention and mitigation.

For more information, see www.itu.int/.

# PARTNERS

### National Science Foundation

The National Science Foundation (NSF) is an independent U.S. government agency whose mission is to promote the progress of science; to advance the national health, prosperity, and welfare; and to secure the national defense. NSF's goals—discovery, learning, research infrastructure, and stewardship—provide an integrated strategy to advance the frontiers of knowledge, cultivate a world-class, broadly inclusive science and engineering workforce, expand the scientific literacy of all citizens, build the nation's research capability through investments in advanced instrumentation and facilities, and support excellence in science and engineering research and education through a capable and responsive organization.

For more information, see www.nsf.gov/.

### Organisation for Economic Co-operation and Development

The Organisation for Economic Co-operation and Development (OECD) includes 30 member countries sharing a commitment to democratic government and the market economy to support sustainable economic growth, boost employment, raise living standards, maintain financial stability, assist other countries' economic development, and contribute to growth in world trade. With active relationships with some 100 other countries it has a global reach. It is best known for its publications and statistics, which cover economic and social issues from macroeconomics to trade, education, development, and science and innovation.

The Development Assistance Committee (DAC, www.oecd.org/dac/) is one of the principal bodies through which the OECD deals with issues related to cooperation with developing countries. The DAC is a key forum of major bilateral donors, who work together to increase the effectiveness of their common efforts to support sustainable development. The DAC concentrates on two key areas: the contribution of international development to the capacity of developing countries to participate in the global economy and the capacity of people to overcome poverty and participate fully in their societies.

For more information, see www.oecd.org/.

### Stockholm International Peace Research Institute

The Stockholm International Peace Research Institute (SIPRI) conducts research on questions of conflict and cooperation of importance for international peace and security, with the aim of contributing to an understanding of the conditions for peaceful solutions to international conflicts and for a stable peace. SIPRI's main publication, *SIPRI Yearbook,* is an authoritive and independent source on armaments and arms control and other conflict and security issues.

For more information, see www.sipri.org/.

### Understanding Children's Work

As part of broader efforts to develop effective and long-term solutions to child labor, the International Labor Organization, the United Nations Children's Fund (UNICEF), and the World Bank initiated the joint interagency research program "Understanding Children's Work and Its Impact" in December 2000. The Understanding Children's Work (UCW) project was located at UNICEF's Innocenti Research Centre in Florence, Italy, until June 2004, when it moved to the Centre for International Studies on Economic Growth in Rome.

The UCW project addresses the crucial need for more and better data on child labor. UCW's online database contains data by country on child labor and the status of children.

For more information, see www.ucw-project.org/.

## United Nations

The United Nations currently has 192 member states. The purposes of the United Nations, as set forth in the Charter, are to maintain international peace and security; to develop friendly relations among nations; to cooperate in solving international economic, social, cultural, and humanitarian problems and in promoting respect for human rights and fundamental freedoms; and to be a center for harmonizing the actions of nations in attaining these ends.

For more information, see www.un.org/.

## United Nations Centre for Human Settlements, Global Urban Observatory

The Urban Indicators Programme of the United Nations Human Settlements Programme was established to address the urgent global need to improve the urban knowledge base by helping countries and cities design, collect, and apply policy-oriented indicators related to development at the city level.

With the Urban Indicators and Best Practices programs, the Global Urban Observatory is establishing a worldwide information, assessment, and capacity building network to help governments, local authorities, the private sector, and nongovernmental and other civil society organizations.

For more information, see www.unhabitat.org/.

## United Nations Children's Fund

The United Nations Children's Fund (UNICEF) works with other UN bodies and with governments and nongovernmental organizations to improve children's lives in more than 190 countries through various programs in education and health. UNICEF focuses primarily on five areas: child survival and development, basic Education and gender equality (including girls' education), child protection, HIV/AIDS, and policy advocacy and partnerships.

For more information, see www.unicef.org/.

## United Nations Conference on Trade and Development

The United Nations Conference on Trade and Development (UNCTAD) is the principal organ of the United Nations General Assembly in the field of trade and development. Its mandate is to accelerate economic growth and development, particularly in developing countries. UNCTAD discharges its mandate through policy analysis; intergovernmental deliberations, consensus building, and negotiation; monitoring, implementation, and follow-up; and technical cooperation.

For more information, see www.unctad.org/.

## United Nations Educational, Scientific, and Cultural Organization, Institute for Statistics

The United Nations Educational, Scientific, and Cultural Organization is a specialized agency of the United Nations that promotes "collaboration among nations through education, science, and culture in order to

# PARTNERS

further universal respect for justice, for the rule of law, and for the human rights and fundamental freedoms . . . for the peoples of the world, without distinction of race, sex, language, or religion."
For more information, see www.uis.unesco.org/.

## United Nations Environment Programme

The mandate of the United Nations Environment Programme is to provide leadership and encourage partnership in caring for the environment by inspiring, informing, and enabling nations and people to improve their quality of life without compromising that of future generations.
For more information, see www.unep.org/.

## United Nations Industrial Development Organization

The United Nations Industrial Development Organization was established to act as the central coordinating body for industrial activities and to promote industrial development and cooperation at the global, regional, national, and sectoral levels. Its mandate is to help develop scientific and technological plans and programs for industrialization in the public, cooperative, and private sectors.
For more information, see www.unido.org/.

## The UN Refugee Agency

The UN Refugee Agency (UNHCR) is mandated to lead and coordinate international action to protect refugees and resolve refugee problems worldwide. Its primary purpose is to safeguard the rights and well-being of refugees. UNHCR also collects and disseminates statistics on refugees.
For more information, see www.unhcr.org

## World Bank Group

The World Bank is one of the world's largest sources of funding and knowledge for developing countries. Its main focus is on helping the poorest people and the poorest countries. It uses its financial resources, staff, and extensive experience to help developing countries reduce poverty, increase economic growth, and improve their quality of life. The Bank brings a mix of money and knowledge to encourage economic and social development and help countries achieve the internationally agreed Millennium Development Goals. The World Bank supports projects that help countries to invest in many different areas: health and education, fighting corruption, boosting agricultural production, building roads and ports, and protecting the environment. Since resources are scarce, assessing the effect of projects the Bank supports is essential in developing countries and is part of its focus on actual results for poor people. The World Bank Group has 185 member countries.
For more information, see www.worldbank.org/data/.

## World Health Organization

The objective of the World Health Organization (WHO), a specialized agency of the United Nations, is the attainment by all people of the highest possible level of health. The WHO carries out a wide range of functions, including coordinating international health work; helping governments strengthen health services;

providing technical assistance and emergency aid; working for the prevention and control of disease; promoting improved nutrition, housing, sanitation, recreation, and economic and working conditions; promoting and coordinating biomedical and health services research; promoting improved standards of teaching and training in health and medical professions; establishing international standards for biological, pharmaceutical, and similar products; and standardizing diagnostic procedures.

For more information, see www.who.int/.

### World Intellectual Property Organization

The World Intellectual Property Organization (WIPO) is a specialized agency of the United Nations dedicated to developing a balanced and accessible international intellectual property (IP) system, which rewards creativity, stimulates innovation, and contributes to economic development while safeguarding the public interest. WIPO carries out a wide variety of tasks related to the protection of IP rights. These include assisting governments and organizations to develop the policies, structures and skills needed to harness the potential of IP for economic development; working with member states to develop international IP law; administering treaties; running global registration systems for trademarks, industrial designs, and appellations of origin and a filing system for patents; delivering dispute resolution services; and providing a forum for informed debate and for the exchange of expertise.

For more information, see www.wipo.int/.

### World Tourism Organization

The World Tourism Organization is an intergovernmental body entrusted by the United Nations with promoting and developing tourism. It serves as a global forum for tourism policy issues and a source of tourism know-how.

For more information, see www.unwto.org/.

### World Trade Organization

The World Trade Organization (WTO) is the only international organization dealing with the global rules of trade between nations. Its main function is to ensure that trade flows as smoothly, predictably, and freely as possible. It does this by administering trade agreements, acting as a forum for trade negotiations, settling trade disputes, reviewing national trade policies, assisting developing countries in trade policy issues—through technical assistance and training programs—and cooperating with other international organizations. At the heart of the system—known as the multilateral trading system—are the WTO's agreements, negotiated and signed by a large majority of the world's trading nations and ratified by their parliaments.

For more information, see www.wto.org/.

### Private and nongovernmental organizations

### Containerisation International

Containerisation International Yearbook is one of the most authoritative reference books on the container industry. The information can be accessed on the Containerisation International Web site, which also provides a comprehensive online daily business news and information service for the container industry.

For more information, see www.ci-online.co.uk/.

# PARTNERS

## International Institute for Strategic Studies

The International Institute for Strategic Studies (IISS) provides information and analysis on strategic trends and facilitates contacts between government leaders, business people, and analysts that could lead to better public policy in international security and international relations. The IISS is a primary source of accurate, objective information on international strategic issues.

For more information, see www.iiss.org/.

## International Road Federation

The International Road Federation (IRF) is a unique global platform that brings together public and private entities committed to road development. Working together with its members and associates, the IRF promotes social and economic benefits that flow from well planned and environmentally sound transportation networks. The IRF serves as a catalyst for public and private partnership to organize, promote, and develop international road programs. The main objectives include promoting the understanding of the social, economic, and environmental benefits derived from developing modern road networks, road transport systems, and road traffic control; improving road safety; planning and executing economically and environmentally sound programs for the improvement and extension of road networks; conducting educational and training programs relating to the development and maintenance of road and road transport systems; facilitating the exchange of experience with national, regional, and international institutions; and harmonizing standards, research, and dissemination of road related information.

For more information, see www.irfnet.org/.

## Netcraft

Netcraft is an Internet services company and a respected authority on the market share of web servers, operating systems, hosting providers, Internet service providers, encrypted transactions, electronic commerce, scripting languages, and content technologies on the Internet. Netcraft provides Internet security services, including antifraud and antiphishing services, application testing, code reviews, and automated penetration testing as well as  research data and analysis on many aspects of the Internet.

For more information, see www.netcraft.com/.

## PricewaterhouseCoopers

PricewaterhouseCoopers provides industry-focused assurance, tax, human resources, transactions, performance improvement, and crisis management services to help address client and stakeholder issues.

For more information, see www.pwc.com/.

## Standard & Poor's

Standard & Poor's is the world's foremost provider of independent credit ratings, indexes, risk evaluation, investment research, and data. S&P's *Global Stock Markets Factbook* draw on data from S&P's Emerging Markets Database (EMDB) and other sources covering data on more than 100 markets with comprehensive market profiles for 82 countries.  Drawing a sample of stocks in each EMDB market, Standard & Poor's calculates indices to serve as benchmarks that are consistent across national boundaries. Standard &

STANDARD
&POOR'S

Poor's calculates one index, the S&P/IFCG (Global) index, that reflects the perspective of local investors and those interested in broad trends in emerging markets and another, the S&P/IFCI (Investable) index, that provides a broad, neutral, and historically consistent benchmark for the growing emerging market investment community.

For more information, see www.standardandpoors.com/.

## World Conservation Monitoring Centre

The World Conservation Monitoring Centre provides information on the conservation and sustainable use of the world's living resources and helps others to develop information systems of their own. It works in close collaboration with a wide range of people and organizations to increase access to the information needed for wise management of the world's living resources.

For more information, see www.unep-wcmc.org/.

WORLD CONSERVATION
MONITORING CENTRE

## World Information Technology and Services Alliance

The World Information Technology and Services Alliance (WITSA) is a consortium of more than 60 information technology (IT) industry associations from economies around the world. WITSA members represent over 90 percent of the world IT market. As the global voice of the IT industry, WITSA has an active role in international public policy issues affecting the creation of a robust global information infrastructure, including advocating policies that advance the industry's growth and development, facilitating international trade and investment in IT products and services, increasing competition through open markets and regulatory reform, strengthening national industry associations through the sharing of knowledge, protecting intellectual property, encouraging cross-industry and government cooperation to enhance information security, bridging the education and skills gap, and safeguarding the viability and continued growth of the Internet and electronic commerce.

For more information, see www.witsa.org/.

## World Resources Institute

The World Resources Institute is an independent center for policy research and technical assistance on global environmental and development issues. The institute provides—and helps other institutions provide—objective information and practical proposals for policy and institutional change that will foster environmentally sound, socially equitable development. The institute's current areas of work include trade, forests, energy, economics, technology, biodiversity, human health, climate change, sustainable agriculture, resource and environmental information, and national strategies for environmental and resource management.

For more information, see www.wri.org/.

# USERS GUIDE

## Tables

The tables are numbered by section and display the identifying icon of the section. Countries and economies are listed alphabetically (except for Hong Kong, China, which appears after China). Data are shown for 153 economies with populations of more than 1 million, as well as for Taiwan, China, in selected tables. Table 1.6 presents selected indicators for 56 other economies—small economies with populations between 30,000 and 1 million and smaller economies if they are members of the International Bank for Reconstruction and Development (IBRD) or, as it is commonly known, the World Bank. The term *country,* used interchangeably with *economy,* does not imply political independence, but refers to any territory for which authorities report separate social or economic statistics. When available, aggregate measures for income and regional groups appear at the end of each table.

Indicators are shown for the most recent year or period for which data are available and, in most tables, for an earlier year or period (usually 1990 or 1995 in this edition). Time-series data are available on the *World Development Indicators* CD-ROM and in *WDI Online.*

Known deviations from standard definitions or breaks in comparability over time or across countries are either footnoted in the tables or noted in *About the data.* When available data are deemed to be too weak to provide reliable measures of levels and trends or do not adequately adhere to international standards, the data are not shown.

## Aggregate measures for income groups

The aggregate measures for income groups include 209 economies (the economies listed in the main tables plus those in table 1.6) whenever data are available. To maintain consistency in the aggregate measures over time and between tables, missing data are imputed where possible. The aggregates are totals (designated by a *t* if the aggregates include gap-filled estimates for missing data and by an *s,* for simple totals, where they do not), median values (*m*), weighted averages (*w*), or simple averages (*u*).

Gap filling of amounts not allocated to countries may result in discrepancies between subgroup aggregates and overall totals. For further discussion of aggregation methods, see *Statistical methods.*

### Aggregate measures for regions

The aggregate measures for regions cover only low- and middle-income economies, including economies with populations of less than 1 million listed in table 1.6.

The country composition of regions is based on the World Bank's analytical regions and may differ from common geographic usage. For regional classifications, see the map on the inside back cover and the list on the back cover flap. For further discussion of aggregation methods, see *Statistical methods.*

## Statistics

Data are shown for economies as they were constituted in 2006, and historical data are revised to reflect current political arrangements. Exceptions are noted throughout the tables.

Additional information about the data is provided in *Primary data documentation.* That section summarizes national and international efforts to improve basic data collection and gives country-level information on primary sources, census years, fiscal years, statistical methods and concepts used, and other background information. *Statistical methods* provides technical information on some of the general calculations and formulas used throughout the book.

### Data consistency, reliability, and comparability

Considerable effort has been made to standardize the data, but full comparability cannot be assured, and care must be taken in interpreting the indicators. Many factors affect data availability, comparability, and reliability: statistical systems in many developing economies are still weak; statistical methods, coverage, practices, and definitions differ widely; and cross-country and intertemporal comparisons involve complex technical and conceptual problems that cannot be resolved unequivocally. Data coverage may not be complete because of special circumstances

affecting the collection and reporting of data, such as problems stemming from conflicts.

For these reasons, although data are drawn from the sources thought to be most authoritative, they should be construed only as indicating trends and characterizing major differences among economies rather than as offering precise quantitative measures of those differences. Discrepancies in data presented in different editions of *World Development Indicators* reflect updates by countries as well as revisions to historical series and changes in methodology. Thus readers are advised not to compare data series between editions of *World Development Indicators* or between different World Bank publications. Consistent time-series data for 1960–2006 are available on the *World Development Indicators* CD-ROM and in *WDI Online.*

Except where otherwise noted, growth rates are in real terms. (See *Statistical methods* for information on the methods used to calculate growth rates.) Data for some economic indicators for some economies are presented in fiscal years rather than calendar years; see *Primary data documentation.* All dollar figures are current U.S. dollars unless otherwise stated. The methods used for converting national currencies are described in *Statistical methods.*

### Country notes

- Unless otherwise noted, data for China do not include data for Hong Kong, China; Macao, China; or Taiwan, China.
- Data for Indonesia include Timor-Leste through 1999 unless otherwise noted
- Montenegro declared independence from Serbia and Montenegro on June 3, 2006. When available, data for each country are shown separately. However, some indicators for Serbia continue to include data for Montenegro through 2005; these data are footnoted in the tables. Moreover, data for most indicators from 1999 onward for Serbia exclude data for Kosovo, a territory within Serbia that is currently under international administration pursuant to UN Security Council Resolution 1244 (1999); any exceptions are noted.

## Classification of economies

For operational and analytical purposes the World Bank's main criterion for classifying economies is gross national income (GNI) per capita (calculated by the *World Bank Atlas* method). Every economy is classified as low income, middle income (subdivided into lower middle and upper middle), or high income. For income classifications see the map on the inside front cover and the list on the front cover flap. Low- and middle-income economies are sometimes referred to as developing economies. The term is used for convenience; it is not intended to imply that all economies in the group are experiencing similar development or that other economies have reached a preferred or final stage of development. Note that classification by income does not necessarily reflect development status. Because GNI per capita changes over time, the country composition of income groups may change from one edition of *World Development Indicators* to the next. Once the classification is fixed for an edition, based on GNI per capita in the most recent year for which data are available (2006 in this edition), all historical data presented are based on the same country grouping.

Low-income economies are those with a GNI per capita of $905 or less in 2006. Middle-income economies are those with a GNI per capita of more than $905 but less than $11,116. Lower middle-income and upper middle-income economies are separated at a GNI per capita of $3,595. High-income economies are those with a GNI per capita of $11,116 or more. The 15 participating member countries of the euro area are presented as a subgroup under high-income economies. Note that Cyprus and Malta joined the euro area on January 1, 2008.

## Symbols

..

means that data are not available or that aggregates cannot be calculated because of missing data in the years shown.

**0 or 0.0**

means zero or small enough that the number would round to zero at the displayed number of decimal places.

**/**

in dates, as in 2003/04, means that the period of time, usually 12 months, straddles two calendar years and refers to a crop year, a survey year, or a fiscal year.

**$**

means current U.S. dollars unless otherwise noted.

**>**

means more than.

**<**

means less than.

## Data presentation conventions

- A blank means not applicable or, for an aggregate, not analytically meaningful.
- A billion is 1,000 million.
- A trillion is 1,000 billion.
- Figures in italics refer to years or periods other than those specified or to growth rates calculated for less than the full period specified.
- Data for years that are more than three years from the range shown are footnoted.

The cutoff date for data is February 1, 2008.

# 1

WORLD VIEW

# Viewing the world at purchasing power parity

Comparable measures of economic activity and living standards are useful for many purposes. Foreign investors, traders, and potential immigrants want to know an economy's market size, productivity, and prices. The globalization of markets for goods, services, finance, labor, and ideas reinforces the interdependence of economies and the need to measure them on a common scale. Countries cannot share responsibilities for global public goods—the environment, security, development assistance, and global governance—without meaningful assessments of the real size of their economies and the well-being of their people.

But comparing the real size of economies is not easy. Even in an integrated global economy large differences in the costs of goods and services persist. Exchange rates can be used to convert values in one currency to another, but since they do not fully reflect differences in price levels they cannot measure the real volume of output. Exchange rates are determined by the demand for and supply of currencies used in international transactions, ignoring domestic economic sectors where prices are set in relative isolation from the rest of the world. Thus the familiar experience of international travelers, who discover that they can buy more, or less, of the same goods in different countries when converting their money using the prevailing exchange rates.

To measure the real size of the world's economy and to compare costs of living across countries, we need to adjust for differences in purchasing power. Finding a way to adjust for those differences has given rise to the efforts to measure purchasing power parties (PPPs), which convert local currencies to a common currency, such as the U.S. dollar.

Since 1970 the International Comparison Program (ICP) has conducted eight rounds of PPP estimates for the major components of countries' gross domestic product (GDP)—the most recent for 2005. The PPP process calls for the systematic collection of price data on hundreds of representative and carefully defined products and services consumed in each country, requiring the full cooperation of national statistical agencies and international organizations.

High-income countries regularly take part in such programs, but 2005 was the first time since 1993 that comprehensive price surveys were carried out in developing economies. An unprecedented number, 101, took part. These new PPPs provide a better and more complete view of the world economy. They show that in 2005 developing country economies were on average 2.2 times larger when measured by PPPs than by exchange rates. They also reveal that past estimates of the real size of the economies of developing countries based on the 1993 ICP round were often too large.

This section reports the major findings of the 2005 ICP round and explores some of the implications. In doing so, it aims to provide a better picture of today's important issues, highlighting the diversity—and the commonality—of development patterns and outcomes.

## Country participation and population coverage

The eighth round of the ICP included 146 economies—101 of them classified by the World Bank as low and middle income based on gross national income per capita at market exchange rates—covering more than 95 percent of the world's people (figure 1a). This was the first global price collection since 1993, although some European economies have carried out regular price comparisons, the last in 2002. Some large economies, such as China, and many smaller ones in Africa, took part for the first time. India took part for the first time since 1985.

Noteworthy is that the two poorest developing regions, South Asia and Sub-Saharan Africa, have the best population coverage—more than 98 percent (figure 1b). Latin America and the Caribbean and the Middle East and North Africa recorded less coverage, both below 87 percent. Caribbean countries and Algeria, Libya, and West Bank and Gaza did not participate in the 2005 round. Many fragile and conflict-beset states were underrepresented (with coverage around 50 percent), with weak statistical capacity and conditions inimical to data collection.

The new ICP round, with its expanded coverage, provides a more complete view of the world economy and, not surprisingly, a different picture of its size and structure.

## Measuring price differences

Purchasing power parities are needed because similar goods and services have widely varying prices across countries when converted to a common currency using market exchange rates. Differences are greatest in sectors not commonly traded internationally, such as housing, construction, and health and education services (figure 1c). Price differences are smaller for widely traded products, such as machinery and equipment, after allowing for taxes, distributor margins, and transport costs. PPPs include the prices of tradable and nontradable goods, using weights that reflect their relative importance in total GDP.

Comparing prices across economies is complicated by tension between comparability and representativeness. Goods and services should have similar characteristics (comparable) and be consumed everywhere (representative). To compensate for noncomparability of representative products, the ICP conducted parallel programs: selecting items at the regional level, where consumption patterns are broadly similar across countries, and selecting items for global comparison among a few countries from each region. The results of the second program were used to link the results of the first into a single set of global PPPs. For details see the *ICP Global Report* (World Bank 2008).

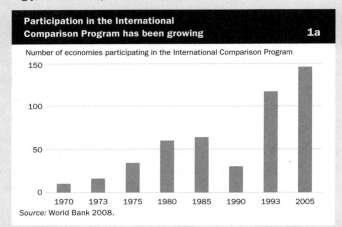

**Participation in the International Comparison Program has been growing**  1a

Number of economies participating in the International Comparison Program

*Source:* World Bank 2008.

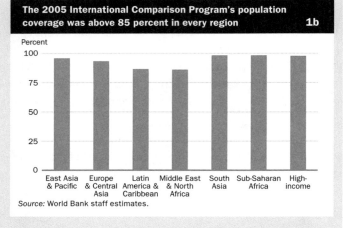

**The 2005 International Comparison Program's population coverage was above 85 percent in every region**  1b

Percent

*Source:* World Bank staff estimates.

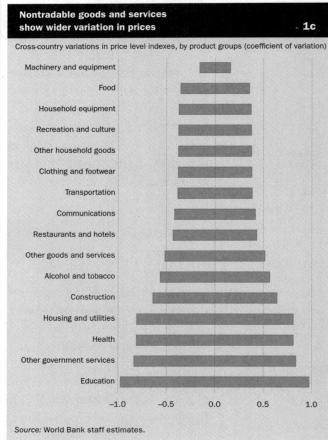

**Nontradable goods and services show wider variation in prices**  1c

Cross-country variations in price level indexes, by product groups (coefficient of variation)

*Source:* World Bank staff estimates.

## The size of the global economy

Converting GDP and its components to a common currency using PPPs leads to dramatic revisions in size and structure of world economies. Generally, the poorer an economy, the greater the upward revision of estimates based on market exchange rates. The GDPs of low-income economies are on average revised upward 160 percent and those of middle-income economies 120 percent (figure 1d). The GDPs of high-income economies are revised upward only 10 percent. But the results are not uniform. Within each group, particularly low-income economies, the diversity of patterns is great.

Viewed through PPPs, low-income economies produced 7 percent of global GDP in 2005, compared with 3 percent at market exchange rates. Middle-income economies produced 33 percent, compared with 19 percent at market exchange rates. High-income economies produced 60 percent of world GDP at PPPs, compared with 78 percent at market exchange rates.

East Asia and Pacific has the largest upward revision—from 7 percent of world GDP to 13 percent (figure 1e). But South Asia and the Middle East and North Africa have the largest relative increases. Sub-Saharan Africa produced 2 percent of world GDP at PPPs in 2005, twice that at market exchange rates.

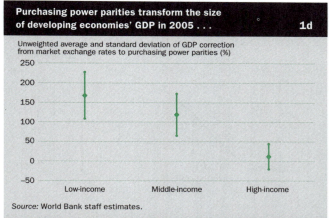

**Purchasing power parities transform the size of developing economies' GDP in 2005 . . .**    **1d**

Unweighted average and standard deviation of GDP correction from market exchange rates to purchasing power parities (%)

*Source:* World Bank staff estimates.

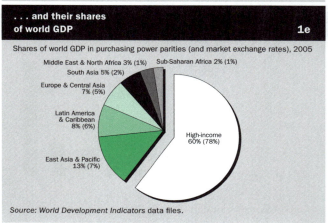

**. . . and their shares of world GDP**    **1e**

Shares of world GDP in purchasing power parities (and market exchange rates), 2005

Middle East & North Africa 3% (1%)    Sub-Saharan Africa 2% (1%)
South Asia 5% (2%)
Europe & Central Asia 7% (5%)
Latin America & Caribbean 8% (6%)
High-income 60% (78%)
East Asia & Pacific 13% (7%)

*Source: World Development Indicators* data files.

## What has changed since the 1993 round?

The PPPs previously published in *World Development Indicators* and used to estimate international poverty rates were extrapolated from the benchmark results of the 1993 ICP. Data for economies participating in the more recent price collection by Eurostat were updated through 2002 and then extrapolated forward and backward. The extrapolation method assumes that an economy's PPP conversion factor adjusts according to the different rates of inflation for its economy and the base economy, the United States. A good approximation in the short run, but over a longer period changes in the relative prices of goods and services and in the structure of economies—what they produce and consume—distort this relationship, and new measurements must be made. New methods of data collection, differences in country participation, and changes in analytical methods all add to the differences between new PPPs and old.

Under the new PPPs the aggregate GDP of developing economies in 2005 is 21 percent smaller than previously estimated, corresponding to a 7 percentage point reduction in their share of world GDP—from 47 percent to 40 percent.

The largest revisions are for developing economies. Among the 20 economies with the largest revisions are 14 Sub-Saharan African countries, 10 fragile states, and 10 economies that did not participate in the 1993 ICP. In absolute terms the largest changes were for China and India, which did not participate in the 1993 ICP. China's estimated GDP in 2005 was revised downward 40 percent and India's 36 percent, accounting for a large part of the net decrease in developing economy GDP (figure 1f). The smaller share of world GDP attributed to developing economies increases high-income economies' shares. The United States—as the base country, unaffected by any revision—increased its share from 20.6 percent to 22.1 percent.

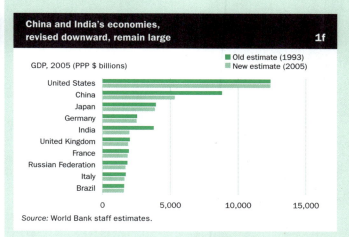

**China and India's economies, revised downward, remain large**    **1f**

GDP, 2005 (PPP $ billions)

■ Old estimate (1993)
■ New estimate (2005)

*Source:* World Bank staff estimates.

## The global distribution of income

From a global perspective income inequality has two sources: inequalities within countries and inequalities between countries. PPPs provide a clearer picture of both.

The distribution of income between economies can be measured by differences in their average GDP per capita. Because PPPs tend to increase the value of output from poorer economies, inequality between economies is less when measured in PPPs.

In 2005 PPP GDP per capita in high-income economies was more than five times higher than that in middle-income economies and more than 19 times higher than that in low-income economies (figure 1g). At market exchange rates the inequalities would have been greater.

The use of PPPs also leads to a reordering of regions by GDP per capita. South Asia, the poorest region at market exchange rates, surpasses Sub-Saharan Africa at PPPs (figure 1h). Average incomes in Europe and Central Asia are higher than those in Latin America and the Caribbean at PPPs, and the gap between the Middle East and North Africa and East Asia and Pacific widens under PPPs compared with the gap under market exchange rates.

## Combining inequalities within and between countries

Inequality within countries is measured using household survey data on income or consumption per capita. Common inequality measures include the Gini coefficient and the ratio of income or consumption of the richest 20 percent of the population to that of the poorest 20 percent (table 2.7). At the low end of the inequality range the Gini may be 25–30 and the ratio of the richest to poorest less than 4 (many countries in Eastern Europe). At the high end the Gini may be as high as 60 and the ratio of the richest to poorest more than 15 (many countries in Latin America and parts of Africa).

Under PPPs both sources of inequalities—between and within countries—can be combined. PPPs are used to compare incomes of individuals from different countries and create a global income distribution curve. Including inequalities within countries widens already highly unequal income distribution between countries. Based on countries with data (90 percent of the world's population), half the world's people consumed less than PPP $1,300 a year and the bottom quarter less than PPP $660 in 2005 (figure 1i). The richest 20 percent of the world's population spent more than 75 percent of the world total, while the poorest 20 percent spent less than 2 percent (figure 1j).

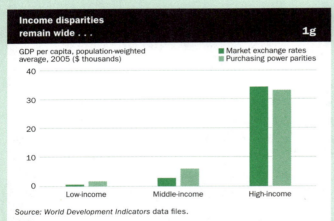

**Income disparities remain wide . . .** 1g

GDP per capita, population-weighted average, 2005 ($ thousands)
- Market exchange rates
- Purchasing power parities

*Source: World Development Indicators data files.*

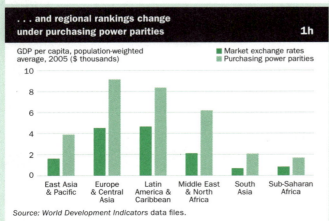

**. . . and regional rankings change under purchasing power parities** 1h

GDP per capita, population-weighted average, 2005 ($ thousands)
- Market exchange rates
- Purchasing power parities

*Source: World Development Indicators data files.*

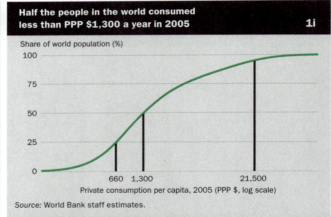

**Half the people in the world consumed less than PPP $1,300 a year in 2005** 1i

Share of world population (%)

Private consumption per capita, 2005 (PPP $, log scale)

*Source: World Bank staff estimates.*

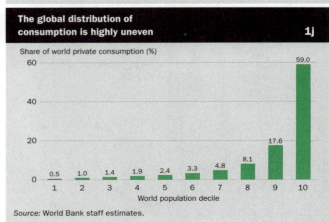

**The global distribution of consumption is highly uneven** 1j

Share of world private consumption (%)

World population decile

*Source: World Bank staff estimates.*

## Regional inequalities

Inequalities between individuals are high in Latin America and the Caribbean and Sub-Saharan Africa, where the income share of the richest 20 percent of the population is at least 18 times that of the poorest 20 percent, and lower in South Asia and Europe and Central Asia, where the ratio falls below 7 (figure 1k). East Asia and Pacific and the Middle East and North Africa stand in between, but the estimate for the Middle East and North Africa is less reliable because many countries have no household surveys for estimating income distribution.

Half of Sub-Saharan Africa's inequalities can be attributed to differences in average incomes between countries, reflecting the region's low economic integration. Its average per capita private consumption is the lowest of all regions, but there are large differences across countries. By contrast, less than 20 percent of inequality in South Asia, East Asia and Pacific, and Latin American and the Caribbean can be attributed to different country patterns (figure 1l). There are different reasons for similar patterns. South Asia and East Asia and Pacific are each dominated by one large economy. In contrast, Latin America and the Caribbean has more equally sized economies with similar consumption per capita.

## Convergence in incomes?

Have income inequalities across countries declined? Although developing economies have grown faster than high-income economies, PPP data show that economies starting from a lower GDP per capita did not systematically grow more rapidly between 1996 and 2006. The reason: large, high-performing economies, such as China and India, raise their group averages.

But after controlling for investment in 1996 (PPP per capita expenditure in education and gross fixed capital formation), initial GDP per capita had a substantial effect on future growth: for the same investment poorer countries grew faster than richer ones over the decade (figure 1m). This emphasizes the importance of improving the investment climate in developing economies; an effectively invested dollar generates much higher growth in poor countries.

Yet low-income countries did not systematically catch up with richer ones, as their investments in human and physical capital were on average much smaller. From 1996 to 2006 the average yield of these expenditures is about 2 percentage points of annual per capita GDP growth in low-income countries, compared with more than 3 percentage points in middle-income countries (figure 1n).

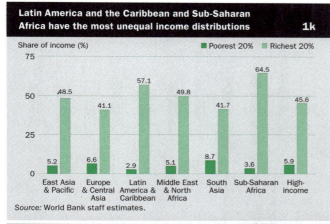

**Latin America and the Caribbean and Sub-Saharan Africa have the most unequal income distributions**   **1k**

Share of income (%)

Poorest 20%   Richest 20%

*Source:* World Bank staff estimates.

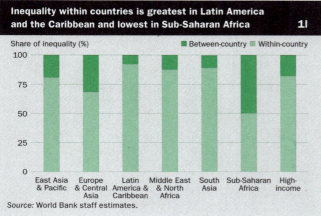

**Inequality within countries is greatest in Latin America and the Caribbean and lowest in Sub-Saharan Africa**   **1l**

Share of inequality (%)

Between-country   Within-country

*Source:* World Bank staff estimates.

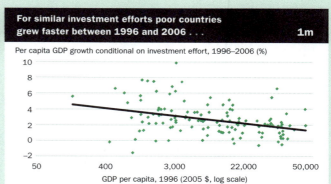

**For similar investment efforts poor countries grew faster between 1996 and 2006 . . .**   **1m**

Per capita GDP growth conditional on investment effort, 1996–2006 (%)

GDP per capita, 1996 (2005 $, log scale)

**Note:** In line with Mankiw, Romer, and Weil (1992), per capita GDP growth rates are regressed on the logarithms of initial per capita GDP, initial per capita investment expenditure, initial per capita education expenditure, and population growth rate.
*Source:* World Bank staff estimates.

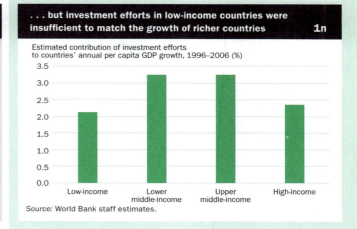

**. . . but investment efforts in low-income countries were insufficient to match the growth of richer countries**   **1n**

Estimated contribution of investment efforts to countries' annual per capita GDP growth, 1996–2006 (%)

*Source:* World Bank staff estimates.

## Comparing standards of living

The 2005 ICP estimated PPPs for subcomponents of GDP, including expenditures on food, health, and education. As has long been observed, differences in spending on food are smaller than differences in income or overall consumption. South Asia's GDP per capita is one-sixteenth that of high-income economies; per capita food consumption, only one-fifth. And despite wide differences in income per capita, food expenditures in South Asia and East Asia and Pacific are almost the same (figure 1o). These two regions also have the smallest range between maximum and minimum average food.

Within developing countries per capita food consumption is strongly correlated with malnutrition, accounting for more than half the differences across countries. But even at similar average food per capita consumption, differences in malnutrition rates remain significant. Average expenditures conceal inequalities in the food consumption measure, specific diets, geographic conditions, and the absence of complementary factors that can prevent malnutrition (micronutrients, health care, education). In South Asia five of seven countries have malnutrition rates much above the average of developing economies at similar food consumption levels.

## Health and education

Similar cross-country comparisons can be made for the relative impact of health and education expenditures on selected outcomes, such as life expectancy at birth and the youth literacy rate. Both public and private expenditures contribute to the improvement of these and of many other indicators. And many factors other than spending affect life expectancy and literacy outcomes. But it is still interesting to observe that among countries with similar expenditures per capita, there is a large range of outcomes.

Among developing economies with similar per capita health spending, Southern African countries have much lower life expectancy, which must to some extent be the consequence of high HIV/AIDS prevalence (figure 1q). In contrast, most developing regions have some countries that record above-average life expectancies.

Compared with developing countries at similar per capita education expenditures, West African countries record particularly low literacy rates for youth ages 15–24 (figure 1r). Again, while worst performers are concentrated geographically, best performers are from diverse regions, including Sub-Saharan Africa.

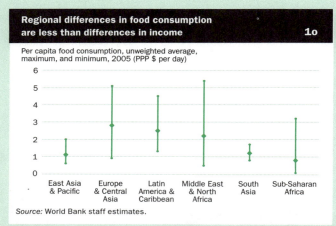

**Regional differences in food consumption are less than differences in income** — 1o

Per capita food consumption, unweighted average, maximum, and minimum, 2005 (PPP $ per day)

*Source:* World Bank staff estimates.

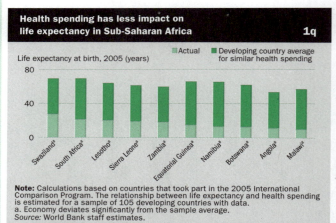

**Health spending has less impact on life expectancy in Sub-Saharan Africa** — 1q

Life expectancy at birth, 2005 (years)

■ Actual ■ Developing country average for similar health spending

**Note:** Calculations based on countries that took part in the 2005 International Comparison Program. The relationship between life expectancy and health spending is estimated for a sample of 105 developing countries with data.
a. Economy deviates significantly from the sample average.
*Source:* World Bank staff estimates.

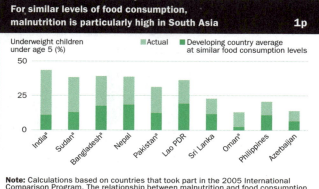

**For similar levels of food consumption, malnutrition is particularly high in South Asia** — 1p

Underweight children under age 5 (%)

■ Actual ■ Developing country average at similar food consumption levels

**Note:** Calculations based on countries that took part in the 2005 International Comparison Program. The relationship between malnutrition and food consumption is estimated for a sample of 77 developing countries with data.
a. Economy deviates significantly from the sample average.
*Source:* World Bank staff estimates.

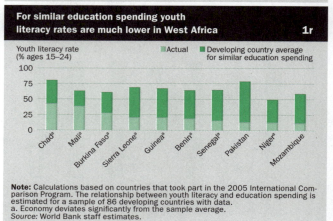

**For similar education spending youth literacy rates are much lower in West Africa** — 1r

Youth literacy rate (% ages 15–24)

■ Actual ■ Developing country average for similar education spending

**Note:** Calculations based on countries that took part in the 2005 International Comparison Program. The relationship between youth literacy and education spending is estimated for a sample of 86 developing countries with data.
a. Economy deviates significantly from the sample average.
*Source:* World Bank staff estimates.

## Public goods

Governments finance the provision of services destined to individuals, such as public health and education, and the provision of public goods, such as security, justice, and the environment. Countries at similar levels of development devote different amounts to collective consumption, most to financing public institutions through recurrent administrative expenditures. While fragile states spend relatively more on collective goods than do nonfragile states at similar levels of development (figure 1s), interpreting this result is difficult. It might reflect a response to the poor quality and prior underfunding of general administration, poor governance that yields less value for money, or the diversion of resources into conflict-related expenditures, such as security and defense.

Energy consumption has a strong impact on the local and global environment. Regions differ in energy efficiency (PPP GDP per unit of energy consumed), but all increased energy efficiency between 1995 and 2005, except the Middle East and North Africa (figure 1t). In 2005 $1 of GDP was produced with 13 percent less energy than in 1995. But the world's GDP grew 42 percent in that same period, for a net increase of 24 percent in global energy consumption.

## Foreign resources

Developing economies receive large financial flows from official development assistance (ODA) and the remittances of workers abroad. Because prices in developing economies are lower, the purchasing power of aid or remittances spent in the local economy is greater than the purchasing power of the same amount spent in the sending country. Adjusting ODA and remittances by the PPP price level index provides better measures of their relative impact.

In 2006 developing countries received PPP $15 per capita in net programmable assistance (net ODA excluding debt relief, humanitarian assistance, and technical cooperation). Low-income countries received PPP $25 per capita, and middle-income countries received PPP $7. Fragile states received PPP $50.

Developing countries received 2006 PPP $62 per capita in net workers' remittances. Middle-income countries received PPP $67, low-income countries PPP $55, and fragile states PPP $16. The Middle East and North Africa is the main recipient of remittances. At the other end Sub-Saharan Africa received PPP $22 in remittances in 2006 (figure 1u), half what it received in programmable aid (figure 1v).

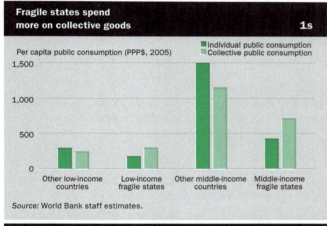

**Fragile states spend more on collective goods** 1s

Source: World Bank staff estimates.

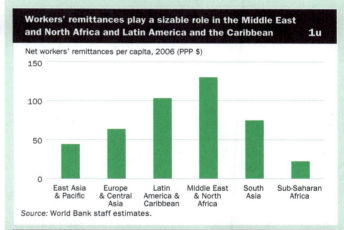

**Workers' remittances play a sizable role in the Middle East and North Africa and Latin America and the Caribbean** 1u

Source: World Bank staff estimates.

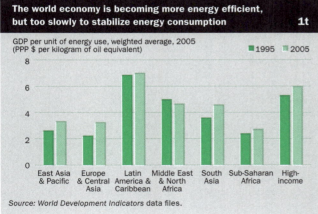

**The world economy is becoming more energy efficient, but too slowly to stabilize energy consumption** 1t

Source: World Development Indicators data files.

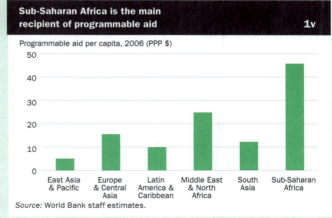

**Sub-Saharan Africa is the main recipient of programmable aid** 1v

Source: World Bank staff estimates.

| | Purchasing power parity (PPP) conversion factor local currency units to international $ 2005 | Market exchange rate local currency units to $ 2005 | Ratio of PPP conversion factor to market exchange rate 2005 | Gross domestic product PPP $ billions 2005 | Gross domestic product per capita PPP $ 2005 | Fixed capital formation per capita PPP $ 2005 | Collective government consumption per capita PPP $ 2005 | Consumption expenditure Individual by household Final 2005 | Consumption expenditure Actual individual 2005 | Consumption expenditure per capita PPP $ Food 2005 | Consumption expenditure per capita PPP $ Individual Education 2005 | Consumption expenditure Health 2005 |
|---|---|---|---|---|---|---|---|---|---|---|---|---|
| Albania | 48.56 | 99.87 | 0.49 | 17.2 | 5,465 | 1,374 | 639 | 3,241 | 4,280 | 650 | 681 | 855 |
| Angola | 44.49 | 87.16 | 0.51 | 60.0 | 3,729 | 850 | 712 | 541 | 692 | 132 | 122 | 75 |
| Argentina | 1.269 | 2.904 | 0.44 | 419.0 | 10,815 | 1,775 | 1,120 | 6,226 | 7,463 | 1,192 | 779 | 1,641 |
| Armenia | 178.6 | 457.7 | 0.39 | 12.6 | 4,162 | 750 | 423 | 2,855 | 3,925 | 1,380 | 1,237 | 510 |
| Australia | 1.388 | 1.309 | 1.06 | 695.8 | 34,106 | 8,133 | 3,297 | 17,487 | 21,915 | 1,613 | 3,421 | 3,449 |
| Austria | 0.8736 | 0.8041 | 1.09 | 280.6 | 34,075 | 6,254 | 2,424 | 18,163 | 23,443 | 1,813 | 2,568 | 3,499 |
| Azerbaijan[a] | 0.3263 | 0.9454 | 0.35 | 38.4 | 4,573 | 1,073 | 334 | 1,795 | 2,669 | 903 | 1,127 | 385 |
| Bahrain | 0.2488 | 0.376 | 0.66 | 24.2 | 33,451 | 6,926 | 2,441 | 10,170 | 12,822 | 2,268 | 2,632 | 2,376 |
| Bangladesh | 22.64 | 61.75 | 0.37 | 163.7 | 1,068 | 254 | 71 | 764 | 903 | 290 | 238 | 112 |
| Belarus | 779.3 | 2154 | 0.36 | 83.5 | 8,541 | 1,351 | 829 | 4,438 | 6,733 | 1,422 | 2,435 | 1,453 |
| Belgium | 0.8988 | 0.8041 | 1.12 | 332.2 | 31,699 | 6,512 | 2,427 | 16,077 | 21,647 | 1,958 | 2,759 | 3,957 |
| Benin | 219.6 | 527.5 | 0.42 | 10.3 | 1,213 | 184 | 232 | 758 | 948 | 197 | 168 | 73 |
| Bhutan | 15.74 | 44.1 | 0.36 | 2.3 | 3,649 | 1,715 | 868 | 1,277 | 1,924 | 417 | 446 | 906 |
| Bolivia | 2.232 | 8.066 | 0.28 | 34.1 | 3,715 | 298 | 557 | 2,151 | 2,972 | 481 | 1,129 | 519 |
| Bosnia and Herzegovina | 0.7268 | 1.573 | 0.46 | 23.3 | 5,949 | 1,157 | 923 | 4,859 | 6,320 | 1,163 | 1,075 | 963 |
| Botswana | 2.421 | 5.110 | 0.47 | 22.0 | 12,010 | 1,981 | 3,491 | 2,228 | 2,895 | 352 | 1,428 | 307 |
| Brazil | 1.357 | 2.434 | 0.56 | 1,583.2 | 8,474 | 1,218 | 1,640 | 4,416 | 5,639 | 712 | 851 | 1,306 |
| Brunei Darussalam | 0.9031 | 1.664 | 0.54 | 17.6 | 46,991 | 4,825 | 14,595 | 9,283 | 12,672 | 1,489 | 6,086 | 1,653 |
| Bulgaria | 0.5928 | 1.574 | 0.38 | 72.2 | 9,328 | 1,418 | 1,563 | 5,234 | 7,285 | 925 | 1,822 | 1,306 |
| Burkina Faso | 200.2 | 527.5 | 0.38 | 14.8 | 1,061 | 136 | 414 | 624 | 778 | 170 | 135 | 51 |
| Burundi | 343.0 | 1082 | 0.32 | 2.5 | 319 | .. | .. | .. | .. | .. | .. | .. |
| Cambodia | 1,279 | 4097 | 0.31 | 20.1 | 1,440 | 146 | 202 | 926 | 1,197 | 324 | 594 | 430 |
| Cameroon | 251.0 | 527.5 | 0.48 | 35.5 | 1,993 | 210 | 268 | 1,211 | 1,499 | 335 | 233 | 72 |
| Canada | 1.214 | 1.212 | 1.00 | 1,130.0 | 34,972 | 7,265 | 2,695 | 18,233 | 23,526 | 1,465 | 2,743 | 3,269 |
| Cape Verde | 69.36 | 88.67 | 0.78 | 1.3 | 2,521 | 936 | 421 | 1,964 | 2,449 | 480 | 766 | 239 |
| Central African Republic | 263.7 | 527.5 | 0.50 | 2.7 | 654 | 36 | 85 | 496 | 607 | 168 | 96 | 22 |
| Chad | 208.0 | 527.5 | 0.39 | 14.9 | 1,471 | 166 | 576 | 548 | 781 | 169 | 469 | 62 |
| Chile | 333.7 | 560.1 | 0.60 | 199.6 | 12,248 | 2,372 | 995 | 6,143 | 7,430 | 917 | 1,084 | 1,323 |
| China[b] | 3.448 | 8.194 | 0.42 | 5,333.2 | 4,088 | 1,581 | 823 | 1,310 | 1,751 | 265 | 582 | 549 |
| Hong Kong, China | 5.688 | 7.777 | 0.73 | 243.2 | 35,690 | 8,326 | 3,078 | 16,320 | 19,622 | 1,266 | 2,923 | 3,632 |
| Macao, China | 5.270 | 7.987 | 0.66 | 17.4 | 36,869 | 8,520 | 2,735 | 8,266 | 10,525 | 963 | 2,181 | 2,164 |
| Taiwan, China | 19.34 | 32.18 | 0.60 | 592.3 | 26,057 | 5,303 | 4,257 | 13,645 | 16,836 | 1,407 | 4,727 | 4,803 |
| Colombia | 1,082 | 2135 | 0.51 | 263.7 | 5,867 | 962 | 1,002 | 3,266 | 4,098 | 610 | 678 | 914 |
| Comoros | 226.2 | 395.6 | 0.57 | 0.7 | 1,127 | 98 | 406 | 762 | 918 | 330 | 171 | 39 |
| Congo, Dem. Rep. | 214.3 | 473.9 | 0.45 | 15.7 | 267 | 52 | 77 | 125 | 151 | 45 | 20 | 16 |
| Congo, Rep. | 268.8 | 527.5 | 0.51 | 11.7 | 3,246 | 252 | 549 | 679 | 943 | 166 | 478 | 135 |
| Côte d'Ivoire | 287.5 | 527.5 | 0.55 | 30.0 | 1,614 | 63 | 279 | 991 | 1,216 | 271 | 118 | 90 |
| Croatia | 3.935 | 5.949 | 0.66 | 58.8 | 13,231 | 3,161 | 1,695 | 6,641 | 9,076 | 1,423 | 1,740 | 1,805 |
| Cyprus | 0.424 | 0.4636 | 0.91 | 18.6 | 24,534 | 4,647 | 2,601 | 14,709 | 17,859 | 2,213 | 2,420 | 1,725 |
| Czech Republic | 14.40 | 23.96 | 0.60 | 207.6 | 20,280 | 3,770 | 2,897 | 9,278 | 13,145 | 1,322 | 2,145 | 2,756 |
| Denmark | 8.517 | 5.997 | 1.42 | 182.2 | 33,645 | 6,955 | 2,960 | 15,082 | 21,490 | 1,583 | 2,895 | 3,283 |
| Djibouti | 84.69 | 177.7 | 0.48 | 1.5 | 1,850 | 240 | 762 | 864 | 1,135 | 187 | 366 | 104 |
| Ecuador | 0.4226 | 1 | 0.42 | 88.0 | 6,737 | 1,329 | 690 | 3,680 | 4,577 | 781 | 781 | 785 |
| Egypt, Arab Rep. | 1.616 | 6.004 | 0.27 | 333.2 | 4,574 | 570 | 887 | 2,835 | 3,662 | 856 | 1,230 | 665 |
| Equatorial Guinea[c] | 287.4 | 527.5 | 0.54 | 13.8 | 13,610 | 2,019 | 860 | 2,359 | 2,912 | 558 | 731 | 612 |
| Estonia | 7.813 | 12.59 | 0.62 | 22.2 | 16,456 | 3,694 | 2,008 | 7,811 | 11,291 | 1,306 | 2,605 | 1,731 |
| Ethiopia | 2.254 | 8.652 | 0.26 | 43.7 | 581 | 70 | 121 | 373 | 457 | 139 | .. | 29 |
| Fiji | 1.430 | 1.691 | 0.85 | 3.5 | 4,282 | 1,116 | 731 | 2,996 | 3,768 | 750 | 1,016 | 691 |
| Finland | 0.9834 | 0.8041 | 1.22 | 159.8 | 30,462 | 5,969 | 2,475 | 13,761 | 19,501 | 1,672 | 2,473 | 3,234 |
| France | 0.9225 | 0.8041 | 1.15 | 1,862.2 | 30,591 | 5,654 | 2,260 | 16,724 | 23,027 | 2,263 | 2,567 | 4,059 |
| Gabon | 256.2 | 527.5 | 0.49 | 17.8 | 13,821 | 2,428 | 2,304 | 2,641 | 3,620 | 594 | 1,691 | 595 |
| Gambia, The | 7.560 | 28.58 | 0.26 | 1.7 | 1,078 | 62 | 409 | 405 | 550 | 75 | .. | 121 |
| Georgia | 0.7380 | 1.812 | 0.41 | 15.7 | 3,520 | 650 | 366 | 2,200 | 3,063 | 564 | 820 | 836 |
| Germany | 0.8926 | 0.8041 | 1.11 | 2,510.7 | 30,445 | 4,963 | 2,325 | 17,278 | 21,742 | 1,780 | 1,436 | 4,123 |
| Ghana | 3,721 | 9073 | 0.41 | 26.1 | 1,160 | 254 | 118 | 745 | 912 | 189 | 241 | 140 |
| Greece | 0.7022 | 0.8041 | 0.87 | 324.9 | 29,261 | 5,523 | 3,313 | 15,481 | 18,545 | 2,168 | 2,170 | 2,557 |

# New purchasing power parity estimates from the 2005 International Comparison Program

**1.a**

| | Purchasing power parity (PPP) conversion factor | Market exchange rate | Ratio of PPP conversion factor to market exchange rate | Gross domestic product | | Fixed capital formation | Collective government consumption | Consumption expenditure | | | | |
|---|---|---|---|---|---|---|---|---|---|---|---|---|
| | local currency units to international $ | local currency units to $ | | PPP $ billions | per capita PPP $ | per capita PPP $ | per capita PPP $ | Individual by household Final | Actual individual | per capita PPP $ Food | Individual Education | Health |
| | 2005 | 2005 | 2005 | 2005 | 2005 | 2005 | 2005 | 2005 | 2005 | 2005 | 2005 | 2005 |
| Guinea | 1,219 | 3640 | 0.33 | 9.9 | 1,105 | 167 | 95 | 548 | 682 | 123 | 241 | 143 |
| Guinea-Bissau | 217.3 | 527.5 | 0.41 | 0.7 | 458 | 57 | 266 | 295 | 361 | 96 | 49 | 25 |
| Hungary | 128.5 | 199.6 | 0.64 | 171.6 | 17,014 | 2,804 | 2,129 | 8,481 | 12,365 | 1,242 | 2,189 | 2,434 |
| Iceland | 97.06 | 62.98 | 1.54 | 10.5 | 35,465 | 12,207 | 3,245 | 19,100 | 26,816 | 1,808 | 4,118 | 4,394 |
| India | 14.67 | 44.27 | 0.33 | 2,431.9 | 2,222 | 504 | 233 | 1,183 | 1,464 | 317 | 391 | 485 |
| Indonesia | 3,934 | 9705 | 0.41 | 707.9 | 3,209 | 615 | 248 | 1,934 | 2,326 | 607 | 658 | 144 |
| Iran, Islamic Rep. | 2,675 | 8964 | 0.30 | 643.5 | 9,314 | 1,646 | 1,489 | 5,275 | 6,645 | 655 | 1,257 | 2,119 |
| Iraq | 558.7 | .. | .. | .. | .. | 269 | 1,643 | 1,297 | 1,862 | 394 | 543 | 877 |
| Ireland | 1.023 | 0.8041 | 1.27 | 157.6 | 37,886 | 8,864 | 2,183 | 15,560 | 20,997 | 867 | 3,177 | 2,998 |
| Israel | 3.717 | 4.488 | 0.83 | 156.7 | 22,627 | 3,775 | 3,602 | 11,096 | 15,278 | 1,681 | 3,385 | 2,248 |
| Italy | 0.8750 | 0.8041 | 1.09 | 1,626.3 | 27,750 | 6,016 | 2,165 | 15,678 | 19,667 | 2,032 | 1,865 | 2,914 |
| Japan | 129.6 | 110.2 | 1.18 | 3,870.3 | 30,290 | 6,656 | 2,615 | 15,342 | 20,438 | 1,348 | 1,767 | 4,653 |
| Jordan | 0.3805 | 0.709 | 0.54 | 23.5 | 4,342 | 1,552 | 875 | 2,947 | 3,843 | 898 | 1,202 | 724 |
| Kazakhstan | 57.61 | 132.9 | 0.43 | 131.8 | 8,699 | 1,632 | 811 | 3,746 | 5,426 | 735 | 2,768 | 1,728 |
| Kenya | 29.52 | 75.55 | 0.39 | 49.0 | 1,375 | 145 | 177 | 948 | 1,196 | 221 | 351 | 259 |
| Korea, Rep. | 788.9 | 1024 | 0.77 | 1,027.4 | 21,273 | 6,376 | 2,046 | 9,829 | 12,157 | 874 | 2,124 | 2,240 |
| Kuwait | 0.2136 | 0.292 | 0.73 | 110.4 | 43,551 | 9,288 | 5,292 | 10,978 | 13,683 | 2,316 | 2,437 | 1,365 |
| Kyrgyz Republic | 11.35 | 41.02 | 0.28 | 8.9 | 1,728 | 138 | 251 | 1,249 | 1,901 | 403 | 841 | 282 |
| Lao PDR | 2,988 | 10636 | 0.28 | 10.3 | 1,814 | 476 | 678 | 859 | 1,109 | 268 | 575 | 165 |
| Latvia | 0.2980 | 0.5647 | 0.53 | 30.4 | 13,215 | 2,663 | 2,007 | 6,985 | 9,745 | 1,277 | 2,464 | 1,498 |
| Lebanon | 847.5 | 1508 | 0.56 | 38.3 | 9,545 | 2,814 | 1,715 | 6,265 | 7,639 | 1,842 | 3,260 | 1,390 |
| Lesotho | 3.490 | 6.359 | 0.55 | 2.6 | 1,311 | 274 | 219 | 1,319 | 1,686 | 309 | 738 | 446 |
| Liberia[d] | 0.4926 | 1 | 0.49 | 1.1 | 312 | 59 | 60 | 200 | 248 | 31 | 216 | 37 |
| Lithuania | 1.484 | 2.776 | 0.53 | 48.1 | 14,084 | 2,030 | 1,551 | 8,169 | 11,402 | 1,888 | 2,478 | 1,944 |
| Luxembourg | 0.9225 | 0.8041 | 1.15 | 31.9 | 69,776 | 14,390 | 3,898 | 27,061 | 34,295 | 1,849 | 2,853 | 4,345 |
| Macedonia, FYR | 19.06 | 49.29 | 0.39 | 15.0 | 7,394 | 905 | 1,276 | 4,623 | 6,123 | 1,181 | 991 | 1,007 |
| Madagascar | 649.6 | 2003 | 0.32 | 15.5 | 834 | 119 | 249 | 557 | 702 | 189 | 383 | 66 |
| Malawi | 39.46 | 118.4 | 0.33 | 8.6 | 648 | 121 | 124 | 400 | 482 | 53 | 161 | 139 |
| Malaysia | 1.734 | 3.8 | 0.46 | 299.6 | 11,678 | 2,483 | 1,642 | 4,302 | 5,669 | 649 | 1,728 | 779 |
| Maldives | 8.134 | 12.8 | 0.64 | 1.2 | 3,995 | 1,965 | 1,497 | 1,496 | 2,190 | 355 | 2,095 | 932 |
| Mali | 240.1 | 527.5 | 0.46 | 11.7 | 1,004 | 98 | 290 | 616 | 772 | 180 | 176 | 76 |
| Malta | 0.2474 | 0.346 | 0.71 | 8.3 | 20,483 | 3,462 | 2,471 | 11,778 | 15,662 | 1,887 | 2,164 | 2,457 |
| Mauritania | 98.84 | 268.6 | 0.37 | 5.0 | 1,684 | 647 | 556 | 906 | 1,150 | 336 | 222 | 124 |
| Mauritius | 14.68 | 28.94 | 0.51 | 12.4 | 9,975 | 1,524 | 1,768 | 5,837 | 7,621 | 1,158 | 1,778 | 889 |
| Mexico | 7.127 | 10.90 | 0.65 | 1,173.9 | 11,387 | 1,631 | 798 | 7,189 | 8,924 | 1,658 | 2,007 | 910 |
| Moldova | 4.434 | 12.60 | 0.35 | 8.5 | 2,190 | 305 | 237 | 1,854 | 2,688 | 374 | 1,345 | 364 |
| Mongolia | 417.2 | 1205 | 0.35 | 6.7 | 2,609 | 714 | 402 | 1,159 | 1,618 | 353 | 1,137 | 421 |
| Montenegro | 0.3659 | 0.8027 | 0.46 | 4.5 | 7,450 | 980 | 3,144 | 4,201 | 5,739 | 1,112 | 885 | 975 |
| Morocco | 4.8782 | 8.865 | 0.55 | 107.1 | 3,554 | 851 | 540 | 1,801 | 2,254 | 494 | 372 | 191 |
| Mozambique | 10,909 | 23061 | 0.47 | 13.9 | 677 | 104 | 108 | 455 | 574 | 180 | 117 | 53 |
| Namibia | 4.265 | 6.359 | 0.67 | 9.3 | 4,599 | 979 | 1,233 | 2,068 | 2,769 | 483 | 1,046 | 589 |
| Nepal | 22.65 | 72.06 | 0.31 | 26.0 | 960 | 179 | 98 | 706 | 850 | 277 | 183 | 303 |
| Netherlands | 0.8983 | 0.8041 | 1.12 | 562.9 | 34,492 | 5,711 | 3,468 | 16,477 | 22,587 | 1,974 | 2,515 | 3,680 |
| New Zealand | 1.535 | 1.420 | 1.08 | 101.6 | 24,566 | 4,842 | 2,114 | 13,620 | 17,750 | 1,670 | 2,180 | 2,698 |
| Niger | 226.7 | 527.5 | 0.43 | 8.0 | 602 | 80 | 164 | 370 | 453 | 103 | 51 | 43 |
| Nigeria | 60.23 | 131.3 | 0.46 | 214.8 | 1,520 | 150 | 207 | 937 | 1,172 | 269 | 280 | 97 |
| Norway | 8.840 | 6.443 | 1.37 | 219.8 | 47,538 | 8,600 | 3,358 | 17,357 | 24,603 | 1,885 | 2,832 | 4,502 |
| Oman | 0.2324 | 0.3845 | 0.60 | 51.0 | 20,350 | 4,800 | 4,385 | 5,814 | 7,402 | 1,515 | 1,446 | 723 |
| Pakistan | 19.10 | 59.36 | 0.32 | 340.3 | 2,184 | 329 | 266 | 1,663 | 2,026 | 525 | 491 | 511 |
| Paraguay | 2,007 | 6178 | 0.32 | 22.6 | 3,824 | 480 | 353 | 2,763 | 3,350 | 761 | 505 | 348 |
| Peru | 1.487 | 3.296 | 0.45 | 176.0 | 6,452 | 1,070 | 536 | 3,834 | 4,564 | 854 | 799 | 559 |
| Philippines | 21.75 | 55.09 | 0.39 | 250.0 | 2,956 | 382 | 308 | 1,845 | 2,218 | 612 | 811 | 175 |
| Poland | 1.898 | 3.235 | 0.59 | 516.6 | 13,535 | 1,945 | 1,504 | 7,421 | 10,271 | 1,423 | 1,985 | 1,858 |
| Portugal | 0.7074 | 0.8041 | 0.88 | 210.5 | 19,956 | 4,337 | 1,940 | 11,920 | 15,288 | 1,851 | 1,681 | 2,778 |
| Qatar | 2.745 | 3.64 | 0.75 | 56.3 | 70,716 | 29,906 | 7,576 | 9,476 | 12,893 | 2,072 | 3,756 | 2,503 |
| Romania | 1.421 | 2.914 | 0.49 | 202.7 | 9,368 | 1,499 | 1,483 | 5,280 | 7,311 | 1,165 | 1,350 | 1,438 |

| | Purchasing power parity (PPP) conversion factor | Market exchange rate | Ratio of PPP conversion factor to market exchange rate | Gross domestic product | | Fixed capital formation | Collective government consumption | Consumption expenditure | | | | |
|---|---|---|---|---|---|---|---|---|---|---|---|---|
| | local currency units to international $ | local currency units to $ | | PPP $ billions | per capita PPP $ | per capita PPP $ | per capita PPP $ | Individual by household Final | Actual individual | per capita PPP $ Food | Individual Education | Health |
| | 2005 | 2005 | 2005 | 2005 | 2005 | 2005 | 2005 | 2005 | 2005 | 2005 | 2005 | 2005 |
| Russian Federation | 12.736 | 28.28 | 0.45 | 1,697.5 | 11,858 | 1,377 | 1,333 | 5,545 | 7,916 | 1,298 | 1,723 | 1,394 |
| Rwanda | 186.2 | 557.8 | 0.33 | 6.4 | 696 | 109 | 243 | 464 | 592 | 148 | 202 | 59 |
| São Tomé and Principe | 5,558 | 10558 | 0.53 | 0.2 | 1,401 | 199 | 418 | 1,167 | 1,446 | 388 | 300 | 176 |
| Saudi Arabia | 2.410 | 3.747 | 0.64 | 490.6 | 21,220 | 4,657 | 3,376 | 5,037 | 6,976 | 1,108 | 1,924 | 1,229 |
| Senegal | 251.7 | 527.5 | 0.48 | 18.1 | 1,541 | 262 | 250 | 988 | 1,239 | 300 | 181 | 144 |
| Serbia | 27.21 | 66.71 | 0.41 | 64.3 | 8,644 | 1,139 | 1,050 | 4,726 | 6,712 | 1,015 | 1,109 | 1,209 |
| Sierra Leone | 1,074 | 2890 | 0.37 | 3.3 | 584 | 62 | 254 | 523 | 667 | 118 | 240 | 278 |
| Singapore | 1.079 | 1.665 | 0.65 | 180.1 | 41,479 | 10,352 | 5,534 | 12,636 | 15,564 | 929 | 3,159 | 3,043 |
| Slovak Republic | 17.20 | 31.02 | 0.55 | 85.6 | 15,881 | 2,856 | 2,561 | 8,181 | 11,077 | 1,227 | 1,916 | 1,990 |
| Slovenia | 147.0 | 192.7 | 0.76 | 45.0 | 22,506 | 5,638 | 2,094 | 11,305 | 14,970 | 1,457 | 2,075 | 2,628 |
| South Africa | 3.872 | 6.359 | 0.61 | 397.5 | 8,478 | 1,214 | 1,587 | 4,582 | 5,886 | 764 | 1,228 | 1,062 |
| Spain | 0.7676 | 0.8041 | 0.95 | 1,179.6 | 27,180 | 7,020 | 2,265 | 14,826 | 19,232 | 2,117 | 2,156 | 3,280 |
| Sri Lanka | 35.17 | 100.5 | 0.35 | 67.3 | 3,420 | 658 | 499 | 2,126 | 2,735 | 568 | 393 | 341 |
| Sudan | 107.7 | 243.6 | 0.44 | 63.1 | 1,711 | 257 | 234 | 1,493 | 1,799 | 489 | 77 | 69 |
| Swaziland | 3.293 | 6.359 | 0.52 | 5.0 | 4,461 | 678 | 752 | 2,537 | 3,157 | 746 | 625 | 1,057 |
| Sweden | 9.243 | 7.473 | 1.24 | 288.9 | 32,016 | 4,784 | 2,752 | 14,381 | 21,833 | 1,631 | 3,339 | 3,635 |
| Switzerland | 1.741 | 1.245 | 1.40 | 261.7 | 35,182 | 7,609 | 1,779 | 19,472 | 23,235 | 1,871 | 2,413 | 4,294 |
| Syrian Arab Republic | 19.72 | 52.86 | 0.37 | 75.6 | 4,002 | 909 | 542 | 2,210 | 2,881 | 861 | 878 | 664 |
| Tajikistan | 0.7444 | 3.117 | 0.24 | 9.7 | 1,478 | 67 | 209 | 948 | 1,560 | 363 | 1,161 | 236 |
| Tanzania | 395.6 | 1129 | 0.35 | 35.9 | 933 | 132 | 126 | 618 | 750 | 261 | .. | 40 |
| Thailand | 15.93 | 40.22 | 0.40 | 444.9 | 7,061 | 1,908 | 747 | 3,638 | 4,616 | 448 | 1,451 | 1,072 |
| Togo | 240.4 | 527.5 | 0.46 | 4.6 | 742 | 75 | 170 | 618 | 767 | 174 | 168 | 41 |
| Tunisia | 0.5813 | 1.297 | 0.45 | 64.0 | 6,382 | 1,149 | 894 | 3,463 | 4,371 | 697 | 553 | 519 |
| Turkey | 0.8683 | 1.341 | 0.65 | 561.1 | 7,786 | 1,192 | 1,057 | 4,612 | 5,715 | 888 | 913 | 346 |
| Uganda | 619.6 | 1737 | 0.36 | 24.5 | 848 | 115 | 181 | 583 | 748 | 155 | .. | 98 |
| Ukraine | 1.678 | 5.125 | 0.33 | 263.0 | 5,583 | 732 | 512 | 3,138 | 4,657 | 953 | 2,081 | 922 |
| United Kingdom | 0.6489 | 0.5493 | 1.18 | 1,889.4 | 31,371 | 4,937 | 2,841 | 19,187 | 25,155 | 1,586 | 1,955 | 3,665 |
| United States | 1 | 1 | 1.00 | 12,397.9 | 41,813 | 8,018 | 3,962 | 29,368 | 32,045 | 1,998 | 2,725 | 5,853 |
| Uruguay | 13.28 | 24.48 | 0.54 | 30.6 | 9,266 | 1,111 | 933 | 5,886 | 7,074 | 1,071 | 716 | 1,506 |
| Venezuela, RB | 1,153 | 2090 | 0.55 | 262.5 | 9,877 | 1,287 | 985 | 4,290 | 5,364 | 844 | 1,026 | 866 |
| Vietnam | 4,713 | 15804 | 0.30 | 178.1 | 2,143 | 634 | 367 | 990 | 1,310 | 238 | 1,009 | 466 |
| Yemen, Rep. | 69.49 | 191.5 | 0.36 | 46.2 | 2,188 | 472 | 386 | 1,073 | 1,405 | 376 | 454 | 190 |
| Zambia | 2,415 | 4464 | 0.54 | 13.4 | 1,171 | 211 | 275 | 672 | 894 | 59 | .. | 233 |
| Zimbabwe | 33,068 | 22364 | 1.48 | 2.3 | 176 | 45 | 169 | 284 | 381 | 90 | 159 | 9 |

a. Original data collected in old manat are converted to new manat at 1 new manat = 5,000 old manat. b. Results for China were based on national average prices extrapolated by the World Bank and Asian Development Bank using price data for 11 cities submitted by the National Bureau of Statistics for China. The data for China do not include Hong Kong, China; Macao, China; and Taiwan, China. c. Per capita figures derived using population from the International Comparison Program. d. Data in U.S. dollars.

# New purchasing power parity estimates from the 2005 International Comparison Program

## 1.a

The International Comparison Program (ICP) is a worldwide statistical initiative to collect comparative price data and estimate purchasing power parities (PPPs) of the world's economies. Using PPPs instead of market exchange rates to convert currencies allows the output of economies and the welfare of their inhabitants to be compared in real terms—that is, controlling for differences in price levels. PPPs are the preferred means of converting gross domestic product (GDP) and its components to a common currency. They enable cross-country comparison of the size of economies, average consumption levels, poverty rates, productivity, and use of resources. The ratio of the PPP conversion factor to the market exchange rate (also referred to as the price level index) allows the cost of the goods and services that make up GDP to be compared across countries.

The new estimates of PPP, published for the first time in *World Development Indicators,* are the result of a global program of price surveys carried out using similar methods in 146 countries. New methods of data collection and analysis were used to overcome problems encountered in previous rounds of the ICP. Teams in each region identified characteristic goods and services to be priced. Surveys conducted by each country in 2005 and 2006 yielded prices for more than 1,000 goods and services. Many countries participated for the first time, including China. (Previous estimates of China's PPPs came from a research study using data for 1986.) India participated for the first time since 1985.

The ICP Global Office within the World Bank coordinated the collection of data and calculation of PPPs in more than 100 (mostly developing) economies. The program was organized in five geographic areas: Africa, Asia-Pacific, Commonwealth of Independent States, South America, and Western Asia. Regional agencies coordinated the work in the five regions. In parallel the Statistical Office of the European Communities (Eurostat) and the Organisation for Economic Co-operation and Development (OECD) conducted its 2005 PPP program, which included 46 countries.

Each region and the Eurostat-OECD group differ in the size and structure of their economies and their statistical capacity. To ensure the most consistent comparisons of countries within regions, different methods were used in each region. Three methods were used to compute housing PPPs. Asia and Africa used reference volumes, Eurostat and West Asia used a combination of rentals and quantities, and the CIS and Latin America used the quantity method. In Africa, Asia-Pacific, and Western Asia government expenditures were adjusted to account for productivity differences. There were other differences in

methodology, such as how basic heading PPPs were computed and aggregated. Annex F of the 2005 ICP report (available at www.worldbank.org/data/ICP) provides a review of the methods used.

For the 2005 ICP GDP data were compiled using the expenditure approach, with its components allocated to 155 basic headings for the year 2005. The detailed breakdown of GDP expenditure used by the ICP may differ from other national accounts data presented in *World Development Indicators 2008* because of the timing of data collection and differences in methodology. In table 1.a gross fixed capital formation and consumption data are from the ICP, and GDP data are collected by World Bank staff from national and international sources and in some cases differ from ICP data. All per capita figures are estimated using the World Bank's population data, except where otherwise noted.

### Definitions

• **Purchasing power parity (PPP) conversion factor** is the number of units of a country's currency required to buy the same amount of goods and services in the domestic market as a U.S. dollar would buy in the United States. • **Market exchange rate** is the exchange rate determined by national authorities or the rate determined in the legally sanctioned exchange market. When the official exchange rate diverges by an exceptionally large margin from the rate effectively applied to domestic transactions of foreign currencies and traded products, the market exchange rate is an estimated alternative conversion factor. It is calculated as an annual average based on monthly averages (local currency units relative to the U.S. dollar). • **Ratio of PPP conversion factor to market exchange rate,** also known as the price level index, is obtained by dividing the PPP conversion factor by the market exchange rate. • **PPP gross domestic product (GDP)** is GDP converted to U.S. dollars using PPP rates. GDP is the sum of value added by all resident producers plus any product taxes (less subsidies) not included in the valuation of output. • **PPP GDP per capita** is PPP GDP divided by midyear population. Population is based on the de facto definition of population, which counts all residents regardless of legal status or citizenship, except refugees not permanently settled in the country of asylum, who are generally considered part of the population of their country of origin. • **PPP gross fixed capital formation per capita** is outlays on additions to the fixed assets of an economy converted to U.S. dollars using PPP rates and divided by midyear population. • **PPP collective government consumption per capita** is all government current expenditures for purchases of goods and services (including

compensation of employees). Data are converted to U.S. dollars using PPP rates and divided by midyear population. • **PPP individual by household final consumption expenditure per capita** is the market value of all goods and services, including durable products, purchased by households. It excludes purchases of dwellings but includes imputed rent for owner-occupied dwellings. Data are converted to U.S. dollars using PPP rates and divided by midyear population. • **PPP actual individual consumption expenditure per capita** is household final consumption expenditure plus the individual component of government consumption expenditure and the final consumption expenditure by nonprofit institutions serving households. The individual component of government consumption expenditure relates to services provided to specific individuals, such as health and education. Data are converted to U.S. dollars using PPP rates and divided by midyear population. • **PPP individual consumption expenditure on food per capita** is expenditure on food products and nonalcoholic beverages purchased for consumption at home. It excludes food products and beverages sold for immediate consumption away from home, cooked dishes prepared by restaurants and catering contractors, and products sold as pet foods. Data are converted to U.S. dollars using PPP rates and divided by midyear population. • **PPP individual consumption expenditure on education per capita** is expenditures by households on pre-primary, primary, secondary, post-secondary, and tertiary education. Data are converted to U.S. dollars using PPP rates and divided by midyear population. • **PPP individual consumption expenditure on health per capita** is expenditures by households on medical products, appliances and equipment, outpatient services, and hospital services. Data are converted to U.S. dollars using PPP rates and divided by midyear population.

### Data sources

PPP conversion factors are estimates by World Bank staff based on data collected by the International Comparison Program (www.worldbank.org/data/ICP). Data on GDP are estimated by World Bank staff based on national accounts data collected by World Bank staff during economic missions or reported to other international organizations such as the OECD. Population estimates are prepared by World Bank staff from a variety of sources (see *Data sources* for table 2.1). Data on gross fixed capital formation, government consumption, and household consumption expenditures are based on data collected by the International Comparison Program.

# Millennium Development Goals

## Goals and targets from the Millennium Declaration | Indicators for monitoring progress

### Goal 1    Eradicate extreme poverty and hunger

| | |
|---|---|
| Target 1.A   Halve, between 1990 and 2015, the proportion of people whose income is less than $1 a day | 1.1   Proportion of population below $1 purchasing power parity (PPP) a day[1] <br> 1.2   Poverty gap ratio [incidence × depth of poverty] <br> 1.3   Share of poorest quintile in national consumption |
| Target 1.B   Achieve full and productive employment and decent work for all, including women and young people | 1.4   Growth rate of GDP per person employed <br> 1.5   Employment to population ratio <br> 1.6   Proportion of employed people living below $1 (PPP) a day <br> 1.7   Proportion of own-account and contributing family workers in total employment |
| Target 1.C   Halve, between 1990 and 2015, the proportion of people who suffer from hunger | 1.8   Prevalence of underweight children under-five years of age <br> 1.9   Proportion of population below minimum level of dietary energy consumption |

### Goal 2    Achieve universal primary education

| | |
|---|---|
| Target 2.A   Ensure that by 2015 children everywhere, boys and girls alike, will be able to complete a full course of primary schooling | 2.1   Net enrolment ratio in primary education <br> 2.2   Proportion of pupils starting grade 1 who reach last grade of primary education <br> 2.3   Literacy rate of 15- to 24-year-olds, women and men |

### Goal 3    Promote gender equality and empower women

| | |
|---|---|
| Target 3.A   Eliminate gender disparity in primary and secondary education, preferably by 2005, and in all levels of education no later than 2015 | 3.1   Ratios of girls to boys in primary, secondary, and tertiary education <br> 3.2   Share of women in wage employment in the nonagricultural sector <br> 3.3   Proportion of seats held by women in national parliament |

### Goal 4    Reduce child mortality

| | |
|---|---|
| Target 4.A   Reduce by two-thirds, between 1990 and 2015, the under-five mortality rate | 4.1   Under-five mortality rate <br> 4.2   Infant mortality rate <br> 4.3   Proportion of one-year-old children immunized against measles |

### Goal 5    Improve maternal health

| | |
|---|---|
| Target 5.A   Reduce by three-quarters, between 1990 and 2015, the maternal mortality ratio | 5.1   Maternal mortality ratio <br> 5.2   Proportion of births attended by skilled health personnel |
| Target 5.B   Achieve by 2015 universal access to reproductive health | 5.3   Contraceptive prevalence rate <br> 5.4   Adolescent birth rate <br> 5.5   Antenatal care coverage (at least one visit and at least four visits) <br> 5.6   Unmet need for family planning |

### Goal 6    Combat HIV/AIDS, malaria, and other diseases

| | |
|---|---|
| Target 6.A   Have halted by 2015 and begun to reverse the spread of HIV/AIDS | 6.1   HIV prevalence among population ages 15–24 years <br> 6.2   Condom use at last high-risk sex <br> 6.3   Proportion of population ages 15–24 years with comprehensive, correct knowledge of HIV/AIDS <br> 6.4   Ratio of school attendance of orphans to school attendance of nonorphans ages 10–14 years |
| Target 6.B   Achieve by 2010 universal access to treatment for HIV/AIDS for all those who need it | 6.5   Proportion of population with advanced HIV infection with access to antiretroviral drugs |
| Target 6.C   Have halted by 2015 and begun to reverse the incidence of malaria and other major diseases | 6.6   Incidence and death rates associated with malaria <br> 6.7   Proportion of children under age five sleeping under insecticide-treated bednets <br> 6.8   Proportion of children under age five with fever who are treated with appropriate antimalarial drugs <br> 6.9   Incidence, prevalence, and death rates associated with tuberculosis <br> 6.10   Proportion of tuberculosis cases detected and cured under directly observed treatment short course |

The **Millennium Development Goals and targets come from the Millennium Declaration,** signed by 189 countries, including 147 heads of state and government, in September 2000 (www. un.org/millennium/declaration/ares552e.htm) as updated by the 60th UN General Assembly in September 2005. The revised Millennium Development Goal (MDG) monitoring framework shown here, including new targets and indicators, was presented to the 62nd General Assembly, with new numbering as recommended by the Inter-agency and Expert Group on MDG Indicators at its 12th meeting on 14 November 2007. The goals and targets are interrelated and should be seen as a whole. They represent a partnership between the developed countries and the developing countries "to create an environment—at the national and global levels alike—which is conducive to development and the elimination of poverty." All indicators should be disaggregated by sex and urban-rural location as far as possible.

## Goal 7    Ensure environmental sustainability

| | |
|---|---|
| **Target 7.A** Integrate the principles of sustainable development into country policies and programs and reverse the loss of environmental resources | 7.1   Proportion of land area covered by forest<br>7.2   Carbon dioxide emissions, total, per capita and per \$1 GDP (PPP)<br>7.3   Consumption of ozone-depleting substances |
| **Target 7.B** Reduce biodiversity loss, achieving, by 2010, a significant reduction in the rate of loss | 7.4   Proportion of fish stocks within safe biological limits<br>7.5   Proportion of total water resources used<br>7.6   Proportion of terrestrial and marine areas protected<br>7.7   Proportion of species threatened with extinction |
| **Target 7.C** Halve by 2015 the proportion of people without sustainable access to safe drinking water and basic sanitation | 7.8   Proportion of population using an improved drinking water source<br>7.9   Proportion of population using an improved sanitation facility |
| **Target 7.D** Achieve by 2020 a significant improvement in the lives of at least 100 million slum dwellers | 7.10 Proportion of urban population living in slums[2] |

## Goal 8    Develop a global partnership for development

| | |
|---|---|
| **Target 8.A** Develop further an open, rule-based, predictable, nondiscriminatory trading and financial system<br><br>(Includes a commitment to good governance, development, and poverty reduction—both nationally and internationally.) | Some of the indicators listed below are monitored separately for the least developed countries (LDCs), Africa, landlocked developing countries, and small island developing states.<br><br>**Official development assistance (ODA)**<br>8.1   Net ODA, total and to the least developed countries, as percentage of OECD/DAC donors' gross national income<br>8.2   Proportion of total bilateral, sector-allocable ODA of OECD/DAC donors to basic social services (basic education, primary health care, nutrition, safe water, and sanitation) |
| **Target 8.B** Address the special needs of the least developed countries<br><br>(Includes tariff and quota-free access for the least developed countries' exports; enhanced program of debt relief for heavily indebted poor countries (HIPC) and cancellation of official bilateral debt; and more generous ODA for countries committed to poverty reduction.) | 8.3   Proportion of bilateral official development assistance of OECD/DAC donors that is untied<br>8.4   ODA received in landlocked developing countries as a proportion of their gross national incomes<br>8.5   ODA received in small island developing states as a proportion of their gross national incomes |
| **Target 8.C** Address the special needs of landlocked developing countries and small island developing states (through the Programme of Action for the Sustainable Development of Small Island Developing States and the outcome of the 22nd special session of the General Assembly) | **Market access**<br>8.6   Proportion of total developed country imports (by value and excluding arms) from developing countries and least developed countries, admitted free of duty<br>8.7   Average tariffs imposed by developed countries on agricultural products and textiles and clothing from developing countries<br>8.8   Agricultural support estimate for OECD countries as a percentage of their GDP<br>8.9   Proportion of ODA provided to help build trade capacity |
| **Target 8.D** Deal comprehensively with the debt problems of developing countries through national and international measures in order to make debt sustainable in the long term | **Debt sustainability**<br>8.10 Total number of countries that have reached their HIPC decision points and number that have reached their HIPC completion points (cumulative)<br>8.11 Debt relief committed under HIPC Initiative and Multilateral Debt Relief Initiative (MDRI)<br>8.12 Debt service as a percentage of exports of goods and services |
| **Target 8.E** In cooperation with pharmaceutical companies, provide access to affordable essential drugs in developing countries | 8.13 Proportion of population with access to affordable essential drugs on a sustainable basis |
| **Target 8.F** In cooperation with the private sector, make available the benefits of new technologies, especially information and communications | 8.14 Telephone lines per 100 population<br>8.15 Cellular subscribers per 100 population<br>8.16 Internet users per 100 population |

1. Where available, indicators based on national poverty lines should be used for monitoring country poverty trends.

2. The proportion of people living in slums is measured by a proxy, represented by the urban population living in households with at least one of these characteristics: lack of access to improved water supply, lack of access to improved sanitation, overcrowding (3 or more persons per room), and dwellings made of nondurable material.

# 1.1 Size of the economy

| | Population | Surface area | Population density | Gross national income | | Gross national income per capita | | PPP gross national income[a] | | | Gross domestic product | |
|---|---|---|---|---|---|---|---|---|---|---|---|---|
| | | | | | | | | | Per capita | | % growth | Per capita % growth |
| | millions 2006 | thousand sq. km 2006 | people per sq. km 2006 | $ billions 2006[b] | Rank 2005 | $ 2006[b] | Rank 2006 | $ billions 2006 | $ 2006 | Rank 2006 | % growth 2005–06 | % growth 2005–06 |
| Afghanistan | .. | 652 | .. | 8.1 | 117 | ..[c] | .. | 23.9[d] | ..[d] | .. | 5.3 | .. |
| Albania | 3 | 29 | 116 | 9.3 | 109 | 2,930 | 116 | 19.0 | 6,000 | 118 | 5.0 | 4.4 |
| Algeria | 33 | 2,382 | 14 | 101.2 | 49 | 3,030 | 111 | 198.0[d] | 5,940[d] | 119 | 3.0 | 1.5 |
| Angola | 17 | 1,247 | 13 | 32.7 | 69 | 1,970 | 131 | 64.5 | 3,890 | 139 | 18.6 | 15.3 |
| Argentina | 39 | 2,780 | 14 | 201.4 | 31 | 5,150 | 88 | 456.8 | 11,670 | 78 | 8.5 | 7.4 |
| Armenia | 3 | 30 | 107 | 5.8 | 132 | 1,920 | 133 | 14.9 | 4,950 | 127 | 13.3 | 13.6 |
| Australia | 21 | 7,741 | 3 | 742.3 | 15 | 35,860 | 25 | 702.5 | 33,940 | 26 | 2.5 | 1.0 |
| Austria | 8 | 84 | 100 | 329.2 | 22 | 39,750 | 18 | 298.4 | 36,040 | 18 | 3.1 | 2.5 |
| Azerbaijan | 8 | 87 | 103 | 15.6 | 95 | 1,840 | 134 | 46.1 | 5,430 | 123 | 34.5 | 33.0 |
| Bangladesh | 156 | 144 | 1,198 | 70.5 | 55 | 450 | 182 | 191.9 | 1,230 | 180 | 6.6 | 4.8 |
| Belarus | 10 | 208 | 47 | 33.8 | 66 | 3,470 | 105 | 94.4 | 9,700 | 88 | 9.9 | 10.4 |
| Belgium | 11 | 31 | 349 | 405.4 | 18 | 38,460 | 20 | 356.9 | 33,860 | 27 | 3.2 | 2.6 |
| Benin | 9 | 113 | 79 | 4.7 | 138 | 530 | 176 | 10.9 | 1,250 | 178 | 4.1 | 0.9 |
| Bolivia | 9 | 1,099 | 9 | 10.3 | 105 | 1,100 | 149 | 35.6 | 3,810 | 142 | 4.6 | 2.7 |
| Bosnia and Herzegovina | 4 | 51 | 77 | 12.7 | 102 | 3,230 | 106 | 26.6 | 6,780 | 109 | 6.0 | 5.7 |
| Botswana | 2 | 582 | 3 | 10.4 | 104 | 5,570 | 81 | 21.8 | 11,730 | 77 | 2.1 | 0.9 |
| Brazil | 189 | 8,515 | 22 | 892.6 | 11 | 4,710 | 93 | 1,647.5 | 8,700 | 96 | 3.7 | 2.4 |
| Bulgaria | 8 | 111 | 71 | 30.7 | 71 | 3,990 | 98 | 79.0 | 10,270 | 84 | 6.1 | 6.7 |
| Burkina Faso | 14 | 274 | 52 | 6.3 | 129 | 440 | 184 | 16.2 | 1,130 | 184 | 6.4 | 3.2 |
| Burundi | 8 | 28 | 318 | 0.8 | 189 | 100 | 209 | 2.6 | 320 | 206 | 5.1 | 1.1 |
| Cambodia | 14 | 181 | 80 | 7.0 | 123 | 490 | 180 | 22.1 | 1,550 | 174 | 10.8 | 9.0 |
| Cameroon | 18 | 475 | 39 | 18.1 | 87 | 990 | 154 | 37.4 | 2,060 | 163 | 3.8 | 1.6 |
| Canada | 33 | 9,985 | 4 | 1,196.6 | 9 | 36,650 | 22 | 1,184.4 | 36,280 | 16 | 2.8 | 1.7 |
| Central African Republic | 4 | 623 | 7 | 1.5 | 173 | 350 | 188 | 2.9 | 690 | 196 | 4.1 | 2.3 |
| Chad | 10 | 1,284 | 8 | 4.7 | 137 | 450 | 182 | 12.3 | 1,170 | 181 | 0.5 | −2.6 |
| Chile | 16 | 757 | 22 | 111.9 | 46 | 6,810 | 76 | 185.6 | 11,300 | 80 | 4.0 | 3.1 |
| China | 1,312 | 9,635[e] | 141 | 2,621.0 | 4 | 2,000 | 130 | 6,119.1 | 4,660 | 133 | 10.7 | 10.1 |
| Hong Kong, China | 7 | 1 | 6,581 | 199.1 | 32 | 29,040 | 31 | 268.8 | 39,200 | 12 | 6.8 | 6.1 |
| Colombia | 46 | 1,142 | 41 | 142.0 | 39 | 3,120 | 108 | 279.2 | 6,130 | 114 | 6.8 | 5.3 |
| Congo, Dem. Rep. | 61 | 2,345 | 27 | 7.7 | 119 | 130 | 207 | 16.2 | 270 | 207 | 5.1 | 1.8 |
| Congo, Rep. | 4 | 342 | 11 | 3.8 | .. | 1,050 | .. | 8.7 | 2,420 | .. | 6.4 | 4.1 |
| Costa Rica | 4 | 51 | 86 | 21.9 | 82 | 4,980 | 90 | 40.6[d] | 9,220[d] | 91 | 8.2 | 6.4 |
| Côte d'Ivoire | 19 | 322 | 59 | 16.6 | 91 | 880 | 158 | 29.8 | 1,580 | 171 | 0.9 | −0.9 |
| Croatia | 4 | 57 | 79 | 41.4 | 62 | 9,310 | 65 | 61.5 | 13,850 | 72 | 4.8 | 4.8 |
| Cuba | 11 | 111 | 103 | .. | .. | ..[f] | .. | .. | .. | .. | 5.4 | 5.2 |
| Czech Republic | 10 | 79 | 133 | 131.4 | 40 | 12,790 | 56 | 214.9 | 20,920 | 55 | 6.1 | 5.7 |
| Denmark | 5 | 43 | 128 | 283.3 | 27 | 52,110 | 7 | 196.7 | 36,190 | 17 | 3.2 | 2.8 |
| Dominican Republic | 10 | 49 | 199 | 28.0 | 77 | 2,910 | 118 | 53.3[d] | 5,550[d] | 121 | 10.7 | 9.0 |
| Ecuador | 13 | 284 | 48 | 38.5 | 63 | 2,910 | 118 | 89.9 | 6,810 | 108 | 3.9 | 2.8 |
| Egypt, Arab Rep. | 74 | 1,001 | 75 | 100.9 | 50 | 1,360 | 143 | 366.5 | 4,940 | 128 | 6.8 | 4.9 |
| El Salvador | 7 | 21 | 326 | 18.1 | 86 | 2,680 | 121 | 37.9[d] | 5,610[d] | 120 | 4.2 | 2.7 |
| Eritrea | 5 | 118 | 46 | 0.9 | 183 | 190 | 202 | 3.2[d] | 680[d] | 198 | −1.0 | −4.5 |
| Estonia | 1 | 45 | 32 | 15.3 | 96 | 11,400 | 60 | 24.3 | 18,090 | 58 | 11.4 | 11.7 |
| Ethiopia | 77 | 1,104 | 77 | 12.9 | 101 | 170 | 204 | 49.0 | 630 | 200 | 9.0 | 6.2 |
| Finland | 5 | 338 | 17 | 217.8 | 29 | 41,360 | 16 | 174.7 | 33,170 | 30 | 5.5 | 5.1 |
| France | 61 | 552 | 111 | 2,306.7[g] | 6 | 36,560[g] | 24 | 1,974.9 | 32,240 | 34 | 2.0 | 1.4 |
| Gabon | 1 | 268 | 5 | 7.0 | 121 | 5,360 | 85 | 14.7 | 11,180 | 81 | 1.2 | −0.4 |
| Gambia, The | 2 | 11 | 166 | 0.5 | 194 | 290 | 196 | 1.8 | 1,110 | 186 | 4.5 | 1.6 |
| Georgia | 4 | 70 | 64 | 7.0 | 122 | 1,580 | 137 | 17.2 | 3,880 | 140 | 9.4 | 10.4 |
| Germany | 82 | 357 | 236 | 3,032.6 | 3 | 36,810 | 21 | 2,692.3 | 32,680 | 32 | 2.8 | 2.9 |
| Ghana | 23 | 239 | 101 | 11.8 | 103 | 510 | 177 | 28.4 | 1,240 | 179 | 6.2 | 4.0 |
| Greece | 11 | 132 | 86 | 305.3 | 26 | 27,390 | 34 | 344.1 | 30,870 | 36 | 4.3 | 3.9 |
| Guatemala | 13 | 109 | 120 | 33.7 | 67 | 2,590 | 123 | 66.7[d] | 5,120[d] | 124 | 4.5 | 1.9 |
| Guinea | 9 | 246 | 37 | 3.7 | 147 | 400 | 186 | 10.4 | 1,130 | 184 | 2.8 | 0.8 |
| Guinea-Bissau | 2 | 36 | 59 | 0.3 | 203 | 190 | 202 | 0.8 | 460 | 205 | 4.2 | 1.1 |
| Haiti | 9 | 28 | 343 | 4.0 | 144 | 430 | 185 | 10.1[d] | 1,070[d] | 187 | 2.3 | 0.7 |

| | Population | Surface area | Population density | Gross national income | | Gross national income per capita | | PPP gross national income[a] | | | Gross domestic product | |
|---|---|---|---|---|---|---|---|---|---|---|---|---|
| | millions 2006 | thousand sq. km 2006 | people per sq. km 2006 | $ billions 2006[b] | Rank 2005 | $ 2006[b] | Rank 2006 | $ billions 2006 | Per capita $ 2006 | Rank 2006 | % growth 2005–06 | Per capita % growth 2005–06 |
| Honduras | 7 | 112 | 62 | 8.8 | 113 | 1,270 | 146 | 23.9[d] | 3,420[d] | 147 | 6.0 | 4.0 |
| Hungary | 10 | 93 | 112 | 109.5 | 47 | 10,870 | 62 | 170.8 | 16,970 | 61 | 3.9 | 4.1 |
| India | 1,110 | 3,287 | 373 | 909.1 | 10 | 820 | 161 | 2,726.3 | 2,460 | 155 | 9.2 | 7.7 |
| Indonesia | 223 | 1,905 | 123 | 315.9 | 24 | 1,420 | 140 | 737.2 | 3,310 | 149 | 5.5 | 4.3 |
| Iran, Islamic Rep. | 70 | 1,745 | 43 | 205.0 | 30 | 2,930 | 116 | 686.9 | 9,800 | 87 | 4.6 | 3.1 |
| Iraq | .. | 438 | .. | | | ..[f] | | .. | .. | .. | 46.5 | .. |
| Ireland | 4 | 70 | 62 | 191.3 | 34 | 44,830 | 10 | 148.2 | 34,730 | 19 | 5.7 | 3.0 |
| Israel | 7 | 22 | 326 | 142.2 | 38 | 20,170 | 44 | 168.1 | 23,840 | 49 | 5.1 | 3.2 |
| Italy | 59 | 301 | 200 | 1,882.5 | 7 | 31,990 | 28 | 1,704.9 | 28,970 | 38 | 1.9 | 1.5 |
| Jamaica | 3 | 11 | 246 | 9.5 | 107 | 3,560 | 104 | 18.8[d] | 7,050[d] | 107 | 2.5 | 2.0 |
| Japan | 128 | 378 | 350 | 4,934.7 | 2 | 38,630 | 19 | 4,195.9 | 32,840 | 31 | 2.2 | 2.2 |
| Jordan | 6 | 89 | 63 | 14.7 | 99 | 2,650 | 122 | 26.7 | 4,820 | 129 | 5.7 | 3.3 |
| Kazakhstan | 15 | 2,725 | 6 | 59.2 | 57 | 3,870 | 99 | 133.2 | 8,700 | 96 | 10.7 | 9.5 |
| Kenya | 37 | 580 | 64 | 21.3 | 83 | 580 | 175 | 53.8 | 1,470 | 176 | 6.1 | 3.3 |
| Korea, Dem. Rep. | 24 | 121 | 197 | .. | .. | ..[c] | .. | .. | .. | .. | .. | .. |
| Korea, Rep. | 48 | 99 | 490 | 856.6 | 12 | 17,690 | 51 | 1,113.0 | 22,990 | 50 | 5.0 | 4.7 |
| Kuwait | 3 | 18 | 146 | 77.7 | | 30,630 | .. | 122.5 | 48,310 | .. | 8.5 | 5.3 |
| Kyrgyz Republic | 5 | 200 | 27 | 2.6 | 157 | 500 | 178 | 9.3 | 1,790 | 167 | 2.7 | 1.7 |
| Lao PDR | 6 | 237 | 25 | 2.9 | 155 | 500 | 178 | 10.0 | 1,740 | 169 | 7.6 | 5.8 |
| Latvia | 2 | 65 | 37 | 18.5 | 85 | 8,100 | 71 | 33.9 | 14,840 | 67 | 11.9 | 12.6 |
| Lebanon | 4 | 10 | 396 | 22.6 | 81 | 5,580 | 80 | 38.9 | 9,600 | 89 | 0.0 | −1.1 |
| Lesotho | 2 | 30 | 66 | 2.0 | 167 | 980 | 155 | 3.6 | 1,810 | 166 | 7.2 | 6.4 |
| Liberia | 4 | 111 | 37 | 0.5 | 195 | 130 | 207 | 0.9 | 260 | 208 | 7.8 | 3.7 |
| Libya | 6 | 1,760 | 3 | 44.0 | 61 | 7,290 | 75 | 70.2[d] | 11,630[d] | 79 | 5.6 | 3.5 |
| Lithuania | 3 | 65 | 54 | 26.9 | 78 | 7,930 | 73 | 49.4 | 14,550 | 68 | 7.7 | 8.3 |
| Macedonia, FYR | 2 | 26 | 80 | 6.3 | 128 | 3,070 | 109 | 16.0 | 7,850 | 102 | 3.0 | 2.9 |
| Madagascar | 19 | 587 | 33 | 5.3 | 134 | 280 | 197 | 16.6 | 870 | 193 | 4.9 | 2.1 |
| Malawi | 14 | 118 | 144 | 3.1 | 152 | 230 | 201 | 9.4 | 690 | 196 | 7.4 | 4.7 |
| Malaysia | 26 | 330 | 79 | 146.8 | 37 | 5,620 | 79 | 317.4 | 12,160 | 75 | 5.9 | 4.0 |
| Mali | 12 | 1,240 | 10 | 5.6 | 133 | 460 | 181 | 11.9 | 1,000 | 189 | 5.3 | 2.2 |
| Mauritania | 3 | 1,031 | 3 | 2.3 | 163 | 760 | 165 | 6.0 | 1,970 | 164 | 11.7 | 8.7 |
| Mauritius | 1 | 2 | 617 | 6.8 | 124 | 5,430 | 82 | 13.3 | 10,640 | 83 | 3.5 | 2.7 |
| Mexico | 104 | 1,964 | 54 | 815.7 | 14 | 7,830 | 74 | 1,249.2 | 11,990 | 76 | 4.8 | 3.6 |
| Moldova | 4 | 34 | 117 | 3.7[h] | 149 | 1,080[h] | 151 | 10.2 | 2,660 | 152 | 4.0 | 5.2 |
| Mongolia | 3 | 1,567 | 2 | 2.6 | 158 | 1,000[i] | 153 | 7.3 | 2,810 | 150 | 8.6 | 7.3 |
| Morocco | 30 | 447 | 68 | 65.8 | 56 | 2,160 | 128 | 117.7 | 3,860 | 141 | 8.0 | 6.7 |
| Mozambique | 21 | 799 | 27 | 6.5 | 126 | 310 | 193 | 13.9 | 660 | 199 | 8.0 | 5.7 |
| Myanmar | 48 | 677 | 74 | .. | .. | ..[c] | .. | .. | .. | .. | 5.0 | 4.1 |
| Namibia | 2 | 824 | 2 | 6.6 | 125 | 3,210 | 107 | 9.8 | 4,770 | 130 | 2.9 | 1.6 |
| Nepal | 28 | 147 | 193 | 8.8 | 114 | 320 | 192 | 27.8 | 1,010 | 188 | 2.8 | 0.8 |
| Netherlands | 16 | 42 | 482 | 703.5 | 16 | 43,050 | 13 | 620.0 | 37,940 | 15 | 2.9 | 2.7 |
| New Zealand | 4 | 268 | 16 | 112.0 | 45 | 26,750 | 37 | 107.7 | 25,750 | 44 | 1.9 | 0.7 |
| Nicaragua | 6 | 130 | 46 | 5.2 | 135 | 930 | 156 | 15.1[d] | 2,720[d] | 151 | 3.7 | 2.4 |
| Niger | 14 | 1,267 | 11 | 3.7 | 148 | 270 | 198 | 8.6 | 630 | 200 | 4.8 | 1.2 |
| Nigeria | 145 | 924 | 159 | 90.0 | 52 | 620 | 173 | 203.7 | 1,410 | 177 | 5.2 | 2.8 |
| Norway | 5 | 324 | 15 | 318.9 | 23 | 68,440 | 2 | 233.3 | 50,070 | 4 | 2.9 | 2.1 |
| Oman | 3 | 310 | 8 | 27.9 | .. | 11,120[j] | .. | 49.5 | 19,740 | .. | 5.8 | 4.6 |
| Pakistan | 159 | 796 | 206 | 126.7 | 42 | 800 | 162 | 382.8 | 2,410 | 156 | 6.9 | 4.7 |
| Panama | 3 | 76 | 44 | 16.4 | 93 | 5,000 | 89 | 28.6[d] | 8,690[d] | 98 | 8.1 | 6.3 |
| Papua New Guinea | 6 | 463 | 14 | 4.6 | 141 | 740 | 168 | 10.1[d] | 1,630[d] | 170 | 2.6 | 0.4 |
| Paraguay | 6 | 407 | 15 | 8.5 | 115 | 1,410 | 141 | 24.3 | 4,040 | 137 | 4.3 | 2.2 |
| Peru | 28 | 1,285 | 22 | 82.2 | 54 | 2,980 | 113 | 179.2 | 6,490 | 110 | 7.7 | 6.5 |
| Philippines | 86 | 300 | 289 | 120.2 | 44 | 1,390 | 142 | 296.2 | 3,430 | 146 | 5.4 | 3.4 |
| Poland | 38 | 313 | 124 | 313.0 | 25 | 8,210 | 70 | 543.4 | 14,250 | 71 | 6.1 | 6.2 |
| Portugal | 11 | 92 | 116 | 189.0 | 35 | 17,850 | 50 | 211.3 | 19,960 | 57 | 1.3 | 0.9 |
| Puerto Rico | 4 | 9 | 443 | .. | .. | ..[k] | .. | .. | .. | .. | .. | .. |

# 1.1 Size of the economy

| | Population | Surface area | Population density | Gross national income | | Gross national income per capita | | PPP gross national income[a] | | | Gross domestic product | |
|---|---|---|---|---|---|---|---|---|---|---|---|---|
| | millions 2006 | thousand sq. km 2006 | people per sq. km 2006 | $ billions 2006[b] | Rank 2005 | $ 2006[b] | Rank 2006 | $ billions 2006 | Per capita $ 2006 | Rank 2006 | % growth 2005–06 | Per capita % growth 2005–06 |
| Romania | 22 | 238 | 94 | 104.4 | 48 | 4,830 | 91 | 219.2 | 10,150 | 85 | 7.7 | 7.9 |
| Russian Federation | 143 | 17,098 | 9 | 822.3 | 13 | 5,770 | 78 | 1,814.9 | 12,740 | 74 | 6.7 | 7.2 |
| Rwanda | 9 | 26 | 384 | 2.3 | 162 | 250 | 199 | 6.9 | 730 | 195 | 5.3 | 2.7 |
| Saudi Arabia | 24 | 2,000[l] | 12 | 331.0 | 21 | 13,980 | 55 | 528.0 | 22,300 | 52 | 4.3 | 1.8 |
| Senegal | 12 | 197 | 63 | 9.1 | 110 | 760 | 165 | 18.8 | 1,560 | 172 | 2.3 | −0.3 |
| Serbia | 7[m] | 88 | 96[m] | 30.0[m] | 75 | 4,030[m] | 97 | 69.3 | 9,320 | 90 | 5.7 | 5.8 |
| Sierra Leone | 6 | 72 | 80 | 1.4 | 175 | 240 | 200 | 3.5 | 610 | 202 | 7.4 | 4.4 |
| Singapore | 4 | 1 | 6,508 | 128.8 | 41 | 28,730 | 33 | 194.1 | 43,300 | 9 | 7.9 | 4.5 |
| Slovak Republic | 5 | 49 | 112 | 51.8 | 60 | 9,610 | 64 | 91.9 | 17,060 | 60 | 8.3 | 8.2 |
| Slovenia | 2 | 20 | 100 | 37.4 | 64 | 18,660 | 49 | 48.1 | 23,970 | 48 | 5.2 | 4.9 |
| Somalia | 8 | 638 | 13 | .. | .. | ..[c] | .. | .. | .. | .. | .. | .. |
| South Africa | 47 | 1,219 | 39 | 255.4 | 28 | 5,390 | 84 | 421.7 | 8,900 | 94 | 5.0 | 3.9 |
| Spain | 44 | 505 | 88 | 1,206.2 | 8 | 27,340 | 35 | 1,244.2 | 28,200 | 39 | 3.9 | 2.2 |
| Sri Lanka | 20 | 66 | 308 | 26.0 | 79 | 1,310 | 144 | 74.2 | 3,730 | 143 | 7.4 | 6.2 |
| Sudan | 38 | 2,506 | 16 | 30.1 | 74 | 800 | 162 | 67.2 | 1,780 | 168 | 11.8 | 9.4 |
| Swaziland | 1 | 17 | 66 | 2.7 | 156 | 2,400 | 124 | 5.3 | 4,700 | 132 | 2.1 | 1.5 |
| Sweden | 9 | 450 | 22 | 395.4 | 19 | 43,530 | 12 | 311.7 | 34,310 | 20 | 4.2 | 3.5 |
| Switzerland | 7 | 41 | 187 | 434.8 | 17 | 58,050 | 6 | 305.9 | 40,840 | 11 | 3.2 | 2.5 |
| Syrian Arab Republic | 19 | 185 | 106 | 30.3 | 72 | 1,560 | 138 | 79.7 | 4,110 | 136 | 5.1 | 2.3 |
| Tajikistan | 7 | 143 | 47 | 2.6 | 159 | 390 | 187 | 10.3 | 1,560 | 172 | 7.0 | 5.6 |
| Tanzania | 39 | 947 | 45 | 13.4[n] | 100 | 350[n] | 188 | 38.8 | 980 | 190 | 5.9 | 3.3 |
| Thailand | 63 | 513 | 124 | 193.7 | 33 | 3,050 | 110 | 472.2 | 7,440 | 104 | 5.0 | 4.3 |
| Timor-Leste | 1 | 15 | 69 | 0.9 | 185 | 840 | 160 | 5.2[d] | 5,100[d] | 125 | −1.6 | −6.7 |
| Togo | 6 | 57 | 118 | 2.3 | 165 | 350 | 188 | 4.9 | 770 | 194 | 4.1 | 1.3 |
| Trinidad and Tobago | 1 | 5 | 259 | 16.6 | 90 | 12,500 | 57 | 22.3[d] | 16,800[d] | 62 | 12.0 | 11.6 |
| Tunisia | 10 | 164 | 65 | 30.1 | 73 | 2,970 | 115 | 65.7 | 6,490 | 110 | 5.2 | 4.2 |
| Turkey | 73 | 784 | 95 | 393.9 | 20 | 5,400 | 83 | 613.7 | 8,410 | 99 | 6.1 | 4.8 |
| Turkmenistan | 5 | 488 | 10 | .. | .. | ..[f] | .. | 19.3[d] | 3,990[d] | .. | .. | .. |
| Uganda | 30 | 241 | 152 | 9.0 | 112 | 300 | 195 | 26.3 | 880 | 192 | 5.4 | 2.1 |
| Ukraine | 47 | 604 | 81 | 90.7 | 51 | 1,940 | 132 | 286.0 | 6,110 | 115 | 7.1 | 7.8 |
| United Arab Emirates | 4 | 84 | 51 | 103.5 | .. | 26,210 | .. | 123.1[d] | 31,190[d] | .. | 8.5 | 4.3 |
| United Kingdom | 61 | 244 | 250 | 2,455.7 | 5 | 40,560 | 17 | 2,037.2 | 33,650 | 29 | 2.8 | 2.2 |
| United States | 299 | 9,632 | 33 | 13,386.6 | 1 | 44,710 | 11 | 13,195.7 | 44,070 | 8 | 2.9 | 1.9 |
| Uruguay | 3 | 176 | 19 | 17.6 | 89 | 5,310 | 86 | 32.9 | 9,940 | 86 | 7.0 | 6.7 |
| Uzbekistan | 27 | 447 | 62 | 16.2 | 94 | 610 | 174 | 58.1[d] | 2,190[d] | 159 | 7.3 | 5.8 |
| Venezuela, RB | 27 | 912 | 31 | 164.0 | 36 | 6,070 | 77 | 296.4 | 10,970 | 82 | 10.3 | 8.5 |
| Vietnam | 84 | 329 | 271 | 58.5 | 58 | 700 | 169 | 194.4 | 2,310 | 157 | 8.2 | 6.9 |
| West Bank and Gaza | 4 | 6 | 627 | 4.5 | .. | 1,230 | .. | 14.0[d] | 3,720[d] | 144 | 1.4 | −2.6 |
| Yemen, Rep. | 22 | 528 | 41 | 16.4 | 92 | 760 | 165 | 45.5 | 2,090 | 162 | 3.3 | 0.3 |
| Zambia | 12 | 753 | 16 | 7.4 | 120 | 630 | 172 | 13.4 | 1,140 | 182 | 6.2 | 4.2 |
| Zimbabwe | 13 | 391 | 34 | 4.5 | .. | 340 | .. | 2.2 | 170 | .. | −5.3 | −6.0 |
| **World** | **6,538 s** | **133,946 s** | **50 w** | **48,694.1 t** | | **7,448 w** | | **60,210 t** | **9,209 w** | | **3.8 w** | **2.6 w** |
| **Low income** | 2,420 | 29,220 | 86 | 1,570.8 | | 649 | | 4,501 | 1,860 | | 8.0 | 6.1 |
| **Middle income** | 3,088 | 70,112 | 45 | 9,426.9 | | 3,053 | | 19,920 | 6,451 | | 7.2 | 6.3 |
| Lower middle income | 2,276 | 28,646 | 81 | 4,639.8 | | 2,038 | | 11,152 | 4,899 | | 8.8 | 7.9 |
| Upper middle income | 811 | 41,466 | 20 | 4,797.3 | | 5,913 | | 8,826 | 10,879 | | 5.7 | 4.9 |
| **Low & middle income** | 5,507 | 99,332 | 57 | 10,997.7 | | 1,997 | | 24,430 | 4,436 | | 7.3 | 6.0 |
| East Asia & Pacific | 1,899 | 16,300 | 120 | 3,524.7 | | 1,856 | | 8,277 | 4,359 | | 9.4 | 8.6 |
| Europe & Central Asia | 461 | 24,114 | 20 | 2,217.1 | | 4,815 | | 4,509 | 9,791 | | 6.8 | 6.7 |
| Latin America & Carib. | 556 | 20,421 | 28 | 2,661.2 | | 4,785 | | 4,828 | 8,682 | | 5.5 | 4.2 |
| Middle East & N. Africa | 311 | 9,087 | 35 | 778.8 | | 2,507 | | 2,084 | 6,710 | | 5.1 | 3.3 |
| South Asia | 1,499 | 5,140 | 314 | 1,151.3 | | 768 | | 3,432 | 2,289 | | 8.7 | 7.0 |
| Sub-Saharan Africa | 782 | 24,270 | 33 | 647.9 | | 829 | | 1,314 | 1,681 | | 5.6 | 3.0 |
| **High income** | 1,031 | 34,614 | 31 | 37,731.7 | | 36,608 | | 36,005 | 34,933 | | 2.9 | 2.2 |
| Euro area | 317 | 2,536 | 128 | 10,864.1 | | 34,307 | | 9,874 | 31,181 | | 2.7 | 2.2 |

a. PPP is purchasing power parity; see *Definitions*. b. Calculated using the *World Bank Atlas* method. c. Estimated to be low income ($905 or less). d. Based on regression; others are extrapolated from the 2005 International Comparison Program benchmark estimates. e. Includes Taiwan, China; Macao, China; and Hong Kong, China. f. Estimated to be lower middle income ($906–$3,595). g. Includes the French overseas departments of French Guiana, Guadeloupe, Martinique, and Réunion. h. Excludes Transnistria. i. Included in the aggregates for low-income economies based on earlier data. j. Included in the aggregates for upper middle-income economies based on earlier data. k. Estimated to be high income ($11,116 or more). l. Provisional estimate. m. Excludes Kosovo and Metohija. n. Covers mainland Tanzania only.

# Size of the economy | 1.1

## About the data

Population, land area, income, output, and growth in output are basic measures of the size of an economy. They also provide a broad indication of actual and potential resources. Population, land area, income (as measured by gross national income, GNI) and output (as measured by gross domestic product, GDP) are therefore used throughout *World Development Indicators* to normalize other indicators.

Population estimates are generally based on extrapolations from the most recent national census. For further discussion of the measurement of population and population growth, see *About the data* for table 2.1 and *Statistical methods*.

The surface area of an economy includes inland bodies of water and some coastal waterways. Surface area thus differs from land area, which excludes bodies of water, and from gross area, which may include offshore territorial waters. Land area is particularly important for understanding an economy's agricultural capacity and the environmental effects of human activity. (For measures of land area and data on rural population density, land use, and agricultural productivity, see tables 3.1–3.3.) Innovations in satellite mapping and computer databases have resulted in more precise measurements of land and water areas.

GNI measures total domestic and foreign value added claimed by residents. GNI comprises GDP plus net receipts of primary income (compensation of employees and property income) from nonresident sources. The World Bank uses GNI per capita in U.S. dollars to classify countries for analytical purposes and to determine borrowing eligibility. For definitions of the income groups in *World Development Indicators,* see *Users guide.* For discussion of the usefulness of national income and output as measures of productivity or welfare, see *About the data* for tables 4.1 and 4.2.

When calculating GNI in U.S. dollars from GNI reported in national currencies, the World Bank follows the *World Bank Atlas* conversion method, using a three-year average of exchange rates to smooth the effects of transitory fluctuations in exchange rates. (For further discussion of the *World Bank Atlas* method, see *Statistical methods*.) GDP and GDP per capita growth rates are calculated from data in constant prices and national currency units.

Because exchange rates do not always reflect differences in price levels between countries, the table also converts GNI and GNI per capita estimates into international dollars using purchasing power parity (PPP) rates. PPP rates provide a standard measure allowing comparison of real levels of expenditure between countries, just as conventional price indexes allow comparison of real values over time. The PPP conversion factors used are derived from the 2005 round of price surveys covering 146 economies conducted by the International Comparison Program. For Organisation for Economic Co-operation and Development (OECD) countries data come from the most recent round of surveys, completed in 2005. Estimates for economies not included in the surveys are derived from statistical models using available data.

For more information on the results of the 2005 International Comparison Program, see the introduction to *World View*. The final report of the program is available at www.worldbank.org/data/icp.

All 209 economies shown in *World Development Indicators* are ranked by size, including those that appear in table 1.6. The ranks are shown only in table 1.1. No rank is shown for economies for which numerical estimates of GNI per capita are not published. Economies with missing data are included in the ranking at their approximate level, so that the relative order of other economies remains consistent.

## Definitions

• **Population** is based on the de facto definition of population, which counts all residents regardless of legal status or citizenship—except for refugees not permanently settled in the country of asylum, who are generally considered part of the population of their country of origin. The values shown are midyear estimates. See also table 2.1. • **Surface area** is a country's total area, including areas under inland bodies of water and some coastal waterways. • **Population density** is midyear population divided by land area in square kilometers. • **Gross national income (GNI)** is the sum of value added by all resident producers plus any product taxes (less subsidies) not included in the valuation of output plus net receipts of primary income (compensation of employees and property income) from abroad. Data are in current U.S. dollars converted using the *World Bank Atlas* method (see *Statistical methods*). • **GNI per capita** is GNI divided by midyear population. GNI per capita in U.S. dollars is converted using the *World Bank Atlas* method. • **Purchasing power parity (PPP) GNI** is GNI converted to international dollars using PPP rates. An international dollar has the same purchasing power over GNI that a U.S. dollar has in the United States. • **Gross domestic product (GDP)** is the sum of value added by all resident producers plus any product taxes (less subsidies) not included in the valuation of output. Growth is calculated from constant price GDP data in local currency. • **GDP per capita** is GDP divided by midyear population.

## Data sources

Population estimates are prepared by World Bank staff from a variety of sources (see *Data sources* for table 2.1). Data on surface and land area are from the Food and Agriculture Organization (see *Data sources* for table 3.1). GNI, GNI per capita, GDP growth, and GDP per capita growth are estimated by World Bank staff based on national accounts data collected by World Bank staff during economic missions or reported by national statistical offices to other international organizations such as the OECD. PPP conversion factors are estimates by World Bank staff based on data collected by the International Comparison Program.

# 1.2 | Millennium Development Goals: eradicating poverty and saving lives

| | Eradicate extreme poverty and hunger | | | | | Achieve universal primary education | | Promote gender equality | | Reduce child mortality | |
|---|---|---|---|---|---|---|---|---|---|---|---|
| | Share of poorest quintile in national consumption or income % 1992–2005[b,c] | Vulnerable employment Unpaid family workers % of total employment | | Prevalence of malnutrition Underweight % of children under age 5 | | Primary completion rate[a] % | | Ratio of girls to boys enrollments in primary and secondary school[a] % | | Under-five mortality rate per 1,000 | |
| | | 1990 | 2005 | 1990 | 2000–06[b] | 1991 | 2006[d] | 1991 | 2006[d] | 1990 | 2006 |
| Afghanistan | .. | .. | .. | .. | .. | .. | .. | 54 | 56 | .. | .. |
| Albania | 8.2 | .. | .. | .. | 17.0 | .. | 96 | 96 | 97 | 45 | 17 |
| Algeria | 7.0 | .. | 29 | .. | 10.2 | 80 | 85 | 83 | 99 | 69 | 38 |
| Angola | .. | .. | .. | .. | 27.5 | 35 | .. | .. | .. | 260 | 260 |
| Argentina | 3.1[e] | .. | 21 | .. | 2.3 | .. | 99 | .. | 104 | 29 | 16 |
| Armenia | 8.5 | .. | .. | .. | 4.2 | 90 | 91 | .. | 104 | 56 | 24 |
| Australia | 5.9 | 10 | 10 | .. | .. | .. | .. | 101 | 97 | 10 | 6 |
| Austria | 8.6 | .. | 9 | .. | .. | .. | 103 | 95 | 97 | 10 | 5 |
| Azerbaijan | 7.4 | .. | .. | .. | 14.0 | .. | 92 | 100 | 96 | 105 | 88 |
| Bangladesh | 8.8 | .. | 63 | .. | 39.2 | 49 | 72 | .. | 103 | 149 | 69 |
| Belarus | 8.8 | .. | .. | .. | .. | 94 | 95 | .. | 101 | 24 | 13 |
| Belgium | 8.5 | .. | 11 | .. | .. | 79 | .. | 101 | 98 | 10 | 4 |
| Benin | 7.4 | .. | .. | .. | 21.5 | 21 | 65 | 49 | 73 | 185 | 148 |
| Bolivia | 1.5 | 40 | 62 | 8.9 | 5.9 | .. | 101 | .. | 98 | 125 | 61 |
| Bosnia and Herzegovina | 7.0 | .. | .. | .. | 4.2 | .. | .. | .. | .. | 22 | 15 |
| Botswana | 3.2 | .. | 12 | .. | 10.7 | 89 | 95 | 109 | 100 | 58 | 124 |
| Brazil | 2.9 | 29 | 29 | .. | 3.7 | 93 | 105 | .. | 102 | 57 | 20 |
| Bulgaria | 8.7 | .. | 10 | .. | 1.6 | 84 | 99 | 99 | 97 | 19 | 14 |
| Burkina Faso | 6.9 | .. | .. | .. | 35.2 | 20 | 31 | 62 | 80 | 206 | 204 |
| Burundi | 5.1 | .. | .. | .. | 38.9 | 46 | 36 | 82 | 89 | 190 | 181 |
| Cambodia | 6.8 | .. | 87 | .. | 28.4 | .. | 87 | 73 | 89 | 116 | 82 |
| Cameroon | 5.6 | .. | .. | .. | 15.1 | 53 | 58 | 83 | 84 | 139 | 149 |
| Canada | 7.2 | .. | .. | .. | .. | .. | .. | 99 | 98 | 8 | 6 |
| Central African Republic | 2.0 | .. | .. | .. | 21.8 | 27 | 24 | 60 | .. | 173 | 175 |
| Chad | .. | 94 | .. | .. | 33.9 | 18 | 31 | 42 | 61 | 201 | 209 |
| Chile | 3.8 | .. | 27 | .. | .. | .. | 123 | 100 | 98 | 21 | 9 |
| China | 4.3 | .. | .. | .. | 6.8 | 105 | .. | 87 | 100 | 45 | 24 |
|   Hong Kong, China | 5.3 | 5 | 8 | .. | .. | 102 | .. | 103 | .. | .. | .. |
| Colombia | 2.9 | 28 | 44 | .. | 5.1 | 70 | 105 | 108 | 104 | 35 | 21 |
| Congo, Dem. Rep. | .. | .. | .. | .. | 33.6 | 46 | 38 | .. | 73 | 205 | 205 |
| Congo, Rep. | .. | .. | .. | .. | 11.8 | 54 | 73 | 85 | 90 | 103 | 126 |
| Costa Rica | 4.1 | 25 | 21 | .. | .. | 79 | 89 | 101 | 102 | 18 | 12 |
| Côte d'Ivoire | 5.2 | .. | .. | .. | .. | 43 | 43 | 65 | .. | 153 | 127 |
| Croatia | 8.8 | .. | 19 | .. | .. | 85 | 92 | 102 | 101 | 12 | 6 |
| Cuba | .. | .. | .. | .. | .. | 99 | 92 | 106 | 100 | 13 | 7 |
| Czech Republic | 10.3 | 7 | 12 | .. | 2.1 | .. | 102 | 98 | 101 | 13 | 4 |
| Denmark | 8.3 | .. | .. | .. | .. | 98 | 99 | 101 | 102 | 9 | 5 |
| Dominican Republic | 4.1 | 39 | 43 | 8.4 | 4.2 | 61 | 83 | .. | 104 | 65 | 29 |
| Ecuador | 3.3 | 36 | 33 | .. | 6.2 | 91 | 106 | .. | 100 | 57 | 24 |
| Egypt, Arab Rep. | 8.9 | 28 | 26 | .. | 5.4 | .. | 98 | 81 | 93 | 91 | 35 |
| El Salvador | 2.7 | 35 | 36 | 7.2 | 6.1 | 41 | 88 | 102 | 99 | 60 | 25 |
| Eritrea | .. | .. | .. | .. | 34.5 | 19 | 48 | .. | 72 | 147 | 74 |
| Estonia | 6.8 | 2 | 5 | .. | .. | 93 | 106 | 103 | 100 | 16 | 7 |
| Ethiopia | 9.1 | .. | 91 | .. | 34.6 | 26 | 49 | 68 | 81 | 204 | 123 |
| Finland | 9.6 | .. | .. | .. | .. | 97 | 100 | 109 | 102 | 7 | 4 |
| France | 7.2 | .. | 7 | .. | .. | 104 | .. | 102 | 100 | 9 | 4 |
| Gabon | .. | 48 | .. | .. | 8.8 | 58 | 75 | .. | .. | 92 | 91 |
| Gambia, The | 4.8 | .. | .. | .. | 15.4 | 44 | 63 | 66 | 102 | 153 | 113 |
| Georgia | 5.4 | .. | 64 | .. | .. | .. | 85 | 98 | 103 | 46 | 32 |
| Germany | 8.5 | .. | 6 | .. | .. | 100 | 95 | 99 | 99 | 9 | 4 |
| Ghana | 5.6 | .. | .. | .. | 18.8 | 61 | 71 | 79 | 95[f] | 120 | 120 |
| Greece | 6.7 | 40 | 28 | .. | .. | 99 | 100 | 99 | 99 | 11 | 4 |
| Guatemala | 3.9 | .. | 55 | 27.8 | 17.7 | .. | 77 | .. | 92 | 82 | 41 |
| Guinea | 7.0 | .. | .. | .. | 22.5 | 17 | 64 | 45 | 74 | 235 | 161 |
| Guinea-Bissau | 5.2 | .. | .. | .. | 21.9 | .. | .. | .. | .. | 240 | 200 |
| Haiti | 2.4 | .. | .. | .. | 18.9 | 27 | .. | 94 | .. | 152 | 80 |

# Millennium Development Goals: eradicating poverty and saving lives

| | Eradicate extreme poverty and hunger | | | | | Achieve universal primary education | | Promote gender equality | | Reduce child mortality | |
|---|---|---|---|---|---|---|---|---|---|---|---|
| | Share of poorest quintile in national consumption or income % 1992–2005[b,c] | Vulnerable employment Unpaid family workers % of total employment | | Prevalence of malnutrition Underweight % of children under age 5 | | Primary completion rate[a] % | | Ratio of girls to boys enrollments in primary and secondary school[a] % | | Under-five mortality rate per 1,000 | |
| | | 1990 | 2005 | 1990 | 2000–06[b] | 1991 | 2006[d] | 1991 | 2006[d] | 1990 | 2006 |
| Honduras | 3.4 | 49 | 49 | .. | 8.6 | 64 | 89 | 106 | 109 | 58 | 27 |
| Hungary | 8.6 | 7 | 8 | 2.3 | .. | 93 | 94 | 100 | 99 | 17 | 7 |
| India | 8.1 | .. | .. | .. | 43.5 | 64 | 85 | 70 | 91 | 115 | 76 |
| Indonesia | 7.1 | .. | .. | 31.0 | 24.4 | 91 | 99 | 93 | 97 | 91 | 34 |
| Iran, Islamic Rep. | 6.5 | .. | .. | .. | .. | 91 | 101 | 85 | 105 | 72 | 34 |
| Iraq | .. | .. | .. | .. | .. | 59 | .. | 78 | 78 | 53 | .. |
| Ireland | 7.4 | 20 | 12 | .. | .. | .. | 97 | 104 | 103 | 9 | 5 |
| Israel | 5.7 | .. | 8 | .. | .. | .. | 101 | 105 | 100 | 12 | 5 |
| Italy | 6.5 | 16 | 13 | .. | .. | 104 | 100 | 100 | 99 | 9 | 4 |
| Jamaica | 5.3 | 42 | 34 | .. | 3.1 | 90 | 82 | 102 | 101 | 33 | 31 |
| Japan | 10.6 | 19 | 12 | .. | .. | 101 | .. | 101 | 100 | 6 | 4 |
| Jordan | 6.7 | .. | .. | .. | 3.6 | 72 | 100 | 101 | 102 | 40 | 25 |
| Kazakhstan | 7.4 | .. | 36 | .. | .. | .. | 101[f] | 102 | 99[f] | 60 | 29 |
| Kenya | 6.0 | .. | .. | 20.1 | 16.5 | .. | 93 | 94 | 96 | 97 | 121 |
| Korea, Dem. Rep. | .. | .. | .. | .. | 17.8 | .. | .. | .. | .. | 55 | 55 |
| Korea, Rep. | 7.9 | .. | 26 | .. | .. | 98 | 101 | 99 | 96 | 9 | 5 |
| Kuwait | .. | .. | .. | .. | .. | .. | 91 | 97 | 102 | 16 | 11 |
| Kyrgyz Republic | 8.9 | .. | 50 | .. | .. | .. | 99 | .. | 100 | 75 | 41 |
| Lao PDR | 8.1 | .. | .. | .. | 36.4 | 43 | 75 | 76 | 85 | 163 | 75 |
| Latvia | 6.8 | .. | 8 | .. | .. | .. | 92 | 101 | 99 | 18 | 9 |
| Lebanon | .. | .. | .. | .. | .. | .. | 80 | .. | 103 | 37 | 30 |
| Lesotho | 1.5 | 38 | .. | .. | 16.6 | 59 | 78 | 123 | 104 | 101 | 132 |
| Liberia | .. | .. | .. | .. | 22.8 | .. | 63 | .. | .. | 235 | 235 |
| Libya | .. | .. | .. | .. | .. | .. | .. | .. | 105 | 41 | 18 |
| Lithuania | 6.8 | .. | .. | .. | .. | 89 | 91 | .. | 100 | 13 | 8 |
| Macedonia, FYR | 6.1 | .. | 22 | .. | 1.2 | 98 | 97 | 99 | 99 | 38 | 17 |
| Madagascar | 4.9 | .. | 82 | 35.5 | 36.8 | 33 | 57 | 98 | 96 | 168 | 115 |
| Malawi | 7.0 | .. | .. | 24.4 | 18.4 | 29 | 55 | 81 | 100 | 221 | 120 |
| Malaysia | 4.4 | .. | 20 | .. | .. | 91 | 95 | 101 | 105 | 22 | 12 |
| Mali | 6.1 | .. | .. | 29.0 | 30.1 | 13 | 49 | 57 | 74 | 250 | 217 |
| Mauritania | 6.2 | .. | .. | .. | 30.4 | 34 | 47 | 71 | 102 | 133 | 125 |
| Mauritius | .. | .. | 17 | .. | .. | 107 | 92 | 102 | 103 | 23 | 14 |
| Mexico | 4.3 | 37 | 31 | 13.9 | 3.4 | 88 | 103 | 97 | 99 | 53 | 35 |
| Moldova | 7.8 | .. | 36 | .. | 3.2 | .. | 90 | 106 | 102 | 37 | 19 |
| Mongolia | 7.5 | .. | 60 | .. | 4.8 | .. | 109 | 109 | 108 | 109 | 43 |
| Morocco | 6.5 | .. | 58 | 8.1 | 9.9 | 48 | 84 | 70 | 87 | 89 | 37 |
| Mozambique | 5.4 | .. | .. | .. | 21.2 | 26 | 42 | 71 | 85 | 235 | 138 |
| Myanmar | .. | .. | .. | .. | 29.6 | .. | 95 | 97 | 101 | 130 | 104 |
| Namibia | 1.4 | .. | .. | .. | 20.3 | 78 | 76 | 106 | 104 | 86 | 61 |
| Nepal | 6.0 | .. | .. | .. | 38.8 | 51 | 76 | 59 | 93 | 142 | 59 |
| Netherlands | 7.6 | .. | .. | .. | .. | .. | 100 | 97 | 98 | 9 | 5 |
| New Zealand | 6.4 | 13 | 12 | .. | .. | 100 | .. | 100 | 104 | 11 | 6 |
| Nicaragua | 5.6 | .. | 38 | .. | 7.8 | 42 | 73 | 109 | 102 | 68 | 36 |
| Niger | 2.6 | .. | .. | 41.0 | 39.9 | 18 | 33 | 53 | 70 | 320 | 253 |
| Nigeria | 5.0 | .. | .. | 35.1 | 27.2 | .. | 76 | 77 | 83 | 230 | 191 |
| Norway | 9.6 | .. | .. | .. | .. | 100 | 99 | 102 | 101 | 9 | 4 |
| Oman | .. | .. | .. | .. | .. | 74 | 94 | 89 | 98 | 32 | 12 |
| Pakistan | 9.1 | .. | 61 | 39.0 | 31.3 | .. | 62 | .. | 78 | 130 | 97 |
| Panama | 2.5 | 34 | 32 | .. | .. | 86 | 94 | .. | 101 | 34 | 23 |
| Papua New Guinea | 4.5 | .. | .. | .. | .. | 46 | .. | 80 | .. | 94 | 73 |
| Paraguay | 2.4 | 23 | 50 | 2.8 | .. | 68 | 94 | 98 | 99 | 41 | 22 |
| Peru | 3.7 | 36 | 36 | 8.8 | 5.2 | .. | 100 | 96 | 101 | 78 | 25 |
| Philippines | 5.4 | .. | 45 | .. | 20.7 | 86 | 96 | 100 | 103 | 62 | 32 |
| Poland | 7.4 | 28 | 22 | .. | .. | 98 | 97 | 101 | 99 | 18 | 7 |
| Portugal | 5.8 | 19 | 19 | .. | .. | 95 | 104 | 103 | 102 | 14 | 5 |
| Puerto Rico | .. | .. | .. | .. | .. | .. | .. | .. | .. | .. | .. |

| | Eradicate extreme poverty and hunger | | | | | Achieve universal primary education | | Promote gender equality | | Reduce child mortality | |
|---|---|---|---|---|---|---|---|---|---|---|---|
| | Share of poorest quintile in national consumption or income % 1992–2005[b,c] | Vulnerable employment Unpaid family workers % of total employment | | Prevalence of malnutrition Underweight % of children under age 5 | | Primary completion rate[a] % | | Ratio of girls to boys enrollments in primary and secondary school[a] % | | Under-five mortality rate per 1,000 | |
| | | 1990 | 2005 | 1990 | 2000–06[b] | 1991 | 2006[d] | 1991 | 2006[d] | 1990 | 2006 |
| Romania | 8.2 | 27 | 33 | .. | 3.5 | 96 | 99 | 99 | 100 | 31 | 18 |
| Russian Federation | 6.1 | 1 | 6 | .. | .. | 93 | 94 | 104 | 99 | 27 | 16 |
| Rwanda | 5.3 | .. | .. | 24.3 | 18.0 | 35 | 35 | 92 | 102 | 176 | 160 |
| Saudi Arabia | .. | .. | .. | .. | .. | 55 | 85 | 84 | 95 | 44 | 25 |
| Senegal | 6.6 | 83 | .. | 21.9 | 14.5 | 39 | 49 | 69 | 91 | 149 | 116 |
| Serbia | 8.3[g] | .. | .. | .. | .. | .. | .. | .. | .. | .. | 8 |
| Sierra Leone | 6.5 | .. | .. | .. | 24.7 | .. | 81[f] | 67 | 86[f] | 290 | 270 |
| Singapore | 5.0 | 8 | 9 | .. | 3.3 | .. | .. | 95 | 101 | 8 | 3 |
| Slovak Republic | 8.8 | .. | 9 | .. | .. | 96 | 94 | .. | 100 | 14 | 8 |
| Slovenia | 8.3 | 12 | 11 | .. | .. | 95 | 99 | .. | 100 | 10 | 4 |
| Somalia | .. | .. | .. | .. | .. | .. | .. | .. | .. | 203 | 145 |
| South Africa | 3.5 | .. | 19 | .. | .. | 76 | 100 | 104 | 100 | 60 | 69 |
| Spain | 7.0 | 22 | 13 | .. | .. | .. | 103 | 104 | 103 | 9 | 4 |
| Sri Lanka | 7.0 | .. | 39 | 29.3 | 22.8 | 102 | 108 | 102 | 104 | 32 | 13 |
| Sudan | .. | .. | .. | .. | 38.4 | 42 | 47 | 77 | 89 | 120 | 89 |
| Swaziland | 4.3 | .. | .. | .. | 9.1 | 60 | 67 | 98 | 95 | 110 | 164 |
| Sweden | 9.1 | .. | .. | .. | .. | 96 | .. | 102 | 100 | 7 | 3 |
| Switzerland | 7.6 | 9 | 10 | .. | .. | 53 | 91 | 97 | 97 | 9 | 5 |
| Syrian Arab Republic | .. | .. | .. | .. | .. | 89 | 115 | 85 | 95 | 38 | 14 |
| Tajikistan | 7.8 | .. | .. | .. | .. | .. | 106 | .. | 88 | 115 | 68 |
| Tanzania | 7.3 | .. | .. | 25.1 | 16.7 | 62 | 85[f] | 97 | .. | 161 | 118 |
| Thailand | 6.3 | 70 | 53 | 17.4 | .. | .. | .. | 97 | 104 | 31 | 8 |
| Timor-Leste | .. | .. | .. | .. | 40.6 | .. | .. | .. | 95 | 177 | 55 |
| Togo | .. | .. | .. | 21.2 | .. | 35 | 67 | 59 | 73 | 149 | 108 |
| Trinidad and Tobago | 5.9 | 22 | 16 | 4.7 | 4.4 | 101 | 88 | 101 | 101 | 34 | 38 |
| Tunisia | 6.0 | .. | .. | 8.5 | .. | 74 | 99 | 86 | 104 | 52 | 23 |
| Turkey | 5.3 | .. | 41 | 8.7 | .. | 90 | 86 | 81 | 89 | 82 | 26 |
| Turkmenistan | 6.1 | .. | .. | .. | .. | .. | .. | .. | .. | 99 | 51 |
| Uganda | 5.7 | .. | 85 | 19.7 | 19.0 | .. | 54 | 82 | 98 | 160 | 134 |
| Ukraine | 9.0 | .. | .. | .. | 4.1 | 94 | 105 | .. | 99 | 25 | 24 |
| United Arab Emirates | .. | .. | .. | .. | .. | 103 | 100 | 104 | 101 | 15 | 8 |
| United Kingdom | 6.1 | .. | .. | .. | .. | .. | .. | 102 | 101 | 10 | 6 |
| United States | 5.4 | .. | .. | .. | 1.1 | .. | .. | 100 | 100 | 11 | 8 |
| Uruguay | 5.0[e] | .. | 25 | .. | 6.0 | 94 | 93 | .. | 106 | 23 | 12 |
| Uzbekistan | 7.2 | .. | .. | .. | .. | .. | 98 | 94 | 98[f] | 74 | 43 |
| Venezuela, RB | 3.3 | .. | 35 | .. | .. | 43 | 96 | 105 | 103 | 33 | 21 |
| Vietnam | 7.1 | .. | 74 | 36.9 | 26.7 | .. | 92 | .. | 97 | 53 | 17 |
| West Bank and Gaza | .. | .. | 38 | .. | .. | .. | 89 | .. | 104 | 40 | 22 |
| Yemen, Rep. | 7.2 | .. | .. | .. | .. | .. | 60 | .. | 66 | 139 | 100 |
| Zambia | 3.6 | 65 | 79 | 21.2 | 23.3 | .. | 84 | .. | 96 | 180 | 182 |
| Zimbabwe | 4.6 | .. | 62 | 8.0 | 14.0 | 97 | 81 | 92 | 96 | 76 | 105 |
| **World** | .. w | .. w | .. w | .. w | 23.5 w | 79 w | 86 w | 86 w | 95 w | 92 w | 73 w |
| **Low income** | .. | .. | | | 35.3 | 57 | 73 | 73 | 89 | 143 | 112 |
| **Middle income** | .. | .. | | | 9.5 | 93 | 97 | 91 | 99 | 56 | 33 |
| Lower middle income | .. | .. | | | 10.7 | 95 | 97 | 89 | 98 | 60 | 36 |
| Upper middle income | .. | .. | 24 | | .. | 88 | 99 | 99 | 100 | 47 | 26 |
| **Low & middle income** | .. | .. | | | 24.5 | 78 | 85 | 84 | 94 | 101 | 79 |
| East Asia & Pacific | .. | .. | | | 12.9 | 101 | 98 | 89 | 99 | 56 | 29 |
| Europe & Central Asia | .. | .. | 18 | | .. | 93 | 95 | 98 | 96 | 49 | 26 |
| Latin America & Carib. | .. | 36 | 32 | | 5.1 | 82 | 99 | 99 | 101 | 55 | 26 |
| Middle East & N. Africa | .. | .. | | | .. | 77 | 91 | 82 | 94 | 77 | 42 |
| South Asia | .. | .. | | | 41.0 | 62 | 80 | 70 | 90 | 123 | 83 |
| Sub-Saharan Africa | .. | .. | | | 27.0 | 51 | 60 | 79 | 86 | 184 | 157 |
| **High income** | .. | .. | | | .. | .. | 97 | 100 | 100 | 12 | 7 |
| Euro area | .. | .. | 12 | | .. | 100 | .. | 101 | .. | 9 | 4 |

a. Because of the change from International Standard Classification of Education 1976 (ISCED76) to ISCED97 in 1998, data before 1998 are not fully comparable with data from 1999 onward. b. Data are for the most recent year available. c. See table 2.8 for survey year and whether share is based on income or consumption expenditure. d. Provisional data. e. Urban data. f. Data are for 2007. g. Includes Montenegro.

# Millennium Development Goals: eradicating poverty and saving lives | 1.2

## About the data

This table and the two following present indicators for 17 of the 21 targets specified by the Millennium Development Goals. Each of the eight goals includes one or more targets, and each target has several associated indicators for monitoring progress toward the target. Most of the targets are set as a value of a specific indicator to be attained by a certain date. In some cases the target value is set relative to a level in 1990. In others it is set at an absolute level. Some of the targets for goals 7 and 8 have not yet been quantified.

The indicators in this table relate to goals 1–4. Goal 1 has three targets between 1990 and 2015: to reduce by half the proportion of people whose income is less than $1 a day, to achieve full and productive employment and decent work for all, and to reduce by half the proportion of people who suffer from hunger. Estimates of poverty rates are in table 2.7. The indicator shown here, the share of the poorest quintile in national consumption, is a distributional measure. Countries with more unequal distributions of consumption (or income) have a higher rate of poverty for a given average income. Vulnerable employment measures the portion of the labor force that receives the lowest wages and least security in employment. No single indicator captures the concept of suffering from hunger. Child malnutrition is a symptom of inadequate food supply, lack of essential nutrients, illnesses that deplete these nutrients, and

undernourished mothers who give birth to underweight children.

Progress toward universal primary education is measured by the primary completion rate. Because many school systems do not record school completion on a consistent basis, it is estimated from the gross enrollment rate in the final grade of primary school, adjusted for repetition. Official enrollments sometimes differ significantly from attendance, and even school systems with high average enrollment ratios may have poor completion rates.

Eliminating gender disparities in education would help to increase the status and capabilities of women. The ratio of female to male enrollments in primary and secondary school provides an imperfect measure of the relative accessibility of schooling for girls.

The targets for reducing under-five mortality rates are among the most challenging. Under-five mortality rates are harmonized estimates produced by a weighted least squares regression model and are available at regular intervals for most countries.

Most of the 60 indicators relating to the Millennium Development Goals can be found in World Development Indicators. Table 1.2a shows where to find the indicators for the first four goals. For more information about data collection methods and limitations, see About the data for the tables listed there. For information about the indicators for goals 5, 6, 7, and 8, see About the data for tables 1.3 and 1.4.

## Definitions

• **Share of poorest quintile in national consumption or income** is the share of the poorest 20 percent of the population in consumption or, in some cases, income. • **Vulnerable employment** is the sum of unpaid family workers and own-account workers as a percentage of total employment. • **Prevalence of malnutrition** is the percentage of children under age five whose weight for age is more than two standard deviations below the median for the international reference population ages 0–59 months. The data are based on the new international child growth standards for infants and young children, called the Child Growth Standards, released in 2006 by the World Health Organization. • **Primary completion rate** is the percentage of students completing the last year of primary school. It is calculated as the total number of students in the last grade of primary school, minus the number of repeaters in that grade, divided by the total number of children of official graduation age. • **Ratio of girls to boys enrollments in primary and secondary school** is the ratio of the female to male gross enrollment rate in primary and secondary school. • **Under-five mortality rate** is the probability that a newborn baby will die before reaching age five, if subject to current age-specific mortality rates. The probability is expressed as a rate per 1,000.

## Location of indicators for Millennium Development Goals 1–4 | 1.2a

**Goal 1. Eradicate extreme poverty and hunger**

| | |
|---|---|
| 1.1 Proportion of population below $1 a day | 2.7* |
| 1.2 Poverty gap ratio | 2.7 |
| 1.3 Share of poorest quintile in national consumption | 1.2, 2.8 |
| 1.4 Growth rate of GDP per person employed | 2.4* |
| 1.5 Employment to population ratio | 2.4 |
| 1.6 Proportion of employed people living below $1 per day | — |
| 1.7 Proportion of own-account and unpaid family workers in total employment | 1.2, 2.4 |
| 1.8 Prevalence of underweight in children under age five | 1.2, 2.18, 2.20 |
| 1.9 Proportion of population below minimum level of dietary energy consumption | 2.18 |

**Goal 2. Achieve universal primary education**

| | |
|---|---|
| 2.1 Net enrollment ratio in primary education | 2.11 |
| 2.2 Proportion of pupils starting grade 1 who reach last grade of primary | 2.12 |
| 2.3 Literacy rate of 15- to 24-year-olds | 2.13 |

**Goal 3. Promote gender equality and empower women**

| | |
|---|---|
| 3.1 Ratio of girls to boys in primary, secondary, and tertiary education | 1.2, 2.11* |
| 3.2 Share of women in wage employment in the nonagricultural sector | 1.5, 2.3* |
| 3.3 Proportion of seats held by women in national parliament | 1.5 |

**Goal 4. Reduce child mortality**

| | |
|---|---|
| 4.1 Under-five mortality rate | 1.2, 2.20, 2.21 |
| 4.2 Infant mortality rate | 2.20, 2.21 |
| 4.3 Proportion of one-year-old children immunized against measles | 2.16, 2.20 |

— No data are available in the World Development Indicators database. * Table shows information on related indicators.

## Data sources

The indicators here and throughout this book have been compiled by World Bank staff from primary and secondary sources. Data on primary school completion rates are provided by the United Nations Educational, Scientific, and Cultural Organization Institute of Statistics and national sources. Efforts have been made to harmonize the data series used to compile this table with those published on the United Nations Millennium Development Goals Web site (www.un.org/ millenniumgoals), but some differences in timing, sources, and definitions remain.

| | Improve maternal health | | Combat HIV/AIDS and other diseases | | Ensure environmental sustainability | | | | | Develop a global partnership for development |
|---|---|---|---|---|---|---|---|---|---|---|
| | Maternal mortality ratio Modeled estimate per 100,000 live births | Contraceptive prevalence rate % of married women ages 15–49 | HIV prevalence % of population ages 15–49 | Incidence of tuberculosis per 100,000 people | Carbon dioxide emissions per capita metric tons | | Proportion of species threatened with extinction % | Access to improved sanitation facilities % of population | | Fixed-line and mobile phone subscribers per 100 people[a] |
| | **2005** | **1990** **2000–06[b]** | **2005** | **2006** | **1990** | **2004** | **2007** | **1990** | **2004** | **2006** |
| Afghanistan | .. | .. .. | .. | .. | .. | .. | 0.8 | .. | .. | 10 |
| Albania | 92 | .. 60 | 0.2 | 19 | 2.2 | 1.2 | 1.3 | .. | 91 | 60 |
| Algeria | 180 | 47 61 | 0.1 | 56 | 3.0 | 6.0 | 2.0 | 88 | 92 | 71 |
| Angola | 1,400 | .. 6 | 3.7 | 285 | 0.4 | 0.5 | 1.4 | 29 | 31 | 14 |
| Argentina | 77 | .. .. | 0.6 | 39 | 3.4 | 3.7 | 1.8 | 81 | 91 | 105 |
| Armenia | 76 | .. 53 | 0.1 | 72 | 1.2 | 1.2 | 0.9 | .. | 83 | 30 |
| Australia | 4 | .. .. | 0.1 | 6 | 16.3 | 16.2 | 3.7 | 100 | 100 | 143 |
| Austria | 4 | .. .. | 0.3 | 13 | 7.5 | 8.5 | 1.8 | 100 | 100 | 155 |
| Azerbaijan | 82 | .. 55 | 0.1 | 77 | 7.5 | 3.8 | 0.8 | .. | 54 | 53 |
| Bangladesh | 570 | 40 58 | <0.1 | 225 | 0.1 | 0.2 | 1.8 | 20 | 39 | 13 |
| Belarus | 18 | .. 73 | 0.3 | 61 | 10.6 | 6.6 | .. | .. | 84 | 96 |
| Belgium | 8 | 78 .. | 0.3 | 13 | 10.1 | 9.7 | 1.4 | .. | .. | 136 |
| Benin | 840 | .. 17 | 1.8 | 90 | 0.1 | 0.3 | 1.5 | 12 | 33 | 13 |
| Bolivia | 290 | 30 58 | 0.1 | 198 | 0.8 | 0.8 | 0.8 | 33 | 46 | 36 |
| Bosnia and Herzegovina | 3 | .. 36 | <0.1 | 51 | 1.6 | 4.0 | 14.4 | .. | 95 | 73 |
| Botswana | 380 | 33 44 | 24.1 | 551 | 1.6 | 2.4 | 0.6 | 38 | 42 | 60 |
| Brazil | 110 | 59 .. | 0.5 | 50 | 1.4 | 1.8 | 1.2 | 71 | 75 | 73 |
| Bulgaria | 11 | .. .. | <0.1 | 40 | 8.6 | 5.5 | 1.2 | 99 | 99 | 138 |
| Burkina Faso | 700 | .. 17 | 2.0 | 248 | 0.1 | 0.1 | 0.9 | 7 | 13 | 8 |
| Burundi | 1,100 | .. 9 | 3.3 | 367 | 0.0 | 0.0 | 1.6 | 44 | 36 | 2 |
| Cambodia | 540 | .. 40 | 1.6 | 500 | 0.0 | 0.0 | 17.4 | .. | 17 | 8 |
| Cameroon | 1,000 | 16 29 | 5.5[c] | 192 | 0.1 | 0.2 | 5.4 | 48 | 51 | 13 |
| Canada | 7 | .. .. | 0.3 | 5 | 15.0 | 20.0 | 2.0 | 100 | 100 | 117 |
| Central African Republic | 980 | .. 19 | 10.7 | 345 | 0.1 | 0.1 | 0.7 | 23 | 27 | 3 |
| Chad | 1,500 | .. 3 | 3.5 | 299 | 0.0 | 0.0 | 1.0 | 7 | 9 | 5 |
| Chile | 16 | 56 .. | 0.3 | 15 | 2.7 | 3.9 | 2.3 | 84 | 91 | 96 |
| China | 45 | 85 87 | 0.1[d] | 99 | 2.1 | 3.9 | 2.3 | 23 | 44 | 63 |
| Hong Kong, China | .. | 86 .. | .. | 62 | 4.6 | 5.5 | 11.8 | .. | .. | 193 |
| Colombia | 130 | 66 78 | 0.6 | 45 | 1.7 | 1.2 | 1.1 | 82 | 86 | 83 |
| Congo, Dem. Rep. | 1,100 | 8 21[e] | 3.2 | 392 | 0.1 | 0.0 | 2.5 | 16 | 30 | 7 |
| Congo, Rep. | 740 | .. 44 | 5.3 | 403 | 0.5 | 1.0 | 1.1 | .. | 27 | 14 |
| Costa Rica | 30 | .. 96 | 0.3 | 14 | 0.9 | 1.5 | 1.8 | .. | 92 | 64 |
| Côte d'Ivoire | 810 | .. 13 | 7.1 | 420 | 0.4 | 0.3 | 3.9 | 21 | 37 | 23 |
| Croatia | 7 | .. 69 | <0.1 | 40 | 5.1 | 5.3 | 1.7 | 100 | 100 | 142 |
| Cuba | 45 | .. 73 | 0.1 | 9 | 3.0 | 2.3 | 4.0 | 98 | 98 | 10 |
| Czech Republic | 4 | 78 .. | 0.1 | 10 | 15.6 | 11.5 | 1.8 | 99 | 98 | 147 |
| Denmark | 3 | 78 .. | 0.2 | 8 | 9.7 | 9.8 | 1.6 | .. | .. | 164 |
| Dominican Republic | 150 | 56 61 | 1.1 | 89 | 1.3 | 2.1 | 1.9 | 52 | 78 | 57 |
| Ecuador | 210 | 53 73 | 0.3 | 128 | 1.6 | 2.3 | 10.3 | 63 | 89 | 78 |
| Egypt, Arab Rep. | 130 | 47 59 | <0.1 | 24 | 1.4 | 2.2 | 2.3 | 54 | 70 | 39 |
| El Salvador | 170 | 47 67 | 0.9 | 50 | 0.5 | 0.9 | 1.6 | 51 | 62 | 72 |
| Eritrea | 450 | .. 8 | 2.4 | 94 | .. | 0.2 | 6.8 | 7 | 9 | 2 |
| Estonia | 25 | .. .. | 1.3 | 39 | 18.1 | 14.0 | 0.7 | 97 | 97 | 164 |
| Ethiopia | 720 | 4 15 | 1.4[f] | 378 | 0.1 | 0.1 | 1.4 | 3 | 13 | 2 |
| Finland | 7 | 77 .. | 0.1 | 5 | 10.3 | 12.6 | 1.2 | 100 | 100 | 144 |
| France | 8 | 81 .. | 0.4 | 14 | 6.4 | 6.2 | 2.3 | .. | .. | 140 |
| Gabon | 520 | .. 33 | 7.9 | 354 | 6.5 | 1.1 | 2.0 | .. | 36 | 61 |
| Gambia, The | 690 | 12 18 | 2.4 | 257 | 0.2 | 0.2 | 2.1 | .. | 53 | 27 |
| Georgia | 66 | .. 47 | 0.2 | 84 | 3.2 | 0.9 | 1.0 | 97 | 94 | 51 |
| Germany | 4 | 75 .. | 0.1 | 6 | 12.3 | 9.8 | 2.2 | 100 | 100 | 168 |
| Ghana | 560 | 13 17 | 2.3 | 203 | 0.2 | 0.3 | 3.7 | 15 | 18 | 24 |
| Greece | 3 | .. .. | 0.2 | 18 | 7.1 | 8.7 | 1.9 | .. | .. | 155 |
| Guatemala | 290 | .. 43 | 0.9 | 79 | 0.6 | 1.0 | 2.3 | 58 | 86 | 65 |
| Guinea | 910 | .. 9 | 1.5 | 265 | 0.2 | 0.2 | 2.2 | 14 | 18 | 2 |
| Guinea-Bissau | 1,100 | .. 10 | 3.8 | 219 | 0.2 | 0.2 | 2.1 | .. | 35 | 7 |
| Haiti | 670 | 10 32 | 2.2[g] | 299 | 0.1 | 0.2 | 2.2 | 24 | 30 | 7 |

# Millennium Development Goals: protecting our common environment | 1.3

| | Improve maternal health | | Combat HIV/AIDS and other diseases | | Ensure environmental sustainability | | | | | Develop a global partnership for development |
|---|---|---|---|---|---|---|---|---|---|---|
| | Maternal mortality ratio Modeled estimate per 100,000 live births | Contraceptive prevalence rate % of married women ages 15–49 | | HIV prevalence % of population ages 15–49 | Incidence of tuberculosis per 100,000 people | Carbon dioxide emissions per capita metric tons | | Proportion of species threatened with extinction % | Access to improved sanitation facilities % of population | | Fixed-line and mobile phone subscribers per 100 people[a] |
| | 2005 | 1990 | 2000–06[b] | 2005 | 2006 | 1990 | 2004 | 2007 | 1990 | 2004 | 2006 |
| Honduras | 280 | 47 | 65 | 1.5 | 76 | 0.5 | 1.1 | 3.2 | 50 | 69 | 42 |
| Hungary | 6 | .. | .. | 0.1 | 19 | 5.8 | 5.7 | 2.1 | .. | 95 | 132 |
| India | 450 | 43 | 56 | 0.9 | 168 | 0.8 | 1.2 | 2.8 | 14 | 33 | 19 |
| Indonesia | 420 | 50 | 57 | 0.1 | 234 | 1.2 | 1.7 | 2.7 | 46 | 55 | 35 |
| Iran, Islamic Rep. | 140 | 49 | 74 | 0.2 | 22 | 4.0 | 6.4 | 0.9 | 83 | .. | 51 |
| Iraq | .. | 14 | .. | .. | .. | 2.6 | | 8.0 | 81 | .. | 6 |
| Ireland | 1 | 60 | .. | 0.2 | 13 | 8.7 | 10.4 | 1.1 | .. | .. | 159 |
| Israel | 4 | 68 | .. | 0.2 | 8 | 7.1 | 10.5 | 2.7 | .. | .. | 162 |
| Italy | 3 | .. | .. | 0.5 | 7 | 6.9 | 7.7 | 2.2 | .. | .. | 165 |
| Jamaica | 170 | 55 | 69 | 1.5 | 7 | 3.3 | 4.0 | 7.4 | 75 | 80 | 118 |
| Japan | 6 | 58 | 56 | <0.1 | 22 | 8.7 | 9.8 | 3.2 | 100 | 100 | 123 |
| Jordan | 62 | 40 | 56 | 0.2 | 5 | 3.2 | 3.1 | 1.7 | 93 | 93 | 90 |
| Kazakhstan | 140 | .. | 51 | 0.1 | 130 | 17.6 | 13.3 | 1.1 | 72 | 72 | 70 |
| Kenya | 560 | 27 | 39 | 6.1 | 384 | 0.2 | 0.3 | 3.4 | 40 | 43 | 19 |
| Korea, Dem. Rep. | 370 | 62 | .. | 0.2 | 178 | 12.1 | 3.4 | 1.4 | .. | 59 | .. |
| Korea, Rep. | 14 | 79 | .. | <0.1 | 88 | 5.6 | 9.7 | 1.6 | .. | .. | 139 |
| Kuwait | 4 | .. | .. | 0.2 | 24 | 20.4 | 40.4 | .. | .. | .. | 114 |
| Kyrgyz Republic | 150 | .. | 48 | 0.1 | 123 | 2.8 | 1.1 | 0.8 | 60 | 59 | 19 |
| Lao PDR | 660 | .. | 32 | 0.1 | 152 | 0.1 | 0.2 | 1.1 | .. | 30 | 13 |
| Latvia | 10 | .. | .. | 0.8 | 57 | 5.4 | 3.1 | 1.5 | .. | 78 | 124 |
| Lebanon | 150 | .. | 58 | 0.1 | 11 | 3.1 | 4.1 | 1.1 | .. | 98 | 44 |
| Lesotho | 960 | 23 | 37 | 23.4[c] | 635 | .. | .. | 0.6 | 37 | 37 | 15 |
| Liberia | 1,200 | .. | 10 | .. | 331 | 0.2 | 0.1 | 3.6 | 39 | 27 | .. |
| Libya | 97 | .. | .. | 0.2 | 18 | 8.7 | 10.3 | 1.4 | 97 | 97 | 73 |
| Lithuania | 11 | .. | .. | 0.2 | 62 | 6.6 | 3.9 | .. | .. | .. | 162 |
| Macedonia, FYR | 10 | .. | 14 | <0.1 | 29 | 8.1 | 5.1 | 0.9 | .. | .. | 94 |
| Madagascar | 510 | 17 | 27 | 0.5 | 248 | 0.1 | 0.2 | 5.5 | 14 | 32 | 6 |
| Malawi | 1,100 | 13 | 42 | 14.1 | 377 | 0.1 | 0.1 | 3.3 | 47 | 61 | 4 |
| Malaysia | 62 | 50 | .. | 0.5 | 103 | 3.1 | 7.0 | 5.5 | .. | 94 | 91 |
| Mali | 970 | .. | 8 | 1.7 | 280 | 0.1 | 0.1 | 1.1 | 36 | 46 | 13 |
| Mauritania | 820 | 3 | 8 | 0.7 | 316 | 1.4 | 0.9 | .. | 31 | 34 | 36 |
| Mauritius | 15 | 75 | 76 | 0.6 | 23 | 1.4 | 2.6 | 17.0 | .. | 94 | 90 |
| Mexico | 60 | .. | 71 | 0.3 | 21 | 5.0 | 4.3 | 3.0 | 58 | 79 | 74 |
| Moldova | 22 | .. | 68 | 1.1 | 141 | 5.4 | 2.0 | 1.4 | .. | 68 | 62 |
| Mongolia | 46 | .. | 66 | <0.1 | 188 | 4.7 | 3.4 | 1.1 | .. | 59 | 28 |
| Morocco | 240 | 42 | 63 | 0.1 | 93 | 1.0 | 1.4 | 1.8 | 56 | 73 | 57 |
| Mozambique | 520 | .. | 17 | 16.1 | 443 | 0.1 | 0.1 | 2.1 | 20 | 32 | 11 |
| Myanmar | 380 | 17 | 34 | 1.3 | 171 | 0.1 | 0.2 | 1.9 | 24 | 77 | 1 |
| Namibia | 210 | 29 | 44 | 19.6 | 767 | 0.0 | 1.2 | 2.0 | 24 | 25 | 31 |
| Nepal | 830 | 23 | 48 | 0.5 | 176 | 0.0 | 0.1 | 1.1 | 11 | 35 | 6 |
| Netherlands | 6 | 76 | .. | 0.2 | 8 | 9.4 | 8.7 | 1.5 | 100 | 100 | 144 |
| New Zealand | 9 | .. | .. | 0.1 | 9 | 6.6 | 7.7 | 5.2 | .. | .. | 127 |
| Nicaragua | 170 | .. | 69 | 0.2 | 58 | 0.6 | 0.7 | 1.2 | 45 | 47 | 38 |
| Niger | 1,800 | 4 | 11 | 1.1 | 174 | 0.1 | 0.1 | 1.1 | 7 | 13 | 3 |
| Nigeria | 1,100 | 6 | 13 | 3.9 | 311 | 0.5 | 0.8 | 4.2 | 39 | 44 | 24 |
| Norway | 7 | 74 | .. | 0.1 | 6 | 7.8 | 19.1 | 1.5 | .. | .. | 152 |
| Oman | 64 | 9 | 32 | 0.2 | 13 | 5.6 | 12.5 | 3.2 | 83 | .. | 82 |
| Pakistan | 320 | 15 | 28 | 0.1 | 181 | 0.6 | 0.8 | 1.4 | 37 | 59 | 25 |
| Panama | 130 | .. | .. | 0.9 | 45 | 1.3 | 1.8 | 2.8 | 71 | 73 | 67 |
| Papua New Guinea | 470 | .. | .. | 1.8 | 250 | 0.6 | 0.4 | 2.4 | 44 | 44 | 2 |
| Paraguay | 150 | 48 | 73 | 0.4 | 71 | 0.5 | 0.7 | 0.6 | 58 | 80 | 59 |
| Peru | 240 | 59 | 46 | 0.6 | 162 | 1.0 | 1.2 | 2.6 | 52 | 63 | 39 |
| Philippines | 230 | 36 | 49 | <0.1 | 287 | 0.7 | 1.0 | 4.8 | 57 | 72 | 54 |
| Poland | 8 | 49 | .. | 0.1 | 25 | 9.1 | 8.0 | 1.4 | .. | .. | 126 |
| Portugal | 11 | .. | .. | 0.4 | 32 | 4.3 | 5.6 | 2.9 | .. | .. | 155 |
| Puerto Rico | 18 | .. | .. | .. | 5 | 3.3 | 0.5 | 3.5 | .. | .. | 112 |

# 1.3 Millennium Development Goals: protecting our common environment

| | Improve maternal health | | | Combat HIV/AIDS and other diseases | | Ensure environmental sustainability | | | | | Develop a global partnership for development |
|---|---|---|---|---|---|---|---|---|---|---|---|
| | Maternal mortality ratio Modeled estimate per 100,000 live births | Contraceptive prevalence rate % of married women ages 15–49 | | HIV prevalence % of population ages 15–49 | Incidence of tuberculosis per 100,000 people | Carbon dioxide emissions per capita metric tons | | Proportion of species threatened with extinction % | Access to improved sanitation facilities % of population | | Fixed-line and mobile phone subscribers per 100 people[a] |
| | 2005 | 1990 | 2000–06[b] | 2005 | 2006 | 1990 | 2004 | 2007 | 1990 | 2004 | 2006 |
| Romania | 24 | .. | 70 | <0.1 | 128 | 6.7 | 4.2 | 1.7 | .. | .. | 100 |
| Russian Federation | 28 | 34 | .. | 1.1 | 107 | 15.3 | 10.6 | 1.3 | 87 | 87 | 112 |
| Rwanda | 1,300 | 21 | 17 | 3.0[f] | 397 | 0.1 | 0.1 | 1.6 | 37 | 42 | 3 |
| Saudi Arabia | 18 | .. | .. | 0.2 | 44 | 15.6 | 13.7 | 1.9 | 91 | 99 | 100 |
| Senegal | 980 | .. | 12 | 0.7[f] | 270 | 0.4 | 0.4 | 2.1 | 33 | 57 | 27 |
| Serbia | 14[h] | .. | 41 | 0.2[h] | 32[h] | 12.4 | 6.6 | 2.0[h] | 87[h] | 87[h] | 99 |
| Sierra Leone | 2,100 | .. | 5 | 1.6 | 517 | 0.1 | 0.2 | 3.3 | .. | 39 | .. |
| Singapore | 14 | 65 | .. | 0.3 | 26 | 14.8 | 12.3 | 3.6 | 100 | 100 | 148 |
| Slovak Republic | 6 | 74 | .. | <0.1 | 15 | 9.7 | 6.7 | 1.3 | 99 | 99 | 112 |
| Slovenia | 6 | .. | .. | <0.1 | 13 | 9.0 | 8.1 | .. | .. | .. | 132 |
| Somalia | 1,400 | 1 | 15 | 0.9 | 218 | 0.0 | .. | 1.9 | .. | 26 | 7 |
| South Africa | 400 | 57 | 60 | 18.8 | 940 | 9.4 | 9.4 | 1.6 | 69 | 65 | 83 |
| Spain | 4 | .. | .. | 0.6 | 30 | 5.5 | 7.7 | 3.8 | 100 | 100 | 146 |
| Sri Lanka | 58 | .. | 70 | <0.1 | 60 | 0.2 | 0.6 | 12.0 | 69 | 91 | 37 |
| Sudan | 450 | 9 | 8 | 1.6 | 242 | 0.2 | 0.3 | 1.5 | 33 | 34 | 14 |
| Swaziland | 390 | 20 | 48 | 33.4 | 1,155 | 0.6 | 0.9 | 0.8 | .. | 48 | 26 |
| Sweden | 3 | .. | .. | 0.2 | 6 | 5.8 | 5.9 | 1.4 | 100 | 100 | 165 |
| Switzerland | 5 | .. | .. | 0.4 | 7 | 6.4 | 5.5 | 1.3 | 100 | 100 | 166 |
| Syrian Arab Republic | 130 | .. | 58 | 0.2 | 32 | 2.8 | 3.7 | 1.7 | 73 | 90 | 41 |
| Tajikistan | 170 | .. | 38 | 0.1 | 204 | 4.4 | 0.8 | 0.8 | .. | 51 | 8 |
| Tanzania | 950 | 10 | 26 | 6.5 | 312 | 0.1 | 0.1 | 4.7 | 47 | 47 | 15 |
| Thailand | 110 | .. | 77 | 1.4 | 142 | 1.8 | 4.3 | 1.9 | 80 | 99 | 75 |
| Timor-Leste | 380 | .. | 10 | 0.2 | 556 | .. | 0.2 | .. | .. | 36 | .. |
| Togo | 510 | 34 | 17 | 3.2 | 389 | 0.2 | 0.4 | 1.1 | 37 | 35 | 12 |
| Trinidad and Tobago | 45 | .. | 43 | 2.6 | 8 | 13.8 | 24.7 | 1.4 | 100 | 100 | 149 |
| Tunisia | 100 | 50 | 63 | 0.1 | 25 | 1.6 | 2.3 | 2.0 | 75 | 85 | 85 |
| Turkey | 44 | 63 | 71 | 0.2 | 29 | 2.6 | 3.2 | 1.3 | 85 | 88 | 98 |
| Turkmenistan | 130 | .. | 48 | <0.1 | 65 | 8.7 | 8.7 | 11.2 | .. | 62 | 10 |
| Uganda | 550 | 5 | 24 | 6.4[i] | 355 | 0.0 | 0.1 | 2.7 | 42 | 43 | 7 |
| Ukraine | 18 | .. | 66 | 1.4 | 106 | 13.2 | 6.9 | 1.1 | .. | 96 | 131 |
| United Arab Emirates | 37 | .. | .. | 0.2 | 16 | 30.8 | 37.8 | .. | 97 | 98 | 161 |
| United Kingdom | 8 | .. | 84 | 0.2 | 15 | 10.1 | 9.8 | 2.2 | .. | .. | 171 |
| United States | 11 | 71 | .. | 0.6 | 4 | 19.3 | 20.6 | 5.7 | 100 | 100 | 135 |
| Uruguay | 20 | .. | .. | 0.5 | 27 | 1.3 | 1.7 | 2.4 | 100 | 100 | 100 |
| Uzbekistan | 24 | .. | 65 | 0.2 | 121 | 6.3 | 5.3 | 0.9 | 51 | 67 | 10 |
| Venezuela, RB | 57 | .. | .. | 0.7 | 41 | 5.9 | 6.6 | 1.0 | .. | 68 | 85 |
| Vietnam | 150 | 53 | 76 | 0.5[f] | 173 | 0.3 | 1.2 | 2.6 | 36 | 61 | 31 |
| West Bank and Gaza | .. | .. | 50 | .. | 20 | .. | .. | .. | .. | 73 | 31 |
| Yemen, Rep. | 430 | 10 | 23 | 0.2 | 78 | 0.8 | 1.0 | 9.8 | 32 | 43 | 14 |
| Zambia | 830 | 15 | 34 | 17.0 | 553 | 0.3 | 0.2 | 0.8 | 44 | 55 | 15 |
| Zimbabwe | 880 | 43 | 60 | 18.1[g] | 557 | 1.6 | 0.8 | 1.0 | 50 | 53 | 9 |
| **World** | **400 w** | **57 w** | **60 w** | **1.0 w** | **139 w** | **4.3 w** | **4.5 w** | | **45 w** | **57 w** | **59 w** |
| **Low income** | 650 | 33 | 44 | 1.7 | 221 | 0.8 | 0.9 | | 21 | 38 | 17 |
| **Middle income** | 160 | 68 | 75 | 0.7 | 114 | 3.6 | 4.0 | | 47 | 62 | 66 |
| Lower middle income | 180 | 73 | 76 | 0.3 | 116 | 2.3 | 3.4 | | 37 | 55 | 60 |
| Upper middle income | 97 | 51 | .. | 1.7 | 109 | 6.9 | 5.6 | | 77 | 81 | 88 |
| **Low & middle income** | 440 | 54 | 60 | 1.1 | 161 | 2.4 | 2.6 | | 36 | 51 | 44 |
| East Asia & Pacific | 150 | 75 | 79 | 0.2 | 135 | 1.9 | 3.3 | | 30 | 51 | 58 |
| Europe & Central Asia | 43 | 46 | 63 | 0.6 | 82 | 10.3 | 7.1 | | 84 | 85 | 88 |
| Latin America & Carib. | 130 | 57 | 69 | 0.6 | 57 | 2.4 | 2.5 | | 67 | 77 | 73 |
| Middle East & N. Africa | 200 | 41 | 60 | 0.1 | 42 | 2.5 | 3.9 | | 70 | 76 | 53 |
| South Asia | 500 | 40 | 53 | 0.7 | 174 | 0.7 | 1.0 | | 17 | 37 | 19 |
| Sub-Saharan Africa | 900 | 15 | 22 | 5.8 | 368 | 0.9 | 0.9 | | 31 | 37 | 15 |
| **High income** | 9 | 71 | .. | 0.4 | 16 | 11.9 | 13.2 | | 100 | 100 | 143 |
| Euro area | 5 | .. | .. | 0.3 | 13 | 8.4 | 8.2 | | 100 | 100 | 153 |

a. Data are from the International Telecommunication Union's World Telecommunication Development Report database. b. Data are for the most recent year available. c. Survey data, 2004. d. Includes Hong Kong, China. e. Data are for 2007. f. Survey data, 2005. g. Survey data, 2005–06. h. Includes Montenegro. i. Survey data, 2004–05.

## About the data

The Millennium Development Goals address concerns common to all economies. Diseases and environmental degradation do not respect national boundaries. Epidemic diseases, wherever they occur, pose a threat to people everywhere. And environmental damage in one location may affect the well-being of plants, animals, and humans far away. The indicators in the table relate to goals 5, 6, and 7 and the targets of goal 8 that address access to new technologies. For the other targets of goal 8, see table 1.4.

The target of achieving universal access to reproductive health has been added to goal 5 to address the importance of family planning and health service in improving maternal health and preventing maternal death. Women with multiple pregnancies are more likely to die in childbirth. Access to contraception is an important way to limit and space births.

Measuring the prevalence or incidence of a disease can be difficult. Most developing economies lack reporting systems for monitoring diseases. Estimates are often derived from surveys and reports from sentinel sites that must be extrapolated to the general population. Tracking diseases such as HIV/AIDS, which has a long latency between contraction of the virus and the appearance of symptoms, or malaria, which has periods of dormancy, can be particularly difficult. The table shows the estimated prevalence of HIV among adults ages 15–49. Prevalence among older populations can be affected by life-prolonging treatment. The incidence of tuberculosis is based on case notifications and estimates of cases detected in the population.

Carbon dioxide emissions are the primary source of greenhouse gases, which contribute to global warming, threatening human and natural habitats. In recognition of the vulnerability of animal and plant species, a new target of reducing biodiversity loss has been added to goal 7.

Access to reliable supplies of safe drinking water and sanitary disposal of excreta are two of the most important means of improving human health and protecting the environment. Improved sanitation facilities prevent human, animal, and insect contact with excreta.

Fixed telephone lines and mobile phones are among the telecommunications technologies that are changing the way the global economy works.

## Location of indicators for Millennium Development Goals 5–7 | 1.3a

**Goal 5. Improve maternal health**

| | | |
|---|---|---|
| 5.1 | Maternal mortality ratio | 1.3, 2.17 |
| 5.2 | Proportion of births attended by skilled health personnel | 2.17, 2.20 |
| 5.3 | Contraceptive prevalence rate | 1.3, 2.17, 2.20 |
| 5.4 | Adolescent fertility rate | 2.17 |
| 5.5 | Antenatal care coverage | 1.5, 2.17, 2.20 |
| 5.6 | Unmet need for family planning | 2.17 |

**Goal 6. Combat HIV/AIDS, malaria, and other diseases**

| | | |
|---|---|---|
| 6.1 | HIV prevalence among pregnant women ages 15–24 | 1.3*, 2.19* |
| 6.2 | Condom use at last high-risk sex | 2.19* |
| 6.3 | Proportion of population ages 15–24 with comprehensive correct knowledge of HIV/AIDS | — |
| 6.4 | Ratio of school attendance of orphans to school attendance of nonorphans ages 10–14 | — |
| 6.5 | Proportion of population with advanced HIV infection with access to antiretroviral drugs | — |
| 6.6 | Incidence and death rates associated with malaria | — |
| 6.7 | Proportion of children under age 5 sleeping under insecticide-treated bednets and proportion of children under age 5 with fever who are treated with appropriate antimalarial drugs | 2.16 |
| 6.8 | Incidence, prevalence, and death rates associated with tuberculosis | 1.3, 2.19 |
| 6.9 | Proportion of tuberculosis cases detected and cured under directly observed treatment short course | 2.16 |

**Goal 7. Ensure environmental sustainability**

| | | |
|---|---|---|
| 7.1 | Proportion of land area covered by forest | 3.1 |
| 7.2 | Carbon dioxide emissions, total, per capita, and per $1 GDP, and consumption of ozone-depleting substances | 3.8 |
| 7.3 | Proportion of fish stocks within safe biological limits | — |
| 7.4 | Proportion of total water resources used | 3.5 |
| 7.5 | Proportion of terrestrial and marine areas protected | 3.4 |
| 7.6 | Proportion of species threatened with extinction | 1.3 |
| 7.7 | Proportion of population using and improved drinking water source | 1.3, 2.16, 3.5 |
| 7.8 | Proportion of population using an improved sanitation facility | 1.3, 2.16, 3.11 |
| 7.9 | Proportion of urban population living in slums | |

— No data are available in the *World Development Indicators* database. * Table shows information on related indicators.

## Definitions

- **Maternal mortality ratio** is the number of women who die from pregnancy-related causes during pregnancy and childbirth, per 100,000 live births. Data are from various years and adjusted to a common 2000 base year. The values are modeled estimates (see *About the data* for table 2.17). • **Contraceptive prevalence rate** is the percentage of women ages 15–49 married or in-union who are practicing, or whose sexual partners are practicing, any form of contraception. • **HIV prevalence** is the percentage of people ages 15–49 who are infected with HIV.
- **Incidence of tuberculosis** is the estimated number of new tuberculosis cases (pulmonary, smear positive, and extrapulmonary). • **Carbon dioxide emissions** are those stemming from the burning of fossil fuels and the manufacture of cement. They include emissions produced during consumption of solid, liquid, and gas fuels and gas flaring (see table 3.8).
- **Proportion of species threatened with extinction** is the total number of threatened mammal (excluding whales and porpoises), bird, and higher native, vascular plant species as a percentage of the total number of known species of the same categories.
- **Access to improved sanitation facilities** is the percentage of the population with at least adequate access to excreta disposal facilities (private or shared, but not public) that can effectively prevent human, animal, and insect contact with excreta (facilities do not have to include treatment to render sewage outflows innocuous). Improved facilities range from simple but protected pit latrines to flush toilets with a sewerage connection. To be effective, facilities must be correctly constructed and properly maintained. • **Fixed-line and mobile phone subscribers** are telephone mainlines connecting a customer's equipment to the public switched telephone network and users of portable telephones subscribing to an automatic public mobile telephone service using cellular technology that provides access to the public switched telephone network.

## Data sources

The indicators here and throughout this book have been compiled by World Bank staff from primary and secondary sources. Efforts have been made to harmonize the data series used to compile this table with those published on the United Nations Millennium Development Goals Web site (www.un.org/millenniumgoals), but some differences in timing, sources, and definitions remain.

# 1.4 Millennium Development Goals: overcoming obstacles

## Development Assistance Committee members

| | Official development assistance (ODA) by donor | | Least developed countries' access to high-income markets | | | | | | | | Support to agriculture |
| | Net % of donor GNI | For basic social services[a] % of total sector-allocable ODA | Goods (excluding arms) admitted free of tariffs % | | Agricultural products % | | Textiles % | | Clothing % | | % of GDP |
| | 2006 | 2006 | 1999 | 2005 | 1999 | 2005 | 1999 | 2005 | 1999 | 2005 | 2006[b] |
|---|---|---|---|---|---|---|---|---|---|---|---|
| Australia | 0.30 | 15.4 | 96.3 | 100.0 | 13.7 | 0.0 | 6.3 | 0.0 | 25.5 | 0.0 | 0.22 |
| Canada | 0.29 | 24.3 | 45.7 | 99.7 | 9.3 | 0.7 | 7.5 | 0.2 | 19.8 | 1.7 | 0.80 |
| European Union | | | 96.9 | 97.8 | 1.0 | 1.2 | 0.0 | 0.1 | 0.0 | 1.2 | 1.10 |
| Austria | 0.47 | 14.9 | | | | | | | | | |
| Belgium | 0.50 | 18.5 | | | | | | | | | |
| Denmark | 0.80 | 26.8 | | | | | | | | | |
| Finland | 0.40 | 15.7 | | | | | | | | | |
| France | 0.47 | 11.1 | | | | | | | | | |
| Germany | 0.36 | 13.3 | | | | | | | | | |
| Greece | 0.17 | 16.4 | | | | | | | | | |
| Ireland | 0.54 | 22.8 | | | | | | | | | |
| Italy | 0.20 | 11.6 | | | | | | | | | |
| Luxembourg | 0.89 | 26.3 | | | | | | | | | |
| Netherlands | 0.81 | 42.6 | | | | | | | | | |
| Portugal | 0.21 | 4.8 | | | | | | | | | |
| Spain | 0.32 | 13.4 | | | | | | | | | |
| Sweden | 1.02 | 13.6 | | | | | | | | | |
| United Kingdom | 0.21 | 12.9 | | | | | | | | | |
| Japan | 0.25 | 18.6 | 58.0 | 23.2 | 3.7 | 2.5 | 5.1 | 2.8 | 0.4 | 0.1 | 1.11 |
| New Zealand[c] | 0.27 | 21.0 | 93.8 | 99.2 | 0.0 | 6.7 | 9.6 | 0.0 | 13.0 | 0.0 | 0.25 |
| Norway | 0.89 | 11.9 | 97.5 | 99.1 | 3.3 | 0.4 | 4.8 | 0.0 | 1.5 | 1.0 | 0.99 |
| Switzerland | 0.39 | 8.8 | 99.9 | 96.7 | 1.5 | 0.9 | 0.0 | 0.0 | 0.0 | 0.0 | 1.46 |
| United States | 0.18 | 13.5 | 53.4 | 76.7 | 9.4 | 7.9 | 7.1 | 5.7 | 14.3 | 11.7 | 0.73 |

## Heavily indebted poor countries (HIPCs)

| | HIPC decision point[d] | HIPC completion point[d] | HIPC Initiative assistance[e] $ millions | MDRI assistance[f] $ millions | | HIPC decision point[d] | HIPC completion point[d] | HIPC Initiative assistance[e] $ millions | MDRI assistance[f] $ millions |
|---|---|---|---|---|---|---|---|---|---|
| Afghanistan | Jul. 2007 | Floating | 546 | .. | Haiti | Nov. 2006 | Floating | 140 | .. |
| Benin | Jul. 2000 | Mar. 2003 | 344 | 570 | Honduras | Jul. 2000 | Apr. 2005 | 729 | 1,474 |
| Bolivia[g] | Feb. 2000 | Jun. 2001 | 1,752 | 1,526 | Madagascar | Dec. 2000 | Oct. 2004 | 1,096 | 1,205 |
| Burkina Faso[g,h] | Jul. 2000 | Apr. 2002 | 725 | 564 | Malawi[h] | Dec. 2000 | Aug. 2006 | 1,278 | 662 |
| Burundi | Aug. 2005 | Floating | 864 | .. | Mali[g] | Sep. 2000 | Mar. 2003 | 707 | 982 |
| Cameroon | Oct. 2000 | Apr. 2006 | 1,662 | 687 | Mauritania | Feb. 2000 | Jun. 2002 | 816 | 422 |
| Central African Republic | Sep. 2007 | Floating | 583 | .. | Mozambique[g] | Apr. 2000 | Sep. 2001 | 2,758 | 1,004 |
| Chad | May 2001 | Floating | 214 | .. | Nicaragua | Dec. 2000 | Jan. 2004 | 4,340 | 900 |
| Congo, Dem. Rep. | Jul. 2003 | Floating | 7,229 | .. | Niger[h] | Dec. 2000 | Apr.2004 | 853 | 477 |
| Congo, Rep. | Apr. 2006 | Floating | 1,757 | .. | Rwanda[h] | Dec. 2000 | Apr. 2005 | 872 | 200 |
| Ethiopia[h] | Nov. 2001 | Apr. 2004 | 2,446 | 1,366 | São Tomé & Principe[h] | Dec. 2000 | Mar. 2007 | 156 | 22 |
| Gambia, The | Dec. 2000 | Dec. 2007 | 81 | 201 | Senegal | Jun. 2000 | Apr. 2004 | 641 | 1,298 |
| Ghana | Feb. 2002 | Jul. 2004 | 2,742 | 1,938 | Sierra Leone | Mar. 2002 | Dec. 2006 | 809 | 316 |
| Guinea | Dec. 2000 | Floating | 716 | .. | Tanzania | Apr. 2000 | Nov. 2001 | 2,658 | 1,907 |
| Guinea-Bissau | Dec. 2000 | Floating | 546 | .. | Uganda[g] | Feb. 2000 | May 2000 | 1,349 | 1,713 |
| Guyana[g] | Nov. 2002 | Dec. 2003 | 824 | 382 | Zambia | Dec. 2000 | Apr. 2005 | 3,279 | 1,437 |

a. Includes basic health, education, nutrition, and water and sanitation services. b. Preliminary. c. Estimates of market access for least developed countries are calculated by World Bank staff using the World Integrated Trade Solution based on the United Nations Conference on Trade and Development's Trade Analysis and Information Systems database. d. Refers to the Enhanced HIPC Initiative. e. Total HIPC assistance (committed debt relief) assuming full participation of creditors, in end-2006 net present value terms. Topping-up assistance and assistance provided under the original HIPC Initiative were committed in net present value terms as of the decision point and are converted to end-2006 terms. f. Multilateral Debt Relief Initiative (MDRI) assistance has been delivered in full to all post-completion point countries, shown in end-2006 net present value terms. g. Also reached completion point under the original HIPC Initiative. The assistance includes original debt relief. h. Assistance includes topping up at completion point.

## About the data

Achieving the Millennium Development Goals requires an open, rule-based global economy in which all countries, rich and poor, participate. Many poor countries, lacking the resources to finance development, burdened by unsustainable debt, and unable to compete globally, need assistance from rich countries. For goal 8—develop a global partnership for development—many indicators therefore monitor the actions of members of the Organisation for Economic Co-operation and Development's (OECD) Development Assistance Committee (DAC).

Official development assistance (ODA) has risen in recent years as a share of donor countries' gross national income (GNI), but the poorest countries need additional assistance to achieve the Millennium Development Goals. After rising to a record $106 billion in 2005, ODA fell 4.5 percent in 2006 to $104 billion in nominal terms.

One important action that high-income economies can take is to reduce barriers to low- and middle-income economy exports. The European Union has begun to eliminate tariffs on developing country exports of "everything but arms," and the United States offers special concessions to Sub-Saharan African exports. However, these programs still have many restrictions.

Average tariffs in the table reflect high-income OECD member tariff schedules for exports of countries designated least developed countries by the United Nations. Agricultural commodities, textiles, and clothing are three of the most important exports of developing economies. Although average tariffs have been falling, averages may disguise high tariffs on specific goods (see table 6.7 for each country's share of tariff lines with "international peaks"). The averages in the table include ad valorem duties and equivalents.

Subsidies to agricultural producers and exporters in OECD countries are another barrier to developing economies' exports. The table shows the total support to agriculture as a share of the economy's gross domestic product (GDP). Agricultural subsidies in OECD economies are estimated at $372 billion in 2006.

The Debt Initiative for Heavily Indebted Poor Countries (HIPCs), an important step in placing debt relief within the framework of poverty reduction, is the first comprehensive approach to reducing the external debt of the world's poorest, most heavily indebted countries. A 1999 review led to an enhancement of the framework. In 2005, to further reduce the debt of HIPCs and provide resources for meeting the Millennium Development Goals, the Multilateral Debt Relief Initiative (MDRI), proposed by the Group of Eight countries, was launched. Under the MDRI the International Development Association (IDA), International Monetary Fund (IMF), and African Development Fund (AfDF) provide 100 percent debt relief on eligible debts due to them from countries that completed the HIPC Initiative process. Debt relief under the two initiatives is expected to reduce the debt stocks of the 32 HIPCs that have reached the decision point by almost 90 percent. Twenty-two countries have reached the completion point and have received nearly $45 billion in HIPC Initiative assistance and $42 billion in MDRI assistance in nominal terms.

## Definitions

- **Net official development assistance (ODA)** is grants and loans (net of repayments of principal) that meet the DAC definition of ODA and are made to countries and territories on the DAC list of recipient countries. • **ODA for basic social services** is aid reported by DAC donors for basic health, education, nutrition, and water and sanitation services.
- **Goods admitted free of tariffs** are exports of goods (excluding arms) from least developed countries admitted without tariff as a share of total exports from least developed countries. • **Average tariff** is the unweighted average of the effectively applied rates for all products subject to tariffs. • **Agricultural products** are plant and animal products, including tree crops but excluding timber and fish products.
- **Textiles** and **clothing** are natural and synthetic fibers and fabrics and articles of clothing made from them. • **Support to agriculture** is the value of gross transfers from taxpayers and consumers arising from policy measures that support agriculture, net of associated budgetary receipts, regardless of their objectives and impacts on farm production and income or consumption of farm products. • **HIPC decision point** is the date when a heavily indebted poor country with an established track record of good performance under adjustment programs supported by the IMF and the World Bank commits to additional reforms and a poverty reduction strategy.
- **HIPC completion point** is the date when a country successfully completes the key structural reforms agreed on at the decision point, including developing and implementing a poverty reduction strategy. The country then receives the bulk of debt relief under the HIPC Initiative without further policy conditions.
- **HIPC Initiative assistance** is the net present value of debt relief committed as of the decision point and converted to end-2006 values. • **MDRI assistance** is the net present value of debt relief from IDA, IMF, and AfDF, delivered to countries having reached the HIPC completion point converted to end-2006 values.

### Location of indicators for Millennium Development Goal 8 — 1.4a

| Goal 8. Develop a global partnership for development | Table |
|---|---|
| 8.1 Net ODA as a percentage of DAC donors' gross national income | 1.4, 6.12 |
| 8.2 Proportion of ODA for basic social services | 1.4, 6.13b* |
| 8.3 Proportion of ODA that is untied | 6.13b |
| 8.4 Proportion of ODA received in landlocked countries as a percentage of GNI | — |
| 8.5 Proportion of ODA received in small island developing states as a percentage of GNI | — |
| 8.6 Proportion of total developed country imports (by value, excluding arms) from least developed countries admitted free of duty | 1.4 |
| 8.7 Average tariffs imposed by developed countries on agricultural products and textiles and clothing from least developed countries | 1.4, 6.7* |
| 8.8 Agricultural support estimate for OECD countries as a percentage of GDP | 1.4 |
| 8.9 Proportion of ODA provided to help build trade capacity | — |
| 8.10 Number of countries reaching HIPC decision and completion points | 1.4 |
| 8.11 Debt relief committed under new HIPC initiative | 1.4 |
| 8.12 Debt services as a percentage of exports of goods and services | 6.9* |
| 8.13 Proportion of population with access to affordable, essential drugs on a sustainable basis | — |
| 8.14 Telephone lines per 100 people | 1.3*, 5.10 |
| 8.15 Cellular subscribers per 100 people | 1.3*, 5.10 |
| 8.16 Internet users per 100 people | 5.11 |

— No data are available in the *World Development Indicators* database. * Table shows information on related indicators.

## Data sources

Data on ODA are from the OECD. Data on goods admitted free of tariffs and average tariffs are from the World Trade Organization, in collaboration with the United Nations Conference on Trade and Development and the International Trade Centre. These data are available electronically at www.mdg-trade.org. Data on subsidies to agriculture are from the OECD's *Producer and Consumer Support Estimates, OECD Database 1986–2006*. Data on the HIPC Initiative and MDRI are from the World Bank's Economic Policy and Debt Department.

# Women in development

| | Female population | Life expectancy at birth | | Pregnant women receiving prenatal care | Teenage mothers | Women in nonagricultural sector | Unpaid family workers | | Women in parliaments | |
|---|---|---|---|---|---|---|---|---|---|---|
| | | years | | | | | Male | Female | | |
| | % of total **2006** | Male **2006** | Female **2006** | % **2000–06[a]** | % of women ages 15–19 **2000–06[a]** | % of nonagricultural wage employment **2005** | % of male employment **2000–05[a]** | % of female employment **2000–05[a]** | % of total seats **1990** | **2007** |
| Afghanistan | .. | .. | .. | 16 | .. | .. | .. | .. | 4 | 27 |
| Albania | 50.0 | 73 | 80 | 97 | .. | 33 | .. | .. | 29 | 7 |
| Algeria | 49.4 | 71 | 73 | 89 | .. | 14 | 7.2 | 7.2 | 2 | 8 |
| Angola | 50.7 | 41 | 44 | 66 | .. | .. | .. | .. | 15 | 15 |
| Argentina | 50.8 | 71 | 79 | 99 | .. | 45 | 0.7[b] | 1.9[b] | 6 | 35 |
| Armenia | 53.2 | 68 | 75 | 93 | 5 | .. | 1.1 | 0.8 | 36 | 9 |
| Australia | 49.7 | 79 | 83 | .. | .. | 49 | 0.2 | 0.4 | 6 | 25 |
| Austria | 50.5 | 77 | 83 | .. | .. | 47 | 1.0 | 1.9 | 12 | 32 |
| Azerbaijan | 51.3 | 70 | 75 | 70 | .. | 49 | .. | .. | .. | 11 |
| Bangladesh | 48.8 | 63 | 65 | 48 | 33 | .. | 9.9 | 48.0 | 10 | 15 |
| Belarus | 53.2 | 63 | 74 | 99 | .. | 53 | .. | .. | .. | 29 |
| Belgium | 50.5 | 77 | 82 | .. | .. | 45 | 0.4 | 3.4 | 9 | 35 |
| Benin | 49.6 | 55 | 57 | 84 | 21 | .. | .. | .. | 3 | 8 |
| Bolivia | 50.1 | 63 | 67 | 79 | 16 | 32 | 12.6 | 34.8 | 9 | 17 |
| Bosnia and Herzegovina | 51.2 | 72 | 77 | 99 | .. | .. | .. | .. | .. | 14 |
| Botswana | 50.3 | 50 | 50 | 97 | .. | 40 | 2.3 | 2.2 | 5 | 11 |
| Brazil | 50.5 | 69 | 76 | 97 | .. | .. | 5.4[b] | 9.1[b] | 5 | 9 |
| Bulgaria | 51.0 | 69 | 76 | .. | .. | 53 | 0.9 | 2.2 | 21 | 22 |
| Burkina Faso | 49.9 | 50 | 53 | 85 | 23 | .. | .. | .. | .. | 15 |
| Burundi | 51.1 | 48 | 50 | 92 | .. | .. | .. | .. | .. | 31 |
| Cambodia | 51.2 | 57 | 61 | 69 | 8 | 52 | 31.6 | 53.3 | .. | 10 |
| Cameroon | 50.0 | 50 | 51 | 82 | 28 | .. | 9.5 | 27.2 | 14 | 14 |
| Canada | 50.0 | 78 | 83 | .. | .. | 49 | 0.1 | 0.2 | 13 | 21 |
| Central African Republic | 51.2 | 43 | 46 | 69 | .. | .. | .. | .. | 4 | 11 |
| Chad | 50.3 | 49 | 52 | 39 | 37 | .. | .. | .. | .. | 7 |
| Chile | 50.3 | 75 | 81 | .. | .. | 38 | 1.4 | 3.2 | .. | 15 |
| China | 48.2 | 70 | 74 | 90 | .. | .. | .. | .. | 21 | 20 |
| Hong Kong, China | 51.6 | 79 | 85 | .. | .. | 48 | 0.2 | 1.4 | .. | .. |
| Colombia | 50.6 | 69 | 76 | 94 | 21 | 48 | 3.5 | 7.7 | 5 | 8 |
| Congo, Dem. Rep. | 50.5 | 45 | 47 | 85[c] | .. | .. | .. | .. | 5 | 8 |
| Congo, Rep. | 50.4 | 54 | 56 | 86 | 27 | .. | .. | .. | 14 | 7 |
| Costa Rica | 49.0 | 76 | 81 | 92 | .. | 40 | 1.7 | 3.5 | 11 | 39 |
| Côte d'Ivoire | 49.2 | 47 | 49 | 85 | .. | .. | .. | .. | 6 | 9 |
| Croatia | 51.5 | 73 | 79 | 100 | 4 | 44 | 1.1[d] | 3.6[d] | .. | 19 |
| Cuba | 49.5 | 76 | 80 | 100 | .. | 43 | .. | .. | 34 | 36 |
| Czech Republic | 50.8 | 73 | 80 | .. | .. | 47 | 0.3 | 1.3 | .. | 16 |
| Denmark | 50.0 | 76 | 80 | .. | .. | 49 | 0.2 | 1.3 | 31 | 37 |
| Dominican Republic | 49.6 | 69 | 75 | 99 | 23 | 38 | 2.8 | 4.9 | 8 | 20 |
| Ecuador | 49.7 | 72 | 78 | 84 | .. | 42 | 3.0[b] | 9.4[b] | 5 | 25 |
| Egypt, Arab Rep. | 49.8 | 69 | 73 | 70 | 9 | 20 | 9.4 | 32.2 | 4 | 2 |
| El Salvador | 50.8 | 69 | 75 | 86 | .. | 35 | 7.7 | 7.7 | 12 | 17 |
| Eritrea | 50.9 | 55 | 60 | 70 | 14 | .. | .. | .. | .. | 22 |
| Estonia | 53.6 | 67 | 78 | .. | .. | 53 | 0.3 | 0.2 | .. | 22 |
| Ethiopia | 50.2 | 51 | 54 | 28 | 17 | 41 | 34.6 | 68.5 | .. | 22 |
| Finland | 50.6 | 76 | 83 | .. | .. | 51 | 0.6 | 0.4 | 32 | 42 |
| France | 50.7 | 77 | 84 | .. | .. | 48 | 0.5 | 1.6 | 7 | 19 |
| Gabon | 49.9 | 56 | 57 | 94 | 33 | .. | .. | .. | 13 | 13 |
| Gambia, The | 49.8 | 58 | 60 | 98 | .. | .. | .. | .. | 8 | 9 |
| Georgia | 52.5 | 67 | 75 | 94 | .. | 49 | 19.0 | 39.0 | .. | 9 |
| Germany | 50.7 | 76 | 82 | .. | .. | 47 | 0.5 | 1.9 | .. | 32 |
| Ghana | 49.3 | 59 | 60 | 92 | 14 | .. | .. | .. | .. | 11 |
| Greece | 49.9 | 77 | 82 | .. | .. | 41 | 3.3 | 11.2 | 7 | 16 |
| Guatemala | 51.1 | 66 | 74 | 84 | .. | .. | 21.3 | 24.5 | 7 | 12 |
| Guinea | 49.5 | 54 | 57 | 82 | 32 | .. | .. | .. | .. | 19 |
| Guinea-Bissau | 50.5 | 45 | 48 | 78 | .. | .. | .. | .. | 20 | 14 |
| Haiti | 50.4 | 59 | 62 | 85 | 14 | .. | .. | .. | .. | 4 |

| | Female population | Life expectancy at birth | | Pregnant women receiving prenatal care | Teenage mothers | Women in nonagricultural sector | Unpaid family workers | | Women in parliaments | |
|---|---|---|---|---|---|---|---|---|---|---|
| | | years | | | | % of nonagricultural wage employment | Male % of male employment | Female % of female employment | % of total seats | |
| | % of total 2006 | Male 2006 | Female 2006 | % 2000–06[a] | % of women ages 15–19 2000–06[a] | 2005 | 2000–05[a] | 2000–05[a] | 1990 | 2007 |
| Honduras | 50.2 | 66 | 73 | 92 | 22 | 45 | 12.1[b] | 8.3[b] | 10 | 23 |
| Hungary | 52.0 | 69 | 77 | .. | .. | 49 | 0.3 | 0.7 | 21 | 10 |
| India | 48.1 | 63 | 66 | 74 | .. | 18 | .. | .. | 5 | 8 |
| Indonesia | 49.9 | 66 | 70 | 92 | 10 | .. | .. | .. | 12 | 11 |
| Iran, Islamic Rep. | 49.2 | 69 | 72 | .. | .. | .. | .. | .. | 2 | 4 |
| Iraq | .. | .. | .. | 84 | .. | .. | .. | .. | 11 | 26 |
| Ireland | 49.8 | 77 | 82 | .. | .. | 48 | 0.6 | 0.9 | 8 | 13 |
| Israel | 50.1 | 78 | 82 | .. | .. | 49 | 0.2 | 0.5 | 7 | 14 |
| Italy | 50.7 | 78 | 84 | .. | .. | 43 | 1.2 | 2.8 | 13 | 17 |
| Jamaica | 50.3 | 70 | 73 | 91 | .. | 47 | 0.4 | 2.5 | 5 | 13 |
| Japan | 50.5 | 79 | 86 | .. | .. | 41 | 1.5 | 8.6 | 1 | 9 |
| Jordan | 48.5 | 71 | 74 | 99 | 4 | .. | .. | .. | 0 | 6 |
| Kazakhstan | 52.1 | 61 | 72 | 100 | 7 | 49 | 1.0 | 1.3 | .. | 16 |
| Kenya | 50.1 | 52 | 55 | 88 | 23 | .. | .. | .. | 1 | 7 |
| Korea, Dem. Rep. | 50.6 | 65 | 69 | .. | .. | .. | .. | .. | 21 | 20 |
| Korea, Rep. | 49.8 | 75 | 82 | .. | .. | 42 | 1.3 | 14.0 | 2 | 13 |
| Kuwait | 39.8 | 76 | 80 | .. | .. | .. | .. | .. | .. | 2 |
| Kyrgyz Republic | 50.6 | 64 | 72 | 97 | .. | 52 | 9.6 | 21.8 | .. | 0 |
| Lao PDR | 50.1 | 63 | 65 | 27 | .. | .. | .. | .. | 6 | 25 |
| Latvia | 53.6 | 65 | 77 | .. | .. | 53 | 2.5 | 2.1 | .. | 19 |
| Lebanon | 50.8 | 70 | 74 | 96 | .. | .. | .. | .. | 0 | 5 |
| Lesotho | 52.9 | 43 | 43 | 90 | 20 | .. | .. | .. | .. | 24 |
| Liberia | 50.0 | 44 | 46 | 85 | .. | .. | .. | .. | .. | 13 |
| Libya | 48.1 | 71 | 77 | .. | .. | .. | .. | .. | .. | 8 |
| Lithuania | 53.1 | 65 | 77 | .. | .. | 51 | 2.1 | 3.9 | .. | 25 |
| Macedonia, FYR | 49.9 | 72 | 76 | 98 | .. | 44 | 6.4 | 16.7 | .. | 28 |
| Madagascar | 50.2 | 57 | 61 | 80 | 34 | 46 | 29.7 | 51.9 | 7 | 8 |
| Malawi | 50.3 | 47 | 48 | 92 | 31 | .. | .. | .. | 10 | 14 |
| Malaysia | 49.1 | 72 | 76 | 79 | .. | 38 | 2.2 | 9.6 | 5 | 9 |
| Mali | 51.2 | 52 | 56 | 57 | 40 | 50 | 18.4 | 10.2 | .. | 10 |
| Mauritania | 49.3 | 62 | 66 | 64 | 16 | .. | .. | .. | .. | 18 |
| Mauritius | 50.2 | 70 | 77 | .. | .. | 37 | 0.9 | 4.7 | 7 | 17 |
| Mexico | 51.0 | 72 | 77 | .. | .. | 39 | 5.5 | 11.0 | 12 | 23 |
| Moldova | 52.0 | 65 | 72 | 98 | 6 | 55 | 0.8 | 1.4 | .. | 22 |
| Mongolia | 50.0 | 66 | 69 | 99 | .. | 53 | 18.4 | 31.7 | 25 | 7 |
| Morocco | 50.7 | 69 | 73 | 68 | 7 | 22 | 22.8 | 55.7 | 0 | 11 |
| Mozambique | 51.5 | 42 | 43 | 85 | 41 | .. | .. | .. | 16 | 35 |
| Myanmar | 50.3 | 59 | 65 | 76 | .. | .. | .. | .. | .. | .. |
| Namibia | 50.6 | 52 | 53 | 91 | 18 | .. | 12.8 | 22.0 | 7 | 27 |
| Nepal | 50.4 | 63 | 64 | 44 | 19 | .. | .. | .. | 6 | 17 |
| Netherlands | 50.1 | 78 | 82 | .. | .. | 47 | 0.2 | 1.0 | 21 | 37 |
| New Zealand | 50.3 | 78 | 82 | .. | .. | 47 | 0.4 | 0.9 | 14 | 32 |
| Nicaragua | 50.0 | 70 | 76 | 86 | 25 | .. | 3.1 | 4.2 | 15 | 19 |
| Niger | 49.2 | 57 | 56 | 46 | 39 | 21 | .. | .. | 5 | 12 |
| Nigeria | 50.0 | 46 | 47 | 58 | 25 | 21 | .. | .. | .. | 7 |
| Norway | 49.7 | 78 | 83 | .. | .. | 49 | 0.2 | 0.3 | 36 | 38 |
| Oman | 44.0 | 74 | 77 | 100 | .. | .. | .. | .. | .. | 0 |
| Pakistan | 48.5 | 65 | 66 | 36 | .. | 10 | 18.3 | 52.8 | 10 | 21 |
| Panama | 49.4 | 73 | 78 | .. | .. | 43 | 2.8 | 5.5 | 8 | 17 |
| Papua New Guinea | 49.2 | 55 | 60 | .. | .. | .. | .. | .. | 0 | 1 |
| Paraguay | 49.3 | 69 | 74 | 94 | .. | .. | 10.9[b] | 8.7[b] | 6 | 10 |
| Peru | 49.8 | 69 | 74 | 92 | 26 | 38 | 1.6[b] | 7.0[b] | 6 | 29 |
| Philippines | 49.6 | 69 | 74 | 88 | 8 | 42 | 8.9 | 18.7 | 9 | 22 |
| Poland | 51.4 | 71 | 80 | .. | .. | 47 | 3.8 | 7.0 | 14 | 20 |
| Portugal | 51.1 | 75 | 82 | .. | .. | 47 | 0.9 | 2.1 | 8 | 21 |
| Puerto Rico | 51.6 | 74 | 83 | .. | .. | 40 | 0.1 | 0.9 | .. | .. |

| | Female population | Life expectancy at birth | | Pregnant women receiving prenatal care | Teenage mothers | Women in nonagricultural sector | Unpaid family workers | | Women in parliaments | |
|---|---|---|---|---|---|---|---|---|---|---|
| | | years | | | % of women ages 15–19 | % of nonagricultural wage employment | Male % of male employment | Female % of female employment | % of total seats | |
| | % of total 2006 | Male 2006 | Female 2006 | % 2000–06[a] | 2000–06[a] | 2005 | 2000–05[a] | 2000–05[a] | 1990 | 2007 |
| Romania | 51.0 | 69 | 76 | 94 | .. | 46 | 7.8 | 21.2 | 34 | 11 |
| Russian Federation | 53.5 | 59 | 73 | .. | .. | 51 | 0.1 | 0.1 | .. | 10 |
| Rwanda | 51.8 | 44 | 47 | 94 | 4 | .. | .. | .. | 17 | 49 |
| Saudi Arabia | 44.8 | 71 | 75 | .. | .. | .. | .. | .. | | 0 |
| Senegal | 50.0 | 61 | 65 | 87 | 19 | .. | .. | .. | 13 | 22 |
| Serbia | 50.2 | 70 | 76 | 98 | .. | .. | .. | .. | | 20 |
| Sierra Leone | 50.7 | 41 | 44 | 81 | .. | 23 | .. | .. | | 13 |
| Singapore | 49.4 | 78 | 82 | .. | .. | 48 | 0.3 | 1.2 | 5 | 25 |
| Slovak Republic | 51.2 | 70 | 78 | .. | .. | 51 | 0.0[b] | 0.1[b] | .. | 19 |
| Slovenia | 50.9 | 74 | 81 | .. | .. | 47 | 3.1 | 6.4 | .. | 12 |
| Somalia | 50.3 | 47 | 49 | 26 | .. | .. | .. | .. | 4 | 8 |
| South Africa | 50.8 | 49 | 53 | 92 | .. | 43 | 0.4 | 1.1 | 3 | 33 |
| Spain | 50.1 | 78 | 84 | .. | .. | 42 | 1.1 | 2.4 | 15 | 36 |
| Sri Lanka | 50.4 | 72 | 78 | 100 | .. | 40 | 4.2[b] | 20.9[b] | 5 | 5 |
| Sudan | 49.6 | 57 | 60 | 70 | .. | .. | .. | .. | .. | 18 |
| Swaziland | 51.6 | 42 | 40 | 90 | .. | .. | .. | .. | 4 | 11 |
| Sweden | 49.6 | 79 | 83 | .. | .. | 51 | 0.2 | 0.2 | 38 | 47 |
| Switzerland | 50.7 | 79 | 84 | .. | .. | 47 | 1.3 | 2.9 | 14 | 30 |
| Syrian Arab Republic | 49.4 | 72 | 76 | 84 | .. | .. | 10.8 | 44.2 | 9 | 12 |
| Tajikistan | 50.3 | 64 | 69 | 77 | .. | .. | .. | .. | .. | 18 |
| Tanzania | 50.2 | 51 | 53 | 78 | 26 | .. | .. | .. | .. | 30 |
| Thailand | 51.1 | 66 | 75 | 98 | .. | 48 | 14.7 | 31.4 | 3 | 9 |
| Timor-Leste | 49.2 | 56 | 58 | 61 | .. | .. | .. | .. | .. | 28 |
| Togo | 50.5 | 56 | 60 | 89 | .. | .. | .. | .. | 5 | 7 |
| Trinidad and Tobago | 50.6 | 68 | 72 | 96 | .. | 44 | 0.3 | 1.7 | 17 | 19 |
| Tunisia | 49.5 | 72 | 76 | 92 | .. | 25 | .. | .. | 4 | 23 |
| Turkey | 49.5 | 69 | 74 | 81 | .. | 20 | 7.0 | 41.7 | 1 | 9 |
| Turkmenistan | 50.7 | 59 | 67 | 99 | 4 | .. | .. | .. | 26 | 16 |
| Uganda | 49.9 | 50 | 51 | 94 | 25 | 39 | 10.3[b] | 40.5[b] | 12 | 30 |
| Ukraine | 53.6 | 62 | 74 | 99 | .. | 55 | 0.5 | 0.5 | .. | 9 |
| United Arab Emirates | 32.2 | 77 | 82 | .. | .. | .. | .. | .. | 0 | 23 |
| United Kingdom | 50.4 | 77 | 81 | .. | .. | 49 | 0.3 | 0.5 | 6 | 20 |
| United States | 50.3 | 75 | 81 | .. | .. | 48 | 0.1 | 0.1 | 7 | 16 |
| Uruguay | 51.3 | 72 | 80 | .. | .. | 48 | 0.7[b] | 2.2[b] | 6 | 11 |
| Uzbekistan | 50.2 | 64 | 71 | 99 | .. | .. | .. | .. | .. | 18 |
| Venezuela, RB | 49.6 | 72 | 77 | 94 | .. | .. | 2.0 | 3.9 | 10 | 19 |
| Vietnam | 49.8 | 68 | 73 | 91 | 3 | 46 | 18.9 | 47.2 | 18 | 26 |
| West Bank and Gaza | 49.1 | 71 | 74 | 99 | .. | 18 | 6.4 | 32.2 | .. | .. |
| Yemen, Rep. | 49.4 | 61 | 64 | 41 | .. | .. | .. | .. | 4 | 0[e] |
| Zambia | 50.1 | 41 | 42 | 93 | 32 | .. | .. | .. | 7 | 15 |
| Zimbabwe | 50.2 | 43 | 42 | 94 | 21 | .. | 10.4 | 13.6 | 11 | 17 |
| **World** | **49.4 w** | **66 w** | **70 w** | **80 w** | | **.. w** | **.. w** | **.. w** | **13 w** | **18 w** |
| **Low income** | 49.0 | 59 | 62 | 69 | | 24 | .. | .. | 11 | 16 |
| **Middle income** | 49.6 | 68 | 73 | 90 | | .. | .. | .. | 14 | 16 |
| Lower middle income | 49.0 | 69 | 73 | 89 | | .. | .. | .. | 14 | 16 |
| Upper middle income | 51.0 | 67 | 74 | .. | | 44 | 3.8 | 7.9 | 12 | 15 |
| **Low & middle income** | 49.3 | 64 | 68 | 80 | | .. | .. | .. | 13 | 16 |
| East Asia & Pacific | 48.7 | 69 | 73 | 89 | | .. | .. | .. | 17 | 18 |
| Europe & Central Asia | 51.9 | 65 | 74 | 91 | | 48 | 2.8 | 6.9 | .. | 15 |
| Latin America & Carib. | 50.4 | 70 | 76 | 95 | | .. | 4.6 | 8.4 | 12 | 20 |
| Middle East & N. Africa | 49.5 | 68 | 72 | 76 | | .. | .. | .. | 4 | 9 |
| South Asia | 48.3 | 63 | 66 | 66 | | 17 | .. | .. | 6 | 14 |
| Sub-Saharan Africa | 50.2 | 49 | 52 | 72 | | .. | .. | .. | .. | 17 |
| **High income** | 50.1 | 76 | 82 | .. | | 46 | 0.6 | 2.6 | 12 | 23 |
| Euro area | 50.5 | 77 | 83 | .. | | 46 | 0.8 | 2.3 | 12 | 25 |

a. Data are for the most recent year available. b. Limited coverage. c. Data are for 2007. d. Data are for 2006. e. Less than 0.5.

# Women in development | **1.5**

Despite much progress in recent decades, gender inequalities remain pervasive in many dimensions of life—worldwide. But while disparities exist throughout the world, they are most prevalent in developing countries. Gender inequalities in the allocation of such resources as education, health care, nutrition, and political voice matter because of the strong association with well-being, productivity, and economic growth. These patterns of inequality begin at an early age, with boys routinely receiving a larger share of education and health spending than do girls, for example.

Because of biological differences girls are expected to experience lower infant and child mortality rates and to have a longer life expectancy than boys. This biological advantage, however, may be overshadowed by gender inequalities in nutrition and medical interventions and by inadequate care during pregnancy and delivery, so that female rates of illness and death sometimes exceed male rates, particularly during early childhood and the reproductive years. In high-income countries women tend to outlive men by four to eight years on average, while in low-income countries the difference is narrower—about two to three years. The difference in child mortality rates (table 2.21) is another good indicator of female social disadvantage because nutrition and medical interventions are particularly important for the 1–4 age group. Female child mortality rates that are as high as or higher than male child mortality rates may indicate discrimination against girls.

Having a child during the teenage years limits girls' opportunities for better education, jobs, and income. Pregnancy is more likely to be unintended during the teenage years, and births are more likely to be premature and are associated with greater risks of complications during delivery and of death. In many countries maternal mortality (tables 1.3 and 2.17) is a leading cause of death among women of reproductive age. Most maternal deaths result from preventable causes—hemorrhage, infection, and complications from unsafe abortions. Prenatal care is essential for recognizing, diagnosing, and promptly treating complications that arise during pregnancy. In high-income countries most women have access to health care during pregnancy, but in developing countries an estimated 200 million women suffer pregnancy-related complications, and over half a million die every year (Glasier and others 2006). This is reflected in the differences in maternal mortality ratios between high- and low-income countries.

Women's wage work is important for economic growth and the well-being of families. But restricted access to education and vocational training, heavy workloads at home and in nonpaid domestic and market activities, and labor market discrimination often limit women's participation in paid economic activities, lower their productivity, and reduce their wages. When women are in salaried employment, they tend to be concentrated in the nonagricultural sector. However, in many developing countries women are a large part of agricultural employment, often as unpaid family workers. Among people who are unsalaried, women are more likely than men to be unpaid family workers, while men are more likely than women to be self-employed or employers. There are several reasons for this.

Few women have access to credit markets, capital, land, training, and education, which may be required to start a business. Cultural norms may prevent women from working on their own or from supervising other workers. Also, women may face time constraints due to their traditional family responsibilities. Because of biases and misclassification substantial numbers of employed women may be underestimated or reported as unpaid family workers even when they work in association or equally with their husbands in the family enterprise.

Women are vastly underrepresented in decision-making positions in government, although there is some evidence of recent improvement. Gender parity in parliamentary representation is still far from being realized. In 2007 women accounted for 18 percent of parliamentarians worldwide, compared with 9 percent in 1987. Without representation at this level, it is difficult for women to influence policy.

For information on other aspects of gender, see tables 1.2 (Millennium Development Goals: eradicating poverty and saving lives), 2.3 (Employment by economic activity), 2.4 (Decent work and productive employment), 2.5 (Unemployment), 2.6 (Children at work), 2.9 (Assessing vulnerability and security), 2.12 (Education efficiency), 2.13 (Education completion and outcomes), 2.14 (Education gaps by income and gender), 2.17 (Reproductive health), 2.19 (Health risk factors and public health challenges), 2.20 (Health gaps by income and gender), and 2.21 (Mortality).

• **Female population** is the percentage of the population that is female. • **Life expectancy at birth** is the number of years a newborn infant would live if prevailing patterns of mortality at the time of its birth were to stay the same throughout its life. • **Pregnant women receiving prenatal care** are the percentage of women attended at least once during pregnancy by skilled health personnel for reasons related to pregnancy. • **Teenage mothers** are the percentage of women ages 15–19 who already have children or are currently pregnant. • **Women in nonagricultural sector** are female wage employees in the nonagricultural sector as a percentage of total nonagricultural wage employment. • **Unpaid family workers** are those who work without pay in a market-oriented establishment or activity operated by a related person living in the same household. • **Women in parliaments** are the percentage of parliamentary seats in a single or lower chamber held by women.

**Data sources**

Data on female population and life expectancy are from the World Bank's population database. Data on pregnant women receiving prenatal care are from household surveys, including Demographic and Health Surveys by Macro International and Multiple Indicator Cluster Surveys by the United Nations Children's Fund (UNICEF), and UNICEF's *State of the World's Children 2008.* Data on teenage mothers are from Demographic and Health Surveys by Macro International. Data on labor force and employment are from the International Labour Organization's *Key Indicators of the Labour Market,* fifth edition. Data on women in parliaments are from the Inter-Parliamentary Union.

| | Population | Surface area | Population density | Gross national income | | | | Gross domestic product | | Life expectancy at birth | Adult literacy rate | Carbon dioxide emissions |
|---|---|---|---|---|---|---|---|---|---|---|---|---|
| | | | | | | PPP[a] | | | | | | |
| | | thousand sq. km | people per sq. km | $ millions | Per capita $ | $ millions | Per capita $ | % growth | Per capita % growth | years | % ages 15 and older | thousand metric tons |
| | thousands 2006 | 2006 | 2006 | 2006[b] | 2006[b] | 2006 | 2006 | 2005–06 | 2005–06 | 2006 | 2005 | 2004 |
| American Samoa | 60 | 0.2 | 298 | .. | ..[c] | .. | .. | .. | .. | .. | .. | 41 |
| Andorra | 67 | 0.5 | 142 | .. | ..[d] | .. | .. | .. | .. | .. | .. | .. |
| Antigua and Barbuda | 84 | 0.4 | 191 | 929 | 11,050[e] | 1,273[f] | 15,130[f] | 11.5 | 10.1 | .. | .. | 414 |
| Aruba | 101 | 0.2 | 562 | .. | ..[d] | .. | .. | .. | .. | .. | .. | 2,154 |
| Bahamas, The | 327 | 13.9 | 33 | .. | ..[d] | ..[f] | ..[f] | .. | .. | 73 | .. | 2,007 |
| Bahrain | 739 | 0.7 | 1,041 | 14,022 | 19,350 | 24,869 | 34,310 | 7.8 | 5.6 | 76 | .. | 16,934 |
| Barbados | 293 | 0.4 | 681 | .. | ..[d] | 4,422[f] | 15,150[f] | .. | .. | 77 | .. | 1,267 |
| Belize | 298 | 23.0 | 13 | 1,114 | 3,740 | 2,108[f] | 7,080[f] | 5.6 | 3.5 | 72 | .. | 791 |
| Bermuda | 64 | 0.1 | 1,276 | .. | ..[d] | .. | .. | .. | .. | 79 | .. | 549 |
| Bhutan | 649 | 47.0 | 14 | 928 | 1,430 | 2,596 | 4,000 | 8.5 | 6.5 | 65 | 60 | 414 |
| Brunei Darussalam | 382 | 5.8 | 72 | 10,287 | 26,930 | 19,059 | 49,900 | 5.1 | 2.9 | 77 | .. | 8,802 |
| Cape Verde | 519 | 4.0 | 129 | 1,105 | 2,130 | 1,344 | 2,590 | 6.1 | 3.7 | 71 | 81 | 275 |
| Cayman Islands | 46 | 0.3 | 177 | .. | ..[d] | .. | .. | .. | .. | .. | .. | 311 |
| Channel Islands | 149 | 0.2 | 784 | .. | ..[d] | .. | .. | .. | .. | 79 | .. | .. |
| Comoros | 614 | 1.9 | 330 | 406 | 660 | 698 | 1,140 | 0.5 | –1.6 | 63 | .. | 88 |
| Cyprus | 771 | 9.3 | 83 | 17,948 | 23,270 | 19,328 | 25,060 | 4.0 | 2.2 | 79 | .. | 6,744 |
| Djibouti | 819 | 23.2 | 35 | 864 | 1,060 | 1,787 | 2,180 | 4.9 | 3.0 | 54 | .. | 366 |
| Dominica | 72 | 0.8 | 97 | 300 | 4,160 | 566[f] | 7,870[f] | 4.0 | 3.4 | .. | .. | 106 |
| Equatorial Guinea | 496 | 28.1 | 18 | 4,216 | 8,510 | 8,238 | 16,620 | –5.6 | –7.8 | 51 | .. | 5,421 |
| Faeroe Islands | 48 | 1.4 | 35 | .. | ..[d] | .. | .. | .. | .. | 79 | .. | 659 |
| Fiji | 833 | 18.3 | 46 | 3,098 | 3,720[g] | 3,707 | 4,450 | 3.6 | 2.9 | 69 | .. | 1,070 |
| French Polynesia | 259 | 4.0 | 71 | .. | ..[d] | .. | .. | .. | .. | 74 | .. | 670 |
| Greenland | 57 | 410.5 | 0[h] | .. | ..[d] | .. | .. | .. | .. | .. | .. | 571 |
| Grenada | 108 | 0.3 | 318 | 495 | 4,650 | 934[f] | 8,770[f] | 0.7 | –0.8 | .. | .. | 216 |
| Guam | 171 | 0.5 | 317 | .. | ..[d] | .. | .. | .. | .. | 75 | .. | 4,081 |
| Guyana | 739 | 215.0 | 4 | 849 | 1,150 | 2,522[f] | 3,410[f] | 4.8 | 4.9 | 66 | .. | 1,443 |
| Iceland | 302 | 103.0 | 3 | 15,078 | 49,960 | 10,181 | 33,740 | 2.6 | 0.9 | 81 | .. | 2,227 |
| Isle of Man | 77 | 0.6 | 135 | 3,088 | 40,600 | .. | .. | 5.9 | 4.9 | .. | .. | .. |

The table shows data for 56 economies with populations between 30,000 and 1 million and smaller economies if they are members of the World Bank. Where data on gross national income (GNI) per capita are not available, the estimated range is given. For more information on the calculation of GNI (gross national product, or GNP, in the System of National Accounts 1968) and purchasing power parity (PPP) conversion factors, see *About the data* for table 1.1. Since 2000 the table has excluded France's overseas departments—French Guiana, Guadeloupe, Martinique, and Réunion—for which GNI and other economic measures are now included in the French national accounts.

• **Population** is based on the de facto definition of population, which counts all residents regardless of legal status or citizenship—except for refugees not permanently settled in the country of asylum, who are generally considered part of the population of their country of origin. The values shown are midyear estimates. See also table 2.1. • **Surface area** is a country's total area, including areas under inland bodies of water and some coastal waterways. • **Population density** is midyear population divided by land area in square kilometers. • **Gross national income (GNI)** is the sum of value added by all resident producers plus any product taxes (less subsidies) not included in the valuation of output plus net receipts of primary income (compensation of employees and property income) from abroad. Data are in current U.S. dollars converted using the *World Bank Atlas* method (see *Statistical methods*). • **GNI per capita** is GNI divided by midyear population. GNI per capita in U.S. dollars is converted using the *World Bank Atlas* method. • **Purchasing power parity (PPP) GNI** is GNI converted to international dollars using PPP rates. An international dollar has the same purchasing power over GNI that a U.S. dollar has in the United States. • **Gross domestic product (GDP)** is the sum of value added by all resident producers plus any product taxes (less subsidies) not included in the valuation of output.

| | Population | Surface area | Population density | Gross national income | | | | Gross domestic product | | Life expectancy at birth | Adult literacy rate | Carbon dioxide emissions |
|---|---|---|---|---|---|---|---|---|---|---|---|---|
| | | | | | | PPP[a] | | | | | | |
| | thousands 2006 | thousand sq. km 2006 | people per sq. km 2006 | $ millions 2006[b] | Per capita $ 2006[b] | $ millions 2006 | Per capita $ 2006 | % growth 2005–06 | Per capita % growth 2005–06 | years 2006 | % ages 15 and older 2005 | thousand metric tons 2004 |
| Kiribati | 100 | 0.8 | 124 | 124 | 1,240 | 624[f] | 6,230[f] | 5.8 | 4.5 | .. | .. | 29 |
| Liechtenstein | 35 | 0.2 | 218 | .. | ..[d] | .. | .. | .. | .. | .. | .. | .. |
| Luxembourg | 462 | 2.6 | 178 | 32,904 | 71,240 | 28,117 | 60,870 | 6.2 | 5.0 | 79 | .. | 11,267 |
| Macao, China | 478 | 0.0 | 16,934 | .. | ..[d] | .. | .. | 16.6 | 15.5 | 80 | .. | 2,205 |
| Maldives | 300 | 0.3 | 1,001 | 903 | 3,010 | 1,424 | 4,740 | 23.5 | 21.5 | 68 | .. | 725 |
| Malta | 406 | 0.3 | 1,269 | 6,216 | 15,310 | 8,523 | 20,990 | 3.4 | 2.8 | 79 | .. | 2,451 |
| Marshall Islands | 65 | 0.2 | 363 | 195 | 2,980 | 525[f] | 8,040[f] | 3.0 | −0.3 | .. | .. | .. |
| Mayotte | 187 | 0.4 | 499 | .. | ..[c] | .. | .. | .. | .. | .. | .. | .. |
| Micronesia, Fed. Sts. | 111 | 0.7 | 158 | 264 | 2,390 | 672[f] | 6,070[f] | −0.7 | −1.2 | 68 | .. | .. |
| Monaco | 33 | 0.0 | 16,718 | .. | ..[d] | .. | .. | .. | .. | .. | .. | .. |
| Montenegro | 601 | 14.0 | 44 | 2,481 | 4,130 | 5,366 | 8,930 | 16.2 | 17.5 | 74 | .. | .. |
| Netherlands Antilles | 189 | 0.8 | 236 | .. | ..[d] | .. | .. | .. | .. | 75 | 96 | 4,084 |
| New Caledonia | 238 | 18.6 | 13 | .. | ..[d] | .. | .. | .. | .. | 75 | .. | 2,575 |
| Northern Mariana Islands | 82 | 0.5 | 178 | .. | ..[c] | .. | .. | .. | .. | .. | .. | .. |
| Palau | 20 | 0.5 | 44 | 161 | 7,990 | 290[f] | 14,340[f] | 5.7 | 5.2 | .. | .. | 238 |
| Qatar | 821 | 11.0 | 75 | .. | ..[d] | .. | .. | 6.1 | 1.8 | 75 | 89 | 52,857 |
| Samoa | 185 | 2.8 | 66 | 421 | 2,270 | 943[f] | 5,090[f] | 2.3 | 1.5 | 71 | 99 | 150 |
| San Marino | 29 | 0.1 | 477 | 1,291 | 45,130 | .. | .. | 5.0 | 3.5 | 82 | .. | .. |
| São Tomé and Principe | 155 | 1.0 | 162 | 124 | 800 | 231 | 1,490 | 7.0 | 5.3 | 65 | .. | 92 |
| Seychelles | 85 | 0.5 | 184 | 751 | 8,870 | 1,215[f] | 14,360[f] | 5.3 | 3.2 | 72 | .. | 546 |
| Solomon Islands | 484 | 28.9 | 17 | 333 | 690 | 896[f] | 1,850[f] | 6.1 | 3.6 | 63 | .. | 176 |
| St. Kitts and Nevis | 48 | 0.3 | 186 | 406 | 8,460 | 597[f] | 12,440[f] | 5.8 | 4.9 | .. | .. | 125 |
| St. Lucia | 166 | 0.6 | 272 | 833 | 5,060 | 1,400[f] | 8,500[f] | 4.5 | 3.7 | 74 | .. | 366 |
| St. Vincent & Grenadines | 120 | 0.4 | 307 | 395 | 3,320 | 741[f] | 6,220[f] | 1.5 | 1.0 | 71 | .. | 198 |
| Suriname | 455 | 163.3 | 3 | 1,918 | 4,210[g] | 3,514[f] | 7,720[f] | 5.8 | 5.1 | 70 | 90 | 2,282 |
| Tonga | 100 | 0.8 | 139 | 225 | 2,250 | 546[f] | 5,470[f] | 1.4 | 0.9 | 73 | .. | 117 |
| Vanuatu | 221 | 12.2 | 18 | 373 | 1,690 | 768[f] | 3,480[f] | 7.2 | 4.6 | 70 | .. | 88 |
| Virgin Islands (U.S.) | 109 | 0.4 | 310 | .. | ..[d] | .. | .. | .. | .. | 79 | .. | 13,524 |

a. PPP is purchasing power parity, see *Definitions*. b. Calculated using the *World Bank Atlas* method. c. Estimated to be upper middle income ($3,596–$11,115). d. Estimated to be high income ($11,116 or more). e. Included in the aggregates for high-income economies based on earlier data. f. Based on regression; others are extrapolated from the 2005 International Comparison Program benchmark estimates. g. Included in the aggregates for lower middle-income economies based on earlier data. h. Less than 0.5.

Growth is calculated from constant price GDP data in local currency. • **GDP per capita** is GDP divided by midyear population. • **Life expectancy at birth** is the number of years a newborn infant would live if prevailing patterns of mortality at the time of its birth were to stay the same throughout its life. • **Adult literacy rate** is the percentage of adults ages 15 and older who can, with understanding, read and write a short, simple statement about their everyday life. • **Carbon dioxide emissions** are those stemming from the burning of fossil fuels and the manufacture of cement. They include carbon dioxide produced during consumption of solid, liquid, and gas fuels and gas flaring.

### Data sources

The indicators here and throughout the book are compiled by World Bank staff from primary and secondary sources. More information about the indicators and their sources can be found in the *About the data*, *Definitions*, and *Data sources* entries that accompany each table in subsequent sections.

2 PEOPLE

# Reproductive health

Keeping mothers alive and healthy is good for women, their families, and society. Prioritizing women's health will help countries meet many of the Millennium Development Goals—first improved maternal and child health, then reduced poverty, universal education, and gender equality. Poor people tend to have large families, suffer disproportionately from illness, and use fewer health services during pregnancy and childbirth. Reproductive health care can enhance poor people's overall health care and help families escape the poverty impact of having many children. When financial resources are divided among fewer family members, more is left for education, health care, and savings, decreasing vulnerability and insecurity (UN Millennium Project 2005a).

This important link between reproductive health and development outcomes was first articulated in 1994 at the International Conference on Population and Development in Cairo. But as fertility declined in many countries and new priorities arose, reproductive health and family planning fell steadily in international priority. Complicating this was the lack of sectoral ownership of reproductive health and the requirement for multisectoral action.

The targets for the Millennium Development Goals, drafted in 2000, ignored the overarching Cairo goal of universal access to sexual and reproductive health services, instead focusing on the target of reducing maternal mortality, a problem of immense magnitude in poor countries (figures 2a and 2b). Millennium Development Goal 5 in 2000 identified two indicators to measure progress: maternal mortality ratios and the proportion of births attended by skilled staff. At an analytical level, however, it is impossible to disentangle maternal health from reproductive health, of which maternal health is just one facet.

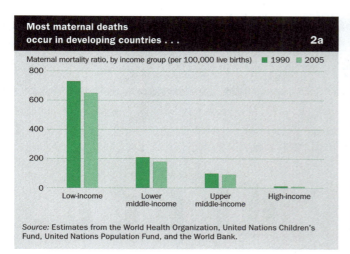

**Most maternal deaths occur in developing countries . . .** 2a

Maternal mortality ratio, by income group (per 100,000 live births) ■ 1990 ■ 2005

*Source:* Estimates from the World Health Organization, United Nations Children's Fund, United Nations Population Fund, and the World Bank.

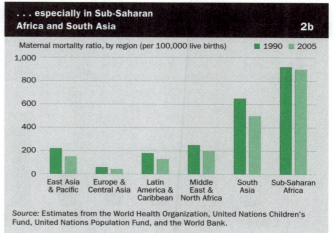

**. . . especially in Sub-Saharan Africa and South Asia** 2b

Maternal mortality ratio, by region (per 100,000 live births) ■ 1990 ■ 2005

*Source:* Estimates from the World Health Organization, United Nations Children's Fund, United Nations Population Fund, and the World Bank.

# Why reproductive health now?

Pregnancy and childbirth are leading causes of death and disability for women of reproductive age in developing countries. In 2005 more than half a million women died from pregnancy-related causes, and about 200 million women suffered life-threatening complications and disabilities (Glasier and others 2006). As a result of reproductive health problems an estimated 250 million years of productive life are lost every year (UNFPA 2005). Over 99 percent of all maternal deaths occur in developing countries, the majority in Sub-Saharan Africa and South Asia (Glasier and others 2006).

In 2005 Millennium Development Goal 5—improved maternal health—was expanded to include family planning and reproductive health services. Reproductive health care was recognized as important for improving maternal health and preventing maternal deaths, but also as essential for achieving all the Millennium Development Goals. A new target was introduced for universal access to reproductive health by 2015, along with indicators measuring adolescent fertility, prenatal care, unmet need for contraception, and contraceptive prevalence.

Poor women disproportionately bear the burden of disability and loss of productive life. Women in low-income countries face a 1 in 40 risk of a pregnancy-related death; those in high-income countries, a 1 in 6,700 risk (figure 2c). The contrast is also large within countries. In Peru the poorest women are about 7 times more likely than the richest to die of pregnancy-related causes (Ronsman and Graham 2006). Even though cheap and easy methods to prevent unintended or unwanted pregnancies are available, 120 million couples hoping to avoid pregnancy did not use contraception. As a result, 80 million women became pregnant against their will, and 45 million sought abortions, about 20 million of them unsafe, performed by untrained providers (Glasier and others 2006).

Progress in maternal and reproductive health in recent years has been mixed in developing countries. Several middle-income countries have made rapid progress in reducing maternal deaths, but maternal mortality ratios and the lifetime risk of dying in childbirth remain unacceptably high in Sub-Saharan Africa and South Asia (figure 2d). Within countries, poorer women are more vulnerable than wealthier women.

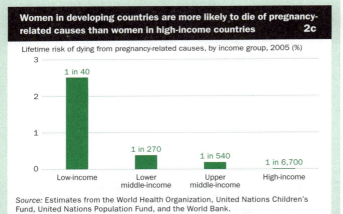

**Women in developing countries are more likely to die of pregnancy-related causes than women in high-income countries** 2c

Lifetime risk of dying from pregnancy-related causes, by income group, 2005 (%)

*Source:* Estimates from the World Health Organization, United Nations Children's Fund, United Nations Population Fund, and the World Bank.

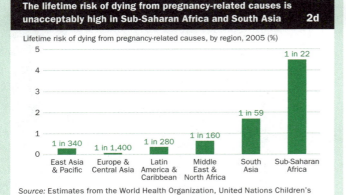

**The lifetime risk of dying from pregnancy-related causes is unacceptably high in Sub-Saharan Africa and South Asia** 2d

Lifetime risk of dying from pregnancy-related causes, by region, 2005 (%)

*Source:* Estimates from the World Health Organization, United Nations Children's Fund, United Nations Population Fund, and the World Bank.

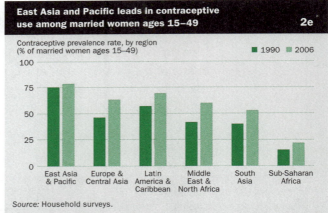

**East Asia and Pacific leads in contraceptive use among married women ages 15–49** 2e

Contraceptive prevalence rate, by region (% of married women ages 15–49)   ■ 1990  ■ 2006

*Source:* Household surveys.

**Women from the richest households are more likely to use contraception—but contraceptive prevalence rates remain low** 2f

Contraceptive prevalence rate, by region and wealth quintile (% of married women ages 15–49)   ■ Poorest 20%  ■ Richest 20%

*Source:* Gwatkin and others 2007.

## Maternal and reproductive health: current status

The vast majority of maternal deaths and disabilities can be prevented through appropriate reproductive health services before, during, and after pregnancy. Key among them is expanding family planning to allow women to space or limit their births.

Contraceptive use among women in developing countries has increased steadily, from about 14 percent of married women ages 15–49 in 1965 to 60 percent in 2006. But use is uneven across and within countries. In Sub-Saharan Africa only 22 percent of married women use contraception, compared with 63 percent in Europe and Central Asia, about 70 percent in Latin America and the Caribbean, and about 80 percent in East Asia and the Pacific (figure 2e).

Contraceptive use follows the distribution of wealth, and the poorest women come up short. Differences are especially stark in South Asia and Sub-Saharan Africa (figure 2f). In Sub-Saharan Africa women from richer households are three times more likely to use contraception, but prevalence is still less than 30 percent of eligible women. In South Asia richer women are twice as likely as poorer women to use contraception.

Despite the benefits, many countries continue to face major challenges in meeting their family planning needs (figure 2g), and rates of unmet need for family planning in developing countries remain high (figure 2h). According to surveys, one married woman in seven in these countries has an unmet need for contraception, and in Sub-Saharan Africa nearly one in four does. Regional aggregates mask wide differences: in Asia only 5 percent of women in Vietnam have an unmet need, compared with 28 percent in Nepal (Sedgh and others 2007b). Preventing unplanned pregnancies alone could avert around one-quarter of maternal deaths, including those from unsafe abortions (Sedgh and others 2007b).

Young girls are particularly vulnerable to maternal death. They have limited information, means, and access to contraception and even less access to good quality maternal health care, especially if they are not married. In regions where the adolescent fertility rate is high (figure 2i), many young women and their children, particularly very young women, face higher risks of death and disability (box 2j). Young girls either continue unintended pregnancies, giving up opportunities

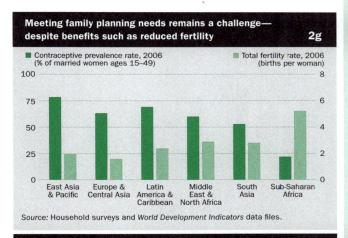

**Meeting family planning needs remains a challenge—despite benefits such as reduced fertility**    **2g**

*Source:* Household surveys and *World Development Indicators* data files.

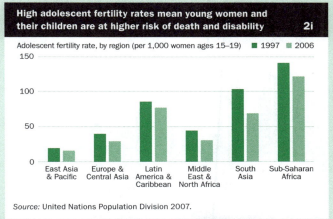

**High adolescent fertility rates mean young women and their children are at higher risk of death and disability**    **2i**

*Source:* United Nations Population Division 2007.

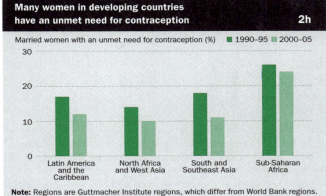

**Many women in developing countries have an unmet need for contraception**    **2h**

**Note:** Regions are Guttmacher Institute regions, which differ from World Bank regions.
*Source:* Sedgh and others 2007b.

**Age-specific fertility for girls ages 15–17**    **Box 2j**

The age below which giving birth is physically risky for a woman varies depending on general health conditions and access to prenatal care. Although the physical risk of giving birth during adolescence is not high for women in countries with good nutritional levels and extensive access to prenatal care, the risk rises in societies where anemia and malnutrition are prevalent and where access to health care is generally poor. The adolescent fertility rate for ages 15–19 is now included as a Millennium Development Goal indicator. However, the fertility rate of girls ages 15–17 is argued to be a better indicator, as this age group is at higher risk of suffering pregnancy-related complications and having very low birthweight babies. Even when very young adolescents deliver their babies in health facilities, they suffer higher rates of mortality than older women do.
*Source:* Lule and others 2005.

for education and employment, or seek unsafe abortions. Forty percent of all the abortions are performed on women under age 25 (Glasier and others 2006).

Prenatal care, long at the core of maternal health services, identifies risks, helps plan for safe delivery, and provides entry into the health care system. All regions but Sub-Saharan Africa have made progress in providing prenatal care to women at least once during pregnancy (figure 2k). In South Asia, with the slowest progress, 66 percent of pregnant women have at least one prenatal care visit. But rich women are three times more likely to get prenatal care than are poor women (figure 2l).

A key factor in lowering maternal mortality is the presence of a skilled attendant during childbirth. Nearly half of maternal deaths in developing countries occur during labor and delivery or just after delivery (Lule and others 2005). The proportion of attended births remains low in South Asia and Sub-Saharan Africa (figure 2m) and is even lower in the poorer segments of these countries (figure 2n). Other regions have made impressive gains, with countries in Europe and Central Asia providing skilled care to nearly all women giving birth.

## An improvement, but is it enough?

Both preventive and strategic interventions are needed to treat the many factors that contribute to maternal mortality. The expanded Millennium Development Goal 5 indicators are mainly process indicators to assess reproductive health and address preventive interventions: preparing for birth, including timing and spacing of births for both adults and adolescents; recognizing danger signs in the prenatal period and responding appropriately; and having skilled health staff at delivery.

Equally important are the strategic interventions, especially during labor and delivery. Among these are obstetric care, including timely and safe transfers of mothers to a hospital or health care center with the necessary staff, equipment, drugs, and other supplies. The World Health Organization (WHO) has proposed that national public health administrators monitor the availability of essential obstetric care and access to emergency obstetric care at the country level (box 2o). An estimated 15 percent of pregnancies result in complications (Nanda, Switlick, and Lule 2005). But data on complications are collected only by ad hoc studies, usually in limited areas of countries, and no standard definition or methodology is followed.

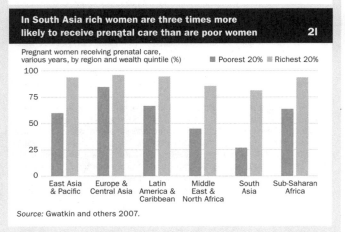

**All regions have made progress in providing prenatal care to women at least once during their pregnancy** **2k**

Pregnant women receiving prenatal care, by region (%)    ■ 1990  ■ 2006

*Source:* Household surveys.

**In South Asia rich women are three times more likely to receive prenatal care than are poor women** **2l**

Pregnant women receiving prenatal care, various years, by region and wealth quintile (%)    ■ Poorest 20%  ■ Richest 20%

*Source:* Gwatkin and others 2007.

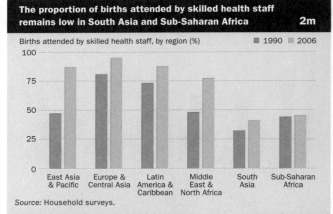

**The proportion of births attended by skilled health staff remains low in South Asia and Sub-Saharan Africa** **2m**

Births attended by skilled health staff, by region (%)    ■ 1990  ■ 2006

*Source:* Household surveys.

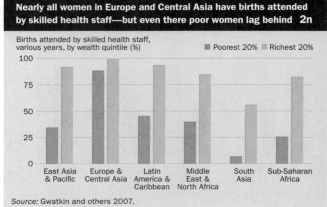

**Nearly all women in Europe and Central Asia have births attended by skilled health staff—but even there poor women lag behind** **2n**

Births attended by skilled health staff, various years, by wealth quintile (%)    ■ Poorest 20%  ■ Richest 20%

*Source:* Gwatkin and others 2007.

Complications from abortion are also now recognized as a major public and reproductive health problem, especially in developing countries. Abortions, especially unsafe ones, account for 13 percent of maternal deaths, and good quality post-abortion services and family planning services to avoid unwanted pregnancies are essential. Of an estimated 20 million unsafe abortions worldwide each year, the majority are in developing countries (Nanda, Switlick, and Lule 2005) (figure 2p). Abortion information is particularly difficult to gather because abortion is restricted and stigmatized in many countries, leading to false reporting by women and service providers. Regional estimates of abortion rates are available from the WHO, UN agencies, national authorities, and nongovernmental organizations. But reliable country data are not routinely collected.

In addition to definitional gaps, data collection for these two indicators faces additional hurdles because the infrastructure for collecting data is weak or because there is political, cultural, or moral hesitation. Obtaining accurate values also requires significant clinical resources and technical skills.

## The importance of emergency obstetric care — Box 2o

Emergency obstetric care encompasses a set of functions performed at health facilities that can prevent the death of women experiencing obstetric complications. Basic emergency obstetric care, usually provided at health centers and small maternity homes, includes administering certain drugs and performing lifesaving procedures, such as for preeclampsia and eclampsia. Comprehensive emergency obstetric care, usually provided at subdistrict or district hospitals, also includes providing Caesarean sections and blood transfusions.

More maternal health programs now recognize that emergency obstetric care is critical to reducing maternal death and disability. Much can be accomplished by upgrading existing facilities. In programming for emergency obstetric care, bottlenecks in accessing services are often assessed using the "three delays" model: delays in the decision to seek care, delays in arrival at a health facility, and delays in the provision of adequate care at the facility.

*Source:* Nanda, Switlick, and Lule 2005.

## Most unsafe abortions take place in developing countries, especially in Latin America and the Caribbean and Africa — 2p

Incidence of unsafe abortion, 2003 (per 1,000 women)

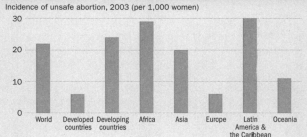

*Note:* Regions are World Health Organization regions, which differ from World Bank regions.
*Source:* WHO 2007.

## Challenges ahead

The interventions to prevent the vast majority of conditions that kill women of reproductive age—and to enable health systems to protect and promote women's health—have already been identified. Some are simple, low-tech, and cost-effective, such as the provision and use of contraception. Yet many people in developing countries, especially in South Asia and Sub-Saharan Africa, do not benefit. Behind the failure of these health systems are weak commitments to improving maternal health, poor management systems, inadequate human and medical resources and equipment, and, for most of the poor, the inability to pay for services.

Underlying the failures of the health system is the lack of reliable data for monitoring progress in maternal and reproductive health and in other safe motherhood indicators. And most developing countries have inadequate health information systems or lack them altogether. So, providing timely and reliable information often depends on local, one-off data collection, such as household surveys, which are both costly and unsustainable because they do not establish permanent health information structures. Ideally, there would be vital registration systems, hospital and health service data, and household surveys.

Least available are data on maternal deaths, needed to monitor the Millennium Development Goal target of cutting maternal mortality ratios by 75 percent. While vital registration systems are a rich and valuable source of health data in developed countries, they are incomplete in developing countries. For example, the share of developing countries with at least 90 percent complete vital registration increased from 45 percent in 1988 to 62 percent in 2006. Still, some of the most populous countries—China, India, Indonesia, Brazil, Pakistan, Bangladesh, Nigeria—do not have complete vital registration systems. Hospital or other health service records are sometimes a source of information. But these record only women who have access to health services, and a large number of women, especially in rural areas, do not. Household surveys for estimating maternal mortality ratios are costly and yield unreliable estimates.

The evidence base should be strong enough to provide crucial information on who dies and why—and to generate insights about interventions that are available, accessible, appropriate, and affordable.

| | Population | | | Average annual population growth | | Population age composition | | | Dependency ratio | | Crude death rate | Crude birth rate |
|---|---|---|---|---|---|---|---|---|---|---|---|---|
| | | | | | | | % | | dependents as proportion of working-age population | | | |
| | | | | | | Ages 0–14 | Ages 15–64 | Ages 65+ | Young | Old | per 1,000 people | per 1,000 people |
| | millions 1990 | 2006 | 2015 | % 1990–2006 | 2006–15 | 2006 | 2006 | 2006 | 2006 | 2006 | 2006 | 2006 |
| Afghanistan | .. | .. | .. | .. | .. | .. | .. | .. | .. | .. | .. | .. |
| Albania | 3.3 | 3.2 | 3.3 | −0.2 | 0.4 | 25.5 | 65.8 | 8.7 | 0.4 | 0.1 | 6 | 16 |
| Algeria | 25.3 | 33.4 | 38.0 | 1.7 | 1.5 | 28.9 | 66.5 | 4.6 | 0.4 | 0.1 | 5 | 21 |
| Angola | 10.5 | 16.6 | 21.2 | 2.8 | 2.8 | 46.3 | 51.3 | 2.4 | 0.9 | 0.0a | 21 | 48 |
| Argentina | 32.6 | 39.1 | 42.5 | 1.1 | 0.9 | 26.1 | 63.6 | 10.3 | 0.4 | 0.2 | 8 | 18 |
| Armenia | 3.5 | 3.0 | 3.0 | −1.0 | −0.2 | 20.0 | 67.9 | 12.1 | 0.3 | 0.2 | 9 | 12 |
| Australia | 17.1 | 20.7 | 22.4 | 1.2 | 0.9 | 19.3 | 67.4 | 13.3 | 0.3 | 0.2 | 7 | 13 |
| Austria | 7.7 | 8.3 | 8.4 | 0.4 | 0.2 | 15.6 | 68.0 | 16.4 | 0.2 | 0.2 | 9 | 9 |
| Azerbaijan | 7.2 | 8.5 | 9.2 | 1.1 | 0.9 | 24.2 | 68.5 | 7.2 | 0.4 | 0.1 | 6 | 18 |
| Bangladesh | 113.0 | 156.0 | 180.0 | 2.0 | 1.6 | 34.7 | 61.7 | 3.6 | 0.6 | 0.1 | 8 | 25 |
| Belarus | 10.2 | 9.7 | 9.2 | −0.3 | −0.6 | 15.3 | 70.4 | 14.3 | 0.2 | 0.2 | 15 | 9 |
| Belgium | 10.0 | 10.5 | 10.7 | 0.3 | 0.1 | 16.9 | 65.8 | 17.3 | 0.3 | 0.3 | 10 | 12 |
| Benin | 5.2 | 8.8 | 11.3 | 3.3 | 2.9 | 44.0 | 53.3 | 2.7 | 0.8 | 0.1 | 11 | 41 |
| Bolivia | 6.7 | 9.4 | 10.9 | 2.1 | 1.6 | 37.7 | 57.7 | 4.6 | 0.7 | 0.1 | 8 | 28 |
| Bosnia and Herzegovina | 4.3 | 3.9 | 3.9 | −0.6 | −0.2 | 17.3 | 68.6 | 14.1 | 0.3 | 0.2 | 9 | 9 |
| Botswana | 1.4 | 1.9 | 2.1 | 1.9 | 1.2 | 35.1 | 61.5 | 3.4 | 0.6 | 0.1 | 15 | 25 |
| Brazil | 149.5 | 189.3 | 209.4 | 1.5 | 1.1 | 27.6 | 66.2 | 6.3 | 0.4 | 0.1 | 6 | 19 |
| Bulgaria | 8.7 | 7.7 | 7.1 | −0.8 | −0.8 | 13.6 | 69.2 | 17.3 | 0.2 | 0.2 | 15 | 9 |
| Burkina Faso | 8.9 | 14.4 | 18.6 | 3.0 | 2.9 | 46.0 | 51.0 | 3.1 | 0.9 | 0.1 | 15 | 44 |
| Burundi | 5.7 | 8.2 | 11.2 | 2.3 | 3.5 | 44.7 | 52.7 | 2.6 | 0.8 | 0.0a | 16 | 47 |
| Cambodia | 9.7 | 14.2 | 16.6 | 2.4 | 1.8 | 36.7 | 60.1 | 3.2 | 0.6 | 0.1 | 9 | 27 |
| Cameroon | 12.2 | 18.2 | 21.5 | 2.5 | 1.9 | 41.5 | 55.0 | 3.5 | 0.8 | 0.1 | 15 | 35 |
| Canada | 27.8 | 32.6 | 35.1 | 1.0 | 0.8 | 17.3 | 69.4 | 13.3 | 0.2 | 0.2 | 7 | 11 |
| Central African Republic | 3.0 | 4.3 | 5.0 | 2.2 | 1.8 | 42.5 | 53.7 | 3.9 | 0.8 | 0.1 | 18 | 37 |
| Chad | 6.1 | 10.5 | 13.4 | 3.4 | 2.7 | 46.2 | 50.9 | 2.9 | 0.9 | 0.1 | 16 | 46 |
| Chile | 13.2 | 16.4 | 17.8 | 1.4 | 0.9 | 24.3 | 67.4 | 8.3 | 0.4 | 0.1 | 5 | 15 |
| China | 1,135.2 | 1,311.8 | 1,382.5 | 0.9 | 0.6 | 21.1 | 71.1 | 7.8 | 0.3 | 0.1 | 7 | 12 |
| Hong Kong, China | 5.7 | 6.9 | 7.4 | 1.2 | 0.9 | 14.8 | 73.2 | 12.1 | 0.2 | 0.2 | 5 | 10 |
| Colombia | 34.9 | 45.6 | 50.6 | 1.7 | 1.2 | 29.8 | 65.0 | 5.2 | 0.5 | 0.1 | 6 | 19 |
| Congo, Dem. Rep. | 37.9 | 60.6 | 78.5 | 2.9 | 2.9 | 47.3 | 50.1 | 2.6 | 0.9 | 0.1 | 18 | 44 |
| Congo, Rep. | 2.4 | 3.7 | 4.5 | 2.6 | 2.1 | 41.9 | 54.9 | 3.2 | 0.8 | 0.1 | 12 | 36 |
| Costa Rica | 3.1 | 4.4 | 5.0 | 2.2 | 1.4 | 27.8 | 66.3 | 5.9 | 0.4 | 0.1 | 4 | 18 |
| Côte d'Ivoire | 12.8 | 18.9 | 22.3 | 2.5 | 1.9 | 41.4 | 55.4 | 3.2 | 0.7 | 0.1 | 16 | 36 |
| Croatia | 4.8 | 4.4 | 4.3 | −0.5 | −0.3 | 15.3 | 67.4 | 17.3 | 0.2 | 0.3 | 11 | 9 |
| Cuba | 10.6 | 11.3 | 11.2 | 0.4 | −0.1 | 18.9 | 69.7 | 11.4 | 0.3 | 0.2 | 8 | 11 |
| Czech Republic | 10.4 | 10.3 | 10.2 | −0.1 | −0.1 | 14.5 | 71.2 | 14.3 | 0.2 | 0.2 | 10 | 10 |
| Denmark | 5.1 | 5.4 | 5.5 | 0.4 | 0.1 | 18.7 | 66.0 | 15.4 | 0.3 | 0.2 | 10 | 12 |
| Dominican Republic | 7.3 | 9.6 | 10.9 | 1.7 | 1.4 | 33.2 | 61.1 | 5.7 | 0.5 | 0.1 | 6 | 24 |
| Ecuador | 10.3 | 13.2 | 14.6 | 1.6 | 1.1 | 32.2 | 61.7 | 6.0 | 0.5 | 0.1 | 5 | 21 |
| Egypt, Arab Rep. | 55.1 | 74.2 | 86.2 | 1.9 | 1.7 | 33.0 | 62.1 | 4.9 | 0.5 | 0.1 | 6 | 24 |
| El Salvador | 5.1 | 6.8 | 7.6 | 1.8 | 1.3 | 33.7 | 60.7 | 5.6 | 0.6 | 0.1 | 6 | 23 |
| Eritrea | 3.2 | 4.7 | 6.2 | 2.5 | 3.0 | 42.9 | 54.8 | 2.3 | 0.8 | 0.0a | 9 | 40 |
| Estonia | 1.6 | 1.3 | 1.3 | −1.0 | −0.4 | 14.9 | 68.4 | 16.7 | 0.2 | 0.2 | 13 | 11 |
| Ethiopia | 51.2 | 77.2 | 96.0 | 2.6 | 2.4 | 44.2 | 52.9 | 2.9 | 0.8 | 0.1 | 13 | 39 |
| Finland | 5.0 | 5.3 | 5.4 | 0.3 | 0.2 | 17.2 | 66.7 | 16.1 | 0.3 | 0.2 | 9 | 11 |
| France | 56.7 | 61.3 | 63.1 | 0.5 | 0.3 | 18.3 | 65.4 | 16.3 | 0.3 | 0.2 | 9 | 13 |
| Gabon | 0.9 | 1.3 | 1.5 | 2.2 | 1.5 | 35.4 | 60.0 | 4.6 | 0.6 | 0.1 | 12 | 26 |
| Gambia, The | 1.0 | 1.7 | 2.1 | 3.4 | 2.5 | 41.0 | 55.2 | 3.8 | 0.7 | 0.1 | 11 | 36 |
| Georgia | 5.5 | 4.4 | 4.2 | −1.3 | −0.7 | 18.4 | 67.3 | 14.4 | 0.3 | 0.2 | 12 | 11 |
| Germany | 79.4 | 82.4 | 81.1 | 0.2 | −0.2 | 14.1 | 66.6 | 19.2 | 0.2 | 0.3 | 10 | 8 |
| Ghana | 15.6 | 23.0 | 27.3 | 2.4 | 1.9 | 38.6 | 57.7 | 3.7 | 0.7 | 0.1 | 9 | 30 |
| Greece | 10.2 | 11.1 | 11.2 | 0.6 | 0.0a | 14.2 | 67.4 | 18.4 | 0.2 | 0.3 | 9 | 10 |
| Guatemala | 8.9 | 13.0 | 16.2 | 2.4 | 2.4 | 42.9 | 52.8 | 4.3 | 0.8 | 0.1 | 6 | 34 |
| Guinea | 6.0 | 9.2 | 11.4 | 2.6 | 2.4 | 43.3 | 53.7 | 3.1 | 0.8 | 0.1 | 12 | 40 |
| Guinea-Bissau | 1.0 | 1.6 | 2.2 | 3.0 | 3.0 | 47.6 | 49.4 | 3.0 | 1.0 | 0.1 | 19 | 50 |
| Haiti | 7.1 | 9.4 | 11.0 | 1.8 | 1.7 | 37.5 | 58.3 | 4.2 | 0.6 | 0.1 | 9 | 28 |

# Population dynamics

| | Population (millions) | | | Average annual population growth (%) | | Population age composition (%) | | | Dependency ratio — dependents as proportion of working-age population | | Crude death rate per 1,000 people | Crude birth rate per 1,000 people |
|---|---|---|---|---|---|---|---|---|---|---|---|---|
| | 1990 | 2006 | 2015 | 1990–2006 | 2006–15 | Ages 0–14 2006 | Ages 15–64 2006 | Ages 65+ 2006 | Young 2006 | Old 2006 | 2006 | 2006 |
| Honduras | 4.9 | 7.0 | 8.2 | 2.2 | 1.8 | 39.4 | 56.4 | 4.2 | 0.7 | 0.1 | 6 | 28 |
| Hungary | 10.4 | 10.1 | 9.7 | −0.2 | −0.4 | 15.5 | 69.1 | 15.4 | 0.2 | 0.2 | 13 | 10 |
| India | 849.5 | 1,109.8 | 1,233.2 | 1.7 | 1.2 | 32.5 | 62.4 | 5.0 | 0.5 | 0.1 | 8 | 24 |
| Indonesia | 178.2 | 223.0 | 245.1 | 1.4 | 1.0 | 28.0 | 66.3 | 5.6 | 0.4 | 0.1 | 7 | 20 |
| Iran, Islamic Rep. | 54.4 | 70.1 | 78.9 | 1.6 | 1.3 | 27.8 | 67.8 | 4.5 | 0.4 | 0.1 | 5 | 18 |
| Iraq | 18.5 | .. | .. | .. | .. | .. | .. | .. | .. | .. | .. | .. |
| Ireland | 3.5 | 4.3 | 4.8 | 1.2 | 1.3 | 20.7 | 68.2 | 11.1 | 0.3 | 0.2 | 6 | 15 |
| Israel | 4.7 | 7.0 | 8.0 | 2.6 | 1.5 | 27.9 | 62.0 | 10.1 | 0.4 | 0.2 | 6 | 21 |
| Italy | 56.7 | 58.8 | 58.4 | 0.2 | −0.1 | 13.9 | 66.1 | 19.9 | 0.2 | 0.3 | 9 | 10 |
| Jamaica | 2.4 | 2.7 | 2.8 | 0.7 | 0.4 | 31.3 | 61.2 | 7.5 | 0.5 | 0.1 | 6 | 17 |
| Japan | 123.5 | 127.8 | 124.5 | 0.2 | −0.3 | 13.8 | 66.0 | 20.3 | 0.2 | 0.3 | 9 | 9 |
| Jordan | 3.2 | 5.5 | 6.8 | 3.5 | 2.2 | 36.5 | 60.2 | 3.3 | 0.6 | 0.1 | 4 | 29 |
| Kazakhstan | 16.3 | 15.3 | 16.4 | −0.4 | 0.8 | 23.9 | 68.2 | 8.0 | 0.4 | 0.1 | 10 | 20 |
| Kenya | 23.4 | 36.6 | 46.1 | 2.8 | 2.6 | 42.6 | 54.7 | 2.7 | 0.8 | 0.0[a] | 12 | 39 |
| Korea, Dem. Rep. | 20.1 | 23.7 | 24.4 | 1.0 | 0.3 | 23.6 | 67.5 | 8.8 | 0.4 | 0.1 | 10 | 14 |
| Korea, Rep. | 42.9 | 48.4 | 49.2 | 0.8 | 0.2 | 18.1 | 72.0 | 9.8 | 0.3 | 0.1 | 5 | 9 |
| Kuwait | 2.1 | 2.6 | 3.2 | 1.3 | 2.2 | 23.6 | 74.6 | 1.9 | 0.3 | 0.0[a] | 2 | 21 |
| Kyrgyz Republic | 4.4 | 5.2 | 5.7 | 1.0 | 1.0 | 30.4 | 63.8 | 5.8 | 0.5 | 0.1 | 7 | 23 |
| Lao PDR | 4.1 | 5.8 | 6.7 | 2.2 | 1.7 | 38.9 | 57.5 | 3.5 | 0.7 | 0.1 | 7 | 27 |
| Latvia | 2.7 | 2.3 | 2.2 | −1.0 | −0.6 | 14.0 | 69.2 | 16.8 | 0.2 | 0.2 | 15 | 10 |
| Lebanon | 3.0 | 4.1 | 4.4 | 1.9 | 1.0 | 28.2 | 64.5 | 7.3 | 0.4 | 0.1 | 7 | 18 |
| Lesotho | 1.6 | 2.0 | 2.1 | 1.4 | 0.6 | 40.1 | 55.1 | 4.7 | 0.7 | 0.1 | 19 | 29 |
| Liberia | 2.1 | 3.6 | 5.1 | 3.2 | 3.9 | 47.0 | 50.8 | 2.2 | 0.9 | 0.0[a] | 19 | 50 |
| Libya | 4.4 | 6.0 | 7.1 | 2.0 | 1.8 | 30.2 | 65.9 | 3.9 | 0.5 | 0.1 | 4 | 24 |
| Lithuania | 3.7 | 3.4 | 3.2 | −0.5 | −0.5 | 16.2 | 68.3 | 15.5 | 0.2 | 0.2 | 13 | 9 |
| Macedonia, FYR | 1.9 | 2.0 | 2.0 | 0.4 | −0.0[b] | 19.2 | 69.5 | 11.3 | 0.3 | 0.2 | 9 | 11 |
| Madagascar | 12.0 | 19.2 | 24.1 | 2.9 | 2.5 | 43.6 | 53.3 | 3.2 | 0.8 | 0.1 | 10 | 37 |
| Malawi | 9.4 | 13.6 | 17.0 | 2.3 | 2.5 | 47.0 | 49.9 | 3.0 | 0.9 | 0.1 | 15 | 41 |
| Malaysia | 18.1 | 26.1 | 30.0 | 2.3 | 1.5 | 31.0 | 64.6 | 4.4 | 0.5 | 0.1 | 4 | 21 |
| Mali | 7.7 | 12.0 | 15.7 | 2.8 | 3.0 | 47.6 | 48.8 | 3.6 | 1.0 | 0.1 | 15 | 48 |
| Mauritania | 1.9 | 3.0 | 3.8 | 2.8 | 2.4 | 40.1 | 56.3 | 3.6 | 0.7 | 0.1 | 8 | 33 |
| Mauritius | 1.1 | 1.3 | 1.3 | 1.1 | 0.7 | 24.0 | 69.3 | 6.7 | 0.3 | 0.1 | 8 | 15 |
| Mexico | 83.2 | 104.2 | 113.7 | 1.4 | 1.0 | 30.2 | 63.8 | 6.0 | 0.5 | 0.1 | 5 | 19 |
| Moldova | 4.4 | 3.8 | 3.6 | −0.8 | −0.8 | 19.4 | 69.5 | 11.1 | 0.3 | 0.2 | 12 | 11 |
| Mongolia | 2.1 | 2.6 | 2.9 | 1.3 | 1.1 | 28.0 | 68.1 | 4.0 | 0.4 | 0.1 | 6 | 18 |
| Morocco | 24.2 | 30.5 | 33.9 | 1.5 | 1.2 | 29.7 | 65.0 | 5.3 | 0.5 | 0.1 | 6 | 22 |
| Mozambique | 13.5 | 21.0 | 24.7 | 2.7 | 1.8 | 44.3 | 52.5 | 3.2 | 0.8 | 0.1 | 20 | 40 |
| Myanmar | 40.1 | 48.4 | 51.9 | 1.2 | 0.8 | 26.7 | 67.7 | 5.6 | 0.4 | 0.1 | 10 | 18 |
| Namibia | 1.4 | 2.0 | 2.3 | 2.3 | 1.2 | 38.3 | 58.2 | 3.5 | 0.7 | 0.1 | 13 | 26 |
| Nepal | 19.1 | 27.6 | 32.2 | 2.3 | 1.7 | 38.5 | 57.8 | 3.7 | 0.7 | 0.1 | 8 | 29 |
| Netherlands | 15.0 | 16.3 | 16.5 | 0.6 | 0.1 | 18.3 | 67.4 | 14.3 | 0.3 | 0.2 | 8 | 11 |
| New Zealand | 3.4 | 4.2 | 4.5 | 1.2 | 0.8 | 21.2 | 66.5 | 12.3 | 0.3 | 0.2 | 7 | 14 |
| Nicaragua | 4.1 | 5.5 | 6.3 | 1.8 | 1.4 | 37.2 | 58.7 | 4.0 | 0.6 | 0.1 | 5 | 25 |
| Niger | 7.8 | 13.7 | 18.5 | 3.5 | 3.3 | 48.0 | 48.8 | 3.2 | 1.0 | 0.1 | 14 | 49 |
| Nigeria | 94.5 | 144.7 | 175.6 | 2.7 | 2.1 | 44.1 | 53.0 | 2.9 | 0.8 | 0.1 | 17 | 40 |
| Norway | 4.2 | 4.7 | 4.9 | 0.6 | 0.6 | 19.4 | 65.9 | 14.7 | 0.3 | 0.2 | 9 | 12 |
| Oman | 1.8 | 2.5 | 3.0 | 2.0 | 2.0 | 33.1 | 64.1 | 2.7 | 0.5 | 0.0[a] | 3 | 22 |
| Pakistan | 108.0 | 159.0 | 191.9 | 2.4 | 2.1 | 36.4 | 59.7 | 3.9 | 0.6 | 0.1 | 7 | 26 |
| Panama | 2.4 | 3.3 | 3.8 | 1.9 | 1.5 | 30.1 | 63.8 | 6.1 | 0.5 | 0.1 | 5 | 21 |
| Papua New Guinea | 4.1 | 6.2 | 7.3 | 2.5 | 1.8 | 40.3 | 57.3 | 2.4 | 0.7 | 0.0[a] | 10 | 30 |
| Paraguay | 4.2 | 6.0 | 7.0 | 2.2 | 1.7 | 35.4 | 59.8 | 4.8 | 0.6 | 0.1 | 6 | 25 |
| Peru | 21.8 | 27.6 | 30.7 | 1.5 | 1.2 | 31.2 | 63.1 | 5.7 | 0.5 | 0.1 | 6 | 21 |
| Philippines | 61.2 | 86.3 | 101.0 | 2.1 | 1.8 | 35.8 | 60.3 | 3.9 | 0.6 | 0.1 | 5 | 26 |
| Poland | 38.1 | 38.1 | 37.4 | 0.0[a] | −0.2 | 15.9 | 70.8 | 13.3 | 0.2 | 0.2 | 10 | 10 |
| Portugal | 9.9 | 10.6 | 10.8 | 0.4 | 0.2 | 15.6 | 67.4 | 17.0 | 0.2 | 0.3 | 10 | 10 |
| Puerto Rico | 3.5 | 3.9 | 4.1 | 0.7 | 0.5 | 21.6 | 65.7 | 12.7 | 0.3 | 0.2 | 8 | 13 |

# 2.1 Population dynamics

| | Population | | | Average annual population growth | | Population age composition | | | Dependency ratio | | Crude death rate | Crude birth rate |
|---|---|---|---|---|---|---|---|---|---|---|---|---|
| | | | | | | | % | | dependents as proportion of working-age population | | per 1,000 people | per 1,000 people |
| | | millions | | % | | Ages 0–14 | Ages 15–64 | Ages 65+ | Young | Old | | |
| | 1990 | 2006 | 2015 | 1990–2006 | 2006–15 | 2006 | 2006 | 2006 | 2006 | 2006 | 2006 | 2006 |
| Romania | 23.2 | 21.6 | 20.5 | −0.5 | −0.6 | 15.4 | 69.8 | 14.9 | 0.2 | 0.2 | 12 | 10 |
| Russian Federation | 148.3 | 142.5 | 135.2 | −0.2 | −0.6 | 14.9 | 71.4 | 13.7 | 0.2 | 0.2 | 15 | 10 |
| Rwanda | 7.3 | 9.5 | 12.1 | 1.6 | 2.8 | 43.1 | 54.5 | 2.5 | 0.8 | 0.0[a] | 17 | 44 |
| Saudi Arabia | 16.4 | 23.7 | 28.5 | 2.3 | 2.1 | 34.0 | 63.2 | 2.8 | 0.5 | 0.0[a] | 4 | 25 |
| Senegal | 7.9 | 12.1 | 15.4 | 2.7 | 2.7 | 41.9 | 53.8 | 4.3 | 0.8 | 0.1 | 9 | 36 |
| Serbia | 7.5[c] | 7.4[c] | 7.3[c] | −0.1[c] | −0.2[c] | 18.4[d] | 66.9[d] | 14.7[d] | 0.3[d] | 0.2[d] | 14[c] | 10[c] |
| Sierra Leone | 4.1 | 5.7 | 6.9 | 2.1 | 2.1 | 42.8 | 53.9 | 3.3 | 0.8 | 0.1 | 22 | 46 |
| Singapore | 3.0 | 4.5 | 4.8 | 2.4 | 0.8 | 18.8 | 72.4 | 8.8 | 0.3 | 0.1 | 4 | 10 |
| Slovak Republic | 5.3 | 5.4 | 5.4 | 0.1 | −0.0[b] | 16.3 | 71.8 | 11.8 | 0.2 | 0.2 | 10 | 10 |
| Slovenia | 2.0 | 2.0 | 2.0 | 0.0[a] | −0.1 | 13.9 | 70.3 | 15.8 | 0.2 | 0.2 | 9 | 9 |
| Somalia | 6.7 | 8.4 | 10.9 | 1.4 | 2.8 | 44.2 | 53.2 | 2.6 | 0.8 | 0.0[a] | 17 | 43 |
| South Africa | 35.2 | 47.4 | 49.1 | 1.9 | 0.4 | 31.9 | 63.7 | 4.4 | 0.5 | 0.1 | 21 | 23 |
| Spain | 38.8 | 44.1 | 45.7 | 0.8 | 0.4 | 14.5 | 68.7 | 16.9 | 0.2 | 0.2 | 9 | 11 |
| Sri Lanka | 17.0 | 19.9 | 20.5 | 1.0 | 0.3 | 23.7 | 69.7 | 6.6 | 0.3 | 0.1 | 6 | 19 |
| Sudan | 25.9 | 37.7 | 45.6 | 2.3 | 2.1 | 40.3 | 56.1 | 3.6 | 0.7 | 0.1 | 10 | 32 |
| Swaziland | 0.8 | 1.1 | 1.2 | 2.4 | 0.5 | 39.2 | 57.5 | 3.3 | 0.7 | 0.1 | 22 | 33 |
| Sweden | 8.6 | 9.1 | 9.4 | 0.4 | 0.4 | 17.1 | 65.5 | 17.4 | 0.3 | 0.3 | 10 | 12 |
| Switzerland | 6.7 | 7.5 | 7.6 | 0.7 | 0.2 | 16.5 | 67.9 | 15.7 | 0.2 | 0.2 | 8 | 10 |
| Syrian Arab Republic | 12.7 | 19.4 | 23.5 | 2.6 | 2.1 | 36.0 | 60.8 | 3.2 | 0.6 | 0.1 | 3 | 27 |
| Tajikistan | 5.3 | 6.6 | 7.7 | 1.4 | 1.6 | 38.7 | 57.4 | 3.9 | 0.7 | 0.1 | 6 | 28 |
| Tanzania | 25.5 | 39.5 | 48.9 | 2.7 | 2.4 | 44.4 | 52.6 | 3.0 | 0.8 | 0.1 | 13 | 40 |
| Thailand | 54.3 | 63.4 | 66.6 | 1.0 | 0.5 | 21.4 | 70.6 | 8.0 | 0.3 | 0.1 | 8 | 15 |
| Timor-Leste | 0.7 | 1.0 | 1.4 | 2.0 | 3.7 | 44.7 | 52.6 | 2.7 | 0.8 | 0.1 | 15 | 51 |
| Togo | 4.0 | 6.4 | 8.0 | 3.0 | 2.5 | 43.0 | 53.9 | 3.1 | 0.8 | 0.1 | 10 | 37 |
| Trinidad and Tobago | 1.2 | 1.3 | 1.4 | 0.5 | 0.4 | 21.7 | 71.7 | 6.6 | 0.3 | 0.1 | 8 | 15 |
| Tunisia | 8.2 | 10.1 | 11.2 | 1.4 | 1.1 | 25.4 | 68.3 | 6.3 | 0.4 | 0.1 | 6 | 17 |
| Turkey | 56.2 | 73.0 | 81.0 | 1.6 | 1.2 | 27.9 | 66.5 | 5.7 | 0.4 | 0.1 | 6 | 19 |
| Turkmenistan | 3.7 | 4.9 | 5.5 | 1.8 | 1.3 | 30.9 | 64.5 | 4.6 | 0.5 | 0.1 | 8 | 22 |
| Uganda | 17.8 | 29.9 | 40.7 | 3.2 | 3.4 | 49.3 | 48.3 | 2.5 | 1.0 | 0.1 | 14 | 47 |
| Ukraine | 51.9 | 46.8 | 43.4 | −0.6 | −0.8 | 14.3 | 69.5 | 16.2 | 0.2 | 0.2 | 16 | 10 |
| United Arab Emirates | 1.8 | 4.2 | 5.3 | 5.5 | 2.4 | 19.6 | 79.3 | 1.1 | 0.2 | 0.0[a] | 1 | 15 |
| United Kingdom | 57.6 | 60.6 | 62.4 | 0.3 | 0.3 | 17.8 | 66.1 | 16.1 | 0.3 | 0.2 | 10 | 12 |
| United States | 249.6 | 299.4 | 323.9 | 1.1 | 0.9 | 20.7 | 67.0 | 12.3 | 0.3 | 0.2 | 8 | 14 |
| Uruguay | 3.1 | 3.3 | 3.4 | 0.4 | 0.2 | 23.6 | 62.8 | 13.6 | 0.4 | 0.2 | 9 | 15 |
| Uzbekistan | 20.5 | 26.5 | 29.6 | 1.6 | 1.2 | 32.4 | 62.9 | 4.7 | 0.5 | 0.1 | 6 | 19 |
| Venezuela, RB | 19.8 | 27.0 | 31.1 | 2.0 | 1.5 | 30.9 | 64.0 | 5.1 | 0.5 | 0.1 | 5 | 22 |
| Vietnam | 66.2 | 84.1 | 93.7 | 1.5 | 1.2 | 28.9 | 65.6 | 5.6 | 0.4 | 0.1 | 5 | 17 |
| West Bank and Gaza | 2.0 | 3.8 | 4.7 | 4.1 | 2.5 | 45.6 | 51.4 | 3.0 | 0.9 | 0.1 | 3 | 32 |
| Yemen, Rep. | 12.3 | 21.7 | 28.2 | 3.6 | 2.9 | 45.4 | 52.2 | 2.3 | 0.9 | 0.0[a] | 8 | 38 |
| Zambia | 8.1 | 11.7 | 13.8 | 2.3 | 1.9 | 45.6 | 51.4 | 2.9 | 0.9 | 0.1 | 19 | 40 |
| Zimbabwe | 10.5 | 13.2 | 14.8 | 1.5 | 1.3 | 39.0 | 57.5 | 3.5 | 0.7 | 0.1 | 18 | 28 |
| **World** | **5,263.9 s** | **6,538.1 s** | **7,200.7 s** | **1.4 w** | **1.1 w** | **28.0 w** | **64.6 w** | **7.4 w** | **0.4 w** | **0.1 w** | **8 w** | **20 w** |
| **Low income** | 1,747.9 | 2,419.7 | 2,815.3 | 2.0 | 1.7 | 36.3 | 59.4 | 4.3 | 0.6 | 0.1 | 10 | 29 |
| **Middle income** | 2,599.1 | 3,087.7 | 3,313.9 | 1.1 | 0.8 | 24.7 | 67.9 | 7.4 | 0.4 | 0.1 | 8 | 16 |
| Lower middle income | 1,899.6 | 2,276.5 | 2,456.3 | 1.1 | 0.8 | 24.7 | 68.3 | 7.0 | 0.4 | 0.1 | 7 | 16 |
| Upper middle income | 699.5 | 811.3 | 857.7 | 0.9 | 0.6 | 24.6 | 66.9 | 8.6 | 0.4 | 0.1 | 9 | 17 |
| **Low & middle income** | 4,347.0 | 5,507.4 | 6,129.2 | 1.5 | 1.2 | 29.8 | 64.2 | 6.0 | 0.5 | 0.1 | 8 | 22 |
| East Asia & Pacific | 1,595.9 | 1,898.9 | 2,032.7 | 1.1 | 0.8 | 23.5 | 69.4 | 7.1 | 0.3 | 0.1 | 7 | 14 |
| Europe & Central Asia | 451.8 | 460.5 | 460.7 | 0.1 | 0.0[a] | 19.4 | 68.9 | 11.6 | 0.3 | 0.2 | 12 | 13 |
| Latin America & Carib. | 436.9 | 556.1 | 616.5 | 1.5 | 1.1 | 29.6 | 64.1 | 6.3 | 0.5 | 0.1 | 6 | 20 |
| Middle East & N. Africa | 225.6 | 310.7 | 361.9 | 2.0 | 1.7 | 32.7 | 63.0 | 4.3 | 0.5 | 0.1 | 6 | 24 |
| South Asia | 1,120.1 | 1,499.4 | 1,694.9 | 1.8 | 1.4 | 33.4 | 61.9 | 4.7 | 0.5 | 0.1 | 8 | 24 |
| Sub-Saharan Africa | 516.7 | 781.8 | 962.6 | 2.6 | 2.3 | 43.3 | 53.6 | 3.1 | 0.8 | 0.1 | 15 | 39 |
| **High income** | 916.9 | 1,030.7 | 1,071.5 | 0.7 | 0.4 | 17.9 | 67.1 | 14.9 | 0.3 | 0.2 | 8 | 12 |
| Euro area | 296.2 | 316.7 | 319.7 | 0.4 | 0.1 | 15.5 | 66.7 | 17.8 | 0.2 | 0.3 | 9 | 10 |

a. Less than 0.05. b. More than −0.05. c. Excludes Kosovo and Metohija. d. Includes Kosovo and Metohija.

# Population dynamics | 2.1

Population estimates are usually based on national population censuses, but their frequency and quality vary by country. Most countries conduct a complete enumeration no more than once a decade. Estimates for the years before and after the census are interpolations or extrapolations based on demographic models. Errors and undercounting occur even in high-income countries; in developing countries errors may be substantial because of limits in the transport, communications, and other resources required to conduct and analyze a full census.

The quality and reliability of official demographic data are also affected by public trust in the government, government commitment to accurate enumeration, confidentiality and protection against misuse of census data, and census agencies' independence from political influence. Moreover, comparability of population indicators is limited by differences in the concepts, definitions, collection procedures, and estimation methods used by national statistical agencies and other organizations that collect the data.

Of the 153 economies in the table, 131 (about 86 percent) conducted a census between 1995 and 2006. The currentness of censuses and the availability of complementary data from surveys or registration systems are objective ways to judge demographic data quality. Some European countries' registration systems offer complete information on population in the absence of a census. See *Primary data documentation* for the most recent census or survey year and for the completeness of registration.

Current population estimates for developing countries that lack recent census-based data and pre- and post-census estimates for countries with census data are provided by the United Nations Population Division and other agencies. The standard estimation method requires fertility, mortality, and net migration data, often collected from sample surveys, which can be small or limited in coverage. Population estimates are from demographic modeling and so are susceptible to biases and errors from shortcomings in the model as well as in the data. Population projections use the cohort component method. Because of a drastic reduction in estimated mortality due partly to revised lower estimates of HIV prevalence, populations of several countries, notably in Sub-Saharan Africa, have been revised upward from previous estimates.

The growth rate of the total population conceals the fact that different age groups may grow at different rates. In many developing countries the under-15 population was growing rapidly but has begun to shrink. Previously high fertility rates and declining

mortality rates are now reflected in the larger share of the working-age population.

Dependency ratios account for variations in the proportions of children, elderly people, and working-age people in the population. Calculations of young and old-age dependency suggest the dependency burden that the working-age population must bear in relation to children and the elderly. But dependency ratios show only the age composition of a population, not economic dependency. Some children and elderly people are part of the labor force; many working-age people are not.

The vital rates in the table are based on data from birth and death registration systems, censuses, and sample surveys by national statistical offices and other organizations, or on demographic analysis. The 2006 estimates for many countries are projections based on extrapolations of levels and trends from earlier years or interpolations of population estimates and projections from the United Nations Population Division.

Vital registers are the preferred source for these data, but in many developing countries systems for registering births and deaths are absent or incomplete because of deficiencies in the coverage of events or geographic areas. Many developing countries carry out special household surveys that ask respondents about births and deaths in the recent past. Estimates derived in this way are subject to sampling errors and errors due to inaccurate recall.

The United Nations Statistics Division monitors the completeness of vital registration systems. The share of countries with at least 90 percent complete vital registration rose from 45 percent in 1988 to 62 percent in 2006. Still, some of the most populous developing countries—China, India, Indonesia, Brazil, Pakistan, Bangladesh, Nigeria—lack complete vital registration systems. From 2003 to 2006, 51 percent of births and deaths and 48 percent of infant deaths worldwide were registered and reported.

International migration is the only other factor besides birth and death rates that directly determines a country's population growth. From 1990 to 2005 the number of immigrants in high-income countries rose by 40 million. About 190 million people (3 percent of the world's population) currently live outside their home country. Estimating international migration is difficult. At any time many people are located outside their home country as tourists, workers, or refugees or for other reasons. Standards for the duration and purpose of international moves that qualify as migration vary, and estimates require information on flows into and out of countries that is difficult to collect.

• **Population** is based on the de facto definition of population, which counts all residents regardless of legal status or citizenship—except for refugees not permanently settled in the country of asylum, who are generally considered part of the population of their country of origin. The values shown are mid-year estimates for 1990 and 2006 and projections for 2015. • **Average annual population growth** is the exponential change for the period indicated. See *Statistical methods* for more information. • **Population age composition** is the percentage of the total population that is in specific age groups. • **Dependency ratio** is the ratio of dependents—people younger than 15 or older than 64—to the working-age population—those ages 15–64. • **Crude death rate** and **crude birth rate** are the number of deaths and the number of live births occurring during the year, per 1,000 population, estimated at midyear. Subtracting the crude death rate from the crude birth rate provides the rate of natural increase, which is equal to the population growth rate in the absence of migration.

The World Bank's population estimates are compiled and produced by its Human Development Network and Development Data Group in consultation with its operational staff and country offices. Important inputs to the World Bank's demographic work come from the United Nations Population Division's *World Population Prospects: The 2006 Revision;* census reports and other statistical publications from national statistical offices; household surveys conducted by national agencies, Macro International, and the U.S. Centers for Disease Control and Prevention; Eurostat, *Demographic Statistics* (various years); Centro Latinoamericano de Demografía, *Boletín Demográfico* (various years); and U.S. Bureau of the Census, International Database.

| | Labor force participation rate | | | | Labor force | | | | |
|---|---|---|---|---|---|---|---|---|---|
| | % ages 15 and older | | | | Total millions | | Ages 15 and older average annual % growth | Female % of labor force | |
| | Male | | Female | | | | | | |
| | 1990 | 2006 | 1990 | 2006 | 1990 | 2006 | 1990–2006 | 1990 | 2006 |
| Afghanistan | .. | .. | .. | .. | .. | .. | .. | .. | .. |
| Albania | 83 | 70 | 58 | 49 | 1.6 | 1.4 | −0.7 | 40.2 | 41.8 |
| Algeria | 78 | 80 | 23 | 37 | 7.2 | 13.9 | 4.1 | 22.6 | 31.0 |
| Angola | 90 | 92 | 74 | 74 | 4.5 | 7.3 | 3.0 | 46.4 | 45.8 |
| Argentina | 78 | 76 | 38 | 54 | 13.0 | 18.8 | 2.3 | 34.4 | 43.1 |
| Armenia | 87 | 60 | 72 | 48 | 1.9 | 1.3 | −2.6 | 47.7 | 48.9 |
| Australia | 75 | 70 | 52 | 56 | 8.4 | 10.5 | 1.4 | 41.3 | 44.8 |
| Austria | 70 | 66 | 43 | 50 | 3.5 | 4.0 | 0.8 | 40.8 | 44.4 |
| Azerbaijan | 78 | 73 | 64 | 61 | 3.3 | 4.3 | 1.6 | 47.4 | 47.7 |
| Bangladesh | 89 | 86 | 63 | 52 | 51.2 | 71.0 | 2.0 | 40.2 | 36.7 |
| Belarus | 76 | 64 | 61 | 53 | 5.3 | 4.8 | −0.7 | 48.8 | 49.1 |
| Belgium | 61 | 60 | 37 | 44 | 3.9 | 4.5 | 0.9 | 39.1 | 43.6 |
| Benin | 90 | 86 | 58 | 54 | 2.0 | 3.4 | 3.3 | 40.8 | 38.3 |
| Bolivia | 80 | 84 | 49 | 63 | 2.5 | 4.3 | 3.3 | 39.2 | 43.5 |
| Bosnia and Herzegovina | 78 | 68 | 60 | 59 | 2.2 | 2.0 | −0.6 | 44.4 | 48.4 |
| Botswana | 77 | 70 | 57 | 46 | 0.5 | 0.7 | 2.1 | 44.5 | 40.3 |
| Brazil | 85 | 79 | 45 | 57 | 62.5 | 93.1 | 2.5 | 35.0 | 42.9 |
| Bulgaria | 68 | 52 | 60 | 40 | 4.4 | 3.1 | −2.3 | 48.0 | 45.0 |
| Burkina Faso | 91 | 89 | 77 | 78 | 3.9 | 6.5 | 3.2 | 47.5 | 47.1 |
| Burundi | 90 | 93 | 91 | 92 | 2.8 | 4.2 | 2.5 | 52.5 | 51.4 |
| Cambodia | 85 | 80 | 78 | 75 | 4.4 | 6.9 | 2.9 | 52.4 | 50.7 |
| Cameroon | 82 | 80 | 56 | 52 | 4.6 | 7.0 | 2.6 | 41.3 | 39.6 |
| Canada | 76 | 72 | 58 | 61 | 14.7 | 17.9 | 1.2 | 44.0 | 46.1 |
| Central African Republic | 89 | 89 | 71 | 71 | 1.4 | 2.0 | 2.3 | 47.0 | 46.0 |
| Chad | 80 | 78 | 64 | 66 | 2.4 | 4.0 | 3.3 | 45.7 | 46.8 |
| Chile | 77 | 70 | 32 | 37 | 5.0 | 6.6 | 1.7 | 30.5 | 35.4 |
| China | 85 | 82 | 73 | 69 | 650.6 | 780.5 | 1.1 | 44.8 | 44.1 |
| Hong Kong, China | 80 | 70 | 47 | 54 | 2.9 | 3.6 | 1.5 | 36.3 | 45.5 |
| Colombia | 81 | 81 | 46 | 62 | 14.0 | 22.8 | 3.0 | 37.0 | 44.8 |
| Congo, Dem. Rep. | 91 | 91 | 61 | 61 | 15.2 | 24.2 | 2.9 | 41.6 | 41.3 |
| Congo, Rep. | 86 | 88 | 58 | 57 | 1.0 | 1.5 | 2.9 | 41.3 | 40.1 |
| Costa Rica | 84 | 81 | 33 | 46 | 1.2 | 2.0 | 3.5 | 27.6 | 35.6 |
| Côte d'Ivoire | 90 | 89 | 44 | 39 | 4.7 | 7.1 | 2.6 | 30.0 | 29.3 |
| Croatia | 71 | 60 | 47 | 45 | 2.2 | 1.9 | −0.8 | 42.1 | 44.8 |
| Cuba | 73 | 73 | 39 | 44 | 4.6 | 5.3 | 0.9 | 34.6 | 37.3 |
| Czech Republic | 73 | 67 | 61 | 52 | 5.4 | 5.2 | −0.3 | 47.5 | 44.9 |
| Denmark | 75 | 69 | 62 | 59 | 2.9 | 2.8 | −0.2 | 46.1 | 46.4 |
| Dominican Republic | 84 | 82 | 36 | 47 | 2.7 | 4.1 | 2.5 | 29.6 | 36.4 |
| Ecuador | 85 | 82 | 33 | 61 | 3.7 | 6.4 | 3.5 | 27.8 | 42.7 |
| Egypt, Arab Rep. | 75 | 73 | 27 | 20 | 16.5 | 23.1 | 2.1 | 26.3 | 21.7 |
| El Salvador | 80 | 75 | 51 | 48 | 2.0 | 2.7 | 2.1 | 41.2 | 40.7 |
| Eritrea | 92 | 90 | 61 | 58 | 1.3 | 2.0 | 2.7 | 41.8 | 41.0 |
| Estonia | 77 | 65 | 64 | 52 | 0.9 | 0.7 | −1.6 | 49.8 | 48.9 |
| Ethiopia | 91 | 89 | 72 | 71 | 22.6 | 34.4 | 2.6 | 44.9 | 44.9 |
| Finland | 70 | 66 | 58 | 57 | 2.6 | 2.7 | 0.2 | 47.2 | 47.4 |
| France | 65 | 61 | 46 | 48 | 24.8 | 27.3 | 0.6 | 43.3 | 45.5 |
| Gabon | 84 | 83 | 63 | 62 | 0.4 | 0.6 | 2.7 | 43.8 | 42.7 |
| Gambia, The | 86 | 86 | 63 | 59 | 0.4 | 0.7 | 3.5 | 42.6 | 40.8 |
| Georgia | 72 | 76 | 69 | 49 | 2.9 | 2.2 | −1.6 | 52.3 | 42.7 |
| Germany | 72 | 65 | 44 | 51 | 38.3 | 41.0 | 0.4 | 40.4 | 45.1 |
| Ghana | 80 | 75 | 76 | 70 | 6.7 | 10.3 | 2.6 | 48.8 | 47.8 |
| Greece | 67 | 65 | 36 | 44 | 4.2 | 5.2 | 1.4 | 36.2 | 40.7 |
| Guatemala | 89 | 83 | 29 | 34 | 2.9 | 4.2 | 2.4 | 24.7 | 31.3 |
| Guinea | 90 | 87 | 80 | 80 | 2.8 | 4.4 | 2.7 | 47.3 | 47.5 |
| Guinea-Bissau | 91 | 93 | 58 | 61 | 0.4 | 0.7 | 2.9 | 40.3 | 40.8 |
| Haiti | 83 | 84 | 58 | 56 | 2.8 | 4.1 | 2.4 | 42.7 | 41.3 |

| | Labor force participation rate | | | | Labor force | | | | |
|---|---|---|---|---|---|---|---|---|---|
| | % ages 15 and older | | | | Total millions | | Ages 15 and older average annual % growth | Female % of labor force | |
| | Male | | Female | | | | | | |
| | 1990 | 2006 | 1990 | 2006 | 1990 | 2006 | 1990–2006 | 1990 | 2006 |
| Honduras | 87 | 89 | 33 | 55 | 1.6 | 3.0 | 4.0 | 27.9 | 39.4 |
| Hungary | 64 | 58 | 46 | 42 | 4.5 | 4.2 | −0.5 | 44.5 | 45.0 |
| India | 85 | 82 | 37 | 34 | 325.6 | 438.0 | 1.9 | 28.4 | 28.1 |
| Indonesia | 81 | 85 | 50 | 51 | 75.3 | 109.2 | 2.3 | 38.4 | 37.9 |
| Iran, Islamic Rep. | 81 | 74 | 22 | 40 | 15.6 | 29.1 | 3.9 | 20.2 | 34.3 |
| Iraq | 76 | .. | 16 | .. | 4.7 | .. | .. | 16.8 | .. |
| Ireland | 70 | 72 | 36 | 54 | 1.3 | 2.1 | 2.9 | 34.3 | 43.0 |
| Israel | 62 | 59 | 41 | 51 | 1.6 | 2.8 | 3.3 | 40.5 | 47.0 |
| Italy | 66 | 61 | 36 | 38 | 23.9 | 24.8 | 0.2 | 37.1 | 39.9 |
| Jamaica | 80 | 74 | 66 | 54 | 1.1 | 1.2 | 0.2 | 46.8 | 43.3 |
| Japan | 77 | 73 | 50 | 48 | 63.9 | 66.2 | 0.2 | 40.6 | 40.8 |
| Jordan | 69 | 77 | 18 | 28 | 0.8 | 1.9 | 5.7 | 18.8 | 25.4 |
| Kazakhstan | 78 | 75 | 61 | 65 | 7.7 | 8.1 | 0.3 | 46.3 | 49.4 |
| Kenya | 90 | 90 | 75 | 70 | 9.8 | 16.7 | 3.3 | 45.9 | 44.2 |
| Korea, Dem. Rep. | 82 | 78 | 52 | 48 | 9.9 | 11.4 | 0.9 | 40.6 | 39.3 |
| Korea, Rep. | 73 | 74 | 47 | 50 | 19.1 | 24.5 | 1.6 | 39.3 | 40.8 |
| Kuwait | 82 | 85 | 35 | 50 | 0.9 | 1.4 | 3.2 | 21.8 | 25.7 |
| Kyrgyz Republic | 74 | 74 | 59 | 55 | 1.8 | 2.3 | 1.5 | 46.2 | 44.0 |
| Lao PDR | 80 | 80 | 53 | 54 | 1.5 | 2.4 | 2.8 | 40.6 | 41.0 |
| Latvia | 77 | 64 | 63 | 49 | 1.5 | 1.1 | −1.8 | 49.7 | 48.0 |
| Lebanon | 78 | 80 | 32 | 34 | 1.0 | 1.6 | 2.9 | 31.2 | 31.0 |
| Lesotho | 86 | 74 | 57 | 46 | 0.6 | 0.7 | 0.8 | 46.5 | 43.5 |
| Liberia | 85 | 83 | 55 | 55 | 0.8 | 1.3 | 3.2 | 39.4 | 39.7 |
| Libya | 79 | 82 | 19 | 35 | 1.3 | 2.5 | 4.2 | 16.9 | 27.8 |
| Lithuania | 75 | 64 | 59 | 52 | 1.9 | 1.6 | −1.0 | 48.1 | 49.0 |
| Macedonia, FYR | 73 | 65 | 48 | 41 | 0.9 | 0.9 | 0.1 | 40.0 | 39.0 |
| Madagascar | 83 | 86 | 79 | 79 | 5.4 | 8.9 | 3.2 | 49.2 | 48.3 |
| Malawi | 91 | 90 | 85 | 86 | 4.4 | 6.3 | 2.2 | 50.2 | 50.0 |
| Malaysia | 81 | 81 | 44 | 47 | 7.1 | 11.6 | 3.0 | 34.8 | 36.0 |
| Mali | 89 | 82 | 72 | 72 | 3.2 | 4.8 | 2.5 | 46.9 | 49.2 |
| Mauritania | 86 | 84 | 56 | 54 | 0.8 | 1.3 | 3.1 | 40.2 | 39.2 |
| Mauritius | 82 | 79 | 42 | 43 | 0.5 | 0.6 | 1.4 | 33.9 | 35.7 |
| Mexico | 84 | 80 | 34 | 40 | 29.9 | 43.1 | 2.3 | 30.0 | 35.2 |
| Moldova | 75 | 68 | 61 | 54 | 2.1 | 1.9 | −0.8 | 48.5 | 46.8 |
| Mongolia | 82 | 82 | 56 | 54 | 0.8 | 1.3 | 2.5 | 41.0 | 40.1 |
| Morocco | 81 | 80 | 24 | 27 | 7.6 | 11.3 | 2.5 | 23.7 | 26.1 |
| Mozambique | 88 | 83 | 88 | 85 | 6.4 | 9.8 | 2.7 | 54.0 | 53.4 |
| Myanmar | 88 | 86 | 69 | 68 | 20.2 | 27.3 | 1.9 | 44.7 | 44.9 |
| Namibia | 65 | 63 | 49 | 47 | 0.4 | 0.7 | 2.7 | 45.0 | 43.8 |
| Nepal | 80 | 78 | 48 | 50 | 7.1 | 10.8 | 2.6 | 37.9 | 40.5 |
| Netherlands | 71 | 73 | 44 | 57 | 6.9 | 8.6 | 1.3 | 39.1 | 44.4 |
| New Zealand | 74 | 74 | 53 | 61 | 1.7 | 2.2 | 1.8 | 43.1 | 46.1 |
| Nicaragua | 86 | 86 | 35 | 36 | 1.3 | 2.1 | 2.8 | 29.7 | 30.0 |
| Niger | 95 | 95 | 71 | 71 | 3.3 | 5.9 | 3.6 | 43.7 | 42.4 |
| Nigeria | 86 | 85 | 48 | 46 | 33.9 | 52.7 | 2.8 | 36.5 | 35.3 |
| Norway | 73 | 73 | 57 | 64 | 2.2 | 2.6 | 0.9 | 44.7 | 46.8 |
| Oman | 83 | 81 | 15 | 24 | 0.6 | 1.0 | 3.3 | 11.1 | 17.3 |
| Pakistan | 86 | 83 | 28 | 33 | 35.0 | 59.6 | 3.3 | 23.3 | 27.3 |
| Panama | 79 | 79 | 39 | 52 | 0.9 | 1.5 | 3.0 | 32.5 | 39.2 |
| Papua New Guinea | 75 | 75 | 72 | 72 | 1.8 | 2.7 | 2.7 | 46.7 | 48.7 |
| Paraguay | 83 | 84 | 52 | 65 | 1.7 | 2.9 | 3.5 | 38.1 | 43.3 |
| Peru | 80 | 82 | 47 | 60 | 8.5 | 13.4 | 2.8 | 37.0 | 42.5 |
| Philippines | 83 | 83 | 47 | 56 | 23.5 | 38.4 | 3.1 | 36.5 | 40.2 |
| Poland | 74 | 61 | 57 | 47 | 18.6 | 17.2 | −0.5 | 45.8 | 45.7 |
| Portugal | 73 | 70 | 50 | 56 | 4.8 | 5.6 | 1.0 | 42.7 | 46.2 |
| Puerto Rico | 61 | 59 | 31 | 38 | 1.2 | 1.5 | 1.5 | 35.8 | 41.4 |

## 2.2 Labor force structure

| | Labor force participation rate | | | | Labor force | | | | |
|---|---|---|---|---|---|---|---|---|---|
| | % ages 15 and older | | | | Total millions | | Ages 15 and older average annual % growth | Female % of labor force | |
| | Male | | Female | | | | | | |
| | **1990** | **2006** | **1990** | **2006** | **1990** | **2006** | **1990–2006** | **1990** | **2006** |
| Romania | 71 | 62 | 54 | 50 | 11.0 | 10.1 | −0.5 | 44.3 | 45.9 |
| Russian Federation | 77 | 68 | 60 | 55 | 77.3 | 73.5 | −0.3 | 48.4 | 48.8 |
| Rwanda | 87 | 84 | 86 | 80 | 3.1 | 4.4 | 2.1 | 51.8 | 51.4 |
| Saudi Arabia | 80 | 80 | 15 | 18 | 5.1 | 8.4 | 3.2 | 11.4 | 14.2 |
| Senegal | 87 | 81 | 61 | 56 | 3.2 | 4.8 | 2.5 | 40.8 | 41.2 |
| Serbia | 72[a] | 70[a] | 50[a] | 51[a] | 3.5[b] | 3.6[b] | 0.2[b] | 41.8[b] | 42.9[b] |
| Sierra Leone | 90 | 94 | 53 | 56 | 1.7 | 2.5 | 2.3 | 38.5 | 38.5 |
| Singapore | 80 | 76 | 50 | 50 | 1.6 | 2.3 | 2.4 | 38.8 | 39.9 |
| Slovak Republic | 75 | 68 | 60 | 52 | 2.6 | 2.7 | 0.1 | 46.3 | 44.9 |
| Slovenia | 70 | 67 | 54 | 54 | 1.0 | 1.0 | 0.4 | 45.5 | 46.0 |
| Somalia | 96 | 95 | 61 | 59 | 2.9 | 3.6 | 1.5 | 39.9 | 39.2 |
| South Africa | 79 | 79 | 54 | 46 | 14.4 | 20.0 | 2.1 | 41.6 | 37.9 |
| Spain | 69 | 67 | 34 | 45 | 15.9 | 21.1 | 1.8 | 34.4 | 40.6 |
| Sri Lanka | 79 | 76 | 45 | 35 | 7.2 | 8.4 | 1.0 | 36.0 | 32.3 |
| Sudan | 79 | 71 | 27 | 24 | 7.7 | 10.7 | 2.0 | 26.0 | 24.9 |
| Swaziland | 78 | 75 | 38 | 32 | 0.2 | 0.4 | 2.9 | 38.0 | 32.3 |
| Sweden | 72 | 67 | 63 | 59 | 4.7 | 4.7 | 0.0 | 47.7 | 46.6 |
| Switzerland | 80 | 75 | 52 | 61 | 3.7 | 4.2 | 0.9 | 40.4 | 46.1 |
| Syrian Arab Republic | 82 | 88 | 29 | 39 | 3.6 | 7.9 | 4.9 | 26.0 | 30.5 |
| Tajikistan | 74 | 62 | 52 | 46 | 1.9 | 2.2 | 0.9 | 42.2 | 43.7 |
| Tanzania | 91 | 90 | 88 | 86 | 12.4 | 19.3 | 2.8 | 50.2 | 49.7 |
| Thailand | 88 | 81 | 75 | 66 | 31.4 | 36.5 | 0.9 | 46.9 | 46.7 |
| Timor-Leste | 79 | 83 | 50 | 56 | 0.3 | 0.4 | 1.9 | 37.5 | 39.5 |
| Togo | 90 | 90 | 54 | 50 | 1.5 | 2.5 | 3.2 | 38.5 | 36.7 |
| Trinidad and Tobago | 75 | 77 | 42 | 47 | 0.5 | 0.6 | 2.0 | 37.0 | 38.9 |
| Tunisia | 76 | 75 | 21 | 29 | 2.4 | 3.9 | 3.0 | 21.6 | 27.9 |
| Turkey | 82 | 76 | 34 | 28 | 21.0 | 27.4 | 1.7 | 29.4 | 26.5 |
| Turkmenistan | 77 | 73 | 64 | 61 | 1.5 | 2.3 | 2.4 | 46.9 | 46.5 |
| Uganda | 92 | 86 | 80 | 80 | 8.0 | 12.6 | 2.9 | 47.2 | 48.4 |
| Ukraine | 73 | 64 | 58 | 50 | 26.3 | 22.5 | −1.0 | 49.3 | 48.1 |
| United Arab Emirates | 92 | 93 | 25 | 41 | 0.9 | 2.7 | 6.7 | 9.8 | 14.6 |
| United Kingdom | 75 | 69 | 53 | 55 | 29.7 | 30.8 | 0.2 | 43.3 | 45.4 |
| United States | 76 | 73 | 57 | 60 | 129.3 | 157.0 | 1.2 | 44.3 | 45.9 |
| Uruguay | 76 | 78 | 46 | 57 | 1.4 | 1.7 | 1.3 | 39.9 | 44.4 |
| Uzbekistan | 76 | 73 | 60 | 57 | 8.2 | 11.6 | 2.2 | 45.4 | 44.6 |
| Venezuela, RB | 81 | 84 | 38 | 59 | 7.3 | 13.3 | 3.8 | 31.8 | 41.3 |
| Vietnam | 81 | 78 | 74 | 72 | 31.3 | 44.8 | 2.2 | 48.4 | 48.2 |
| West Bank and Gaza | 64 | 66 | 9 | 10 | 0.4 | 0.8 | 4.4 | 11.9 | 13.2 |
| Yemen, Rep. | 74 | 75 | 28 | 30 | 3.0 | 6.3 | 4.6 | 27.5 | 28.2 |
| Zambia | 90 | 91 | 66 | 66 | 3.4 | 5.0 | 2.3 | 43.1 | 42.6 |
| Zimbabwe | 80 | 85 | 70 | 64 | 4.2 | 6.0 | 2.2 | 47.0 | 43.6 |
| **World** | **81 w** | **79 w** | **54 w** | **53 w** | **2,386.6 t** | **3,081.8 t** | **1.6 w** | **39.7 w** | **39.9 w** |
| **Low income** | 85 | 83 | 48 | 46 | 694.0 | 995.4 | 2.3 | 35.1 | 35.0 |
| **Middle income** | 82 | 79 | 59 | 57 | 1,258.0 | 1,582.6 | 1.4 | 41.7 | 41.9 |
| Lower middle income | 83 | 81 | 63 | 60 | 954.4 | 1,208.6 | 1.5 | 42.4 | 42.0 |
| Upper middle income | 79 | 74 | 48 | 49 | 303.7 | 374.0 | 1.3 | 39.5 | 41.5 |
| **Low & middle income** | 83 | 81 | 55 | 53 | 1,952.1 | 2,578.0 | 1.7 | 39.4 | 39.2 |
| East Asia & Pacific | 85 | 82 | 69 | 66 | 858.7 | 1,074.1 | 1.4 | 44.1 | 43.5 |
| Europe & Central Asia | 75 | 68 | 56 | 49 | 216.4 | 214.6 | −0.1 | 45.7 | 44.7 |
| Latin America & Carib. | 83 | 80 | 41 | 53 | 171.1 | 257.4 | 2.6 | 33.9 | 40.8 |
| Middle East & N. Africa | 78 | 77 | 23 | 30 | 64.9 | 111.8 | 3.4 | 22.9 | 28.0 |
| South Asia | 85 | 82 | 39 | 36 | 430.6 | 597.1 | 2.0 | 29.7 | 29.3 |
| Sub-Saharan Africa | 87 | 85 | 63 | 61 | 210.3 | 323.0 | 2.7 | 43.0 | 42.2 |
| **High income** | 73 | 70 | 49 | 52 | 434.5 | 503.8 | 0.9 | 41.4 | 43.4 |
| Euro area | 68 | 64 | 41 | 47 | 131.8 | 148.8 | 0.8 | 39.6 | 43.4 |

a. Includes Montenegro. b. Excludes Kosovo and Metohija.

The labor force is the supply of labor available for producing goods and services in an economy. It includes people who are currently employed and people who are unemployed but seeking work as well as first-time job-seekers. Not everyone who works is included, however. Unpaid workers, family workers, and students are often omitted, and some countries do not count members of the armed forces. Labor force size tends to vary during the year as seasonal workers enter and leave.

Data on the labor force are collected from labor force surveys, censuses, establishment censuses and surveys, and administrative records such as employment exchange registers and unemployment insurance schemes. For some countries a combination of these sources is used. Labor force surveys are the most comprehensive source for internationally comparable labor force data. They can cover all noninstitutionalized civilians, all branches and sectors of the economy, and all categories of workers, including people holding multiple jobs. By contrast, labor force data from population censuses are often based on a limited number of questions on the economic characteristics of individuals, with little scope to probe. The resulting data often differ from labor force survey data and vary considerably by country, depending on the census scope and coverage. Establishment censuses and surveys provide data only on the employed population, not unemployed workers, workers in small establishments, or workers in the informal sector (International Labour Organization, *Key Indicators of the Labour Market 2001–2002).*

The reference period of a census or survey is another important source of differences: in some countries data refer to people's status on the day of the census or survey or during a specific period before the inquiry date, while in others data are recorded without reference to any period. In developing countries, where the household is often the basic unit of production and all members contribute to output, but some at low intensity or irregularly, the estimated labor force may be much smaller than the numbers actually working.

Differing definitions of employment age also affect comparability. For most countries the working age is 15 and older, but in some developing countries children younger than 15 work full- or part-time and are included in the estimates. Similarly, some countries have an upper age limit. As a result, calculations may systematically over- or underestimate actual rates. For further information on source, reference period, or definition, consult the original source.

The labor force participation rates in the table are from *Key Indicators of the Labour Market,* 5th edition. These harmonized estimates use strict data selection criteria and enhanced methods to ensure comparability across countries and over time, including collection and tabulation methodologies and methods applied to such country-specific factors as military service requirements. Estimates are based mainly on labor force surveys, with other sources (population censuses and nationally reported estimates) used only when no survey data are available.

Participation rates indicate the relative size of the labor supply. The indicator in this edition is for the population ages 15 and older, to include people who continue working past age 65. In previous editions the indicator was for the population ages 15–64, so participation rates are not comparable across editions.

The labor force estimates in the table were calculated by applying labor force participation rates from the International Labour Organization (ILO) database to World Bank population estimates to create a series consistent with these population estimates. This procedure sometimes results in labor force estimates that differ slightly from those in the ILO's *Yearbook of Labour Statistics* and its database Key Indicators of the Labour Market.

Estimates of women in the labor force and employment are generally lower than those of men and are not comparable internationally, reflecting that demographic, social, legal, and cultural trends and norms determine whether women's activities are regarded as economic. In many countries many women work on farms or in other family enterprises without pay, and others work in or near their homes, mixing work and family activities during the day.

• **Labor force participation rate** is the proportion of the population ages 15 and older that is economically active: all people who supply labor for the production of goods and services during a specified period. • **Total labor force** comprises people ages 15 and older who meet the ILO definition of the economically active population. It includes both the employed and the unemployed. • **Average annual percentage growth of the labor force** is calculated using the exponential endpoint method (see *Statistical methods* for more information). • **Females as a percentage of the labor force** show the extent to which women are active in the labor force.

Data on labor force participation rates are from the ILO database Key Indicators of the Labour Market, 5th edition. Labor force numbers were calculated by World Bank staff, applying labor force participation rates from the ILO database to population estimates.

# Employment by economic activity

| | Agriculture | | | | Industry | | | | Services | | | |
|---|---|---|---|---|---|---|---|---|---|---|---|---|
| | Male % of male employment | | Female % of female employment | | Male % of male employment | | Female % of female employment | | Male % of male employment | | Female % of female employment | |
| | 1990–92[a] | 2003–06[a] | 1990–92[a] | 2003–06[a] | 1990–92[a] | 2003–06[a] | 1990–92[a] | 2003–06[a] | 1990–92[a] | 2003–06[a] | 1990–92[a] | 2003–06[a] |
| Afghanistan | .. | .. | .. | .. | .. | .. | .. | .. | .. | .. | .. | .. |
| Albania | .. | .. | .. | .. | .. | .. | .. | .. | .. | .. | .. | .. |
| Algeria | .. | 23 | .. | 11 | .. | 24 | .. | 25 | .. | 53 | .. | 64 |
| Angola | .. | .. | .. | .. | .. | .. | .. | .. | .. | .. | .. | .. |
| Argentina | 0[b,c] | 2[c] | 0[b,c] | 1[c] | 40[c] | 33[c] | 18[c] | 11[c] | 59[c] | 66[c] | 81[c] | 88[c] |
| Armenia | .. | .. | .. | .. | .. | .. | .. | .. | .. | .. | .. | .. |
| Australia | 6 | 5 | 4 | 3 | 32 | 31 | 12 | 9 | 61 | 65 | 84 | 88 |
| Austria | 6 | 6[c] | 8 | 6[c] | 47 | 40[c] | 20 | 13[c] | 46 | 55[c] | 72 | 81[c] |
| Azerbaijan | .. | 41 | .. | 37 | .. | 15 | .. | 9 | .. | 44 | .. | 54 |
| Bangladesh | 54 | 50 | 85 | 59 | 16 | 12 | 9 | 18 | 25 | 38 | 2 | 23 |
| Belarus | .. | .. | .. | .. | .. | .. | .. | .. | .. | .. | .. | .. |
| Belgium | 3[c] | 2[c] | 2[c] | 2[c] | 41[c] | 35[c] | 16[c] | 11[c] | 56[c] | 62[c] | 81[c] | 86[c] |
| Benin | .. | .. | .. | .. | .. | .. | .. | .. | .. | .. | .. | .. |
| Bolivia | 3[c] | .. | 1[c] | .. | 42[c] | .. | 17[c] | .. | 55[c] | .. | 82[c] | .. |
| Bosnia and Herzegovina | .. | .. | .. | .. | .. | .. | .. | .. | .. | .. | .. | .. |
| Botswana | .. | 29 | .. | 13 | .. | 28 | .. | 17 | .. | 43 | .. | 71 |
| Brazil | 31[c] | 25[c] | 25[c] | 16[c] | 27[c] | 27[c] | 10[c] | 13[c] | 43[c] | 48[c] | 65[c] | 71[c] |
| Bulgaria | .. | 11 | .. | 7 | .. | 39 | .. | 29 | .. | 50 | .. | 64 |
| Burkina Faso | .. | .. | .. | .. | .. | .. | .. | .. | .. | .. | .. | .. |
| Burundi | .. | .. | .. | .. | .. | .. | .. | .. | .. | .. | .. | .. |
| Cambodia | .. | .. | .. | .. | .. | .. | .. | .. | .. | .. | .. | .. |
| Cameroon | 53 | .. | 68 | .. | 14 | .. | 4 | .. | 26 | .. | 23 | .. |
| Canada | 6[c] | 4[c] | 2[c] | 2[c] | 31[c] | 32[c] | 11[c] | 11[c] | 64[c] | 64[c] | 87[c] | 88[c] |
| Central African Republic | .. | .. | .. | .. | .. | .. | .. | .. | .. | .. | .. | .. |
| Chad | .. | .. | .. | .. | .. | .. | .. | .. | .. | .. | .. | .. |
| Chile | 24 | 17 | 6 | 6 | 32 | 29 | 15 | 12 | 45 | 54 | 79 | 83 |
| China | .. | .. | .. | .. | .. | .. | .. | .. | .. | .. | .. | .. |
|   Hong Kong, China | 1 | 0[b] | 0[b] | 0[b] | 37 | 22 | 27 | 7 | 63 | 77 | 73 | 93 |
| Colombia | 2 | 32[b] | 1[b,c] | 8[b,c] | 35 | 21 | 25 | 16 | 63 | 48 | 74 | 76 |
| Congo, Dem. Rep. | .. | .. | .. | .. | .. | .. | .. | .. | .. | .. | .. | .. |
| Congo, Rep. | .. | .. | .. | .. | .. | .. | .. | .. | .. | .. | .. | .. |
| Costa Rica | 32 | 21 | 5 | 5 | 27 | 26 | 25 | 13 | 41 | 52 | 69 | 82 |
| Côte d'Ivoire | .. | .. | .. | .. | .. | .. | .. | .. | .. | .. | .. | .. |
| Croatia | .. | 16[c] | .. | 19[c] | .. | 37[c] | .. | 18[c] | .. | 47[c] | .. | 63[c] |
| Cuba | .. | 28 | .. | 10 | .. | 23 | .. | 14 | .. | 50 | .. | 76 |
| Czech Republic | 9 | 5 | 7 | 3 | 55 | 49 | 33 | 27 | 36 | 46 | 61 | 71 |
| Denmark | 7 | 4 | 3 | 2 | 37 | 34 | 16 | 12 | 56 | 62 | 81 | 86 |
| Dominican Republic | 26 | 21 | 3 | 3 | 23 | 26 | 21 | 15 | 52 | 53 | 76 | 82 |
| Ecuador | 10[c] | 11[c] | 2[c] | 4[c] | 29[c] | 27[c] | 17[c] | 12[c] | 62[c] | 62[c] | 81[c] | 84[c] |
| Egypt, Arab Rep. | 35 | 28 | 52 | 39 | 25 | 23 | 10 | 6 | 41 | 49 | 37 | 55 |
| El Salvador | 48[c] | 28 | 15[c] | 5 | 23[c] | 25 | 23[c] | 22 | 29[c] | 45 | 63[c] | 75 |
| Eritrea | .. | .. | .. | .. | .. | .. | .. | .. | .. | .. | .. | .. |
| Estonia | 23 | 7 | 13 | 4 | 42 | 44 | 30 | 24 | 36 | 49 | 57 | 72 |
| Ethiopia | .. | 84[c] | .. | 76[c] | .. | 5[c] | .. | 8[c] | .. | 10[c] | .. | 16[c] |
| Finland | 11 | 7 | 6 | 3 | 38 | 38 | 15 | 12 | 51 | 56 | 78 | 84 |
| France | .. | 5 | .. | 2 | .. | 35 | .. | 12 | .. | 60 | .. | 85 |
| Gabon | .. | .. | .. | .. | .. | .. | .. | .. | .. | .. | .. | .. |
| Gambia, The | .. | .. | .. | .. | .. | .. | .. | .. | .. | .. | .. | .. |
| Georgia | .. | 52 | .. | 57 | .. | 14 | .. | 4 | .. | 34 | .. | 38 |
| Germany | 4 | 3 | 4 | 2 | 50 | 41 | 24 | 16 | 47 | 56 | 72 | 82 |
| Ghana | 66 | .. | 59 | .. | 10 | .. | 10 | .. | 23 | .. | 32 | .. |
| Greece | 20[c] | 12[c] | 26[c] | 14[c] | 32[c] | 30[c] | 17[c] | 10[c] | 48[c] | 58[c] | 56[c] | 76[c] |
| Guatemala | .. | .. | .. | .. | .. | .. | .. | .. | .. | .. | .. | .. |
| Guinea | .. | .. | .. | .. | .. | .. | .. | .. | .. | .. | .. | .. |
| Guinea-Bissau | .. | .. | .. | .. | .. | .. | .. | .. | .. | .. | .. | .. |
| Haiti | .. | .. | .. | .. | .. | .. | .. | .. | .. | .. | .. | .. |

| | Agriculture | | | | Industry | | | | Services | | | |
|---|---|---|---|---|---|---|---|---|---|---|---|---|
| | Male % of male employment | | Female % of female employment | | Male % of male employment | | Female % of female employment | | Male % of male employment | | Female % of female employment | |
| | 1990–92[a] | 2003–06[a] | 1990–92[a] | 2003–06[a] | 1990–92[a] | 2003–06[a] | 1990–92[a] | 2003–06[a] | 1990–92[a] | 2003–06[a] | 1990–92[a] | 2003–06[a] |
| Honduras | 53 | 51 | 6 | 13 | 18 | 20 | 25 | 23 | 29 | 29 | 69 | 63 |
| Hungary | .. | 7[c] | .. | 3[c] | .. | 42[c] | .. | 21[c] | .. | 51[c] | .. | 76[c] |
| India | .. | .. | .. | .. | .. | .. | .. | .. | .. | .. | .. | .. |
| Indonesia | 54 | 43 | 57 | 41 | 15 | 20 | 13 | 15 | 31 | 37 | 31 | 44 |
| Iran, Islamic Rep. | .. | 23 | .. | 34 | .. | 31 | .. | 28 | .. | 46 | .. | 37 |
| Iraq | .. | .. | .. | .. | .. | .. | .. | .. | .. | .. | .. | .. |
| Ireland | 19 | 9 | 3 | 1 | 33 | 39 | 18 | 12 | 48 | 51 | 78 | 86 |
| Israel | 5 | 3 | 2 | 1 | 38 | 31 | 15 | 11 | 57 | 65 | 83 | 88 |
| Italy | 8 | 5 | 9 | 3 | 37 | 39 | 22 | 18 | 55 | 56 | 70 | 79 |
| Jamaica | 36 | 25 | 16 | 9 | 25 | 27 | 12 | 5 | 39 | 48 | 72 | 86 |
| Japan | 6 | 4 | 7 | 5 | 40 | 35 | 27 | 18 | 54 | 59 | 65 | 77 |
| Jordan | .. | 4 | .. | 2 | .. | 23 | .. | 12 | .. | 73 | .. | 84 |
| Kazakhstan | .. | 33 | .. | 30 | .. | 25 | .. | 12 | .. | 42 | .. | 58 |
| Kenya | 19[c] | .. | 20[c] | .. | 23[c] | .. | 9[c] | .. | 58[c] | .. | 71[c] | .. |
| Korea, Dem. Rep. | .. | .. | .. | .. | .. | .. | .. | .. | .. | .. | .. | .. |
| Korea, Rep. | 14 | 7 | 18 | 9 | 40 | 34 | 28 | 17 | 46 | 59 | 54 | 74 |
| Kuwait | .. | .. | .. | .. | .. | .. | .. | .. | .. | .. | .. | .. |
| Kyrgyz Republic | .. | 39 | .. | 39 | .. | 23 | .. | 11 | .. | 38 | .. | 50 |
| Lao PDR | .. | .. | .. | .. | .. | .. | .. | .. | .. | .. | .. | .. |
| Latvia | .. | 15[c] | .. | 8[c] | .. | 35[c] | .. | 16[c] | .. | 49[c] | .. | 75[c] |
| Lebanon | .. | .. | .. | .. | .. | .. | .. | .. | .. | .. | .. | .. |
| Lesotho | .. | .. | .. | .. | .. | .. | .. | .. | .. | .. | .. | .. |
| Liberia | .. | .. | .. | .. | .. | .. | .. | .. | .. | .. | .. | .. |
| Libya | .. | .. | .. | .. | .. | .. | .. | .. | .. | .. | .. | .. |
| Lithuania | 25 | 17[c] | 15 | 11[c] | 46 | 37[c] | 31 | 21[c] | 29 | 46[c] | 54 | 68[c] |
| Macedonia, FYR | .. | 20 | .. | 19 | .. | 34 | .. | 30 | .. | 46 | .. | 51 |
| Madagascar | .. | 77 | .. | 79 | .. | 7 | .. | 6 | .. | 16 | .. | 15 |
| Malawi | .. | .. | .. | .. | .. | .. | .. | .. | .. | .. | .. | .. |
| Malaysia | 23 | 16 | 20 | 11 | 31 | 35 | 32 | 27 | 46 | 49 | 48 | 62 |
| Mali | .. | 50 | .. | 30 | .. | 18 | .. | 15 | .. | 32 | .. | 55 |
| Mauritania | .. | .. | .. | .. | .. | .. | .. | .. | .. | .. | .. | .. |
| Mauritius | 15 | 11 | 13 | 9 | 36 | 34 | 48 | 29 | 48 | 55 | 39 | 62 |
| Mexico | 34 | 21 | 11 | 5 | 25 | 30 | 19 | 19 | 41 | 49 | 70 | 76 |
| Moldova | .. | 41 | .. | 40 | .. | 21 | .. | 12 | .. | 38 | .. | 48 |
| Mongolia | .. | 43 | .. | 37 | .. | 19 | .. | 15 | .. | 38 | .. | 48 |
| Morocco | .. | 38 | .. | 63 | .. | 22 | .. | 14 | .. | 40 | .. | 23 |
| Mozambique | .. | .. | .. | .. | .. | .. | .. | .. | .. | .. | .. | .. |
| Myanmar | .. | .. | .. | .. | .. | .. | .. | .. | .. | .. | .. | .. |
| Namibia | 45 | .. | 52 | .. | 21 | .. | 8 | .. | 34 | .. | 40 | .. |
| Nepal | 75 | .. | 91 | .. | 4 | .. | 1 | .. | 20 | .. | 8 | .. |
| Netherlands | 5 | 4 | 3 | 2 | 33 | 30 | 10 | 8 | 60 | 62 | 82 | 86 |
| New Zealand | 13 | 9 | 8 | 5 | 31 | 32 | 13 | 11 | 56 | 59 | 80 | 84 |
| Nicaragua | .. | 41 | .. | 10 | .. | 19 | .. | 17 | .. | 33 | .. | 52 |
| Niger | .. | .. | .. | .. | .. | .. | .. | .. | .. | .. | .. | .. |
| Nigeria | .. | .. | .. | .. | .. | .. | .. | .. | .. | .. | .. | .. |
| Norway | 7 | 5 | 3 | 2 | 34 | 32 | 10 | 8 | 58 | 63 | 86 | 90 |
| Oman | .. | .. | .. | .. | .. | .. | .. | .. | .. | .. | .. | .. |
| Pakistan | 45 | 38 | 69 | 67 | 20 | 21 | 15 | 15 | 35 | 41 | 16 | 18 |
| Panama | 35 | 22 | 3 | 4 | 20 | 22 | 11 | 9 | 45 | 56 | 85 | 86 |
| Papua New Guinea | .. | .. | .. | .. | .. | .. | .. | .. | .. | .. | .. | .. |
| Paraguay | 3[c] | 39[c] | 0[b,c] | 20[c] | 33[c] | 19[c] | 19[c] | 10[c] | 64[c] | 42[c] | 80[c] | 70[c] |
| Peru | 1[c] | 1[c] | 0[b,c] | 0[b,c] | 30[c] | 31[c] | 13[c] | 13[c] | 69[c] | 68[c] | 87[c] | 86[c] |
| Philippines | 53[c] | 45 | 32[c] | 25 | 17[c] | 17 | 14[c] | 12 | 29[c] | 39 | 55[c] | 64 |
| Poland | .. | 18[c] | .. | 17[c] | .. | 39[c] | .. | 17[c] | .. | 43[c] | .. | 66[c] |
| Portugal | 10[c] | 11[c] | 13[c] | 13[c] | 39[c] | 41[c] | 24[c] | 19[c] | 51[c] | 48[c] | 63[c] | 68[c] |
| Puerto Rico | 5 | 3 | 0[b] | 0[b] | 27 | 25 | 19 | 11 | 67 | 72 | 80 | 89 |

| | Agriculture | | | | Industry | | | | Services | | | |
|---|---|---|---|---|---|---|---|---|---|---|---|---|
| | Male % of male employment | | Female % of female employment | | Male % of male employment | | Female % of female employment | | Male % of male employment | | Female % of female employment | |
| | 1990–92[a] | 2003–06[a] | 1990–92[a] | 2003–06[a] | 1990–92[a] | 2003–06[a] | 1990–92[a] | 2003–06[a] | 1990–92[a] | 2003–06[a] | 1990–92[a] | 2003–06[a] |
| Romania | 29[c] | 31 | 38[c] | 33 | 44[c] | 35 | 30[c] | 25 | 28[c] | 34 | 33[c] | 42 |
| Russian Federation | .. | 12 | .. | 8 | .. | 38 | .. | 21 | .. | 50 | .. | 71 |
| Rwanda | .. | .. | .. | .. | .. | .. | .. | .. | .. | .. | .. | .. |
| Saudi Arabia | .. | 5 | .. | 0[b] | .. | 11 | .. | 1 | .. | 85 | .. | 99 |
| Senegal | .. | .. | .. | .. | .. | .. | .. | .. | .. | .. | .. | .. |
| Serbia | .. | .. | .. | .. | .. | .. | .. | .. | .. | .. | .. | .. |
| Sierra Leone | .. | .. | .. | .. | .. | .. | .. | .. | .. | .. | .. | .. |
| Singapore | 1 | 0 | 0[b] | 0 | 36 | 36 | 32 | 21 | 63 | 63 | 68 | 79 |
| Slovak Republic | .. | 6[c] | .. | 3[c] | .. | 50[c] | .. | 25[c] | .. | 44[c] | .. | 72[c] |
| Slovenia | .. | 9 | .. | 9 | .. | 47 | .. | 25 | .. | 43 | .. | 65 |
| Somalia | .. | .. | .. | .. | .. | .. | .. | .. | .. | .. | .. | .. |
| South Africa | .. | 13 | .. | 7 | .. | 33 | .. | 14 | .. | 54 | .. | 79 |
| Spain | 11[c] | 6[c] | 8[c] | 4[c] | 41[c] | 41[c] | 16[c] | 12[c] | 49[c] | 52[c] | 76[c] | 84[c] |
| Sri Lanka | .. | .. | .. | .. | .. | .. | .. | .. | .. | .. | .. | .. |
| Sudan | .. | .. | .. | .. | .. | .. | .. | .. | .. | .. | .. | .. |
| Swaziland | .. | .. | .. | .. | .. | .. | .. | .. | .. | .. | .. | .. |
| Sweden | 5[c] | 3[c] | 2[c] | 1[c] | 40[c] | 34[c] | 12[c] | 9[c] | 55[c] | 63[c] | 86[c] | 90[c] |
| Switzerland | 4[c] | 5[c] | 4[c] | 3[c] | 37[c] | 32[c] | 15[c] | 11[c] | 59[c] | 63[c] | 81[c] | 86[c] |
| Syrian Arab Republic | 23 | 23 | 54 | 49 | 28 | 29 | 8 | 8 | 49 | 48 | 38 | 43 |
| Tajikistan | .. | .. | .. | .. | .. | .. | .. | .. | .. | .. | .. | .. |
| Tanzania | 78[c] | .. | 90[c] | .. | 7[c] | .. | 1[c] | .. | 15[c] | .. | 8[c] | .. |
| Thailand | 60 | 44 | 62 | 41 | 18 | 22 | 13 | 19 | 22 | 34 | 25 | 41 |
| Timor-Leste | .. | .. | .. | .. | .. | .. | .. | .. | .. | .. | .. | .. |
| Togo | .. | .. | .. | .. | .. | .. | .. | .. | .. | .. | .. | .. |
| Trinidad and Tobago | 15 | 6 | 6 | 2 | 34 | 41 | 14 | 16 | 51 | 52 | 80 | 82 |
| Tunisia | .. | .. | .. | .. | .. | .. | .. | .. | .. | .. | .. | .. |
| Turkey | 33 | 22 | 72 | 52 | 26 | 28 | 11 | 15 | 41 | 50 | 17 | 33 |
| Turkmenistan | .. | .. | .. | .. | .. | .. | .. | .. | .. | .. | .. | .. |
| Uganda | 91 | 60[c] | 91 | 77[c] | 4 | 11[c] | 6 | 5[c] | 5 | 29[c] | 3 | 18[c] |
| Ukraine | .. | .. | .. | .. | .. | .. | .. | .. | .. | .. | .. | .. |
| United Arab Emirates | .. | .. | .. | .. | .. | .. | .. | .. | .. | .. | .. | .. |
| United Kingdom | 3 | 2 | 1 | 1 | 41 | 33 | 16 | 9 | 55 | 65 | 82 | 90 |
| United States | 4 | 2 | 1 | 1 | 34 | 30 | 14 | 10 | 62 | 68 | 85 | 90 |
| Uruguay | 7[c] | 7[c] | 1[c] | 2[c] | 36[c] | 29[c] | 21[c] | 13[c] | 57[c] | 64[c] | 78[c] | 86[c] |
| Uzbekistan | .. | .. | .. | .. | .. | .. | .. | .. | .. | .. | .. | .. |
| Venezuela, RB | 17 | 16[c] | 2 | 2[c] | 32 | 25[c] | 16 | 11[c] | 52 | 59[c] | 82 | 86[c] |
| Vietnam | .. | 56 | .. | 60 | .. | 21 | .. | 14 | .. | 23 | .. | 26 |
| West Bank and Gaza | .. | 12 | .. | 34 | .. | 28 | .. | 8 | .. | 59 | .. | 56 |
| Yemen, Rep. | 44 | .. | 83 | .. | 14 | .. | 2 | .. | 38 | .. | 13 | .. |
| Zambia | .. | .. | .. | .. | .. | .. | .. | .. | .. | .. | .. | .. |
| Zimbabwe | .. | .. | .. | .. | .. | .. | .. | .. | .. | .. | .. | .. |
| **World** | .. w | .. w | .. w | .. w | .. w | .. w | .. w | .. w | .. w | .. w | .. w | .. w |
| **Low income** | .. | .. | .. | .. | .. | .. | .. | .. | .. | .. | .. | .. |
| **Middle income** | .. | .. | .. | .. | .. | .. | .. | .. | .. | .. | .. | .. |
| Lower middle income | .. | .. | .. | .. | .. | .. | .. | .. | .. | .. | .. | .. |
| Upper middle income | .. | 20 | .. | 14 | .. | 31 | .. | 17 | .. | 49 | .. | 68 |
| **Low & middle income** | .. | .. | .. | .. | .. | .. | .. | .. | .. | .. | .. | .. |
| East Asia & Pacific | .. | .. | .. | .. | .. | .. | .. | .. | .. | .. | .. | .. |
| Europe & Central Asia | .. | 19 | .. | 18 | .. | 34 | .. | 19 | .. | 47 | .. | 62 |
| Latin America & Carib. | 20 | 21 | 14 | 10 | 30 | 27 | 14 | 15 | 50 | 52 | 72 | 76 |
| Middle East & N. Africa | .. | .. | .. | .. | .. | .. | .. | .. | .. | .. | .. | .. |
| South Asia | .. | .. | .. | .. | .. | .. | .. | .. | .. | .. | .. | .. |
| Sub-Saharan Africa | .. | .. | .. | .. | .. | .. | .. | .. | .. | .. | .. | .. |
| **High income** | 6 | 4 | 5 | 3 | 38 | 34 | 19 | 13 | 56 | 62 | 76 | 85 |
| Euro area | 7 | 5 | 7 | 3 | 42 | 38 | 20 | 14 | 50 | 56 | 72 | 82 |

**Note:** Data across sectors may not sum to 100 percent because of workers not classified by sectors.
a. Data are for the most recent year available. b. Less than 0.5. c. Limited coverage.

# Employment by economic activity | **2.3**

The International Labour Organization (ILO) classifies economic activity using the International Standard Industrial Classification (ISIC) of All Economic Activities, revision 2 (1968) and revision 3 (1990). Because this classification is based on where work is performed (industry) rather than type of work performed (occupation), all of an enterprise's employees are classified under the same industry, regardless of their trade or occupation. The categories should sum to 100 percent. Where they do not, the differences are due to workers who cannot be classified by economic activity.

Data on employment are drawn from labor force surveys, household surveys, official estimates, censuses and administrative records of social insurance schemes, and establishment surveys when no other information is available. The concept of employment generally refers to people above a certain age who worked, or who held a job, during a reference period. Employment data include both full-time and part-time workers.

There are many differences in how countries define and measure employment status, particularly, members of the armed forces, self-employed workers, and unpaid family workers. Where members of the armed forces are included, they are allocated to the service sector, causing that sector to be somewhat overstated relative to the service sector in economies where they are excluded. Where data are obtained from establishment surveys, data cover only employees; thus self-employed and unpaid family workers are excluded. In such cases the employment share of the agricultural sector is severely underreported. Caution should be also used where the data refer only to urban areas, which record little or no agricultural work. Moreover, the age group and area covered could differ by country or change over time within a country. For detailed information on breaks in series, consult the original source.

Countries also take different approaches to the treatment of unemployed people. In most countries unemployed people with previous job experience are classified according to their last job. But in some countries the unemployed and people seeking their first job are not classifiable by economic activity. Because of these differences, the size and distribution of employment by economic activity may not be fully comparable across countries.

The ILO's *Yearbook of Labour Statistics* and its database Key Indicators of the Labour Market report data by major divisions of the ISIC revision 2 or revision 3. In the table the reported divisions or categories are aggregated into three broad groups: agriculture, industry, and services. Such broad classification may obscure fundamental shifts within countries' industrial patterns. A slight majority of countries report economic activity according to the ISIC revision 2 instead of revision 3. The use of one classification or the other should not have a significant impact on the information for the three broad sectors presented in the table.

The distribution of economic wealth in the world remains strongly correlated with employment by economic activity. The wealthier economies are those with the largest share of total employment in services, whereas the poorer economies are largely agriculture based.

The distribution of economic activity by gender reveals some clear patterns. Men still make up the majority of people employed in all three sectors, but the gender gap is biggest in industry. Employment in agriculture is also male-dominated, although not as much as industry. Segregating one sex in a narrow range of occupations significantly reduces economic efficiency by reducing labor market flexibility and thus the economy's ability to adapt to change. This segregation is particularly harmful for women, who have a much narrower range of labor market choices and lower levels of pay than men. But it is also detrimental to men when job losses are concentrated in industries dominated by men and job growth is centered in service occupations, where women have better chances, as has been the recent experience in many countries.

There are several explanations for the rising importance of service jobs for women. Many service jobs—such as nursing and social and clerical work—are considered "feminine" because of a perceived similarity to women's traditional roles. Women often do not receive the training needed to take advantage of changing employment opportunities. And the greater availability of part-time work in service industries may lure more women, although it is unclear whether this is a cause or an effect.

• **Agriculture** corresponds to division 1 (ISIC revision 2) or tabulation categories A and B (ISIC revision 3) and includes hunting, forestry, and fishing. • **Industry** corresponds to divisions 2–5 (ISIC revision 2) or tabulation categories C–F (ISIC revision 3) and includes mining and quarrying (including oil production), manufacturing, construction, and public utilities (electricity, gas, and water). • **Services** correspond to divisions 6–9 (ISIC revision 2) or tabulation categories G–P (ISIC revision 3) and include wholesale and retail trade and restaurants and hotels; transport, storage, and communications; financing, insurance, real estate, and business services; and community, social, and personal services.

Data on employment are from the ILO database Key Indicators of the Labour Market, 5th edition.

# 2.4 Decent work and productive employment

| | Employment to population ratio | | | | Vulnerable employment | | | | Labor productivity | | | |
|---|---|---|---|---|---|---|---|---|---|---|---|---|
| | | | | | Unpaid family workers and own-account workers | | | | GDP per person employed | | | |
| | % ages 15 and older | | % ages 15–24 | | Male % of male employment | | Female % of female employment | | 1990 PPP $[a] | | Index 1980 = 100 | |
| | 1991 | 2006 | 1991 | 2006 | 1990 | 2005 | 1990 | 2005 | 1990 | 2006 | 1990 | 2006 |
| Afghanistan | .. | .. | .. | .. | .. | .. | .. | .. | .. | .. | .. | .. |
| Albania | 62 | 51 | 45 | 37 | .. | .. | .. | .. | 2,499 | 3,502 | 107 | 149 |
| Algeria | 37 | 50 | 22 | 33 | .. | 29 | .. | 32 | 2,946 | 3,401 | 94 | 108 |
| Angola | 74 | 75 | 64 | 66 | .. | .. | .. | .. | 869 | 1,143 | 90 | 119 |
| Argentina | 54 | 60 | 45 | 46 | .. | 23[b] | .. | 19[b] | 6,436 | 8,915 | 78 | 109 |
| Armenia | 68 | 49 | 51 | 19 | .. | .. | .. | .. | 6,066 | 8,428 | .. | .. |
| Australia | 57 | 60 | 56 | 63 | 12 | 12 | 8 | 7 | 17,106 | 24,603 | 119 | 171 |
| Austria | 54 | 55 | 61 | 50 | .. | 9 | .. | 8 | 16,895 | 22,708 | 123 | 165 |
| Azerbaijan | 59 | 61 | 39 | 41 | .. | .. | .. | .. | 4,639 | 5,954 | .. | .. |
| Bangladesh | 73 | 67 | 64 | 57 | .. | 60 | .. | 73 | 640 | 1,014 | 117 | 185 |
| Belarus | 59 | 52 | 40 | 36 | .. | .. | .. | .. | 7,184 | 9,491 | .. | .. |
| Belgium | 46 | 48 | 32 | 28 | .. | 11 | .. | 10 | 17,197 | 22,582 | 119 | 156 |
| Benin | 67 | 64 | 55 | 49 | .. | .. | .. | .. | .. | .. | .. | .. |
| Bolivia | 61 | 70 | 44 | 51 | 32[b] | .. | 50[b] | .. | 2,197 | 2,764 | 85 | 107 |
| Bosnia and Herzegovina | 58 | 55 | 37 | 37 | .. | .. | .. | .. | 3,737 | 6,469 | .. | .. |
| Botswana | 57 | 44 | 38 | 21 | .. | 7 | .. | 17 | .. | .. | .. | .. |
| Brazil | 60 | 61 | 54 | 49 | 29[b] | 34[b] | 30[b] | 32[b] | 4,923 | 5,812 | 95 | 112 |
| Bulgaria | 50 | 41 | 31 | 20 | .. | 11 | .. | 9 | 5,597 | 7,780 | 93 | 129 |
| Burkina Faso | 81 | 82 | 74 | 73 | .. | .. | .. | .. | 810 | 1,135 | 111 | 155 |
| Burundi | 83 | 84 | 67 | 71 | .. | .. | .. | .. | .. | .. | .. | .. |
| Cambodia | 79 | 76 | 69 | 63 | .. | .. | .. | .. | 880 | 1,827 | 106 | 220 |
| Cameroon | 63 | 61 | 48 | 44 | .. | .. | .. | .. | 1,222 | 1,155 | 102 | 97 |
| Canada | 59 | 62 | 57 | 59 | .. | .. | .. | .. | 18,872 | 24,633 | 117 | 152 |
| Central African Republic | 73 | 72 | 56 | 57 | .. | .. | .. | .. | .. | .. | .. | .. |
| Chad | 66 | 65 | 44 | 45 | .. | .. | .. | .. | .. | .. | .. | .. |
| Chile | 51 | 49 | 34 | 22 | .. | 29 | .. | 24 | 6,402 | 12,207 | 113 | 215 |
| China | 76 | 73 | 73 | 65 | .. | .. | .. | .. | 1,871 | 6,352 | 176 | 599 |
| Hong Kong, China | 63 | 58 | 54 | 39 | .. | 10 | .. | 5 | 17,541 | 27,769 | 167 | 264 |
| Colombia | 54 | 63 | 41 | 46 | 30[b] | 44 | 26[b] | 44 | 4,840 | 5,767 | 114 | 135 |
| Congo, Dem. Rep. | 67 | 68 | 56 | 58 | .. | .. | .. | .. | 510 | 224 | 85 | 38 |
| Congo, Rep. | 66 | 66 | 49 | 48 | .. | .. | .. | .. | .. | .. | .. | .. |
| Costa Rica | 55 | 60 | 48 | 44 | 26 | 20 | 20 | 23 | 4,747 | 7,321 | 97 | 149 |
| Côte d'Ivoire | 62 | 58 | 47 | 45 | .. | .. | .. | .. | 1,363 | 1,310 | 65 | 63 |
| Croatia | 52 | 45 | 34 | 27 | .. | 19 | .. | 21 | 7,351 | 8,326 | .. | .. |
| Cuba | 54 | 58 | 39 | 37 | .. | .. | .. | .. | 2,948 | 3,008 | 112 | 114 |
| Czech Republic | 62 | 55 | 51 | 30 | .. | 15 | .. | 8 | 8,895 | 11,688 | .. | .. |
| Denmark | 62 | 61 | 65 | 61 | .. | .. | .. | .. | 18,452 | 24,816 | 121 | 163 |
| Dominican Republic | 49 | 53 | 32 | 32 | 42 | 49 | 30 | 31 | 2,473 | 4,344 | 104 | 183 |
| Ecuador | 55 | 66 | 43 | 48 | 33[b] | 30[b] | 41[b] | 39[b] | 3,903 | 4,831 | 95 | 117 |
| Egypt, Arab Rep. | 43 | 42 | 22 | 20 | .. | 21 | .. | 46 | 2,522 | 3,386 | 122 | 164 |
| El Salvador | 58 | 57 | 41 | 37 | .. | 29 | .. | 45 | .. | .. | .. | .. |
| Eritrea | 68 | 66 | 60 | 56 | .. | .. | .. | .. | .. | .. | .. | .. |
| Estonia | 68 | 54 | 51 | 29 | 2 | 7 | 3 | 4 | 10,820 | 20,795 | .. | .. |
| Ethiopia | 77 | 76 | 74 | 71 | .. | 89 | .. | 93 | 578 | 702 | 89 | 108 |
| Finland | 59 | 56 | 45 | 43 | .. | .. | .. | .. | 16,866 | 23,358 | 130 | 180 |
| France | 50 | 49 | 28 | 23 | .. | 8 | .. | 5 | 18,093 | 22,402 | 120 | 148 |
| Gabon | 60 | 59 | 42 | 39 | .. | .. | .. | .. | .. | .. | .. | .. |
| Gambia, The | 68 | 66 | 52 | 51 | .. | .. | .. | .. | .. | .. | .. | .. |
| Georgia | 60 | 53 | 37 | 24 | .. | 64 | .. | 65 | 7,616 | 4,721 | .. | .. |
| Germany | 56 | 52 | 58 | 41 | .. | 7 | .. | 6 | 16,306 | 20,018 | .. | .. |
| Ghana | 72 | 66 | 51 | 42 | .. | .. | .. | .. | 1,063 | 1,485 | 92 | 128 |
| Greece | 46 | 50 | 31 | 28 | .. | 29 | .. | 28 | 10,015 | 15,440 | 112 | 172 |
| Guatemala | 58 | 55 | 52 | 49 | .. | .. | .. | .. | 3,631 | 4,554 | 83 | 104 |
| Guinea | 82 | 81 | 72 | 70 | .. | .. | .. | .. | .. | .. | .. | .. |
| Guinea-Bissau | 67 | 69 | 56 | 60 | .. | .. | .. | .. | .. | .. | .. | .. |
| Haiti | 60 | 65 | 39 | 50 | .. | .. | .. | .. | .. | .. | .. | .. |

# Decent work and productive employment

| | Employment to population ratio | | | | Vulnerable employment | | | | Labor productivity | | | |
|---|---|---|---|---|---|---|---|---|---|---|---|---|
| | | | | | Unpaid family workers and own-account workers | | | | GDP per person employed | | | |
| | % ages 15 and older | | % ages 15–24 | | Male % of male employment | | Female % of female employment | | 1990 PPP $[a] | | Index 1980 = 100 | |
| | 1991 | 2006 | 1991 | 2006 | 1990 | 2005 | 1990 | 2005 | 1990 | 2006 | 1990 | 2006 |
| Honduras | 57 | 69 | 48 | 60 | 48[b] | 48[b] | 50[b] | 51[b] | .. | .. | .. | .. |
| Hungary | 49 | 46 | 39 | 24 | 8 | 9 | 7 | 6 | 6,459 | 9,291 | 102 | 147 |
| India | 59 | 56 | 46 | 40 | .. | .. | .. | .. | 1,309 | 2,611 | 140 | 278 |
| Indonesia | 63 | 61 | 45 | 37 | .. | .. | .. | .. | 2,526 | 4,126 | 135 | 220 |
| Iran, Islamic Rep. | 46 | 51 | 33 | 34 | .. | .. | .. | .. | 3,503 | 5,786 | 89 | 146 |
| Iraq | 33 | .. | 20 | .. | .. | .. | .. | .. | 2,458 | | 39 | |
| Ireland | 45 | 60 | 38 | 48 | 25 | 17 | 9 | 5 | 11,818 | 27,768 | 138 | 325 |
| Israel | 46 | 50 | 24 | 25 | .. | 9 | .. | 5 | 12,968 | 17,548 | 118 | 160 |
| Italy | 44 | 46 | 30 | 26 | .. | 15 | .. | 11 | 16,313 | 19,653 | 124 | 150 |
| Jamaica | 61 | 57 | 39 | 30 | 46 | 37 | 37 | 31 | 3,786 | 3,751 | 121 | 120 |
| Japan | 63 | 58 | 43 | 41 | 15 | 11 | 26 | 14 | 18,789 | 22,461 | 140 | 167 |
| Jordan | 39 | 47 | 26 | 31 | .. | .. | .. | .. | 3,792 | 4,591 | 85 | 103 |
| Kazakhstan | 63 | 65 | 45 | 44 | .. | 33 | .. | 39 | 7,458 | 8,954 | .. | .. |
| Kenya | 64 | 63 | 44 | 43 | .. | .. | .. | .. | 1,117 | 1,060 | 106 | 101 |
| Korea, Dem. Rep. | 64 | 60 | 49 | 33 | .. | .. | .. | .. | .. | .. | .. | .. |
| Korea, Rep. | 59 | 60 | 36 | 34 | .. | 24 | .. | 29 | 8,704 | 18,086 | 212 | 440 |
| Kuwait | 65 | 71 | 34 | 38 | .. | .. | .. | .. | 6,121 | 11,806 | 46 | 89 |
| Kyrgyz Republic | 59 | 59 | 41 | 41 | .. | 50 | .. | 50 | 3,602 | 2,464 | .. | .. |
| Lao PDR | 65 | 66 | 53 | 54 | .. | .. | .. | .. | .. | .. | .. | .. |
| Latvia | 61 | 51 | 46 | 31 | .. | 9 | .. | 7 | 9,916 | 13,514 | .. | .. |
| Lebanon | 47 | 51 | 32 | 32 | .. | .. | .. | .. | .. | .. | .. | .. |
| Lesotho | 54 | 37 | 40 | 25 | .. | .. | .. | .. | .. | .. | .. | .. |
| Liberia | 63 | 63 | 48 | 47 | .. | .. | .. | .. | .. | .. | .. | .. |
| Libya | 47 | 54 | 30 | 33 | .. | .. | .. | .. | .. | .. | .. | .. |
| Lithuania | 55 | 53 | 35 | 24 | .. | .. | .. | .. | 8,663 | 10,309 | .. | .. |
| Macedonia, FYR | 40 | 33 | 20 | 13 | .. | 23 | .. | 21 | 3,972 | 3,538 | .. | .. |
| Madagascar | 77 | 78 | 61 | 63 | .. | 79 | .. | 86 | 799 | 675 | 76 | 64 |
| Malawi | 80 | 80 | 66 | 66 | .. | .. | .. | .. | 554 | 620 | 86 | 96 |
| Malaysia | 61 | 62 | 47 | 44 | .. | 20 | .. | 21 | 5,132 | 9,782 | 140 | 268 |
| Mali | 75 | 70 | 67 | 58 | .. | .. | .. | .. | 747 | 1,026 | 102 | 140 |
| Mauritania | 64 | 64 | 49 | 48 | .. | .. | .. | .. | .. | .. | .. | .. |
| Mauritius | 53 | 55 | 39 | 35 | .. | 18 | .. | 15 | .. | .. | .. | .. |
| Mexico | 57 | 57 | 50 | 40 | 37 | 30 | 36 | 34 | 6,085 | 7,816 | 96 | 124 |
| Moldova | 58 | 56 | 36 | 36 | .. | 37 | .. | 36 | 6,165 | 3,057 | .. | .. |
| Mongolia | 50 | 59 | 39 | 44 | .. | 62 | .. | 57 | .. | .. | .. | .. |
| Morocco | 46 | 47 | 39 | 36 | .. | 54 | .. | 67 | 2,596 | 2,998 | 114 | 132 |
| Mozambique | 80 | 77 | 62 | 55 | .. | .. | .. | .. | 1,115 | 1,783 | 91 | 146 |
| Myanmar | 75 | 75 | 63 | 58 | .. | .. | .. | .. | 778 | 2,387 | 95 | 291 |
| Namibia | 46 | 38 | 23 | 18 | .. | .. | .. | .. | .. | .. | .. | .. |
| Nepal | 59 | 58 | 48 | 44 | .. | .. | .. | .. | .. | .. | .. | .. |
| Netherlands | 53 | 61 | 55 | 69 | .. | .. | .. | .. | 17,262 | 23,385 | 117 | 159 |
| New Zealand | 57 | 65 | 54 | 58 | 15 | 15 | 10 | 9 | 13,909 | 18,306 | 113 | 148 |
| Nicaragua | 56 | 56 | 45 | 44 | .. | .. | .. | .. | .. | .. | .. | .. |
| Niger | 78 | 79 | 68 | 71 | .. | .. | .. | .. | 540 | 514 | 67 | 64 |
| Nigeria | 60 | 59 | 44 | 43 | .. | .. | .. | .. | 1,214 | 1,329 | 85 | 93 |
| Norway | 60 | 66 | 49 | 60 | .. | .. | .. | .. | 18,466 | 28,044 | 123 | 186 |
| Oman | 52 | 52 | 28 | 28 | .. | .. | .. | .. | 6,479 | 7,528 | 159 | 185 |
| Pakistan | 54 | 55 | 44 | 44 | .. | 60 | .. | 69 | 1,589 | 2,278 | 137 | 196 |
| Panama | 50 | 59 | 34 | 36 | 44 | 35 | 19 | 26 | .. | .. | .. | .. |
| Papua New Guinea | 71 | 71 | 58 | 58 | .. | .. | .. | .. | .. | .. | .. | .. |
| Paraguay | 62 | 69 | 51 | 58 | 17[b] | 50[b] | 31[b] | 52[b] | .. | .. | .. | .. |
| Peru | 56 | 64 | 40 | 43 | 30[b] | 34[b] | 45[b] | 39[b] | 3,021 | 4,272 | 71 | 100 |
| Philippines | 59 | 64 | 42 | 44 | .. | 43 | .. | 48 | 2,224 | 2,734 | 94 | 115 |
| Poland | 55 | 46 | 35 | 22 | .. | 23 | .. | 20 | 5,113 | 8,999 | 89 | 157 |
| Portugal | 59 | 58 | 53 | 38 | 18[b] | 18 | 21[b] | 20 | 10,826 | 14,174 | 135 | 176 |
| Puerto Rico | 38 | 43 | 21 | 30 | .. | .. | .. | .. | 10,539 | 15,026 | 129 | 184 |

| | Employment to population ratio | | | | Vulnerable employment | | | | Labor productivity | | | |
|---|---|---|---|---|---|---|---|---|---|---|---|---|
| | | | | | Unpaid family workers and own-account workers | | | | GDP per person employed | | | |
| | | | | | Male % of male employment | | Female % of female employment | | 1990 PPP \$[a] | | Index 1980 = 100 | |
| | % ages 15 and older | | % ages 15–24 | | | | | | | | | |
| | 1991 | 2006 | 1991 | 2006 | 1990 | 2005 | 1990 | 2005 | 1990 | 2006 | 1990 | 2006 |
| Romania | 58 | 52 | 47 | 22 | 7[b] | 33 | 10[b] | 34 | 3,511 | 4,305 | 85 | 104 |
| Russian Federation | 58 | 56 | 36 | 33 | 1 | 6 | 1 | 6 | 7,779 | 7,297 | .. | .. |
| Rwanda | 79 | 73 | 63 | 58 | .. | .. | .. | .. | .. | .. | .. | .. |
| Saudi Arabia | 51 | 51 | 26 | 25 | .. | .. | .. | .. | 8,993 | 8,691 | 68 | 66 |
| Senegal | 67 | 62 | 55 | 47 | 77 | | 91 | .. | 1,279 | 1,433 | 101 | 113 |
| Serbia | 49[c] | 51[c] | 28[c] | 33[c] | .. | .. | .. | .. | 5,160[c] | 2,935[c] | .. | .. |
| Sierra Leone | 64 | 68 | 51 | 60 | .. | .. | .. | .. | .. | .. | .. | .. |
| Singapore | 64 | 60 | 56 | 41 | 10 | 12 | 6 | 6 | 14,220 | 24,688 | 157 | 273 |
| Slovak Republic | 56 | 52 | 41 | 30 | .. | 13[b] | .. | 5[b] | 7,763 | 11,057 | .. | .. |
| Slovenia | 55 | 57 | 37 | 33 | .. | 12 | .. | 10 | 10,860 | 16,136 | .. | .. |
| Somalia | 70 | 69 | 64 | 63 | .. | .. | .. | .. | .. | .. | .. | .. |
| South Africa | 48 | 45 | 31 | 27 | .. | 18 | .. | 20 | 3,842 | 4,821 | 88 | 110 |
| Spain | 43 | 51 | 37 | 36 | 20 | 14 | 24 | 11 | 12,055 | 17,110 | 131 | 186 |
| Sri Lanka | 52 | 52 | 32 | 37 | .. | 39[b] | .. | 39[b] | 2,448 | 4,193 | 132 | 227 |
| Sudan | 47 | 43 | 33 | 26 | .. | .. | .. | .. | 743 | 947 | 80 | 102 |
| Swaziland | 42 | 39 | 26 | 22 | .. | .. | .. | .. | .. | .. | .. | .. |
| Sweden | 65 | 59 | 59 | 44 | .. | .. | .. | .. | 17,609 | 23,831 | 118 | 160 |
| Switzerland | 65 | 65 | 68 | 63 | 8 | 9 | 11 | 10 | 21,487 | 23,475 | 114 | 125 |
| Syrian Arab Republic | 51 | 56 | 40 | 43 | .. | .. | .. | .. | 5,701 | 7,015 | 88 | 108 |
| Tajikistan | 54 | 48 | 37 | 28 | .. | .. | .. | .. | 2,979 | 1,318 | .. | .. |
| Tanzania | 87 | 84 | 77 | 72 | .. | .. | .. | .. | 551 | 690 | 92 | 115 |
| Thailand | 77 | 72 | 70 | 46 | 67 | 51 | 74 | 55 | 4,633 | 7,888 | 181 | 309 |
| Timor-Leste | 62 | 67 | 46 | 57 | .. | .. | .. | .. | .. | .. | .. | .. |
| Togo | 65 | 63 | 53 | 51 | .. | .. | .. | .. | .. | .. | .. | .. |
| Trinidad and Tobago | 48 | 58 | 33 | 46 | 22 | 17 | 21 | 13 | 9,272 | 23,233 | 75 | 188 |
| Tunisia | 41 | 45 | 29 | 29 | .. | .. | .. | .. | 3,337 | 5,362 | 113 | 182 |
| Turkey | 53 | 47 | 48 | 39 | .. | 36 | .. | 55 | 5,445 | 8,080 | 136 | 201 |
| Turkmenistan | 58 | 60 | 36 | 37 | .. | .. | .. | .. | 3,626 | 2,609 | .. | .. |
| Uganda | 83 | 81 | 74 | 71 | .. | 77[b] | .. | 92[b] | 598 | 889 | 104 | 154 |
| Ukraine | 60 | 52 | 43 | 34 | .. | .. | .. | .. | 6,027 | 4,154 | .. | .. |
| United Arab Emirates | 72 | 76 | 43 | 47 | .. | .. | .. | .. | 13,070 | 22,700 | 47 | 82 |
| United Kingdom | 58 | 59 | 66 | 59 | .. | .. | .. | .. | 16,430 | 22,967 | 127 | 178 |
| United States | 61 | 63 | 56 | 55 | .. | .. | .. | .. | 23,201 | 31,245 | 125 | 168 |
| Uruguay | 55 | 62 | 49 | 50 | .. | 27[b] | .. | 22[b] | 6,474 | 8,313 | 98 | 126 |
| Uzbekistan | 56 | 58 | 36 | 37 | .. | .. | .. | .. | 4,241 | 4,202 | .. | .. |
| Venezuela, RB | 55 | 60 | 38 | 41 | .. | 33 | .. | 40 | 8,313 | 8,815 | 82 | 87 |
| Vietnam | 75 | 73 | 75 | 66 | .. | 70 | .. | 79 | 1,025 | 2,458 | 135 | 325 |
| West Bank and Gaza | 29 | 28 | 18 | 15 | .. | 37 | .. | 43 | .. | .. | .. | .. |
| Yemen, Rep. | 44 | 47 | 32 | 32 | .. | .. | .. | .. | 2,272 | 2,861 | 99 | 125 |
| Zambia | 63 | 70 | 48 | 61 | 56 | .. | 81 | .. | 810 | 719 | 89 | 79 |
| Zimbabwe | 71 | 70 | 50 | 52 | .. | .. | .. | .. | 1,356 | 910 | 105 | 70 |
| **World** | **63 w** | **62 w** | **53 w** | **47 w** | **.. w** | **.. w** | **.. w** | **.. w** | **5,408 w** | **7,629 w** | **106 m** | **146 m** |
| **Low income** | 63 | 61 | 51 | 47 | .. | .. | .. | .. | 1,175 | 1,937 | 95 | 115 |
| **Middle income** | 66 | 64 | 57 | 48 | .. | .. | .. | .. | 3,208 | 5,775 | 97 | 120 |
| Lower middle income | 69 | 67 | 61 | 52 | .. | .. | .. | .. | 2,353 | 5,348 | 103 | 120 |
| Upper middle income | 57 | 55 | 44 | 38 | .. | 26 | .. | 24 | 6,099 | 7,245 | 96 | 123 |
| **Low & middle income** | 65 | 63 | 54 | 48 | .. | .. | .. | .. | 2,507 | 4,356 | 96 | 120 |
| East Asia & Pacific | 74 | 71 | 68 | 58 | .. | .. | .. | .. | 2,006 | 6,352 | 135 | 279 |
| Europe & Central Asia | 57 | 53 | 40 | 33 | .. | 19 | .. | 17 | 6,359 | 6,704 | .. | .. |
| Latin America & Carib. | 57 | 60 | 47 | 45 | .. | 33 | .. | 34 | 5,186 | 6,452 | 96 | 117 |
| Middle East & N. Africa | 43 | 46 | 29 | 30 | .. | .. | .. | .. | 3,110 | 4,253 | 96 | 125 |
| South Asia | 60 | 57 | 47 | 43 | .. | .. | .. | .. | 1,266 | 2,611 | 135 | 212 |
| Sub-Saharan Africa | 67 | 66 | 54 | 52 | .. | .. | .. | .. | 1,061 | 1,192 | 90 | 102 |
| **High income** | 57 | 57 | 47 | 45 | .. | .. | .. | .. | 18,145 | 24,534 | 123 | 167 |
| Euro area | 50 | 51 | 41 | 35 | .. | 13 | .. | 10 | 15,772 | 20,101 | 123 | 169 |

a. Based on extrapolated PPPs from the 1993 ICP. b. Limited coverage. c. Includes Montenegro.

# Decent work and productive employment | **2.4**

At the 2005 World Summit four targets were added to the UN Millennium Declaration. One was full and productive employment and decent work for all, which is seen as the main route for people to escape poverty. The four indicators for this target have an economic focus, and three of them are presented in the table.

The employment to population ratio indicates how efficiently an economy provides jobs for people who want to work. A high ratio means that a large proportion of the population is employed. But this indicator has a gender bias because women who do not consider their work employment or who are not perceived as working tend to be undercounted. This bias has different effects across countries.

Comparability of employment ratios across countries is also affected by variations in definitions of employment and population (see *About the data* for table 2.3). The biggest difference results from the age range used to define labor force activity. The population base for employment ratios can also vary (see table 2.1). Most countries use the resident, noninstitutionalized population of working age living in private households, excluding members of the armed forces and individuals residing in mental, penal, or other types of institutions. But some countries include members of the armed forces in the population base of their employment ratio while still excluding them from employment data (International Labour Organization, *Key Indicators of the Labour Market,* 5th edition).

The proportion of unpaid family workers and own-account workers in total employment is derived from information on status in employment. Each status group faces different economic risks, and unpaid family workers and own-account workers are the most vulnerable—and therefore the most likely to fall into poverty. They are the least likely to have formal work arrangements, are the least likely to have social protection and safety nets to guard against economic shocks, and often are incapable of generating sufficient savings to offset these shocks. A high proportion of unpaid family workers in a country indicates weak development, little job growth, and often a large rural economy.

Data on employment by status are drawn from labor force surveys and household surveys, supplemented by official estimates and censuses for a small group of countries. The labor force survey is the most comprehensive source for international comparable employment, but there are still some limitations for comparing data across countries and over time even within a country. Information from labor force surveys is not always consistent in terms of what is included in employment. For example, information provided by the Organisation for Economic Co-operation and Development relates only to civilian employment, which can result in an underestimation of "employees" and "workers not classified by status," especially in countries with large armed forces. While the categories of unpaid family workers and self-employed workers, which include own-account workers, would not be affected, their relative shares would be. Geographic coverage is another factor that can limit cross-country comparisons. The employment by status data for most Latin American countries covers urban areas only. Similarly, in some countries in Sub-Saharan Africa, where limited information is available anyway, the members of producer cooperatives are usually excluded from the self-employed category. For detailed information on definitions and coverage, consult the original source.

Labor productivity, measured as output per person employed, can be used to assess a country's economic ability to create and sustain decent employment opportunities with fair and equitable remuneration. For comparability of individual sectors labor productivity is estimated according to national accounts conventions. However, there are still significant limitations on the availability of reliable data, as the information on consistent series of output in both national currencies and purchasing power parity U.S. dollars is not easily available, especially in developing countries, because the definition, coverage, and methodology are not always consistent across countries. For example, countries employ different methodologies for estimating the missing values for the nonmarket service sectors and use different definitions of the informal sector (see *About the data* for tables 4.1 and 4.14).

• **Employment to population ratio** is the proportion of a country's population that is employed. Ages 15 and older are generally considered the working-age population. Ages 15–24 are generally considered the youth population. • **Vulnerable employment** is unpaid family workers and own-account workers as a percentage of total employment • **Labor productivity** is gross domestic product (GDP) divided by total employment in the economy. Purchasing power parity (PPP) GDP is GDP converted to 1990 constant international dollars using PPP rates. An international dollar has the same purchasing power over GDP that a U.S. dollar has in the United States.

Data on decent work and productive employment are from the International Labour Organization database Key Indicators of the Labour Market, 5th edition.

# Unemployment

| | Unemployment | | | | | | Long-term unemployment | | | Unemployment by educational attainment | | |
|---|---|---|---|---|---|---|---|---|---|---|---|---|
| | Total % of total labor force | | Male % of male labor force | | Female % of female labor force | | % of total unemployment | | | % of total unemployment | | |
| | 1990–92[a] | 2003–05[a] | 1990–92[a] | 2003–05[a] | 1990–92[a] | 2003–05[a] | Total 2000–05[a] | Male 2000–05[a] | Female 2000–05[a] | Primary 2003–05[a] | Secondary 2003–05[a] | Tertiary 2003–05[a] |
| Afghanistan | .. | .. | .. | .. | .. | .. | .. | .. | .. | .. | .. | .. |
| Albania | .. | 14.4 | .. | 12.4 | .. | 17.5 | .. | .. | .. | 98.3 | .. | 1.7 |
| Algeria | .. | 15.3 | .. | 14.9 | .. | 17.5 | .. | .. | .. | 59.3 | 23.0 | 11.4 |
| Angola | .. | .. | .. | .. | .. | .. | .. | .. | .. | .. | .. | .. |
| Argentina | 6.6[b] | 10.2[b] | 6.8[b] | 9.2[b] | 6.3[b] | 12.5[b] | .. | .. | .. | 40.3[b] | 39.8[b] | 18.4[b] |
| Armenia | .. | .. | .. | .. | .. | .. | 71.6[b] | 72.2[b] | 70.8[b] | 6.2 | 79.8 | 14.0 |
| Australia | 10.8 | 5.1 | 11.4 | 4.9 | 10.0 | 5.3 | 17.7[b] | 20.2[b] | 14.9[b] | 51.4 | 29.1 | 19.3 |
| Austria | 3.6 | 5.2 | 3.5 | 4.9 | 3.8 | 5.5 | 25.3 | 25.6 | 24.9 | 35.2[b] | 55.0[b] | 9.6[b] |
| Azerbaijan | .. | 8.6 | .. | 7.6 | .. | 9.5 | .. | .. | .. | 4.4 | 30.2 | 65.4 |
| Bangladesh | 1.9 | 4.3 | 2.0 | 4.2 | 1.9 | 4.9 | .. | .. | .. | .. | .. | .. |
| Belarus | .. | .. | .. | .. | .. | .. | .. | .. | .. | 10.2 | 40.6 | 49.1 |
| Belgium | 6.7 | 8.1 | 4.8 | 7.4 | 9.5 | 9.0 | 51.6 | 50.4 | 52.7 | 42.1 | 38.4 | 19.6 |
| Benin | .. | .. | .. | .. | .. | .. | .. | .. | .. | .. | .. | .. |
| Bolivia | 5.5[b] | .. | 5.5[b] | .. | 5.6[b] | .. | .. | .. | .. | .. | .. | .. |
| Bosnia and Herzegovina | .. | .. | .. | .. | .. | .. | .. | .. | .. | .. | .. | .. |
| Botswana | 14.2 | 23.8 | 12.1 | 21.4 | 17.5 | 26.3 | .. | .. | .. | 65.5 | 27.3 | |
| Brazil | 6.4[b] | 8.9[b] | 5.4[b] | 6.8[b] | 7.9[b] | 11.7[b] | .. | .. | .. | 53.4[b] | 30.4[b] | 3.0[b] |
| Bulgaria | .. | 10.1 | .. | 10.3 | .. | 9.9 | .. | .. | .. | 38.6 | 51.0 | 10.3 |
| Burkina Faso | .. | .. | .. | .. | .. | .. | .. | .. | .. | .. | .. | .. |
| Burundi | .. | .. | .. | .. | .. | .. | .. | .. | .. | .. | .. | .. |
| Cambodia | .. | .. | .. | .. | .. | .. | .. | .. | .. | .. | .. | .. |
| Cameroon | .. | .. | .. | .. | .. | .. | .. | .. | .. | .. | .. | .. |
| Canada | 11.2[b] | 6.8[b] | 12.0[b] | 7.0[b] | 10.2[b] | 6.5[b] | 9.6[b] | 10.1[b] | 9.1[b] | 27.1[b] | 31.2[b] | 41.7[b] |
| Central African Republic | .. | .. | .. | .. | .. | .. | .. | .. | .. | .. | .. | .. |
| Chad | .. | .. | .. | .. | .. | .. | .. | .. | .. | .. | .. | .. |
| Chile | 4.4 | 6.9 | 3.9 | 6.1 | 5.3 | 8.5 | .. | .. | .. | 16.1 | 58.9 | 24.5 |
| China | 2.3[b] | 4.2[b] | .. | .. | .. | .. | .. | .. | .. | .. | .. | .. |
| Hong Kong, China | 2.0 | 5.6 | 2.0 | 6.5 | 1.9 | 4.4 | .. | .. | .. | 46.3[b] | 39.7[b] | 12.6[b] |
| Colombia | 9.4[b] | 9.5 | 6.7[b] | 7.4 | 13.0[b] | 12.3 | .. | .. | .. | 58.4 | .. | 15.6 |
| Congo, Dem. Rep. | .. | .. | .. | .. | .. | .. | .. | .. | .. | .. | .. | .. |
| Congo, Rep. | .. | .. | .. | .. | .. | .. | .. | .. | .. | .. | .. | .. |
| Costa Rica | 4.0 | 6.6 | 3.4 | 5.0 | 5.4 | 9.6 | 10.9 | 8.9 | 13.3 | 64.0 | 20.5 | 12.0 |
| Côte d'Ivoire | 6.7 | .. | .. | .. | .. | .. | .. | .. | .. | .. | .. | .. |
| Croatia | .. | 11.2[c] | .. | 10.1[c] | .. | 13.2[c] | 53.7[c] | 52.7[c] | 54.5[c] | 22.0[c] | 69.1[c] | 9.8[c] |
| Cuba | .. | 1.9 | .. | 1.7 | .. | 2.2 | .. | .. | .. | 50.6 | 44.7 | 4.7 |
| Czech Republic | .. | 7.9 | .. | 6.5 | .. | 9.8 | 53.6 | 52.9 | 54.2 | 24.1 | 72.0 | 4.1 |
| Denmark | 9.0 | 4.8 | 8.3 | 4.1 | 9.9 | 5.6 | 25.9 | 29.7 | 22.7 | 27.7 | 44.8 | 27.5 |
| Dominican Republic | 20.7 | 17.9 | 12.0 | 11.3 | 35.2 | 28.8 | 1.6 | 2.2 | 1.3 | .. | .. | .. |
| Ecuador | 8.9[b] | 7.7[b] | 6.0[b] | 5.6[b] | 13.2[b] | 10.8[b] | .. | .. | .. | 76.0[b] | .. | 22.5[b] |
| Egypt, Arab Rep. | 9.1 | 10.7 | 6.5 | 6.8 | 17.3 | 24.4 | .. | .. | .. | .. | .. | .. |
| El Salvador | 7.9[b] | 6.6 | 8.4[b] | 8.5 | 7.2[b] | 3.9 | .. | .. | .. | .. | .. | .. |
| Eritrea | .. | .. | .. | .. | .. | .. | .. | .. | .. | .. | .. | .. |
| Estonia | 3.7 | 7.9 | 3.9 | 8.8 | 3.5 | 7.1 | .. | .. | .. | 15.7 | 64.4 | 19.9 |
| Ethiopia | .. | 5.4 | .. | 2.7 | .. | 8.2 | 24.4 | 24.3 | 24.4 | 35.9 | 13.3 | 3.2 |
| Finland | 11.7 | 8.4 | 13.6 | 8.2 | 9.7 | 8.7 | 24.9 | 27.9 | 21.9 | 35.5 | 46.8 | 17.7 |
| France | 10.0[b] | 9.8[b] | 7.9[b] | 9.0[b] | 12.7[b] | 10.8[b] | 42.5 | 41.8 | 43.2 | 40.6 | 39.4 | 18.7 |
| Gabon | .. | .. | .. | .. | .. | .. | .. | .. | .. | .. | .. | .. |
| Gambia, The | .. | .. | .. | .. | .. | .. | .. | .. | .. | .. | .. | .. |
| Georgia | .. | 13.8 | .. | 14.8 | .. | 12.7 | .. | .. | .. | 4.8 | 56.0 | 38.8 |
| Germany | 6.6 | 11.1 | 5.3 | 11.3 | 8.4 | 10.9 | 54.0 | 53.8 | 54.4 | 27.1 | 60.5 | 12.4 |
| Ghana | .. | .. | .. | .. | .. | .. | .. | .. | .. | .. | .. | .. |
| Greece | 7.8 | 9.6 | 4.9 | 5.8 | 12.9 | 15.2 | 53.7 | 43.1 | 59.6 | 30.8 | 49.7 | 19.1 |
| Guatemala | 3.2[b] | 3.4 | 2.6[b] | 2.5 | 4.6[b] | 4.9 | .. | .. | .. | .. | .. | .. |
| Guinea | .. | .. | .. | .. | .. | .. | .. | .. | .. | .. | .. | .. |
| Guinea-Bissau | .. | .. | .. | .. | .. | .. | .. | .. | .. | .. | .. | .. |
| Haiti | 12.2 | .. | 11.2 | .. | 13.6 | .. | .. | .. | .. | .. | .. | .. |

| | Unemployment | | | | | | Long-term unemployment | | | Unemployment by educational attainment | | |
|---|---|---|---|---|---|---|---|---|---|---|---|---|
| | Total % of total labor force | | Male % of male labor force | | Female % of female labor force | | % of total unemployment | | | % of total unemployment | | |
| | 1990–92[a] | 2003–05[a] | 1990–92[a] | 2003–05[a] | 1990–92[a] | 2003–05[a] | Total 2000–05[a] | Male 2000–05[a] | Female 2000–05[a] | Primary 2003–05[a] | Secondary 2003–05[a] | Tertiary 2003–05[a] |
| Honduras | 3.2[b] | 4.2[b] | 3.3[b] | 3.2[b] | 3.0[b] | 6.2[b] | .. | .. | .. | .. | .. | .. |
| Hungary | 9.9 | 7.2 | 11.0 | 7.0 | 8.7 | 7.5 | 46.1 | 47.9 | 44.2 | 30.2 | 62.2 | 7.6 |
| India | .. | 5.0[b] | .. | 4.9[b] | .. | 5.3[b] | .. | .. | .. | 27.0 | 41.1 | 31.9 |
| Indonesia | 2.8 | 10.3[c] | 2.7 | 8.5[c] | 3.0 | 13.4[c] | .. | .. | .. | 48.7[c] | 38.0[c] | 6.2[c] |
| Iran, Islamic Rep. | 11.1 | 11.5 | 9.5 | 10.1 | 24.4 | 17.1 | .. | .. | .. | 41.8 | 34.7 | 19.6 |
| Iraq | .. | .. | .. | .. | .. | .. | .. | .. | .. | .. | .. | .. |
| Ireland | 15.2 | 4.3 | 15.2 | 4.6 | 15.2 | 3.8 | 34.3 | 42.4 | 21.1 | 45.0 | 25.6 | 26.1 |
| Israel | 11.2[b] | 9.0[b] | 9.2[b] | 8.5[b] | 13.9[b] | 9.5[b] | .. | .. | .. | 20.6 | 48.7 | 25.9 |
| Italy | 11.5 | 7.7 | 8.1 | 6.2 | 17.3 | 10.1 | 52.2 | 50.5 | 53.8 | 48.1 | 39.4 | 10.7 |
| Jamaica | 15.7 | 10.9 | 9.5 | 7.4 | 22.8 | 15.3 | 31.7 | 24.4 | 36.2 | 12.9 | 4.2 | 9.2 |
| Japan | 2.2 | 4.4 | 2.1 | 4.6 | 2.2 | 4.2 | 33.3 | 40.3 | 22.6 | 67.7 | .. | 29.9 |
| Jordan | .. | 12.4 | .. | 11.8 | .. | 16.5 | .. | .. | .. | .. | .. | .. |
| Kazakhstan | .. | 7.8[c] | .. | 6.4[c] | .. | 9.2[c] | .. | .. | .. | 7.1[c] | 49.0[c] | 43.9[c] |
| Kenya | .. | .. | .. | .. | .. | .. | .. | .. | .. | .. | .. | .. |
| Korea, Dem. Rep. | .. | .. | .. | .. | .. | .. | .. | .. | .. | .. | .. | .. |
| Korea, Rep. | 2.5 | 3.7 | 2.8 | 4.0 | 2.1 | 3.4 | 0.8 | 1.0 | 0.4 | 17.4 | 53.2 | 29.4 |
| Kuwait | .. | 1.7 | .. | .. | .. | .. | .. | .. | .. | .. | .. | .. |
| Kyrgyz Republic | .. | 8.5 | .. | 8.0 | .. | 9.3 | .. | .. | .. | 9.9 | 79.5 | 10.7 |
| Lao PDR | .. | 1.4 | .. | 1.3 | .. | 1.4 | .. | .. | .. | .. | .. | .. |
| Latvia | .. | 8.7 | .. | 9.0 | .. | 8.4 | .. | .. | .. | 23.6 | 65.6 | 10.7 |
| Lebanon | .. | .. | .. | .. | .. | .. | .. | .. | .. | .. | .. | .. |
| Lesotho | .. | .. | .. | .. | .. | .. | .. | .. | .. | .. | .. | .. |
| Liberia | .. | .. | .. | .. | .. | .. | .. | .. | .. | .. | .. | .. |
| Libya | .. | .. | .. | .. | .. | .. | .. | .. | .. | .. | .. | .. |
| Lithuania | .. | 8.3 | .. | 8.2 | .. | 8.3 | 57.8 | .. | .. | 16.4 | 69.5 | 14.1 |
| Macedonia, FYR | .. | 37.3 | .. | 36.5 | .. | 38.4 | .. | .. | .. | .. | .. | .. |
| Madagascar | .. | 5.0 | .. | 3.8 | .. | 6.2 | .. | .. | .. | 61.5 | .. | 6.1 |
| Malawi | .. | .. | .. | .. | .. | .. | .. | .. | .. | .. | .. | .. |
| Malaysia | 3.7 | 3.5 | .. | 3.6 | .. | 3.6 | .. | .. | .. | 32.0 | 48.8 | 15.6 |
| Mali | .. | 8.8 | .. | 7.2 | .. | 10.9 | .. | .. | .. | .. | .. | .. |
| Mauritania | .. | .. | .. | .. | .. | .. | .. | .. | .. | .. | .. | .. |
| Mauritius | 3.1 | 9.6 | 3.2 | 5.8 | 3.1 | 16.5 | .. | .. | .. | 48.6 | 44.9 | 5.4 |
| Mexico | 3.1 | 3.5 | 2.7 | 3.4 | 4.0 | 3.6 | 2.4[b] | 2.3[b] | 2.6[b] | 51.7 | 24.4 | 21.5 |
| Moldova | .. | 7.3 | .. | 8.7 | .. | 6.0 | .. | .. | .. | .. | .. | .. |
| Mongolia | .. | 14.2 | .. | 14.3 | .. | 14.1 | .. | .. | .. | 35.1 | 45.8 | 18.5 |
| Morocco | 16.0[b] | 9.7[c] | 13.0[b] | 9.7[c] | 25.3[b] | 9.7[c] | .. | .. | .. | 51.1[b] | 22.4[b] | 21.6[b] |
| Mozambique | .. | .. | .. | .. | .. | .. | .. | .. | .. | .. | .. | .. |
| Myanmar | 6.0 | .. | 4.7 | .. | 8.8 | .. | .. | .. | .. | .. | .. | .. |
| Namibia | 19.1 | .. | 19.6 | .. | 18.6 | .. | .. | .. | .. | .. | .. | .. |
| Nepal | .. | .. | .. | .. | .. | .. | .. | .. | .. | .. | .. | .. |
| Netherlands | 5.5 | 5.2 | 4.3 | 4.9 | 7.3 | 5.6 | 40.1 | 44.7 | 35.0 | 40.7 | 39.1 | 17.9 |
| New Zealand | 10.4[b] | 3.7[b] | 11.0[b] | 3.4[b] | 9.6[b] | 4.0[b] | 9.4[b] | 12.6[b] | 6.2[b] | 0.0 | 52.7 | 14.4 |
| Nicaragua | 14.4 | 8.0 | 11.3 | 7.9 | 19.4 | 8.1 | .. | .. | .. | .. | .. | .. |
| Niger | .. | .. | .. | .. | .. | .. | .. | .. | .. | .. | .. | .. |
| Nigeria | .. | .. | .. | .. | .. | .. | .. | .. | .. | .. | .. | .. |
| Norway | 5.9 | 4.6 | 6.6 | 4.8 | 5.1 | 4.4 | 9.5 | 10.4 | 8.5 | 24.3 | 54.1 | 18.9 |
| Oman | .. | .. | .. | .. | .. | .. | .. | .. | .. | .. | .. | .. |
| Pakistan | 5.2 | 7.7 | 3.8 | 6.6 | 14.0 | 12.8 | .. | .. | .. | 13.1 | 12.3 | 29.1 |
| Panama | 14.7 | 10.3 | 10.8 | 8.1 | 22.3 | 14.0 | 29.3 | 24.0 | 35.7 | 31.7 | 38.4 | 29.1 |
| Papua New Guinea | 7.7 | .. | 9.0 | .. | 5.9 | .. | .. | .. | .. | .. | .. | .. |
| Paraguay | 5.0[b] | 7.9[b] | 6.0[b] | 6.6[b] | 3.7[b] | 10.0[b] | .. | .. | .. | .. | .. | .. |
| Peru | 9.4[b] | 11.4[b] | 7.5[b] | 9.7[b] | 12.5[b] | 13.7[b] | .. | .. | .. | 69.6[b] | .. | 30.0[b] |
| Philippines | 8.6 | 7.4 | 7.9 | 7.4 | 9.9 | 7.3 | .. | .. | .. | 15.2 | 45.2 | 38.9 |
| Poland | 13.3 | 17.7 | 12.2 | 16.6 | 14.7 | 19.1 | 52.2 | 51.3 | 53.1 | 17.7 | 74.8 | 7.6 |
| Portugal | 4.1[b] | 7.6 | 3.5[b] | 6.7 | 5.0[b] | 8.7 | 48.6 | 47.1 | 49.9 | 70.2 | 15.3 | 10.9 |
| Puerto Rico | 17.0 | 11.3 | 19.3 | 12.2 | 13.3 | 10.2 | .. | .. | .. | .. | .. | .. |

# 2.5 | Unemployment

| | Unemployment | | | | | | Long-term unemployment | | | Unemployment by educational attainment | | |
| | Total % of total labor force | | Male % of male labor force | | Female % of female labor force | | % of total unemployment | | | % of total unemployment | | |
| | | | | | | | Total | Male | Female | Primary | Secondary | Tertiary |
| | 1990–92[a] | 2003–05[a] | 1990–92[a] | 2003–05[a] | 1990–92[a] | 2003–05[a] | 2000–05[a] | 2000–05[a] | 2000–05[a] | 2003–05[a] | 2003–05[a] | 2003–05[a] |
|---|---|---|---|---|---|---|---|---|---|---|---|---|
| Romania | .. | 7.2 | .. | 7.7 | .. | 6.4 | .. | .. | .. | 23.1 | 69.1 | 6.6 |
| Russian Federation | 5.3 | 7.9 | 5.4 | 7.8 | 5.2 | 8.0 | .. | .. | .. | .. | .. | .. |
| Rwanda | .. | .. | .. | .. | .. | .. | .. | .. | .. | .. | .. | .. |
| Saudi Arabia | .. | 6.2 | .. | 4.7 | .. | 14.7 | .. | .. | .. | 12.3 | 43.9 | 40.0 |
| Senegal | .. | .. | .. | .. | .. | .. | .. | .. | .. | .. | .. | .. |
| Serbia | .. | 15.2[d] | .. | 14.4[d] | .. | 16.4[d] | .. | .. | .. | .. | .. | .. |
| Sierra Leone | .. | .. | .. | .. | .. | .. | .. | .. | .. | .. | .. | .. |
| Singapore | 2.7 | 4.2 | 2.7 | 3.7 | 2.6 | 5.0 | .. | .. | .. | 20.2 | 25.7 | 59.2 |
| Slovak Republic | .. | 16.2 | .. | 15.4 | .. | 17.2 | 68.1 | 68.7 | 67.4 | 27.1[b] | 68.3[b] | 4.5[b] |
| Slovenia | .. | 5.8 | .. | 5.5 | .. | 6.0 | .. | .. | .. | 22.4 | 69.0 | 8.6 |
| Somalia | .. | .. | .. | .. | .. | .. | .. | .. | .. | .. | .. | .. |
| South Africa | .. | 26.7 | .. | 26.8 | .. | 26.6 | .. | .. | .. | 50.2 | 41.0 | 5.1 |
| Spain | 18.1 | 9.2 | 13.9 | 7.0 | 25.8 | 12.2 | 32.6 | 28.2 | 36.0 | 53.9 | 22.1 | 23.1 |
| Sri Lanka | 13.3[b] | 7.6[b] | 10.1[b] | 5.5[b] | 19.9[b] | 11.9[b] | .. | .. | .. | 41.7[b] | .. | 58.3[b] |
| Sudan | .. | .. | .. | .. | .. | .. | .. | .. | .. | .. | .. | .. |
| Swaziland | .. | .. | .. | .. | .. | .. | .. | .. | .. | .. | .. | .. |
| Sweden | 5.7 | 7.7 | 6.7 | 7.8 | 4.6 | 7.6 | 18.9 | 20.9 | 16.4 | 25.9 | 54.4 | 17.8 |
| Switzerland | 2.8 | 4.4 | 2.3 | 3.9 | 3.5 | 5.1 | 38.8 | 37.1 | 40.4 | 28.6 | 53.5 | 17.3 |
| Syrian Arab Republic | .. | 12.3 | .. | 9.0 | .. | 28.3 | .. | .. | .. | .. | .. | .. |
| Tajikistan | .. | .. | .. | .. | .. | .. | .. | .. | .. | .. | .. | .. |
| Tanzania | 3.6[b] | .. | 2.8[b] | .. | 4.3[b] | .. | .. | .. | .. | 39.7 | 46.3 | 0.2 |
| Thailand | 1.4 | 1.3 | 1.3 | 1.5 | 1.5 | 1.2 | .. | .. | .. | .. | .. | .. |
| Timor-Leste | .. | .. | .. | .. | .. | .. | .. | .. | .. | .. | .. | .. |
| Togo | .. | .. | .. | .. | .. | .. | .. | .. | .. | .. | .. | .. |
| Trinidad and Tobago | 19.6 | 8.0 | 17.0 | 5.8 | 23.9 | 11.0 | 27.6 | 20.3 | 34.7 | .. | .. | .. |
| Tunisia | .. | 14.2 | .. | 13.1 | .. | 17.3 | .. | .. | .. | 79.1 | .. | 13.6 |
| Turkey | 8.5 | 10.3 | 8.8 | 10.3 | 7.8 | 10.3 | 39.6 | 36.9 | 47.4 | 54.3 | 28.1 | 11.4 |
| Turkmenistan | .. | .. | .. | .. | .. | .. | .. | .. | .. | .. | .. | .. |
| Uganda | .. | 3.2 | .. | 2.5 | .. | 3.9 | .. | .. | .. | .. | .. | .. |
| Ukraine | .. | 7.2 | .. | 7.5 | .. | 6.8 | .. | .. | .. | 10.9 | 53.2 | 35.8 |
| United Arab Emirates | .. | .. | .. | .. | .. | .. | .. | .. | .. | .. | .. | .. |
| United Kingdom | 9.7 | 4.6 | 11.5 | 5.0 | 7.3 | 4.1 | 22.4 | 26.2 | 16.9 | 36.7 | 46.1 | 16.2 |
| United States | 7.5[b] | 5.1[b] | 7.9[b] | 5.1[b] | 7.0[b] | 5.1[b] | 11.8[b] | 12.6[b] | 10.8[b] | 19.1[b] | 35.5[b] | 45.4[b] |
| Uruguay | 9.0[b] | 12.2[b] | 6.8[b] | 9.5[b] | 11.8[b] | 15.3[b] | .. | .. | .. | .. | .. | .. |
| Uzbekistan | .. | .. | .. | .. | .. | .. | .. | .. | .. | .. | .. | .. |
| Venezuela, RB | 7.7 | 15.0 | 8.2 | 13.4 | 6.8 | 17.6 | .. | .. | .. | .. | .. | .. |
| Vietnam | .. | 2.1 | .. | 1.9 | .. | 2.4 | .. | .. | .. | .. | .. | .. |
| West Bank and Gaza | .. | 26.8 | .. | 28.1 | .. | 20.1 | .. | .. | .. | 58.5 | 13.1 | 18.9 |
| Yemen, Rep. | .. | .. | .. | .. | .. | .. | .. | .. | .. | .. | .. | .. |
| Zambia | 18.9 | .. | 16.3 | .. | 22.4 | .. | .. | .. | .. | .. | .. | .. |
| Zimbabwe | .. | .. | .. | .. | .. | .. | .. | .. | .. | .. | .. | .. |
| **World** | .. w | **6.7 w** | .. w | .. w | .. w | .. w | .. w | .. w | .. w | .. w | .. w | .. w |
| **Low income** | .. | .. | .. | .. | .. | .. | .. | .. | .. | .. | .. | .. |
| **Middle income** | 3.9 | 6.4 | .. | .. | .. | .. | .. | .. | .. | .. | .. | .. |
| Lower middle income | 3.2 | 5.7 | .. | .. | .. | .. | .. | .. | .. | .. | .. | .. |
| Upper middle income | 6.3 | 9.8 | 6.0 | 9.0 | 7.0 | 11.4 | .. | .. | .. | 44.0 | 41.2 | 8.7 |
| **Low & middle income** | .. | 6.8 | .. | .. | .. | .. | .. | .. | .. | .. | .. | .. |
| East Asia & Pacific | 2.5 | 4.9 | .. | .. | .. | .. | .. | .. | .. | .. | .. | .. |
| Europe & Central Asia | .. | 10.0 | .. | 10.0 | .. | 9.9 | .. | .. | .. | .. | .. | .. |
| Latin America & Carib. | 6.7 | 8.9 | 5.5 | 7.1 | 8.4 | 11.5 | .. | .. | .. | 56.6 | 31.9 | 12.7 |
| Middle East & N. Africa | .. | 13.8 | .. | 12.8 | .. | 18.7 | .. | .. | .. | .. | .. | .. |
| South Asia | .. | 5.3 | .. | 5.1 | .. | 6.3 | .. | .. | .. | .. | .. | .. |
| Sub-Saharan Africa | .. | .. | .. | .. | .. | .. | .. | .. | .. | .. | .. | .. |
| **High income** | 7.4 | 6.2 | 7.0 | 6.0 | 7.9 | 6.6 | 26.4 | 28.0 | 24.0 | 36.3 | 38.1 | 29.1 |
| Euro area | 9.5 | 9.0 | 7.5 | 8.1 | 12.5 | 10.3 | 45.8 | 44.6 | 46.5 | 45.8 | 35.5 | 17.2 |

a. Data are for the most recent year available. b. Limited coverage. c. Data are for 2006. d. Includes Montenegro and excludes Kosovo and Metohija.

Unemployment and total employment are the broadest indicators of economic activity as reflected by the labor market. The International Labour Organization (ILO) defines the unemployed as members of the economically active population who are without work but available for and seeking work, including people who have lost their jobs or who have voluntarily left work. Some unemployment is unavoidable. At any time some workers are temporarily unemployed—between jobs as employers look for the right workers and workers search for better jobs. Such unemployment, often called frictional unemployment, results from the normal operation of labor markets.

Changes in unemployment over time may reflect changes in the demand for and supply of labor; they may also reflect changes in reporting practices. Paradoxically, low unemployment rates can disguise substantial poverty in a country, while high unemployment rates can occur in countries with a high level of economic development and low rates of poverty. In countries without unemployment or welfare benefits people eke out a living in the informal sector. In countries with well developed safety nets workers can afford to wait for suitable or desirable jobs. But high and sustained unemployment indicates serious inefficiencies in resource allocation.

The ILO definition of unemployment notwithstanding, reference periods, the criteria for people considered to be seeking work, and the treatment of people temporarily laid off or seeking work for the first time vary across countries. In many developing countries it is especially difficult to measure employment and unemployment in agriculture. The timing of a survey, for example, can maximize the effects of seasonal unemployment in agriculture. And informal sector employment is difficult to quantify where informal activities are not tracked.

Data on unemployment are drawn from labor force sample surveys and general household sample surveys, censuses, and official estimates, which are generally based on information from different sources and can be combined in many ways. Administrative records, such as social insurance statistics and employment office statistics, are not included in the table because of their limitations in coverage. Labor force surveys generally yield the most comprehensive data because they include groups not covered in other unemployment statistics, particularly people seeking work for the first time. These surveys generally use a definition of unemployment that follows the international recommendations more closely than that used by other sources and therefore generate statistics that are more comparable internationally. But the age group, geographic coverage, and collection methods could differ by country or change over time within a country. For detailed information, consult the original source.

Women tend to be excluded from the unemployment count for various reasons. Women suffer more from discrimination and from structural, social, and cultural barriers that impede them from seeking work. Also, women are often responsible for the care of children and the elderly and for household affairs. They may not be available for work during the short reference period, as they need to make arrangements before starting work. Furthermore, women are considered to be employed when they are working part-time or in temporary jobs in the informal sector, despite the instability of these jobs or their active search for more secure employment.

Long-term unemployment is measured by the length of time that an unemployed person has been without work and looking for a job. The data in the table are from labor force surveys. The underlying assumption is that shorter periods of joblessness are of less concern, especially when the unemployed are covered by unemployment benefits or similar forms of support. The length of time that a person has been unemployed is difficult to measure, because the ability to recall that time diminishes as the period of joblessness extends. Women's long-term unemployment is likely to be lower in countries where women constitute a large share of the unpaid family workforce.

Unemployment by level of educational attainment provides insights into the relation between the educational attainment of workers and unemployment and may be used to draw inferences about changes in employment demand. Information on educational attainment is the best available indicator of skill levels of the labor force. Besides the limitations to comparability raised for measuring unemployment, the different ways of classifying the education level may also cause inconsistency. Education level is supposed to be classified according to International Standard Classification of Education 1997 (ISCED97). For more information on ISCED97, see *About the data* for table 2.10.

• **Unemployment** is the share of the labor force without work but available for and seeking employment. Definitions of labor force and unemployment may differ by country (see *About the data*). • **Long-term unemployment** is the number of people with continuous periods of unemployment extending for a year or longer, expressed as a percentage of the total unemployed. • **Unemployment by educational attainment** is the unemployed by level of educational attainment as a percentage of the total unemployed. The levels of educational attainment accord with the ISCED97 of the United Nations Educational, Scientific, and Cultural Organization.

Data on unemployment are from the ILO database Key Indicators of the Labour Market, 5th edition.

| | Survey year | Economically active children | | | | | Employment by economic activity[a] | | | | | |
|---|---|---|---|---|---|---|---|---|---|---|---|---|
| | | % of children ages 7–14 | | | % of economically active children ages 7–14 | | Agriculture | | % of economically active children ages 7–14 Manufacturing | | Services | |
| | | Total | Male | Female | Work only | Study and work | Male | Female | Male | Female | Male | Female |
| Afghanistan | | .. | .. | .. | .. | .. | .. | .. | .. | .. | .. | .. |
| Albania | 2000 | 36.6 | 41.1 | 31.8 | 43.1 | 56.9 | .. | .. | .. | .. | .. | .. |
| Algeria | | .. | .. | .. | .. | .. | .. | .. | .. | .. | .. | .. |
| Angola[b] | 2001 | 30.1 | 30.0 | 30.1 | 26.6 | 73.4 | .. | .. | .. | .. | .. | .. |
| Argentina | 2004 | 15.1 | 18.0 | 12.0 | 4.1 | 95.9 | .. | .. | .. | .. | .. | .. |
| Armenia | | .. | .. | .. | .. | .. | .. | .. | .. | .. | .. | .. |
| Australia | | | | | | | | | | | | |
| Austria | | .. | .. | .. | .. | .. | .. | .. | .. | .. | .. | .. |
| Azerbaijan | 2000 | 9.7 | 12.0 | 7.3 | 4.2 | 95.8 | .. | .. | .. | .. | .. | .. |
| Bangladesh | 2003 | 17.5 | 20.9 | 13.9 | 63.3 | 36.7 | 61.4 | 64.0 | 11.6 | 15.5 | 25.2 | 18.3 |
| Belarus | | .. | .. | .. | .. | .. | .. | .. | .. | .. | .. | .. |
| Belgium | | .. | .. | .. | .. | .. | .. | .. | .. | .. | .. | .. |
| Benin | | .. | .. | .. | .. | .. | .. | .. | .. | .. | .. | .. |
| Bolivia | 2002 | 23.2 | 24.0 | 22.5 | 15.2 | 84.8 | 78.8 | 73.4 | 4.5 | 3.8 | 15.5 | 22.6 |
| Bosnia and Herzegovina | 2000 | 20.2 | 22.8 | 17.6 | 4.0 | 96.0 | .. | .. | .. | .. | .. | .. |
| Botswana | | | | | | | | | | | | |
| Brazil | 2004 | 7.0 | 9.4 | 4.6 | 7.2 | 92.8 | 66.2 | 48.9 | 5.2 | 9.7 | 26.4 | 40.8 |
| Bulgaria | | .. | .. | .. | .. | .. | .. | .. | .. | .. | .. | .. |
| Burkina Faso | 2004 | 50.0 | 49.0 | 51.0 | 98.1 | 1.9 | 98.4 | 96.1 | 0.2 | 0.5 | 1.3 | 3.1 |
| Burundi | 2000 | 37.0 | 38.4 | 35.7 | 48.3 | 51.7 | .. | .. | .. | .. | .. | .. |
| Cambodia | 2001 | 52.3 | 52.4 | 52.1 | 16.5 | 83.5 | 78.5 | 73.6 | 4.7 | 5.4 | 15.7 | 20.4 |
| Cameroon[c] | 2001 | 15.9 | 14.5 | 17.4 | 52.5 | 47.5 | 90.4 | 86.3 | 1.9 | 2.3 | 5.1 | 8.8 |
| Canada | | .. | .. | .. | .. | .. | .. | .. | .. | .. | .. | .. |
| Central African Republic | 2000 | 67.0 | 66.5 | 67.6 | 54.9 | 45.1 | .. | .. | .. | .. | .. | .. |
| Chad | 2004 | 60.4 | 64.4 | 56.2 | 59.0 | 41.0 | .. | .. | .. | .. | .. | .. |
| Chile | 2003 | 4.1 | 5.1 | 3.1 | 3.2 | 96.8 | 31.0 | 12.2 | 8.2 | 4.5 | 57.8 | 81.5 |
| China | | .. | .. | .. | .. | .. | .. | .. | .. | .. | .. | .. |
| Hong Kong, China | | .. | .. | .. | .. | .. | .. | .. | .. | .. | .. | .. |
| Colombia | 2005 | 4.0 | 6.2 | 1.8 | 32.8 | 67.2 | .. | .. | .. | .. | .. | .. |
| Congo, Dem. Rep. | 2000 | 39.8 | 39.9 | 39.8 | 35.7 | 64.3 | .. | .. | .. | .. | .. | .. |
| Congo, Rep. | | .. | .. | .. | .. | .. | .. | .. | .. | .. | .. | .. |
| Costa Rica[c] | 2004 | 5.7 | 8.1 | 3.5 | 44.6 | 55.4 | 48.0 | 19.4 | 9.5 | 9.6 | 40.8 | 71.1 |
| Côte d'Ivoire | 2000 | 40.7 | 40.9 | 40.5 | 46.4 | 53.6 | .. | .. | .. | .. | .. | .. |
| Croatia | | .. | .. | .. | .. | .. | .. | .. | .. | .. | .. | .. |
| Cuba | | .. | .. | .. | .. | .. | .. | .. | .. | .. | .. | .. |
| Czech Republic | | .. | .. | .. | .. | .. | .. | .. | .. | .. | .. | .. |
| Denmark | | .. | .. | .. | .. | .. | .. | .. | .. | .. | .. | .. |
| Dominican Republic[c] | 2002 | 3.5 | 5.9 | 0.9 | 11.4 | 88.6 | .. | .. | .. | .. | .. | .. |
| Ecuador | 2004 | 12.0 | 14.6 | 9.3 | 27.0 | 73.0 | 71.2 | 68.0 | 5.0 | 4.1 | 21.1 | 27.8 |
| Egypt, Arab Rep. | 2005 | 7.9 | 11.5 | 4.3 | 21.0 | 79.0 | .. | .. | .. | .. | .. | .. |
| El Salvador | 2003 | 12.7 | 17.1 | 8.1 | 19.5 | 80.5 | 66.4 | 17.6 | 10.8 | 16.1 | 21.2 | 66.3 |
| Eritrea | | .. | .. | .. | .. | .. | .. | .. | .. | .. | .. | .. |
| Estonia | | .. | .. | .. | .. | .. | .. | .. | .. | .. | .. | .. |
| Ethiopia | 2005 | 56.0 | 64.3 | 47.1 | 69.4 | 30.6 | 96.8 | 91.4 | 0.6 | 2.8 | 2.4 | 5.6 |
| Finland | | .. | .. | .. | .. | .. | .. | .. | .. | .. | .. | .. |
| France | | .. | .. | .. | .. | .. | .. | .. | .. | .. | .. | .. |
| Gabon | | .. | .. | .. | .. | .. | .. | .. | .. | .. | .. | .. |
| Gambia, The | 2000 | 25.3 | 25.4 | 25.3 | 41.6 | 58.4 | .. | .. | .. | .. | .. | .. |
| Georgia | | .. | .. | .. | .. | .. | .. | .. | .. | .. | .. | .. |
| Germany | | .. | .. | .. | .. | .. | .. | .. | .. | .. | .. | .. |
| Ghana | 2003 | 6.0 | 6.0 | 5.9 | 71.2 | 28.8 | 89.0 | 67.9 | 1.5 | 4.1 | 7.5 | 23.5 |
| Greece | | .. | .. | .. | .. | .. | .. | .. | .. | .. | .. | .. |
| Guatemala | 2003 | 21.1 | 26.2 | 16.0 | 33.8 | 66.2 | 74.2 | 43.0 | 6.0 | 20.1 | 16.5 | 36.9 |
| Guinea | 1994 | 48.3 | 47.2 | 49.5 | 98.6 | 1.4 | .. | .. | .. | .. | .. | .. |
| Guinea-Bissau | 2000 | 67.5 | 67.4 | 67.5 | 63.7 | 36.3 | .. | .. | .. | .. | .. | .. |
| Haiti | 2005 | 33.4 | 37.3 | 29.6 | 17.7 | 82.3 | .. | .. | .. | .. | .. | .. |

| | Survey year | Economically active children | | | | | Employment by economic activity[a] | | | | | |
|---|---|---|---|---|---|---|---|---|---|---|---|---|
| | | % of children ages 7–14 | | | % of economically active children ages 7–14 | | Agriculture | | % of economically active children ages 7–14 Manufacturing | | Services | |
| | | Total | Male | Female | Work only | Study and work | Male | Female | Male | Female | Male | Female |
| Honduras | 2004 | 6.8 | 10.4 | 3.2 | 48.6 | 51.4 | 76.9 | 20.2 | 5.3 | 17.9 | 13.9 | 59.4 |
| Hungary | | .. | .. | .. | .. | .. | .. | .. | .. | .. | .. | .. |
| India | 2000 | 5.2 | 5.3 | 5.1 | 89.8 | 10.2 | 70.5 | 76.6 | 10.0 | 15.4 | 15.9 | 6.5 |
| Indonesia | 2000 | 8.9 | 8.8 | 9.1 | 24.9 | 75.1 | .. | .. | .. | .. | .. | .. |
| Iran, Islamic Rep. | | .. | .. | .. | .. | .. | .. | .. | .. | .. | .. | .. |
| Iraq | | .. | .. | .. | .. | .. | .. | .. | .. | .. | .. | .. |
| Ireland | | .. | .. | .. | .. | .. | .. | .. | .. | .. | .. | .. |
| Israel | | .. | .. | .. | .. | .. | .. | .. | .. | .. | .. | .. |
| Italy | | .. | .. | .. | .. | .. | .. | .. | .. | .. | .. | .. |
| Jamaica | 2002 | 1.1 | 1.5 | 0.6 | 17.1 | 82.9 | 36.8 | 17.1 | 6.2 | 11.6 | 43.6 | 71.3 |
| Japan | | .. | .. | .. | .. | .. | .. | .. | .. | .. | .. | .. |
| Jordan | | .. | .. | .. | .. | .. | .. | .. | .. | .. | .. | .. |
| Kazakhstan | 1996 | 29.7 | 30.3 | 29.1 | 4.4 | 95.6 | .. | .. | .. | .. | .. | .. |
| Kenya | 1999 | 6.7 | 6.9 | 6.4 | 44.8 | 55.2 | 87.3 | 74.4 | 2.5 | 0.3 | 8.8 | 25.3 |
| Korea, Dem. Rep. | | .. | .. | .. | .. | .. | .. | .. | .. | .. | .. | .. |
| Korea, Rep. | | .. | .. | .. | .. | .. | .. | .. | .. | .. | .. | .. |
| Kuwait | | .. | .. | .. | .. | .. | .. | .. | .. | .. | .. | .. |
| Kyrgyz Republic | 1998 | 8.6 | 9.7 | 7.6 | 7.0 | 93.0 | 93.0 | 96.3 | 0.0 | 0.0 | 7.0 | 2.7 |
| Lao PDR | | .. | .. | .. | .. | .. | .. | .. | .. | .. | .. | .. |
| Latvia | | .. | .. | .. | .. | .. | .. | .. | .. | .. | .. | .. |
| Lebanon | | .. | .. | .. | .. | .. | .. | .. | .. | .. | .. | .. |
| Lesotho | 2000 | 30.8 | 34.2 | 27.5 | 17.6 | 82.4 | .. | .. | .. | .. | .. | .. |
| Liberia | | .. | .. | .. | .. | .. | .. | .. | .. | .. | .. | .. |
| Libya | | .. | .. | .. | .. | .. | .. | .. | .. | .. | .. | .. |
| Lithuania | | .. | .. | .. | .. | .. | .. | .. | .. | .. | .. | .. |
| Macedonia, FYR | | .. | .. | .. | .. | .. | .. | .. | .. | .. | .. | .. |
| Madagascar | 2001 | 25.6 | 26.1 | 25.1 | 85.1 | 14.9 | 94.1 | 93.9 | 0.6 | 1.4 | 2.0 | 2.9 |
| Malawi | 2004 | 42.6 | 45.0 | 40.3 | 13.9 | 86.1 | .. | .. | .. | .. | .. | .. |
| Malaysia | | .. | .. | .. | .. | .. | .. | .. | .. | .. | .. | .. |
| Mali | 2005 | 70.9 | 71.2 | 70.7 | 53.3 | 46.7 | 78.4 | 41.8 | 1.4 | 3.2 | 19.6 | 54.6 |
| Mauritania | | .. | .. | .. | .. | .. | .. | .. | .. | .. | .. | .. |
| Mauritius | | .. | .. | .. | .. | .. | .. | .. | .. | .. | .. | .. |
| Mexico[d] | 2004 | 8.9 | 12.2 | 5.6 | 34.1 | 65.9 | 46.4 | 20.6 | 12.6 | 11.5 | 38.6 | 68.0 |
| Moldova | 2000 | 33.5 | 34.1 | 32.8 | 3.8 | 96.2 | .. | .. | .. | .. | .. | .. |
| Mongolia | 2000 | 22.0 | 23.5 | 20.6 | 28.2 | 71.8 | .. | .. | .. | .. | .. | .. |
| Morocco | 1998–99 | 13.2 | 13.5 | 12.8 | 93.2 | 6.8 | 60.8 | 60.3 | 8.1 | 8.5 | 13.5 | 6.4 |
| Mozambique | | .. | .. | .. | .. | .. | .. | .. | .. | .. | .. | .. |
| Myanmar | | .. | .. | .. | .. | .. | .. | .. | .. | .. | .. | .. |
| Namibia | 1999 | 15.4 | 16.2 | 14.7 | 9.5 | 90.5 | 91.5 | 91.7 | 0.4 | 0.4 | 8.1 | 8.0 |
| Nepal | 1999 | 47.2 | 42.2 | 52.4 | 35.6 | 64.4 | 89.0 | 86.1 | 1.2 | 1.5 | 9.7 | 12.3 |
| Netherlands | | .. | .. | .. | .. | .. | .. | .. | .. | .. | .. | .. |
| New Zealand | | .. | .. | .. | .. | .. | .. | .. | .. | .. | .. | .. |
| Nicaragua | 2001 | 12.1 | 17.5 | 6.5 | 33.3 | 66.7 | 73.2 | 32.0 | 3.0 | 10.2 | 23.3 | 57.8 |
| Niger | | .. | .. | .. | .. | .. | .. | .. | .. | .. | .. | .. |
| Nigeria | | .. | .. | .. | .. | .. | .. | .. | .. | .. | .. | .. |
| Norway | | .. | .. | .. | .. | .. | .. | .. | .. | .. | .. | .. |
| Oman | | .. | .. | .. | .. | .. | .. | .. | .. | .. | .. | .. |
| Pakistan | | .. | .. | .. | .. | .. | .. | .. | .. | .. | .. | .. |
| Panama[c] | 2003 | 5.1 | 7.7 | 2.2 | 38.4 | 61.6 | 62.0 | 41.3 | 2.5 | 5.2 | 34.0 | 53.5 |
| Papua New Guinea | | .. | .. | .. | .. | .. | .. | .. | .. | .. | .. | .. |
| Paraguay[c] | 2005 | 15.3 | 22.6 | 7.7 | 24.2 | 75.7 | 69.8 | 33.9 | 6.0 | 6.9 | 34.0 | 59.3 |
| Peru | 2000 | 24.1 | 25.7 | 22.3 | 4.8 | 95.2 | 75.4 | 69.1 | 3.1 | 2.5 | 21.2 | 28.4 |
| Philippines | 2001 | 13.3 | 16.3 | 10.0 | 14.8 | 85.2 | 72.6 | 53.6 | 3.6 | 5.3 | 22.1 | 41.0 |
| Poland | | .. | .. | .. | .. | .. | .. | .. | .. | .. | .. | .. |
| Portugal | 2001 | 3.6 | 4.6 | 2.6 | 3.6 | 96.4 | 52.7 | 40.7 | 11.4 | 10.7 | 25.6 | 47.7 |
| Puerto Rico | | .. | .. | .. | .. | .. | .. | .. | .. | .. | .. | .. |

| | Survey year | Economically active children | | | | | Employment by economic activity[a] | | | | | |
|---|---|---|---|---|---|---|---|---|---|---|---|---|
| | | % of children ages 7–14 | | | % of economically active children ages 7–14 | | Agriculture | | % of economically active children ages 7–14 Manufacturing | | Services | |
| | | Total | Male | Female | Work only | Study and work | Male | Female | Male | Female | Male | Female |
| Romania | 2000 | 1.4 | 1.7 | 1.1 | 20.7 | 79.3 | 96.4 | 98.1 | 0.0 | 0.0 | 2.6 | 1.9 |
| Russian Federation | | .. | .. | .. | .. | .. | .. | .. | .. | .. | .. | .. |
| Rwanda | 2000 | 33.1 | 36.1 | 30.3 | 27.5 | 72.5 | .. | .. | .. | .. | .. | .. |
| Saudi Arabia | | .. | .. | .. | .. | .. | .. | .. | .. | .. | .. | .. |
| Senegal | 2005 | 18.5 | 24.4 | 12.6 | 61.9 | 38.1 | 85.2 | 67.0 | 6.5 | 2.3 | 6.7 | 28.5 |
| Serbia | | .. | .. | .. | .. | .. | .. | .. | .. | .. | .. | .. |
| Sierra Leone | 2000 | 65.0 | 64.7 | 65.4 | 53.8 | 46.2 | .. | .. | .. | .. | .. | .. |
| Singapore | | .. | .. | .. | .. | .. | .. | .. | .. | .. | .. | .. |
| Slovak Republic | | .. | .. | .. | .. | .. | .. | .. | .. | .. | .. | .. |
| Slovenia | | .. | .. | .. | .. | .. | .. | .. | .. | .. | .. | .. |
| Somalia | | .. | .. | .. | .. | .. | .. | .. | .. | .. | .. | .. |
| South Africa | 1999 | 27.7 | 29.0 | 26.4 | 5.1 | 94.9 | .. | .. | .. | .. | .. | .. |
| Spain | | .. | .. | .. | .. | .. | .. | .. | .. | .. | .. | .. |
| Sri Lanka | 1998 | 17.0 | 20.4 | 13.4 | 5.4 | 94.6 | 71.1 | 71.4 | 12.0 | 15.0 | 15.8 | 13.5 |
| Sudan[e] | 2000 | 19.1 | 21.5 | 16.8 | 55.9 | 44.1 | .. | .. | .. | .. | .. | .. |
| Swaziland | 2000 | 11.2 | 11.4 | 10.9 | 14.0 | 86.0 | .. | .. | .. | .. | .. | .. |
| Sweden | | .. | .. | .. | .. | .. | .. | .. | .. | .. | .. | .. |
| Switzerland | | .. | .. | .. | .. | .. | .. | .. | .. | .. | .. | .. |
| Syrian Arab Republic | | .. | .. | .. | .. | .. | .. | .. | .. | .. | .. | .. |
| Tajikistan[f] | 1999 | 7.3 | 7.9 | 6.8 | 11.2 | 88.8 | 23.8 | 35.3 | .. | .. | 76.2 | 64.7 |
| Tanzania | 2001 | 40.4 | 41.5 | 39.2 | 40.0 | 60.0 | 83.5 | 73.1 | 0.1 | 0.2 | 16.3 | 26.7 |
| Thailand | | .. | .. | .. | .. | .. | .. | .. | .. | .. | .. | .. |
| Timor-Leste | | .. | .. | .. | .. | .. | .. | .. | .. | .. | .. | .. |
| Togo | 2006 | 39.6 | 40.5 | 38.5 | 30.2 | 69.8 | 89.7 | 77.2 | 0.9 | 1.5 | 8.3 | 20.8 |
| Trinidad and Tobago | 2000 | 3.9 | 5.2 | 2.8 | 12.8 | 87.2 | .. | .. | .. | .. | .. | .. |
| Tunisia | | .. | .. | .. | .. | .. | .. | .. | .. | .. | .. | .. |
| Turkey | 1999 | 4.5 | 5.2 | 3.8 | 66.8 | 33.2 | 52.7 | 83.4 | 19.9 | 10.2 | 10.2 | 1.8 |
| Turkmenistan | | .. | .. | .. | .. | .. | .. | .. | .. | .. | .. | .. |
| Uganda | 2005–06 | 38.2 | 39.8 | 36.5 | 7.7 | 92.3 | 96.0 | 94.9 | 1.0 | 1.7 | 2.7 | 3.3 |
| Ukraine | | .. | .. | .. | .. | .. | .. | .. | .. | .. | .. | .. |
| United Arab Emirates | | .. | .. | .. | .. | .. | .. | .. | .. | .. | .. | .. |
| United Kingdom | | .. | .. | .. | .. | .. | .. | .. | .. | .. | .. | .. |
| United States | | .. | .. | .. | .. | .. | .. | .. | .. | .. | .. | .. |
| Uruguay | | .. | .. | .. | .. | .. | .. | .. | .. | .. | .. | .. |
| Uzbekistan | 2000 | 18.1 | 22.0 | 14.0 | 4.1 | 95.9 | .. | .. | .. | .. | .. | .. |
| Venezuela, RB[c] | 2003 | 9.1 | 11.4 | 6.6 | 17.6 | 82.4 | 35.2 | 9.2 | 7.3 | 9.5 | 53.9 | 81.0 |
| Vietnam | | .. | .. | .. | .. | .. | .. | .. | .. | .. | .. | .. |
| West Bank and Gaza | | .. | .. | .. | .. | .. | .. | .. | .. | .. | .. | .. |
| Yemen, Rep. | 1999 | 13.1 | 12.4 | 14.0 | 64.3 | 35.7 | 87.2 | 96.6 | 1.2 | 0.8 | 10.8 | 1.8 |
| Zambia | 2005 | 47.9 | 48.9 | 46.8 | 25.9 | 74.1 | 96.5 | 95.3 | 0.7 | 0.5 | 2.8 | 4.2 |
| Zimbabwe | 1999 | 14.3 | 15.3 | 13.3 | 12.0 | 88.0 | .. | .. | .. | .. | .. | .. |

a. Shares by major industrial category may not sum to 100 percent because of a residual category not included in the table. b. Covers only Angola-secured territory. c. Covers children ages 10–14. d. Covers children ages 12–14. e. Covers northern Sudan only. f. Covers children ages 11–14.

# Children at work | 2.6

## About the data

The indicators in the table refer to children's economic activity, a broader concept than child labor. According to a gradually emerging consensus, child labor is a subset of children's economic activity. Based on International Labour Organization (ILO) Conventions 138 and 182, child labor is work that is damaging to the child and therefore targeted for elimination.

In line with the definition of economic activity adopted by the Thirteenth International Conference of Labour Statisticians and set by the 1993 United Nations System of National Accounts, the threshold for classifying a person as employed is spending at least one hour during the reference period in the production of goods and services. Economic activity covers all market production and certain types of nonmarket production, including the production of goods for own use. It excludes household chores performed in one's own household.

The data used to develop the indicators are from household surveys conducted by the ILO, the United Nations Children's Fund (UNICEF), the World Bank, and national statistical offices. These surveys yield data on education, employment, health, expenditure, and consumption that relate to child work.

Household survey data generally include information on work type—for example, whether a child is working for pay in cash or in kind or is involved in unpaid work, whether a child is working for someone who is not a member of the household, whether a child is involved in any type of family work (on the farm or in a business), and the like. The age used in country surveys to define child labor ranges from 5 to 17 years old. The data in the table have been recalculated to present statistics for children ages 7–14.

Although efforts are made to harmonize the definition of employment and the questions on employment used in survey questionnaires, substantial differences remain among the survey instruments used to collect data on working children and the sampling design underlying these surveys. Differences exist not only among different household surveys in the same country, but also within the same type of survey carried out in different countries.

Because of differences in the underlying survey instruments and survey dates, estimates of working children are not fully comparable across countries. Great caution should be exercised in drawing conclusions concerning relative levels of child economic activity across countries or regions based on the published data.

The table aggregates the distribution of working children by the industrial categories of the International Standard Industrial Classification (ISIC): agriculture, industry, and services. A residual category, which includes mining and quarrying; electricity, gas, and water; construction; extraterritorial organization; and other inadequately defined activities, is not presented in the table, and so the broad groups do not add up to 100 percent. The use of either ISIC revision 2 or revision 3 is strictly related to the codification applied by each country in describing the economic activity. The use of two different classifications does not affect the definition of the groups presented in the table.

## Definitions

• **Survey year** is the year in which the underlying data were collected. • **Economically active children** are children involved in economic activity for at least one hour in the reference week of the survey. • **Work only** refers to children involved in economic activity and not attending school. • **Study and work** refer to children attending school in combination with economic activity. • **Employment by economic activity** is the distribution of economically active children by the major industrial categories (ISIC revision 2 or revision 3). • **Agriculture** corresponds to division 1 (ISIC revision 2) or categories A and B (ISIC revision 3) and includes agriculture and hunting, forestry and logging, and fishing. • **Manufacturing** corresponds to division 3 (ISIC revision 2) or category D (ISIC revision 3). • **Services** correspond to divisions 6–9 (ISIC revision 2) or categories G–P (ISIC revision 3) and include wholesale and retail trade, hotels and restaurants, transport, financial intermediation, real estate, public administration, education, health and social work, other community services, and private household activity.

---

### In developing countries the majority of child workers ages 5–14 are involved in unpaid family work | 2.6a

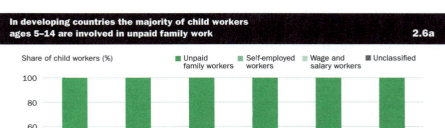

The incidence of child work varies substantially by country, as does status in employment for working children. A majority of children are unpaid family workers, with self-employed workers the next largest group.

*Source:* Understanding Children's Work.

### Data sources

Data on children at work are estimates produced by the Understanding Children's Work project based on household survey data sets made available by the ILO's International Programme on the Elimination of Child Labour under its Statistical Monitoring Programme on Child Labour, UNICEF under its Multiple Indicator Cluster Survey program, the World Bank under its Living Standards Measurement Study program, and national statistical offices. Information on how the data were collected and some indication of their reliability can be found at www.ilo.org/public/english/standards/ipec/simpoc/, www.childinfo.org, and www.worldbank.org/lsms. Detailed country statistics can be found at www.ucw-project.org.

| | Population below national poverty line | | | | | | | Poverty gap at national poverty line | | | |
|---|---|---|---|---|---|---|---|---|---|---|---|
| | Survey year | Rural | % Urban | National | Survey year | Rural | % Urban | National | Survey year | Rural | % Urban | National |
| Afghanistan | .. | .. | .. | .. | | .. | .. | .. | | .. | .. | .. |
| Albania | 2002 | 29.6 | 19.8 | 25.4 | | .. | .. | .. | 2002 | 6.6 | .. | 5.7 |
| Algeria | 1988 | 16.6 | 7.3 | 12.2 | 1995 | 30.3 | 14.7 | 22.6 | 1995 | 4.5 | 1.8 | 3.2 |
| Angola | .. | .. | .. | .. | | .. | .. | .. | | .. | .. | .. |
| Argentina | 1995 | .. | 28.4 | .. | 1998 | .. | 29.9 | .. | 1998 | .. | 11.6 | .. |
| Armenia | 1998–99 | 50.8 | 58.3 | 55.1 | 2001 | 48.7 | 51.9 | 50.9 | 2001 | .. | .. | 15.1 |
| Australia | .. | .. | .. | .. | | .. | .. | .. | | .. | .. | .. |
| Austria | .. | .. | .. | .. | | .. | .. | .. | | .. | .. | .. |
| Azerbaijan | 1995 | .. | .. | 68.1 | 2001 | 42.0 | 55.0 | 49.6 | 2001 | .. | .. | 15.5 |
| Bangladesh | 1995–96 | 55.2 | 29.4 | 51.0 | 2000 | 53.0 | 36.6 | 49.8 | 2000 | 13.8 | 9.5 | 12.9 |
| Belarus | 2000 | .. | .. | 41.9 | 2002 | .. | .. | 18.5 | 2002 | .. | .. | 20.0 |
| Belgium | .. | .. | .. | .. | | .. | .. | .. | | .. | .. | .. |
| Benin | 1995 | 25.2 | 28.5 | 26.5 | 1999 | 33.0 | 23.3 | 29.0 | 1999 | 9.4 | 6.9 | .. |
| Bolivia | 1999 | 84.0 | 51.4 | 63.5 | 2002 | 83.5 | 53.9 | 65.2 | 2002 | 43.4 | 23.8 | 31.2 |
| Bosnia and Herzegovina | 2001–02 | 19.9 | 13.8 | 19.5 | | .. | .. | .. | 2001–02 | 4.9 | 2.8 | 4.6 |
| Botswana | .. | .. | .. | .. | | .. | .. | .. | | .. | .. | .. |
| Brazil | 1998 | 51.4 | 14.7 | 22.0 | 2002–03 | 41.0 | 17.5 | 21.5 | 2002–03 | 28.4 | 17.8 | 19.6 |
| Bulgaria | 1997 | .. | .. | 36.0 | 2001 | .. | .. | 12.8 | 2001 | .. | .. | 4.2 |
| Burkina Faso | 1998 | 61.1 | 22.4 | 54.6 | 2003 | 52.4 | 19.2 | 46.4 | 2003 | 17.6 | 5.1 | 15.3 |
| Burundi | 1998 | 64.6 | 66.5 | 68.0 | | .. | .. | .. | | .. | .. | .. |
| Cambodia | 1994 | .. | .. | 47.0 | 2004 | 38.0 | 18.0 | 35.0 | 2004 | 7.8 | 1.2 | 6.7 |
| Cameroon | 1996 | 59.6 | 41.4 | 53.3 | 2001 | 49.9 | 22.1 | 40.2 | | .. | .. | .. |
| Canada | .. | .. | .. | .. | | .. | .. | .. | | .. | .. | .. |
| Central African Republic | .. | .. | .. | .. | | .. | .. | .. | | .. | .. | .. |
| Chad | 1995–96 | 48.6 | .. | 43.4 | | .. | .. | .. | 1995–96 | 26.3 | .. | 27.5 |
| Chile | 1996 | .. | .. | 19.9 | 1998 | .. | .. | 17.0 | 1998 | .. | .. | 5.7 |
| China | 1998 | 4.6 | .. | 4.6 | 2004 | .. | .. | 2.8 | | .. | .. | .. |
| Hong Kong, China | .. | .. | .. | .. | | .. | .. | .. | | .. | .. | .. |
| Colombia | 1995 | 79.0 | 48.0 | 60.0 | 1999 | 79.0 | 55.0 | 64.0 | 1999 | 44.0 | 26.0 | 34.0 |
| Congo, Dem. Rep. | .. | .. | .. | .. | | .. | .. | .. | | .. | .. | .. |
| Congo, Rep. | .. | .. | .. | .. | | .. | .. | .. | | .. | .. | .. |
| Costa Rica | 1992 | 25.5 | 19.2 | 22.0 | 2004 | 28.3 | 20.8 | 23.9 | 2004 | 10.8 | 7.0 | 8.6 |
| Côte d'Ivoire | .. | .. | .. | .. | | .. | .. | .. | | .. | .. | .. |
| Croatia | .. | .. | .. | .. | | .. | .. | .. | | .. | .. | .. |
| Cuba | .. | .. | .. | .. | | .. | .. | .. | | .. | .. | .. |
| Czech Republic | .. | .. | .. | .. | | .. | .. | .. | | .. | .. | .. |
| Denmark | .. | .. | .. | .. | | .. | .. | .. | | .. | .. | .. |
| Dominican Republic | 2000 | 45.3 | 18.2 | 27.7 | 2004 | 55.7 | 34.7 | 42.2 | 2004 | 24.0 | 12.9 | 16.8 |
| Ecuador | 1995 | 56.0 | 19.0 | 34.0 | 1998 | 69.0 | 30.0 | 46.0 | 1998 | 29.0 | 9.0 | 18.0 |
| Egypt, Arab Rep. | 1995–96 | 23.3 | 22.5 | 22.9 | 1999–2000 | .. | .. | 16.7 | 1999–2000 | .. | .. | 3.0 |
| El Salvador | 1995 | 64.8 | 38.9 | 50.6 | 2002 | 49.8 | 28.5 | 37.2 | 2002 | 24.2 | 11.1 | 16.5 |
| Eritrea | 1993–94 | .. | .. | 53.0 | | .. | .. | .. | | .. | .. | .. |
| Estonia | 1995 | 14.7 | 6.8 | 8.9 | | .. | .. | .. | 1995 | 6.6 | 1.8 | 3.1 |
| Ethiopia | 1995–96 | 47.0 | 33.3 | 45.5 | 1999–2000 | 45.0 | 37.0 | 44.2 | 1999–2000 | 12.0 | 10.0 | 12.0 |
| Finland | .. | .. | .. | .. | | .. | .. | .. | | .. | .. | .. |
| France | .. | .. | .. | .. | | .. | .. | .. | | .. | .. | .. |
| Gabon | .. | .. | .. | .. | | .. | .. | .. | | .. | .. | .. |
| Gambia, The | 1998 | 61.0 | 48.0 | 57.6 | 2003 | 63.0 | 57.0 | 61.3 | 2003 | .. | .. | 25.9 |
| Georgia | 2002 | 55.4 | 48.5 | 52.1 | 2003 | 52.7 | 56.2 | 54.5 | | .. | .. | .. |
| Germany | .. | .. | .. | .. | | .. | .. | .. | | .. | .. | .. |
| Ghana | 1998–99 | 49.6 | 19.4 | 39.5 | 2005–06 | 39.2 | 10.8 | 28.5 | 2005–06 | 13.5 | 3.1 | 9.6 |
| Greece | .. | .. | .. | .. | | .. | .. | .. | | .. | .. | .. |
| Guatemala | 1989 | 71.9 | 33.7 | 57.9 | 2000 | 74.5 | 27.1 | 56.2 | 2000 | .. | .. | 22.6 |
| Guinea | 1994 | .. | .. | 40.0 | | .. | .. | .. | | .. | .. | .. |
| Guinea-Bissau | 2002 | .. | 52.6 | 65.7 | | .. | .. | .. | 2000 | .. | 17.5 | 25.7 |
| Haiti | 1987 | .. | .. | 65.0 | 1995 | 66.0 | .. | .. | | .. | .. | .. |

# Poverty | 2.7

|  | Population below national poverty line | | | | | | | Poverty gap at national poverty line | | | |
|---|---|---|---|---|---|---|---|---|---|---|---|
|  | Survey year | Rural | % Urban | National | Survey year | Rural | % Urban | National | Survey year | Rural | % Urban | National |
| Honduras | 1998–99 | 71.2 | 28.6 | 52.5 | 2004 | 70.4 | 29.5 | 50.7 | 2004 | 34.5 | 9.1 | 22.3 |
| Hungary | 1993 | .. | .. | 14.5 | 1997 | .. | .. | 17.3 | 1997 | 4.1 | .. | .. |
| India | 1993–94 | 37.3 | 32.4 | 36.0 | 1999–2000 | 30.2 | 24.7 | 28.6 | 1999–2000 | 5.6 | 6.9 | .. |
| Indonesia | 1996 | .. | .. | 17.5 | 2004 | .. | .. | 16.7 | 2004 | .. | .. | 2.9 |
| Iran, Islamic Rep. |  | .. | .. | .. |  | .. | .. | .. |  | .. | .. | .. |
| Iraq |  | .. | .. | .. |  | .. | .. | .. |  | .. | .. | .. |
| Ireland |  | .. | .. | .. |  | .. | .. | .. |  | .. | .. | .. |
| Israel |  | .. | .. | .. |  | .. | .. | .. |  | .. | .. | .. |
| Italy |  | .. | .. | .. |  | .. | .. | .. |  | .. | .. | .. |
| Jamaica | 1995 | 37.0 | 18.7 | 27.5 | 2000 | 25.1 | 12.8 | 18.7 |  |  |  |  |
| Japan |  | .. | .. | .. |  | .. | .. | .. |  | .. | .. | .. |
| Jordan | 1997 | 27.0 | 19.7 | 21.3 | 2002 | 18.7 | 12.9 | 14.2 | 2002 | 4.7 | 2.9 | 3.3 |
| Kazakhstan | 2001 | .. | .. | 17.6 | 2002 | .. | .. | 15.4 | 2002 | 4.5 | 2.0 | 3.1 |
| Kenya | 1994 | 47.0 | 29.0 | 40.0 | 1997 | 53.0 | 49.0 | 52.0 |  | .. | .. | .. |
| Korea, Dem. Rep. |  | .. | .. | .. |  | .. | .. | .. |  | .. | .. | .. |
| Korea, Rep. |  | .. | .. | .. |  | .. | .. | .. |  | .. | .. | .. |
| Kuwait |  | .. | .. | .. |  | .. | .. | .. |  | .. | .. | .. |
| Kyrgyz Republic | 2003 | 57.5 | 35.7 | 49.9 | 2005 | 50.8 | 29.8 | 43.1 | 2005 | 12.0 | 7.0 | 10.0 |
| Lao PDR | 1997–98 | 41.0 | 26.9 | 38.6 | 2002–03 | .. | .. | 33.0 | 2002–03 | .. | .. | 8.0 |
| Latvia | 2002 | 11.6 | .. | 7.5 | 2004 | 12.7 | .. | 5.9 | 2004 | .. | .. | 1.2 |
| Lebanon |  | .. | .. | .. |  | .. | .. | .. |  | .. | .. | .. |
| Lesotho | 1993 | 53.9 | 27.8 | 49.2 | 1999 | .. | .. | 68.0 |  | .. | .. | .. |
| Liberia |  | .. | .. | .. |  | .. | .. | .. |  | .. | .. | .. |
| Libya |  | .. | .. | .. |  | .. | .. | .. |  | .. | .. | .. |
| Lithuania |  | .. | .. | .. |  | .. | .. | .. |  | .. | .. | .. |
| Macedonia, FYR | 2002 | 25.3 | .. | 21.4 | 2003 | 22.3 | .. | 21.7 | 2003 | 6.5 | .. | 6.7 |
| Madagascar | 1997 | 76.0 | 63.2 | 73.3 | 1999 | 76.7 | 52.1 | 71.3 | 1999 | 36.1 | 21.4 | 32.8 |
| Malawi | 1990–91 | .. | .. | 54.0 | 1997–98 | 66.5 | 54.9 | 65.3 |  | .. | .. | .. |
| Malaysia | 1989 | .. | .. | 15.5 |  | .. | .. | .. |  | .. | .. | .. |
| Mali | 1998 | 75.9 | 30.1 | 63.8 |  | .. | .. | .. |  | .. | .. | .. |
| Mauritania | 1996 | 65.5 | 30.1 | 50.0 | 2000 | 61.2 | 25.4 | 46.3 |  | .. | .. | .. |
| Mauritius |  | .. | .. | .. |  | .. | .. | .. |  | .. | .. | .. |
| Mexico | 2002 | 34.8 | 11.4 | 20.3 | 2004 | 27.9 | 11.3 | 17.6 | 2002 | 12.2 | 2.8 | 6.3 |
| Moldova | 2001 | 64.1 | 58.0 | 62.4 | 2002 | 67.2 | 42.6 | 48.5 | 2002 | .. | .. | 16.5 |
| Mongolia | 1998 | 32.6 | 39.4 | 35.6 | 2002 | 43.4 | 30.3 | 36.1 | 2002 | 13.2 | 9.2 | 11.0 |
| Morocco | 1990–91 | 18.0 | 7.6 | 13.1 | 1998–99 | 27.2 | 12.0 | 19.0 | 1998–99 | 6.7 | 2.5 | 4.4 |
| Mozambique | 1996–97 | 71.3 | 62.0 | 69.4 | 2002–03 | 55.3 | 51.5 | 54.1 | 2002–03 | 20.9 | 19.7 | 20.5 |
| Myanmar |  | .. | .. | .. |  | .. | .. | .. |  | .. | .. | .. |
| Namibia |  | .. | .. | .. |  | .. | .. | .. |  | .. | .. | .. |
| Nepal | 1995–96 | 43.3 | 21.6 | 41.8 | 2003–04 | 34.6 | 9.6 | 30.9 | 2003–04 | 8.5 | 2.2 | 7.5 |
| Netherlands |  | .. | .. | .. |  | .. | .. | .. |  | .. | .. | .. |
| New Zealand |  | .. | .. | .. |  | .. | .. | .. |  | .. | .. | .. |
| Nicaragua | 1998 | 68.5 | 30.5 | 47.9 | 2001 | 64.3 | 28.7 | 45.8 | 2001 | 25.9 | 8.7 | 17.0 |
| Niger | 1989–93 | 66.0 | 52.0 | 63.0 |  | .. | .. | .. |  | .. | .. | .. |
| Nigeria | 1985 | 49.5 | 31.7 | 43.0 | 1992–93 | 36.4 | 30.4 | 34.1 |  | .. | .. | .. |
| Norway |  | .. | .. | .. |  | .. | .. | .. |  | .. | .. | .. |
| Oman |  | .. | .. | .. |  | .. | .. | .. |  | .. | .. | .. |
| Pakistan | 1993 | 33.4 | 17.2 | 28.6 | 1998–99 | 35.9 | 24.2 | 32.6 | 1998–99 | 7.9 | 5.0 | 7.0 |
| Panama | 1997 | 64.9 | 15.3 | 37.3 |  | .. | .. | .. | 1997 | 32.1 | 3.9 | 16.4 |
| Papua New Guinea | 1996 | 41.3 | 16.1 | 37.5 |  | .. | .. | .. | 1996 | 13.8 | 4.3 | 12.4 |
| Paraguay[a] | 1990 | 28.5 | 19.7 | 20.5 |  | .. | .. | .. | 1990 | 10.5 | 5.6 | 6.0 |
| Peru | 2001 | 77.1 | 42.0 | 54.3 | 2004 | 72.1 | 42.9 | 53.1 | 2004 | 28.3 | 12.4 | 18.0 |
| Philippines | 1994 | 45.4 | 18.6 | 32.1 | 1997 | 36.9 | 11.9 | 25.1 | 1997 | 10.0 | 2.6 | 6.4 |
| Poland | 1996 | .. | .. | 14.6 | 2001 | .. | .. | 14.8 |  | .. | .. | .. |
| Portugal |  | .. | .. | .. |  | .. | .. | .. |  | .. | .. | .. |
| Puerto Rico |  | .. | .. | .. |  | .. | .. | .. |  | .. | .. | .. |

# 2.7 Poverty

| | Population below national poverty line | | | | | | | | Poverty gap at national poverty line | | | |
|---|---|---|---|---|---|---|---|---|---|---|---|---|
| | Survey year | Rural | % Urban | National | Survey year | Rural | % Urban | National | Survey year | Rural | % Urban | National |
| Romania | 1995 | .. | .. | 25.4 | 2002 | .. | .. | 28.9 | 2002 | .. | .. | 7.6 |
| Russian Federation | 1998 | .. | .. | 31.4 | 2002 | .. | .. | 19.6 | 2002 | .. | .. | 5.1 |
| Rwanda | 1993 | .. | .. | 51.2 | 1999–2000 | 65.7 | 14.3 | 60.3 | | .. | .. | .. |
| Saudi Arabia | | .. | .. | .. | | .. | .. | .. | | .. | .. | .. |
| Senegal | 1992 | 40.4 | 23.7 | 33.4 | | .. | .. | .. | 1992 | 16.4 | 3.1 | 13.9 |
| Serbia | | .. | .. | .. | | .. | .. | .. | | .. | .. | .. |
| Sierra Leone | 1989 | .. | .. | 82.8 | 2003–04 | 79.0 | 56.4 | 70.2 | 2003–04 | 34.0 | .. | 29.0 |
| Singapore | | .. | .. | .. | | .. | .. | .. | | .. | .. | .. |
| Slovak Republic | | .. | .. | .. | | .. | .. | .. | | .. | .. | .. |
| Slovenia | | .. | .. | .. | | .. | .. | .. | | .. | .. | .. |
| Somalia | | .. | .. | .. | | .. | .. | .. | | .. | .. | .. |
| South Africa | | .. | .. | .. | | .. | .. | .. | | .. | .. | .. |
| Spain | | .. | .. | .. | | .. | .. | .. | | .. | .. | .. |
| Sri Lanka | 1995–96 | 27.0 | 15.0 | 25.0 | 2002 | 7.9 | 24.7 | 22.7 | 2002 | .. | .. | 5.1 |
| Sudan | | .. | .. | .. | | .. | .. | .. | | .. | .. | .. |
| Swaziland | 2000–01 | 75.0 | 49.0 | 69.2 | | .. | .. | .. | 2000–01 | .. | .. | 32.9 |
| Sweden | | .. | .. | .. | | .. | .. | .. | | .. | .. | .. |
| Switzerland | | .. | .. | .. | | .. | .. | .. | | .. | .. | .. |
| Syrian Arab Republic | | .. | .. | .. | | .. | .. | .. | | .. | .. | .. |
| Tajikistan | 1999 | .. | .. | 74.9 | 2003 | .. | .. | 44.4 | 2003 | .. | .. | 12.7 |
| Tanzania | 1991 | 40.8 | 31.2 | 38.6 | 2000–01 | 38.7 | 29.5 | 35.7 | | .. | .. | .. |
| Thailand | 1994 | .. | .. | 9.8 | 1998 | .. | .. | 13.6 | 1998 | .. | .. | 3.0 |
| Timor-Leste | 2001 | .. | .. | 39.7 | | .. | .. | .. | 2001 | .. | .. | 11.9 |
| Togo | 1987–89 | .. | .. | 32.3 | | .. | .. | .. | 1987–89 | .. | .. | 10.0 |
| Trinidad and Tobago | 1992 | 20.0 | 24.0 | 21.0 | | .. | .. | .. | 1992 | 6.2 | 7.4 | 7.3 |
| Tunisia | 1990 | 13.1 | 3.5 | 7.4 | 1995 | 13.9 | 3.6 | 7.6 | 1990 | 3.3 | 0.9 | 1.7 |
| Turkey | 1994 | .. | .. | 28.3 | 2002 | 34.5 | 22.0 | 27.0 | 2002 | .. | .. | 0.3 |
| Turkmenistan | | .. | .. | .. | | .. | .. | .. | | .. | .. | .. |
| Uganda | 1999–2000 | 37.4 | 9.6 | 33.8 | 2002–03 | 41.7 | 12.2 | 37.7 | 2002–03 | 12.6 | 3.0 | 11.3 |
| Ukraine | 2000 | 34.9 | .. | 31.5 | 2003 | 28.4 | .. | 19.5 | | .. | .. | .. |
| United Arab Emirates | | .. | .. | .. | | .. | .. | .. | | .. | .. | .. |
| United Kingdom | | .. | .. | .. | | .. | .. | .. | | .. | .. | .. |
| United States | | .. | .. | .. | | .. | .. | .. | | .. | .. | .. |
| Uruguay | 1994 | .. | 20.2 | .. | 1998 | .. | 24.7 | .. | 1998 | .. | 8.6 | .. |
| Uzbekistan | 2000 | 30.5 | 22.5 | 27.5 | | .. | .. | .. | | .. | .. | .. |
| Venezuela, RB | 1989 | .. | .. | 31.3 | | .. | .. | .. | 1989 | .. | 24.0 | .. |
| Vietnam | 1998 | 45.5 | 9.2 | 37.4 | 2002 | 35.6 | 6.6 | 28.9 | 2002 | 8.7 | 1.3 | 6.9 |
| West Bank and Gaza | | .. | .. | .. | | .. | .. | .. | | .. | .. | .. |
| Yemen, Rep. | 1998 | 45.0 | 30.8 | 41.8 | | .. | .. | .. | 1998 | 14.7 | 8.2 | 13.2 |
| Zambia | 1998 | 83.1 | 56.0 | 72.9 | 2004 | 78.0 | 53.0 | 68.0 | 2004 | 44.0 | 22.0 | 36.0 |
| Zimbabwe | 1990–91 | 35.8 | 3.4 | 25.8 | 1995–96 | 48.0 | 7.9 | 34.9 | | .. | .. | .. |

a. Covers Asunción metropolitan area only.

## About the data

The World Bank periodically prepares poverty assessments for member countries in which it has an active program in close collaboration with national institutions, other development agencies, and civil society groups, including poor people's organizations. Poverty assessments assess the extent and causes of poverty and propose strategies to reduce it. Since 1992 the World Bank has conducted about 180 poverty assessments, which are the source of all poverty estimates based on national poverty lines presented in the table.

The World Bank published its first systematic review of poverty for developing countries in *World Development Report 1990* using household survey data for 22 countries (Ravallion, Datt, and van de Walle 1991). Since then the number of countries that field such surveys has increased considerably, as have the frequency of the surveys and the quality of the data. Household survey data sets rose dramatically from 10 between 1979 and 1981 to 111 between 2000 and 2002. Fewer surveys are available after 2002, reflecting the lag between data collection and availability for analysis, not a reduction in collection effort. Coverage is improving in all regions, but Sub-Saharan Africa continues to lag, with only 21 of 48 countries having at least one data set available since 2000. Overall more than 550 surveys representing about 100 developing countries are now included in the World Bank's data sets. Some 1.1 million randomly sampled households were interviewed in these surveys, representing 93 percent of the population of developing countries. A complete overview of data availability by year and country is available at http://iresearch.worldbank.org/povcalnet/.

These household surveys ask detailed questions on sources of income and how income was spent and on household characteristics such as the number of people sharing that income. Most interviews are conducted by staff of government statistics offices. As data coverage and quality have improved, so has the underlying methodology, resulting in more comprehensive estimates.

Estimating poverty and comparing poverty rates is difficult. In addition to survey data availability are data quality issues that arise in measuring household living standards. One concerns the choice of income or consumption as a welfare indicator. Income is generally more difficult to measure accurately, and consumption comes closer to the notion of living standards. And income can vary over time even if living standards do not. But consumption data are not always available. Another issue is that household

surveys can differ widely. Even similar surveys may not be strictly comparable because of differences in timing or in the quality and training of enumerators.

Comparisons of countries at different levels of development also pose a potential problem because of differences in the relative importance of consumption of nonmarket goods. The local market value of all consumption in kind (including own production, particularly important in underdeveloped rural economies) should be included in total consumption expenditure. Similarly, imputed profit from the production of nonmarket goods should be included in income. This is not always done, though such omissions were a far bigger problem in surveys before the 1980s. Most survey data now include valuations for consumption or income from own production, but valuation methods vary.

The statistics reported here are based on consumption data or, when unavailable, on income surveys. Analysis of some 20 countries for which income and consumption expenditure data were both available from the same surveys found income to yield a higher mean than consumption but also found higher inequality. When poverty measures based on consumption and income were compared, the two effects roughly cancelled each other out: there was no significant statistical difference.

### International poverty lines and the 2005 International Comparison Project

This year's table does not include poverty estimates using the international poverty lines of $1 a day and $2 a day, which were based on 1993 purchasing power parities (PPPs). The International Comparison Program recently released new PPP estimates benchmarked to 2005 (see introduction to *World View*). Poverty estimates using new international poverty lines based on PPPs will be published later as a supplement to *World Development Indicators*.

### Do it yourself: PovcalNet

The World Bank's Development Research Group developed *PovcalNet*, an interactive Web-based tool that allows users to replicate the calculations by the World Bank's researchers in estimating absolute poverty in the world. *PovcalNet* is self-contained and powered by built-in software that performs the calculations from a primary database. The underlying software can also be downloaded from the *PovcalNet* site and used with distributional data of various formats. The *PovcalNet* primary database consists of distributional data calculated directly

from household survey data. Detailed information is available from the site.

Estimation from distributional data requires an interpolation method. The method chosen was Lorenz curves with flexible functional forms, which have proved reliable in past work. The Lorenz curve can be graphed as the cumulative percentages of total consumption or income against the cumulative number of people, starting with the poorest individual. The empirical Lorenz curves estimated by *PovcalNet* are weighted by household size, so they are based on percentiles of population, not households.

*PovcalNet* also allows users to calculate poverty measures under different assumptions. For example, users can specify different poverty lines and aggregate the estimates using alternative country groupings (for example, UN groupings or groupings based on average incomes) or a selected set of individual countries. *PovcalNet* is available online at http://iresearch.worldbank.org/povcalnet/. It will be updated using the 2005 PPP results along with the *World Development Indicators* supplemental publication later this year.

### Definitions

• **Survey year** is the year in which the underlying data were collected. • **Rural population below national poverty line** is the percentage of the rural population living below the national rural poverty line. • **Urban population below national poverty line** is the percentage of the urban population living below the national urban poverty line. • **National population below national poverty line** is the percentage of the country's population living below the national poverty line. National estimates are based on population-weighted subgroup estimates from household surveys. • **Poverty gap at national poverty line** is the mean shortfall from the poverty line (counting the nonpoor as having zero shortfall) as a percentage of the poverty line. This measure reflects the depth of poverty as well as its incidence.

### Data sources

The poverty measures are prepared by the World Bank's Development Research Group. The national poverty lines are based on the World Bank's country poverty assessments. For details on data sources and methods used in deriving the World Bank's latest estimates, see Chen and Ravallion's "How Have the World's Poorest Fared Since the Early 1980s?"

| | Survey year | Gini index | Percentage share of income or consumption[a] | | | | | | |
|---|---|---|---|---|---|---|---|---|---|
| | | | Lowest 10% | Lowest 20% | Second 20% | Third 20% | Fourth 20% | Highest 20% | Highest 10% |
| Afghanistan | | .. | .. | .. | .. | .. | .. | .. | .. |
| Albania | 2004[b] | 31.1 | 3.4 | 8.2 | 12.6 | 17.0 | 22.6 | 39.5 | 24.4 |
| Algeria | 1995[b] | 35.3 | 2.8 | 7.0 | 11.6 | 16.1 | 22.7 | 42.6 | 26.8 |
| Angola | | .. | .. | .. | .. | .. | .. | .. | .. |
| Argentina[c] | 2004[d] | 51.3 | 0.9 | 3.1 | 7.6 | 12.8 | 21.1 | 55.4 | 38.2 |
| Armenia | 2003[b] | 33.8 | 3.6 | 8.5 | 12.3 | 15.7 | 20.6 | 42.8 | 29.0 |
| Australia | 1994[d] | 35.2 | 2.0 | 5.9 | 12.0 | 17.2 | 23.6 | 41.3 | 25.4 |
| Austria | 2000[d] | 29.1 | 3.3 | 8.6 | 13.3 | 17.4 | 22.9 | 37.8 | 23.0 |
| Azerbaijan | 2001[b] | 36.5 | 3.1 | 7.4 | 11.5 | 15.3 | 21.2 | 44.5 | 29.5 |
| Bangladesh | 2005[b] | 33.2 | 3.8 | 8.8 | 12.2 | 15.6 | 20.9 | 42.5 | 28.0 |
| Belarus | 2005[b] | 28.0 | 3.6 | 8.8 | 13.7 | 17.7 | 23.0 | 36.8 | 22.1 |
| Belgium | 2000[d] | 33.0 | 3.4 | 8.5 | 13.0 | 16.3 | 20.8 | 41.4 | 28.1 |
| Benin | 2003[b] | 36.5 | 3.1 | 7.4 | 11.3 | 15.4 | 21.5 | 44.5 | 29.0 |
| Bolivia | 2002[d] | 60.1 | 0.3 | 1.5 | 5.9 | 10.9 | 18.7 | 63.0 | 47.2 |
| Bosnia and Herzegovina | 2005[b] | 35.8 | 2.7 | 7.0 | 11.6 | 15.9 | 22.3 | 43.2 | 27.5 |
| Botswana | 1993[b] | 60.5 | 1.2 | 3.2 | 6.0 | 9.7 | 16.0 | 65.1 | 51.0 |
| Brazil | 2005[d] | 56.6 | 0.9 | 2.9 | 6.5 | 11.1 | 18.7 | 60.8 | 44.9 |
| Bulgaria | 2003[b] | 29.2 | 3.4 | 8.7 | 13.7 | 17.2 | 22.1 | 38.3 | 23.9 |
| Burkina Faso | 2003[b] | 39.5 | 2.8 | 6.9 | 10.9 | 14.5 | 20.5 | 47.2 | 32.2 |
| Burundi | 1998[b] | 42.4 | 1.7 | 5.1 | 10.3 | 15.1 | 21.5 | 48.0 | 32.8 |
| Cambodia | 2004[b] | 41.7 | 2.9 | 6.8 | 10.2 | 13.7 | 19.6 | 49.6 | 34.8 |
| Cameroon | 2001[b] | 44.6 | 2.3 | 5.6 | 9.3 | 13.7 | 20.4 | 50.9 | 35.4 |
| Canada | 2000[d] | 32.6 | 2.6 | 7.2 | 12.7 | 17.2 | 23.0 | 39.9 | 24.8 |
| Central African Republic | 1993[b] | 61.3 | 0.7 | 2.0 | 4.9 | 9.6 | 18.5 | 65.0 | 47.7 |
| Chad | | .. | .. | .. | .. | .. | .. | .. | .. |
| Chile | 2003[d] | 54.9 | 1.4 | 3.8 | 7.3 | 11.1 | 17.8 | 60.0 | 45.0 |
| China | 2004[d] | 46.9 | 1.6 | 4.3 | 8.5 | 13.7 | 21.7 | 51.9 | 34.9 |
| Hong Kong, China | 1996[d] | 43.4 | 2.0 | 5.3 | 9.4 | 13.9 | 20.7 | 50.7 | 34.9 |
| Colombia | 2004[d] | 56.2 | 0.8 | 2.9 | 6.9 | 11.0 | 18.3 | 60.9 | 45.0 |
| Congo, Dem. Rep. | | .. | .. | .. | .. | .. | .. | .. | .. |
| Congo, Rep. | | .. | .. | .. | .. | .. | .. | .. | .. |
| Costa Rica | 2004[d] | 48.2 | 1.4 | 4.1 | 8.5 | 13.2 | 20.9 | 53.3 | 36.7 |
| Côte d'Ivoire | 2002[b] | 44.6 | 2.0 | 5.2 | 9.1 | 13.7 | 21.3 | 50.7 | 34.0 |
| Croatia | 2005[b] | 29.0 | 3.6 | 8.8 | 13.3 | 17.3 | 22.7 | 37.9 | 23.1 |
| Cuba | | .. | .. | .. | .. | .. | .. | .. | .. |
| Czech Republic | 1996[d] | 25.4 | 4.3 | 10.3 | 14.5 | 17.7 | 21.7 | 35.9 | 22.4 |
| Denmark | 1997[d] | 24.7 | 2.6 | 8.3 | 14.7 | 18.2 | 22.9 | 35.8 | 21.3 |
| Dominican Republic | 2005[d] | 49.9 | 1.5 | 4.1 | 8.1 | 12.6 | 19.9 | 55.3 | 39.0 |
| Ecuador | 1998[b] | 53.6 | 0.9 | 3.3 | 7.5 | 11.7 | 19.4 | 58.0 | 41.6 |
| Egypt, Arab Rep. | 2004–05[b] | 34.4 | 3.8 | 8.9 | 12.7 | 16.0 | 20.8 | 41.5 | 27.6 |
| El Salvador | 2002[d] | 52.4 | 0.7 | 2.7 | 7.5 | 12.8 | 21.2 | 55.9 | 38.8 |
| Eritrea | | .. | .. | .. | .. | .. | .. | .. | .. |
| Estonia | 2004[b] | 36.0 | 2.6 | 6.8 | 11.7 | 16.2 | 22.0 | 43.3 | 27.8 |
| Ethiopia | 1999–2000[b] | 30.0 | 3.9 | 9.1 | 13.2 | 16.8 | 21.5 | 39.4 | 25.5 |
| Finland | 2000[d] | 26.9 | 4.0 | 9.6 | 14.1 | 17.5 | 22.1 | 36.7 | 22.6 |
| France | 1995[d] | 32.7 | 2.8 | 7.2 | 12.6 | 17.2 | 22.8 | 40.2 | 25.1 |
| Gabon | | .. | .. | .. | .. | .. | .. | .. | .. |
| Gambia, The | 2003–04[b] | 47.4 | 1.8 | 4.8 | 8.7 | 13.0 | 20.7 | 52.9 | 36.9 |
| Georgia | 2005[b] | 40.8 | 1.9 | 5.4 | 10.5 | 15.3 | 22.2 | 46.7 | 30.6 |
| Germany | 2000[d] | 28.3 | 3.2 | 8.5 | 13.7 | 17.8 | 23.1 | 36.9 | 22.1 |
| Ghana | 1998–99[b] | 40.8 | 2.1 | 5.6 | 10.1 | 14.9 | 22.9 | 46.6 | 30.0 |
| Greece | 2000[d] | 34.3 | 2.5 | 6.7 | 11.9 | 16.8 | 23.0 | 41.5 | 26.0 |
| Guatemala | 2004[d] | 49.4 | 1.3 | 3.9 | 8.2 | 13.1 | 20.6 | 54.1 | 38.0 |
| Guinea | 2003[b] | 38.6 | 2.9 | 7.0 | 10.8 | 14.7 | 21.4 | 46.1 | 30.7 |
| Guinea-Bissau | 1993[b] | 47.0 | 2.1 | 5.2 | 8.8 | 13.1 | 19.4 | 53.4 | 39.3 |
| Haiti | 2001[d] | 59.2 | 0.7 | 2.4 | 6.2 | 10.4 | 17.7 | 63.4 | 47.7 |

| | Survey year | Gini index | Percentage share of income or consumption[a] | | | | | | |
|---|---|---|---|---|---|---|---|---|---|
| | | | Lowest 10% | Lowest 20% | Second 20% | Third 20% | Fourth 20% | Highest 20% | Highest 10% |
| Honduras | 2003[d] | 53.8 | 1.2 | 3.4 | 7.1 | 11.6 | 19.6 | 58.3 | 42.2 |
| Hungary | 2004[b] | 30.1 | 3.5 | 8.6 | 13.1 | 17.1 | 22.3 | 38.9 | 24.2 |
| India | 2004–05[b] | 36.8 | 3.6 | 8.1 | 11.3 | 14.9 | 20.4 | 45.3 | 31.1 |
| Indonesia | 2005[b] | 39.4 | 3.0 | 7.1 | 10.7 | 14.4 | 20.5 | 47.3 | 32.3 |
| Iran, Islamic Rep. | 2005[b] | 38.4 | 2.5 | 6.5 | 10.9 | 15.4 | 22.1 | 45.1 | 29.6 |
| Iraq | | .. | .. | .. | .. | .. | .. | .. | .. |
| Ireland | 2000[d] | 34.3 | 2.9 | 7.4 | 12.3 | 16.3 | 21.9 | 42.0 | 27.2 |
| Israel | 2001[d] | 39.2 | 2.1 | 5.7 | 10.5 | 15.9 | 23.0 | 44.9 | 28.8 |
| Italy | 2000[d] | 36.0 | 2.3 | 6.5 | 12.0 | 16.8 | 22.8 | 42.0 | 26.8 |
| Jamaica | 2004[b] | 45.5 | 2.1 | 5.3 | 9.2 | 13.2 | 20.6 | 51.6 | 35.8 |
| Japan | 1993[d] | 24.9 | 4.8 | 10.6 | 14.2 | 17.6 | 22.0 | 35.7 | 21.7 |
| Jordan | 2002–03[b] | 38.8 | 2.7 | 6.7 | 10.8 | 14.9 | 21.3 | 46.3 | 30.6 |
| Kazakhstan | 2003[b] | 33.9 | 3.0 | 7.4 | 11.9 | 16.4 | 22.8 | 41.5 | 25.9 |
| Kenya | 1997[b] | 42.5 | 2.5 | 6.0 | 9.8 | 14.3 | 20.8 | 49.1 | 33.9 |
| Korea, Dem. Rep. | | .. | .. | .. | .. | .. | .. | .. | .. |
| Korea, Rep. | 1998[d] | 31.6 | 2.9 | 7.9 | 13.6 | 18.0 | 23.1 | 37.5 | 22.5 |
| Kuwait | | .. | .. | .. | .. | .. | .. | .. | .. |
| Kyrgyz Republic | 2003[b] | 30.3 | 3.8 | 8.9 | 12.8 | 16.4 | 22.5 | 39.4 | 24.3 |
| Lao PDR | 2002[b] | 34.6 | 3.4 | 8.1 | 11.9 | 15.6 | 21.1 | 43.3 | 28.5 |
| Latvia | 2004[b] | 35.8 | 2.6 | 6.8 | 11.7 | 16.2 | 22.3 | 42.9 | 27.5 |
| Lebanon | | .. | .. | .. | .. | .. | .. | .. | .. |
| Lesotho | 1995[b] | 63.2 | 0.5 | 1.5 | 4.3 | 8.9 | 18.8 | 66.5 | 48.3 |
| Liberia | | .. | .. | .. | .. | .. | .. | .. | .. |
| Libya | | .. | .. | .. | .. | .. | .. | .. | .. |
| Lithuania | 2004[b] | 35.8 | 2.6 | 6.8 | 11.7 | 16.1 | 22.4 | 43.0 | 27.5 |
| Macedonia, FYR | 2003[b] | 39.0 | 2.4 | 6.1 | 10.8 | 15.5 | 22.2 | 45.5 | 29.6 |
| Madagascar | 2001[b] | 47.5 | 1.9 | 4.9 | 8.5 | 12.7 | 20.4 | 53.5 | 36.6 |
| Malawi | 2004–05[b] | 39.0 | 2.9 | 7.0 | 10.8 | 14.8 | 20.7 | 46.6 | 31.8 |
| Malaysia | 1997[d] | 49.2 | 1.7 | 4.4 | 8.1 | 12.9 | 20.3 | 54.3 | 38.4 |
| Mali | 2001[b] | 40.1 | 2.4 | 6.1 | 10.2 | 14.7 | 22.2 | 46.6 | 30.2 |
| Mauritania | 2000[b] | 39.0 | 2.5 | 6.2 | 10.6 | 15.2 | 22.3 | 45.7 | 29.5 |
| Mauritius | | .. | .. | .. | .. | .. | .. | .. | .. |
| Mexico | 2004[b] | 46.1 | 1.6 | 4.3 | 8.3 | 12.6 | 19.7 | 55.1 | 39.4 |
| Moldova | 2003[b] | 33.2 | 3.2 | 7.8 | 12.2 | 16.5 | 22.1 | 41.4 | 26.4 |
| Mongolia | 2002[b] | 32.8 | 3.0 | 7.5 | 12.2 | 16.8 | 23.1 | 40.5 | 24.6 |
| Morocco | 1998–99[b] | 39.5 | 2.6 | 6.5 | 10.6 | 14.8 | 21.3 | 46.6 | 30.9 |
| Mozambique | 2002–03[b] | 47.3 | 2.1 | 5.4 | 9.3 | 13.0 | 18.7 | 53.6 | 39.4 |
| Myanmar | | .. | .. | .. | .. | .. | .. | .. | .. |
| Namibia | 1993[d] | 74.3 | 0.5 | 1.4 | 3.0 | 5.4 | 11.5 | 78.7 | 64.5 |
| Nepal | 2003–04[b] | 47.2 | 2.6 | 6.0 | 9.0 | 12.4 | 18.0 | 54.6 | 40.6 |
| Netherlands | 1999[d] | 30.9 | 2.5 | 7.6 | 13.2 | 17.2 | 23.3 | 38.7 | 22.9 |
| New Zealand | 1997[d] | 36.2 | 2.2 | 6.4 | 11.4 | 15.8 | 22.6 | 43.8 | 27.8 |
| Nicaragua | 2001[b] | 43.1 | 2.2 | 5.6 | 9.8 | 14.2 | 21.1 | 49.3 | 33.8 |
| Niger | 1995[b] | 50.5 | 0.8 | 2.6 | 7.1 | 13.9 | 23.1 | 53.3 | 35.4 |
| Nigeria | 2003[b] | 43.7 | 1.9 | 5.0 | 9.6 | 14.5 | 21.7 | 49.2 | 33.2 |
| Norway | 2000[d] | 25.8 | 3.9 | 9.6 | 14.0 | 17.2 | 22.0 | 37.2 | 23.4 |
| Oman | | .. | .. | .. | .. | .. | .. | .. | .. |
| Pakistan | 2005[b] | 31.2 | 3.9 | 9.1 | 12.9 | 16.1 | 21.1 | 40.8 | 26.5 |
| Panama | 2003[d] | 56.1 | 0.7 | 2.5 | 6.6 | 11.4 | 19.6 | 59.9 | 43.0 |
| Papua New Guinea | 1996[b] | 50.9 | 1.7 | 4.5 | 7.9 | 11.9 | 19.2 | 56.5 | 40.5 |
| Paraguay | 2003[d] | 58.4 | 0.7 | 2.4 | 6.3 | 10.8 | 18.6 | 61.9 | 46.1 |
| Peru | 2003[d] | 52.0 | 1.3 | 3.7 | 7.7 | 12.2 | 19.7 | 56.7 | 40.9 |
| Philippines | 2003[b] | 44.5 | 2.2 | 5.4 | 9.1 | 13.6 | 21.3 | 50.6 | 34.2 |
| Poland | 2005[b] | 34.9 | 3.0 | 7.4 | 11.7 | 16.1 | 22.3 | 42.5 | 27.2 |
| Portugal | 1997[d] | 38.5 | 2.0 | 5.8 | 11.0 | 15.5 | 21.9 | 45.9 | 29.8 |
| Puerto Rico | | .. | .. | .. | .. | .. | .. | .. | .. |

| | Survey year | Gini index | Percentage share of income or consumption[a] | | | | | | |
|---|---|---|---|---|---|---|---|---|---|
| | | | Lowest 10% | Lowest 20% | Second 20% | Third 20% | Fourth 20% | Highest 20% | Highest 10% |
| Romania | 2005[b] | 31.5 | 3.3 | 8.2 | 12.8 | 16.9 | 22.1 | 40.0 | 25.4 |
| Russian Federation | 2002[b] | 39.9 | 2.4 | 6.1 | 10.5 | 14.9 | 21.8 | 46.6 | 30.6 |
| Rwanda | 2000[b] | 46.8 | 2.1 | 5.3 | 9.1 | 13.2 | 19.4 | 53.0 | 38.2 |
| Saudi Arabia | | .. | .. | .. | .. | .. | .. | .. | .. |
| Senegal | 2001[b] | 41.3 | 2.7 | 6.6 | 10.3 | 14.2 | 20.6 | 48.4 | 33.4 |
| Serbia[e] | 2003[b] | 30.0 | 3.4 | 8.3 | 13.0 | 17.3 | 23.0 | 38.4 | 23.4 |
| Sierra Leone | 2003[b] | 40.0 | 2.6 | 6.5 | 10.5 | 14.5 | 21.2 | 47.3 | 31.2 |
| Singapore | 1998[d] | 42.5 | 1.9 | 5.0 | 9.4 | 14.6 | 22.0 | 49.0 | 32.8 |
| Slovak Republic | 1996[d] | 25.8 | 3.1 | 8.8 | 14.9 | 18.7 | 22.8 | 34.8 | 20.9 |
| Slovenia | 2004[b] | 30.9 | 3.4 | 8.3 | 12.8 | 16.7 | 22.6 | 39.6 | 24.6 |
| Somalia | | .. | .. | .. | .. | .. | .. | .. | .. |
| South Africa | 2000[b] | 57.8 | 1.4 | 3.5 | 6.3 | 10.0 | 18.0 | 62.2 | 44.7 |
| Spain | 2000[d] | 34.7 | 2.6 | 7.0 | 12.1 | 16.4 | 22.5 | 42.0 | 26.6 |
| Sri Lanka | 2002[b] | 40.2 | 3.0 | 7.0 | 10.5 | 14.2 | 20.4 | 48.0 | 32.7 |
| Sudan | | .. | .. | .. | .. | .. | .. | .. | .. |
| Swaziland | 2000–01[d] | 50.4 | 1.6 | 4.3 | 8.2 | 12.3 | 18.9 | 56.3 | 40.7 |
| Sweden | 2000[d] | 25.0 | 3.6 | 9.1 | 14.0 | 17.6 | 22.7 | 36.6 | 22.2 |
| Switzerland | 2000[d] | 33.7 | 2.9 | 7.6 | 12.2 | 16.3 | 22.6 | 41.3 | 25.9 |
| Syrian Arab Republic | | .. | .. | .. | .. | .. | .. | .. | .. |
| Tajikistan | 2004[b] | 33.6 | 3.2 | 7.8 | 12.0 | 16.4 | 21.9 | 41.9 | 26.6 |
| Tanzania | 2000–01[b] | 34.6 | 2.9 | 7.3 | 12.0 | 16.1 | 22.3 | 42.4 | 26.9 |
| Thailand | 2002[b] | 42.0 | 2.7 | 6.3 | 9.9 | 14.0 | 20.8 | 49.0 | 33.4 |
| Timor-Leste | | .. | .. | .. | .. | .. | .. | .. | .. |
| Togo | | .. | .. | .. | .. | .. | .. | .. | .. |
| Trinidad and Tobago | 1992[d] | 38.9 | 2.2 | 5.9 | 10.8 | 15.3 | 23.1 | 44.9 | 28.8 |
| Tunisia | 2000[b] | 39.8 | 2.3 | 6.0 | 10.3 | 14.8 | 21.7 | 47.3 | 31.5 |
| Turkey | 2003[b] | 43.6 | 2.0 | 5.3 | 9.7 | 14.2 | 21.0 | 49.7 | 34.1 |
| Turkmenistan | 1998[b] | 40.8 | 2.6 | 6.1 | 10.2 | 14.7 | 21.5 | 47.5 | 31.7 |
| Uganda | 2002[b] | 45.7 | 2.3 | 5.7 | 9.4 | 13.2 | 19.1 | 52.5 | 37.7 |
| Ukraine | 2005[b] | 28.2 | 3.8 | 9.0 | 13.5 | 17.4 | 22.7 | 37.4 | 22.6 |
| United Arab Emirates | | .. | .. | .. | .. | .. | .. | .. | .. |
| United Kingdom | 1999[d] | 36.0 | 2.1 | 6.1 | 11.4 | 16.0 | 22.5 | 44.0 | 28.5 |
| United States | 2000[d] | 40.8 | 1.9 | 5.4 | 10.7 | 15.7 | 22.4 | 45.8 | 29.9 |
| Uruguay[c] | 2003[d] | 44.9 | 1.9 | 5.0 | 9.1 | 14.0 | 21.5 | 50.5 | 34.0 |
| Uzbekistan | 2003[b] | 36.8 | 2.8 | 7.2 | 11.7 | 15.4 | 21.0 | 44.7 | 29.6 |
| Venezuela, RB | 2003[d] | 48.2 | 0.7 | 3.3 | 8.7 | 13.9 | 22.0 | 52.1 | 35.2 |
| Vietnam | 2004[b] | 37.0 | 2.9 | 7.1 | 11.1 | 15.1 | 21.8 | 44.8 | 28.9 |
| West Bank and Gaza | | .. | .. | .. | .. | .. | .. | .. | .. |
| Yemen, Rep. | 2005[b] | 37.7 | 2.9 | 7.2 | 11.4 | 15.3 | 20.8 | 45.3 | 30.9 |
| Zambia | 2004[b] | 50.8 | 1.2 | 3.6 | 7.9 | 12.6 | 20.8 | 55.1 | 38.8 |
| Zimbabwe | 1995[b] | 50.1 | 1.8 | 4.6 | 8.1 | 12.2 | 19.3 | 55.7 | 40.3 |

a. Percentage shares by quintile may not sum to 100 percent because of rounding. b. Refers to expenditure shares by percentiles of population, ranked by per capita expenditure. c. Urban data. d. Refers to income shares by percentiles of population, ranked by per capita income. e. Includes Montenegro.

# Distribution of income or consumption

## 2.8

PEOPLE

## About the data

Inequality in the distribution of income is reflected in the percentage shares of income or consumption accruing to portions of the population ranked by income or consumption levels. The portions ranked lowest by personal income receive the smallest shares of total income. The Gini index provides a convenient summary measure of the degree of inequality. Data on the distribution of income or consumption come from nationally representative household surveys. Where the original data from the household survey were available, they have been used to directly calculate the income or consumption shares by quintile. Otherwise, shares have been estimated from the best available grouped data.

The distribution data have been adjusted for household size, providing a more consistent measure of per capita income or consumption. No adjustment has been made for spatial differences in cost of living within countries, because the data needed for such calculations are generally unavailable. For further details on the estimation method for low- and middle-income economies, see Ravallion and Chen (1996).

Because the underlying household surveys differ in method and type of data collected, the distribution data are not strictly comparable across countries. These problems are diminishing as survey methods improve and become more standardized,

but achieving strict comparability is still impossible (see *About the data* for table 2.7).

Two sources of noncomparability should be noted in particular. First, the surveys can differ in many respects, including whether they use income or consumption expenditure as the living standard indicator. The distribution of income is typically more unequal than the distribution of consumption. In addition, the definitions of income used differ more often among surveys. Consumption is usually a much better welfare indicator, particularly in developing countries. Second, households differ in size (number of members) and in the extent of income sharing among members. And individuals differ in age and consumption needs. Differences among countries in these respects may bias comparisons of distribution.

World Bank staff have made an effort to ensure that the data are as comparable as possible. Wherever possible, consumption has been used rather than income. Income distribution and Gini indexes for high-income economies are calculated directly from the Luxembourg Income Study database, using an estimation method consistent with that applied for developing countries.

## Definitions

• **Survey year** is the year in which the underlying data were collected. • **Gini index** measures the extent to which the distribution of income (or consumption expenditure) among individuals or households within an economy deviates from a perfectly equal distribution. A Lorenz curve plots the cumulative percentages of total income received against the cumulative number of recipients, starting with the poorest individual. The Gini index measures the area between the Lorenz curve and a hypothetical line of absolute equality, expressed as a percentage of the maximum area under the line. Thus a Gini index of 0 represents perfect equality, while an index of 100 implies perfect inequality. • **Percentage share of income or consumption** is the share of total income or consumption that accrues to subgroups of population indicated by deciles or quintiles.

---

**The Gini coefficient and ratio of income or consumption of the richest quintile to the poorest quintiles are closely correlated**                    2.8a

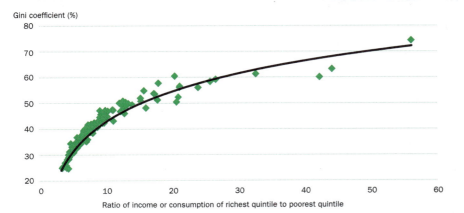

There are many ways to measure income or consumption inequality. The Gini coefficient shows inequality over the entire population; the ratio of income or consumption of the richest quintile to the poorest quintiles shows differences only at the tails of the population distribution. Both measures are closely correlated and provide similar information. At low levels of inequality the Gini coefficient is a more sensitive measure, but above a Gini value of 45–55 percent the inequality ratio rises faster.

*Source: World Development Indicators data files.*

## Data sources

Data on distribution are compiled by the World Bank's Development Research Group using primary household survey data obtained from government statistical agencies and World Bank country departments. Data for high-income economies are from the Luxembourg Income Study database.

| | Urban informal sector employment | | Youth unemployment | | Female-headed households | Pension contributors | | | Public expenditure on pensions | | | |
|---|---|---|---|---|---|---|---|---|---|---|---|---|
| | % of urban employment | | Male % of male labor force ages 15–24 | Female % of female labor force ages 15–24 | % of total | | % of labor force | % of working-age population | | % of GDP | | Average pension % of per capita income |
| | Male 1998–2005[a] | Female 1998–2005[a] | 2003–05[a] | 2003–05[a] | 2003–05[a] | Year | | | Year | | Year | |
| Afghanistan | .. | .. | .. | .. | .. | | .. | .. | 2005 | 0.5 | | .. |
| Albania | .. | .. | .. | .. | .. | 2004 | 48.9 | 33.0 | 2004 | 4.6 | | .. |
| Algeria | .. | .. | 43 | 46 | .. | 2002 | 36.7 | 22.1 | 2002 | 3.2 | 2002 | 89.1 |
| Angola | .. | .. | .. | .. | .. | | .. | .. | | .. | | .. |
| Argentina | .. | .. | 22[b] | 28[b] | .. | 2004 | 35.0 | 25.9 | 1994 | 6.2 | 2002 | 73.7 |
| Armenia | .. | .. | .. | .. | 36 | 2002 | 64.4 | 48.3 | 2004 | 3.4 | | .. |
| Australia | .. | .. | 11[b] | 11[b] | .. | 2005 | 92.6 | 69.6 | 2003 | 5.4 | 2002 | 52.4 |
| Austria | .. | .. | 11 | 10 | .. | 2005 | 96.4 | 68.7 | 2003 | 14.6 | 2002 | 93.2 |
| Azerbaijan | .. | .. | .. | .. | .. | 1996 | 52.0 | 46.0 | 1996 | 2.5 | | .. |
| Bangladesh | .. | .. | 7 | 6 | 10 | 2004 | 2.8 | 2.1 | 1992 | 0.0 | | .. |
| Belarus | .. | .. | .. | .. | 54 | 1992 | 97.0 | 94.0 | 1997 | 7.7 | | .. |
| Belgium | .. | .. | 21 | 19 | .. | 2005 | 94.2 | 61.6 | 2003 | 11.3 | 2002 | 62.8 |
| Benin | 50[b] | 41[b] | .. | .. | 23 | 1996 | 4.8 | .. | 1993 | 0.4 | | .. |
| Bolivia | .. | .. | .. | .. | 20 | 2002 | 10.1 | 7.8 | 2000 | 4.5 | | .. |
| Bosnia and Herzegovina | .. | .. | .. | .. | .. | 2004 | 36.0 | 27.0 | 2004 | 8.8 | | .. |
| Botswana | .. | .. | .. | .. | .. | | .. | .. | | .. | | .. |
| Brazil | .. | .. | 14[b] | 23[b] | .. | 2004 | 52.6 | 39.1 | 2004 | 12.6 | | .. |
| Bulgaria | .. | .. | 23 | 21 | .. | 1994 | 64.0 | 63.0 | 2005 | 8.9 | 2002 | 75.2 |
| Burkina Faso | .. | .. | .. | .. | 9 | 1993 | 3.1 | 3.0 | 1992 | 0.3 | | .. |
| Burundi | .. | .. | .. | .. | .. | 1993 | 3.3 | 3.0 | 1991 | 0.2 | | .. |
| Cambodia | .. | .. | .. | .. | 24 | | .. | .. | | .. | | .. |
| Cameroon | .. | .. | .. | .. | 24 | 1993 | 13.7 | 11.5 | 2001 | 0.8 | | .. |
| Canada | .. | .. | 14[b] | 11[b] | .. | 2005 | 90.5 | 71.4 | 2003 | 5.4 | 2002 | 57.1 |
| Central African Republic | .. | .. | .. | .. | .. | | .. | .. | 1990 | 0.3 | | .. |
| Chad | .. | .. | .. | .. | 20 | 1990 | 1.1 | 1.0 | 1997 | 0.1 | | .. |
| Chile | .. | .. | 15 | 21 | .. | 2003 | 58.0 | 35.2 | 2001 | 2.9 | 2002 | 53.5 |
| China | .. | .. | .. | .. | .. | 2005 | 20.5 | 17.2 | 1996 | 2.7 | | .. |
| Hong Kong, China | .. | .. | 14 | 8 | .. | | .. | .. | | .. | | .. |
| Colombia | .. | .. | 12 | 19 | 30 | 2000 | 19.0 | 14.0 | 1994 | 1.1 | 2002 | 54.4 |
| Congo, Dem. Rep. | .. | .. | .. | .. | .. | | .. | .. | | .. | | .. |
| Congo, Rep. | .. | .. | .. | .. | 23 | 1992 | 5.8 | 5.6 | 1992 | 0.9 | | .. |
| Costa Rica | .. | .. | 11 | 22 | .. | 2004 | 55.3 | 37.6 | 1997 | 4.2 | 2002 | 103.1 |
| Côte d'Ivoire | .. | .. | .. | .. | .. | 1997 | 9.3 | 9.1 | 1997 | 0.3 | | .. |
| Croatia | .. | .. | 27[c] | 31[c] | .. | 2005 | 77.0 | 50.0 | 2005 | 12.3 | 2002 | 61.6 |
| Cuba | .. | .. | .. | .. | 46 | | .. | .. | 1992 | 12.6 | | .. |
| Czech Republic | .. | .. | 19 | 19 | .. | 2003 | 86.3 | 61.5 | 2003 | 8.7 | 2002 | 58.2 |
| Denmark | .. | .. | 6 | 10 | .. | 2005 | 94.6 | 75.0 | 2003 | 11.0 | 2002 | 54.1 |
| Dominican Republic | .. | .. | .. | .. | 28 | 2005 | 27.2 | 18.6 | 2000 | 0.8 | 2002 | 55.9 |
| Ecuador | 32[b] | 42[b] | 12[b] | 21[b] | .. | 2004 | 27.0 | 20.8 | 2002 | 2.5 | | .. |
| Egypt, Arab Rep. | .. | .. | .. | .. | 12 | 2004 | 55.5 | 27.7 | 2004 | 4.1 | 2002 | 119.8 |
| El Salvador | 43[c] | 55[c] | 13[c] | 10[c] | .. | 2005 | 29.8 | 19.7 | 1997 | 1.3 | 2002 | 39.3 |
| Eritrea | .. | .. | .. | .. | 47 | | .. | .. | 2001 | 0.3 | | .. |
| Estonia | .. | .. | 16 | 15 | .. | 2004 | 95.2 | 68.6 | 2003 | 6.0 | 2002 | 60.9 |
| Ethiopia | 33[b] | 46[b] | 4 | 11 | 23 | | .. | .. | 1993 | 0.9 | | .. |
| Finland | .. | .. | 21 | 19 | .. | 2005 | 88.7 | 67.2 | 2003 | 11.2 | 2002 | 78.8 |
| France | .. | .. | 21 | 25[b] | .. | 2005 | 89.9 | 61.4 | 2003 | 13.1 | 2002 | 65.0 |
| Gabon | .. | .. | .. | .. | 26 | 1995 | 15.0 | 14.0 | | .. | | .. |
| Gambia, The | .. | .. | .. | .. | .. | 2003 | 3.8 | 2.9 | | .. | | .. |
| Georgia | 21[b] | 7[b] | 27 | 31 | .. | 2004 | 29.9 | 22.7 | 2004 | 3.0 | | .. |
| Germany | .. | .. | 16 | 14 | .. | 2005 | 88.2 | 65.5 | 2003 | 13.3 | 2002 | 71.8 |
| Ghana | .. | .. | .. | .. | 34 | 2003 | 9.1 | 7.1 | 2002 | 1.3 | | .. |
| Greece | .. | .. | 18 | 35 | .. | 2005 | 85.2 | 58.5 | 2003 | 12.8 | 2002 | 99.9 |
| Guatemala | .. | .. | .. | .. | .. | 2000 | 19.0 | 11.7 | 1995 | 0.7 | | .. |
| Guinea | .. | .. | .. | .. | 17 | 1993 | 1.5 | 1.8 | | .. | | .. |
| Guinea-Bissau | .. | .. | .. | .. | .. | 2004 | 1.9 | 1.5 | 2005 | 2.1 | | .. |
| Haiti | .. | .. | .. | .. | 44 | | .. | .. | | .. | | .. |

# Assessing vulnerability and security

| | Urban informal sector employment | | Youth unemployment | | Female-headed households | Pension contributors | | | Public expenditure on pensions | | | |
|---|---|---|---|---|---|---|---|---|---|---|---|---|
| | % of urban employment | | Male % of male labor force ages 15–24 | Female % of female labor force ages 15–24 | % of total | | % of labor force | % of working-age population | | % of GDP | | Average pension % of per capita income |
| | Male 1998–2005[a] | Female 1998–2005[a] | 2003–05[a] | 2003–05[a] | 2003–05[a] | Year | | | Year | | Year | |
| Honduras | .. | .. | 5[b] | 11[b] | 26 | 1999 | 20.6 | 17.7 | 1994 | 0.6 | | .. |
| Hungary | .. | .. | 20 | 19 | .. | 2002 | 56.3 | 34.0 | 2003 | 9.1 | 2002 | 90.5 |
| India | 54[b] | 41[b] | 10[b] | 11[b] | .. | 2004 | 9.0 | 5.7 | | .. | | |
| Indonesia | .. | .. | 25 | 34 | 12 | 2002 | 15.5 | 11.3 | | .. | | |
| Iran, Islamic Rep. | .. | .. | 20 | 32 | .. | 2001 | 35.0 | 20.0 | 2000 | 1.1 | 2002 | 124.2 |
| Iraq | .. | .. | .. | .. | 11 | .. | .. | .. | | .. | | |
| Ireland | .. | .. | 9 | 7 | .. | 2005 | 88.0 | 63.9 | 2003 | 4.1 | 2002 | 36.6 |
| Israel | .. | .. | 17 | 19 | .. | 1992 | 82.0 | 63.0 | 1996 | 5.9 | | .. |
| Italy | .. | .. | 22 | 27 | .. | 2005 | 92.4 | 58.4 | 2003 | 14.7 | 2002 | 88.8 |
| Jamaica | .. | .. | 22 | 36 | .. | 2004 | 17.4 | 12.6 | | .. | | .. |
| Japan | .. | .. | 10[b] | 7[b] | .. | 2005 | 95.3 | 75.0 | 2003 | 8.9 | 2002 | 59.1 |
| Jordan | .. | .. | .. | .. | 12 | 2003 | 30.3 | 17.4 | 2001 | 2.2 | 2002 | 76.1 |
| Kazakhstan | .. | .. | 10[c] | 15[c] | .. | 2004 | 33.8 | 26.4 | 2004 | 4.9 | | .. |
| Kenya | .. | .. | .. | .. | 32 | 2005 | 8.0 | 6.7 | 1993 | 0.5 | | .. |
| Korea, Dem. Rep. | .. | .. | .. | .. | .. | .. | .. | .. | | .. | | .. |
| Korea, Rep. | .. | .. | 12 | 9 | .. | 2005 | 74.3 | 52.0 | 2003 | 1.3 | 2002 | 43.3 |
| Kuwait | .. | .. | .. | .. | .. | .. | .. | .. | 1990 | 3.5 | | .. |
| Kyrgyz Republic | 33[b] | 25[b] | 14 | 18 | .. | 2006 | 42.2 | 28.9 | 2006 | 4.8 | | .. |
| Lao PDR | .. | .. | .. | .. | .. | .. | .. | .. | | .. | | .. |
| Latvia | .. | .. | 12 | 14 | .. | 2003 | 92.4 | 66.5 | 2002 | 7.5 | 2002 | 81.8 |
| Lebanon | .. | .. | .. | .. | .. | 2003 | 33.1 | 19.9 | 2003 | 2.1 | | .. |
| Lesotho | .. | .. | .. | .. | 37 | 2005 | 5.7 | 3.6 | | .. | | .. |
| Liberia | .. | .. | .. | .. | .. | .. | .. | .. | | .. | | .. |
| Libya | .. | .. | .. | .. | .. | 2003 | 65.5 | 38.1 | 2001 | 2.1 | 2002 | 91.2 |
| Lithuania | 50[b] | 27[b] | 16 | 15 | .. | 2004 | 79.7 | 56.0 | 2003 | 6.2 | 2002 | 71.3 |
| Macedonia, FYR | .. | .. | 63 | 62 | 8 | 2000 | 63.8 | 38.9 | 1998 | 8.7 | | .. |
| Madagascar | .. | .. | 7 | 7 | 22 | 1993 | 5.4 | 4.8 | 1990 | 0.2 | | .. |
| Malawi | .. | .. | .. | .. | 25 | .. | .. | .. | | .. | | .. |
| Malaysia | .. | .. | .. | .. | .. | 1993 | 48.7 | 37.8 | 1999 | 6.5 | | .. |
| Mali | .. | .. | .. | .. | 11 | 1990 | 2.5 | 2.0 | 1991 | 0.4 | | .. |
| Mauritania | .. | .. | .. | .. | 29 | 1995 | 5.0 | 4.0 | 1992 | 0.2 | | .. |
| Mauritius | .. | .. | 21 | 34 | .. | 2000 | 51.4 | 33.6 | 1999 | 4.4 | | .. |
| Mexico | 18[b] | 22[b] | 6 | 7 | .. | 2002 | 34.5 | 22.7 | 2003 | 1.3 | 2002 | 45.1 |
| Moldova | .. | .. | 19 | 18 | .. | 2000 | 60.6 | 43.1 | 2003 | 8.0 | | .. |
| Mongolia | .. | .. | 20 | 21 | .. | 2002 | 61.4 | 49.1 | 2002 | 5.8 | | .. |
| Morocco | .. | .. | 18[c] | 14[c] | 17 | 2003 | 22.4 | 12.8 | 2003 | 1.9 | 2002 | 74.1 |
| Mozambique | .. | .. | .. | .. | 26 | 1995 | 2.0 | 2.1 | 1996 | 0.0 | | .. |
| Myanmar | .. | .. | .. | .. | .. | .. | .. | .. | | .. | | .. |
| Namibia | .. | .. | .. | .. | 42 | .. | .. | .. | | .. | | .. |
| Nepal | 60[b] | 76[b] | .. | .. | 23 | 2003 | 2.1 | 1.4 | 2003 | 0.3 | | .. |
| Netherlands | .. | .. | 10 | 10 | .. | 2005 | 90.3 | 70.4 | 2003 | 12.8 | 2002 | 84.1 |
| New Zealand | .. | .. | 9[b] | 10[b] | .. | .. | .. | .. | 2003 | 7.4 | 2002 | 39.5 |
| Nicaragua | .. | .. | 11 | 16 | 31 | 2005 | 17.9 | 11.5 | 1996 | 2.5 | | .. |
| Niger | .. | .. | .. | .. | 19 | 1992 | 1.3 | 1.5 | 2005 | 0.2 | | .. |
| Nigeria | .. | .. | .. | .. | 17 | 2005 | 1.7 | 1.2 | 1991 | 0.1 | | .. |
| Norway | .. | .. | 13 | 12 | .. | 2005 | 90.8 | 75.7 | 2003 | 10.7 | 2002 | 65.1 |
| Oman | .. | .. | .. | .. | .. | .. | .. | .. | | .. | | .. |
| Pakistan | 44[b] | 22[b] | 11 | 15 | .. | 2004 | 6.4 | 4.0 | 1993 | 0.9 | | .. |
| Panama | .. | .. | 19 | 30 | .. | 1998 | 51.6 | 40.7 | 1996 | 4.3 | | .. |
| Papua New Guinea | .. | .. | .. | .. | .. | .. | .. | .. | | .. | | .. |
| Paraguay | .. | .. | 12[b] | 21[b] | .. | 2004 | 11.6 | 9.1 | 2001 | 1.2 | | .. |
| Peru | 56[b] | 55[b] | 21[b] | 21[b] | 22 | 2003 | 16.3 | 12.3 | 2000 | 2.6 | 2002 | 43.9 |
| Philippines | .. | .. | 15 | 19 | 15 | 2000 | 27.1 | 18.7 | 1993 | 1.0 | | .. |
| Poland | .. | .. | 37 | 39 | .. | 2005 | 84.9 | 54.5 | 2003 | 13.9 | 2002 | 69.7 |
| Portugal | .. | .. | 14 | 19 | .. | 2005 | 91.4 | 71.9 | 2003 | 11.9 | 2002 | 79.8 |
| Puerto Rico | .. | .. | 25[b] | 21[b] | .. | .. | .. | .. | | .. | | .. |

# Assessing vulnerability and security

| | Urban informal sector employment | | Youth unemployment | | Female-headed households | Pension contributors | | | Public expenditure on pensions | | | |
|---|---|---|---|---|---|---|---|---|---|---|---|---|
| | % of urban employment | | Male % of male labor force ages 15–24 | Female % of female labor force ages 15–24 | % of total | | % of labor force | % of working-age population | | % of GDP | | Average pension % of per capita income |
| | Male 1998–2005[a] | Female 1998–2005[a] | 2003–05[a] | 2003–05[a] | 2003–05[a] | Year | | | Year | | Year | |
| Romania | .. | .. | 21 | 18 | .. | 2005 | 57.6 | 39.1 | 2003 | 6.9 | | .. |
| Russian Federation | .. | .. | .. | .. | .. | | .. | | 2004 | 5.8 | | .. |
| Rwanda | .. | .. | .. | .. | 34 | 2004 | 4.8 | 4.1 | | .. | | .. |
| Saudi Arabia | .. | .. | .. | .. | .. | | .. | .. | | .. | | .. |
| Senegal | .. | .. | .. | .. | 23 | 2003 | 5.3 | 3.9 | 2003 | 1.3 | | .. |
| Serbia | .. | .. | .. | .. | 26 | 2003 | 46.0[d] | 32.2[d] | 2003 | 12.4[d] | | .. |
| Sierra Leone | .. | .. | .. | .. | .. | 2004 | 4.6 | 3.6 | | .. | | .. |
| Singapore | .. | .. | 4 | 6 | .. | 1995 | 73.0 | 56.0 | 1996 | 1.4 | | .. |
| Slovak Republic | .. | .. | 31 | 29 | .. | 2003 | 78.5 | 55.3 | 2003 | 8.5 | 2002 | 60.2 |
| Slovenia | .. | .. | 11 | 12 | .. | 1995 | 86.0 | 68.7 | 2003 | 10.1 | | .. |
| Somalia | .. | .. | .. | .. | .. | | .. | .. | | .. | | .. |
| South Africa | 16 | 28 | 56 | 65 | .. | | .. | .. | | .. | | .. |
| Spain | .. | .. | 17 | 24 | .. | 2005 | 91.0 | 63.2 | 2003 | 9.2 | 2002 | 88.3 |
| Sri Lanka | .. | .. | 20[b] | 37[b] | .. | 2004 | 35.6 | 22.2 | 1996 | 2.4 | | .. |
| Sudan | .. | .. | .. | .. | 19 | 1995 | 12.1 | 12.0 | | .. | | .. |
| Swaziland | .. | .. | .. | .. | .. | | .. | .. | | .. | | .. |
| Sweden | .. | .. | 23 | 22 | .. | 2005 | 91.0 | 72.3 | 2003 | 12.7 | 2002 | 68.2 |
| Switzerland | .. | .. | 9 | 9 | .. | 2005 | 100.0 | 79.1 | 2003 | 12.1 | 2002 | 67.3 |
| Syrian Arab Republic | .. | .. | .. | .. | .. | 2004 | 17.4 | 11.4 | 2004 | 1.3 | | .. |
| Tajikistan | .. | .. | .. | .. | .. | | .. | .. | 1996 | 3.0 | | .. |
| Tanzania | .. | .. | .. | .. | 25 | 1996 | 2.0 | 2.0 | | .. | | .. |
| Thailand | .. | .. | 5 | 5 | 30 | 2003 | 22.5 | 18.0 | | .. | | .. |
| Timor-Leste | .. | .. | .. | .. | .. | | .. | .. | | .. | | .. |
| Togo | .. | .. | .. | .. | .. | 1997 | 15.9 | 15.0 | 1997 | 0.6 | | .. |
| Trinidad and Tobago | .. | .. | .. | .. | .. | 2004 | 55.6 | .. | 1996 | 0.6 | | .. |
| Tunisia | .. | .. | 31 | 29 | .. | 2004 | 45.3 | 25.4 | 2003 | 4.3 | 2002 | 72.7 |
| Turkey | 10[b] | 6[b] | 19 | 19 | .. | 2002 | 45.0 | 24.3 | 2002 | 7.1 | 2002 | 103.3 |
| Turkmenistan | .. | .. | .. | .. | 27 | | .. | .. | 1996 | 2.3 | | .. |
| Uganda | .. | .. | .. | .. | 30 | 2004 | 10.7 | 9.3 | 2003 | 0.3 | | .. |
| Ukraine | 3[b] | 3[b] | 15 | 14 | .. | 2005 | 76.0 | 52.3 | 2005 | 15.4 | | .. |
| United Arab Emirates | .. | .. | .. | .. | .. | | .. | .. | | .. | | .. |
| United Kingdom | .. | .. | 13 | 10 | .. | 2005 | 92.7 | 71.4 | 2003 | 10.9 | 2002 | 47.6 |
| United States | .. | .. | 12[b] | 10[b] | .. | 2005 | 92.5 | 72.5 | 2003 | 7.5 | 2002 | 51.0 |
| Uruguay | .. | .. | 25 | 35 | .. | 2004 | 55.0 | 44.3 | 1996 | 15.0 | 2002 | 125.4 |
| Uzbekistan | .. | .. | .. | .. | .. | | .. | .. | 1995 | 5.3 | | .. |
| Venezuela, RB | .. | .. | 24 | 35 | .. | 2004 | 31.8 | 23.8 | 2001 | 2.7 | | .. |
| Vietnam | .. | .. | 4 | 5 | 27 | 2005 | 13.2 | 10.8 | 1998 | 1.6 | | .. |
| West Bank and Gaza | .. | .. | 39 | 45 | .. | 2000 | 18.8 | 7.8 | 2001 | 0.8 | | .. |
| Yemen, Rep. | .. | .. | .. | .. | .. | 2005 | 10.0 | 5.5 | 1994 | 0.1 | 2002 | 106.3 |
| Zambia | .. | .. | .. | .. | 23 | 2000 | 5.9 | 4.9 | 1993 | 0.1 | | .. |
| Zimbabwe | .. | .. | .. | .. | 38 | 1995 | 12.0 | 10.0 | 2002 | 2.3 | | .. |
| **World** | | | .. w | .. w | | | | | | | | |
| **Low income** | | | .. | .. | | | | | | | | |
| **Middle income** | | | .. | .. | | | | | | | | |
| Lower middle income | | | .. | .. | | | | | | | | |
| Upper middle income | | | 21 | 26 | | | | | | | | |
| **Low & middle income** | | | .. | .. | | | | | | | | |
| East Asia & Pacific | | | .. | .. | | | | | | | | |
| Europe & Central Asia | | | .. | .. | | | | | | | | |
| Latin America & Carib. | | | 14 | 20 | | | | | | | | |
| Middle East & N. Africa | | | .. | .. | | | | | | | | |
| South Asia | | | 11 | 12 | | | | | | | | |
| Sub-Saharan Africa | | | .. | .. | | | | | | | | |
| **High income** | | | 14 | 13 | | | | | | | | |
| Euro area | | | 18 | 20 | | | | | | | | |

a. Data are for the most recent year available. b. Limited coverage. c. Data are for 2006. d. Includes Montenegro.

# Assessing vulnerability and security

## About the data

As traditionally measured, poverty is a static concept, and vulnerability a dynamic one. Vulnerability reflects a household's resilience in the face of shocks and the likelihood that a shock will lead to a decline in well-being. Thus, it depends primarily on the household's assets and insurance mechanisms. Because poor people have fewer assets and less diversified sources of income than do the better-off, fluctuations in income affect them more.

Enhancing security for poor people means reducing their vulnerability to such risks as ill health, providing them the means to manage risk themselves, and strengthening market or public institutions for managing risk. Tools include microfinance programs, public provision of education and basic health care, and old age assistance (see tables 2.10 and 2.15).

Poor households face many risks, and vulnerability is thus multidimensional. The indicators in the table focus on individual risks—informal sector employment, youth unemployment, female-headed households, income insecurity in old age—and the extent to which publicly provided services may be capable of mitigating some of these risks. Poor people face labor market risks, often having to take up precarious, low-quality jobs in the informal sector and to increase their household's labor market participation by sending their children to work (see table 2.6). Income security is a prime concern for the elderly.

Data on informal sector employment are from a variety of sources, including labor force and special informal sector surveys, household surveys, surveys of household industries or economic activities, surveys of small enterprises and microenterprises, and official estimates. In most countries data on the informal economy are collected on an ad hoc basis or less frequently than annually. The international comparability of the data is affected by differences among countries in definitions and coverage and in treatment of domestic workers. The data in the table are based on national definitions of informal sector and urban areas established by countries, and therefore data may not be comparable across countries. For details on these definitions, consult the original source.

Youth unemployment is an important policy issue for many economies. Experiencing unemployment may permanently impair a young person's productive potential and future employment opportunities. The table presents unemployment among youth ages 15–24, but the lower age limit for young people in a country could be determined by the minimum age for leaving school, so age groups could differ across countries. Also, since this age group is

likely to include school leavers, the level of youth unemployment varies considerably over the year as a result of different school opening and closing dates. The youth unemployment rate shares similar limitations on comparability as the general unemployment rate. For further information, see *About the data* for table 2.5 and the original source.

The definition of female-headed household differs greatly across countries, making cross-country comparison difficult. In some cases it is assumed that a woman cannot be the head of any household with an adult male, because of sex-biased stereotype. Caution should be exercised in interpreting the data.

Pension scheme coverage may be broad or even universal where eligibility is determined by citizenship, residency, or income status. In contribution-related schemes, however, eligibility is usually restricted to individuals who have contributed for a minimum number of years. Definitional issues—relating to the labor force, for example—may arise in comparing coverage by contribution-related schemes over time and across countries (for country-specific information, see Palacios and Pallares-Miralles 2000). The share of the labor force covered by a pension scheme may be overstated in countries that do not try to count informal sector workers as part of the labor force.

Public interventions and institutions can provide services directly to poor people, although whether these interventions and institutions work well for the poor is debated. State action is often ineffective, in part because governments can influence only a few of the many sources of well-being and in part because of difficulties in delivering goods and services. The effectiveness of public provision is further constrained by the fiscal resources at governments' disposal and the fact that state institutions may not be responsive to the needs of poor people.

The data on public pension spending cover non-contributory pensions or social assistance targeted to the elderly and disabled and spending by social insurance schemes for which contributions had previously been made. A country's pattern of spending is correlated with its demographic structure—spending increases as the population ages.

## Definitions

• **Urban informal sector employment** is all people who, during a given reference period, were employed in at least one informal enterprise, irrespective of their status in employment and whether it was their main or secondary job. • **Youth unemployment** is the share of the labor force ages 15–24 without work but available for and seeking employment. • **Female-headed households** are the percentage of households with a female head. • **Pension contributors** are the share of the labor force or working-age population (here defined as ages 15–64) covered by a pension scheme. • **Public expenditure on pensions** is all government expenditures on cash transfers to the elderly, the disabled, and survivors and the administrative costs of these programs. • **Average pension** is estimated by dividing total pension expenditure by the number of pensioners.

## Data sources

Data on urban informal sector employment and youth unemployment are from the ILO database Key Indicators of the Labour Market, 5th edition. Data on female-headed household are from Demographic and Health Surveys by Macro International. Data on pension contributors and pension spending are from the World Bank Pensions Database (available June 2008).

# 2.10 Education inputs

| | Public expenditure per student[a] | | | | | | Public expenditure on education | | Trained teachers in primary education | Primary school pupil-teacher ratio |
|---|---|---|---|---|---|---|---|---|---|---|
| | Primary | | % of GDP per capita Secondary | | Tertiary | | % of GDP | % of total government expenditure | % of total | pupils per teacher |
| | 1991 | 2006[b] | 1999 | 2006[b] | 1999 | 2006[b] | 2006[b] | 2006[b] | 2006[b] | 2006[b] |
| Afghanistan | .. | .. | .. | .. | .. | .. | .. | .. | 36.5 | 83 |
| Albania | .. | .. | .. | .. | .. | .. | .. | .. | .. | 21 |
| Algeria | 26.5 | .. | .. | .. | .. | .. | .. | .. | 99.3 | 24 |
| Angola | .. | .. | .. | .. | .. | 65.5 | 2.4 | .. | .. | .. |
| Argentina | .. | 11.3 | 16.4 | 15.7 | 17.7 | 11.8 | 3.8 | 13.1 | .. | 17 |
| Armenia | .. | .. | 12.4 | .. | 29.1 | .. | .. | .. | 77.5 | 21 |
| Australia | .. | 15.9 | 14.5 | 14.5 | 25.7 | 22.5 | 4.6 | .. | .. | .. |
| Austria | 18.2 | 22.5 | 29.9 | 27.2 | 51.6 | 48.5 | 5.4 | 10.8 | .. | 12 |
| Azerbaijan | .. | 5.5 | 17.0 | 8.5 | 19.1 | 9.4 | 2.1 | 17.4 | 100.0 | 13 |
| Bangladesh | .. | 7.6 | 12.4 | 14.6 | 46.3 | 49.4 | 2.5 | 14.2 | 48.3 | 51 |
| Belarus | .. | 14.3 | .. | 27.0 | .. | 29.0 | 6.1 | 12.9 | 99.6 | 16 |
| Belgium | 15.8 | 20.0 | 23.7 | 33.5 | 38.3 | 35.1 | 6.0 | 12.2 | .. | 11 |
| Benin | .. | 11.5 | 26.1 | .. | 202.9 | .. | 4.4 | 17.1 | 72.2 | 47 |
| Bolivia | .. | .. | 11.7 | .. | 44.1 | .. | .. | .. | .. | 24 |
| Bosnia and Herzegovina | .. | .. | .. | .. | .. | .. | .. | .. | .. | .. |
| Botswana | .. | 15.7 | .. | 40.2 | .. | 438.4 | 8.7[c] | 21.0[c] | 96.7 | 25 |
| Brazil | .. | 12.8 | 9.5 | 11.5 | 57.0 | 32.6 | 4.0 | .. | .. | 21 |
| Bulgaria | .. | 11.9 | 18.8 | 10.8 | 17.9 | 17.8 | 2.5 | .. | .. | 16 |
| Burkina Faso | .. | 27.4 | .. | 20.5 | .. | 208.1 | 4.2 | 15.4 | 86.9 | 46 |
| Burundi | 13.4 | 19.1 | .. | 74.5 | 1,051.9 | 348.8 | 5.1 | 17.7 | 87.5 | 54 |
| Cambodia | .. | 5.6 | 11.4 | .. | 43.8 | .. | 1.7 | .. | 98.3 | 50 |
| Cameroon | .. | 6.3 | 16.5 | 22.8 | 63.0 | 94.1 | 3.3 | 16.8 | 61.8 | 44 |
| Canada | .. | .. | .. | .. | 47.9 | .. | .. | .. | .. | .. |
| Central African Republic | 11.9 | 10.5 | .. | .. | .. | 291.3 | 1.4 | .. | 49.7 | .. |
| Chad | 8.0 | 6.8 | 27.5 | 28.0 | .. | 333.9 | 1.9 | 10.1 | 26.8 | 63 |
| Chile | .. | 11.9 | 14.8 | 13.1 | 19.4 | 11.6 | 3.4 | 18.5 | .. | 26 |
| China | .. | .. | 11.5 | .. | 90.1 | .. | .. | .. | .. | 18 |
|   Hong Kong, China | .. | 14.1 | 17.7 | 18.2 | .. | 58.3 | 3.9 | 23.9 | 94.8 | 18 |
| Colombia | .. | 19.2 | 16.9 | 18.0 | 39.6 | 23.6 | 4.7 | 11.1 | .. | 28 |
| Congo, Dem. Rep. | .. | .. | .. | .. | .. | .. | .. | .. | .. | .. |
| Congo, Rep. | .. | 3.4 | .. | .. | 404.9 | .. | 1.9 | 8.1 | 89.0 | 55 |
| Costa Rica | 7.8 | 17.0 | 23.2 | 17.1 | 55.0 | 35.9 | 4.7 | 29.8 | 88.0 | 20 |
| Côte d'Ivoire | .. | .. | 54.5 | .. | 212.8 | .. | .. | .. | .. | 46 |
| Croatia | .. | 23.7 | .. | 22.5 | 41.5 | 27.9 | 4.4 | 9.1 | 100.0 | 15 |
| Cuba | 21.6 | 33.8 | 41.3 | 43.0 | 86.4 | 34.5 | 9.1 | 14.2 | 100.0 | 10 |
| Czech Republic | .. | 12.8 | 21.7 | 23.3 | 33.7 | 30.4 | 4.4 | 10.0 | .. | 16 |
| Denmark | .. | 24.8 | 38.1 | 35.3 | 65.9 | 62.5 | 8.4 | 15.3 | .. | .. |
| Dominican Republic | .. | 8.2 | .. | 5.9 | .. | .. | 3.6 | 16.8 | 88.3 | 23 |
| Ecuador | .. | .. | 9.7 | .. | .. | .. | .. | .. | 71.1 | 23 |
| Egypt, Arab Rep. | .. | .. | .. | .. | .. | .. | .. | .. | .. | 26 |
| El Salvador | .. | 10.0 | 7.9 | 9.3 | 9.4 | 16.6 | 3.1 | 20.0 | 94.0 | 40 |
| Eritrea | .. | 9.3 | 37.3 | 9.3 | 429.4 | 1,082.5 | 5.3 | .. | 87.5 | 47 |
| Estonia | .. | 19.2 | 27.9 | 25.5 | 32.6 | 18.2 | 5.1 | 14.9 | .. | .. |
| Ethiopia | 22.1 | 14.1 | .. | 13.7 | .. | 747.7 | 6.0 | 17.5 | .. | 59 |
| Finland | 21.7 | 18.8 | 26.2 | 32.9 | 40.9 | 36.7 | 6.5 | 12.8 | .. | 16 |
| France | 11.8 | 17.8 | 28.6 | 29.0 | 29.7 | 34.0 | 5.8 | 10.9 | .. | 19 |
| Gabon | .. | .. | .. | .. | .. | .. | .. | .. | .. | 36 |
| Gambia, The | 13.2 | 7.4 | .. | 9.1 | .. | 238.0 | 2.0 | .. | 76.3 | 35 |
| Georgia | .. | .. | .. | .. | .. | .. | 3.1 | 9.3 | .. | 15 |
| Germany | .. | 16.3 | 20.5 | 21.7 | .. | .. | 4.6 | 9.8 | .. | 14 |
| Ghana | .. | 17.8 | .. | 28.0 | .. | 209.4 | 5.4 | .. | 53.0[c] | 32[c] |
| Greece | 7.5 | 16.5 | 17.0 | 22.6 | 28.7 | 27.1 | 4.2 | 8.5 | .. | 11 |
| Guatemala | .. | 9.2 | 4.2 | 4.1 | .. | 34.9 | 2.6 | .. | .. | 31 |
| Guinea | .. | .. | .. | .. | .. | 188.8 | 1.6 | .. | 67.7 | 44 |
| Guinea-Bissau | .. | .. | .. | .. | .. | .. | .. | .. | .. | .. |
| Haiti | 9.1 | .. | .. | .. | .. | .. | .. | .. | .. | .. |

| | Public expenditure per student[a] | | | | | | Public expenditure on education | | Trained teachers in primary education | Primary school pupil-teacher ratio |
|---|---|---|---|---|---|---|---|---|---|---|
| | Primary | | Secondary | | Tertiary | | % of GDP | % of total government expenditure | % of total | pupils per teacher |
| | | | % of GDP per capita | | | | | | | |
| | **1991** | **2006[b]** | **1999** | **2006[b]** | **1999** | **2006[b]** | **2006[b]** | **2006[b]** | **2006[b]** | **2006[b]** |
| Honduras | .. | .. | .. | .. | .. | .. | .. | .. | 87.2 | 28 |
| Hungary | 21.2 | 23.3 | 19.1 | 23.5 | 34.2 | 24.3 | 5.4 | 11.1 | .. | 10 |
| India | .. | 9.2 | 24.9 | 27.0 | 90.8 | 61.0 | 3.8 | .. | .. | 40 |
| Indonesia | .. | .. | 7.3 | .. | 21.3 | .. | .. | .. | .. | 20 |
| Iran, Islamic Rep. | .. | 13.6 | 9.8 | 11.1 | 34.6 | 30.0 | 5.1 | 18.6 | 70.4 | 19 |
| Iraq | .. | .. | .. | .. | .. | .. | .. | .. | 100.0 | 17 |
| Ireland | 11.5 | 14.3 | 16.8 | 21.1 | 28.5 | 23.9 | 4.7 | 14.0 | .. | 18 |
| Israel | 12.6 | 22.3 | 23.3 | 22.7 | 32.9 | 25.6 | 6.9 | .. | .. | 13 |
| Italy | 14.9 | 24.9 | 27.7 | 27.2 | 27.6 | 22.7 | 4.6 | 9.6 | .. | 10 |
| Jamaica | 9.9 | 14.6 | 23.6 | 21.5 | 79.0 | .. | 5.3 | 8.8 | .. | 28 |
| Japan | .. | 22.7 | 21.0 | 22.7 | 15.2 | 20.8 | 3.7 | 9.8 | .. | 19 |
| Jordan | .. | 14.6 | 15.8 | 17.6 | .. | .. | .. | .. | .. | 20 |
| Kazakhstan | .. | 9.8 | .. | 7.7 | .. | 5.6 | 3.2 | 15.8 | .. | 17[c] |
| Kenya | 12.9 | 21.0 | 14.8 | 20.7 | 204.8 | 284.5 | 6.9 | 17.9 | 98.8 | 40 |
| Korea, Dem. Rep. | .. | .. | .. | .. | .. | .. | .. | .. | .. | .. |
| Korea, Rep. | 11.8 | 19.2 | 15.7 | 25.0 | 8.4 | 8.9 | 4.6 | 16.5 | .. | 28 |
| Kuwait | 35.4 | 9.6 | .. | 13.9 | .. | 80.5 | 3.8 | 12.9 | 100.0 | 10 |
| Kyrgyz Republic | .. | .. | 11.9 | .. | 27.7 | 21.8 | 4.9 | .. | 61.3 | 24 |
| Lao PDR | .. | 9.1 | 4.3 | 4.7 | 66.5 | 25.2 | 3.0 | 14.0 | 85.8 | 31 |
| Latvia | .. | 20.7 | 23.7 | 24.0 | 27.9 | 12.4 | 5.1 | 14.2 | .. | 12 |
| Lebanon | .. | 8.3 | .. | 8.8 | 14.2 | 17.2 | 2.7 | 11.0 | 12.6 | 14 |
| Lesotho | .. | 22.2 | 69.0 | 44.2 | 1,247.8 | 1,012.0 | 13.0 | 29.8 | 66.1 | 40 |
| Liberia | .. | .. | .. | .. | .. | .. | .. | .. | .. | 19 |
| Libya | .. | .. | .. | .. | 23.8 | .. | .. | .. | .. | .. |
| Lithuania | .. | 15.0 | .. | 21.2 | 34.2 | 20.0 | 5.2 | 15.6 | .. | 14 |
| Macedonia, FYR | .. | .. | .. | .. | .. | .. | .. | .. | .. | 19 |
| Madagascar | .. | 8.1 | 39.9 | 15.3 | 180.9 | 187.8 | 3.1 | 25.3 | 36.5 | 48 |
| Malawi | 7.2 | .. | .. | .. | .. | .. | .. | .. | .. | .. |
| Malaysia | 10.1 | 14.5 | 22.3 | 21.1 | 83.3 | 71.0 | 6.2 | 25.2 | .. | 17 |
| Mali | .. | 24.5 | 61.6 | 36.4 | 265.0 | .. | 4.5 | 16.8 | .. | 56 |
| Mauritania | .. | 10.0 | 36.4 | 25.1 | 80.1 | 40.6 | 2.9 | 10.1 | 100.0 | 41 |
| Mauritius | 10.1 | 10.3 | 15.3 | 17.4 | 40.4 | 29.8 | 3.9 | 12.7 | 100.0 | 22 |
| Mexico | 4.8 | 14.9 | 14.2 | 15.7 | 47.8 | 41.3 | 5.4 | 25.6 | .. | 28 |
| Moldova | .. | .. | .. | .. | .. | 43.8 | 7.6 | 20.2 | .. | 17 |
| Mongolia | .. | 14.0 | .. | 13.0 | .. | 22.4 | 5.2 | .. | .. | 33 |
| Morocco | 15.4 | 22.9 | 50.1 | 39.7 | 107.0 | 84.3 | 6.8 | 27.2 | 100.0 | 27 |
| Mozambique | .. | 15.0 | .. | 94.8 | .. | 361.2 | 5.0 | 19.5 | 64.6 | 67 |
| Myanmar | .. | .. | 7.0 | .. | 28.6 | .. | .. | .. | 98.3 | 30 |
| Namibia | .. | 20.0 | 36.4 | 19.9 | 157.6 | .. | .. | .. | 92.4 | 31 |
| Nepal | .. | .. | 13.1 | .. | 141.7 | .. | .. | .. | 30.5 | 40 |
| Netherlands | 12.1 | 17.9 | 20.9 | 24.0 | 42.3 | 40.6 | 5.2 | 11.2 | .. | .. |
| New Zealand | 17.2 | 19.3 | 24.3 | 22.5 | 41.6 | 25.2 | 6.5 | .. | .. | 16 |
| Nicaragua | .. | 9.2 | .. | 4.2 | .. | .. | .. | .. | 73.6 | 33 |
| Niger | .. | 32.4 | 64.4 | 49.1 | .. | 384.9 | 3.6 | 15.0 | 91.9 | 40 |
| Nigeria | .. | .. | .. | .. | .. | .. | .. | .. | 49.8 | 37 |
| Norway | 32.7 | 20.3 | 27.0 | 30.5 | 46.1 | 52.2 | 7.6 | 16.6 | .. | 11 |
| Oman | 10.5 | 15.4 | 22.2 | 12.9 | .. | 14.2 | 4.7 | 31.1 | 100.0 | 14 |
| Pakistan | .. | .. | .. | .. | .. | .. | 2.6 | 12.2 | 84.6 | 39 |
| Panama | 11.3 | 9.7 | 19.1 | 12.3 | 33.6 | 26.5 | 3.8 | 8.9 | 91.1 | 25 |
| Papua New Guinea | .. | .. | .. | .. | .. | .. | .. | .. | .. | 36 |
| Paraguay | .. | .. | 18.4 | .. | 58.9 | .. | .. | .. | .. | 28 |
| Peru | .. | 6.6 | 10.8 | 8.9 | 21.2 | 9.0 | 2.7 | 17.0 | .. | 23 |
| Philippines | .. | 9.2 | 10.7 | 9.0 | 15.0 | 12.4 | 2.7 | 16.4 | .. | 35 |
| Poland | 12.9 | 22.8 | 16.5 | 21.6 | 21.1 | 21.5 | 5.4 | 12.7 | .. | 12 |
| Portugal | 16.3 | 23.2 | 27.5 | 34.9 | 28.1 | 23.5 | 5.4 | 11.5 | .. | 11 |
| Puerto Rico | .. | .. | .. | .. | .. | .. | .. | .. | .. | .. |

# 2.10 | Education inputs

| | Public expenditure per student[a] | | | | | | Public expenditure on education | | Trained teachers in primary education | Primary school pupil-teacher ratio |
|---|---|---|---|---|---|---|---|---|---|---|
| | % of GDP per capita | | | | | | % of GDP | % of total government expenditure | % of total | pupils per teacher |
| | Primary | | Secondary | | Tertiary | | | | | |
| | 1991 | 2006[b] | 1999 | 2006[b] | 1999 | 2006[b] | 2006[b] | 2006[b] | 2006[b] | 2006[b] |
| Romania | .. | 9.9 | 16.0 | 14.7 | 32.6 | 22.1 | 3.3 | 8.6 | .. | 17 |
| Russian Federation | .. | .. | .. | .. | .. | 10.8 | 3.5 | 12.9 | .. | 17 |
| Rwanda | .. | 10.4 | 28.4 | 18.4 | 657.6 | 404.5 | 3.8 | 19.0[c] | 98.3 | 66 |
| Saudi Arabia | .. | .. | .. | .. | .. | .. | 6.8 | 27.6 | .. | 15 |
| Senegal | 18.9 | 18.3 | .. | 35.0 | .. | 235.3 | 5.0 | 26.3 | 100.0 | 39 |
| Serbia | .. | .. | .. | .. | .. | .. | .. | .. | .. | .. |
| Sierra Leone | .. | .. | .. | .. | .. | .. | 3.8 | .. | 50.1[c] | 44[c] |
| Singapore | .. | .. | 17.9 | .. | .. | .. | .. | .. | .. | 24 |
| Slovak Republic | .. | 11.9 | 18.3 | 16.7 | 32.6 | 32.2 | 4.2 | 10.8 | .. | 18 |
| Slovenia | 17.4 | 25.9 | 26.5 | 30.6 | 28.8 | 25.8 | 6.0 | .. | .. | 15 |
| Somalia | .. | .. | .. | .. | .. | .. | .. | .. | .. | .. |
| South Africa | 20.2 | 14.3 | 20.0 | 17.6 | 60.7 | 50.1 | 5.4 | 17.6 | .. | 36 |
| Spain | 11.3 | 19.0 | 24.4 | 23.8 | 19.6 | 22.7 | 4.3 | 11.0 | .. | 14 |
| Sri Lanka | .. | .. | .. | .. | .. | .. | .. | .. | .. | 22 |
| Sudan | .. | .. | .. | .. | .. | .. | .. | .. | 58.7 | 34 |
| Swaziland | 6.7 | 14.2 | 26.1 | 38.8 | 388.4 | 320.6 | 7.0 | .. | 90.8 | 33 |
| Sweden | 45.8 | 25.7 | 26.1 | 34.5 | 52.7 | 43.7 | 7.3 | 12.9 | .. | 10 |
| Switzerland | 36.1 | 25.0 | 27.7 | 28.0 | 54.5 | 63.1 | 6.0 | .. | .. | 13 |
| Syrian Arab Republic | .. | .. | 22.1 | .. | .. | .. | .. | .. | .. | .. |
| Tajikistan | .. | 8.8 | .. | 11.4 | .. | 11.2 | 3.4 | 19.0 | 93.0 | 22 |
| Tanzania | .. | .. | .. | .. | .. | .. | .. | .. | 100.0[c] | 53[c] |
| Thailand | 11.6 | 14.1 | 15.7 | 15.5 | 35.5 | 25.0 | 4.2 | 25.0 | .. | 18 |
| Timor-Leste | .. | .. | .. | .. | .. | .. | .. | .. | .. | 34 |
| Togo | .. | .. | 30.9 | .. | 317.9 | .. | .. | .. | 36.8 | 38 |
| Trinidad and Tobago | .. | .. | 12.2 | .. | 147.6 | .. | .. | .. | 81.0 | 17 |
| Tunisia | .. | 21.1 | 27.1 | 24.4 | 89.4 | 56.4 | 7.3 | 20.8 | .. | 20 |
| Turkey | 10.7 | 14.1 | 14.3 | 17.8 | 45.5 | 40.7 | 4.0 | .. | .. | .. |
| Turkmenistan | .. | .. | .. | .. | .. | .. | .. | .. | .. | .. |
| Uganda | .. | 11.3 | .. | 34.0 | .. | 188.9 | 5.2 | 18.3 | 84.8 | 49 |
| Ukraine | .. | 16.0 | 11.2 | 24.5 | 36.5 | 31.5 | 6.3 | 19.3 | 99.6 | 17 |
| United Arab Emirates | .. | 7.1 | 11.5 | 9.2 | 41.5 | .. | 1.3 | 27.4 | 60.0 | 15 |
| United Kingdom | 15.0 | 18.0 | 24.4 | 27.0 | 26.2 | 27.6 | 5.4 | 11.7 | .. | 17 |
| United States | .. | 22.0 | 22.5 | 24.7 | 27.0 | 23.5 | 5.6 | 14.4 | .. | 14 |
| Uruguay | 7.8 | 7.6 | 11.3 | 8.7 | 19.1 | 20.1 | 2.6 | 14.1 | .. | 21 |
| Uzbekistan | .. | .. | .. | .. | .. | .. | .. | .. | 100.0[c] | 18[c] |
| Venezuela, RB | .. | 8.0 | .. | 8.3 | .. | 34.3 | 3.7 | .. | 83.1 | 17 |
| Vietnam | .. | .. | .. | .. | .. | .. | .. | .. | 95.6 | 21 |
| West Bank and Gaza | .. | .. | .. | .. | .. | .. | .. | .. | 100.0 | 32 |
| Yemen, Rep. | .. | .. | .. | .. | .. | .. | .. | .. | .. | .. |
| Zambia | .. | 5.4 | 19.9 | 8.2 | 168.2 | .. | 2.0 | 14.8 | .. | 51 |
| Zimbabwe | 20.7 | .. | 19.5 | .. | 195.2 | .. | .. | .. | .. | .. |
| **World** | .. m | 14.5 m | .. m | 21.1 m | .. m | .. m | 4.6 m | .. m | .. m | 30 w |
| **Low income** | .. | .. | .. | .. | .. | .. | .. | .. | .. | 41 |
| **Middle income** | .. | 13.0 | 16.6 | 17.1 | 37.2 | 25.9 | 4.3 | .. | .. | .. |
| Lower middle income | .. | .. | .. | .. | .. | .. | .. | .. | .. | 19 |
| Upper middle income | .. | 13.2 | 17.1 | 16.7 | 31.8 | 23.3 | 4.1 | 14.1 | .. | 21 |
| **Low & middle income** | .. | .. | .. | .. | .. | .. | 4.1 | .. | .. | 33 |
| East Asia & Pacific | .. | .. | 7.0 | .. | 32.2 | .. | 3.5 | .. | .. | 19 |
| Europe & Central Asia | .. | 13.6 | .. | 18.2 | .. | 21.8 | 4.2 | 13.1 | .. | 16 |
| Latin America & Carib. | .. | 11.4 | 14.8 | 14.1 | 37.1 | .. | 4.0 | .. | .. | 24 |
| Middle East & N. Africa | .. | .. | .. | .. | .. | .. | .. | .. | .. | 23 |
| South Asia | .. | .. | 13.1 | .. | 90.8 | .. | 2.2 | .. | .. | 41 |
| Sub-Saharan Africa | .. | 11.8 | .. | .. | .. | .. | 4.2 | .. | .. | 47 |
| **High income** | 15.8 | 19.2 | 24.3 | 24.8 | 32.8 | 29.0 | 5.4 | 12.5 | .. | 16 |
| Euro area | 14.9 | 18.9 | 25.3 | 27.2 | 28.7 | 27.1 | 5.3 | 11.0 | .. | 14 |

a. Because of the change from International Standard Classification of Education 1976 (ISCED76) to ISCED97 in 1998, data for 1991 are not fully comparable with data from 1999 onward. b. Provisional data. c. Data are for 2007.

Data on education are compiled by the United Nations Educational, Scientific, and Cultural Organization (UNESCO) Institute for Statistics from official responses to surveys and from reports provided by education authorities in each country. The data are used for monitoring, policymaking, and resource allocation. For a variety of reasons, however, education statistics generally fail to provide a complete and accurate picture of a country's education system. Statistics often lag by one to two years, though efforts have been made to shorten the delay. Moreover, coverage and data collection methods vary across countries and over time within countries, so comparisons should be interpreted with caution.

For most countries the data on education spending in the table refer to public spending—government spending on public education plus subsidies for private education—and generally exclude foreign aid for education. They may also exclude spending by religious schools, which play a significant role in many developing countries. Data for some countries and some years refer to ministry of education spending only and exclude education expenditures by other ministries and local authorities.

Many developing countries seek to supplement public funds for education, some with tuition fees to recover part of the cost of providing education services or to encourage development of private schools. Fees raise difficult questions of equity, efficiency, access, and taxation, however, and some governments have used scholarships, vouchers, and other public finance methods to counter criticism. For most countries the data reflect only public spending. Data for a few countries include private spending, although countries vary on whether parents or schools pay for books, uniforms, and other supplies. For greater detail, consult the country- and indicator-specific notes in the original source.

The share of public expenditure devoted to education allows an assessment of the priority a government assigns to education relative to other public investments, as well as a government's commitment to investing in human capital development. It also reflects the development status of a country's education system relative to that of others. However, returns on investment to education, especially primary and lower secondary education, cannot be understood simply by comparing current education indicators with national income. It takes a long time before currently enrolled children can productively contribute to the national economy (Hanushek 2002).

The general quality of the data on education finance is poor. This is partly because ministries of education, from which the UNESCO Institute for Statistics collects data, are not necessarily the best source for education finance data. Other agencies, particularly ministries of finance, need to be consulted, but coordination is not easy. It is also difficult to track actual spending from the central government to local institutions. And private spending adds to the complexity of collecting accurate data on public spending.

The share of trained teachers in primary education measures the quality of the teaching staff. It does not take account of competencies acquired by teachers through their professional experience or self-instruction or of such factors as work experience, teaching methods and materials, or classroom conditions, which may affect the quality of teaching. Since the training teachers receive varies greatly (pre-service or in-service), care should be taken in making comparisons across countries.

The primary school pupil-teacher ratio reflects the average number of pupils per teacher. It differs from the average class size because of the different practices countries employ, such as part-time teachers, school shifts, and multigrade classes. The comparability of pupil-teacher ratios across countries is affected by the definition of teachers and by differences in class size by grade and in the number of hours taught, as well as the different practices mentioned above. Moreover, the underlying enrollment levels are subject to a variety of reporting errors (for further discussion of enrollment data, see *About the data* for table 2.11). While the pupil-teacher ratio is often used to compare the quality of schooling across countries, it is often weakly related to the value added of schooling systems.

In 1998 UNESCO introduced the new International Standard Classification of Education 1997. Thus the time-series data for the years through 1997 are not comparable with those for 1999 onward. Any time-series analysis should therefore be undertaken with extreme caution.

In 2006 the UNESCO Institute for Statistics also changed its convention for citing the reference year of education data and indicators to the calendar year in which the academic or financial year ends. Data that used to be listed for 2005/06, for example, are now listed for 2006. This change was implemented to present the most recent data available and to align the data reporting with that of other international organizations (in particular the Organisation for Economic Co-operation and Development and Eurostat).

• **Public expenditure per student** is public current and capital spending on education divided by the number of students by level as a percentage of gross domestic product (GDP) per capita. • **Public expenditure on education** is current and capital public expenditure on education as a percentage of GDP and as a percentage of total government expenditure. • **Trained teachers in primary education** are the percentage of primary school teachers who have received the minimum organized teacher training (pre-service or in-service) required for teaching in their country. • **Primary school pupil-teacher ratio** is the number of pupils enrolled in primary school divided by the number of primary school teachers (regardless of their teaching assignment).

Data on education inputs are from the UNESCO Institute for Statistics, which compiles international data on education in cooperation with national commissions and national statistical services.

# Participation in education

| | Gross enrollment ratio | | | | Net enrollment ratio[a] | | | | Total net enrollment ratio, primary | | Children out of school | |
|---|---|---|---|---|---|---|---|---|---|---|---|---|
| | | % of relevant age group | | | | % of relevant age group | | | % of primary-school-age children | | thousand primary-school-age children | |
| | Preprimary | Primary | Secondary | Tertiary | Primary | | Secondary | | Male | Female | Male | Female |
| | 2006[b] | 2006[b] | 2006[b] | 2006[b] | 1991 | 2006[b] | 1991 | 2006[b] | 2006[b] | 2006[b] | 2006[b] | 2006[b] |
| Afghanistan | .. | .. | .. | . | .. | .. | .. | .. | .. | .. | .. | .. |
| Albania | 49 | 105 | 77 | 19 | 95 | 94 | .. | 73 | 94 | 93 | 8 | 8 |
| Algeria | 14 | 110 | 83 | 22 | 89 | 95 | 53 | 66 | 100 | 98 | 26 | 62 |
| Angola | .. | .. | .. | 3 | 50 | .. | .. | .. | .. | .. | .. | .. |
| Argentina | 64 | 113 | 86 | 65 | .. | 99 | .. | 79 | .. | .. | .. | .. |
| Armenia | 36 | 98 | 90 | 32 | .. | 82 | .. | 86 | 84 | 88 | 7 | 4 |
| Australia | 104 | 104 | 149 | 73 | 99 | 96 | 80 | 86 | 96 | 97 | 35 | 27 |
| Austria | 88 | 102 | 102 | 49 | 88 | 97 | .. | .. | 96 | 98 | 8 | 4 |
| Azerbaijan | 32 | 96 | 83 | 15 | 89 | 85 | .. | 78 | 87 | 84 | 38 | 43 |
| Bangladesh | 10 | 103 | 44 | 6 | .. | 89 | .. | 41 | 91 | 94 | 842 | 529 |
| Belarus | 103 | 96 | 96 | 66 | 85 | 89 | .. | 88 | 91 | 88 | 18 | 21 |
| Belgium | 120 | 102 | 109 | 62 | 96 | 98 | 86 | 97 | 98 | 98 | 9 | 7 |
| Benin | 5 | 96 | 32 | .. | 41 | 78 | .. | .. | 89 | 71 | 79 | 198 |
| Bolivia | 50 | 109 | 82 | 41 | .. | 95 | .. | 71 | 96 | 97 | 30 | 22 |
| Bosnia and Herzegovina | .. | .. | .. | .. | .. | .. | .. | .. | .. | .. | .. | .. |
| Botswana | .. | 108 | 75 | 5 | 88 | 86 | 39 | 61 | 88 | 89 | 19 | 17 |
| Brazil | 63 | 140 | 106 | 24 | 85 | 95 | 17 | 78 | 95 | 97 | 336 | 224 |
| Bulgaria | 80 | 102 | 105 | 44 | 85 | 93 | 63 | 89 | 95 | 94 | 8 | 8 |
| Burkina Faso | 2 | 60 | 15 | 2 | 27 | 47 | .. | 12 | 49 | 39 | 562 | 653 |
| Burundi | 2 | 103 | 14 | 2 | 53 | 75 | .. | .. | 61 | 56 | 154 | 170 |
| Cambodia | 11 | 122 | 38 | 5 | 72 | 90 | .. | 24 | 97 | 96 | 98 | 114 |
| Cameroon | 22 | 106 | 41 | 7 | 69 | .. | .. | .. | .. | .. | .. | .. |
| Canada | 68 | 100 | 117 | 62 | 98 | .. | 89 | .. | .. | .. | 0 | .. |
| Central African Republic | 2 | 61 | .. | 1 | 52 | 45 | .. | .. | .. | .. | 160 | 212 |
| Chad | 1 | 76 | 15 | 1 | 34 | .. | .. | .. | .. | .. | .. | .. |
| Chile | 55 | 104 | 91 | 48 | 89 | .. | 55 | .. | 95 | 94 | 44 | 53 |
| China | 39 | 111 | 76 | 22 | 98 | .. | .. | .. | .. | .. | .. | .. |
| Hong Kong, China | .. | .. | 85 | 33 | .. | .. | .. | 78 | 97 | 93 | .. | .. |
| Colombia | 40 | 116 | 82 | 31 | 68 | 88 | 34 | 65 | 92 | 92 | 193 | 174 |
| Congo, Dem. Rep. | .. | .. | .. | .. | 54 | .. | .. | .. | .. | .. | .. | .. |
| Congo, Rep. | 9 | 108 | 43 | .. | 82 | 55 | .. | .. | 49 | 60 | 116 | 133 |
| Costa Rica | 70 | 111 | 86 | 25 | 87 | .. | 38 | .. | .. | .. | .. | .. |
| Côte d'Ivoire | 3 | 71 | .. | .. | 45 | .. | .. | .. | .. | .. | .. | .. |
| Croatia | 53 | 93 | 89 | 46 | 79 | .. | 63 | .. | .. | .. | .. | .. |
| Cuba | 113 | 101 | 94 | 88 | 94 | 97 | 73 | 87 | 97 | 97 | 15 | 12 |
| Czech Republic | 114 | 102 | 96 | 48 | 87 | 93 | .. | .. | 91 | 94 | 22 | 15 |
| Denmark | 94 | 99 | 124 | 81 | 98 | 96 | 87 | 91 | 96 | 97 | 9 | 6 |
| Dominican Republic | 32 | 98 | 69 | 35 | 56 | 77 | .. | 52 | 78 | 81 | 139 | 116 |
| Ecuador | 80 | 117 | 65 | .. | 98 | 97 | .. | 55 | 99 | 100 | 12 | 0 |
| Egypt, Arab Rep. | 17 | 102 | 86 | 35 | 86 | 94 | .. | 83 | 100 | 94 | 10 | 256 |
| El Salvador | 51 | 114 | 64 | 21 | .. | 94 | .. | 54 | 96 | 97 | 21 | 18 |
| Eritrea | 14 | 62 | 31 | 1 | 15 | 47 | .. | 25 | 53 | 45 | 145 | 163 |
| Estonia | 116 | 100 | 100 | 66 | 100 | 95 | .. | 91 | 97 | 97 | 1 | 1 |
| Ethiopia | 2 | 83 | 27 | 2 | 22 | 65 | .. | 24 | 70 | 65 | 2,047 | 2,426 |
| Finland | 59 | 100 | 111 | 92 | 98 | 99 | 93 | 95 | 99 | 99 | 3 | 2 |
| France | 117 | 110 | 114 | 56 | 100 | 99 | .. | 99 | 99 | 99 | 19 | 9 |
| Gabon | .. | 152 | .. | .. | 94 | .. | .. | .. | .. | .. | .. | .. |
| Gambia, The | 17 | 74 | 45 | 1 | 46 | 62 | .. | 38 | .. | .. | 49 | 41 |
| Georgia | 55 | 96 | 85 | 38 | 97 | 89 | .. | 79 | 87 | 88 | 19 | 14 |
| Germany | 97 | 101 | 100 | .. | 84 | .. | .. | .. | .. | .. | .. | .. |
| Ghana | 55 | 98[c] | 47[c] | 5 | 54 | 66[c] | .. | 38 | 64 | 65 | 572[c] | 569[c] |
| Greece | 68 | 102 | 102 | 90 | 95 | 100 | 83 | 91 | 100 | 100 | 0 | 1 |
| Guatemala | 29 | 114 | 53 | 9 | .. | 94 | .. | 38 | 97 | 93 | 21 | 62 |
| Guinea | 7 | 88 | 35 | 3 | 27 | 72 | .. | 28 | 76 | 64 | 159 | 230 |
| Guinea-Bissau | .. | .. | .. | .. | 38 | .. | .. | .. | .. | .. | .. | .. |
| Haiti | .. | .. | .. | .. | 21 | .. | .. | .. | .. | .. | .. | .. |

# Participation in education | 2.11

| | Gross enrollment ratio | | | | Net enrollment ratio[a] | | | | Total net enrollment ratio, primary | | Children out of school | |
|---|---|---|---|---|---|---|---|---|---|---|---|---|
| | | % of relevant age group | | | | % of relevant age group | | | % of primary-school-age children | | thousand primary-school-age children | |
| | Preprimary | Primary | Secondary | Tertiary | Primary | | Secondary | | Male | Female | Male | Female |
| | 2006[b] | 2006[b] | 2006[b] | 2006[b] | 1991 | 2006[b] | 1991 | 2006[b] | 2006[b] | 2006[b] | 2006[b] | 2006[b] |
| Honduras | 38 | 118 | 76 | 17 | 88 | 96 | 21 | .. | 96 | 97 | 21 | 11 |
| Hungary | 84 | 98 | 96 | 65 | 91 | 89 | 75 | 90 | 96 | 96 | 10 | 9 |
| India | 39 | 115 | 54 | 11 | .. | 88 | .. | .. | 96 | 92 | 2,780 | 4,713 |
| Indonesia | 33 | 115 | 62 | 17 | 96 | 95 | 39 | 57 | 99 | 96 | 142 | 544 |
| Iran, Islamic Rep. | 53 | 118 | 81 | 27 | 92 | 94 | .. | 77 | 91 | 100 | 305 | 0 |
| Iraq | .. | .. | .. | .. | 94 | .. | .. | .. | .. | .. | .. | .. |
| Ireland | .. | 104 | 112 | 58 | 90 | 95 | 80 | 87 | 94 | 95 | 13 | 11 |
| Israel | 93 | 110 | 93 | 58 | 92 | 97 | .. | 89 | 97 | 98 | 11 | 7 |
| Italy | 104 | 102 | 99 | 65 | 100 | 99 | .. | 92 | 100 | 99 | 4 | 12 |
| Jamaica | 92 | 95 | 87 | .. | 96 | 90 | 64 | 78 | 91 | 91 | 16 | 15 |
| Japan | 85 | 100 | 102 | 55 | 100 | 100 | 97 | 100 | 100 | 100 | 12 | 0 |
| Jordan | 32 | 97 | 89 | 40 | 94 | 91 | .. | 79 | 95 | 96 | 23 | 17 |
| Kazakhstan | 36 | 105[c] | 93[c] | 51[c] | 88 | 90[c] | .. | 86[c] | 98 | 99 | 6[c] | 3[c] |
| Kenya | 50 | 108 | 48 | 3 | .. | 76 | .. | 42 | 76 | 77 | 670 | 649 |
| Korea, Dem. Rep. | .. | .. | .. | .. | .. | .. | .. | .. | .. | .. | .. | .. |
| Korea, Rep. | 96 | 105 | 96 | 91 | 100 | 98 | 86 | 94 | .. | .. | .. | .. |
| Kuwait | 75 | 96 | 89 | 18 | 49 | 83 | .. | .. | 89 | 88 | 12 | 12 |
| Kyrgyz Republic | 14 | 97 | 86 | 43 | 92 | 86 | .. | 80 | 94 | 93 | 14 | 14 |
| Lao PDR | 11 | 116 | 43 | 9 | 62 | 84 | .. | 35 | 85 | 80 | 54 | 71 |
| Latvia | 87 | 95 | 99 | 75 | 94 | 90 | .. | .. | 90 | 94 | 4 | 3 |
| Lebanon | 64 | 94 | 81 | 48 | 66 | 82 | .. | 73 | 83 | 83 | 40 | 40 |
| Lesotho | 18 | 114 | 37 | 4 | 72 | 72 | 15 | 24 | 73 | 78 | 55 | 48 |
| Liberia | 100 | 91 | .. | .. | .. | 39 | .. | .. | .. | .. | 177 | 179 |
| Libya | 9 | 110 | 111 | .. | 93 | .. | .. | .. | .. | .. | .. | .. |
| Lithuania | 65 | 94 | 100 | 76 | .. | 88 | .. | 94 | 90 | 91 | 8 | 7 |
| Macedonia, FYR | 33 | 98 | 84 | 30 | 94 | 92 | .. | 81 | 97 | 97 | 2 | 1 |
| Madagascar | 8 | 139 | 24 | 3 | 64 | 96 | .. | .. | 93 | 93 | 54 | 52 |
| Malawi | .. | 119 | 29 | 0[d] | 49 | 91 | .. | 24 | 91 | 96 | 136 | 66 |
| Malaysia | 122 | 100 | 72 | 31 | .. | 99 | .. | 72 | 99 | 99 | 11 | 15 |
| Mali | 3 | 80 | 28 | 3 | 25 | 61 | 6 | .. | 67 | 52 | 328 | 466 |
| Mauritania | 2 | 102 | 22 | 4 | 36 | 79 | .. | 16 | 75 | 79 | 52 | 40 |
| Mauritius | 101 | 102 | 86 | 17 | 91 | 95 | .. | 79 | 94 | 96 | 3 | 2 |
| Mexico | 96 | 112 | 85 | 25 | 98 | 98 | 45 | 69 | 100 | 99 | 15 | 52 |
| Moldova | 68 | 91 | 82 | 36 | 88 | 83 | .. | 75 | 85 | 85 | 14 | 13 |
| Mongolia | 54 | 101 | 89 | 47 | 90 | 91 | .. | 82 | 95 | 99 | 6 | 1 |
| Morocco | 59 | 106 | 52 | 12 | 56 | 88 | .. | .. | 90 | 85 | 168 | 261 |
| Mozambique | .. | 105 | 16 | 1 | 42 | 69 | .. | 4 | 80 | 73 | 568 | 662 |
| Myanmar | 6 | 114 | 49 | .. | 99 | 100 | .. | 46 | 98 | 100 | 16 | 0 |
| Namibia | 31 | 107 | 57 | 6 | .. | 76 | .. | 35 | 74 | 79 | 49 | 40 |
| Nepal | 27 | 126 | 43 | 6 | .. | 79 | .. | .. | 85 | 75 | 267 | 436 |
| Netherlands | 90 | 107 | 118 | 59 | 95 | 98 | 84 | 87 | 99 | 97 | 8 | 15 |
| New Zealand | 93 | 102 | 121 | 82 | 98 | 99 | 85 | .. | 99 | 99 | 1 | 1 |
| Nicaragua | 52 | 116 | 66 | .. | 70 | 90 | .. | 43 | 93 | 94 | 38 | 34 |
| Niger | 2 | 51 | 11 | 1 | 24 | 43 | 6 | 9 | 49 | 36 | 565 | 680 |
| Nigeria | 14 | 96 | 32 | 10 | 55 | 63 | .. | 26 | 70 | 60 | 3,550 | 4,547 |
| Norway | 88 | 98 | 113 | 78 | 100 | 98 | 88 | 96 | 98 | 98 | 5 | 4 |
| Oman | 8 | 82 | 89 | 25 | 69 | 74 | .. | 77 | 76 | 77 | 44 | 38 |
| Pakistan | 52 | 84 | 30 | 5 | 33 | 66 | .. | 30 | 76 | 58 | 2,705 | 4,116 |
| Panama | 67 | 112 | 70 | 45 | .. | 98 | .. | 64 | 99 | 99 | 1 | 2 |
| Papua New Guinea | .. | 55 | .. | .. | .. | .. | .. | .. | .. | .. | .. | .. |
| Paraguay | 34 | 112 | 67 | 25 | 94 | 94 | 26 | .. | 94 | 95 | 24 | 21 |
| Peru | 66 | 116 | 92 | 34 | .. | 96 | .. | 70 | 98 | 100 | 30 | 2 |
| Philippines | 40 | 111 | 85 | 28 | 96 | 93 | .. | 60 | 92 | 95 | 463 | 315 |
| Poland | 55 | 98 | 100 | 64 | 97 | 97 | 76 | 93 | 97 | 97 | 50 | 38 |
| Portugal | 79 | 116 | 97 | 55 | 98 | 98 | .. | 82 | 100 | 99 | 1 | 3 |
| Puerto Rico | .. | .. | .. | .. | .. | .. | .. | .. | .. | .. | .. | .. |

# Participation in education

| | Gross enrollment ratio | | | | Net enrollment ratio[a] | | | | Total net enrollment ratio, primary | | Children out of school | |
|---|---|---|---|---|---|---|---|---|---|---|---|---|
| | | % of relevant age group | | | | % of relevant age group | | | % of primary-school-age children | | thousand primary-school-age children | |
| | Preprimary | Primary | Secondary | Tertiary | Primary | | Secondary | | Male | Female | Male | Female |
| | 2006[b] | 2006[b] | 2006[b] | 2006[b] | 1991 | 2006[b] | 1991 | 2006[b] | 2006[b] | 2006[b] | 2006[b] | 2006[b] |
| Romania | 74 | 105 | 86 | 45 | 81 | 91 | .. | 81 | 95 | 95 | 24 | 24 |
| Russian Federation | 88 | 129 | 91 | 70 | 98 | 92 | .. | .. | 92 | 93 | 170 | 140 |
| Rwanda | .. | 140 | 13 | 3 | 67 | 91 | 8 | .. | 72 | 75 | 78 | 45 |
| Saudi Arabia | 12 | 108 | 96 | 27 | 87 | 93 | 39 | 60 | 87 | 87 | 110 | 108 |
| Senegal | 9 | 80 | 22 | 6 | 45 | 71 | .. | 17 | 75 | 71 | 250 | 262 |
| Serbia | .. | .. | .. | .. | .. | .. | .. | .. | .. | .. | .. | .. |
| Sierra Leone | .. | 145[c] | 32[c] | .. | 43 | .. | .. | 23[c] | .. | .. | .. | .. |
| Singapore | .. | 78 | 63 | .. | .. | .. | .. | .. | .. | .. | .. | .. |
| Slovak Republic | 95 | 99 | 96 | 41 | .. | 92 | .. | .. | 92 | 92 | 10 | 9 |
| Slovenia | 78 | 98 | 96 | 79 | 96 | 96 | .. | 91 | 97 | 97 | 1 | 1 |
| Somalia | .. | .. | .. | .. | 9 | 19 | .. | .. | .. | .. | .. | .. |
| South Africa | 38 | 106 | 95 | 15 | 90 | 88 | 45 | .. | 93 | 94 | 262 | 207 |
| Spain | 119 | 105 | 118 | 66 | 100 | 100 | .. | 94 | 100 | 99 | 3 | 6 |
| Sri Lanka | .. | 108 | 87 | .. | .. | 97 | .. | .. | .. | .. | .. | .. |
| Sudan | 24 | 66 | 34 | .. | 40 | 54 | .. | 19 | .. | .. | .. | .. |
| Swaziland | 17 | 106 | 47 | 4 | 75 | 78 | 30 | 32 | 76 | 77 | 23 | 22 |
| Sweden | 93 | 98 | 103 | 82 | 100 | 97 | 85 | 99 | 97 | 97 | 10 | 10 |
| Switzerland | 96 | 98 | 93 | 45 | 84 | 90 | 80 | 82 | 94 | 94 | 16 | 14 |
| Syrian Arab Republic | 11 | 126 | 70 | .. | 91 | .. | 43 | 63 | .. | .. | 2 | 17 |
| Tajikistan | 9 | 100 | 83 | 19 | 77 | 97 | .. | 80 | 99 | 95 | .. | .. |
| Tanzania | 28 | 112[c] | .. | 1 | 51 | 100[c] | .. | .. | 99 | 97 | 0[c] | 10[c] |
| Thailand | 92 | 108 | 78 | 46 | 88 | 94 | .. | 71 | 100 | 100 | 0 | 1 |
| Timor-Leste | 10 | 99 | 53 | .. | .. | 68 | .. | .. | 70 | 67 | 28 | 29 |
| Togo | 2 | 102 | 40 | .. | 64 | 80 | 15 | .. | 87 | 74 | 58 | 120 |
| Trinidad and Tobago | 85 | 95 | 76 | 11 | 89 | 85 | .. | 65 | 89 | 90 | 8 | 7 |
| Tunisia | .. | 110 | 83 | 30 | 93 | 97 | .. | .. | 98 | 99 | 12 | 6 |
| Turkey | 10 | 94 | 74 | 31 | 89 | 90 | 42 | 66 | 92 | 88 | 329 | 499 |
| Turkmenistan | .. | .. | .. | .. | .. | .. | .. | .. | .. | .. | .. | .. |
| Uganda | 3 | 117 | 18 | 3 | .. | .. | .. | 16 | .. | .. | .. | .. |
| Ukraine | 90 | 102 | 93 | 73 | 81 | 90 | .. | 84 | 91 | 91 | 81 | 79 |
| United Arab Emirates | 78 | 104 | 90 | .. | 99 | 88 | 60 | 79 | 93 | 92 | 7 | 6 |
| United Kingdom | 71 | 107 | 105 | 59 | 98 | 99 | 80 | 95 | 100 | 100 | 3 | 0[d] |
| United States | 61 | 98 | 94 | 82 | 97 | 92 | 84 | 88 | 93 | 94 | 954 | 750 |
| Uruguay | 67 | 113 | 107 | 42 | 91 | 94 | .. | .. | 97 | 98 | 5 | 4 |
| Uzbekistan | 27 | 95[c] | 102[c] | 10[c] | 78 | .. | .. | .. | .. | .. | .. | .. |
| Venezuela, RB | 60 | 104 | 78 | 52 | 87 | 91 | 18 | 67 | 91 | 91 | 123 | 103 |
| Vietnam | 60 | 90 | 76 | 16 | 90 | 84 | .. | 69 | .. | .. | .. | .. |
| West Bank and Gaza | 30 | 83 | 94 | 41 | .. | 76 | .. | 90 | 80 | 80 | 48 | 45 |
| Yemen, Rep. | 1 | 87 | 46 | 9 | 50 | 75 | .. | 37 | 86 | 62 | 275 | 632 |
| Zambia | .. | 117 | 36 | .. | .. | 92 | .. | 28 | 92 | 94 | 96 | 54 |
| Zimbabwe | .. | .. | .. | .. | .. | .. | .. | .. | .. | .. | .. | .. |
| **World** | **40 w** | **106 w** | **65 w** | **24 w** | **84 w** | **86 w** | **.. w** | **58 w** | **90 w** | **87 w** | | |
| **Low income** | 34 | 102 | 45 | 9 | .. | 78 | .. | 39 | 84 | 78 | | |
| **Middle income** | .. | 112 | 78 | 27 | 93 | 93 | .. | 70 | 95 | 94 | | |
| Lower middle income | 41 | 112 | 73 | 23 | 93 | 93 | .. | 68 | 94 | 94 | | |
| Upper middle income | 63 | 113 | 92 | 40 | 91 | 94 | .. | 76 | 96 | 95 | | |
| **Low & middle income** | 34 | 107 | 61 | 19 | 82 | 85 | .. | 54 | 89 | 86 | | |
| East Asia & Pacific | 41 | 111 | 72 | 20 | 96 | 93 | .. | 68 | 94 | 94 | | |
| Europe & Central Asia | 54 | 103 | 89 | 51 | 90 | 91 | .. | 81 | 93 | 91 | | |
| Latin America & Carib. | 62 | 119 | 89 | 30 | 85 | 94 | 31 | 69 | 96 | 96 | | |
| Middle East & N. Africa | 23 | 104 | 74 | 24 | 82 | 91 | .. | 67 | 94 | 90 | | |
| South Asia | 41 | 110 | 49 | 9 | .. | 85 | .. | .. | 92 | 87 | | |
| Sub-Saharan Africa | 16 | 93 | 31 | 5 | 49 | 68 | .. | 25 | 72 | 66 | | |
| **High income** | 78 | 101 | 101 | 67 | 95 | 95 | 85 | 91 | 96 | 96 | | |
| Euro area | 103 | .. | .. | .. | 95 | .. | .. | .. | .. | .. | | |

a. Because of the change from International Standard Classification of Education 1976 (ISCED76) to ISCED97 in 1998, data for 1991 are not fully comparable with data from 1999 onward. b. Provisional data. c. Data are for 2007. d. Less than 0.5.

## About the data

School enrollment data are reported to the United Nations Educational, Scientific, and Cultural Organization (UNESCO) Institute for Statistics by national education authorities and statistical offices. Enrollment ratios help monitor whether a country is on track to achieve the Millennium Development Goal of universal primary education by 2015, which implies achieving a net primary enrollment ratio of 100 percent, and whether an education system has the capacity to meet the needs of universal primary education, as indicated in part by its gross enrollment ratios.

Enrollment ratios, while a useful measure of participation in education, have limitations. They are based on data from annual school surveys, which are typically conducted at the beginning of the school year. They do not reflect actual attendance or dropout rates during the year. And school administrators may exaggerate enrollments, especially if there is a financial incentive to do so.

Also, as international indicators, the gross and net primary enrollment ratios have an inherent weakness: the length of primary education differs across countries, although the International Standard Classification of Education tries to minimize the difference. A relatively short duration for primary education tends to increase the ratio; a relatively long one to decrease it (in part because more older children drop out).

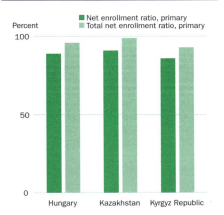

**In some countries close to 10 percent of primary-school-age children are enrolled in secondary school** **2.11a**

Percent
- Net enrollment ratio, primary
- Total net enrollment ratio, primary

Hungary  Kazakhstan  Kyrgyz Republic

The difference between net enrollment and total primary net enrollment is small in most countries. But it is larger in some countries because many children start primary school earlier than the official entrance age and are younger than the official age when they reach secondary school.

*Source:* United Nations Educational, Scientific, and Cultural Organization Institute for Statistics.

Overage or underage enrollments are frequent, particularly when, for cultural or economic reasons, parents prefer children to start school at other than the official age. Age at enrollment may be inaccurately estimated or misstated, especially in communities where registration of births is not strictly enforced.

Other problems of cross-country comparison of enrollment data stem from errors in school-age population estimates. Age-sex structures drawn from censuses or vital registrations, the primary data sources on school-age population, commonly underenumerate (especially young children) to circumvent laws or regulations. Errors are also introduced when parents round children's ages. While census data are often adjusted for age bias, adjustments are rarely made for inadequate vital registration systems. Compounding these problems, pre- and postcensus estimates of school-age children are model interpolations or projections that may miss important demographic events (see discussion of demographic data in *About the data* for table 2.1).

Gross enrollment ratios indicate the capacity of each level of the education system, but a high ratio may reflect a substantial number of overage children enrolled in each grade because of repetition rather than a successful education system. The net enrollment ratio excludes overage and underage students to capture more accurately the system's coverage and internal efficiency but does not account for children who fall outside the official school age because of late or early entry rather than grade repetition. Differences between gross and net enrollment ratios show the incidence of overage and underage enrollments.

Total net primary enrollment was recently added as a Millennium Development Goal indicator. It captures the children of primary-school age who have progressed to secondary education, which the traditional net enrollment ratio excludes.

Children out of school are primary-school-age children not enrolled in primary or secondary education. The data are calculated by the UNESCO Institute for Statistics using administrative data. Children out of school include dropouts, children never enrolled, and children of primary age enrolled in preprimary education. Large numbers of children out of school create pressure to enroll children and provide classrooms, teachers, and educational materials, a task made difficult in many developing countries by limited education budgets. However, getting children into school is a high priority for countries and crucial for achieving the Millennium Development Goal of universal primary education.

In 2006 the UNESCO Institute for Statistics changed its convention for citing the reference year. For more information, see *About the data* for table 2.10.

## Definitions

- **Gross enrollment ratio** is the ratio of total enrollment, regardless of age, to the population of the age group that officially corresponds to the level of education shown. • **Preprimary education** refers to the initial stage of organized instruction, designed primarily to introduce very young children to a school-type environment. • **Primary education** provides children with basic reading, writing, and mathematics skills along with an elementary understanding of such subjects as history, geography, natural science, social science, art, and music. • **Secondary education** completes the provision of basic education that began at the primary level and aims at laying the foundations for lifelong learning and human development by offering more subject- or skill-oriented instruction using more specialized teachers. • **Tertiary education** refers to a wide range of post-secondary education institutions, including technical and vocational education, colleges, and universities, whether or not leading to an advanced research qualification, that normally require as a minimum condition of admission the successful completion of education at the secondary level. • **Net enrollment ratio** is the ratio of total enrollment of children of official school age based on the International Standard Classification of Education 1997 to the population of the age group that officially corresponds to the level of education shown. • **Total net enrollment ratio, primary,** is the ratio of total enrollment of children of official school age for primary education who are enrolled in primary or secondary education to the total primary-school-age population. • **Children out of school** are the number of primary-school-age children not enrolled in primary or secondary school.

## Data sources

Data on gross and net enrollment ratios and out of school children are from the UNESCO Institute for Statistics.

# 2.12 Education efficiency

| | Gross intake rate in grade 1 | | Cohort survival rate | | | | | | Repeaters in primary school | | Transition to secondary school | |
|---|---|---|---|---|---|---|---|---|---|---|---|---|
| | | | | | % of grade 1 students | | | | | | | |
| | % of relevant age group | | Reaching grade 5[a] | | | | Reaching last grade of primary education | | % of enrollment | | % | |
| | Male | Female | Male | | Female | | Male | Female | Male | Female | Male | Female |
| | 2006[b] | 2006[b] | 1991 | 2005[b] | 1991 | 2005[b] | 2005[b] | 2005[b] | 2006[b] | 2006[b] | 2005[b] | 2005[b] |
| Afghanistan | .. | .. | .. | .. | .. | .. | .. | .. | 18 | 14 | .. | .. |
| Albania | 100 | 99 | .. | .. | .. | .. | 89 | 91 | 3 | 2 | 100 | 99 |
| Algeria | 99 | 97 | 95 | 95 | 94 | 96 | 90 | 92 | 14 | 9 | 74 | 79 |
| Angola | .. | .. | .. | .. | .. | .. | .. | .. | .. | .. | .. | .. |
| Argentina | 110 | 109 | .. | 96 | .. | 98 | 94 | 97 | 8 | 5 | 93 | 96 |
| Armenia | 102 | 106 | .. | .. | .. | .. | 100 | 99 | 0[c] | 0[c] | 100 | 99 |
| Australia | 106 | 105 | 98 | .. | 99 | .. | .. | .. | .. | .. | .. | .. |
| Austria | 102 | 100 | .. | .. | .. | .. | 97 | 100 | 1 | 1 | .. | .. |
| Azerbaijan | 99 | 97 | .. | .. | .. | .. | 100 | 94 | 0[c] | 0[c] | 100 | 98 |
| Bangladesh | 122 | 124 | .. | 63 | .. | 67 | 63 | 67 | 7 | 7 | 86 | 92 |
| Belarus | 102 | 100 | .. | .. | .. | .. | 99 | 100 | 0[c] | 0[c] | 99 | 100 |
| Belgium | 97 | 99 | 90 | .. | 92 | .. | .. | .. | 3 | 3 | .. | .. |
| Benin | 109 | 96 | 54 | 53 | 56 | 50 | 48 | 44 | 17 | 17 | .. | .. |
| Bolivia | 122 | 122 | .. | 85 | .. | 85 | 83 | 81 | 1 | 1 | 90 | 90 |
| Bosnia and Herzegovina | .. | .. | .. | .. | .. | .. | .. | .. | .. | .. | .. | .. |
| Botswana | 111 | 104 | 81 | 89 | 87 | 92 | 83 | 88 | 5 | 4 | 95 | 95 |
| Brazil | 106 | 97 | .. | .. | .. | .. | .. | .. | 20 | 20 | .. | .. |
| Bulgaria | 97 | 94 | 91 | .. | 90 | .. | 91 | 93 | 3 | 2 | 95 | 96 |
| Burkina Faso | 79 | 67 | 71 | 71 | 68 | 74 | 63 | 66 | 12 | 12 | 45 | 43 |
| Burundi | 164 | 164 | 65 | 66 | 58 | 68 | 57 | 61 | 29 | 28 | 37 | 31 |
| Cambodia | 135 | 127 | .. | 61 | .. | 64 | 54 | 57 | 14 | 11 | 83 | 80 |
| Cameroon | 111 | 97 | .. | .. | .. | .. | .. | .. | 28 | 23 | 43 | 47 |
| Canada | 97 | 95 | 95 | .. | 98 | .. | .. | .. | .. | .. | .. | .. |
| Central African Republic | 73 | 55 | 24 | .. | 22 | .. | .. | .. | 29 | 30 | 46 | 52 |
| Chad | 109 | 79 | 56 | 34 | 41 | 32 | 27 | 23 | 22 | 24 | 56 | 42 |
| Chile | 101 | 99 | 94 | 100 | 91 | 99 | 98 | 98 | 3 | 2 | 96 | 98 |
| China | 88 | 87 | 58 | .. | 78 | .. | .. | .. | 0[c] | 0[c] | .. | .. |
| Hong Kong, China | .. | .. | .. | 99 | .. | 100 | 99 | 100 | 1 | 1 | 100 | 100 |
| Colombia | 127 | 123 | .. | 78 | .. | 86 | 78 | 86 | 4 | 3 | 99 | 100 |
| Congo, Dem. Rep. | .. | .. | 58 | .. | 50 | .. | .. | .. | .. | .. | .. | .. |
| Congo, Rep. | 78 | 78 | 56 | .. | 65 | .. | .. | .. | 21 | 21 | 58 | 58 |
| Costa Rica | 108 | 108 | 83 | 93 | 85 | 95 | 89 | 92 | 8 | 6 | 100 | 97 |
| Côte d'Ivoire | 73 | 61 | 75 | .. | 70 | .. | .. | .. | 23 | 24 | .. | .. |
| Croatia | .. | .. | .. | .. | .. | .. | .. | .. | 0[c] | 1 | 100[d] | 100[d] |
| Cuba | 102 | 104 | .. | 96 | .. | 98 | 96 | 98 | 1 | 0[c] | 98 | 99 |
| Czech Republic | 102 | 103 | .. | 98 | .. | 99 | 98 | 99 | 1 | 1 | 99 | 100 |
| Denmark | 98 | 97 | 94 | 93 | 94 | 93 | 92 | 92 | .. | .. | 100 | 99 |
| Dominican Republic | 102 | 100 | .. | 66 | .. | 71 | 58 | 65 | 10 | 6 | 81 | 87 |
| Ecuador | 133 | 131 | .. | 75 | .. | 77 | 75 | 77 | 2 | 1 | 81 | 76 |
| Egypt, Arab Rep. | 106 | 102 | .. | 98 | .. | 99 | 98 | 99 | 3 | 2 | 72 | 82 |
| El Salvador | 121 | 116 | 56 | 70 | 60 | 74 | 65 | 70 | 9 | 6 | 91 | 92 |
| Eritrea | 53 | 45 | .. | 77 | .. | 69 | 77 | 69 | 15 | 15 | 86 | 79 |
| Estonia | 100 | 97 | .. | 98 | .. | 99 | 99 | 99 | 2 | 1 | 96 | 99 |
| Ethiopia | 125 | 113 | 16 | 57[d] | 23 | 59[d] | 62 | 63 | 6 | 5 | 91 | 91 |
| Finland | 98 | 98 | 100 | 99 | 100 | 100 | 99 | 100 | 1 | 0[c] | 100 | 100 |
| France | .. | .. | 69 | .. | 95 | .. | .. | .. | .. | .. | .. | .. |
| Gabon | .. | .. | .. | .. | .. | .. | .. | .. | .. | .. | .. | .. |
| Gambia, The | 65 | 71 | .. | .. | .. | .. | .. | .. | 6 | 6 | .. | .. |
| Georgia | 97 | 103 | .. | 86 | .. | 90 | 83 | 89 | 0[c] | 0[c] | 98 | 100 |
| Germany | 104 | 103 | .. | .. | .. | .. | 99 | 100 | 1 | 1 | 99 | 99 |
| Ghana | 105 | 110 | 81 | .. | 79 | .. | .. | .. | 6 | 6 | .. | .. |
| Greece | 100 | 100 | 100 | 98 | 100 | 100 | 98 | 100 | 1 | 0[c] | 99 | 100 |
| Guatemala | 125 | 122 | .. | 70 | .. | 68 | 65 | 62 | 13 | 11 | 92 | 90 |
| Guinea | 94 | 87 | 64 | 83 | 48 | 78 | 79 | 72 | 8 | 9 | 75 | 66 |
| Guinea-Bissau | .. | .. | .. | .. | .. | .. | .. | .. | .. | .. | .. | .. |
| Haiti | .. | .. | .. | .. | .. | .. | .. | .. | .. | .. | .. | .. |

# Education efficiency

| | Gross intake rate in grade 1 | | Cohort survival rate | | | | | | Repeaters in primary school | | Transition to secondary school | |
|---|---|---|---|---|---|---|---|---|---|---|---|---|
| | % of relevant age group | | % of grade 1 students | | | | | | % of enrollment | | % | |
| | | | Reaching grade 5[a] | | | | Reaching last grade of primary education | | | | | |
| | Male | Female | Male | | Female | | Male | Female | Male | Female | Male | Female |
| | 2006[b] | 2006[b] | 1991 | 2005[b] | 1991 | 2005[b] | 2005[b] | 2005[b] | 2006[b] | 2006[b] | 2005[b] | 2005[b] |
| Honduras | 139 | 134 | .. | 80 | .. | 87 | 77 | 85 | 8 | 6 | 68 | 74 |
| Hungary | 97 | 95 | 77 | .. | 98 | .. | 98 | 98 | 3 | 2 | 99 | 99 |
| India | 132 | 125 | .. | 73 | .. | 73 | 73 | 73 | 3 | 3 | 87 | 83 |
| Indonesia | 120 | 116 | 34 | 92 | 78 | 87 | 88 | 83 | 6 | 4 | 79 | 78 |
| Iran, Islamic Rep. | 112 | 150 | 91 | .. | 89 | .. | .. | .. | 3 | 1 | 93 | 83 |
| Iraq | .. | .. | .. | 87 | .. | 73 | 78 | 61 | 9 | 7 | 73 | 66 |
| Ireland | 99 | 99 | 99 | 100 | 100 | 100 | .. | .. | 1 | 1 | .. | .. |
| Israel | 96 | 99 | .. | 100 | .. | 100 | 100 | 100 | 2 | 1 | 74 | 73 |
| Italy | 104 | 102 | .. | 100 | .. | 100 | 100 | 100 | 0[c] | 0[c] | 100 | 99 |
| Jamaica | 94 | 92 | .. | .. | .. | .. | .. | .. | 3 | 2 | 100 | 97 |
| Japan | 98 | 99 | 100 | .. | 100 | .. | .. | .. | .. | .. | .. | .. |
| Jordan | 92 | 92 | .. | 97 | .. | 96 | 96 | 95 | 1 | 1 | 96 | 97 |
| Kazakhstan | 107 | 107 | .. | .. | .. | .. | 100[d] | 100[d] | 0[c,e] | 0[c,e] | 100[d] | 100[d] |
| Kenya | 112 | 108 | 75 | 81 | 78 | 85 | 74 | 71 | 6 | 6 | .. | .. |
| Korea, Dem. Rep. | .. | .. | .. | .. | .. | .. | .. | .. | .. | .. | .. | .. |
| Korea, Rep. | 105 | 106 | 99 | 99 | 100 | 99 | 99 | 99 | 0[c] | 0[c] | 99 | 99 |
| Kuwait | 96 | 93 | .. | 95 | .. | 97 | 95 | 97 | 2 | 2 | 95 | 100 |
| Kyrgyz Republic | 98 | 97 | .. | .. | .. | .. | 97 | 100 | 0[c] | 0[c] | 100 | 100 |
| Lao PDR | 129 | 120 | .. | 62 | .. | 62 | 62 | 62 | 19 | 17 | 79 | 75 |
| Latvia | 94 | 93 | .. | .. | .. | .. | 99 | 98 | 4 | 2 | 97 | 98 |
| Lebanon | 86 | 86 | .. | 88 | .. | 94 | 83 | 91 | 11 | 8 | 83 | 88 |
| Lesotho | 105 | 99 | 58 | 68 | 73 | 80 | 53 | 71 | 21 | 16 | 67 | 65 |
| Liberia | 109 | 106 | .. | .. | .. | .. | .. | .. | 6 | 6 | .. | .. |
| Libya | .. | .. | .. | .. | .. | .. | .. | .. | .. | .. | .. | .. |
| Lithuania | 94 | 93 | .. | .. | .. | .. | 98 | 98 | 1 | 0[c] | 98 | 99 |
| Macedonia, FYR | 99 | 99 | .. | .. | .. | .. | 98 | 99 | 0[c] | 0[c] | 100 | 99 |
| Madagascar | 181 | 176 | 22 | 35 | 21 | 37 | 35 | 37 | 20 | 19 | 56 | 54 |
| Malawi | 145 | 156 | 71 | 44 | 57 | 44 | 36 | 36 | 21 | 20 | 74 | 71 |
| Malaysia | 102 | 101 | 97 | .. | 97 | .. | .. | .. | .. | .. | .. | .. |
| Mali | 89 | 76 | 71 | 83 | 67 | 79 | 75 | 70 | 17 | 17 | 63 | 48 |
| Mauritania | 124 | 129 | 76 | 59 | 75 | 56 | 46 | 43 | 10 | 10 | 51 | 45 |
| Mauritius | 104 | 104 | 97 | 98 | 98 | 100 | 97 | 100 | 5 | 4 | 61 | 72 |
| Mexico | 111 | 109 | 35 | 93 | 71 | 94 | 91 | 92 | 6 | 4 | 95 | 93 |
| Moldova | 90 | 87 | .. | .. | .. | .. | 96 | 98 | 0[c] | 0[c] | 98 | 99 |
| Mongolia | 117 | 119 | .. | .. | .. | .. | 91 | 91 | 0[c] | 0[c] | 95 | 99 |
| Morocco | 104 | 100 | 75 | 82 | 76 | 79 | 76 | 72 | 15 | 10 | 78 | 77 |
| Mozambique | 153 | 143 | 36 | 60 | 32 | 55 | 41 | 39 | 5 | 5 | 52 | 56 |
| Myanmar | 139 | 136 | .. | 71 | .. | 72 | 71 | 72 | 1 | 0[c] | 76 | 72 |
| Namibia | 104 | 105 | 60 | 84 | 65 | 90 | 73 | 80 | 19 | 14 | 72 | 77 |
| Nepal | 160 | 160 | 51 | 75 | 51 | 83 | 75 | 83 | 21 | 20 | 79 | 74 |
| Netherlands | 101 | 100 | .. | 99 | .. | 100 | .. | .. | .. | .. | 96 | 100 |
| New Zealand | 105 | 104 | .. | .. | .. | .. | .. | .. | .. | .. | .. | .. |
| Nicaragua | 173 | 163 | 11 | 50 | 37 | 57 | 46 | 55 | 11 | 8 | .. | .. |
| Niger | 76 | 59 | 61 | 58 | 65 | 54 | 55 | 50 | 5 | 5 | 61 | 58 |
| Nigeria | 116 | 99 | .. | 71 | .. | 75 | 61 | 64 | 3 | 3 | .. | .. |
| Norway | 97 | 97 | 99 | 100 | 100 | 100 | 100 | 100 | .. | .. | 100 | 100 |
| Oman | 76 | 76 | 97 | 100 | 96 | 100 | 100 | 99 | 0[c] | 1 | 99 | 98 |
| Pakistan | 125 | 100 | .. | 68 | .. | 72 | 68 | 72 | 2 | 2 | 69 | 75 |
| Panama | 116 | 114 | .. | 87 | .. | 89 | 84 | 86 | 7 | 5 | 92 | 95 |
| Papua New Guinea | .. | .. | 70 | .. | 68 | .. | .. | .. | .. | .. | .. | .. |
| Paraguay | 117 | 114 | 73 | 79 | 75 | 83 | 74 | 79 | 8 | 5 | 90 | 90 |
| Peru | 110 | 112 | .. | 91 | .. | 90 | 86 | 85 | 9 | 9 | 96 | 94 |
| Philippines | 137 | 128 | .. | 71 | .. | 80 | 66 | 77 | 3 | 2 | 91 | 92 |
| Poland | 97 | 98 | 89 | .. | 96 | .. | .. | .. | 1 | 0[c] | .. | .. |
| Portugal | 106 | 106 | .. | .. | .. | .. | .. | .. | 13 | 7 | .. | .. |
| Puerto Rico | .. | .. | .. | .. | .. | .. | .. | .. | .. | .. | .. | .. |

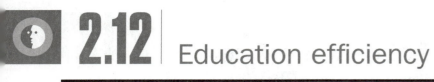

# 2.12 | Education efficiency

| | Gross intake rate in grade 1 | | Cohort survival rate | | | | | | Repeaters in primary school | | Transition to secondary school | |
|---|---|---|---|---|---|---|---|---|---|---|---|---|
| | % of relevant age group | | % of grade 1 students | | | | | | % of enrollment | | % | |
| | | | Reaching grade 5a | | | | Reaching last grade of primary education | | | | | |
| | Male | Female | Male | | Female | | Male | Female | Male | Female | Male | Female |
| | 2006b | 2006b | 1991 | 2005b | 1991 | 2005b | 2005b | 2005b | 2006b | 2006b | 2005b | 2005b |
| Romania | 97 | 96 | .. | .. | .. | .. | 94 | 95 | 3 | 2 | 98 | 98 |
| Russian Federation | .. | .. | .. | .. | .. | .. | .. | .. | .. | .. | .. | .. |
| Rwanda | 209 | 206 | 61 | 43 | 59 | 49 | 30 | 32 | 15 | 15 | .. | .. |
| Saudi Arabia | 102 | 105 | 82 | 100 | 84 | 93 | 100 | 94 | 6 | 4 | 93 | 97 |
| Senegal | 95 | 98 | .. | 65 | .. | 65 | 54 | 53 | 11 | 10 | 52 | 48 |
| Serbia | .. | .. | .. | .. | .. | .. | .. | .. | .. | .. | .. | .. |
| Sierra Leone | .. | .. | .. | .. | .. | .. | .. | .. | 10e | 10e | .. | .. |
| Singapore | .. | .. | .. | .. | .. | .. | .. | .. | .. | .. | .. | .. |
| Slovak Republic | 100 | 98 | .. | .. | .. | .. | 97 | 98 | 3 | 2 | 98 | 99 |
| Slovenia | 98 | 96 | .. | .. | .. | .. | .. | .. | 1 | 0c | .. | .. |
| Somalia | .. | .. | .. | .. | .. | .. | .. | .. | .. | .. | .. | .. |
| South Africa | 118 | 112 | .. | 82 | .. | 83 | 75 | 79 | 8 | 8 | 89 | 91 |
| Spain | 103 | 101 | .. | 100 | .. | 100 | 100 | 100 | 3 | 2 | .. | .. |
| Sri Lanka | 109 | 109 | 92 | .. | 93 | .. | .. | .. | 1 | 1 | .. | .. |
| Sudan | 67 | 58 | 90 | 78 | 99 | 79 | 73 | 75 | 1 | 2 | 94 | 100 |
| Swaziland | 111 | 103 | 74 | 81 | 80 | 87 | 66 | 75 | 19 | 15 | 88 | 89 |
| Sweden | 96 | 95 | 100 | .. | 100 | .. | .. | .. | .. | .. | .. | .. |
| Switzerland | 86 | 91 | .. | .. | .. | .. | .. | .. | 2 | 1 | 99 | 100 |
| Syrian Arab Republic | 125 | 122 | 97 | .. | 95 | .. | 92 | 93 | 7 | 5 | 95 | 97 |
| Tajikistan | 103 | 99 | .. | .. | .. | .. | 100 | 97 | 0c | 0c | 98 | 97 |
| Tanzania | 105 | 104 | 81 | 85d | 82 | 89d | 81d | 85d | 4e | 4e | 47 | 45 |
| Thailand | .. | .. | .. | .. | .. | .. | .. | .. | .. | .. | .. | .. |
| Timor-Leste | 118 | 105 | .. | .. | .. | .. | .. | .. | .. | .. | .. | .. |
| Togo | 101 | 95 | 52 | 79 | 42 | 70 | 74 | 62 | 23 | 23 | 68 | 61 |
| Trinidad and Tobago | 96 | 92 | .. | 90 | .. | 92 | 80 | 87 | 6 | 4 | 94 | 92 |
| Tunisia | 100 | 101 | 94 | 97 | 77 | 97 | 93 | 95 | 10 | 7 | 86 | 90 |
| Turkey | 97 | 93 | 98 | 97 | 97 | 97 | 95 | 93 | 3 | 3 | 93 | 90 |
| Turkmenistan | .. | .. | .. | .. | .. | .. | .. | .. | .. | .. | .. | .. |
| Uganda | 145 | 147 | .. | 49 | .. | 49 | 26 | 25 | 30 | 29 | 42 | 43 |
| Ukraine | 99 | 99 | .. | .. | .. | .. | .. | .. | 0c | 0c | 100 | 100 |
| United Arab Emirates | 103 | 101 | 80 | 98 | 80 | 100 | 98 | 100 | 2 | 2 | 99 | 100 |
| United Kingdom | .. | .. | .. | .. | .. | .. | .. | .. | 0 | 0 | .. | .. |
| United States | 102 | 100 | .. | .. | .. | .. | .. | .. | .. | .. | .. | .. |
| Uruguay | 107 | 105 | 96 | 90 | 98 | 93 | 88 | 91 | 9 | 6 | 75 | 87 |
| Uzbekistan | 97 | 94 | .. | .. | .. | .. | .. | .. | 0e | 0e | .. | .. |
| Venezuela, RB | 102 | 99 | 82 | 90 | 90 | 94 | 87 | 93 | 8 | 5 | 99 | 99 |
| Vietnam | 99 | 94 | .. | .. | .. | .. | .. | .. | .. | .. | .. | .. |
| West Bank and Gaza | 78 | 78 | .. | .. | .. | .. | 97 | 100 | 1 | 1 | 98 | 99 |
| Yemen, Rep. | 122 | 102 | .. | 67 | .. | 65 | 61 | 57 | 5 | 4 | 83 | 82 |
| Zambia | 119 | 125 | .. | 92 | .. | 87 | 79 | 73 | 7 | 6 | 49 | 60 |
| Zimbabwe | .. | .. | 72 | .. | 81 | .. | .. | .. | .. | .. | .. | .. |
| **World** | **116 w** | **111 w** | **.. w** | **.. w** | **.. w** | **.. w** | **.. w** | **.. w** | **.. w** | **.. w** | **.. w** | **.. w** |
| **Low income** | 126 | 116 | .. | 71 | .. | 71 | 69 | 69 | 6 | 6 | 79 | 77 |
| **Middle income** | .. | .. | 61 | .. | 80 | .. | .. | .. | .. | .. | .. | .. |
| Lower middle income | 94 | 95 | 59 | .. | 79 | .. | .. | .. | 3 | 2 | .. | .. |
| Upper middle income | 105 | 101 | .. | .. | .. | .. | .. | .. | 10 | 9 | .. | .. |
| **Low & middle income** | .. | .. | .. | .. | .. | .. | .. | .. | .. | .. | .. | .. |
| East Asia & Pacific | 91 | 90 | 55 | .. | 78 | .. | .. | .. | 1 | 1 | .. | .. |
| Europe & Central Asia | .. | .. | .. | .. | .. | .. | .. | .. | .. | .. | .. | .. |
| Latin America & Carib. | 112 | 108 | .. | .. | .. | .. | .. | .. | 10 | 9 | .. | .. |
| Middle East & N. Africa | 108 | 110 | .. | 90 | .. | 87 | 87 | 84 | 7 | 4 | 82 | 83 |
| South Asia | 130 | 120 | .. | 72 | .. | 73 | 72 | 73 | 4 | 4 | 84 | 82 |
| Sub-Saharan Africa | 117 | 108 | .. | .. | .. | .. | .. | .. | 9 | 9 | .. | .. |
| **High income** | 101 | 101 | .. | .. | .. | .. | .. | .. | .. | .. | .. | .. |
| Euro area | 103 | 102 | .. | .. | .. | .. | .. | .. | 1 | 1 | .. | .. |

a. Because of the change from International Standard Classification of Education 1976 (ISCED76) to ISCED97 in 1998, data for 1991 are not fully comparable with data from 1999 onward. b. Provisional data. c. Less than 0.5. d. Data are for 2006. e. Data are for 2007.

## About the data

The United Nations Educational, Scientific, and Cultural Organization (UNESCO) Institute for Statistics estimates indicators of students' progress through school. These indicators measure an education system's success in reaching all students, efficiently moving students from one grade to the next, and imparting a particular level of education.

The gross intake rate indicates the level of access to primary education and the education system's capacity to provide access to primary education. Low gross intake rates in grade 1 reflect the fact that many children do not enter primary school even though school attendance, at least through the primary level, is mandatory in all countries. Because the gross intake rate includes all new entrants regardless of age, it can exceed 100 percent. Once enrolled, students drop out for a variety of reasons, including low quality schooling, relevance of curriculum (real or perceived by parents or students), repetition, discouragement over poor performance, and direct and indirect schooling costs. Students' progress to higher grades may also be limited by the availability of teachers, classrooms, and materials.

The cohort survival rate is the estimated proportion of an entering cohort of grade 1 students that eventually reaches grade 5 or the last grade of primary education. It measures an education system's holding

power and internal efficiency. Rates approaching 100 percent indicate high retention and low dropout levels. Cohort survival rates are typically estimated from data on enrollment and repetition by grade for two consecutive years. This procedure, called the reconstructed cohort method, makes three simplifying assumptions: dropouts never return to school; promotion, repetition, and dropout rates remain constant over the period in which the cohort is enrolled in school; and the same rates apply to all pupils enrolled in a grade, regardless of whether they previously repeated a grade (Fredricksen 1993). Cross-country comparisons should thus be made with caution, because other flows—caused by new entrants, reentrants, grade skipping, migration, or transfers during the school year—are not considered.

Research suggests that five to six years of schooling, which is how long primary education lasts in most countries, is a critical threshold for achieving sustainable basic literacy and numeracy skills. But the indicator only indirectly reflects the quality of schooling, and a high rate does not guarantee these learning outcomes. Measuring actual learning outcomes requires setting curriculum standards and measuring students' learning progress against those standards through standardized assessments, actions that many countries do not systematically undertake.

Data on repeaters are often used to indicate an education system's internal efficiency. Repeaters not only increase the cost of education for the family and the school system, but also use limited school resources. Country policies on repetition and promotion differ; in some cases the number of repeaters is controlled because of limited capacity. Care should be taken in interpreting this indicator.

The transition rate from primary to secondary school conveys the degree of access or transition between the two levels. As completing primary education is a prerequisite for participating in lower secondary school, growing numbers of primary completers will inevitably create pressure for more available places at the secondary level. A low transition rate can signal such problems as an inadequate examination and promotion system or insufficient secondary school capacity. The quality of data on the transition rate is affected when new entrants and repeaters are not correctly distinguished in the first grade of secondary school. Students who interrupt their studies after completing primary school could also affect data quality.

In 2006 the UNESCO Institute for Statistics changed its convention for citing the reference year. For more information, see *About the data* for table 2.10.

## Definitions

- **Gross intake rate in grade 1** is the number of new entrants in the first grade of primary education regardless of age as a percentage of the population of the official primary school entrance age. • **Cohort survival rate** is the percentage of children enrolled in the first grade of primary school who eventually reach grade 5 or the last grade of primary education. The estimate is based on the reconstructed cohort method (see *About the data*). • **Repeaters in primary school** are the number of students enrolled in the same grade as in the previous year as a percentage of all students enrolled in primary school. • **Transition to secondary school** is the number of new entrants to the first grade of secondary school in a given year as a percentage of the number of students enrolled in the final grade of primary school in the previous year.

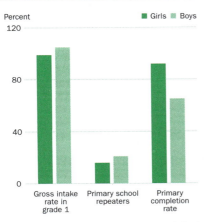

**In Lesotho more girls who enroll in primary school stay in and complete school than boys do**    2.12a

In many developing countries, especially in Sub-Saharan Africa, fewer girls than boys enroll and stay in school. But in Lesotho more girls complete primary school because they repeat grades less often and are less likely to drop out.

*Source:* United Nations Educational, Scientific, and Cultural Organization Institute for Statistics.

## Data sources

Data on education efficiency are from the UNESCO Institute for Statistics.

# 2.13 | Education completion and outcomes

| | Primary completion rate[a] | | | | | | Youth literacy rate | | | | Adult literacy rate | |
|---|---|---|---|---|---|---|---|---|---|---|---|---|
| | % of relevant age group | | | | | | % ages 15–24 | | | | % ages 15 and older | |
| | Total | | Male | | Female | | Male | | Female | | Male | Female |
| | **1991** | **2006**[b] | **1991** | **2006**[b] | **1991** | **2006**[b] | **1990** | **2005** | **1990** | **2005** | **2005** | **2005** |
| Afghanistan | .. | .. | .. | .. | .. | .. | .. | .. | .. | .. | .. | .. |
| Albania | .. | 96 | .. | 97 | .. | 96 | .. | 99 | .. | 99 | 99 | 98 |
| Algeria | 80 | 85 | 86 | 86 | 73 | 84 | 86 | 94 | 62 | 86 | 80 | 60 |
| Angola | 35 | .. | .. | .. | .. | .. | .. | 84 | .. | 63 | 83 | 54 |
| Argentina | .. | 99 | .. | 97 | .. | 102 | 98 | 99 | 99 | 99 | 97 | 97 |
| Armenia | 90 | 91 | .. | 90 | .. | 93 | 100 | 100 | 100 | 100 | 100 | 99 |
| Australia | .. | .. | .. | .. | .. | .. | .. | .. | .. | .. | .. | .. |
| Austria | .. | 103 | .. | 103 | .. | 102 | .. | .. | .. | .. | .. | .. |
| Azerbaijan | .. | 92 | .. | 94 | .. | 90 | .. | .. | .. | .. | .. | .. |
| Bangladesh | 49 | 72 | .. | 70 | .. | 74 | 52 | 67 | 38 | 60 | 54 | 41 |
| Belarus | 94 | 95 | 95 | 96 | 96 | 93 | 100 | .. | 100 | .. | .. | .. |
| Belgium | 79 | .. | 76 | .. | 82 | .. | .. | .. | .. | .. | .. | .. |
| Benin | 21 | 65 | 28 | 78 | 13 | 51 | 55 | 59 | 27 | 33 | 48 | 23 |
| Bolivia | .. | 101 | .. | 102 | .. | 100 | 96 | 99 | 92 | 96 | 93 | 81 |
| Bosnia and Herzegovina | .. | .. | .. | .. | .. | .. | .. | 100 | .. | 100 | 99 | 94 |
| Botswana | 89 | 95 | 82 | 75 | 97 | 115 | 86 | 92 | 92 | 96 | 80 | 82 |
| Brazil | 93 | 105 | .. | .. | .. | .. | .. | 96 | .. | 98 | 88 | 89 |
| Bulgaria | 84 | 99 | 86 | 98 | 83 | 99 | .. | 98 | .. | 98 | 99 | 98 |
| Burkina Faso | 20 | 31 | 24 | 35 | 15 | 28 | 27 | 40 | 14 | 26 | 31 | 17 |
| Burundi | 46 | 36 | 49 | 40 | 43 | 32 | 59 | 77 | 48 | 70 | 67 | 52 |
| Cambodia | .. | 87 | .. | 87 | .. | 86 | .. | 88 | .. | 79 | 85 | 64 |
| Cameroon | 53 | 58 | 57 | 65 | 49 | 51 | .. | .. | .. | .. | 77 | 60 |
| Canada | .. | .. | .. | .. | .. | .. | .. | .. | .. | .. | .. | .. |
| Central African Republic | 27 | 24 | 35 | 31 | 18 | 18 | 63 | 70 | 35 | 47 | 65 | 33 |
| Chad | 18 | 31 | 29 | 41 | 7 | 21 | .. | 56 | .. | 23 | 41 | 13 |
| Chile | .. | 123 | .. | 130 | .. | 116 | 98 | 99 | 99 | 99 | 96 | 96 |
| China | 105 | .. | .. | .. | .. | .. | 97 | 99 | 91 | 99 | 95 | 87 |
|   Hong Kong, China | 102 | .. | .. | .. | .. | .. | .. | .. | .. | .. | .. | .. |
| Colombia | 70 | 105 | 67 | 103 | 73 | 107 | 89 | 98 | 92 | 98 | 93 | 93 |
| Congo, Dem. Rep. | 46 | 38 | 58 | 46 | 34 | 31 | .. | 78 | .. | 63 | 81 | 54 |
| Congo, Rep. | 54 | 73 | 59 | 77 | 49 | 69 | .. | 98 | .. | 97 | 91 | 79 |
| Costa Rica | 79 | 89 | 77 | 87 | 81 | 91 | .. | 97 | .. | 98 | 95 | 95 |
| Côte d'Ivoire | 43 | 43 | 55 | 53 | 32 | 33 | 60 | 71 | 38 | 52 | 61 | 39 |
| Croatia | 85 | 92 | .. | 93 | .. | 92 | 100 | 100 | 100 | 100 | 99 | 97 |
| Cuba | 99 | 92 | .. | 92 | .. | 91 | .. | 100 | .. | 100 | 100 | 100 |
| Czech Republic | .. | 102 | .. | 102 | .. | 102 | .. | .. | .. | .. | .. | .. |
| Denmark | 98 | 99 | 98 | 99 | 98 | 99 | .. | .. | .. | .. | .. | .. |
| Dominican Republic | 61 | 83 | .. | 80 | .. | 87 | .. | 93 | .. | 95 | 87 | 87 |
| Ecuador | 91 | 106 | 91 | 105 | 92 | 106 | 97 | 96 | 96 | 96 | 92 | 90 |
| Egypt, Arab Rep. | .. | 98 | .. | 102 | .. | 94 | .. | 90 | .. | 79 | 83 | 59 |
| El Salvador | 41 | 88 | 38 | 88 | 43 | 88 | 85 | 87 | 85 | 90 | 82 | 79 |
| Eritrea | 19 | 48 | 22 | 56 | 17 | 41 | .. | .. | .. | .. | .. | .. |
| Estonia | 93 | 106 | 93 | 107 | 94 | 104 | 100 | 100 | 100 | 100 | 100 | 100 |
| Ethiopia | 26 | 49 | 32 | 55 | 19 | 42 | .. | 62 | .. | 39 | 50 | 23 |
| Finland | 97 | 100 | 98 | 101 | 97 | 99 | .. | .. | .. | .. | .. | .. |
| France | 104 | .. | .. | .. | .. | .. | .. | .. | .. | .. | .. | .. |
| Gabon | 58 | 75 | 55 | 73 | 61 | 76 | 94 | 97 | 92 | 95 | 88 | 80 |
| Gambia, The | 44 | 63 | 55 | 62 | 33 | 64 | .. | .. | .. | .. | .. | .. |
| Georgia | .. | 85 | .. | 83 | .. | 86 | .. | .. | .. | .. | .. | .. |
| Germany | 100 | 95 | 99 | 94 | 100 | 95 | .. | .. | .. | .. | .. | .. |
| Ghana | 61 | 71 | 69 | 73 | 54 | 68 | .. | 76 | .. | 65 | 66 | 50 |
| Greece | 99 | 100 | 99 | 100 | 98 | 100 | 99 | 99 | 99 | 99 | 98 | 94 |
| Guatemala | .. | 77 | .. | 80 | .. | 73 | .. | 86 | .. | 78 | 75 | 63 |
| Guinea | 17 | 64 | 25 | 74 | 9 | 53 | .. | 59 | .. | 34 | 43 | 18 |
| Guinea-Bissau | .. | .. | .. | .. | .. | .. | .. | .. | .. | .. | .. | .. |
| Haiti | 27 | .. | 29 | .. | 26 | .. | .. | .. | .. | .. | .. | .. |

# Education completion and outcomes

| | Primary completion rate[a] | | | | | | Youth literacy rate | | | | Adult literacy rate | |
|---|---|---|---|---|---|---|---|---|---|---|---|---|
| | % of relevant age group | | | | | | % ages 15–24 | | | | % ages 15 and older | |
| | Total | | Male | | Female | | Male | | Female | | Male | Female |
| | 1991 | 2006[b] | 1991 | 2006[b] | 1991 | 2006[b] | 1990 | 2005 | 1990 | 2005 | 2005 | 2005 |
| Honduras | 64 | 89 | 67 | 86 | 61 | 91 | .. | 87 | .. | 91 | 80 | 80 |
| Hungary | 93 | 94 | 88 | 94 | 90 | 94 | .. | .. | .. | .. | .. | .. |
| India | 64 | 85 | 75 | 87 | 52 | 82 | 74 | 84[c] | 49 | 68[c] | 73[c] | 48[c] |
| Indonesia | 91 | 99 | .. | 99 | .. | 100 | 97 | 99 | 95 | 99 | 94 | 87 |
| Iran, Islamic Rep. | 91 | 101 | 97 | 95 | 85 | 108 | 92 | 98 | 81 | 97 | 88 | 77 |
| Iraq | 59 | .. | 64 | .. | 53 | .. | .. | .. | .. | .. | .. | .. |
| Ireland | .. | 97 | .. | 96 | .. | 97 | .. | .. | .. | .. | .. | .. |
| Israel | .. | 101 | .. | 101 | .. | 101 | .. | .. | .. | .. | .. | .. |
| Italy | 104 | 100 | 104 | 100 | 104 | 99 | .. | 100 | .. | 100 | 99 | 98 |
| Jamaica | 90 | 82 | 86 | 81 | 94 | 84 | .. | .. | .. | .. | .. | .. |
| Japan | 101 | .. | 101 | .. | 102 | .. | .. | .. | .. | .. | .. | .. |
| Jordan | 72 | 100 | 69 | 100 | 77 | 101 | .. | 99 | .. | 99 | 95 | 87 |
| Kazakhstan | .. | 101[d] | .. | 100[d] | .. | 101[d] | 100 | .. | 100 | .. | .. | .. |
| Kenya | .. | 93 | .. | 94 | .. | 92 | .. | 80 | .. | 81 | 78 | 70 |
| Korea, Dem. Rep. | .. | .. | .. | .. | .. | .. | .. | .. | .. | .. | .. | .. |
| Korea, Rep. | 98 | 101 | 98 | 107 | 98 | 95 | .. | .. | .. | .. | .. | .. |
| Kuwait | .. | 91 | .. | 90 | .. | 92 | .. | 100 | .. | 100 | 94 | 91 |
| Kyrgyz Republic | .. | 99 | .. | 99 | .. | 100 | .. | .. | .. | .. | .. | .. |
| Lao PDR | 43 | 75 | 48 | 80 | 38 | 70 | .. | 83 | .. | 75 | 77 | 61 |
| Latvia | .. | 92 | .. | 93 | .. | 92 | 100 | 100 | 100 | 100 | 100 | 100 |
| Lebanon | .. | 80 | .. | 79 | .. | 82 | .. | .. | .. | .. | .. | .. |
| Lesotho | 59 | 78 | 42 | 65 | 76 | 92 | .. | .. | .. | .. | 74 | 90 |
| Liberia | .. | 63 | .. | 69 | .. | 58 | .. | 65 | .. | 69 | 58 | 46 |
| Libya | .. | .. | .. | .. | .. | .. | .. | 100 | .. | 96 | 93 | 75 |
| Lithuania | 89 | 91 | .. | 91 | .. | 91 | 100 | 100 | 100 | 100 | 100 | 100 |
| Macedonia, FYR | 98 | 97 | .. | 96 | .. | 98 | .. | 99 | .. | 98 | 98 | 94 |
| Madagascar | 33 | 57 | 33 | 57 | 34 | 57 | .. | 73 | .. | 68 | 77 | 65 |
| Malawi | 29 | 55 | 36 | 55 | 21 | 55 | 70 | .. | 49 | .. | .. | .. |
| Malaysia | 91 | 95 | 91 | 95 | 91 | 95 | 96 | 97 | 95 | 97 | 92 | 85 |
| Mali | 13 | 49 | 15 | 59 | 10 | 40 | .. | .. | .. | .. | 33 | 16 |
| Mauritania | 34 | 47 | 41 | 47 | 27 | 47 | .. | 68 | .. | 55 | 60 | 43 |
| Mauritius | 107 | 92 | 107 | 91 | 107 | 94 | 91 | 94 | 92 | 95 | 88 | 81 |
| Mexico | 88 | 103 | 89 | 102 | 90 | 103 | 96 | 98 | 95 | 98 | 93 | 90 |
| Moldova | .. | 90 | .. | 90 | .. | 91 | 100 | 100 | 100 | 100 | 100 | 99 |
| Mongolia | .. | 109 | .. | 108 | .. | 110 | .. | 97 | .. | 98 | 98 | 98 |
| Morocco | 48 | 84 | 57 | 88 | 39 | 80 | .. | 81 | .. | 60 | 66 | 40 |
| Mozambique | 26 | 42 | 32 | 49 | 21 | 35 | .. | .. | .. | .. | .. | .. |
| Myanmar | .. | 95 | .. | 93 | .. | 98 | .. | 96 | .. | 93 | 94 | 86 |
| Namibia | 78 | 76 | 70 | 73 | 86 | 80 | 86 | 91 | 90 | 93 | 87 | 83 |
| Nepal | 51 | 76 | 68 | 80 | 40 | 72 | 68 | 81 | 33 | 60 | 63 | 35 |
| Netherlands | .. | 100 | .. | 101 | .. | 99 | .. | .. | .. | .. | .. | .. |
| New Zealand | 100 | .. | 101 | .. | 99 | .. | .. | .. | .. | .. | .. | .. |
| Nicaragua | 42 | 73 | 43 | 70 | 59 | 77 | .. | 84 | .. | 89 | 77 | 77 |
| Niger | 18 | 33 | 22 | 39 | 13 | 26 | .. | 52 | .. | 23 | 43 | 15 |
| Nigeria | .. | 76 | .. | 83 | .. | 68 | 81 | 87 | 62 | 81 | 78 | 60 |
| Norway | 100 | 99 | 100 | 99 | 100 | 98 | .. | .. | .. | .. | .. | .. |
| Oman | 74 | 94 | 78 | 95 | 70 | 92 | .. | 98 | .. | 97 | 87 | 74 |
| Pakistan | .. | 62 | .. | 70 | .. | 53 | .. | 77 | .. | 53 | 64 | 35 |
| Panama | 86 | 94 | 86 | 94 | 86 | 95 | 95 | 97 | 95 | 96 | 93 | 91 |
| Papua New Guinea | 46 | .. | 51 | .. | 42 | .. | .. | 69 | .. | 64 | 63 | 51 |
| Paraguay | 68 | 94 | 68 | 94 | 69 | 95 | 96 | 96 | 95 | 96 | 94 | 93 |
| Peru | .. | 100 | .. | 100 | .. | 100 | 97 | 98 | 94 | 96 | 94 | 82 |
| Philippines | 86 | 96 | 84 | 92 | 84 | 100 | 96 | 94 | 97 | 97 | 92 | 94 |
| Poland | 98 | 97 | .. | .. | .. | .. | .. | .. | .. | .. | .. | .. |
| Portugal | 95 | 104 | 94 | 102 | 95 | 107 | 99 | 100 | 99 | 100 | 96 | 92 |
| Puerto Rico | .. | .. | .. | .. | .. | .. | 92 | 86 | 94 | 86 | 90 | 90 |

# 2.13 Education completion and outcomes

| | Primary completion rate[a] | | | | | | Youth literacy rate | | | | Adult literacy rate | |
|---|---|---|---|---|---|---|---|---|---|---|---|---|
| | % of relevant age group | | | | | | % ages 15–24 | | | | % ages 15 and older | |
| | Total | | Male | | Female | | Male | | Female | | Male | Female |
| | 1991 | 2006[b] | 1991 | 2006[b] | 1991 | 2006[b] | 1990 | 2005 | 1990 | 2005 | 2005 | 2005 |
| Romania | 96 | 99 | 96 | 99 | 96 | 98 | 99 | 98 | 99 | 98 | 98 | 96 |
| Russian Federation | 93 | 94 | 92 | .. | 93 | .. | 100 | 100 | 100 | 100 | 100 | 99 |
| Rwanda | 35 | 35 | 40 | 36 | 31 | 35 | .. | 79 | .. | 77 | 71 | 60 |
| Saudi Arabia | 55 | 85 | 60 | .. | 51 | .. | 94 | 97 | 81 | 95 | 88 | 78 |
| Senegal | 39 | 49 | 47 | 51 | 30 | 47 | 49 | 58 | 28 | 41 | 51 | 29 |
| Serbia | .. | .. | .. | .. | .. | .. | .. | 99[e] | .. | 99[e] | 99[e] | 94[e] |
| Sierra Leone | .. | 81[d] | .. | 92[d] | .. | 70[d] | .. | 60 | .. | 37 | 47 | 24 |
| Singapore | .. | .. | .. | .. | .. | .. | 99 | 99 | 99 | 100 | 97 | 89 |
| Slovak Republic | 96 | 94 | 95 | 95 | 96 | 94 | .. | .. | .. | .. | .. | .. |
| Slovenia | 95 | 99 | .. | 100 | .. | 99 | 100 | 100 | 100 | 100 | 100 | 100 |
| Somalia | .. | .. | .. | .. | .. | .. | .. | .. | .. | .. | .. | .. |
| South Africa | 76 | 100 | 71 | 100 | 80 | 100 | .. | .. | .. | .. | .. | .. |
| Spain | .. | 103 | .. | 103 | .. | 103 | 100 | .. | 100 | .. | .. | .. |
| Sri Lanka | 102 | 108 | 103 | 107 | 102 | 108 | .. | 95[f] | .. | 96[f] | 92[f] | 89[f] |
| Sudan | 42 | 47 | 47 | 50 | 37 | 43 | .. | 85[g] | .. | 71[g] | 71[g] | 52[g] |
| Swaziland | 60 | 67 | 57 | 64 | 63 | 69 | .. | 87 | .. | 90 | 81 | 78 |
| Sweden | 96 | .. | 96 | .. | 96 | .. | .. | .. | .. | .. | .. | .. |
| Switzerland | 53 | 91 | 53 | 91 | 54 | 92 | .. | .. | .. | .. | .. | .. |
| Syrian Arab Republic | 89 | 115 | 94 | 116 | 84 | 113 | .. | 95 | .. | 90 | 88 | 74 |
| Tajikistan | .. | 106 | .. | 108 | .. | 104 | 100 | 100 | 100 | 100 | 100 | 99 |
| Tanzania | 62 | 85[d] | 62 | 87[d] | 63 | 83[d] | 86 | 81 | 78 | 76 | 78 | 62 |
| Thailand | .. | .. | .. | .. | .. | .. | .. | 98 | .. | 98 | 95 | 91 |
| Timor-Leste | .. | .. | .. | .. | .. | .. | .. | .. | .. | .. | .. | .. |
| Togo | 35 | 67 | 48 | 78 | 22 | 56 | .. | 84 | .. | 64 | 69 | 38 |
| Trinidad and Tobago | 101 | 88 | 98 | 86 | 104 | 90 | .. | 99 | .. | 99 | 99 | 98 |
| Tunisia | 74 | 99 | 79 | 98 | 70 | 100 | .. | 96 | .. | 92 | 83 | 65 |
| Turkey | 90 | 86 | 93 | 90 | 86 | 82 | 97 | 98 | 88 | 93 | 95 | 80 |
| Turkmenistan | .. | .. | .. | .. | .. | .. | .. | .. | .. | .. | .. | .. |
| Uganda | .. | 54 | .. | 57 | .. | 51 | 77 | 83 | 63 | 71 | 77 | 58 |
| Ukraine | 94 | 105 | 98 | 105 | 97 | 105 | .. | 100 | .. | 100 | 100 | 99 |
| United Arab Emirates | 103 | 100 | 104 | 101 | 103 | 100 | .. | 98 | .. | 95 | 89 | 88 |
| United Kingdom | .. | .. | .. | .. | .. | .. | .. | .. | .. | .. | .. | .. |
| United States | .. | .. | .. | .. | .. | .. | .. | .. | .. | .. | .. | .. |
| Uruguay | 94 | 93 | 91 | 92 | 96 | 93 | .. | .. | .. | .. | .. | .. |
| Uzbekistan | .. | 98 | .. | 98 | .. | 98 | .. | .. | .. | .. | .. | .. |
| Venezuela, RB | 43 | 96 | 37 | 93 | 49 | 98 | 95 | 96 | 96 | 98 | 93 | 93 |
| Vietnam | .. | 92 | .. | 103 | .. | 97 | 94 | .. | 93 | .. | .. | .. |
| West Bank and Gaza | .. | 89 | .. | 89 | .. | 89 | .. | 99 | .. | 99 | 97 | 88 |
| Yemen, Rep. | .. | 60 | .. | 74 | .. | 46 | .. | 91 | .. | 59 | 73 | 35 |
| Zambia | .. | 84 | .. | 89 | .. | 79 | 67 | .. | 66 | .. | .. | .. |
| Zimbabwe | 97 | 81 | 99 | 83 | 96 | 79 | 97 | 97 | 94 | 98 | 93 | 86 |
| **World** | **79 w** | **86 w** | **85 w** | **88 w** | **74 w** | **84 w** | **88 w** | **91 w** | **79 w** | **84 w** | **87 w** | **77 w** |
| **Low income** | 57 | 73 | 68 | 77 | 48 | 69 | 72 | 80 | 54 | 66 | 72 | 50 |
| **Middle income** | 93 | 97 | 96 | 98 | 90 | 97 | 95 | 97 | 91 | 96 | 93 | 87 |
| Lower middle income | 95 | 97 | 98 | 97 | 90 | 96 | 95 | 97 | 90 | 95 | 93 | 85 |
| Upper middle income | 88 | 99 | 88 | 99 | 88 | 99 | 97 | 98 | 96 | 98 | 94 | 92 |
| **Low & middle income** | 78 | 85 | 84 | 87 | 72 | 83 | 86 | 90 | 76 | 82 | 85 | 73 |
| East Asia & Pacific | 101 | 98 | 103 | 98 | 95 | 98 | 97 | 98 | 92 | 98 | 95 | 87 |
| Europe & Central Asia | 93 | 95 | 94 | 96 | 91 | 94 | 99 | 99 | 98 | 98 | 99 | 96 |
| Latin America & Carib. | 82 | 99 | 82 | 98 | 83 | 100 | 93 | 96 | 94 | 96 | 91 | 89 |
| Middle East & N. Africa | 77 | 91 | 83 | 93 | 71 | 88 | 84 | 93 | 68 | 84 | 83 | 63 |
| South Asia | 62 | 80 | 75 | 83 | 52 | 76 | 71 | 81 | 48 | 65 | 70 | 46 |
| Sub-Saharan Africa | 51 | 60 | 56 | 65 | 46 | 55 | 71 | 76 | 58 | 64 | 69 | 50 |
| **High income** | .. | 97 | .. | 99 | .. | 96 | 99 | 99 | 99 | 99 | 99 | 98 |
| Euro area | 100 | .. | .. | .. | .. | .. | .. | .. | .. | .. | .. | .. |

a. Because of the change from International Standard Classification of Education 1976 (ISCED76) to ISCED97 in 1998, data for 1991 are not fully comparable with data from 1999 onward. b. Provisional data. c. Excludes Mao Maram, Paomata, and Purul of Senapati district of Manipur. d. Data are for 2007. e. Includes Montenegro and excludes Kosovo and Metohija. f. Covers 18 of 25 districts. g. Covers northern Sudan only.

## About the data

Many governments publish statistics that indicate how their education systems are working and developing—statistics on enrollment and such efficiency indicators as repetition rates, pupil-teacher ratios, and cohort progression. The World Bank and the United Nations Educational, Scientific, and Cultural Organization (UNESCO) Institute for Statistics jointly developed the primary completion rate indicator. Increasingly used as a core indicator of an education system's performance, it reflects an education system's coverage and the educational attainment of students. The indicator is a key measure of educational outcome at the primary level and of progress on the Millennium Development Goals and the Education for All initiative. However, because curricula and standards for school completion vary across countries, a high primary completion rate does not necessarily mean high levels of student learning.

The primary completion rate reflects the primary cycle as defined by the International Standard Classification of Education, ranging from three or four years of primary education (in a very small number of countries) to five or six years (in most countries) and seven (in a small number of countries).

The table shows the proxy primary completion rate, calculated by subtracting the number of repeaters in the last grade of primary school from the total number of students in that grade and dividing by the total number of children of official graduation age. Data limitations preclude adjusting for students who drop out during the final year of primary school. Thus proxy rates should be taken as an upper estimate of the actual primary completion rate.

There are many reasons why the primary completion rate can exceed 100 percent. The numerator may include late entrants and overage children who have repeated one or more grades of primary school as well as children who entered school early, while the denominator is the number of children of official completing age. Other data limitations contribute to completion rates exceeding 100 percent, such as the use of estimates for the population of varying reliability, the conduct of school and population surveys at different times of year, and other discrepancies in the numbers used in the calculation.

Basic student outcomes include achievements in reading and mathematics judged against established standards. National assessments are enabling many countries' ministries of education to monitor progress in these outcomes. International comparable assessments are not yet available, although a few exist for some countries. The UNESCO Institute for Statistics has established literacy as an outcome indicator based on an internationally agreed definition.

The literacy rate is the percentage of people who can, with understanding, both read and write a short, simple statement about their everyday life. In practice, literacy is difficult to measure. To estimate literacy using such a definition requires census or survey measurements under controlled conditions. Many countries estimate the number of literate people from self-reported data. Some use educational attainment data as a proxy but apply different lengths of school attendance or levels of completion. Because definitions and methodologies of data collection differ across countries, data should be used cautiously.

The reported literacy data are compiled by the UNESCO Institute for Statistics based on national censuses and household surveys during 1985–2005. For detailed information on sources and definitions, consult the original source.

Literacy statistics for most countries cover the population ages 15 and older, but some include younger ages or are confined to age ranges that tend to inflate literacy rates. The literacy data in the narrower age range of 15–24 captures the ability of participants in the formal education system better and reflects recent progress in education. The youth literacy rate reported in the table measures the accumulated outcomes of primary education over the previous 10 years or so by indicating the proportion of people who have passed through the primary education system and acquired basic literacy and numeracy skills.

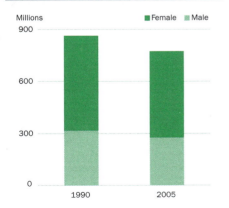

Source: United Nations Educational, Scientific, and Cultural Organization Institute for Statistics.

## Definitions

• **Primary completion rate** is the percentage of students completing the last year of primary school. It is calculated by taking the total number of students in the last grade of primary school, minus the number of repeaters in that grade, divided by the total number of children of official completing age. • **Youth literacy rate** is the percentage of people ages 15–24 that can, with understanding, both read and write a short, simple statement about their everyday life. • **Adult literacy rate** is the literacy rate among people ages 15 and older.

## Data sources

Data on primary completion rates and literacy rates are from the UNESCO Institute for Statistics.

# Education gaps by income and gender

| | Survey year | Gross intake rate in grade 1 | | Gross primary participation rate | | Average years of schooling | | Primary completion rate | | | | Children out of school | |
|---|---|---|---|---|---|---|---|---|---|---|---|---|---|
| | | % of relevant age group | | % of relevant age group | | Ages 15–24 | | | % of relevant age group | | | % of children ages 6–11 | |
| | | Poorest quintile | Richest quintile | Poorest quintile | Richest quintile | Poorest quintile | Richest quintile | Poorest quintile | Richest quintile | Male | Female | Poorest quintile | Richest quintile |
| Armenia | 2000 | 105 | 93 | 177 | 181 | 9 | 11 | 96 | 98 | 96 | 98 | 14 | 13 |
| Bangladesh | 2004 | 193 | 156 | 107 | 120 | 3 | 8 | 26 | 70 | 47 | 58 | 25 | 10 |
| Benin | 2001 | 74 | 112 | 51 | 115 | 1 | 6 | 7 | 45 | 23 | 15 | 66 | 21 |
| Bolivia | 2003 | 98 | 95 | 92 | 98 | 6 | 11 | 48 | 90 | 75 | 75 | 24 | 5 |
| Burkina Faso | 2003 | 24 | 97 | 20 | 98 | 1 | 6 | 8 | 52 | 24 | 20 | 87 | 32 |
| Cambodia | 2000 | 146 | 187 | 78 | 134 | 2 | 7 | 4 | 45 | 18 | 17 | 50 | 12 |
| Cameroon | 2004 | 115 | 100 | 94 | 122 | 3 | 9 | 12 | 69 | 36 | 37 | 42 | 4 |
| Central African Republic | 1994–95 | 103 | 118 | 57 | 130 | 2 | 6 | 0ᵃ | 18 | 8 | 6 | 65 | 21 |
| Chad | 2004 | 3 | 14 | 15 | 98 | 0ᵃ | 5 | 1 | 36 | 15 | 8 | 91 | 36 |
| Colombia | 2005 | 157 | 85 | 126 | 99 | 6 | 11 | 50 | 90 | 70 | 77 | 8 | 1 |
| Comoros | 1996 | 84 | 119 | 56 | 147 | 2 | 6 | 4 | 29 | 12 | 12 | 72 | 26 |
| Côte d'Ivoire | 1994 | 26 | 39 | 41 | 103 | 2 | 6 | 6 | 41 | 25 | 17 | 70 | 23 |
| Dominican Republic | 2002 | 170 | 103 | 149 | 156 | 6 | 11 | 38 | 87 | 57 | 69 | 14 | 4 |
| Egypt, Arab Rep. | 2003 | 87 | 120 | 96 | 103 | 6 | 11 | 58 | 87 | 77 | 71 | 24 | 5 |
| Eritrea | 1995 | 55 | 117 | 42 | 154 | 1 | 7 | 3 | 65 | 21 | 24 | 84 | 10 |
| Ethiopia | 2000 | 87 | 257 | 61 | 186 | 1 | 5 | 4 | 44 | 15 | 12 | 87 | 42 |
| Gabon | 2000 | .. | .. | 155 | 140 | 5 | 8 | 12 | 60 | 35 | 40 | 8 | 3 |
| Ghana | 2003 | 90 | 90 | 71 | 108 | 4 | 9 | 15 | 66 | 38 | 41 | 57 | 20 |
| Guatemala | 1995 | 114 | 124 | 62 | 122 | 2 | 9 | 9 | 76 | 41 | 40 | 58 | 8 |
| Guinea | 1999 | 13 | 39 | 10 | 38 | 1 | 5 | 3 | 27 | 18 | 9 | 95 | 77 |
| Haiti | 2000 | 141 | 200 | 94 | 152 | 3 | 8 | 1 | 40 | 13 | 18 | 64 | 21 |
| India | 1999 | 99 | 72 | 87 | 122 | 3 | 10 | 31 | 87 | 64 | 55 | 35 | 2 |
| Indonesia | 2002–03 | 85 | 92 | 103 | 104 | 7 | 11 | 75 | 97 | 86 | 89 | 19 | 6 |
| Jordan | 2002 | .. | .. | 101 | 99 | 10 | 12 | 93 | 98 | 97 | 97 | 11 | 9 |
| Kazakhstan | 1999 | .. | .. | 125 | 130 | 10 | 11 | 98 | 100 | 98 | 99 | 24 | 18 |
| Kenya | 2003 | 128 | 123 | 104 | 118 | 5 | 9 | 14 | 57 | 30 | 36 | 24 | 4 |
| Kyrgyz Republic | 1997 | .. | .. | 133 | 138 | 10 | 10 | 86 | 88 | 85 | 87 | 21 | 18 |
| Madagascar | 1997 | 84 | 87 | 59 | 134 | 2 | 7 | 1 | 47 | 13 | 16 | 60 | 6 |
| Malawi | 2002 | 180 | 226 | 103 | 126 | 4 | 8 | 10 | 52 | 32 | 14 | 29 | 9 |
| Mali | 2001 | 45 | 89 | 36 | 101 | 1 | 5 | 3 | 37 | 16 | 11 | 75 | 29 |
| Morocco | 2003–04 | 109 | 85 | 98 | 116 | 2 | 9 | 17 | 78 | 47 | 46 | 26 | 2 |
| Mozambique | 2003 | 104 | 134 | 79 | 150 | 2 | 5 | 2 | 17 | 8 | 7 | 59 | 13 |
| Namibia | 1992 | .. | .. | 138 | 116 | 5 | 8 | 15 | 65 | 25 | 34 | 22 | 9 |
| Nepal | 2001 | 240 | 249 | 116 | 160 | 3 | 7 | 18 | 59 | 37 | 28 | 33 | 6 |
| Nicaragua | 2001 | 127 | 108 | 79 | 104 | 3 | 10 | 14 | 88 | 47 | 59 | 46 | 5 |
| Niger | 1998 | 11 | 69 | 15 | 77 | 1 | 4 | 8 | 46 | 22 | 13 | 90 | 44 |
| Nigeria | 2003 | 77 | 106 | 67 | 111 | 4 | 10 | 16 | 70 | 39 | 37 | 56 | 5 |
| Pakistan | 1990–91 | 68 | 173 | 45 | 127 | 2 | 8 | 11 | 55 | 32 | 22 | 72 | 13 |
| Paraguay | 1990 | 137 | 106 | 103 | 114 | 5 | 10 | 29 | 77 | 49 | 54 | 21 | 10 |
| Peru | 2000 | 114 | 94 | 112 | 109 | 6 | 11 | 41 | 93 | 72 | 72 | 9 | 1 |
| Philippines | 2003 | 131 | 102 | 103 | 102 | 6 | 11 | 46 | 88 | 67 | 79 | 17 | 2 |
| Rwanda | 2000 | 216 | 197 | 100 | 126 | 3 | 6 | 7 | 28 | 14 | 14 | 43 | 23 |
| Tanzania | 1999 | 95 | 231 | 63 | 119 | 4 | 7 | 27 | 55 | 34 | 34 | 74 | 27 |
| Uganda | 2000–01 | 145 | 127 | 106 | 120 | 4 | 8 | 7 | 43 | 19 | 21 | 28 | 6 |
| Uzbekistan | 1996 | .. | .. | 102 | 114 | 10 | 10 | 84 | 87 | 84 | 86 | 29 | 23 |
| Vietnam | 2002 | 121 | 105 | 139 | 127 | 5 | 10 | 58 | 97 | 84 | 84 | 8 | 2 |
| Zambia | 2001–02 | 83 | 119 | 74 | 112 | 4 | 9 | 16 | 79 | 38 | 43 | 61 | 18 |
| Zimbabwe | 1994 | 138 | 114 | 104 | 109 | 7 | 10 | 36 | 80 | 51 | 57 | 22 | 8 |

a. Less than 0.5.

# Education gaps by income and gender

**2.14** PEOPLE

## About the data

The data in the table describe basic information on school participation and attainment by individuals in different socioeconomic groups within countries. The data are from Demographic and Health Surveys conducted by Macro International with the support of the U.S. Agency for International Development. These large-scale household sample surveys, conducted periodically in developing countries, collect information on a large number of health, nutrition, and population measures as well as on respondents' social, demographic, and economic characteristics using a standard set of questionnaires. The data presented here draw on responses to individual and household questionnaires.

Typically, Demographic and Health Surveys collect basic information on educational attainment and enrollment levels from every household member ages 5 or 6 and older as background characteristics. As the surveys are intended for the collection of demographic and health information, the education section of the survey is not as robust and detailed as the health section; however, it still provides useful micro-level information on education that cannot be explained by aggregate national-level data.

Socioeconomic status as displayed in the table is based on a household's assets, including ownership of consumer items, features of the household's dwelling, and other characteristics related to wealth. Each household asset on which information was collected was assigned a weight generated through principal-component analysis. The resulting scores were standardized in relation to a standard normal distribution with a mean of zero and a standard deviation of one. The standardized scores were then used to create break-points defining wealth quintiles, expressed as quintiles of individuals in the population.

The choice of the asset index for defining socioeconomic status was based on pragmatic rather than conceptual considerations: Demographic and Health Surveys do not collect income or consumption data but do have detailed information on households' ownership of consumer goods and access to a variety of goods and services. Like income or consumption, the asset index defines disparities primarily in economic terms. It therefore excludes other possibilities of disparities among groups, such as those based on gender, education, ethnic background, or other facets of social exclusion. To that extent the index provides only a partial view of the multidimensional concepts of poverty, inequality, and inequity.

Creating one index that includes all asset indicators limits the types of analysis that can be performed. In particular, the use of a unified index does not permit a disaggregated analysis to examine which asset indicators have a more or less important association with education status. In addition, some asset indicators may reflect household wealth better in some countries than in others—or reflect different degrees of wealth in different countries. Taking such information into account and creating country-specific asset indexes with country-specific choices of asset indicators might produce a more effective and accurate index for each country. The asset index used in the table does not have this flexibility.

The analysis was carried out for 48 countries. The table shows the estimates for the poorest and richest quintiles only; the full set of estimates for 32 indicators is available in the country reports (see *Data sources*). The data in the table differ from data for similar indicators in preceding tables either because the indicator refers to a period a few years preceding the survey date or because the indicator definition or methodology is different. Findings should be interpreted with caution because of measurement error inherent in the use of survey data.

## Definitions

• **Survey year** is the year in which the underlying data were collected. • **Gross intake rate in grade 1** is the number of students in the first grade of primary education regardless of age as a percentage of the population of the official primary school entrance age. These data may differ from those in table 2.12. • **Gross primary participation rate** is the ratio of total students attending primary school regardless of age to the population of the age group that officially corresponds to primary education. • **Average years of schooling** are the years of formal schooling received, on average, by youths and adults ages 15–24. • **Primary completion rate** is the percentage of children of the official primary school completing age to the official primary school completing age plus four who have completed the last year of primary school or higher. These data differ from those in table 2.13 because the definition and methodology are different. • **Children out of school** are the percentage of children ages 6–11 who are not in school. These data differ from those in table 2.11 because the definition and methodology are different.

## Data sources

Data on education gaps by income and gender are from an analysis of Demographic and Health Surveys by Macro International and the World Bank. Country reports are available at www.worldbank.org/education/edstats/.

That the asset index defines

# 2.15 Health expenditure, services, and use

| | Health expenditure | | | | | | | Health workers | | | Hospital beds |
| | | | | | | | | per 1,000 people | | | |
| | Total % of GDP | % of GDP | Public % of total | % of government expenditure | Out of pocket % of private | External resources[a] % of total | Per capita $ | Physicians | Nurses and midwives | Community health workers | per 1,000 people |
| | 2005 | 2005 | 2005 | 2005 | 2005 | 2005 | 2005 | 2000–06[b] | 2000–06[b] | 2000–06[b] | 2000–06[b] |
|---|---|---|---|---|---|---|---|---|---|---|---|
| Afghanistan | 5.2 | 1.0 | 20.0 | 3.3 | 97.4 | 13.1 | .. | .. | .. | .. | .. |
| Albania | 6.5 | 2.6 | 40.3 | 8.6 | 97.0 | 1.9 | 169 | 1.2 | 4.7 | .. | 3.0 |
| Algeria | 3.5 | 2.6 | 75.3 | 9.5 | 94.6 | 0.1 | 108 | 1.1 | 2.2 | 0.0[c] | 1.7 |
| Angola | 1.8 | 1.5 | 81.5 | 4.7 | 100.0 | 7.3 | 36 | 0.1 | 1.4 | .. | .. |
| Argentina | 10.2 | 4.5 | 43.9 | 14.2 | 43.4 | 0.0 | 484 | .. | .. | .. | 4.1 |
| Armenia | 5.4 | 1.8 | 32.9 | 8.2 | 89.2 | 12.7 | 88 | 3.7 | 4.9 | .. | 4.5 |
| Australia | 8.8 | 5.9 | 67.0 | 17.0 | 55.2 | 0.0 | 3,181 | 2.5 | 9.7 | 0.2 | 4.0 |
| Austria | 10.2 | 7.7 | 75.7 | 15.5 | 67.4 | 0.0 | 3,788 | 3.7 | 6.6 | .. | 7.7 |
| Azerbaijan | 3.9 | 1.0 | 24.8 | 3.8 | 84.6 | 0.4 | 62 | 3.6 | 8.4 | .. | 8.2 |
| Bangladesh | 2.8 | 0.8 | 29.1 | 5.5 | 88.3 | 12.2 | 12 | 0.3 | 0.3 | 0.2 | 0.3 |
| Belarus | 6.6 | 5.0 | 75.8 | 10.5 | 69.0 | .. | 204 | 4.8 | 12.5 | .. | 11.1 |
| Belgium | 9.6 | 6.9 | 71.4 | 13.9 | 78.7 | 0.0 | 3,451 | 4.2 | 14.2 | .. | 5.3 |
| Benin | 5.4 | 3.0 | 55.6 | 13.5 | 99.9 | 19.7 | 28 | 0.0[c] | 0.8 | 0.0[c] | 0.5 |
| Bolivia | 6.9 | 4.3 | 61.6 | 12.4 | 81.4 | 6.8 | 71 | 1.2 | 2.1 | 0.1 | 1.0 |
| Bosnia and Herzegovina | 8.8 | 5.2 | 58.7 | 14.0 | 100.0 | 0.6 | 243 | 1.4 | 4.7 | .. | 3.0 |
| Botswana | 7.0 | 4.5 | 63.6 | 12.4 | 26.2 | 4.7 | 362 | 0.4 | 2.7 | .. | 2.2 |
| Brazil | 7.9 | 3.5 | 44.1 | 6.7 | 54.6 | 0.0 | 371 | 1.2 | 3.8 | .. | 2.6 |
| Bulgaria | 7.7 | 4.7 | 60.6 | 12.1 | 96.3 | 1.1 | 272 | 0.3 | 4.6 | .. | 6.4 |
| Burkina Faso | 6.7 | 4.0 | 59.5 | 18.4 | 94.2 | 29.5 | 27 | 0.1 | 0.5 | 0.1 | .. |
| Burundi | 3.4 | 1.0 | 28.6 | 2.3 | 100.0 | 50.9 | 3 | 0.0[c] | 0.2 | 0.1 | 0.7 |
| Cambodia | 6.4 | 1.5 | 24.2 | 12.0 | 79.3 | 25.7 | 29 | 0.2 | 0.9 | .. | 0.6 |
| Cameroon | 5.2 | 1.5 | 28.0 | 11.0 | 94.6 | 5.3 | 49 | 0.2 | 1.6 | .. | .. |
| Canada | 9.7 | 6.8 | 70.3 | 17.5 | 48.7 | 0.0 | 3,430 | 1.9 | 10.1 | .. | 3.6 |
| Central African Republic | 4.0 | 1.5 | 37.5 | 10.9 | 95.3 | 38.5 | 13 | 0.1 | 0.4 | 0.1 | .. |
| Chad | 3.7 | 1.5 | 39.8 | 9.5 | 96.2 | 12.5 | 22 | 0.0[c] | 0.3 | 0.0[c] | 0.4 |
| Chile | 5.4 | 2.8 | 51.4 | 13.2 | 54.3 | 0.1 | 397 | 1.1 | 0.6 | .. | 2.4 |
| China | 4.7 | 1.8 | 38.8 | 1.0 | 85.3 | 0.1 | 81 | 1.5 | 1.0 | 0.1 | 2.5 |
|   Hong Kong, China | .. | .. | .. | .. | .. | .. | .. | .. | .. | .. | .. |
| Colombia | 7.3 | 6.2 | 84.8 | 17.7 | 45.1 | 0.0 | 201 | 1.4 | 0.6 | .. | 1.2 |
| Congo, Dem. Rep. | 4.2 | 1.5 | 34.6 | 7.2 | 100.0 | 23.6 | 5 | 0.1 | 0.5 | .. | .. |
| Congo, Rep. | 1.9 | 0.9 | 47.1 | 4.0 | 100.0 | 4.7 | 31 | 0.2 | 1.0 | 0.0[c] | .. |
| Costa Rica | 7.1 | 5.4 | 76.0 | 21.0 | 79.4 | 0.2 | 327 | 1.3 | 0.9 | 1.3 | 1.4 |
| Cote d'Ivoire | 3.9 | 0.8 | 21.5 | 4.2 | 87.8 | 6.6 | 34 | 0.1 | 0.6 | .. | .. |
| Croatia | 8.4[d] | 6.3[d] | 75.5[d] | 13.1[d] | 93.6 | 0.0 | 812[d] | 2.5 | 5.5 | .. | 5.5 |
| Cuba | 7.6 | 6.9 | 90.8 | 11.7 | 93.2 | 0.3 | 310 | 5.9 | 7.4 | .. | 4.9 |
| Czech Republic | 7.1 | 6.3 | 88.6 | 14.4 | 95.3 | 0.0 | 868 | 3.6 | 8.9 | .. | 8.4 |
| Denmark | 9.1 | 7.7 | 84.1 | 14.4 | 90.1 | 0.0 | 4,350 | 3.6 | 10.1 | .. | 3.8 |
| Dominican Republic | 5.4 | 1.7 | 31.1 | 9.3 | 86.4 | 2.5 | 197 | 1.9 | 1.8 | .. | 2.2 |
| Ecuador | 5.3 | 2.1 | 40.0 | 8.0 | 85.0 | 0.4 | 147 | 1.5 | 1.7 | .. | 1.4 |
| Egypt, Arab Rep. | 6.1 | 2.3 | 38.0 | 7.3 | 94.9 | 0.9 | 78 | 2.4 | 3.4 | .. | 2.2 |
| El Salvador | 8.1[d] | 4.0[d] | 50.0[d] | 22.0[d] | 94.0[d] | 2.7[d] | 220[d] | 1.5 | 0.8 | .. | 0.9 |
| Eritrea | 3.7 | 1.7 | 44.9 | 4.2 | 100.0 | 50.5 | 8 | 0.1 | 0.6 | .. | .. |
| Estonia | 5.0 | 3.8 | 76.9 | 11.5 | 88.7 | 0.3 | 516 | 3.3 | 7.0 | 0.0[c] | 5.8 |
| Ethiopia | 4.9 | 3.0 | 61.0 | 10.8 | 80.6 | 37.9 | 6 | 0.0[c] | 0.2 | 0.3 | 0.2 |
| Finland | 7.5 | 5.8 | 77.8 | 11.6 | 80.0 | 0.0 | 2,824 | 3.3 | 8.9 | .. | 7.0 |
| France | 11.1 | 8.9 | 79.8 | 16.5 | 34.2 | 0.0 | 3,807 | 3.4 | 8.0 | .. | 7.5 |
| Gabon | 4.1 | 3.0 | 74.0 | 13.9 | 100.0 | 1.5 | 276 | 0.3 | 5.0 | .. | .. |
| Gambia, The | 5.2 | 3.4 | 65.4 | 11.2 | 70.3 | 29.3 | 15 | 0.1 | 1.3 | 0.7 | 0.8 |
| Georgia | 8.6 | 1.7 | 19.5 | 6.7 | 95.7 | 5.1 | 123 | 4.7 | 4.0 | .. | 3.8 |
| Germany | 10.7 | 8.2 | 76.9 | 17.6 | 56.8 | 0.0 | 3,628 | 3.4 | 8.0 | .. | 8.4 |
| Ghana | 6.2 | 2.1 | 34.1 | 6.9 | 79.1 | 26.0 | 30 | 0.2 | 0.9 | .. | 0.9 |
| Greece | 10.1 | 4.3 | 42.8 | 11.5 | 62.0 | .. | 2,580 | 5.0 | 3.6 | .. | 4.7 |
| Guatemala | 5.2 | 2.0 | 37.9 | 15.7 | 92.2 | 1.1 | 132 | .. | .. | .. | 0.7 |
| Guinea | 5.6 | 0.7 | 11.9 | 4.7 | 99.5 | 12.2 | 21 | 0.1 | 0.5 | 0.0[c] | .. |
| Guinea-Bissau | 5.2 | 1.7 | 31.9 | 4.0 | 85.7 | 31.8 | 10 | 0.1 | 0.7 | 2.9 | .. |
| Haiti | 6.2 | 3.2 | 51.3 | 27.7 | 90.1 | 18.9 | 28 | .. | .. | .. | 0.8 |

| | Health expenditure | | | | | | | Health workers | | | Hospital beds |
|---|---|---|---|---|---|---|---|---|---|---|---|
| | Total % of GDP | % of GDP | Public % of total | % of government expenditure | Out of pocket % of private | External resources[a] % of total | Per capita $ | | per 1,000 people | | per 1,000 people |
| | | | | | | | | Physicians | Nurses and midwives | Community health workers | |
| | 2005 | 2005 | 2005 | 2005 | 2005 | 2005 | 2005 | 2000–06[b] | 2000–06[b] | 2000–06[b] | 2000–06[b] |
| Honduras | 7.5 | 3.8 | 50.6 | 16.1 | 87.0 | 6.8 | 91 | 0.6 | 1.3 | .. | 1.0 |
| Hungary | 7.8 | 5.5 | 70.8 | 11.1 | 86.8 | .. | 855 | 3.0 | 9.2 | .. | 7.9 |
| India | 5.0 | 1.0 | 19.0 | 3.5 | 94.0 | 0.4 | 36 | 0.6 | 1.3 | 0.1 | 0.9 |
| Indonesia | 2.1 | 1.0 | 46.6 | 5.1 | 66.4 | 4.6 | 26 | 0.1 | 0.8 | 0.0 | .. |
| Iran, Islamic Rep. | 7.8 | 4.4 | 55.8 | 9.2 | 94.8 | 0.1 | 212 | 0.9 | 1.6 | 0.4 | 1.7 |
| Iraq | 4.1[e] | 3.1[e] | 74.4[e] | 3.4[e] | 100.0[e] | 4.9[e] | .. | .. | .. | .. | .. |
| Ireland | 8.2 | 6.5 | 79.5 | 19.0 | 59.3 | 0.0 | 3,993 | 2.9 | 19.5 | .. | 5.7 |
| Israel | 7.9 | 4.8 | 61.3 | 10.4 | 61.0 | 0.0 | 1,533 | 3.7 | 6.2 | .. | 6.3 |
| Italy | 8.9 | 6.8 | 76.6 | 14.1 | 86.6 | 0.0 | 2,692 | 3.7 | 7.2 | .. | 4.0 |
| Jamaica | 4.7 | 2.3 | 48.8 | 3.5 | 63.6 | 1.8 | 170 | 0.9 | 1.7 | .. | 1.7 |
| Japan | 8.2 | 6.7 | 82.2 | 17.8 | 83.5 | 0.0 | 2,936 | 2.1 | 9.5 | .. | 14.3 |
| Jordan | 10.5[f] | 4.8[f] | 45.3[f] | 9.5[f] | 76.1 | 4.5 | 241 | 2.4 | 3.2 | 0.2 | 1.7 |
| Kazakhstan | 4.1[d] | 2.2[d] | 67.4[d] | 10.8[d] | 100.0[d] | 0.3[d] | 204[d] | 3.9 | 7.6 | .. | 7.7 |
| Kenya | 4.5 | 2.1 | 46.6 | 6.1 | 80.0 | 18.1 | 24 | 0.1 | 1.2 | .. | 1.9 |
| Korea, Dem. Rep. | 3.5 | 3.0 | 85.6 | 6.0 | 100.0 | 36.6 | 0[g] | 3.3 | 4.1 | .. | 13.2 |
| Korea, Rep. | 5.9 | 3.1 | 53.0 | 10.9 | 80.1 | 0.0 | 973 | 1.6 | 1.9 | .. | 7.1 |
| Kuwait | 2.2 | 1.7 | 77.2 | 6.2 | 91.6 | 0.0 | 687 | 1.8 | 3.7 | .. | 1.9 |
| Kyrgyz Republic | 6.1 | 2.5 | 40.3 | 8.6 | 95.0 | 7.5 | 29 | 2.4 | 5.8 | .. | 5.1 |
| Lao PDR | 3.6 | 0.7 | 20.6 | 4.1 | 92.7 | 11.3 | 18 | 0.4 | 1.0 | .. | 0.9 |
| Latvia | 6.4 | 3.9 | 60.5 | 10.8 | 97.7 | 0.3 | 443 | 3.1 | 5.6 | .. | 7.7 |
| Lebanon | 8.7 | 3.8 | 43.5 | 11.9 | 74.7 | 2.3 | 460 | 2.4 | 1.3 | .. | 3.6 |
| Lesotho | 9.4 | 8.5 | 90.1 | 18.2 | 18.3 | 10.7 | 69 | 0.1 | 0.6 | .. | .. |
| Liberia | 6.4 | 4.4 | 68.2 | 36.3 | 98.7 | 41.2 | 10 | 0.0[c] | 0.3 | 0.0[c] | .. |
| Libya | 3.2 | 2.2 | 69.5 | 6.5 | 100.0 | 0.0 | 223 | 1.3 | 4.8 | .. | 3.4 |
| Lithuania | 5.9 | 4.0 | 67.3 | 11.9 | 98.6 | 0.0 | 448 | 4.0 | 7.7 | .. | 8.1 |
| Macedonia, FYR | 7.8 | 5.5 | 70.4 | 15.8 | 100.0 | 1.0 | 224 | 2.6 | 4.3 | .. | 4.7 |
| Madagascar | 3.2 | 2.0 | 62.5 | 9.6 | 52.6 | 46.1 | 9 | 0.3 | 0.3 | 0.0[c] | 0.4 |
| Malawi | 12.2 | 8.7 | 71.3 | 16.6 | 30.6 | 61.2 | 19 | 0.0[c] | 0.6 | .. | .. |
| Malaysia | 4.2 | 1.9 | 44.8 | 7.0 | 75.7 | 0.0 | 222 | 0.7 | 1.8 | .. | 1.8 |
| Mali | 5.8 | 2.9 | 50.6 | 12.0 | 99.5 | 15.6 | 28 | 0.1 | 0.6 | 0.0[c] | .. |
| Mauritania | 2.7 | 1.7 | 63.2 | 5.0 | 100.0 | 26.1 | 17 | 0.1 | 0.6 | 0.1 | 0.6 |
| Mauritius | 4.3 | 2.2 | 51.5 | 9.2 | 81.4 | 1.1 | 218 | 1.1 | 3.7 | 0.2 | 3.0 |
| Mexico | 6.4 | 2.9 | 45.5 | 12.5 | 93.9 | 0.0 | 474 | 1.5 | 0.9 | .. | 1.0 |
| Moldova | 7.5 | 4.2 | 55.5 | 11.3 | 96.4 | 2.6 | 58 | 2.7 | 6.2 | .. | 6.4 |
| Mongolia | 4.3 | 3.3 | 77.5 | 11.0 | 86.5 | 1.5 | 35 | 2.6 | 3.5 | 1.5 | 7.5 |
| Morocco | 5.3 | 1.9 | 36.6 | 5.5 | 76.0 | 1.0 | 89 | 0.5 | 0.8 | .. | 0.9 |
| Mozambique | 4.3 | 2.7 | 63.6 | 12.6 | 40.5 | 66.5 | 14 | 0.0[c] | 0.3 | .. | .. |
| Myanmar | 2.2 | 0.3 | 11.6 | 1.2 | 99.4 | 12.7 | 4 | 0.4 | 1.0 | 1.0 | 0.6 |
| Namibia | 5.3 | 3.5 | 65.2 | 10.1 | 15.5 | 13.5 | 165 | 0.3 | 3.1 | .. | .. |
| Nepal | 5.8 | 1.6 | 28.1 | 8.4 | 87.0 | 16.4 | 16 | 0.2 | 0.5 | 0.6 | 0.2 |
| Netherlands | 9.2 | 6.0 | 64.9 | 13.2 | 21.9 | 0.0 | 3,560 | 3.7 | 14.6 | .. | 5.0 |
| New Zealand | 8.9 | 6.9 | 77.4 | 18.0 | 74.4 | 0.0 | 2,403 | 2.2 | 8.9 | 1.4 | 6.0 |
| Nicaragua | 8.3 | 4.1 | 49.6 | 13.7 | 96.2 | 9.2 | 75 | 0.4 | 1.1 | .. | 0.9 |
| Niger | 3.8 | 1.9 | 50.5 | 10.2 | 85.2 | 17.0 | 9 | 0.0[c] | 0.2 | .. | .. |
| Nigeria | 3.9 | 1.2 | 30.9 | 3.5 | 90.4 | 4.8 | 27 | 0.3 | 1.7 | 0.9 | 1.2 |
| Norway | 9.0 | 7.5 | 83.6 | 17.9 | 95.3 | 0.0 | 5,910 | 3.8 | 16.2 | .. | 4.2 |
| Oman | 2.5 | 2.1 | 85.0 | 6.1 | 64.4 | 0.0 | 312 | 1.7 | 3.7 | .. | 2.1 |
| Pakistan | 2.1 | 0.4 | 17.5 | 1.5 | 98.0 | 3.6 | 15 | 0.8 | 0.5 | 0.4 | 0.7 |
| Panama | 7.3 | 5.0 | 68.9 | 12.3 | 80.8 | 0.2 | 351 | 1.5 | 2.8 | 0.5 | 2.4 |
| Papua New Guinea | 4.2 | 3.6 | 86.2 | 9.6 | 42.5 | 37.0 | 34 | 0.1 | 0.5 | .. | .. |
| Paraguay | 7.3 | 2.7 | 36.5 | 15.3 | 87.7 | 0.6 | 92 | 1.1 | 1.8 | 1.2 | 1.2 |
| Peru | 4.3 | 2.1 | 49.0 | 8.4 | 80.0 | 1.7 | 125 | .. | .. | .. | 1.1 |
| Philippines | 3.2 | 1.2 | 36.6 | 5.5 | 80.3 | 5.1 | 37 | 1.2 | 6.1 | .. | 1.2 |
| Poland | 6.2 | 4.3 | 69.3 | 9.9 | 85.1 | 0.1 | 495 | 2.0 | 5.2 | .. | 5.3 |
| Portugal | 10.2 | 7.4 | 72.3 | 15.5 | 79.8 | 0.0 | 1,800 | 3.4 | 4.7 | .. | 3.7 |
| Puerto Rico | .. | .. | .. | .. | .. | .. | .. | .. | .. | .. | .. |

# Health expenditure, services, and use

| | Health expenditure | | | | | | | Health workers (per 1,000 people) | | | Hospital beds |
|---|---|---|---|---|---|---|---|---|---|---|---|
| | Total % of GDP | Public % of GDP | Public % of total | % of government expenditure | Out of pocket % of private | External resources[a] % of total | Per capita $ | Physicians | Nurses and midwives | Community health workers | per 1,000 people |
| | 2005 | 2005 | 2005 | 2005 | 2005 | 2005 | 2005 | 2000–06[b] | 2000–06[b] | 2000–06[b] | 2000–06[b] |
| Romania | 5.5 | 3.9 | 70.3 | 12.4 | 85.0 | 0.8 | 250 | 1.9 | 4.2 | .. | 6.6 |
| Russian Federation | 5.2 | 3.2 | 62.0 | 10.1 | 82.4 | 0.0 | 277 | 4.3 | 8.5 | 3.0 | 9.7 |
| Rwanda | 7.2 | 4.1 | 56.9 | 16.9 | 36.9 | 43.9 | 19 | 0.1 | 0.4 | 1.4 | 1.7 |
| Saudi Arabia | 3.4 | 2.6 | 76.2 | 8.7 | 16.5 | 0.0 | 448 | 1.7 | 3.0 | .. | 2.3 |
| Senegal | 5.4 | 1.7 | 31.7 | 6.7 | 90.3 | 13.0 | 38 | 0.1 | 0.3 | .. | .. |
| Serbia | 8.0[h] | 5.8[h] | 71.9[h] | 15.1[h] | 86.7[h] | 0.5[h] | 212[h] | 2.0 | 4.3 | .. | 5.9 |
| Sierra Leone | 3.7 | 1.9 | 51.5 | 7.8 | 100.0 | 41.0 | 8 | 0.0[c] | 0.5 | 0.1 | 0.4 |
| Singapore | 3.5 | 1.1 | 31.9 | 5.6 | 93.8 | 0.0 | 944 | 1.5 | 4.5 | .. | 2.8 |
| Slovak Republic | 7.0 | 5.2 | 74.4 | 13.9 | 88.1 | 0.0 | 626 | 3.1 | 6.6 | .. | 6.9 |
| Slovenia | 8.5 | 6.2 | 72.4 | 13.4 | 45.0 | 0.1 | 1,495 | 2.4 | 8.0 | .. | 4.8 |
| Somalia | .. | .. | .. | .. | .. | .. | .. | .. | .. | .. | .. |
| South Africa | 8.7 | 3.6 | 41.7 | 9.9 | 17.4 | 0.5 | 437 | 0.8 | 4.1 | 0.2 | .. |
| Spain | 8.2 | 5.9 | 71.4 | 15.4 | 73.1 | 0.0 | 2,152 | 3.3 | 7.6 | .. | 3.5 |
| Sri Lanka | 4.1 | 1.9 | 46.2 | 7.8 | 86.0 | 1.2 | 51 | 0.6 | 1.7 | .. | 3.1 |
| Sudan | 3.8 | 1.4 | 37.6 | 7.0 | 98.3 | 6.8 | 29 | 0.3 | 0.9 | 0.2 | 0.7 |
| Swaziland | 6.3 | 4.0 | 64.1 | 10.9 | 41.7 | 5.6 | 146 | 0.2 | 6.3 | 4.3 | .. |
| Sweden | 8.9 | 7.5 | 84.6 | 13.6 | 89.6 | 0.0 | 3,598 | 3.3 | 10.9 | .. | 3.6 |
| Switzerland | 11.4 | 6.8 | 59.7 | 18.7 | 75.7 | 0.0 | 5,694 | 4.0 | 11.0 | .. | 5.7 |
| Syrian Arab Republic | 4.2 | 2.1 | 50.5 | 6.8 | 100.0 | 0.5 | 61 | 0.5 | 1.4 | .. | 1.3 |
| Tajikistan | 5.0 | 1.1 | 22.8 | 5.0 | 96.6 | 11.8 | 18 | 2.0 | 5.0 | .. | 6.2 |
| Tanzania | 5.1 | 2.9 | 56.9 | 12.6 | 83.4 | 27.8 | 17 | 0.0[c] | 0.4 | .. | .. |
| Thailand | 3.5 | 2.2 | 63.9 | 11.3 | 76.6 | 0.2 | 98 | 0.4 | 2.8 | 0.1 | 2.2 |
| Timor-Leste | 13.7 | 11.9 | 86.6 | 19.1 | 37.2 | 57.2 | 45 | 0.1 | 2.2 | 2.0 | .. |
| Togo | 5.3 | 1.4 | 25.5 | 6.9 | 84.7 | 13.3 | 18 | 0.0[c] | 0.4 | 0.1 | 0.9 |
| Trinidad and Tobago | 4.5 | 2.4 | 53.7 | 8.3 | 87.8 | 2.4 | 513 | .. | .. | .. | 3.3 |
| Tunisia | 5.5 | 2.4 | 44.3 | 6.5 | 82.2 | 0.8 | 158 | 1.3 | 2.9 | .. | 1.8 |
| Turkey | 7.6 | 5.4 | 71.4 | 13.9 | 69.5 | 0.0 | 383 | 1.6 | 2.9 | .. | 2.6 |
| Turkmenistan | 4.8 | 3.2 | 66.7 | 14.9 | 100.0 | 0.3 | 156 | 2.5 | 4.7 | .. | 4.9 |
| Uganda | 7.0 | 2.0 | 28.6 | 10.0 | 51.8 | 33.1 | 22 | 0.1 | 0.7 | .. | 0.7 |
| Ukraine | 7.0 | 3.7 | 52.8 | 8.4 | 84.8 | 0.6 | 128 | 3.1 | 8.5 | .. | 8.7 |
| United Arab Emirates | 2.6 | 1.9 | 71.6 | 8.6 | 77.9 | 0.0 | 833 | 1.7 | 3.5 | .. | 2.2 |
| United Kingdom | 8.2 | 7.1 | 87.1 | 16.2 | 92.1 | 0.0 | 3,064 | 2.2 | .. | .. | 3.9 |
| United States | 15.9 | 7.2 | 45.4 | 0.7 | 23.9 | 0.0 | 6,657 | 2.3 | 9.4 | .. | 3.3 |
| Uruguay | 8.1 | 3.4 | 42.5 | 10.1 | 31.1 | 0.6 | 404 | 3.7 | 0.9 | .. | 2.4 |
| Uzbekistan | 5.0 | 2.4 | 47.7 | 7.4 | 97.1 | 3.5 | 26 | 2.7 | 10.9 | .. | 5.2 |
| Venezuela, RB | 4.7 | 2.1 | 45.3 | 7.9 | 88.2 | 0.1 | 247 | 1.9 | 1.1 | .. | 0.9 |
| Vietnam | 6.0 | 1.5 | 25.7 | 5.1 | 86.1 | 2.0 | 37 | 0.6 | 0.8 | .. | 1.4 |
| West Bank and Gaza | .. | .. | .. | .. | .. | .. | .. | 0.8 | .. | .. | .. |
| Yemen, Rep. | 5.1 | 2.1 | 41.8 | 5.6 | 95.2 | 15.0 | 39 | 0.3 | 0.7 | 0.3 | 0.6 |
| Zambia | 5.6 | 2.7 | 49.0 | 10.7 | 71.5 | 40.5 | 36 | 0.1 | 2.0 | .. | 2.0 |
| Zimbabwe | 8.1 | 3.6 | 44.8 | 8.9 | 52.0 | 20.6 | 21 | 0.2 | 0.7 | 0.0[c] | .. |
| **World** | 10.1 w | 6.0 w | 59.3 w | 10.4 w | 43.5 w | 0.1 w | 703 w | .. w | .. w | .. w | .. w |
| **Low income** | 4.6 | 1.2 | 24.9 | 6.9 | 92.0 | 5.6 | 27 | 0.5 | .. | 0.2 | .. |
| **Middle income** | 5.8 | 2.9 | 51.1 | 8.2 | 74.5 | 0.4 | 162 | 1.6 | .. | .. | 3.1 |
| Lower middle income | 4.8 | 2.2 | 46.9 | 5.9 | 84.9 | 0.8 | 86 | 1.3 | 1.0 | .. | 2.7 |
| Upper middle income | 6.7 | 3.6 | 53.8 | .. | 66.8 | 0.1 | 374 | 2.3 | .. | .. | .. |
| **Low & middle income** | 5.6 | 2.7 | 48.1 | 7.3 | 77.4 | 1.0 | 104 | .. | .. | .. | .. |
| East Asia & Pacific | 4.3 | 1.8 | 40.3 | 2.1 | 83.8 | 0.7 | 70 | 1.5 | 1.0 | 0.1 | 2.5 |
| Europe & Central Asia | 6.2 | 4.1 | 66.2 | 10.5 | 82.8 | 0.2 | 279 | 3.1 | 6.8 | .. | 7.2 |
| Latin America & Carib. | 7.1 | 3.3 | 47.9 | .. | 68.0 | 0.2 | 329 | .. | .. | .. | .. |
| Middle East & N. Africa | 5.8 | 3.0 | 53.4 | 8.2 | 90.5 | 1.1 | 123 | .. | .. | .. | .. |
| South Asia | 4.5 | 0.9 | 20.2 | 3.5 | 93.9 | 1.3 | 31 | 0.6 | 1.3 | 0.1 | 0.9 |
| Sub-Saharan Africa | 6.1 | 2.6 | 42.9 | .. | 45.7 | 7.4 | 49 | .. | .. | .. | .. |
| **High income** | 11.4 | 7.0 | 60.9 | 10.9 | 36.8 | 0.0 | 3,979 | 2.6 | .. | .. | 6.2 |
| Euro area | 9.9 | 7.4 | 75.1 | 15.6 | 58.2 | 0.0 | 3,155 | 3.5 | .. | .. | 6.6 |

a. 0.0 is not applicable or less than 0.05. b. Data are for the most recent year available. c. Less than 0.05. d. Data are for 2006. e. Excludes northern Iraq. f. Includes contributions from the United Nations Relief and Works Agency for Palestine Refugees. g. Less than 0.5. h. Excludes Kosovo and Metohija.

## About the data

National health accounts track financial flows in the health sector, including public and private expenditures, by source of funding. In contrast with high-income countries, few developing countries have health accounts that are methodologically consistent with national accounting approaches. Efforts are needed to standardize and harmonize the various competing national health account methodologies. The difficulties in creating national health accounts go beyond data collection. To establish a national health accounting system, a country needs to define the boundaries of the health care system and to define a taxonomy of health care delivery institutions. The accounting system should be comprehensive and standardized, providing not only accurate measures of financial flows but also information on the equity and efficiency of health financing to inform health policy.

The absence of consistent national health accounting systems in most developing countries makes cross-country comparisons of health spending difficult. Compiling estimates of public health expenditures is complicated in countries where state or provincial and local governments are involved in financing and delivering health care, often because the data on public spending are not aggregated. There are a number of potential data sources related to external resources for health, including government expenditure accounts, government records on external assistance, routine surveys of external financing assistance, and special surveys. Survey data are the major source of information about out of pocket expenditure on health. The data in the table are the product of an effort by the World Health Organization (WHO), the Organisation for Economic Co-operation and Development (OECD), and the World Bank to collect all available information on health expenditures from national and local government budgets, national accounts, household surveys, insurance publications, international donors, and existing tabulations.

Indicators on health services (physicians, nurses and midwives, community health workers, and hospital beds) are compiled by the WHO based on household and labor force surveys, censuses, and professional and administrative records. Data comparability is limited by differences in definitions. In estimates of health personnel, for example, some countries incorrectly include retired physicians (because deletions to physician rosters are made only periodically) or physicians working outside the health sector. Caution must be exercised in using the data for nurses and midwives, because for some countries the available information does not clearly distinguish between the two groups. There is no universally accepted definition of hospital beds. Moreover, figures on physicians and hospital beds are indicators of availability, not of quality or use. They do not show how well trained the physicians are or how well equipped the hospitals or medical centers are. And physicians and hospital beds tend to be concentrated in urban areas, so these indicators give only a partial view of health services available to the entire population.

Meeting the minimum of 2.5 physicians, nurses, and midwives per 1,000 people is critical for countries to provide the adequate primary health care interventions needed to achieve the health-related Millennium Development Goals (WHO, World Health Report 2006).

## Definitions

• **Total health expenditure** is the sum of public and private health expenditure. It covers the provision of health services (preventive and curative), family planning and nutrition activities, and emergency aid for health but excludes provision of water and sanitation. • **Public health expenditure** is recurrent and capital spending from central and local governments, external borrowing and grants (including donations from international agencies and nongovernmental organizations), and social (or compulsory) health insurance funds. • **Out of pocket health expenditure,** part of private health expenditure, is direct household outlays including gratuities and in-kind payments to health practitioners and pharmaceutical suppliers, therapeutic appliances, and other goods and services whose primary intent is to contribute to health restoration or enhancement. • **External resources for health,** part of total health expenditure, are funds or services in kind provided by entities not part of the country. Resources may come from international organizations, other countries, or foreign nongovernmental organizations. • **Health expenditure per capita** is total health expenditure divided by population. • **Physicians** are graduates of any faculty or school of medicine working in the country in any medical field (practice, teaching, or research). • **Nurses and midwives** are professional nurses, auxiliary nurses, enrolled nurses, and other nurses, such as dental nurses and primary care nurses, and professional midwives, auxiliary midwives, and enrolled midwives. • **Community health workers** are traditional medicine practitioners, faith healers, assistant and community health education workers, community health officers, family health workers, lady health visitors, health extension package workers, community midwives, and traditional birth attendants. • **Hospital beds** are inpatient beds for both acute and chronic care available in public, private, general, and specialized hospitals and rehabilitation centers.

### Data sources

Data on health expenditure come mostly from the WHO's National Health Account database (www.who.int/nha/en) and from the OECD for its member countries, supplemented by country data. Data on physicians, nurses and midwives, community health workers, and hospital beds are from the WHO, OECD, and TransMONEE, supplemented by country data.

# Disease prevention coverage and quality

| | Access to an improved water source | | Access to improved sanitation facilities | | Child immunization rate | | Children with acute respiratory infection taken to health provider | Children with diarrhea who received oral rehydration and continuous feeding | Children sleeping under treated bednets[a] | Children with fever receiving antimalarial drugs | Tuberculosis treatment success rate | DOTS detection rate |
|---|---|---|---|---|---|---|---|---|---|---|---|---|
| | % of population | | % of population | | % of children ages 12–23 months[b] | | % of children under age 5 with ARI | % of children under age 5 with diarrhea | % of children under age 5 | % of children under age 5 with fever | % of new registered cases | % of new estimated cases |
| | | | | | Measles | DTP3 | | | | | | |
| | 1990 | 2004 | 1990 | 2004 | 2006 | 2006 | 2000–06[c] | 2000–06[c] | 2000–06[c] | 2000–06[c] | 2005 | 2006 |
| Afghanistan | .. | .. | .. | .. | .. | .. | .. | .. | .. | .. | 90 | 66 |
| Albania | 96 | 96 | .. | 91 | 97 | 98 | 45 | 50 | .. | .. | 77 | 37 |
| Algeria | 94 | 85 | 88 | 92 | 91 | 95 | 53 | 24 | .. | .. | 87 | 102 |
| Angola | 36 | 53 | 29 | 31 | 48 | 44 | 58 | 32 | 2.3 | 63.0 | 72 | 76 |
| Argentina | 94 | 96 | 81 | 91 | 97 | 91 | .. | .. | .. | .. | 53 | 71 |
| Armenia | .. | 92 | .. | 83 | 92 | 87 | 36 | 59 | .. | .. | 72 | 59 |
| Australia | 100 | 100 | 100 | 100 | 94 | 92 | .. | .. | .. | .. | 80 | 40 |
| Austria | 100 | 100 | 100 | 100 | 80 | 83 | .. | .. | .. | .. | 75 | 46 |
| Azerbaijan | 68 | 77 | .. | 54 | 96 | 95 | 36 | 40 | 1.4 | 0.8 | 59 | 50 |
| Bangladesh | 72 | 74 | 20 | 39 | 81 | 88 | 30 | 49 | .. | .. | 91 | 65 |
| Belarus | 100 | 100 | .. | 84 | 97 | 99 | 90 | 54 | .. | .. | 73 | 40 |
| Belgium | .. | .. | .. | .. | 88 | 97 | .. | 42 | .. | .. | 66 | 55 |
| Benin | 63 | 67 | 12 | 33 | 89 | 93 | 36 | 42 | 20.1 | 54.0 | 87 | 86 |
| Bolivia | 72 | 85 | 33 | 46 | 81 | 81 | 52 | 54 | .. | .. | 78 | 69 |
| Bosnia and Herzegovina | 97 | 97 | .. | 95 | 90 | 87 | 91 | 53 | .. | .. | 97 | 62 |
| Botswana | 93 | 95 | 38 | 42 | 90 | 97 | 14 | 7 | .. | .. | 70 | 80 |
| Brazil | 83 | 90 | 71 | 75 | 99 | 99 | .. | .. | .. | .. | 77 | 55 |
| Bulgaria | 99 | 99 | 99 | 99 | 96 | 95 | .. | .. | .. | .. | 86 | 94 |
| Burkina Faso | 38 | 61 | 7 | 13 | 88 | 95 | 39 | 42 | 9.6 | 48.0 | 71 | 17 |
| Burundi | 69 | 79 | 44 | 36 | 75 | 74 | 38 | 23 | 8.3 | 30.0 | 79 | 24 |
| Cambodia | .. | 41 | .. | 17 | 78 | 80 | 48 | 59 | 4.2 | 0.2 | 93 | 62 |
| Cameroon | 50 | 66 | 48 | 51 | 73 | 81 | 35 | 22 | 13.1 | 57.8 | 74 | 91 |
| Canada | 100 | 100 | 100 | 100 | 94 | 94 | .. | .. | .. | .. | 68 | 55 |
| Central African Republic | 52 | 75 | 23 | 27 | 35 | 40 | 32 | 47 | 15.1 | 57.0 | 65 | 69 |
| Chad | 19 | 42 | 7 | 9 | 23 | 20 | 7 | 27 | 0.6 | 44.0 | 69 | 19 |
| Chile | 90 | 95 | 84 | 91 | 91 | 94 | .. | .. | .. | .. | 78 | 141 |
| China | 70 | 77 | 23 | 44 | 93 | 93 | .. | .. | .. | .. | 94 | 79 |
| Hong Kong, China | .. | .. | .. | .. | .. | .. | .. | .. | .. | .. | 77 | 56 |
| Colombia | 92 | 93 | 82 | 86 | 88 | 86 | 62 | 39 | 0.7 | .. | 71 | 83 |
| Congo, Dem. Rep. | 43 | 46 | 16 | 30 | 73 | 77 | 36 | 17 | 5.8[d] | 29.8[d] | 85 | 61 |
| Congo, Rep. | .. | 58 | .. | 27 | 66 | 79 | 48 | 39 | 6.1 | 48.0 | 28 | 51 |
| Costa Rica | .. | 97 | .. | 92 | 89 | 91 | .. | .. | .. | .. | 89 | 102 |
| Côte d'Ivoire | 69 | 84 | 21 | 37 | 73 | 77 | 35 | 45 | 5.9 | 36.0 | 75 | 37 |
| Croatia | 100 | 100 | 100 | 100 | 96 | 96 | .. | .. | .. | .. | .. | .. |
| Cuba | .. | 91 | 98 | 98 | 96 | 89 | .. | .. | .. | .. | 91 | 94 |
| Czech Republic | 100 | 100 | 99 | 98 | 97 | 98 | .. | .. | .. | .. | 72 | 57 |
| Denmark | 100 | 100 | .. | .. | 99 | 93 | .. | .. | .. | .. | 83 | 62 |
| Dominican Republic | 84 | 95 | 52 | 78 | 99 | 81 | 64 | 42 | .. | .. | 85 | 66 |
| Ecuador | 73 | 94 | 63 | 89 | 97 | 98 | .. | .. | .. | .. | 83 | 34 |
| Egypt, Arab Rep. | 94 | 98 | 54 | 70 | 98 | 98 | 63 | 27 | .. | .. | 79 | 59 |
| El Salvador | 67 | 84 | 51 | 62 | 98 | 96 | 62 | .. | .. | .. | 91 | 61 |
| Eritrea | 43 | 60 | 7 | 9 | 95 | 97 | 44 | 54 | 4.2 | 3.6 | 88 | 35 |
| Estonia | 100 | 100 | 97 | 97 | 96 | 95 | .. | .. | .. | .. | 72 | 66 |
| Ethiopia | 23 | 22 | 3 | 13 | 63 | 72 | 19 | 15 | 1.5 | 3.0 | 78 | 27 |
| Finland | 100 | 100 | 100 | 100 | 97 | 97 | .. | .. | .. | .. | .. | .. |
| France | 100 | 100 | .. | .. | 87 | 98 | .. | .. | .. | .. | .. | .. |
| Gabon | .. | 88 | .. | 36 | 55 | 38 | 48 | 44 | .. | .. | 46 | 58 |
| Gambia, The | .. | 82 | .. | 53 | 95 | 95 | 69 | 38 | 49.0 | 62.6 | 87 | 64 |
| Georgia | 80 | 82 | 97 | 94 | 95 | 87 | 99 | .. | .. | .. | 73 | 109 |
| Germany | 100 | 100 | 100 | 100 | 94 | 90 | .. | .. | .. | .. | 71 | 54 |
| Ghana | 55 | 75 | 15 | 18 | 85 | 84 | 59 | 29 | 21.8 | 60.8 | 73 | 38 |
| Greece | .. | .. | .. | .. | 88 | 88 | .. | .. | .. | .. | .. | .. |
| Guatemala | 79 | 95 | 58 | 86 | 95 | 80 | 64 | .. | .. | .. | 85 | 56 |
| Guinea | 44 | 50 | 14 | 18 | 67 | 71 | 42 | 38 | 0.3 | 43.5 | 72 | 55 |
| Guinea-Bissau | .. | 59 | .. | 35 | 60 | 77 | 57 | 25 | 39.0 | 45.7 | 69 | 64 |
| Haiti | 47 | 54 | 24 | 30 | 58 | 53 | 35 | 43 | .. | 5.1 | 81 | 55 |

| | Access to an improved water source | | Access to improved sanitation facilities | | Child immunization rate | | Children with acute respiratory infection taken to health provider | Children with diarrhea who received oral rehydration and continuous feeding | Children sleeping under treated bednets[a] | Children with fever receiving antimalarial drugs | Tuberculosis treatment success rate | DOTS detection rate |
|---|---|---|---|---|---|---|---|---|---|---|---|---|
| | % of population | | % of population | | % of children ages 12–23 months[b] | | % of children under age 5 with ARI | % of children under age 5 with diarrhea | % of children under age 5 | % of children under age 5 with fever | % of new registered cases | % of new estimated cases |
| | | | | | Measles | DTP3 | | | | | | |
| | 1990 | 2004 | 1990 | 2004 | 2006 | 2006 | 2000–06[c] | 2000–06[c] | 2000–06[c] | 2000–06[c] | 2005 | 2006 |
| Honduras | 84 | 87 | 50 | 69 | 91 | 87 | 56 | 49 | .. | 0.5 | 88 | 85 |
| Hungary | 99 | 99 | .. | 95 | 99 | 99 | .. | .. | .. | .. | 45 | 49 |
| India | 70 | 86 | 14 | 33 | 59 | 55 | 69 | 32 | .. | 12.0 | 86 | 64 |
| Indonesia | 72 | 77 | 46 | 55 | 72 | 70 | 61 | 56 | 0.1 | 0.7 | 91 | 73 |
| Iran, Islamic Rep. | 92 | 94 | 83 | .. | 99 | 99 | 93 | .. | .. | .. | 83 | 69 |
| Iraq | 83 | .. | 81 | .. | .. | .. | .. | .. | .. | .. | 86 | 40 |
| Ireland | .. | .. | .. | .. | 86 | 91 | .. | .. | .. | .. | .. | .. |
| Israel | 100 | 100 | .. | .. | 95 | 95 | .. | .. | .. | .. | 78 | 31 |
| Italy | .. | .. | .. | .. | 87 | 96 | .. | .. | .. | .. | 74 | 71 |
| Jamaica | 92 | 93 | 75 | 80 | 87 | 85 | 75 | 39 | .. | .. | 57 | 73 |
| Japan | 100 | 100 | 100 | 100 | 99 | 99 | .. | .. | .. | .. | 60 | 79 |
| Jordan | 97 | 97 | 93 | 93 | 99 | 98 | 72 | 44 | .. | .. | 83 | 76 |
| Kazakhstan | 87 | 86 | 72 | 72 | 99 | 99 | 71 | 48 | .. | .. | 74[e] | 69 |
| Kenya | 45 | 61 | 40 | 43 | 77 | 80 | 49 | 33 | 4.6 | 26.5 | 82 | 70 |
| Korea, Dem. Rep. | 100 | 100 | .. | 59 | 96 | 89 | 93 | .. | .. | .. | 89 | 97 |
| Korea, Rep. | .. | 92 | .. | .. | 99 | 98 | .. | .. | .. | .. | 83 | 18 |
| Kuwait | .. | .. | .. | .. | 99 | 99 | .. | .. | .. | .. | 63 | 95 |
| Kyrgyz Republic | 78 | 77 | 60 | 59 | 97 | 92 | 62 | 22 | .. | .. | 85 | 63 |
| Lao PDR | .. | 51 | .. | 30 | 48 | 57 | 36 | 37 | 17.7 | 8.7 | 90 | 77 |
| Latvia | 99 | 99 | .. | 78 | 95 | 98 | .. | .. | .. | .. | 74 | 85 |
| Lebanon | 100 | 100 | .. | 98 | 96 | 92 | 74 | .. | .. | .. | 92 | 55 |
| Lesotho | .. | 79 | 37 | 37 | 85 | 83 | 59 | 53 | .. | .. | 73 | 79 |
| Liberia | 55 | 61 | 39 | 27 | 94 | 88 | 70 | .. | 2.6 | .. | 76 | 55 |
| Libya | 71 | .. | 97 | 97 | 98 | 98 | .. | .. | .. | .. | 69 | 156 |
| Lithuania | .. | .. | .. | .. | 97 | 94 | .. | .. | .. | .. | 70 | 109 |
| Macedonia, FYR | .. | .. | .. | .. | 94 | 93 | 93 | 45 | .. | .. | 84 | 66 |
| Madagascar | 40 | 46 | 14 | 32 | 59 | 61 | 48 | 47 | 0.2 | 34.2 | 74 | 73 |
| Malawi | 40 | 73 | 47 | 61 | 85 | 99 | 51 | 26 | 23.0 | 23.9 | 73 | 42 |
| Malaysia | 98 | 99 | .. | 94 | 90 | 96 | .. | .. | .. | .. | 70 | 80 |
| Mali | 34 | 50 | 36 | 46 | 86 | 85 | 43 | 45 | 8.4 | 38.0 | 75 | 26 |
| Mauritania | 38 | 53 | 31 | 34 | 62 | 68 | 41 | 9 | 2.1 | 33.4 | 55 | 34 |
| Mauritius | 100 | 100 | .. | 94 | 99 | 97 | .. | .. | .. | .. | 86 | 67 |
| Mexico | 82 | 97 | 58 | 79 | 96 | 98 | .. | .. | .. | .. | 77 | 118 |
| Moldova | .. | 92 | .. | 68 | 96 | 97 | 60 | 48 | .. | .. | 62 | 69 |
| Mongolia | 63 | 62 | .. | 59 | 99 | 99 | 63 | 47 | .. | .. | 88 | 97 |
| Morocco | 75 | 81 | 56 | 73 | 95 | 97 | 38 | 46 | .. | .. | 81 | 95 |
| Mozambique | 36 | 43 | 20 | 32 | 77 | 72 | 55 | 47 | .. | 15.0 | 79 | 47 |
| Myanmar | 57 | 78 | 24 | 77 | 78 | 82 | 66 | 65 | .. | .. | 85 | 109 |
| Namibia | 57 | 87 | 24 | 25 | 63 | 74 | 53 | 39 | 3.4 | 14.4 | 75 | 83 |
| Nepal | 70 | 90 | 11 | 35 | 85 | 89 | 43 | 43 | .. | .. | 88 | 64 |
| Netherlands | 100 | 100 | 100 | 100 | 96 | 98 | .. | .. | .. | .. | 84 | 36 |
| New Zealand | 97 | .. | .. | .. | 82 | 89 | .. | .. | .. | .. | 60 | 61 |
| Nicaragua | 70 | 79 | 45 | 47 | 99 | 87 | 57 | 49 | .. | 1.8 | 85 | 89 |
| Niger | 39 | 46 | 7 | 13 | 47 | 39 | 47 | 43 | 7.4 | 33.0 | 74 | 49 |
| Nigeria | 49 | 48 | 39 | 44 | 62 | 54 | 33 | 28 | 1.2 | 33.9 | 75 | 20 |
| Norway | 100 | 100 | .. | .. | 91 | 93 | .. | .. | .. | .. | 91 | 39 |
| Oman | 80 | .. | 83 | .. | 96 | 98 | .. | .. | .. | .. | 90 | 122 |
| Pakistan | 83 | 91 | 37 | 59 | 80 | 83 | .. | .. | .. | .. | 83 | 50 |
| Panama | 90 | 90 | 71 | 73 | 94 | 99 | .. | .. | .. | .. | 80 | 134 |
| Papua New Guinea | 39 | 39 | 44 | 44 | 65 | 75 | .. | .. | .. | .. | 71 | 21 |
| Paraguay | 62 | 86 | 58 | 80 | 88 | 73 | .. | .. | .. | .. | 91 | 48 |
| Peru | 74 | 83 | 52 | 63 | 99 | 94 | 68 | 71 | .. | .. | 91 | 96 |
| Philippines | 87 | 85 | 57 | 72 | 92 | 88 | 55 | 76 | .. | .. | 89 | 77 |
| Poland | .. | .. | .. | .. | 99 | 99 | .. | .. | .. | .. | 77 | 67 |
| Portugal | .. | .. | .. | .. | 93 | 93 | .. | .. | .. | .. | 89 | 88 |
| Puerto Rico | .. | .. | .. | .. | .. | .. | .. | .. | .. | .. | 75 | 82 |

# Disease prevention coverage and quality

| | Access to an improved water source | | Access to improved sanitation facilities | | Child immunization rate | | Children with acute respiratory infection taken to health provider | Children with diarrhea who received oral rehydration and continuous feeding | Children sleeping under treated bednets[a] | Children with fever receiving antimalarial drugs | Tuberculosis treatment success rate | DOTS detection rate |
|---|---|---|---|---|---|---|---|---|---|---|---|---|
| | % of population | | % of population | | % of children ages 12–23 months[b] | | % of children under age 5 with ARI | % of children under age 5 with diarrhea | % of children under age 5 | % of children under age 5 with fever | % of new registered cases | % of new estimated cases |
| | | | | | Measles | DTP3 | | | | | | |
| | 1990 | 2004 | 1990 | 2004 | 2006 | 2006 | 2000–06[c] | 2000–06[c] | 2000–06[c] | 2000–06[c] | 2005 | 2006 |
| Romania | .. | 57 | .. | .. | 95 | 97 | .. | .. | .. | .. | 82 | 79 |
| Russian Federation | 94 | 97 | 87 | 87 | 99 | 99 | .. | .. | 13.0 | .. | 58 | 44 |
| Rwanda | 59 | 74 | 37 | 42 | 95 | 99 | 28 | 24 | 5.0 | 12.3 | 83 | 27 |
| Saudi Arabia | 94 | 96 | 91 | 99 | 95 | 96 | .. | .. | .. | .. | 65 | 40 |
| Senegal | 65 | 76 | 33 | 57 | 80 | 89 | 47 | 43 | 7.1 | 26.8 | 74 | 48 |
| Serbia | 93[f] | 93[f] | 87[f] | 87[f] | 88 | 92 | 93 | 31 | .. | .. | 85 | 79 |
| Sierra Leone | .. | 57 | .. | 39 | 67 | 64 | 48 | 31 | 5.3 | 51.9 | 86 | 35 |
| Singapore | 100 | 100 | 100 | 100 | 93 | 95 | .. | .. | .. | .. | 83 | 107 |
| Slovak Republic | 100 | 100 | 99 | 99 | 98 | 99 | .. | .. | .. | .. | 92 | 43 |
| Slovenia | .. | .. | .. | .. | 96 | 97 | .. | .. | .. | .. | 84 | 71 |
| Somalia | .. | 29 | .. | 26 | 35 | 35 | 13 | 7 | 9.2 | 7.9 | 89 | 83 |
| South Africa | 83 | 88 | 69 | 65 | 85 | 99 | .. | .. | .. | .. | 71 | 71 |
| Spain | 100 | 100 | 100 | 100 | 97 | 98 | .. | .. | .. | .. | .. | .. |
| Sri Lanka | 68 | 79 | 69 | 91 | 99 | 99 | .. | .. | .. | .. | 86 | 85 |
| Sudan | 64 | 70 | 33 | 34 | 73 | 78 | 57 | 56 | 27.6 | 54.2 | 82 | 30 |
| Swaziland | .. | 62 | .. | 48 | 57 | 68 | 60 | 24 | 0.1 | 25.5 | 42 | 49 |
| Sweden | 100 | 100 | 100 | 100 | 95 | 99 | .. | .. | .. | .. | 64 | 58 |
| Switzerland | 100 | 100 | 100 | 100 | 86 | 95 | .. | .. | .. | .. | .. | .. |
| Syrian Arab Republic | 80 | 93 | 73 | 90 | 98 | 99 | 77 | 34 | .. | .. | 89 | 48 |
| Tajikistan | .. | 59 | .. | 51 | 87 | 86 | 64 | 22 | 1.3 | 1.2 | 86 | 33 |
| Tanzania | 46 | 62 | 47 | 47 | 93 | 90 | 57 | 53 | 16.0 | 58.2 | 82 | 46 |
| Thailand | 95 | 99 | 80 | 99 | 96 | 98 | 84 | 46 | .. | .. | 75 | 73 |
| Timor-Leste | .. | 58 | .. | 36 | 64 | 67 | 24 | .. | 8.0 | 47.4 | 82 | 33 |
| Togo | 50 | 52 | 37 | 35 | 83 | 87 | 23 | 22 | 38.4 | 47.7 | 71 | 19 |
| Trinidad and Tobago | 92 | 91 | 100 | 100 | 89 | 92 | 74 | 32 | .. | .. | .. | .. |
| Tunisia | 81 | 93 | 75 | 85 | 98 | 99 | 43 | .. | .. | .. | 90 | 81 |
| Turkey | 85 | 96 | 85 | 88 | 98 | 90 | 41 | .. | .. | .. | 89 | 80 |
| Turkmenistan | .. | 72 | .. | 62 | 99 | 98 | 83 | 25 | .. | .. | 81 | 58 |
| Uganda | 44 | 60 | 42 | 43 | 89 | 80 | 74 | 28 | 9.7 | 61.8 | 73 | 44 |
| Ukraine | .. | 96 | .. | 96 | 98 | 98 | .. | .. | .. | .. | .. | 65 |
| United Arab Emirates | 100 | 100 | 97 | 98 | 92 | 94 | .. | .. | .. | .. | 73 | 17 |
| United Kingdom | 100 | 100 | .. | .. | 85 | 92 | .. | .. | .. | .. | .. | .. |
| United States | 100 | 100 | 100 | 100 | 93 | 96 | .. | .. | .. | .. | 64 | 88 |
| Uruguay | 100 | 100 | 100 | 100 | 94 | 95 | .. | .. | .. | .. | 84 | 77 |
| Uzbekistan | 94 | 82 | 51 | 67 | 95 | 95 | 68 | 28 | .. | .. | 81 | 48 |
| Venezuela, RB | .. | 83 | .. | 68 | 55 | 71 | 72 | 51 | .. | .. | 83 | 71 |
| Vietnam | 65 | 85 | 36 | 61 | 93 | 94 | 71 | 65 | 5.1 | 2.6 | 92 | 85 |
| West Bank and Gaza | .. | 92 | .. | 73 | .. | .. | 65 | .. | .. | .. | 100 | 5 |
| Yemen, Rep. | 71 | 67 | 32 | 43 | 80 | 85 | 47 | 18 | .. | .. | 80 | 43 |
| Zambia | 50 | 58 | 44 | 55 | 84 | 80 | 69 | 48 | 22.8 | 57.9 | 84 | 53 |
| Zimbabwe | 78 | 81 | 50 | 53 | 90 | 90 | 26 | .. | 2.9 | 4.7 | 68 | 42 |
| **World** | **76 w** | **83 w** | **45 w** | **57 w** | **80 w** | **80 w** | | | | **.. w** | **85 w** | **62 w** |
| **Low income** | 64 | 75 | 21 | 38 | 69 | 68 | | | | 21.1 | 84 | 54 |
| **Middle income** | 78 | 84 | 47 | 62 | 91 | 91 | | | | .. | 86 | 74 |
| Lower middle income | 74 | 81 | 37 | 55 | 90 | 89 | | | | .. | 90 | 77 |
| Upper middle income | 88 | 93 | 77 | 81 | 94 | 95 | | | | .. | 71 | 66 |
| **Low & middle income** | 72 | 80 | 36 | 51 | 79 | 79 | | | | .. | 85 | 62 |
| East Asia & Pacific | 72 | 79 | 30 | 51 | 89 | 89 | | | | .. | 91 | 78 |
| Europe & Central Asia | 92 | 92 | 84 | 85 | 97 | 95 | | | | .. | 70 | 56 |
| Latin America & Carib. | 83 | 91 | 67 | 77 | 93 | 92 | | | | .. | 79 | 69 |
| Middle East & N. Africa | 88 | 89 | 70 | 76 | 92 | 93 | | | | .. | 83 | 69 |
| South Asia | 71 | 84 | 17 | 37 | 65 | 64 | | | | 12.0 | 86 | 63 |
| Sub-Saharan Africa | 49 | 56 | 31 | 37 | 71 | 72 | | | | 34.5 | 76 | 46 |
| **High income** | 100 | 99 | 100 | 100 | 93 | 96 | | | | .. | 68 | 52 |
| Euro area | 100 | 100 | 100 | 100 | 91 | 95 | | | | .. | .. | 33 |

a. For malaria prevention only. b. Refers to children who were immunized before age 12 months or in some cases at any time before the survey (12–23 months). c. Data are for the most recent year available. d. Data are for 2007. e. Data are for 2006. f. Includes Montenegro.

## About the data

People's health is influenced by the environment in which they live. Lack of clean water and basic sanitation is the main reason diseases transmitted by feces are so common in developing countries. Access to drinking water from an improved source and access to improved sanitation do not ensure safety or adequacy, as these characteristics are not tested at the time of the surveys. But improved drinking water technologies and improved sanitation facilities are more likely than those characterized as unimproved to provide safe drinking water and to prevent contact with human excreta. The data are derived by the Joint Monitoring Programme (JMP) of the World Health Organization (WHO) and United Nations Children's Fund (UNICEF) based on national censuses and nationally representative household surveys. The coverage rates for water and sanitation are based on information from service users on the facilities their households actually use rather than on information from service providers, which may include nonfunctioning systems. While the estimates are based on use, the JMP reports use as access, because access is the term used in the Millennium Development Goal target for drinking water and sanitation.

Governments in developing countries usually finance immunization against measles and diphtheria, pertussis (whooping cough), and tetanus (DTP) as part of the basic public health package. In many developing countries lack of precise information on the size of the cohort of one-year-old children makes immunization coverage difficult to estimate from program statistics. The data shown here are based on an assessment of national immunization coverage rates by the WHO and UNICEF. The assessment considered both administrative data from service providers and household survey data on children's immunization histories. Based on the data available, consideration of potential biases, and contributions of local experts, the most likely true level of immunization coverage was determined for each year.

Acute respiratory infection continues to be a leading cause of death among young children, killing about 2 million children under age 5 in developing countries each year. An estimated 60 percent of these deaths can be prevented by the selective use of antibiotics by appropriate health care providers. Data are drawn mostly from household health surveys in which mothers report on number of episodes and treatment for acute respiratory infection.

Since 1990 diarrhea-related deaths among children have declined tremendously. Most diarrhea-related deaths are due to dehydration, and many of these deaths can be prevented with the use of oral rehydration salts at home. However, recommendations for the use of oral rehydration therapy have changed over time based on scientific progress, so it is difficult to accurately compare use rates across countries. Until the current recommended method for home management of diarrhea is adopted and applied in all countries, the data should be used with caution. Also, the prevalence of diarrhea may vary by season. Since country surveys are administered at different times, data comparability is further affected.

Malaria is endemic to the poorest countries in the world, mainly in tropical and subtropical regions of Africa, Asia, and the Americas. An estimated 300–500 million clinical malaria cases and more than 1 million malaria deaths occur each year—the vast majority in Sub-Saharan Africa and among children under age 5. Insecticide-treated bednets, if properly used and maintained, are one of the most important malaria-preventive strategies to limit human-mosquito contact. Studies have emphasized that mortality rates could be reduced by about 25–30 percent if every child under age 5 in malaria-risk areas such as Africa slept under a treated bednet every night.

Prompt and effective treatment of malaria is a critical element of malaria control. It is vital that sufferers, especially children under age 5, start treatment within 24 hours of the onset of symptoms, to prevent progression—often rapid—to severe malaria and death.

Data on the success rate of tuberculosis treatment are provided for countries that have implemented DOTS, the internationally recommended tuberculosis control strategy. The treatment success rate for tuberculosis provides a useful indicator of the quality of health services. A low rate or no success suggests that infectious patients may not be receiving adequate treatment. An essential complement to the tuberculosis treatment success rate is the DOTS detection rate, which indicates whether there is adequate coverage by the recommended case detection and treatment strategy. A country with a high treatment success rate may still face big challenges if its DOTS detection rate remains low.

For indicators that are from household surveys, the year in the table refers to the survey year. For more information, consult the original sources.

## Definitions

• **Access to an improved water source** is the percentage of people with reasonable access to water from an improved source, such as piped water into a dwelling; public tap; tubewell; protected dug well; and rainwater collection. Reasonable access is the availability of at least 20 liters a person a day from a source within 1 kilometer of the dwelling. • **Access to improved sanitation facilities** is the percentage of people with at least adequate access to excreta disposal facilities that can effectively prevent human, animal, and insect contact with excreta. Improved facilities range from protected pit latrines to flush toilets. • **Child immunization rate** is the percentage of children ages 12–23 months who, before 12 months or at any time before the survey, had received measles vaccine and three doses of diphtheria, pertussis (whooping cough), and tetanus (DTP3) vaccine. One dose of measles vaccine and three doses of DTP vaccine are considered adequate. • **Children with acute respiratory infection taken to a health provider** are the percentage of children under age 5 with acute respiratory infection in the two weeks before the survey who were taken to an appropriate health provider. • **Children with diarrhea who received oral rehydration and continuous feeding** are the percentage of children under age 5 with diarrhea in the two weeks before the survey who received either oral rehydration therapy or increased fluids, with continuous feeding. • **Children sleeping under treated bednets** are the percentage of children under age 5 who slept under an insecticide-treated bednet to prevent malaria in the two weeks before the survey. • **Children with fever receiving antimalarial drugs** are the percentage of children under age 5 who were ill with fever in the two weeks before the survey and received any appropriate (locally defined) antimalarial drugs. • **Tuberculosis treatment success rate** is the percentage of new registered infectious tuberculosis cases that were cured or completed a full course of treatment. • **DOTS detection rate** is the percentage of estimated new infectious tuberculosis cases detected under the internationally recommended tuberculosis detection and treatment strategy.

## Data sources

Data on access to water and sanitation are from the WHO and UNICEF's *Meeting the MDG Drinking Water and Sanitation Target* (www.who.int/water_sanitation_health/monitoring). Data on immunization are from WHO and UNICEF estimates (www.who.int/immunization_monitoring). Data on children with acute respiratory infection, with diarrhea, sleeping under treated bednets, and receiving antimalarial drugs are from UNICEF's *State of the World's Children 2008*, Childinfo, and Demographic and Health Surveys by Macro International. Data on tuberculosis are from the WHO's *Global Tuberculosis Control Report 2008: Surveillance, Planning, Financing*.

# Reproductive health

| | Total fertility rate | | Adolescent fertility rate | Unmet need for contraception | Contraceptive prevalence rate | Newborns protected against tetanus | Pregnant women receiving prenatal care | Births attended by skilled health staff | | Maternal mortality ratio | |
|---|---|---|---|---|---|---|---|---|---|---|---|
| | births per woman | | births per 1,000 women ages 15–19 | % of married women ages 15–49 | % of married women ages 15–49 | % of births | % | % of total | | per 100,000 live births | |
| | | | | | | | | | | National estimates | Modeled estimates |
| | 1990 | 2006 | 2006 | 2000–06[a] | 2000–06[a] | 2006 | 2000–06[a] | 1990 | 2000–06[a] | 1990–2006[a] | 2005 |
| Afghanistan | .. | .. | .. | .. | .. | .. | 16 | .. | 14 | .. | .. |
| Albania | 2.9 | 1.4 | 16 | .. | 60 | 87 | 97 | .. | 100 | 16 | 92 |
| Algeria | 4.6 | 2.4 | 8 | .. | 61 | 70 | 89 | 77 | 95 | 117 | 180 |
| Angola | 7.1 | 6.5 | 139 | .. | 6 | 80 | 66 | .. | 45 | .. | 1,400 |
| Argentina | 3.0 | 2.3 | 58 | .. | .. | .. | 99 | 96 | 99 | 39 | 77 |
| Armenia | 2.5 | 1.3 | 30 | 13 | 53 | .. | 93 | .. | 98 | 16 | 76 |
| Australia | 1.9 | 1.8 | 15 | .. | .. | .. | .. | 100 | 100 | .. | 4 |
| Austria | 1.5 | 1.4 | 12 | .. | .. | .. | .. | .. | .. | .. | 4 |
| Azerbaijan | 2.7 | 2.3 | 29 | .. | 55 | .. | 70 | .. | 100 | 26 | 82 |
| Bangladesh | 4.3 | 2.9 | 129 | 11 | 58 | 92 | 48 | .. | 20 | 322 | 570 |
| Belarus | 1.9 | 1.3 | 22 | .. | 73 | .. | 99 | .. | 100 | 10 | 18 |
| Belgium | 1.6 | 1.7 | 7 | .. | .. | 94 | .. | .. | .. | .. | 8 |
| Benin | 6.7 | 5.5 | 123 | 30 | 17 | 84 | 84 | .. | 79 | 498 | 840 |
| Bolivia | 4.9 | 3.6 | 79 | 23 | 58 | .. | 79 | 43 | 67 | 230 | 290 |
| Bosnia and Herzegovina | 1.7 | 1.2 | 21 | 23 | 36 | 85 | 99 | 97 | 100 | 3 | 3 |
| Botswana | 4.6 | 3.0 | 54 | .. | 44 | 71 | 97 | 77 | 94 | 326 | 380 |
| Brazil | 2.8 | 2.3 | 89 | .. | .. | 84 | 97 | 72 | 97 | 76 | 110 |
| Bulgaria | 1.8 | 1.4 | 41 | .. | .. | 65 | .. | .. | 99 | 10 | 11 |
| Burkina Faso | 7.3 | 6.1 | 129 | 29 | 17 | .. | 85 | .. | 54 | 484 | 700 |
| Burundi | 6.8 | 6.8 | 55 | .. | 9 | 84 | 92 | .. | 34 | 615 | 1,100 |
| Cambodia | 5.7 | 3.3 | 43 | 25 | 40 | 80 | 69 | .. | 44 | 472 | 540 |
| Cameroon | 5.9 | 4.4 | 122 | 20 | 29 | 52 | 82 | 58 | 63 | 669 | 1,000 |
| Canada | 1.8 | 1.5 | 14 | .. | .. | 82 | .. | .. | 100 | .. | 7 |
| Central African Republic | 5.6 | 4.7 | 119 | .. | 19 | 74 | 69 | .. | 53 | 543 | 980 |
| Chad | 6.7 | 6.3 | 169 | 21 | 3 | 60 | 39 | .. | 14 | 1,099 | 1,500 |
| Chile | 2.6 | 2.0 | 60 | .. | .. | .. | .. | .. | 100 | 17 | 16 |
| China | 2.1 | 1.8 | 7 | .. | 87 | .. | 90 | 50 | 98 | 48 | 45 |
| Hong Kong, China | 1.3 | 1.0 | 5 | .. | .. | .. | .. | .. | 100 | .. | .. |
| Colombia | 3.0 | 2.3 | 67 | 6 | 78 | 88 | 94 | 82 | 96 | 78 | 130 |
| Congo, Dem. Rep. | 6.7 | 6.3 | 224 | .. | 21[b] | 77 | 85[b] | .. | 74[b] | 1,289 | 1,100 |
| Congo, Rep. | 5.3 | 4.6 | 118 | 16 | 44 | 84 | 86 | .. | 86 | 781 | 740 |
| Costa Rica | 3.1 | 2.1 | 73 | .. | 96 | .. | 92 | 98 | 99 | 36 | 30 |
| Cote d'Ivoire | 6.5 | 4.6 | 112 | 29 | 13 | .. | 85 | .. | 57 | 543 | 810 |
| Croatia | 1.6 | 1.4 | 13 | .. | 69 | .. | 100 | 100 | 100 | 7 | 7 |
| Cuba | 1.7 | 1.5 | 48 | 8 | 73 | .. | 100 | .. | 100 | 37 | 45 |
| Czech Republic | 1.9 | 1.3 | 11 | .. | .. | .. | .. | .. | 100 | 5 | 4 |
| Denmark | 1.7 | 1.9 | 6 | .. | .. | .. | .. | .. | .. | 10 | 3 |
| Dominican Republic | 3.3 | 2.8 | 109 | 11 | 61 | 85 | 99 | 93 | 96 | 92 | 150 |
| Ecuador | 3.6 | 2.6 | 83 | .. | 73 | 66 | 84 | .. | 75 | 107 | 210 |
| Egypt, Arab Rep. | 4.3 | 2.9 | 41 | 10 | 59 | 86 | 70 | 37 | 74 | 84 | 130 |
| El Salvador | 3.7 | 2.7 | 82 | .. | 67 | 91 | 86 | 52 | 92 | 71 | 170 |
| Eritrea | 6.2 | 5.1 | 75 | 27 | 8 | 79 | 70 | .. | 28 | 998 | 450 |
| Estonia | 2.0 | 1.5 | 22 | .. | .. | .. | .. | .. | 100 | 29 | 25 |
| Ethiopia | 6.8 | 5.3 | 97 | 34 | 15 | 80 | 28 | .. | 6 | 673 | 720 |
| Finland | 1.8 | 1.8 | 10 | .. | .. | .. | .. | .. | 100 | 6 | 7 |
| France | 1.8 | 2.0 | 7 | .. | .. | .. | .. | .. | .. | 10 | 8 |
| Gabon | 4.7 | 3.1 | 85 | 28 | 33 | 63 | 94 | .. | 86 | 519 | 520 |
| Gambia, The | 6.0 | 4.8 | 106 | .. | 18 | 94 | 98 | 44 | 57 | 730 | 690 |
| Georgia | 2.1 | 1.4 | 31 | .. | 47 | 87 | 94 | .. | 92 | 23 | 66 |
| Germany | 1.5 | 1.3 | 10 | .. | .. | .. | .. | .. | 100 | 8 | 4 |
| Ghana | 5.7 | 3.9 | 58 | 34 | 17 | .. | 92 | 40 | 50 | .. | 560 |
| Greece | 1.4 | 1.4 | 9 | .. | .. | 69 | .. | .. | .. | 1 | 3 |
| Guatemala | 5.6 | 4.2 | 109 | .. | 43 | 91 | 84 | .. | 41 | 153 | 290 |
| Guinea | 6.6 | 5.5 | 153 | 21 | 9 | 79 | 82 | 31 | 38 | 980 | 910 |
| Guinea-Bissau | 7.1 | 7.1 | 190 | .. | 10 | 91 | 78 | .. | 39 | 405 | 1,100 |
| Haiti | 5.4 | 3.6 | 48 | 38 | 32 | 94 | 85 | 23 | 26 | 630 | 670 |

| | Total fertility rate | | Adolescent fertility rate | Unmet need for contraception | Contraceptive prevalence rate | Newborns protected against tetanus | Pregnant women receiving prenatal care | Births attended by skilled health staff | | Maternal mortality ratio | |
|---|---|---|---|---|---|---|---|---|---|---|---|
| | births per woman | | births per 1,000 women ages 15–19 | % of married women ages 15–49 | % of married women ages 15–49 | % of births | % | % of total | | per 100,000 live births National estimates | Modeled estimates |
| | 1990 | 2006 | 2006 | 2000–06[a] | 2000–06[a] | 2006 | 2000–06[a] | 1990 | 2000–06[a] | 1990–2006[a] | 2005 |
| Honduras | 5.1 | 3.4 | 95 | 17 | 65 | .. | 92 | 45 | 67 | 108 | 280 |
| Hungary | 1.8 | 1.4 | 20 | .. | .. | .. | .. | .. | 100 | 4 | 6 |
| India | 3.8 | 2.5 | 63 | .. | 56 | 83 | 74 | .. | 47 | 301 | 450 |
| Indonesia | 3.1 | 2.2 | 41 | 9 | 57 | 87 | 92 | 32 | 72 | 307 | 420 |
| Iran, Islamic Rep. | 4.8 | 2.1 | 21 | .. | 74 | .. | .. | .. | 90 | 37 | 140 |
| Iraq | 5.9 | .. | .. | .. | .. | .. | 84 | 54 | 89 | .. | .. |
| Ireland | 2.1 | 1.9 | 17 | .. | .. | .. | .. | .. | 100 | 6 | 1 |
| Israel | 2.8 | 2.7 | 14 | .. | .. | .. | .. | .. | .. | 5 | 4 |
| Italy | 1.3 | 1.4 | 6 | .. | .. | 52 | .. | .. | 99 | 7 | 3 |
| Jamaica | 2.9 | 2.3 | 80 | .. | 69 | 72 | 91 | 79 | 97 | 95 | 170 |
| Japan | 1.5 | 1.3 | 3 | .. | 56 | 86 | .. | 100 | 100 | 8 | 6 |
| Jordan | 5.4 | 3.2 | 25 | 11 | 56 | .. | 99 | 87 | 100 | 41 | 62 |
| Kazakhstan | 2.7 | 2.1 | 30 | .. | 51 | .. | 100 | .. | 100 | 70 | 140 |
| Kenya | 5.8 | 5.0 | 104 | 25 | 39 | 74 | 88 | 50 | 42 | 414 | 560 |
| Korea, Dem. Rep. | 2.4 | 1.9 | 1 | .. | .. | .. | .. | .. | 97 | 105 | 370 |
| Korea, Rep. | 1.6 | 1.1 | 4 | .. | .. | .. | .. | 98 | 100 | 20 | 14 |
| Kuwait | 3.5 | 2.3 | 13 | .. | .. | 90 | .. | .. | 100 | 5 | 4 |
| Kyrgyz Republic | 3.7 | 2.4 | 31 | 1 | 48 | 82 | 97 | .. | 98 | 104 | 150 |
| Lao PDR | 6.1 | 3.3 | 75 | .. | 32 | 52 | 27 | .. | 19 | 405 | 660 |
| Latvia | 2.0 | 1.4 | 15 | .. | .. | .. | .. | .. | 100 | 10 | 10 |
| Lebanon | 3.1 | 2.2 | 25 | .. | 58 | 72 | 96 | .. | 98 | .. | 150 |
| Lesotho | 4.9 | 3.5 | 77 | 31 | 37 | 72 | 90 | .. | 55 | 762 | 960 |
| Liberia | 6.9 | 6.8 | 220 | .. | 10 | .. | 85 | .. | 51 | .. | 1,200 |
| Libya | 4.7 | 2.8 | 3 | .. | .. | .. | .. | .. | .. | 77 | 97 |
| Lithuania | 2.0 | 1.3 | 19 | .. | .. | .. | .. | .. | 100 | 16 | 11 |
| Macedonia, FYR | 2.0 | 1.5 | 22 | 34 | 14 | .. | 98 | .. | 98 | 21 | 10 |
| Madagascar | 6.2 | 4.9 | 136 | 24 | 27 | 67 | 80 | 57 | 51 | 469 | 510 |
| Malawi | 6.9 | 5.7 | 140 | 28 | 42 | 84 | 92 | 55 | 54 | 984 | 1,100 |
| Malaysia | 3.7 | 2.7 | 13 | .. | .. | 88 | 79 | .. | 98 | 28 | 62 |
| Mali | 7.4 | 6.6 | 183 | 29 | 8 | .. | 57 | .. | 41 | 582 | 970 |
| Mauritania | 5.8 | 4.5 | 88 | 32 | 8 | 94 | 64 | 40 | 57 | 747 | 820 |
| Mauritius | 2.3 | 2.0 | 41 | .. | 76 | .. | .. | 91 | 99 | 22 | 15 |
| Mexico | 3.4 | 2.2 | 66 | .. | 71 | 87 | .. | .. | 83 | 62 | 60 |
| Moldova | 2.3 | 1.2 | 33 | .. | 68 | .. | 98 | .. | 100 | 19 | 22 |
| Mongolia | 4.0 | 2.3 | 46 | 14 | 66 | 87 | 99 | .. | 99 | 93 | 46 |
| Morocco | 4.0 | 2.4 | 19 | 10 | 63 | .. | 68 | 31 | 63 | 227 | 240 |
| Mozambique | 6.2 | 5.2 | 155 | 18 | 17 | 85 | 85 | .. | 48 | 408 | 520 |
| Myanmar | 3.4 | 2.1 | 17 | .. | 34 | 87 | 76 | .. | 68 | 316 | 380 |
| Namibia | 5.7 | 3.3 | 61 | 22 | 44 | 81 | 91 | 68 | 76 | 271 | 210 |
| Nepal | 5.1 | 3.1 | 116 | 25 | 48 | 83 | 44 | 7 | 19 | 281 | 830 |
| Netherlands | 1.6 | 1.7 | 5 | .. | .. | .. | .. | .. | 100 | 7 | 6 |
| New Zealand | 2.2 | 2.1 | 23 | .. | .. | .. | .. | .. | 97 | 15 | 9 |
| Nicaragua | 4.7 | 2.8 | 114 | 15 | 69 | 94 | 86 | .. | 67 | 87 | 170 |
| Niger | 7.9 | 7.0 | 201 | 16 | 11 | 53 | 46 | 15 | 18 | 648 | 1,800 |
| Nigeria | 6.7 | 5.4 | 131 | 17 | 13 | 71 | 58 | 33 | 36 | .. | 1,100 |
| Norway | 1.9 | 1.9 | 9 | .. | .. | .. | .. | 100 | .. | 6 | 7 |
| Oman | 6.5 | 3.1 | 11 | .. | 32 | 94 | 100 | .. | 98 | 15 | 64 |
| Pakistan | 5.8 | 3.9 | 33 | .. | 28 | 80 | 36 | 19 | 31 | 533 | 320 |
| Panama | 3.0 | 2.6 | 84 | .. | .. | .. | .. | .. | 91 | 40 | 130 |
| Papua New Guinea | 4.8 | 3.9 | 55 | .. | .. | 81 | .. | .. | 42 | .. | 470 |
| Paraguay | 4.7 | 3.2 | 74 | .. | 73 | 82 | 94 | 66 | 77 | 174 | 150 |
| Peru | 3.9 | 2.6 | 61 | 8 | 46 | 64 | 92 | 80 | 87 | 185 | 240 |
| Philippines | 4.3 | 3.3 | 48 | 17 | 49 | 57 | 88 | .. | 60 | 172 | 230 |
| Poland | 2.0 | 1.3 | 13 | .. | .. | .. | .. | .. | 100 | 4 | 8 |
| Portugal | 1.4 | 1.4 | 14 | .. | .. | .. | .. | 98 | 100 | 8 | 11 |
| Puerto Rico | 2.2 | 1.8 | 50 | .. | .. | .. | .. | .. | 100 | .. | 18 |

# Reproductive health

| | Total fertility rate | | Adolescent fertility rate | Unmet need for contraception | Contraceptive prevalence rate | Newborns protected against tetanus | Pregnant women receiving prenatal care | Births attended by skilled health staff | | Maternal mortality ratio | |
|---|---|---|---|---|---|---|---|---|---|---|---|
| | births per woman | | births per 1,000 women ages 15–19 | % of married women ages 15–49 | % of married women ages 15–49 | % of births | % | % of total | | per 100,000 live births | |
| | | | | | | | | | | National estimates | Modeled estimates |
| | 1990 | 2006 | 2006 | 2000–06[a] | 2000–06[a] | 2006 | 2000–06[a] | 1990 | 2000–06[a] | 1990–2006[a] | 2005 |
| Romania | 1.8 | 1.3 | 33 | .. | 70 | .. | 94 | .. | 98 | 17 | 24 |
| Russian Federation | 1.9 | 1.3 | 28 | .. | .. | .. | .. | .. | 99 | 23 | 28 |
| Rwanda | 7.4 | 5.9 | 41 | 38 | 17 | 82 | 94 | 26 | 39 | 750 | 1,300 |
| Saudi Arabia | 5.9 | 3.4 | 29 | .. | .. | 56 | .. | .. | 96 | 10 | 18 |
| Senegal | 6.5 | 5.3 | 91 | 32 | 12 | 86 | 87 | .. | 52 | 434 | 980 |
| Serbia | 1.8 | 1.4 | 25 | 29 | 41 | .. | 98 | .. | 99 | 7[c] | 14[c] |
| Sierra Leone | 6.5 | 6.5 | 166 | .. | 5 | .. | 81 | .. | 43 | 1,800 | 2,100 |
| Singapore | 1.9 | 1.3 | 5 | .. | .. | 4 | .. | .. | 100 | 6 | 14 |
| Slovak Republic | 2.1 | 1.2 | 20 | .. | .. | 73 | .. | .. | 100 | 6 | 6 |
| Slovenia | 1.5 | 1.3 | 7 | .. | .. | 74 | .. | 100 | 100 | 17 | 6 |
| Somalia | 6.8 | 6.1 | 67 | .. | 15 | .. | 26 | .. | 33 | 1,044 | 1,400 |
| South Africa | 3.3 | 2.7 | 63 | .. | 60 | 88 | 92 | .. | 92 | 150 | 400 |
| Spain | 1.3 | 1.4 | 9 | .. | .. | 72 | .. | .. | .. | 6 | 4 |
| Sri Lanka | 2.5 | 1.9 | 26 | .. | 70 | 93 | 100 | .. | 96 | 43 | 58 |
| Sudan | 5.9 | 4.3 | 59 | 6 | 8 | .. | 70 | 69 | 49 | .. | 450 |
| Swaziland | 5.3 | 3.5 | 34 | .. | 48 | .. | 90 | .. | 74 | 229 | 390 |
| Sweden | 2.1 | 1.9 | 4 | .. | .. | 86 | .. | .. | .. | 5 | 3 |
| Switzerland | 1.6 | 1.4 | 4 | .. | .. | 93 | .. | .. | 100 | 5 | 5 |
| Syrian Arab Republic | 5.4 | 3.2 | 38 | .. | 58 | 87 | 84 | .. | 93 | 65 | 130 |
| Tajikistan | 5.1 | 3.4 | 28 | .. | 38 | 88 | 77 | .. | 83 | 97 | 170 |
| Tanzania | 6.1 | 5.3 | 123 | 22 | 26 | .. | 78 | 53 | 46 | 578 | 950 |
| Thailand | 2.1 | 1.8 | 42 | .. | 77 | .. | 98 | .. | 97 | 24 | 110 |
| Timor-Leste | 4.9 | 7.3 | 56 | .. | 10 | 63 | 61 | .. | 18 | .. | 380 |
| Togo | 6.4 | 4.9 | 92 | .. | 17 | 84 | 89 | 31 | 62 | 480 | 510 |
| Trinidad and Tobago | 2.4 | 1.6 | 35 | .. | 43 | .. | 96 | .. | 98 | 45 | 45 |
| Tunisia | 3.5 | 2.0 | 7 | .. | 63 | 89 | 92 | 69 | 90 | 69 | 100 |
| Turkey | 3.0 | 2.2 | 39 | .. | 71 | 67 | 81 | .. | 83 | 29 | 44 |
| Turkmenistan | 4.2 | 2.6 | 16 | 10 | 48 | .. | 99 | .. | 100 | 14 | 130 |
| Uganda | 7.1 | 6.7 | 156 | 41 | 24 | 88 | 94 | 38 | 42 | 505 | 550 |
| Ukraine | 1.8 | 1.3 | 28 | .. | 66 | .. | 99 | .. | 100 | 13 | 18 |
| United Arab Emirates | 4.3 | 2.3 | 19 | .. | .. | .. | .. | .. | 100 | 3 | 37 |
| United Kingdom | 1.8 | 1.9 | 24 | .. | 84 | .. | .. | .. | .. | 7 | 8 |
| United States | 2.1 | 2.1 | 43 | .. | .. | .. | .. | 99 | 99 | 8 | 11 |
| Uruguay | 2.5 | 2.0 | 62 | .. | .. | .. | .. | .. | 99 | 26 | 20 |
| Uzbekistan | 4.1 | 2.4 | 34 | 8 | 65 | 87 | 99 | .. | 100 | 28 | 24 |
| Venezuela, RB | 3.4 | 2.6 | 90 | .. | .. | 88 | 94 | .. | 95 | 60 | 57 |
| Vietnam | 3.6 | 2.1 | 18 | 5 | 76 | 61 | 91 | .. | 88 | 162 | 150 |
| West Bank and Gaza | 6.3 | 4.6 | 82 | .. | 50 | .. | 99 | .. | 99 | .. | .. |
| Yemen, Rep. | 8.0 | 5.6 | 73 | .. | 23 | .. | 41 | 16 | 27 | 365 | 430 |
| Zambia | 6.4 | 5.3 | 130 | 27 | 34 | 90 | 93 | 51 | 43 | 729 | 830 |
| Zimbabwe | 5.1 | 3.8 | 62 | 13 | 60 | 80 | 94 | 70 | 80 | 555 | 880 |
| **World** | **3.1 w** | **2.5 w** | **52 w** | | **60 w** | **.. w** | **80 w** | **.. w** | **65 w** | | **400 w** |
| **Low income** | 4.7 | 3.5 | 82 | | 44 | 81 | 69 | | 43 | | 650 |
| **Middle income** | 2.7 | 2.1 | 32 | | 75 | .. | 90 | 53 | 88 | | 160 |
| Lower middle income | 2.6 | 2.1 | 24 | | 76 | .. | 89 | 50 | 86 | | 180 |
| Upper middle income | 2.7 | 2.0 | 56 | | .. | .. | .. | .. | 94 | | 97 |
| **Low & middle income** | 3.4 | 2.7 | 56 | | 60 | .. | 80 | .. | 62 | | 440 |
| East Asia & Pacific | 2.4 | 2.0 | 16 | | 79 | .. | 89 | 47 | 87 | | 150 |
| Europe & Central Asia | 2.3 | 1.6 | 29 | | 63 | .. | 91 | 81 | 95 | | 43 |
| Latin America & Carib. | 3.2 | 2.4 | 77 | | 69 | 84 | 95 | 73 | 88 | | 130 |
| Middle East & N. Africa | 4.8 | 2.9 | 30 | | 60 | .. | 76 | 48 | 77 | | 200 |
| South Asia | 4.1 | 2.8 | 69 | | 53 | 84 | 66 | 32 | 41 | | 500 |
| Sub-Saharan Africa | 6.2 | 5.2 | 122 | | 22 | 76 | 72 | 44 | 45 | | 900 |
| **High income** | 1.8 | 1.7 | 22 | | .. | .. | .. | .. | 99 | | 9 |
| Euro area | 1.5 | 1.5 | 8 | | .. | .. | .. | .. | .. | | 5 |

a. Data are for most recent year available. b. Data are for 2007. c. Includes Montenegro.

Reproductive health is a state of physical and mental well-being in relation to the reproductive system and its functions and processes. Means of achieving reproductive health include education and services during pregnancy and childbirth, safe and effective contraception, and prevention and treatment of sexually transmitted diseases. Pregnancy and childbirth complications are the leading cause of death and disability among women of reproductive age in developing countries.

Total and adolescent fertility rates are based on data on registered live births from vital registration systems or, in the absence of such systems, from censuses or sample surveys. The estimated rates are generally considered reliable measures of fertility in the recent past. Where no empirical information on age-specific fertility rates is available, a model is used to estimate the share of births to adolescents. For countries without vital registration systems fertility rates are generally based on extrapolations from trends observed in censuses or surveys from earlier years.

More couples in developing countries want to limit or postpone childbearing but are not using effective contraception. These couples have an unmet need for contraception. Common reasons are lack of knowledge about contraceptive methods and concerns about possible side effects. This indicator excludes women not exposed to the risk of unintended pregnancy because of menopause, infertility, or postpartum anovulation.

Contraceptive prevalence reflects all methods—ineffective traditional methods as well as highly effective modern methods. Contraceptive prevalence rates are obtained mainly from household surveys, including Demographic and Health Surveys, Multiple Indicator Cluster Surveys, and contraceptive prevalence surveys (see *Primary data documentation* for the most recent survey year). Unmarried women are often excluded from such surveys, which may bias the estimates.

An important cause of infant mortality in some developing countries, neonatal tetanus can be prevented through immunization of the mother during pregnancy. The data on tetanus in this year's edition are estimated by the "protection at birth" model, which tracks the immunization status of women of child-bearing age. The estimates account for the number of doses received and the time since the mother's last immunization. A currently immune woman's child is considered protected. Because the methodology behind this indicator has changed,

these data cannot be compared with those in previous editions.

. Good prenatal and postnatal care improve maternal health and reduce maternal and infant mortality. But data may not reflect such improvements because health information systems are often weak, maternal deaths are underreported, and rates of maternal mortality are difficult to measure.

The share of births attended by skilled health staff is an indicator of a health system's ability to provide adequate care for pregnant women. Maternal mortality ratios are generally of unknown reliability, as are many other cause-specific mortality indicators. Household surveys such as Demographic and Health Surveys attempt to measure maternal mortality by asking respondents about survivorship of sisters. The main disadvantage of this method is that the estimates of maternal mortality that it produces pertain to 12 years or so before the survey, making them unsuitable for monitoring recent changes or observing the impact of interventions. In addition, measurement of maternal mortality is subject to many types of errors. Even in high-income countries with vital registration systems, misclassification of maternal deaths has been found to lead to serious underestimation.

The national estimates of maternal mortality ratios in the table are based on national surveys, vital registration records, and surveillance data or are derived from community and hospital records. The modeled estimates are based on an exercise by the World Health Organization (WHO), United Nations Children's Fund (UNICEF), United Nations Population Fund (UNFPA), and World Bank. For countries with complete vital registration systems with good attribution of cause of death information, the data are used as reported. For countries with national data, either from complete vital registration systems with uncertain or poor attribution of cause of death information, or from household surveys, reported maternal mortality was adjusted usually by a factor of underenumeration and misclassification. For countries with no empirical national data (about 35 percent of countries), maternal mortality was estimated with a regression model using socioeconomic information, including fertility, birth attendants, and GDP. Neither set of ratios can be assumed to provide an exact estimate of maternal mortality for any of the countries in the table.

For the indicators that are from household surveys, the year in the table refers to the survey year. For more information, consult the original sources.

• **Total fertility rate** is the number of children that would be born to a woman if she were to live to the end of her childbearing years and bear children in accordance with current age-specific fertility rates. • **Adolescent fertility rate** is the number of births per 1,000 women ages 15–19. • **Unmet need for contraception** is the percentage of fertile, married women of reproductive age who do not want to become pregnant and are not using contraception. • **Contraceptive prevalence rate** is the percentage of women married or in-union ages 15–49 who are practicing, or whose sexual partners are practicing, any form of contraception. • **Newborns protected against tetanus** are the percentage of births by women of child-bearing age who are immunized against tetanus. • **Pregnant women receiving prenatal care** are the percentage of women attended at least once during pregnancy by skilled health personnel for reasons related to pregnancy. • **Births attended by skilled health staff** are the percentage of deliveries attended by personnel trained to give the necessary care to women during pregnancy, labor, and postpartum; to conduct deliveries on their own; and to care for newborns. • **Maternal mortality ratio** is the number of women who die from pregnancy-related causes during pregnancy and childbirth per 100,000 live births.

Data on fertility rates are compiled and estimated by the World Bank's Development Data Group. Inputs come from the United Nations Population Division's *World Population Prospects: The 2006 Revision*, census reports and other statistical publications from national statistical offices, and household surveys such as Demographic and Health Surveys. Data on women with unmet need for contraception and contraceptive prevalence rates are from household surveys, including Demographic and Health Surveys by Macro International and Multiple Indicator Cluster Surveys by UNICEF. Data on tetanus vaccinations, pregnant women receiving prenatal care, births attended by skilled health staff, and national estimates of maternal mortality ratios are from UNICEF's *State of the World's Children 2008* and Childinfo and Demographic and Health Surveys by Macro International. Modeled estimates for maternal mortality ratios are from "Maternal Mortality in 2005: Estimates Developed by WHO, UNICEF, UNFPA and the World Bank" (2007).

| | Prevalence of undernourishment | | Prevalence of child malnutrition | | Prevalence of overweight children | Low-birthweight babies | Exclusive breastfeeding | Consumption of iodized salt | Vitamin A supplementation |
|---|---|---|---|---|---|---|---|---|---|
| | % of population | | % of children under age 5 | | % of children under age 5 | % of births | % of children under 6 months | % of households | % of children 6–59 months |
| | 1990–92 | 2002–04[a] | Underweight 2000–06[b] | Stunting 2000–06[b] | 2000–06[b] | 2000–06[b] | 2000–06[b] | 2000–06[b] | 2005 |
| Afghanistan | .. | .. | .. | .. | .. | .. | .. | 28 | .. |
| Albania | 5[c] | 6 | 17.0 | 39.2 | 30.0 | 7 | 2 | 62 | .. |
| Algeria | 5 | 4 | 10.2 | 21.6 | 15.4 | 6 | 7 | 61 | .. |
| Angola | 58 | 35 | 27.5 | 50.8 | 5.3 | 12 | 11 | 35 | 79 |
| Argentina | <2.5 | 3 | 2.3 | 8.2 | 9.9 | 7 | .. | .. | .. |
| Armenia | 52[c] | 24 | 4.2 | 18.2 | 11.7 | 8 | 33 | 97 | .. |
| Australia | <2.5 | <2.5 | .. | .. | .. | 7 | .. | .. | .. |
| Austria | <2.5 | <2.5 | .. | .. | .. | 7 | .. | .. | .. |
| Azerbaijan | 34[c] | 7 | 14.0 | 24.1 | 6.2 | 12 | 7 | 26 | 29[d] |
| Bangladesh | 35 | 30 | 39.2 | 47.8 | 0.9 | 22 | 37 | 84 | 83 |
| Belarus | <2.5[c] | 4 | .. | .. | .. | 4 | 9 | 55 | .. |
| Belgium | <2.5 | <2.5 | .. | .. | .. | .. | .. | .. | .. |
| Benin | 20 | 12 | 21.5 | 39.1 | 3.0 | 13 | 70 | 55 | 94 |
| Bolivia | 28 | 23 | 5.9 | 32.5 | 9.2 | 7 | 54 | 90 | 39 |
| Bosnia and Herzegovina | 9[c] | 9 | 4.2 | 12.1 | 16.3 | 5 | 18 | 62 | .. |
| Botswana | 23 | 32 | 10.7 | 29.1 | 10.4 | 10 | 34 | 66 | 62 |
| Brazil | 12 | 7 | 3.7 | .. | .. | 8 | .. | 88 | .. |
| Bulgaria | 8[c] | 8 | 1.6 | 8.8 | 13.6 | 10 | .. | 100 | .. |
| Burkina Faso | 21 | 15 | 35.2 | 43.1 | 5.4 | 16 | 7 | 34 | 95 |
| Burundi | 48 | 66 | 38.9 | 63.1 | 1.4 | 11 | 45 | 98 | 69 |
| Cambodia | 43 | 33 | 28.4 | 43.7 | 1.7 | 11 | 60 | 73 | 79 |
| Cameroon | 33 | 26 | 15.1 | 35.4 | 8.7 | 11 | 21 | 49 | 95 |
| Canada | <2.5 | <2.5 | .. | .. | .. | 6 | .. | .. | .. |
| Central African Republic | 50 | 44 | 21.8 | 44.6 | 10.8 | 13 | 23 | 62 | 79 |
| Chad | 58 | 35 | 33.9 | 44.8 | 4.4 | 22 | 2 | 56 | 95 |
| Chile | 8 | 4 | .. | .. | .. | 6 | 63 | 100 | .. |
| China | 16 | 12 | 6.8 | 21.8 | 9.2 | 2 | 51 | 90 | .. |
| Hong Kong, China | .. | .. | .. | .. | .. | 5 | .. | .. | .. |
| Colombia | 17 | 13 | 5.1 | 16.2 | 4.2 | 6 | 47 | 90 | .. |
| Congo, Dem. Rep. | 31 | 74 | 33.6 | 44.4 | 6.5 | 12 | 36[e] | 72 | 92 |
| Congo, Rep. | 54 | 33 | 11.8 | 31.2 | 8.5 | 13 | 19 | 82 | 90 |
| Costa Rica | 6 | 5 | .. | .. | .. | 7 | .. | .. | 60 |
| Côte d'Ivoire | 18 | 13 | .. | .. | .. | 17 | 4 | 84 | 95 |
| Croatia | 16[c] | 7 | .. | .. | .. | 6 | .. | .. | .. |
| Cuba | 7 | <2.5 | .. | .. | .. | 5 | 26 | 88 | .. |
| Czech Republic | <2.5[c] | <2.5 | 2.1 | 2.6 | 4.4 | 7 | .. | .. | .. |
| Denmark | <2.5 | <2.5 | .. | .. | .. | 5 | .. | .. | .. |
| Dominican Republic | 27 | 29 | 4.2 | 11.7 | 8.6 | 11 | 4 | 19 | 40 |
| Ecuador | 8 | 6 | 6.2 | 29.0 | 5.1 | .. | 40 | .. | .. |
| Egypt, Arab Rep. | 4 | 4 | 5.4 | 23.8 | 14.1 | 14 | 38 | 78 | .. |
| El Salvador | 12 | 11 | 6.1 | 24.6 | 5.8 | 7 | 24 | 62 | .. |
| Eritrea | 70[c] | 75 | 34.5 | 43.7 | 1.6 | 14 | 52 | 68 | 57 |
| Estonia | 9[c] | <2.5 | .. | .. | .. | 4 | .. | .. | .. |
| Ethiopia | 69[c] | 46 | 34.6 | 50.7 | 5.1 | 14 | 49 | 20 | 59 |
| Finland | <2.5 | <2.5 | .. | .. | .. | 4 | .. | .. | .. |
| France | <2.5 | <2.5 | .. | .. | .. | .. | .. | .. | .. |
| Gabon | 10 | 5 | 8.8 | 26.3 | 5.6 | 14 | 6 | 36 | 30 |
| Gambia, The | 22 | 29 | 15.4 | 24.1 | 3.0 | 20 | 41 | 7 | 95 |
| Georgia | 44[c] | 9 | .. | .. | .. | 7 | .. | 91 | .. |
| Germany | <2.5 | <2.5 | .. | .. | .. | .. | .. | .. | .. |
| Ghana | 37 | 11 | 18.8 | 35.6 | 4.5 | 9 | 54 | 32 | 95 |
| Greece | <2.5 | <2.5 | .. | .. | .. | .. | .. | .. | .. |
| Guatemala | 16 | 22 | 17.7 | 54.3 | 5.6 | 12 | 51 | 67 | 44[d] |
| Guinea | 39 | 24 | 22.5 | 39.3 | 5.1 | 12 | 27 | 51 | 95 |
| Guinea-Bissau | 24 | 39 | 21.9 | 36.1 | 5.1 | 24 | 16 | 1 | 64 |
| Haiti | 65 | 46 | 18.9 | 29.7 | 3.9 | 25 | 41 | 3 | 42 |

| | Prevalence of undernourishment | | Prevalence of child malnutrition | | Prevalence of overweight children | Low-birthweight babies | Exclusive breastfeeding | Consumption of iodized salt | Vitamin A supplementation |
|---|---|---|---|---|---|---|---|---|---|
| | % of population | | % of children under age 5 | | % of children under age 5 | % of births | % of children under 6 months | % of households | % of children 6–59 months |
| | 1990–92 | 2002–04[a] | Underweight 2000–06[b] | Stunting 2000–06[b] | 2000–06[b] | 2000–06[b] | 2000–06[b] | 2000–06[b] | 2005 |
| Honduras | 23 | 23 | 8.6 | 29.9 | 5.8 | 10 | 30 | .. | 40 |
| Hungary | <2.5[c] | <2.5 | .. | .. | .. | 9 | .. | .. | .. |
| India | 25 | 20 | 43.5 | 47.9 | 1.9 | .. | 46 | 51 | 64[d] |
| Indonesia | 9 | 6 | 24.4 | 28.6 | 5.1 | 9 | 40 | 73 | 76 |
| Iran, Islamic Rep. | 4 | 4 | .. | .. | .. | .. | 44 | 99 | .. |
| Iraq | .. | .. | .. | .. | .. | .. | .. | 28 | .. |
| Ireland | <2.5 | <2.5 | .. | .. | .. | .. | .. | .. | .. |
| Israel | <2.5 | <2.5 | .. | .. | .. | 8 | .. | .. | .. |
| Italy | <2.5 | <2.5 | .. | .. | .. | .. | .. | .. | .. |
| Jamaica | 14 | 9 | 3.1 | 4.5 | 7.5 | 12 | 15 | .. | .. |
| Japan | <2.5 | <2.5 | .. | .. | .. | 8 | .. | .. | .. |
| Jordan | 4 | 6 | 3.6 | 12.0 | 4.7 | 12 | 27 | 88 | .. |
| Kazakhstan | <2.5[c] | 6 | .. | .. | .. | 6 | 17 | 92 | .. |
| Kenya | 39 | 31 | 16.5 | 35.8 | 5.8 | 10 | 13 | 91 | 69 |
| Korea, Dem. Rep. | 18 | 33 | 17.8 | 44.7 | 0.9 | 7 | 65 | 40 | 95 |
| Korea, Rep. | <2.5 | <2.5 | .. | .. | .. | 4 | .. | .. | .. |
| Kuwait | 24 | 5 | .. | .. | .. | .. | .. | .. | .. |
| Kyrgyz Republic | 21[c] | 4 | .. | .. | .. | 5 | 32 | 76 | 88 |
| Lao PDR | 29 | 19 | 36.4 | 48.2 | 2.7 | 14 | 23 | 75 | 63 |
| Latvia | 3[c] | 3 | .. | .. | .. | 5 | .. | .. | .. |
| Lebanon | <2.5 | 3 | .. | .. | .. | 6 | 27 | 92 | .. |
| Lesotho | 17 | 13 | 16.6 | 45.2 | 6.8 | 13 | 36 | 91 | 9 |
| Liberia | 34 | 50 | 22.8 | 45.3 | 4.6 | .. | 35 | .. | 95 |
| Libya | <2.5 | <2.5 | .. | .. | .. | .. | .. | .. | .. |
| Lithuania | 4[c] | <2.5 | .. | .. | .. | 4 | .. | .. | .. |
| Macedonia, FYR | 15[c] | 5 | 1.2 | 1.2 | 7.9 | 6 | 16 | 94 | 95 |
| Madagascar | 35 | 38 | 36.8 | 52.8 | 6.2 | 17 | 67 | 75 | 95 |
| Malawi | 50 | 35 | 18.4 | 52.5 | 10.2 | 13 | 56 | 48 | 94 |
| Malaysia | 3 | 3 | .. | .. | .. | 9 | .. | .. | .. |
| Mali | 29 | 29 | 30.1 | 42.7 | 3.1 | 23 | 25 | 74 | 66 |
| Mauritania | 15 | 10 | 30.4 | 39.5 | 3.8 | .. | 20 | 2 | 96 |
| Mauritius | 6 | 5 | .. | .. | .. | 14 | 21 | .. | .. |
| Mexico | 5 | 5 | 3.4 | 15.5 | 7.6 | 8 | .. | 91 | 68 |
| Moldova | 5[c] | 11 | 3.2 | 11.3 | 9.1 | 6 | 46 | 60 | .. |
| Mongolia | 34 | 27 | 4.8 | 23.5 | 6.1 | 6 | 57 | 83 | 92 |
| Morocco | 6 | 6 | 9.9 | 23.1 | 13.3 | 15 | 31 | 59 | .. |
| Mozambique | 66 | 44 | 21.2 | 47.0 | 6.3 | 15 | 30 | 54 | 95 |
| Myanmar | 10 | 5 | 29.6 | 40.6 | 2.4 | 15 | 15 | 60 | 95 |
| Namibia | 34 | 24 | 20.3 | 29.5 | 3.3 | 14 | 19 | 63 | 68 |
| Nepal | 20 | 17 | 38.8 | 49.3 | 0.6 | 21 | 53 | 63 | 96 |
| Netherlands | <2.5 | <2.5 | .. | .. | .. | .. | .. | .. | .. |
| New Zealand | <2.5 | <2.5 | .. | .. | .. | 6 | .. | .. | .. |
| Nicaragua | 30 | 27 | 7.8 | 25.2 | 7.1 | 12 | 31 | 97 | 98 |
| Niger | 41 | 32 | 39.9 | 54.8 | 3.5 | 13 | 14 | 46 | 94 |
| Nigeria | 13 | 9 | 27.2 | 43.0 | 6.2 | 14 | 17 | 97 | 73 |
| Norway | <2.5 | <2.5 | .. | .. | .. | 5 | .. | .. | .. |
| Oman | .. | .. | .. | .. | .. | 8 | .. | .. | 95 |
| Pakistan | 24 | 24 | 31.3 | 41.5 | 4.8 | .. | .. | 17 | 95 |
| Panama | 21 | 23 | .. | .. | .. | 10 | .. | .. | 4 |
| Papua New Guinea | .. | .. | .. | .. | .. | .. | .. | .. | 90 |
| Paraguay | 18 | 15 | .. | .. | .. | 9 | 22 | 88 | .. |
| Peru | 42 | 12 | 5.2 | 31.3 | 11.8 | 7 | 63 | 91 | .. |
| Philippines | 26 | 18 | 20.7 | 33.8 | 2.4 | 20 | 34 | 56 | 85 |
| Poland | <2.5[c] | <2.5 | .. | .. | .. | 6 | .. | .. | .. |
| Portugal | <2.5 | <2.5 | .. | .. | .. | 8 | .. | .. | .. |
| Puerto Rico | .. | .. | .. | .. | .. | .. | .. | .. | .. |

| | Prevalence of undernourishment | | Prevalence of child malnutrition | | Prevalence of overweight children | Low-birthweight babies | Exclusive breastfeeding | Consumption of iodized salt | Vitamin A supplementation |
|---|---|---|---|---|---|---|---|---|---|
| | % of population | | % of children under age 5 | | % of children under age 5 | % of births | % of children under 6 months | % of households | % of children 6–59 months |
| | 1990–92 | 2002–04[a] | Underweight 2000–06[b] | Stunting 2000–06[b] | 2000–06[b] | 2000–06[b] | 2000–06[b] | 2000–06[b] | 2005 |
| Romania | <2.5[c] | <2.5 | 3.5 | 12.8 | 8.3 | 8 | 16 | 74 | .. |
| Russian Federation | 4[c] | 3 | .. | .. | .. | 6 | .. | 35 | .. |
| Rwanda | 43 | 33 | 18.0 | 51.7 | 6.7 | 6 | 88 | 88 | 100 |
| Saudi Arabia | 4 | 4 | .. | .. | .. | .. | .. | .. | .. |
| Senegal | 23 | 20 | 14.5 | 20.1 | 2.4 | 19 | 34 | 41 | 95 |
| Serbia | 5[c,f] | 9[f] | .. | .. | .. | 5 | 15 | .. | .. |
| Sierra Leone | 46 | 51 | 24.7 | 38.4 | 4.7 | 24 | 8 | 45 | 95 |
| Singapore | .. | .. | 3.3 | 4.4 | 2.6 | 8 | .. | .. | .. |
| Slovak Republic | 4[c] | 7 | .. | .. | .. | 7 | .. | .. | .. |
| Slovenia | 3[c] | 3 | .. | .. | .. | 6 | .. | .. | .. |
| Somalia | .. | .. | .. | .. | .. | 11 | 9 | 1 | 6 |
| South Africa | <2.5 | <2.5 | .. | .. | .. | .. | 7 | .. | 33 |
| Spain | <2.5 | <2.5 | .. | .. | .. | .. | .. | .. | .. |
| Sri Lanka | 28 | 22 | 22.8 | 18.4 | 1.0 | 22 | 53 | 94 | 64[d] |
| Sudan | 31 | 26 | 38.4 | 47.6 | 5.2 | .. | 34 | 11 | 90 |
| Swaziland | 14 | 22 | 9.1 | 36.6 | 14.9 | 9 | 24 | 59 | 59 |
| Sweden | <2.5 | <2.5 | .. | .. | .. | .. | .. | .. | .. |
| Switzerland | <2.5 | <2.5 | .. | .. | .. | .. | .. | .. | .. |
| Syrian Arab Republic | 5 | 4 | .. | .. | .. | 9 | 29 | 79 | .. |
| Tajikistan | 22[c] | 56 | .. | .. | .. | 10 | 25 | 46 | 98 |
| Tanzania | 37 | 44 | 16.7 | 44.4 | 4.9 | 10 | 41 | 43 | 95 |
| Thailand | 30 | 22 | .. | .. | .. | 9 | 5 | 58 | .. |
| Timor-Leste | 11 | 9 | 40.6 | 55.7 | 5.7 | 12 | 31 | 72 | 91 |
| Togo | 33 | 24 | .. | .. | .. | 12 | 28 | 25 | 95 |
| Trinidad and Tobago | 13 | 10 | 4.4 | 5.3 | 4.9 | 19 | 13 | 28 | .. |
| Tunisia | <2.5 | <2.5 | .. | .. | .. | 7 | 47 | 97 | .. |
| Turkey | <2.5 | 3 | .. | .. | .. | .. | 21 | 64 | .. |
| Turkmenistan | 12[c] | 7 | .. | .. | .. | 4 | 11 | 87 | .. |
| Uganda | 24 | 19 | 19.0 | 44.8 | 4.9 | 12 | 60 | 96 | 78 |
| Ukraine | <2.5[c] | <2.5 | 4.1 | 22.9 | 26.5 | 4 | 6 | 18 | .. |
| United Arab Emirates | 4 | 3 | .. | .. | .. | 8 | .. | .. | .. |
| United Kingdom | <2.5 | <2.5 | .. | .. | .. | 8 | .. | .. | .. |
| United States | <2.5 | <2.5 | 1.1 | 3.3 | 7.0 | 8 | .. | .. | .. |
| Uruguay | 7 | <2.5 | 6.0 | 13.9 | 9.4 | 8 | .. | .. | .. |
| Uzbekistan | 8[c] | 25 | .. | .. | .. | 5 | 26 | 53 | 82 |
| Venezuela, RB | 11 | 18 | .. | .. | .. | 9 | .. | .. | .. |
| Vietnam | 31 | 16 | 26.7 | 43.4 | 2.5 | 7 | 17 | 93 | 99[d] |
| West Bank and Gaza | .. | 16 | .. | .. | .. | 7 | 27 | 86 | .. |
| Yemen, Rep. | 34 | 38 | .. | .. | .. | .. | 12 | 30 | 15[d] |
| Zambia | 48 | 46 | 23.3 | 52.5 | 5.9 | 12 | 40 | 77 | 66 |
| Zimbabwe | 45 | 47 | 14.0 | 35.8 | 9.1 | .. | 22 | .. | 81 |
| **World** | **17 w** | **14 w** | **23.5 w** | **.. w** | **5.5 w** | **10 w** | **39 w** | **68 w** | **.. w** |
| **Low income** | 27 | 24 | 35.3 | 45.9 | 3.4 | .. | 38 | 55 | 76 |
| **Middle income** | 14 | 10 | 9.5 | 23.8 | 8.5 | 7 | 40 | 79 | .. |
| Lower middle income | 16 | 11 | 10.7 | 24.8 | 8.5 | 7 | 41 | 81 | .. |
| Upper middle income | .. | 5 | .. | .. | .. | 8 | .. | 72 | .. |
| **Low & middle income** | 20 | 16 | 24.5 | 37.1 | 5.4 | 10 | 39 | 68 | .. |
| East Asia & Pacific | 17 | 12 | 12.9 | 26.2 | 7.3 | 6 | 44 | 84 | .. |
| Europe & Central Asia | 6[c] | 6 | .. | .. | .. | 6 | .. | 50 | .. |
| Latin America & Carib. | 13 | 10 | 5.1 | .. | .. | 9 | .. | 85 | .. |
| Middle East & N. Africa | 6 | 7 | .. | .. | .. | 12 | 30 | 72 | .. |
| South Asia | 26 | 21 | 41.0 | 46.7 | 2.1 | .. | 45 | 51 | 72 |
| Sub-Saharan Africa | 29 | 30 | 27.0 | 44.5 | 5.7 | 13 | 31 | 61 | 79 |
| **High income** | 3 | 3 | .. | .. | .. | .. | .. | .. | .. |
| Euro area | 3 | 3 | .. | .. | .. | .. | .. | .. | .. |

a. Preliminary data. b. Data are for the most recent year available. c. Data are for 1993–95. d. Country's vitamin A supplementation programs do not target children all the way up to 59 months of age. e. Data are for 2007. f. Includes Montenegro.

Data on undernourishment are produced by the Food and Agriculture Organization (FAO) of the United Nations based on the calories available from local food production, trade, and stocks; the number of calories needed by different age and gender groups; the proportion of the population represented by each age group; and a coefficient of distribution to account for inequality in access to food (FAO, *State of Food Insecurity in the World 2000*). From a policy and program standpoint, however, this measure has its limits. First, food insecurity exists even where food availability is not a problem because of inadequate access of poor households to food. Second, food insecurity is an individual or household phenomenon, and the average food available to each person, even corrected for possible effects of low income, is not a good predictor of food insecurity among the population. And third, nutrition security is determined not only by food security but also by the quality of care of mothers and children and the quality of the household's health environment (Smith and Haddad 2000).

Estimates of child malnutrition, based on weight for age (underweight) and height for age (stunting), are from national survey data. The proportion of children who are underweight is the most common indicator of malnutrition. Being underweight, even mildly, increases the risk of death and inhibits cognitive development in children. Moreover, it perpetuates the problem from one generation to the next, as malnourished women are more likely to have low-birthweight babies. Height for age reflects linear growth achieved pre- and postnatally, and a deficit indicates long-term, cumulative effects of inadequacies of health, diet, or care. It is often argued that stunting is a proxy for multifaceted deprivation and is a better indicator of long-term changes in malnutrition.

Estimates of children who are overweight are also from national survey data. Overweight children have become a growing concern in developing countries. Researchers show an association between obesity in childhood and a high prevalence of diabetes, respiratory disease, high blood pressure, and psychosocial and orthopedic disorders (de Onis and Blössner 2000).

New international child growth reference standards for infants and young children were released in 2006 by the World Health Organization (WHO) as a tool for monitoring the nutritional status of children. They are also key in measuring and monitoring health targets for the Millennium Development Goals. The differences in children's growth to age 5 are influenced more by nutrition, feeding practices, environment, and healthcare than by genetics or ethnicity. The data reported previously were based on the U.S. National Center for Health Statistics–WHO growth reference. Because of the change in standards, the data in this edition should not be compared with data in previous editions.

Low birthweight, which is associated with maternal malnutrition, raises the risk of infant mortality and stunts growth in infancy and childhood. There is also emerging evidence that low-birthweight babies are more prone to noncommunicable diseases such as diabetes and cardiovascular diseases. Estimates of low-birthweight infants are drawn mostly from hospital records and household surveys. Many births in developing countries take place at home, and these births are seldom recorded. A hospital birth may indicate higher income and therefore better nutrition, or it could indicate a higher risk birth, possibly skewing the data on birthweights downward. The data should therefore be used with caution.

Improved breastfeeding practice can save an estimated 1.3 million children a year. Breast milk alone contains all the nutrients, antibodies, hormones, and antioxidants an infant needs to thrive. It protects babies from diarrhea and acute respiratory infections, stimulates their immune systems and response to vaccination, and according to some studies confers cognitive benefits as well. The data on breastfeeding are derived from national surveys.

Iodine deficiency is the single most important cause of preventable mental retardation, and it contributes significantly to the risk of stillbirth and miscarriage. Widely used and inexpensive, iodized salt is the best source of iodine, and a global campaign to iodize edible salt is significantly reducing the risks (UNICEF, *Childinfo 2006*). The data on iodized salt are derived from household surveys.

Vitamin A is essential for the functioning of the immune system. Besides being a leading cause of blindness, vitamin A deficiency causes a 23 percent greater risk of dying from a range of childhood ailments such as measles, malaria, and diarrhea. Giving vitamin A to new mothers who are breastfeeding helps protect their children during the first months of life. Food fortification with vitamin A is being introduced in many developing countries.

For indicators from household surveys, the year in the table refers to the survey year. For more information, consult the original sources.

• **Prevalence of undernourishment** is the percentage of the population that is undernourished—whose dietary energy consumption is continuously below a minimum dietary energy requirement for maintaining a healthy life and carrying out light physical activity. • **Prevalence of child malnutrition** is the percentage of children under age 5 whose weight for age (underweight) or height for age (stunting) is more than two standard deviations below the median for the international reference population ages 0–59 months. For children up to two years old height is measured by recumbent length. For older children height is measured by stature while standing. The table presents data for the WHO's new child growth standards released in 2006. • **Prevalence of overweight children** is the percentage of children under age 5 whose weight for height is more than two standard deviations above the median for the international reference population of the corresponding age as established by the WHO's new child growth standards released in 2006. • **Low-birthweight babies** are the percentage of newborns weighing less than 2.5 kilograms, with the measurement taken within the first hours of life, before significant postnatal weight loss has occurred. • **Exclusive breastfeeding** is the percentage of children less than six months old who were fed breast milk alone (no other liquids) in the past 24 hours. • **Consumption of iodized salt** is the percentage of households that use edible salt fortified with iodine. • **Vitamin A supplementation** is the percentage of children ages 6–59 months old who received at least one dose of vitamin A in the previous six months, as reported by mothers.

**Data sources**

Data on undernourishment are from www.fao. org/faostat/foodsecurity/index_en.htm. Data on malnutrition and overweight children are from the WHO's Global Database on Child Growth and Malnutrition (www.who.int/nutgrowthdb). Data on low-birthweight babies, breastfeeding, iodized salt consumption, and vitamin A supplementation are from the United Nations Children's Fund's *State of the World's Children 2008* and Childinfo.

| | Prevalence of smoking | | Incidence of tuberculosis | Prevalence of diabetes | Prevalence of HIV | | | | | | Condom use | |
|---|---|---|---|---|---|---|---|---|---|---|---|---|
| | % of adults | | per 100,000 people | % of population ages 20–79 | Total % of population ages 15–49 | | Female % of total population with HIV | | Youth % of population ages 15–24 | | % of population ages 15–24 | |
| | Male | Female | | | | | | | Male | Female | Male | Female |
| | 2000–05[a] | 2000–05[a] | 2006 | 2007 | 2003 | 2005 | 2003 | 2005 | 2005 | 2005 | 2000–06[a] | 2000–06[a] |
| Afghanistan | .. | .. | .. | .. | .. | .. | .. | .. | .. | .. | .. | .. |
| Albania | 60 | 18 | 19 | 4.5 | 0.2 | 0.2 | .. | .. | .. | .. | .. | .. |
| Algeria | 32 | 0[b] | 56 | 8.4 | 0.1 | 0.1 | 20.6 | 21.6 | .. | .. | .. | .. |
| Angola | .. | .. | 285 | 3.3 | 3.7 | 3.7 | 59.3 | 60.7 | 0.9 | 2.5 | .. | .. |
| Argentina | 32 | 25 | 39 | 5.6 | 0.6 | 0.6 | 26.7 | 27.7 | .. | .. | 32 | 7 |
| Armenia | 62 | 2 | 72 | 7.7 | 0.1 | 0.1 | .. | .. | .. | .. | .. | .. |
| Australia | 19 | 16 | 6 | 5.0 | 0.1 | 0.1 | .. | .. | .. | .. | .. | .. |
| Austria | .. | .. | 13 | 7.9 | 0.3 | 0.3 | 19.2 | 19.2 | .. | .. | .. | .. |
| Azerbaijan | .. | 1 | 77 | 7.3 | <0.1 | 0.1 | .. | .. | .. | .. | .. | .. |
| Bangladesh | 55 | 27 | 225 | 5.3 | <0.1 | <0.1 | .. | 12.7 | .. | .. | .. | .. |
| Belarus | 53 | 7 | 61 | 7.6 | 0.3 | 0.3 | 24.4 | 25.5 | .. | .. | .. | .. |
| Belgium | 30 | 25 | 13 | 5.2 | 0.2 | 0.3 | 45.5 | 38.6 | .. | .. | .. | .. |
| Benin | .. | .. | 90 | 4.4 | 2.0 | 1.8 | 59.3 | 58.4 | 0.4 | 1.1 | 32 | 8 |
| Bolivia | .. | .. | 198 | 5.8 | 0.1 | 0.1 | 27.0 | 27.9 | .. | .. | 29 | 10 |
| Bosnia and Herzegovina | 49 | 30 | 51 | 7.0 | .. | <0.1 | .. | .. | .. | .. | .. | .. |
| Botswana | .. | .. | 551 | 5.2 | 24.0 | 24.1 | 56.0 | 53.8 | 5.7 | 15.3 | .. | .. |
| Brazil | 22 | 14 | 50 | 6.2 | 0.5 | 0.5 | 34.5 | 36.1 | .. | .. | .. | .. |
| Bulgaria | 44 | 23 | 40 | 7.6 | .. | <0.1 | .. | .. | .. | .. | .. | .. |
| Burkina Faso | .. | .. | 248 | 3.7 | 1.8[c] | 2.0 | 59.2 | 57.1 | 0.5 | 1.4 | 54 | 17 |
| Burundi | .. | .. | 367 | 1.7 | 3.3 | 3.3 | 60.8 | 60.8 | 0.8 | 2.3 | .. | .. |
| Cambodia | .. | .. | 500 | 5.0 | 2.0 | 1.6 | 46.4 | 45.4 | 1.4 | 4.9 | .. | 3 |
| Cameroon | .. | .. | 192 | 3.7 | 5.5 | 5.5[d] | 62.2 | 61.7 | 1.4 | 4.9 | 52 | 24 |
| Canada | 22 | 17 | 5 | 7.4 | 0.3 | 0.3 | 12.2 | 16.3 | .. | .. | .. | .. |
| Central African Republic | .. | .. | 345 | 4.4 | 10.8 | 10.7 | 59.1 | 56.5 | 2.5 | 7.3 | .. | .. |
| Chad | .. | .. | 299 | 3.6 | 3.4 | 3.5 | 54.7 | 56.3 | 0.9 | 2.2 | 18 | 7 |
| Chile | 48 | 37 | 15 | 5.6 | 0.3 | 0.3 | 26.4 | 27.1 | .. | .. | .. | .. |
| China | 67 | 4 | 99 | 4.1 | 0.1[e] | 0.1[e] | 24.5[e] | 27.7[e] | .. | .. | .. | .. |
| Hong Kong, China | 22 | 4 | 62 | 8.2 | .. | .. | .. | .. | .. | .. | .. | 23 |
| Colombia | .. | .. | 45 | 5.0 | 0.5 | 0.6 | 26.4 | 28.1 | .. | .. | .. | .. |
| Congo, Dem. Rep. | .. | .. | 392 | 3.0 | 3.2 | 3.2 | 59.0 | 58.4 | 0.8 | 2.2 | .. | .. |
| Congo, Rep. | .. | .. | 403 | 5.0 | 5.4 | 5.3 | 58.6 | 61.0 | 1.2 | 3.7 | 36 | 16 |
| Costa Rica | 29 | 10 | 14 | 9.3 | 0.3 | 0.3 | 27.0 | 27.4 | .. | .. | .. | .. |
| Côte d'Ivoire | .. | .. | 420 | 4.6 | 7.0 | 7.1 | 57.8 | 58.8 | 1.7 | 5.1 | .. | .. |
| Croatia | 32 | 23 | 40 | 7.1 | .. | <0.1 | .. | .. | .. | .. | .. | .. |
| Cuba | .. | .. | 9 | 9.3 | 0.1 | 0.1 | 54.8 | 55.3 | .. | .. | .. | .. |
| Czech Republic | 31 | 20 | 10 | 7.6 | <0.1 | 0.1 | .. | .. | .. | .. | .. | .. |
| Denmark | 31 | 25 | 8 | 5.5 | <0.1 | 0.2 | 24.0 | 23.6 | .. | .. | .. | .. |
| Dominican Republic | 16 | 11 | 89 | 8.7 | 1.0[f] | 1.1 | 49.2 | 50.0 | .. | .. | 40 | 10 |
| Ecuador | .. | .. | 128 | 5.7 | 0.3 | 0.3 | 52.4 | 54.5 | .. | .. | .. | .. |
| Egypt, Arab Rep. | 40 | 18 | 24 | 11.0 | <0.1 | <0.1 | .. | .. | .. | .. | .. | .. |
| El Salvador | 42 | 15 | 50 | 9.0 | 0.9 | 0.9 | 27.1 | 28.3 | 0.6 | 0.4 | .. | .. |
| Eritrea | .. | .. | 94 | 2.3 | 2.4 | 2.4 | 59.2 | 58.5 | 0.6 | 1.6 | .. | 2 |
| Estonia | 45 | 18 | 39 | 7.6 | 1.1 | 1.3 | 22.1 | 24.0 | .. | .. | .. | .. |
| Ethiopia | 6 | 0[b] | 378 | 2.3 | .. | 1.4[g] | .. | .. | 0.2 | 1.1 | 18 | 2 |
| Finland | 26 | 19 | 5 | 5.9 | 0.1 | 0.1 | .. | .. | .. | .. | .. | .. |
| France | 30 | 21 | 14 | 5.9 | 0.4 | 0.4 | 33.3 | 34.6 | .. | .. | .. | .. |
| Gabon | .. | .. | 354 | 4.9 | 7.7 | 7.9 | 59.6 | 58.9 | 1.8 | 5.4 | .. | .. |
| Gambia, The | .. | .. | 257 | 4.1 | 2.2 | 2.4 | 58.8 | 57.9 | 0.6 | 1.7 | .. | .. |
| Georgia | 53 | 6 | 84 | 7.4 | 0.1 | 0.2 | .. | .. | .. | .. | .. | .. |
| Germany | 37 | 28 | 6 | 7.9 | 0.1 | 0.1 | 29.5 | 30.6 | .. | .. | .. | .. |
| Ghana | 7 | 1 | 203 | 4.2 | 2.2[c] | 2.3 | 60.7 | 60.0 | 0.2 | 1.3 | 45 | 19 |
| Greece | 47 | 29 | 18 | 5.9 | 0.2 | 0.2 | 20.7 | 21.5 | .. | .. | .. | .. |
| Guatemala | 21 | 2 | 79 | 8.6 | 0.9 | 0.9 | 26.4 | 27.1 | .. | .. | .. | .. |
| Guinea | .. | .. | 265 | 4.1 | 1.6 | 1.5 | 68.9 | 67.9 | 0.6 | 1.2 | 35 | 10 |
| Guinea-Bissau | .. | .. | 219 | 3.8 | 3.8 | 3.8 | 59.3 | 58.6 | 0.9 | 2.5 | .. | .. |
| Haiti | 15 | 6 | 299 | 9.0 | 3.8 | 2.2[h] | 52.9 | 53.3 | 0.6 | 1.5 | 28 | 20 |

# Health risk factors and public health challenges 2.19

| | Prevalence of smoking | | Incidence of tuberculosis | Prevalence of diabetes | Prevalence of HIV | | | | | | Condom use | |
|---|---|---|---|---|---|---|---|---|---|---|---|---|
| | % of adults | | per 100,000 people | % of population ages 20–79 | Total % of population ages 15–49 | | Female % of total population with HIV | | Youth % of population ages 15–24 | | % of population ages 15–24 | |
| | Male 2000–05[a] | Female 2000–05[a] | 2006 | 2007 | 2003 | 2005 | 2003 | 2005 | Male 2005 | Female 2005 | Male 2000–06[a] | Female 2000–06[a] |
| Honduras | .. | .. | 76 | 9.1 | 1.5 | 1.5 | 25.0 | 26.2 | .. | .. | .. | 7 |
| Hungary | 41 | 28 | 19 | 7.6 | 0.1 | 0.1 | .. | .. | .. | .. | .. | .. |
| India | 47 | 17 | 168 | 6.7 | 0.9 | 0.9 | 28.8 | 28.6 | .. | .. | .. | .. |
| Indonesia | 58 | 3 | 234 | 2.3 | 0.1 | 0.1 | 13.6 | 17.1 | .. | .. | .. | .. |
| Iran, Islamic Rep. | 22 | 2 | 22 | 7.8 | 0.1 | 0.2 | 13.0 | 16.7 | .. | .. | .. | 1 |
| Iraq | .. | .. | .. | .. | .. | .. | .. | .. | .. | .. | .. | .. |
| Ireland | 28 | 26 | 13 | 5.1 | 0.2 | 0.2 | 32.0 | 36.0 | .. | .. | .. | .. |
| Israel | 32 | 18 | 8 | 6.9 | 0.2 | 0.2 | .. | .. | .. | .. | .. | .. |
| Italy | 31 | 17 | 7 | 5.8 | 0.5 | 0.5 | 33.6 | 33.3 | .. | .. | .. | .. |
| Jamaica | .. | .. | 7 | 10.3 | 1.5 | 1.5 | 27.1 | 27.6 | .. | .. | .. | .. |
| Japan | 47 | 15 | 22 | 4.9 | <0.1 | <0.1 | 56.5 | 58.2 | .. | .. | .. | .. |
| Jordan | 51 | 8 | 5 | 9.8 | 0.2 | 0.2 | .. | .. | .. | .. | .. | 4 |
| Kazakhstan | 65 | 9 | 130 | 5.6 | 0.1 | 0.1 | 56.0 | 56.7 | .. | .. | .. | .. |
| Kenya | 21 | 1 | 384 | 3.3 | 6.7[c] | 6.1 | 64.2 | 61.7 | 1.0 | 5.2 | 39 | 9 |
| Korea, Dem. Rep. | .. | .. | 178 | 5.2 | 0.2 | 0.2 | .. | .. | .. | .. | .. | .. |
| Korea, Rep. | .. | .. | 88 | 7.8 | <0.1 | <0.1 | 59.1 | 56.9 | .. | .. | .. | .. |
| Kuwait | .. | .. | 24 | 14.4 | 0.2 | 0.2 | .. | .. | .. | .. | .. | .. |
| Kyrgyz Republic | 51 | 5 | 123 | 5.1 | <0.1 | 0.1 | .. | .. | .. | .. | .. | .. |
| Lao PDR | 59 | 13 | 152 | 3.1 | 0.1 | 0.1 | .. | .. | .. | .. | .. | .. |
| Latvia | 51 | 19 | 57 | 7.6 | 0.6 | 0.8 | 20.3 | 22.0 | .. | .. | .. | .. |
| Lebanon | 42 | 31 | 11 | 7.7 | 0.1 | 0.1 | .. | .. | .. | .. | .. | .. |
| Lesotho | .. | .. | 635 | 3.8 | 23.7 | 23.4[d] | 56.0 | 60.0 | 5.9 | 14.1 | 44 | 26 |
| Liberia | .. | .. | 331 | 4.6 | .. | .. | .. | .. | .. | .. | .. | .. |
| Libya | .. | .. | 18 | 4.4 | 0.2 | 0.2 | .. | .. | .. | .. | .. | .. |
| Lithuania | 44 | 13 | 62 | 7.6 | 0.1 | 0.2 | .. | .. | .. | .. | .. | .. |
| Macedonia, FYR | .. | .. | 29 | 7.1 | <0.1 | <0.1 | .. | .. | .. | .. | .. | .. |
| Madagascar | .. | .. | 248 | 3.0 | 0.5 | 0.5 | 28.2 | 27.7 | 0.6 | 0.3 | 8 | 2 |
| Malawi | 21 | 5 | 377 | 2.1 | 14.2 | 14.1 | 59.3 | 58.8 | 3.4 | 9.6 | 28 | 9 |
| Malaysia | 43 | 2 | 103 | 10.7 | 0.4 | 0.5 | 25.0 | 25.4 | .. | .. | .. | .. |
| Mali | .. | .. | 280 | 4.1 | 1.8[i] | 1.7 | 57.3 | 60.0 | 0.4 | 1.2 | 32 | 9 |
| Mauritania | .. | .. | 316 | 4.6 | 0.7 | 0.7 | 59.2 | 57.3 | 0.2 | 0.5 | .. | .. |
| Mauritius | 32 | 1 | 23 | 11.1 | 0.2 | 0.6 | .. | .. | .. | .. | .. | .. |
| Mexico | 13 | 5 | 21 | 10.6 | 0.3 | 0.3 | 20.0 | 23.3 | .. | .. | .. | .. |
| Moldova | 34 | 2 | 141 | 7.6 | 0.9 | 1.1 | 56.5 | 57.1 | .. | .. | 55 | 22 |
| Mongolia | 68 | 26 | 188 | 1.9 | <0.1 | <0.1 | .. | .. | .. | .. | .. | .. |
| Morocco | 29 | 0[b] | 93 | 8.1 | 0.1 | 0.1 | 18.2 | 21.1 | .. | .. | .. | .. |
| Mozambique | .. | .. | 443 | 3.7 | 16.0 | 16.1 | 57.5 | 60.0 | 3.6 | 10.7 | 27 | 12 |
| Myanmar | 36 | 12 | 171 | 3.2 | 1.4 | 1.3 | 31.6 | 31.4 | .. | .. | .. | .. |
| Namibia | 23 | 10 | 767 | 4.2 | 19.5 | 19.6 | 60.0 | 61.9 | 4.4 | 13.4 | 65 | 42 |
| Nepal | 49 | 24 | 176 | 4.2 | 0.5 | 0.5 | 20.3 | 21.6 | .. | .. | 24 | 8 |
| Netherlands | 36 | 28 | 8 | 5.2 | 0.2 | 0.2 | 33.8 | 34.7 | .. | .. | .. | .. |
| New Zealand | 24 | 22 | 9 | 6.4 | 0.1 | 0.1 | .. | .. | .. | .. | .. | .. |
| Nicaragua | .. | 5 | 58 | 10.1 | 0.2 | 0.2 | 22.4 | 23.6 | .. | .. | .. | 7 |
| Niger | .. | .. | 174 | 3.7 | 1.1 | 1.1 | 59.7 | 59.2 | 0.2 | 0.8 | .. | .. |
| Nigeria | .. | 1 | 311 | 4.5 | 3.7 | 3.9 | 58.3 | 61.5 | 0.9 | 2.7 | 38 | 8 |
| Norway | 27 | 25 | 6 | 3.6 | 0.1 | 0.1 | .. | .. | .. | .. | .. | .. |
| Oman | .. | .. | 13 | 13.1 | 0.2 | 0.2 | .. | .. | .. | .. | .. | .. |
| Pakistan | .. | .. | 181 | 9.6 | 0.1 | 0.1 | 13.3 | 16.7 | .. | .. | .. | .. |
| Panama | .. | .. | 45 | 9.7 | 0.9 | 0.9 | 26.0 | 25.3 | .. | .. | .. | .. |
| Papua New Guinea | .. | .. | 250 | 2.9 | 1.6 | 1.8 | 59.2 | 59.6 | .. | .. | .. | .. |
| Paraguay | 23 | 7 | 71 | 4.8 | 0.4 | 0.4 | 27.3 | 26.9 | .. | .. | .. | .. |
| Peru | .. | .. | 162 | 6.0 | 0.5 | 0.6 | 26.8 | 28.6 | .. | .. | .. | 9 |
| Philippines | 41 | 8 | 287 | 7.6 | <0.1 | <0.1 | 20.2 | 28.3 | .. | .. | 13 | 3 |
| Poland | 40 | 25 | 25 | 7.6 | 0.1 | 0.1 | 30.0 | 30.0 | .. | .. | .. | .. |
| Portugal | .. | .. | 32 | 5.7 | 0.4 | 0.4 | 3.9 | 4.1 | .. | .. | .. | .. |
| Puerto Rico | 17 | 10 | 5 | 10.7 | .. | .. | .. | .. | .. | .. | .. | .. |

# 2.19 Health risk factors and public health challenges

| | Prevalence of smoking | | Incidence of tuberculosis | Prevalence of diabetes | Prevalence of HIV | | | | | | Condom use | |
|---|---|---|---|---|---|---|---|---|---|---|---|---|
| | % of adults | | per 100,000 people | % of population ages 20–79 | Total % of population ages 15–49 | | Female % of total population with HIV | | Youth % of population ages 15–24 | | % of population ages 15–24 | |
| | Male 2000–05a | Female 2000–05a | 2006 | 2007 | 2003 | 2005 | 2003 | 2005 | Male 2005 | Female 2005 | Male 2000–06a | Female 2000–06a |
| Romania | 32 | 10 | 128 | 7.6 | .. | <0.1 | .. | .. | .. | .. | .. | .. |
| Russian Federation | 60 | 16 | 107 | 7.6 | 0.9 | 1.1 | 21.1 | 22.3 | .. | .. | .. | .. |
| Rwanda | .. | .. | 397 | 1.5 | 3.8 | 3.0g | 52.6 | 56.9 | 0.4 | 1.5 | 19 | 5 |
| Saudi Arabia | 19 | 8 | 44 | 16.7 | 0.2 | 0.2 | .. | .. | .. | .. | .. | .. |
| Senegal | .. | .. | 270 | 4.6 | 0.9 | 0.7g | 58.5 | 58.9 | 0.1 | 0.4 | 48 | 5 |
| Serbia | 48j | 34j | 32j | 7.1j | 0.2j | 0.2j | 22.2j | 20.0j | .. | .. | .. | .. |
| Sierra Leone | .. | .. | 517 | 4.3 | 1.6 | 1.6 | 60.0 | 60.5 | 0.4 | 1.1 | .. | .. |
| Singapore | 24 | 4 | 26 | 10.1 | 0.3 | 0.3 | 25.5 | 27.3 | .. | .. | .. | .. |
| Slovak Republic | .. | .. | 15 | 7.6 | <0.1 | <0.1 | .. | .. | .. | .. | .. | .. |
| Slovenia | 28 | 20 | 13 | 7.6 | <0.1 | <0.1 | .. | .. | .. | .. | .. | .. |
| Somalia | .. | .. | 218 | 2.8 | 0.9 | 0.9 | 60.5 | 57.5 | 0.2 | 0.6 | .. | .. |
| South Africa | 23 | 8 | 940 | 4.4 | 15.6f | 18.8 | 56.9 | 58.5 | 4.5 | 14.8 | 57 | 46 |
| Spain | 39 | 25 | 30 | 5.7 | 0.7 | 0.6 | 22.9 | 22.9 | .. | .. | .. | .. |
| Sri Lanka | 23 | 2 | 60 | 8.4 | <0.1 | <0.1 | .. | .. | .. | .. | .. | .. |
| Sudan | .. | .. | 242 | 4.0 | 1.6 | 1.6 | 56.7 | 56.3 | .. | .. | .. | .. |
| Swaziland | 11 | 3 | 1,155 | 4.0 | 32.4 | 33.4 | 63.2 | 57.1 | 7.7 | 22.7 | .. | .. |
| Sweden | 17 | 18 | 6 | 5.2 | 0.2 | 0.2 | 31.3 | 31.3 | .. | .. | .. | .. |
| Switzerland | 27 | 23 | 7 | 7.9 | 0.4 | 0.4 | 36.0 | 36.9 | .. | .. | .. | .. |
| Syrian Arab Republic | .. | .. | 32 | 10.6 | 0.2 | 0.2 | .. | .. | .. | .. | .. | .. |
| Tajikistan | .. | .. | 204 | 4.9 | <0.1 | 0.1 | .. | .. | .. | .. | .. | .. |
| Tanzania | .. | .. | 312 | 2.9 | 7.0k | 6.5 | 52.3 | 54.6 | 2.8 | 3.8 | 36 | 13 |
| Thailand | 49 | 3 | 142 | 6.9 | 1.4 | 1.4 | 38.6 | 39.3 | .. | .. | .. | .. |
| Timor-Leste | .. | .. | 556 | 1.7 | 0.2 | 0.2 | .. | .. | .. | .. | .. | .. |
| Togo | .. | .. | 389 | 4.1 | 3.2 | 3.2 | 58.9 | 61.0 | 0.8 | 2.2 | .. | .. |
| Trinidad and Tobago | .. | .. | 8 | 11.5 | 2.6 | 2.6 | 56.0 | 57.7 | .. | .. | .. | .. |
| Tunisia | 50 | 2 | 25 | 5.2 | 0.1 | 0.1 | .. | 22.1 | .. | .. | .. | .. |
| Turkey | 49 | 18 | 29 | 7.8 | 0.2 | 0.2 | .. | .. | .. | .. | .. | .. |
| Turkmenistan | .. | .. | 65 | 5.2 | .. | <0.1 | .. | .. | .. | .. | .. | 1 |
| Uganda | 25 | 3 | 355 | 2.0 | 6.8 | 6.4l | 57.6 | 57.8 | 1.1 | 4.3 | 38 | 15 |
| Ukraine | 53 | 11 | 106 | 7.6 | 1.3 | 1.4 | 47.4 | 48.8 | .. | .. | .. | .. |
| United Arab Emirates | 17 | 1 | 16 | 19.5 | 0.2 | 0.2 | .. | .. | .. | .. | .. | .. |
| United Kingdom | 27 | 25 | 15 | 2.9 | 0.2 | 0.2 | .. | .. | .. | .. | .. | .. |
| United States | 24 | 19 | 4 | 7.8 | 0.6 | 0.6 | 25.5 | 25.0 | .. | .. | .. | .. |
| Uruguay | 35 | 24 | 27 | 5.6 | 0.4 | 0.5 | 55.6 | 55.8 | .. | .. | .. | .. |
| Uzbekistan | 24 | 1 | 121 | 5.1 | 0.1 | 0.2 | .. | 13.2 | .. | .. | 18 | 2 |
| Venezuela, RB | .. | .. | 41 | 5.4 | 0.6 | 0.7 | 27.7 | 28.2 | .. | .. | .. | .. |
| Vietnam | 35 | 2 | 173 | 2.9 | 0.4 | 0.5g | 30.5 | 33.6 | 0.8 | .. | .. | 8 |
| West Bank and Gaza | .. | .. | 20 | 8.4 | .. | .. | .. | .. | .. | .. | .. | .. |
| Yemen, Rep. | .. | .. | 78 | 2.9 | 0.2 | 0.2 | .. | .. | .. | .. | .. | .. |
| Zambia | 16 | 1 | 553 | 3.8 | 15.6m | 17.0 | 56.3 | 57.0 | 3.8 | 12.7 | 36 | 19 |
| Zimbabwe | 20 | 2 | 557 | 4.0 | 22.1 | 18.1h | 58.1 | 59.3 | 4.4 | 14.7 | 52 | 9 |
| **World** | .. w | .. w | 139 w | 5.8 w | 1.0 w | 1.0 w | 30.4 w | 31.4 w | | | | |
| **Low income** | .. | 15 | 221 | 5.7 | 1.7 | 1.7 | 35.8 | 34.3 | | | | |
| **Middle income** | .. | .. | 114 | 5.6 | 0.6 | 0.7 | 26.1 | 28.7 | | | | |
| Lower middle income | .. | .. | 116 | 5.0 | 0.3 | 0.3 | 24.9 | 27.9 | | | | |
| Upper middle income | .. | .. | 109 | 7.3 | 1.6 | 1.7 | 29.9 | 31.3 | | | | |
| **Low & middle income** | .. | .. | 161 | 5.6 | 1.1 | 1.1 | 29.9 | 31.1 | | | | |
| East Asia & Pacific | 67 | 4 | 135 | 4.2 | 0.2 | 0.2 | 24.3 | 27.4 | | | | |
| Europe & Central Asia | .. | .. | 82 | 7.3 | 0.5 | 0.6 | .. | .. | | | | |
| Latin America & Carib. | .. | .. | 57 | 7.1 | 0.5 | 0.6 | 30.3 | 31.9 | | | | |
| Middle East & N. Africa | .. | .. | 42 | 8.7 | 0.1 | 0.1 | .. | .. | | | | |
| South Asia | 47 | 18 | 174 | 6.9 | 0.7 | 0.7 | 26.9 | 25.4 | | | | |
| Sub-Saharan Africa | .. | .. | 368 | 3.6 | 6.4 | 5.8 | 57.6 | 58.5 | | | | |
| **High income** | .. | .. | 16 | 6.8 | 0.4 | 0.4 | 33.1 | 33.3 | | | | |
| Euro area | .. | .. | 13 | 6.4 | 0.4 | 0.3 | 29.3 | 29.7 | | | | |

a. Data are for the most recent year available. b. Less than 0.5. c. Survey data, 2003. d Survey data, 2004. e. Includes Hong Kong, China. f. Survey data, 2002. g. Survey data, 2005. h. Survey data, 2005–06. i. Survey data, 2001. j. Includes Montenegro. k. Survey data, 2003–04. l. Survey data, 2004–05. m. Survey data, 2001–02.

## About the data

The limited availability of data on health status is a major constraint in assessing the health situation in developing countries. Surveillance data are lacking for many major public health concerns. Estimates of prevalence and incidence are available for some diseases but are often unreliable and incomplete. National health authorities differ widely in their capacity and willingness to collect or report information. To compensate for the paucity of data and ensure reasonable reliability and international comparability, the World Health Organization (WHO) prepares estimates in accordance with epidemiological models and statistical standards.

Smoking is the most common form of tobacco use in many countries, and the prevalence of smoking is therefore a good measure of the extent of the tobacco epidemic (Corrao and others 2000). Tobacco use causes heart and other vascular diseases and cancers of the lung and other organs. Given the long delay between starting to smoke and the onset of disease, the health impact of smoking in developing countries will increase rapidly in the next few decades. Because the data present a one-time estimate, with no information on the intensity or duration of smoking, and because the definition of adult varies across countries, the data should be interpreted with caution.

Tuberculosis is one of the main causes of death from a single infectious agent among adults in developing countries. In high-income countries tuberculosis has reemerged largely as a result of cases among immigrants. The estimates of tuberculosis incidence in the table are based on a new approach in which reported cases are adjusted using the ratio of case notifications to the estimated share of cases detected by panels of 80 epidemiologists convened by the WHO.

Diabetes, an important cause of ill health and a risk factor for other diseases in developed countries, is spreading rapidly in developing countries. While diabetes is most common among the elderly, prevalence rates are rising among younger and productive populations in developing countries. Economic development has led to the spread of Western lifestyles and diet to developing countries, resulting in a substantial increase in diabetes. Without effective prevention and control programs, diabetes will likely continue to increase. Data are estimated based on sample surveys.

Adult HIV prevalence rates reflect the rate of HIV infection in each country's population. Low national prevalence rates can be very misleading, however.

They often disguise serious epidemics that are initially concentrated in certain localities or among specific population groups and threaten to spill over into the wider population. In many developing countries most new infections occur in young adults, with young women especially vulnerable.

The current HIV estimates from the Joint United Nations Programme on HIV/AIDS (UNAIDS) and the WHO are lower than the previous estimates, due mostly to increased availability of reliable data, including more population-based HIV prevalence surveys, new and improved HIV surveillance data, and improved quality and coverage of sentinel surveillance in many countries, including rural areas, where prevalence is known to be lower.

Estimates from recent Demographic and Health Surveys that have collected data on HIV/AIDS differ somewhat from those of UNAIDS and the WHO, which are based on surveillance systems that focus on pregnant women who attend sentinel antenatal clinics. Caution should be exercised in about comparing the two sets of estimates. Demographic and Health Surveys are household surveys that use a representative sample from the whole population, whereas surveillance data from antenatal clinics are limited to pregnant women. Representative household surveys also frequently provide better coverage of rural populations. However, the fact that some respondents refuse to participate or are absent from the household adds considerable uncertainty to survey-based HIV estimates, because the possible association of absence or refusal with higher HIV prevalence is unknown. UNAIDS and the WHO use a methodology to estimate HIV prevalence for the adult population (ages 15–49) that assumes that prevalence among pregnant women is a good approximation of prevalence among men and women. However, this assumption might not apply to all countries or over time. There are also other potential biases associated with the use of antenatal clinic data, such as differences among women who attend antenatal clinics and those who do not.

Data on condom use are from household surveys and refer to condom use at last intercourse. However, condoms are not as effective at preventing the transmission of HIV unless used consistently. Some surveys have tried to ask directly about consistent use, but the question is subject to recall and other biases. Caution should be used in interpreting the data.

For indicators from household surveys, the year in the table refers to the survey year. For more information, consult the original sources.

## Definitions

• **Prevalence of smoking** is the percentage of men and women who smoke cigarettes. The age range varies, but in most countries is 18 and older or 15 and older. • **Incidence of tuberculosis** is the estimated number of new tuberculosis cases (pulmonary, smear positive, extrapulmonary). • **Prevalence of diabetes** refers to the percentage of people ages 20–79 who have type 1 or type 2 diabetes. • **Prevalence of HIV** is the percentage of people who are infected with HIV. Total and youth rates are as a percentage of the relevant age group. Female rate is as a percentage of the total population with HIV. • **Condom use** is the percentage of the population ages 15–24 who used condom at last intercourse in the last 12 months.

## Data sources

Data on smoking are from J. McCay, M. Erkson, and O. Shafey's *Tobacco Atlas,* 2nd edition (2006). Data on tuberculosis are from the WHO's *Global Tuberculosis Control Report 2008: Surveillance, Planning, Financing.* Data on diabetes are from the International Diabetes Federation's *Diabetes Atlas,* 3rd edition. Data on prevalence of HIV are from UNAIDS and the WHO's *2006 Report on the Global AIDS Epidemic.* Data on condom use are from Demographic and Health Surveys by Macro International.

# Health gaps by income and gender

| | Survey year | Prevalence of child malnutrition | | | | Child immunization rate | | | | Infant mortality rate | | Under-five mortality rate | |
|---|---|---|---|---|---|---|---|---|---|---|---|---|---|
| | | Moderate underweight % of children under age 5 | | | | % of children ages 12–23 months[a] | | | | per 1,000 live births | | per 1,000 | |
| | | New reference | | Old reference | | Measles | | DTP3 | | | | | |
| | | Poorest quintile | Richest quintile | Poorest quintile | Richest quintile | Poorest quintile | Richest quintile | Poorest quintile | Richest quintile | Poorest quintile | Richest quintile | Poorest quintile | Richest quintile |
| Armenia | 2000 | 3 | 2 | 3 | 1 | 68 | 74[b] | 89 | 84[b] | 52 | 27 | 61 | 30 |
| Bangladesh | 2004 | 36 | 19 | 41 | 24 | 60 | 91 | 71 | 91 | 90 | 65 | 121 | 71 |
| Benin | 2001 | 18 | 6 | 21 | 9 | 57 | 83 | 63 | 89 | 112 | 50 | 198 | 93 |
| Bolivia | 2003 | 7 | 1 | 10 | 1 | 62 | 74 | 64 | 85 | 87 | 32 | 119 | 37 |
| Brazil | 1996 | 7 | 2 | 10 | 3 | 78 | 90 | 66 | 82 | 83 | 29 | 99 | 33 |
| Burkina Faso | 2003 | 19 | 13 | 26 | 16 | 48 | 71 | 45 | 73 | 97 | 78 | 206 | 144 |
| Cambodia | 2000 | 27 | 23 | 35 | 28 | 44 | 82 | 39 | 75 | 110 | 50 | 155 | 64 |
| Cameroon | 2004 | .. | .. | .. | .. | 57 | 86 | 55 | 86 | 101 | 52 | 189 | 88 |
| Central African Republic | 1994–95 | 20 | 11 | 25 | 15 | 31 | 80 | 27 | 76 | 132 | 54 | 193 | 98 |
| Chad | 2004 | 24 | 16 | 27 | 19 | 8 | 38 | 5 | 42 | 109 | 101 | 176 | 187 |
| Colombia | 2005 | 7 | 2 | 11 | 3 | 70 | 91 | 73 | 91 | 32 | 14 | 39 | 16 |
| Côte d'Ivoire | 1994 | 17 | 7 | 21 | 10 | 31 | 79 | 26 | 74 | 117 | 63 | 190 | 97 |
| Dominican Republic | 2002 | 7 | 1 | 9 | 1 | 83 | 94 | 46 | 66 | 50 | 20 | 66 | 22 |
| Egypt, Arab Rep. | 2000 | 4 | 2 | 5 | 2 | 95 | 99 | 94 | 93 | 76 | 30 | 98 | 34 |
| Eritrea | 1995 | .. | .. | .. | .. | 37 | 92 | 30 | 89 | 74 | 68 | 152 | 104 |
| Ethiopia | 2000 | 25 | 22 | 32 | 29 | 18 | 52 | 14 | 43 | 93 | 95 | 159 | 147 |
| Gabon | 2000 | 10 | 4 | 14 | 7 | 34 | 71 | 18 | 49 | 57 | 36 | 93 | 55 |
| Ghana | 2003 | 17 | 6 | 22 | 10 | 74 | 88 | 64 | 87 | 61 | 58 | 128 | 88 |
| Guatemala | 1998–99 | 21 | 9 | 26 | 10 | 80 | 91 | 74 | 76 | 58 | 39 | 78 | 39 |
| Guinea | 1999 | 17 | 9 | 22 | 13 | 33 | 73 | 30 | 69 | 119 | 70 | 230 | 133 |
| Haiti | 2000 | 14 | 4 | 18 | 6 | 43 | 63 | 31 | 58 | 100 | 97 | 164 | 109 |
| India | 1998–99 | 28 | 16 | 33 | 21 | 28 | 81 | 36 | 85 | 97 | 38 | 141 | 46 |
| Indonesia | 2002–03 | .. | .. | .. | .. | 59 | 85 | 42 | 72 | 61 | 17 | 77 | 22 |
| Jordan | 1997 | .. | .. | .. | .. | 90 | 93 | 98 | 93 | 35 | 23 | 42 | 25 |
| Kazakhstan | 1999 | 3 | 5 | 5 | 6 | 74 | 76[b] | 90 | 82[b] | 68 | 42 | 82 | 45 |
| Kenya | 2003 | 17 | 6 | 22 | 7 | 54 | 88 | 56 | 73 | 96 | 62 | 149 | 91 |
| Kyrgyz Republic | 1997 | 6 | 5 | 10 | 7 | 82 | 81 | 82 | 87 | 83 | 46 | 96 | 49 |
| Madagascar | 1997 | 24 | 18 | 29 | 24 | 32 | 79 | 32 | 81 | 119 | 58 | 195 | 101 |
| Malawi | 2000 | 18 | 9 | 24 | 12 | 80 | 90 | 79 | 93 | 132 | 86 | 231 | 149 |
| Mali | 2001 | 20 | 10 | 26 | 13 | 40 | 77 | 28 | 71 | 137 | 90 | 248 | 148 |
| Mauritania | 2000–01 | 18 | 11 | 23 | 15 | 42 | 86 | 18 | 61 | 61 | 62 | 98 | 79 |
| Morocco | 2003–04 | 11 | 2 | 13 | 3 | 83 | 98 | 89 | 98 | 62 | 24 | 78 | 26 |
| Mozambique | 2003 | 16 | 5 | 21 | 7 | 61 | 96 | 52 | 96 | 143 | 71 | 196 | 108 |
| Namibia | 2000 | 17 | 6 | 22 | 9 | 76 | 86 | 76 | 83 | 36 | 23 | 55 | 31 |
| Nepal | 2001 | 34 | 20 | 40 | 26 | 61 | 83 | 62 | 85 | 86 | 53 | 130 | 68 |
| Nicaragua | 2001 | 9 | 2 | 13 | 2 | 76 | 94 | 77 | 83 | 50 | 16 | 64 | 19 |
| Niger | 1998 | 27 | 18 | 30 | 26 | 23 | 66 | 9 | 68 | 131 | 86 | 282 | 184 |
| Nigeria | 2003 | 20 | 9 | 24 | 10 | 16 | 71 | 7 | 61 | 133 | 52 | 257 | 79 |
| Pakistan | 1990–91 | 28 | 14 | 33 | 19 | 28 | 75 | 24 | 64 | 89 | 63 | 125 | 74 |
| Paraguay | 1990 | 3 | 1 | 5 | 1 | 48 | 69 | 40 | 69 | 43 | 16 | 57 | 20 |
| Peru | 2000 | 9 | 1 | 13 | 1 | 81 | 92 | 76 | 93 | 64 | 14 | 93 | 18 |
| Philippines | 2003 | .. | .. | .. | .. | 70 | 89 | 64 | 92 | 42 | 19 | 66 | 21 |
| Rwanda | 2000 | 15 | 8 | 19 | 12 | 84 | 89 | 80 | 89 | 139 | 88 | 246 | 154 |
| Senegal | 1997 | .. | .. | .. | .. | .. | .. | .. | .. | 85 | 45 | 181 | 70 |
| South Africa | 1998 | .. | .. | .. | .. | 74 | 85 | 64 | 85 | 62 | 17 | 87 | 22 |
| Tanzania | 2004 | 14 | 8 | 20 | 11 | 65 | 91 | 34 | 36 | 88 | 64 | 137 | 93 |
| Togo | 1998 | 17 | 8 | 23 | 10 | 35 | 63 | 29 | 68 | 84 | 66 | 168 | 97 |
| Turkey | 1998 | .. | .. | .. | .. | 64 | 89 | 45 | 81 | 68 | 30 | 85 | 33 |
| Turkmenistan | 2000 | .. | .. | .. | .. | 91 | 80 | 97 | 86 | 89 | 58 | 106 | 70 |
| Uganda | 2000–01 | 16 | 7 | 21 | 10 | 49 | 65 | 35 | 55 | 106 | 60 | 192 | 106 |
| Uzbekistan | 1996 | 11 | 8 | 15 | 10 | 96 | 93 | 89 | 82 | 54 | 46 | 70 | 50 |
| Vietnam | 2002 | .. | .. | .. | .. | 64 | 98 | 53 | 94 | 39 | 14 | 53 | 16 |
| Yemen, Rep. | 1997 | .. | .. | 36 | 24 | 16 | 73 | 14 | 71 | 109 | 60 | 163 | 73 |
| Zambia | 2001–02 | 18 | 12 | 24 | 17 | 81 | 88 | 74 | 89 | 115 | 57 | 192 | 92 |
| Zimbabwe | 1999 | 10 | 5 | 16 | 6 | 80 | 86 | 81 | 86 | 59 | 44 | 100 | 62 |

a. Refers to children who were immunized at any time before the survey. b. The data contain large sampling errors because of the small number of cases.

# Health gaps by income and gender

| | Survey year | Prevalence of child malnutrition | | Child immunization rate | | | | Infant mortality rate | | Under-five mortality rate | |
|---|---|---|---|---|---|---|---|---|---|---|---|
| | | Old reference Moderate underweight % of children under age 5 | | % of children ages 12–23 months[a] | | | | per 1,000 live births | | per 1,000 | |
| | | | | Measles | | DTP3 | | | | | |
| | | Male | Female | Male | Female | Male | Female | Male | Female | Male | Female |
| Armenia | 2000 | 2 | 3 | 71 | 79 | 90 | 89 | 46 | 42 | 51 | 45 |
| Bangladesh | 2004 | 34 | 35 | 76 | 76 | 81 | 81 | 80 | 64 | 102 | 91 |
| Benin | 2001 | 19 | 17 | 69 | 67 | 74 | 71 | 98 | 92 | 162 | 163 |
| Bolivia | 2003 | 6 | 6 | 65 | 63 | 70 | 73 | 71 | 64 | 94 | 91 |
| Brazil | 1996 | 6 | 5 | 87 | 87 | 82 | 80 | 52 | 44 | 60 | 53 |
| Burkina Faso | 2003 | 25 | 23 | 54 | 58 | 57 | 57 | 95 | 89 | 195 | 192 |
| Cambodia | 2000 | 32 | 33 | 57 | 54 | 50 | 47 | 103 | 82 | 133 | 110 |
| Cameroon | 2004 | 14 | 15 | 65 | 66 | 65 | 68 | 88 | 74 | 154 | 141 |
| Central African Republic | 1994–95 | 21 | 19 | 52 | 53 | 49 | 46 | 109 | 94 | 165 | 152 |
| Chad | 2004 | 23 | 23 | 23 | 23 | 20 | 21 | 122 | 108 | 207 | 198 |
| Colombia | 2005 | 6 | 6 | 83 | 82 | 84 | 81 | 26 | 18 | 30 | 21 |
| Côte d'Ivoire | 1994 | 19 | 16 | 54 | 52 | 49 | 45 | 99 | 83 | 163 | 137 |
| Dominican Republic | 2002 | 5 | 5 | 89 | 88 | 54 | 61 | 38 | 31 | 46 | 40 |
| Egypt, Arab Rep. | 2000 | 4 | 3 | 97 | 97 | 94 | 94 | 55 | 55 | 69 | 70 |
| Eritrea | 1995 | 26 | 27 | 52 | 50 | 49 | 49 | 82 | 69 | 163 | 141 |
| Ethiopia | 2000 | 32 | 31 | 28 | 26 | 22 | 19 | 124 | 101 | 197 | 178 |
| Gabon | 2000 | 10 | 9 | 55 | 55 | 40 | 33 | 74 | 49 | 103 | 80 |
| Ghana | 2003 | 17 | 17 | 82 | 83 | 81 | 77 | 70 | 59 | 111 | 108 |
| Guatemala | 1998–99 | 21 | 18 | 82 | 87 | 73 | 74 | 50 | 48 | 64 | 65 |
| Guinea | 1999 | 17 | 19 | 52 | 52 | 46 | 47 | 112 | 101 | 202 | 188 |
| Haiti | 2000 | 14 | 13 | 54 | 54 | 43 | 43 | 97 | 83 | 143 | 132 |
| India | 1998–99 | 28 | 30 | 52 | 50 | 56 | 54 | 75 | 71 | 98 | 105 |
| Indonesia | 2002–03 | .. | .. | 73 | 71 | 58 | 59 | 46 | 40 | 58 | 51 |
| Jordan | 1997 | 4 | 5 | 90 | 90 | 96 | 96 | 34 | 23 | 38 | 30 |
| Kazakhstan | 1999 | 4 | 4 | 79 | 78 | 89 | 88 | 62 | 47 | 72 | 53 |
| Kenya | 2003 | 18 | 14 | 73 | 72 | 71 | 74 | 84 | 67 | 122 | 103 |
| Kyrgyz Republic | 1997 | 11 | 8 | 84 | 85 | 83 | 81 | 72 | 60 | 81 | 70 |
| Madagascar | 1997 | 27 | 27 | 47 | 45 | 48 | 49 | 109 | 90 | 176 | 152 |
| Malawi | 2000 | 20 | 19 | 83 | 83 | 84 | 85 | 117 | 108 | 207 | 199 |
| Mali | 2001 | 24 | 21 | 49 | 48 | 41 | 38 | 136 | 116 | 250 | 226 |
| Mauritania | 2000–01 | 22 | 22 | 61 | 63 | 39 | 41 | 74 | 59 | 110 | 94 |
| Morocco | 2003–04 | 9 | 8 | 88 | 92 | 95 | 95 | 51 | 37 | 59 | 48 |
| Mozambique | 2003 | 18 | 17 | 77 | 76 | 73 | 71 | 127 | 120 | 181 | 176 |
| Namibia | 2000 | 19 | 18 | 79 | 82 | 78 | 81 | 45 | 34 | 67 | 54 |
| Nepal | 2001 | 35 | 36 | 73 | 69 | 74 | 70 | 79 | 75 | 105 | 112 |
| Nicaragua | 2001 | 9 | 7 | 87 | 86 | 84 | 81 | 39 | 32 | 48 | 41 |
| Niger | 1998 | 29 | 30 | 36 | 34 | 25 | 25 | 141 | 131 | 299 | 306 |
| Nigeria | 2003 | 19 | 20 | 34 | 38 | 19 | 24 | 116 | 102 | 222 | 212 |
| Pakistan | 1990–91 | 27 | 27 | 55 | 46 | 45 | 40 | 102 | 86 | 122 | 119 |
| Paraguay | 1990 | 3 | 4 | 56 | 61 | 50 | 57 | 39 | 33 | 49 | 45 |
| Peru | 2000 | 6 | 6 | 84 | 85 | 85 | 84 | 46 | 40 | 64 | 57 |
| Philippines | 2003 | .. | .. | 78 | 81 | 78 | 80 | 35 | 25 | 48 | 34 |
| Rwanda | 2000 | 19 | 19 | 86 | 88 | 85 | 87 | 123 | 112 | 215 | 198 |
| Senegal | 1997 | .. | .. | .. | .. | .. | .. | 74 | 65 | 144 | 134 |
| South Africa | 1998 | .. | .. | 84 | 81 | 74 | 78 | 49 | 35 | 66 | 48 |
| Tanzania | 2004 | 18 | 18 | 80 | 80 | 37 | 33 | 83 | 82 | 135 | 130 |
| Togo | 1998 | 19 | 18 | 45 | 40 | 43 | 41 | 89 | 71 | 156 | 132 |
| Turkey | 1998 | 7 | 7 | 79 | 78 | 60 | 57 | 51 | 46 | 61 | 58 |
| Turkmenistan | 2000 | 11 | 10 | 87 | 88 | 93 | 92 | 83 | 60 | 101 | 76 |
| Uganda | 2000–01 | 18 | 17 | 56 | 57 | 45 | 48 | 93 | 85 | 164 | 149 |
| Uzbekistan | 1996 | 15 | 13 | 91 | 92 | 87 | 90 | 50 | 37 | 65 | 46 |
| Vietnam | 2002 | .. | .. | 84 | 82 | 72 | 73 | 25 | 25 | 34 | 31 |
| Yemen, Rep. | 1997 | 33 | 30 | 45 | 40 | 41 | 39 | 98 | 80 | 128 | 114 |
| Zambia | 2001–02 | 21 | 21 | 83 | 86 | 78 | 82 | 95 | 93 | 176 | 160 |
| Zimbabwe | 1999 | 12 | 11 | 77 | 81 | 80 | 82 | 63 | 56 | 95 | 85 |

a. Refers to children who were immunized at any time before the survey.

| | Survey year | Pregnant women receiving prenatal care | | Contraceptive prevalence rate | | Births attended by skilled health staff[a] | | Total fertility rate | | Exclusive breastfeeding | |
|---|---|---|---|---|---|---|---|---|---|---|---|
| | | % | | modern methods % of married women ages 15–49 | | % of total | | births per woman | | % of children under 4 months | |
| | | Poorest quintile | Richest quintile | Poorest quintile | Richest quintile | Poorest quintile | Richest quintile | Poorest quintile | Richest quintile | Poorest quintile | Richest quintile |
| Armenia | 2000 | 85 | 97 | 16 | 29 | 93 | 100 | 2.5 | 1.6 | .. | .. |
| Bangladesh | 2004 | 25 | 81 | 45 | 50 | 3 | 39 | 4.1 | 2.2 | 62 | 31 |
| Benin | 2001 | 73 | 100 | 4 | 15 | 50 | 99 | 7.2 | 3.5 | 50 | 42[b] |
| Bolivia | 2003 | 62 | 98 | 23 | 49 | 27 | 98 | 6.7 | 2.0 | 79 | 31 |
| Brazil | 1996 | 72 | 98 | 56 | 77 | 72 | 99 | 4.8 | 1.7 | 33 | 60[b] |
| Burkina Faso | 2003 | 56 | 96 | 2 | 27 | 19 | 84 | 6.6 | 3.6 | 17 | 28 |
| Cambodia | 2000 | 22 | 80 | 13 | 25 | 15 | 81 | 4.7 | 2.2 | 14 | 18 |
| Cameroon | 2004 | 65 | 97 | 2 | 27 | 29 | 95 | 6.5 | 3.2 | 33 | 30[b] |
| Central African Republic | 1994–95 | 39 | 91 | 1 | 9 | 14 | 82 | 5.1 | 4.9 | 9 | 4 |
| Chad | 2004 | 9 | 77 | 0 | 7 | 1 | 51 | 5.1 | 6.0 | 1 | 2 |
| Colombia | 2005 | 84 | 99 | 60 | 72 | 72 | 99 | 4.1 | 1.4 | 60 | 64 |
| Côte d'Ivoire | 1994 | 62 | 98 | 1 | 13 | 17 | 84 | 6.4 | 3.7 | 0 | 5 |
| Dominican Republic | 2002 | 97 | 99 | 59 | 70 | 94 | 100 | 4.5 | 2.1 | 18 | 6 |
| Egypt, Arab Rep. | 2000 | 31 | 84 | 43 | 61 | 31 | 94 | 4.0 | 2.9 | 72 | 57 |
| Eritrea | 1995 | 34 | 90 | 0[c] | 19 | 5 | 74 | 8.0 | 3.7 | 64 | 73 |
| Ethiopia | 2000 | 15 | 60 | 3 | 23 | 1 | 25 | 6.3 | 3.6 | 63 | 46 |
| Gabon | 2000 | 85 | 98 | 6 | 18 | 67 | 97 | 6.3 | 3.0 | 6 | 5[b] |
| Ghana | 2003 | 83 | 98 | 9 | 26 | 21 | 90 | 6.4 | 2.8 | 62[b] | .. |
| Guatemala | 1998–99 | 37 | 97 | 5 | 60 | 9 | 92 | 7.6 | 2.9 | 62 | .. |
| Guinea | 1999 | 58 | 97 | 1 | 9 | 12 | 82 | 5.8 | 4.0 | 9 | 8 |
| Haiti | 2000 | 65 | 91 | 17 | 24 | 4 | 70 | 6.8 | 2.7 | 40 | 15[b] |
| India | 1998–99 | 44 | 93 | 29 | 55 | 16 | 84 | 3.4 | 1.8 | 64 | 37 |
| Indonesia | 2002–03 | 78 | 99 | 49 | 58 | 40 | 94 | 3.0 | 2.2 | 58 | 35 |
| Jordan | 1997 | 93 | 97 | 28 | 47 | 91 | 99 | 5.2 | 3.1 | 14 | 14[b] |
| Kazakhstan | 1999 | 97 | 91 | 49 | 55 | 99 | 99 | 3.4 | 1.2 | .. | .. |
| Kenya | 2003 | 75 | 94 | 12 | 44 | 17 | 75 | 7.6 | 3.1 | 22 | 17 |
| Kyrgyz Republic | 1997 | 96 | 99 | 44 | 54 | 96 | 100 | 4.6 | 2.0 | 18[b] | .. |
| Madagascar | 1997 | 67 | 96 | 2 | 24 | 30 | 89 | 8.1 | 3.4 | 57 | 65 |
| Malawi | 2000 | 89 | 98 | 20 | 40 | 43 | 83 | 7.1 | 4.8 | 53 | 72 |
| Mali | 2001 | 42 | 92 | 4 | 18 | 22 | 89 | 7.3 | 5.3 | 38 | 18 |
| Mauritania | 2000–01 | 33 | 89 | 0[c] | 17 | 15 | 93 | 5.4 | 3.5 | 28 | 30 |
| Morocco | 2003–04 | 40 | 93 | 51 | 57 | 29 | 95 | 3.3 | 1.9 | 53 | 36 |
| Mozambique | 2003 | 67 | 98 | 14 | 37 | 25 | 89 | 6.3 | 3.8 | 47 | 27 |
| Namibia | 2000 | 81 | 96 | 29 | 64 | 55 | 97 | 6.0 | 2.7 | 100[b] | 85[b] |
| Nepal | 2001 | 30 | 80 | 24 | 55 | 4 | 45 | 5.3 | 2.3 | 76 | 67 |
| Nicaragua | 2001 | 69 | 97 | 50 | 71 | 78 | 99 | 5.6 | 2.1 | 53 | 15[b] |
| Niger | 1998 | 24 | 85 | 1 | 18 | 4 | 63 | 8.4 | 5.7 | 1 | 3 |
| Nigeria | 2003 | 37 | 96 | 4 | 21 | 13 | 85 | 6.5 | 4.2 | 15 | 34 |
| Pakistan | 1990–91 | 8 | 72 | 1 | 23 | 5 | 55 | 5.1 | 4.0 | 36 | 9 |
| Paraguay | 1990 | 73 | 98 | 21 | 46 | 41 | 98 | 7.9 | 2.7 | 7 | 0 |
| Peru | 2000 | 41 | 74 | 37 | 58 | 13 | 88 | 5.5 | 1.6 | 88 | 59 |
| Philippines | 2003 | 72 | 97 | 24 | 35 | 25 | 92 | 5.9 | 2.0 | 60 | 20 |
| Rwanda | 2000 | 90 | 95 | 2 | 15 | 17 | 60 | 6.0 | 5.4 | 89 | 79 |
| Senegal | 1997 | 67 | 97 | 1 | 24 | 20 | 86 | 7.4 | 3.6 | 13 | 19 |
| South Africa | 1998 | 96 | 94 | 34 | 70 | 68 | 98 | 4.8 | 1.9 | 15 | 11[b] |
| Tanzania | 2004 | 91 | 97 | 11 | 36 | 31 | 87 | 7.3 | 3.3 | 58 | 55 |
| Togo | 1998 | 69 | 97 | 3 | 13 | 25 | 91 | 7.3 | 2.9 | 7 | 34 |
| Turkey | 1998 | 38 | 96 | 24 | 48 | 53 | 98 | 3.9 | 1.7 | 10 | 4[b] |
| Turkmenistan | 2000 | 98 | 97 | 51 | 50 | 97 | 98 | 3.4 | 2.1 | 11 | 28[b] |
| Uganda | 2000–01 | 88 | 98 | 11 | 41 | 20 | 77 | 8.5 | 4.1 | 73 | 59 |
| Uzbekistan | 1996 | 93 | 96 | 46 | 52 | 92 | 100 | 4.4 | 2.2 | .. | .. |
| Vietnam | 2002 | 68 | 100 | 58 | 52 | 58 | 100 | 2.2 | 1.4 | 18 | .. |
| Yemen, Rep. | 1997 | 17 | 68 | 1 | 24 | 7 | 50 | 7.3 | 4.7 | 20 | 13 |
| Zambia | 2001–02 | 89 | 99 | 11 | 53 | 20 | 91 | 7.3 | 3.6 | 39 | 70[b] |
| Zimbabwe | 1999 | 94 | 97 | 41 | 67 | 57 | 94 | 4.9 | 2.6 | 36 | 46[b] |

a. Based on births in the five years before the survey. b. The data contain large sampling errors because of the small number of cases. c. Less than 0.5.

## About the data

The data in the table describe the health status and use of health services by individuals in different socioeconomic groups within countries. The data are from Demographic and Health Surveys conducted by Macro International with the support of the U.S. Agency for International Development. These large-scale household sample surveys, conducted periodically in developing countries, collect information on a large number of health, nutrition, and population measures as well as on respondents' social, demographic, and economic characteristics using a standard set of questionnaires. The data presented here draw on responses to individual and household questionnaires.

Socioeconomic status as displayed in the table is based on a household's assets, including ownership of consumer items, features of the household's dwelling, and other characteristics related to wealth. Each household asset on which information was collected was assigned a weight generated through principal-component analysis. The resulting scores were standardized in relation to a standard normal distribution with a mean of zero and a standard deviation of one. The standardized scores were then used to create break-points defining wealth quintiles, expressed as quintiles of individuals in the population rather than quintiles of individuals at risk with respect to any one health indicator.

The choice of the asset index for defining socioeconomic status was based on pragmatic rather than conceptual considerations: Demographic and Health Surveys do not collect income or consumption data but do have detailed information on households' ownership of consumer goods and access to a variety of goods and services. Like income or consumption, the asset index defines disparities primarily in economic terms. It therefore excludes other possibilities of disparities among groups, such as those based on gender, education, ethnic background, or other facets of social exclusion. To that extent the index provides only a partial view of the multidimensional concepts of poverty, inequality, and inequity.

Creating one index that includes all asset indicators limits the types of analysis that can be performed. In particular, the use of a unified index does not permit a disaggregated analysis to examine which asset indicators have a more or less important association with health status or use of health services. In addition, some asset indicators may reflect household wealth better in some countries than in others—or reflect different degrees of wealth in different countries. Taking such information into account and creating country-specific asset indexes with country-specific choices of asset indicators might produce a more effective and accurate index for each country. The asset index used in the table does not have this flexibility.

The analysis was carried out for 56 countries, with the results issued in country reports. The table shows the estimates for the poorest and richest quintiles and by sex only; the full set of estimates for up to 117 indicators is available in the country reports (see Data sources).

Demographic and Health Surveys try to collect cross-country comparable data, but the age group of the reference population could differ across countries. Caution should be exercised when comparing the data. The estimates in the table are based on survey data, which refer to a period preceding the survey date, or use a definition or methodology different from the estimates in tables 2.16–2.18 and 2.21. Thus the estimates may differ from those in the other tables, and caution should be exercised in using the data.

## Definitions

• **Survey year** is the year in which the underlying data were collected. • **Prevalence of child malnutrition** is the percentage of children under age 5 whose weight for age is two to three standard deviations below the median reference standard for their age. New international child growth standards were released in 2006 by the World Health Organization. The table presents malnutrition data using both the new and old reference standards. For more information about the change in standards, see About the data for table 2.18. • **Child immunization rate** is the percentage of children ages 12–23 months at the time of the survey who, at any time before the survey, had received measles vaccine and three doses of diphtheria, tetanus, and pertussis (whooping cough) vaccine (DTP3). • **Infant mortality rate** is the number of infants dying before reaching one year of age, per 1,000 live births. • **Under-five mortality rate** is the probability that a newborn baby will die before reaching age 5, per 1,000, if subject to current age-specific mortality rates. • **Pregnant women receiving prenatal care** are the percentage of women with one or more births during the five years preceding the survey who were attended at least once during pregnancy by skilled health personnel for reasons related to pregnancy. • **Contraceptive prevalence rate** is the percentage of women married or in-union ages 15–49 who are practicing, or whose sexual partners are practicing, any modern method of contraception. • **Births attended by skilled health staff** are the percentage of deliveries attended by personnel trained to give the necessary supervision, care, and advice to women during pregnancy, labor, and the postpartum period; to conduct deliveries on their own; and to care for newborns. Skilled health staff include doctors, nurses, and trained midwives, but exclude trained or untrained traditional birth attendants. • **Total fertility rate** is the number of children that would be born to a woman if she were to live to the end of her childbearing years and bear children in accordance with current age-specific fertility rates. • **Exclusive breastfeeding** refers to the percentage of children ages 0–3 months who received only breast milk in the 24 hours preceding the survey.

### Data sources

Data on health gaps by income and gender are from an analysis of Demographic and Health Surveys by the World Bank and Macro International. Country reports are available at www.worldbank.org/povertyandhealth/countrydata.

# 2.21 | Mortality

| | Life expectancy at birth | | Infant mortality rate | | Under-five mortality rate | | Child mortality rate | | Adult mortality rate | | Survival to age 65 | |
|---|---|---|---|---|---|---|---|---|---|---|---|---|
| | | | | | | | per 1,000 | | per 1,000 | | % of cohort | |
| | years | | per 1,000 live births | | per 1,000 | | Male | Female | Male | Female | Male | Female |
| | 1990 | 2006 | 1990 | 2006 | 1990 | 2006 | 1997–2006[a] | 1997–2006[a] | 2004–06[a] | 2004–06[a] | 2006 | 2006 |
| Afghanistan | .. | .. | .. | .. | .. | .. | .. | .. | .. | .. | .. | .. |
| Albania | 72 | 76 | 37 | 15 | 45 | 17 | .. | .. | 108 | 52 | 81 | 90 |
| Algeria | 67 | 72 | 54 | 33 | 69 | 38 | .. | .. | 123 | 105 | 77 | 81 |
| Angola | 40 | 42 | 154 | 154 | 260 | 260 | .. | .. | 486 | 437 | 30 | 35 |
| Argentina | 72 | 75 | 25 | 14 | 29 | 16 | .. | .. | 168 | 80 | 74 | 87 |
| Armenia | 68 | 72 | 47 | 21 | 56 | 24 | 8 | 3 | 197 | 88 | 68 | 83 |
| Australia | 77 | 81 | 8 | 5 | 10 | 6 | .. | .. | 85 | 49 | 87 | 93 |
| Austria | 76 | 80 | 8 | 4 | 10 | 5 | .. | .. | 111 | 55 | 84 | 92 |
| Azerbaijan | 71 | 72 | 84 | 73 | 105 | 88 | .. | .. | 218 | 103 | 62 | 77 |
| Bangladesh | 55 | 64 | 100 | 52 | 149 | 69 | 24 | 29 | 235 | 203 | 61 | 66 |
| Belarus | 71 | 69 | 20 | 12 | 24 | 13 | .. | .. | 368 | 128 | 52 | 82 |
| Belgium | 76 | 79 | 8 | 4 | 10 | 4 | .. | .. | 114 | 62 | 84 | 92 |
| Benin | 53 | 56 | 111 | 88 | 185 | 148 | 64 | 65 | 287 | 239 | 52 | 58 |
| Bolivia | 59 | 65 | 89 | 50 | 125 | 61 | 25 | 29 | 238 | 178 | 63 | 71 |
| Bosnia and Herzegovina | 72 | 75 | 18 | 13 | 22 | 15 | .. | .. | 148 | 77 | 76 | 86 |
| Botswana | 63 | 50 | 45 | 90 | 58 | 124 | .. | .. | 586 | 575 | 31 | 35 |
| Brazil | 67 | 72 | 48 | 19 | 57 | 20 | .. | .. | 234 | 123 | 66 | 80 |
| Bulgaria | 72 | 73 | 15 | 12 | 19 | 14 | .. | .. | 221 | 92 | 69 | 86 |
| Burkina Faso | 50 | 52 | 123 | 122 | 206 | 204 | 110 | 113 | 288 | 187 | 46 | 57 |
| Burundi | 46 | 49 | 114 | 109 | 190 | 181 | .. | .. | 412 | 377 | 39 | 44 |
| Cambodia | 55 | 59 | 85 | 65 | 116 | 82 | 20 | 20 | 359 | 248 | 49 | 61 |
| Cameroon | 55 | 50 | 85 | 87 | 139 | 149 | 73 | 72 | 416 | 420 | 41 | 43 |
| Canada | 77 | 80 | 7 | 5 | 8 | 6 | .. | .. | 95 | 57 | 86 | 91 |
| Central African Republic | 50 | 44 | 114 | 115 | 173 | 175 | .. | .. | 566 | 536 | 28 | 33 |
| Chad | 51 | 51 | 120 | 124 | 201 | 209 | 96 | 101 | 352 | 303 | 43 | 50 |
| Chile | 74 | 78 | 18 | 8 | 21 | 9 | .. | .. | 130 | 62 | 80 | 89 |
| China | 69 | 72 | 36 | 20 | 45 | 24 | .. | .. | 153 | 92 | 75 | 82 |
|   Hong Kong, China | 77 | 82 | .. | .. | .. | .. | .. | .. | 78 | 34 | 87 | 94 |
| Colombia | 68 | 73 | 26 | 17 | 35 | 21 | 4 | 3 | 206 | 97 | 71 | 83 |
| Congo, Dem. Rep. | 46 | 46 | 129 | 129 | 205 | 205 | .. | .. | 439 | 401 | 35 | 40 |
| Congo, Rep. | 57 | 55 | 67 | 79 | 103 | 126 | 49 | 43 | 402 | 377 | 44 | 50 |
| Costa Rica | 76 | 79 | 16 | 11 | 18 | 12 | .. | .. | 116 | 62 | 82 | 89 |
| Côte d'Ivoire | 53 | 48 | 105 | 90 | 153 | 127 | 83 | 58 | 429 | 408 | 38 | 42 |
| Croatia | 72 | 76 | 11 | 5 | 12 | 6 | .. | .. | 159 | 62 | 75 | 89 |
| Cuba | 75 | 78 | 11 | 5 | 13 | 7 | .. | .. | 119 | 74 | 82 | 88 |
| Czech Republic | 71 | 76 | 11 | 3 | 13 | 4 | .. | .. | 139 | 60 | 78 | 90 |
| Denmark | 75 | 78 | 8 | 4 | 9 | 5 | .. | .. | 116 | 68 | 83 | 88 |
| Dominican Republic | 68 | 72 | 50 | 25 | 65 | 29 | 9 | 9 | 222 | 134 | 68 | 78 |
| Ecuador | 69 | 75 | 43 | 21 | 57 | 24 | .. | .. | 171 | 91 | 75 | 85 |
| Egypt, Arab Rep. | 62 | 71 | 67 | 29 | 91 | 35 | 10 | 10 | 158 | 94 | 72 | 82 |
| El Salvador | 66 | 72 | 47 | 22 | 60 | 25 | .. | .. | 209 | 127 | 70 | 80 |
| Eritrea | 49 | 57 | 88 | 48 | 147 | 74 | 55 | 50 | 430 | 326 | 41 | 54 |
| Estonia | 69 | 73 | 12 | 5 | 16 | 7 | .. | .. | 282 | 100 | 59 | 84 |
| Ethiopia | 48 | 52 | 122 | 77 | 204 | 123 | 56 | 56 | 367 | 329 | 44 | 49 |
| Finland | 75 | 79 | 6 | 3 | 7 | 4 | .. | .. | 132 | 57 | 83 | 92 |
| France | 77 | 81 | 7 | 4 | 9 | 4 | .. | .. | 127 | 57 | 84 | 93 |
| Gabon | 61 | 57 | 60 | 60 | 92 | 91 | 32 | 33 | 378 | 374 | 49 | 51 |
| Gambia, The | 51 | 59 | 103 | 84 | 153 | 113 | .. | .. | 221 | 180 | 57 | 62 |
| Georgia | 70 | 71 | 39 | 28 | 46 | 32 | .. | .. | 214 | 82 | 67 | 83 |
| Germany | 75 | 79 | 7 | 4 | 9 | 4 | .. | .. | 112 | 58 | 84 | 92 |
| Ghana | 57 | 60 | 76 | 76 | 120 | 120 | 44 | 52 | 289 | 283 | 56 | 58 |
| Greece | 77 | 79 | 9 | 4 | 11 | 4 | .. | .. | 93 | 42 | 85 | 92 |
| Guatemala | 63 | 70 | 60 | 31 | 82 | 41 | 15 | 18 | 237 | 131 | 67 | 79 |
| Guinea | 47 | 56 | 139 | 98 | 235 | 161 | 89 | 86 | 275 | 236 | 52 | 58 |
| Guinea-Bissau | 42 | 46 | 142 | 119 | 240 | 200 | .. | .. | 447 | 396 | 35 | 41 |
| Haiti | 55 | 60 | 105 | 60 | 152 | 80 | 33 | 36 | 309 | 245 | 54 | 62 |

| | Life expectancy at birth | | Infant mortality rate | | Under-five mortality rate | | Child mortality rate | | Adult mortality rate | | Survival to age 65 | |
|---|---|---|---|---|---|---|---|---|---|---|---|---|
| | years | | per 1,000 live births | | per 1,000 | | per 1,000 | | per 1,000 | | % of cohort | |
| | | | | | | | Male | Female | Male | Female | Male | Female |
| | 1990 | 2006 | 1990 | 2006 | 1990 | 2006 | 1997–2006[a] | 1997–2006[a] | 2004–06[a] | 2004–06[a] | 2006 | 2006 |
| Honduras | 66 | 70 | 45 | 23 | 58 | 27 | 8 | 9 | 245 | 141 | 65 | 78 |
| Hungary | 69 | 73 | 15 | 6 | 17 | 7 | .. | .. | 256 | 107 | 66 | 85 |
| India | 59 | 64 | 80 | 57 | 115 | 76 | 25 | 37 | 260 | 168 | 59 | 69 |
| Indonesia | 62 | 68 | 60 | 26 | 91 | 34 | 13 | 11 | 172 | 123 | 71 | 79 |
| Iran, Islamic Rep. | 65 | 71 | 54 | 30 | 72 | 34 | .. | .. | 155 | 104 | 73 | 81 |
| Iraq | 62 | .. | 42 | .. | 53 | .. | .. | .. | .. | .. | .. | .. |
| Ireland | 75 | 79 | 8 | 4 | 9 | 5 | .. | .. | 90 | 52 | 85 | 91 |
| Israel | 77 | 80 | 10 | 4 | 12 | 5 | .. | .. | 82 | 39 | 87 | 93 |
| Italy | 77 | 81 | 8 | 4 | 9 | 4 | .. | .. | 86 | 45 | 85 | 93 |
| Jamaica | 71 | 71 | 28 | 26 | 33 | 31 | .. | .. | 222 | 140 | 70 | 79 |
| Japan | 79 | 82 | 5 | 3 | 6 | 4 | .. | .. | 93 | 45 | 87 | 94 |
| Jordan | 68 | 72 | 33 | 21 | 40 | 25 | 5 | 5 | 167 | 116 | 73 | 80 |
| Kazakhstan | 68 | 66 | 51 | 26 | 60 | 29 | 11 | 6 | 369 | 147 | 49 | 76 |
| Kenya | 59 | 53 | 64 | 79 | 97 | 121 | 42 | 39 | 432 | 408 | 42 | 47 |
| Korea, Dem. Rep. | 70 | 67 | 42 | 42 | 55 | 55 | .. | .. | 182 | 128 | 65 | 75 |
| Korea, Rep. | 71 | 78 | 8 | 5 | 9 | 5 | .. | .. | 114 | 47 | 81 | 92 |
| Kuwait | 75 | 78 | 14 | 9 | 16 | 11 | .. | .. | 87 | 53 | 85 | 89 |
| Kyrgyz Republic | 68 | 68 | 63 | 36 | 75 | 41 | 10 | 11 | 281 | 132 | 57 | 75 |
| Lao PDR | 55 | 64 | 120 | 59 | 163 | 75 | .. | .. | 238 | 196 | 61 | 67 |
| Latvia | 69 | 71 | 14 | 8 | 18 | 9 | .. | .. | 311 | 111 | 63 | 86 |
| Lebanon | 69 | 72 | 32 | 26 | 37 | 30 | .. | .. | 155 | 103 | 73 | 82 |
| Lesotho | 59 | 43 | 81 | 102 | 101 | 132 | 22 | 19 | 715 | 698 | 20 | 24 |
| Liberia | 43 | 45 | 157 | 157 | 235 | 235 | .. | .. | 466 | 430 | 33 | 37 |
| Libya | 68 | 74 | 35 | 17 | 41 | 18 | .. | .. | 152 | 94 | 74 | 83 |
| Lithuania | 71 | 71 | 10 | 7 | 13 | 8 | .. | .. | 326 | 110 | 62 | 86 |
| Macedonia, FYR | 71 | 74 | 33 | 15 | 38 | 17 | .. | .. | 137 | 81 | 77 | 85 |
| Madagascar | 51 | 59 | 103 | 72 | 168 | 115 | 45 | 45 | 289 | 231 | 54 | 61 |
| Malawi | 49 | 48 | 131 | 76 | 221 | 120 | 101 | 67 | 540 | 525 | 32 | 37 |
| Malaysia | 70 | 74 | 16 | 10 | 22 | 12 | .. | .. | 156 | 89 | 75 | 85 |
| Mali | 48 | 54 | 140 | 119 | 250 | 217 | 132 | 125 | 263 | 184 | 48 | 58 |
| Mauritania | 58 | 64 | 85 | 78 | 133 | 125 | 38 | 38 | 177 | 111 | 64 | 73 |
| Mauritius | 69 | 73 | 20 | 13 | 23 | 14 | .. | .. | 210 | 108 | 68 | 82 |
| Mexico | 71 | 74 | 42 | 29 | 53 | 35 | .. | .. | 144 | 81 | 78 | 86 |
| Moldova | 67 | 69 | 30 | 16 | 37 | 19 | 7 | 4 | 296 | 140 | 58 | 77 |
| Mongolia | 63 | 67 | 79 | 34 | 109 | 43 | .. | .. | 268 | 175 | 59 | 70 |
| Morocco | 64 | 71 | 69 | 34 | 89 | 37 | 9 | 11 | 151 | 101 | 73 | 82 |
| Mozambique | 44 | 42 | 158 | 96 | 235 | 138 | 61 | 64 | 609 | 589 | 25 | 29 |
| Myanmar | 59 | 62 | 91 | 74 | 130 | 104 | .. | .. | 304 | 192 | 54 | 66 |
| Namibia | 62 | 52 | 60 | 45 | 86 | 61 | 22 | 20 | 523 | 508 | 37 | 41 |
| Nepal | 54 | 63 | 99 | 46 | 142 | 59 | 21 | 19 | 235 | 211 | 61 | 65 |
| Netherlands | 77 | 80 | 7 | 4 | 9 | 5 | .. | .. | 83 | 53 | 86 | 91 |
| New Zealand | 75 | 80 | 8 | 5 | 11 | 6 | .. | .. | 81 | 53 | 86 | 91 |
| Nicaragua | 64 | 72 | 52 | 29 | 68 | 36 | 10 | 9 | 214 | 124 | 70 | 80 |
| Niger | 47 | 56 | 191 | 148 | 320 | 253 | 138 | 136 | 169 | 182 | 59 | 57 |
| Nigeria | 47 | 47 | 120 | 99 | 230 | 191 | 120 | 123 | 432 | 410 | 37 | 40 |
| Norway | 77 | 80 | 7 | 3 | 9 | 4 | .. | .. | 86 | 53 | 86 | 92 |
| Oman | 70 | 76 | 25 | 10 | 32 | 12 | .. | .. | 103 | 76 | 82 | 87 |
| Pakistan | 59 | 65 | 100 | 78 | 130 | 97 | .. | .. | 177 | 145 | 66 | 69 |
| Panama | 72 | 75 | 27 | 18 | 34 | 23 | .. | .. | 140 | 75 | 78 | 87 |
| Papua New Guinea | 55 | 57 | 69 | 54 | 94 | 73 | .. | .. | 422 | 305 | 41 | 55 |
| Paraguay | 68 | 72 | 33 | 19 | 41 | 22 | .. | .. | 176 | 129 | 72 | 79 |
| Peru | 66 | 71 | 58 | 21 | 78 | 25 | 19 | 8 | 201 | 125 | 70 | 79 |
| Philippines | 66 | 71 | 41 | 24 | 62 | 32 | 14 | 9 | 161 | 107 | 73 | 81 |
| Poland | 71 | 75 | 19 | 6 | 18 | 7 | .. | .. | 190 | 66 | 71 | 89 |
| Portugal | 74 | 78 | 11 | 3 | 14 | 5 | .. | .. | 139 | 58 | 83 | 91 |
| Puerto Rico | 75 | 78 | .. | .. | .. | .. | .. | .. | 138 | 54 | 79 | 91 |

| | Life expectancy at birth | | Infant mortality rate | | Under-five mortality rate | | Child mortality rate | | Adult mortality rate | | Survival to age 65 | |
|---|---|---|---|---|---|---|---|---|---|---|---|---|
| | years | | per 1,000 live births | | per 1,000 | | per 1,000 Male | Female | per 1,000 Male | Female | % of cohort Male | Female |
| | 1990 | 2006 | 1990 | 2006 | 1990 | 2006 | 1997–2006[a] | 1997–2006[a] | 2004–06[a] | 2004–06[a] | 2006 | 2006 |
| Romania | 70 | 72 | 27 | 16 | 31 | 18 | .. | .. | 205 | 87 | 69 | 85 |
| Russian Federation | 69 | 66 | 23 | 14 | 27 | 16 | .. | .. | 429 | 158 | 43 | 77 |
| Rwanda | 32 | 46 | 106 | 98 | 176 | 160 | 90 | 87 | 471 | 422 | 33 | 39 |
| Saudi Arabia | 68 | 73 | 35 | 21 | 44 | 25 | 3 | 4 | 143 | 93 | 75 | 84 |
| Senegal | 57 | 63 | 72 | 60 | 149 | 116 | 69 | 69 | 174 | 106 | 63 | 72 |
| Serbia | 71 | 73 | .. | 7 | .. | 8 | .. | .. | 159 | 85 | 74 | 85 |
| Sierra Leone | 39 | 42 | 169 | 159 | 290 | 270 | .. | .. | 412 | 349 | 33 | 39 |
| Singapore | 74 | 80 | 7 | 2 | 8 | 3 | .. | .. | 83 | 47 | 86 | 92 |
| Slovak Republic | 71 | 74 | 12 | 7 | 14 | 8 | .. | .. | 196 | 76 | 71 | 88 |
| Slovenia | 73 | 78 | 8 | 3 | 10 | 4 | .. | .. | 149 | 57 | 80 | 91 |
| Somalia | 42 | 48 | 121 | 90 | 203 | 145 | .. | .. | 389 | 339 | 39 | 44 |
| South Africa | 62 | 51 | 45 | 56 | 60 | 69 | 18 | 13 | 605 | 568 | 29 | 36 |
| Spain | 77 | 81 | 8 | 4 | 9 | 4 | .. | .. | 110 | 45 | 85 | 94 |
| Sri Lanka | 71 | 75 | 26 | 11 | 32 | 13 | .. | .. | 241 | 102 | 66 | 83 |
| Sudan | 53 | 58 | 74 | 61 | 120 | 89 | 38 | 30 | 311 | 270 | 52 | 58 |
| Swaziland | 57 | 41 | 78 | 112 | 110 | 164 | .. | .. | 750 | 727 | 17 | 21 |
| Sweden | 78 | 81 | 6 | 3 | 7 | 3 | .. | .. | 78 | 49 | 88 | 93 |
| Switzerland | 77 | 82 | 7 | 4 | 9 | 5 | .. | .. | 80 | 47 | 87 | 93 |
| Syrian Arab Republic | 68 | 74 | 31 | 12 | 38 | 14 | .. | .. | 126 | 86 | 78 | 85 |
| Tajikistan | 63 | 67 | 91 | 56 | 115 | 68 | .. | .. | 213 | 141 | 63 | 73 |
| Tanzania | 51 | 52 | 102 | 74 | 161 | 118 | 56 | 52 | 444 | 412 | 40 | 45 |
| Thailand | 67 | 70 | 26 | 7 | 31 | 8 | .. | .. | 276 | 162 | 63 | 77 |
| Timor-Leste | 46 | 57 | 133 | 47 | 177 | 55 | .. | .. | 272 | 237 | 56 | 61 |
| Togo | 58 | 58 | 88 | 69 | 149 | 108 | 73 | 65 | 280 | 235 | 54 | 61 |
| Trinidad and Tobago | 70 | 70 | 30 | 33 | 34 | 38 | .. | .. | 243 | 191 | 66 | 73 |
| Tunisia | 70 | 74 | 41 | 19 | 52 | 23 | .. | .. | 126 | 73 | 78 | 86 |
| Turkey | 66 | 71 | 67 | 24 | 82 | 26 | 10 | 13 | 154 | 87 | 73 | 84 |
| Turkmenistan | 63 | 63 | 81 | 45 | 99 | 51 | 19 | 17 | 300 | 144 | 53 | 72 |
| Uganda | 50 | 51 | 93 | 78 | 160 | 134 | 71 | 61 | 446 | 433 | 39 | 43 |
| Ukraine | 70 | 68 | 22 | 20 | 25 | 24 | .. | .. | 375 | 132 | 51 | 80 |
| United Arab Emirates | 73 | 79 | 13 | 8 | 15 | 8 | .. | .. | 75 | 50 | 86 | 91 |
| United Kingdom | 76 | 79 | 8 | 5 | 10 | 6 | .. | .. | 88 | 56 | 85 | 90 |
| United States | 75 | 78 | 9 | 6 | 11 | 8 | .. | .. | 140 | 82 | 81 | 88 |
| Uruguay | 73 | 76 | 20 | 11 | 23 | 12 | .. | .. | 145 | 68 | 76 | 88 |
| Uzbekistan | 69 | 67 | 61 | 38 | 74 | 43 | .. | .. | 242 | 138 | 61 | 74 |
| Venezuela, RB | 71 | 74 | 27 | 18 | 33 | 21 | .. | .. | 181 | 96 | 73 | 84 |
| Vietnam | 65 | 71 | 38 | 15 | 53 | 17 | 10 | 7 | 139 | 93 | 78 | 84 |
| West Bank and Gaza | 69 | 73 | 34 | 20 | 40 | 22 | .. | .. | 131 | 95 | 77 | 83 |
| Yemen, Rep. | 54 | 62 | 98 | 75 | 139 | 100 | 33 | 36 | 259 | 210 | 58 | 65 |
| Zambia | 48 | 42 | 101 | 102 | 180 | 182 | 89 | 74 | 636 | 632 | 23 | 26 |
| Zimbabwe | 61 | 43 | 52 | 68 | 76 | 105 | 21 | 21 | 706 | 729 | 21 | 21 |
| **World** | **65 w** | **68 w** | **63 w** | **50 w** | **92 w** | **73 w** | | | **226 w** | **155 w** | **67 w** | **76 w** |
| **Low income** | 57 | 60 | 93 | 74 | 143 | 112 | | | 285 | 223 | 56 | 63 |
| **Middle income** | 68 | 71 | 43 | 26 | 56 | 33 | | | 195 | 116 | 70 | 80 |
| Lower middle income | 67 | 71 | 44 | 27 | 60 | 36 | | | 173 | 108 | 72 | 81 |
| Upper middle income | 69 | 70 | 38 | 22 | 47 | 26 | | | 260 | 137 | 64 | 80 |
| **Low & middle income** | 63 | 66 | 69 | 54 | 101 | 79 | | | 232 | 159 | 64 | 73 |
| East Asia & Pacific | 67 | 71 | 42 | 24 | 56 | 29 | | | 165 | 104 | 73 | 81 |
| Europe & Central Asia | 69 | 69 | 40 | 22 | 49 | 26 | | | 298 | 122 | 58 | 81 |
| Latin America & Carib. | 68 | 73 | 43 | 22 | 55 | 26 | | | 197 | 107 | 71 | 82 |
| Middle East & N. Africa | 64 | 70 | 58 | 34 | 77 | 42 | | | 166 | 115 | 71 | 79 |
| South Asia | 59 | 64 | 86 | 62 | 123 | 83 | | | 251 | 172 | 60 | 68 |
| Sub-Saharan Africa | 50 | 50 | 109 | 94 | 184 | 157 | | | 421 | 391 | 40 | 45 |
| **High income** | 76 | 79 | 9 | 6 | 12 | 7 | | | 117 | 63 | 83 | 91 |
| Euro area | 76 | 80 | 8 | 4 | 9 | 4 | | | 112 | 54 | 84 | 92 |

a. Data are for the most recent year available.

## About the data

Mortality rates for different age groups (infants, children, and adults) and overall mortality indicators (life expectancy at birth or survival to a given age) are important indicators of a country's health status. Because data on disease incidence and prevalence are frequently unavailable, mortality rates are often used to identify vulnerable populations. They are among the indicators most frequently used to compare socioeconomic development across countries.

The main sources of mortality data are vital registration systems and direct or indirect estimates based on sample surveys or censuses. A "complete" vital registration system—covering at least 90 percent of vital events in the population—is the best source of age-specific mortality data. Where reliable age-specific mortality data are available, life expectancy at birth is directly estimated from the life table constructed based on age-specific mortality data. But "complete" vital registration systems are fairly uncommon in developing countries. Thus estimates must be obtained from sample surveys or derived by applying indirect estimation techniques to registration, census, or survey data (see *Primary data documentation*). Survey data are subject to recall error, and surveys estimating infant deaths require large samples because households in which a birth or an infant death has occurred during a given year cannot ordinarily be preselected for sampling. Indirect estimates rely on estimated actuarial "life" tables that may be inappropriate for the population concerned. Because life expectancy at birth is estimated using infant mortality data and model life tables for many developing countries, similar reliability issues arise for this indicator. Extrapolations based on outdated surveys may not be reliable for monitoring changes in health status or for comparative analytical work.

To produce harmonized estimates of infant and under-five mortality rates that transparently use all available information, the United Nations Children's Fund (UNICEF) and the World Bank developed a methodology that fits a regression line to the relationship between mortality rates and their reference dates using weighted least squares. (For further discussion of childhood mortality estimates, see UNICEF, WHO, World Bank, and United Nations Population Division 2007.)

Infant and child mortality rates are higher for boys than for girls in countries in which parental gender preferences are insignificant. Child mortality captures the effect of gender discrimination better than does infant mortality, as malnutrition and medical interventions are more important in this age group. Where female child mortality is higher, as in some countries in South Asia, girls probably have unequal access to resources. Child mortality rates in the table are not compatible with infant mortality and under-five mortality rates because of differences in methodologies and reference years. Child mortality data were directly estimated from surveys, based on vital events that occurred during the 10 years preceding the survey. The reference year for the child mortality data is the survey year.

Adult mortality rates increased in many countries in Sub-Saharan Africa and in Europe and Central Asia. In Sub-Saharan Africa the increase stems from AIDS-related mortality and affects both men and women. In Europe and Central Asia the causes are more diverse (high prevalence of smoking, high-fat diet, excessive alcohol use, stressful conditions related to the economic transition) and affect men more.

The percentage of a cohort surviving to age 65 reflects both child and adult mortality rates. Like life expectancy, it is a synthetic measure based on current age-specific mortality rates. It shows that even in countries where mortality is high, a certain share of the current birth cohort will live well beyond the life expectancy at birth, while in low-mortality countries close to 90 percent will reach at least age 65.

Revised lower estimates of HIV prevalence have led adult mortality estimates for many countries, notably in Sub-Saharan Africa, to be revised drastically downward from previous estimates from 1990 onward and life expectancy at birth and survival to age 65 to be revised upward.

## Definitions

• **Life expectancy at birth** is the number of years a newborn infant would live if prevailing patterns of mortality at the time of its birth were to stay the same throughout its life. • **Infant mortality rate** is the number of infants dying before reaching one year of age per 1,000 live births in a given year. • **Under-five mortality rate** is the probability per 1,000 that a newborn baby will die before reaching age 5, if subject to current age-specific mortality rates. • **Child mortality rate** is the probability per 1,000 of dying between ages 1 and 5—that is, the probability of a 1-year-old dying before reaching age 5—if subject to current age-specific mortality rates. • **Adult mortality rate** is the probability per 1,000 of dying between the ages of 15 and 60—that is, the probability of a 15-year-old dying before reaching age 60—if subject to current age-specific mortality rates between those ages. • **Survival to age 65** refers to the percentage of a cohort of newborn infants that would survive to age 65, if subject to current age-specific mortality rates.

## Data sources

Data on infant and under-five mortality rates are the harmonized estimates of the World Health Organization, UNICEF, and the World Bank, based mainly on household surveys, censuses, and vital registration data, supplemented by the World Bank's estimates based on household surveys and vital registration and sample registration data. Data on child mortality rates are from Demographic and Health Surveys by Macro International. Other estimates are compiled and produced by the World Bank's Human Development Network and Development Data Group in consultation with its operational staff and country offices. Important inputs to the World Bank's demographic work come from the United Nations Population Division's *World Population Prospects: The 2006 Revision,* census reports and other statistical publications from national statistical offices, Eurostat, Demographic and Health Surveys by Macro International, and the Human Mortality Database by the University of California, Berkeley, and the Max Planck Institute for Demographic Research (www.mortality.org).

3 ENVIRONMENT

# Climate change by the numbers

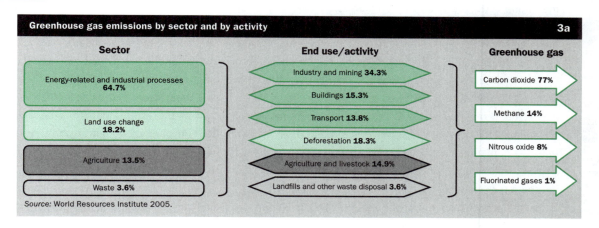

**Greenhouse gas emissions by sector and by activity**     3a

| Sector | End use/activity | Greenhouse gas |
|---|---|---|
| Energy-related and industrial processes **64.7%** | Industry and mining **34.3%** | Carbon dioxide **77%** |
| | Buildings **15.3%** | Methane **14%** |
| Land use change **18.2%** | Transport **13.8%** | Nitrous oxide **8%** |
| | Deforestation **18.3%** | Fluorinated gases **1%** |
| Agriculture **13.5%** | Agriculture and livestock **14.9%** | |
| Waste **3.6%** | Landfills and other waste disposal **3.6%** | |

*Source:* World Resources Institute 2005.

Numbers tell the story. The natural climate has changed, and the change is accelerating as our planet warms. The rate of warming has been nearly twice as fast in the last 50 years as in the last 100 years, with the 13 warmest years since 1880 experienced in the last 15 years. Since 1978 annual mean arctic sea ice has been declining. Temperatures at the top of the permafrost have increased by up to 3 degrees centigrade. Sea levels rose more from 1993 to 2003 than in the previous 30 years. Concentration of atmospheric carbon dioxide, the main cause of global warming, increased one-third faster in the last decade than over the last 50 years (IPCC 2007a).

Climate change poses risks for the environment and for development in most economies, disproportionately affecting those with the lowest capacity to adapt to such impacts. That makes climate change a development issue critical to poverty reduction. It is also an environmental issue vital to sustaining growth and preserving the ecosystem. Countries need measures to mitigate it—and to adapt to its unavoidable outcomes.

Knowledge about climate change has grown greatly in the last few years. The most comprehensive treatment is in the Fourth Assessment Report of the Intergovernmental Panel on Climate Change (IPCC), which presents the findings of hundreds of experts in the field:

- All greenhouse gas concentrations—the main causes of climate change—have increased since the start of the industrial revolution. From 1750 to 2005 carbon dioxide grew from 280 parts per million to 379, methane from 715 parts per billion to 1,774, and nitrous oxide from 270 parts per billion to 319.
- Warming of the climate system is unequivocal—now evident in global averages of air, surface, and ocean temperatures; in widespread melting of snow and ice; and in rising global mean sea level.
- The likely consequences of climate change are uneven across regions, with more profound negative impacts for developing countries and for more vulnerable socioeconomic groups.
- It is very likely (90+ percent confidence) that human activities are causing global warming.
- Changes in technology, management, and behavior can mitigate climate change.
- Even with mitigation, climate change will continue, and adaptation will be needed.

## Why the natural climate has changed

The IPCC's assessment concluded that global greenhouse gas emissions have drastically increased since preindustrial times, with a 70 percent increase between 1970 and 2004. More than 75 percent of these emissions come from carbon dioxide, mainly from burning fossil fuels, manufacturing cement, and cutting forests. Carbon dioxide emissions grew by about 80 percent, accelerating in recent years (a 28 percent increase since 1990).

The other major greenhouse gases are methane and nitrous oxide, mainly from agriculture, energy use, industrial processes, waste, and savannah burning (see figure 3a for a schematic representation of greenhouse gas emissions). Their emissions have grown as well (table 3.9). But emissions of ozone-depleting substances, also greenhouse gases, have declined significantly since the 1990s, controlled under the international treaty known as the Montreal Protocol. By 2005 consumption of these substances was less than 10 percent of their 1990 level (figure 3b).

Global energy intensity declined 33 percent during 1970–2004. But the favorable impact on carbon dioxide emissions has been more than offset by per capita income growth (67 percent) and population growth (73 percent).

Country trends and contributions to climate change vary substantially, with the United States and China contributing most (figure 3c and tables 3.7 and 3.8). The average resident of a rich country produces far more carbon dioxide than does the average resident of a low- and middle-income country. Per capita emissions of carbon dioxide in 2004 averaged 0.9 metric tons in low-income countries, 4.0 metric tons in middle-income countries, and 13.2 metric tons in high-income countries (figure 3d). High-income economies, with 15 percent of the world's people, produced 55 percent of global GDP (in purchasing power parity terms) and emitted nearly half of the global carbon dioxide emissions in 2004 (figure 3e and table 3.8).

Global trends in emissions of greenhouse gas sources also vary substantially. The power sector contributes almost a quarter of global greenhouse gases, and transport, industry, buildings, and other energy-related activities account for another 41 percent (figure 3f). The biggest growth between

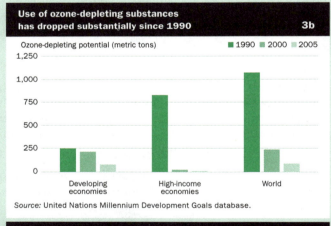

**Use of ozone-depleting substances has dropped substantially since 1990** — 3b

Source: United Nations Millennium Development Goals database.

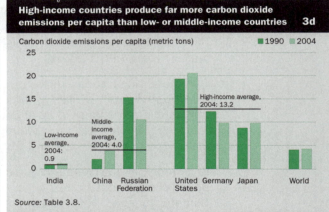

**High-income countries produce far more carbon dioxide emissions per capita than low- or middle-income countries** — 3d

Source: Table 3.8.

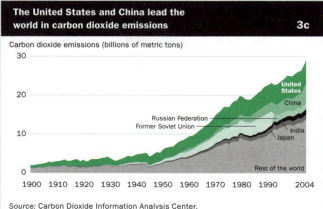

**The United States and China lead the world in carbon dioxide emissions** — 3c

Source: Carbon Dioxide Information Analysis Center.

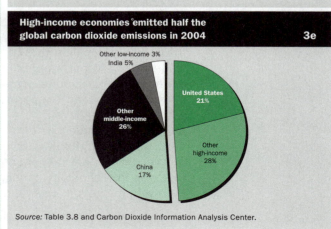

**High-income economies emitted half the global carbon dioxide emissions in 2004** — 3e

Source: Table 3.8 and Carbon Dioxide Information Analysis Center.

1970 and 2004 was from power generation (145 percent) followed by transport (120 percent). Fossil fuels account for three-quarters of the energy used in the power sector, with coal dominant (figure 3g and table 3.10 ). Coal is responsible for the majority of emissions from the power sector (figure 3h). Almost half the electricity and heat produced is used in buildings (residential and commercial), and around one-third in industry (WRI 2006).

North America accounts for by far the largest amount of power sector emissions (3 gigatons of carbon dioxide equivalent), followed by China (1.7 gigatons), European Union (1.6 gigatons), and transition economies (1.4 gigatons). North America also has among the highest emissions per capita (7 tons of carbon dioxide per person), more than twice those of the European Union and six times those of China (WRI 2006).

Transport accounts for 14 percent of global greenhouse gas emissions, behind power and land use change but about the same as agriculture (see figure 3f). Most of these emissions are from road transport (76 percent) and aviation

(12 percent; figure 3i). By far the largest source of transport emissions is North America, producing 37 percent of the global total. This partly reflects the fact that the United States has the highest vehicle ownership in the world (814 vehicles per 1,000 people, compared with 604 in the European Union and 15 in China) and also lags in fuel efficiency, which is about two-thirds that in the European Union (An and Sauer 2004).

Agriculture and deforestation are responsible for one-third of greenhouse gas emissions. In many countries soil degradation, along with the loss of agricultural land through urbanization and population growth, has led to substantial deforestation. The global forested area in 2005 was about 4 billion hectares, covering 30 percent of total land area (table 3.4). But deforestation continues at about 13 million hectares a year. Reforestation reduced the net loss of forest areas to 7.3 million hectares a year during 2000–05, an improvement from losses of 8.9 million hectares a year during 1990–2000. Sub-Saharan Africa and Latin America continued to have the largest forest loss after 1990.

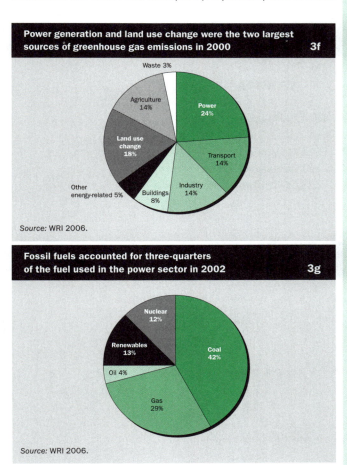

**Power generation and land use change were the two largest sources of greenhouse gas emissions in 2000**     **3f**

Source: WRI 2006.

**Fossil fuels accounted for three-quarters of the fuel used in the power sector in 2002**     **3g**

Source: WRI 2006.

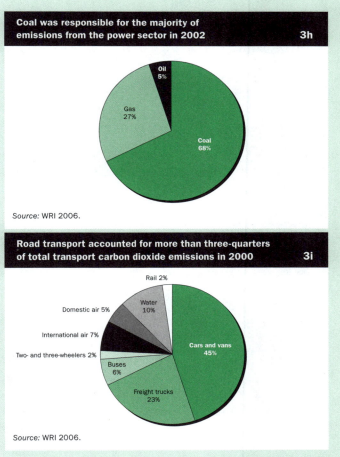

**Coal was responsible for the majority of emissions from the power sector in 2002**     **3h**

Source: WRI 2006.

**Road transport accounted for more than three-quarters of total transport carbon dioxide emissions in 2000**     **3i**

Source: WRI 2006.

# Climate change and vulnerable people and regions

Climate change will have different effects on different regions (depending on geography) and different income groups (depending on livelihoods and adaptive capacity). The effects will also vary by the extent of adaptation, exposure to temperature change, and socioeconomic conditions. Potential impacts could include:

- *Lower agricultural productivity.* Climate change has the potential to drastically affect food production (figure 3j). In parts of Sub-Saharan Africa and South and East Asia losses in agricultural productivity are linked to drought and rainfall variation. Drought has already become more frequent in Sub-Saharan Africa (figure 3k). Because a large share of the world's poor people depend directly on agriculture, drought and other negative effects of climate change put poverty reduction efforts at risk. But global warming could potentially benefit agriculture in some temperate areas—mostly in developed countries.
- *Greater water scarcity.* The rise in global temperature is accelerating (figure 3l). If it exceeds the 2° C threshold (as some scenarios project), the distribution of the world's water resources will change drastically. While water's availability could increase in the moist tropics and in high latitudes, it will decline in the midlatitudes and in semiarid low altitudes, increasing droughts and water shortages. Accelerated glacial melt in the Himalayas will compound severe ecological problems in northern China, India, and Pakistan, increasing floods but reducing water flow to major river systems vital for irrigation. In Latin America accelerated melting of tropical glaciers will threaten water supplies for urban populations, agriculture, and hydroelectricity, especially in the Andean region. Water shortages could contribute to regional conflicts.
- *Heightened health risks.* Climate change will affect human health. Globally, 220–400 million more people could be at increased risk of malaria, particularly in Sub-Saharan Africa, where exposure to malaria is projected to increase 16–28 percent (UNDP 2007b; IPCC 2007b). Climate change could also increase the incidence of malnutrition, diarrhea, and infectious diseases—and change the distribution of disease vectors, adding to the burden on health services.

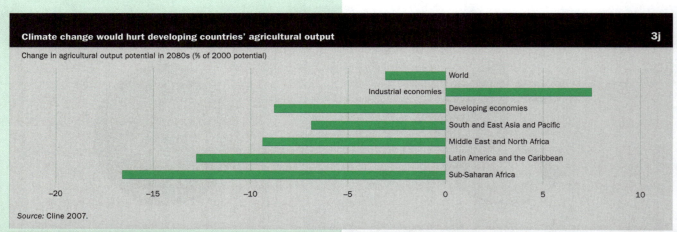

**Climate change would hurt developing countries' agricultural output** 3j

Change in agricultural output potential in 2080s (% of 2000 potential)

*Source:* Cline 2007.

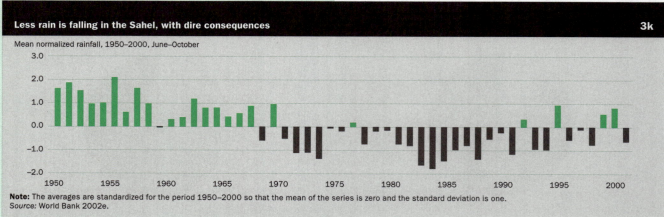

**Less rain is falling in the Sahel, with dire consequences** 3k

Mean normalized rainfall, 1950–2000, June–October

**Note:** The averages are standardized for the period 1950–2000 so that the mean of the series is zero and the standard deviation is one.
*Source:* World Bank 2002e.

- *More exposure to climate disasters.* Climate-related disasters, mainly floods and droughts, have already increased. On average 262 million people a year were affected between 2000 and 2004, more than twice the number in the 1980s (figure 3m), and most of them (98 percent) live in developing countries (figure 3n). Temperature increases greater than 2° C would accelerate the rise in sea level, causing widespread displacement of people in countries such as Bangladesh, Egypt, and Vietnam and the inundation of several small-island economies. Rising sea levels and more intense tropical storm activity could raise the number of people experiencing coastal flooding by 180–230 million (Dasgupta and others 2007; Anthoff and others 2006; UNDP 2007b).

- *Harm to ecosystems.* Coral reef systems, already in decline, would suffer extensive bleaching, transforming marine ecologies, with large losses of biodiversity and ecosystem services. This would adversely affect hundreds of millions of people dependent on fish for their livelihoods and nutrition (UNDP 2007b).

The negative impacts will not occur everywhere (IPCC 2007a). These impacts depend on two main factors: exposure to the effects of climate change and capacity to adapt to them.

Exposure is partly determined by environmental factors. People, flora, and fauna in areas prone to flooding or facing water scarcity have far greater exposure. The level of exposure also depends on the population density or the infrastructure in environmentally sensitive areas. Adaptive capacity is the ability to deal with climate change, such as by building levies to combat flooding or irrigation systems to deal with drought. It is closely associated with a society's wealth, education, institutional strength, and access to technology (Burton, Diringer, and Smith 2006; IPCC 2007e).

High exposure and low adaptive capacity occur mostly in developing countries, making them highly vulnerable to climate change.

Poverty and political instability make the negative impacts of climate change more severe and weaken the ability to adapt.

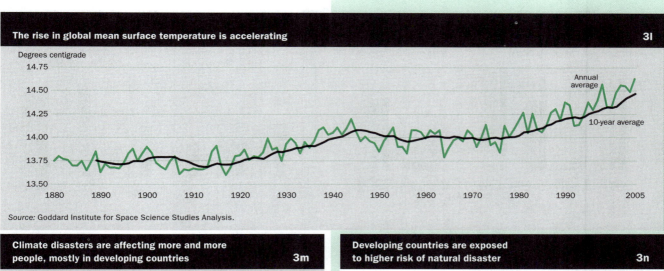

**The rise in global mean surface temperature is accelerating** 3l

Degrees centigrade

Annual average

10-year average

*Source:* Goddard Institute for Space Science Studies Analysis.

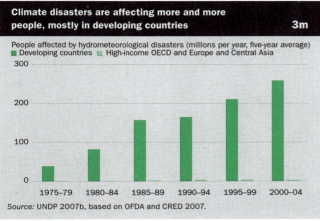

**Climate disasters are affecting more and more people, mostly in developing countries** 3m

People affected by hydrometeorological disasters (millions per year, five-year average)
■ Developing countries ■ High-income OECD and Europe and Central Asia

*Source:* UNDP 2007b, based on OFDA and CRED 2007.

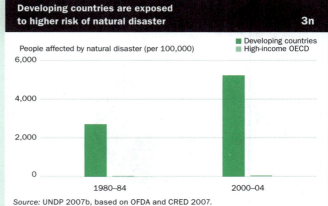

**Developing countries are exposed to higher risk of natural disaster** 3n

People affected by natural disaster (per 100,000)
■ Developing countries
■ High-income OECD

*Source:* UNDP 2007b, based on OFDA and CRED 2007.

## The enormous costs of inaction

The impacts of climate change are costly—so is mitigating the causes of the climate change or adapting to the unavoidable outcomes of change. There is substantial economic and social justification for mitigating global greenhouse gases emissions over the coming decades (IPCC 2007d), offsetting the projected growth of global emissions or even reducing emissions below current levels. The costs of mitigation depend on the level at which emissions stabilize.

But the cost of inaction is significantly higher. The range of estimates is wide, depending on underlying assumptions, on which consensus is lacking. For example, the Stern Review (Stern 2006) estimates that without action the overall costs of climate change will be equivalent to losing at least 5 percent of global GDP each year, now and forever. They would be much higher under a wider range of risks and impacts.

Some steps to reduce carbon dioxide are economically and socially desirable, regardless of their mitigating impact. Conserving energy and promoting new technologies and energy alternatives (such as capturing and storing carbon and shifting to renewable and cleaner sources of energy) would reduce pollution while economizing on exhaustible resources. Preventing deforestation is important because forests protect biodiversity and provide livelihood for millions of poor people (figure 3o). But taking a low carbon path by shifting to alternative energy may be difficult for many developing countries that need to grow but can afford to use only fossil fuels—particularly coal, the "dirtiest" of energy sources.

With some 1.6 billion people lacking electricity (figure 3p; IEA 2006b), cheap and abundant coal is the fuel of choice in much of the world, powering economic booms in most developing economies, notably China and India, that have lifted millions of people out of poverty. Low-income countries use coal to generate 47 percent of their electricity. Coal generates 78 percent of China's electricity and 69 percent of India's (figure 3q). Worldwide, coal demand is projected to rise about 60 percent by 2030, to 6.9 billion metric tons a year, most of it going to electrical plants. So, greater coal efficiency can reduce carbon dioxide emissions (figure 3r).

Burning coal does more than add to global warming—it is also linked to other environmental and health issues,

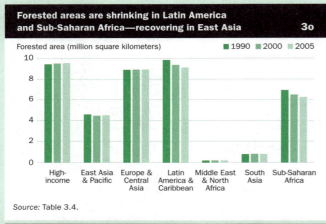

**Forested areas are shrinking in Latin America and Sub-Saharan Africa—recovering in East Asia** 3o

Forested area (million square kilometers)  ■ 1990 ■ 2000 ■ 2005

*Source:* Table 3.4.

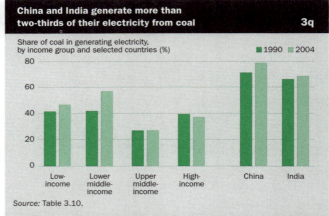

**China and India generate more than two-thirds of their electricity from coal** 3q

Share of coal in generating electricity, by income group and selected countries (%)  ■ 1990 ■ 2004

*Source:* Table 3.10.

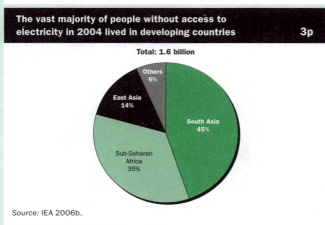

**The vast majority of people without access to electricity in 2004 lived in developing countries** 3p

Total: 1.6 billion

Others 6%
East Asia 14%
South Asia 45%
Sub-Saharan Africa 35%

*Source:* IEA 2006b.

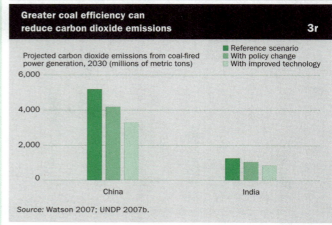

**Greater coal efficiency can reduce carbon dioxide emissions** 3r

Projected carbon dioxide emissions from coal-fired power generation, 2030 (millions of metric tons)
■ Reference scenario
■ With policy change
■ With improved technology

China    India

*Source:* Watson 2007; UNDP 2007b.

including acid rain and asthma. Air pollution prematurely kills more than 2 million people a year. In China the health costs attributable to air pollution are estimated at $68 billion a year, nearly 4 percent of its economic output (World Bank 2007c). And acid rain has contaminated one-third of the country, destroying some $4 billion worth of crops every year. Chinese authorities have closed some polluting factories and by 2010 will retire 50 gigawatts of inefficient power plants (about 8 percent of the power grid; Pew Center on Global Climate Change 2007). The authorities have also mandated that solar, wind, hydroelectric, and other forms of renewable energy provide 10 percent of the nation's power by 2010—and ordered key industries to reduce energy consumption by 20 percent.

There is considerable agreement and much evidence that, even with current mitigation policies, global greenhouse gas emissions will continue to grow over the coming decades (IPCC 2007d). So, countries need to adapt to the unavoidable effects of climate change that are already affecting the well-being of their people, particularly those who are poor, the unintended victims of industrialized economies' past energy consumption.

With poor adaptive capacity, inadequate social protection, and gaps in climate information, developing countries will find it difficult to respond (figures 3s and 3t). Because climate change crosses national borders, a coordinated program of funding and new technologies is required. But the funding needed for adaptation is enormous, and the amount available for climate adaptation in developing countries is still insufficient. In June 2007 pledges totaled less than $220 million, with even smaller amounts allocated and disbursed (figure 3u). The Netherlands has already spent $2.2 billion for flood protection, and Austria has a $1.3 billion project to deal with water scarcity and extreme weather (WRI 2007).

There is still a window of opportunity to act before the economic and human costs become insurmountable (Stern 2006; IPCC 2007c). But action requires measuring and monitoring the state of the environment and human well-being and how they are changing. There are still information gaps, and many of the available data are not up to date. The impacts of carbon dioxide emissions are not well quantified, especially in developing countries. The impacts of extreme climate events are poorly tracked. Local impacts are not widely researched. Few projections on aquatic resources are available. Research on adaptation is still not comprehensive across a range of climate and socioeconomic futures. There is much to be learned about the impacts on biofuel and industrial crops.

Numbers tell the story. But we still lack many of the numbers to tell the whole story.

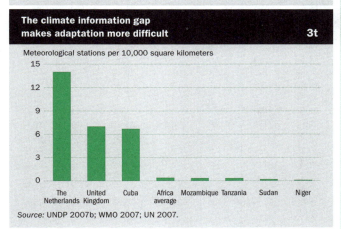

**Social insurance spending is lower in developing countries, where people are exposed to higher risk of climate change impact**   **3s**

Social insurance spending (% of GDP)

*Source:* World Bank 2005d.

**The climate information gap makes adaptation more difficult**   **3t**

Meteorological stations per 10,000 square kilometers

*Source:* UNDP 2007b; WMO 2007; UN 2007.

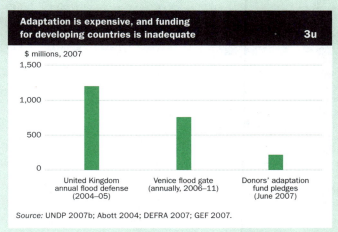

**Adaptation is expensive, and funding for developing countries is inadequate**   **3u**

$ millions, 2007

*Source:* UNDP 2007b; Abott 2004; DEFRA 2007; GEF 2007.

# Rural population and land use

| | Rural population | | | Land area | Land use | | | | | | | |
|---|---|---|---|---|---|---|---|---|---|---|---|---|
| | % of total | | average annual % growth | thousand sq. km | Forest area | | % of land area | | | | Arable land hectares per 100 people | |
| | | | | | | | Permanent cropland | | Arable land | | | |
| | 1990 | 2006 | 1990–2006 | 2006 | 1990 | 2005 | 1990 | 2005 | 1990 | 2005 | 1990–92 | 2003–05 |
| Afghanistan | .. | .. | .. | 652.1 | 2.0 | 1.3 | 0.2 | 0.2 | 12.1 | 12.1 | .. | .. |
| Albania | 63.6 | 53.9 | −1.3 | 27.4 | 28.8 | 29.0 | 4.6 | 4.5 | 21.1 | 21.1 | 18.7 | 18.4 |
| Algeria | 47.9 | 36.1 | 0.0 | 2,381.7 | 0.8 | 1.0 | 0.2 | 0.4 | 3.0 | 3.1 | 24.5 | 23.1 |
| Angola | 62.9 | 46.0 | 0.9 | 1,246.7 | 48.9 | 47.4 | 0.4 | 0.2 | 2.3 | 2.6 | 21.2 | 21.1 |
| Argentina | 13.0 | 9.7 | −0.7 | 2,736.7 | 12.9 | 12.1 | 0.4 | 0.4 | 9.6 | 10.4 | 75.2 | 74.0 |
| Armenia | 32.5 | 36.0 | −0.4 | 28.2 | 12.3 | 10.0 | 2.7 | 2.1 | 17.7 | 17.6 | 16.1c | 16.4 |
| Australia | 14.6 | 11.6 | −0.2 | 7,682.3 | 21.9 | 21.3 | 0.0 | 0.0 | 6.2 | 6.4 | 248.9 | 240.6 |
| Austria | 34.2 | 33.9 | 0.4 | 82.5 | 45.8 | 46.8 | 1.0 | 0.8 | 17.3 | 16.8 | 17.3 | 17.0 |
| Azerbaijan | 46.3 | 48.4 | 1.3 | 82.7 | 11.3 | 11.3 | 3.7 | 2.7 | 20.5 | 22.3 | 22.6 | 22.2 |
| Bangladesh | 80.2 | 74.5 | 1.5 | 130.2 | 6.8 | 6.7 | 2.3 | 3.5 | 70.2 | 61.1 | 5.7 | 5.3 |
| Belarus | 33.6 | 27.3 | −1.6 | 207.5 | 35.6 | 38.0 | 0.9 | 0.6 | 29.3 | 26.3 | 58.4c | 56.2 |
| Belgium | 3.6 | 2.8 | −1.3 | 30.2 | 22.4 | 22.1 | .. | 0.8 | .. | 27.9 | 8.2 | 8.1 |
| Benin | 65.5 | 59.5 | 2.7 | 110.6 | 30.0 | 21.3 | 0.9 | 2.4 | 14.6 | 24.9 | 33.0 | 33.0 |
| Bolivia | 44.4 | 35.3 | 0.7 | 1,084.4 | 57.9 | 54.2 | 0.1 | 0.2 | 1.9 | 2.8 | 34.9 | 33.9 |
| Bosnia and Herzegovina | 60.8 | 53.7 | −1.4 | 51.2 | 43.2 | 42.7 | 2.9 | 1.9 | 16.6 | 19.5 | 26.1c | 25.9 |
| Botswana | 58.1 | 41.8 | −0.1 | 566.7 | 24.2 | 21.1 | 0.0 | 0.0 | 0.7 | 0.7 | 21.5 | 20.8 |
| Brazil | 25.2 | 15.3 | −1.6 | 8,459.4 | 61.5 | 56.5 | 0.8 | 0.9 | 6.0 | 7.0 | 33.1 | 32.0 |
| Bulgaria | 33.6 | 29.7 | −1.5 | 108.6 | 30.1 | 33.4 | 2.7 | 1.9 | 34.9 | 29.2 | 43.4 | 42.0 |
| Burkina Faso | 86.2 | 81.3 | 2.6 | 273.6 | 26.1 | 24.8 | 0.2 | 0.2 | 12.9 | 17.7 | 35.9 | 35.9 |
| Burundi | 93.7 | 89.7 | 2.0 | 25.7 | 11.3 | 5.9 | 14.0 | 14.2 | 36.2 | 37.8 | 14.2 | 13.0 |
| Cambodia | 87.4 | 79.7 | 1.8 | 176.5 | 73.3 | 59.2 | 0.6 | 0.9 | 20.9 | 21.0 | 28.4 | 27.0 |
| Cameroon | 59.3 | 44.5 | 0.7 | 465.4 | 52.7 | 45.6 | 2.6 | 2.6 | 12.8 | 12.8 | 36.7 | 34.2 |
| Canada | 23.4 | 19.8 | 0.0 | 9,093.5 | 34.1 | 34.1 | 0.7 | 0.7 | 5.0 | 5.0 | 147.4 | 142.8 |
| Central African Republic | 63.2 | 61.8 | 2.0 | 623.0 | 37.2 | 36.5 | 0.1 | 0.1 | 3.1 | 3.1 | 49.1 | 46.8 |
| Chad | 79.2 | 74.2 | 3.0 | 1,259.2 | 10.4 | 9.5 | 0.0 | 0.0 | 2.6 | 3.3 | 40.7 | 40.1 |
| Chile | 16.7 | 12.1 | −0.6 | 748.8 | 20.4 | 21.5 | 0.3 | 0.5 | 3.7 | 2.6 | 12.7 | 12.2 |
| China | 72.6 | 58.7 | −0.4 | 9,360.8a | 16.8 | 21.2 | 0.8 | 1.4 | 13.3 | 15.4 | 11.1 | 11.0 |
| Hong Kong, China | 0.5 | 0.0 | .. | 1.0 | .. | .. | .. | .. | .. | .. | .. | .. |
| Colombia | 31.3 | 27.0 | 0.7 | 1,109.5 | 55.4 | 54.7 | 1.5 | 1.5 | 3.0 | 1.8 | 5.9 | 4.9 |
| Congo, Dem. Rep. | 72.2 | 67.3 | 2.5 | 2,267.1 | 62.0 | 58.9 | 0.5 | 0.5 | 2.9 | 3.0 | 12.9 | 11.8 |
| Congo, Rep. | 45.7 | 39.4 | 1.7 | 341.5 | 66.5 | 65.8 | 0.1 | 0.1 | 1.4 | 1.4 | 15.0 | 14.0 |
| Costa Rica | 49.3 | 37.8 | 0.6 | 51.1 | 50.2 | 46.8 | 4.9 | 6.5 | 5.1 | 4.4 | 5.6 | 5.3 |
| Côte d'Ivoire | 60.3 | 54.6 | 1.8 | 318.0 | 32.1 | 32.7 | 11.0 | 11.3 | 7.6 | 11.0 | 18.2 | 18.8 |
| Croatia | 46.0 | 43.2 | −0.8 | 55.9 | 37.8 | 38.2 | 2.0 | 2.1 | 21.7 | 19.8 | 32.7c | 27.6 |
| Cuba | 26.6 | 24.6 | −0.1 | 109.8 | 18.7 | 24.7 | 7.4 | 6.1 | 27.6 | 33.4 | 32.8 | 32.7 |
| Czech Republic | 24.8 | 26.5 | 0.4 | 77.3 | 34.0 | 34.3 | .. | 3.1 | .. | 39.4 | 30.1 | 29.9 |
| Denmark | 15.2 | 14.3 | 0.0 | 42.4 | 10.5 | 11.8 | 0.2 | 0.2 | 60.4 | 52.7 | 42.6 | 41.8 |
| Dominican Republic | 44.8 | 32.5 | −0.3 | 48.4 | 28.4 | 28.4 | 9.3 | 10.3 | 18.6 | 16.9 | 9.2 | 8.8 |
| Ecuador | 44.9 | 36.7 | 0.3 | 276.8 | 49.9 | 39.2 | 4.8 | 4.4 | 5.8 | 4.9 | 12.0 | 10.1 |
| Egypt, Arab Rep. | 56.5 | 57.0 | 1.9 | 995.5 | 0.0 | 0.1 | 0.4 | 0.5 | 2.3 | 3.0 | 4.2 | 4.1 |
| El Salvador | 50.8 | 39.9 | 0.2 | 20.7 | 18.1 | 14.4 | 12.5 | 12.1 | 26.5 | 31.9 | 10.4 | 10.0 |
| Eritrea | 84.2 | 80.2 | 2.2 | 101.0 | 16.0 | 15.4 | .. | 0.0 | .. | 6.3 | 14.6 | 14.0 |
| Estonia | 28.9 | 30.9 | −0.6 | 42.4 | 51.0 | 53.9 | 0.3 | 0.3 | 26.3 | 13.9 | 52.1c | 40.9 |
| Ethiopia | 87.4 | 83.7 | 2.3 | 1,000.0 | 13.7 | 13.0 | 0.6 | 0.8 | 9.8 | 13.1 | 15.1 | 16.7 |
| Finland | 38.6 | 38.8 | 0.4 | 304.6 | 72.9 | 73.9 | 0.0 | 0.0 | 7.4 | 7.3 | 42.2 | 42.5 |
| France | 25.9 | 23.1 | −0.2 | 550.1 | 26.4 | 28.3 | 2.2 | 2.1 | 32.7 | 33.6 | 31.1 | 30.5 |
| Gabon | 30.9 | 15.9 | −1.9 | 257.7 | 85.1 | 84.5 | 0.6 | 0.7 | 1.1 | 1.3 | 27.0 | 25.6 |
| Gambia, The | 61.7 | 45.3 | 1.5 | 10.0 | 44.2 | 47.1 | 0.5 | 0.5 | 18.2 | 35.0 | 21.3 | 21.9 |
| Georgia | 44.8 | 47.7 | −0.9 | 69.5 | 39.7 | 39.7 | 4.8 | 3.8 | 11.4 | 11.5 | 17.1c | 17.8 |
| Germany | 26.6 | 24.7 | −0.2 | 348.8 | 30.8 | 31.8 | 1.3 | 0.6 | 34.3 | 34.1 | 14.3 | 14.4 |
| Ghana | 63.5 | 51.5 | 1.1 | 227.5 | 32.7 | 24.2 | 6.6 | 9.7 | 11.9 | 18.4 | 19.7 | 19.0 |
| Greece | 41.2 | 40.9 | 0.5 | 128.9 | 25.6 | 29.1 | 8.3 | 8.8 | 22.5 | 20.4 | 24.9 | 24.1 |
| Guatemala | 58.9 | 52.3 | 1.6 | 108.4 | 43.8 | 36.3 | 4.5 | 5.6 | 12.0 | 13.3 | 12.2 | 11.6 |
| Guinea | 72.0 | 66.5 | 2.1 | 245.7 | 30.1 | 27.4 | 2.0 | 2.7 | 3.0 | 4.9 | 12.1 | 13.2 |
| Guinea-Bissau | 71.9 | 70.3 | 2.9 | 28.1 | 78.8 | 73.7 | 4.2 | 8.9 | 10.7 | 10.7 | 21.2 | 19.4 |
| Haiti | 70.5 | 60.5 | 0.8 | 27.6 | 4.2 | 3.8 | 11.6 | 11.6 | 28.3 | 28.3 | 8.9 | 8.5 |

| | Rural population | | | Land area | Land use | | | | | | | |
|---|---|---|---|---|---|---|---|---|---|---|---|---|
| | % of total | | average annual % growth | thousand sq. km | Forest area | | Permanent cropland | | Arable land | | Arable land hectares per 100 people | |
| | 1990 | 2006 | 1990–2006 | 2006 | 1990 | 2005 | 1990 | 2005 | 1990 | 2005 | 1990–92 | 2003–05 |
| Honduras | 59.7 | 53.0 | 1.5 | 111.9 | 66.0 | 41.5 | 3.2 | 3.2 | 13.1 | 9.5 | 16.9 | 15.9 |
| Hungary | 34.2 | 33.3 | −0.4 | 89.6 | 20.0 | 22.1 | 2.6 | 2.3 | 56.2 | 51.3 | 45.2 | 45.5 |
| India | 74.5 | 71.0 | 1.4 | 2,973.2 | 21.5 | 22.8 | 2.2 | 3.4 | 54.8 | 53.7 | 15.5 | 14.8 |
| Indonesia | 69.4 | 50.8 | −0.6 | 1,811.6 | 64.3 | 48.8 | 6.5 | 7.5 | 11.2 | 12.7 | 10.3 | 10.6 |
| Iran, Islamic Rep. | 43.7 | 32.6 | −0.3 | 1,628.6 | 6.8 | 6.8 | 0.8 | 1.0 | 9.3 | 10.2 | 24.0 | 24.0 |
| Iraq | 30.3 | .. | .. | 437.4 | 1.8 | 1.9 | 0.7 | 0.6 | 12.1 | 13.1 | 22.0 | .. |
| Ireland | 43.1 | 39.2 | 0.6 | 68.9 | 6.4 | 9.7 | 0.0 | 0.0 | 15.1 | 17.6 | 29.7 | 29.5 |
| Israel | 9.6 | 8.4 | 1.7 | 21.6 | 7.1 | 7.9 | 4.1 | 3.5 | 15.9 | 14.6 | 5.3 | 4.8 |
| Italy | 33.3 | 32.2 | 0.0 | 294.1 | 28.5 | 33.9 | 10.1 | 8.6 | 30.6 | 26.3 | 14.7 | 13.6 |
| Jamaica | 50.6 | 46.6 | 0.2 | 10.8 | 31.9 | 31.3 | 9.2 | 10.2 | 11.0 | 16.1 | 6.7 | 6.6 |
| Japan | 36.9 | 34.0 | −0.3 | 364.5 | 68.4 | 68.2 | 1.3 | 0.9 | 13.1 | 12.0 | 3.5 | 3.4 |
| Jordan | 27.8 | 17.4 | 0.6 | 88.2 | 0.9 | 0.9 | 0.8 | 1.0 | 2.0 | 2.1 | 3.9 | 3.6 |
| Kazakhstan | 43.7 | 42.4 | −0.6 | 2,699.7 | 1.3 | 1.2 | 0.1 | 0.1 | 13.0 | 8.3 | 148.7 | 149.3 |
| Kenya | 81.8 | 79.0 | 2.6 | 569.1 | 6.5 | 6.2 | 0.8 | 0.8 | 8.8 | 9.2 | 15.7 | 15.1 |
| Korea, Dem. Rep. | 41.6 | 38.0 | 0.5 | 120.4 | 68.1 | 51.4 | 1.5 | 1.7 | 19.0 | 23.3 | 11.4 | 11.7 |
| Korea, Rep. | 26.2 | 19.0 | −1.3 | 98.7 | 64.5 | 63.5 | 1.6 | 2.0 | 19.8 | 16.4 | 3.6 | 3.4 |
| Kuwait | 2.0 | 1.7 | 0.2 | 17.8 | 0.2 | 0.2 | 0.1 | 0.2 | 0.2 | 0.8 | 0.6c | 0.6 |
| Kyrgyz Republic | 62.2 | 64.0 | 1.2 | 191.8 | 4.4 | 4.5 | 0.4 | 0.4 | 6.9 | 6.7 | 27.2c | 25.9 |
| Lao PDR | 84.6 | 79.0 | 1.7 | 230.8 | 75.0 | 69.9 | 0.3 | 0.4 | 3.5 | 4.3 | 17.0 | 17.8 |
| Latvia | 30.7 | 32.1 | −0.7 | 62.3 | 44.7 | 47.2 | 0.4 | 0.2 | 27.2 | 17.5 | 41.0c | 44.1 |
| Lebanon | 16.9 | 13.3 | 0.4 | 10.2 | 11.8 | 13.3 | 11.9 | 13.9 | 17.9 | 18.2 | 4.7 | 4.7 |
| Lesotho | 82.8 | 81.0 | 1.2 | 30.4 | 0.2 | 0.3 | 0.1 | 0.1 | 10.4 | 10.9 | 17.3 | 16.8 |
| Liberia | 54.7 | 41.2 | 1.5 | 96.3 | 42.1 | 32.7 | 2.2 | 2.3 | 4.2 | 4.0 | 12.0 | 11.4 |
| Libya | 21.4 | 14.9 | −0.2 | 1,759.5 | 0.1 | 0.1 | 0.2 | 0.2 | 1.0 | 1.0 | 33.3 | 30.6 |
| Lithuania | 32.4 | 33.4 | −0.3 | 62.7 | 31.0 | 33.5 | 0.7 | 0.6 | 46.0 | 30.4 | 58.8c | 49.0 |
| Macedonia, FYR | 42.2 | 30.4 | −1.6 | 25.4 | 35.6 | 35.6 | 2.2 | 1.8 | 23.8 | 22.3 | 27.9c | 27.9 |
| Madagascar | 76.4 | 72.9 | 2.6 | 581.5 | 23.5 | 22.1 | 1.0 | 1.0 | 4.7 | 5.1 | 17.6 | 16.3 |
| Malawi | 88.4 | 82.3 | 1.8 | 94.1 | 41.4 | 36.2 | 1.2 | 1.5 | 19.3 | 27.6 | 18.4 | 19.8 |
| Malaysia | 50.2 | 31.8 | −0.6 | 328.6 | 68.1 | 63.6 | 16.0 | 17.6 | 5.2 | 5.5 | 7.6 | 7.1 |
| Mali | 76.7 | 68.9 | 2.1 | 1,220.2 | 11.5 | 10.3 | 0.0 | 0.0 | 1.7 | 3.9 | 45.3 | 42.6 |
| Mauritania | 60.3 | 59.4 | 2.7 | 1,030.7 | 0.4 | 0.3 | 0.0 | 0.0 | 0.4 | 0.5 | 18.5 | 17.1 |
| Mauritius | 56.1 | 57.5 | 1.2 | 2.0 | 19.2 | 18.2 | 3.0 | 3.0 | 49.3 | 49.3 | 8.3 | 8.1 |
| Mexico | 27.5 | 23.7 | 0.5 | 1,944.0 | 35.5 | 33.0 | 1.0 | 1.3 | 12.5 | 12.9 | 25.4 | 24.6 |
| Moldova | 53.2 | 53.0 | −0.9 | 32.9 | 9.7 | 10.0 | 14.2 | 9.1 | 52.8 | 56.2 | 45.1c | 47.1 |
| Mongolia | 43.0 | 43.1 | 1.3 | 1,566.5 | 7.3 | 6.5 | 0.0 | 0.0 | 0.9 | 0.7 | 49.1 | 46.7 |
| Morocco | 51.6 | 40.7 | 0.0 | 446.3 | 9.6 | 9.8 | 1.6 | 2.1 | 19.5 | 19.0 | 29.7 | 28.4 |
| Mozambique | 78.9 | 64.7 | 1.5 | 786.4 | 25.4 | 24.5 | 0.3 | 0.3 | 4.4 | 5.6 | 21.6 | 21.8 |
| Myanmar | 75.1 | 68.7 | 0.6 | 657.6 | 59.6 | 49.0 | 0.8 | 1.4 | 14.5 | 15.3 | 21.4 | 21.1 |
| Namibia | 72.3 | 64.3 | 1.6 | 823.3 | 10.6 | 9.3 | 0.0 | 0.0 | 0.8 | 1.0 | 42.7 | 40.9 |
| Nepal | 91.1 | 83.7 | 1.8 | 143.0 | 33.7 | 25.4 | 0.5 | 0.9 | 16.0 | 16.5 | 9.4 | 8.9 |
| Netherlands | 31.3 | 19.3 | −2.5 | 33.9 | 10.2 | 10.8 | 0.9 | 1.0 | 25.9 | 26.8 | 5.7 | 5.6 |
| New Zealand | 15.3 | 13.7 | 0.5 | 267.7 | 28.8 | 31.0 | 5.1 | 7.1 | 9.9 | 5.6 | 38.5 | 36.7 |
| Nicaragua | 46.9 | 40.6 | 0.9 | 121.4 | 53.9 | 42.7 | 1.6 | 1.9 | 10.7 | 15.9 | 37.1 | 35.7 |
| Niger | 84.6 | 83.0 | 3.4 | 1,266.7 | 1.5 | 1.0 | 0.0 | 0.0 | 8.7 | 11.4 | 125.7 | 113.1 |
| Nigeria | 65.0 | 51.0 | 1.2 | 910.8 | 18.9 | 12.2 | 2.8 | 3.3 | 32.4 | 35.1 | 22.6 | 22.6 |
| Norway | 28.0 | 22.5 | −0.8 | 304.3 | 30.0 | 30.8 | .. | .. | 2.8 | 2.8 | 19.6 | 19.0 |
| Oman | 34.6 | 28.5 | 0.8 | 309.5 | 0.0 | 0.0 | 0.1 | 0.1 | 0.1 | 0.2 | 1.6 | 2.2 |
| Pakistan | 69.4 | 64.7 | 2.0 | 770.9 | 3.3 | 2.5 | 0.6 | 1.0 | 26.6 | 27.6 | 15.2 | 14.1 |
| Panama | 46.1 | 28.4 | −1.1 | 74.4 | 58.8 | 57.7 | 2.1 | 2.0 | 6.7 | 7.4 | 18.1 | 17.3 |
| Papua New Guinea | 86.9 | 86.5 | 2.5 | 452.9 | 69.6 | 65.0 | 1.3 | 1.4 | 0.4 | 0.5 | 3.8 | 3.9 |
| Paraguay | 51.3 | 40.9 | 0.8 | 397.3 | 53.3 | 46.5 | 0.2 | 0.2 | 5.3 | 10.6 | 61.2 | 70.2 |
| Peru | 31.1 | 27.2 | 0.6 | 1,280.0 | 54.8 | 53.7 | 0.3 | 0.5 | 2.7 | 2.9 | 14.2 | 13.7 |
| Philippines | 51.2 | 36.6 | 0.0 | 298.2 | 35.5 | 24.0 | 14.8 | 16.8 | 18.4 | 19.1 | 7.3 | 6.9 |
| Poland | 38.7 | 37.8 | −0.2 | 306.3 | 29.2 | 30.0 | 1.1 | 1.2 | 47.3 | 39.6 | 35.3 | 32.6 |
| Portugal | 52.1 | 41.8 | −1.0 | 91.5 | 33.9 | 41.3 | 8.5 | 7.1 | 25.6 | 13.8 | 15.4 | 13.3 |
| Puerto Rico | 27.8 | 2.2 | −15.3 | 8.9 | 45.5 | 46.0 | 5.6 | 4.7 | 7.3 | 8.0 | 1.7 | 1.8 |

# 3.1 Rural population and land use

| | Rural population | | | Land area | Land use | | | | | | | |
|---|---|---|---|---|---|---|---|---|---|---|---|---|
| | % of total | | average annual % growth | thousand sq. km | Forest area | | Permanent cropland | | Arable land | | Arable land hectares per 100 people | |
| | | | | | | | % of land area | | | | | |
| | 1990 | 2006 | 1990–2006 | 2006 | 1990 | 2005 | 1990 | 2005 | 1990 | 2005 | 1990–92 | 2003–05 |
| Romania | 45.7 | 46.1 | −0.4 | 230.0 | 27.8 | 27.7 | 2.6 | 2.3 | 41.2 | 40.4 | 42.4 | 43.2 |
| Russian Federation | 26.6 | 27.1 | −0.1 | 16,381.4 | 49.4 | 49.4 | 0.1 | 0.1 | 8.1 | 7.4 | 84.9ᶜ | 84.9 |
| Rwanda | 94.6 | 79.8 | 0.6 | 24.7 | 12.9 | 19.5 | 12.4 | 11.1 | 35.7 | 48.6 | 11.8 | 13.2 |
| Saudi Arabia | 23.4 | 18.8 | 0.9 | 2,000.0ᵇ | 1.4 | 1.4 | 0.0 | 0.1 | 1.7 | 1.8 | 17.0 | 15.7 |
| Senegal | 61.0 | 58.1 | 2.4 | 192.5 | 48.6 | 45.0 | 0.1 | 0.2 | 12.1 | 13.2 | 22.9 | 21.8 |
| Serbiaᵈ | 49.1 | 47.6 | .. | 102.0 | 25.1 | 26.4 | 3.5 | 3.1 | 36.5 | 34.4 | 41.9ᶜ | 42.4 |
| Sierra Leone | 69.9 | 58.6 | 1.0 | 71.6 | 42.5 | 38.5 | 0.8 | 1.1 | 6.8 | 8.4 | 10.8 | 11.0 |
| Singapore | 0.0 | 0.0 | .. | 0.7 | 3.0 | 2.9 | 1.5 | 0.3 | 1.5 | 0.9 | 0.0 | 0.0 |
| Slovak Republic | 43.5 | 43.7 | 0.2 | 48.1 | 40.0 | 40.1 | .. | 0.5 | .. | 28.9 | 27.1 | 26.0 |
| Slovenia | 49.6 | 48.8 | −0.1 | 20.1 | 59.0 | 62.8 | 1.8 | 1.3 | 9.9 | 8.7 | 8.6ᶜ | 8.7 |
| Somalia | 70.3 | 64.3 | 0.9 | 627.3 | 13.2 | 11.4 | 0.0 | 0.0 | 1.6 | 2.2 | 15.1 | 16.5 |
| South Africa | 48.0 | 40.2 | 0.8 | 1,214.5 | 7.6 | 7.6 | 0.7 | 0.8 | 11.1 | 12.1 | 33.0 | 31.8 |
| Spain | 24.6 | 23.2 | 0.4 | 499.2 | 27.0 | 35.9 | 9.7 | 9.9 | 30.7 | 27.4 | 32.2 | 32.0 |
| Sri Lanka | 82.8 | 84.9 | 1.1 | 64.6 | 36.4 | 29.9 | 15.9 | 15.5 | 13.5 | 14.2 | 4.7 | 4.7 |
| Sudan | 73.4 | 58.3 | 0.9 | 2,376.0 | 32.1 | 28.4 | 0.0 | 0.1 | 5.4 | 8.2 | 48.1 | 51.2 |
| Swaziland | 77.1 | 75.6 | 2.3 | 17.2 | 27.4 | 31.5 | 0.7 | 0.8 | 10.5 | 10.3 | 16.7 | 15.9 |
| Sweden | 16.9 | 15.7 | −0.1 | 410.3 | 66.7 | 67.1 | 0.0 | 0.0 | 6.9 | 6.6 | 30.3 | 29.8 |
| Switzerland | 31.6 | 24.4 | −0.9 | 40.0 | 28.9 | 30.5 | 0.5 | 0.6 | 9.8 | 10.3 | 5.7 | 5.5 |
| Syrian Arab Republic | 51.1 | 49.2 | 2.4 | 183.8 | 2.0 | 2.5 | 4.0 | 4.7 | 26.6 | 26.5 | 27.1 | 25.9 |
| Tajikistan | 68.5 | 75.4 | 2.0 | 140.0 | 2.9 | 2.9 | 0.9 | 0.9 | 6.1 | 6.6 | 14.9ᶜ | 14.4 |
| Tanzania | 81.1 | 75.4 | 2.3 | 885.8 | 46.8 | 39.8 | 1.1 | 1.3 | 10.2 | 10.4 | 25.9 | 24.5 |
| Thailand | 70.6 | 67.4 | 0.7 | 510.9 | 31.2 | 28.4 | 6.1 | 7.0 | 34.2 | 27.8 | 25.9 | 22.7 |
| Timor-Leste | 79.2 | 73.1 | 1.5 | 14.9 | 65.0 | 53.7 | 3.9 | 4.6 | 7.4 | 8.2 | 15.2 | 13.2 |
| Togo | 69.9 | 59.2 | 2.0 | 54.4 | 12.6 | 7.1 | 1.7 | 2.6 | 38.6 | 45.8 | 45.1 | 41.2 |
| Trinidad and Tobago | 91.5 | 87.5 | 0.2 | 5.1 | 45.8 | 44.1 | 9.0 | 9.2 | 14.4 | 14.6 | 5.7 | 5.7 |
| Tunisia | 40.4 | 34.3 | 0.3 | 155.4 | 4.1 | 6.8 | 12.5 | 13.9 | 18.7 | 17.6 | 29.0 | 27.9 |
| Turkey | 40.8 | 32.2 | 0.2 | 769.6 | 12.6 | 13.2 | 3.9 | 3.6 | 32.0 | 31.0 | 34.8 | 33.2 |
| Turkmenistan | 54.9 | 53.4 | 1.6 | 469.9 | 8.8 | 8.8 | 0.1 | 0.1 | 2.9 | 4.9 | 40.5ᶜ | 46.9 |
| Uganda | 88.9 | 87.3 | 3.1 | 197.1 | 25.0 | 18.4 | 9.4 | 11.2 | 25.4 | 27.4 | 20.0 | 18.9 |
| Ukraine | 33.2 | 32.0 | −0.9 | 579.4 | 16.0 | 16.5 | 1.9 | 1.6 | 57.6 | 56.0 | 66.9ᶜ | 68.4 |
| United Arab Emirates | 20.9 | 23.3 | 6.1 | 83.6 | 2.9 | 3.7 | 0.2 | 2.3 | 0.4 | 0.8 | 2.0 | 1.6 |
| United Kingdom | 11.3 | 10.2 | −0.3 | 241.9 | 10.8 | 11.8 | 0.3 | 0.2 | 27.4 | 23.7 | 9.7 | 9.6 |
| United States | 24.7 | 18.9 | −0.5 | 9,161.9 | 32.6 | 33.1 | 0.2 | 0.3 | 20.3 | 19.0 | 61.6 | 59.6 |
| Uruguay | 11.0 | 7.9 | −1.7 | 175.0 | 5.2 | 8.6 | 0.3 | 0.2 | 7.2 | 7.8 | 41.5 | 41.5 |
| Uzbekistan | 59.9 | 63.3 | 2.0 | 425.4 | 7.2 | 7.7 | 0.9 | 0.8 | 10.5 | 11.0 | 18.0ᶜ | 18.2 |
| Venezuela, RB | 16.0 | 6.3 | −3.9 | 882.1 | 59.0 | 54.1 | 0.9 | 0.9 | 3.2 | 3.0 | 10.5 | 10.1 |
| Vietnam | 79.7 | 73.1 | 1.0 | 310.1 | 28.8 | 41.7 | 3.2 | 7.6 | 16.4 | 21.3 | 8.2 | 8.0 |
| West Bank and Gaza | 32.1 | 28.3 | 3.3 | 6.0 | 1.5 | 1.5 | 19.1 | 19.1 | 18.4 | 17.8 | 3.4 | 3.0 |
| Yemen, Rep. | 79.1 | 72.3 | 3.0 | 528.0 | 1.0 | 1.0 | 0.2 | 0.3 | 2.9 | 2.9 | 8.1 | 7.4 |
| Zambia | 60.6 | 64.9 | 2.7 | 743.4 | 66.1 | 57.1 | 0.0 | 0.0 | 7.1 | 7.1 | 49.3 | 46.7 |
| Zimbabwe | 71.0 | 63.6 | 0.8 | 386.9 | 57.5 | 45.3 | 0.3 | 0.3 | 7.5 | 8.3 | 25.2 | 24.7 |
| **World** | **57.0 w** | **50.9 w** | **0.6 w** | **129,644.6 w** | **31.5 w** | **30.5 w** | **1.1 w** | **1.1 w** | **10.9 w** | **11.0 w** | **23.0 w** | **22.3 w** |
| **Low income** | 74.6 | 69.6 | 1.6 | 28,147.5 | 26.2 | 23.9 | 1.0 | 1.3 | 13.2 | 14.1 | 17.4 | 16.9 |
| **Middle income** | 55.8 | 45.5 | −0.2 | 68,468.3 | 34.8 | 33.8 | 1.4 | 1.2 | 9.1 | 9.7 | 22.4 | 21.8 |
| Lower middle income | 64.9 | 52.7 | −0.2 | 27,976.6 | 27.0 | 26.5 | 1.6 | 1.9 | 9.4 | 11.4 | 14.5 | 14.2 |
| Upper middle income | 30.6 | 25.0 | −0.3 | 40,491.7 | 40.2 | 38.8 | 1.1 | 0.7 | 8.9 | 8.5 | 44.6 | 43.2 |
| **Low & middle income** | 63.3 | 56.1 | 0.7 | 96,615.8 | 32.2 | 30.9 | 1.2 | 1.2 | 10.6 | 11.0 | 20.3 | 19.7 |
| East Asia & Pacific | 71.2 | 57.6 | −0.2 | 15,871.1 | 28.8 | 28.4 | 2.2 | 2.9 | 12.1 | 13.5 | 11.6 | 11.4 |
| Europe & Central Asia | 37.0 | 36.2 | 0.0 | 23,247.6 | 38.2 | 38.3 | 0.4 | 0.4 | 12.3 | 11.1 | 57.7 | 57.0 |
| Latin America & Carib. | 29.0 | 22.3 | −0.1 | 20,156.5 | 48.8 | 45.4 | 0.9 | 1.0 | 6.5 | 7.2 | 27.5 | 26.7 |
| Middle East & N. Africa | 48.0 | 42.5 | 1.2 | 8,953.2 | 2.2 | 2.4 | 0.8 | 0.9 | 5.6 | 5.9 | 18.1 | 17.5 |
| South Asia | 75.1 | 71.2 | 1.5 | 4,781.3 | 16.5 | 16.8 | 1.8 | 2.6 | 42.6 | 41.9 | 14.5 | 13.8 |
| Sub-Saharan Africa | 72.0 | 64.2 | 1.9 | 23,606.1 | 29.2 | 26.5 | 0.8 | 0.9 | 6.7 | 8.0 | 25.5 | 25.0 |
| **High income** | 26.4 | 22.4 | −0.3 | 33,028.8 | 29.1 | 29.5 | 0.7 | 0.7 | 11.4 | 11.0 | 37.3 | 36.4 |
| Euro area | 29.0 | 26.5 | −0.2 | 2,464.9 | 33.4 | 37.2 | 4.7 | 4.4 | 27.1 | 25.4 | 20.4 | 20.1 |

a. Includes Taiwan, China; Macao, China; and Hong Kong, China. b. Provisional estimate. c. Data for all three years are not available. d. Includes Montenegro.

## About the data

With 3 billion people, including 70 percent of the world's poor people, living in rural areas, adequate indicators to monitor progress in rural areas are essential. However, few indicators are disaggregated between rural and urban areas (for some that are, see tables 2.7, 3.5, and 3.11). The table shows indicators of rural population and land use. Rural population is approximated as the midyear nonurban population. While a practical means of identifying the rural population, it is not precise (see box 3.1a for further discussion).

The data in the table show that land use patterns are changing. They also indicate major differences in resource endowments and uses among countries. True comparability of the data is limited, however, by variations in definitions, statistical methods, and quality of data. Countries use different definitions of rural and urban population and land use. The Food and Agriculture Organization of the United Nations (FAO), the primary compiler of the data, occasionally adjusts its definitions of land use categories and revises earlier data. Because the data reflect changes in reporting procedures as well as actual changes in land use, apparent trends should be interpreted cautiously.

Satellite images show land use that differs from that of ground-based measures in area under cultivation and type of land use. Moreover, land use data in some countries (India is an example) are based on reporting systems designed for collecting tax revenue. With land taxes no longer a major source of government revenue, the quality and coverage of land use data have declined. Data on forest area may be particularly unreliable because of irregular surveys and differences in definitions (see *About the data* for table 3.4). FAO's *Global Forest Resources Assessment 2005* aims to address this limitation. The FAO has been coordinating global forest resources assessments every 5–10 years since 1946. *Global Forest Resources Assessment 2005,* conducted during 2003–05, covers 229 countries and territories at three points: 1990, 2000, and 2005. The most comprehensive assessment of forests, forestry, and the benefits of forest resources in both scope and number of countries and people involved, it examines status and trends for about 40 variables on the extent, condition, uses, and values of forests and other wooded land.

## Definitions

• **Rural population** is calculated as the difference between the total population and the urban population (see *Definitions* for tables 2.1 and 3.11). • **Land area** is a country's total area, excluding area under inland water bodies and national claims to the continental shelf and to exclusive economic zones. In most cases definitions of inland water bodies includes major rivers and lakes. (See table 1.1 for the total surface area of countries.) • **Land use** can be broken into several categories, three of which are presented in the table (not shown are land used as permanent pasture and land under urban developments). • **Forest area** is land under natural or planted stands of trees, whether productive or not. • **Permanent cropland** is land cultivated with crops that occupy the land for long periods and need not be replanted after each harvest, such as cocoa, coffee, and rubber. Land under flowering shrubs, fruit trees, nut trees, and vines is included, but land under trees grown for wood or timber is not. • **Arable land** is land defined by the FAO as under temporary crops (double-cropped areas are counted once), temporary meadows for mowing or for pasture, land under market or kitchen gardens, and land temporarily fallow. Land abandoned as a result of shifting cultivation is excluded.

## What is rural? Urban? | 3.1a

The rural population identified in table 3.1 is approximated as the difference between total population and urban population, calculated using the urban share reported by the United Nations Population Division. There is no universal standard for distinguishing rural from urban areas, and any urban-rural dichotomy is an oversimplification (see *About the data* for table 3.11). The two distinct images—isolated farm, thriving metropolis—represent poles on a continuum. Life changes along a variety of dimensions, moving from the most remote forest outpost through fields and pastures, past tiny hamlets, through small towns with weekly farm markets, into intensively cultivated areas near large towns and small cities, eventually reaching the center of a megacity. Along the way access to infrastructure, social services, and nonfarm employment increase, and with them population density and income. Because rurality has many dimensions, for policy purposes the rural-urban dichotomy presented in tables 3.1 and 3.11 is inadequate.

A recent World Bank Policy Research Paper proposes an operational definition of rurality based on population density and distance to large cities (Chomitz, Buys, and Thomas 2005). The report argues that these criteria are important gradients along which economic behavior and appropriate development interventions vary substantially. Where population densities are low, markets of all kinds are thin, and the unit cost of delivering most social services and many types of infrastructure is high. Where large urban areas are distant, farm-gate or factory-gate prices of outputs will be low and input prices will be high, and it will be difficult to recruit skilled people to public service or private enterprises. Thus, low population density and remoteness together define a set of rural areas that face special development challenges.

Using these criteria and the Gridded Population of the World (CIESIN 2005), the authors' estimates of the rural population for Latin America and the Caribbean differ substantially from those in table 3.1. Their estimates range from 13 percent of the population, based on a population density of less than 20 people per square kilometer, to 64 percent, based on a population density of more than 500 people per square kilometer. Taking remoteness into account, the estimated rural population would be 13–52 percent. The estimate for Latin America and the Caribbean in table 3.1 is 22 percent.

## Data sources

Data on urban population shares used to estimate rural population come from the United Nations Population Division's *World Urbanization Prospects: The 2005 Revision.* The total population figures are World Bank estimates. Data on land area and land use are from the FAO's electronic files. The FAO gathers these data from national agencies through annual questionnaires and by analyzing the results of national agricultural censuses. Data on forest area are from the FAO's *Global Forest Resources Assessment 2005.*

# 3.2 Agricultural inputs

| | Agricultural land[a] | | Irrigated land | | Land under cereal production | | Fertilizer consumption | | Agricultural employment | | Agricultural machinery | |
|---|---|---|---|---|---|---|---|---|---|---|---|---|
| | % of land area | | % of cropland | | thousand hectares | | hundred grams per hectare of arable land | | % of total employment | | Tractors per 100 sq. km of arable land | |
| | 1990–92 | 2003–05 | 1990–92[b] | 2003–05[b,c] | 1990–92 | 2004–06 | 1990–92[b] | 2003–05[b] | 1990–92 | 2003–05 | 1990–92 | 2001–03 |
| Afghanistan | 58.3 | 58.3 | 33.9 | 33.8 | 2,283 | 2,702 | 59 | .. | .. | .. | 1 | 1 |
| Albania | 41.1 | 40.9 | 55.6 | 49.5 | 243 | 145 | 903 | 924 | .. | 58.3 | 177 | 141 |
| Algeria | 16.3 | 17.1 | 6.4 | 6.9 | 3,105 | 2,675 | 144 | 137 | .. | 21.1 | 128 | 129 |
| Angola | 46.1 | 46.2 | 2.3 | 2.3 | 893 | 1,441 | 29 | 29 | .. | .. | 35 | 33 |
| Argentina | 46.6 | 47.2 | 5.6 | 4.7[d] | 8,510 | 9,309 | 73 | 480 | 0.4 | 1.2 | 103 | 107 |
| Armenia | 44.7[d] | 49.3 | 49.9[d] | 51.2 | 163[d] | 171 | 502[d] | 232 | .. | 46.5 | 293 | 289 |
| Australia | 60.5 | 57.5 | 4.2 | 4.9 | 12,814 | 19,004 | 275 | 469 | 5.5 | 3.8 | 67 | 65 |
| Austria | 42.5 | 40.0 | 0.3 | 2.5[d,e] | 903 | 798 | 1,995 | 2,309 | 7.5 | 5.4 | 2,367 | 2,380 |
| Azerbaijan | 53.4[d] | 57.5 | 68.0[d] | 69.1 | 627 | 791 | 440[d] | 134 | 32.5 | 39.6 | 195[d] | 164 |
| Bangladesh | 73.5 | 69.2 | 33.8 | 54.3 | 10,985 | 11,312 | 1,136 | 2,094 | 66.4 | 51.7 | 6 | 7 |
| Belarus | 45.3[d] | 42.7 | 2.1[d] | 2.0 | 2,578[d] | 2,186 | 2,293[d] | 1,886 | 21.7 | .. | 207[d] | 111 |
| Belgium | .. | 46.0 | .. | 4.6 | .. | 320 | .. | .. | 2.8 | 1.9 | .. | 1,146 |
| Benin | 20.6 | 31.9 | 0.6 | 0.4 | 660 | 937 | 78 | 3 | .. | .. | 1 | 1 |
| Bolivia | 32.9 | 34.6 | 5.5 | 4.1 | 633 | 846 | 42 | 62 | 1.7 | .. | 25 | 20 |
| Bosnia and Herzegovina | 43.0[d] | 42.1 | 0.2[d] | 0.3 | 305[d] | 318 | .. | 453 | .. | .. | 235[d] | 289 |
| Botswana | 45.9 | 45.8 | 0.2 | 0.3 | 140 | 75 | 22 | .. | .. | 21.2 | 143 | 159 |
| Brazil | 28.9 | 31.2 | 4.6 | 4.4 | 19,633 | 19,368 | 656 | 1,539 | 25.6 | 20.9 | 142 | 137 |
| Bulgaria | 55.7 | 48.5 | 29.6 | 16.5 | 2,174 | 1,701 | 1,194 | 1,541 | 19.7 | 9.6 | 128 | 95 |
| Burkina Faso | 34.9 | 39.8 | 0.6 | 0.5 | 2,725 | 3,249 | 60 | 75 | .. | .. | 3 | 4 |
| Burundi | 82.9 | 90.9 | 1.2 | 1.6 | 219 | 209 | 34 | 16 | .. | .. | 2 | 2 |
| Cambodia | 25.5 | 29.6 | 6.6 | 7.0 | 1,801 | 2,431 | 19 | 50[c] | .. | .. | 3 | 7 |
| Cameroon | 19.7 | 19.7 | 0.3 | 0.4 | 816 | 1,107 | 34 | 94 | 60.6 | .. | 1 | 1 |
| Canada | 7.5 | 7.4 | 1.4 | 1.5 | 20,864 | 16,772 | 476 | 581 | 4.2 | 2.7 | 162 | 160 |
| Central African Republic | 8.0 | 8.4 | 0.0 | 0.1 | 104 | 177 | 5 | .. | .. | .. | 0 | 0 |
| Chad | 38.4 | 38.9 | 0.5 | 0.8 | 1,242 | 2,264 | 25 | .. | .. | .. | 1 | 0 |
| Chile | 21.0 | 20.4 | 57.1 | 81.1 | 742 | 663 | 1,215 | 2,910 | 18.8 | 13.4 | 144 | 272 |
| China | 57.0 | 59.5 | 36.9 | 35.5 | 93,430 | 81,957 | 2,321 | 3,214 | 53.5 | .. | 64 | 65 |
| Hong Kong, China | .. | .. | .. | .. | .. | .. | .. | .. | 0.8 | 0.3 | .. | .. |
| Colombia | 40.5 | 38.2 | 14.3 | 23.3 | 1,598 | 1,210 | 1,822 | 2,940 | 1.4 | 21.3 | 98 | 91 |
| Congo, Dem. Rep. | 10.1 | 10.1 | 0.1 | 0.1 | 1,868 | 1,964 | 8 | .. | .. | .. | 4 | 4 |
| Congo, Rep. | 30.8 | 30.9 | 0.3 | 0.4 | 9 | 12 | 35 | .. | .. | .. | 15 | 14 |
| Costa Rica | 55.7 | 56.5 | 15.2 | 20.4 | 83 | 62 | 4,522 | 8,528 | 25.2 | 15.0 | 259 | 311 |
| Côte d'Ivoire | 59.8 | 63.4 | 1.1 | 1.1 | 1,434 | 842 | 151 | 203 | .. | .. | 15 | 12 |
| Croatia | 43.0[d] | 50.8 | 0.2[d] | 0.4 | 593[d] | 598 | 1,514[d] | 1,337 | .. | 16.8 | 35[d] | 25 |
| Cuba | 61.5 | 60.0 | 22.6 | 19.5 | 235 | 286 | 1,288 | 156 | 25.1 | 21.5 | 250 | 209 |
| Czech Republic | .. | 55.2 | .. | 0.7 | .. | 1,589 | .. | 1,404 | 10.1 | 4.3 | .. | 305 |
| Denmark | 65.4 | 62.0 | 16.9 | 9.7 | 1,581 | 1,499 | 2,249 | 1,159 | 5.4 | 3.0 | 625 | 540 |
| Dominican Republic | 71.6 | 70.7 | 16.5 | 20.9 | 134 | 156 | 1,003 | .. | 19.5 | 14.4 | 25 | 23 |
| Ecuador | 28.6 | 26.9 | 27.9 | 28.3 | 861 | 881 | 508 | 1,731 | 7.0 | 8.9 | 67 | 106 |
| Egypt, Arab Rep. | 2.7 | 3.5 | 100.0 | 100.0 | 2,410 | 2,918 | 3,977 | 6,707 | 36.2 | 29.9 | 251 | 309 |
| El Salvador | 71.1 | 82.2 | 4.9 | 4.9 | 453 | 335 | 1,336 | 904 | 17.9 | 18.7 | 60 | 52 |
| Eritrea | .. | 75.1 | .. | 3.6 | .. | 371 | .. | 13 | .. | .. | .. | 8 |
| Estonia | 32.4[d] | 19.1 | 0.5[d] | 0.6 | 454 | 274 | 1,011[d] | 4,846 | 19.5 | 5.8 | 419[d] | 889 |
| Ethiopia | 51.0 | 33.0 | 1.4 | 2.6 | 4,586 | 9,126 | .. | 32 | .. | 44.1 | 4 | 3 |
| Finland | 7.9 | 7.4 | 2.8 | 2.9 | 1,050 | 1,154 | 1,647 | 1,286 | 8.8 | 4.9 | 1,040 | 882 |
| France | 55.3 | 53.9 | 11.0 | 13.3 | 9,212 | 9,226 | 2,918 | 2,162 | .. | 4.0 | 784 | 685 |
| Gabon | 20.0 | 20.0 | 1.1 | 1.4 | 14 | 20 | 25 | 38 | .. | .. | 50 | 46 |
| Gambia, The | 63.2 | 80.7 | 0.9 | 0.6 | 90 | 200 | 44 | .. | .. | .. | 2 | 1 |
| Georgia | 46.5[d] | 43.3 | 39.9[d] | 44.1 | 249 | 314 | 906[d] | 319 | .. | 54.4 | 296[d] | 254 |
| Germany | 49.8 | 48.8 | 4.0 | 4.0 | 6,673 | 6,829 | 2,616 | 2,208 | 4.0 | 2.4 | 1,253 | 801 |
| Ghana | 55.7 | 64.8 | 0.7 | 0.5 | 1,078 | 1,377 | 38 | 63 | 62.0 | .. | 15 | 9 |
| Greece | 71.3 | 65.2 | 31.1 | 37.4 | 1,455 | 1,156 | 2,289 | 1,691 | 22.7 | 13.4 | 774 | 939 |
| Guatemala | 39.5 | 42.9 | 6.8 | 6.4 | 768 | 790 | 1,072 | 1,285 | .. | .. | 33 | 30 |
| Guinea | 48.9 | 51.0 | 7.0 | 5.6 | 774 | 1,398 | 16 | 27 | .. | .. | 5 | 5 |
| Guinea-Bissau | 53.2 | 58.0 | 4.1 | 4.6 | 112 | 139 | 15 | .. | .. | .. | 1 | 1 |
| Haiti | 57.9 | 57.7 | 8.0 | 8.4 | 406 | 444 | 35 | .. | .. | .. | 2 | 2 |

| | Agricultural land[a] | | Irrigated land | | Land under cereal production | | Fertilizer consumption | | Agricultural employment | | Agricultural machinery | |
|---|---|---|---|---|---|---|---|---|---|---|---|---|
| | % of land area | | % of cropland | | thousand hectares | | hundred grams per hectare of arable land | | % of total employment | | Tractors per 100 sq. km of arable land | |
| | 1990–92 | 2003–05 | 1990–92[b] | 2003–05[b,c] | 1990–92 | 2004–06 | 1990–92[b] | 2003–05[b] | 1990–92 | 2003–05 | 1990–92 | 2001–03 |
| Honduras | 29.8 | 26.2 | 3.8 | 5.6 | 502 | 354 | 203 | 545 | 42.1 | 37.2 | 31 | 49 |
| Hungary | 70.7 | 65.4 | 4.1 | 2.5 | 2,803 | 2,939 | 796 | 1,197 | 11.3 | 5.3 | 158 | 247 |
| India | 60.9 | 60.6 | 28.3 | 32.7 | 100,760 | 97,347 | 758 | 1,140 | 68.1 | .. | 65 | 141 |
| Indonesia | 23.5 | 26.3 | 14.5 | 12.7 | 13,861 | 15,151 | 1,330 | 1,449 | 54.9 | 44.5 | 18 | 41 |
| Iran, Islamic Rep. | 38.5 | 36.1 | 39.9 | 47.2 | 9,612 | 9,056 | 750 | 571 | 25.6 | 24.9 | 136 | 158 |
| Iraq | 21.9 | 22.9 | 63.0 | 58.6 | 3,506 | 3,509 | 347 | .. | .. | 17.0 | 72 | 80 |
| Ireland | 70.2 | 62.4 | .. | .. | 298 | 287 | 6,591 | 4,529 | 14.1 | 6.3 | 1,667 | 1,324 |
| Israel | 26.7 | 24.4 | 44.4 | 40.9 | 108 | 88 | 2,836 | 20,008 | 3.7 | 2.0 | 763 | 714 |
| Italy | 55.4 | 50.7 | 22.9 | 25.8[d] | 4,347 | 4,025 | 2,195 | 1,817 | 8.4 | 4.6 | 1,619 | 2,031 |
| Jamaica | 44.0 | 47.4 | 11.0 | 8.8 | 3 | 1 | 1,737 | 432 | 27.3 | 19.0 | 242 | 177 |
| Japan | 15.5 | 12.9 | 54.3 | 35.8 | 2,439 | 2,015 | 3,779 | 3,924 | 6.8 | 4.5 | 4,297 | 4,588 |
| Jordan | 12.0 | 11.5 | 25.0 | 27.5 | 112 | 57 | 969 | 7,295 | .. | 3.6 | 352 | 308 |
| Kazakhstan | 82.0[d] | 76.9 | 9.8[d] | 15.7 | 22,152[d] | 14,517 | 136[d] | 68 | .. | 33.7 | 62[d] | 22 |
| Kenya | 47.3 | 47.4 | 1.1 | 1.7 | 1,766 | 2,103 | 209 | 442 | 19.0 | .. | 20 | 25 |
| Korea, Dem. Rep. | 21.0 | 24.9 | 58.2 | 50.9 | 1,569 | 1,282 | 3,522 | .. | .. | .. | 297 | 241 |
| Korea, Rep. | 21.9 | 19.2 | 47.1 | 47.1 | 1,368 | 1,072 | 4,932 | 4,379 | 16.7 | 8.3 | 275 | 1,239 |
| Kuwait | 7.9 | 8.6 | 60.0 | 77.0 | 0 | 1 | 2,000[d] | 15,602[c,e] | .. | 0.0 | 215 | 69 |
| Kyrgyz Republic | 52.6[d] | 56.2 | 72.6[d] | 73.1 | 579[d] | 611 | 242[d] | 152 | 35.5 | 43.4 | 189[d] | 167 |
| Lao PDR | 7.2 | 8.5 | 16.2 | 17.2 | 630 | 770 | 31 | .. | .. | .. | 11 | 12 |
| Latvia | 40.8[d] | 26.5 | 1.1[d] | 2.1 | 699[d] | 475 | 995[d] | 876 | .. | 13.0 | 364[d] | 580 |
| Lebanon | 31.1 | 38.1 | 28.1 | 32.3 | 41 | 64 | 1,639 | 1,619 | .. | .. | 188 | 465 |
| Lesotho | 76.7 | 76.9 | 0.6 | 0.9 | 178 | 182 | 167 | .. | .. | .. | 57 | 61 |
| Liberia | 27.1 | 27.0 | 0.5 | 0.5 | 135 | .. | 8 | .. | .. | .. | 8 | 9 |
| Libya | 8.8 | 8.8 | 21.8 | 21.9 | 355 | 356 | 458 | 506 | .. | .. | 187 | 219 |
| Lithuania | 54.1[d] | 42.5 | 0.5[d] | 0.4 | 1,134[d] | 933 | 541[d] | 1,470 | 18.8 | 15.9 | 256[d] | 641 |
| Macedonia, FYR | 51.4[d] | 48.8 | 12.1[d] | 9.0 | 235[d] | 192 | .. | 200 | .. | 19.4 | 730[d] | 954 |
| Madagascar | 62.5 | 70.2 | 30.7 | 30.6 | 1,321 | 1,486 | 34 | 32 | .. | 78.0 | 11 | 12 |
| Malawi | 40.2 | 48.3 | 1.2 | 2.3 | 1,443 | 1,491 | 351 | 236 | .. | .. | 8 | 6 |
| Malaysia | 22.7 | 24.0 | 4.8 | 4.8 | 699 | 692 | 5,264 | 8,536 | 23.9 | 14.6 | 161 | 241 |
| Mali | 26.3 | 32.4 | 3.7 | 5.0 | 2,393 | 3,206 | 91 | .. | .. | 41.5 | 11 | 6 |
| Mauritania | 38.5 | 38.6 | 11.8 | 9.8 | 133 | 203 | 132 | .. | .. | .. | 8 | 8 |
| Mauritius | 55.7 | 55.7 | 16.0 | 20.1 | 1 | 0 | 2,732 | 2,301 | 14.7 | 10.0 | 36 | 37 |
| Mexico | 53.8 | 55.3 | 22.0 | 22.8 | 10,075 | 9,941 | 686 | 733 | 24.7 | 15.9 | 128 | 129 |
| Moldova | 77.9[d] | 76.7 | 14.2[d] | 11.5 | 676[d] | 969 | 776[d] | 122 | .. | 41.4 | 310[d] | 221 |
| Mongolia | 79.9 | 83.3 | 5.8 | 7.0 | 620 | 153 | 111 | 38 | .. | 40.6 | 73 | 42 |
| Morocco | 68.2 | 68.1 | 13.2 | 15.5 | 5,374 | 5,584 | 353 | 570 | .. | 45.0 | 46 | 58 |
| Mozambique | 60.7 | 61.8 | 2.8 | 2.7 | 1,509 | 2,046 | 12 | 51 | .. | .. | 16 | 14 |
| Myanmar | 15.8 | 17.1 | 10.1 | 17.9 | 5,283 | 7,670 | 79 | 11 | 69.4 | .. | 12 | 10 |
| Namibia | 47.0 | 47.2 | 0.7 | 1.0 | 215 | 290 | .. | 22 | 48.2 | .. | 47 | 39 |
| Nepal | 29.0 | 29.5 | 43.0 | 47.0 | 2,957 | 3,352 | 340 | 124 | 81.9 | .. | 23 | 24 |
| Netherlands | 58.9 | 56.8 | 61.0 | 60.0 | 185 | 215 | 6,298 | 5,839 | 4.3 | 2.9 | 2,056 | 1,645 |
| New Zealand | 65.0 | 64.5 | 7.6 | 11.4[d] | 153 | 114 | 1,911 | 6,741 | 10.7 | 7.6 | 324 | 507 |
| Nicaragua | 33.5 | 43.5 | 4.0 | 2.8 | 299 | 484 | 270 | 317 | 38.7 | 29.0 | 20 | 15 |
| Niger | 27.0 | 30.4 | 0.5 | 0.5 | 7,011 | 7,666 | 1 | 4 | .. | .. | 0 | 0 |
| Nigeria | 79.4 | 80.4 | 0.7 | 0.8 | 16,417 | 18,399 | 142 | 64 | .. | .. | 8 | 10 |
| Norway | 3.3 | 3.4 | .. | .. | 361 | 324 | 2,362 | 1,886 | 5.9 | 3.5 | 1,723 | 1,486 |
| Oman | 3.5 | 5.1 | 71.6 | 88.4 | 4 | 5 | 2,441 | 3,424 | .. | .. | 42 | 50 |
| Pakistan | 33.7 | 35.2 | 78.5 | 84.2 | 11,777 | 12,714 | 962 | 1,621[c,e] | 48.9 | 42.7 | 133 | 149 |
| Panama | 28.7 | 30.0 | 4.8 | 6.2 | 182 | 188 | 666 | 421 | 25.8 | 16.4 | 103 | 148 |
| Papua New Guinea | 2.0 | 2.3 | .. | .. | 2 | 3 | 622 | 1,806 | .. | .. | 59 | 53 |
| Paraguay | 56.0 | 60.7 | 2.9 | 1.8 | 455 | 791 | 92 | 581 | 1.7 | 31.5 | 72 | 46 |
| Peru | 17.1 | 16.6 | 29.9 | 27.9 | 683 | 1,110 | 246 | 854 | 1.0 | 0.7 | 36 | 36 |
| Philippines | 37.4 | 40.9 | 15.7 | 14.5 | 6,957 | 6,632 | 935 | 1,579 | 45.3 | 37.1 | 20 | 20 |
| Poland | 61.6 | 52.8 | 0.7 | 0.6[d,e] | 8,523 | 8,362 | 895 | 1,297 | 25.2 | 17.9 | 821 | 1,034 |
| Portugal | 42.8 | 41.2 | 20.5 | 23.8[d] | 780 | 403 | 1,123 | 1,884 | 15.6 | 12.1 | 569 | 1,100 |
| Puerto Rico | 47.5 | 25.1 | 36.8 | 15.7[d] | 0 | 0 | .. | .. | 3.5 | 2.1 | 478 | 449 |

# 3.2 | Agricultural inputs

| | Agricultural land[a] (% of land area) | | Irrigated land (% of cropland) | | Land under cereal production (thousand hectares) | | Fertilizer consumption (hundred grams per hectare of arable land) | | Agricultural employment (% of total employment) | | Agricultural machinery (Tractors per 100 sq. km of arable land) | |
|---|---|---|---|---|---|---|---|---|---|---|---|---|
| | 1990–92 | 2003–05 | 1990–92[b] | 2003–05[b,c] | 1990–92 | 2004–06 | 1990–92[b] | 2003–05[b] | 1990–92 | 2003–05 | 1990–92 | 2001–03 |
| Romania | 64.4 | 63.8 | 31.0 | 3.2 | 5,842 | 5,663 | 788 | 429 | 30.6 | 33.1 | 146 | 179 |
| Russian Federation | 13.5[d] | 13.2 | 4.2[d] | 3.6 | 59,541[d] | 40,742 | 417 | 137 | .. | 10.4 | 98[d] | 52 |
| Rwanda | 75.6 | 78.6 | 0.3 | 0.7 | 258 | 336 | 20 | .. | .. | .. | 1 | 1 |
| Saudi Arabia | .. | .. | 44.2 | 42.7 | 1,062 | 666 | 1,446 | 1,060 | .. | .. | 20 | 28 |
| Senegal | 41.9 | 42.6 | 3.3 | 4.6 | 1,154 | 1,133 | 65 | 221 | .. | .. | 2 | 3 |
| Serbia | .. | .. | .. | .. | .. | 1,856[d] | .. | .. | .. | .. | .. | .. |
| Sierra Leone | 38.3 | 40.0 | 5.2 | 5.0 | 452 | 576 | 23 | .. | .. | .. | 3 | 2 |
| Singapore | 2.2 | 1.2 | .. | .. | .. | .. | 54,333 | 160,533 | 0.3 | 0.2 | 637 | 794 |
| Slovak Republic | .. | 42.3 | .. | 3.8 | 1[d] | 782 | .. | 965 | .. | 5.2 | .. | 159 |
| Slovenia | 28.0[d] | 25.0 | 0.8[d] | 1.2 | 112[d] | 97 | 3,168 | 3,835 | .. | 8.9 | .. | .. |
| Somalia | 70.2 | 70.7 | 19.2 | 16.9 | 531 | 704 | 26[d] | .. | .. | .. | 21 | 15 |
| South Africa | 80.2 | 82.0 | 8.3 | 9.5 | 5,736 | 3,875 | 549 | 521 | .. | 10.3 | 101 | 46 |
| Spain | 60.8 | 58.3 | 16.9 | 20.6 | 7,588 | 6,485 | 1,186 | 1,472 | 10.7 | 5.5 | 494 | 712 |
| Sri Lanka | 36.2 | 36.5 | 28.0 | 34.4 | 834 | 879 | 2,016 | 2,873 | 44.3 | 33.9 | 71 | 113 |
| Sudan | 51.9 | 57.2 | 14.1 | 10.9 | 6,267 | 7,883 | 51 | 36 | .. | .. | 8 | 7 |
| Swaziland | 75.8 | 80.9 | 24.1 | 26.0 | 69 | 54 | 688 | .. | .. | .. | 251 | 222 |
| Sweden | 8.2 | 7.8 | 4.1 | 4.3 | 1,184 | 1,040 | 1,112 | 1,051 | 3.3 | 2.1 | 604 | 615 |
| Switzerland | 46.9 | 38.1 | 6.0 | 5.8 | 207 | 164 | 4,032 | 2,100 | 4.2 | 4.0 | 2,870 | 2,649 |
| Syrian Arab Republic | 73.7 | 75.6 | 14.3 | 24.0 | 3,812 | 3,214 | 621 | 857 | 28.2 | 27.0 | 137 | 224 |
| Tajikistan | 32.1[d] | 30.4 | 72.9[d] | 68.2 | 266[d] | 392 | 1,488[d] | .. | 57.9 | .. | 415[d] | 233 |
| Tanzania | 38.4 | 38.8 | 1.4 | 1.8 | 3,003 | 3,519 | 53 | 70 | 84.2 | .. | 7 | 8 |
| Thailand | 41.9 | 36.3 | 21.0 | 26.6 | 10,594 | 11,252 | 598 | 1,411 | 61.7 | 43.3 | 39 | 144 |
| Timor-Leste | 21.9 | 22.9 | .. | .. | 84 | 115 | .. | .. | .. | .. | 10 | 9 |
| Togo | 58.7 | 66.7 | 0.3 | 0.3 | 610 | 729 | 56 | 61 | .. | .. | 0 | 0 |
| Trinidad and Tobago | 25.7 | 25.9 | 3.3 | 3.3 | 6 | 2 | 1,111 | 6,764 | 11.8 | 4.9 | 354 | 360 |
| Tunisia | 58.4 | 63.0 | 7.3 | 7.2 | 1,525 | 1,457 | 330 | 461 | .. | .. | 88 | 126 |
| Turkey | 51.8 | 53.3 | 14.8 | 19.7 | 13,760 | 13,929 | 757 | 836 | 46.5 | 32.5 | 287 | 410 |
| Turkmenistan | 68.6[d] | 70.2 | 106.1[d] | 89.2 | 331[d] | 1,013 | 1,296[d] | .. | .. | .. | 465[d] | 256 |
| Uganda | 61.0 | 63.9 | 0.1 | 0.1 | 1,098 | 1,611 | 1 | 15 | 91.5 | 69.1 | 9 | 9 |
| Ukraine | 72.4[d] | 71.4 | 7.6[d] | 6.8 | 12,542[d] | 14,144 | 807[d] | 157 | 20.0 | 19.8 | 153[d] | 124 |
| United Arab Emirates | 3.7 | 6.7 | 106.7 | 29.2 | 1 | 0 | 4,810 | 5,531 | .. | .. | 50 | 55 |
| United Kingdom | 75.0 | 70.2 | 2.5 | 3.0 | 3,549 | 2,970 | 3,323 | 3,020 | 2.2 | 1.3 | 762 | 878 |
| United States | 46.6 | 45.3 | 11.3 | 12.5 | 64,547 | 56,333 | 1,015 | 1,153 | 2.9 | 1.6 | 245 | 270 |
| Uruguay | 84.7 | 85.4 | 10.2 | 14.3 | 509 | 557 | 610 | 1,257 | 1.5 | 4.6 | 259 | 241 |
| Uzbekistan | 65.2[d] | 65.6 | 87.3[d] | 87.4 | 1,225[d] | 1,632 | 1,632 | .. | .. | .. | 402[d] | 373 |
| Venezuela, RB | 24.7 | 24.6 | 13.9 | 16.9 | 799 | 1,119 | 1,388 | 1,747 | 12.6 | 10.7 | 176 | 189 |
| Vietnam | 21.0 | 30.8 | 44.6 | 33.9 | 6,730 | 8,393 | 1,299 | 3,309 | 73.8 | 58.8 | 60 | 247 |
| West Bank and Gaza | 62.5 | 61.8 | .. | 6.9 | 31 | 33 | .. | .. | .. | 15.8 | 441 | 710 |
| Yemen, Rep. | 33.4 | 33.6 | 24.3 | 31.4 | 738 | 710 | 127 | 25 | 52.6 | .. | 40 | 43 |
| Zambia | 31.4 | 34.4 | 0.7 | 2.8 | 813 | 647 | 131 | .. | .. | .. | 11 | 11 |
| Zimbabwe | 34.1 | 39.9 | 3.6 | 5.2 | 1,431 | 1,606 | 508 | 316 | .. | .. | 61 | 75 |
| **World** | **38.6 w** | **37.5 w** | **17.4 w** | **18.1 w** | **632,022 s** | **677,485 s** | **958 w** | **1,145 w** | **42.5 w** | **.. w** | **189 w** | **191 w** |
| **Low income** | 43.3 | 45.0 | 21.5 | 24.0 | 209,966 | 229,649 | 522 | .. | 66.5 | .. | 46 | 82 |
| **Middle income** | 37.3 | 35.3 | 19.4 | 18.2 | 279,067 | 312,815 | 1,096 | 1,289 | 45.9 | .. | 125 | 123 |
| Lower middle income | 40.5 | 42.4 | 27.1 | 26.3 | 170,383 | 175,242 | 1,502 | 1,949 | 49.5 | .. | 75 | 90 |
| Upper middle income | 34.5 | 30.5 | 8.5 | 9.0 | 108,684 | 137,573 | 644 | 694 | .. | 17.1 | 187 | 153 |
| **Low & middle income** | 39.3 | 38.2 | 20.2 | 20.4 | 489,033 | 542,464 | 851 | 1,104 | 51.9 | .. | 91 | 108 |
| East Asia & Pacific | 48.3 | 50.7 | .. | .. | 142,273 | 136,511 | .. | .. | 54.3 | .. | 56 | 72 |
| Europe & Central Asia | 47.8 | 28.4 | 10.5 | 10.9 | 67,977 | 114,139 | 782 | 371 | .. | 20.0 | 175 | 171 |
| Latin America & Carib. | 34.4 | 35.7 | 11.3 | 12.5 | 47,713 | 49,115 | 586 | 1,091 | 17.4 | 16.5 | 123 | 122 |
| Middle East & N. Africa | 22.8 | 22.9 | 29.6 | 33.8 | 30,625 | 29,638 | 643 | 928 | .. | .. | 116 | 143 |
| South Asia | 54.7 | 54.7 | 33.9 | 39.2 | 129,690 | 128,361 | 767 | 1,220 | 66.1 | .. | 67 | 129 |
| Sub-Saharan Africa | 42.5 | 43.8 | 3.3 | 3.5 | 70,755 | 84,700 | 130 | .. | .. | .. | 17 | 13 |
| **High income** | 36.9 | 35.5 | 10.9 | .. | 142,990 | 135,021 | 1,206 | 1,260 | 5.8 | 3.4 | 415 | 434 |
| Euro area | 49.9 | 47.4 | 14.9 | 16.8 | 32,589 | 31,089 | 2,303 | 2,027 | 7.3 | 4.5 | 986 | 1,003 |

a. Includes permanent pastures, arable land, and land under permanent crops. b. Time series have been revised but are available only from 2001 onward; data for earlier years are from the Food and Agriculture Organization's previous release of time series data. c. The averages in italics are for years other than those specified. d. Data for all three years are not available. e. The average is not for consecutive years.

## About the data

Agriculture is still a major sector in many economies, and agricultural activities provide developing countries with food and revenue. But agricultural activities also can degrade natural resources. Poor farming practices can cause soil erosion and loss of soil fertility. Efforts to increase productivity through the use of chemical fertilizers, pesticides, and intensive irrigation have environmental costs and health impacts. Excessive use of chemical fertilizers can alter the chemistry of soil. Pesticide poisoning is common in developing countries. And salinization of irrigated land diminishes soil fertility. Thus inappropriate use of inputs for agricultural production has far-reaching effects.

The table provides indicators of major inputs to agricultural production: land, fertilizer, labor, and machinery. There is no single correct mix of inputs: appropriate levels and application rates vary by country and over time and depend on the type of crops, the climate and soils, and the production process used.

The data shown here and in table 3.3 are collected by the Food and Agriculture Organization of the United Nations (FAO) through annual questionnaires. The FAO tries to impose standard definitions and reporting methods, but complete consistency across countries and over time is not possible. For example, despite standard definitions, data on agricultural land in different climates may not be comparable. For example, permanent pastures are quite different in nature and intensity in African countries and dry Middle Eastern countries. Data on agricultural employment, in particular, should be used with caution. In many countries much agricultural employment is informal and unrecorded, including substantial work performed by women and children.

Fertilizer consumption measures the quantity of plant nutrients. Consumption is calculated as production plus imports minus exports. Because some chemical compounds used for fertilizers have other industrial applications, the consumption data may overstate the quantity available for crops. The FAO recently revised the time series for fertilizer consumption and irrigation but only for 2001 onward. The data for earlier years are from the FAO's previous releases and are not necessarily comparable with later data. Caution should thus be exercised when comparing data over time.

To smooth annual fluctuations in agricultural activity, the indicators in the table have been averaged over three years.

Total land area in 2005: 130 million sq. km

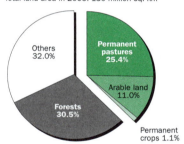

Others 32.0%
Permanent pastures 25.4%
Arable land 11.0%
Forests 30.5%
Permanent crops 1.1%

**Note:** Agricultural land includes permanent pastures, arable land, and land under permanent crops.
*Source:* Tables 3.1 and 3.2.

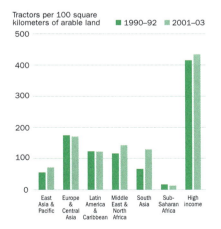

Tractors per 100 square kilometers of arable land ■ 1990–92 ■ 2001–03

| | |
|---|---|
| 500 | |
| 400 | |
| 300 | |
| 200 | |
| 100 | |
| 0 | |

East Asia & Pacific | Europe & Central Asia | Latin America & Caribbean | Middle East & North Africa | South Asia | Sub-Saharan Africa | High income

*Source:* Table 3.2.

| | Crop production index | | Food production index | | Livestock production index | | Cereal yield | | Agricultural productivity | |
|---|---|---|---|---|---|---|---|---|---|---|
| | | | | | | | | | Agriculture value added per worker 2000 $ | |
| | | | | | | | kilograms per hectare | | | |
| | 1999–2001 = 100 | | 1999–2001 = 100 | | 1999–2001 = 100 | | | | | |
| | **1990–92** | **2002–04** | **1990–92** | **2004–06ᵃ** | **1990–92** | **2002–04** | **1990–92** | **2004–06** | **1990–92** | **2003–05** |
| Afghanistan | .. | .. | .. | .. | .. | .. | 1,153 | 1,571 | .. | .. |
| Albania | 86.2 | 100.6 | 74.2 | 105.1 | 66.6 | 108.9 | 2,372 | 3,492 | 778 | 1,449 |
| Algeria | 85.4 | 122.9 | 81.7 | 116.8 | 80.7 | 103.3 | 915 | 1,449 | 1,911 | 2,225 |
| Angola | 60.5 | 119.4 | 65.0 | 112.9 | 75.6 | 100.0 | 378 | 522 | 165 | 174 |
| Argentina | 67.2 | 106.4 | 73.6 | 102.0 | 89.2 | 92.0 | 2,652 | 3,857 | 6,767 | 10,072 |
| Armenia | 106.5 | 119.2 | 112.9 | 140.6 | 118.9 | 123.2 | 1,843ᵇ | 2,036 | 1,476 | 3,692 |
| Australia | 59.7 | 81.6 | 69.2 | 91.9 | 83.3 | 96.9 | 1,739 | 1,560 | 22,523 | 34,880 |
| Austria | 93.4 | 99.1 | 89.8 | 102.2 | 92.5 | 99.6 | 5,400 | 6,128 | 12,048 | 22,203 |
| Azerbaijan | 137.4 | 122.7 | 104.8 | 121.1 | 98.2 | 113.6 | 2,112ᵇ | 2,594 | 1,084 | 1,143 |
| Bangladesh | 75.4 | 104.7 | 73.8 | 104.6 | 73.8 | 103.2 | 2,567 | 3,648 | 254 | 338 |
| Belarus | 107.3 | 124.7 | 136.1ᵇ | 116.0 | 146.5 | 99.7 | 2,739ᵇ | 2,801 | 1,977ᵇ | 3,153 |
| Belgium | 77.6 | 106.0 | 91.3 | 101.0 | 94.3 | 99.7 | .. | 8,680 | 21,479 | 41,631 |
| Benin | 57.7 | 125.4 | 62.7 | 137.4 | 89.1 | 109.2 | 880 | 1,136 | 326 | 519 |
| Bolivia | 63.6 | 116.4 | 70.0 | 110.3 | 77.2 | 107.9 | 1,385 | 1,865 | 670 | 773 |
| Bosnia and Herzegovina | 107.2 | 101.1 | 120.3ᵇ | 98.0 | 122.7ᵇ | 86.6 | 3,548ᵇ | 4,326 | .. | 8,270 |
| Botswana | 96.2 | 111.5 | 114.8 | 104.3 | 118.8 | 103.4 | 312 | 363 | 536 | 390 |
| Brazil | 77.2 | 119.6 | 70.4 | 124.3 | 65.5 | 116.8 | 1,916 | 3,076 | 1,506 | 3,126 |
| Bulgaria | 149.2 | 110.9 | 137.5 | 107.7 | 147.1 | 96.2 | 3,639 | 3,679 | 2,500 | 7,159 |
| Burkina Faso | 67.0 | 126.6 | 68.7 | 115.2 | 70.7 | 108.1 | 783 | 1,065 | 110 | 173 |
| Burundi | 112.4 | 107.0 | 112.1 | 104.4 | 135.1 | 100.2 | 1,370 | 1,328 | 108 | 70 |
| Cambodia | 65.2 | 105.8 | 65.1 | 105.4 | 65.7 | 103.5 | 1,356 | 2,356 | .. | 306 |
| Cameroon | 71.2 | 103.0 | 73.9 | 104.7 | 84.1 | 103.1 | 1,166 | 1,459 | 389 | 652 |
| Canada | 87.9 | 93.8 | 84.1 | 101.6 | 78.3 | 103.6 | 2,559 | 3,114 | 28,243 | 43,055 |
| Central African Republic | 74.4 | 97.7 | 69.9 | 108.2 | 68.1 | 113.5 | 884 | 1,033 | 287 | 381 |
| Chad | 69.0 | 110.9 | 72.5 | 112.2 | 84.5 | 105.4 | 636 | 727 | 173 | 215 |
| Chile | 78.2 | 110.5 | 74.0 | 112.8 | 68.0 | 107.0 | 3,949 | 5,822 | 3,600 | 5,308 |
| China | 69.6 | 110.6 | 60.1 | 117.8 | 49.4 | 116.1 | 4,307 | 5,237 | 254 | 401 |
| Hong Kong, China | .. | .. | .. | .. | .. | .. | .. | .. | .. | .. |
| Colombia | 98.4 | 107.4 | 83.9 | 109.7 | 80.6 | 107.1 | 2,492 | 3,725 | 3,405 | 2,847 |
| Congo, Dem. Rep. | 124.7 | 97.2 | 121.4 | 97.5 | 100.8 | 99.2 | 794 | 776 | 184 | 149 |
| Congo, Rep. | 80.2 | 105.1 | 79.0 | 108.8 | 76.0 | 114.5 | 688 | 794 | .. | .. |
| Costa Rica | 71.4 | 99.6 | 72.2 | 99.4 | 79.9 | 101.4 | 3,188 | 3,135 | 3,143 | 4,499 |
| Côte d'Ivoire | 73.0 | 96.2 | 72.9 | 101.2 | 74.9 | 110.9 | 869 | 1,708 | 598 | 795 |
| Croatia | 79.9 | 97.2 | 99.0 | 96.7 | 126.6ᵇ | 108.2 | 3,975ᵇ | 5,233 | 4,921ᵇ | 9,987 |
| Cuba | 112.1 | 112.6 | 111.5 | 109.6 | 130.0 | 92.7 | 2,092 | 2,755 | .. | .. |
| Czech Republic | .. | 94.8 | .. | 104.6 | .. | 95.8 | .. | 4,785 | .. | 5,423 |
| Denmark | 103.5 | 97.7 | 97.6 | 101.4 | 89.0 | 102.8 | 5,448 | 5,976 | 15,190 | 40,780 |
| Dominican Republic | 119.1 | 110.0 | 104.0 | 102.6 | 79.5 | 103.7 | 4,078 | 4,262 | 2,268 | 4,586 |
| Ecuador | 80.1 | 95.9 | 72.4 | 107.2 | 65.1 | 115.3 | 1,724 | 2,779 | 1,686 | 1,676 |
| Egypt, Arab Rep. | 69.2 | 104.2 | 67.5 | 110.9 | 65.4 | 115.3 | 5,738 | 7,536 | 1,528 | 2,072 |
| El Salvador | 102.2 | 90.6 | 86.4 | 104.8 | 74.5 | 108.5 | 1,871 | 2,639 | 1,633 | 1,638 |
| Eritrea | .. | 67.7 | .. | 86.3ᵇ | .. | 97.1 | .. | 343 | .. | 61 |
| Estonia | 121.4 | 89.9 | 181.3ᵇ | 102.1 | 193.3 | 101.7 | 1,304ᵇ | 2,412 | 2,747 | 3,235 |
| Ethiopia | .. | 106.7 | .. | 112.1 | .. | 117.7 | 1,234 | 1,374 | 135 | 145 |
| Finland | 97.5 | 102.4 | 104.0 | 103.6 | 106.5 | 104.3 | 3,246 | 3,309 | 18,822 | 31,214 |
| France | 94.0 | 98.8 | 97.4 | 101.6 | 97.3 | 100.4 | 6,370 | 7,099 | 22,234 | 44,017 |
| Gabon | 87.2 | 101.9 | 89.1 | 101.7 | 86.5 | 100.5 | 1,712 | 1,574 | 1,176 | 1,592 |
| Gambia, The | 55.8 | 65.2 | 60.2 | 69.0 | 98.8 | 102.6 | 1,114 | 1,145 | 224 | 233 |
| Georgia | 120.6 | 91.9 | 102.7 | 100.8 | 78.9 | 110.3 | 1,998ᵇ | 1,858 | 2,443ᵇ | 1,790 |
| Germany | 83.7 | 95.1 | 98.0 | 102.9 | 107.5 | 101.0 | 5,578 | 6,855 | 13,724 | 26,549 |
| Ghana | 59.1 | 117.0 | 61.1 | 121.0 | 89.8 | 108.7 | 1,084 | 1,380 | 293 | 320 |
| Greece | 86.9 | 90.4 | 93.7 | 95.3 | 101.5 | 98.2 | 3,589 | 3,951 | 7,668 | 9,011 |
| Guatemala | 77.6 | 102.6 | 75.4 | 104.4 | 76.6 | 100.6 | 1,882 | 1,542 | 2,120 | 2,547 |
| Guinea | 73.7 | 107.5 | 72.9 | 113.8 | 60.5 | 111.8 | 1,423 | 1,599 | 142 | 190 |
| Guinea-Bissau | 71.1 | 104.9 | 73.1 | 109.7 | 81.2 | 106.6 | 1,529 | 1,460 | 205 | 238 |
| Haiti | 108.5 | 98.8 | 99.8 | 100.6 | 69.8 | 111.6 | 997 | 882 | .. | .. |

# Agricultural output and productivity | **3.3**

| | Crop production index | | Food production index | | Livestock production index | | Cereal yield | | Agricultural productivity | |
|---|---|---|---|---|---|---|---|---|---|---|
| | | | | | | | | | Agriculture value added per worker 2000 $ | |
| | 1999–2001 = 100 | | 1999–2001 = 100 | | 1999–2001 = 100 | | kilograms per hectare | | | |
| | 1990–92 | 2002–04 | 1990–92 | 2004–06[a] | 1990–92 | 2002–04 | 1990–92 | 2004–06 | 1990–92 | 2003–05 |
| Honduras | 92.9 | 118.9 | 86.5 | 111.0 | 69.3 | 105.8 | 1,371 | 1,471 | 977 | 1,197 |
| Hungary | 114.0 | 99.7 | 117.0 | 111.9 | 125.5 | 101.9 | 4,551 | 5,403 | 4,105 | 6,987 |
| India | 79.6 | 100.0 | 75.9 | 104.7 | 69.4 | 110.5 | 1,947 | 2,428 | 324 | 392 |
| Indonesia | 82.8 | 112.7 | 83.8 | 117.4 | 85.8 | 127.3 | 3,826 | 4,354 | 484 | 583 |
| Iran, Islamic Rep. | 73.8 | 118.1 | 72.2 | 115.4 | 68.8 | 103.3 | 1,523 | 2,462 | 1,954 | 2,542 |
| Iraq | .. | .. | .. | .. | .. | .. | 872 | 1,014 | .. | 1,756 |
| Ireland | 92.7 | 100.3 | 95.3 | 98.4 | 94.3 | 96.1 | 6,653 | 7,473 | .. | 17,879 |
| Israel | 97.8 | 103.3 | 82.8 | 108.2 | 72.4 | 113.1 | 3,132 | 3,096 | .. | .. |
| Italy | 97.3 | 92.6 | 97.0 | 98.1 | 95.1 | 99.4 | 4,340 | 5,368 | 11,542 | 23,967 |
| Jamaica | 84.9 | 96.7 | 85.7 | 99.4 | 87.2 | 102.8 | 1,298 | 1,099 | 2,016 | 1,889 |
| Japan | 112.9 | 95.0 | 108.4 | 97.7 | 106.8 | 100.2 | 5,713 | 5,983 | 20,445 | 35,517 |
| Jordan | 100.1 | 136.6 | 85.4 | 118.2 | 71.2 | 94.1 | 1,168 | 1,267 | 1,892 | 1,360 |
| Kazakhstan | 163.8 | 108.4 | 163.0[b] | 103.1 | 178.5 | 111.6 | 1,338[b] | 975 | 1,795[b] | 1,557 |
| Kenya | 86.9 | 103.2 | 85.7 | 104.3 | 83.9 | 110.4 | 1,645 | 1,709 | 335 | 333 |
| Korea, Dem. Rep. | 126.2 | 108.4 | 119.6 | 109.7 | 145.1 | 114.2 | 5,073 | 3,787 | .. | .. |
| Korea, Rep. | 88.2 | 91.3 | 79.8 | 92.1 | 68.1 | 100.4 | 5,885 | 6,400 | 5,679 | 11,286 |
| Kuwait | 33.6 | 110.6 | 26.4 | 125.9 | 27.9 | 115.7 | 3,112 | 2,440 | .. | 13,521[b] |
| Kyrgyz Republic | 68.5 | 102.9 | 74.0[b] | 97.9 | 106.9 | 98.4 | 2,771[b] | 2,696 | 675[b] | 979 |
| Lao PDR | 62.2 | 115.3 | 59.1 | 116.8[b] | 60.6 | 107.5 | 2,341 | 3,804 | 360 | 458 |
| Latvia | 128.7 | 119.4 | 222.3[b] | 117.4 | 273.8 | 101.1 | 1,641[b] | 2,499 | 1,790[b] | 2,704 |
| Lebanon | 109.7 | 94.1 | 100.4 | 100.8 | 65.6 | 120.4 | 2,001 | 2,708 | .. | 30,099 |
| Lesotho | 67.5 | 100.8 | 87.8 | 106.0[b] | 115.0 | 100.0 | 716 | 589 | 422 | 418 |
| Liberia | 62.3 | 97.7 | 80.5 | 97.3 | 90.4 | 107.8 | 951 | .. | .. | .. |
| Libya | 79.2 | 96.9 | 77.1 | 104.3 | 75.9 | 101.0 | 706 | 619 | .. | .. |
| Lithuania | 80.2 | 113.1 | 159.9[b] | 112.2 | 187.0 | 107.8 | 1,938[b] | 2,708 | .. | 4,703 |
| Macedonia, FYR | 107.4 | 93.3 | 107.8 | 108.5 | 105.1[b] | 103.3 | 2,652[b] | 3,345 | 2,256[b] | 3,487 |
| Madagascar | 93.6 | 103.5 | 90.4 | 107.6 | 93.3 | 97.1 | 1,935 | 2,440 | 186 | 174 |
| Malawi | 57.5 | 84.3 | 49.6 | 95.6 | 85.4 | 101.8 | 871 | 1,099 | 72 | 116 |
| Malaysia | 74.4 | 114.0 | 70.5 | 120.0 | 81.3 | 115.1 | 2,827 | 3,317 | 3,803 | 5,126 |
| Mali | 73.8 | 107.4 | 78.6 | 109.6[b] | 81.3 | 112.9 | 840 | 1,008 | 208 | 241 |
| Mauritania | 63.2 | 97.2 | 84.2 | 108.8[b] | 87.4 | 109.3 | 802 | 771 | 574 | 356 |
| Mauritius | 110.7 | 101.6 | 101.1 | 105.9 | 71.1 | 116.8 | 4,117 | 7,269 | 3,942 | 5,011 |
| Mexico | 82.8 | 103.8 | 77.7 | 107.8 | 71.4 | 107.8 | 2,520 | 3,083 | 2,256 | 2,792 |
| Moldova | 136.6 | 112.2 | 153.3[b] | 115.7 | 198.7 | 103.2 | 2,928[b] | 2,721 | 1,286[b] | 816 |
| Mongolia | 246.9 | 107.3 | 98.3 | 93.6 | 93.9 | 95.9 | 967 | 791 | 870 | 907 |
| Morocco | 101.1 | 133.4 | 94.3 | 132.1 | 81.3 | 102.0 | 1,095 | 1,307 | 1,430 | 1,775 |
| Mozambique | 64.7 | 106.1 | 70.5 | 104.0 | 94.8 | 100.9 | 330 | 938 | 109 | 153 |
| Myanmar | 61.5 | 114.7 | 62.3 | 115.4 | 65.0 | 115.1 | 2,739 | 3,424 | .. | .. |
| Namibia | 71.9 | 111.4 | 99.5 | 114.0 | 104.1 | 109.3 | 381 | 403 | 820 | 1,103 |
| Nepal | 73.5 | 111.2 | 75.2 | 110.5 | 80.1 | 107.3 | 1,831 | 2,304 | 192 | 209 |
| Netherlands | 93.7 | 97.9 | 105.5 | 95.1 | 105.3 | 92.6 | 7,145 | 8,287 | 24,914 | 42,198 |
| New Zealand | 78.9 | 101.9 | 77.8 | 116.4 | 80.7 | 112.1 | 5,257 | 6,876 | 19,869 | 25,978 |
| Nicaragua | 76.6 | 115.3 | 64.0 | 123.1 | 57.5 | 119.9 | 1,529 | 1,808 | .. | 2,071 |
| Niger | 71.4 | 119.5 | 75.4 | 118.4 | 82.0 | 104.7 | 323 | 463 | 152 | 157[b] |
| Nigeria | 68.9 | 103.4 | 69.1 | 106.2 | 76.9 | 106.6 | 1,135 | 1,420 | 562 | 950 |
| Norway | 120.7 | 103.4 | 104.1 | 99.5 | 98.2 | 97.3 | 3,744 | 4,085 | 19,500 | 37,776 |
| Oman | 62.8 | 87.3 | 60.2 | 92.1[b] | 65.7 | 94.0 | 2,411 | 2,621 | 1,005 | 1,302 |
| Pakistan | 80.6 | 102.5 | 70.6 | 110.6 | 67.6 | 109.1 | 1,818 | 2,533 | 594 | 696 |
| Panama | 110.9 | 104.2 | 94.8 | 103.7 | 76.3 | 101.1 | 1,862 | 1,845 | 2,363 | 3,914 |
| Papua New Guinea | 78.5 | 101.6 | 79.9 | 107.7[b] | 80.8 | 110.1 | 2,504 | 3,848 | 390 | 490[b] |
| Paraguay | 85.8 | 120.7 | 77.4 | 115.0 | 87.3 | 98.2 | 1,905 | 2,283 | 1,596 | 2,052 |
| Peru | 52.6 | 108.1 | 57.1 | 110.2 | 68.3 | 114.1 | 2,463 | 3,433 | 930 | 1,498 |
| Philippines | 84.2 | 109.6 | 77.9 | 115.5 | 62.1 | 120.7 | 2,070 | 3,074 | 905 | 1,075 |
| Poland | 109.1 | 91.6 | 110.0 | 106.7 | 114.8 | 105.0 | 2,958 | 3,123 | 1,502[b] | 2,182 |
| Portugal | 103.1 | 98.6 | 98.7 | 98.9 | 85.7 | 98.2 | 1,939 | 2,744 | 4,612 | 5,980 |
| Puerto Rico | 167.7 | 114.6 | 127.6 | 98.2 | 118.4 | 94.1 | 1,100 | 2,119 | .. | .. |

# 3.3 Agricultural output and productivity

| | Crop production index | | Food production index | | Livestock production index | | Cereal yield | | Agricultural productivity | |
|---|---|---|---|---|---|---|---|---|---|---|
| | 1999–2001 = 100 | | 1999–2001 = 100 | | 1999–2001 = 100 | | kilograms per hectare | | Agriculture value added per worker 2000 $ | |
| | 1990–92 | 2002–04 | 1990–92 | 2004–06[a] | 1990–92 | 2002–04 | 1990–92 | 2004–06 | 1990–92 | 2003–05 |
| Romania | 92.2 | 112.2 | 97.7 | 123.2 | 114.5 | 107.6 | 2,777 | 3,478 | 2,196 | 4,646 |
| Russian Federation | 125.8 | 116.0 | 132.6[b] | 111.4 | 152.1 | 103.2 | 1,743[b] | 1,879 | 1,825[b] | 2,518 |
| Rwanda | 111.4 | 117.6 | 107.3 | 113.2 | 77.7 | 107.3 | 1,088 | 1,087 | 191 | 214 |
| Saudi Arabia | 120.7 | 114.8 | 105.2 | 118.6 | 67.8 | 104.9 | 4,212 | 4,545 | 7,875 | 15,780 |
| Senegal | 73.0 | 68.3 | 71.9 | 81.6 | 74.8 | 98.2 | 803 | 1,018 | 225 | 215 |
| Serbia[c] | 97.6 | 110.0 | 109.2 | 114.2 | 103.8 | 94.9 | 2,926 | 4,910 | .. | 1,679 |
| Sierra Leone | 128.1 | 113.5 | 118.9 | 113.5 | 86.1 | 105.2 | 1,223 | 1,971 | .. | .. |
| Singapore | 157.1 | 100.0 | 352.1 | 70.2[b] | 396.3 | 74.2 | .. | .. | 22,695 | 40,323 |
| Slovak Republic | .. | .. | .. | .. | .. | .. | 1,031[b] | 4,383 | .. | 5,026 |
| Slovenia | 93.1 | 110.2 | 77.2[b] | 108.5 | 73.6 | 103.6 | 3,270[b] | 5,668 | 11,531[b] | .. |
| Somalia | .. | .. | .. | .. | .. | .. | 622 | 558 | .. | .. |
| South Africa | 79.6 | 102.4 | 84.2 | 105.9 | 94.6 | 108.2 | 1,602 | 3,076 | 1,786 | 2,484 |
| Spain | 87.9 | 106.1 | 87.1 | 105.9 | 79.5 | 107.2 | 2,310 | 3,008 | 9,511 | 19,030 |
| Sri Lanka | 86.2 | 98.8 | 88.9 | 95.6 | 94.6 | 109.9 | 2,950 | 3,550 | 679 | 700 |
| Sudan | 68.9 | 110.8 | 66.7 | 107.8 | 67.6 | 106.3 | 596 | 663 | 418 | 666 |
| Swaziland | 106.6 | 100.1 | 108.9 | 105.9 | 130.3 | 111.9 | 1,299 | 1,030 | 1,225 | 1,243 |
| Sweden | 102.2 | 102.1 | 97.9 | 99.4 | 95.7 | 97.7 | 4,272 | 4,711 | 21,463 | 33,023 |
| Switzerland | 112.4 | 95.3 | 104.9 | 99.6 | 104.8 | 101.9 | 6,102 | 6,393 | 22,344 | 23,418 |
| Syrian Arab Republic | 73.6 | 117.1 | 75.1 | 121.7 | 75.0 | 115.6 | 947 | 1,711 | 2,344 | 3,261 |
| Tajikistan | 123.6 | 132.9 | 138.1 | 145.8 | 192.6 | 139.2 | 1,037[b] | 2,211 | 397[b] | 465 |
| Tanzania | 92.7 | 103.6 | 88.7 | 105.6 | 82.9 | 109.4 | 1,276 | 1,477 | 238 | 295 |
| Thailand | 82.0 | 106.1 | 84.1 | 104.7 | 86.8 | 105.5 | 2,186 | 2,976 | 497 | 621 |
| Timor-Leste | 93.5 | 107.2 | 102.2 | 112.9 | 101.6 | 117.9 | 1,694 | 1,322 | .. | 281 |
| Togo | 73.4 | 110.3 | 74.1 | 104.2 | 87.9 | 106.7 | 791 | 1,155 | 312 | 347 |
| Trinidad and Tobago | 116.3 | 91.9 | 88.7 | 117.5 | 73.5 | 142.6 | 3,159 | 3,341 | 1,666 | 1,989 |
| Tunisia | 104.6 | 104.2 | 91.2 | 101.6 | 60.3 | 99.9 | 1,401 | 1,360 | 2,422 | 2,719 |
| Turkey | 88.0 | 104.0 | 89.5 | 103.9 | 92.2 | 101.6 | 2,192 | 2,514 | 1,890 | 1,891 |
| Turkmenistan | 111.4 | 116.5 | 57.1[b] | 131.0 | 64.0 | 121.7 | 2,210[b] | 3,057 | 1,222[b] | .. |
| Uganda | 78.0 | 106.6 | 79.5 | 109.2 | 82.3 | 112.9 | 1,487 | 1,508 | 184 | 229 |
| Ukraine | 130.6 | 114.0 | 146.0[b] | 115.4 | 170.0 | 108.1 | 2,834[b] | 2,636 | 1,195[b] | 1,702 |
| United Arab Emirates | 23.4 | 56.0 | 26.5 | 63.7[b] | 57.5 | 116.9 | 2,042 | 7,333 | 10,454 | 25,841 |
| United Kingdom | 104.9 | 100.3 | 107.2 | 98.0 | 105.6 | 98.5 | 6,321 | 7,169 | 22,659 | 26,933 |
| United States | 88.4 | 101.5 | 84.8 | 107.5 | 83.4 | 102.6 | 4,875 | 6,538 | 20,793 | 41,797 |
| Uruguay | 70.4 | 112.7 | 76.7 | 115.5 | 84.2 | 98.3 | 2,445 | 4,203 | 5,714 | 7,973 |
| Uzbekistan | 107.8 | 109.0 | 91.3[b] | 105.2 | 99.7 | 104.7 | 1,777 | 3,839 | 1,272[b] | 1,800 |
| Venezuela, RB | 79.5 | 96.0 | 73.9 | 98.3 | 73.5 | 100.4 | 2,561 | 3,401 | 4,483 | 6,292 |
| Vietnam | 60.1 | 116.6 | 63.1 | 124.4 | 57.9 | 124.9 | 3,096 | 4,717 | 214 | 305 |
| West Bank and Gaza | .. | .. | .. | .. | .. | .. | 1,105 | 2,037 | .. | .. |
| Yemen, Rep. | 75.0 | 100.1 | 71.5 | 110.5 | 66.3 | 115.5 | 906 | 798 | 271 | 328[b] |
| Zambia | 80.7 | 102.4 | 84.3 | 108.0 | 80.1 | 99.2 | 1,251 | 1,822 | 159 | 206 |
| Zimbabwe | 69.2 | 69.3 | 77.3 | 86.4 | 90.1 | 100.1 | 1,123 | 663 | 240 | 222 |
| **World** | **82.5 w** | **105.7 w** | **82.0 w** | **106.2 w** | **83.4 w** | **107.0 w** | **2,866 w** | **3,306 w** | **742 w** | **914 w** |
| **Low income** | 78.5 | 103.5 | 76.1 | 105.2 | 73.5 | 109.6 | 1,752 | 2,105 | 303 | 376 |
| **Middle income** | 80.9 | 110.2 | 79.8 | 110.5 | 81.2 | 111.0 | 2,986 | 3,354 | 531 | 763 |
| Lower middle income | 77.5 | 111.7 | 72.8 | 112.5 | 67.9 | 114.1 | 3,424 | 3,956 | 388 | 561 |
| Upper middle income | 93.1 | 104.9 | 101.8 | 104.2 | 115.8 | 102.7 | 2,318 | 2,602 | 2,163 | 2,999 |
| **Low & middle income** | 80.1 | 108.1 | 78.7 | 108.9 | 79.3 | 110.6 | 2,451 | 2,827 | 438 | 591 |
| East Asia & Pacific | 71.8 | 110.8 | 64.5 | 112.4 | 52.4 | 116.6 | 3,816 | 4,518 | 303 | 445 |
| Europe & Central Asia | 113.2 | 107.1 | 127.1 | 106.1 | 149.3 | 104.1 | 2,652 | 2,359 | 1,903 | 2,195 |
| Latin America & Carib. | 78.2 | 111.5 | 74.4 | 110.4 | 72.9 | 108.9 | 2,234 | 3,194 | 2,151 | 3,057 |
| Middle East & N. Africa | 78.8 | 113.7 | 75.7 | 112.5 | 70.4 | 107.7 | 1,632 | 2,360 | 1,576 | 2,198 |
| South Asia | 79.9 | 101.0 | 75.5 | 103.5 | 69.1 | 109.8 | 1,992 | 2,513 | 335 | 406 |
| Sub-Saharan Africa | 75.9 | 103.9 | 77.6 | 105.1 | 84.5 | 107.1 | 984 | 1,120 | 277 | 335 |
| **High income** | 89.9 | 98.2 | 89.7 | 99.9 | 90.1 | 101.2 | 4,254 | 5,160 | 15,072 | 26,940 |
| Euro area | 91.5 | 97.8 | 94.6 | 98.8 | 97.9 | 99.7 | 4,632 | 5,664 | 12,701 | 23,097 |

a. Aggregates are for 2002–04. b. Data for all three years are not available. c. Includes Montenegro.

# Agricultural output and productivity

**3.3**

ENVIRONMENT

## About the data

The agricultural production indexes in the table are prepared by the Food and Agriculture Organization of the United Nations (FAO). The FAO obtains data from official and semiofficial reports of crop yields, area under production, and livestock numbers. If data are unavailable, the FAO makes estimates. The indexes are calculated using the Laspeyres formula: production quantities of each commodity are weighted by average international commodity prices in the base period and summed for each year. Because the FAO's indexes are based on the concept of agriculture as a

single enterprise, estimates of the amounts retained for seed and feed are subtracted from the production data to avoid double counting. The resulting aggregate represents production available for any use except as seed and feed. The FAO's indexes may differ from those from other sources because of differences in coverage, weights, concepts, time periods, calculation methods, and use of international prices.

To facilitate cross-country comparisons, the FAO uses international commodity prices to value production. These prices, expressed in international dollars (equivalent in purchasing power to the U.S. dollar), are derived using a Geary-Khamis formula applied to agricultural outputs (see Inter-Secretariat Working Group on National Accounts 1993, sections 16.93–96). This method assigns a single price to each commodity so that, for example, one metric ton of wheat has the same price regardless of where it was produced. The use of international prices eliminates fluctuations in the value of output due to transitory movements of nominal exchange rates unrelated to the purchasing power of the domestic currency.

Data on cereal yield may be affected by a variety of reporting and timing differences. Millet and sorghum, which are grown as feed for livestock and poultry in Europe and North America, are used as food in Africa, Asia, and countries of the former Soviet Union. So some cereal crops are excluded from the data for some countries and included elsewhere, depending on their use. To smooth annual fluctuations in agricultural activity, the indicators in the table have been averaged over three years.

## Definitions

• **Crop production index** is agricultural production for each period relative to the base period 1999–2001. It includes all crops except fodder crops. The regional and income group aggregates for the FAO's production indexes are calculated from the underlying values in international dollars, normalized to the base period 1999–2001. • **Food production index** covers food crops that are considered edible and that contain nutrients. Coffee and tea are excluded because, although edible, they have no nutritive value. • **Livestock production index** includes meat and milk from all sources, dairy products such as cheese, and eggs, honey, raw silk, wool, and hides and skins. • **Cereal yield,** measured in kilograms per hectare of harvested land, includes wheat, rice, maize, barley, oats, rye, millet, sorghum, buckwheat, and mixed grains. Production data on cereals refer to crops harvested for dry grain only. Cereal crops harvested for hay or harvested green for food, feed, or silage, and those used for grazing, are excluded. The FAO allocates production data to the calendar year in which the bulk of the harvest took place. But most of a crop harvested near the end of a year will be used in the following year. • **Agricultural productivity** is the ratio of agricultural value added, measured in 2000 U.S. dollars, to the number of workers in agriculture. Agricultural productivity is measured by value added per unit of input. (For further discussion of the calculation of value added in national accounts, see *About the data* for tables 4.1 and 4.2.) Agricultural value added includes that from forestry and fishing. Thus interpretations of land productivity should be made with caution.

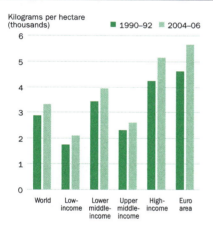

**Cereal yield in low-income countries was only 40 percent of the yield in high-income countries** **3.3a**

*Source:* Table 3.3.

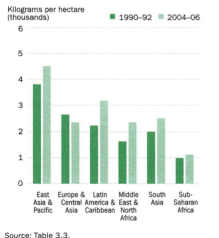

**Sub-Saharan Africa had the lowest yield, while East Asia and Pacific is closing the gap with high-income countries** **3.3b**

*Source:* Table 3.3.

## Data sources

Data on agricultural production indexes, cereal yield, and agricultural employment are from electronic files that the FAO makes available to the World Bank. The files may contain more recent information than published versions. Data on agricultural value added are from the World Bank's national accounts files.

| | Forest area | | Average annual deforestation[a] | | Animal species | | Higher plants[b] | | GEF benefits index for biodiversity | Nationally protected areas | | Marine protected areas | |
|---|---|---|---|---|---|---|---|---|---|---|---|---|---|
| | thousand sq. km | | % | | Total known species | Threatened species | Total known species | Threatened species | 0–100 (no biodiversity to maximum biodiversity) | thousand sq. km | % of total land area | thousand sq. km | % of surface area |
| | 1990 | 2005 | 1990–2000 | 2000–05 | 2004 | 2007 | 2004 | 2007 | 2005 | 2004[c] | 2004[c] | 2004 | 2004 |
| Afghanistan | 13 | 9 | 2.5 | 3.1 | 578 | 33 | 4,000 | 2 | 3.6 | 2.2 | 0.3 | .. | .. |
| Albania | 8 | 8 | 0.3 | −0.6 | 376 | 45 | 3,031 | 0 | 0.2 | 0.7 | 2.7 | 0.3 | 1.0 |
| Algeria | 18 | 23 | −1.8 | −1.2 | 472 | 71 | 3,164 | 3 | 3.0 | 118.6 | 5.0 | 0.9 | 0.0 |
| Angola | 610 | 591 | 0.2 | 0.2 | 1,226 | 62 | 5,185 | 26 | 9.6 | 125.5 | 10.1 | 29.1 | 2.3 |
| Argentina | 353 | 330 | 0.4 | 0.4 | 1,413 | 152 | 9,372 | 42 | 18.5 | 174.5 | 6.4 | 7.8 | 0.3 |
| Armenia | 3 | 3 | 1.3 | 1.5 | 380 | 35 | 3,553 | 1 | 0.3 | 3.0 | 10.6 | .. | .. |
| Australia | 1,679 | 1,637 | 0.2 | 0.1 | 1,227 | 568 | 15,638 | 55 | 95.8 | 745.3 | 9.7 | 680.8 | 8.8 |
| Austria | 38 | 39 | −0.2 | −0.1 | 513 | 62 | 3,100 | 4 | 0.3 | 23.5 | 28.5 | .. | .. |
| Azerbaijan | 9 | 9 | 0.0 | 0.0 | 446 | 38 | 4,300 | 0 | 0.9 | 4.0 | 4.8 | 1.2 | 1.4 |
| Bangladesh | 9 | 9 | 0.0 | 0.3 | 735 | 89 | 5,000 | 12 | 1.6 | 0.7 | 0.5 | 0.3 | 0.2 |
| Belarus | 74 | 79 | −0.6 | −0.1 | 297 | 17 | 2,100 | .. | 0.0 | 13.2 | 6.3 | .. | .. |
| Belgium[d] | 7 | 7 | 0.1 | 0.0 | 519 | 29 | 1,550 | 1 | 0.0 | 1.0 | 3.5 | 0.0 | 0.0 |
| Benin | 33 | 24 | 2.1 | 2.5 | 644 | 34 | 2,500 | 14 | 0.2 | 26.4 | 23.9 | .. | .. |
| Bolivia | 628 | 587 | 0.4 | 0.5 | 1,775 | 80 | 17,367 | 71 | 13.8 | 211.0 | 19.5 | .. | .. |
| Bosnia and Herzegovina | 22 | 22 | 0.1 | 0.0 | 390 | 55 | .. | 1 | 0.4 | 0.3 | 0.5 | .. | .. |
| Botswana | 137 | 119 | 0.9 | 1.0 | 739 | 18 | 2,151 | 0 | 1.5 | 174.9 | 30.9 | .. | .. |
| Brazil | 5,200 | 4,777 | 0.5 | 0.6 | 2,290 | 343 | 56,215 | 382 | 100.0 | 1,532.6 | 18.1 | 47.4 | 0.6 |
| Bulgaria | 33 | 36 | −0.1 | −1.4 | 485 | 47 | 3,572 | 0 | 0.9 | 11.2 | 10.3 | 0.0 | 0.0 |
| Burkina Faso | 72 | 68 | 0.3 | 0.3 | 581 | 13 | 1,100 | 2 | 0.3 | 42.1 | 15.4 | .. | .. |
| Burundi | 3 | 2 | 3.7 | 5.2 | 713 | 48 | 2,500 | 2 | 0.5 | 1.5 | 5.7 | .. | .. |
| Cambodia | 129 | 104 | 1.1 | 2.0 | 648 | 82 | .. | 31 | 3.9 | 41.5 | 23.5 | 1.9 | 1.1 |
| Cameroon | 245 | 212 | 0.9 | 1.0 | 1,258 | 157 | 8,260 | 355 | 13.3 | 37.4 | 8.0 | 3.9 | 0.8 |
| Canada | 3,101 | 3,101 | 0.0 | 0.0 | 683 | 77 | 3,270 | 1 | 22.2 | 628.7 | 6.9 | 362.7 | 3.6 |
| Central African Republic | 232 | 228 | 0.1 | 0.1 | 850 | 17 | 3,602 | 15 | 1.7 | 103.3 | 16.6 | .. | .. |
| Chad | 131 | 119 | 0.6 | 0.7 | 635 | 21 | 1,600 | 2 | 2.1 | 119.8 | 9.5 | .. | .. |
| Chile | 153 | 161 | −0.4 | −0.4 | 604 | 95 | 5,284 | 39 | 16.2 | 26.9 | 3.6 | 114.5 | 15.1 |
| China | 1,571 | 1,973 | −1.2 | −2.2 | 1,801 | 351 | 32,200 | 446 | 64.8 | 1,100.7 | 11.8 | 16.0 | 0.2 |
| Hong Kong, China | .. | .. | .. | .. | 363 | 37 | .. | 6 | .. | 0.3 | 24.7 | 0.3 | .. |
| Colombia | 614 | 607 | 0.1 | 0.1 | 2,288 | 382 | 51,220 | 222 | 57.3 | 825.3 | 74.4 | 8.1 | 0.7 |
| Congo, Dem. Rep. | 1,405 | 1,336 | 0.4 | 0.2 | 1,578 | 126 | 11,007 | 65 | 17.0 | 194.4 | 8.6 | .. | .. |
| Congo, Rep. | 227 | 225 | 0.1 | 0.1 | 763 | 37 | 6,000 | 35 | 3.4 | 61.3 | 18.0 | .. | .. |
| Costa Rica | 26 | 24 | 0.8 | −0.1 | 1,070 | 131 | 12,119 | 111 | 11.1 | 12.1 | 23.6 | 4.8 | 9.4 |
| Côte d'Ivoire | 102 | 104 | −0.1 | −0.1 | 931 | 73 | 3,660 | 105 | 3.9 | 54.5 | 17.1 | 0.3 | 0.1 |
| Croatia | 21 | 21 | −0.1 | −0.1 | 461 | 78 | 4,288 | 1 | 0.5 | 3.6 | 6.5 | 2.5 | 4.4 |
| Cuba | 21 | 27 | −1.7 | −2.2 | 423 | 115 | 6,522 | 163 | 13.5 | 1.5 | 1.4 | 31.7 | 28.6 |
| Czech Republic | 26 | 26 | 0.0 | −0.1 | 474 | 39 | 1,900 | 4 | 0.1 | 14.4 | 18.7 | .. | .. |
| Denmark | 4 | 5 | −0.9 | −0.6 | 508 | 28 | 1,450 | 3 | 0.2 | 10.9 | 25.7 | 5.1 | 11.8 |
| Dominican Republic | 14 | 14 | 0.0 | 0.0 | 260 | 81 | 5,657 | 30 | 6.8 | 11.9 | 24.6 | 8.6 | 17.6 |
| Ecuador | 138 | 109 | 1.5 | 1.7 | 1,856 | 340 | 19,362 | 1,838 | 30.0 | 67.2 | 24.3 | 141.0 | 49.7 |
| Egypt, Arab Rep. | 0 | 1 | −3.0 | −2.6 | 599 | 59 | 2,076 | 2 | 3.2 | 56.0 | 5.6 | 76.7 | 7.7 |
| El Salvador | 4 | 3 | 1.5 | 1.7 | 571 | 29 | 2,911 | 26 | 0.8 | 0.4 | 1.9 | 0.1 | 0.4 |
| Eritrea | 16 | 16 | 0.3 | 0.3 | 607 | 38 | .. | 3 | 0.9 | 5.0 | 5.0 | .. | .. |
| Estonia | 22 | 23 | −0.4 | −0.4 | 334 | 14 | 1,630 | 0 | 0.0 | 8.9 | 21.1 | .. | .. |
| Ethiopia | 151 | 130 | 1.0 | 1.1 | 1,127 | 86 | 6,603 | 22 | 8.5 | 186.2 | 18.6 | .. | .. |
| Finland | 222 | 225 | −0.1 | 0.0 | 501 | 19 | 1,102 | 1 | 0.2 | 29.5 | 9.7 | 1.1 | 0.3 |
| France | 145 | 156 | −0.5 | −0.3 | 665 | 117 | 4,630 | 7 | 3.9 | 16.2 | 3.0 | 0.5 | 0.1 |
| Gabon | 219 | 218 | 0.0 | 0.0 | 798 | 43 | 6,651 | 108 | 3.4 | 8.8 | 3.4 | 1.0 | 0.4 |
| Gambia, The | 4 | 5 | −0.4 | −0.4 | 668 | 31 | 974 | 4 | 0.1 | 0.3 | 3.5 | 0.2 | 1.9 |
| Georgia | 28 | 28 | 0.0 | 0.0 | 366 | 46 | 4,350 | 0 | 0.7 | 3.0 | 4.3 | 0.0 | 0.1 |
| Germany | 107 | 111 | −0.3 | 0.0 | 613 | 59 | 2,682 | 12 | 0.7 | 111.5 | 32.0 | 9.1 | 2.6 |
| Ghana | 74 | 55 | 2.0 | 2.0 | 978 | 56 | 3,725 | 117 | 2.0 | 36.9 | 16.2 | .. | .. |
| Greece | 33 | 38 | −0.9 | −0.8 | 530 | 95 | 4,992 | 11 | 3.0 | 4.3 | 3.3 | 2.5 | 1.9 |
| Guatemala | 47 | 39 | 1.2 | 1.3 | 877 | 133 | 8,681 | 84 | 8.9 | 25.4 | 23.4 | 0.1 | 0.1 |
| Guinea | 74 | 67 | 0.7 | 0.5 | 855 | 61 | 3,000 | 22 | 2.6 | 15.6 | 6.4 | .. | .. |
| Guinea-Bissau | 22 | 21 | 0.4 | 0.5 | 560 | 29 | 1,000 | 4 | 0.7 | 0.0 | 0.0 | .. | .. |
| Haiti | 1 | 1 | 0.6 | 0.7 | 312 | 91 | 5,242 | 29 | 5.8 | 0.1 | 0.3 | .. | .. |

| | Forest area (thousand sq. km) | | Average annual deforestation[a] (%) | | Animal species | | Higher plants[b] | | GEF benefits index for biodiversity (0–100 (no biodiversity to maximum biodiversity)) | Nationally protected areas | | Marine protected areas | |
|---|---|---|---|---|---|---|---|---|---|---|---|---|---|
| | | | | | Total known species | Threatened species | Total known species | Threatened species | | thousand sq. km | % of total land area | thousand sq. km | % of surface area |
| | 1990 | 2005 | 1990–2000 | 2000–05 | 2004 | 2007 | 2004 | 2007 | 2005 | 2004[c] | 2004[c] | 2004 | 2004 |
| Honduras | 74 | 46 | 3.0 | 3.1 | 900 | 102 | 5,680 | 110 | 7.9 | 23.4 | 21.0 | 1.9 | 1.7 |
| Hungary | 18 | 20 | −0.6 | −0.7 | 455 | 55 | 2,214 | 1 | 0.2 | 8.3 | 9.3 | .. | .. |
| India | 639 | 677 | −0.6 | 0.0 | 1,602 | 313 | 18,664 | 247 | 43.9 | 156.3 | 5.3 | 16.1 | 0.5 |
| Indonesia | 1,166 | 885 | 1.7 | 2.0 | 2.271 | 464 | 29,375 | 386 | 90.0 | 259.9 | 14.3 | 130.1 | 6.8 |
| Iran, Islamic Rep. | 111 | 111 | 0.0 | 0.0 | 656 | 75 | 8,000 | 1 | 7.9 | 105.5 | 6.5 | 6.2 | 0.4 |
| Iraq | 8 | 8 | −0.2 | −0.1 | 498 | 40 | .. | 0 | 1.7 | 0.0 | 0.0 | .. | .. |
| Ireland | 4 | 7 | −3.3 | −1.9 | 471 | 15 | 950 | 1 | 0.7 | 0.8 | 1.1 | 0.0 | 0.0 |
| Israel | 2 | 2 | −0.6 | −0.8 | 649 | 79 | 2,317 | 0 | 0.9 | 4.6 | 21.3 | 0.1 | 0.6 |
| Italy | 84 | 100 | −1.2 | −1.1 | 610 | 119 | 5,599 | 19 | 4.4 | 32.4 | 11.0 | 1.5 | 0.5 |
| Jamaica | 3 | 3 | 0.1 | 0.1 | 333 | 61 | 3,308 | 209 | 4.9 | 1.8 | 16.2 | 8.2 | 74.5 |
| Japan | 250 | 249 | 0.0 | 0.0 | 763 | 190 | 5,565 | 12 | 41.4 | 52.2 | 14.3 | 10.6 | 2.8 |
| Jordan | 1 | 1 | 0.0 | 0.0 | 490 | 43 | 2,100 | 0 | 0.3 | 9.7 | 11.0 | 0.0 | 0.0 |
| Kazakhstan | 34 | 33 | 0.2 | 0.2 | 642 | 55 | 6,000 | 16 | 5.4 | 77.4 | 2.9 | 0.5 | 0.0 |
| Kenya | 37 | 35 | 0.3 | 0.3 | 1,510 | 172 | 6,506 | 103 | 9.9 | 71.9 | 12.6 | 3.1 | 0.5 |
| Korea, Dem. Rep. | 82 | 62 | 1.8 | 1.9 | 474 | 44 | 2,898 | 3 | 0.7 | 3.2 | 2.6 | .. | .. |
| Korea, Rep. | 64 | 63 | 0.1 | 0.1 | 512 | 54 | 2,898 | 0 | 1.8 | 3.5 | 3.6 | 3.5 | 3.5 |
| Kuwait | 0 | 0 | −5.2 | −3.7 | 381 | 23 | 234 | .. | 0.1 | 0.0 | 0.0 | 0.3 | 1.5 |
| Kyrgyz Republic | 8 | 9 | −0.3 | −0.3 | 265 | 22 | 4,500 | 14 | 1.2 | 7.2 | 3.7 | .. | .. |
| Lao PDR | 173 | 161 | 0.5 | 0.5 | 919 | 77 | 8,286 | 21 | 5.4 | 37.4 | 16.2 | .. | .. |
| Latvia | 28 | 29 | −0.4 | −0.4 | 393 | 23 | 1,153 | 0 | 0.0 | 9.7 | 15.6 | 0.2 | 0.2 |
| Lebanon | 1 | 1 | −0.8 | −0.8 | 447 | 38 | 3,000 | 0 | 0.2 | 0.1 | 0.7 | 0.0 | 0.0 |
| Lesotho | 0 | 0 | −3.4 | −2.7 | 370 | 11 | 1,591 | 1 | 0.3 | 0.1 | 0.2 | .. | .. |
| Liberia | 41 | 32 | 1.6 | 1.8 | 759 | 60 | 2,200 | 46 | 2.9 | 15.2 | 15.8 | 0.6 | 0.5 |
| Libya | 2 | 2 | 0.0 | 0.0 | 413 | 31 | 1,825 | 1 | 1.7 | 1.2 | 0.1 | 0.5 | 0.0 |
| Lithuania | 19 | 21 | −0.4 | −0.8 | 298 | 20 | 1,796 | .. | 0.0 | 5.9 | 9.5 | 0.5 | 0.8 |
| Macedonia, FYR | 9 | 9 | 0.0 | 0.0 | 380 | 34 | 3,500 | 0 | 0.2 | 2.0 | 7.9 | .. | .. |
| Madagascar | 137 | 128 | 0.5 | 0.3 | 427 | 262 | 9,505 | 280 | 31.4 | 18.3 | 3.1 | 0.2 | 0.0 |
| Malawi | 39 | 34 | 0.9 | 0.9 | 865 | 141 | 3,765 | 14 | 3.9 | 19.4 | 20.6 | .. | .. |
| Malaysia | 224 | 209 | 0.4 | 0.7 | 1,083 | 225 | 15,500 | 686 | 14.8 | 100.8 | 30.7 | 5.0 | 1.5 |
| Mali | 141 | 126 | 0.7 | 0.8 | 758 | 21 | 1,741 | 6 | 1.6 | 46.7 | 3.8 | .. | .. |
| Mauritania | 4 | 3 | 2.7 | 3.4 | 615 | 44 | 1,100 | .. | 1.4 | 2.5 | 0.2 | 15.0 | 1.5 |
| Mauritius | 0 | 0 | 0.3 | 0.5 | 151 | 65 | 750 | 88 | 4.2 | 0.1 | 3.3 | 0.1 | 4.4 |
| Mexico | 690 | 642 | 0.5 | 0.4 | 1,570 | 579 | 26,071 | 261 | 75.8 | 99.0 | 5.1 | 82.1 | 4.2 |
| Moldova | 3 | 3 | −0.2 | −0.2 | 253 | 28 | 1,752 | 0 | 0.0 | 0.5 | 1.4 | .. | .. |
| Mongolia | 115 | 103 | 0.7 | 0.8 | 527 | 38 | 2,823 | 0 | 4.4 | 217.9 | 13.9 | .. | .. |
| Morocco | 43 | 44 | −0.1 | −0.2 | 559 | 76 | 3,675 | 2 | 4.0 | 4.7 | 1.1 | 0.5 | 0.1 |
| Mozambique | 200 | 193 | 0.3 | 0.3 | 913 | 93 | 5,692 | 46 | 8.2 | 45.3 | 5.8 | 22.5 | 2.8 |
| Myanmar | 392 | 322 | 1.3 | 1.4 | 1,335 | 118 | 7,000 | 38 | 10.6 | 35.3 | 5.4 | 0.2 | 0.0 |
| Namibia | 88 | 77 | 0.9 | 0.9 | 811 | 55 | 3,174 | 24 | 5.9 | 46.0 | 5.6 | 74.0 | 9.0 |
| Nepal | 48 | 36 | 2.1 | 1.4 | 477 | 72 | 6,973 | 7 | 2.2 | 26.6 | 18.6 | .. | .. |
| Netherlands | 3 | 4 | −0.4 | −0.3 | 539 | 26 | 1,221 | 0 | 0.1 | 9.5 | 28.0 | 0.8 | 1.9 |
| New Zealand | 77 | 83 | −0.6 | −0.2 | 424 | 124 | 2,382 | 21 | 22.3 | 64.7 | 24.2 | 22.7 | 8.4 |
| Nicaragua | 65 | 52 | 1.6 | 1.3 | 813 | 59 | 7,590 | 39 | 3.6 | 28.1 | 23.1 | 1.3 | 1.0 |
| Niger | 19 | 13 | 3.7 | 1.0 | 616 | 20 | 1,460 | 2 | 0.9 | 96.9 | 7.7 | .. | .. |
| Nigeria | 172 | 111 | 2.7 | 3.3 | 1,189 | 79 | 4,715 | 171 | 6.6 | 55.0 | 6.0 | .. | .. |
| Norway | 91 | 94 | −0.2 | −0.2 | 525 | 32 | 1,715 | 2 | 1.6 | 19.7 | 6.5 | 1.3 | 0.4 |
| Oman | 0 | 0 | 0.0 | 0.0 | 557 | 50 | 1,204 | 6 | 4.4 | 0.2 | 0.1 | 29.6 | 9.6 |
| Pakistan | 25 | 19 | 1.8 | 2.1 | 820 | 78 | 4,950 | 2 | 5.1 | 73.1 | 9.5 | 2.2 | 0.3 |
| Panama | 44 | 43 | 0.2 | 0.1 | 1,145 | 121 | 9,915 | 194 | 11.7 | 13.1 | 17.6 | 10.0 | 13.3 |
| Papua New Guinea | 315 | 294 | 0.5 | 0.5 | 980 | 158 | 11,544 | 142 | 27.7 | 7.3 | 1.6 | 3.5 | 0.8 |
| Paraguay | 212 | 185 | 0.9 | 0.9 | 864 | 39 | 7,851 | 10 | 3.3 | 16.6 | 4.2 | .. | .. |
| Peru | 702 | 687 | 0.1 | 0.1 | 2,222 | 238 | 17,144 | 274 | 36.3 | 216.1 | 16.9 | 3.4 | 0.3 |
| Philippines | 106 | 72 | 2.8 | 2.1 | 812 | 253 | 8,931 | 213 | 33.7 | 24.3 | 8.2 | 16.6 | 5.5 |
| Poland | 89 | 92 | −0.2 | −0.3 | 534 | 38 | 2,450 | 4 | 0.6 | 70.3 | 23.1 | 0.7 | 0.2 |
| Portugal | 31 | 38 | −1.5 | −1.1 | 606 | 147 | 5,050 | 16 | 3.8 | 4.7 | 5.1 | 2.0 | 2.2 |
| Puerto Rico | 4 | 4 | −0.1 | 0.0 | 348 | 47 | 2,493 | 53 | 3.8 | 0.3 | 3.5 | 1.7 | 19.1 |

# 3.4 Deforestation and biodiversity

| | Forest area (thousand sq. km) | | Average annual deforestation[a] (%) | | Animal species | | Higher plants[b] | | GEF benefits index for biodiversity (0–100 (no biodiversity to maximum biodiversity)) | Nationally protected areas | | Marine protected areas | |
|---|---|---|---|---|---|---|---|---|---|---|---|---|---|
| | | | | | Total known species | Threatened species | Total known species | Threatened species | | thousand sq. km | % of total land area | thousand sq. km | % of surface area |
| | 1990 | 2005 | 1990–2000 | 2000–05 | 2004 | 2007 | 2004 | 2007 | 2005 | 2004[c] | 2004[c] | 2004 | 2004 |
| Romania | 64 | 64 | 0.0 | 0.0 | 466 | 64 | 3,400 | 1 | .. | 5.8 | 2.5 | 6.1 | 2.6 |
| Russian Federation | 8,090 | 8,088 | 0.0 | 0.0 | 941 | 153 | 11,400 | 7 | 37.1 | 1,287.0 | 7.9 | 301.8 | 1.8 |
| Rwanda | 3 | 5 | −0.8 | −6.9 | 871 | 49 | 2,288 | 3 | 1.1 | 1.9 | 7.9 | .. | .. |
| Saudi Arabia | 27 | 27 | 0.0 | 0.0 | 527 | 45 | 2,028 | 3 | 3.4 | 819.1 | 41.0 | 5.2 | 0.2 |
| Senegal | 93 | 87 | 0.5 | 0.5 | 803 | 55 | 2,086 | 7 | 1.3 | 21.6 | 11.2 | 0.9 | 0.4 |
| Serbia[e] | 26 | 27 | −0.3 | −0.3 | 477 | 91 | 4,082 | 1 | .. | 3.8 | 3.7 | 0.1 | 0.1 |
| Sierra Leone | 30 | 28 | 0.7 | 0.7 | 823 | 48 | 2,090 | 47 | 1.5 | 3.2 | 4.5 | .. | .. |
| Singapore | 0 | 0 | 0.0 | 0.0 | 473 | 44 | 2,282 | 54 | 0.1 | 0.0 | 4.2 | 0.0 | 0.1 |
| Slovak Republic | 19 | 19 | 0.0 | −0.1 | 419 | 44 | 3,124 | 2 | 0.1 | 11.0 | 22.8 | .. | .. |
| Slovenia | 12 | 13 | −0.4 | −0.4 | 437 | 80 | 3,200 | .. | 0.2 | 2.9 | 14.5 | 0.0 | 0.0 |
| Somalia | 83 | 71 | 1.0 | 1.0 | 824 | 55 | 3,028 | 17 | 6.7 | 1.9 | 0.3 | 3.3 | 0.5 |
| South Africa | 92 | 92 | 0.0 | 0.0 | 1,149 | 323 | 23,420 | 73 | 23.5 | 74.0 | 6.1 | 3.4 | 0.3 |
| Spain | 135 | 179 | −2.0 | −1.7 | 647 | 170 | 5,050 | 49 | 6.6 | 46.2 | 9.3 | 1.8 | 0.4 |
| Sri Lanka | 24 | 19 | 1.2 | 1.5 | 504 | 177 | 3,314 | 280 | 6.6 | 17.7 | 27.3 | 2.3 | 3.5 |
| Sudan | 764 | 675 | 0.8 | 0.8 | 1,254 | 47 | 3,137 | 17 | 5.5 | 123.0 | 5.2 | 0.3 | 0.0 |
| Swaziland | 5 | 5 | −0.9 | −0.9 | 614 | 16 | 2,715 | 11 | 0.1 | 0.6 | 3.5 | .. | .. |
| Sweden | 274 | 275 | 0.0 | 0.0 | 542 | 30 | 1,750 | 3 | 0.3 | 44.8 | 10.9 | 4.3 | 1.0 |
| Switzerland | 12 | 12 | −0.4 | −0.4 | 475 | 44 | 3,030 | 3 | 0.2 | 11.9 | 29.6 | .. | .. |
| Syrian Arab Republic | 4 | 5 | −1.5 | −1.3 | 432 | 59 | 3,000 | 0 | 0.9 | 2.7 | 1.5 | .. | .. |
| Tajikistan | 4 | 4 | 0.0 | 0.0 | 427 | 27 | 5,000 | 14 | 0.7 | 26.0 | 18.6 | .. | .. |
| Tanzania | 414 | 353 | 1.0 | 1.1 | 1,431 | 299 | 10,008 | 240 | 15.1 | 374.3 | 42.3 | 2.3 | 0.2 |
| Thailand | 160 | 145 | 0.7 | 0.4 | 1,271 | 157 | 11,625 | 86 | 8.0 | 80.3 | 15.7 | 5.8 | 1.1 |
| Timor-Leste | 10 | 8 | 1.2 | 1.3 | .. | .. | .. | .. | .. | 1.9 | 12.6 | .. | .. |
| Togo | 7 | 4 | 3.4 | 4.5 | 740 | 33 | 3,085 | 10 | 0.4 | 6.5 | 11.9 | .. | .. |
| Trinidad and Tobago | 2 | 2 | 0.3 | 0.2 | 551 | 38 | 2,259 | 1 | 2.4 | 0.2 | 4.7 | 0.1 | 1.3 |
| Tunisia | 6 | 11 | −4.1 | −1.9 | 438 | 52 | 2,196 | 0 | 0.5 | 2.3 | 1.5 | 0.2 | 0.1 |
| Turkey | 97 | 102 | −0.4 | −0.2 | 581 | 121 | 8,650 | 3 | 6.0 | 20.3 | 2.6 | 4.5 | 0.6 |
| Turkmenistan | 41 | 41 | 0.0 | 0.0 | 421 | 44 | .. | 3 | 2.0 | 19.8 | 4.2 | .. | .. |
| Uganda | 49 | 36 | 1.9 | 2.2 | 1,375 | 131 | 4,900 | 38 | 3.3 | 64.3 | 32.6 | .. | .. |
| Ukraine | 93 | 96 | −0.3 | −0.1 | 445 | 58 | 5,100 | 1 | 0.4 | 19.4 | 3.3 | 3.1 | 0.5 |
| United Arab Emirates | 2 | 3 | −2.4 | −0.1 | 298 | 27 | .. | .. | 0.2 | 0.2 | 0.2 | .. | .. |
| United Kingdom | 26 | 28 | −0.7 | −0.4 | 660 | 38 | 1,623 | 13 | 2.1 | 60.5 | 25.0 | 22.5 | 9.2 |
| United States | 2,986 | 3,031 | −0.1 | −0.1 | 1,356 | 937 | 19,473 | 242 | 90.3 | 1,490.1 | 16.3 | 909.5 | 9.4 |
| Uruguay | 9 | 15 | −4.5 | −1.3 | 532 | 66 | 2,278 | 1 | 1.4 | 0.7 | 0.4 | 0.1 | 0.0 |
| Uzbekistan | 30 | 33 | −0.5 | −0.5 | 434 | 33 | 4,800 | 15 | 1.2 | 20.5 | 4.8 | .. | .. |
| Venezuela, RB | 520 | 477 | 0.6 | 0.6 | 1,745 | 166 | 21,073 | 68 | 26.8 | 644.4 | 73.1 | 21.3 | 2.3 |
| Vietnam | 94 | 129 | −2.3 | −2.0 | 1,116 | 152 | 10,500 | 146 | 11.7 | 13.6 | 4.4 | 0.7 | 0.2 |
| West Bank and Gaza | 0 | 0 | 0.0 | 0.0 | .. | .. | .. | .. | .. | .. | .. | .. | .. |
| Yemen, Rep. | 5 | 5 | 0.0 | 0.0 | 459 | 47 | 1,650 | 159 | 3.4 | 0.0 | 0.0 | .. | .. |
| Zambia | 491 | 425 | 0.9 | 1.0 | 1,025 | 38 | 4,747 | 8 | 5.0 | 312.3 | 42.0 | .. | .. |
| Zimbabwe | 222 | 175 | 1.5 | 1.7 | 883 | 35 | 4,440 | 17 | 2.1 | 57.5 | 14.9 | .. | .. |
| **World** | **40,679 s** | **39,426 s** | **0.2 w** | **0.2 w** | | | | | | **15,050.8 s** | **11.6 w** | **4,348.9 s** | **3.8 w** |
| **Low income** | 7,392 | 6,714 | 0.6 | 0.7 | | | | | | 2,794.9 | 9.9 | 73.8 | .. |
| **Middle income** | 23,770 | 23,086 | 0.2 | 0.1 | | | | | | 7,975.0 | 11.7 | 1,233.1 | 1.9 |
| Lower middle income | 7,550 | 7,413 | 0.2 | −0.1 | | | | | | 3,585.7 | 12.8 | 632.6 | 1.7 |
| Upper middle income | 16,220 | 15,673 | 0.2 | 0.3 | | | | | | 4,389.3 | 10.9 | 600.6 | 2.1 |
| **Low & middle income** | 31,161 | 29,799 | 0.3 | 0.3 | | | | | | 10,769.9 | 11.2 | 1,307.0 | 1.6 |
| East Asia & Pacific | 4,581 | 4,507 | 0.3 | −0.2 | | | | | | 1,926.6 | 12.1 | 192.1 | 1.3 |
| Europe & Central Asia | 8,845 | 8,869 | 0.0 | 0.0 | | | | | | 1,630.1 | 7.0 | 321.6 | 1.4 |
| Latin America & Carib. | 9,834 | 9,147 | 0.5 | 0.5 | | | | | | 3,966.0 | 19.7 | 495.7 | 2.7 |
| Middle East & N. Africa | 200 | 211 | −0.4 | −0.3 | | | | | | 301.1 | 3.4 | 114.7 | 1.5 |
| South Asia | 789 | 801 | −0.2 | 0.1 | | | | | | 288.6 | 6.0 | 20.9 | 0.5 |
| Sub-Saharan Africa | 6,913 | 6,263 | 0.7 | 0.6 | | | | | | 2,657.5 | 11.3 | 162.0 | .. |
| **High income** | 9,492 | 9,600 | −0.1 | −0.1 | | | | | | 4,277.1 | 13.0 | 3,042.0 | 8.8 |
| Euro area | 822 | 915 | −0.8 | −0.6 | | | | | | 283.9 | 11.5 | 19.5 | 0.8 |

a. Negative values indicate an increase in forest area. b. Flowering plants only. c. Data may refer to earlier years. They are the most recent reported by the World Conservation Monitoring Centre in 2004. d. Includes Luxembourg. e. Includes Montenegro.

# Deforestation and biodiversity | 3.4

ENVIRONMENT

## About the data

Biological diversity is defined in terms of variability in genes, species, and ecosystems. As threats to biodiversity mount, the international community is increasingly focusing on conserving diversity. Deforestation is a major cause of loss of biodiversity, and habitat conservation is vital for stemming this loss. Conservation efforts have focused on protecting areas of high biodiversity.

The Food and Agriculture Organization's (FAO) *Global Forest Resources Assessment 2005* provides detailed information on forest cover in 2005 and adjusted estimates of forest cover in 1990 and 2000. The current survey uses a uniform definition of forest. Because of space limitations, the table does not break down forest cover between natural forest and plantation, a breakdown the FAO provides for developing countries. Thus the deforestation data in the table may underestimate the rate at which natural forest is disappearing in some countries.

Measures of species richness are a straightforward way to indicate an area's importance for biodiversity. The number of threatened species is also an important measure of the immediate need for conservation in an area. Global analyses of the status of threatened species have been carried out for few groups of organisms. Only for mammals, birds, and amphibians has the status of virtually all known species been assessed. Threatened species are defined using the World Conservation Union's (IUCN) classification: *endangered* (in danger of extinction and unlikely to survive if causal factors continue operating); *vulnerable* (likely to move into the endangered category in the near future if causal factors continue operating); *rare* (not endangered or vulnerable but at risk); *indeterminate* (known to be endangered, vulnerable, or rare but not enough information is available to say which); *out of danger* (formerly included in one of the above categories but now considered relatively secure because appropriate conservation measures are in effect); and *insufficiently known* (suspected but not definitely known to belong to one of the above categories).

Unlike birds and mammals, it is difficult to accurately count plants. The number of plant species is highly debated. The IUCN's *2007 IUCN Red List of Threatened Species*, the result of more than 20 years' work by botanists worldwide, is the most comprehensive list of threatened species on a global scale. Only 5 percent of plant species have been evaluated, and 70 percent are threatened with extinction. Plant species data may not be comparable across countries because of differences in taxonomic concepts and coverage and so should be interpreted with caution. However, the data identify countries that are major sources of global biodiversity and that show national commitments to habitat protection.

More than information about species richness is needed to set priorities for conserving biodiversity. The Global Environment Facility's (GEF) benefits index for biodiversity is a comprehensive indicator of national biodiversity status and is used to guide its biodiversity priorities. The indicator incorporates information on individual species range maps available from the IUCN for virtually all mammals (4,863), amphibians (5,915), and endangered birds (1,098); country data from the World Resources Institute for reptiles and vascular plants; country data from FishBase for 31,190 fish species; and the ecological characteristics of 867 world terrestrial ecoregions from WWF International. For each country the biodiversity indicator incorporates the best available and comparable information in four relevant dimensions: represented species, threatened species, represented ecoregions, and threatened ecoregions. To combine these dimensions into one measure, the indicator uses dimensional weights that reflect the consensus of conservation scientists at the GEF, IUCN, WWF International, and other nongovernmental organizations.

The World Conservation Monitoring Centre (WCMC) compiles data on protected areas, numbers of certain species, and numbers of those species under threat from various sources. Because of differences in definitions, reporting practices, and reporting periods, cross-country comparability is limited.

Nationally protected areas are defined using the six IUCN management categories for areas of at least 1,000 hectares: *scientific reserves* and strict nature reserves with limited public access; *national parks* of national or international significance and not materially affected by human activity; *natural monuments* and natural landscapes with unique aspects; *managed nature reserves* and wildlife sanctuaries; *protected landscapes* (which may include cultural landscapes); and *areas managed mainly for the sustainable use* of natural systems to ensure long-term protection and maintenance of biological diversity. Designating land as a protected area does not mean that protection is in force. And for small countries that only have protected areas smaller than 1,000 hectares, the size limit in the definition leads to an underestimate of protected areas.

Due to variations in consistency and methods of collection, data quality is highly variable across countries. Some countries update their information more frequently than others, some have more accurate data on extent of coverage, and many underreport the number or extent of protected areas.

## Definitions

• **Forest area** is land under natural or planted stands of trees, whether productive or not. • **Average annual deforestation** is the permanent conversion of natural forest area to other uses, including agriculture, ranching, settlements, and infrastructure. Deforested areas do not include areas logged but intended for regeneration or areas degraded by fuelwood gathering, acid precipitation, or forest fires. • **Animal species** are mammals (excluding whales and porpoises) and birds (included within a country's breeding or wintering ranges). • **Higher plants** are native vascular plant species. • **Threatened species** are the number of species classified by the IUCN as endangered, vulnerable, rare, indeterminate, out of danger, or insufficiently known. • **GEF benefits index for biodiversity** is a composite index of relative biodiversity potential based on the species represented in each country and their threat status and diversity of habitat types. The index has been normalized from 0 (no biodiversity potential) to 100 (maximum biodiversity potential). • **Nationally protected areas** are totally or partially protected areas of at least 1,000 hectares that are designated as scientific reserves with limited public access, national parks, natural monuments, nature reserves or wildlife sanctuaries, and protected landscapes. Marine areas, unclassified areas, littoral (intertidal) areas, and sites protected under local or provincial law are excluded. Total area protected is a percentage of total land area (see table 3.1). • **Marine protected areas** are areas of intertidal or subtidal terrain—and overlying water and associated flora and fauna and historical and cultural features—that have been reserved to protect part or all of the enclosed environment.

## Data sources

Data on forest area and deforestation are from the FAO's *Global Forest Resources Assessment 2005*. Data on species are from the electronic files of the United Nations Environmental Program and WCMC and *2007 IUCN Red List of Threatened Species*. The GEF benefits index for biodiversity is from Kiran Dev Pandey, Piet Buys, Ken Chomitz, and David Wheeler's, "Biodiversity Conservation Indicators: New Tools for Priority Setting at the Global Environment Facility" (2006). Data on protected areas are from the United Nations Environment Programme and WCMC, as compiled by the World Resources Institute.

# 3.5 | Freshwater

| | Renewable internal freshwater resources[a] | | Annual freshwater withdrawals | | | | | Water productivity | Access to an improved water source | |
|---|---|---|---|---|---|---|---|---|---|---|
| | Flows billion cu. m 2005 | Per capita cu. m 2005 | billion cu. m 1987–2002[b] | % of internal resources 1987–2002[b] | % for agriculture 1987–2002[b] | % for industry 1987–2002[b] | % for domestic 1987–2002[b] | GDP/water use 2000 $ per cu. m 2002 | % of urban population 2004 | % of rural population 2004 |
| Afghanistan | 55 | .. | 23.3 | 42.3 | 98 | 0 | 2 | .. | .. | .. |
| Albania | 27 | 8,530 | 1.7 | 6.4 | 62 | 11 | 27 | 2.4 | 99 | 94 |
| Algeria | 11 | 341 | 6.1 | 54.2 | 65 | 13 | 22 | 9.7 | 88 | 80 |
| Angola | 148 | 9,195 | 0.4 | 0.2 | 60 | 17 | 23 | 30.8 | 75 | 40 |
| Argentina | 276 | 7,123 | 29.2 | 10.6 | 74 | 9 | 17 | 8.3 | 98 | 80 |
| Armenia | 9 | 3,016 | 3.0 | 32.4 | 66 | 4 | 30 | 0.8 | 99 | 80 |
| Australia | 492 | 24,118 | 23.9 | 4.9 | 75 | 10 | 15 | 17.9 | 100 | 100 |
| Austria | 55 | 6,680 | 2.1 | 3.8 | 1 | 64 | 35 | 93.4 | 100 | 100 |
| Azerbaijan | 8 | 965 | 17.3 | 213.0 | 68 | 28 | 5 | 0.4 | 95 | 59 |
| Bangladesh | 105 | 685 | 79.4 | 75.6 | 96 | 1 | 3 | 0.7 | 82 | 72 |
| Belarus | 37 | 3,805 | 2.8 | 7.5 | 30 | 47 | 23 | 5.0 | 100 | 100 |
| Belgium | 12 | 1,145 | .. | .. | .. | .. | .. | .. | 100 | .. |
| Benin | 10 | 1,213 | 0.1 | 1.3 | 45 | 23 | 32 | 19.0 | 78 | 57 |
| Bolivia | 304 | 33,054 | 1.4 | 0.5 | 81 | 7 | 13 | 6.1 | 95 | 68 |
| Bosnia and Herzegovina | 36 | 9,067 | .. | .. | .. | .. | .. | .. | 99 | 96 |
| Botswana | 2 | 1,307 | 0.2 | 8.1 | 41 | 18 | 41 | 35.4 | 100 | 90 |
| Brazil | 5,418 | 29,000 | 59.3 | 1.1 | 62 | 18 | 20 | 11.3 | 96 | 57 |
| Bulgaria | 21 | 2,713 | 10.5 | 50.0 | 19 | 78 | 3 | 1.3 | 100 | 97 |
| Burkina Faso | 13 | 897 | 0.8 | 6.4 | 86 | 1 | 13 | 3.6 | 94 | 54 |
| Burundi | 10 | 1,285 | 0.3 | 2.9 | 77 | 6 | 17 | 2.6 | 92 | 77 |
| Cambodia | 121 | 8,642 | 4.1 | 3.4 | 98 | 0 | 1 | 1.0 | 64 | 35 |
| Cameroon | 273 | 15,341 | 1.0 | 0.4 | 74 | 8 | 18 | 11.1 | 86 | 44 |
| Canada | 2,850 | 88,203 | 46.0 | 1.6 | 12 | 69 | 20 | 16.5 | 100 | 99 |
| Central African Republic | 141 | 33,640 | 0.0 | 0.0 | 4 | 16 | 80 | 38.3 | 93 | 61 |
| Chad | 15 | 1,478 | 0.2 | 1.5 | 83 | 0 | 17 | 7.3 | 41 | 43 |
| Chile | 884 | 54,249 | 12.6 | 1.4 | 64 | 25 | 11 | 6.4 | 100 | 58 |
| China | 2,812 | 2,156 | 630.3 | 22.4 | 68 | 26 | 7 | 2.2 | 93 | 67 |
| Hong Kong, China | .. | .. | .. | .. | .. | .. | .. | .. | .. | .. |
| Colombia | 2,112 | 46,990 | 10.7 | 0.5 | 46 | 4 | 50 | 8.1 | 99 | 71 |
| Congo, Dem. Rep. | 900 | 15,322 | 0.4 | 0.0 | 31 | 17 | 53 | 12.1 | 82 | 29 |
| Congo, Rep. | 222 | 61,498 | 0.0 | 0.0 | 9 | 22 | 70 | 76.1 | 84 | 27 |
| Costa Rica | 112 | 25,975 | 2.7 | 2.4 | 53 | 17 | 29 | 6.2 | 100 | 92 |
| Côte d'Ivoire | 77 | 4,132 | 0.9 | 1.2 | 65 | 12 | 24 | 11.0 | 97 | 74 |
| Croatia | 38 | 8,485 | .. | .. | .. | .. | .. | .. | 100 | 100 |
| Cuba | 38 | 3,384 | 8.2 | 21.5 | 69 | 12 | 19 | .. | 95 | 78 |
| Czech Republic | 13 | 1,290 | 2.6 | 19.5 | 2 | 57 | 41 | 23.0 | 100 | 100 |
| Denmark | 6 | 1,108 | 1.3 | 21.2 | 43 | 25 | 32 | 127.5 | 100 | 100 |
| Dominican Republic | 21 | 2,218 | 3.4 | 16.1 | 66 | 2 | 32 | 6.3 | 97 | 91 |
| Ecuador | 432 | 33,076 | 17.0 | 3.9 | 82 | 5 | 12 | 1.0 | 97 | 89 |
| Egypt, Arab Rep. | 2 | 25 | 68.3 | 3,794.4 | 86 | 6 | 8 | 1.6 | 99 | 97 |
| El Salvador | 18 | 2,669 | 1.3 | 7.2 | 59 | 16 | 25 | 10.7 | 94 | 70 |
| Eritrea | 3 | 619 | 0.3 | 10.7 | 97 | 0 | 3 | 2.3 | 74 | 57 |
| Estonia | 13 | 9,435 | 0.2 | 1.2 | 5 | 38 | 57 | 41.4 | 100 | 99 |
| Ethiopia | 122 | 1,623 | 5.6 | 4.6 | 94 | 0 | 6 | 1.6 | 81 | 11 |
| Finland | 107 | 20,396 | 2.5 | 2.3 | 3 | 84 | 14 | 51.3 | 100 | 100 |
| France | 179 | 2,932 | 40.0 | 22.4 | 10 | 74 | 16 | 34.2 | 100 | 100 |
| Gabon | 164 | 127,064 | 0.1 | 0.1 | 42 | 8 | 50 | 43.0 | 95 | 47 |
| Gambia, The | 3 | 1,855 | 0.0 | 1.0 | 65 | 12 | 23 | 14.1 | 95 | 77 |
| Georgia | 58 | 12,988 | 3.6 | 6.2 | 59 | 21 | 20 | 0.9 | 96 | 67 |
| Germany | 107 | 1,297 | 47.1 | 44.0 | 20 | 68 | 12 | 40.9 | 100 | 100 |
| Ghana | 30 | 1,345 | 1.0 | 3.2 | 66 | 10 | 24 | 5.5 | 88 | 64 |
| Greece | 58 | 5,223 | 7.8 | 13.4 | 80 | 3 | 16 | 20.1 | .. | .. |
| Guatemala | 109 | 8,592 | 2.0 | 1.8 | 80 | 13 | 6 | 10.0 | 99 | 92 |
| Guinea | 226 | 25,104 | 1.5 | 0.7 | 90 | 2 | 8 | 2.2 | 78 | 35 |
| Guinea-Bissau | 16 | 10,019 | 0.2 | 1.1 | 82 | 5 | 13 | 1.1 | 79 | 49 |
| Haiti | 13 | 1,398 | 1.0 | 7.6 | 94 | 1 | 5 | 3.8 | 52 | 56 |

| | Renewable internal freshwater resources[a] | | Annual freshwater withdrawals | | | | | Water productivity | Access to an improved water source | |
|---|---|---|---|---|---|---|---|---|---|---|
| | Flows billion cu. m **2005** | Per capita cu. m **2005** | billion cu. m **1987–2002[b]** | % of internal resources **1987–2002[b]** | % for agriculture **1987–2002[b]** | % for industry **1987–2002[b]** | % for domestic **1987–2002[b]** | GDP/water use 2000 $ per cu. m **2002** | % of urban population **2004** | % of rural population **2004** |
| Honduras | 96 | 14,033 | 0.9 | 0.9 | 80 | 12 | 8 | 7.3 | 95 | 81 |
| Hungary | 6 | 595 | 7.6 | 127.3 | 32 | 59 | 9 | 6.8 | 100 | 98 |
| India | 1,261 | 1,152 | 645.8 | 51.2 | 86 | 5 | 8 | 0.8 | 95 | 83 |
| Indonesia | 2,838 | 12,867 | 82.8 | 2.9 | 91 | 1 | 8 | 2.2 | 87 | 69 |
| Iran, Islamic Rep. | 129 | 1,860 | 72.9 | 56.7 | 91 | 2 | 7 | 1.5 | 99 | 84 |
| Iraq | 35 | .. | 42.7 | 121.3 | 92 | 5 | 3 | 0.5 | .. | .. |
| Ireland | 49 | 11,781 | 1.1 | 2.3 | 0 | 77 | 23 | 95.7 | 100 | .. |
| Israel | 1 | 116 | 2.1 | 256.3 | 62 | 7 | 31 | 58.1 | 100 | 100 |
| Italy | 183 | 3,114 | 44.4 | 24.3 | 45 | 37 | 18 | 25.3 | 100 | .. |
| Jamaica | 9 | 3,541 | 0.4 | 4.4 | 49 | 17 | 34 | 20.2 | 98 | 88 |
| Japan | 430 | 3,365 | 88.4 | 20.6 | 62 | 18 | 20 | 53.0 | 100 | 100 |
| Jordan | 1 | 129 | 1.0 | 144.3 | 75 | 4 | 21 | 9.3 | 99 | 91 |
| Kazakhstan | 75 | 4,978 | 35.0 | 46.4 | 82 | 17 | 2 | 0.7 | 97 | 73 |
| Kenya | 21 | 581 | 1.6 | 7.6 | 64 | 6 | 30 | 8.4 | 83 | 46 |
| Korea, Dem. Rep. | 67 | 2,837 | 9.0 | 13.5 | 55 | 25 | 20 | .. | 100 | 100 |
| Korea, Rep. | 65 | 1,344 | 18.6 | 28.6 | 48 | 16 | 36 | 30.6 | 97 | 71 |
| Kuwait | .. | .. | 0.4 | .. | 52 | 2 | 45 | 90.8 | .. | .. |
| Kyrgyz Republic | 47 | 9,041 | 10.1 | 21.7 | 94 | 3 | 3 | 0.1 | 98 | 66 |
| Lao PDR | 190 | 33,616 | 3.0 | 1.6 | 90 | 6 | 4 | 0.6 | 79 | 43 |
| Latvia | 17 | 7,259 | 0.3 | 1.8 | 13 | 33 | 53 | 30.0 | 100 | 96 |
| Lebanon | 5 | 1,197 | 1.4 | 28.8 | 67 | 1 | 33 | 13.2 | 100 | 100 |
| Lesotho | 5 | 2,625 | 0.1 | 1.0 | 20 | 40 | 40 | 17.9 | 92 | 76 |
| Liberia | 200 | 58,109 | 0.1 | 0.1 | 55 | 18 | 27 | 5.4 | 72 | 52 |
| Libya | 1 | 101 | 4.3 | 711.3 | 83 | 3 | 14 | 8.7 | 72 | 68 |
| Lithuania | 16 | 4,569 | 0.3 | 1.7 | 7 | 15 | 78 | 48.2 | .. | .. |
| Macedonia, FYR | 5 | 2,655 | .. | .. | .. | .. | .. | .. | .. | .. |
| Madagascar | 337 | 18,077 | 15.0 | 4.4 | 96 | 2 | 3 | 0.2 | 77 | 35 |
| Malawi | 16 | 1,217 | 1.0 | 6.3 | 80 | 5 | 15 | 1.6 | 98 | 68 |
| Malaysia | 580 | 22,609 | 9.0 | 1.6 | 62 | 21 | 17 | 10.5 | 100 | 96 |
| Mali | 60 | 5,167 | 6.5 | 10.9 | 90 | 1 | 9 | 0.4 | 78 | 36 |
| Mauritania | 0 | 135 | 1.7 | 425.0 | 88 | 3 | 9 | 0.7 | 59 | 44 |
| Mauritius | 3 | 2,252 | 0.6 | 21.8 | .. | .. | .. | 7.9 | 100 | 100 |
| Mexico | 409 | 3,967 | 78.2 | 19.1 | 77 | 5 | 17 | 7.5 | 100 | 87 |
| Moldova | 1 | 258 | 2.3 | 231.0 | 33 | 58 | 10 | 0.6 | 97 | 88 |
| Mongolia | 35 | 13,626 | 0.4 | 1.3 | 52 | 27 | 20 | 2.7 | 87 | 30 |
| Morocco | 29 | 962 | 12.6 | 43.4 | 87 | 3 | 10 | 3.3 | 99 | 56 |
| Mozambique | 100 | 4,885 | 0.6 | 0.6 | 87 | 2 | 11 | 8.2 | 72 | 26 |
| Myanmar | 881 | 18,358 | 33.2 | 3.8 | 98 | 1 | 1 | .. | 80 | 77 |
| Namibia | 6 | 3,070 | 0.3 | 4.8 | 71 | 5 | 24 | 12.4 | 98 | 81 |
| Nepal | 198 | 7,315 | 10.2 | 5.1 | 96 | 1 | 3 | 0.6 | 96 | 89 |
| Netherlands | 11 | 674 | 7.9 | 72.2 | 34 | 60 | 6 | 49.5 | 100 | 100 |
| New Zealand | 327 | 79,102 | 2.1 | 0.6 | 42 | 9 | 48 | 27.0 | 100 | .. |
| Nicaragua | 190 | 34,727 | 1.3 | 0.7 | 83 | 2 | 15 | 3.1 | 90 | 63 |
| Niger | 4 | 264 | 2.2 | 62.3 | 95 | 0 | 4 | 0.9 | 80 | 36 |
| Nigeria | 221 | 1,563 | 8.0 | 3.6 | 69 | 10 | 21 | 6.0 | 67 | 31 |
| Norway | 382 | 82,625 | 2.2 | 0.6 | 11 | 67 | 23 | 79.6 | 100 | 100 |
| Oman | 1 | 399 | 1.4 | 136.0 | 90 | 2 | 7 | 16.1 | 85 | 73 |
| Pakistan | 52 | 336 | 169.4 | 323.3 | 96 | 2 | 2 | 0.5 | 96 | 89 |
| Panama | 147 | 45,613 | 0.8 | 0.6 | 28 | 5 | 67 | 14.6 | 99 | 79 |
| Papua New Guinea | 801 | 131,967 | .. | .. | .. | .. | .. | .. | 88 | 32 |
| Paraguay | 94 | 15,936 | 0.5 | 0.5 | 71 | 8 | 20 | 14.7 | 99 | 68 |
| Peru | 1,616 | 59,250 | 20.1 | 1.2 | 82 | 10 | 8 | 2.8 | 89 | 65 |
| Philippines | 479 | 5,664 | 28.5 | 6.0 | 74 | 9 | 17 | 2.8 | 87 | 82 |
| Poland | 54 | 1,404 | 16.2 | 30.2 | 8 | 79 | 13 | 10.9 | 100 | .. |
| Portugal | 38 | 3,602 | 11.3 | 29.6 | 78 | 12 | 10 | 10.3 | .. | .. |
| Puerto Rico | 7 | 1,815 | .. | .. | .. | .. | .. | .. | .. | .. |

| | Renewable internal freshwater resources[a] | | Annual freshwater withdrawals | | | | | Water productivity | Access to an improved water source | |
|---|---|---|---|---|---|---|---|---|---|---|
| | Flows billion cu. m | Per capita cu. m | billion cu. m | % of internal resources | % for agriculture | % for industry | % for domestic | GDP/water use 2000 $ per cu. m | % of urban population | % of rural population |
| | **2005** | **2005** | **1987–2002[b]** | **1987–2002[b]** | **1987–2002[b]** | **1987–2002[b]** | **1987–2002[b]** | **2002** | **2004** | **2004** |
| Romania | 42 | 1,955 | 23.2 | 54.8 | 57 | 34 | 9 | 1.8 | 91 | 16 |
| Russian Federation | 4,313 | 30,127 | 76.7 | 1.8 | 18 | 63 | 19 | 3.7 | 100 | 88 |
| Rwanda | 10 | 1,029 | 0.2 | 1.6 | 68 | 8 | 24 | 14.1 | 92 | 69 |
| Saudi Arabia | 2 | 104 | 17.3 | 721.7 | 89 | 1 | 10 | 11.0 | 97 | 63 |
| Senegal | 26 | 2,192 | 2.2 | 8.6 | 93 | 3 | 4 | 2.2 | 92 | 60 |
| Serbia[c] | 44 | 5,456 | .. | .. | .. | .. | .. | .. | 99 | 86 |
| Sierra Leone | 160 | 28,641 | 0.4 | 0.2 | 92 | 3 | 5 | 2.5 | 75 | 46 |
| Singapore | 1 | 138 | .. | .. | .. | .. | .. | .. | 100 | .. |
| Slovak Republic | 13 | 2,339 | .. | .. | .. | .. | .. | .. | 100 | 99 |
| Slovenia | 19 | 9,348 | .. | .. | .. | .. | .. | .. | .. | .. |
| Somalia | 6 | 732 | 3.3 | 54.8 | 100 | 0 | 0 | .. | 32 | 27 |
| South Africa | 45 | 955 | 12.5 | 27.9 | 63 | 6 | 31 | 11.3 | 99 | 73 |
| Spain | 111 | 2,562 | 35.6 | 32.0 | 68 | 19 | 13 | 17.3 | 100 | 100 |
| Sri Lanka | 50 | 2,542 | 12.6 | 25.2 | 95 | 2 | 2 | 1.3 | 98 | 74 |
| Sudan | 30 | 813 | 37.3 | 124.4 | 97 | 1 | 3 | 0.4 | 78 | 64 |
| Swaziland | 3 | 2,299 | 1.0 | 40.1 | 97 | 1 | 2 | 1.4 | 87 | 54 |
| Sweden | 171 | 18,949 | 3.0 | 1.7 | 9 | 54 | 37 | 84.3 | 100 | 100 |
| Switzerland | 40 | 5,432 | 2.6 | 6.4 | 2 | 74 | 24 | 97.0 | 100 | 100 |
| Syrian Arab Republic | 7 | 370 | 20.0 | 285.0 | 95 | 2 | 3 | 1.1 | 98 | 87 |
| Tajikistan | 66 | 10,122 | 12.0 | 18.0 | 92 | 5 | 4 | 0.1 | 92 | 48 |
| Tanzania | 84 | 2,183 | 5.2 | 6.2 | 89 | 0 | 10 | 2.0 | 85 | 49 |
| Thailand | 210 | 3,333 | 87.1 | 41.5 | 95 | 2 | 2 | 1.5 | 98 | 100 |
| Timor-Leste | .. | .. | .. | .. | .. | .. | .. | .. | .. | .. |
| Togo | 12 | 1,843 | 0.2 | 1.5 | 45 | 2 | 53 | 8.2 | 80 | 36 |
| Trinidad and Tobago | 4 | 2,871 | 0.3 | 8.2 | 6 | 26 | 68 | 29.6 | 92 | 88 |
| Tunisia | 4 | 419 | 2.6 | 62.9 | 82 | 4 | 14 | 7.9 | 99 | 82 |
| Turkey | 227 | 3,150 | 37.5 | 16.5 | 74 | 11 | 15 | 5.3 | 98 | 93 |
| Turkmenistan | 1 | 290 | 24.7 | 1,760.7 | 98 | 1 | 2 | .. | 93 | 54 |
| Uganda | 39 | 1,347 | 0.3 | 0.8 | 40 | 17 | 43 | 22.1 | 87 | 56 |
| Ukraine | 53 | 1,127 | 37.5 | 70.7 | 52 | 35 | 12 | 1.0 | 99 | 91 |
| United Arab Emirates | 0 | 49 | 2.3 | 1,150.0 | 68 | 9 | 23 | 34.0 | 100 | 100 |
| United Kingdom | 145 | 2,408 | 9.5 | 6.6 | 3 | 75 | 22 | 157.9 | 100 | 100 |
| United States | 2,800 | 9,443 | 479.3 | 17.1 | 41 | 46 | 13 | 20.9 | 100 | 100 |
| Uruguay | 59 | 17,848 | 3.2 | 5.3 | 96 | 1 | 3 | 5.6 | 100 | 100 |
| Uzbekistan | 16 | 623 | 58.3 | 357.9 | 93 | 2 | 5 | 0.3 | 95 | 75 |
| Venezuela, RB | 723 | 27,185 | 8.4 | 1.2 | 47 | 7 | 46 | 13.2 | 85 | 70 |
| Vietnam | 367 | 4,410 | 71.4 | 19.5 | 68 | 24 | 8 | 0.5 | 99 | 80 |
| West Bank and Gaza | .. | .. | .. | .. | .. | .. | .. | .. | 94 | 88 |
| Yemen, Rep. | 4 | 194 | 6.6 | 161.7 | 95 | 1 | 4 | 1.5 | 71 | 65 |
| Zambia | 80 | 6,987 | 1.7 | 2.2 | 76 | 7 | 17 | 2.0 | 90 | 40 |
| Zimbabwe | 12 | 938 | 4.2 | 34.2 | 79 | 7 | 14 | 1.6 | 98 | 72 |
| **World** | **43,507 s** | **6,778 w** | **3,807.4 s** | **9.1 w** | **70 w** | **20 w** | **10 w** | **8.6 w** | **94 w** | **72 w** |
| **Low income** | 7,404 | 3,077 | 1,240.7 | 18.9 | 89 | 5 | 6 | 0.8 | 88 | 69 |
| **Middle income** | 26,662 | 8,754 | 1,667.0 | 6.3 | 71 | 19 | 10 | 3.3 | 95 | 72 |
| Lower middle income | 18,455 | 5,769 | 1,337.3 | 7.3 | 75 | 17 | 8 | 2.1 | 93 | 71 |
| Upper middle income | 8,207 | 17,199 | 329.6 | 4.0 | 54 | 29 | 18 | 6.7 | 98 | 78 |
| **Low & middle income** | 34,066 | 6,268 | 2,907.6 | 8.8 | 78 | 13 | 8 | 2.3 | 93 | 70 |
| East Asia & Pacific | 9,454 | 5,022 | 958.8 | 11.1 | 74 | 20 | 7 | 2.1 | 92 | 70 |
| Europe & Central Asia | 5,255 | 11,473 | 383.2 | 7.5 | 59 | 31 | 10 | 2.5 | 99 | 80 |
| Latin America & Carib. | 13,429 | 24,471 | 265.3 | 2.0 | 71 | 10 | 19 | 7.8 | 96 | 73 |
| Middle East & N. Africa | 228 | 757 | 239.8 | 105.0 | 89 | 4 | 7 | 2.0 | 96 | 81 |
| South Asia | 1,816 | 1,230 | 941.1 | 51.8 | 90 | 4 | 6 | 0.7 | 94 | 81 |
| Sub-Saharan Africa | 3,884 | 5,093 | 119.3 | 3.1 | 87 | 3 | 10 | 3.1 | 80 | 42 |
| **High income** | 9,441 | 9,579 | 899.7 | 10.2 | 42 | 42 | 15 | 28.3 | 100 | 98 |
| Euro area | 929 | 2,951 | 199.7 | 22.3 | 38 | 48 | 15 | 30.7 | 100 | 100 |

a. Excludes river flows from other countries because of data unreliability. b. Data are for the most recent year available (see *Primary data documentation*). c. Includes Montenegro.

## About the data

The data on freshwater resources are based on estimates of runoff into rivers and recharge of groundwater. These estimates are based on different sources and refer to different years, so cross-country comparisons should be made with caution. Because the data are collected intermittently, they may hide significant variations in total renewable water resources from year to year. The data also fail to distinguish between seasonal and geographic variations in water availability within countries. Data for small countries and countries in arid and semiarid zones are less reliable than those for larger countries and countries with greater rainfall.

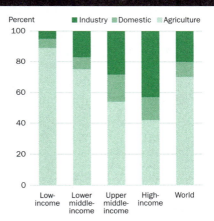

**Agriculture is still the largest user of water, accounting for some 70 percent of global withdrawals**    3.5a

*Source:* Table 3.5.

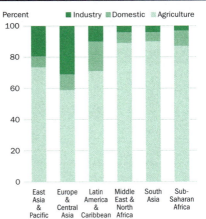

**The share of withdrawals for agriculture approaches 90 percent in some developing regions**    3.5b

*Source:* Table 3.5.

Caution should also be exercised in comparing data on annual freshwater withdrawals, which are subject to variations in collection and estimation methods. In addition, inflows and outflows are estimated at different times and at different levels of quality and precision, requiring caution in interpreting the data, particularly for water-short countries, notably in the Middle East and North Africa.

Water productivity is an indication only of the efficiency by which each country uses its water resources. Given the different economic structure of each country, these indicators should be used carefully, taking into account the countries' sectoral activities and natural resource endowments.

The data on access to an improved water source measure the percentage of the population with ready access to water for domestic purposes. The data are based on surveys and estimates provided by governments to the Joint Monitoring Programme of the World Health Organization (WHO) and the United Nations Children's Fund (UNICEF). The coverage rates are based on information from service users on actual household use rather than on information from service providers, which may include nonfunctioning systems. Access to drinking water from an improved source does not ensure that the water is safe or adequate, as these characteristics are not tested at the time of survey. While information on access to an improved water source is widely used, it is extremely subjective, and such terms as *safe, improved, adequate,* and *reasonable* may have different meaning in different countries despite official WHO definitions (see *Definitions*). Even in high-income countries treated water may not always be safe to drink. Access to an improved water source is equated with connection to a supply system; it does not take into account variations in the quality and cost (broadly defined) of the service.

## Definitions

• **Renewable internal freshwater resources flows** are internal renewable resources (internal river flows and groundwater from rainfall) in the country. • **Renewable internal freshwater resources per capita** are calculated using the World Bank's population estimates (see table 2.1). • **Annual freshwater withdrawals** are total water withdrawals, not counting evaporation losses from storage basins. Withdrawals also include water from desalination plants in countries where they are a significant source. Withdrawals can exceed 100 percent of total renewable resources where extraction from nonrenewable aquifers or desalination plants is considerable or where water reuse is significant. Withdrawals for agriculture and industry are total withdrawals for irrigation and livestock production and for direct industrial use (including for cooling thermoelectric plants). Withdrawals for domestic uses include drinking water, municipal use or supply, and use for public services, commercial establishments, and homes. • **Water productivity** is calculated as GDP in constant prices divided by annual total water withdrawal. • **Access to an improved water source** is the percentage of the population with reasonable access to an adequate amount of water from an improved source, such as piped water into a dwelling, plot, or yard; public tap or standpipe; tubewell or borehole; protected dug well or spring; and rainwater collection. Unimproved sources include unprotected dug wells or springs, carts with small tank or drum, bottled water, and tanker trucks. Reasonable access is defined as the availability of at least 20 liters a person a day from a source within 1 kilometer of the dwelling.

### Data sources

Data on freshwater resources and withdrawals are compiled by the World Resources Institute from various sources and published in *World Resources 2005* (produced in collaboration with the United Nations Environment Programme, United Nations Development Programme, and World Bank). These data are supplemented by the Food and Agriculture Organization's AQUASTAT data. The GDP estimates used to calculate water productivity are from the World Bank national accounts database. Data on access to water are from WHO and UNICEF's *Meeting the MDG Drinking Water and Sanitation Target* (www.unicef.org/wes/mdgreport).

| | Emissions of organic water pollutants | | | | Industry shares of emissions of organic water pollutants | | | | | | | |
|---|---|---|---|---|---|---|---|---|---|---|---|---|
| | thousand kilograms per day | | kilograms per day per worker | | Primary metals | Paper and pulp | Chemicals | Food and beverages | Stone, ceramics, and glass | Textiles | Wood | Other |
| | | | | | | | | | % of total | | | |
| | 1990 | 2004[a] | 1990 | 2004[a] | 2004[a] | 2004[a] | 2004[a] | 2004[a] | 2004[a] | 2004[a] | 2004[a] | 2004[a] |
| Afghanistan | 5.9 | 0.2 | 0.16 | 0.21 | .. | 37.7 | 17.5 | 31.1 | 0.4 | 13.2 | .. | .. |
| Albania | 34.8 | 2.0 | 0.14 | 0.20 | 0.0 | 0.0 | 0.0 | 25.0 | 0.0 | 75.0 | 0.0 | 0.0 |
| Algeria | 107.0 | .. | 0.25 | .. | .. | .. | .. | .. | .. | .. | .. | .. |
| Angola | 4.5 | .. | 0.19 | .. | .. | .. | .. | .. | .. | .. | .. | .. |
| Argentina | 186.7 | 164.3 | 0.20 | 0.23 | 5.6 | 14.6 | 8.6 | 58.9 | 0.1 | 7.6 | 1.1 | 3.5 |
| Armenia | 37.9 | 7.1 | 0.11 | 0.28 | .. | .. | .. | 77.6 | .. | 22.4 | .. | .. |
| Australia | 186.1 | 111.7 | 0.18 | 0.18 | 12.4 | 22.8 | 6.7 | 43.5 | 0.2 | 5.3 | 2.8 | 6.3 |
| Austria | 94.1 | 36.9 | 0.15 | 0.08 | 14.6 | 21.0 | 7.8 | 34.9 | 0.3 | 3.3 | 6.1 | 12.1 |
| Azerbaijan | 53.3 | 16.1 | 0.15 | 0.17 | 9.9 | 2.4 | 21.0 | 15.0 | 5.9 | 14.3 | 1.0 | 30.4 |
| Bangladesh | 171.1 | .. | 0.17 | .. | .. | .. | .. | .. | .. | .. | .. | .. |
| Belarus | .. | .. | .. | .. | .. | .. | .. | .. | .. | .. | .. | .. |
| Belgium | 118.0 | 102.3 | 0.16 | 0.17 | 13.6 | 18.4 | 11.2 | 40.3 | 0.2 | 5.9 | 2.2 | 8.2 |
| Benin | .. | .. | .. | .. | .. | .. | .. | .. | .. | .. | .. | .. |
| Bolivia | 8.4 | 11.5 | 0.24 | 0.25 | 1.2 | 15.1 | 6.8 | 64.9 | 0.2 | 8.7 | 2.3 | 0.7 |
| Bosnia and Herzegovina | 50.7 | .. | 0.14 | .. | .. | .. | .. | .. | .. | .. | .. | .. |
| Botswana | 4.5 | 3.3 | 0.19 | 0.34 | 0.0 | 3.4 | 0.0 | 69.5 | 0.0 | 5.6 | 0.0 | 21.4 |
| Brazil | 780.4 | .. | 0.19 | .. | .. | .. | .. | .. | .. | .. | .. | .. |
| Bulgaria | 149.4 | 101.9 | 0.11 | 0.17 | 7.9 | 9.5 | 6.6 | 46.1 | 0.2 | 22.2 | 2.3 | 5.2 |
| Burkina Faso | .. | .. | .. | .. | .. | .. | .. | .. | .. | .. | .. | .. |
| Burundi | 1.6 | .. | 0.24 | .. | .. | .. | .. | .. | .. | .. | .. | .. |
| Cambodia | 11.8 | .. | 0.14 | .. | .. | .. | .. | .. | .. | .. | .. | .. |
| Cameroon | 14.0 | 10.0 | 0.28 | 0.19 | 0.4 | 5.2 | 36.1 | 48.8 | 0.0 | 3.8 | 5.0 | 0.8 |
| Canada | 321.5 | 312.5 | 0.17 | 0.16 | 9.6 | 22.1 | 8.6 | 39.5 | 0.1 | 5.8 | 5.4 | 8.9 |
| Central African Republic | 1.0 | .. | 0.18 | .. | .. | .. | .. | .. | .. | .. | .. | .. |
| Chad | .. | .. | .. | .. | .. | .. | .. | .. | .. | .. | .. | .. |
| Chile | 66.8 | 72.9 | 0.22 | 0.24 | 6.9 | 11.3 | 8.9 | 62.7 | 0.1 | 5.0 | 2.6 | 2.5 |
| China | 7,038.1 | 6,088.7 | 0.14 | 0.14 | 20.4 | 10.9 | 14.8 | 28.1 | 0.5 | 15.5 | 0.9 | 8.8 |
| Hong Kong, China | 86.1 | 34.3 | 0.12 | 0.20 | 1.2 | 43.5 | 3.9 | 30.5 | 0.1 | 16.2 | 0.2 | 4.6 |
| Colombia | 93.3 | 93.9 | 0.19 | 0.21 | 3.1 | 16.2 | 9.7 | 53.2 | 0.2 | 14.2 | 1.0 | 2.4 |
| Congo, Dem. Rep. | .. | .. | .. | .. | .. | .. | .. | .. | .. | .. | .. | .. |
| Congo, Rep. | 2.5 | .. | 0.32 | .. | .. | .. | .. | .. | .. | .. | .. | .. |
| Costa Rica | 27.2 | 31.2 | 0.20 | 0.22 | 1.6 | 10.0 | 8.2 | 65.7 | 0.1 | 10.2 | 1.3 | 2.9 |
| Côte d'Ivoire | 7.9 | .. | 0.22 | .. | .. | .. | .. | .. | .. | .. | .. | .. |
| Croatia | 80.0 | 42.9 | 0.15 | 0.17 | 6.1 | 15.9 | 7.5 | 48.4 | 0.2 | 12.0 | 3.6 | 6.3 |
| Cuba | 173.0 | .. | 0.25 | .. | .. | .. | .. | .. | .. | .. | .. | .. |
| Czech Republic | 205.1 | .. | 0.13 | .. | .. | .. | .. | .. | .. | .. | .. | .. |
| Denmark | 91.9 | .. | 0.18 | .. | .. | .. | .. | .. | .. | .. | .. | .. |
| Dominican Republic | 47.9 | .. | 0.36 | .. | .. | .. | .. | .. | .. | .. | .. | .. |
| Ecuador | 25.6 | 41.5 | 0.23 | 0.28 | 1.9 | 7.5 | 12.6 | 45.4 | 4.6 | 12.9 | 2.6 | 12.5 |
| Egypt, Arab Rep. | 211.5 | 186.1 | 0.20 | 0.20 | 10.8 | 8.2 | 9.0 | 50.7 | 0.3 | 17.7 | 0.6 | 2.8 |
| El Salvador | 5.5 | .. | 0.22 | .. | .. | .. | .. | .. | .. | .. | .. | .. |
| Eritrea | .. | .. | .. | .. | .. | .. | .. | .. | .. | .. | .. | .. |
| Estonia | .. | .. | .. | .. | .. | .. | .. | .. | .. | .. | .. | .. |
| Ethiopia | 18.6 | 22.1 | 0.23 | 0.23 | 2.3 | 11.0 | 5.5 | 61.0 | 0.3 | 17.3 | 2.0 | 0.7 |
| Finland | 79.5 | 67.4 | 0.18 | 0.16 | 8.7 | 40.1 | 7.6 | 26.6 | 0.2 | 2.4 | 3.9 | 10.6 |
| France | 653.5 | 564.6 | 0.15 | 0.15 | 7.2 | 13.8 | 12.9 | 49.5 | 0.2 | 2.9 | 2.3 | 11.1 |
| Gabon | 2.0 | .. | 0.25 | .. | .. | .. | .. | .. | .. | .. | .. | .. |
| Gambia, The | 0.8 | .. | 0.34 | .. | .. | .. | .. | .. | .. | .. | .. | .. |
| Georgia | .. | .. | .. | .. | .. | .. | .. | .. | .. | .. | .. | .. |
| Germany | 835.0 | 966.7 | 0.12 | 0.14 | 9.3 | 20.4 | 11.8 | 38.7 | 0.2 | 2.3 | 2.1 | 15.1 |
| Ghana | 16.5 | .. | 0.20 | .. | .. | .. | .. | .. | .. | .. | .. | .. |
| Greece | 63.5 | .. | 0.18 | .. | .. | .. | .. | .. | .. | .. | .. | .. |
| Guatemala | 21.6 | .. | 0.23 | .. | .. | .. | .. | .. | .. | .. | .. | .. |
| Guinea | .. | .. | .. | .. | .. | .. | .. | .. | .. | .. | .. | .. |
| Guinea-Bissau | .. | .. | .. | .. | .. | .. | .. | .. | .. | .. | .. | .. |
| Haiti | 5.4 | .. | 0.20 | .. | .. | .. | .. | .. | .. | .. | .. | .. |

|  | Emissions of organic water pollutants | | | | Industry shares of emissions of organic water pollutants | | | | | | | |
|---|---|---|---|---|---|---|---|---|---|---|---|---|
|  | thousand kilograms per day | | kilograms per day per worker | | | | | | % of total | | | | |
|  | | | | | Primary metals | Paper and pulp | Chemicals | Food and beverages | Stone, ceramics, and glass | Textiles | Wood | Other |
|  | 1990 | 2004a | 1990 | 2004a | 2004a | 2004a | 2004a | 2004a | 2004a | 2004a | 2004a | 2004a |
| Honduras | 17.8 | .. | 0.23 | .. | .. | .. | .. | .. | .. | .. | .. | .. |
| Hungary | 178.0 | 60.7 | 0.16 | 0.10 | 6.4 | 11.8 | 7.6 | 49.1 | 0.2 | 12.8 | 2.4 | 9.8 |
| India | 1,410.6 | 1,519.8 | 0.20 | 0.20 | 12.2 | 7.6 | 9.2 | 53.7 | 0.3 | 12.7 | 0.3 | 3.9 |
| Indonesia | 495.6 | 733.0 | 0.19 | 0.18 | 2.5 | 8.2 | 9.2 | 53.7 | 0.1 | 19.4 | 4.5 | 2.4 |
| Iran, Islamic Rep. | 102.7 | 164.8 | 0.16 | 0.15 | 15.6 | 8.0 | 10.7 | 46.7 | 0.7 | 9.5 | 0.9 | 8.1 |
| Iraq | 26.7 | .. | 0.19 | .. | .. | .. | .. | .. | .. | .. | .. | .. |
| Ireland | 34.6 | 11.6 | 0.18 | 0.21 | .. | 58.5 | 10.4 | 22.9 | 0.7 | .. | 7.5 | .. |
| Israel | 46.4 | 54.0 | 0.16 | 0.16 | 3.6 | 22.3 | 10.5 | 45.5 | 0.1 | 6.0 | 1.9 | 10.1 |
| Italy | 358.1 | 488.9 | 0.13 | 0.12 | 9.4 | 16.6 | 10.7 | 30.8 | 0.3 | 15.0 | 3.9 | 13.3 |
| Jamaica | 18.7 | .. | 0.29 | .. | .. | .. | .. | .. | .. | .. | .. | .. |
| Japan | 1,556.6 | 1,184.7 | 0.14 | 0.15 | 7.1 | 19.0 | 9.4 | 45.7 | 0.2 | 4.8 | 1.6 | 12.3 |
| Jordan | 8.3 | 25.3 | 0.19 | 0.18 | 2.7 | 6.5 | 15.5 | 21.8 | 11.6 | 16.9 | 2.4 | 22.7 |
| Kazakhstan | .. | .. | .. | .. | .. | .. | .. | .. | .. | .. | .. | .. |
| Kenya | 42.6 | 56.1 | 0.23 | 0.24 | .. | 11.5 | 5.4 | 66.8 | 0.1 | 12.8 | 1.7 | 1.8 |
| Korea, Dem. Rep. | .. | .. | .. | .. | .. | .. | .. | .. | .. | .. | .. | .. |
| Korea, Rep. | 369.2 | 315.2 | 0.12 | 0.12 | 11.4 | 18.9 | 13.0 | 25.8 | 0.2 | 13.6 | 1.5 | 15.7 |
| Kuwait | 9.1 | 11.9 | 0.16 | 0.17 | 2.1 | 16.6 | 11.1 | 50.2 | 0.4 | 11.6 | 2.8 | 5.2 |
| Kyrgyz Republic | 30.9 | 19.1 | 0.12 | 0.21 | 7.3 | 7.8 | 3.5 | 65.4 | 0.4 | 11.0 | 0.9 | 3.7 |
| Lao PDR | .. | .. | .. | .. | .. | .. | .. | .. | .. | .. | .. | .. |
| Latvia | 39.9 | 29.2 | 0.12 | 0.19 | 4.1 | 15.4 | 3.6 | 53.8 | 0.1 | 9.6 | 9.7 | 3.7 |
| Lebanon | .. | .. | .. | .. | .. | .. | .. | .. | .. | .. | .. | .. |
| Lesotho | 3.0 | .. | 0.16 | .. | .. | .. | .. | .. | .. | .. | .. | .. |
| Liberia | 0.6 | .. | 0.30 | .. | .. | .. | .. | .. | .. | .. | .. | .. |
| Libya | .. | .. | .. | .. | .. | .. | .. | .. | .. | .. | .. | .. |
| Lithuania | 53.8 | 43.9 | 0.13 | 0.17 | 0.8 | 4.8 | 6.8 | 20.5 | 3.8 | 22.9 | 11.2 | 29.2 |
| Macedonia, FYR | 32.4 | .. | 0.18 | .. | .. | .. | .. | .. | .. | .. | .. | .. |
| Madagascar | 11.0 | 67.2 | 0.27 | 0.14 | 0.3 | 1.7 | 12.4 | 7.6 | 2.8 | 58.9 | 6.3 | 10.0 |
| Malawi | 10.0 | .. | 0.29 | .. | .. | .. | .. | .. | .. | .. | .. | .. |
| Malaysia | 104.7 | 183.8 | 0.13 | 0.12 | 7.8 | 14.9 | 15.5 | 33.7 | 0.2 | 8.3 | 6.8 | 12.8 |
| Mali | .. | .. | .. | .. | .. | .. | .. | .. | .. | .. | .. | .. |
| Mauritania | .. | .. | .. | .. | .. | .. | .. | .. | .. | .. | .. | .. |
| Mauritius | 17.8 | 17.7 | 0.16 | 0.15 | 0.9 | 6.6 | 2.6 | 32.8 | 0.1 | 55.4 | 0.6 | 1.1 |
| Mexico | 174.3 | 296.1 | 0.18 | 0.20 | 7.8 | 12.5 | 10.4 | 55.6 | 0.2 | 7.5 | 0.9 | 5.1 |
| Moldova | 55.9 | 21.6 | 0.15 | 0.45 | .. | 2.2 | .. | 97.7 | .. | .. | .. | 0.1 |
| Mongolia | 10.2 | .. | 0.18 | .. | .. | .. | .. | .. | .. | .. | .. | .. |
| Morocco | 41.7 | 91.0 | 0.14 | 0.18 | 1.2 | 3.0 | 8.5 | 21.8 | 6.0 | 43.2 | 1.8 | 14.5 |
| Mozambique | 20.4 | 10.2 | 0.27 | 0.31 | 1.1 | 7.1 | 2.7 | 81.2 | 0.1 | 5.8 | 1.4 | 0.7 |
| Myanmar | 7.7 | 6.2 | 0.17 | 0.18 | 56.5 | 4.6 | 13.2 | 14.9 | 0.4 | 2.9 | 1.7 | 5.8 |
| Namibia | 7.4 | .. | 0.35 | .. | .. | .. | .. | .. | .. | .. | .. | .. |
| Nepal | 20.9 | 26.9 | 0.13 | 0.16 | 3.5 | 9.7 | 5.9 | 55.1 | 1.4 | 21.7 | 1.7 | 1.0 |
| Netherlands | 136.7 | .. | 0.18 | .. | .. | .. | .. | .. | .. | .. | .. | .. |
| New Zealand | 50.2 | 46.1 | 0.22 | 0.22 | 3.2 | 21.7 | 5.2 | 57.3 | 0.1 | 4.6 | 3.6 | 4.2 |
| Nicaragua | 10.5 | .. | 0.27 | .. | .. | .. | .. | .. | .. | .. | .. | .. |
| Niger | .. | 0.4 | .. | 0.32 | .. | 17.0 | 4.4 | 76.9 | 0.3 | .. | 0.8 | 0.6 |
| Nigeria | 70.8 | .. | 0.22 | .. | .. | .. | .. | .. | .. | .. | .. | .. |
| Norway | 55.0 | 51.7 | 0.20 | 0.20 | 9.0 | 31.3 | 4.7 | 42.8 | 0.1 | 1.4 | 3.1 | 7.5 |
| Oman | 0.4 | 5.8 | 0.11 | 0.17 | 7.3 | 13.3 | 10.1 | 54.3 | 0.9 | 8.3 | 2.4 | 3.4 |
| Pakistan | 104.1 | .. | 0.18 | .. | .. | .. | .. | .. | .. | .. | .. | .. |
| Panama | 9.7 | 11.7 | 0.26 | 0.32 | 1.5 | 13.2 | 4.6 | 76.6 | 0.2 | 3.2 | 0.4 | 0.4 |
| Papua New Guinea | 5.7 | .. | 0.25 | .. | .. | .. | .. | .. | .. | .. | .. | .. |
| Paraguay | 3.3 | .. | 0.28 | .. | .. | .. | .. | .. | .. | .. | .. | .. |
| Peru | 56.1 | .. | 0.20 | .. | .. | .. | .. | .. | .. | .. | .. | .. |
| Philippines | 228.3 | .. | 0.21 | .. | .. | .. | .. | .. | .. | .. | .. | .. |
| Poland | 428.9 | 329.4 | 0.14 | 0.17 | 7.5 | 11.7 | 7.6 | 52.2 | 0.2 | 9.1 | 4.3 | 7.3 |
| Portugal | 147.9 | 127.5 | 0.15 | 0.15 | 3.1 | 16.4 | 4.9 | 37.8 | 0.4 | 26.1 | 5.3 | 6.0 |
| Puerto Rico | 19.0 | 9.2 | 0.15 | 0.18 | 1.9 | 14.9 | 21.9 | 34.4 | 0.2 | 15.5 | 1.4 | 9.7 |

| | Emissions of organic water pollutants | | | | Industry shares of emissions of organic water pollutants | | | | | | | |
|---|---|---|---|---|---|---|---|---|---|---|---|---|
| | thousand kilograms per day | | kilograms per day per worker | | Primary metals | Paper and pulp | Chemicals | Food and beverages | % of total Stone, ceramics, and glass | Textiles | Wood | Other |
| | 1990 | 2004ᵃ | 1990 | 2004ᵃ | 2004ᵃ | 2004ᵃ | 2004ᵃ | 2004ᵃ | 2004ᵃ | 2004ᵃ | 2004ᵃ | 2004ᵃ |
| Romania | 413.9 | 241.5 | 0.12 | 0.14 | 4.8 | 3.0 | 6.6 | 12.2 | 4.2 | 30.9 | 5.4 | 32.9 |
| Russian Federation | 1,911.3 | 1,470.8 | 0.13 | 0.18 | 9.9 | 4.4 | 11.5 | 18.5 | 8.0 | 7.7 | 4.6 | 35.4 |
| Rwanda | 1.6 | .. | 0.25 | .. | .. | .. | .. | .. | .. | .. | .. | .. |
| Saudi Arabia | 18.5 | .. | 0.15 | .. | .. | .. | .. | .. | .. | .. | .. | .. |
| Senegal | 10.3 | 6.6 | 0.32 | 0.30 | 5.8 | 8.4 | 10.7 | 70.1 | 0.1 | 4.2 | 0.4 | 0.3 |
| Serbia | .. | .. | .. | .. | .. | .. | .. | .. | .. | .. | .. | .. |
| Sierra Leone | 4.2 | .. | 0.32 | .. | .. | .. | .. | .. | .. | .. | .. | .. |
| Singapore | 32.4 | 34.3 | 0.09 | 0.10 | 1.4 | 24.6 | 16.0 | 25.4 | 0.1 | 3.9 | 1.6 | 26.9 |
| Slovak Republic | 77.2 | 43.3 | 0.13 | 0.14 | 2.9 | 16.9 | 8.4 | 43.7 | 0.3 | 12.2 | 4.0 | 11.6 |
| Slovenia | 55.6 | 38.4 | 0.16 | 0.16 | 33.7 | 14.7 | 8.3 | 23.7 | 0.2 | 10.8 | 2.0 | 6.7 |
| Somalia | 6.2 | .. | 0.38 | .. | .. | .. | .. | .. | .. | .. | .. | .. |
| South Africa | 261.6 | 181.7 | 0.17 | 0.17 | 6.8 | 7.4 | 10.4 | 16.7 | 5.0 | 7.1 | 4.7 | 41.9 |
| Spain | 320.3 | 352.9 | 0.17 | 0.15 | 7.5 | 20.6 | 9.5 | 39.6 | 0.4 | 8.6 | 4.3 | 9.6 |
| Sri Lanka | 53.0 | 78.4 | 0.19 | 0.18 | 0.5 | 7.2 | 6.6 | 51.5 | 0.2 | 31.6 | 1.1 | 1.2 |
| Sudan | .. | 38.6 | .. | 0.29 | 0.7 | 2.5 | 3.1 | 88.6 | 0.4 | 3.2 | 0.6 | 1.1 |
| Swaziland | 6.6 | .. | 0.33 | .. | .. | .. | .. | .. | .. | .. | .. | .. |
| Sweden | 109.6 | 103.9 | 0.15 | 0.14 | 11.3 | 35.0 | 7.8 | 26.6 | 0.1 | 1.3 | 3.0 | 14.9 |
| Switzerland | 146.0 | .. | 0.16 | .. | .. | .. | .. | .. | .. | .. | .. | .. |
| Syrian Arab Republic | 21.7 | .. | 0.22 | .. | .. | .. | .. | .. | .. | .. | .. | .. |
| Tajikistan | .. | .. | .. | .. | .. | .. | .. | .. | .. | .. | .. | .. |
| Tanzania | 31.1 | 35.2 | 0.24 | 0.25 | 1.5 | 9.4 | 2.7 | 69.3 | 0.1 | 14.0 | 1.5 | 1.4 |
| Thailand | 291.6 | .. | 0.17 | .. | .. | .. | .. | .. | .. | .. | .. | .. |
| Timor-Leste | .. | .. | .. | .. | .. | .. | .. | .. | .. | .. | .. | .. |
| Togo | .. | .. | .. | .. | .. | .. | .. | .. | .. | .. | .. | .. |
| Trinidad and Tobago | 10.0 | 7.9 | 0.26 | 0.23 | 6.5 | 18.8 | 11.9 | 55.3 | 0.2 | 3.8 | 2.0 | 1.5 |
| Tunisia | 44.6 | 55.8 | 0.18 | 0.14 | 2.5 | 6.1 | 5.5 | 35.8 | 0.4 | 43.3 | 1.9 | 4.6 |
| Turkey | 177.3 | 172.2 | 0.18 | 0.16 | 11.4 | 4.8 | 8.0 | 43.7 | 0.3 | 26.4 | 0.4 | 5.0 |
| Turkmenistan | .. | .. | .. | .. | .. | .. | .. | .. | .. | .. | .. | .. |
| Uganda | 16.7 | .. | 0.30 | .. | .. | .. | .. | .. | .. | .. | .. | .. |
| Ukraine | 692.4 | 525.1 | 0.14 | 0.19 | 14.3 | 4.1 | 9.7 | 18.9 | 6.4 | 7.0 | 2.3 | 37.2 |
| United Arab Emirates | 5.6 | .. | 0.14 | .. | .. | .. | .. | .. | .. | .. | .. | .. |
| United Kingdom | 739.6 | 331.0 | 0.15 | 0.12 | 9.0 | 48.0 | 17.5 | 0.6 | 0.3 | 5.2 | 4.0 | 15.4 |
| United States | 2,565.2 | 1,805.9 | 0.15 | 0.13 | 9.6 | 10.6 | 14.0 | 42.1 | 0.2 | 5.4 | 4.2 | 13.9 |
| Uruguay | 38.7 | 15.8 | 0.23 | 0.28 | 1.2 | 3.7 | 6.6 | 79.2 | 0.1 | 7.4 | 0.6 | 1.2 |
| Uzbekistan | .. | .. | .. | .. | .. | .. | .. | .. | .. | .. | .. | .. |
| Venezuela, RB | 96.5 | .. | 0.21 | .. | .. | .. | .. | .. | .. | .. | .. | .. |
| Vietnam | .. | .. | .. | .. | .. | .. | .. | .. | .. | .. | .. | .. |
| West Bank and Gaza | .. | .. | .. | .. | .. | .. | .. | .. | .. | .. | .. | .. |
| Yemen, Rep. | 6.9 | 15.4 | 0.27 | 0.23 | .. | 7.7 | 6.8 | 74.6 | 0.4 | 7.6 | 0.9 | 2.0 |
| Zambia | 15.9 | .. | 0.23 | .. | .. | .. | .. | .. | .. | .. | .. | .. |
| Zimbabwe | 37.1 | .. | 0.20 | .. | .. | .. | .. | .. | .. | .. | .. | .. |

a. Data are derived using the United Nations Industrial Development Organization's (UNIDO) industry database four-digit International Standard Industrial Classification (ISIC). Data in italics are for the most recent year available and are derived using UNIDO's industry database at the three-digit ISIC.

## About the data

Emissions of organic pollutants from industrial activities are a major cause of degradation of water quality. Water quality and pollution levels are generally measured as concentration or load—the rate of occurrence of a substance in an aqueous solution. Polluting substances include organic matter, metals, minerals, sediment, bacteria, and toxic chemicals. The table focuses on organic water pollution resulting from industrial activities. Because water pollution tends to be sensitive to local conditions, the national-level data in the table may not reflect the quality of water in specific locations.

The data in the table come from an international study of industrial emissions that may be the first to include data from developing countries (Hettige, Mani, and Wheeler 1998). These data were updated through 2004 by the World Bank's Development Research Group. Unlike estimates from earlier studies based on engineering or economic models, these estimates are based on actual measurements of plant-level water pollution. The focus is on organic water pollution caused by organic waste, measured in terms of biochemical oxygen demand (BOD), because the data for this indicator are the most plentiful and reliable for cross-country comparisons of emissions. BOD measures the strength of an organic waste by the amount of oxygen consumed in breaking it down. A sewage overload in natural waters exhausts the water's dissolved oxygen content. Wastewater treatment, by contrast, reduces BOD.

Data on water pollution are more readily available than are other emissions data because most industrial pollution control programs start by regulating emissions of organic water pollutants. Such data

are fairly reliable because sampling techniques for measuring water pollution are more widely understood and much less expensive than those for air pollution.

Hettige, Mani, and Wheeler (1998) used plant- and sector-level information on emissions and employment from 13 national environmental protection agencies and sector-level information on output and employment from the United Nations Industrial Development Organization (UNIDO). Their econometric analysis found that the ratio of BOD to employment in each industrial sector is about the same across countries. This finding allowed the authors to estimate BOD loads across countries and over time. The estimated BOD intensities per unit of employment were multiplied by sectoral employment numbers from UNIDO's industry database for 1980–98. These estimates of sectoral emissions were then used to calculate kilograms of emissions of organic water pollutants per day for each country and year. The data in the table were derived by updating these estimates through 2004.

## Definitions

• **Emissions of organic water pollutants** are measured as biochemical oxygen demand, or the amount of oxygen that bacteria in water will consume in breaking down waste, a standard water treatment test for the presence of organic pollutants. Emissions per worker are total emissions divided by the number of industrial workers. • **Industry shares of emissions of organic water pollutants** are emissions from manufacturing activities as defined by two-digit divisions of the International Standard Industrial Classification (ISIC) revision 3.

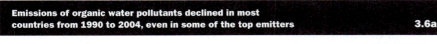

**Emissions of organic water pollutants declined in most countries from 1990 to 2004, even in some of the top emitters**  **3.6a**

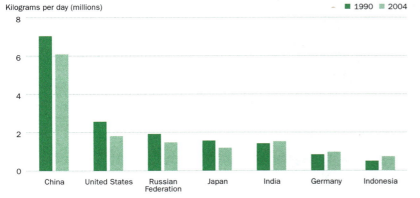

Kilograms per day (millions)

■ 1990  ■ 2004

China, United States, Russian Federation, Japan, India, Germany, Indonesia

*Source:* Table 3.6.

## Data sources

Data on water pollutants come from the 1998 study by Hemamala Hettige, Muthukumara Mani, and David Wheeler, "Industrial Pollution in Economic Development: Kuznets Revisited" (available at www.worldbank.org/nipr). The data were updated through 2004 by the World Bank's Development Research Group using the same methodology as the initial study. Data on industrial sectoral employment are from UNIDO's industry database.

# 3.7 | Energy production and use

| | Total energy production | | Energy use | | | | | | | | | |
|---|---|---|---|---|---|---|---|---|---|---|---|---|
| | | | Total | | Per capita | | % of total | | | | | |
| | million metric tons of oil equivalent | | million metric tons of oil equivalent | | kilograms of oil equivalent | | Fossil fuel | | Combustible renewables and waste | | Clean energy | |
| | 1990 | 2005 | 1990 | 2005 | 1990 | 2005 | 1990 | 2005 | 1990 | 2005 | 1990 | 2005 |
| Afghanistan | .. | .. | .. | .. | .. | .. | .. | .. | .. | .. | .. | .. |
| Albania | 2.4 | 1.2 | 2.7 | 2.4 | 809 | 762 | 76.5 | 69.8 | 13.6 | 9.6 | 9.2 | 19.2 |
| Algeria | 104.4 | 175.1 | 23.9 | 34.8 | 944 | 1,058 | 99.8 | 99.6 | 0.1 | 0.2 | 0.1 | 0.1 |
| Angola | 28.7 | 70.7 | 6.3 | 9.9 | 597 | 615 | 30.2 | 34.7 | 68.8 | 63.8 | 1.0 | 1.5 |
| Argentina | 48.5 | 81.0 | 46.1 | 63.7 | 1,415 | 1,644 | 88.6 | 88.5 | 3.7 | 3.5 | 7.5 | 7.4 |
| Armenia | 0.1 | 0.9 | 7.9 | 2.6 | 2,240 | 848 | 97.3 | 66.4 | 0.1 | 0.0 | 1.7 | 33.6 |
| Australia | 157.5 | 271.0 | 87.5 | 122.0 | 5,130 | 5,978 | 94.0 | 94.5 | 4.5 | 4.3 | 1.4 | 1.1 |
| Austria | 8.1 | 9.8 | 25.1 | 34.4 | 3,251 | 4,174 | 79.4 | 78.1 | 9.8 | 11.6 | 10.8 | 9.1 |
| Azerbaijan | 21.3 | 27.3 | 26.0 | 13.8 | 3,637 | 1,649 | 98.8 | 97.3 | 0.0 | 0.0 | 0.2 | 1.9 |
| Bangladesh | 10.8 | 19.3 | 12.8 | 24.2 | 113 | 158 | 45.9 | 65.2 | 53.5 | 34.3 | 0.6 | 0.5 |
| Belarus | 3.3 | 3.8 | 42.2 | 26.6 | 4,139 | 2,720 | 97.6 | 93.9 | 0.5 | 4.8 | 0.0 | 0.0 |
| Belgium | 13.1 | 13.9 | 49.2 | 56.7 | 4,932 | 5,407 | 75.8 | 74.1 | 1.5 | 2.8 | 22.7 | 21.9 |
| Benin | 1.8 | 1.7 | 1.7 | 2.6 | 324 | 304 | 5.8 | 33.3 | 93.2 | 64.7 | 0.0 | 0.0 |
| Bolivia | 4.9 | 13.9 | 2.8 | 5.3 | 416 | 578 | 69.1 | 81.9 | 27.2 | 14.0 | 3.6 | 4.1 |
| Bosnia and Herzegovina | 4.6 | 3.3 | 7.0 | 5.0 | 1,633 | 1,268 | 93.9 | 86.6 | 2.3 | 3.7 | 3.7 | 9.4 |
| Botswana | 0.9 | 1.1 | 1.3 | 1.9 | 930 | 1,032 | 66.3 | 68.0 | 33.1 | 24.1 | 0.0 | 0.0 |
| Brazil | 98.1 | 187.8 | 134.0 | 209.5 | 896 | 1,122 | 53.5 | 56.7 | 31.1 | 26.5 | 13.7 | 15.1 |
| Bulgaria | 9.6 | 10.6 | 28.8 | 20.1 | 3,306 | 2,592 | 84.5 | 70.0 | 0.6 | 3.7 | 13.8 | 26.3 |
| Burkina Faso | .. | .. | .. | .. | .. | .. | .. | .. | .. | .. | .. | .. |
| Burundi | .. | .. | .. | .. | .. | .. | .. | .. | .. | .. | .. | .. |
| Cambodia | .. | .. | .. | .. | .. | .. | .. | .. | .. | .. | .. | .. |
| Cameroon | 12.1 | 11.9 | 5.0 | 7.0 | 411 | 392 | 19.5 | 16.6 | 75.9 | 78.6 | 4.5 | 4.8 |
| Canada | 273.7 | 401.3 | 209.4 | 272.0 | 7,535 | 8,417 | 74.7 | 75.1 | 3.9 | 4.6 | 21.4 | 20.3 |
| Central African Republic | .. | .. | .. | .. | .. | .. | .. | .. | .. | .. | .. | .. |
| Chad | .. | .. | .. | .. | .. | .. | .. | .. | .. | .. | .. | .. |
| Chile | 7.6 | 9.1 | 14.1 | 29.6 | 1,067 | 1,815 | 74.8 | 76.9 | 19.0 | 15.5 | 6.2 | 7.0 |
| China | 886.3 | 1,640.9 | 863.2 | 1,717.2 | 760 | 1,316 | 75.5 | 84.2 | 23.2 | 13.0 | 1.3 | 2.8 |
| Hong Kong, China | 0.0 | 0.0 | 10.7 | 18.1 | 1,869 | 2,653 | 99.5 | 96.6 | 0.5 | 0.3 | 0.0 | 0.0 |
| Colombia | 48.2 | 79.5 | 24.7 | 28.6 | 710 | 636 | 68.1 | 73.6 | 22.3 | 14.4 | 9.6 | 12.0 |
| Congo, Dem. Rep. | 12.0 | 17.4 | 11.9 | 17.0 | 314 | 289 | 11.9 | 3.8 | 84.0 | 92.5 | 4.1 | 3.7 |
| Congo, Rep. | 9.0 | 13.7 | 1.1 | 1.2 | 436 | 332 | 26.4 | 38.2 | 69.4 | 56.3 | 4.0 | 2.6 |
| Costa Rica | 1.0 | 1.8 | 2.0 | 3.8 | 658 | 883 | 48.3 | 51.9 | 36.6 | 7.0 | 14.4 | 40.6 |
| Côte d'Ivoire | 3.4 | 8.2 | 4.4 | 7.8 | 345 | 422 | 24.8 | 40.1 | 72.1 | 58.3 | 2.6 | 1.6 |
| Croatia | 5.1 | 3.8 | 9.1 | 8.9 | 1,897 | 2,000 | 86.6 | 84.9 | 3.4 | 4.0 | 3.6 | 6.1 |
| Cuba | 6.6 | 5.5 | 16.8 | 10.2 | 1,587 | 906 | 65.1 | 79.6 | 34.9 | 20.3 | 0.0 | 0.1 |
| Czech Republic | 40.1 | 32.9 | 49.0 | 45.2 | 4,728 | 4,417 | 93.1 | 81.3 | 0.0 | 3.9 | 6.9 | 14.8 |
| Denmark | 10.0 | 31.3 | 17.9 | 19.6 | 3,482 | 3,621 | 89.9 | 83.2 | 6.4 | 13.2 | 0.0 | 0.0 |
| Dominican Republic | 1.0 | 1.5 | 4.1 | 7.4 | 567 | 777 | 75.1 | 79.2 | 24.2 | 18.6 | 0.7 | 2.2 |
| Ecuador | 16.5 | 28.6 | 6.1 | 10.4 | 597 | 799 | 79.5 | 87.9 | 13.5 | 5.1 | 7.0 | 5.7 |
| Egypt, Arab Rep. | 54.9 | 76.0 | 31.9 | 61.3 | 578 | 841 | 94.0 | · 95.9 | 3.3 | 2.3 | 2.7 | 1.8 |
| El Salvador | 1.7 | 2.5 | 2.5 | 4.6 | 496 | 694 | 32.0 | 44.4 | 48.2 | 32.4 | 19.8 | 22.6 |
| Eritrea | .. | .. | .. | .. | .. | .. | .. | .. | .. | .. | .. | .. |
| Estonia | 5.0 | 3.7 | 9.6 | 5.1 | 6,107 | 3,786 | 98.0 | 87.9 | 2.0 | 12.1 | 0.0 | 0.0 |
| Ethiopia | 14.2 | 19.9 | 15.2 | 21.6 | 296 | 288 | 6.6 | 8.2 | 92.8 | 90.6 | 0.6 | 1.1 |
| Finland | 12.1 | 16.6 | 29.2 | 35.0 | 5,851 | 6,664 | 60.9 | 55.0 | 15.6 | 19.6 | 20.4 | 20.7 |
| France | 112.4 | 136.9 | 227.8 | 276.0 | 4,015 | 4,534 | 56.9 | 51.4 | 5.1 | 4.3 | 38.0 | 44.3 |
| Gabon | 14.6 | 12.1 | 1.2 | 1.7 | 1,354 | 1,333 | 35.3 | 37.2 | 59.8 | 58.7 | 4.9 | 4.1 |
| Gambia, The | .. | .. | .. | .. | .. | .. | .. | .. | .. | .. | .. | .. |
| Georgia | 1.8 | 1.3 | 12.3 | 3.2 | 2,259 | 718 | 88.8 | 59.3 | 3.7 | 20.1 | 5.3 | 17.0 |
| Germany | 186.2 | 134.5 | 356.2 | 344.7 | 4,485 | 4,180 | 87.0 | 82.9 | 1.3 | 3.5 | 11.6 | 12.9 |
| Ghana | 4.4 | 6.4 | 5.3 | 8.9 | 343 | 397 | 17.7 | 28.7 | 73.1 | 66.0 | 9.2 | 5.1 |
| Greece | 9.2 | 10.3 | 22.2 | 31.0 | 2,183 | 2,790 | 94.7 | 93.6 | 4.0 | 3.3 | 0.7 | 1.4 |
| Guatemala | 3.4 | 5.4 | 4.5 | 8.0 | 503 | 628 | 28.8 | 43.3 | 67.8 | 53.2 | 3.4 | 3.5 |
| Guinea | .. | .. | .. | .. | .. | .. | .. | .. | .. | .. | .. | .. |
| Guinea-Bissau | .. | .. | .. | .. | .. | .. | .. | .. | .. | .. | .. | .. |
| Haiti | 1.3 | 1.9 | 1.6 | 2.5 | 223 | 269 | 20.9 | 23.2 | 76.5 | 75.9 | 2.5 | 0.9 |

| | Total energy production | | Energy use | | | | | | | | | |
|---|---|---|---|---|---|---|---|---|---|---|---|---|
| | million metric tons of oil equivalent | | Total million metric tons of oil equivalent | | Per capita kilograms of oil equivalent | | % of total | | | | | |
| | | | | | | | Fossil fuel | | Combustible renewables and waste | | Clean energy | |
| | **1990** | **2005** | **1990** | **2005** | **1990** | **2005** | **1990** | **2005** | **1990** | **2005** | **1990** | **2005** |
| Honduras | 1.7 | 1.8 | 2.4 | 3.9 | 494 | 566 | 29.9 | 53.9 | 62.0 | 42.0 | 8.1 | 4.0 |
| Hungary | 14.3 | 10.3 | 28.6 | 27.8 | 2,753 | 2,752 | 82.4 | 80.6 | 1.3 | 4.0 | 12.9 | 13.4 |
| India | 291.1 | 419.0 | 319.9 | 537.3 | 377 | 491 | 55.8 | 68.0 | 41.7 | 29.4 | 2.4 | 2.4 |
| Indonesia | 170.3 | 263.4 | 103.2 | 179.5 | 579 | 814 | 54.9 | 67.8 | 43.6 | 28.5 | 1.5 | 3.7 |
| Iran, Islamic Rep. | 179.7 | 303.8 | 68.8 | 162.5 | 1,264 | 2,352 | 98.2 | 98.6 | 1.0 | 0.5 | 0.8 | 0.9 |
| Iraq | 104.9 | 96.0 | 19.1 | 30.8 | 1,029 | .. | 98.7 | 99.4 | 0.1 | 0.1 | 1.2 | 0.1 |
| Ireland | 3.5 | 1.7 | 10.4 | 15.3 | 2,957 | 3,676 | 98.4 | 96.3 | 1.0 | 1.6 | 0.6 | 0.4 |
| Israel | 0.4 | 2.1 | 12.1 | 19.5 | 2,599 | 2,816 | 97.3 | 97.0 | 0.0 | 0.0 | 0.0 | 0.0 |
| Italy | 25.3 | 27.6 | 148.0 | 185.2 | 2,609 | 3,160 | 93.5 | 91.2 | 0.6 | 2.3 | 3.8 | 4.1 |
| Jamaica | 0.5 | 0.5 | 2.9 | 3.8 | 1,231 | 1,445 | 83.5 | 87.4 | 16.2 | 12.2 | 0.3 | 0.3 |
| Japan | 75.2 | 99.8 | 444.5 | 530.5 | 3,598 | 4,152 | 84.7 | 81.9 | 1.1 | 1.2 | 13.9 | 16.8 |
| Jordan | 0.2 | 0.3 | 3.5 | 7.1 | 1,103 | 1,311 | 98.3 | 98.1 | 0.1 | 0.0 | 0.0 | 0.1 |
| Kazakhstan | 90.5 | 121.7 | 73.7 | 52.4 | 4,506 | 3,462 | 97.0 | 98.6 | 0.2 | 0.1 | 0.9 | 1.3 |
| Kenya | 10.3 | 13.9 | 12.5 | 17.2 | 532 | 484 | 17.6 | 19.5 | 78.4 | 74.6 | 4.0 | 5.9 |
| Korea, Dem. Rep. | 28.7 | 20.2 | 32.9 | 21.2 | 1,632 | 898 | 93.0 | 89.8 | 2.9 | 4.9 | 4.1 | 5.3 |
| Korea, Rep. | 22.6 | 42.9 | 93.4 | 213.8 | 2,178 | 4,426 | 83.9 | 80.9 | 0.8 | 1.0 | 15.3 | 18.0 |
| Kuwait | 50.4 | 146.3 | 8.5 | 28.1 | 3,984 | 11,100 | 99.9 | 100.0 | 0.1 | 0.0 | 0.0 | 0.0 |
| Kyrgyz Republic | 2.5 | 1.4 | 7.6 | 2.8 | 1,723 | 544 | 88.6 | 56.1 | 0.1 | 0.1 | 11.3 | 43.8 |
| Lao PDR | .. | .. | .. | .. | .. | .. | .. | .. | .. | .. | .. | .. |
| Latvia | 1.2 | 2.3 | 7.8 | 4.7 | 2,916 | 2,050 | 82.2 | 59.8 | 8.5 | 30.2 | 5.0 | 6.1 |
| Lebanon | 0.1 | 0.2 | 2.3 | 5.6 | 776 | 1,391 | 93.6 | 95.3 | 4.5 | 2.3 | 1.9 | 1.6 |
| Lesotho | .. | .. | .. | .. | .. | .. | .. | .. | .. | .. | .. | .. |
| Liberia | .. | .. | .. | .. | .. | .. | .. | .. | .. | .. | .. | .. |
| Libya | 73.2 | 95.0 | 11.5 | 19.0 | 2,645 | 3,218 | 98.9 | 99.2 | 1.1 | 0.8 | 0.0 | 0.0 |
| Lithuania | 4.9 | 3.9 | 16.2 | 8.6 | 4,377 | 2,515 | 70.2 | 59.3 | 1.8 | 8.3 | 28.0 | 32.4 |
| Macedonia, FYR | 1.5 | 1.5 | 2.7 | 2.7 | 1,421 | 1,346 | 98.2 | 84.2 | 0.0 | 5.6 | 1.5 | 5.1 |
| Madagascar | .. | .. | .. | .. | .. | .. | .. | .. | .. | .. | .. | .. |
| Malawi | .. | .. | .. | .. | .. | .. | .. | .. | .. | .. | .. | .. |
| Malaysia | 50.3 | 93.9 | 23.3 | 61.3 | 1,288 | 2,389 | 89.4 | 94.6 | 9.1 | 4.5 | 1.5 | 0.8 |
| Mali | .. | .. | .. | .. | .. | .. | .. | .. | .. | .. | .. | .. |
| Mauritania | .. | .. | .. | .. | .. | .. | .. | .. | .. | .. | .. | .. |
| Mauritius | .. | .. | .. | .. | .. | .. | .. | .. | .. | .. | .. | .. |
| Mexico | 194.8 | 259.2 | 124.3 | 176.5 | 1,494 | 1,712 | 88.3 | 88.8 | 5.9 | 4.7 | 5.8 | 6.5 |
| Moldova | 0.1 | 0.1 | 10.0 | 3.6 | 2,277 | 917 | 99.4 | 90.1 | 0.4 | 2.1 | 0.2 | 0.1 |
| Mongolia | .. | .. | .. | .. | .. | .. | .. | .. | .. | .. | .. | .. |
| Morocco | 0.8 | 1.0 | 6.7 | 13.8 | 278 | 458 | 93.6 | 95.2 | 4.7 | 3.3 | 1.6 | 0.9 |
| Mozambique | 6.8 | 11.7 | 7.2 | 10.2 | 532 | 497 | 5.1 | 3.4 | 94.4 | 85.4 | 0.3 | 11.2 |
| Myanmar | 10.7 | 22.1 | 10.7 | 14.7 | 266 | 307 | 14.6 | 28.6 | 84.4 | 69.6 | 1.0 | 1.8 |
| Namibia | 0.0 | 0.3 | 0.0 | 1.4 | 0 | 683 | 62.0 | 66.9 | 16.0 | 13.5 | 17.5 | 10.4 |
| Nepal | 5.5 | 8.2 | 5.8 | 9.2 | 304 | 338 | 5.3 | 11.1 | 93.4 | 86.6 | 1.3 | 2.3 |
| Netherlands | 60.5 | 61.9 | 66.8 | 81.8 | 4,464 | 5,015 | 96.0 | 93.3 | 1.4 | 3.2 | 1.4 | 1.3 |
| New Zealand | 12.0 | 12.2 | 13.8 | 16.9 | 3,990 | 4,090 | 65.3 | 71.1 | 4.0 | 5.1 | 30.7 | 23.4 |
| Nicaragua | 1.5 | 2.0 | 2.1 | 3.3 | 512 | 611 | 29.2 | 41.3 | 53.2 | 50.5 | 17.3 | 8.1 |
| Niger | .. | .. | .. | .. | .. | .. | .. | .. | .. | .. | .. | .. |
| Nigeria | 150.5 | 231.8 | 70.9 | 103.8 | 751 | 734 | 19.7 | 21.3 | 79.8 | 78.0 | 0.5 | 0.7 |
| Norway | 120.3 | 233.7 | 21.5 | 32.1 | 5,072 | 6,948 | 46.8 | 59.5 | 4.8 | 4.1 | 48.4 | 36.4 |
| Oman | 38.3 | 59.6 | 4.6 | 14.0 | 2,475 | 5,570 | 100.0 | 100.0 | 0.0 | 0.0 | 0.0 | 0.0 |
| Pakistan | 34.4 | 61.3 | 43.4 | 76.3 | 402 | 490 | 53.3 | 60.2 | 43.2 | 35.5 | 3.5 | 4.3 |
| Panama | 0.6 | 0.7 | 1.5 | 2.6 | 618 | 804 | 58.4 | 71.6 | 28.3 | 16.1 | 12.8 | 12.3 |
| Papua New Guinea | .. | .. | .. | .. | .. | .. | .. | .. | .. | .. | .. | .. |
| Paraguay | 4.6 | 6.6 | 3.1 | 4.0 | 731 | 674 | 21.6 | 29.2 | 72.3 | 54.8 | .. | .. |
| Peru | 10.6 | 10.8 | 10.0 | 13.8 | 457 | 506 | 64.1 | 70.7 | 26.9 | 16.4 | 9.0 | 12.4 |
| Philippines | 13.7 | 24.2 | 26.2 | 44.7 | 427 | 528 | 50.8 | 54.9 | 29.2 | 24.4 | 20.0 | 20.7 |
| Poland | 99.4 | 78.6 | 99.9 | 93.0 | 2,620 | 2,436 | 97.7 | 94.7 | 2.2 | 5.1 | 0.1 | 0.2 |
| Portugal | 3.4 | 3.6 | 17.7 | 27.2 | 1,793 | 2,575 | 81.5 | 84.7 | 14.0 | 10.8 | 4.5 | 1.7 |
| Puerto Rico | .. | .. | .. | .. | .. | .. | .. | .. | .. | .. | .. | .. |

| | Total energy production | | Energy use | | | | | | | | | | |
|---|---|---|---|---|---|---|---|---|---|---|---|---|---|
| | | | Total | | Per capita | | % of total | | | | | | |
| | million metric tons of oil equivalent | | million metric tons of oil equivalent | | kilograms of oil equivalent | | Fossil fuel | | Combustible renewables and waste | | Clean energy | | |
| | 1990 | 2005 | 1990 | 2005 | 1990 | 2005 | 1990 | 2005 | 1990 | 2005 | 1990 | 2005 |
| Romania | 40.8 | 27.9 | 62.4 | 38.3 | 2,689 | 1,772 | 96.2 | 83.0 | 1.0 | 8.5 | 1.6 | 8.5 |
| Russian Federation | 1,280.3 | 1,184.9 | 878.3 | 646.7 | 5,923 | 4,517 | 93.4 | 90.5 | 1.4 | 1.1 | 5.2 | 8.4 |
| Rwanda | .. | .. | .. | .. | .. | .. | .. | .. | .. | .. | .. | .. |
| Saudi Arabia | 370.8 | 576.7 | 61.3 | 140.3 | 3,744 | 6,068 | 100.0 | 100.0 | 0.0 | 0.0 | 0.0 | 0.0 |
| Senegal | 1.4 | 1.3 | 2.2 | 3.0 | 283 | 258 | 39.4 | 58.8 | 60.6 | 39.2 | 0.0 | 0.8 |
| Serbia[a] | 13.2 | 11.5 | 21.5 | 16.2 | 2,044 | 2,004 | .. | .. | 1.8 | 4.9 | .. | .. |
| Sierra Leone | .. | .. | .. | .. | .. | .. | .. | .. | .. | .. | .. | .. |
| Singapore | 0.0 | 0.0 | 13.4 | 30.1 | 4,384 | 6,933 | 100.0 | 100.0 | 0.0 | 0.0 | 0.0 | 0.0 |
| Slovak Republic | 5.3 | 6.6 | 21.3 | 18.8 | 4,035 | 3,496 | 81.6 | 70.6 | 0.8 | 2.4 | 15.5 | 27.0 |
| Slovenia | 2.9 | 3.4 | 5.6 | 7.3 | 2,801 | 3,657 | 69.1 | 68.3 | 4.8 | 6.7 | 26.1 | 25.0 |
| Somalia | .. | .. | .. | .. | .. | .. | .. | .. | .. | .. | .. | .. |
| South Africa | 114.5 | 158.6 | 91.2 | 127.6 | 2,592 | 2,722 | 86.1 | 87.0 | 11.4 | 10.5 | 2.5 | 2.5 |
| Spain | 34.6 | 30.3 | 91.1 | 145.2 | 2,345 | 3,346 | 77.6 | 83.8 | 4.5 | 3.5 | 17.9 | 11.5 |
| Sri Lanka | 4.2 | 5.3 | 5.5 | 9.4 | 324 | 477 | 24.1 | 43.9 | 71.0 | 52.9 | 4.9 | 3.2 |
| Sudan | 8.8 | 31.1 | 10.6 | 18.4 | 410 | 499 | 17.5 | 19.9 | 81.7 | 79.5 | 0.8 | 0.6 |
| Swaziland | .. | .. | .. | .. | .. | .. | .. | .. | .. | .. | .. | .. |
| Sweden | 29.8 | 34.8 | 47.6 | 52.2 | 5,557 | 5,782 | 37.9 | 34.6 | 11.6 | 17.2 | 50.5 | 48.2 |
| Switzerland | 9.7 | 10.9 | 25.0 | 27.2 | 3,723 | 3,651 | 61.1 | 57.9 | 3.7 | 7.1 | 35.2 | 32.9 |
| Syrian Arab Republic | 22.3 | 29.1 | 11.7 | 17.9 | 918 | 948 | 98.0 | 98.3 | 0.0 | 0.0 | 2.0 | 1.7 |
| Tajikistan | 2.0 | 1.5 | 5.6 | 3.5 | 1,055 | 528 | 72.8 | 57.9 | 0.0 | 0.0 | 25.4 | 41.5 |
| Tanzania | 9.1 | 19.1 | 9.8 | 20.4 | 385 | 530 | 7.6 | 7.1 | 91.0 | 92.1 | 1.4 | 0.7 |
| Thailand | 26.5 | 54.0 | 43.9 | 100.0 | 808 | 1,588 | 65.5 | 82.7 | 33.4 | 16.5 | 1.0 | 0.5 |
| Timor-Leste | .. | .. | .. | .. | .. | .. | .. | .. | .. | .. | .. | .. |
| Togo | 1.2 | 1.6 | 1.4 | 2.0 | 365 | 320 | 15.5 | 18.1 | 82.6 | 79.4 | 0.6 | 0.3 |
| Trinidad and Tobago | 12.6 | 31.4 | 6.0 | 12.7 | 4,934 | 9,599 | 99.2 | 99.8 | 0.8 | 0.2 | 0.0 | 0.0 |
| Tunisia | 6.1 | 6.7 | 5.5 | 8.5 | 679 | 843 | 81.2 | 86.5 | 18.7 | 13.3 | 0.1 | 0.1 |
| Turkey | 25.8 | 23.6 | 53.0 | 85.2 | 943 | 1,182 | 81.8 | 88.2 | 13.6 | 6.3 | 4.6 | 5.2 |
| Turkmenistan | 74.9 | 61.1 | 19.6 | 16.3 | 5,353 | 3,381 | 99.7 | 100.0 | 0.0 | 0.0 | 0.3 | 0.0 |
| Uganda | .. | .. | .. | .. | .. | .. | .. | .. | .. | .. | .. | .. |
| Ukraine | 133.7 | 81.0 | 251.7 | 143.2 | 4,851 | 3,041 | 91.7 | 82.9 | 0.1 | 0.2 | 8.2 | 16.9 |
| United Arab Emirates | 109.4 | 167.9 | 22.5 | 46.9 | 12,716 | 11,436 | 100.0 | 100.0 | 0.0 | 0.0 | 0.0 | 0.0 |
| United Kingdom | 208.0 | 204.3 | 212.2 | 233.9 | 3,686 | 3,884 | 90.9 | 88.6 | 0.3 | 1.7 | 8.3 | 9.3 |
| United States | 1,650.3 | 1,630.7 | 1,927.5 | 2,340.3 | 7,721 | 7,893 | 86.5 | 86.2 | 3.2 | 3.2 | 10.2 | 10.4 |
| Uruguay | 1.1 | 1.0 | 2.3 | 2.9 | 725 | 875 | 58.7 | 62.5 | 24.3 | 15.4 | 26.8 | 19.9 |
| Uzbekistan | 38.6 | 56.6 | 46.4 | 47.0 | 2,262 | 1,798 | 98.8 | 98.9 | 0.0 | 0.0 | 1.2 | 1.1 |
| Venezuela, RB | 148.9 | 204.7 | 43.9 | 60.9 | 2,224 | 2,293 | 91.5 | 88.5 | 1.2 | 0.9 | 7.2 | 10.6 |
| Vietnam | 24.7 | 69.5 | 24.3 | 51.3 | 367 | 617 | 20.4 | 49.7 | 77.7 | 46.7 | 1.9 | 3.6 |
| West Bank and Gaza | .. | .. | .. | .. | .. | .. | .. | .. | .. | .. | .. | .. |
| Yemen, Rep. | 9.4 | 20.4 | 2.6 | 6.7 | 208 | 319 | 97.0 | 98.8 | 3.0 | 1.1 | 0.0 | 0.0 |
| Zambia | 4.9 | 6.5 | 5.5 | 7.1 | 673 | 621 | 14.1 | 10.6 | 73.4 | 78.7 | 12.5 | 10.7 |
| Zimbabwe | 8.6 | 8.9 | 9.4 | 9.7 | 895 | 741 | 45.3 | 30.3 | 50.4 | 61.9 | 4.0 | 5.2 |
| **World** | **8,804.7 t** | **11,441.1 t** | **8,610.9 t** | **11,209.7 t** | **1,682 w** | **1,796 w** | **81.3 w** | **81.1 w** | **10.0 w** | **9.7 w** | **8.7 w** | **9.1 w** |
| **Low income** | 739.4 | 1,147.0 | 723.3 | 1,110.7 | 426 | 486 | 49.1 | 55.5 | 48.3 | 41.7 | 2.6 | 2.8 |
| **Middle income** | 4,367.6 | 5,790.6 | 3,495.9 | 4,544.6 | 1,346 | 1,486 | 83.9 | 84.1 | 11.7 | 10.3 | 4.4 | 5.6 |
| Lower middle income | 1,982.3 | 3,133.1 | 1,701.7 | 2,747.8 | 894 | 1,216 | 78.6 | 83.3 | 18.4 | 12.8 | 3.0 | 3.9 |
| Upper middle income | 2,385.3 | 2,657.5 | 1,794.2 | 1,796.9 | 2,586 | 2,248 | 88.7 | 85.4 | 5.3 | 6.5 | 5.8 | 8.0 |
| **Low & middle income** | 5,106.5 | 6,929.5 | 4,213.0 | 5,639.6 | 993 | 1,071 | 78.2 | 78.8 | 17.7 | 16.2 | 4.1 | 5.0 |
| East Asia & Pacific | 1,222.6 | 2,209.1 | 1,138.3 | 2,210.7 | 717 | 1,182 | 71.7 | 81.4 | 26.5 | 15.5 | 1.8 | 3.1 |
| Europe & Central Asia | 1,879.2 | 1,729.1 | 1,734.7 | 1,287.5 | 3,878 | 2,826 | 93.2 | 89.1 | 1.5 | 2.2 | 5.3 | 8.7 |
| Latin America & Carib. | 604.3 | 908.0 | 452.9 | 656.9 | 1,039 | 1,198 | 72.4 | 74.3 | 18.4 | 14.8 | 9.2 | 10.8 |
| Middle East & N. Africa | 601.9 | 874.1 | 194.4 | 386.8 | 861 | 1,270 | 97.1 | 98.0 | 1.8 | 1.1 | 1.0 | 0.8 |
| South Asia | 348.8 | 517.3 | 390.7 | 661.9 | 350 | 453 | 54.0 | 65.9 | 43.5 | 31.5 | 2.5 | 2.6 |
| Sub-Saharan Africa | 481.8 | 748.0 | 317.4 | 462.6 | 685 | 681 | 41.2 | 41.3 | 56.6 | 56.3 | 2.2 | 2.4 |
| **High income** | 3,723.0 | 4,545.8 | 4,426.7 | 5,609.3 | 4,841 | 5,498 | 84.2 | 83.4 | 2.8 | 3.2 | 13.0 | 13.2 |
| Euro area | 471.3 | 450.5 | 1,052.7 | 1,244.4 | 3,562 | 3,961 | 80.2 | 77.5 | 3.2 | 4.3 | 16.4 | 17.5 |

a. Includes Montenegro.

## About the data

In developing countries growth in energy use is closely related to growth in the modern sectors—industry, motorized transport, and urban areas—but energy use also reflects climatic, geographic, and economic factors (such as the relative price of energy). Energy use has been growing rapidly in low- and middle-income countries, but high-income countries still use more than five times as much energy on a per capita basis.

Energy data are compiled by the International Energy Agency (IEA). IEA data for countries that are not members of the Organisation for Economic Co-operation and Development (OECD) are based on national energy data adjusted to conform to annual questionnaires completed by OECD member governments.

Total energy use refers to the use of primary energy before transformation to other end-use fuels (such as electricity and refined petroleum products). It includes energy from combustible renewables and waste—solid biomass and animal products, gas and liquid from biomass, and industrial and municipal waste. Biomass is any plant matter used directly as fuel or converted into fuel, heat, or electricity. (The data series published in *World Development Indicators 1998* and earlier editions did not include energy from combustible renewables and waste.) Data for combustible renewables and waste are often based on small surveys or other incomplete information and thus give only a broad impression of developments and are not strictly comparable across countries. The IEA reports include country notes that explain some of these differences (see *Data sources*). All forms of energy—primary energy and primary electricity—are converted into oil equivalents. A notional thermal efficiency of 33 percent is assumed to convert nuclear electricity into oil equivalents and 100 percent efficiency to convert hydroelectric power.

The IEA makes these estimates in consultation with national statistical offices, oil companies, electric utilities, and national energy experts. The IEA occasionally revises its time series to reflect political changes, and energy statistics undergo continual changes in coverage or methodology as more detailed energy accounts become available. Breaks in series are therefore unavoidable.

## Definitions

• **Total energy production** refers to forms of primary energy—petroleum (crude oil, natural gas liquids, and oil from nonconventional sources), natural gas, solid fuels (coal, lignite, and other derived fuels), and combustible renewables and waste—and primary electricity, all converted into oil equivalents (see *About the data*). • **Energy use** refers to the use of primary energy before transformation to other end-use fuels, which is equal to indigenous production plus imports and stock changes, minus exports and fuels supplied to ships and aircraft engaged in international transport (see *About the data*). • **Fossil fuel** comprises coal, oil, petroleum, and natural gas products. • **Combustible renewables and waste** comprise solid biomass, liquid biomass, biogas, industrial waste, and municipal waste. • **Clean energy** is noncarbohydrate energy that does not produce carbon dioxide when generated. It includes hydropower and nuclear, geothermal, and solar power, among others.

---

**A person in a high-income economy uses an average of more than 11 times as much energy as a person in a low-income economy** — 3.7a

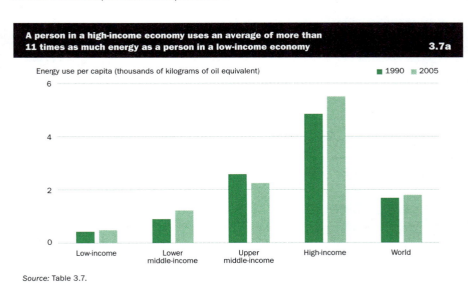

Energy use per capita (thousands of kilograms of oil equivalent) — ■ 1990 ■ 2005

*Source:* Table 3.7.

## Data sources

Data on energy production and use are from IEA electronic files and are published in IEA's annual publications, *Energy Statistics and Balances of Non-OECD Countries*, *Energy Statistics of OECD Countries*, and *Energy Balances of OECD Countries*.

| | Net energy imports[a] | | Energy use | GDP per unit of energy use | | Carbon dioxide emissions | | | | | | | |
|---|---|---|---|---|---|---|---|---|---|---|---|---|---|
| | | | average annual % growth | 2005 PPP $ per kilogram of oil equivalent | | Total million metric tons | | From solid fuel consumption % of total | | Per capita metric tons | | kilograms per 2005 PPP $ of GDP | |
| | % of energy use | | | | | | | | | | | | |
| | 1990 | 2005 | 1990–2005 | 1990 | 2005 | 1990 | 2004 | 1990 | 2004 | 1990 | 2004 | 1990 | 2004 |
| Afghanistan | .. | .. | .. | .. | .. | 2.6 | 0.7 | 10.7 | 13.2 | .. | .. | .. | 0.0 |
| Albania | 8 | 51 | 2.0 | 4.3 | 7.2 | 7.3 | 3.7 | 38.2 | 3.0 | 2.2 | 1.2 | 0.6 | 0.2 |
| Algeria | –338 | –404 | 2.4 | 5.6 | 5.7 | 77.0 | 193.8 | 3.9 | 1.0 | 3.0 | 6.0 | 0.6 | 1.0 |
| Angola | –356 | –614 | 3.1 | 5.4 | 6.1 | 4.6 | 7.9 | 0.0 | 0.0 | 0.4 | 0.5 | 0.1 | 0.2 |
| Argentina | –5 | –27 | 1.9 | 5.3 | 6.6 | 109.7 | 141.7 | 2.8 | 1.2 | 3.4 | 3.7 | 0.5 | 0.4 |
| Armenia | 98 | 66 | –5.8 | 1.3 | 4.9 | 4.2 | 3.6 | 10.2 | 0.0 | 1.2 | 1.2 | 0.4 | 0.3 |
| Australia | –80 | –122 | 2.2 | 4.8 | 5.7 | 278.4 | 326.5 | 52.4 | 50.3 | 16.3 | 16.2 | 0.7 | 0.5 |
| Austria | 68 | 71 | 2.0 | 8.1 | 8.2 | 57.6 | 69.8 | 28.3 | 21.0 | 7.5 | 8.5 | 0.3 | 0.3 |
| Azerbaijan | 18 | –97 | –4.0 | 1.3 | 2.8 | 53.7 | 31.3 | 0.1 | 0.0 | 7.5 | 3.8 | 1.5 | 1.0 |
| Bangladesh | 16 | 20 | 4.5 | 6.1 | 6.8 | 15.4 | 37.1 | 6.9 | 3.6 | 0.1 | 0.2 | 0.2 | 0.2 |
| Belarus | 92 | 86 | –2.8 | 1.6 | 3.1 | 107.8 | 64.8 | 8.3 | 3.4 | 10.6 | 6.6 | 1.6 | 0.9 |
| Belgium | 73 | 75 | 1.2 | 5.1 | 5.9 | 100.6 | 100.6 | 40.8 | 22.9 | 10.1 | 9.7 | 0.4 | 0.3 |
| Benin | –6 | 35 | 2.8 | 3.2 | 4.0 | 0.7 | 2.4 | 0.0 | 0.0 | 0.1 | 0.3 | 0.1 | 0.2 |
| Bolivia | –77 | –161 | 4.0 | 7.3 | 6.4 | 5.5 | 7.0 | 0.0 | 0.0 | 0.8 | 0.8 | 0.3 | 0.2 |
| Bosnia and Herzegovina | 35 | 33 | 0.9 | .. | 4.7 | 6.9 | 15.6 | 52.1 | 70.7 | 1.6 | 4.0 | .. | 0.7 |
| Botswana | 28 | 45 | 2.7 | 7.3 | 11.6 | 2.2 | 4.3 | 100.0 | 57.3 | 1.6 | 2.4 | 0.2 | 0.2 |
| Brazil | 27 | 10 | 3.2 | 8.1 | 7.6 | 209.5 | 331.5 | 20.4 | 18.2 | 1.4 | 1.8 | 0.2 | 0.2 |
| Bulgaria | 67 | 47 | –1.8 | 2.3 | 3.6 | 75.3 | 42.5 | 46.8 | 63.8 | 8.6 | 5.5 | 1.1 | 0.6 |
| Burkina Faso | .. | .. | .. | .. | .. | 1.0 | 1.1 | 0.0 | 0.0 | 0.1 | 0.1 | 0.2 | 0.1 |
| Burundi | .. | .. | .. | .. | .. | 0.2 | 0.2 | 7.5 | 3.3 | 0.0 | 0.0 | 0.1 | 0.1 |
| Cambodia | .. | .. | .. | .. | .. | 0.5 | 0.5 | 0.0 | 0.0 | 0.0 | 0.0 | .. | 0.0 |
| Cameroon | –140 | –71 | 2.4 | 5.1 | 5.1 | 1.6 | 3.8 | 0.2 | 0.0 | 0.1 | 0.2 | 0.1 | 0.1 |
| Canada | –31 | –48 | 1.7 | 3.6 | 4.2 | 415.7 | 638.8 | 22.0 | 15.6 | 15.0 | 20.0 | 0.6 | 0.6 |
| Central African Republic | .. | .. | .. | .. | .. | 0.2 | 0.3 | 0.0 | 0.0 | 0.1 | 0.1 | 0.1 | 0.1 |
| Chad | .. | .. | .. | .. | .. | 0.1 | 0.1 | 0.0 | 0.0 | 0.0 | 0.0 | 0.0 | 0.0 |
| Chile | 46 | 69 | 5.2 | 6.2 | 6.7 | 35.6 | 62.4 | 30.3 | 23.6 | 2.7 | 3.9 | 0.4 | 0.3 |
| China | –3 | 4 | 3.9 | 1.5 | 3.1 | 2,398.2 | 5,005.7 | 80.5 | 71.9 | 2.1 | 3.9 | 1.9 | 1.0 |
|   Hong Kong, China | 100 | 100 | 3.2 | 12.0 | 13.5 | 26.2 | 37.4 | 69.2 | 53.2 | 4.6 | 5.5 | 0.2 | 0.2 |
| Colombia | –95 | –178 | 0.4 | 7.0 | 9.2 | 58.0 | 53.6 | 23.9 | 13.7 | 1.7 | 1.2 | 0.3 | 0.2 |
| Congo, Dem. Rep. | –1 | –2 | 2.4 | 1.9 | 0.9 | 4.0 | 2.1 | 19.3 | 45.1 | 0.1 | 0.0 | 0.2 | 0.1 |
| Congo, Rep. | –753 | –1,041 | 0.1 | 7.8 | 9.8 | 1.2 | 3.5 | 0.0 | 0.0 | 0.5 | 1.0 | 0.1 | 0.3 |
| Costa Rica | 49 | 52 | 4.6 | 9.1 | 9.9 | 2.9 | 6.4 | 0.0 | 2.3 | 0.9 | 1.5 | 0.2 | 0.2 |
| Côte d'Ivoire | 23 | –5 | 3.6 | 5.4 | 3.8 | 5.4 | 5.2 | 0.0 | 0.0 | 0.4 | 0.3 | 0.2 | 0.2 |
| Croatia | 43 | 57 | 1.2 | 6.0 | 6.6 | 24.6 | 23.5 | 10.0 | 13.2 | 5.1 | 5.3 | 0.5 | 0.4 |
| Cuba | 61 | 46 | –1.5 | .. | .. | 32.0 | 25.8 | 1.2 | 0.1 | 3.0 | 2.3 | .. | .. |
| Czech Republic | 18 | 27 | –0.1 | 3.4 | 4.6 | 161.7 | 116.9 | 77.6 | 66.7 | 15.6 | 11.5 | 1.0 | 0.6 |
| Denmark | 44 | –60 | 0.3 | 7.4 | 9.3 | 49.7 | 52.9 | 47.2 | 37.1 | 9.7 | 9.8 | 0.4 | 0.3 |
| Dominican Republic | 75 | 79 | 4.6 | 5.6 | 6.7 | 9.6 | 19.6 | 0.3 | 10.5 | 1.3 | 2.1 | 0.4 | 0.4 |
| Ecuador | –169 | –174 | 3.6 | 9.2 | 8.4 | 16.7 | 29.2 | 0.0 | 0.0 | 1.6 | 2.3 | 0.3 | 0.4 |
| Egypt, Arab Rep. | –72 | –24 | 4.6 | 5.7 | 5.4 | 75.4 | 158.1 | 4.5 | 2.1 | 1.4 | 2.2 | 0.4 | 0.5 |
| El Salvador | 32 | 45 | 3.9 | 8.2 | 7.8 | 2.6 | 6.2 | 0.0 | 0.0 | 0.5 | 0.9 | 0.1 | 0.2 |
| Eritrea | .. | .. | .. | .. | .. | .. | 0.8 | .. | 0.0 | .. | 0.2 | .. | 0.2 |
| Estonia | 47 | 27 | –3.1 | 1.7 | 4.3 | 28.3 | 18.9 | 76.9 | 75.1 | 18.1 | 14.0 | 1.8 | 0.9 |
| Ethiopia | 7 | 8 | 2.6 | 1.7 | 2.0 | 3.0 | 8.0 | 0.0 | 0.0 | 0.1 | 0.1 | 0.1 | 0.2 |
| Finland | 59 | 53 | 1.8 | 4.0 | 4.6 | 51.2 | 65.7 | 39.6 | 44.9 | 10.3 | 12.6 | 0.4 | 0.4 |
| France | 51 | 50 | 1.2 | 6.2 | 6.7 | 363.7 | 373.4 | 21.7 | 15.1 | 6.4 | 6.2 | 0.3 | 0.2 |
| Gabon | –1,077 | –604 | 2.1 | 11.2 | 10.4 | 6.0 | 1.4 | 0.0 | 0.0 | 6.5 | 1.1 | 0.4 | 0.1 |
| Gambia, The | .. | .. | .. | .. | .. | 0.2 | 0.3 | 0.0 | 0.0 | 0.2 | 0.2 | 0.2 | 0.2 |
| Georgia | 85 | 60 | –9.2 | 2.4 | 4.9 | 17.3 | 3.9 | 6.4 | 0.7 | 3.2 | 0.9 | 0.6 | 0.3 |
| Germany | 48 | 61 | 0.0 | 5.5 | 7.3 | 980.3 | 808.0 | 48.6 | 41.4 | 12.3 | 9.8 | 0.5 | 0.3 |
| Ghana | 18 | 29 | 3.6 | 2.5 | 2.9 | 3.8 | 7.2 | 0.2 | 0.0 | 0.2 | 0.3 | 0.3 | 0.3 |
| Greece | 59 | 67 | 2.5 | 9.4 | 10.5 | 72.4 | 96.6 | 43.8 | 39.8 | 7.1 | 8.7 | 0.3 | 0.3 |
| Guatemala | 24 | 32 | 4.2 | 8.2 | 7.8 | 5.1 | 12.2 | 0.0 | 10.0 | 0.6 | 1.0 | 0.1 | 0.2 |
| Guinea | .. | .. | .. | .. | .. | 1.0 | 1.3 | 0.0 | 0.0 | 0.2 | 0.2 | 0.2 | 0.1 |
| Guinea-Bissau | .. | .. | .. | .. | .. | 0.2 | 0.3 | 0.0 | 0.0 | 0.2 | 0.2 | 0.3 | 0.4 |
| Haiti | 21 | 23 | 3.3 | 8.1 | 4.4 | 1.0 | 1.8 | 3.3 | 0.0 | 0.1 | 0.2 | 0.1 | 0.2 |

| | Net energy imports[a] | | Energy use | GDP per unit of energy use | | Carbon dioxide emissions | | | | | | | |
|---|---|---|---|---|---|---|---|---|---|---|---|---|---|
| | % of energy use | | average annual % growth | 2005 PPP $ per kilogram of oil equivalent | | Total million metric tons | | From solid fuel consumption % of total | | Per capita metric tons | | kilograms per 2005 PPP $ of GDP | |
| | 1990 | 2005 | 1990–2005 | 1990 | 2005 | 1990 | 2004 | 1990 | 2004 | 1990 | 2004 | 1990 | 2004 |
| Honduras | 30 | 54 | 3.0 | 5.7 | 5.8 | 2.6 | 7.6 | 0.0 | 6.1 | 0.5 | 1.1 | 0.2 | 0.4 |
| Hungary | 50 | 63 | 0.0 | 4.5 | 6.2 | 60.1 | 57.1 | 31.2 | 22.3 | 5.8 | 5.7 | 0.5 | 0.3 |
| India | 9 | 22 | 3.5 | 3.2 | 4.5 | 681.5 | 1,341.8 | 69.9 | 69.6 | 0.8 | 1.2 | 0.7 | 0.6 |
| Indonesia | −65 | −47 | 3.6 | 3.6 | 3.9 | 213.8 | 377.9 | 3.7 | 10.0 | 1.2 | 1.7 | 0.6 | 0.6 |
| Iran, Islamic Rep. | −161 | −87 | 5.5 | 5.0 | 4.0 | 218.2 | 433.2 | 2.1 | 1.0 | 4.0 | 6.4 | 0.6 | 0.7 |
| Iraq | −451 | −212 | 3.3 | | | 48.5 | 81.6 | 0.0 | 0.0 | 2.6 | .. | .. | .. |
| Ireland | 67 | 89 | 3.3 | 5.9 | 10.3 | 30.6 | 42.3 | 43.0 | 22.6 | 8.7 | 10.4 | 0.5 | 0.3 |
| Israel | 96 | 89 | 3.6 | 6.8 | 8.0 | 33.1 | 71.2 | 29.7 | 48.5 | 7.1 | 10.5 | 0.4 | 0.5 |
| Italy | 83 | 85 | 1.6 | 9.1 | 8.8 | 389.6 | 449.5 | 13.1 | 14.5 | 6.9 | 7.7 | 0.3 | 0.3 |
| Jamaica | 84 | 87 | 2.3 | 4.9 | 5.0 | 8.0 | 10.6 | 1.7 | 1.7 | 3.3 | 4.0 | 0.6 | 0.6 |
| Japan | 83 | 81 | 1.2 | 7.2 | 7.3 | 1,070.4 | 1,256.8 | 28.5 | 38.0 | 8.7 | 9.8 | 0.3 | 0.3 |
| Jordan | 95 | 96 | 4.0 | 3.0 | 3.3 | 10.2 | 16.5 | 0.0 | 0.0 | 3.2 | 3.1 | 1.0 | 0.8 |
| Kazakhstan | −23 | −132 | −3.8 | 1.6 | 2.5 | 288.1 | 200.1 | 56.9 | 54.4 | 17.6 | 13.3 | 2.5 | 1.7 |
| Kenya | 18 | 19 | 2.2 | 2.7 | 2.8 | 5.8 | 10.6 | 6.9 | 2.7 | 0.2 | 0.3 | 0.2 | 0.2 |
| Korea, Dem. Rep. | 13 | 5 | −2.8 | .. | .. | 244.6 | 79.0 | 91.2 | 92.1 | 12.1 | 3.4 | .. | .. |
| Korea, Rep. | 76 | 80 | 5.6 | 4.9 | 4.8 | 241.1 | 465.2 | 38.7 | 43.8 | 5.6 | 9.7 | 0.5 | 0.5 |
| Kuwait | −495 | −420 | 8.3 | 3.0 | 3.9 | 43.4 | 99.3 | 0.0 | 0.0 | 20.4 | 40.4 | 0.6 | 1.0 |
| Kyrgyz Republic | 67 | 48 | −5.6 | 1.5 | 3.2 | 12.6 | 5.7 | 31.4 | 37.1 | 2.8 | 1.1 | 1.1 | 0.6 |
| Lao PDR | .. | .. | .. | .. | .. | 0.2 | 1.3 | 1.6 | 60.2 | 0.1 | 0.2 | 0.1 | 0.1 |
| Latvia | 85 | 51 | −3.0 | 3.5 | 6.4 | 14.5 | 7.1 | 10.6 | 2.7 | 5.4 | 3.1 | 0.5 | 0.3 |
| Lebanon | 94 | 96 | 5.4 | 6.7 | 6.9 | 9.1 | 16.2 | 0.0 | 3.3 | 3.1 | 4.1 | 0.6 | 0.4 |
| Lesotho | .. | .. | .. | .. | .. | .. | .. | .. | .. | .. | .. | .. | .. |
| Liberia | .. | .. | .. | .. | .. | 0.5 | 0.5 | 0.0 | 0.0 | 0.2 | 0.1 | 0.4 | 0.5 |
| Libya | −534 | −399 | 2.8 | .. | 3.4 | 37.8 | 59.9 | 0.0 | 0.0 | 8.7 | 10.3 | .. | 1.0 |
| Lithuania | 70 | 54 | −3.1 | 2.9 | 5.6 | 24.3 | 13.3 | 8.5 | 5.9 | 6.6 | 3.9 | 0.5 | 0.3 |
| Macedonia, FYR | 46 | 47 | −0.4 | 5.7 | 5.5 | 15.5 | 10.4 | 67.7 | 77.6 | 8.1 | 5.1 | 1.0 | 0.7 |
| Madagascar | .. | .. | .. | .. | .. | 0.9 | 2.7 | 3.5 | 0.9 | 0.1 | 0.2 | 0.1 | 0.2 |
| Malawi | .. | .. | .. | .. | .. | 0.6 | 1.0 | 7.9 | 14.4 | 0.1 | 0.1 | 0.1 | 0.1 |
| Malaysia | −116 | −53 | 6.0 | 5.2 | 4.9 | 55.3 | 177.4 | 9.8 | 19.8 | 3.1 | 7.0 | 0.5 | 0.6 |
| Mali | .. | .. | .. | .. | .. | 0.4 | 0.6 | 0.0 | 0.0 | 0.1 | 0.1 | 0.1 | 0.1 |
| Mauritania | .. | .. | .. | .. | .. | 2.6 | 2.6 | 0.6 | 0.7 | 1.4 | 0.9 | 0.9 | 0.5 |
| Mauritius | .. | .. | .. | .. | .. | 1.5 | 3.2 | 13.5 | 24.0 | 1.4 | 2.6 | 0.2 | 0.3 |
| Mexico | −57 | −47 | 2.0 | 6.1 | 6.6 | 413.1 | 437.6 | 2.2 | 4.5 | 5.0 | 4.3 | 0.5 | 0.4 |
| Moldova | 99 | 98 | −6.7 | 1.7 | 2.4 | 23.8 | 7.7 | 19.2 | 4.1 | 5.4 | 2.0 | 1.4 | 1.0 |
| Mongolia | .. | .. | .. | .. | .. | 10.0 | 8.5 | 73.2 | 79.5 | 4.7 | 3.4 | 2.0 | 1.4 |
| Morocco | 89 | 93 | 4.2 | 9.9 | 7.8 | 23.5 | 41.1 | 19.9 | 35.3 | 1.0 | 1.4 | 0.4 | 0.4 |
| Mozambique | 5 | −15 | 2.8 | 0.8 | 1.4 | 1.0 | 2.2 | 15.4 | 2.9 | 0.1 | 0.1 | 0.2 | 0.2 |
| Myanmar | 0 | −50 | 2.0 | 1.3 | 2.7 | 4.3 | 9.8 | 6.4 | 3.9 | 0.1 | 0.2 | 0.3 | 0.3 |
| Namibia | 67 | 76 | 5.1 | 8.1 | 6.7 | 0.0 | 2.5 | 0.0 | 0.4 | 0.0 | 1.2 | 0.0 | 0.3 |
| Nepal | 5 | 11 | 3.2 | 2.3 | 2.8 | 0.6 | 3.0 | 5.2 | 26.3 | 0.0 | 0.1 | 0.0 | 0.1 |
| Netherlands | 9 | 24 | 1.2 | 5.8 | 6.9 | 141.0 | 141.9 | 28.7 | 22.2 | 9.4 | 8.7 | 0.4 | 0.3 |
| New Zealand | 13 | 28 | 1.6 | 4.7 | 6.0 | 22.6 | 31.5 | 14.6 | 14.5 | 6.6 | 7.7 | 0.3 | 0.3 |
| Nicaragua | 29 | 41 | 3.1 | 4.2 | 4.3 | 2.6 | 4.0 | 0.0 | 0.0 | 0.6 | 0.7 | 0.3 | 0.3 |
| Niger | .. | .. | .. | .. | .. | 1.0 | 1.2 | 43.7 | 39.0 | 0.1 | 0.1 | 0.2 | 0.2 |
| Nigeria | −112 | −123 | 2.3 | 1.7 | 2.1 | 45.3 | 113.9 | 0.3 | 0.0 | 0.5 | 0.8 | 0.4 | 0.6 |
| Norway | −459 | −627 | 2.0 | 6.4 | 6.8 | 33.2 | 87.5 | 9.9 | 4.0 | 7.8 | 19.1 | 0.2 | 0.4 |
| Oman | −740 | −327 | 7.0 | 5.7 | 3.7 | 10.3 | 30.9 | 0.0 | 0.0 | 5.6 | 12.5 | 0.4 | 0.6 |
| Pakistan | 21 | 20 | 3.7 | 4.2 | 4.5 | 68.0 | 125.6 | 12.5 | 13.5 | 0.6 | 0.8 | 0.4 | 0.4 |
| Panama | 59 | 72 | 3.8 | 9.1 | 10.5 | 3.1 | 5.7 | 2.9 | 0.1 | 1.3 | 1.8 | 0.2 | 0.2 |
| Papua New Guinea | .. | .. | .. | .. | .. | 2.4 | 2.4 | 0.2 | 0.1 | 0.6 | 0.4 | 0.4 | 0.2 |
| Paraguay | −48 | −66 | 1.7 | 5.4 | 5.7 | 2.3 | 4.2 | 0.0 | 0.0 | 0.5 | 0.7 | 0.1 | 0.2 |
| Peru | −6 | 22 | 2.1 | 9.8 | 12.7 | 21.0 | 31.5 | 2.6 | 9.0 | 1.0 | 1.2 | 0.2 | 0.2 |
| Philippines | 48 | 46 | 4.0 | 5.7 | 5.6 | 43.9 | 80.4 | 13.0 | 28.7 | 0.7 | 1.0 | 0.3 | 0.3 |
| Poland | 1 | 15 | −0.8 | 3.1 | 5.6 | 347.5 | 307.0 | 82.9 | 71.0 | 9.1 | 8.0 | 1.1 | 0.6 |
| Portugal | 81 | 87 | 3.2 | 8.6 | 7.7 | 42.3 | 58.9 | 26.0 | 22.0 | 4.3 | 5.6 | 0.3 | 0.3 |
| Puerto Rico | .. | .. | .. | .. | .. | 11.8 | 2.1 | .. | .. | 3.3 | 0.5 | .. | .. |

| | Net energy imports[a] | | Energy use | GDP per unit of energy use | | Carbon dioxide emissions | | | | | | | |
|---|---|---|---|---|---|---|---|---|---|---|---|---|---|
| | | | average annual % growth | 2005 PPP $ per kilogram of oil equivalent | | Total million metric tons | | From solid fuel consumption % of total | | Per capita metric tons | | kilograms per 2005 PPP $ of GDP | |
| | % of energy use | | | | | | | | | | | | |
| | 1990 | 2005 | 1990–2005 | 1990 | 2005 | 1990 | 2004 | 1990 | 2004 | 1990 | 2004 | 1990 | 2004 |
| Romania | 35 | 27 | −2.6 | 2.9 | 5.3 | 155.0 | 90.3 | 30.9 | 35.1 | 6.7 | 4.2 | 0.9 | 0.5 |
| Russian Federation | −46 | −83 | −1.8 | 2.1 | 2.6 | 2,261.7 | 1,523.6 | 24.9 | 22.2 | 15.3 | 10.6 | 1.2 | 1.0 |
| Rwanda | .. | .. | .. | .. | .. | 0.5 | 0.6 | 0.0 | 0.0 | 0.1 | 0.1 | 0.1 | 0.1 |
| Saudi Arabia | −505 | −311 | 4.7 | 5.1 | 3.5 | 254.7 | 308.1 | 0.0 | 0.0 | 15.6 | 13.7 | 0.8 | 0.7 |
| Senegal | 39 | 58 | 2.4 | 4.8 | 6.0 | 3.1 | 5.0 | 0.0 | 0.4 | 0.4 | 0.4 | 0.3 | 0.3 |
| Serbia[b] | 38 | 29 | −0.5 | .. | .. | 130.4 | 53.3 | 54.7 | 68.7 | 12.4 | 6.6 | .. | .. |
| Sierra Leone | .. | .. | .. | .. | .. | 0.3 | 1.0 | 0.0 | 0.0 | 0.1 | 0.2 | 0.1 | 0.3 |
| Singapore | 100 | 100 | 3.6 | 5.3 | 6.0 | 45.1 | 52.2 | 0.2 | 0.0 | 14.8 | 12.3 | 0.6 | 0.3 |
| Slovak Republic | 75 | 65 | −0.2 | 3.1 | 4.5 | 51.4 | 36.3 | 49.0 | 43.4 | 9.7 | 6.7 | 0.8 | 0.4 |
| Slovenia | 48 | 53 | 2.3 | 5.7 | 6.2 | 18.0 | 16.2 | 42.9 | 41.3 | 9.0 | 8.1 | 0.6 | 0.4 |
| Somalia | .. | .. | .. | .. | .. | 0.0 | .. | 0.0 | .. | 0.0 | .. | .. | .. |
| South Africa | −26 | −24 | 2.1 | 3.0 | 3.1 | 331.7 | 436.6 | 79.9 | 82.2 | 9.4 | 9.4 | 1.2 | 1.2 |
| Spain | 62 | 79 | 3.4 | 8.4 | 8.1 | 212.1 | 330.2 | 35.6 | 25.2 | 5.5 | 7.7 | 0.3 | 0.3 |
| Sri Lanka | 24 | 44 | 3.8 | 6.0 | 7.2 | 3.8 | 11.5 | 0.1 | 2.2 | 0.2 | 0.6 | 0.1 | 0.2 |
| Sudan | 18 | −69 | 3.8 | 2.5 | 3.4 | 5.4 | 10.4 | 0.0 | 0.0 | 0.2 | 0.3 | 0.2 | 0.2 |
| Swaziland | .. | .. | .. | .. | .. | 0.4 | 1.0 | 100.0 | 100.0 | 0.6 | 0.9 | 0.1 | 0.2 |
| Sweden | 37 | 33 | 0.6 | 4.5 | 5.5 | 49.4 | 53.0 | 21.3 | 20.9 | 5.8 | 5.9 | 0.2 | 0.2 |
| Switzerland | 61 | 60 | 0.7 | 8.9 | 9.6 | 42.7 | 40.4 | 3.3 | 1.3 | 6.4 | 5.5 | 0.2 | 0.2 |
| Syrian Arab Republic | −91 | −63 | 2.9 | 3.2 | 4.2 | 35.9 | 68.4 | 0.0 | 0.0 | 2.8 | 3.7 | 1.0 | 0.9 |
| Tajikistan | 64 | 56 | −3.3 | 2.9 | 2.8 | 23.4 | 5.0 | 3.5 | 5.7 | 4.4 | 0.8 | 1.4 | 0.6 |
| Tanzania | 8 | 6 | 4.9 | 2.0 | 1.8 | 2.3 | 4.3 | 0.5 | 4.0 | 0.1 | 0.1 | 0.1 | 0.1 |
| Thailand | 40 | 46 | 5.2 | 5.1 | 4.4 | 95.7 | 267.8 | 14.2 | 21.6 | 1.8 | 4.3 | 0.4 | 0.6 |
| Timor-Leste | .. | .. | .. | .. | .. | .. | 0.2 | .. | 0.0 | .. | 0.2 | .. | 0.1 |
| Togo | 17 | 20 | 2.3 | 2.3 | 2.3 | 0.8 | 2.3 | 0.0 | 0.0 | 0.2 | 0.4 | 0.2 | 0.5 |
| Trinidad and Tobago | −109 | −147 | 5.7 | 1.6 | 1.6 | 16.9 | 32.5 | 0.0 | 0.0 | 13.8 | 24.7 | 1.7 | 1.7 |
| Tunisia | −11 | 21 | 3.3 | 5.8 | 7.6 | 13.3 | 22.9 | 2.0 | 0.0 | 1.6 | 2.3 | 0.4 | 0.4 |
| Turkey | 51 | 72 | 3.4 | 6.0 | 6.6 | 146.1 | 225.9 | 42.1 | 38.6 | 2.6 | 3.2 | 0.5 | 0.4 |
| Turkmenistan | −281 | −274 | 0.8 | .. | .. | 32.0 | 41.7 | 2.5 | 0.0 | 8.7 | 8.7 | .. | .. |
| Uganda | .. | .. | .. | .. | .. | 0.8 | 1.8 | 0.0 | 0.0 | 0.0 | 0.1 | 0.1 | 0.1 |
| Ukraine | 47 | 43 | −3.7 | 1.7 | 1.8 | 684.0 | 329.7 | 45.9 | 38.0 | 13.2 | 6.9 | 1.6 | 1.3 |
| United Arab Emirates | −385 | −258 | 4.8 | 2.7 | 2.9 | 54.7 | 149.1 | 0.0 | 0.0 | 30.8 | 37.8 | 0.9 | 1.2 |
| United Kingdom | 2 | 13 | 0.6 | 6.2 | 8.1 | 579.2 | 586.7 | 41.5 | 25.8 | 10.1 | 9.8 | 0.4 | 0.3 |
| United States | 14 | 30 | 1.4 | 4.1 | 5.3 | 4,816.9 | 6,044.0 | 37.1 | 35.7 | 19.3 | 20.6 | 0.6 | 0.5 |
| Uruguay | 49 | 65 | 1.1 | 9.7 | 10.6 | 3.9 | 5.5 | 0.1 | 0.1 | 1.3 | 1.7 | 0.2 | 0.2 |
| Uzbekistan | 17 | −20 | 0.7 | 0.9 | 1.1 | 129.2 | 137.8 | 6.0 | 2.0 | 6.3 | 5.3 | 3.1 | 2.8 |
| Venezuela, RB | −239 | −236 | 1.6 | 4.3 | 4.3 | 117.3 | 172.5 | 1.0 | 0.0 | 5.9 | 6.6 | 0.6 | 0.7 |
| Vietnam | −2 | −36 | 5.2 | 2.5 | 3.5 | 21.4 | 98.6 | 51.5 | 40.1 | 0.3 | 1.2 | 0.4 | 0.6 |
| West Bank and Gaza | .. | .. | .. | .. | .. | .. | .. | .. | .. | .. | .. | .. | .. |
| Yemen, Rep. | −266 | −203 | 6.3 | 8.6 | 6.9 | 9.6 | 21.1 | 0.0 | 0.0 | 0.8 | 1.0 | 0.4 | 0.5 |
| Zambia | 10 | 9 | 1.7 | 1.8 | 1.9 | 2.4 | 2.3 | 34.0 | 14.9 | 0.3 | 0.2 | 0.2 | 0.2 |
| Zimbabwe | 9 | 9 | −0.1 | 0.3 | 0.2 | 16.6 | 10.5 | 87.5 | 80.8 | 1.6 | 0.8 | 6.0 | 4.3 |
| **World** | **−2[c] w** | **−2[c] w** | **1.7 w** | **4.1 w** | **5.0 w** | **22,695.9[d] t** | **28,974.3[d] t** | **38.5[d] w** | **35.9[d] w** | **4.3[d] w** | **4.5[d] w** | **0.6[d] w** | **0.5[d] w** |
| **Low income** | −2 | −3 | 2.9 | 2.8 | 3.8 | 1,337.9 | 2,082.9 | 63.1 | 58.5 | 0.8 | 0.9 | 0.6 | 0.5 |
| **Middle income** | −25 | −27 | 1.6 | 3.0 | 4.0 | 9,187.1 | 11,936.3 | 42.2 | 46.0 | 3.6 | 4.0 | 0.9 | 0.7 |
| Lower middle income | −17 | −14 | 2.9 | 2.5 | 3.6 | 4,388.4 | 7,508.5 | 55.1 | 55.5 | 2.3 | 3.4 | 1.1 | 0.8 |
| Upper middle income | −33 | −48 | 0.1 | 3.4 | 4.6 | 4,798.7 | 4,427.8 | 33.1 | 31.1 | 6.9 | 5.6 | 0.8 | 0.6 |
| **Low & middle income** | −21 | −23 | 1.8 | 2.9 | 4.0 | 10,525.0 | 14,019.1 | 44.6 | 47.7 | 2.4 | 2.6 | 0.8 | 0.7 |
| East Asia & Pacific | −7 | 0 | 3.9 | 2.0 | 3.3 | 3,091.4 | 6,111.6 | 71.6 | 63.6 | 1.9 | 3.3 | 1.3 | 0.9 |
| Europe & Central Asia | −8 | −34 | −1.8 | 2.3 | 3.3 | 4,566.4 | 3,187.7 | 35.5 | 31.9 | 10.3 | 7.1 | 1.2 | 0.8 |
| Latin America & Carib. | −33 | −38 | 2.4 | 6.7 | 7.0 | 1,066.0 | 1,381.8 | 7.9 | 8.3 | 2.4 | 2.5 | 0.4 | 0.3 |
| Middle East & N. Africa | −210 | −126 | 4.4 | 5.4 | 4.7 | 569.0 | 1,143.9 | 3.9 | 3.0 | 2.5 | 3.9 | 0.6 | 0.7 |
| South Asia | 11 | 22 | 3.5 | 3.4 | 4.6 | 772.2 | 1,520.8 | 63.0 | 62.8 | 0.7 | 1.0 | 0.6 | 0.5 |
| Sub-Saharan Africa | −52 | −62 | 2.4 | 2.5 | 2.7 | 460.0 | 673.2 | 88.4 | 79.2 | 0.9 | 0.9 | 0.6 | 0.6 |
| **High income** | 16 | 19 | 1.6 | 5.2 | 6.0 | 10,929.8 | 13,382.1 | 34.7 | 32.7 | 11.9 | 13.2 | 0.5 | 0.4 |
| Euro area | 55 | 64 | 1.2 | 6.6 | 7.5 | 2,469.2 | 2,564.5 | 33.8 | 27.5 | 8.4 | 8.2 | 0.4 | 0.3 |

a. Negative values indicate that a country is a net exporter. b. Includes Montenegro. c. Deviation from zero is due to statistical errors and changes in stock. d. Includes emissions not allocated to specific countries.

## About the data

Because commercial energy is widely traded, its production and use need to be distinguished. Net energy imports show the extent to which an economy's use exceeds its production. High-income countries are net energy importers; middle-income countries are their main suppliers.

The ratio of gross domestic product (GDP) to energy use indicates energy efficiency. To produce comparable and consistent estimates of real GDP across countries relative to physical inputs to GDP—that is, units of energy use—GDP is converted to 2005 constant international dollars using purchasing power parity (PPP) rates. Differences in this ratio over time and across countries reflect structural changes in the economy, changes in sectoral energy efficiency, and differences in fuel mixes.

Carbon dioxide emissions, largely byproducts of energy production and use (see table 3.7), account for the largest share of greenhouse gases, which are associated with global warming. Anthropogenic carbon dioxide emissions result primarily from fossil fuel combustion and cement manufacturing. In

combustion different fossil fuels release different amounts of carbon dioxide for the same level of energy use: oil releases about 50 percent more carbon dioxide than natural gas, and coal releases about twice as much. Cement manufacturing releases about half a metric ton of carbon dioxide for each metric ton of cement produced.

The U.S. Department of Energy's Carbon Dioxide Information Analysis Center (CDIAC) calculates annual anthropogenic emissions from data on fossil fuel consumption (from the United Nations Statistics Division's World Energy Data Set) and world cement manufacturing (from the U.S. Bureau of Mines's Cement Manufacturing Data Set). Carbon dioxide emissions are often calculated and reported as elemental carbon. For the table these values were converted to actual carbon dioxide mass by multiplying them by 3.664 (the ratio of the mass of carbon to that of carbon dioxide). Although estimates of global carbon dioxide emissions are probably accurate within 10 percent (as calculated from global average fuel chemistry and use), country estimates may

have larger error bounds. Trends estimated from a consistent time series tend to be more accurate than individual values. Each year the CDIAC recalculates the entire time series since 1949, incorporating recent findings and corrections to its database. Estimates exclude fuels supplied to ships and aircraft in international transport because of the difficulty of apportioning these fuels among the benefiting countries.

### Definitions

• **Net energy imports** are estimated as energy use less production, both measured in oil equivalents. • **Energy use** refers to the use of primary energy before transformation to other end-use fuel, which is equal to indigenous production plus imports and stock changes minus exports and fuel supplied to ships and aircraft engaged in international transport (see *About the data* for table 3.7). • **GDP per unit of energy use** is the ratio of gross domestic product (GDP) per kilogram of oil equivalent of energy use, with GDP converted to 2005 constant international dollars using purchasing power parity (PPP) rates. An international dollar has the same purchasing power over GDP that a U.S. dollar has in the United States. • **Carbon dioxide emissions** are emissions from the burning of fossil fuels and the manufacture of cement and include carbon dioxide produced during consumption of solid, liquid, and gas fuels and gas flaring. • **Carbon dioxide emissions from solid fuel consumption** refer mainly to emissions from use of coal as an energy source.

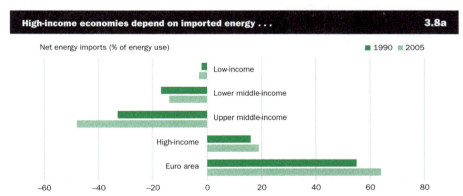

**High-income economies depend on imported energy . . .**   **3.8a**

Net energy imports (% of energy use)   ■ 1990   ■ 2005

**Note:** Negative values indicate that the income group is a net energy exporter.
*Source:* Table 3.8.

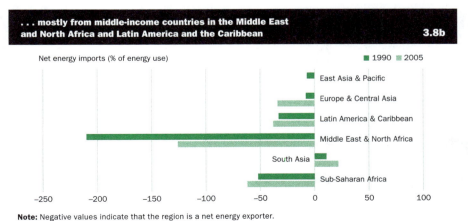

**. . . mostly from middle-income countries in the Middle East and North Africa and Latin America and the Caribbean**   **3.8b**

Net energy imports (% of energy use)   ■ 1990   ■ 2005

**Note:** Negative values indicate that the region is a net energy exporter.
*Source:* Table 3.8.

### Data sources

Data on energy use are from the electronic files of the International Energy Agency. Data on carbon dioxide emissions are from the CDIAC, Environmental Sciences Division, Oak Ridge National Laboratory, in Tennessee, United States.

# Trends in greenhouse gas emissions

| | Carbon dioxide emissions | | Methane emissions | | | | Nitrous oxide emissions | | | | Other greenhouse gas emissions | |
|---|---|---|---|---|---|---|---|---|---|---|---|---|
| | average annual % growth | | Total thousand metric tons of carbon dioxide equivalent | | Industrial % of total | Agricultural % of total | Total thousand metric tons of carbon dioxide equivalent | | Industrial % of total | Agricultural % of total | thousand metric tons of carbon dioxide equivalent | |
| | 1970–90 | 1990–2004 | 1990 | 2005 | 2005 | 2005 | 1990 | 2005 | 2005 | 2005 | 1990 | 2005 |
| Afghanistan | 3.2 | −11.0 | .. | .. | .. | .. | .. | .. | .. | .. | .. | .. |
| Albania | 3.5 | −2.0 | 2,230 | 2,170 | 11.5 | 70.0 | 2,340 | 1,390 | 0.0 | 97.1 | 0 | 50 |
| Algeria | 7.3 | 8.8 | 18,570 | 24,310 | 66.3 | 15.3 | 8,780 | 10,330 | 7.2 | 89.1 | 230 | 110 |
| Angola | 1.5 | 4.1 | 13,630 | 37,020 | 11.6 | 39.1 | 5,110 | 28,350 | 0.0 | 35.9 | 0 | 0 |
| Argentina | 1.3 | 1.4 | 82,110 | 94,340 | 13.0 | 63.9 | 65,060 | 83,410 | 0.2 | 97.7 | 1,880 | 930 |
| Armenia | 2.6 | −0.5 | 3,090 | 2,300 | 25.2 | 50.9 | 910 | 450 | 0.0 | 93.3 | 0 | 10 |
| Australia | 3.1 | 1.2 | 104,050 | 116,840 | 24.6 | 61.5 | 106,090 | 114,500 | 1.3 | 94.9 | 2,620 | 4,580 |
| Austria | −0.1 | 1.4 | 8,210 | 7,210 | 14.6 | 50.1 | 5,740 | 4,620 | 9.1 | 85.3 | 1,210 | 3,310 |
| Azerbaijan | 2.6 | −4.5 | 14,510 | 11,550 | 45.2 | 45.4 | 4,060 | 4,040 | 0.0 | 93.6 | 180 | 50 |
| Bangladesh | 7.8 | 6.9 | 81,620 | 92,530 | 11.6 | 69.2 | 22,420 | 37,100 | 0.0 | 91.9 | 0 | 0 |
| Belarus | 2.6 | −3.8 | 19,230 | 16,620 | 43.0 | 38.8 | 15,270 | 10,360 | 32.3 | 65.6 | 0 | 440 |
| Belgium | −1.9 | −0.4 | 10,230 | 7,610 | 17.0 | 59.7 | 11,250 | 9,650 | 12.0 | 65.4 | 130 | 9,380 |
| Benin | 4.3 | 7.9 | 2,730 | 4,840 | 8.9 | 47.5 | 2,120 | 4,660 | 0.0 | 68.0 | 0 | 0 |
| Bolivia | 1.9 | 2.6 | 15,550 | 27,120 | 2.8 | 34.5 | 14,310 | 28,300 | 0.0 | 43.3 | 0 | 0 |
| Bosnia and Herzegovina | 3.4 | 12.5 | 2,000 | 2,850 | 51.9 | 32.6 | 1,140 | 1,020 | 0.0 | 82.4 | 460 | 850 |
| Botswana | 21.1 | 4.3 | 130 | 4,480 | 17.9 | 71.9 | 0 | 2,460 | 0.0 | 96.3 | 0 | 0 |
| Brazil | 3.9 | 3.6 | 285,650 | 421,820 | 3.0 | 67.1 | 227,790 | 300,300 | 3.2 | 74.4 | 5,290 | 7,760 |
| Bulgaria | 1.7 | −3.4 | 9,560 | 6,140 | 31.9 | 32.7 | 13,250 | 5,880 | 29.9 | 64.5 | 0 | 650 |
| Burkina Faso | 8.7 | 1.3 | .. | .. | .. | .. | .. | .. | .. | .. | .. | .. |
| Burundi | 7.4 | 1.2 | .. | .. | .. | .. | .. | .. | .. | .. | .. | .. |
| Cambodia | 7.2 | 1.1 | .. | 14,890 | 5.4 | 71.5 | .. | 3,820 | 0.0 | 74.1 | 0 | 0 |
| Cameroon | 9.3 | 5.0 | 10,500 | 15,110 | 17.9 | 56.0 | 8,290 | 14,540 | 0.0 | 85.0 | 810 | 890 |
| Canada | 0.7 | 3.6 | 83,000 | 103,830 | 46.6 | 22.2 | 50,700 | 51,390 | 4.5 | 86.7 | 12,810 | 11,010 |
| Central African Republic | 1.9 | 2.0 | .. | .. | .. | .. | .. | .. | .. | .. | .. | .. |
| Chad | −0.5 | 2.7 | .. | .. | .. | .. | .. | .. | .. | .. | .. | .. |
| Chile | 0.2 | 4.8 | 14,190 | 19,560 | 12.1 | 29.9 | 8,170 | 12,590 | 6.9 | 88.7 | 0 | 10 |
| China | 5.7 | 4.0 | 895,350 | 995,760 | 34.2 | 50.0 | 455,150 | 566,680 | 3.0 | 92.7 | 8,640 | 119,720 |
| Hong Kong, China | 6.9 | 2.5 | 1,180 | 1,090 | 40.4 | 0.9 | 210 | 200 | 0.0 | 5.0 | 0 | 330 |
| Colombia | 3.7 | −0.8 | 49,180 | 61,690 | 15.7 | 55.1 | 21,140 | 24,530 | 0.9 | 78.0 | 190 | 330 |
| Congo, Dem. Rep. | 1.5 | −6.1 | 2,670 | 5,750 | 49.6 | 11.8 | 820 | 2,250 | 0.0 | 15.6 | 0 | 0 |
| Congo, Rep. | 2.9 | 8.8 | 27,720 | 50,320 | 7.7 | 26.3 | 19,390 | 38,680 | 0.0 | 23.2 | 0 | 0 |
| Costa Rica | 2.8 | 5.0 | 3,720 | 2,450 | 1.6 | 58.0 | 3,440 | 2,850 | 0.0 | 98.9 | 0 | 0 |
| Côte d'Ivoire | 5.3 | 0.5 | 5,410 | 15,320 | 11.2 | 20.6 | 2,460 | 12,350 | 0.0 | 25.0 | 0 | 0 |
| Croatia | 3.4 | 1.8 | 3,950 | 3,690 | 44.2 | 29.8 | 3,390 | 3,590 | 22.3 | 63.8 | 670 | 720 |
| Cuba | 3.0 | −1.8 | 9,890 | 9,490 | 6.4 | 62.4 | 13,650 | 8,330 | 8.0 | 87.4 | 0 | 110 |
| Czech Republic | 0.6 | −2.0 | 22,250 | 14,930 | 58.7 | 17.2 | 10,740 | 6,570 | 16.4 | 75.0 | 20 | 3,530 |
| Denmark | −0.5 | −1.0 | 5,650 | 4,920 | 16.3 | 67.7 | 10,000 | 7,380 | 7.7 | 78.6 | 260 | 1,460 |
| Dominican Republic | 4.6 | 6.1 | 5,280 | 5,960 | 4.0 | 62.1 | 4,140 | 2,850 | 0.0 | 96.1 | 0 | 0 |
| Ecuador | 8.8 | 2.8 | 12,170 | 12,890 | 16.3 | 57.4 | 8,840 | 8,500 | 0.0 | 97.6 | 0 | 0 |
| Egypt, Arab Rep. | 7.3 | 5.6 | 23,250 | 32,960 | 31.2 | 44.2 | 16,980 | 27,810 | 11.5 | 85.6 | 2,250 | 1,820 |
| El Salvador | 1.7 | 5.8 | 2,740 | 3,200 | 12.5 | 48.1 | 2,050 | 2,250 | 0.0 | 95.1 | 0 | 0 |
| Eritrea | .. | 12.3 | 2,090 | 2,410 | 7.5 | 77.6 | 1,340 | 2,350 | 0.0 | 99.1 | 0 | 0 |
| Estonia | 2.6 | −3.3 | 2,610 | 1,230 | 43.1 | 35.0 | 1,630 | 610 | 0.0 | 83.6 | 0 | 60 |
| Ethiopia | 3.5 | 8.1 | 39,110 | 47,740 | 10.0 | 77.2 | 50,730 | 63,130 | 0.0 | 98.6 | 0 | 0 |
| Finland | 0.7 | 1.5 | 7,400 | 5,470 | 10.2 | 30.3 | .. | .. | 27.0 | 59.5 | 220 | 1,030 |
| France | −1.6 | 0.1 | 56,710 | 43,520 | 10.7 | 71.1 | 88,450 | 78,090 | 12.1 | 77.3 | 10,740 | 27,010 |
| Gabon | 4.5 | −9.0 | 3,120 | 2,040 | 79.9 | 4.4 | 1,850 | 420 | 0.0 | 57.1 | 0 | 0 |
| Gambia, The | 7.0 | 3.3 | .. | .. | .. | .. | .. | .. | .. | .. | .. | .. |
| Georgia | 2.6 | −10.2 | 5,790 | 4,330 | 29.6 | 51.7 | 3,390 | 3,390 | 17.4 | 49.3 | 0 | 10 |
| Germany | −0.2 | −1.0 | 109,870 | 58,100 | 45.7 | 39.2 | 77,470 | 69,470 | 13.3 | 74.2 | 11,230 | 41,980 |
| Ghana | 1.7 | 5.3 | 5,310 | 8,630 | 10.7 | 49.6 | 4,540 | 10,520 | 0.0 | 88.6 | 190 | 170 |
| Greece | 4.8 | 2.5 | 6,390 | 7,410 | 9.7 | 39.1 | 13,060 | 13,090 | 3.3 | 91.3 | 790 | 1,620 |
| Guatemala | 2.6 | 6.7 | 5,920 | 8,990 | 11.3 | 42.7 | 4,780 | 7,980 | 0.0 | 70.8 | 0 | 0 |
| Guinea | 1.4 | 2.1 | .. | .. | .. | .. | .. | .. | .. | .. | .. | .. |
| Guinea-Bissau | 5.4 | 2.0 | .. | .. | .. | .. | .. | .. | .. | .. | .. | .. |
| Haiti | 5.3 | 7.0 | 2,870 | 3,740 | 6.4 | 61.2 | 2,470 | 4,290 | 0.0 | 98.4 | 0 | 0 |

| | Carbon dioxide emissions | | Methane emissions | | | | Nitrous oxide emissions | | | | Other greenhouse gas emissions | |
|---|---|---|---|---|---|---|---|---|---|---|---|---|
| | average annual % growth | | Total thousand metric tons of carbon dioxide equivalent | | Industrial % of total | Agricultural % of total | Total thousand metric tons of carbon dioxide equivalent | | Industrial % of total | Agricultural % of total | thousand metric tons of carbon dioxide equivalent | |
| | 1970–90 | 1990–2004 | 1990 | 2005 | 2005 | 2005 | 1990 | 2005 | 2005 | 2005 | 1990 | 2005 |
| Honduras | 3.0 | 7.7 | 5,020 | 5,380 | 5.8 | 71.9 | 3,550 | 3,860 | 0.0 | 97.9 | 0 | 0 |
| Hungary | 0.1 | −0.4 | 14,220 | 11,050 | 52.6 | 18.3 | 11,950 | 8,760 | 20.7 | 76.0 | 760 | 1,540 |
| India | 6.6 | 4.8 | 625,420 | 712,330 | 14.7 | 64.8 | 225,250 | 300,680 | 0.5 | 93.0 | 8,010 | 9,510 |
| Indonesia | 8.0 | 3.8 | 180,250 | 224,330 | 36.2 | 41.2 | 60,220 | 69,910 | 0.3 | 72.6 | 1,380 | 900 |
| Iran, Islamic Rep. | 2.6 | 5.0 | 54,730 | 95,060 | 64.7 | 21.8 | 48,620 | 66,140 | 0.9 | 97.6 | 2,130 | 1,560 |
| Iraq | 3.5 | 3.7 | 11,120 | 10,980 | 48.7 | 14.7 | 6,570 | 3,990 | 0.0 | 93.0 | 390 | 470 |
| Ireland | 2.0 | 2.8 | 11,560 | 3,660 | 24.3 | 32.0 | 12,840 | 12,320 | 0.2 | 92.6 | 110 | 2,050 |
| Israel | 3.2 | 5.6 | 1,010 | 1,170 | 9.4 | 36.8 | 1,900 | 1,820 | 0.0 | 83.5 | 840 | 1,140 |
| Italy | 1.0 | 1.0 | 42,310 | 36,670 | 19.1 | 37.7 | 35,560 | 37,200 | 23.7 | 70.5 | 4,770 | 27,710 |
| Jamaica | −1.0 | 2.3 | 1,220 | 1,160 | 3.4 | 47.4 | 1,220 | 1,020 | 0.0 | 96.1 | 0 | 0 |
| Japan | 1.0 | 1.1 | 57,690 | 53,480 | 30.0 | 13.4 | 31,970 | 23,590 | 8.4 | 49.3 | 26,560 | 70,570 |
| Jordan | 11.3 | 3.5 | 1,080 | 1,610 | 13.0 | 24.2 | 1,160 | 1,240 | 0.0 | 93.5 | 0 | 10 |
| Kazakhstan | 2.6 | −3.8 | 55,300 | 28,270 | 49.1 | 37.9 | 23,600 | 5,530 | 0.0 | 90.2 | 0 | 0 |
| Kenya | 1.6 | 4.9 | 19,410 | 20,310 | 18.0 | 65.0 | 21,830 | 19,060 | 0.0 | 96.4 | 0 | 0 |
| Korea, Dem. Rep. | 5.1 | −11.2 | 9,800 | 10,650 | 29.0 | 36.4 | 9,190 | 23,160 | 0.0 | 97.5 | 300 | 860 |
| Korea, Rep. | 7.8 | 4.4 | 27,430 | 31,280 | 18.5 | 31.1 | 9,480 | 22,020 | 56.6 | 36.1 | 5,400 | 8,700 |
| Kuwait | 2.7 | 12.2 | 6,800 | 11,200 | 93.9 | 1.5 | 250 | 540 | 0.0 | 81.5 | 250 | 390 |
| Kyrgyz Republic | 2.6 | −6.3 | 4,680 | 3,520 | 10.5 | 72.2 | 4,240 | 3,260 | 0.0 | 98.8 | 0 | 60 |
| Lao PDR | −4.2 | 15.8 | .. | .. | .. | .. | .. | .. | .. | .. | .. | .. |
| Latvia | 2.6 | −6.1 | 4,320 | 2,290 | 40.6 | 29.3 | 2,690 | 1,390 | 0.0 | 88.5 | 0 | 110 |
| Lebanon | 2.4 | 4.5 | 730 | 980 | 12.2 | 18.4 | 740 | 1,020 | 0.0 | 93.1 | 0 | 0 |
| Lesotho | .. | .. | .. | .. | .. | .. | .. | .. | .. | .. | .. | .. |
| Liberia | −5.4 | 3.2 | .. | .. | .. | .. | .. | .. | .. | .. | .. | .. |
| Libya | 4.4 | 4.0 | 8,750 | 8,540 | 77.6 | 8.9 | 2,860 | 2,050 | 0.0 | 91.7 | 100 | 290 |
| Lithuania | 2.6 | −4.7 | 7,740 | 3,650 | 44.1 | 38.1 | 4,160 | 2,860 | 0.0 | 90.2 | 0 | 150 |
| Macedonia, FYR | 3.4 | −0.8 | .. | .. | .. | .. | .. | .. | .. | .. | .. | .. |
| Madagascar | −0.2 | 8.6 | .. | .. | .. | .. | .. | .. | .. | .. | .. | .. |
| Malawi | 0.6 | 4.4 | .. | .. | .. | .. | .. | .. | .. | .. | .. | .. |
| Malaysia | 6.4 | 6.9 | 21,300 | 25,510 | 57.2 | 22.3 | 11,600 | 9,920 | 3.9 | 64.3 | 960 | 530 |
| Mali | 2.9 | 2.2 | .. | .. | .. | .. | .. | .. | .. | .. | .. | .. |
| Mauritania | 9.6 | −1.1 | .. | .. | .. | .. | .. | .. | .. | .. | .. | .. |
| Mauritius | 3.4 | 6.3 | .. | .. | .. | .. | .. | .. | .. | .. | .. | .. |
| Mexico | 7.1 | 0.3 | 95,840 | 120,100 | 22.2 | 39.6 | 70,240 | 75,500 | 1.2 | 90.1 | 1,930 | 3,160 |
| Moldova | 2.6 | −9.1 | 4,780 | 2,590 | 43.6 | 30.9 | 3,270 | 970 | 0.0 | 94.8 | 0 | 360 |
| Mongolia | 7.4 | −2.1 | 7,380 | 4,840 | 2.9 | 83.9 | 10,000 | 22,850 | 0.0 | 99.6 | 0 | 0 |
| Morocco | 5.9 | 3.7 | 9,070 | 13,240 | 2.6 | 41.6 | 14,380 | 15,510 | 0.0 | 75.2 | 0 | 0 |
| Mozambique | −6.8 | 4.2 | 9,430 | 11,630 | 16.9 | 64.3 | 2,950 | 9,930 | 0.0 | 99.7 | 0 | 0 |
| Myanmar | 1.2 | 6.2 | 40,170 | 60,840 | 6.8 | 70.0 | 14,390 | 25,900 | 0.0 | 66.8 | 0 | 10 |
| Namibia | .. | 57.6 | 4,320 | 4,260 | 4.7 | 89.9 | 4,240 | 4,620 | 0.0 | 99.1 | 0 | 0 |
| Nepal | 6.9 | 10.3 | 33,810 | 36,040 | 10.4 | 80.5 | 5,700 | 7,100 | 0.0 | 88.5 | 0 | 0 |
| Netherlands | −0.4 | 0.2 | 19,320 | 15,180 | 23.6 | 49.2 | 19,320 | 16,800 | 33.8 | 51.5 | 5,950 | 5,300 |
| New Zealand | 1.9 | 3.1 | 27,370 | 27,490 | 10.4 | 82.3 | 33,920 | 27,960 | 0.1 | 99.4 | 400 | 820 |
| Nicaragua | 1.4 | 4.7 | 4,690 | 6,350 | 4.7 | 80.2 | 3,750 | 3,210 | 0.0 | 96.9 | 0 | 0 |
| Niger | 9.4 | 1.1 | .. | .. | .. | .. | .. | .. | .. | .. | .. | .. |
| Nigeria | 2.7 | 6.8 | 59,690 | 78,290 | 45.5 | 33.7 | 28,050 | 39,030 | 0.0 | 87.1 | 120 | 80 |
| Norway | 2.4 | 7.4 | 7,620 | 12,080 | 61.8 | 14.3 | 5,290 | 4,680 | 37.8 | 53.0 | 4,980 | 1,770 |
| Oman | 11.2 | 8.6 | 2,020 | 4,260 | 76.1 | 12.9 | 870 | 1,140 | 0.0 | 96.5 | 0 | 0 |
| Pakistan | 6.6 | 4.0 | 82,830 | 110,300 | 14.1 | 66.3 | 55,400 | 80,040 | 0.8 | 96.4 | 700 | 620 |
| Panama | 0.3 | 4.9 | 2,970 | 3,040 | 4.3 | 72.4 | 2,520 | 2,070 | 0.0 | 95.7 | 0 | 0 |
| Papua New Guinea | 4.7 | 0.0 | .. | .. | .. | .. | .. | .. | .. | .. | .. | .. |
| Paraguay | 6.4 | 4.3 | 11,690 | 17,750 | 1.7 | 70.9 | 9,980 | 12,870 | 0.0 | 81.8 | 0 | 0 |
| Peru | 0.9 | 2.7 | 17,260 | 21,510 | 6.4 | 48.1 | 14,300 | 18,720 | 0.0 | 89.4 | 0 | 80 |
| Philippines | 1.6 | 4.6 | 38,830 | 44,860 | 8.0 | 66.7 | 17,990 | 18,940 | 0.1 | 95.6 | 100 | 350 |
| Poland | 1.6 | −1.2 | 90,010 | 60,060 | 67.0 | 18.4 | 31,570 | 26,110 | 22.3 | 72.5 | 460 | 1,270 |
| Portugal | 5.0 | 2.8 | 7,450 | 7,140 | 8.0 | 52.9 | 6,920 | 7,000 | 9.9 | 80.7 | 130 | 1,050 |
| Puerto Rico | 0.7 | −4.1 | .. | .. | .. | .. | .. | .. | .. | .. | .. | .. |

| | Carbon dioxide emissions | | Methane emissions | | | | Nitrous oxide emissions | | | | Other greenhouse gas emissions | |
|---|---|---|---|---|---|---|---|---|---|---|---|---|
| | average annual % growth | | Total thousand metric tons of carbon dioxide equivalent | | Industrial % of total | Agricultural % of total | Total thousand metric tons of carbon dioxide equivalent | | Industrial % of total | Agricultural % of total | thousand metric tons of carbon dioxide equivalent | |
| | 1970–90 | 1990–2004 | 1990 | 2005 | 2005 | 2005 | 1990 | 2005 | 2005 | 2005 | 1990 | 2005 |
| Romania | 2.4 | –3.7 | 42,300 | 23,260 | 52.4 | 30.1 | 24,700 | 11,790 | 25.9 | 69.6 | 1,500 | 2,220 |
| Russian Federation | 2.6 | –2.7 | 631,450 | 501,380 | 77.3 | 7.9 | 129,210 | 42,650 | 8.0 | 76.2 | 19,380 | 56,600 |
| Rwanda | 14.2 | 1.6 | .. | .. | .. | .. | .. | .. | .. | .. | .. | .. |
| Saudi Arabia | 8.9 | –1.1 | 39,710 | 63,500 | 91.8 | 1.9 | 8,230 | 7,720 | 0.0 | 92.1 | 2,260 | 1,530 |
| Senegal | 4.4 | 2.4 | 5,550 | 6,340 | 4.7 | 75.9 | 6,220 | 10,250 | 0.0 | 99.0 | 0 | 10 |
| Serbia[a] | 3.4 | –3.1 | 12,860 | 6,720 | 16.4 | 59.2 | 9,070 | 4,700 | 11.1 | 81.5 | 340 | 840 |
| Sierra Leone | –0.7 | 5.0 | .. | .. | .. | .. | .. | .. | .. | .. | .. | .. |
| Singapore | 3.6 | 1.0 | 740 | 1,260 | 27.0 | 4.8 | 180 | 7,970 | 95.7 | 0.8 | 400 | 1,300 |
| Slovak Republic | 0.6 | –1.8 | 7,450 | 5,290 | 54.3 | 19.5 | 4,650 | 2,760 | 32.2 | 58.0 | 10 | 710 |
| Slovenia | 3.4 | 1.5 | 1,740 | 1,630 | 20.9 | 47.9 | 1,070 | 1,100 | 0.0 | 88.2 | 580 | 210 |
| Somalia | 2.5 | .. | .. | .. | .. | .. | .. | .. | .. | .. | .. | .. |
| South Africa | 4.6 | 1.8 | 52,260 | 59,200 | 54.3 | 23.8 | 26,460 | 29,250 | 7.3 | 82.7 | 1,450 | 2,600 |
| Spain | 2.2 | 3.3 | 31,640 | 38,010 | 11.3 | 44.1 | 35,290 | 48,520 | 3.5 | 85.7 | 4,440 | 15,050 |
| Sri Lanka | 1.0 | 8.5 | 10,280 | 10,280 | 12.3 | 61.8 | 2,410 | 3,130 | 0.0 | 89.1 | 0 | 0 |
| Sudan | –1.3 | 5.9 | 39,760 | 67,310 | 21.5 | 73.3 | 39,400 | 59,750 | 0.0 | 96.2 | 0 | 0 |
| Swaziland | 1.0 | 11.5 | .. | .. | .. | .. | .. | .. | .. | .. | .. | .. |
| Sweden | –2.9 | 0.1 | 7,670 | 6,460 | 6.5 | 41.5 | 6,330 | 6,070 | 8.4 | 76.8 | 990 | 1,620 |
| Switzerland | –0.1 | –0.2 | 4,790 | 4,150 | 8.7 | 68.0 | 3,170 | 2,840 | 8.1 | 78.2 | 760 | 3,310 |
| Syrian Arab Republic | 9.7 | 2.6 | 5,810 | 7,960 | 33.8 | 34.7 | 7,860 | 9,430 | 2.8 | 94.9 | 0 | 0 |
| Tajikistan | 2.6 | –11.1 | 3,690 | 3,270 | 10.1 | 68.5 | 3,110 | 1,590 | 0.0 | 99.4 | 80 | 120 |
| Tanzania | 0.0 | 3.4 | 26,860 | 39,460 | 20.3 | 63.5 | 23,300 | 31,690 | 0.0 | 84.3 | 0 | 0 |
| Thailand | 7.6 | 6.3 | 68,930 | 78,840 | 9.4 | 76.1 | 21,330 | 27,990 | 0.7 | 87.9 | 1,580 | 940 |
| Timor-Leste | .. | .. | .. | .. | .. | .. | .. | .. | .. | .. | .. | .. |
| Togo | 4.7 | 8.3 | 1,790 | 2,840 | 14.8 | 48.6 | 1,990 | 5,470 | 0.0 | 88.8 | 0 | 0 |
| Trinidad and Tobago | 4.5 | 4.7 | 2,510 | 3,820 | 78.0 | 1.0 | 340 | 360 | 0.0 | 91.7 | 0 | 0 |
| Tunisia | 7.0 | 3.3 | 3,740 | 4,390 | 32.1 | 34.2 | 4,260 | 7,230 | 4.1 | 94.2 | 0 | 30 |
| Turkey | 5.8 | 3.5 | 27,050 | 23,140 | 15.3 | 59.5 | 44,270 | 47,950 | 9.0 | 88.0 | 2,840 | 1,480 |
| Turkmenistan | 2.6 | 3.0 | 33,230 | 23,060 | 81.8 | 15.2 | 4,150 | 3,200 | 20.0 | 78.8 | 0 | 250 |
| Uganda | –3.5 | 7.1 | .. | .. | .. | .. | .. | .. | .. | .. | .. | .. |
| Ukraine | 2.6 | –5.6 | 146,380 | 75,640 | 68.9 | 15.7 | 69,380 | 23,270 | 41.6 | 54.2 | 60 | 1,390 |
| United Arab Emirates | 4.6 | 9.3 | 19,110 | 34,250 | 96.8 | 1.7 | 930 | 2,730 | 0.0 | 90.5 | 220 | 480 |
| United Kingdom | –0.6 | –0.2 | 67,750 | 39,400 | 35.7 | 50.7 | 68,470 | 65,480 | 37.1 | 52.2 | 5,880 | 14,030 |
| United States | 0.3 | 1.9 | 857,660 | 810,280 | 56.4 | 18.4 | 412,740 | 456,210 | 5.5 | 74.7 | 91,230 | 108,420 |
| Uruguay | –2.7 | 1.1 | 14,110 | 17,700 | 0.6 | 90.3 | 15,170 | 15,630 | 0.0 | 99.6 | 0 | 20 |
| Uzbekistan | 2.6 | 0.9 | 41,610 | 51,480 | 70.1 | 23.2 | 14,330 | 14,660 | 0.3 | 98.3 | 0 | 760 |
| Venezuela, RB | 3.7 | 1.8 | 41,520 | 65,730 | 42.0 | 33.6 | 21,700 | 26,460 | 0.1 | 77.8 | 1,330 | 2,300 |
| Vietnam | –0.3 | 11.9 | 52,990 | 75,080 | 17.8 | 66.8 | 13,920 | 37,470 | 0.0 | 94.9 | 0 | 10 |
| West Bank and Gaza | .. | .. | .. | .. | .. | .. | .. | .. | .. | .. | .. | .. |
| Yemen, Rep. | 10.0 | 5.1 | 4,620 | 9,040 | 44.5 | 27.7 | 5,110 | 7,080 | 0.0 | 98.9 | 0 | 10 |
| Zambia | –2.5 | –1.6 | 9,820 | 16,770 | 5.7 | 68.6 | 4,800 | 11,410 | 3.7 | 65.1 | 0 | 0 |
| Zimbabwe | 3.3 | –3.1 | 10,850 | 10,400 | 24.8 | 60.4 | 8,970 | 10,160 | 0.0 | 97.1 | 0 | 20 |
| **World** | **1.8 w** | **1.6 w** | **6,174,140 s** | **6,607,490 s** | **34.8 w** | **43.1 w** | **3,323,000 s** | **3,787,800 s** | **82.6 w** | **47.9 w** | **265,210 s** | **601,890 s** |
| **Low income** | 4.9 | 2.8 | 1,231,970 | 1,526,640 | 18.1 | 62.6 | 585,050 | 861,010 | 91.5 | 63.3 | 9,400 | 12,240 |
| **Middle income** | 3.6 | 1.4 | 3,270,800 | 3,491,860 | 36.1 | 41.9 | 1,660,270 | 1,809,370 | 82.8 | 48.4 | 56,960 | 213,780 |
| Lower middle income | 4.6 | 3.1 | 1,749,030 | 1,973,890 | 32.8 | 46.1 | 908,360 | 1,085,030 | 84.0 | 46.1 | 18,400 | 130,730 |
| Upper middle income | 2.9 | –0.6 | 1,521,770 | 1,517,970 | 40.4 | 36.5 | 751,910 | 724,340 | 81.1 | 51.8 | 38,560 | 83,050 |
| **Low & middle income** | 3.8 | 1.6 | 4,502,770 | 5,018,500 | 30.6 | 48.2 | 2,245,320 | 2,670,380 | 85.6 | 53.2 | 66,360 | 226,020 |
| East Asia & Pacific | 5.7 | 3.6 | .. | .. | 30.5 | 51.9 | .. | .. | 90.0 | 52.3 | .. | .. |
| Europe & Central Asia | 2.5 | –2.6 | 1,174,570 | 867,600 | 68.8 | 16.2 | 419,030 | 226,870 | 77.2 | 30.6 | 26,400 | 69,800 |
| Latin America & Carib. | 4.1 | 1.7 | 683,590 | 929,970 | 10.7 | 57.9 | 518,270 | 645,520 | 80.8 | 59.0 | 10,620 | 14,700 |
| Middle East & N. Africa | 4.7 | 5.3 | 143,490 | 213,330 | 52.5 | 25.7 | 118,190 | 152,970 | 92.0 | 28.7 | 5,100 | 4,300 |
| South Asia | 6.6 | 4.8 | 833,960 | 961,480 | 14.1 | 66.0 | 311,180 | 428,050 | 93.4 | 65.7 | 8,710 | 10,130 |
| Sub-Saharan Africa | 3.9 | 2.6 | .. | .. | 24.4 | 49.4 | .. | .. | 78.5 | 54.4 | .. | .. |
| **High income** | 0.6 | 1.5 | 1,671,370 | 1,588,990 | 47.8 | 27.1 | 1,077,680 | 1,117,420 | 75.3 | 35.3 | 198,850 | 375,870 |
| Euro area | 0.0 | 0.4 | 313,430 | 232,220 | 22.2 | 47.6 | 313,640 | 303,960 | 76.4 | 49.3 | 40,300 | 135,750 |

a. Includes Montenegro.

## About the data

Greenhouse gases—which include carbon dioxide, methane, nitrous oxide, hydrofluorocarbons, perfluorocarbons, and sulfur hexafluoride—contribute to climate change.

Carbon dioxide emissions, largely a by-product of energy production and use (see table 3.7), account for the largest share of greenhouse gases. Anthropogenic carbon dioxide emissions result primarily from fossil fuel combustion and cement manufacturing. Burning oil releases more carbon dioxide than burning natural gas, and burning coal releases even more for the same level of energy use. Cement manufacturing releases about half a metric ton of carbon dioxide for each metric ton of cement produced.

Methane emissions result largely from agricultural activities, industrial production landfills and wastewater treatment, and other sources such as tropical forest and other vegetation fires. The emissions are usually expressed in carbon dioxide equivalents using the global warming potential, which allows the effective contributions of different gases to be compared. A kilogram of methane is 21 times as effective at trapping heat in the earth's atmosphere as a kilogram of carbon dioxide within 100 years.

Nitrous oxide emissions are mainly from fossil fuel combustion, fertilizers, rainforest fires, and animal waste. Nitrous oxide is a powerful greenhouse gas, with an estimated atmospheric lifetime of 114 years, compared with 12 years for methane. The per kilogram global warming potential of nitrous oxide is nearly 310 times that of carbon dioxide within 100 years.

Other greenhouse gases covered under the Kyoto Protocol are hydrofluorocarbons, perfluorocarbons, and sulfur hexafluoride. Although emissions of these artificial gases are small, they are more powerful greenhouse gases than carbon dioxide, with much higher atmospheric lifetime and high global warming potential.

The Carbon Dioxide Information Analysis Center (CDIAC), sponsored by the U.S. Department of Energy, calculates annual anthropogenic emissions of carbon dioxide from fossil fuel consumption data (from the United Nations Statistics Division's World Energy Data Set) and data on world cement manufacturing data (from the U.S. Bureau of Mines's Cement Manufacturing Data Set). Carbon dioxide emissions are often calculated and reported as elemental carbon. For the table these values were converted to actual carbon dioxide mass by multiplying by 3.664 (the ratio of the mass of carbon to that of carbon dioxide). Although estimates of global carbon dioxide emissions are probably accurate within 10 percent, country estimates may have larger error bounds. Trends estimated from a consistent time series tend to be more accurate than individual values. Each year the CDIAC recalculates the entire time series, incorporating recent findings and corrections to the database. Estimates exclude fuels supplied to ships and aircraft in international transport because of the difficulty of apportioning these fuels among benefiting countries.

### Definitions

• **Carbon dioxide emissions** are emissions from the burning of fossil fuels and the manufacture of cement and include carbon dioxide produced during consumption of solid, liquid, and gas fuels and gas flaring. • **Methane emissions** are emissions from human activities such as agriculture and from industrial methane production. • **Industrial methane emissions** are emissions from the handling, transmission, and combustion of fossil fuels and biofuels. • **Agricultural methane emissions** are emissions from animals, animal waste, rice production, agricultural waste burning (nonenergy, on-site), and savannah burning. • **Nitrous oxide emissions** are emissions from agricultural biomass burning, industrial activities, and livestock management. • **Industrial nitrous oxide emissions** are emissions produced during the manufacturing of adipic acid and nitric acid. • **Agricultural nitrous oxide emissions** are emissions produced through fertilizer use (synthetic and animal manure), animal waste management, agricultural waste burning (nonenergy, on-site), and savannah burning. • **Other greenhouse gas emissions** are by-product emissions of hydrofluorocarbons, perfluorocarbons, and sulfur hexafluoride.

---

### The 10 largest contributors to methane emissions account for about 62 percent of emissions | 3.9a

Methane emissions, 2005 (million metric tons of carbon dioxide equivalent)

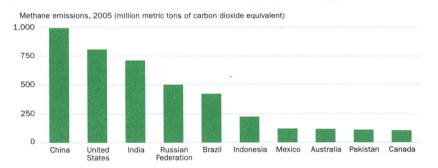

*Source:* Table 3.9.

### The 10 largest contributors to nitrous oxide emissions account for about 56 percent of emissions | 3.9b

Nitrous oxide emissions, 2005 (million metric tons of carbon dioxide equivalent)

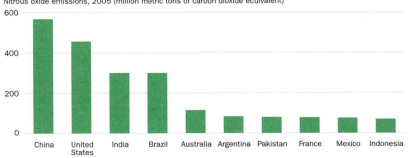

*Source:* Table 3.9.

### Data sources

Data on carbon dioxide emissions are from the CDIAC, Environmental Sciences Division, Oak Ridge National Laboratory, Tennessee, United States. Data on methane, nitrous oxide, and other greenhouse gases emissions are compiled by the International Energy Agency.

# Sources of electricity

| | Electricity production | | Sources of electricity[a] | | | | | | | | | |
|---|---|---|---|---|---|---|---|---|---|---|---|---|
| | | | | | | | % of total | | | | | |
| | billion kilowatt hours | | Coal | | Gas | | Oil | | Hydropower | | Nuclear power | |
| | 1990 | 2005 | 1990 | 2005 | 1990 | 2005 | 1990 | 2005 | 1990 | 2005 | 1990 | 2005 |
| Afghanistan | .. | .. | .. | .. | .. | .. | .. | .. | .. | .. | .. | .. |
| Albania | 3.2 | 5.4 | 0.0 | 0.0 | 0.0 | 0.0 | 10.9 | 1.3 | 89.1 | 98.7 | 0.0 | 0.0 |
| Algeria | 16.1 | 33.9 | 0.0 | 0.0 | 93.7 | 96.2 | 5.4 | 2.2 | 0.8 | 1.6 | 0.0 | 0.0 |
| Angola | 0.8 | 2.7 | 0.0 | 0.0 | 0.0 | 0.0 | 13.8 | 34.2 | 86.2 | 65.8 | 0.0 | 0.0 |
| Argentina | 51.0 | 105.8 | 1.3 | 2.1 | 39.0 | 52.3 | 9.7 | 5.4 | 35.6 | 32.4 | 14.3 | 6.5 |
| Armenia | 10.4 | 6.3 | 0.0 | 0.0 | 16.4 | 28.9 | 68.6 | 0.0 | 15.0 | 28.1 | 0.0 | 43.0 |
| Australia | 154.3 | 250.9 | 77.1 | 80.1 | 10.6 | 11.7 | 2.7 | 0.8 | 9.2 | 6.3 | 0.0 | 0.0 |
| Austria | 49.3 | 63.0 | 14.2 | 13.5 | 15.7 | 20.7 | 3.8 | 2.6 | 63.9 | 57.0 | 0.0 | 0.0 |
| Azerbaijan | 23.2 | 21.2 | 0.0 | 0.0 | 0.0 | 58.1 | 97.0 | 27.7 | 3.0 | 14.2 | 0.0 | 0.0 |
| Bangladesh | 7.7 | 22.6 | 0.0 | 0.0 | 84.3 | 87.6 | 4.3 | 6.7 | 11.4 | 5.7 | 0.0 | 0.0 |
| Belarus | 29.5 | 31.0 | 0.0 | 0.0 | 44.0 | 91.4 | 55.9 | 8.4 | 0.1 | 0.1 | 0.0 | 0.0 |
| Belgium | 70.3 | 85.7 | 28.2 | 12.2 | 7.7 | 26.7 | 1.9 | 2.0 | 0.4 | 0.3 | 60.8 | 55.5 |
| Benin | 0.0 | 0.1 | 0.0 | 0.0 | 0.0 | 0.0 | 100.0 | 99.1 | 0.0 | 0.9 | 0.0 | 0.0 |
| Bolivia | 2.1 | 5.2 | 0.0 | 0.0 | 37.6 | 32.3 | 5.3 | 16.7 | 55.3 | 47.8 | 0.0 | 0.0 |
| Bosnia and Herzegovina | 14.6 | 12.7 | 71.8 | 56.0 | 0.0 | 0.0 | 7.3 | 1.1 | 20.9 | 42.9 | 0.0 | 0.0 |
| Botswana | 0.9 | 1.0 | 88.1 | 99.4 | 0.0 | 0.0 | 11.9 | 0.6 | 0.0 | 0.0 | 0.0 | 0.0 |
| Brazil | 222.8 | 403.0 | 2.0 | 2.5 | 0.0 | 4.7 | 2.2 | 2.9 | 92.8 | 83.7 | 1.0 | 2.4 |
| Bulgaria | 42.1 | 44.0 | 50.3 | 42.4 | 7.6 | 3.9 | 2.9 | 1.4 | 4.5 | 9.9 | 34.8 | 42.4 |
| Burkina Faso | .. | .. | .. | .. | .. | .. | .. | .. | .. | .. | .. | .. |
| Burundi | .. | .. | .. | .. | .. | .. | .. | .. | .. | .. | .. | .. |
| Cambodia | .. | 0.9 | .. | .. | .. | .. | .. | 41.0 | .. | 1.9 | .. | .. |
| Cameroon | 2.7 | 4.1 | 0.0 | 0.0 | 0.0 | 0.0 | 1.5 | 5.6 | 98.5 | 94.4 | 0.0 | 0.0 |
| Canada | 481.9 | 628.1 | 17.1 | 16.9 | 2.0 | 5.8 | 3.4 | 3.1 | 61.6 | 57.9 | 15.1 | 14.7 |
| Central African Republic | .. | .. | .. | .. | .. | .. | .. | .. | .. | .. | .. | .. |
| Chad | .. | .. | .. | .. | .. | .. | .. | .. | .. | .. | .. | .. |
| Chile | 18.4 | 49.9 | 34.3 | 16.7 | 1.3 | 29.9 | 7.6 | 3.4 | 55.3 | 48.1 | 0.0 | 0.0 |
| China | 621.2 | 2,497.4 | 71.3 | 79.0 | 0.4 | 0.5 | 7.9 | 2.4 | 20.4 | 15.9 | 0.0 | 2.1 |
|   Hong Kong, China | 28.9 | 38.5 | 98.3 | 62.6 | 0.0 | 36.8 | 1.7 | 0.6 | 0.0 | 0.0 | 0.0 | 0.0 |
| Colombia | 36.4 | 51.6 | 10.1 | 8.2 | 12.4 | 13.3 | 1.0 | 0.2 | 75.6 | 77.2 | 0.0 | 0.0 |
| Congo, Dem. Rep. | 5.7 | 7.4 | 0.0 | 0.0 | 0.0 | 0.0 | 0.4 | 0.3 | 99.6 | 99.7 | 0.0 | 0.0 |
| Congo, Rep. | 0.5 | 0.4 | 0.0 | 0.0 | 0.0 | 0.0 | 0.6 | 0.3 | 99.4 | 99.7 | 0.0 | 0.0 |
| Costa Rica | 3.5 | 8.3 | 0.0 | 0.0 | 0.0 | 0.0 | 2.5 | 3.3 | 97.5 | 79.6 | 0.0 | 0.0 |
| Côte d'Ivoire | 2.0 | 5.6 | 0.0 | 0.0 | 0.0 | 74.1 | 33.3 | 0.1 | 66.7 | 25.8 | 0.0 | 0.0 |
| Croatia | 9.2 | 12.4 | 6.8 | 18.8 | 20.2 | 14.7 | 31.6 | 15.0 | 41.3 | 51.3 | 0.0 | 0.0 |
| Cuba | 15.0 | 15.3 | 0.0 | 0.0 | 0.2 | 0.0 | 91.5 | 97.5 | 0.6 | 0.6 | 0.0 | 0.0 |
| Czech Republic | 62.3 | 81.9 | 76.4 | 60.8 | 0.6 | 4.8 | 0.9 | 0.4 | 1.9 | 2.9 | 20.2 | 30.2 |
| Denmark | 26.0 | 36.3 | 90.7 | 42.6 | 2.7 | 24.3 | 3.4 | 3.8 | 0.1 | 0.1 | 0.0 | 0.0 |
| Dominican Republic | 3.7 | 12.9 | 1.2 | 10.0 | 0.0 | 0.3 | 88.6 | 74.6 | 9.4 | 14.7 | 0.0 | 0.0 |
| Ecuador | 6.3 | 13.4 | 0.0 | 0.0 | 0.0 | 7.7 | 21.5 | 41.0 | 78.5 | 51.4 | 0.0 | 0.0 |
| Egypt, Arab Rep. | 42.3 | 108.7 | 0.0 | 0.0 | 39.6 | 74.3 | 36.9 | 13.6 | 23.5 | 11.6 | 0.0 | 0.0 |
| El Salvador | 2.2 | 4.8 | 0.0 | 0.0 | 0.0 | 0.0 | 6.9 | 42.6 | 73.5 | 35.0 | 0.0 | 0.0 |
| Eritrea | .. | .. | .. | .. | .. | .. | .. | .. | .. | .. | .. | .. |
| Estonia | 17.2 | 10.2 | 86.8 | 91.2 | 4.8 | 7.4 | 8.4 | 0.3 | 0.0 | 0.2 | 0.0 | 0.0 |
| Ethiopia | 1.2 | 2.9 | 0.0 | 0.0 | 0.0 | 0.0 | 11.6 | 0.7 | 88.4 | 99.3 | 0.0 | 0.0 |
| Finland | 54.4 | 70.6 | 33.0 | 16.5 | 8.6 | 15.9 | 3.1 | 0.7 | 20.0 | 19.5 | 35.3 | 33.0 |
| France | 417.2 | 570.6 | 8.5 | 5.4 | 0.7 | 4.0 | 2.1 | 1.3 | 12.9 | 9.1 | 75.3 | 79.1 |
| Gabon | 1.0 | 1.6 | 0.0 | 0.0 | 16.4 | 15.9 | 11.2 | 31.7 | 72.1 | 51.9 | 0.0 | 0.0 |
| Gambia, The | .. | .. | .. | .. | .. | .. | .. | .. | .. | .. | .. | .. |
| Georgia | 13.7 | 7.3 | 0.0 | 0.0 | 15.6 | 13.3 | 29.2 | 0.9 | 55.2 | 85.8 | 0.0 | 0.0 |
| Germany | 547.7 | 613.2 | 58.7 | 49.8 | 7.4 | 11.3 | 1.9 | 1.7 | 3.2 | 3.2 | 27.8 | 26.6 |
| Ghana | 5.7 | 6.8 | 0.0 | 0.0 | 0.0 | 0.0 | 0.0 | 21.5 | 100.0 | 78.5 | 0.0 | 0.0 |
| Greece | 34.8 | 59.4 | 72.4 | 59.8 | 0.3 | 13.7 | 22.3 | 15.5 | 5.1 | 8.4 | 0.0 | 0.0 |
| Guatemala | 2.3 | 7.6 | 0.0 | 13.9 | 0.0 | 0.0 | 9.0 | 31.4 | 76.0 | 42.8 | 0.0 | 0.0 |
| Guinea | .. | .. | .. | .. | .. | .. | .. | .. | .. | .. | .. | .. |
| Guinea-Bissau | .. | .. | .. | .. | .. | .. | .. | .. | .. | .. | .. | .. |
| Haiti | 0.6 | 0.6 | 0.0 | 0.0 | 0.0 | 0.0 | 20.6 | 52.3 | 76.5 | 47.7 | 0.0 | 0.0 |

| | Electricity production | | Sources of electricity[a] | | | | | | | | | |
|---|---|---|---|---|---|---|---|---|---|---|---|---|
| | | | % of total | | | | | | | | | |
| | billion kilowatt hours | | Coal | | Gas | | Oil | | Hydropower | | Nuclear power | |
| | 1990 | 2005 | 1990 | 2005 | 1990 | 2005 | 1990 | 2005 | 1990 | 2005 | 1990 | 2005 |
| Honduras | 2.3 | 5.6 | 0.0 | 0.0 | 0.0 | 0.0 | 1.7 | 66.4 | 98.3 | 32.3 | 0.0 | 0.0 |
| Hungary | 28.4 | 35.8 | 30.5 | 20.0 | 15.7 | 34.6 | 4.8 | 1.3 | 0.6 | 0.6 | 48.3 | 38.7 |
| India | 289.4 | 699.0 | 66.2 | 68.7 | 3.4 | 8.9 | 3.5 | 4.5 | 24.8 | 14.3 | 2.1 | 2.5 |
| Indonesia | 33.3 | 127.4 | 31.5 | 40.7 | 2.3 | 13.8 | 42.7 | 31.9 | 20.2 | 8.4 | 0.0 | 0.0 |
| Iran, Islamic Rep. | 59.1 | 180.4 | 0.0 | 0.0 | 52.5 | 73.0 | 37.3 | 18.0 | 10.3 | 8.9 | 0.0 | 0.0 |
| Iraq | 24.0 | 34.0 | 0.0 | 0.0 | 0.0 | 0.0 | 89.2 | 98.5 | 10.8 | 1.5 | 0.0 | 0.0 |
| Ireland | 14.2 | 25.6 | 57.4 | 34.5 | 27.7 | 45.2 | 10.0 | 13.0 | 4.9 | 2.5 | 0.0 | 0.0 |
| Israel | 20.9 | 49.8 | 50.1 | 71.1 | 0.0 | 11.4 | 49.9 | 17.5 | 0.0 | 0.1 | 0.0 | 0.0 |
| Italy | 213.1 | 294.4 | 16.8 | 16.8 | 18.6 | 50.7 | 48.2 | 16.0 | 14.8 | 11.4 | 0.0 | 0.0 |
| Jamaica | 2.5 | 7.4 | 0.0 | 0.0 | 0.0 | 0.0 | 92.4 | 96.6 | 3.6 | 2.0 | 0.0 | 0.0 |
| Japan | 836.7 | 1,094.2 | 14.0 | 28.3 | 19.9 | 21.1 | 18.2 | 9.5 | 10.7 | 7.1 | 24.2 | 27.9 |
| Jordan | 3.6 | 9.7 | 0.0 | 0.0 | 11.9 | 57.3 | 87.8 | 42.1 | 0.3 | 0.6 | 0.0 | 0.0 |
| Kazakhstan | 87.4 | 67.9 | 71.1 | 70.3 | 10.5 | 10.7 | 10.0 | 7.4 | 8.4 | 11.6 | 0.0 | 0.0 |
| Kenya | 3.0 | 6.0 | 0.0 | 0.0 | 0.0 | 0.0 | 7.6 | 29.5 | 81.6 | 50.4 | 0.0 | 0.0 |
| Korea, Dem. Rep. | 27.7 | 22.9 | 40.1 | 39.0 | 0.0 | 0.0 | 3.6 | 3.6 | 56.3 | 57.3 | 0.0 | 0.0 |
| Korea, Rep. | 105.4 | 387.9 | 16.8 | 38.4 | 9.1 | 16.0 | 17.9 | 6.3 | 6.0 | 0.9 | 50.2 | 37.8 |
| Kuwait | 18.5 | 43.7 | 0.0 | 0.0 | 45.7 | 17.9 | 54.3 | 82.1 | 0.0 | 0.0 | 0.0 | 0.0 |
| Kyrgyz Republic | 15.7 | 16.4 | 13.1 | 3.6 | 23.5 | 9.5 | 0.0 | 0.0 | 63.5 | 86.9 | 0.0 | 0.0 |
| Lao PDR | .. | .. | .. | .. | .. | .. | .. | .. | .. | .. | .. | .. |
| Latvia | 6.6 | 4.9 | 0.9 | 0.0 | 26.1 | 30.3 | 5.4 | 0.1 | 67.6 | 67.8 | 0.0 | 0.0 |
| Lebanon | 1.5 | 10.1 | 0.0 | 0.0 | 0.0 | 0.0 | 66.7 | 89.7 | 33.3 | 10.3 | 0.0 | 0.0 |
| Lesotho | .. | .. | .. | .. | .. | .. | .. | .. | .. | .. | .. | .. |
| Liberia | .. | .. | .. | .. | .. | .. | .. | .. | .. | .. | .. | .. |
| Libya | 10.2 | 22.5 | 0.0 | 0.0 | 0.0 | 28.2 | 100.0 | 71.8 | 0.0 | 0.0 | 0.0 | 0.0 |
| Lithuania | 28.4 | 14.4 | 0.0 | 0.0 | 23.8 | 20.9 | 14.6 | 2.8 | 1.5 | 3.1 | 60.0 | 71.7 |
| Macedonia, FYR | 5.8 | 6.9 | 89.7 | 78.3 | 0.0 | 0.0 | 1.8 | 0.2 | 8.5 | 21.5 | 0.0 | 0.0 |
| Madagascar | .. | .. | .. | .. | .. | .. | .. | .. | .. | .. | .. | .. |
| Malawi | .. | .. | .. | .. | .. | .. | .. | .. | .. | .. | .. | .. |
| Malaysia | 23.0 | 87.3 | 12.3 | 26.5 | 22.0 | 64.0 | 48.4 | 2.9 | 17.3 | 6.6 | 0.0 | 0.0 |
| Mali | .. | .. | .. | .. | .. | .. | .. | .. | .. | .. | .. | .. |
| Mauritania | .. | .. | .. | .. | .. | .. | .. | .. | .. | .. | .. | .. |
| Mauritius | .. | .. | .. | .. | .. | .. | .. | .. | .. | .. | .. | .. |
| Mexico | 124.1 | 234.9 | 6.3 | 14.0 | 11.6 | 36.1 | 56.7 | 29.3 | 18.9 | 11.8 | 2.4 | 4.6 |
| Moldova | 15.5 | 3.9 | 32.3 | 0.0 | 39.5 | 98.1 | 26.6 | 0.2 | 1.7 | 1.6 | 0.0 | 0.0 |
| Mongolia | .. | .. | .. | .. | .. | .. | .. | .. | .. | .. | .. | .. |
| Morocco | 9.6 | 22.6 | 23.0 | 69.2 | 0.0 | 0.0 | 64.4 | 23.6 | 12.7 | 6.3 | 0.0 | 0.0 |
| Mozambique | 0.5 | 13.3 | 13.9 | 0.0 | 0.0 | 0.1 | 23.6 | 0.1 | 62.6 | 99.8 | 0.0 | 0.0 |
| Myanmar | 2.5 | 6.0 | 1.6 | 0.0 | 39.3 | 39.8 | 10.9 | 10.3 | 48.1 | 49.8 | 0.0 | 0.0 |
| Namibia | 0.0 | 1.7 | 1.5 | 0.4 | 0.0 | 0.0 | 3.3 | 2.6 | 95.2 | 97.0 | 0.0 | 0.0 |
| Nepal | 0.9 | 2.4 | 0.0 | 0.0 | 0.0 | 0.0 | 0.1 | 0.2 | 99.9 | 99.8 | 0.0 | 0.0 |
| Netherlands | 71.9 | 100.2 | 38.3 | 26.9 | 50.9 | 57.7 | 4.3 | 2.3 | 0.1 | 0.1 | 4.9 | 4.0 |
| New Zealand | 32.3 | 43.0 | 1.9 | 13.5 | 17.6 | 22.0 | 0.0 | 0.0 | 72.3 | 54.6 | 0.0 | 0.0 |
| Nicaragua | 1.4 | 2.9 | 0.0 | 0.0 | 0.0 | 0.0 | 39.8 | 69.8 | 28.8 | 15.1 | 0.0 | 0.0 |
| Niger | .. | .. | .. | .. | .. | .. | .. | .. | .. | .. | .. | .. |
| Nigeria | 13.5 | 23.5 | 0.1 | 0.0 | 53.7 | 53.6 | 13.7 | 12.7 | 32.6 | 33.8 | 0.0 | 0.0 |
| Norway | 121.6 | 137.3 | 0.1 | 0.1 | 0.0 | 0.3 | 0.0 | 0.0 | 99.6 | 98.9 | 0.0 | 0.0 |
| Oman | 4.5 | 12.6 | 0.0 | 0.0 | 81.6 | 82.0 | 18.4 | 18.0 | 0.0 | 0.0 | 0.0 | 0.0 |
| Pakistan | 37.7 | 93.8 | 0.1 | 0.1 | 33.6 | 44.0 | 20.6 | 20.3 | 44.9 | 32.9 | 0.8 | 2.6 |
| Panama | 2.7 | 5.8 | 0.0 | 0.0 | 0.0 | 0.0 | 14.7 | 35.7 | 83.2 | 63.9 | 0.0 | 0.0 |
| Papua New Guinea | .. | .. | .. | .. | .. | .. | .. | .. | .. | .. | .. | .. |
| Paraguay | 27.2 | 51.2 | 0.0 | 0.0 | 0.0 | 0.0 | 0.0 | 0.0 | 99.9 | 100.0 | 0.0 | 0.0 |
| Peru | 13.8 | 25.5 | 0.0 | 3.2 | 1.7 | 9.7 | 21.5 | 8.2 | 75.8 | 78.3 | 0.0 | 0.0 |
| Philippines | 25.2 | 56.5 | 7.7 | 27.0 | 0.0 | 29.8 | 46.7 | 10.9 | 24.0 | 14.8 | 0.0 | 0.0 |
| Poland | 134.4 | 155.4 | 97.5 | 93.4 | 0.1 | 2.3 | 1.2 | 1.5 | 1.1 | 1.4 | 0.0 | 0.0 |
| Portugal | 28.4 | 46.2 | 32.1 | 33.0 | 0.0 | 29.5 | 33.1 | 19.0 | 32.3 | 10.2 | 0.0 | 0.0 |
| Puerto Rico | .. | .. | .. | .. | .. | .. | .. | .. | .. | .. | .. | .. |

| | Electricity production | | Sources of electricity[a] | | | | | | | | | |
| | | | % of total | | | | | | | | | |
| | billion kilowatt hours | | Coal | | Gas | | Oil | | Hydropower | | Nuclear power | |
| | 1990 | 2005 | 1990 | 2005 | 1990 | 2005 | 1990 | 2005 | 1990 | 2005 | 1990 | 2005 |
|---|---|---|---|---|---|---|---|---|---|---|---|---|
| Romania | 64.3 | 59.4 | 28.8 | 37.3 | 35.1 | 16.2 | 18.4 | 3.2 | 17.7 | 34.0 | 0.0 | 9.3 |
| Russian Federation | 1,082.2 | 951.2 | 14.5 | 17.4 | 47.3 | 46.2 | 11.9 | 2.2 | 15.3 | 18.2 | 10.9 | 15.7 |
| Rwanda | .. | .. | .. | .. | .. | .. | .. | .. | .. | .. | .. | .. |
| Saudi Arabia | 69.2 | 176.1 | 0.0 | 0.0 | 48.1 | 49.1 | 51.9 | 50.9 | 0.0 | 0.0 | 0.0 | 0.0 |
| Senegal | 0.9 | 2.5 | 0.0 | 0.0 | 2.4 | 2.4 | 97.6 | 79.4 | 0.0 | 10.5 | 0.0 | 0.0 |
| Serbia[b] | 43.2 | 35.4 | 79.8 | 69.9 | 1.6 | 1.5 | 1.2 | 0.8 | 22.3 | 27.9 | 0.0 | 0.0 |
| Sierra Leone | .. | .. | .. | .. | .. | .. | .. | .. | .. | .. | .. | .. |
| Singapore | 15.7 | 38.2 | 0.0 | 0.0 | 0.0 | 74.4 | 100.0 | 25.6 | 0.0 | 0.0 | 0.0 | 0.0 |
| Slovak Republic | 25.5 | 31.4 | 31.9 | 19.1 | 7.1 | 7.0 | 6.4 | 2.4 | 7.4 | 14.8 | 47.2 | 56.5 |
| Slovenia | 12.0 | 15.1 | 31.9 | 34.9 | 0.0 | 2.2 | 4.8 | 0.3 | 24.7 | 22.9 | 38.7 | 38.9 |
| Somalia | .. | .. | .. | .. | .. | .. | .. | .. | .. | .. | .. | .. |
| South Africa | 165.4 | 242.9 | 94.3 | 94.1 | 0.0 | 0.0 | 0.0 | 0.0 | 0.6 | 0.9 | 5.1 | 4.6 |
| Spain | 151.2 | 290.6 | 40.1 | 27.8 | 1.0 | 27.2 | 5.7 | 8.4 | 16.8 | 6.7 | 35.9 | 19.8 |
| Sri Lanka | 3.2 | 8.8 | 0.0 | 0.0 | 0.0 | 0.0 | 0.2 | 60.6 | 99.8 | 39.4 | 0.0 | 0.0 |
| Sudan | 1.5 | 4.1 | 0.0 | 0.0 | 0.0 | 0.0 | 36.8 | 70.0 | 63.2 | 30.0 | 0.0 | 0.0 |
| Swaziland | .. | .. | .. | .. | .. | .. | .. | .. | .. | .. | .. | .. |
| Sweden | 146.0 | 158.4 | 1.1 | 1.2 | 0.3 | 0.4 | 0.9 | 0.9 | 49.7 | 46.0 | 46.7 | 45.7 |
| Switzerland | 55.0 | 57.8 | 0.1 | 0.0 | 0.6 | 1.5 | 0.7 | 0.3 | 54.2 | 54.1 | 43.0 | 40.4 |
| Syrian Arab Republic | 11.6 | 34.9 | 0.0 | 0.0 | 20.5 | 37.1 | 56.0 | 53.0 | 23.5 | 9.9 | 0.0 | 0.0 |
| Tajikistan | 18.1 | 17.1 | 0.0 | 0.0 | 9.1 | 2.3 | 0.0 | 0.0 | 90.9 | 97.7 | 0.0 | 0.0 |
| Tanzania | 1.6 | 3.0 | 0.0 | 3.3 | 0.0 | 0.0 | 4.9 | 38.2 | 95.1 | 58.6 | 0.0 | 0.0 |
| Thailand | 44.2 | 132.2 | 25.0 | 15.1 | 40.2 | 71.4 | 23.5 | 6.6 | 11.3 | 4.4 | 0.0 | 0.0 |
| Timor-Leste | .. | .. | .. | .. | .. | .. | .. | .. | .. | .. | .. | .. |
| Togo | 0.2 | 0.2 | 0.0 | 0.0 | 0.0 | 0.0 | 39.9 | 60.4 | 60.1 | 39.6 | 0.0 | 0.0 |
| Trinidad and Tobago | 3.6 | 7.1 | 0.0 | 0.0 | 99.0 | 99.5 | 0.1 | 0.2 | 0.0 | 0.0 | 0.0 | 0.0 |
| Tunisia | 5.8 | 13.7 | 0.0 | 0.0 | 63.7 | 90.4 | 35.5 | 8.2 | 0.8 | 1.1 | 0.0 | 0.0 |
| Turkey | 57.5 | 162.0 | 35.1 | 26.7 | 17.7 | 45.3 | 6.9 | 3.4 | 40.2 | 24.4 | 0.0 | 0.0 |
| Turkmenistan | 14.6 | 12.8 | 0.0 | 0.0 | 95.2 | 100.0 | 0.0 | 0.0 | 4.8 | 0.0 | 0.0 | 0.0 |
| Uganda | .. | .. | .. | .. | .. | .. | .. | .. | .. | .. | .. | .. |
| Ukraine | 298.6 | 185.9 | 38.2 | 26.7 | 16.8 | 18.7 | 16.1 | 0.3 | 3.5 | 6.7 | 25.5 | 47.7 |
| United Arab Emirates | 17.1 | 60.7 | 0.0 | 0.0 | 96.3 | 97.9 | 3.7 | 2.1 | 0.0 | 0.0 | 0.0 | 0.0 |
| United Kingdom | 317.8 | 397.6 | 65.0 | 34.3 | 1.6 | 38.5 | 10.9 | 1.4 | 1.6 | 1.2 | 20.7 | 20.5 |
| United States | 3,202.8 | 4,268.4 | 53.1 | 50.5 | 11.9 | 18.3 | 4.1 | 3.3 | 8.5 | 6.4 | 19.1 | 19.0 |
| Uruguay | 7.4 | 7.7 | 0.0 | 0.0 | 0.0 | 0.0 | 5.1 | 12.5 | 94.2 | 87.0 | 0.0 | 0.0 |
| Uzbekistan | 56.3 | 47.7 | 7.4 | 4.7 | 76.4 | 68.8 | 4.4 | 13.6 | 11.8 | 12.8 | 0.0 | 0.0 |
| Venezuela, RB | 59.3 | 101.5 | 0.0 | 0.0 | 26.2 | 15.6 | 11.5 | 10.5 | 62.3 | 73.9 | 0.0 | 0.0 |
| Vietnam | 8.7 | 53.5 | 23.1 | 16.7 | 0.1 | 38.5 | 15.0 | 4.6 | 61.8 | 40.1 | 0.0 | 0.0 |
| West Bank and Gaza | .. | .. | .. | .. | .. | .. | .. | .. | .. | .. | .. | .. |
| Yemen, Rep. | 1.7 | 4.7 | 0.0 | 0.0 | 0.0 | 0.0 | 100.0 | 100.0 | 0.0 | 0.0 | 0.0 | 0.0 |
| Zambia | 8.0 | 8.9 | 0.5 | 0.2 | 0.0 | 0.0 | 0.3 | 0.4 | 99.2 | 99.4 | 0.0 | 0.0 |
| Zimbabwe | 9.4 | 10.3 | 53.3 | 43.0 | 0.0 | 0.0 | 0.0 | 0.2 | 46.7 | 56.8 | 0.0 | 0.0 |
| **World** | **11,735.9 s** | **18,155.6 s** | **37.5 w** | **40.3 w** | **14.6 w** | **19.8 w** | **10.4 w** | **6.2 w** | **18.1 w** | **16.0 w** | **17.2 w** | **15.2 w** |
| **Low income** | 520.1 | 1,082.4 | 41.5 | 46.7 | 16.5 | 18.3 | 5.7 | 7.4 | 35.0 | 24.8 | 1.2 | 1.8 |
| **Middle income** | 3,709.5 | 6,599.4 | 32.7 | 44.1 | 22.0 | 20.3 | 15.4 | 7.1 | 22.0 | 21.5 | 7.4 | 6.0 |
| Lower middle income | 1,447.7 | 3,765.8 | 41.9 | 56.9 | 12.6 | 13.9 | 20.2 | 7.8 | 19.3 | 16.8 | 5.3 | 3.8 |
| Upper middle income | 2,261.8 | 2,833.5 | 26.8 | 27.0 | 28.0 | 28.9 | 12.3 | 6.1 | 23.7 | 27.8 | 8.7 | 9.0 |
| **Low & middle income** | 4,229.7 | 7,681.8 | 33.8 | 44.4 | 21.3 | 20.0 | 14.2 | 7.1 | 23.6 | 22.0 | 6.6 | 5.5 |
| East Asia & Pacific | 785.8 | 2,984.2 | 61.4 | 70.4 | 3.5 | 7.4 | 12.6 | 4.1 | 21.7 | 15.6 | 0.0 | 1.8 |
| Europe & Central Asia | 2,085.5 | 1,913.2 | 27.3 | 27.3 | 34.0 | 35.8 | 13.1 | 2.9 | 13.6 | 17.5 | 12.1 | 16.0 |
| Latin America & Carib. | 605.1 | 1,120.8 | 3.8 | 5.4 | 9.2 | 18.0 | 18.9 | 13.6 | 63.9 | 57.6 | 2.1 | 2.5 |
| Middle East & N. Africa | 190.0 | 487.9 | 1.2 | 3.2 | 38.4 | 60.0 | 48.2 | 29.3 | 12.2 | 7.4 | 0.0 | 0.0 |
| South Asia | 338.9 | 826.7 | 56.6 | 58.1 | 8.6 | 14.9 | 5.4 | 6.9 | 27.6 | 16.7 | 1.9 | 2.4 |
| Sub-Saharan Africa | 224.4 | 349.0 | 72.1 | 67.1 | 3.3 | 4.9 | 2.2 | 4.1 | 18.4 | 20.1 | 3.8 | 3.2 |
| **High income** | 7,506.2 | 10,473.9 | 39.5 | 37.3 | 10.8 | 19.6 | 8.2 | 5.6 | 15.1 | 11.5 | 23.1 | 22.4 |
| Euro area | 1,665.0 | 2,238.0 | 34.4 | 26.3 | 8.6 | 20.7 | 9.5 | 5.2 | 11.1 | 8.4 | 35.5 | 33.6 |

a. Shares may not sum to 100 percent because some sources of generated electricity (such as wind, solar, and geothermal) are not shown. b. Includes Montenegro.

# 3.10

## About the data

Use of energy is important in improving people's standard of living. But electricity generation also can damage the environment. Whether such damage occurs depends largely on how electricity is generated. For example, burning coal releases twice as much carbon dioxide—a major contributor to global warming—as does burning an equivalent amount of natural gas (see *About the data* for table 3.8). Nuclear energy does not generate carbon dioxide emissions, but it produces other dangerous waste products. The table provides information on electricity production by source.

The International Energy Agency (IEA) compiles data on energy inputs used to generate electricity. IEA data for countries that are not members of the Organisation for Economic Co-operation and Development (OECD) are based on national energy data adjusted to conform to annual questionnaires completed by OECD member governments. In addition, estimates are sometimes made to complete major aggregates from which key data are missing, and

adjustments are made to compensate for differences in definitions. The IEA makes these estimates in consultation with national statistical offices, oil companies, electric utilities, and national energy experts. It occasionally revises its time series to reflect political changes. Since 1990, for example, the IEA has constructed energy statistics for countries of the former Soviet Union. In addition, energy statistics for other countries have undergone continuous changes in coverage or methodology in recent years as more detailed energy accounts have become available. Breaks in series are therefore unavoidable.

## Definitions

• **Electricity production** is measured at the terminals of all alternator sets in a station. In addition to hydropower, coal, oil, gas, and nuclear power generation, it covers generation by geothermal, solar, wind, and tide and wave energy as well as that from combustible renewables and waste. Production includes the output of electric plants designed to produce electricity only, as well as that of combined heat and power plants. • **Sources of electricity** are the inputs used to generate electricity: coal, gas, oil, hydropower, and nuclear power. • **Coal** is all coal and brown coal, both primary (including hard coal and lignite-brown coal) and derived fuels (including patent fuel, coke oven coke, gas coke, coke oven gas, and blast furnace gas). Peat is also included in this category. • **Gas** is natural gas but not natural gas liquids. • **Oil** is crude oil and petroleum products. • **Hydropower** is electricity produced by hydroelectric power plants. • **Nuclear power** is electricity produced by nuclear power plants.

## Sources of electricity generation have shifted since 1990 . . .                    3.10a

### World

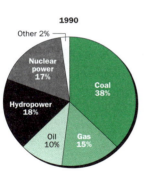
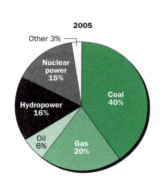

*Source:* Table 3.10.

## . . . with low-income countries relying more on coal                    3.10b

### Low-income countries

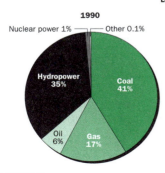
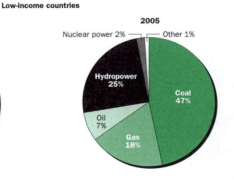

*Source:* Table 3.10.

## Data sources

Data on electricity production are from the IEA's electronic files and its annual publications *Energy Statistics and Balances of Non-OECD Countries*, *Energy Statistics of OECD Countries*, and *Energy Balances of OECD Countries*.

# 3.11 Urbanization

| | Urban population | | | | | Population in urban agglomerations of more than 1 million | | Population in largest city | | Access to improved sanitation facilities | | | |
|---|---|---|---|---|---|---|---|---|---|---|---|---|---|
| | millions | | % of total population | | average annual % growth | % of total population | | % of urban population | | % of urban population | | % of rural population | |
| | 1990 | 2006 | 1990 | 2006 | 1990–2006 | 1990 | 2005 | 1990 | 2005 | 1990 | 2004 | 1990 | 2004 |
| Afghanistan | .. | .. | .. | .. | .. | .. | .. | .. | .. | .. | .. | .. | .. |
| Albania | 1.2 | 1.5 | 36 | 46 | 1.3 | .. | .. | .. | .. | 99 | 99 | .. | 84 |
| Algeria | 13.2 | 21.3 | 52 | 64 | 3.0 | 8 | 10 | 14 | 15 | 99 | 99 | 77 | 82 |
| Angola | 3.9 | 8.9 | 37 | 54 | 5.2 | 15 | 17 | 40 | 32 | 61 | 56 | 18 | 16 |
| Argentina | 28.3 | 35.3 | 87 | 90 | 1.4 | 39 | 39 | 37 | 36 | 86 | 92 | 45 | 83 |
| Armenia | 2.4 | 1.9 | 68 | 64 | −1.4 | 33 | 37 | 49 | 57 | 96 | 96 | .. | 61 |
| Australia | 14.6 | 18.3 | 85 | 88 | 1.4 | 60 | 60 | 25 | 24 | 100 | 100 | 100 | 100 |
| Austria | 5.1 | 5.5 | 66 | 66 | 0.5 | 27 | 27 | 41 | 42 | 100 | 100 | 100 | 100 |
| Azerbaijan | 3.8 | 4.4 | 54 | 52 | 0.8 | 24 | 22 | 45 | 43 | .. | 73 | .. | 36 |
| Bangladesh | 22.4 | 39.8 | 20 | 26 | 3.6 | 8 | 12 | 29 | 32 | 55 | 51 | 12 | 35 |
| Belarus | 6.8 | 7.1 | 66 | 73 | 0.3 | 16 | 18 | 24 | 25 | .. | 93 | .. | 61 |
| Belgium | 9.6 | 10.2 | 96 | 97 | 0.4 | 10 | 10 | 10 | 10 | .. | .. | .. | .. |
| Benin | 1.8 | 3.5 | 35 | 41 | 4.3 | .. | .. | .. | .. | 32 | 59 | 2 | 11 |
| Bolivia | 3.7 | 6.0 | 56 | 65 | 3.1 | 25 | 31 | 29 | 26 | 49 | 60 | 14 | 22 |
| Bosnia and Herzegovina | 1.7 | 1.8 | 39 | 46 | 0.5 | .. | .. | .. | .. | 99 | 99 | .. | 92 |
| Botswana | 0.6 | 1.1 | 42 | 58 | 4.0 | .. | .. | .. | .. | 61 | 57 | 21 | 25 |
| Brazil | 111.8 | 160.3 | 75 | 85 | 2.2 | 34 | 37 | 13 | 12 | 82 | 83 | 37 | 37 |
| Bulgaria | 5.8 | 5.4 | 66 | 70 | −0.4 | 14 | 14 | 21 | 20 | 100 | 100 | 96 | 96 |
| Burkina Faso | 1.2 | 2.7 | 14 | 19 | 4.9 | .. | .. | 49 | 36 | 32 | 42 | 3 | 6 |
| Burundi | 0.4 | 0.8 | 6 | 10 | 5.3 | .. | .. | .. | .. | 42 | 47 | 44 | 35 |
| Cambodia | 1.2 | 2.9 | 13 | 20 | 5.4 | 6 | 10 | 49 | 50 | .. | 53 | .. | 8 |
| Cameroon | 5.0 | 10.1 | 41 | 55 | 4.4 | 14 | 18 | 19 | 18 | 59 | 58 | 40 | 43 |
| Canada | 21.3 | 26.2 | 77 | 80 | 1.3 | 40 | 44 | 18 | 21 | 100 | 100 | 99 | 99 |
| Central African Republic | 1.1 | 1.6 | 37 | 38 | 2.4 | .. | .. | .. | .. | 34 | 47 | 17 | 12 |
| Chad | 1.3 | 2.7 | 21 | 26 | 4.7 | .. | .. | 38 | 35 | 28 | 24 | 2 | 4 |
| Chile | 11.0 | 14.4 | 83 | 88 | 1.7 | 35 | 35 | 42 | 40 | 91 | 95 | 52 | 62 |
| China | 311.0 | 541.8 | 27 | 41 | 3.5 | 13 | 18 | 3 | 3 | 64 | 69 | 7 | 28 |
| Hong Kong, China | 5.7 | 6.9 | 100 | 100 | 1.2 | 100 | 100 | 100 | 100 | .. | .. | .. | .. |
| Colombia | 24.0 | 33.3 | 69 | 73 | 2.0 | 30 | 36 | 20 | 24 | 95 | 96 | 52 | 54 |
| Congo, Dem. Rep. | 10.5 | 19.8 | 28 | 33 | 3.9 | 15 | 16 | 35 | 32 | 53 | 42 | 1 | 25 |
| Congo, Rep. | 1.3 | 2.2 | 54 | 61 | 3.3 | 29 | 32 | 53 | 54 | .. | 28 | .. | 25 |
| Costa Rica | 1.6 | 2.7 | 51 | 62 | 3.5 | 24 | 28 | 47 | 46 | .. | 89 | 97 | 97 |
| Côte d'Ivoire | 5.1 | 8.6 | 40 | 45 | 3.3 | 16 | 19 | 41 | 43 | 37 | 46 | 10 | 29 |
| Croatia | 2.6 | 2.5 | 54 | 57 | −0.1 | .. | .. | .. | .. | 100 | 100 | 100 | 100 |
| Cuba | 7.8 | 8.5 | 73 | 75 | 0.5 | 20 | 19 | 27 | 26 | 99 | 99 | 95 | 95 |
| Czech Republic | 7.8 | 7.5 | 75 | 74 | −0.2 | 12 | 11 | 16 | 16 | 99 | 99 | 97 | 97 |
| Denmark | 4.4 | 4.7 | 85 | 86 | 0.4 | 26 | 20 | 31 | 23 | .. | .. | .. | .. |
| Dominican Republic | 4.0 | 6.5 | 55 | 68 | 3.0 | 21 | 21 | 38 | 32 | 60 | 81 | 43 | 73 |
| Ecuador | 5.7 | 8.4 | 55 | 63 | 2.4 | 26 | 30 | 28 | 29 | 77 | 94 | 45 | 82 |
| Egypt, Arab Rep. | 24.0 | 31.9 | 44 | 43 | 1.8 | 22 | 20 | 38 | 36 | 70 | 86 | 42 | 58 |
| El Salvador | 2.5 | 4.1 | 49 | 60 | 3.0 | 19 | 23 | 39 | 38 | 70 | 77 | 33 | 39 |
| Eritrea | 0.5 | 0.9 | 16 | 20 | 3.9 | .. | .. | .. | .. | 44 | 32 | 0 | 3 |
| Estonia | 1.1 | 0.9 | 71 | 69 | −1.2 | .. | .. | .. | .. | 97 | 97 | 96 | 96 |
| Ethiopia | 6.4 | 12.6 | 13 | 16 | 4.2 | 3 | 4 | 28 | 24 | 13 | 44 | 2 | 7 |
| Finland | 3.1 | 3.2 | 61 | 61 | 0.3 | 17 | 21 | 28 | 34 | 100 | 100 | 100 | 100 |
| France | 42.0 | 47.1 | 74 | 77 | 0.7 | 23 | 22 | 22 | 21 | .. | .. | .. | .. |
| Gabon | 0.6 | 1.1 | 69 | 84 | 3.5 | .. | .. | .. | .. | .. | 37 | .. | 30 |
| Gambia, The | 0.4 | 0.9 | 38 | 55 | 5.7 | .. | .. | .. | .. | .. | 72 | .. | 46 |
| Georgia | 3.0 | 2.3 | 55 | 52 | −1.6 | 22 | 23 | 41 | 45 | 99 | 96 | 94 | 91 |
| Germany | 58.3 | 62.0 | 73 | 75 | 0.4 | 8 | 8 | 6 | 5 | 100 | 100 | 100 | 100 |
| Ghana | 5.7 | 11.2 | 37 | 49 | 4.2 | 12 | 16 | 21 | 18 | 23 | 27 | 10 | 11 |
| Greece | 6.0 | 6.6 | 59 | 59 | 0.6 | 30 | 29 | 51 | 49 | .. | .. | .. | .. |
| Guatemala | 3.7 | 6.2 | 41 | 48 | 3.3 | .. | .. | 22 | 16 | 73 | 90 | 47 | 82 |
| Guinea | 1.7 | 3.1 | 28 | 33 | 3.7 | 15 | 16 | 53 | 48 | 27 | 31 | 10 | 11 |
| Guinea-Bissau | 0.3 | 0.5 | 28 | 30 | 3.4 | .. | .. | .. | .. | .. | 57 | .. | 23 |
| Haiti | 2.1 | 3.7 | 30 | 39 | 3.6 | 16 | 23 | 54 | 59 | 25 | 57 | 23 | 14 |

| | Urban population | | | | | Population in urban agglomerations of more than 1 million | | Population in largest city | | Access to improved sanitation facilities | | | |
|---|---|---|---|---|---|---|---|---|---|---|---|---|---|
| | millions | | % of total population | | average annual % growth | % of total population | | % of urban population | | % of urban population | | % of rural population | |
| | 1990 | 2006 | 1990 | 2006 | 1990–2006 | 1990 | 2005 | 1990 | 2005 | 1990 | 2004 | 1990 | 2004 |
| Honduras | 2.0 | 3.3 | 40 | 47 | 3.2 | .. | .. | 29 | 29 | 77 | 87 | 31 | 54 |
| Hungary | 6.8 | 6.7 | 66 | 67 | −0.1 | 19 | 17 | 29 | 25 | 100 | 100 | .. | 85 |
| India | 216.6 | 321.6 | 26 | 29 | 2.5 | 10 | 12 | 6 | 6 | 45 | 59 | 3 | 22 |
| Indonesia | 54.5 | 109.8 | 31 | 49 | 4.4 | 9 | 12 | 14 | 12 | 65 | 73 | 37 | 40 |
| Iran, Islamic Rep. | 30.6 | 47.3 | 56 | 67 | 2.7 | 23 | 23 | 21 | 16 | 86 | .. | 78 | .. |
| Iraq | 12.9 | .. | 70 | .. | .. | 26 | .. | 32 | .. | 95 | .. | 48 | .. |
| Ireland | 2.0 | 2.6 | 57 | 61 | 1.6 | 26 | 25 | 46 | 41 | .. | .. | .. | .. |
| Israel | 4.2 | 6.5 | 90 | 92 | 2.7 | 43 | 44 | 48 | 47 | 100 | 100 | .. | .. |
| Italy | 37.8 | 39.9 | 67 | 68 | 0.3 | 19 | 17 | 9 | 8 | .. | .. | .. | .. |
| Jamaica | 1.2 | 1.4 | 49 | 53 | 1.2 | .. | .. | .. | .. | 86 | 91 | 64 | 69 |
| Japan | 78.0 | 84.3 | 63 | 66 | 0.5 | 46 | 48 | 42 | 42 | 100 | 100 | 100 | 100 |
| Jordan | 2.3 | 4.6 | 72 | 83 | 4.3 | 27 | 24 | 37 | 29 | 97 | 94 | 82 | 87 |
| Kazakhstan | 9.2 | 8.8 | 56 | 58 | −0.3 | 7 | 8 | 12 | 13 | 87 | 87 | 52 | 52 |
| Kenya | 4.3 | 7.7 | 18 | 21 | 3.7 | 6 | 8 | 32 | 38 | 48 | 46 | 37 | 41 |
| Korea, Dem. Rep. | 11.8 | 14.7 | 58 | 62 | 1.4 | 15 | 19 | 21 | 23 | .. | 58 | .. | 60 |
| Korea, Rep. | 31.6 | 39.2 | 74 | 81 | 1.3 | 51 | 51 | 33 | 25 | .. | .. | .. | .. |
| Kuwait | 2.1 | 2.6 | 98 | 98 | 1.3 | 65 | 71 | 67 | 73 | .. | .. | .. | .. |
| Kyrgyz Republic | 1.7 | 1.9 | 38 | 36 | 0.7 | .. | .. | 38 | 43 | 75 | 75 | 51 | 51 |
| Lao PDR | 0.6 | 1.2 | 15 | 21 | 4.1 | .. | .. | .. | .. | .. | 67 | .. | 20 |
| Latvia | 1.9 | 1.6 | 69 | 68 | −1.1 | .. | .. | .. | .. | .. | 82 | .. | 71 |
| Lebanon | 2.5 | 3.5 | 83 | 87 | 2.2 | 43 | 44 | 52 | 51 | 100 | 100 | .. | 87 |
| Lesotho | 0.3 | 0.4 | 17 | 19 | 2.0 | .. | .. | .. | .. | 61 | 61 | 32 | 32 |
| Liberia | 1.0 | 2.1 | 45 | 59 | 4.9 | .. | .. | 55 | 47 | 59 | 49 | 24 | 7 |
| Libya | 3.4 | 5.1 | 79 | 85 | 2.5 | 48 | 54 | 44 | 42 | 97 | 97 | 96 | 96 |
| Lithuania | 2.5 | 2.3 | 68 | 67 | −0.6 | .. | .. | .. | .. | .. | .. | .. | .. |
| Macedonia, FYR | 1.1 | 1.4 | 58 | 70 | 1.6 | .. | .. | .. | .. | .. | .. | .. | .. |
| Madagascar | 2.8 | 5.2 | 24 | 27 | 3.8 | 8 | 9 | 33 | 32 | 27 | 48 | 10 | 26 |
| Malawi | 1.1 | 2.4 | 12 | 18 | 4.9 | .. | .. | .. | .. | 64 | 62 | 45 | 61 |
| Malaysia | 9.0 | 17.8 | 50 | 68 | 4.3 | 6 | 5 | 12 | 8 | 95 | 95 | .. | 93 |
| Mali | 1.8 | 3.7 | 23 | 31 | 4.6 | 10 | 12 | 42 | 39 | 50 | 59 | 32 | 39 |
| Mauritania | 0.8 | 1.2 | 40 | 41 | 2.9 | .. | .. | .. | .. | 42 | 49 | 22 | 8 |
| Mauritius | 0.5 | 0.5 | 44 | 42 | 0.9 | .. | .. | .. | .. | 95 | 95 | .. | 94 |
| Mexico | 60.3 | 79.5 | 73 | 76 | 1.7 | 32 | 35 | 25 | 25 | 75 | 91 | 13 | 41 |
| Moldova | 2.1 | 1.8 | 47 | 47 | −0.8 | .. | .. | .. | .. | .. | 86 | .. | 52 |
| Mongolia | 1.2 | 1.5 | 57 | 57 | 1.3 | .. | .. | 48 | 60 | .. | 75 | .. | 37 |
| Morocco | 11.7 | 18.1 | 48 | 59 | 2.7 | 16 | 16 | 23 | 18 | 87 | 88 | 27 | 52 |
| Mozambique | 2.9 | 7.4 | 21 | 35 | 5.9 | 6 | 6 | 27 | 19 | 49 | 53 | 12 | 19 |
| Myanmar | 10.0 | 15.1 | 25 | 31 | 2.6 | 7 | 9 | 29 | 28 | 48 | 88 | 16 | 72 |
| Namibia | 0.4 | 0.7 | 28 | 36 | 3.9 | .. | .. | .. | .. | 70 | 50 | 8 | 13 |
| Nepal | 1.7 | 4.5 | 9 | 16 | 6.1 | .. | .. | 23 | 19 | 48 | 62 | 7 | 30 |
| Netherlands | 10.3 | 13.2 | 69 | 81 | 1.6 | 14 | 14 | 10 | 9 | 100 | 100 | 100 | 100 |
| New Zealand | 2.9 | 3.6 | 85 | 86 | 1.3 | 25 | 28 | 30 | 32 | .. | .. | 88 | .. |
| Nicaragua | 2.2 | 3.3 | 53 | 59 | 2.5 | 18 | 21 | 33 | 36 | 64 | 56 | 24 | 34 |
| Niger | 1.2 | 2.3 | 15 | 17 | 4.1 | .. | .. | 36 | 38 | 35 | 43 | 2 | 4 |
| Nigeria | 33.1 | 70.9 | 35 | 49 | 4.8 | 11 | 13 | 14 | 16 | 51 | 53 | 33 | 36 |
| Norway | 3.1 | 3.6 | 72 | 78 | 1.0 | .. | .. | 22 | 22 | .. | .. | .. | .. |
| Oman | 1.2 | 1.8 | 65 | 72 | 2.6 | .. | .. | .. | .. | 97 | 97 | 61 | .. |
| Pakistan | 33.0 | 56.2 | 31 | 35 | 3.3 | 16 | 18 | 22 | 21 | 82 | 92 | 17 | 41 |
| Panama | 1.3 | 2.4 | 54 | 72 | 3.7 | 35 | 38 | 65 | 53 | 89 | 89 | 51 | 51 |
| Papua New Guinea | 0.5 | 0.8 | 13 | 14 | 2.7 | .. | .. | .. | .. | 67 | 67 | 41 | 41 |
| Paraguay | 2.1 | 3.6 | 49 | 59 | 3.4 | 22 | 31 | 45 | 54 | 72 | 94 | 45 | 61 |
| Peru | 15.0 | 20.1 | 69 | 73 | 1.8 | 27 | 26 | 39 | 36 | 69 | 74 | 15 | 32 |
| Philippines | 29.9 | 54.7 | 49 | 63 | 3.8 | 14 | 14 | 27 | 20 | 66 | 80 | 48 | 59 |
| Poland | 23.4 | 23.7 | 61 | 62 | 0.1 | 4 | 4 | 7 | 7 | .. | .. | .. | .. |
| Portugal | 4.7 | 6.2 | 48 | 58 | 1.6 | 37 | 39 | 54 | 45 | .. | .. | .. | .. |
| Puerto Rico | 2.6 | 3.8 | 72 | 98 | 2.6 | 44 | 67 | 60 | 68 | .. | .. | .. | .. |

| | Urban population | | | | | Population in urban agglomerations of more than 1 million | | Population in largest city | | Access to improved sanitation facilities | | | |
|---|---|---|---|---|---|---|---|---|---|---|---|---|---|
| | millions | | % of total population | | average annual % growth | % of total population | | % of urban population | | % of urban population | | % of rural population | |
| | 1990 | 2006 | 1990 | 2006 | 1990–2006 | 1990 | 2005 | 1990 | 2005 | 1990 | 2004 | 1990 | 2004 |
| Romania | 12.6 | 11.6 | 54 | 54 | −0.5 | 8 | 9 | 14 | 17 | .. | 89 | .. | .. |
| Russian Federation | 108.8 | 103.9 | 73 | 73 | −0.3 | 18 | 19 | 8 | 10 | 93 | 93 | 70 | 70 |
| Rwanda | 0.4 | 1.9 | 5 | 20 | 9.9 | .. | .. | 56 | 44 | 49 | 56 | 36 | 38 |
| Saudi Arabia | 12.5 | 19.2 | 77 | 81 | 2.7 | 30 | 36 | 19 | 22 | 100 | 100 | .. | .. |
| Senegal | 3.1 | 5.1 | 39 | 42 | 3.1 | 18 | 18 | 45 | 44 | 53 | 79 | 19 | 34 |
| Serbia[a] | 5.4 | 4.2 | 51 | 52 | .. | 11 | 14 | 22 | 26 | 97 | 97 | 77 | 77 |
| Sierra Leone | 1.2 | 2.4 | 30 | 41 | 4.1 | .. | .. | 43 | 35 | .. | 53 | .. | 30 |
| Singapore | 3.0 | 4.5 | 100 | 100 | 2.4 | 99 | 100 | 99 | 100 | 100 | 100 | .. | .. |
| Slovak Republic | 3.0 | 3.0 | 57 | 56 | 0.1 | .. | .. | .. | .. | 100 | 100 | 98 | 98 |
| Slovenia | 1.0 | 1.0 | 50 | 51 | 0.1 | .. | .. | .. | .. | .. | .. | .. | .. |
| Somalia | 2.0 | 3.0 | 30 | 36 | 2.6 | 14 | 16 | 47 | 46 | .. | 48 | .. | 14 |
| South Africa | 18.3 | 28.3 | 52 | 60 | 2.7 | 25 | 30 | 10 | 12 | 85 | 79 | 53 | 46 |
| Spain | 29.3 | 33.9 | 75 | 77 | 0.9 | 22 | 24 | 15 | 17 | 100 | 100 | 100 | 100 |
| Sri Lanka | 2.9 | 3.0 | 17 | 15 | 0.2 | .. | .. | .. | .. | 89 | 98 | 64 | 89 |
| Sudan | 6.9 | 15.7 | 27 | 42 | 5.1 | 9 | 12 | 34 | 30 | 53 | 50 | 26 | 24 |
| Swaziland | 0.2 | 0.3 | 23 | 24 | 2.8 | .. | .. | .. | .. | .. | 59 | .. | 44 |
| Sweden | 7.1 | 7.7 | 83 | 84 | 0.5 | 17 | 19 | 21 | 22 | 100 | 100 | 100 | 100 |
| Switzerland | 4.6 | 5.7 | 68 | 76 | 1.3 | 14 | 15 | 20 | 20 | 100 | 100 | 100 | 100 |
| Syrian Arab Republic | 6.2 | 9.9 | 49 | 51 | 2.9 | 26 | 25 | 25 | 26 | 97 | 99 | 50 | 81 |
| Tajikistan | 1.7 | 1.6 | 32 | 25 | −0.1 | .. | .. | .. | .. | .. | 70 | .. | 45 |
| Tanzania | 4.8 | 9.7 | 19 | 25 | 4.4 | 5 | 7 | 27 | 29 | 52 | 53 | 45 | 43 |
| Thailand | 16.0 | 20.7 | 29 | 33 | 1.6 | 11 | 10 | 37 | 32 | 95 | 98 | 74 | 99 |
| Timor-Leste | 0.2 | 0.3 | 21 | 27 | 3.6 | .. | .. | .. | .. | .. | 66 | .. | 33 |
| Togo | 1.2 | 2.6 | 30 | 41 | 4.9 | 16 | 21 | 52 | 53 | 71 | 71 | 24 | 15 |
| Trinidad and Tobago | 0.1 | 0.2 | 9 | 13 | 2.9 | .. | .. | .. | .. | 100 | 100 | 100 | 100 |
| Tunisia | 4.9 | 6.7 | 60 | 66 | 2.0 | .. | .. | .. | .. | 95 | 96 | 47 | 65 |
| Turkey | 33.2 | 49.4 | 59 | 68 | 2.5 | 22 | 26 | 20 | 20 | 96 | 96 | 70 | 72 |
| Turkmenistan | 1.7 | 2.3 | 45 | 47 | 2.0 | .. | .. | .. | .. | .. | 77 | .. | 50 |
| Uganda | 2.0 | 3.8 | 11 | 13 | 4.1 | 4 | 5 | 38 | 36 | 54 | 54 | 41 | 41 |
| Ukraine | 34.7 | 31.8 | 67 | 68 | −0.5 | 12 | 13 | 7 | 8 | 98 | 98 | .. | 93 |
| United Arab Emirates | 1.4 | 3.3 | 79 | 77 | 5.3 | 27 | 32 | 34 | 42 | 98 | 98 | 95 | 95 |
| United Kingdom | 51.1 | 54.4 | 89 | 90 | 0.4 | 26 | 26 | 15 | 16 | .. | .. | .. | .. |
| United States | 188.0 | 242.8 | 75 | 81 | 1.6 | 41 | 43 | 9 | 8 | 100 | 100 | 100 | 100 |
| Uruguay | 2.8 | 3.1 | 89 | 92 | 0.6 | 41 | 38 | 46 | 42 | 100 | 100 | 99 | 99 |
| Uzbekistan | 8.2 | 9.8 | 40 | 37 | 1.1 | 10 | 8 | 25 | 23 | 69 | 78 | 39 | 61 |
| Venezuela, RB | 16.6 | 25.3 | 84 | 94 | 2.6 | 34 | 37 | 17 | 12 | .. | 71 | .. | 48 |
| Vietnam | 13.4 | 22.6 | 20 | 27 | 3.3 | 13 | 13 | 30 | 23 | 58 | 92 | 30 | 50 |
| West Bank and Gaza | 1.3 | 2.7 | 68 | 72 | 4.4 | .. | .. | .. | .. | .. | 78 | .. | 61 |
| Yemen, Rep. | 2.6 | 6.0 | 21 | 28 | 5.3 | 5 | 9 | 25 | 31 | 82 | 86 | 19 | 28 |
| Zambia | 3.2 | 4.1 | 39 | 35 | 1.6 | 9 | 11 | 24 | 31 | 63 | 59 | 31 | 52 |
| Zimbabwe | 3.0 | 4.8 | 29 | 36 | 2.9 | 10 | 12 | 34 | 32 | 69 | 63 | 42 | 47 |
| **World** | **2,250.7 s** | **3,197.7 s** | **43 w** | **49 w** | **2.2 w** | **18 w** | **20 w** | **17 w** | **16 w** | **77 w** | **79 w** | **23 w** | **38 w** |
| **Low income** | 444.5 | 735.8 | 25 | 30 | 3.1 | 10 | 12 | 17 | 18 | 50 | 60 | 12 | 28 |
| **Middle income** | 1,146.2 | 1,679.3 | 44 | 55 | 2.4 | .. | .. | 15 | 14 | 78 | 81 | 24 | 41 |
| Lower middle income | 666.2 | 1,077.3 | 35 | 47 | 3.0 | 14 | 18 | 14 | 12 | 73 | 76 | 20 | 39 |
| Upper middle income | 480.0 | 602.1 | 69 | 75 | 1.4 | .. | .. | 17 | 17 | 87 | 89 | 53 | 60 |
| **Low & middle income** | 1,590.7 | 2,415.1 | 37 | 44 | 2.6 | 14 | 17 | 16 | 15 | 70 | 74 | 18 | 34 |
| East Asia & Pacific | 459.9 | 804.8 | 29 | 42 | 3.5 | .. | .. | 9 | 8 | 65 | 72 | 15 | 36 |
| Europe & Central Asia | 279.7 | 288.6 | 63 | 64 | 0.2 | 15 | 17 | 13 | 15 | 94 | 93 | .. | 70 |
| Latin America & Carib. | 310.3 | 432.2 | 71 | 78 | 2.1 | 32 | 34 | 24 | 22 | 81 | 86 | 35 | 49 |
| Middle East & N. Africa | 117.2 | 178.6 | 52 | 57 | 2.6 | 20 | 20 | 27 | 25 | 87 | 92 | 52 | 58 |
| South Asia | 279.1 | 431.4 | 25 | 29 | 2.7 | 10 | 12 | 10 | 11 | 50 | 63 | 6 | 27 |
| Sub-Saharan Africa | 144.5 | 279.6 | 28 | 36 | 4.1 | .. | .. | 26 | 25 | 52 | 53 | 24 | 28 |
| **High income** | 660.0 | 782.6 | 74 | 78 | 1.1 | .. | .. | 20 | 19 | 100 | 100 | .. | .. |
| Euro area | 210.2 | 232.7 | 71 | 73 | 0.6 | 18 | 18 | 15 | 15 | .. | .. | .. | .. |

a. Includes Montenegro.

# Urbanization

Urbanization **3.11** | ENVIRONMENT

## About the data

There is no consistent and universally accepted standard for distinguishing urban from rural areas, in part because of the wide variety of situations across countries. Most countries use an urban classification related to the size or characteristics of settlements. Some define urban areas based on the presence of certain infrastructure and services. And other countries designate urban areas based on administrative arrangements.

The population of a city or metropolitan area depends on the boundaries chosen. For example, in 1990 Beijing, China, contained 2.3 million people in 87 square kilometers of "inner city" and 5.4 million in 158 square kilometers of "core city." The population of "inner city and inner suburban districts" was 6.3 million and that of "inner city, inner and outer suburban districts, and inner and outer counties" was 10.8 million. (Most countries use the last definition.) For further discussion of urban-rural issues see box 3.1a in *About the data* for table 3.1.

Estimates of the world's urban population would change significantly if China, India, and a few other populous nations were to change their definition of urban centers. According to China's State Statistical Bureau, by the end of 1996 urban residents accounted for about 43 percent of China's population, more than double the 20 percent considered urban in 1994. In addition to the continuous migration of people from rural to urban areas, one of the main reasons for this shift was the rapid growth in the hundreds of towns reclassified as cities in recent years. Because the estimates in the table are based on national definitions of what constitutes a city or metropolitan area, cross-country comparisons should be made with caution. To estimate urban populations, UN ratios of urban to total population were applied to the World Bank's estimates of total population (see table 2.1).

The table shows access to improved sanitation facilities for both urban and rural populations to allow comparison of access. Definitions of access and urban areas vary, however, so comparisons between countries can be misleading.

## Definitions

• **Urban population** is the midyear population of areas defined as urban in each country and reported to the United Nations (see *About the data*). • **Population in urban agglomerations of more than 1 million** is the percentage of a country's population living in metropolitan areas that in 2005 had a population of more than 1 million. • **Population in largest city** is the percentage of a country's urban population living in that country's largest metropolitan area. • **Access to improved sanitation facilities** is the percentage of the urban or rural population with access to at least adequate excreta disposal facilities (private or shared but not public) that can effectively prevent human, animal, and insect contact with excreta. Improved facilities range from simple but protected pit latrines to flush toilets with a sewerage connection. To be effective, facilities must be correctly constructed and properly maintained.

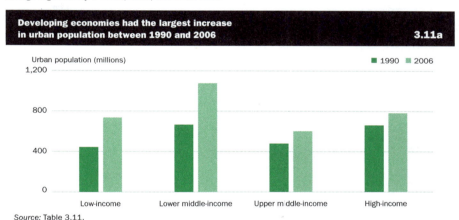

**Developing economies had the largest increase in urban population between 1990 and 2006**  3.11a

Source: Table 3.11.

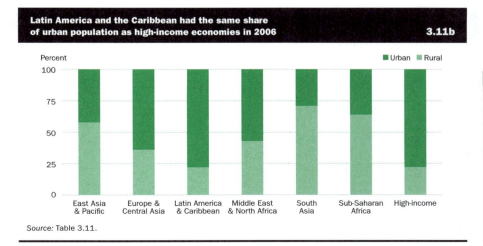

**Latin America and the Caribbean had the same share of urban population as high-income economies in 2006**  3.11b

Source: Table 3.11.

### Data sources

Data on urban population and the population in urban agglomerations and in the largest city are from the United Nations Population Division's *World Urbanization Prospects: The 2005 Revision*. Data on total population are World Bank estimates. Data on access to sanitation are from the World Health Organization and United Nations Children's Fund's *Meeting the MDG Drinking Water and Sanitation Target*.

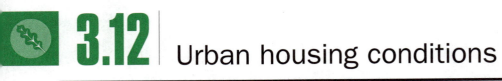

# 3.12 Urban housing conditions

| | Census year | Household size (number of people) | | Overcrowding (Households living in overcrowded dwellings[a] % of total) | | Durable dwelling units (Buildings with durable structure % of total) | | Home ownership (Privately owned dwellings % of total) | | Multiunit dwellings (% of total) | | Vacancy rate (Unoccupied dwellings % of total) | |
|---|---|---|---|---|---|---|---|---|---|---|---|---|---|
| | | National | Urban | National | Urban | National | Urban | National | Urban | National | Urban | National | Urban |
| Afghanistan | | .. | .. | .. | .. | .. | .. | .. | .. | .. | .. | .. | .. |
| Albania | 2001 | 4.2 | 3.9 | .. | .. | .. | .. | 65[b] | 30[b] | .. | .. | 12 | 13 |
| Algeria | 1998 | 4.9 | .. | .. | .. | .. | .. | 67 | .. | .. | .. | 19 | .. |
| Angola | | .. | .. | .. | .. | .. | .. | .. | .. | .. | .. | .. | .. |
| Argentina | 2001 | 3.6 | .. | 19 | .. | 97 | .. | .. | .. | 4 | .. | 16[b] | .. |
| Armenia | 2001 | 4.1 | 4.0 | 4 | 6 | 93 | 93 | 95 | 90 | 1 | 1 | .. | .. |
| Australia | 2001 | 3.8 | .. | 1 | .. | .. | .. | .. | .. | .. | .. | .. | .. |
| Austria | 1991 | 2.6 | .. | 2 | .. | .. | .. | .. | .. | 50 | .. | 13 | .. |
| Azerbaijan | 1999 | 4.7 | 4.4 | .. | .. | .. | .. | 74 | 62 | 4 | 5 | .. | .. |
| Bangladesh | 2001 | 4.8 | 4.8 | .. | .. | 21[b] | 42[b] | 88[b] | 61[b] | .. | .. | .. | .. |
| Belarus | 1999 | .. | .. | .. | .. | .. | .. | .. | .. | .. | .. | .. | .. |
| Belgium | 2001 | 2.6 | .. | 0[b] | .. | .. | .. | 67 | .. | 32[b] | .. | .. | .. |
| Benin | 1992 | 5.9 | .. | .. | .. | 26 | .. | 59 | .. | .. | .. | .. | .. |
| Bolivia | 2001 | 4.2 | 4.3 | 40 | .. | 43 | 58 | 70 | 59 | 3[b] | 5[b] | 6 | 4 |
| Bosnia and Herzegovina | | .. | .. | .. | .. | .. | .. | .. | .. | .. | .. | .. | .. |
| Botswana | 2001 | 4.2 | 3.9 | 27 | 47 | 88 | 90[b] | 61 | 47 | 1 | .. | .. | .. |
| Brazil | 2000 | 3.8 | 3.7 | .. | .. | .. | .. | 74 | 75 | .. | .. | .. | .. |
| Bulgaria | 2001 | 2.7 | 2.7 | .. | .. | 79 | 89 | 98 | 98 | .. | .. | 23 | 17 |
| Burkina Faso | 1996 | 6.2 | 5.8 | 30 | 53 | .. | .. | .. | .. | .. | .. | .. | .. |
| Burundi | 1990 | 4.7 | .. | .. | .. | .. | .. | .. | .. | .. | .. | .. | .. |
| Cambodia | 1998 | 5.2 | .. | .. | .. | .. | .. | .. | .. | .. | .. | .. | .. |
| Cameroon | 1987 | 5.2 | 5.1 | 67 | 77 | 77 | .. | 73 | 48 | 27 | 42 | .. | .. |
| Canada | 2001 | 2.6 | .. | .. | .. | .. | .. | 64 | .. | 32 | .. | 8 | .. |
| Central African Republic | 2003 | 5.2 | 5.8 | 32 | 36[b] | 78 | 92 | 85 | 74 | .. | .. | .. | .. |
| Chad | 1993 | 5.1 | 5.1 | .. | .. | .. | .. | .. | .. | .. | .. | .. | .. |
| Chile | 2002 | 3.4 | 3.5 | .. | .. | 91 | 92 | 66 | 65 | 13 | 15 | 11 | 10 |
| China | 2000 | 3.4 | 3.2 | .. | .. | 82 | .. | 88 | 74 | .. | .. | 1 | .. |
| Hong Kong, China | | .. | .. | .. | .. | .. | .. | .. | .. | .. | .. | .. | .. |
| Colombia | 1993 | 4.8 | .. | 27[b] | .. | 83[b] | .. | 68[b] | .. | 13 | .. | 10[b] | .. |
| Congo Dem Rep | 1984 | 5.4 | .. | 55 | .. | .. | .. | .. | .. | .. | .. | .. | .. |
| Congo Rep | 1984 | 10.5 | .. | .. | .. | .. | .. | 76 | .. | .. | .. | .. | .. |
| Costa Rica | 2000 | 4.0 | .. | 22 | .. | 88 | .. | 72 | .. | 2 | 3 | 9 | 6 |
| Côte d'Ivoire | 1998 | 5.4 | .. | .. | .. | .. | .. | .. | .. | .. | .. | .. | .. |
| Croatia | 2001 | 3.0 | .. | .. | .. | .. | .. | .. | .. | .. | .. | 12 | .. |
| Cuba | 1981 | 4.2 | 4.2 | .. | .. | .. | .. | .. | .. | 15 | 21 | 0 | 0 |
| Czech Republic | 2001 | 2.4 | .. | .. | .. | .. | .. | 52 | .. | 49 | .. | 12 | .. |
| Denmark | 2001 | 2.2 | .. | .. | .. | .. | .. | .. | .. | .. | .. | .. | .. |
| Dominican Republic | 2002 | 3.9 | .. | .. | .. | 97 | .. | .. | .. | 8 | .. | 11 | .. |
| Ecuador | 2001 | 3.5 | 3.7 | 30 | .. | 81 | 88 | 68[b] | 58[b] | 9 | 14 | 12 | 7 |
| Egypt | 1996 | 4.7 | .. | .. | .. | .. | .. | .. | .. | 75 | .. | .. | .. |
| El Salvador | 1992 | .. | .. | 63 | .. | 67 | 83 | 70 | 68 | 3 | 6 | 11 | 11 |
| Eritrea | | .. | .. | .. | .. | .. | .. | .. | .. | .. | .. | .. | .. |
| Estonia | 2000 | 2.4 | 2.3 | 3 | .. | .. | .. | .. | .. | 72 | .. | 13 | .. |
| Ethiopia | 1994 | 4.8 | 4.7 | .. | .. | .. | 23 | .. | 54 | .. | .. | .. | .. |
| Finland | 2000 | 2.2 | .. | .. | .. | .. | .. | 64 | .. | 44 | .. | .. | .. |
| France | 1999 | 2.5 | .. | .. | .. | .. | .. | 55 | .. | .. | .. | 7 | .. |
| Gabon | 2003 | 5.2 | .. | .. | .. | .. | .. | .. | .. | .. | .. | .. | .. |
| Gambia | 1993 | 8.9 | .. | .. | .. | 18 | .. | 68 | .. | .. | .. | .. | .. |
| Georgia | 2002 | 3.5 | 3.5 | .. | .. | .. | .. | .. | .. | .. | .. | .. | .. |
| Germany | 2001 | 2.3 | .. | .. | .. | .. | .. | 43 | .. | .. | .. | 7 | .. |
| Ghana | 2000 | 5.1 | 5.1 | .. | .. | 45 | .. | 57 | .. | 53 | .. | 5 | .. |
| Greece | 2001 | 3.0 | .. | 1 | .. | .. | .. | .. | .. | .. | .. | .. | .. |
| Guatemala | 2002 | 4.4 | 4.7 | .. | .. | 67 | 80 | 81 | 74 | 2 | 4 | 13 | 11 |
| Guinea | | .. | .. | .. | .. | .. | .. | .. | .. | .. | .. | .. | .. |
| Guinea-Bissau | | .. | .. | .. | .. | .. | .. | .. | .. | .. | .. | .. | .. |
| Haiti | 1982 | 4.2 | .. | 26 | .. | .. | .. | 92 | 68 | .. | .. | 9 | 19 |

| | Census year | Household size | | Overcrowding | | Durable dwelling units | | Home ownership | | Multiunit dwellings | | Vacancy rate | |
|---|---|---|---|---|---|---|---|---|---|---|---|---|---|
| | | number of people | | Households living in overcrowded dwellings[a] % of total | | Buildings with durable structure % of total | | Privately owned dwellings % of total | | % of total | | Unoccupied dwellings % of total | |
| | | National | Urban | National | Urban | National | Urban | National | Urban | National | Urban | National | Urban |
| Honduras | 2001 | 4.4 | .. | .. | .. | 69 | 85 | .. | .. | .. | .. | 14 | .. |
| Hungary | 1990 | 2.7 | .. | .. | .. | .. | .. | .. | .. | .. | .. | 4 | .. |
| India | 2001 | 5.3 | 5.3 | 77 | 71 | 83 | 81 | 87 | 67 | .. | .. | 6 | 9 |
| Indonesia | 2000 | 4.0 | .. | .. | .. | .. | .. | .. | .. | .. | .. | .. | .. |
| Iran, Islamic Rep. | 1996 | 4.8 | 4.6 | 33[b] | 26[b] | 72 | 76 | 73 | 67 | .. | .. | .. | .. |
| Iraq | 1997 | 7.7 | 7.2 | .. | .. | 88 | 96 | 70 | 66 | 4 | 5 | 13 | 15 |
| Ireland | 2002 | 3.0 | .. | .. | .. | .. | .. | .. | .. | 8[b] | .. | .. | .. |
| Israel | 1995 | 3.5 | .. | .. | .. | .. | .. | .. | .. | .. | .. | .. | .. |
| Italy | 2001 | 2.8 | .. | .. | .. | .. | .. | .. | .. | .. | .. | 21 | .. |
| Jamaica | 2001 | 3.5 | .. | .. | .. | 98[b] | .. | 58[b] | .. | 2[b] | .. | .. | .. |
| Japan | 2000 | 2.7 | .. | .. | .. | .. | .. | 61 | .. | 37 | .. | .. | .. |
| Jordan | 1994 | 6.2 | 6.0 | 1 | .. | 97 | 97 | 69 | 64 | 57 | 67 | .. | .. |
| Kazakhstan | | .. | .. | .. | .. | .. | .. | .. | .. | .. | .. | .. | .. |
| Kenya | 1999 | 4.6 | 3.4 | .. | .. | 35 | 72 | 72 | 25 | .. | .. | 39 | 17 |
| Korea, Dem Rep | 2000 | 3.8 | .. | 23 | .. | .. | .. | 50 | .. | 15 | .. | .. | .. |
| Korea, Rep. | 1993 | 4.4 | .. | .. | .. | .. | .. | .. | .. | .. | .. | .. | .. |
| Kuwait | 1995 | 6.4 | .. | .. | .. | .. | .. | .. | .. | 9[b] | .. | 11 | .. |
| Kyrgyz Republic | 1999 | 4.4 | 3.6 | .. | .. | .. | .. | .. | .. | .. | .. | .. | .. |
| Laos | 1995 | 6.1 | 6.1 | .. | .. | 49 | 77 | 96 | 86 | .. | .. | .. | .. |
| Latvia | 2000 | 3.0 | 2.6 | 4 | .. | 88 | .. | 58 | .. | 74 | .. | 0 | .. |
| Lebanon | | .. | .. | .. | .. | .. | .. | .. | .. | .. | .. | .. | .. |
| Lesotho | 2001 | 5.0 | .. | 10[b] | .. | .. | .. | 84 | .. | 0 | .. | .. | .. |
| Liberia | 1974 | 4.8 | .. | 31 | .. | 20 | .. | 1 | .. | .. | .. | .. | .. |
| Libya | | 6.4 | .. | .. | .. | .. | .. | .. | .. | .. | .. | 7 | .. |
| Lithuania | 2001 | 2.6 | .. | 7 | .. | .. | .. | .. | .. | .. | .. | .. | .. |
| Macedonia, FYR | 2002 | 3.6 | 3.6[b] | 8[b] | .. | 95[b] | 95[b] | 48[b] | .. | .. | .. | 7[b] | 3[b] |
| Madagascar | 1993 | 4.9 | 4.8 | 64 | 57 | .. | .. | 81 | 59 | .. | .. | .. | .. |
| Malawi | 1998 | 4.4 | 4.4 | 30 | .. | 48 | 84 | 86 | 47 | .. | .. | .. | .. |
| Malaysia | 2000 | 4.5 | 4.4 | .. | .. | .. | .. | .. | .. | 10[b] | 16[b] | .. | .. |
| Mali | 1998 | 5.6 | .. | .. | .. | .. | .. | .. | .. | .. | .. | .. | .. |
| Mauritania | 1988 | .. | .. | .. | .. | .. | .. | .. | .. | .. | .. | .. | .. |
| Mauritius | 2000 | 3.9 | 3.8 | 6 | 7 | 91 | 94 | 87 | 81 | .. | .. | 7 | 6 |
| Mexico | 2000 | 4.4 | .. | 27[b] | .. | 87 | .. | 78 | .. | 6 | .. | .. | .. |
| Moldova | 2003 | .. | .. | .. | .. | .. | .. | .. | .. | .. | .. | .. | .. |
| Mongolia | 2000 | 4.4 | 4.5 | .. | .. | .. | .. | .. | .. | 48 | 56 | .. | .. |
| Morocco | 1982 | 5.9 | 5.3 | .. | .. | .. | .. | .. | .. | .. | .. | .. | .. |
| Mozambique | 1997 | 4.4 | 4.9 | 37 | 28 | 7 | 20 | 92 | 83 | 1 | 1 | 0 | .. |
| Myanmar | | .. | .. | .. | .. | .. | .. | .. | .. | .. | .. | .. | .. |
| Namibia | 2001 | 5.3 | .. | .. | .. | .. | .. | .. | .. | .. | .. | .. | .. |
| Nepal | 2001 | 5.4 | 4.9 | .. | .. | .. | .. | 88 | .. | .. | .. | 0 | .. |
| Netherlands | | .. | .. | .. | .. | .. | .. | .. | .. | .. | .. | .. | .. |
| New Zealand | 2001 | 2.8 | .. | 1[b] | .. | .. | .. | 65 | .. | 17 | .. | 10 | .. |
| Nicaragua | 1995 | 5.3 | .. | .. | .. | 79 | 87 | 84 | 86 | 0 | 0 | 8 | .. |
| Niger | 2001 | 6.4 | 6.0 | .. | .. | .. | .. | 77 | 40 | .. | .. | .. | .. |
| Nigeria | 1991 | 5.0 | 4.7 | .. | .. | .. | .. | .. | .. | .. | .. | .. | .. |
| Norway | 1980 | 2.7 | .. | 1 | .. | .. | .. | 67 | .. | 38 | .. | .. | .. |
| Oman | 2003 | 7.1 | .. | .. | .. | .. | .. | .. | .. | .. | .. | .. | .. |
| Pakistan | 1998 | 6.8 | 6.8 | .. | .. | 58 | 86 | 81 | .. | .. | .. | .. | .. |
| Panama | 2000 | 4.1 | .. | 28[b] | .. | 88 | 98[b] | 80 | 66[b] | 10[b] | 10[b] | 14 | .. |
| Papua New Guinea | 1990 | 4.5[b] | 6.5 | .. | .. | .. | .. | .. | 44 | .. | 8 | .. | .. |
| Paraguay | 2002 | 4.6 | 4.5 | 38[b] | ..[b] | 95[b] | 98[b] | 79 | 75 | 1[b] | 2[b] | 6[b] | 6[b] |
| Peru | 1993 | .. | .. | .. | .. | 49 | 64 | .. | .. | .. | .. | 7 | 3 |
| Philippines | 1990 | 5.3 | 5.3 | .. | .. | 62 | .. | 83 | 76 | 6 | 11 | 4 | 4 |
| Poland | 1988 | 3.2 | .. | .. | .. | .. | .. | .. | .. | .. | .. | 1 | .. |
| Portugal | 2001 | 2.8 | .. | .. | .. | .. | .. | 76 | .. | 86 | .. | .. | .. |
| Puerto Rico | 1990 | 3.3 | .. | .. | .. | .. | .. | 72 | .. | .. | .. | 11 | .. |

| | Census year | Household size number of people | | Overcrowding Households living in overcrowded dwellings[a] % of total | | Durable dwelling units Buildings with durable structure % of total | | Home ownership Privately owned dwellings % of total | | Multiunit dwellings % of total | | Vacancy rate Unoccupied dwellings % of total | |
|---|---|---|---|---|---|---|---|---|---|---|---|---|---|
| | | National | Urban | National | Urban | National | Urban | National | Urban | National | Urban | National | Urban |
| Romania | 1992 | 3.1 | 3.1 | .. | .. | 58 | .. | 87 | 77 | 39 | 71 | 6 | 4 |
| Russia | 2002 | 2.8 | 2.7 | 7 | 5 | .. | .. | .. | .. | 73 | 86 | .. | .. |
| Rwanda | 1991 | 4.7 | .. | .. | .. | 79 | 78 | 92 | 73 | 19 | 25 | .. | .. |
| Saudi Arabia | 2004 | 5.5 | .. | .. | .. | 92[b] | .. | 43 | .. | .. | .. | .. | .. |
| Senegal | | .. | .. | .. | .. | .. | .. | .. | .. | .. | .. | .. | .. |
| Serbia | 2001 | 2.9 | 2.2 | .. | .. | .. | .. | .. | .. | .. | .. | .. | .. |
| Sierra Leone | 1985 | 6.8 | .. | .. | .. | 34 | .. | 68 | .. | .. | .. | .. | .. |
| Singapore | 2000 | 4.4 | .. | .. | .. | .. | .. | .. | .. | .. | .. | .. | .. |
| Slovak Republic | | .. | .. | .. | .. | .. | .. | .. | .. | .. | .. | .. | .. |
| Slovenia | 1991 | 3.1 | .. | .. | .. | .. | .. | 69 | .. | 37 | .. | 9 | .. |
| Somalia | 1975 | .. | .. | .. | .. | .. | .. | .. | .. | .. | .. | .. | .. |
| South Africa | 2001 | 4.0 | .. | .. | .. | .. | .. | .. | .. | 7 | .. | .. | .. |
| Spain | 1991 | 3.3 | .. | 0 | .. | .. | .. | 78 | .. | .. | .. | .. | .. |
| Sri Lanka | 2001 | 3.8 | .. | .. | .. | 93[b] | 92[b] | 70[b] | 58[b] | 1 | 14[b] | 13 | 1[b] |
| Sudan | 1993 | 5.8 | 6.0 | .. | .. | .. | .. | 86[b] | 58[b] | 0[b] | 1[b] | .. | .. |
| Swaziland | 1997 | 5.4 | 3.7 | .. | .. | .. | .. | .. | .. | .. | .. | .. | .. |
| Sweden | 1990 | 2.0 | .. | .. | .. | .. | .. | .. | .. | 54 | .. | 1 | .. |
| Switzerland | 1990 | 2.4 | 2.1 | .. | .. | .. | .. | 31 | 24 | 28 | 32 | 11 | 7 |
| Syrian Arab Republic | 1981 | 6.3 | 6.0 | .. | .. | .. | .. | .. | .. | .. | .. | .. | .. |
| Tajikistan | 2000 | .. | .. | .. | .. | .. | .. | .. | .. | .. | .. | .. | .. |
| Tanzania | 2002 | 4.9 | 4.5[b] | 33[b] | 7[b] | .. | .. | 82[b] | 43[b] | .. | .. | .. | .. |
| Thailand | 2000 | 3.8 | .. | .. | .. | 93 | 93 | 81 | 62 | 3 | .. | 3 | .. |
| Timor-Leste | | .. | .. | .. | .. | .. | .. | .. | .. | .. | .. | .. | .. |
| Togo | | .. | .. | .. | .. | .. | .. | .. | .. | .. | .. | .. | .. |
| Trinidad and Tobago | 2000 | 3.7 | .. | 9[b] | .. | 98[b] | .. | 74[b] | .. | 17[b] | .. | .. | .. |
| Tunisia | 1994 | 8.0 | .. | .. | .. | 99 | .. | 71 | 89[b] | 6 | 10[b] | 15 | 12[b] |
| Turkey | 1990 | 5.0 | .. | .. | .. | .. | .. | 70 | .. | .. | .. | .. | .. |
| Turkmenistan | | .. | .. | .. | .. | .. | .. | .. | .. | .. | .. | .. | .. |
| Uganda | 1991 | 4.9 | 4.0[b] | .. | .. | 21[b] | .. | 80[b] | 24[b] | 0[b] | 2[b] | .. | .. |
| Ukraine | 2003 | .. | .. | .. | .. | .. | .. | .. | .. | .. | .. | .. | .. |
| United Arab Emirates | | .. | .. | .. | .. | .. | .. | .. | .. | .. | .. | .. | .. |
| United Kingdom | 2001 | .. | 2.4 | .. | .. | .. | .. | .. | 69 | .. | 19 | .. | .. |
| United States | 2000 | 2.7 | .. | .. | .. | .. | .. | 66 | .. | .. | .. | 9 | 7 |
| Uruguay | 1996 | 3.3 | 3.4[b] | 22[b] | .. | .. | .. | 57[b] | 57[b] | .. | .. | 13[b] | 13[b] |
| Uzbekistan | | .. | .. | .. | .. | .. | .. | .. | .. | .. | .. | .. | .. |
| Venezuela. RB | 2001 | 4.4 | .. | .. | .. | .. | .. | 78 | .. | 14 | .. | 16 | .. |
| Vietnam | 1999 | 4.6 | 4.5 | .. | .. | 77 | 89 | 95 | 86 | .. | .. | .. | .. |
| West Bank and Gaza | 1997 | 7.1 | .. | .. | .. | .. | .. | 78 | .. | 45 | .. | .. | .. |
| Yemen | 1994 | 6.7 | 6.8 | 54[b] | 6[b] | .. | .. | 88[b] | 68[b] | 3[b] | 11[b] | .. | .. |
| Zambia | 2000 | 5.3 | 5.9 | .. | .. | .. | .. | 94 | 30 | .. | .. | .. | .. |
| Zimbabwe | 1992 | 4.8 | 4.2 | .. | .. | .. | .. | 94 | 30 | 6 | .. | .. | .. |

a. More than two people per room. b. Data are from a previous census.

## About the data

Urbanization can yield important social benefits, improving access to public services and the job market. It also leads to significant demands for services. Inadequate living quarters and demand for housing and shelter are major concerns for policymakers.

The unmet demand for affordable housing, along with urban poverty, has led to the emergence of slums in many poor countries. Improving the shelter situation requires a better understanding of the mechanisms governing housing markets and the processes governing housing availability. That requires good data and adequate policy-oriented analysis so that housing policy can be formulated in a global comparative perspective and drawn from lessons learned in other countries. Housing policies and outcomes affect such broad socioeconomic conditions as the infant mortality rate, performance in school, household saving, productivity levels, capital formation, and government budget deficits. A good understanding of housing conditions thus requires an extensive set of indicators within a reasonable framework.

There is a strong demand for quantitative indicators that can measure housing conditions on a regular basis to monitor progress. However, data deficiencies and lack of rigorous quantitative analysis hamper informed decisionmaking on desirable policies to improve housing conditions. The data in the table are from housing and population censuses, collected using similar definitions. The table will incorporate household survey data in future editions. The table focuses attention on urban areas, where housing conditions are typically most severe. Not all the compiled indicators are presented in the table because of space limitations.

## Definitions

• **Census year** is the year in which the underlying data were collected. • **Household size** is the average number of people within a household, calculated by dividing total population by the number of households in the country and in urban areas. • **Overcrowding** refers to the number of households living in dwellings with two or more people per room as a percentage of total households in the country and in urban areas. • **Durable dwelling units** are the number of housing units in structures made of durable building materials (concrete, stone, cement, brick, asbestos, zinc, and stucco) expected to maintain their stability for 20 years or longer under local conditions with normal maintenance and repair, taking into account location and environmental hazards such as floods, mudslides, and earthquakes, as a percentage of total dwellings. • **Home ownership** refers to the number of privately owned dwellings as a percentage of total dwellings. When the number of private dwellings is not available from the census data, the share of households that own their housing unit is used. Privately owned and owner-occupied units are included, depending on the definition used in the census data. State- and community-owned units and rented, squatted, and rent-free units are excluded. • **Multiunit dwellings** are the number of multiunit dwellings, such as apartments, flats, condominiums, barracks, boardinghouses, orphanages, retirement houses, hostels, hotels, and collective dwellings, as a percentage of total dwellings. • **Vacancy rate** is the percentage of completed dwelling units that are currently unoccupied. It includes all vacant units, whether on the market or not (such as second homes).

### Selected housing indicators for smaller economies — 3.12a

| | Census year | Household size | Overcrowding | Durable dwelling units | Home ownership | Multiunit dwellings | Vacancy rate |
|---|---|---|---|---|---|---|---|
| | | number of people | Households living in overcrowded dwellings[a] % of total | Buildings with durable structure % of total | Privately owned dwellings % of total | % of total | Unoccupied dwellings % of total |
| Antigua and Barbuda | 2001 | 3.0 | .. | 99[b] | 65[b] | 3[b] | 22 |
| Bahamas | 1990 | 3.8 | 12 | 99 | 55 | 13 | 14 |
| Bahrain | 2001 | 5.9 | .. | 94[b] | 51 | 28 | 6 |
| Barbados | 1990 | 3.5 | 3 | 100 | 76 | 9 | 9 |
| Belize | 2000 | 4.6 | .. | 93 | 63 | 4 | .. |
| Cape Verde | 1990 | 5.1 | 28 | 78 | 72 | 2 | .. |
| Cayman Islands | 1999 | 3.1 | .. | 100 | 53 | 38 | 19 |
| Equatorial Guinea | 1993 | 7.5 | 14 | 56[b] | 75 | 14 | .. |
| Fiji | 1996 | 5.4 | .. | 60 | 65 | 7 | .. |
| Guam | 2000 | 4.0 | 2[b] | 93 | 48 | 29 | 19 |
| Isle of Man | 2001 | 2.4 | 0 | .. | 68 | 16 | .. |
| Maldives | 2000 | 6.6 | .. | 93 | .. | 1 | 15 |
| Marshall Islands | 1999 | 7.8 | .. | 95 | 72 | 12 | 8 |
| Netherlands Antilles | 2001 | 2.9 | 24[b] | 99 | 60 | 16 | 12 |
| New Caledonia | 1989 | 4.1 | .. | 77 | 53 | 9 | 13 |
| Northern Mariana Islands | 1995 | 4.9 | 9[b] | 99 | 33 | 27 | 17 |
| Palau | 2000 | 5.7 | 8 | 76 | 79 | 11 | 3 |
| Seychelles | 1997 | 4.2 | 15[b] | 97 | 78 | .. | 0 |
| Solomon Islands | 1999 | 6.3 | 51 | 23 | 85 | 1 | .. |
| St. Vincent & Grenadines | 1991 | 3.9 | .. | 98 | 71 | 7 | .. |
| Turks and Caicos | 1990 | 3.3 | 4 | 96 | 66 | 11 | .. |
| Virgin Islands (UK) | 1991 | 3.0 | 2 | 99 | 40 | 46 | .. |
| Western Samoa | 1991 | 7.3 | .. | 42 | 90 | 47 | 30 |

a. More than two people per room. b. Data are from a previous census.
*Source:* National population and housing censuses.

## Data sources

Data on urban housing conditions are from national population and housing censuses.

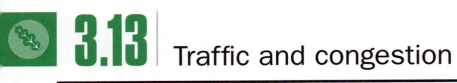

# 3.13 Traffic and congestion

| | Motor vehicles | | | | Passenger cars | | Road density | Fuel prices | | Particulate matter concentration | |
|---|---|---|---|---|---|---|---|---|---|---|---|
| | per 1,000 people | | per kilometer of road | | per 1,000 people | | km. of road per 100 sq. km. of land area | \$ per liter | | Urban-population-weighted PM10 micrograms per cubic meter | |
| | | | | | | | | Gasoline | Diesel | | |
| | 1990 | 2005 | 1990 | 2005 | 1990 | 2005 | 2005 | 2006 | 2006 | 1990 | 2005 |
| Afghanistan | .. | .. | 3 | 9 | .. | .. | 5 | 0.68 | 0.65 | 79 | 44 |
| Albania | 11 | 85 | 3 | 15 | 2 | 61 | 66 | 1.44 | 1.29 | 92 | 50 |
| Algeria | 55 | 91 | 15 | 27 | 26 | 58 | 5 | 0.32 | 0.19 | 115 | 71 |
| Angola | 19 | .. | 3 | .. | .. | 8 | 4 | 0.50 | 0.36 | 142 | 80 |
| Argentina | 181 | .. | 27 | .. | 134 | 146 | 8 | 0.62 | 0.48 | 105 | 76 |
| Armenia | 5 | .. | 2 | .. | 1 | 1 | 27 | 0.96 | 0.77 | 456 | 68 |
| Australia | 530 | 671 | 11 | 17 | 450 | 542 | 11 | 0.93 | 0.94 | 22 | 15 |
| Austria | 421 | 599 | 30 | 36 | 387 | 503 | 162 | 1.32 | 1.26 | 38 | 34 |
| Azerbaijan | 52 | 61 | 7 | 10 | 36 | 57 | 72 | 0.46 | 0.41 | 169 | 59 |
| Bangladesh | 1 | 1 | 0 | 1 | 0 | 0 | 184 | 0.79 | 0.45 | 231 | 140 |
| Belarus | 61 | .. | 13 | 21 | 59 | 181 | 46 | 0.79 | 0.55 | 23 | 7 |
| Belgium | 423 | 529 | 30 | 37 | 385 | 468 | 498 | 1.63 | 1.34 | 31 | 23 |
| Benin | 3 | .. | 2 | .. | 2 | 13 | 17 | 0.81 | 0.81 | 75 | 41 |
| Bolivia | 41 | 49 | 6 | 7 | .. | 15 | 6 | 0.54 | 0.47 | 120 | 97 |
| Bosnia and Herzegovina | 114 | .. | 24 | .. | 101 | .. | 43 | 1.34 | 1.24 | 36 | 19 |
| Botswana | 18 | 113 | 3 | 8 | 10 | 47 | 4 | 0.78 | 0.74 | 95 | 68 |
| Brazil | 88 | 170 | 8 | 18 | 84 | 136 | 21 | 1.26 | 0.84 | 40 | 26 |
| Bulgaria | 163 | 360 | 39 | 63 | 146 | 314 | 40 | 1.05 | 1.08 | 111 | 60 |
| Burkina Faso | 4 | 7 | 3 | 7 | 2 | 5 | 34 | 1.15 | 1.12 | 149 | 94 |
| Burundi | .. | .. | 3 | .. | .. | 1 | 48 | 1.20 | 1.22 | 56 | 30 |
| Cambodia | .. | 36 | 0 | 37 | .. | 25 | 22 | 1.01 | 0.78 | 116 | 62 |
| Cameroon | 10 | 11 | 3 | 3 | 6 | 11 | 11 | 1.14 | 1.07 | 116 | 65 |
| Canada | .. | 582 | 20 | 13 | 468 | 561 | 15 | 0.84 | 0.78 | 25 | 19 |
| Central African Republic | 1 | .. | 0 | .. | 1 | 1 | 4 | 1.37 | 1.27 | 61 | 49 |
| Chad | 2 | .. | 0 | .. | 1 | .. | 3 | 1.31 | 1.20 | 215 | 123 |
| Chile | 81 | 135 | 13 | 26 | 52 | 88 | 11 | 1.09 | 0.86 | 88 | 53 |
| China | 5 | 24 | 4 | 16 | 1 | 15 | 21 | 0.69 | 0.61 | 114 | 75 |
| Hong Kong, China | 66 | 72 | 253 | 254 | 42 | 53 | 188 | 1.69 | 1.06 | .. | .. |
| Colombia | 39 | 59 | 13 | 16 | 21 | 35 | 15 | 0.98 | 0.57 | 39 | 23 |
| Congo, Dem. Rep. | .. | .. | 9 | .. | 17 | .. | 7 | 0.94 | 1.00 | 73 | 50 |
| Congo, Rep. | 18 | .. | 3 | .. | .. | 8 | 5 | 0.96 | 0.67 | 132 | 91 |
| Costa Rica | 87 | 198 | 7 | 24 | 55 | 146 | 69 | 0.98 | 0.67 | 45 | 37 |
| Côte d'Ivoire | 24 | .. | 6 | .. | .. | 7 | 25 | 1.20 | 1.06 | 94 | 48 |
| Croatia | .. | 349 | 34 | 55 | 185 | 312 | 51 | 1.34 | 1.22 | 50 | 31 |
| Cuba | 37 | .. | 16 | .. | 18 | .. | 55 | 1.10 | 0.91 | 44 | 17 |
| Czech Republic | 246 | 394 | 46 | 31 | 228 | 363 | 165 | 1.30 | 1.29 | 68 | 22 |
| Denmark | 368 | 437 | 27 | 33 | 320 | 354 | 170 | 1.58 | 1.45 | 30 | 19 |
| Dominican Republic | 75 | 115 | 48 | .. | 21 | 78 | 26 | 1.03 | 0.75 | 44 | 23 |
| Ecuador | 35 | 55 | 8 | 17 | 31 | 32 | 16 | 0.47 | 0.39 | 38 | 26 |
| Egypt, Arab Rep. | 29 | .. | 33 | .. | 21 | 27 | 9 | 0.30 | 0.12 | 222 | 128 |
| El Salvador | 33 | .. | 14 | .. | 17 | 24 | 48 | 0.82 | 0.80 | 46 | 35 |
| Eritrea | 1 | .. | 1 | .. | 1 | .. | 4 | 1.90 | 0.81 | 121 | 61 |
| Estonia | 211 | 477 | 22 | 11 | 154 | 367 | 135 | 1.23 | 1.22 | 45 | 14 |
| Ethiopia | 1 | 2 | 2 | 4 | 1 | 1 | 4 | 0.93 | 0.62 | 112 | 74 |
| Finland | 441 | 531 | 29 | 35 | 386 | 460 | 26 | 1.55 | 1.26 | 24 | 18 |
| France | 494 | 596 | 32 | 38 | 405 | 494 | 173 | 1.48 | 1.33 | 18 | 14 |
| Gabon | 32 | .. | 4 | .. | 19 | .. | 4 | 0.64 | 0.39 | 10 | 7 |
| Gambia, The | .. | 7 | .. | 3 | .. | 5 | 37 | 1.08 | 1.01 | 142 | 95 |
| Georgia | .. | 71 | .. | 16 | .. | 56 | 29 | 0.86 | 0.89 | 208 | 51 |
| Germany | 405 | 585 | 53 | 208 | 386 | 550 | .. | 1.55 | 1.38 | 27 | 19 |
| Ghana | 8 | 21 | 4 | 9 | 5 | 5 | 25 | 0.86 | 0.84 | 39 | 34 |
| Greece | 248 | 497 | 22 | 47 | 171 | 388 | 91 | 1.16 | 1.19 | 64 | 36 |
| Guatemala | 21 | 68 | 16 | 53 | 11 | 53 | 13 | 0.78 | 0.64 | 63 | 62 |
| Guinea | 4 | 14 | 1 | 4 | 2 | 8 | 18 | 0.79 | 0.82 | 107 | 77 |
| Guinea-Bissau | .. | .. | .. | .. | .. | .. | 12 | 0.00 | 0.00 | 118 | 80 |
| Haiti | 8 | .. | 14 | .. | 5 | .. | 15 | 0.88 | 0.60 | 70 | 39 |

| | Motor vehicles | | | | Passenger cars | | Road density | Fuel prices | | Particulate matter concentration | |
|---|---|---|---|---|---|---|---|---|---|---|---|
| | per 1,000 people | | per kilometer of road | | per 1,000 people | | km. of road per 100 sq. km. of land area | $ per liter | | Urban-population-weighted PM10 micrograms per cubic meter | |
| | | | | | | | | Gasoline | Diesel | | |
| | 1990 | 2005 | 1990 | 2005 | 1990 | 2005 | 2005 | 2006 | 2006 | 1990 | 2005 |
| Honduras | 22 | 67 | 10 | 31 | 5 | 52 | 12 | 0.89 | 0.73 | 45 | 46 |
| Hungary | 212 | 316 | 21 | 20 | 188 | 274 | 178 | 1.30 | 1.31 | 36 | 18 |
| India | 4 | 12 | 2 | 3 | 2 | 8 | 114 | 1.01 | 0.75 | 112 | 68 |
| Indonesia | 16 | 109 | 10 | 62 | 7 | .. | 21 | 0.57 | 0.44 | 138 | 96 |
| Iran, Islamic Rep. | 34 | .. | 14 | .. | .. | 24 | 11 | 0.09 | 0.03 | 86 | 55 |
| Iraq | 14 | .. | 6 | .. | 1 | .. | 10 | 0.03 | 0.01 | 146 | 126 |
| Ireland | 270 | 447 | 10 | 20 | 227 | 382 | 140 | 1.34 | 1.35 | 26 | 17 |
| Israel | 210 | 293 | 74 | 115 | 174 | 239 | 81 | 1.47 | 1.27 | 71 | 31 |
| Italy | 529 | 667 | 99 | 81 | 476 | 595 | 165 | 1.56 | 1.49 | 42 | 28 |
| Jamaica | 52 | .. | 7 | .. | 43 | 135 | 199 | 0.82 | 0.75 | 58 | 38 |
| Japan | 469 | 586 | 52 | 63 | 283 | 441 | 323 | 1.09 | 0.90 | 43 | 31 |
| Jordan | 60 | 115 | 26 | 83 | 44 | 78 | 9 | 0.86 | 0.45 | 110 | 52 |
| Kazakhstan | 76 | 116 | 8 | 17 | 50 | 93 | 3 | 0.70 | 0.45 | 43 | 19 |
| Kenya | 12 | 18 | 5 | 10 | .. | 9 | 11 | 1.12 | 0.98 | 66 | 38 |
| Korea, Dem. Rep. | .. | .. | .. | .. | .. | .. | 26 | 0.71 | 0.79 | 181 | 73 |
| Korea, Rep. | 79 | 319 | 60 | 151 | 48 | 230 | 104 | 1.65 | 1.33 | 51 | 37 |
| Kuwait | .. | 422 | .. | 181 | .. | 349 | 32 | 0.22 | 0.21 | 82 | 101 |
| Kyrgyz Republic | .. | 39 | .. | 10 | .. | 39 | 10 | 0.64 | 0.54 | 76 | 24 |
| Lao PDR | 9 | 57 | 3 | 10 | 6 | .. | 14 | 0.86 | 0.73 | 73 | 47 |
| Latvia | 135 | 377 | 6 | 12 | 106 | 323 | 112 | 1.20 | 1.15 | 38 | 15 |
| Lebanon | 321 | .. | 183 | .. | 300 | 403 | 68 | 0.74 | 0.62 | 43 | 40 |
| Lesotho | 11 | .. | 4 | .. | 3 | .. | 20 | 0.89 | 0.88 | 85 | 42 |
| Liberia | 14 | .. | 4 | .. | .. | 6 | 11 | 0.79 | 0.85 | 60 | 45 |
| Libya | 165 | 257 | 10 | .. | 96 | 232 | 5 | 0.13 | 0.13 | 106 | 94 |
| Lithuania | 160 | 467 | 12 | 20 | 133 | 426 | 127 | 1.08 | 1.09 | 53 | 19 |
| Macedonia, FYR | 132 | 163 | 30 | 25 | 121 | 150 | 52 | 1.23 | 1.09 | 46 | 20 |
| Madagascar | 6 | .. | 2 | .. | 4 | .. | 9 | 1.15 | 1.00 | 77 | 35 |
| Malawi | 4 | .. | 4 | .. | 2 | .. | 16 | 1.17 | 1.12 | 75 | 34 |
| Malaysia | 124 | 272 | 26 | 72 | 101 | 225 | 30 | 0.53 | 0.40 | 37 | 25 |
| Mali | 3 | .. | 2 | .. | 2 | .. | 2 | 1.22 | 1.04 | 271 | 171 |
| Mauritania | 10 | .. | 3 | .. | 7 | .. | 1 | 0.97 | 0.84 | 145 | 104 |
| Mauritius | 59 | 130 | 35 | 79 | 44 | 96 | 99 | 0.74 | 0.56 | 23 | 17 |
| Mexico | 119 | 208 | 41 | 90 | 82 | 137 | 18 | 0.74 | 0.52 | 69 | 40 |
| Moldova | 53 | 94 | 17 | 31 | 48 | 70 | 39 | 0.45 | 0.31 | 98 | 38 |
| Mongolia | 21 | 43 | 1 | 2 | 6 | 28 | 3 | 0.88 | 0.87 | 65 | 64 |
| Morocco | 37 | 59 | 15 | 29 | 28 | 46 | 13 | 1.22 | 0.87 | 32 | 22 |
| Mozambique | 4 | .. | 2 | .. | 3 | .. | 4 | 1.15 | 1.06 | 110 | 28 |
| Myanmar | 2 | 5 | 3 | .. | 1 | 4 | 4 | 0.66 | 0.75 | 116 | 63 |
| Namibia | 71 | 85 | 1 | 4 | 39 | 42 | 5 | 0.87 | 0.87 | 74 | 42 |
| Nepal | .. | .. | .. | .. | .. | 3 | 12 | 0.94 | 0.73 | 67 | 36 |
| Netherlands | 405 | 486 | 58 | 62 | 368 | 429 | 372 | 1.70 | 1.32 | 46 | 35 |
| New Zealand | 524 | 720 | 19 | 32 | 436 | 607 | 35 | 0.98 | 0.70 | 16 | 15 |
| Nicaragua | 19 | 46 | 5 | 13 | 10 | 18 | 15 | 0.67 | 0.58 | 49 | 30 |
| Niger | 6 | 5 | .. | 4 | 5 | 4 | 1 | 1.14 | 1.11 | 217 | 149 |
| Nigeria | 30 | .. | 21 | .. | 12 | 17 | 21 | 0.51 | 0.66 | 176 | 62 |
| Norway | 458 | 546 | 22 | 27 | 380 | 439 | 31 | 1.80 | 1.66 | 24 | 20 |
| Oman | 130 | .. | 9 | .. | 83 | 156 | 11 | 0.31 | 0.39 | 148 | 132 |
| Pakistan | 6 | 14 | 4 | 8 | 4 | 10 | 34 | 1.01 | 0.64 | 212 | 120 |
| Panama | 75 | 103 | 18 | 27 | 60 | 73 | 16 | 0.70 | 0.60 | 58 | 35 |
| Papua New Guinea | 27 | .. | 6 | .. | .. | 5 | 4 | 0.94 | 0.64 | 34 | 24 |
| Paraguay | 27 | 85 | 4 | 15 | 16 | 50 | 7 | 0.97 | 0.77 | 106 | 84 |
| Peru | .. | 47 | 43 | 16 | .. | 30 | 6 | 1.22 | 0.86 | 98 | 61 |
| Philippines | 10 | 34 | 4 | 14 | 7 | 9 | 67 | 0.76 | 0.67 | 55 | 26 |
| Poland | 168 | 386 | 18 | 35 | 138 | 323 | 138 | 1.30 | 1.30 | 59 | 37 |
| Portugal | 222 | 507 | 34 | 67 | 162 | 471 | 86 | 1.56 | 1.10 | 52 | 28 |
| Puerto Rico | 295 | .. | 79 | .. | 242 | .. | 289 | 0.65 | 0.78 | 27 | 21 |

| | Motor vehicles | | | | Passenger cars | | Road density | Fuel prices | | Particulate matter concentration | |
|---|---|---|---|---|---|---|---|---|---|---|---|
| | per 1,000 people | | per kilometer of road | | per 1,000 people | | km. of road per 100 sq. km. of land area | $ per liter | | Urban-population-weighted PM10 micrograms per cubic meter | |
| | | | | | | | | Gasoline | Diesel | | |
| | 1990 | 2005 | 1990 | 2005 | 1990 | 2005 | 2005 | 2006 | 2006 | 1990 | 2005 |
| Romania | 72 | 185 | 11 | 20 | 56 | 149 | 86 | 1.26 | 1.24 | 36 | 14 |
| Russian Federation | 87 | 174 | 14 | 48 | 65 | 161 | 3 | 0.77 | 0.66 | 41 | 19 |
| Rwanda | 2 | 3 | 1 | .. | 1 | 1 | 57 | 1.11 | 1.08 | 49 | 28 |
| Saudi Arabia | 165 | .. | 19 | .. | 98 | 415 | 8 | 0.16 | 0.07 | 161 | 120 |
| Senegal | 11 | 14 | 6 | 9 | 8 | 10 | 7 | 1.31 | 1.09 | 95 | 95 |
| Serbia[a] | 137 | 199 | 31 | 102 | 133 | 181 | 44 | 1.48 | 1.31 | 30 | 14 |
| Sierra Leone | .. | 4 | .. | 2 | .. | 2 | 16 | 0.98 | 0.98 | 91 | 57 |
| Singapore | 130 | 137 | 142 | 183 | 89 | 101 | 469 | 0.92 | 0.63 | 106 | 40 |
| Slovak Republic | 194 | 256 | 57 | 32 | 163 | 222 | 89 | 1.35 | 1.43 | 41 | 16 |
| Slovenia | 306 | 523 | 42 | 27 | 289 | 471 | 191 | 1.23 | 1.21 | 40 | 31 |
| Somalia | 2 | .. | 1 | .. | 1 | .. | 4 | 0.74 | 0.67 | 78 | 32 |
| South Africa | 139 | 143 | 26 | 16 | 97 | 98 | 30 | 0.85 | 0.84 | 34 | 22 |
| Spain | 360 | 550 | 43 | 35 | 309 | 445 | 133 | 1.15 | 1.10 | 42 | 34 |
| Sri Lanka | 21 | 42 | 4 | 9 | 7 | 13 | 151 | 0.88 | 0.55 | 95 | 94 |
| Sudan | 9 | .. | 22 | .. | 8 | .. | 1 | 0.72 | 0.49 | 326 | 173 |
| Swaziland | 66 | 84 | 18 | 25 | 35 | 40 | 21 | 0.80 | 0.85 | 60 | 31 |
| Sweden | 464 | 513 | 29 | 11 | 426 | 460 | 104 | 1.46 | 1.44 | 15 | 12 |
| Switzerland | 491 | 563 | 46 | 59 | 449 | 520 | 178 | 1.27 | 1.36 | 37 | 25 |
| Syrian Arab Republic | 26 | 36 | 10 | 7 | 10 | 12 | 52 | 0.60 | 0.13 | 159 | 79 |
| Tajikistan | 3 | .. | 1 | .. | 0 | 19 | 20 | 0.80 | 0.74 | 104 | 52 |
| Tanzania | 5 | .. | 2 | .. | 1 | 1 | 9 | 1.04 | 0.99 | 57 | 24 |
| Thailand | 46 | .. | 36 | .. | 14 | 54 | 11 | 0.70 | 0.65 | 88 | 77 |
| Timor-Leste | .. | .. | .. | .. | .. | .. | .. | .. | .. | .. | .. |
| Togo | 24 | .. | 11 | .. | .. | 10 | 14 | 1.03 | 1.01 | 56 | 36 |
| Trinidad and Tobago | 117 | .. | 19 | .. | 98 | .. | 162 | 0.43 | 0.24 | 142 | 107 |
| Tunisia | 48 | 95 | 19 | 49 | 23 | 83 | 12 | 0.83 | 0.57 | 71 | 32 |
| Turkey | 50 | 117 | 8 | 20 | 34 | 80 | 55 | 1.88 | 1.62 | 75 | 43 |
| Turkmenistan | .. | .. | .. | .. | .. | .. | 5 | 0.02 | 0.01 | 177 | 56 |
| Uganda | 2 | 5 | .. | 4 | 1 | 2 | 36 | 1.17 | 1.01 | 27 | 12 |
| Ukraine | 63 | 128 | 20 | 36 | 63 | 118 | 29 | 0.81 | 0.87 | 72 | 23 |
| United Arab Emirates | 121 | .. | 52 | .. | 97 | 228 | 5 | 0.37 | 0.53 | 264 | 135 |
| United Kingdom | 400 | 517 | 64 | 80 | 341 | 457 | 160 | 1.63 | 1.73 | 25 | 16 |
| United States | 756[b] | 814[b] | 30 | 31 | 536[b] | 461[b,c] | 71 | 0.63 | 0.69 | 30 | 22 |
| Uruguay | 138 | 176 | 45 | .. | 122 | 151 | 44 | 1.23 | 0.94 | 237 | 161 |
| Uzbekistan | .. | .. | .. | .. | .. | .. | 19 | 0.85 | 0.54 | 84 | 61 |
| Venezuela, RB | 93 | .. | 25 | .. | 73 | 94 | 11 | 0.03 | 0.02 | 22 | 11 |
| Vietnam | .. | 8 | .. | .. | .. | .. | 72 | 0.67 | 0.53 | 124 | 61 |
| West Bank and Gaza | .. | 36 | .. | 26 | .. | 29 | 83 | 1.29 | 0.98 | .. | .. |
| Yemen, Rep. | 34 | .. | 8 | .. | 14 | 19 | 14 | 0.30 | 0.28 | 141 | 82 |
| Zambia | 14 | .. | 3 | .. | 8 | .. | 12 | 1.31 | 1.22 | 95 | 44 |
| Zimbabwe | 32 | .. | 4 | .. | 29 | 45 | 25 | 0.61 | 0.65 | 35 | 27 |
| **World** | **117 w** | **148 w** | **.. ** | **.. ** | **91 w** | **118 w** | **23 w** | **0.97 m** | **0.84 m** | **80 w** | **53 w** |
| **Low income** | 5 | 9 | .. | .. | 3 | 8 | 21 | 0.98 | 0.84 | 130 | 74 |
| **Middle income** | 36 | 66 | .. | .. | 22 | 50 | 13 | 0.86 | 0.74 | 85 | 56 |
| Lower middle income | 14 | 31 | .. | .. | 8 | 21 | 16 | 0.85 | 0.70 | 107 | 69 |
| Upper middle income | 111 | 174 | .. | .. | 87 | 140 | 12 | 0.92 | 0.79 | 54 | 33 |
| **Low & middle income** | 24 | 39 | .. | .. | 15 | 39 | 15 | 0.89 | 0.79 | 98 | 61 |
| East Asia & Pacific | 9 | 24 | .. | .. | 4 | 14 | 22 | 0.53 | 0.40 | 112 | 73 |
| Europe & Central Asia | 93 | 167 | .. | .. | 75 | 152 | 9 | 1.14 | 1.09 | 62 | 29 |
| Latin America & Carib. | 100 | 155 | .. | .. | 71 | 115 | 18 | 0.82 | 0.67 | 59 | 37 |
| Middle East & N. Africa | 37 | .. | .. | .. | 25 | 34 | 7 | 0.46 | 0.34 | 124 | 77 |
| South Asia | 4 | 12 | .. | .. | 2 | 8 | 110 | 0.91 | 0.65 | 132 | 81 |
| Sub-Saharan Africa | 21 | .. | .. | .. | 14 | .. | 7 | 1.03 | 0.98 | 115 | 60 |
| **High income** | 496 | 600 | .. | .. | 388 | 467 | 55 | 1.33 | 1.24 | 37 | 27 |
| Euro area | 428 | 604 | .. | .. | 379 | 418[d] | 139 | 1.52 | 1.29 | 33 | 24 |

a. Includes Montenegro. b. Data are from the U.S. Federal Highway Administration. c. Excludes personal passenger vans, passenger minivans, and utility-type vehicles, which are all treated as trucks. d. Data are from the European Commission and the European Road Federation.

**About the data**

Traffic congestion in urban areas constrains economic productivity, damages people's health, and degrades the quality of life. The particulate air pollution emitted by motor vehicles—the dust and soot in exhaust—is far more damaging to human health than once believed. (For information on particulate matter and other air pollutants, see table 3.14.)

In recent years ownership of passenger cars has increased, and the expansion of economic activity has led to the transport by road of more goods and services over greater distances (see table 5.9). These developments have increased demand for roads and vehicles, adding to urban congestion, air pollution, health hazards, and traffic accidents and injuries. Congestion, the most visible cost of expanding vehicle ownership, is reflected in the indicators in the table. Other relevant indicators—such as average vehicle speed in major cities and the cost of traffic congestion, which takes a heavy toll on economic productivity—are not included because data are incomplete or difficult to compare.

The data in the table—except those on fuel prices and particulate matter—are compiled by the International Road Federation (IRF) through questionnaires sent to national organizations. The IRF uses a hierarchy of sources to gather as much information as possible. Primary sources are national road associations. Where an association lacks data or does not respond, other agencies are contacted, including road directorates, ministries of transport or public works, and central statistical offices. As a result, data are of uneven quality. The coverage of each indicator may differ across countries because of different definitions. Comparability is also limited when time series data are reported. The IRF is taking steps to improve the quality of the data in its 2006 *World Road Statistics*.

Because this effort covers data for 1999–2005 only, data in the table for 1990 and 2005 may not be comparable. Another reason is coverage. For example, for the United States the 2005 estimate for passenger cars from the U.S. Federal Highway Administration excludes personal passenger vans, passenger minivans, and utility-type vehicles, which are all treated as trucks. Moreover, the data do not cover vehicle quality or age. Road density is a rough indicator of accessibility and does not capture the width, type, or condition of roads. Thus comparisons over time and across countries should be made with caution.

Data on fuel prices are compiled by the German Agency for Technical Cooperation (GTZ), from its global network of regional offices and representatives, and other sources, including the Allgemeiner Deutscher Automobile Club (for Europe) and a project of the Latin American Energy Organization for Latin America. Local prices are converted to U.S. dollars using the exchange rate in the *Financial Times* international monetary table on the survey date. When multiple exchange rates exist, the market, parallel, or black market rate is used.

Considerable uncertainty surrounds estimates of particulate matter concentrations, and caution should be used in interpreting them. They allow for cross-country comparisons of the relative risk of particulate matter pollution facing urban residents. Major sources of urban outdoor particulate matter pollution are traffic and industrial emissions, but nonanthropogenic sources such as dust storms may also be a substantial contributor for some cities. Country technology and pollution controls are important determinants of particulate matter. Data on particulate matter for selected cities are in table 3.14. Estimates of economic damages from death and illness due to particulate matter pollution are in table 3.16.

**Definitions**

• **Motor vehicles** include cars, buses, and freight vehicles but not two-wheelers. Population figures refer to the midyear population in the year for which data are available. Roads refer to motorways, highways, main or national roads, and secondary or regional roads. A motorway is a road designed and built for motor traffic that separates the traffic flowing in opposite directions. • **Passenger cars** are road motor vehicles, other than two-wheelers, intended for the carriage of passengers and designed to seat no more than nine people (including the driver). • **Road density** is the ratio of the length of the country's total road network to the country's land area. The road network includes all roads in the country—motorways, highways, main or national roads, secondary or regional roads, and other urban and rural roads. • **Fuel prices** are the pump prices of the most widely sold grade of gasoline and of diesel fuel. Prices are converted from the local currency to U.S. dollars (see *About the data*). • **Particulate matter concentration** is fine suspended particulates of less than 10 microns in diameter (PM10) that are capable of penetrating deep into the respiratory tract and causing significant health damage. Data are urban-population-weighted PM10 levels in residential areas of cities with more than 100,000 residents. The estimates represent the average annual exposure level of the average urban resident to outdoor particulate matter.

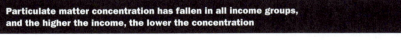

**Particulate matter concentration has fallen in all income groups, and the higher the income, the lower the concentration**

3.13a

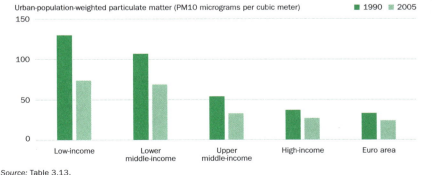

Urban-population-weighted particulate matter (PM10 micrograms per cubic meter)  ■ 1990  ■ 2005

*Source:* Table 3.13.

**Data sources**

Data on vehicles and road density are from the IRF's electronic files and its annual *World Road Statistics*, except where footnoted. Data on fuel prices are from the GTZ's electronic files. Data on particulate matter concentrations are from Kiran Dev Pandey, David Wheeler, Bart Ostro, Uwe Deichmann, Kirk Hamilton, and Katie Bolt's "Ambient Particulate Matter Concentrations in Residential and Pollution Hotspot Areas of World Cities: New Estimates Based on the Global Model of Ambient Particulates (GMAPS)" (2006).

| | City | City population | Particulate matter concentration | Sulfur dioxide | Nitrogen dioxide |
|---|---|---|---|---|---|
| | | | Urban-population-weighted PM10 micrograms per cubic meter | micrograms per cubic meter | micrograms per cubic meter |
| | | thousands 2005 | 2004 | 2001[a] | 2001[a] |
| Argentina | Córdoba | 1,423 | 58 | .. | 97 |
| Australia | Melbourne | 3,626 | 12 | .. | 30 |
| | Perth | 1,474 | 12 | 5 | 19 |
| | Sydney | 4,331 | 20 | 28 | 81 |
| Austria | Vienna | 2,260 | 41 | 14 | 42 |
| Belgium | Brussels | 1,012 | 28 | 20 | 48 |
| Brazil | Rio de Janeiro | 11,469 | 35 | 129 | .. |
| | São Paulo | 18,333 | 40 | 43 | 83 |
| Bulgaria | Sofia | 1,093 | 61 | 39 | 122 |
| Canada | Montréal | 3,640 | 19 | 10 | 42 |
| | Toronto | 5,312 | 22 | 17 | 43 |
| | Vancouver | 2,188 | 13 | 14 | 37 |
| Chile | Santiago | 5,683 | 61 | 29 | 81 |
| China | Anshan | 1,611 | 82 | 115 | 88 |
| | Beijing | 10,717 | 89 | 90 | 122 |
| | Changchun | 3,046 | 74 | 21 | 64 |
| | Chengdu | 4,065 | 86 | 77 | 74 |
| | Chongqing | 6,363 | 123 | 340 | 70 |
| | Dalian | 3,073 | 50 | 61 | 100 |
| | Guangzhou | 8,425 | 63 | 57 | 136 |
| | Guiyang | 3,447 | 70 | 424 | 53 |
| | Harbin | 3,695 | 77 | 23 | 30 |
| | Jinan | 2,743 | 94 | 132 | 45 |
| | Kunming | 2,837 | 70 | 19 | 33 |
| | Lanzhou | 2,411 | 91 | 102 | 104 |
| | Liupanshui | 1,149 | 59 | 102 | .. |
| | Nanchang | 2,188[b] | 78 | 69 | 29 |
| | Pingxiang | 905 | 67 | 75 | .. |
| | Quingdao | 2,817 | 68 | 190 | 64 |
| | Shanghai | 14,503 | 73 | 53 | 73 |
| | Shenyang | 4,720 | 101 | 99 | 73 |
| | Taiyuan | 2,794 | 88 | 211 | 55 |
| | Tianjin | 7,040 | 125 | 82 | 50 |
| | Wulumqi | 2,025 | 57 | 60 | 70 |
| | Wuhan | 7,093 | 79 | 40 | 43 |
| | Zhengzhou | 2,590 | 97 | 63 | 95 |
| | Zibo | 2,982 | 74 | 198 | 43 |
| Colombia | Bogotá | 7,747 | 31 | .. | .. |
| Croatia | Zagreb | 908[b] | 33 | 31 | .. |
| Cuba | Havana | 2,189 | 21 | 1 | 5 |
| Czech Republic | Prague | 1,171 | 23 | 14 | 33 |
| Denmark | Copenhagen | 1,088 | 21 | 7 | 54 |
| Ecuador | Guayaquil | 2,387 | 23 | 15 | .. |
| | Quito | 1,514 | 30 | 22 | .. |
| Egypt, Arab Rep. | Cairo | 11,128 | 169 | 69 | .. |
| Finland | Helsinki | 1,091 | 21 | 4 | 35 |
| France | Paris | 9,820 | 11 | 14 | 57 |
| Germany | Berlin | 3,389 | 22 | 18 | 26 |
| | Frankfurt | 668[b] | 19 | 11 | 45 |
| | Munich | 1,263 | 20 | 8 | 53 |
| Ghana | Accra | 1,981 | 33 | .. | .. |
| Greece | Athens | 3,230 | 43 | 34 | 64 |
| Hungary | Budapest | 1,693 | 19 | 39 | 51 |
| Iceland | Reykjavik | 164[b] | 18 | 5 | 42 |
| India | Ahmadabad | 5,120 | 83 | 30 | 21 |
| | Bengaluru | 6,462 | 45 | .. | .. |

## About the data

Indoor and outdoor air pollution place a major burden on world health. More than half the world's people rely on dung, wood, crop waste, or coal to meet basic energy needs. Cooking and heating with these fuels on open fires or stoves without chimneys lead to indoor air pollution, which is responsible for 1.6 million deaths a year—one every 20 seconds. In many urban areas air pollution exposure is the main environmental threat to health. Long-term exposure to high levels of soot and small particles contributes to a range of health effects, including respiratory diseases, lung cancer, and heart disease. Particulate pollution, alone or with sulfur dioxide, creates an enormous burden of ill health.

Sulfur dioxide and nitrogen dioxide emissions lead to deposition of acid rain and other acidic compounds over long distances, which can lead to the leaching of trace minerals and nutrients critical to trees and plants. Sulfur dioxide emissions can damage human health, particularly that of the young and old. Nitrogen dioxide is emitted by bacteria, motor vehicles, industrial activities, nitrogen fertilizers, fuel and biomass combustion, and aerobic decomposition of organic matter in soils and oceans.

Where coal is the primary fuel for power plants without effective dust controls, steel mills, industrial boilers, and domestic heating, high levels of urban air pollution are common—especially particulates and sulfur dioxide. Elsewhere the worst emissions are from petroleum product combustion.

Sulfur dioxide and nitrogen dioxide concentration data are based on average observed concentrations at urban monitoring sites, which not all cities have.

The data on particulate matter are estimated average annual concentrations in residential areas away from air pollution "hotspots," such as industrial districts and transport corridors. The data are from the World Bank's Development Research Group and Environment Department estimates of annual ambient concentrations of particulate matter in cities with populations exceeding 100,000 (Pandey and others 2006b). A country's technology and pollution controls are important determinants of particulate matter concentrations.

Pollutant concentrations are sensitive to local conditions, and even monitoring sites in the same city may register different levels. Thus these data should be considered only a general indication of air quality, and comparisons should be made with caution. Current World Health Organization (WHO) air quality guidelines are annual mean concentrations of 20 micrograms per cubic meter for particulate matter less than 10 microns in diameter and 40 micrograms for nitrogen dioxide and daily mean concentrations of 20 micrograms per cubic meter for sulfur dioxide.

| | City | City population | Particulate matter concentration | Sulfur dioxide | Nitrogen dioxide |
|---|---|---|---|---|---|
| | | thousands 2005 | Urban-population-weighted PM10 micrograms per cubic meter 2004 | micrograms per cubic meter 2001[a] | micrograms per cubic meter 2001[a] |
| India | Chennai | 6,916 | 37 | 15 | 17 |
| | Delhi | 15,048 | 150 | 24 | 41 |
| | Hyderabad | 6,115 | 41 | 12 | 17 |
| | Kanpur | 3,018 | 109 | 15 | 14 |
| | Kolkata | 14,277 | 128 | 49 | 34 |
| | Lucknow | 2,566 | 109 | 26 | 25 |
| | Mumbai | 18,196 | 63 | 33 | 39 |
| | Nagpur | 2,350 | 56 | 6 | 13 |
| | Pune | 4,409 | 47 | .. | .. |
| Indonesia | Jakarta | 13,215 | 104 | .. | .. |
| Iran, Islamic Rep. | Tehran | 7,314 | 58 | 209 | .. |
| Ireland | Dublin | 1,037 | 19 | 20 | .. |
| Italy | Milan | 2,953 | 30 | 31 | 248 |
| | Rome | 3,348 | 29 | .. | .. |
| | Turin | 1,660 | 44 | .. | .. |
| Japan | Osaka-Kobe | 11,268 | 35 | 19 | 63 |
| | Tokyo | 35,197 | 40 | 18 | 68 |
| | Yokohama | 3,366[b] | 31 | 100 | 13 |
| Kenya | Nairobi | 2,773 | 43 | .. | .. |
| Korea, Rep. | Pusan | 3,554 | 44 | 60 | 51 |
| | Seoul | 9,645 | 41 | 44 | 60 |
| | Taegu | 2,511 | 50 | 81 | 62 |
| Malaysia | Kuala Lumpur | 1,405 | 29 | 24 | .. |
| Mexico | Mexico City | 19,411 | 51 | 74 | 130 |
| Netherlands | Amsterdam | 1,147 | 34 | 10 | 58 |
| New Zealand | Auckland | 1,148 | 14 | 3 | 20 |
| Norway | Oslo | 802 | 14 | 8 | 43 |
| Philippines | Manila | 10,686 | 39 | 33 | .. |
| Poland | Katowice | 2,914[b] | 39 | 83 | 79 |
| | Lódz | 776 | 39 | 21 | 43 |
| | Warsaw | 1,680 | 43 | 16 | 32 |
| Portugal | Lisbon | 2,761 | 23 | 8 | 52 |
| Romania | Bucharest | 1,934 | 18 | 10 | 71 |
| Russian Federation | Moscow | 10,654 | 21 | 109 | .. |
| | Omsk | 1,132 | 22 | 20 | 34 |
| Singapore | Singapore | 4,326 | 44 | 20 | 30 |
| Slovak Republic | Bratislava | 456[b] | 15 | 21 | 27 |
| South Africa | Cape Town | 3,083 | 16 | 21 | 72 |
| | Durban | 2,631 | 32 | 31 | .. |
| | Johannesburg | 3,254 | 33 | 19 | 31 |
| Spain | Barcelona | 4,795 | 35 | 11 | 43 |
| | Madrid | 5,608 | 30 | 24 | 66 |
| Sweden | Stockholm | 1,708 | 11 | 3 | 20 |
| Switzerland | Zurich | 1,144 | 23 | 11 | 39 |
| Thailand | Bangkok | 6,593 | 79 | 11 | 23 |
| Turkey | Ankara | 3,573 | 46 | 55 | 46 |
| | Istanbul | 9,712 | 55 | 120 | .. |
| Ukraine | Kiev | 2,672 | 35 | 14 | 51 |
| United Kingdom | Birmingham | 2,280 | 25 | 9 | 45 |
| | London | 8,505 | 21 | 25 | 77 |
| | Manchester | 2,228 | 15 | 26 | 49 |
| United States | Chicago | 8,814 | 25 | 14 | 57 |
| | Los Angeles | 12,298 | 34 | 9 | 74 |
| | New York-Newark | 18,718 | 21 | 26 | 79 |
| Venezuela, RB | Caracas | 2,913 | 10 | 33 | 57 |

a. Data are for the most recent year available. b. Data are for 2000.

### Definitions

• **City population** is the number of residents of the city or metropolitan area as defined by national authorities and reported to the United Nations. • **Particulate matter concentration** is fine suspended particulates of less than 10 microns in diameter (PM10) that are capable of penetrating deep into the respiratory tract and causing significant health damage. Data are urban-population-weighted PM10 levels in residential areas of cities with more than 100,000 residents. The estimates represent the average annual exposure level of the average urban resident to outdoor particulate matter. • **Sulfur dioxide** is an air pollutant produced when fossil fuels containing sulfur are burned. • **Nitrogen dioxide** is a poisonous, pungent gas formed when nitric oxide combines with hydrocarbons and sunlight, producing a photochemical reaction. These conditions occur in both natural and anthropogenic activities.

### Data sources

Data on city population are from the United Nations Population Division. Data on particulate matter concentrations are from Kiran D. Pandey, David Wheeler, Bart Ostro, Uwe Deichman, Kirk Hamilton, and Kathrine Bolt's "Ambient Particulate Matter Concentration in Residential and Pollution Hotspot Areas of World Cities: New Estimates Based on the Global Model of Ambient Particulates (GMAPS)" (2006). Data on sulfur dioxide and nitrogen dioxide concentrations are from the WHO's Healthy Cities Air Management Information System and the World Resources Institute.

| | Environmental strategies or action plans | Biodiversity assessments, strategies, or action plans | Participation in treaties[a] | | | | | | | | |
|---|---|---|---|---|---|---|---|---|---|---|---|
| | | | Climate change[b] | Ozone layer | CFC control | Law of the Sea[c] | Biological diversity[b] | Kyoto Protocol | CITES | CCD | Stockholm Convention |
| | | | **1992** | **1985** | **1987** | **1982** | **1992** | **1997** | **1973** | **1994** | **2004** |
| Afghanistan | | | 2002 | 2004[f] | 2004[f] | | 2002 | | 1985[f] | 1995[f] | |
| Albania | 1993 | | 1995 | 1999[f] | 1999[f] | 2003[f] | 1994[f] | 2005[f] | 2003[f] | 2000[f] | 2004 |
| Algeria | 2001 | | 1994 | 1992[f] | 1992[f] | 1996 | 1995 | 2005[f] | 1983[f] | 1996 | 2006 |
| Angola | | | 2000 | 2000[f] | 2000[f] | 1994 | 1998 | 2007 | | 1997 | 2006 |
| Argentina | 1992 | | 1994 | 1990 | 1990 | 1995 | 1994 | 2001 | 1981 | 1997 | 2005 |
| Armenia | | | 1994 | 1999[f] | 1999[f] | 2002[f] | 1993[d] | 2003[f] | | 1997 | 2003 |
| Australia | 1992 | 1994 | 1994 | 1987[f] | 1989 | 1994 | 1993 | 2007[d] | 1976 | 2000 | 2002 |
| Austria | | | 1994 | 1987 | 1989 | 1995 | 1994 | 2002 | 1982[f] | 1997[f] | 2002 |
| Azerbaijan | 1998 | | 1995 | 1996[f] | 1996[f] | | 2000[e] | 2000[f] | 1998[f] | 1998[f] | 2004[f] |
| Bangladesh | 1991 | 1990 | 1994 | 1990[f] | 1990[f] | 2001 | 1994 | 2001[f] | 1981 | 1996 | 2007 |
| Belarus | | | 2000 | 1986[d] | 1988[d] | 2006[f] | 1993 | 2005[d] | 1995[f] | 2001[f] | 2004[f] |
| Belgium | | | 1996 | 1988 | 1988 | 1998 | 1996 | 2002 | 1983 | 1997[f] | 2006 |
| Benin | 1993 | | 1994 | 1993[f] | 1993[f] | 1997 | 1994 | 2002[f] | 1984[f] | 1996 | 2004 |
| Bolivia | 1994 | 1988 | 1995 | 1994[f] | 1994[f] | 1995 | 1994 | 1999 | 1979 | 1996 | 2003 |
| Bosnia and Herzegovina | | | 2000 | 1992[g] | 1992[g] | 1994[g] | 2002[f] | 2007 | 2002 | 2002[f] | |
| Botswana | 1990 | 1991 | 1994 | 1991[f] | 1991[f] | 1994 | 1995 | 2003[f] | 1977[f] | 1996 | 2002[f] |
| Brazil | | 1988 | 1994 | 1990[f] | 1990[f] | 1994 | 1994 | 2002 | 1975 | 1997 | 2004 |
| Bulgaria | | 1994 | 1995 | 1990[f] | 1990[f] | 1996 | 1996 | 2002 | 1991[f] | 2001[f] | 2004 |
| Burkina Faso | 1993 | | 1994 | 1989 | 1989 | 2005 | 1993 | 2005[f] | 1989[f] | 1996 | 2004 |
| Burundi | 1994 | 1989 | 1997 | 1997[f] | 1997[f] | | 1997 | 2001[f] | 1988[f] | 1997 | 2005 |
| Cambodia | 1999 | | 1996 | 2001[f] | 2001[f] | | 1995[f] | 2002[f] | 1997 | 1997 | 2006 |
| Cameroon | | 1989 | 1995 | 1989[f] | 1989[f] | 1994 | 1994 | 2002[f] | 1981[f] | 1997 | |
| Canada | 1990 | 1994 | 1994 | 1986 | 1988 | 2003 | 1992 | 2002 | 1975 | 1995 | 2001 |
| Central African Republic | | | 1995 | 1993[f] | 1993[f] | | 1995 | | 1980[f] | 1996 | |
| Chad | 1990 | | 1994 | 1989[f] | 1994 | | 1994 | | 1989[f] | 1996 | 2004 |
| Chile | | 1993 | 1995 | 1990 | 1990 | 1997 | 1994 | 2002 | 1975 | 1997 | 2005 |
| China | 1994 | 1994 | 1994 | 1989[f] | 1991[f] | 1996 | 1993 | 2002[e] | 1981[f] | 1997 | 2004 |
|   Hong Kong, China | | | | | | | | | | | |
| Colombia | 1998 | 1988 | 1995 | 1990[f] | 1993[f] | | 1994 | 2001[f] | 1981 | 1999 | |
| Congo, Dem. Rep. | | 1990 | 1995 | 1994[f] | 1994[f] | 1995 | 1996 | 2005[f] | 1976[f] | 1997 | 2005[f] |
| Congo, Rep. | | 1990 | 1997 | 1994[f] | 1994[f] | | 1994 | 2007 | 1983[f] | 1999 | 2007 |
| Costa Rica | 1990 | 1992 | 1994 | 1991[f] | 1991[f] | 1994 | 1994 | 2002 | 1975 | 1998 | 2007 |
| Côte d'Ivoire | 1994 | 1991 | 1995 | 1993[f] | 1993[f] | 1994 | 1994 | 2007 | 1994[f] | 1997 | 2004 |
| Croatia | 2001 | 2000 | 1996 | 1991[d] | 1991[d] | 1994[g] | 1996 | 2007[d] | 2000[f] | 2000[d] | 2007 |
| Cuba | | | 1994 | 1992[f] | 1992[f] | 1994 | 1994 | 2002 | 1990[f] | 1997 | |
| Czech Republic | 1994 | | 1994 | 1993[d] | 1993[d] | 1996 | 1993[e] | 2001[e] | 993[g] | 2000[f] | 2002 |
| Denmark | 1994 | | 1994 | 1988 | 1988 | 2004 | 1993 | 2002 | 1977 | 1995[f] | 2003 |
| Dominican Republic | | 1995 | 1999 | 1993[f] | 1993[f] | | 1996 | 2002[f] | 1986[f] | 1997[f] | 2007 |
| Ecuador | 1993 | 1995 | 1994 | 1990[f] | 1990[f] | | 1993 | 2000 | 1975 | 1995 | 2004 |
| Egypt, Arab Rep. | 1992 | 1988 | 1995 | 1988 | 1988 | 1994 | 1994 | 2005[f] | 1978 | 1995 | 2003 |
| El Salvador | 1994 | 1988 | 1996 | 1992 | 1992 | | 1994 | 1998 | 1987[f] | 1997[f] | |
| Eritrea | 1995 | | 1995 | 2005[f] | 2005[f] | | 1996[f] | 2005[f] | 1994[f] | 1996 | 2005[f] |
| Estonia | 1998 | | 1994 | 1996[f] | 1996[f] | 2005[f] | 1994 | 2002 | 1992[f] | | |
| Ethiopia | 1994 | 1991 | 1994 | 1994[f] | 1994[f] | | 1994 | 2005[f] | 1989[f] | 1997 | 2003 |
| Finland | 1995 | | 1994 | 1986 | 1988 | 1996 | 1994[d] | 2002 | 1976[f] | 1995[d] | 2002[d] |
| France | 1990 | | 1994 | 1987[e] | 1988[e] | 1996 | 1994 | 2002[e] | 978 | 1997 | 2004[e] |
| Gabon | | 1990 | 1998 | 1994[f] | 1994[f] | 1998 | 1997 | 2006[d] | 1989[f] | 1996[f] | 2007 |
| Gambia, The | 1992 | 1989 | 1994 | 1990[f] | 1990[f] | 1994 | 1994 | 2001[f] | 1977[f] | 1996 | 2006 |
| Georgia | 1998 | | 1994 | 1996[f] | 1996[f] | 1996[f] | 1994[f] | 1999[f] | 1996[f] | 1999 | 2006 |
| Germany | | | 1994 | 1988 | 1988 | 1994[f] | 1993 | 2002 | 1976 | 1996 | 2002 |
| Ghana | 1992 | 1988 | 1995 | 1989[f] | 1989 | 1994 | 1994 | 2003[f] | 1975 | 1996 | 2003 |
| Greece | | | 1994 | 1988 | 1988 | 1995 | 1994 | 2002 | 1992[f] | 1997 | 2006 |
| Guatemala | 1994 | 1988 | 1996 | 1987[f] | 1989[f] | 1997 | 1995 | 1999 | 1979 | 1998[f] | |
| Guinea | 1994 | 1988 | 1994 | 1992[f] | 1992[f] | 1994 | 1993 | 2000[f] | 1981[f] | 1997 | |
| Guinea-Bissau | 1993 | 1991 | 1996 | 2002[f] | 2002[f] | 1994 | 1995 | 2005[d] | 1990[f] | 1995 | |
| Haiti | 1999 | | 1996 | 2000[f] | 2000[f] | 1996 | 1996 | 2005[f] | | 1996 | |

| | Environ-mental strategies or action plans | Biodiversity assessments, strategies, or action plans | Participation in treaties[a] | | | | | | | | |
|---|---|---|---|---|---|---|---|---|---|---|---|
| | | | Climate change[b] 1992 | Ozone layer 1985 | CFC control 1987 | Law of the Sea[c] 1982 | Biological diversity[b] 1992 | Kyoto Protocol 1997 | CITES 1973 | CCD 1994 | Stockholm Convention 2004 |
| Honduras | 1993 | | 1996 | 1993[f] | 1993[f] | 1994 | 1995 | 2000 | 1985[f] | 1997 | 2005 |
| Hungary | 1995 | | 1994 | 1988[f] | 1989[f] | 2002 | 1994 | 2002[f] | 1985[f] | 1999[f] | |
| India | 1993 | 1994 | 1994 | 1991[f] | 1992[f] | 1995 | 1994 | 2002[f] | 1976 | 1996 | 2006 |
| Indonesia | 1993 | 1993 | 1994 | 1992[f] | 1992 | 1994 | 1994 | 2004 | 1978[f] | 1998 | |
| Iran, Islamic Rep. | | | 1996 | 1990[f] | 1990[f] | | 1996 | 2005[f] | 1976 | 1997 | 2006 |
| Iraq | | | | | | 1994 | | | | | |
| Ireland | | | 1994 | 1988[f] | 1988 | 1996 | 1996 | 2002 | 2002 | 1997 | |
| Israel | | | 1996 | 1992[f] | 1992 | | 1995 | 2004 | 1979 | 1996 | |
| Italy | | | 1994 | 1988 | 1988 | 1995 | 1994 | 2002 | 1979 | 1997 | |
| Jamaica | 1994 | | 1995 | 1993[f] | 1993[f] | 1994 | 1995 | 1999[f] | 1997[f] | 1997[f] | 2007 |
| Japan | | | 1994 | 1988[f] | 1988 | 1996 | 1993[d] | 2002[d] | 1980 | 1998[d] | 2002[f] |
| Jordan | 1991 | | 1994 | 1989[f] | 1989[f] | 1995[f] | 1993 | 2003[f] | 1978[f] | 1996 | 2004 |
| Kazakhstan | | | 1995 | 1998[f] | 1998[f] | | 1994 | | 2000[f] | 1997 | |
| Kenya | 1994 | 1992 | 1994 | 1988[f] | 1988 | 1994 | 1994 | 2005[f] | 1978 | 1997 | 2004 |
| Korea, Dem. Rep. | | | 1995 | 1995[f] | 1995[f] | | 1994[e] | 2005[f] | | 2003[f] | 2002[f] |
| Korea, Rep. | | | 1994 | 1992 | 1992 | 1996 | 1994 | 2002 | 1993[f] | 1999 | 2007 |
| Kuwait | | | 1995 | 1992[f] | 1992[f] | 1994 | 2002 | 2005[f] | 2002 | 1997 | 2006 |
| Kyrgyz Republic | 1995 | | 2000 | 2000[f] | 2000[f] | | 1996[e] | 2003[f] | | 1997[f] | 2006 |
| Lao PDR | 1995 | | 1995 | 1998[f] | 1998[f] | 1998 | 1996[e] | 2003[f] | 2004[f] | 1996[d] | 2006 |
| Latvia | | | 1995 | 1995[f] | 1995[f] | 2004[f] | 1995 | 2002 | 1997[f] | 2002[f] | 2004 |
| Lebanon | | | 1995 | 1993[f] | 1993[f] | 1995 | 1994 | 2006 | | 1996 | 2003 |
| Lesotho | 1989 | | 1995 | 1994[f] | 1994[f] | | 1995 | 2000[f] | 2003 | 1995 | 2002 |
| Liberia | | | 2003 | 1996[f] | 1996[f] | | 2000 | 2002[f] | 2005[f] | 1998[f] | 2002[f] |
| Libya | | | 1999 | 1990[f] | 1990[f] | | 2001 | 2006 | 2003[f] | 1996 | 2005[f] |
| Lithuania | | | 1995 | 1995[f] | 1995[f] | 2003[f] | 1996 | 2003 | 2001[f] | 2003[f] | 2006 |
| Macedonia, FYR | | | 1998 | 1994[g] | 1994[g] | 1994[g] | 1997[f] | 2004[f] | 2000[f] | 2002[f] | 2004 |
| Madagascar | 1988 | 1991 | 1999 | 1996[f] | 1996[f] | 2001 | 1996 | 2003[f] | 1975 | 1997 | |
| Malawi | 1994 | | 1994 | 1991[f] | 1991[f] | | 1994 | 2001[f] | 1982[f] | 1996 | |
| Malaysia | 1991 | 1988 | 1994 | 1989[f] | 1989[f] | 1996 | 1994 | 2002 | 1977[f] | 1997 | |
| Mali | | 1989 | 1995 | 1994[f] | 1994[f] | 1994 | 1995 | 2002 | 1994[f] | 1995 | 2003 |
| Mauritania | 1988 | | 1994 | 1994[f] | 1994[f] | 1996 | 1996 | 2005[f] | 1998[f] | 1996 | 2005 |
| Mauritius | 1990 | | 1994 | 1992[f] | 1992[f] | 1994 | 1992 | 2001[f] | 1975 | 1996 | 2004 |
| Mexico | | 1988 | 1994 | 1987 | 1988 | 1994 | 1993 | 2000 | 1991[f] | 1995 | 2003 |
| Moldova | 2002 | | 1995 | 1996[f] | 1996[f] | 2007 | 1995 | 2003[f] | 2001[f] | 1999[f] | 2004 |
| Mongolia | 1995 | | 1994 | 1996[f] | 1996[f] | 1996 | 1993 | 1999[f] | 1996[f] | 1996 | 2004 |
| Morocco | | 1988 | 1996 | 1995 | 1995 | | 1995 | 2002[f] | 1975 | 1996 | 2004 |
| Mozambique | 1994 | | 1995 | 1994[f] | 1994[f] | 1997 | 1995 | 2005[f] | 1981[f] | 1997 | 2005 |
| Myanmar | | 1989 | 1995 | 1993[f] | 1993[f] | 1996 | 1995 | 2003[f] | 1997[f] | 1997[f] | 2004[f] |
| Namibia | 1992 | | 1995 | 1993[f] | 1993[f] | 1994 | 1997 | 2003[f] | 1990[f] | 1997 | 2005[f] |
| Nepal | 1993 | | 1994 | 1994[f] | 1994[f] | 1998 | 1993 | 2005[f] | 1975[f] | 1996 | 2007 |
| Netherlands | 1994 | | 1994 | 1988[f] | 1988[d] | 1996 | 1994[d] | 2002[f] | 1984 | 1995[d] | 2002[d] |
| New Zealand | 1994 | | 1994 | 1987 | 1988 | 1996 | 1993 | 2002 | 1989[f] | 2000[f] | 2004 |
| Nicaragua | 1994 | | 1996 | 1993[f] | 1993[f] | 2000 | 1995 | 1999 | 1977[f] | 1998 | |
| Niger | | 1991 | 1995 | 1992[f] | 1992[f] | | 1995 | 2004 | 1975 | 1996 | 2006 |
| Nigeria | 1990 | 1992 | 1994 | 1988[f] | 1988[f] | 1994 | 1994 | 2004[f] | 1974 | 1997 | 2004 |
| Norway | | 1994 | 1994 | 1986 | 1988 | 1996 | 1993 | 2002 | 1976 | 1996 | 2002 |
| Oman | | | 1995 | 1999[f] | 1999[f] | 1994 | 1995 | 2005[f] | | 1996[f] | 2005 |
| Pakistan | 1994 | 1991 | 1994 | 1992[f] | 1992[f] | 1997 | 1994 | 2005[f] | 1976[f] | 1997 | |
| Panama | 1990 | | 1995 | 1989[f] | 1989 | 1996 | 1995 | 1999 | 1978 | 1996 | 2003 |
| Papua New Guinea | 1992 | 1993 | 1994 | 1992[f] | 1992[f] | 1997 | 1993 | 2002 | 1975[f] | 2000[f] | 2003 |
| Paraguay | | | 1994 | 1992[f] | 1992[f] | 1994 | 1994 | 1999 | 1976 | 1997 | 2004 |
| Peru | | 1988 | 1994 | 1989 | 1993[f] | | 1993 | 2002 | 1975 | 1995 | 2005 |
| Philippines | 1989 | 1989 | 1994 | 1991[f] | 1991 | 1994 | 1993 | 2003 | 1981 | 2000 | 2004 |
| Poland | 1993 | 1991 | 1994 | 1990[f] | 1990[f] | 1998 | 1996 | 2002 | 1989 | 2001[f] | |
| Portugal | 1995 | | 1994 | 1988[f] | 1988 | 1997 | 1993 | 2002[e] | 1980 | 1996 | 2004[d] |
| Puerto Rico | | | | | | | | | | | |

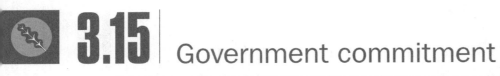

# 3.15 | Government commitment

| | Environ-mental strategies or action plans | Biodiversity assessments, strategies, or action plans | Participation in treaties[a] | | | | | | | | |
|---|---|---|---|---|---|---|---|---|---|---|---|
| | | | Climate change[b] 1992 | Ozone layer 1985 | CFC control 1987 | Law of the Sea[c] 1982 | Biological diversity[b] 1992 | Kyoto Protocol 1997 | CITES 1973 | CCD 1994 | Stockholm Convention 2004 |
| Romania | 1995 | | 1994 | 1993[f] | 1993[f] | 1996 | 1994 | 2001 | 1994[f] | 1998[f] | 2004 |
| Russian Federation | 1999 | 1994 | 1995 | 1986[d] | 1988[d] | 1997 | 1995 | 2004 | 1992 | 2003[f] | |
| Rwanda | 1991 | | 1998 | 2001[f] | 2001[f] | | 1996 | 2004[f] | 1980[f] | 1998 | 2002[f] |
| Saudi Arabia | | | 1995 | 1993[f] | 1993[f] | 1996 | 2001[e] | 2005[f] | 1996[f] | 1997[f] | |
| Senegal | 1984 | 1991 | 1995 | 1993[f] | 1993 | 1994 | 1994 | 2001[f] | 1977[f] | 1995 | 2003 |
| Serbia | | | 2001 | 2001[g] | 2001[g] | 2001[g] | 2002 | | 2002 | | 2002 |
| Sierra Leone | 1994 | | 1995 | 2001[f] | 2001[f] | 1994 | 1994[e] | 2006[f] | 1994[f] | 1997 | 2003[f] |
| Singapore | 1993 | 1995 | 1997 | 1989[f] | 1989[f] | 1994 | 1995 | 2006[f] | 1986[f] | 1999[f] | 2005 |
| Slovak Republic | | | 1994 | 1993[g] | 1993[g] | 1996 | 1994[e] | 2002 | 1993 | 2001[f] | 2002 |
| Slovenia | 1994 | | 1996 | 1992[g] | 1992[g] | 1995[g] | 1996 | 2002 | 2000[f] | 2001[f] | 2004 |
| Somalia | | | | 2001[f] | 2001[f] | 1994 | | | 1985[f] | 2002[f] | |
| South Africa | 1993 | | 1997 | 1990[f] | 1990[f] | 1997 | 1995 | 2002[f] | 1975 | 1997 | 2002 |
| Spain | | | 1994 | 1988[f] | 1988 | 1997 | 1995 | 2002 | 1986[f] | 1996 | 2004 |
| Sri Lanka | 1994 | 1991 | 1994 | 1989[f] | 1989[f] | 1994 | 1994 | 2002[f] | 1979[f] | 1998[f] | |
| Sudan | | | 1994 | 1993[f] | 1993[f] | 1994 | 1995 | 2004[f] | 1982 | 1995 | 2006 |
| Swaziland | | | 1997 | 1992[f] | 1992[f] | | 1994 | | 1997[f] | 1996 | 2006 |
| Sweden | | | 1994 | 1986 | 1988 | 1996 | 1993 | 2002 | 1974 | 1995 | 2002 |
| Switzerland | | | 1994 | 1987 | 1988 | | 1994 | 2006[f] | 1974 | 1996 | 2003 |
| Syrian Arab Republic | 1999 | | 1996 | 1989[f] | 1989[f] | | 1996 | 2006[f] | 2003[f] | 1997 | 2005 |
| Tajikistan | | | 1998 | 1996[f] | 1998[f] | | 1997[e] | | | 1997[f] | 2007 |
| Tanzania | 1994 | 1988 | 1996 | 1993[f] | 1993[f] | 1994 | 1996 | 2002[f] | 1979 | 1997 | 2004 |
| Thailand | | | 1995 | 1989[f] | 1989 | | 2004 | 2002 | 1983 | 2001[f] | 2005 |
| Timor-Leste | | | | | | | | | | | |
| Togo | 1991 | | 1995 | 1991[f] | 1991 | 1994 | 1995[d] | 2004[f] | 1978 | 1995[d] | 2004 |
| Trinidad and Tobago | | | 1994 | 1989[f] | 1989[f] | 1994 | 1996 | 1999 | 1984[f] | 2000[f] | 2002[f] |
| Tunisia | 1994 | 1988 | 1994 | 1989[f] | 1989[f] | 1994 | 1993 | 2003[f] | 1974 | 1995 | 2004 |
| Turkey | 1998 | | 2004 | 1991[f] | 1991[f] | | 1997 | | 1996[f] | 1998 | |
| Turkmenistan | | | 1995 | 1993[f] | 1993[f] | | 1996[e] | 1999 | | 1996 | |
| Uganda | 1994 | 1988 | 1994 | 1988[f] | 1988 | 1994 | 1993 | 2002[f] | 1991[f] | 1997 | 2004[f] |
| Ukraine | 1999 | | 1997 | 1986[d] | 1988[d] | 1999 | 1995 | 2004 | 1999[f] | 2002[f] | |
| United Arab Emirates | | | 1996 | 1989[f] | 1989[f] | | 2000 | 2005[f] | 1990[f] | 1998[f] | 2002 |
| United Kingdom | 1995 | 1994 | 1994 | 1987 | 1988 | 1997[f] | 1994 | 2002 | 1976 | 1996 | 2005 |
| United States | 1995 | 1995 | 1994 | 1986 | 1988 | | | | 1974 | 2000 | |
| Uruguay | | | 1994 | 1989[f] | 1991[f] | 1994 | 1993 | 2001 | 1975 | 1999[f] | 2004 |
| Uzbekistan | | | 1994 | 1993[f] | 1993[f] | | 1995[e] | 1999 | 1997[f] | 1995 | |
| Venezuela | | | 1995 | 1988[f] | 1989 | | 1994 | | 1977 | 1998[f] | 2005 |
| Vietnam | | 1993 | 1995 | 1994[f] | 1994[f] | 2006[f] | 1994 | 2002 | 1994[f] | 1998[f] | 2002 |
| West Bank and Gaza | | | | | | | | | | | |
| Yemen, Rep. | 1996 | 1992 | 1996 | 1996[f] | 1996[f] | 1994 | 1996 | 2004[f] | 1997[f] | 1997[f] | 2004 |
| Zambia | 1994 | | 1994 | 1990[f] | 1990[f] | 1994 | 1993 | 2006[f] | 1980[f] | 1996 | 2006 |
| Zimbabwe | 1987 | | 1994 | 1992[f] | 1992[f] | 1994 | 1994 | | 1981[f] | 1997 | |

a. Ratification of the treaty. b. Year the treaty entered into force in the country. c. Convention became effective November 16, 1994. d. Acceptance. e. Approval. f. Accession. g. Succession.

## About the data

National environmental strategies and participation in international treaties on environmental issues provide some evidence of government commitment to sound environmental management. But the signing of these treaties does not always imply ratification, nor does it guarantee that governments will comply with treaty obligations.

In many countries efforts to halt environmental degradation have failed, primarily because governments have neglected to make this issue a priority, a reflection of competing claims on scarce resources. To address this problem, many countries are preparing national environmental strategies—some focusing narrowly on environmental issues, and others integrating environmental, economic, and social concerns. Among such initiatives are conservation strategies and environmental action plans. Some countries have also prepared country environmental profiles and biodiversity strategies and profiles.

National conservation strategies—promoted by the World Conservation Union (IUCN)—provide a comprehensive, cross-sectoral analysis of conservation and resource management issues to help integrate environmental concerns with the development process. Such strategies discuss current and future needs, institutional capabilities, prevailing technical conditions, and the status of natural resources in a country.

National environmental action plans, supported by the World Bank and other development agencies, describe a country's main environmental concerns, identify the principal causes of environmental problems, and formulate policies and actions to deal with them. These plans are a continuing process in which governments develop comprehensive environmental policies, recommend specific actions, and outline the investment strategies, legislation, and institutional arrangements required to implement them.

Biodiversity profiles—prepared by the World Conservation Monitoring Centre and the IUCN—provide basic background on species diversity, protected areas, major ecosystems and habitat types, and legislative and administrative support. In an effort to establish a scientific baseline for measuring progress in biodiversity conservation, the United Nations Environment Programme (UNEP) coordinates global biodiversity assessments.

To address global issues, many governments have also signed international treaties and agreements launched in the wake of the 1972 United Nations Conference on the Human Environment in Stockholm and the 1992 United Nations Conference on

Environment and Development (the Earth Summit) in Rio de Janeiro, which produced Agenda 21—an array of actions to address environmental challenges:

· The Framework Convention on Climate Change aims to stabilize atmospheric concentrations of greenhouse gases at levels that will prevent human activities from interfering dangerously with the global climate.
· The Vienna Convention for the Protection of the Ozone Layer aims to protect human health and the environment by promoting research on the effects of changes in the ozone layer and on alternative substances (such as substitutes for chlorofluorocarbon) and technologies, monitoring the ozone layer, and taking measures to control the activities that produce adverse effects.
· The Montreal Protocol for Chlorofluorocarbon Control requires that countries help protect the earth from excessive ultraviolet radiation by cutting chlorofluorocarbon consumption by 20 percent over their 1986 level by 1994 and by 50 percent over their 1986 level by 1999, with allowances for increases in consumption by developing countries.
· The United Nations Convention on the Law of the Sea, which became effective in November 1994, establishes a comprehensive legal regime for seas and oceans, establishes rules for environmental standards and enforcement provisions, and develops international rules and national legislation to prevent and control marine pollution.
· The Convention on Biological Diversity promotes conservation of biodiversity through scientific and technological cooperation among countries, access to financial and genetic resources, and transfer of ecologically sound technologies.

But 10 years after the Earth Summit in Rio de Janeiro the World Summit on Sustainable Development in Johannesburg recognized that many of the proposed actions had yet to materialize. To help developing countries comply with their obligations under these agreements, the Global Environment Facility (GEF) was created to focus on global improvement in biodiversity, climate change, international waters, and ozone layer depletion. The UNEP, United Nations Development Programme, and World Bank manage the GEF according to the policies of its governing body of country representatives. The World Bank is responsible for the GEF Trust Fund and chairs the GEF.

## Definitions

· **Environmental strategies or action plans** provide a comprehensive analysis of conservation and resource management issues that integrate environmental concerns with development. They include national conservation strategies, environmental action plans, environmental management strategies, and sustainable development strategies. The date is the year a country adopted a strategy or action plan. · **Biodiversity assessments, strategies, or action plans** include biodiversity profiles (see *About the data*). · **Participation in treaties** covers nine international treaties (see *About the data*). · **Climate change** refers to the Framework Convention on Climate Change (signed in 1992). · **Ozone layer** refers to the Vienna Convention for the Protection of the Ozone Layer (signed in 1985). · **CFC control** refers to the Protocol on Substances That Deplete the Ozone Layer (the Montreal Protocol for Chlorofluorocarbon Control) (signed in 1987). · **Law of the Sea** refers to the United Nations Convention on the Law of the Sea (signed in 1982). · **Biological diversity** refers to the Convention on Biological Diversity (signed at the Earth Summit in 1992). · **Kyoto Protocol** refers to the protocol on climate change adopted at the third conference of the parties to the United Nations Framework Convention on Climate Change in December 1997. · **CITES** is the Convention on International Trade in Endangered Species of Wild Fauna and Flora, an agreement among governments to ensure that the survival of wild animals and plants is not threatened by uncontrolled exploitation. Adopted in 1973, it entered into force in 1975. · **CCD** is the United Nations Convention to Combat Desertification, an international convention addressing the problems of land degradation in the world's drylands. Adopted in 1994, it entered into force in 1996. · **Stockholm Convention** is an international legally binding instrument to protect human health and the environment from persistent organic pollutants. Adopted in 2001, it entered into force in 2004.

## Data sources

Data on environmental strategies and participation in international environmental treaties are from the Secretariat of the United Nations Framework Convention on Climate Change, the Ozone Secretariat of the UNEP, the World Resources Institute, the UNEP, the Center for International Earth Science Information Network, and the United Nations Treaty Series.

# 3.16 | Toward a broader measure of savings

| | Gross savings | Consumption of fixed capital | Net national savings | Education expenditure | Energy depletion | Mineral depletion | Net forest depletion | Carbon dioxide damage | Particulate emission damage | Adjusted net savings |
|---|---|---|---|---|---|---|---|---|---|---|
| | % of GNI 2006 | % of GNI 2006 | % of GNI 2006 | % of GNI 2006 | % of GNI 2006 | % of GNI 2006 | % of GNI 2006 | % of GNI 2006 | % of GNI 2006 | % of GNI 2006 |
| Afghanistan | .. | 7.7 | .. | .. | 0.0 | .. | 0.9 | 0.1 | 0.9 | .. |
| Albania | 16.7 | 10.5 | 6.1 | 2.8 | 2.0 | 0.0 | 0.0 | 0.2 | 0.2 | 6.5 |
| Algeria | .. | 11.8 | .. | 4.5 | 58.1 | 0.1 | 0.1 | 1.3 | 0.3 | .. |
| Angola | 42.2 | 12.2 | 30.0 | 3.0 | 68.8 | 0.0 | 0.0 | 0.2 | 1.6 | −37.6 |
| Argentina | 27.1 | 12.0 | 15.1 | 4.0 | 12.8 | 1.0 | 0.0 | 0.5 | 1.6 | 3.2 |
| Armenia | 29.3 | 10.2 | 19.2 | 3.0 | 0.0 | 2.2 | 0.0 | 0.6 | 1.8 | 17.6 |
| Australia | 21.9[a] | 15.1 | 6.8 | 4.7 | 3.6 | 5.1 | 0.0 | 0.4 | 0.1 | 2.4 |
| Austria | 25.8 | 14.2 | 11.6 | 5.3 | 0.3 | 0.0 | 0.0 | 0.2 | 0.3 | 16.1 |
| Azerbaijan | 57.0 | 12.1 | 44.9 | 2.8 | 83.8 | 0.0 | 0.0 | 2.4 | 1.1 | −39.7 |
| Bangladesh | 31.6 | 8.1 | 23.6 | 1.9 | 5.6 | 0.0 | 0.7 | 0.4 | 0.5 | 18.3 |
| Belarus | 26.4 | 11.2 | 15.2 | 5.7 | 2.1 | 0.0 | 0.0 | 1.6 | .. | 17.2[b] |
| Belgium | 23.9 | 15.4 | 8.5 | 5.9 | 0.0 | 0.0 | 0.0 | 0.2 | 0.2 | 14.1 |
| Benin | .. | 8.5 | .. | 3.6 | 0.0 | 0.0 | 0.9 | 0.3 | 0.4 | .. |
| Bolivia | 26.9 | 9.8 | 17.1 | 6.3 | 40.6 | 4.9 | 0.0 | 0.7 | 1.4 | −24.2 |
| Bosnia and Herzegovina | 6.0 | 10.4 | −4.4 | .. | 0.3 | 0.0 | .. | 1.3 | 0.1 | .. |
| Botswana | 55.8 | 12.5 | 43.3 | 8.6 | 0.3 | 7.0 | 0.0 | 0.3 | .. | 44.2[b,c] |
| Brazil | 17.8 | 12.0 | 5.8 | 4.3 | 3.7 | 2.3 | 0.0 | 0.2 | 0.3 | 3.5 |
| Bulgaria | 15.5 | 11.9 | 3.6 | 4.2 | 0.9 | 2.0 | 0.0 | 1.2 | 1.6 | 2.1 |
| Burkina Faso | .. | 8.1 | .. | 4.5 | 0.0 | 0.0 | 0.9 | 0.1 | 1.4 | .. |
| Burundi | 2.0 | 6.4 | −4.4 | 5.1 | 0.0 | 0.8 | 10.5 | 0.2 | 0.1 | −10.9 |
| Cambodia | 18.1 | 8.7 | 9.5 | 1.8 | 0.0 | 0.0 | 0.3 | 0.1 | 0.4 | 10.5 |
| Cameroon | 17.5 | 9.4 | 8.1 | 1.6 | 14.9 | 0.1 | 0.0 | 0.2 | 0.8 | −6.2 |
| Canada | 23.7[a] | 14.6 | 9.1 | 5.2 | 7.4 | 1.1 | 0.0 | 0.3 | 0.1 | 5.4 |
| Central African Republic | .. | 7.8 | .. | 1.6 | 0.0 | 0.0 | 0.0 | 0.1 | 0.4 | .. |
| Chad | 29.5 | 10.9 | 18.6 | 1.3 | 65.4 | 0.0 | 0.0 | 0.0 | 1.1 | −46.6 |
| Chile | 27.6 | 14.2 | 13.4 | 3.7 | 0.6 | 27.5 | 0.0 | 0.4 | 0.6 | −12.1 |
| China | 53.8 | 10.2 | 43.6 | 1.8 | 5.8 | 0.7 | 0.0 | 1.3 | 1.5 | 36.1 |
| Hong Kong, China | 31.9 | 13.9 | 18.1 | 3.4 | 0.0 | 0.0 | 0.0 | 0.2 | .. | 21.3[b] |
| Colombia | 20.9 | 11.4 | 9.5 | 5.0 | 9.7 | 1.7 | 0.0 | 0.3 | 0.1 | 2.5 |
| Congo, Dem. Rep. | 9.3 | 6.8 | 2.5 | 0.9 | 4.8 | 4.2 | 0.0 | 0.2 | 0.6 | −6.3 |
| Congo, Rep. | .. | .. | .. | 2.6 | .. | .. | .. | .. | 1.0 | .. |
| Costa Rica | 19.4 | 6.2 | 13.2 | 4.0 | 0.0 | 0.0 | 0.2 | 0.2 | 0.3 | 16.5 |
| Côte d'Ivoire | 15.1 | 9.6 | 5.6 | 4.7 | 12.5 | 0.0 | 0.0 | 0.3 | 0.4 | −3.0 |
| Croatia | 24.7 | 12.9 | 11.8 | 4.5 | 2.1 | 0.0 | 0.2 | 0.4 | 0.5 | 13.0 |
| Cuba | .. | .. | .. | 7.1 | .. | .. | .. | .. | 0.1 | .. |
| Czech Republic | 25.4 | 13.7 | 11.7 | 4.2 | 0.3 | 0.0 | 0.1 | 0.7 | 0.1 | 14.7 |
| Denmark | 25.0 | 15.0 | 10.0 | 8.1 | 3.4 | 0.0 | 0.0 | 0.1 | 0.1 | 14.4 |
| Dominican Republic | 20.7 | 11.6 | 9.1 | 1.9 | 0.0 | 3.4 | 0.0 | 0.6 | 0.1 | 6.9 |
| Ecuador | 28.1 | 11.4 | 16.7 | 1.4 | 28.8 | 0.4 | 0.0 | 0.5 | 0.1 | −11.8 |
| Egypt, Arab Rep. | 22.1 | 9.8 | 12.3 | 4.4 | 24.4 | 0.2 | 0.2 | 1.1 | 1.0 | −10.2 |
| El Salvador | 11.9 | 11.0 | 0.9 | 2.8 | 0.0 | 0.0 | 0.5 | 0.3 | 0.3 | 2.7 |
| Eritrea | 8.7 | 7.2 | 1.5 | 4.0 | 0.0 | 0.0 | 1.1 | 0.4 | 0.4 | 3.5 |
| Estonia | 25.7 | 12.9 | 12.8 | 5.1 | 37.6 | 0.0 | 0.0 | 1.1 | 0.0 | −20.9 |
| Ethiopia | 9.4 | 6.9 | 2.5 | 4.0 | 0.0 | 0.6 | 6.8 | 0.5 | 0.3 | −1.7 |
| Finland | 26.5 | 15.8 | 10.8 | 6.0 | 0.0 | 0.2 | 0.0 | 0.2 | 0.1 | 16.3 |
| France | 18.8 | 12.5 | 6.3 | 5.3 | 0.0 | 0.0 | 0.0 | 0.1 | 0.0 | 11.4 |
| Gabon | 52.4 | 15.3 | 37.1 | 3.3 | 60.8 | 0.0 | 0.0 | 0.2 | .. | −20.6[b] |
| Gambia, The | 10.3 | 7.8 | 2.5 | 2.0 | 0.0 | 0.0 | 0.6 | 0.5 | 0.8 | 2.7 |
| Georgia | 7.7 | 10.4 | −2.7 | 2.8 | 0.4 | 0.0 | 0.0 | 0.5 | 1.4 | −2.2 |
| Germany | 22.9 | 14.7 | 8.2 | 4.5 | 0.3 | 0.0 | 0.0 | 0.2 | 0.1 | 12.1 |
| Ghana | 27.4 | 8.5 | 18.9 | 4.7 | 0.0 | 7.7 | 1.6 | 0.5 | 0.1 | 13.8 |
| Greece | 16.4 | 6.9 | 9.5 | 3.4 | 0.2 | 0.2 | 0.0 | 0.3 | 0.7 | 11.6 |
| Guatemala | 14.5 | 10.8 | 3.7 | 1.6 | 1.1 | 0.0 | 0.7 | 0.2 | 0.4 | 2.9 |
| Guinea | 8.6 | 7.9 | 0.7 | 2.0 | 0.0 | 9.5 | 2.1 | 0.3 | 0.4 | −9.7 |
| Guinea-Bissau | 23.5 | 7.1 | 16.4 | 2.3 | 0.0 | 0.0 | 0.0 | 0.7 | 1.0 | 17.0 |
| Haiti | .. | 9.6 | .. | 1.5 | 0.0 | 0.0 | 0.8 | 0.3 | 0.4 | .. |

| | Gross savings | Consumption of fixed capital | Net national savings | Education expenditure | Energy depletion | Mineral depletion | Net forest depletion | Carbon dioxide damage | Particulate emission damage | Adjusted net savings |
|---|---|---|---|---|---|---|---|---|---|---|
| | % of GNI 2006 | % of GNI 2006 | % of GNI 2006 | % of GNI 2006 | % of GNI 2006 | % of GNI 2006 | % of GNI 2006 | % of GNI 2006 | % of GNI 2006 | % of GNI 2006 |
| Honduras | 32.3 | 10.0 | 22.3 | 3.5 | 0.0 | 2.4 | 0.0 | 0.5 | 0.4 | 22.5 |
| Hungary | 20.3 | 13.6 | 6.6 | 5.5 | 1.3 | 0.0 | 0.0 | 0.4 | 0.1 | 10.3 |
| India | 33.7 | 9.0 | 24.7 | 3.9 | 4.3 | 1.2 | 0.5 | 1.3 | 0.7 | 20.6 |
| Indonesia | 27.6 | 10.4 | 17.2 | 0.9 | 11.4 | 3.1 | 0.0 | 0.7 | 1.2 | 1.7 |
| Iran, Islamic Rep. | 40.7 | 11.0 | 29.7 | 4.4 | 54.2 | 0.5 | 0.0 | 1.3 | 0.8 | −22.7 |
| Iraq | .. | .. | .. | .. | .. | .. | .. | .. | .. | .. |
| Ireland | 37.7[a] | 10.7 | 27.0 | 5.3 | 3.4 | 0.4 | 0.0 | 0.2 | 0.0 | 28.2 |
| Israel | .. | 16.7 | .. | 6.7 | 0.3 | 0.0 | 0.0 | 0.4 | 0.4 | .. |
| Italy | 19.3 | 13.4 | 5.9 | 4.5 | 0.3 | 0.0 | 0.0 | 0.2 | 0.2 | 9.7 |
| Jamaica | .. | 7.6 | .. | 4.5 | 0.0 | 3.5 | 0.0 | 0.8 | 0.2 | .. |
| Japan | 27.3[a] | 13.9 | 13.4 | 3.1 | 0.0 | 0.0 | 0.0 | 0.2 | 0.5 | 15.8 |
| Jordan | 13.8 | 10.2 | 3.6 | 5.6 | 0.4 | 0.0 | 0.0 | 1.0 | 0.7 | 7.1 |
| Kazakhstan | 34.5 | 13.1 | 21.3 | 4.4 | 52.4 | 4.2 | 0.0 | 2.1 | 0.3 | −33.2 |
| Kenya | 10.1 | 9.6 | 0.5 | 6.3 | 0.0 | 0.1 | 1.0 | 0.4 | 0.1 | 5.2 |
| Korea, Dem. Rep. | .. | .. | .. | .. | .. | .. | .. | .. | .. | .. |
| Korea, Rep. | 30.5 | 13.3 | 17.1 | 4.0 | 0.1 | 0.0 | 0.0 | 0.4 | 0.6 | 20.0 |
| Kuwait | .. | .. | .. | 4.2 | .. | .. | 0.0 | .. | 1.4 | .. |
| Kyrgyz Republic | 4.5 | 8.5 | −4.0 | 4.4 | 1.1 | 0.0 | 0.0 | 1.3 | 0.3 | −2.3 |
| Lao PDR | 21.8 | 9.7 | 12.1 | 1.1 | 0.0 | 0.0 | 0.0 | 0.4 | 0.8 | 12.1 |
| Latvia | 17.5 | 18.2 | −0.7 | 5.6 | 0.0 | 0.0 | 0.7 | 0.3 | 0.0 | 3.8 |
| Lebanon | −4.5 | 11.9 | −16.4 | 2.5 | 0.0 | 0.0 | 0.0 | 0.6 | 0.9 | −15.4 |
| Lesotho | 21.8 | 7.1 | 14.7 | 9.3 | 0.0 | 0.0 | 1.4 | 0.0 | 0.2 | 22.4 |
| Liberia | .. | 8.7 | .. | .. | 0.0 | 0.1 | 6.0 | 0.6 | 0.5 | .. |
| Libya | .. | 12.2 | .. | .. | 81.3 | 0.0 | 0.0 | 0.8 | .. | .. |
| Lithuania | 14.5 | 13.0 | 1.5 | 5.1 | 0.3 | 0.0 | 0.1 | 0.4 | 0.2 | 5.6 |
| Macedonia, FYR | 22.1 | 10.8 | 11.3 | 4.9 | 0.0 | 0.0 | 0.2 | 1.4 | 0.1 | 14.5 |
| Madagascar | 16.3 | 7.6 | 8.7 | 2.7 | 0.0 | 0.0 | 0.0 | 0.3 | 0.2 | 10.9 |
| Malawi | 15.7 | 7.3 | 8.4 | 4.9 | 0.0 | 0.0 | 0.6 | 0.2 | 0.2 | 12.2 |
| Malaysia | 32.7 | 12.1 | 20.6 | 5.8 | 22.1 | 0.0 | 0.0 | 0.8 | 0.1 | 3.3 |
| Mali | 13.8 | 8.8 | 5.0 | 3.6 | 0.0 | 0.0 | 0.0 | 0.1 | 1.6 | 7.0 |
| Mauritania | 27.5 | 8.7 | 18.8 | 2.4 | 0.0 | 24.2 | 0.4 | 0.8 | 2.8 | −7.0 |
| Mauritius | 18.9 | 11.5 | 7.4 | 3.8 | 0.0 | 0.0 | 0.0 | 0.4 | .. | 10.8[b] |
| Mexico | 22.2 | 12.4 | 9.8 | 5.3 | 10.6 | 0.6 | 0.0 | 0.4 | 0.4 | 3.1 |
| Moldova | 20.3 | 8.1 | 12.2 | 3.6 | 0.1 | 0.0 | 0.0 | 1.7 | 0.7 | 13.3 |
| Mongolia | 45.3 | 7.9 | 37.3 | 5.1 | 2.8 | 26.4 | 0.0 | 2.5 | 1.1 | 9.7 |
| Morocco | 35.0 | 10.5 | 24.5 | 6.5 | 0.2 | 0.8 | 0.0 | 0.5 | 0.1 | 29.4 |
| Mozambique | 3.5 | 8.5 | −5.1 | 3.7 | 11.5 | 0.0 | 0.5 | 0.2 | 0.2 | −13.8 |
| Myanmar | .. | .. | .. | 0.8 | .. | .. | .. | .. | 0.6 | .. |
| Namibia | 42.7 | 11.0 | 31.6 | 7.3 | 0.0 | 5.2 | 0.0 | 0.3 | 0.1 | 33.4 |
| Nepal | 28.0 | 7.6 | 20.4 | 2.6 | 0.0 | 0.0 | 2.1 | 0.3 | 0.1 | 20.5 |
| Netherlands | 28.7 | 14.5 | 14.2 | 5.2 | 2.5 | 0.0 | 0.0 | 0.2 | 0.6 | 16.0 |
| New Zealand | 21.2[a] | 13.7 | 7.5 | 7.0 | 1.5 | 0.3 | 0.0 | 0.3 | 0.0 | 12.4 |
| Nicaragua | 13.6 | 9.5 | 4.1 | 3.0 | 0.0 | 1.1 | 0.0 | 0.6 | 0.1 | 5.3 |
| Niger | .. | 7.4 | .. | 2.3 | 0.0 | 0.0 | 2.6 | 0.3 | 0.9 | .. |
| Nigeria | 38.8 | 10.2 | 28.5 | 0.9 | 57.7 | 0.0 | 0.2 | 0.4 | 0.7 | −29.6 |
| Norway | 38.8[a] | 13.3 | 25.4 | 7.0 | 23.0 | 0.0 | 0.0 | 0.1 | 0.1 | 9.2 |
| Oman | .. | .. | .. | 3.7 | .. | .. | 0.0 | .. | 1.4 | .. |
| Pakistan | 23.1 | 8.4 | 14.7 | 1.8 | 7.2 | 0.0 | 0.4 | 0.8 | 1.5 | 6.8 |
| Panama | 18.6 | 12.3 | 6.3 | 4.4 | 0.0 | 0.0 | 0.0 | 0.3 | 0.2 | 10.2 |
| Papua New Guinea | .. | 10.2 | .. | .. | 23.8 | 48.5 | 0.0 | 0.4 | 0.0 | .. |
| Paraguay | 7.3[a] | 9.9 | −2.6 | 4.1 | 0.0 | 0.0 | 0.0 | 0.3 | 0.7 | 0.5 |
| Peru | 25.1 | 12.0 | 13.1 | 2.5 | 3.2 | 14.8 | 0.0 | 0.3 | 0.7 | −3.4 |
| Philippines | 30.5 | 8.4 | 22.1 | 2.4 | 0.7 | 1.2 | 0.1 | 0.5 | 0.3 | 21.7 |
| Poland | 18.8 | 12.8 | 6.0 | 5.4 | 1.3 | 1.1 | 0.0 | 0.8 | 0.4 | 7.8 |
| Portugal | 12.7 | 17.4 | −4.7 | 5.7 | 0.0 | 0.2 | 0.0 | 0.2 | 0.4 | 0.1 |
| Puerto Rico | .. | .. | .. | .. | .. | .. | .. | .. | .. | .. |

# 3.16 | Toward a broader measure of savings

| | Gross savings | Consumption of fixed capital | Net national savings | Education expenditure | Energy depletion | Mineral depletion | Net forest depletion | Carbon dioxide damage | Particulate emission damage | Adjusted net savings |
|---|---|---|---|---|---|---|---|---|---|---|
| | % of GNI | % of GNI | % of GNI | % of GNI | % of GNI | % of GNI | % of GNI | % of GNI | % of GNI | % of GNI |
| | 2006 | 2006 | 2006 | 2006 | 2006 | 2006 | 2006 | 2006 | 2006 | 2006 |
| Romania | 13.0 | 12.0 | 0.9 | 3.3 | 4.5 | 0.2 | 0.0 | 0.7 | 0.0 | –1.2 |
| Russian Federation | 30.7 | 7.0 | 23.7 | 3.5 | 37.5 | 1.9 | 0.0 | 1.4 | 0.3 | –13.8 |
| Rwanda | 13.9 | 7.4 | 6.4 | 3.5 | 0.0 | 0.0 | 2.3 | 0.2 | 0.1 | 7.3 |
| Saudi Arabia | .. | .. | .. | 7.2 | .. | .. | 0.0 | .. | 1.4 | .. |
| Senegal | 18.8 | 9.0 | 9.8 | 4.6 | 0.0 | 0.1 | 0.0 | 0.4 | 1.1 | 12.6 |
| Serbia[d] | 9.0 | .. | .. | .. | 2.2 | 0.1 | .. | 1.5 | .. | .. |
| Sierra Leone | 9.7 | 7.5 | 2.2 | 4.5 | 0.0 | 0.0 | 1.7 | 0.5 | 1.1 | 3.5[c] |
| Singapore | 47.8[a] | 15.0 | 32.8 | 2.5 | 0.0 | 0.0 | 0.0 | 0.4 | 0.8 | 34.0 |
| Slovak Republic | 21.2 | 21.9 | –0.8 | 4.1 | 0.1 | 0.0 | 0.4 | 0.6 | 0.0 | 2.2 |
| Slovenia | 26.3 | 13.5 | 12.8 | 5.6 | 5.1 | 0.0 | 0.2 | 0.3 | 0.2 | 12.5 |
| Somalia | .. | .. | .. | .. | .. | .. | .. | .. | .. | .. |
| South Africa | 14.2 | 11.9 | 2.3 | 5.3 | 3.5 | 3.1 | 0.1 | 1.1 | 0.1 | –0.3 |
| Spain | 22.4 | 14.5 | 7.9 | 3.9 | 0.0 | 0.0 | 0.0 | 0.2 | 0.4 | 11.2 |
| Sri Lanka | 24.9 | 9.7 | 15.1 | 2.6 | 0.0 | 0.0 | 0.3 | 0.3 | 0.4 | 16.7 |
| Sudan | 15.5 | 10.0 | 5.4 | 0.9 | 21.6 | 0.2 | 0.0 | 0.2 | 0.4 | –16.2 |
| Swaziland | 18.6 | 10.4 | 8.2 | 6.2 | 0.0 | 0.0 | 0.0 | 0.3 | 0.1 | 14.1 |
| Sweden | 24.8 | 12.1 | 12.7 | 7.3 | 0.0 | 0.5 | 0.0 | 0.1 | 0.1 | 19.4 |
| Switzerland | .. | 13.5 | .. | 5.1 | 0.0 | 0.0 | 0.0 | 0.1 | 0.2 | .. |
| Syrian Arab Republic | 17.6 | 10.3 | 7.3 | 2.6 | 31.7 | 0.0 | 0.0 | 1.2 | 0.9 | –24.0 |
| Tajikistan | 12.2 | 8.3 | 3.9 | 3.2 | 0.6 | 0.0 | 0.0 | 1.6 | 0.4 | 4.5 |
| Tanzania | 11.4 | 7.8 | 3.6 | 2.4 | 0.3 | 4.7 | 0.0 | 0.2 | 0.1 | 0.6 |
| Thailand | 32.1 | 11.2 | 20.9 | 4.7 | 5.8 | 0.0 | 0.2 | 1.0 | 0.4 | 18.1 |
| Timor-Leste | 104.5 | 3.3 | 101.3 | .. | .. | .. | .. | .. | .. | .. |
| Togo | .. | 7.8 | .. | 2.5 | 0.0 | 0.3 | 2.8 | 0.6 | 0.2 | .. |
| Trinidad and Tobago | .. | 12.1 | .. | 4.0 | 71.7 | 0.0 | 0.0 | 1.6 | 0.2 | .. |
| Tunisia | 26.9 | 11.4 | 15.5 | 6.7 | 7.4 | 0.4 | 0.1 | 0.6 | 0.3 | 13.4 |
| Turkey | 16.6 | 11.7 | 4.9 | 3.5 | 0.4 | 0.1 | 0.0 | 0.5 | 1.2 | 6.2 |
| Turkmenistan | .. | 11.0 | .. | .. | .. | 0.0 | .. | 2.9 | 1.0 | .. |
| Uganda | 14.7 | 7.7 | 7.0 | 4.0 | 0.0 | 0.0 | 4.5 | 0.2 | .. | 6.3[b] |
| Ukraine | 23.2 | 10.6 | 12.6 | 4.4 | 9.7 | 0.0 | 0.0 | 2.8 | 0.5 | 4.1 |
| United Arab Emirates | .. | .. | .. | .. | .. | .. | .. | .. | .. | .. |
| United Kingdom | 14.2 | 10.2 | 4.0 | 5.3 | 2.2 | 0.0 | 0.0 | 0.2 | 0.0 | 6.9 |
| United States | 14.1[a] | 12.2 | 1.9 | 4.8 | 1.8 | 0.1 | 0.0 | 0.3 | 0.3 | 4.1 |
| Uruguay | 14.3 | 12.1 | 2.3 | 2.6 | 0.0 | 0.0 | 0.2 | 0.2 | 1.9 | 2.6 |
| Uzbekistan | 36.0 | 8.7 | 27.4 | 9.4 | .. | 0.0 | 0.0 | 6.3 | 0.9 | .. |
| Venezuela, RB | 39.8 | 12.0 | 27.8 | 4.4 | 39.8 | 1.1 | 0.0 | 0.7 | 0.0 | –9.5 |
| Vietnam | 37.7 | 9.0 | 28.7 | 2.8 | 17.9 | 0.1 | 0.4 | 1.1 | 0.6 | 11.6 |
| West Bank and Gaza | 10.0 | 9.1 | 1.0 | .. | 0.0 | 0.0 | .. | .. | .. | .. |
| Yemen, Rep. | .. | 9.8 | .. | .. | 42.8 | 0.0 | 0.0 | 0.7 | 0.9 | .. |
| Zambia | 25.3 | 10.1 | 15.3 | 2.2 | 0.1 | 31.0 | 0.0 | 0.2 | 0.7 | –14.4 |
| Zimbabwe | .. | .. | .. | 6.9 | .. | .. | .. | .. | 0.1 | .. |
| **World** | **21.8 w** | **12.4 w** | **9.3 w** | **4.4 w** | **4.1 w** | **0.5 w** | **0.0 w** | **0.4 w** | **0.4 w** | **8.3 w** |
| **Low income** | 30.5 | 9.0 | 21.5 | 3.4 | 9.4 | 1.3 | 0.6 | 1.0 | 0.7 | 11.9 |
| **Middle income** | 30.5 | 10.9 | 19.6 | 3.5 | 12.8 | 1.6 | 0.0 | 0.9 | 0.8 | 7.0 |
| Lower middle income | 41.4 | 10.4 | 31.0 | 2.5 | 11.1 | 1.1 | 0.0 | 1.2 | 1.1 | 18.9 |
| Upper middle income | 22.3 | 11.4 | 10.9 | 4.4 | 14.4 | 2.0 | 0.0 | 0.7 | 0.4 | –2.2 |
| **Low & middle income** | 30.5 | 10.7 | 19.8 | 3.5 | 12.3 | 1.5 | 0.1 | 0.9 | 0.8 | 7.6 |
| East Asia & Pacific | 47.2 | 10.3 | 36.9 | 2.1 | 7.1 | 0.9 | 0.0 | 1.2 | 1.3 | 28.5 |
| Europe & Central Asia | 22.6 | 10.3 | 12.3 | 4.1 | 18.4 | 1.1 | 0.0 | 1.1 | 0.5 | –4.9 |
| Latin America & Carib. | 22.4 | 12.1 | 10.4 | 4.4 | 9.1 | 3.0 | 0.0 | 0.4 | 0.4 | 1.8 |
| Middle East & N. Africa | .. | 10.9 | .. | 4.6 | 40.0 | 0.3 | 0.1 | 1.1 | 0.6 | .. |
| South Asia | 32.1 | 8.9 | 23.2 | 3.5 | 4.5 | 0.9 | 0.5 | 1.1 | 0.8 | 18.8 |
| Sub-Saharan Africa | 19.4 | 10.7 | 8.7 | 3.8 | 18.7 | 2.3 | 0.4 | 0.6 | 0.4 | –10.0 |
| **High income** | 19.9 | 13.0 | 6.9 | 4.7 | 1.5 | 0.2 | 0.0 | 0.3 | 0.3 | 9.3 |
| Euro area | 21.8 | 13.8 | 8.0 | 4.8 | 0.4 | 0.0 | 0.0 | 0.2 | 0.2 | 12.0 |

a. World Bank staff estimates. b. Excludes particulate emissions damage. c. Likely to be overestimated because mineral depletion excludes diamonds. d. Includes Montenegro.

**About the data**

Adjusted net savings measure the change in value of a specified set of assets, excluding capital gains. If a country's net savings are positive and the accounting includes a sufficiently broad range of assets, economic theory suggests that the present value of social welfare is increasing. Conversely, persistently negative adjusted net savings indicate that an economy is on an unsustainable path.

The table provides a test to check the extent to which today's rents from a number of natural resources and changes in human capital are balanced by net savings, that is, this generation's bequest to future generations.

Adjusted net savings are derived from standard national accounting measures of gross savings by making four adjustments. First, estimates of capital consumption of produced assets are deducted to obtain net savings. Second, current public expenditures on education are added to net savings (in standard national accounting these expenditures are treated as consumption). Third, estimates of the depletion of a variety of natural resources are deducted to reflect the decline in asset values associated with their extraction and harvest. And fourth, deductions are made for damages from carbon dioxide and particulate emissions.

The exercise treats public education expenditures as an addition to savings effort. However, because of the wide variability in the effectiveness of government education expenditures, these figures cannot be construed as the value of investments in human capital. Current expenditure of $1 on education does not necessarily yield $1 of human capital. The calculation should also consider private education expenditure, but data are not available for a large number of countries.

While extensive, the accounting of natural resource depletion and pollution costs still has some gaps. Key estimates missing on the resource side include the value of fossil water extracted from aquifers, net depletion of fish stocks, and depletion and degradation of soils. Important pollutants affecting human health and economic assets are excluded because no internationally comparable data are widely available on damage from ground-level ozone or sulfur oxides.

Estimates of resource depletion are based on the calculation of unit resource rents. An economic rent represents an excess return to a given factor of production—in this case the returns from resource extraction or harvest are higher than the normal rate of return on capital. Natural resources give rise to

rents because they are not produced; in contrast, for produced goods and services competitive forces will expand supply until economic profits are driven to zero. For each type of resource and each country, unit resource rents are derived by taking the difference between world prices and the average unit extraction or harvest costs (including a "normal" return on capital). Unit rents are then multiplied by the physical quantity extracted or harvested in order to arrive at a depletion figure. This figure is one of a range of possible depletion estimates, depending on the assumptions made about future quantities, prices, and costs, and there is reason to believe that it is at the high end of the range. World prices are used in order to reflect the social opportunity cost of depleting minerals and energy.

A positive net depletion figure for forest resources implies that the harvest rate exceeds the rate of natural growth; this is not the same as deforestation, which represents a change in land use (see *Definitions* for table 3.4). In principle, there should be an addition to savings in countries where growth exceeds harvest, but empirical estimates suggest that most of this net growth is in forested areas that cannot currently be exploited economically. Because the depletion estimates reflect only timber values, they ignore all the external and nontimber benefits associated with standing forests.

Pollution damage from emissions of carbon dioxide is calculated as the marginal social cost per unit multiplied by the increase in the stock of carbon dioxide. The unit damage figure represents the present value of global damage to economic assets and to human welfare over the time the unit of pollution remains in the atmosphere.

Pollution damage from particulate emissions is estimated by valuing the human health effects from exposure to particulate matter pollution in urban areas. The estimates are calculated as willingness to pay to avoid illness and death from cardiopulmonary disease and lung cancer in adults and acute respiratory infections in children that is attributable to particulate emissions.

For a detailed note on methodology, see www.worldbank.org/data.

**Definitions**

• **Gross savings** are the difference between gross national income and public and private consumption, plus net current transfers. • **Consumption of fixed capital** is the replacement value of capital used up in production. • **Net national savings** are gross savings minus consumption of fixed capital. • **Education expenditure** is public current operating expenditures in education, including wages and salaries and excluding capital investments in buildings and equipment. • **Energy depletion** is unit resource rents times the physical quantities of extracted coal, crude oil, and natural gas. • **Mineral depletion** is unit resource rents times the physical quantities of extracted tin, gold, lead, zinc, iron, copper, nickel, silver, bauxite, and phosphate. • **Net forest depletion** is unit resource rents times the excess of roundwood harvest over natural growth. • **Carbon dioxide damage** is estimated at $20 per ton of carbon (in 1995 U.S. dollars) times tons of carbon emitted. • **Particulate emission damage** is the willingness to pay to avoid illness and death attributable to particulate emissions.• **Adjusted net savings** are net savings plus education expenditure minus energy depletion, mineral depletion, net forest depletion, and carbon dioxide and particulate emissions damage.

**Data sources**

Data on gross savings are from World Bank national accounts data files, described in the *Economy* section. Data on consumption of fixed capital are from the United Nations Statistics Division's *National Accounts Statistics: Main Aggregates and Detailed Tables, 1997,* extrapolated to 2006. Data on education expenditure are from the United Nations Statistics Division's *Statistical Yearbook 1997* and from the United Nations Educational, Scientific, and Cultural Organization Institute for Statistics' online database. The data sources and methods used to estimate resource depletion are described in Kunte and others' "Estimating National Wealth" (1998). The unit damage figure for carbon dioxide emissions is from Frankhauser's "Fractales, tissues urbains et reseaux de transport" (1994). The estimates of particulate emissions damage are from Pandey and others' "The Human Costs of Air Pollution: New Estimates for Developing Countries" (2006). The conceptual underpinnings of the savings measure appear in Hamilton and Clemens' "Genuine Savings Rates in Developing Countries" (1999).

# 4 ECONOMY

# A portrait of the global economy

The world's output grew 4.8 percent in 2006, half a percentage point faster than in 2005, to reach nearly $59 trillion. That was an increase of almost 50 percent since 1995, measured in purchasing power parity and 2005 prices (figure 4a). Low- and middle-income economies—whose share of global output increased from 34 percent to 41 percent—grew faster on average than high-income economies. Setting the pace were East Asia and Pacific, whose developing economies more than doubled their output and increased their share of global output from 9 percent to 14 percent, and South Asia, whose share increased from 4 percent to 6 percent. Dominating the growth in these two regions were China and India. Growing less rapidly, Europe and Central Asia gained a percentage point, Sub-Saharan Africa and the Middle East and North Africa saw their shares stay the same, while Latin America and the Caribbean saw its share of global output decline from 9 percent to 8 percent.

The statistics in this section measure the size and structure of the world's economies and how they are managed. The national accounts record the sources of economic growth. The balance of payments tracks the flow of goods and services between countries. The fiscal and monetary accounts, interest rates, and exchange rates reflect the domestic and international forces acting on the economy and the responses of politicians and policymakers.

Viewed over time, macroeconomic statistics show the health of an economy and the quality of macroeconomic management. Viewed across countries, they reveal the many varied patterns of development. Together they inform citizens, businesses, and governments of the results of their efforts and guide them in their future choices.

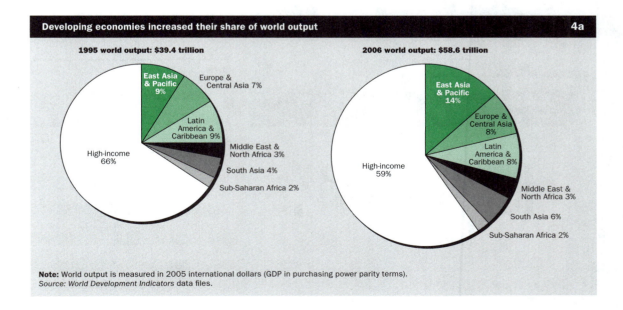

**Developing economies increased their share of world output**　　4a

1995 world output: $39.4 trillion

- East Asia & Pacific 9%
- Europe & Central Asia 7%
- Latin America & Caribbean 9%
- Middle East & North Africa 3%
- South Asia 4%
- Sub-Saharan Africa 2%
- High-income 66%

2006 world output: $58.6 trillion

- East Asia & Pacific 14%
- Europe & Central Asia 8%
- Latin America & Caribbean 8%
- Middle East & North Africa 3%
- South Asia 6%
- Sub-Saharan Africa 2%
- High-income 59%

**Note:** World output is measured in 2005 international dollars (GDP in purchasing power parity terms).
*Source: World Development Indicators* data files.

## Long-term trends

Developing economies are expected to continue growing faster than high-income economies thanks to labor surpluses, higher returns to physical capital, and ready access to technology already developed and amortized in high-income economies. With adequate investment in physical and human capital, developing economies should close the gap with richer economies in the long run.

Average growth of low- and lower middle-income economies has been rising, surpassing that of upper middle-income and high-income economies in the last three decades (figure 4b). Since 2000 annual GDP growth in low-income economies has averaged 6.5 percent, compared with 5.6 percent in middle-income economies and 2.3 percent in high-income economies. A few large countries drive these averages: China, India, and the Russian Federation, which have performed exceptionally well and carry large weights in the aggregates. Growth remains uneven across regions (figure 4c) and economies. In the last decade 20, mostly small, economies graduated from the World Bank's low- and middle-income economies classification. Some of the most successful economies are now classified as high-income. But poverty traps, exclusion from global markets, internal conflicts, resource constraints, poor policies, and market failures have limited growth and poverty reduction in low-income economies, especially in Africa.

## Better policies to achieve macroeconomic stability

Developing economies are running lower fiscal and external deficits, accumulating larger reserves, and pursuing more prudent monetary and fiscal policies. These policies mean less vulnerability and volatility and increased investor confidence. Since the high inflation and the debt crises of the 1970s and 1980s—and the rapid inflation in Europe and Central Asia after the Soviet Union's collapse—better fiscal, monetary, and exchange rate policies have reduced inflation in most developing countries. These shocks also revealed the importance of reliable, publicly available data for monitoring governments and private agents. The number of countries with double-digit inflation dropped from 61 in the 1990s to 27 in 2000–06, and inflation averaged less than 9 percent in all developing regions in 2006 (table 4d). But higher prices for oil and other commodities pushed inflation back up in three regions in 2006.

Better macroeconomic management has also lowered real interest rates in many developing economies, encouraging investment and faster growth. For the poorest and most indebted, Heavily Indebted Poor Country and Multilateral Debt Relief Initiatives led by the World Bank and International Monetary Fund have reduced debt burdens. Reforms under these programs have improved Sub-Saharan Africa's growth prospects.

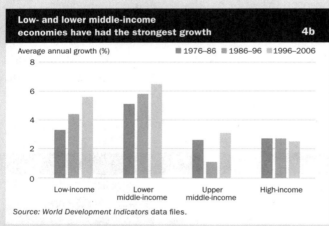

**Low- and lower middle-income economies have had the strongest growth** — **4b**

Average annual growth (%) — ■ 1976–86 ■ 1986–96 ■ 1996–2006

*Source: World Development Indicators data files.*

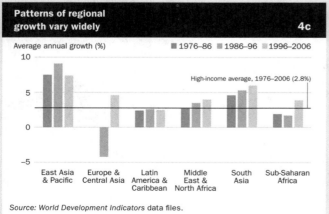

**Patterns of regional growth vary widely** — **4c**

Average annual growth (%) — ■ 1976–86 ■ 1986–96 ■ 1996–2006

High-income average, 1976–2006 (2.8%)

*Source: World Development Indicators data files.*

**Inflation is now less than 9 percent in all developing regions** — **4d**

| Region | 1975 | 1985 | 1995 | 2000 | 2005 | 2006 |
|---|---|---|---|---|---|---|
| East Asia & Pacific | .. | 3 | 8 | 3 | 6 | 5 |
| Europe & Central Asia | .. | .. | 56 | 13 | 7 | 8 |
| Latin America & Caribbean | 15 | 16 | 12 | 7 | 6 | 7 |
| Middle East & North Africa | 5 | 4 | 8 | 7 | 6 | 7 |
| South Asia | 24 | 7 | 9 | 4 | 6 | 6 |
| Sub-Saharan Africa | 11 | 10 | 10 | 6 | 8 | 7 |

*Source: World Development Indicators data files.*

**Real interest rates have fallen in many developing economies** — **4e**

| Economy | 1985 | 1990 | 1995 | 2000 | 2005 | 2006 |
|---|---|---|---|---|---|---|
| Argentina | .. | .. | 14 | 10 | −2 | −4 |
| Algeria | .. | .. | −8 | −12 | −7 | −1 |
| Brazil | .. | .. | .. | 48 | 45 | 45 |
| China | −2 | 3 | −1 | 4 | 1 | 2 |
| India | 9 | 5 | 6 | 8 | 6 | 5 |
| Indonesia | .. | 12 | 8 | −2 | −1 | 2 |
| Nigeria | 6 | 17 | −23 | −12 | −6 | 8 |
| Russian Federation | .. | .. | 72 | −10 | −7 | −5 |
| South Africa | 4 | 5 | 7 | 5 | 6 | 4 |
| Ukraine | .. | .. | −57 | 15 | −7 | 1 |

*Source: World Development Indicators and International Monetary Fund data files.*

# The contribution of trade

Globalization has elevated the importance of trade for developing economies. The rapid industrialization of many large developing economies has increased demand for primary commodities. The prices of oil, metals, and minerals have increased rapidly since 2002, allowing commodity producers to invest and produce more (figure 4f).

As a result, many primary commodity–exporting economies have experienced strong GDP growth, while oil- and metal-importing economies have seen price increases (figure 4g).

Such changes in the terms of trade affect the real growth of GDP. When export prices rise faster than import prices, the terms of trade improve, an economy's capacity to import rises, and the real value of its output increases.

One commonly used measure of the terms of trade effect is the difference between the value of exports deflated by the import price index and the value of exports in constant prices. Adding the terms of trade adjustment to GDP in constant prices yields real gross domestic income (GDI).

For some countries the terms of trade effect can be quite large. The terms of trade adjustment accounted for 33 percent of Zambia's GDI between 2000 and 2006 (table 4h). Real growth rates, taking account of the terms of trade effect, may differ substantially from constant price growth rates. Tajikistan's GDP increased 9.1 percent a year from 2000 to 2006, but the real growth of GDI was only 0.6 percent. This represented a terms-of-trade loss of 8.5 percent, the largest of any economy over the period.

Most oil-exporting economies have seen rising terms of trade in recent years. Some metal-exporting economies, such as Chile and Zambia, have also experienced favorable terms of trade thanks to recent increases in copper prices. But some oil-importing economies have weathered the worsening terms of trade by rapidly expanding manufactured goods exports (China) or services (India). Of 147 economies with data, 65 experienced a loss in income due to the terms of trade effect (6 greater than 2 percent), 68 economies gained (18 more than 2 percent), and 14 economies had no appreciable terms of trade effect.

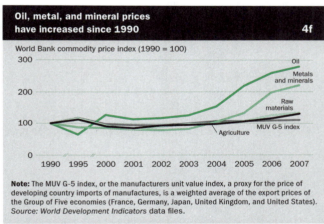

## Oil, metal, and mineral prices have increased since 1990 — 4f

World Bank commodity price index (1990 = 100)

**Note:** The MUV G-5 index, or the manufacturers unit value index, a proxy for the price of developing country imports of manufactures, is a weighted average of the export prices of the Group of Five economies (France, Germany, Japan, United Kingdom, and United States). *Source: World Development Indicators data files.*

## Oil-exporting economies have experienced gains — 4g

Terms of trade index (2000 = 100)

*Source: World Development Indicators data files.*

## Terms of trade, gross domestic product, and gross domestic income growth for selected economies — 4h

| Economy | Terms of trade | | Gross domestic product | Gross domestic income | Terms of trade gain or loss | |
|---|---|---|---|---|---|---|
| | 2000 = 100 | average annual % growth | average annual % growth | | % | % of GDI |
| | **2006** | **2000–06** | **2000–06** | **2000–06** | **2000–06** | **2000–06** |
| *Oil-exporting economies* | | | | | | |
| Azerbaijan | 214 | 14.2 | 15.6 | 23.5 | 7.9 | 13.5 |
| Equatorial Guinea | 168 | 9.3 | 19.4 | 30.1 | 10.7 | 16.1 |
| Iran, Islamic Rep. | 172 | 11.1 | 5.6 | 8.7 | 3.1 | 7.6 |
| Russian Federation | 149 | 7.8 | 6.4 | 10.7 | 4.4 | 6.9 |
| Venezuela, RB | 215 | 15.8 | 3.4 | 8.9 | 5.4 | 18.5 |
| *Metal- and primary commodity-exporting economies* | | | | | | |
| Burkina Faso | 96 | −1.5 | 6.2 | 6.0 | −0.2 | −0.8 |
| Chile | 174 | 10.2 | 4.3 | 8.6 | 4.3 | 5.5 |
| Côte d'Ivoire | 82 | −3.0 | 0.1 | −2.3 | −2.3 | −17.7 |
| Tajikistan | 42 | −11.7 | 9.1 | 0.6 | −8.5 | 1.7 |
| Zambia | 142 | 4.7 | 5.0 | 15.7 | 10.8 | 32.8 |
| *Oil-importing economies* | | | | | | |
| China | 87 | −2.7 | 9.8 | 8.5 | −1.3 | −2.9 |
| Costa Rica | 87 | −2.4 | 4.8 | 3.4 | −1.4 | −2.5 |
| Brazil | 110 | 1.5 | 3.0 | 3.2 | 0.2 | −3.5 |
| India | 87 | −2.8 | 7.4 | 6.9 | −0.5 | 0.3 |
| South Africa | 113 | 2.0 | 4.1 | 4.7 | 0.6 | 1.7 |

*Source: World Development Indicators data files.*

## 4.a

| | Gross domestic product | | Exports of goods and services | | Imports of goods and services | | GDP deflator | | Current account balance | | Gross international reserves | |
|---|---|---|---|---|---|---|---|---|---|---|---|---|
| | average annual % growth | | average annual % growth | | average annual % growth | | % growth | | % of GDP | | $ millions | months of import coverage |
| | 2006 | 2007ª | 2006 | 2007ª | 2006 | 2007ª | 2006 | 2007ª | 2006 | 2007ª | 2007 | 2007ª |
| Algeria | 3.0 | 3.0 | .. | −0.1 | .. | 38.8 | 9.1 | 7.8 | .. | 23.6 | 110,600 | 41.3 |
| Angola | 18.6 | 23.4 | .. | .. | .. | .. | 14.7 | 0.2 | 23.7 | 6.4 | .. | .. |
| Argentina | 8.5 | 8.5 | 7.4 | .. | 15.2 | .. | 13.5 | 12.8 | 3.8 | 2.6 | 44,779 | 12.0 |
| Armenia | 13.3 | 13.7 | −4.3 | 2.0 | 6.7 | 25.0 | 4.6 | 3.9 | −1.8 | −5.0 | 1,657 | 5.1 |
| Azerbaijan | 34.5 | 25.0 | 29.3 | 37.4 | 12.3 | 19.8 | 5.3 | 7.7 | 18.7 | 30.1 | 4,273 | 5.8 |
| Bangladesh | 6.6 | 6.5 | 25.8 | 27.0 | 18.2 | 23.6 | 5.2 | 5.6 | 1.9 | 1.4 | 5,077 | 3.3 |
| Belarus | 9.9 | 8.1 | 9.9 | 8.2 | 9.9 | 6.1 | 10.8 | 11.1 | −4.1 | −6.6 | 4,182 | 1.7 |
| Bolivia | 4.6 | 4.2 | 9.6 | −3.2 | 4.2 | 2.7 | 12.2 | 14.0 | 11.8 | 9.1 | 4,636 | 11.8 |
| Bosnia and Herzegovina | 6.0 | 6.0 | 13.7 | 12.6 | −6.9 | 14.2 | 6.5 | 2.5 | −10.1 | 12.1 | 5,621 | 17.3 |
| Botswana | 2.1 | 4.3 | 8.0 | 12.6 | −4.4 | 16.5 | 13.5 | 8.4 | 18.3 | 20.4 | 9,907 | 24.4 |
| Brazil | 3.7 | 5.3 | 4.6 | 6.3 | 18.1 | 20.0 | 4.3 | 4.4 | 1.3 | 0.3 | 179,433 | 13.4 |
| Bulgaria | 6.1 | 6.0 | 9.0 | 6.0 | 15.2 | 11.0 | 8.1 | 8.0 | −15.9 | −20.2 | 15,876 | 6.0 |
| Cameroon | 3.8 | 2.7 | 1.9 | 7.7 | 10.4 | 39.9 | 3.7 | 1.8 | .. | −1.4 | 1,896 | 16.9 |
| Chile | 4.0 | 5.2 | 4.2 | 8.1 | 9.4 | 15.1 | 11.7 | 5.5 | 3.6 | 3.8 | .. | .. |
| China | 10.7 | 11.4 | 23.3 | 21.2 | 14.3 | 16.5 | 3.6 | 5.2 | 9.4 | 11.0 | 8,249 | 17.8 |
| Colombia | 6.8 | 6.6 | 7.8 | 15.2 | 20.8 | 27.3 | 5.4 | 5.1 | −2.0 | −3.9 | 20,955 | 5.6 |
| Congo, Dem. Rep. | 4.9 | 6.5 | 2.5 | 9.9 | 5.7 | 9.2 | 13.1 | 17.0 | 0.0 | −7.8 | 522 | 1.5 |
| Congo, Rep. | 6.4 | 3.7 | .. | .. | .. | .. | 15.2 | −16.4 | .. | .. | 2,362 | 5.8 |
| Costa Rica | 8.2 | 6.8 | 9.9 | 14.2 | 8.9 | 11.8 | 10.1 | 9.0 | −5.0 | −5.9 | 4,114 | 3.6 |
| Côte d'Ivoire | 0.9 | 1.7 | −1.6 | −0.4 | 2.4 | 2.6 | 5.6 | 1.7 | 3.0 | 2.3 | .. | .. |
| Croatia | 4.8 | 5.8 | 6.9 | 6.9 | 7.3 | 7.4 | 3.4 | 3.2 | −7.5 | −8.2 | 12,210 | 4.7 |
| Dominican Republic | 10.7 | 8.0 | 5.8 | 7.6 | 12.6 | 6.7 | 7.6 | 7.0 | −2.5 | −2.0 | 2,946 | 1.8 |
| Ecuador | 3.9 | 2.2 | 8.6 | 2.6 | 9.2 | 6.5 | 7.2 | 4.7 | 3.6 | 3.3 | 3,521 | 3.5 |
| Egypt, Arab Rep. | 6.8 | 7.1 | 21.3 | 23.3 | 21.8 | 28.8 | 7.4 | 10.5 | 2.5 | 2.1 | 28,589 | 7.3 |
| El Salvador | 4.2 | 4.2 | 8.1 | 7.8 | 8.4 | 9.6 | 4.9 | 4.1 | −4.6 | 5.9 | 2,158 | 3.0 |
| Gabon | 1.2 | 5.6 | −9.7 | 4.2 | 8.6 | 118.3 | 7.9 | 1.1 | .. | 13.2 | 1,689 | 5.2 |
| Ghana | 6.2 | 6.3 | 10.3 | 10.0 | 8.9 | 14.0 | 14.6 | 13.0 | −8.1 | −13.6 | 2,500 | 2.7 |
| Guatemala | 4.5 | 5.7 | 6.5 | 12.5 | 5.2 | 7.5 | 6.3 | 5.4 | −4.5 | −5.1 | 4,320 | 4.0 |
| Honduras | 6.0 | 6.0 | 4.8 | 7.9 | 13.5 | 15.6 | 5.1 | 9.4 | −2.1 | −10.0 | 2,733 | 3.1 |
| Hungary | 3.9 | 1.7 | 18.9 | 15.5 | 14.5 | 13.2 | 3.7 | 6.4 | −6.6 | −4.9 | 24,121 | 2.9 |
| India | 9.2 | 8.7 | 8.6 | 6.4 | 11.4 | 6.4 | 5.9 | 4.5 | −1.0 | −1.4 | 295,000 | 12.0 |
| Indonesia | 5.5 | 6.3 | 9.2 | 8.4 | 7.6 | 7.4 | 13.6 | 10.5 | 2.7 | 2.5 | 56,920 | 5.7 |
| Iran, Islamic Rep. | 4.6 | 6.2 | 36.7 | 3.3 | 38.9 | −6.5 | 11.0 | 21.4 | .. | 11.1 | 78,112 | 14.2 |
| Jamaica | 2.5 | 1.4 | .. | .. | .. | .. | 6.3 | 6.6 | −11.7 | −17.0 | 1,878 | 3.8 |
| Jordan | 5.7 | 6.5 | 6.7 | 4.1 | −0.2 | 0.0 | 5.8 | 4.4 | −13.5 | −13.8 | 7,585 | 6.0 |
| Kazakhstan | 10.7 | 8.7 | 6.9 | 9.3 | 12.1 | 9.6 | 21.6 | 18.6 | −2.2 | −7.3 | 17,392 | 4.9 |
| Kenya | 6.1 | 5.5 | 0.7 | 12.5 | 18.1 | 9.6 | 7.1 | −0.6 | −2.3 | −13.3 | 3,015 | 3.7 |
| Latvia | 11.9 | 11.9 | 5.3 | 9.5 | 17.5 | 22.1 | 11.1 | 12.3 | −22.5 | −24.8 | 5,758 | 4.6 |
| Lebanon | 0.0 | 1.0 | 8.5 | 13.2 | −4.9 | 15.7 | 5.6 | 3.4 | −5.9 | −15.0 | 14,649 | 15.4 |
| Lesotho | 7.2 | 4.9 | 7.9 | 6.6 | 1.8 | 19.7 | 4.2 | 6.2 | 4.5 | 1.7 | 829 | 6.3 |

| | Gross domestic product | | Exports of goods and services | | Imports of goods and services | | GDP deflator | | Current account balance | | Gross international reserves | |
|---|---|---|---|---|---|---|---|---|---|---|---|---|
| | average annual % growth | | average annual % growth | | average annual % growth | | % growth | | % of GDP | | $ millions | months of import coverage |
| | 2006 | 2007[a] | 2006 | 2007[a] | 2006 | 2007[a] | 2006 | 2007[a] | 2006 | 2007[a] | 2007 | 2007[a] |
| Lithuania | 7.7 | 8.7 | 12.2 | 8.6 | 13.8 | 16.0 | 6.6 | 6.1 | −10.8 | −14.0 | 7,721 | 3.8 |
| Macedonia, FYR | 3.0 | 5.1 | 12.9 | 16.5 | 12.0 | 12.1 | 2.7 | 4.2 | −0.4 | −2.3 | 2,239 | 5.3 |
| Malawi | 7.4 | 7.4 | −11.8 | 15.8 | −13.1 | 5.7 | 18.5 | 7.6 | .. | −16.3 | 215 | 2.5 |
| Malaysia | 5.9 | 5.7 | 7.4 | 6.0 | 8.6 | 5.0 | 4.1 | 2.6 | 16.9 | 15.9 | 92,791 | 6.5 |
| Mauritius | 3.5 | 4.9 | 8.0 | 6.2 | 9.0 | 5.6 | 4.1 | 5.0 | −9.6 | −7.4 | 1,273 | 3.0 |
| Mexico | 4.8 | 3.2 | 11.1 | 5.1 | 12.2 | 7.7 | 4.4 | 2.0 | −0.2 | −0.8 | 77,990 | 3.3 |
| Moldova | 4.0 | 5.0 | 3.0 | 28.0 | 16.7 | 32.0 | 12.6 | 10.9 | −11.5 | −9.7 | 1,334 | 3.0 |
| Morocco | 8.0 | 2.0 | 10.5 | 3.5 | 6.7 | 11.0 | 1.9 | 2.0 | 2.8 | 1.0 | 24,760 | 8.3 |
| Montenegro | 16.2 | 7.5 | .. | 15.2 | .. | 38.1 | 2.6 | 2.4 | .. | −45.9 | 515 | 2.0 |
| Nicaragua | 3.7 | 3.8 | 10.5 | 8.9 | 6.1 | 8.1 | 10.6 | 12.5 | −16.1 | −15.8 | 930 | 2.5 |
| Nigeria | 5.2 | 6.3 | .. | .. | .. | .. | 7.9 | 4.8 | | 0.9 | 51,000 | 11.0 |
| Pakistan | 6.9 | 6.4 | 9.9 | 0.4 | 18.7 | 1.3 | 9.3 | 7.8 | −5.4 | −4.9 | 14,287 | 4.4 |
| Panama | 8.1 | 9.5 | 11.1 | 8.6 | 10.0 | 10.5 | 2.1 | 3.7 | −3.2 | −6.2 | 1,628 | 1.2 |
| Papua New Guinea | 2.6 | 6.2 | .. | 18.8 | .. | 19.2 | 9.7 | 2.4 | .. | 4.3 | 2,109 | 4.7 |
| Paraguay | 4.3 | 6.4 | 14.2 | .. | 33.3 | .. | 10.8 | 8.6 | −2.3 | 5.1 | 2,462 | 4.2 |
| Peru | 7.7 | 8.5 | 1.1 | 6.0 | 11.8 | 19.0 | 7.3 | 0.6 | 2.8 | 1.0 | 27,720 | 17.0 |
| Philippines | 5.4 | 6.5 | 11.2 | 5.4 | 1.9 | 2.5 | 5.2 | 3.3 | 5.0 | 4.6 | 30,249 | 5.3 |
| Poland | 6.1 | 6.5 | 14.5 | 11.7 | 15.8 | 12.3 | 1.0 | 1.4 | −3.3 | −5.1 | 61,236 | 3.8 |
| Romania | 7.7 | 6.1 | 10.3 | 8.0 | 8.6 | 18.6 | 10.1 | 6.8 | −10.5 | −14.6 | 39,423 | 6.5 |
| Russian Federation | 6.7 | 8.1 | 7.2 | 7.4 | 21.7 | −30.4 | 16.1 | 12.8 | 9.6 | 6.0 | 476,391 | 20.3 |
| Senegal | 2.3 | 5.0 | −8.6 | 3.6 | 1.0 | 3.0 | 2.9 | 5.9 | .. | −8.1 | 1,686 | 4.1 |
| Serbia | 5.7 | 7.5 | 5.7 | 33.2 | 2.8 | 32.5 | 15.6 | 8.9 | .. | −16.1 | 14,218 | 8.0 |
| Seychelles | 5.3 | 5.3 | 17.8 | −8.8 | 11.9 | 16.9 | 2.2 | 7.3 | −21.2 | −38.7 | 41 | 0.4 |
| Slovak Republic | 8.3 | 10.3 | 20.7 | 16.6 | 17.8 | 12.6 | 2.7 | 3.6 | .. | −4.0 | 22,148 | 4.3 |
| South Africa | 5.0 | 4.8 | 5.5 | 7.0 | 18.4 | 7.6 | 6.9 | 8.1 | −6.5 | −6.7 | 28,613 | 3.3 |
| Sri Lanka | 7.4 | 6.5 | 4.8 | 5.9 | 8.3 | 5.8 | 10.3 | 11.5 | −4.9 | −4.2 | 3,238 | 2.8 |
| Sudan | 11.8 | 10.5 | 0.4 | 15.5 | 8.2 | −4.1 | 7.0 | 3.8 | −12.6 | −11.8 | 1,000 | 1.0 |
| Swaziland | 2.1 | 2.3 | 6.0 | 10.0 | 5.5 | 15.0 | 5.7 | 8.3 | 3.7 | −0.7 | 637 | 3.4 |
| Syrian Arab Republic | 5.1 | 3.9 | −10.0 | 2.5 | −4.5 | 8.4 | 9.1 | 3.8 | 2.8 | 2.5 | 2,689 | 2.1 |
| Thailand | 5.0 | 4.3 | 8.6 | 6.5 | 1.6 | 3.2 | 5.0 | 3.0 | 1.1 | 2.2 | 92,574 | 6.5 |
| Tunisia | 5.2 | 5.7 | 3.9 | 4.2 | 1.4 | 5.3 | 3.0 | 1.8 | −2.1 | −1.4 | 7,348 | 4.5 |
| Turkey | 6.1 | 5.0 | 8.5 | 11.2 | 7.1 | 10.7 | 11.5 | 7.0 | −8.1 | −7.7 | 74,692 | 5.9 |
| Uganda | 5.4 | 6.2 | 4.0 | 15.6 | 7.0 | 12.8 | 7.3 | 8.9 | −2.5 | −6.8 | 2,160 | 6.0 |
| Ukraine | 7.1 | 7.3 | −4.9 | 3.3 | 6.5 | 15.2 | 13.7 | 21.4 | −1.5 | −3.2 | 32,500 | 5.6 |
| Uruguay | 7.0 | 7.3 | 7.6 | 19.0 | 16.0 | 16.0 | 6.8 | 9.5 | −2.3 | −1.7 | 4,121 | 7.4 |
| Uzbekistan | 7.3 | 9.5 | 2.0 | 17.6 | 1.2 | 10.0 | 21.5 | 23.9 | .. | 21.1 | 6,500 | 14.9 |
| Venezuela, RB | 10.3 | 8.4 | −4.2 | −5.3 | 31.4 | 31.9 | 16.9 | 23.4 | 14.9 | 11.1 | 33,477 | 5.7 |
| Vietnam | 8.2 | 8.5 | 22.7 | 21.1 | 21.5 | 34.0 | 7.3 | 8.2 | .. | −9.0 | 21,565 | 4.3 |
| Zambia | 6.2 | 5.7 | 21.0 | 10.8 | 14.3 | 20.0 | 12.2 | 10.1 | 8.8 | −4.0 | 1,080 | 3.6 |

a. Data are preliminary estimates.
**Source:** *World Development Indicators* data files.

# 4.1 Growth of output

| | Gross domestic product | | Agriculture | | Industry | | Manufacturing | | Services | |
|---|---|---|---|---|---|---|---|---|---|---|
| | average annual % growth | | average annual % growth | | average annual % growth | | average annual % growth | | average annual % growth | |
| | 1990–2000 | 2000–06 | 1990–2000 | 2000–06 | 1990–2000 | 2000–06 | 1990–2000 | 2000–06 | 1990–2000 | 2000–06 |
| Afghanistan | .. | 10.7 | .. | 0.4 | .. | 21.1 | .. | 13.8 | .. | 21.9 |
| Albania | 3.5 | 5.3 | 4.3 | 1.4 | −0.5 | 2.9 | .. | −0.2 | 6.9 | 7.6 |
| Algeria | 1.9 | 5.0 | 3.6 | 7.3 | 1.8 | 4.4 | −2.1 | 2.4 | 1.8 | 5.2 |
| Angola[a] | 1.6 | 11.5 | −1.4 | 13.8 | 4.4 | 12.2 | −0.3 | 17.1 | −2.2 | 6.7 |
| Argentina | 4.3 | 3.6 | 3.5 | 3.0 | 3.8 | 5.3 | 2.7 | 5.0 | 4.5 | 2.4 |
| Armenia | −1.9 | 12.5 | 0.5 | 7.8 | −7.8 | 16.4 | −4.3 | 7.7 | 6.4 | 13.4 |
| Australia | 4.0 | 3.2 | 3.7 | 1.7 | 2.8 | 2.7 | 2.1 | 1.1 | 4.4 | 3.6 |
| Austria | 2.4 | 1.7 | 1.6 | 0.0 | 2.7 | 2.2 | 2.7 | 1.3 | 2.3 | 1.6 |
| Azerbaijan | −6.3 | 15.6 | −2.1 | 5.9 | −0.8 | 20.1 | −12.0 | 8.8 | −2.3 | 12.2 |
| Bangladesh | 4.8 | 5.6 | 2.9 | 2.8 | 7.3 | 7.7 | 7.2 | 7.3 | 4.5 | 5.8 |
| Belarus | −1.7 | 8.1 | −4.0 | 6.5 | −1.8 | 11.5 | −0.7 | 11.6 | −0.4 | 6.1 |
| Belgium | 2.1 | 1.7 | 2.7 | 1.0 | 1.8 | 0.8 | 3.1 | 0.4 | 1.9 | 2.0 |
| Benin[a] | 4.8 | 3.8 | 5.8 | 4.6 | 4.1 | 3.8 | 5.8 | 2.7 | 4.2 | 3.2 |
| Bolivia | 4.0 | 3.3 | 2.9 | 3.7 | 4.1 | 3.7 | 3.8 | 3.7 | 4.3 | 2.3 |
| Bosnia and Herzegovina | .. | 5.1 | .. | 4.6 | .. | 6.6 | .. | 7.3 | .. | 3.6 |
| Botswana | 6.0 | 5.1 | −1.2 | −1.6 | 5.8 | 4.8 | 4.4 | 2.1 | 7.8 | 5.4 |
| Brazil | 2.7 | 3.0 | 3.6 | 4.2 | 2.4 | 2.9 | 2.0 | 3.0 | 3.8 | 3.1 |
| Bulgaria | −1.8 | 5.5 | 3.0 | −1.1 | −5.0 | 5.1 | .. | 6.0 | −5.2 | 5.9 |
| Burkina Faso | 5.5 | 6.2 | 5.9 | 6.2 | 5.9 | 7.3 | 5.9 | 6.3 | 3.9 | 5.5 |
| Burundi | −2.9 | 2.5 | −1.9 | −1.5 | −4.3 | −6.2 | −8.7 | .. | −2.8 | 10.4 |
| Cambodia | 7.0 | 9.5 | 3.7 | 5.2 | 14.3 | 14.6 | 18.6 | 14.2 | 7.5 | 10.0 |
| Cameroon | 1.7 | 3.6 | 5.5 | 3.8 | −0.9 | 2.6 | 1.4 | 5.0 | 0.2 | 7.3 |
| Canada | 3.1 | 2.6 | 1.1 | 1.7 | 3.2 | 1.3 | 4.5 | −0.1 | 3.0 | 3.0 |
| Central African Republic | 2.0 | −0.7 | 3.8 | 0.3 | 0.7 | −0.4 | −0.2 | −0.1 | 0.2 | −2.6 |
| Chad | 2.2 | 14.1 | 4.9 | 3.4 | 0.6 | 41.7 | .. | .. | 0.8 | 8.5 |
| Chile | 6.6 | 4.3 | 2.2 | 6.2 | 5.6 | 3.7 | 4.4 | 4.0 | 6.9 | 4.3 |
| China[a] | 10.6 | 9.8 | 4.1 | 4.2 | 13.7 | 11.2 | 12.9 | 11.1 | 10.2 | 10.1 |
| Hong Kong, China | 4.1 | 4.8 | .. | −1.1 | .. | −3.0 | .. | −4.2 | .. | 4.1 |
| Colombia | 2.8 | 3.9 | −2.6 | 1.6 | 1.5 | 5.5 | −2.5 | 4.9 | 4.5 | 3.1 |
| Congo, Dem. Rep. | −4.9 | 4.7 | 1.4 | 0.8 | −8.0 | 9.3 | −8.7 | 5.7 | −12.3 | 6.2 |
| Congo, Rep.[a] | 1.0 | 4.4 | 0.7 | .. | 1.7 | .. | −2.4 | .. | −0.7 | .. |
| Costa Rica | 5.3 | 4.8 | 4.1 | 3.0 | 6.2 | 5.2 | 6.8 | 5.2 | 4.7 | 5.3 |
| Côte d'Ivoire[a] | 3.2 | 0.1 | 3.5 | 1.1 | 6.3 | −1.3 | 5.5 | −3.0 | 2.0 | 0.1 |
| Croatia | 0.6 | 4.8 | −2.1 | 1.1 | −1.1 | 5.9 | −3.5 | 5.5 | 1.3 | 4.6 |
| Cuba[a] | 4.2 | 3.4 | .. | .. | .. | .. | .. | .. | .. | .. |
| Czech Republic | 1.1 | 4.2 | 0.0 | 2.9 | 0.2 | 5.8 | 4.3 | 7.1 | 1.2 | 3.5 |
| Denmark | 2.7 | 1.6 | 4.6 | 2.8 | 2.5 | 0.6 | 2.5 | −0.4 | 2.7 | 1.5 |
| Dominican Republic[a] | 6.0 | 3.9 | 3.9 | 3.8 | 7.0 | 1.0 | 4.9 | 1.7 | 6.0 | 5.6 |
| Ecuador[a] | 1.9 | 5.3 | −1.7 | 4.8 | 2.6 | 6.1 | 1.5 | 5.2 | 2.4 | 4.8 |
| Egypt, Arab Rep. | 4.4 | 4.0 | 3.1 | 3.3 | 5.1 | 3.6 | 6.4 | 3.5 | 4.1 | 4.6 |
| El Salvador | 4.8 | 2.5 | 1.2 | 2.2 | 5.1 | 2.2 | 5.2 | 2.2 | 4.0 | 2.7 |
| Eritrea | 5.7 | 2.7 | 1.5 | 2.0 | 15.0 | 4.1 | 10.6 | 6.6 | 5.7 | 3.5 |
| Estonia | 0.2 | 8.6 | −3.4 | −0.1 | −3.3 | 9.4 | 5.9 | 10.5 | 3.1 | 8.7 |
| Ethiopia | 4.0 | 5.7 | 2.4 | 5.0 | 4.5 | 7.0 | 4.0 | 4.4 | 5.5 | 5.7 |
| Finland | 2.6 | 2.9 | −1.1 | −0.2 | 4.1 | 4.2 | 6.4 | 4.0 | 2.5 | 1.8 |
| France | 1.9 | 1.7 | 2.0 | −0.3 | 1.0 | 1.3 | .. | 1.1 | 2.2 | 1.8 |
| Gabon[a] | 2.3 | 1.7 | 2.0 | 0.8 | 1.6 | 1.3 | 3.0 | 3.5 | 3.1 | 2.1 |
| Gambia, The | 3.0 | 3.9 | 3.3 | 2.5 | 1.0 | 5.9 | 0.9 | 4.2 | 3.7 | 5.4 |
| Georgia | −7.1 | 7.8 | −11.0 | 1.9 | −8.1 | 13.0 | .. | 7.7 | −0.3 | 8.3 |
| Germany | 1.8 | 0.8 | 0.1 | 1.0 | −0.1 | 1.0 | 0.2 | 1.2 | 2.9 | 1.0 |
| Ghana[a] | 4.3 | 5.3 | 3.4 | 3.6 | 2.7 | 7.5 | −4.5 | .. | 5.6 | 6.1 |
| Greece | 2.2 | 4.4 | 0.5 | −3.1 | 1.0 | 2.9 | .. | 1.2 | 2.6 | 4.8 |
| Guatemala[a] | 4.2 | 2.7 | 2.8 | 2.6 | 4.3 | 2.0 | 2.8 | 1.8 | 4.7 | 3.1 |
| Guinea | 4.4 | 2.9 | 4.3 | 4.0 | 4.9 | 3.4 | 4.0 | 2.2 | 3.6 | 1.8 |
| Guinea-Bissau | 1.2 | 0.4 | 3.9 | 4.4 | −3.1 | 3.7 | −2.0 | 3.7 | −0.6 | 0.6 |
| Haiti | −1.5 | −0.3 | .. | .. | .. | .. | .. | .. | .. | .. |

# Growth of output | **4.1**

| | Gross domestic product | | Agriculture | | Industry | | Manufacturing | | Services | |
|---|---|---|---|---|---|---|---|---|---|---|
| | average annual % growth | | average annual % growth | | average annual % growth | | average annual % growth | | average annual % growth | |
| | 1990–2000 | 2000–06 | 1990–2000 | 2000–06 | 1990–2000 | 2000–06 | 1990–2000 | 2000–06 | 1990–2000 | 2000–06 |
| Honduras | 3.2 | 4.0 | 2.2 | 3.7 | 3.6 | 4.0 | 4.0 | 4.3 | 3.8 | 4.7 |
| Hungary | 1.5 | 4.3 | –2.4 | 8.2 | 3.6 | 3.7 | 7.9 | 7.0 | 1.3 | 4.1 |
| India | 5.9 | 7.4 | 3.2 | 2.7 | 6.1 | 8.0 | 6.7 | 7.7 | 7.7 | 8.9 |
| Indonesia[a] | 4.2 | 4.9 | 2.0 | 3.1 | 5.2 | 4.0 | 6.7 | 5.1 | 4.0 | 6.5 |
| Iran, Islamic Rep. | 3.1 | 5.6 | 3.2 | 5.5 | 2.6 | 6.7 | 5.1 | 9.3 | 3.8 | 5.1 |
| Iraq | .. | –11.4 | .. | –3.6 | .. | –17.0 | .. | –12.8 | .. | 5.9 |
| Ireland | 7.5 | 5.1 | 0.8 | –1.8 | 12.7 | 4.9 | .. | .. | 8.1 | 5.6 |
| Israel | 5.4 | 2.6 | .. | .. | .. | .. | .. | .. | .. | .. |
| Italy | 1.5 | 0.7 | 2.1 | –0.4 | 0.8 | –0.3 | 1.4 | –1.2 | 1.7 | 1.1 |
| Jamaica | 1.8 | 1.8 | –0.3 | –1.3 | –1.0 | 1.8 | –2.2 | –0.2 | 2.3 | 1.8 |
| Japan | 1.1 | 1.5 | –1.3 | –1.9 | –0.3 | 0.9 | .. | 1.9 | 2.0 | 1.6 |
| Jordan | 5.0 | 6.1 | –3.0 | 9.4 | 5.2 | 8.8 | 5.6 | 10.8 | 5.0 | 5.5 |
| Kazakhstan | –4.1 | 10.1 | –8.0 | 4.7 | 0.6 | 11.4 | 2.7 | 8.8 | 0.3 | 10.8 |
| Kenya | 2.2 | 3.9 | 1.9 | 3.2 | 1.2 | 4.6 | 1.3 | 3.8 | 3.2 | 3.5 |
| Korea, Dem. Rep. | .. | .. | .. | .. | .. | .. | .. | .. | .. | .. |
| Korea, Rep. | 5.8 | 4.6 | 1.6 | 0.1 | 6.0 | 6.4 | 7.3 | 7.3 | 5.6 | 3.7 |
| Kuwait[a] | 4.9 | 7.3 | 1.0 | 15.1 | 0.3 | 1.9 | –0.1 | 2.5 | 3.5 | 10.2 |
| Kyrgyz Republic | –4.1 | 3.8 | 1.5 | 2.3 | –10.3 | –0.7 | –7.5 | –1.9 | –4.9 | 7.7 |
| Lao PDR | 6.5 | 6.4 | 4.8 | 2.6 | 11.1 | 12.9 | 11.7 | 10.2 | 6.6 | 6.8 |
| Latvia | –1.5 | 8.6 | –5.2 | 3.2 | –8.3 | 8.4 | –7.3 | 7.1 | 2.7 | 9.0 |
| Lebanon | 6.1 | 3.7 | 1.8 | 0.8 | –1.3 | 4.2 | –5.1 | 3.8 | 3.7 | 2.9 |
| Lesotho | 3.9 | 3.4 | 2.4 | –2.7 | 5.0 | 5.2 | 6.6 | 3.2 | 4.4 | 3.9 |
| Liberia[a] | 4.1 | –4.7 | .. | .. | .. | .. | .. | .. | .. | .. |
| Libya | .. | 3.2 | .. | .. | .. | .. | .. | .. | .. | .. |
| Lithuania | –2.7 | 8.0 | –0.3 | 3.3 | 3.3 | 10.2 | 7.0 | 10.1 | 5.4 | 6.6 |
| Macedonia, FYR | –0.8 | 2.2 | 0.2 | 0.8 | –2.3 | 1.4 | –5.3 | 0.6 | 0.5 | 2.3 |
| Madagascar | 2.0 | 2.7 | 1.9 | 1.9 | 2.4 | 1.6 | 2.0 | 1.6 | 2.3 | 2.7 |
| Malawi | 3.7 | 2.4 | 8.6 | –0.8 | 2.0 | 3.9 | 0.5 | 1.5 | 1.6 | 3.6 |
| Malaysia[a] | 7.0 | 5.0 | 0.3 | 3.6 | 8.6 | 4.9 | 9.5 | 5.7 | 7.3 | 5.3 |
| Mali | 4.1 | 5.7 | 2.6 | 5.0 | 6.4 | 4.8 | –1.4 | 5.3 | 3.0 | 6.3 |
| Mauritania | 2.9 | 5.0 | –0.2 | –0.4 | 3.4 | 4.0 | 5.8 | –2.5 | 4.9 | 7.2 |
| Mauritius | 5.2 | 4.0 | –0.5 | 1.1 | 5.5 | 1.4 | 5.3 | 0.2 | 6.4 | 5.9 |
| Mexico | 3.1 | 2.3 | 1.5 | 1.9 | 3.8 | 1.3 | 4.3 | 0.8 | 2.9 | 2.8 |
| Moldova | –9.6 | 6.8 | –11.2 | 1.8 | –13.6 | 1.2 | –7.1 | 5.8 | 0.7 | 10.1 |
| Mongolia | 1.0 | 7.1 | 2.5 | 2.7 | –2.5 | 7.9 | –9.7 | 7.5 | 0.7 | 8.6 |
| Morocco[a] | 2.4 | 5.1 | –0.4 | 8.7 | 3.2 | 4.1 | 2.6 | 3.4 | 3.1 | 4.7 |
| Mozambique | 5.7 | 8.2 | 4.9 | 7.9 | 12.8 | 9.6 | 10.2 | 12.4 | 2.8 | 7.8 |
| Myanmar[a] | 6.9 | 9.2 | 5.7 | .. | 10.5 | .. | 7.9 | .. | 7.2 | .. |
| Namibia | 4.0 | 4.8 | 3.8 | 1.5 | 2.4 | 6.0 | 2.6 | 3.4 | 4.5 | 5.4 |
| Nepal | 4.9 | 3.3 | 2.4 | 3.6 | 7.2 | 2.4 | 8.9 | 0.6 | 6.4 | 3.4 |
| Netherlands | 3.2 | 1.3 | 1.8 | 1.5 | 1.7 | 0.1 | 2.6 | 0.1 | 3.6 | 1.8 |
| New Zealand | 3.2 | 3.3 | 2.9 | 0.3 | 2.4 | 3.2 | 2.2 | 2.6 | 3.5 | 4.0 |
| Nicaragua | 3.7 | 3.3 | 4.7 | 3.0 | 5.5 | 4.2 | 5.3 | 5.2 | 5.0 | 3.4 |
| Niger[a] | 2.4 | 3.9 | 3.0 | 6.4 | 2.0 | 3.1 | 2.6 | 3.9 | 1.9 | 3.7 |
| Nigeria | 2.5 | 6.0 | 3.4 | 5.8 | 1.0 | 5.5 | 1.1 | 8.8 | 3.3 | 6.5 |
| Norway | 3.9 | 2.3 | 2.6 | 4.4 | 3.8 | 0.8 | 1.5 | 2.8 | 3.9 | 2.7 |
| Oman[a] | 4.5 | 4.2 | 5.0 | 2.2 | 3.9 | –0.5 | 6.0 | 9.3 | 5.0 | 7.5 |
| Pakistan | 3.8 | 5.5 | 4.4 | 2.5 | 4.1 | 7.9 | 3.8 | 10.0 | 4.4 | 6.1 |
| Panama | 4.7 | 5.0 | 3.1 | 4.4 | 6.0 | 2.7 | 2.7 | –0.4 | 4.5 | 5.6 |
| Papua New Guinea | 4.3 | 1.9 | 4.0 | 2.2 | 5.6 | –3.6 | 5.5 | –1.1 | 1.5 | 1.4 |
| Paraguay[a] | 2.2 | 2.9 | 3.3 | 4.9 | 0.6 | 1.8 | 1.4 | 1.4 | 2.5 | 2.5 |
| Peru | 4.7 | 4.9 | 5.5 | 3.5 | 5.4 | 5.8 | 3.8 | 5.4 | 4.0 | 4.5 |
| Philippines[a] | 3.3 | 4.9 | 1.7 | 3.8 | 3.5 | 3.5 | 3.0 | 4.5 | 4.0 | 6.3 |
| Poland | 4.7 | 3.7 | 0.5 | 3.4 | 7.1 | 4.3 | 9.9 | 7.0 | 5.1 | 3.2 |
| Portugal | 2.8 | 0.7 | –0.3 | –0.9 | 3.1 | –0.8 | 3.6 | 0.0 | 2.4 | 1.4 |
| Puerto Rico[a] | 4.2 | .. | .. | .. | .. | .. | .. | .. | .. | .. |

# 4.1 Growth of output

| | Gross domestic product | | Agriculture | | Industry | | Manufacturing | | Services | |
|---|---|---|---|---|---|---|---|---|---|---|
| | average annual % growth | | average annual % growth | | average annual % growth | | average annual % growth | | average annual % growth | |
| | 1990–2000 | 2000–06 | 1990–2000 | 2000–06 | 1990–2000 | 2000–06 | 1990–2000 | 2000–06 | 1990–2000 | 2000–06 |
| Romania | −0.6 | 6.0 | −1.9 | 8.1 | −1.2 | 5.6 | .. | .. | 0.9 | 5.4 |
| Russian Federation | −4.7 | 6.4 | −4.9 | 3.9 | −7.1 | 6.0 | .. | .. | −1.7 | 6.6 |
| Rwanda[a] | −0.3 | 5.0 | 2.6 | 3.6 | −3.7 | 6.2 | −6.0 | 3.0 | −1.2 | 6.2 |
| Saudi Arabia[a] | 2.1 | 4.4 | 1.6 | 1.5 | 2.2 | 4.9 | 5.6 | 6.0 | 2.2 | 4.2 |
| Senegal | 3.0 | 4.5 | 2.4 | 1.6 | 3.8 | 3.9 | 3.1 | 1.7 | 3.0 | 5.5 |
| Serbia | .. | 5.3 | .. | .. | .. | .. | .. | .. | .. | .. |
| Sierra Leone | −5.1 | 12.3 | −13.0 | .. | −4.5 | .. | 6.1 | .. | −2.9 | .. |
| Singapore | 7.6 | 5.0 | −2.4 | 1.8 | 7.8 | 4.6 | 7.0 | 6.5 | 7.8 | 5.3 |
| Slovak Republic[a] | 2.1 | 5.1 | 0.4 | 10.0 | 3.8 | 9.6 | 9.3 | 10.7 | 5.3 | 2.1 |
| Slovenia | 2.7 | 3.7 | 0.0 | 0.0 | 1.3 | 4.0 | 1.1 | 4.4 | 3.4 | 2.0 |
| Somalia | .. | .. | .. | .. | .. | .. | .. | .. | .. | .. |
| South Africa | 2.1 | 4.1 | 1.0 | −0.2 | 1.1 | 3.1 | 1.6 | 2.9 | 2.7 | 4.8 |
| Spain | 2.7 | 3.3 | 3.1 | −1.7 | 2.3 | 2.6 | .. | 0.7 | 2.7 | 3.5 |
| Sri Lanka | 5.3 | 4.8 | 1.8 | 1.2 | 6.9 | 4.4 | 8.1 | 3.5 | 5.7 | 6.3 |
| Sudan | 5.6 | 7.0 | 7.4 | 1.7 | 8.6 | 14.2 | 8.9 | 8.8 | 1.9 | 6.2 |
| Swaziland | 3.3 | 2.4 | 1.2 | 0.7 | 3.7 | 1.9 | 2.8 | 1.9 | 3.6 | 2.8 |
| Sweden | 2.1 | 2.7 | −1.1 | 2.0 | 4.2 | 4.3 | 8.6 | 4.4 | 1.9 | 2.1 |
| Switzerland | 1.0 | 1.3 | −2.0 | −1.7 | 0.4 | 1.1 | 1.2 | 0.8 | 1.2 | 0.9 |
| Syrian Arab Republic | 5.1 | 4.2 | 6.0 | 3.8 | 9.2 | 2.2 | .. | 16.1 | 1.5 | 7.3 |
| Tajikistan | −10.4 | 9.1 | −6.9 | 9.4 | −10.8 | 11.2 | −10.0 | 9.8 | −12.6 | 7.4 |
| Tanzania[b] | 2.9 | 6.5 | 3.2 | 4.9 | 3.1 | 9.6 | 2.7 | 8.0 | 2.7 | 6.2 |
| Thailand[a] | 4.2 | 5.4 | 1.0 | 2.4 | 5.7 | 6.8 | 6.9 | 7.0 | 3.7 | 4.6 |
| Timor-Leste | .. | −0.7 | .. | 4.3 | .. | −5.3 | .. | −0.2 | .. | −1.8 |
| Togo[a] | 3.5 | 2.6 | 4.0 | 2.8 | 1.8 | 8.1 | 1.8 | 7.5 | 3.9 | −0.7 |
| Trinidad and Tobago | 3.2 | 9.5 | 2.7 | −5.6 | 3.2 | 13.3 | 4.9 | 9.5 | 3.2 | 5.7 |
| Tunisia[a] | 4.7 | 4.6 | 2.3 | 3.4 | 4.6 | 3.2 | 5.5 | 3.1 | 5.3 | 5.6 |
| Turkey | 3.8 | 5.6 | 1.3 | 1.6 | 4.6 | 6.4 | 4.7 | 6.7 | 3.9 | 5.2 |
| Turkmenistan | −4.8 | .. | −5.7 | .. | −3.4 | .. | .. | .. | −5.4 | .. |
| Uganda | 7.1 | 5.6 | 3.7 | 4.3 | 12.2 | 7.5 | 14.1 | 5.6 | 8.2 | 7.6 |
| Ukraine | −9.3 | 7.8 | −5.6 | 3.2 | −12.6 | 6.3 | −11.2 | 11.4 | −8.1 | 7.3 |
| United Arab Emirates | 4.8 | 8.2 | 13.2 | 2.9 | 3.0 | 5.6 | 11.9 | 8.5 | 7.2 | 9.3 |
| United Kingdom | 2.7 | 2.5 | −0.3 | 0.6 | 1.5 | 0.1 | 1.3 | −0.4 | 3.2 | 3.4 |
| United States | 3.5 | 2.6 | 3.7 | 2.5 | 3.7 | 1.5 | .. | 2.2 | 3.4 | 2.7 |
| Uruguay | 3.4 | 2.3 | 2.8 | 6.3 | 1.1 | 2.5 | −0.1 | 4.2 | 3.7 | 1.2 |
| Uzbekistan | −0.2 | 5.7 | 0.5 | 6.9 | −3.4 | 4.3 | 0.7 | 1.8 | 0.4 | 5.7 |
| Venezuela, RB | 1.6 | 3.4 | 1.2 | 3.0 | 1.2 | 1.6 | 4.5 | 2.5 | −0.1 | 4.9 |
| Vietnam[a] | 7.9 | 7.6 | 4.3 | 3.9 | 11.9 | 10.3 | 11.2 | 11.7 | 7.5 | 7.2 |
| West Bank and Gaza[a] | 7.3 | 0.2 | .. | .. | .. | .. | .. | .. | .. | .. |
| Yemen, Rep. | 6.0 | 3.9 | 5.6 | 0.3 | 8.2 | −0.1 | 5.7 | 3.0 | 5.0 | 8.1 |
| Zambia | 0.5 | 5.0 | 4.2 | 2.1 | −4.2 | 9.2 | 0.8 | 5.4 | 2.5 | 5.9 |
| Zimbabwe | 2.1 | −5.7 | 4.3 | −8.5 | 0.4 | −10.0 | 0.4 | −12.0 | 2.9 | −10.0 |
| **World** | **2.9 w** | **3.0 w** | **2.0 w** | **2.5 w** | **2.4 w** | **2.6 w** | **.. w** | **2.9 w** | **3.1 w** | **2.8 w** |
| **Low income** | 4.7 | 6.5 | 3.3 | 3.1 | 4.9 | 7.6 | 5.9 | 7.7 | 5.8 | 7.6 |
| **Middle income** | 3.8 | 5.6 | 2.0 | 3.7 | 4.6 | 6.6 | 6.3 | 6.9 | 4.0 | 5.4 |
| Lower middle income | 6.2 | 7.6 | 2.7 | 4.0 | 8.0 | 8.7 | 8.6 | 9.4 | 6.0 | 7.7 |
| Upper middle income | 2.2 | 3.9 | 0.8 | 3.3 | 1.6 | 3.9 | 3.8 | 3.8 | 3.0 | 3.8 |
| **Low & middle income** | 3.9 | 5.7 | 2.4 | 3.6 | 4.6 | 6.7 | 6.2 | 6.9 | 4.2 | 5.7 |
| East Asia & Pacific | 8.5 | 8.6 | 3.4 | 3.9 | 11.0 | 9.7 | 10.9 | 9.8 | 8.1 | 8.8 |
| Europe & Central Asia | −0.9 | 5.8 | −1.8 | 3.6 | −2.9 | 6.2 | .. | .. | 0.9 | 5.4 |
| Latin America & Carib. | 3.2 | 3.1 | 2.1 | 3.2 | 3.1 | 2.9 | 2.9 | 2.8 | 3.6 | 3.1 |
| Middle East & N. Africa | 3.8 | 4.2 | 2.9 | 4.7 | 4.1 | 2.5 | 3.8 | 5.7 | 3.5 | 5.0 |
| South Asia | 5.5 | 7.0 | 3.3 | 2.7 | 6.0 | 7.9 | 6.4 | 7.8 | 6.9 | 8.2 |
| Sub-Saharan Africa | 2.5 | 4.7 | 3.3 | 3.5 | 1.7 | 5.4 | 2.1 | 3.4 | 2.5 | 4.7 |
| **High income** | 2.7 | 2.3 | 1.4 | 0.5 | 1.9 | 1.4 | .. | 1.8 | 2.9 | 2.4 |
| Euro area | 2.1 | 1.5 | 1.6 | −0.4 | 1.0 | 1.2 | 2.2 | 0.6 | 2.5 | 1.7 |

a. Components are at producer prices. b. Covers mainland Tanzania only.

# Growth of output | 4.1

An economy's growth is measured by the change in the volume of its output or in the real incomes of its residents. The 1993 United Nations System of National Accounts (1993 SNA) offers three plausible indicators for calculating growth: the volume of gross domestic product (GDP), real gross domestic income, and real gross national income. The volume of GDP is the sum of value added, measured at constant prices, by households, government, and industries operating in the economy.

Each industry's contribution to growth in the economy's output is measured by growth in the industry's value added. In principle, value added in constant prices can be estimated by measuring the quantity of goods and services produced in a period, valuing them at an agreed set of base year prices, and subtracting the cost of intermediate inputs, also in constant prices. This double-deflation method, recommended by the 1993 SNA and its predecessors, requires detailed information on the structure of prices of inputs and outputs.

In many industries, however, value added is extrapolated from the base year using single volume indexes of outputs or, less commonly, inputs. Particularly in the services industries, including most of government, value added in constant prices is often imputed from labor inputs, such as real wages or number of employees. In the absence of well defined measures of output, measuring the growth of services remains difficult.

Moreover, technical progress can lead to improvements in production processes and in the quality of goods and services that, if not properly accounted for, can distort measures of value added and thus of growth. When inputs are used to estimate output, as for nonmarket services, unmeasured technical progress leads to underestimates of the volume of output. Similarly, unmeasured improvements in quality lead to underestimates of the value of output and value added. The result can be underestimates of growth and productivity improvement and overestimates of inflation.

Informal economic activities pose a particular measurement problem, especially in developing countries, where much economic activity is unrecorded. A complete picture of the economy requires estimating household outputs produced for home use, sales in informal markets, barter exchanges, and illicit or deliberately unreported activities. The consistency and completeness of such estimates depend on the skill and methods of the compiling statisticians.

## Rebasing national accounts

When countries rebase their national accounts, they update the weights assigned to various components to better reflect current patterns of production or uses of output. The new base year should represent normal operation of the economy—it should be a year without major shocks or distortions. Some developing countries have not rebased their national accounts for many years. Using an old base year can be misleading because implicit price and volume weights become progressively less relevant and useful.

To obtain comparable series of constant price data, the World Bank rescales GDP and value added by industrial origin to a common reference year. This year's *World Development Indicators* continues to use 2000 as the reference year. Because rescaling changes the implicit weights used in forming regional and income group aggregates, aggregate growth rates in this year's edition are not comparable with those from earlier editions with different base years.

Rescaling may result in a discrepancy between the rescaled GDP and the sum of the rescaled components. Because allocating the discrepancy would cause distortions in the growth rates, the discrepancy is left unallocated. As a result, the weighted average of the growth rates of the components generally will not equal the GDP growth rate.

## Computing growth rates

Growth rates of GDP and its components are calculated using the least squares method and constant price data in the local currency. Constant price U.S. dollar series are used to calculate regional and income group growth rates. Local currency series are converted to constant U.S. dollars using an exchange rate in the common reference year. The growth rates in the table are average annual compound growth rates. Methods of computing growth rates and the alternative conversion factor are described in *Statistical methods*.

## Changes in the System of National Accounts

*World Development Indicators* adopted the terminology of the 1993 SNA in 2001. Although many countries continue to compile their national accounts according to the SNA version 3 (referred to as the 1968 SNA), more and more are adopting the 1993 SNA. Some low-income countries still use concepts from the even older 1953 SNA guidelines, including valuations such as factor cost, in describing major economic aggregates. Countries that use the 1993 SNA are identified in *Primary data documentation*.

• **Gross domestic product (GDP)** at purchaser prices is the sum of gross value added by all resident producers in the economy plus any product taxes (less subsidies) not included in the valuation of output. It is calculated without deducting for depreciation of fabricated capital assets or for depletion and degradation of natural resources. Value added is the net output of an industry after adding up all outputs and subtracting intermediate inputs. The industrial origin of value added is determined by the International Standard Industrial Classification (ISIC) revision 3. • **Agriculture** corresponds to ISIC divisions 1–5 and includes forestry and fishing. • **Industry** corresponds to ISIC divisions 10–45, which cover mining, manufacturing (also reported separately), construction, electricity, water, and gas. • **Manufacturing** corresponds to industries belonging to ISIC divisions 15–37. • **Services** correspond to ISIC divisions 50–99. This sector is derived as a residual (from GDP less agriculture and industry) and may not properly reflect the sum of services output, including banking and financial services. For some countries it includes product taxes (minus subsidies) and may also include statistical discrepancies.

### Data sources

Data on national accounts for most developing countries are collected from national statistical organizations and central banks by visiting and resident World Bank missions. Data for high-income economies come from Organisation for Economic Co-operation and Development (OECD) data files (see *Annual National Accounts for OECD Member Countries: Data from 1970 Onwards*). The World Bank rescales constant price data to a common reference year. The complete national accounts time series is available on the *World Development Indicators 2008* CD-ROM. The United Nations Statistics Division publishes detailed national accounts for UN member countries in *National Accounts Statistics: Main Aggregates and Detailed Tables* and publishes updates in the *Monthly Bulletin of Statistics*.

| | Gross domestic product | | Agriculture | | Industry | | Manufacturing | | Services | |
|---|---|---|---|---|---|---|---|---|---|---|
| | $ millions | | % of GDP | | % of GDP | | % of GDP | | % of GDP | |
| | 1995 | 2006 | 1995 | 2006 | 1995 | 2006 | 1995 | 2006 | 1995 | 2006 |
| Afghanistan | .. | 8,399 | .. | 36 | .. | 24 | .. | 15 | .. | 39 |
| Albania | 2,424 | 9,098 | 56 | 23 | 22 | 22 | 14 | .. | 22 | 56 |
| Algeria | 41,764 | 114,727 | 10 | 8 | 50 | 61 | 11 | 6 | 39 | 30 |
| Angola[a] | 5,040 | 45,163 | 7 | 9 | 66 | 70 | 4 | 4 | 26 | 21 |
| Argentina | 258,032 | 214,241 | 6 | 8 | 28 | 36 | 18 | 22 | 66 | 56 |
| Armenia | 1,468 | 6,387 | 42 | 20 | 32 | 44 | 25 | 17 | 26 | 37 |
| Australia | 384,095 | 780,531 | 4 | 3 | 28 | 28 | 15 | 11 | 68 | 69 |
| Austria | 239,560 | 322,001 | 3 | 2 | 30 | 31 | 19 | 19 | 67 | 67 |
| Azerbaijan | 3,052 | 19,851 | 27 | 7 | 34 | 70 | 13 | 6 | 39 | 22 |
| Bangladesh | 37,940 | 61,897 | 26 | 20 | 25 | 28 | 15 | 17 | 49 | 52 |
| Belarus | 13,973 | 36,945 | 17 | 9 | 37 | 42 | 31 | 33 | 46 | 49 |
| Belgium | 284,321 | 394,033 | 2 | 1 | 28 | 24 | 20 | 17 | 70 | 75 |
| Benin[a] | 2,009 | 4,775 | 34 | 32 | 15 | 13 | 9 | 8 | 51 | 54 |
| Bolivia | 6,715 | 11,162 | 17 | 14 | 33 | 34 | 19 | 15 | 50 | 52 |
| Bosnia and Herzegovina | 1,867 | 12,255 | 21 | 10 | 26 | 25 | 11 | 12 | 54 | 65 |
| Botswana | 4,774 | 10,598 | 4 | 2 | 51 | 53 | 5 | 4 | 45 | 45 |
| Brazil | 768,951 | 1,067,472 | 6 | 5 | 28 | 31 | 19 | 18 | 67 | 64 |
| Bulgaria | 13,107 | 31,483 | 14 | 9 | 35 | 31 | 24 | 19 | 50 | 60 |
| Burkina Faso | 2,380 | 6,173 | 35 | 33 | 21 | 22 | 15 | 14 | 44 | 45 |
| Burundi | 1,000 | 903 | 48 | 35 | 19 | 20 | 9 | 9 | 33 | 45 |
| Cambodia | 3,441 | 7,258 | 48 | 30 | 14 | 26 | 9 | 19 | 38 | 44 |
| Cameroon | 8,733 | 18,323 | 24 | 20 | 31 | 33 | 22 | 18 | 45 | 47 |
| Canada | 590,517 | 1,271,593 | 3 | .. | 31 | .. | 18 | .. | 66 | .. |
| Central African Republic | 1,122 | 1,494 | 46 | 56 | 21 | 15 | 10 | 8 | 33 | 29 |
| Chad | 1,446 | 6,541 | 36 | 21 | 14 | 55 | 11 | 5 | 51 | 25 |
| Chile | 71,349 | 145,843 | 9 | 4 | 35 | 48 | 18 | 14 | 55 | 48 |
| China[a] | 728,011 | 2,644,681 | 20 | 12 | 47 | 48 | 34 | 33 | 33 | 40 |
| Hong Kong, China | 144,230 | 189,799 | 0 | 0 | 15 | 9 | 8 | 3 | 85 | 91 |
| Colombia | 92,503 | 153,405 | 15 | 12 | 32 | 36 | 16 | 17 | 53 | 52 |
| Congo, Dem. Rep. | 5,643 | 8,543 | 57 | 46 | 17 | 28 | 9 | 6 | 26 | 27 |
| Congo, Rep.[a] | 2,116 | 7,385 | 10 | 4 | 45 | 73 | 8 | 5 | 45 | 22 |
| Costa Rica | 11,722 | 22,229 | 14 | 9 | 30 | 29 | 22 | 22 | 57 | 62 |
| Côte d'Ivoire[a] | 11,000 | 17,551 | 25 | 23 | 21 | 26 | 15 | 18 | 55 | 51 |
| Croatia | 18,808 | 42,925 | 11 | 7 | 34 | 32 | 24 | 21 | 55 | 61 |
| Cuba[a] | .. | .. | 6 | .. | 45 | .. | 38 | .. | 49 | .. |
| Czech Republic | 55,257 | 143,018 | 5 | 3 | 38 | 39 | 24 | 27 | 57 | 58 |
| Denmark | 181,984 | 275,366 | 3 | 2 | 25 | 26 | 17 | 14 | 71 | 72 |
| Dominican Republic[a] | 12,585 | 31,846 | 13 | 12 | 33 | 26 | 18 | 14 | 55 | 62 |
| Ecuador[a] | 20,206 | 41,402 | 17 | 7 | 25 | 35 | 14 | 9 | 58 | 59 |
| Egypt, Arab Rep. | 60,159 | 107,484 | 17 | 14 | 32 | 38 | 17 | 17 | 51 | 48 |
| El Salvador | 9,500 | 18,654 | 14 | 11 | 30 | 29 | 23 | 22 | 56 | 60 |
| Eritrea | 578 | 1,085 | 21 | 17 | 17 | 23 | 9 | 9 | 62 | 60 |
| Estonia | 4,331 | 16,410 | 8 | 3 | 29 | 29 | 18 | 17 | 63 | 68 |
| Ethiopia | 7,606 | 13,315 | 57 | 47 | 10 | 13 | 5 | 5 | 33 | 39 |
| Finland | 130,605 | 210,652 | 4 | 3 | 33 | 32 | 25 | 23 | 63 | 65 |
| France | 1,569,983 | 2,248,091 | 3 | 2 | 25 | 21 | .. | 12 | 72 | 77 |
| Gabon[a] | 4,959 | 9,546 | 8 | 5 | 52 | 61 | 5 | 4 | 40 | 34 |
| Gambia, The | 382 | 511 | 30 | 33 | 13 | 13 | 6 | 5 | 57 | 54 |
| Georgia | 2,694 | 7,744 | 52 | 13 | 16 | 25 | 17 | 13 | 32 | 62 |
| Germany | 2,522,792 | 2,896,876 | 1 | 1 | 32 | 30 | 23 | 23 | 67 | 69 |
| Ghana[a] | 6,457 | 12,906 | 39 | 37 | 24 | 25 | 9 | 8 | 37 | 37 |
| Greece | 151,184 | 308,449 | 8 | 3 | 21 | 21 | .. | 10 | 71 | 76 |
| Guatemala[a] | 14,657 | 35,325 | 24 | 22 | 20 | 19 | 14 | 12 | 56 | 59 |
| Guinea | 3,694 | 3,317 | 19 | 13 | 29 | 37 | 4 | 4 | 52 | 50 |
| Guinea-Bissau | 254 | 304 | 55 | 62 | 12 | 11 | 8 | 7 | 33 | 27 |
| Haiti | 2,908 | 4,975 | 25 | .. | 32 | .. | 20 | .. | 44 | .. |

| | Gross domestic product $ millions | | Agriculture % of GDP | | Industry % of GDP | | Manufacturing % of GDP | | Services % of GDP | |
|---|---|---|---|---|---|---|---|---|---|---|
| | 1995 | 2006 | 1995 | 2006 | 1995 | 2006 | 1995 | 2006 | 1995 | 2006 |
| Honduras | 3,911 | 9,235 | 22 | 14 | 31 | 31 | 18 | 20 | 48 | 55 |
| Hungary | 44,656 | 112,920 | 7 | 4 | 32 | 30 | 24 | 23 | 61 | 66 |
| India | 356,299 | 911,813 | 26 | 18 | 28 | 28 | 18 | 16 | 46 | 55 |
| Indonesia[a] | 202,132 | 364,790 | 17 | 13 | 42 | 47 | 24 | 28 | 41 | 40 |
| Iran, Islamic Rep. | 90,829 | 217,898 | 18 | 10 | 34 | 45 | 12 | 12 | 47 | 45 |
| Iraq | 10,114 | .. | 9 | .. | 75 | .. | 1 | .. | 16 | .. |
| Ireland | 67,105 | 220,137 | 7 | 2 | 38 | 36 | 30 | 25 | 55 | 62 |
| Israel | 93,992 | 140,457 | .. | .. | .. | .. | .. | .. | .. | .. |
| Italy | 1,126,042 | 1,850,961 | 3 | 2 | 30 | 27 | 22 | 18 | 66 | 71 |
| Jamaica | 5,813 | 10,023 | 9 | 6 | 37 | 33 | 16 | 13 | 54 | 61 |
| Japan | 5,247,610 | 4,368,435 | 2 | 2 | 34 | 30 | 23 | 21 | 64 | 69 |
| Jordan | 6,727 | 14,101 | 4 | 3 | 29 | 30 | 15 | 19 | 67 | 67 |
| Kazakhstan | 20,374 | 81,003 | 13 | 6 | 32 | 42 | 15 | 12 | 55 | 52 |
| Kenya | 9,046 | 22,779 | 31 | 27 | 16 | 19 | 10 | 11 | 53 | 54 |
| Korea, Dem. Rep. | .. | .. | .. | .. | .. | .. | .. | .. | .. | .. |
| Korea, Rep. | 517,118 | 888,024 | 6 | 3 | 42 | 40 | 28 | 28 | 52 | 57 |
| Kuwait[a] | 27,192 | 80,781 | 0 | .. | 55 | .. | 4 | .. | 45 | .. |
| Kyrgyz Republic | 1,661 | 2,818 | 44 | 33 | 20 | 20 | 9 | 13 | 37 | 47 |
| Lao PDR | 1,764 | 3,437 | 56 | 42 | 19 | 32 | 14 | 21 | 25 | 26 |
| Latvia | 5,236 | 20,116 | 9 | 4 | 30 | 21 | 21 | 12 | 61 | 75 |
| Lebanon | 11,719 | 22,722 | 7 | 7 | 27 | 24 | 15 | 11 | 66 | 70 |
| Lesotho | 931 | 1,494 | 18 | 16 | 39 | 43 | 16 | 18 | 43 | 40 |
| Liberia[a] | 135 | 631 | 82 | 66 | 5 | 16 | 3 | 12 | 13 | 18 |
| Libya | 25,541 | 50,320 | .. | .. | .. | .. | .. | .. | .. | .. |
| Lithuania | 7,621 | 29,766 | 11 | 5 | 32 | 35 | 20 | 18 | 56 | 59 |
| Macedonia, FYR | 4,449 | 6,217 | 13 | 13 | 30 | 29 | 23 | 19 | 57 | 58 |
| Madagascar | 3,160 | 5,499 | 27 | 28 | 9 | 15 | 8 | 13 | 64 | 57 |
| Malawi | 1,397 | 3,164 | 30 | 34 | 20 | 20 | 16 | 14 | 50 | 46 |
| Malaysia[a] | 88,832 | 150,672 | 13 | 9 | 41 | 50 | 26 | 30 | 46 | 41 |
| Mali | 2,466 | 5,866 | 50 | 37 | 19 | 24 | 8 | 3 | 32 | 39 |
| Mauritania | 1,415 | 2,663 | 37 | 13 | 25 | 48 | 8 | 5 | 37 | 39 |
| Mauritius | 3,820 | 6,347 | 10 | 6 | 32 | 27 | 23 | 19 | 58 | 68 |
| Mexico | 286,698 | 839,182 | 6 | 4 | 28 | 27 | 21 | 18 | 66 | 69 |
| Moldova | 1,753 | 3,356 | 33 | 18 | 32 | 15 | 26 | 14 | 35 | 67 |
| Mongolia | 1,227 | 3,132 | 41 | 22 | 29 | 42 | 12 | 4 | 30 | 36 |
| Morocco | 32,986 | 65,401 | 15 | 16 | 34 | 28 | 19 | 16 | 51 | 57 |
| Mozambique | 2,247 | 6,833 | 37 | 28 | 15 | 26 | 8 | 16 | 48 | 46 |
| Myanmar[a] | .. | .. | 60 | .. | 10 | .. | 7 | .. | 30 | .. |
| Namibia | 3,503 | 6,566 | 12 | 11 | 28 | 31 | 13 | 14 | 60 | 58 |
| Nepal | 4,401 | 8,938 | 42 | 34 | 23 | 16 | 10 | 8 | 36 | 49 |
| Netherlands | 418,969 | 662,296 | 3 | 2 | 27 | 25 | 17 | 14 | 69 | 73 |
| New Zealand | 61,281 | 104,519 | 7 | .. | 27 | .. | 19 | .. | 66 | .. |
| Nicaragua | 3,191 | 5,301 | 23 | 20 | 27 | 30 | 19 | 18 | 49 | 51 |
| Niger[a] | 1,881 | 3,663 | 40 | .. | 17 | .. | 6 | .. | 43 | .. |
| Nigeria | 28,109 | 115,338 | 32 | 23 | 47 | 57 | 5 | .. | 22 | 20 |
| Norway | 148,920 | 334,942 | 3 | 2 | 34 | 45 | 13 | 9 | 63 | 54 |
| Oman[a] | 13,803 | 30,835 | 3 | 2 | 46 | 55 | 5 | 8 | 51 | 43 |
| Pakistan | 60,636 | 126,836 | 26 | 19 | 24 | 27 | 16 | 19 | 50 | 53 |
| Panama | 7,906 | 17,097 | 8 | 8 | 18 | 19 | 9 | 8 | 74 | 73 |
| Papua New Guinea | 4,601 | 5,654 | 32 | 42 | 36 | 39 | 10 | 6 | 31 | 19 |
| Paraguay[a] | 8,066 | 9,275 | 21 | 21 | 23 | 18 | 16 | 12 | 56 | 61 |
| Peru | 53,674 | 92,416 | 9 | 7 | 31 | 38 | 17 | 17 | 60 | 55 |
| Philippines[a] | 74,120 | 117,562 | 22 | 14 | 32 | 32 | 23 | 23 | 46 | 54 |
| Poland | 139,095 | 338,733 | 8 | 5 | 35 | 32 | 21 | 19 | 57 | 64 |
| Portugal | 112,960 | 194,726 | 6 | 3 | 28 | 25 | 19 | .. | 66 | 72 |
| Puerto Rico[a] | 42,647 | .. | 1 | .. | 44 | .. | 42 | .. | 55 | .. |

# 4.2 | Structure of output

| | Gross domestic product | | Agriculture | | Industry | | Manufacturing | | Services | |
|---|---|---|---|---|---|---|---|---|---|---|
| | $ millions | | % of GDP | | % of GDP | | % of GDP | | % of GDP | |
| | 1995 | 2006 | 1995 | 2006 | 1995 | 2006 | 1995 | 2006 | 1995 | 2006 |
| Romania | 35,477 | 121,609 | 21 | 11 | 43 | 38 | 29 | 26 | 36 | 52 |
| Russian Federation | 395,529 | 986,940 | 7 | 5 | 37 | 39 | .. | 19 | 56 | 56 |
| Rwanda[a] | 1,293 | 2,494 | 44 | 41 | 16 | 21 | 10 | 8 | 40 | 38 |
| Saudi Arabia[a] | 142,458 | 349,138 | 6 | 3 | 49 | 65 | 10 | 9 | 45 | 32 |
| Senegal | 4,879 | 9,186 | 21 | 16 | 24 | 23 | 17 | 14 | 55 | 61 |
| Serbia | 19,681 | 31,989 | .. | 13 | .. | 26 | .. | .. | .. | 62 |
| Sierra Leone | 871 | 1,450 | 43 | 46 | 39 | 25 | 9 | .. | 18 | 29 |
| Singapore | 84,291 | 132,158 | 0 | 0 | 35 | 35 | 27 | 29 | 65 | 65 |
| Slovak Republic[a] | 19,715 | 55,049 | 5 | 4 | 34 | 32 | 24 | 20 | 61 | 65 |
| Slovenia | 20,288 | 37,303 | 4 | 2 | 35 | 35 | 26 | 25 | 61 | 63 |
| Somalia | .. | .. | .. | .. | .. | .. | .. | .. | .. | .. |
| South Africa | 151,113 | 255,155 | 4 | 3 | 35 | 31 | 21 | 18 | 61 | 66 |
| Spain | 596,751 | 1,224,676 | 5 | 3 | 29 | 30 | .. | 15 | 66 | 67 |
| Sri Lanka | 13,030 | 26,964 | 23 | 16 | 27 | 27 | 16 | 14 | 50 | 56 |
| Sudan | 7,288 | 37,442 | 44 | 32 | 15 | 29 | 9 | 6 | 41 | 39 |
| Swaziland | 1,364 | 2,648 | 15 | 11 | 44 | 46 | 36 | 37 | 40 | 43 |
| Sweden | 250,640 | 383,799 | 3 | 1 | 30 | 29 | 22 | 20 | 67 | 70 |
| Switzerland | 314,799 | 380,412 | 2 | 1 | 31 | 28 | 21 | 20 | 66 | 70 |
| Syrian Arab Republic | 11,397 | 33,407 | 32 | 18 | 20 | 32 | 15 | 7 | 48 | 49 |
| Tajikistan | 1,232 | 2,811 | 38 | 25 | 39 | 27 | 28 | 19 | 22 | 48 |
| Tanzania[b] | 5,255 | 12,784 | 47 | 45 | 14 | 17 | 7 | 7 | 38 | 37 |
| Thailand[a] | 167,896 | 206,338 | 10 | 11 | 41 | 45 | 30 | 35 | 50 | 45 |
| Timor-Leste | .. | 356 | .. | 32 | .. | 13 | .. | 3 | .. | 55 |
| Togo[a] | 1,309 | 2,206 | 38 | 44 | 22 | 24 | 10 | 10 | 40 | 32 |
| Trinidad and Tobago | 5,329 | 18,136 | 2 | 1 | 47 | 62 | 9 | 6 | 51 | 38 |
| Tunisia[a] | 18,031 | 30,298 | 11 | 11 | 29 | 28 | 19 | 17 | 59 | 60 |
| Turkey | 169,708 | 402,710 | 16 | 10 | 27 | 27 | 23 | 22 | 56 | 63 |
| Turkmenistan | 2,482 | 10,496 | 17 | 20 | 63 | 40 | 40 | 22 | 20 | 40 |
| Uganda | 5,756 | 9,419 | 49 | 32 | 14 | 18 | 7 | 9 | 36 | 49 |
| Ukraine | 48,214 | 106,469 | 15 | 9 | 43 | 35 | 35 | 21 | 42 | 57 |
| United Arab Emirates | 42,807 | 129,702 | 3 | 2 | 52 | 56 | 10 | 14 | 45 | 42 |
| United Kingdom | 1,135,785 | 2,376,984 | 2 | 1 | 32 | 24 | 22 | 14 | 66 | 75 |
| United States | 7,342,300 | 13,163,870 | 2 | 1 | 26 | 23 | 19 | 14 | 72 | 76 |
| Uruguay | 18,348 | 19,308 | 9 | 9 | 29 | 32 | 20 | 23 | 62 | 58 |
| Uzbekistan | 13,350 | 17,178 | 32 | 26 | 28 | 27 | 12 | 11 | 40 | 46 |
| Venezuela, RB | 74,889 | 181,862 | 6 | 4 | 41 | 55 | 15 | 18 | 53 | 40 |
| Vietnam[a] | 20,736 | 60,999 | 27 | 20 | 29 | 42 | 15 | 21 | 44 | 38 |
| West Bank and Gaza[a] | 3,220 | 4,059 | .. | .. | .. | .. | .. | .. | .. | .. |
| Yemen, Rep. | 4,236 | 19,057 | 20 | .. | 32 | .. | 14 | .. | 48 | .. |
| Zambia | 3,478 | 10,734 | 18 | 22 | 36 | 33 | 11 | 11 | 46 | 45 |
| Zimbabwe | 7,111 | 3,418 | 15 | 19 | 29 | 24 | 22 | 14 | 56 | 57 |
| **World** | **29,613,549 t** | **48,461,854 t** | **4 w** | **3 w** | **31 w** | **28 w** | **20 w** | **18 w** | **65 w** | **69 w** |
| **Low income** | 665,159 | 1,618,703 | 29 | 20 | 27 | 28 | 16 | 16 | 44 | 52 |
| **Middle income** | 4,510,786 | 10,059,157 | 12 | 8 | 36 | 37 | 23 | 20 | 52 | 54 |
| Lower middle income | 1,814,273 | 4,735,728 | 18 | 12 | 41 | 44 | 27 | 27 | 41 | 45 |
| Upper middle income | 2,695,409 | 5,324,615 | 7 | 6 | 31 | 32 | 20 | 19 | 61 | 62 |
| **Low & middle income** | 5,177,822 | 11,678,579 | 14 | 10 | 34 | 36 | 22 | 19 | 51 | 54 |
| East Asia & Pacific | 1,313,304 | 3,616,708 | 19 | 12 | 44 | 47 | 31 | 32 | 37 | 41 |
| Europe & Central Asia | 987,511 | 2,499,359 | 12 | 7 | 34 | 33 | 23 | 20 | 54 | 60 |
| Latin America & Carib. | 1,751,110 | 2,964,189 | 7 | 6 | 29 | 31 | 19 | 18 | 64 | 62 |
| Middle East & N. Africa | 329,469 | 734,423 | 15 | 12 | 35 | 40 | 14 | 13 | 50 | 48 |
| South Asia | 476,196 | 1,146,716 | 26 | 18 | 27 | 28 | 17 | 17 | 46 | 54 |
| Sub-Saharan Africa | 320,739 | 712,731 | 19 | 15 | 32 | 30 | 15 | 14 | 49 | 55 |
| **High income** | 24,431,143 | 36,794,507 | 2 | 2 | 30 | 26 | 20 | 17 | 68 | 72 |
| Euro area | 7,273,737 | 10,636,418 | 3 | 2 | 29 | 27 | 22 | 18 | 68 | 72 |

a. Components are at producer prices. b. Covers mainland Tanzania only.

## About the data

An economy's gross domestic product (GDP) represents the sum of value added by all producers in the economy. Value added is the value of the gross output of producers less the value of intermediate goods and services consumed in production, before taking account of the consumption of fixed capital in the production process. The United Nations System of National Accounts calls for estimates of value added to be valued at either basic prices (excluding net taxes on products) or producer prices (including net taxes on products paid by producers but excluding sales or value added taxes). Both valuations exclude transport charges that are invoiced separately by producers. Total GDP shown in the table and elsewhere in this volume is measured at purchaser prices. Value added by industry is normally measured at basic prices. When value added is measured at producer prices, this is noted in *Primary data documentation*.

While GDP estimates based on the production approach are generally more reliable than estimates compiled from the income or expenditure side, different countries use different definitions, methods, and reporting standards. World Bank staff review the quality of national accounts data and sometimes make adjustments to improve consistency with international guidelines. Nevertheless, significant discrepancies remain between international standards and actual practice. Many statistical offices, especially those in developing countries, face severe limitations in the resources, time, training, and budgets required to produce reliable and comprehensive series of national accounts statistics.

### Data problems in measuring output

Among the difficulties faced by compilers of national accounts is the extent of unreported economic activity in the informal or secondary economy. In developing countries a large share of agricultural output is either not exchanged (because it is consumed within the household) or not exchanged for money.

Agricultural production often must be estimated indirectly, using a combination of methods involving estimates of inputs, yields, and area under cultivation. This approach sometimes leads to crude approximations that can differ from the true values over time and across crops for reasons other than climate conditions or farming techniques. Similarly, agricultural inputs that cannot easily be allocated to specific outputs are frequently "netted out" using equally crude and ad hoc approximations. For further discussion of the measurement of agricultural production, see *About the data* for table 3.3.

Ideally, industrial output should be measured through regular censuses and surveys of firms. But in most developing countries such surveys are infrequent, so earlier survey results must be extrapolated using an appropriate indicator. The choice of sampling unit, which may be the enterprise (where responses may be based on financial records) or the establishment (where production units may be recorded separately), also affects the quality of the data. Moreover, much industrial production is organized in unincorporated or owner-operated ventures that are not captured by surveys aimed at the formal sector. Even in large industries, where regular surveys are more likely, evasion of excise and other taxes and nondisclosure of income lower the estimates of value added. Such problems become more acute as countries move from state control of industry to private enterprise, because new firms enter business and growing numbers of established firms fail to report. In accordance with the System of National Accounts, output should include all such unreported activity as well as the value of illegal activities and other unrecorded, informal, or small-scale operations. Data on these activities need to be collected using techniques other than conventional surveys of firms.

In industries dominated by large organizations and enterprises, such as public utilities, data on output, employment, and wages are usually readily available and reasonably reliable. But in the services industry the many self-employed workers and one-person businesses are sometimes difficult to locate, and they have little incentive to respond to surveys, let alone to report their full earnings. Compounding these problems are the many forms of economic activity that go unrecorded, including the work that women and children do for little or no pay. For further discussion of the problems of using national accounts data, see Srinivasan (1994) and Heston (1994).

### Dollar conversion

To produce national accounts aggregates that are measured in the same standard monetary units, the value of output must be converted to a single common currency. The World Bank conventionally uses the U.S. dollar and applies the average official exchange rate reported by the International Monetary Fund for the year shown. An alternative conversion factor is applied if the official exchange rate is judged to diverge by an exceptionally large margin from the rate effectively applied to transactions in foreign currencies and traded products.

## Definitions

• **Gross domestic product (GDP)** at purchaser prices is the sum of gross value added by all resident producers in the economy plus any product taxes (less subsidies) not included in the valuation of output. It is calculated without deducting for depreciation of fabricated assets or for depletion and degradation of natural resources. Value added is the net output of an industry after adding up all outputs and subtracting intermediate inputs. The industrial origin of value added is determined by the International Standard Industrial Classification (ISIC) revision 3. • **Agriculture** corresponds to ISIC divisions 1–5 and includes forestry and fishing. • **Industry** corresponds to ISIC divisions 10–45, which cover mining, manufacturing (also reported separately), construction, electricity, water, and gas. • **Manufacturing** corresponds to ISIC divisions 15–37. • **Services** correspond to ISIC divisions 50–99. This sector is derived as a residual (from GDP less agriculture and industry) and may not properly reflect the sum of services output, including banking and financial services. For some countries it includes product taxes (minus subsidies) and may also include statistical discrepancies.

### Data sources

Data on national accounts for most developing countries are collected from national statistical organizations and central banks by visiting and resident World Bank missions. Data for high-income economies come from Organisation for Economic Co-operation and Development (OECD) data files (see *Annual National Accounts for OECD Member Countries: Data from 1970 Onwards*). The complete national accounts time series is available on the *World Development Indicators 2008* CD-ROM. The United Nations Statistics Division publishes detailed national accounts for UN member countries in *National Accounts Statistics: Main Aggregates and Detailed Tables* and publishes updates in the *Monthly Bulletin of Statistics*.

# 4.3 | Structure of manufacturing

| | Manufacturing value added ($ millions) | | Food, beverages, and tobacco (% of total) | | Textiles and clothing[a] (% of total) | | Machinery and transport equipment[a] (% of total) | | Chemicals[a] (% of total) | | Other manufacturing[b] (% of total) | |
|---|---|---|---|---|---|---|---|---|---|---|---|---|
| | 1995 | 2006 | 1995 | 2004 | 1995 | 2004 | 1995 | 2004 | 1995 | 2004 | 1995 | 2004 |
| Afghanistan | .. | 1,053 | .. | .. | .. | .. | .. | .. | .. | .. | .. | .. |
| Albania | 405 | .. | .. | 17 | .. | 27 | .. | 4 | .. | 5 | .. | 48 |
| Algeria | 4,366 | 5,404 | .. | .. | .. | .. | .. | .. | .. | .. | .. | .. |
| Angola | 202 | 1,922 | .. | .. | .. | .. | .. | .. | .. | .. | .. | .. |
| Argentina | 44,502 | 44,048 | 30 | 31 | 7 | 6 | 10 | 8 | 15 | 16 | 38 | 39 |
| Armenia | 356 | 985 | .. | .. | .. | .. | .. | .. | .. | .. | .. | .. |
| Australia | 51,314 | 74,569 | 20 | 19 | 6 | 4 | 11 | 17 | 8 | 7 | 55 | 53 |
| Austria | 41,681 | 52,934 | 11 | 10 | 6 | 3 | 27 | 31 | 2 | 2 | 54 | 54 |
| Azerbaijan | 352 | 1,055 | .. | .. | .. | .. | .. | .. | .. | .. | .. | .. |
| Bangladesh | 5,586 | 10,262 | 28 | .. | 44 | .. | 4 | .. | 11 | .. | 13 | .. |
| Belarus | 3,909 | 10,382 | .. | .. | .. | .. | .. | .. | .. | .. | .. | .. |
| Belgium | 51,721 | 56,400 | 13 | .. | 6 | .. | 22 | .. | 8 | .. | 51 | .. |
| Benin | 174 | 322 | .. | .. | .. | .. | .. | .. | .. | .. | .. | .. |
| Bolivia | 1,123 | 1,286 | 36 | .. | 5 | .. | 1 | .. | 3 | .. | 55 | .. |
| Bosnia and Herzegovina | 213 | 1,176 | .. | .. | .. | .. | .. | .. | .. | .. | .. | .. |
| Botswana | 242 | 352 | 44 | 20 | 9 | 4 | 6 | .. | 4 | .. | 36 | 76 |
| Brazil | 124,976 | 169,164 | 21 | 18 | 8 | 6 | 23 | 22 | 13 | 12 | 35 | 43 |
| Bulgaria | 2,015 | 4,764 | .. | .. | .. | .. | .. | .. | .. | .. | .. | .. |
| Burkina Faso | 336 | 775 | .. | .. | .. | .. | .. | .. | .. | .. | .. | .. |
| Burundi | 83 | 64 | .. | .. | .. | .. | .. | .. | .. | .. | .. | .. |
| Cambodia | 315 | 1,349 | .. | .. | .. | .. | .. | .. | .. | .. | .. | .. |
| Cameroon | 1,758 | 3,084 | .. | .. | .. | .. | .. | .. | .. | .. | .. | .. |
| Canada | 100,393 | .. | 13 | 13 | 4 | 4 | 23 | 25 | 10 | 8 | 50 | 50 |
| Central African Republic | 108 | 106 | .. | .. | .. | .. | .. | .. | .. | .. | .. | .. |
| Chad | 159 | 342 | .. | .. | .. | .. | .. | .. | .. | .. | .. | .. |
| Chile | 10,594 | 18,654 | .. | .. | .. | .. | .. | .. | .. | .. | .. | .. |
| China | 244,997 | 751,172 | .. | .. | .. | .. | .. | .. | .. | .. | .. | .. |
| Hong Kong, China | 10,524 | 5,856 | .. | .. | .. | .. | .. | .. | .. | .. | .. | .. |
| Colombia | 13,506 | 23,047 | .. | .. | .. | .. | .. | .. | .. | .. | .. | .. |
| Congo, Dem. Rep. | 510 | 526 | .. | .. | .. | .. | .. | .. | .. | .. | .. | .. |
| Congo, Rep. | 172 | 360 | .. | .. | .. | .. | .. | .. | .. | .. | .. | .. |
| Costa Rica | 2,339 | 4,344 | .. | .. | .. | .. | .. | .. | .. | .. | .. | .. |
| Côte d'Ivoire | 1,655 | 3,205 | .. | .. | .. | .. | .. | .. | .. | .. | .. | .. |
| Croatia | 3,666 | 7,400 | .. | .. | .. | .. | .. | .. | .. | .. | .. | .. |
| Cuba | .. | .. | .. | .. | .. | .. | .. | .. | .. | .. | .. | .. |
| Czech Republic | 12,124 | 34,965 | .. | .. | .. | .. | .. | .. | .. | .. | .. | .. |
| Denmark | 26,924 | 31,100 | 20 | 14 | 2 | 2 | 25 | 21 | 1 | 2 | 52 | 60 |
| Dominican Republic | 2,286 | 4,444 | .. | .. | .. | .. | .. | .. | .. | .. | .. | .. |
| Ecuador | 2,830 | 3,725 | 26 | 32 | 7 | 3 | 4 | 3 | 4 | 3 | 59 | 58 |
| Egypt, Arab Rep. | 9,829 | 16,737 | 19 | 20 | 13 | 10 | 12 | 10 | 18 | 22 | 38 | 38 |
| El Salvador | 2,026 | 3,845 | .. | .. | .. | .. | .. | .. | .. | .. | .. | .. |
| Eritrea | 47 | 86 | .. | .. | .. | .. | .. | .. | .. | .. | .. | .. |
| Estonia | 684 | 2,410 | .. | .. | .. | .. | .. | .. | .. | .. | .. | .. |
| Ethiopia | 344 | 647 | .. | .. | .. | .. | .. | .. | .. | .. | .. | .. |
| Finland | 28,814 | 39,106 | 10 | 7 | 3 | 2 | 27 | 37 | 4 | 3 | 57 | 51 |
| France | .. | 248,295 | 13 | 14 | 5 | 2 | 28 | 30 | 12 | 12 | 42 | 41 |
| Gabon | 224 | 391 | .. | .. | .. | .. | .. | .. | .. | .. | .. | .. |
| Gambia, The | 20 | 22 | 65 | .. | 8 | .. | 1 | .. | 9 | .. | 17 | .. |
| Georgia | 523 | 862 | .. | .. | .. | .. | .. | .. | .. | .. | .. | .. |
| Germany | 516,542 | 584,442 | .. | 9 | .. | 2 | .. | 42 | .. | 10 | .. | 37 |
| Ghana | 602 | 1,093 | .. | 32 | .. | 6 | .. | 1 | .. | 12 | .. | 49 |
| Greece | .. | 24,626 | 25 | .. | 15 | .. | 13 | .. | 10 | .. | 38 | .. |
| Guatemala | 2,069 | 4,405 | .. | .. | .. | .. | .. | .. | .. | .. | .. | .. |
| Guinea | 142 | 116 | .. | .. | .. | .. | .. | .. | .. | .. | .. | .. |
| Guinea-Bissau | 19 | 22 | .. | .. | .. | .. | .. | .. | .. | .. | .. | .. |
| Haiti | 558 | .. | .. | .. | .. | .. | .. | .. | .. | .. | .. | .. |

| | Manufacturing value added | | Food, beverages, and tobacco | | Textiles and clothing[a] | | Machinery and transport equipment[a] | | Chemicals[a] | | Other manufacturing[b] | |
|---|---|---|---|---|---|---|---|---|---|---|---|---|
| | $ millions | | % of total | | % of total | | % of total | | % of total | | % of total | |
| | **1995** | **2006** | **1995** | **2004** | **1995** | **2004** | **1995** | **2004** | **1995** | **2004** | **1995** | **2004** |
| Honduras | 607 | 1,638 | .. | .. | .. | .. | .. | .. | .. | .. | .. | .. |
| Hungary | 8,839 | 22,028 | 19 | 16 | 3 | 5 | 10 | 34 | 13 | 10 | 55 | 35 |
| India | 57,917 | 134,725 | .. | 10 | .. | 10 | .. | 20 | .. | 17 | .. | 43 |
| Indonesia | 48,781 | 102,323 | .. | 23 | .. | 13 | .. | 18 | .. | 9 | .. | 36 |
| Iran, Islamic Rep. | 10,918 | 25,354 | 15 | 10 | 12 | 5 | 18 | 28 | 15 | 13 | 40 | 44 |
| Iraq | 67 | .. | .. | .. | .. | .. | .. | .. | .. | .. | .. | .. |
| Ireland | 18,096 | 43,393 | .. | .. | .. | .. | .. | .. | .. | .. | .. | .. |
| Israel | | | .. | .. | .. | .. | .. | .. | .. | .. | .. | .. |
| Italy | 225,513 | 299,459 | 9 | 9 | 14 | 11 | 27 | 26 | 8 | 8 | 41 | 46 |
| Jamaica | 865 | 1,163 | .. | .. | .. | .. | .. | .. | .. | .. | .. | .. |
| Japan | 1,077,348 | 954,411 | 11 | 12 | 4 | 3 | 37 | 39 | 10 | 11 | 39 | 35 |
| Jordan | 866 | 2,393 | 30 | 24 | 7 | 12 | 5 | 5 | 15 | 16 | 44 | 42 |
| Kazakhstan | 2,976 | 9,423 | .. | .. | .. | .. | .. | .. | .. | .. | .. | .. |
| Kenya | 757 | 2,316 | .. | 30 | .. | 5 | .. | 5 | .. | 6 | .. | 53 |
| Korea, Dem. Rep. | .. | .. | .. | .. | .. | .. | .. | .. | .. | .. | .. | .. |
| Korea, Rep. | 128,839 | 219,771 | 8 | 8 | 10 | 7 | 39 | 46 | 8 | 9 | 34 | 30 |
| Kuwait | 1,032 | .. | .. | .. | .. | .. | .. | .. | .. | .. | .. | .. |
| Kyrgyz Republic | 142 | 318 | .. | .. | .. | .. | .. | .. | .. | .. | .. | .. |
| Lao PDR | 245 | 711 | .. | .. | .. | .. | .. | .. | .. | .. | .. | .. |
| Latvia | 965 | 2,101 | .. | .. | .. | .. | .. | .. | .. | .. | .. | .. |
| Lebanon | 1,577 | 2,217 | .. | .. | .. | .. | .. | .. | .. | .. | .. | .. |
| Lesotho | 129 | 237 | .. | .. | .. | .. | .. | .. | .. | .. | .. | .. |
| Liberia | 4 | 66 | .. | .. | .. | .. | .. | .. | .. | .. | .. | .. |
| Libya | .. | .. | .. | .. | .. | .. | .. | .. | .. | .. | .. | .. |
| Lithuania | 1,351 | 4,733 | .. | 21 | .. | 12 | .. | 14 | .. | 4 | .. | 49 |
| Macedonia, FYR | 873 | 980 | 35 | .. | 17 | .. | 9 | .. | 8 | .. | 31 | .. |
| Madagascar | 233 | 672 | .. | 42 | .. | 27 | .. | 1 | .. | 2 | .. | 29 |
| Malawi | 195 | 384 | .. | .. | .. | .. | .. | .. | .. | .. | .. | .. |
| Malaysia | 23,432 | 44,884 | .. | 8 | .. | 3 | .. | 39 | .. | 10 | .. | 40 |
| Mali | 174 | 167 | .. | .. | .. | .. | .. | .. | .. | .. | .. | .. |
| Mauritania | 107 | 84 | .. | .. | .. | .. | .. | .. | .. | .. | .. | .. |
| Mauritius | 765 | 1,060 | 25 | 24 | 52 | 51 | 2 | 2 | .. | .. | 21 | 24 |
| Mexico | 54,546 | 135,863 | 26 | .. | 4 | .. | 22 | .. | 15 | .. | 33 | .. |
| Moldova | 400 | 404 | .. | .. | .. | .. | .. | .. | .. | .. | .. | .. |
| Mongolia | 143 | 109 | 23 | .. | 62 | .. | 1 | .. | 1 | .. | 12 | .. |
| Morocco | 6,056 | 9,610 | .. | 32 | .. | 18 | .. | 9 | .. | 14 | .. | 28 |
| Mozambique | 166 | 960 | .. | .. | .. | .. | .. | .. | .. | .. | .. | .. |
| Myanmar | .. | .. | .. | .. | .. | .. | .. | .. | .. | .. | .. | .. |
| Namibia | 403 | 826 | .. | .. | .. | .. | .. | .. | .. | .. | .. | .. |
| Nepal | 393 | 661 | 35 | 45 | 34 | 19 | 2 | 2 | 6 | 10 | 23 | 23 |
| Netherlands | 65,999 | 78,537 | 18 | 19 | 3 | 2 | 15 | 14 | 16 | 9 | 48 | 56 |
| New Zealand | 10,517 | .. | 29 | .. | .. | .. | .. | .. | .. | .. | 71 | .. |
| Nicaragua | 533 | 859 | .. | .. | .. | .. | .. | .. | .. | .. | .. | .. |
| Niger | 120 | .. | .. | .. | .. | .. | .. | .. | .. | .. | .. | .. |
| Nigeria | 1,495 | .. | .. | .. | .. | .. | .. | .. | .. | .. | .. | .. |
| Norway | 17,018 | 28,060 | 17 | .. | 2 | .. | 24 | .. | 9 | .. | 48 | .. |
| Oman | 643 | 2,045 | .. | .. | .. | .. | .. | .. | .. | .. | .. | .. |
| Pakistan | 8,864 | 23,178 | .. | .. | .. | .. | .. | .. | .. | .. | .. | .. |
| Panama | 694 | 1,204 | 54 | .. | 7 | .. | .. | .. | 7 | .. | 32 | .. |
| Papua New Guinea | 388 | 249 | .. | .. | .. | .. | .. | .. | .. | .. | .. | .. |
| Paraguay | 1,280 | 1,094 | .. | .. | .. | .. | .. | .. | .. | .. | .. | .. |
| Peru | 8,105 | 13,743 | 28 | .. | 9 | .. | 7 | .. | 9 | .. | 48 | .. |
| Philippines | 17,043 | 26,916 | 29 | 23 | 6 | 5 | 7 | 13 | 2 | 2 | 57 | 56 |
| Poland | 25,891 | 56,009 | .. | .. | .. | .. | .. | .. | .. | .. | .. | .. |
| Portugal | 18,383 | .. | 13 | 14 | 22 | 18 | 18 | 17 | 6 | 5 | 41 | 46 |
| Puerto Rico | 17,867 | .. | .. | .. | .. | .. | .. | .. | .. | .. | .. | .. |

# 4.3 | Structure of manufacturing

| | Manufacturing value added ($ millions) | | Food, beverages, and tobacco (% of total) | | Textiles and clothing[a] (% of total) | | Machinery and transport equipment[a] (% of total) | | Chemicals[a] (% of total) | | Other manufacturing[b] (% of total) | |
|---|---|---|---|---|---|---|---|---|---|---|---|---|
| | 1995 | 2006 | 1995 | 2004 | 1995 | 2004 | 1995 | 2004 | 1995 | 2004 | 1995 | 2004 |
| Romania | 9,387 | 26,495 | 28 | 13 | 13 | 18 | 19 | 21 | 7 | 5 | 33 | 43 |
| Russian Federation | .. | 163,520 | .. | 16 | .. | 2 | .. | 9 | .. | 2 | .. | 71 |
| Rwanda | 132 | 212 | .. | .. | .. | .. | .. | .. | .. | .. | .. | .. |
| Saudi Arabia | 13,714 | 33,087 | .. | .. | .. | .. | .. | .. | .. | .. | .. | .. |
| Senegal | 730 | 1,104 | .. | 41 | .. | 3 | .. | 2 | .. | 29 | .. | 26 |
| Serbia | .. | .. | .. | .. | .. | .. | .. | .. | .. | .. | .. | .. |
| Sierra Leone | 75 | .. | .. | .. | .. | .. | .. | .. | .. | .. | .. | .. |
| Singapore | 20,799 | 36,496 | 4 | 4 | 1 | 1 | 60 | 50 | 9 | 24 | 26 | 20 |
| Slovak Republic | 4,704 | 10,923 | 11 | 9 | 7 | 6 | 14 | 22 | 9 | 3 | 59 | 60 |
| Slovenia | 4,556 | 8,005 | .. | .. | .. | .. | .. | .. | .. | .. | .. | .. |
| Somalia | .. | .. | .. | .. | .. | .. | .. | .. | .. | .. | .. | .. |
| South Africa | 29,274 | 41,198 | 15 | 17 | 8 | 4 | 19 | 16 | 10 | 7 | 47 | 56 |
| Spain | .. | 156,192 | 16 | 15 | 7 | 6 | 23 | 22 | 10 | 9 | 43 | 48 |
| Sri Lanka | 1,836 | 3,329 | .. | .. | .. | .. | .. | .. | .. | .. | .. | .. |
| Sudan | 799 | 2,173 | .. | .. | .. | .. | .. | .. | .. | .. | .. | .. |
| Swaziland | 398 | 596 | .. | .. | .. | .. | .. | .. | .. | .. | .. | .. |
| Sweden | 48,628 | 60,294 | 7 | 8 | 1 | 1 | 33 | 30 | 3 | 3 | 56 | 58 |
| Switzerland | 63,668 | 66,928 | .. | .. | .. | .. | .. | .. | .. | .. | .. | .. |
| Syrian Arab Republic | 1,574 | 2,687 | .. | .. | .. | .. | .. | .. | .. | .. | .. | .. |
| Tajikistan | 331 | 471 | .. | .. | .. | .. | .. | .. | .. | .. | .. | .. |
| Tanzania[c] | 349 | 819 | .. | .. | .. | .. | .. | .. | .. | .. | .. | .. |
| Thailand | 50,194 | 72,318 | 21 | .. | 9 | .. | 29 | .. | 6 | .. | 35 | .. |
| Timor-Leste | .. | 9 | .. | .. | .. | .. | .. | .. | .. | .. | .. | .. |
| Togo | 130 | 214 | .. | .. | .. | .. | .. | .. | .. | .. | .. | .. |
| Trinidad and Tobago | 439 | 1,029 | .. | 25 | .. | 1 | .. | 1 | .. | 22 | .. | 52 |
| Tunisia | 3,419 | 5,279 | .. | .. | .. | .. | .. | .. | .. | .. | .. | .. |
| Turkey | 38,296 | 84,983 | 15 | .. | 17 | .. | 16 | .. | 10 | .. | 42 | .. |
| Turkmenistan | 948 | 1,399 | .. | .. | .. | .. | .. | .. | .. | .. | .. | .. |
| Uganda | 359 | 786 | .. | .. | .. | .. | .. | .. | .. | .. | .. | .. |
| Ukraine | 14,922 | 19,068 | .. | .. | .. | .. | .. | .. | .. | .. | .. | .. |
| United Arab Emirates | 4,452 | 18,770 | .. | .. | .. | .. | .. | .. | .. | .. | .. | .. |
| United Kingdom | 219,282 | 269,610 | 13 | 14 | 5 | 4 | 28 | 27 | 11 | 11 | 43 | 44 |
| United States | 1,289,100 | 1,662,800 | 12 | .. | 4 | .. | 33 | .. | 12 | .. | 38 | .. |
| Uruguay | 3,614 | 4,484 | .. | 40 | .. | 12 | .. | 4 | .. | 11 | .. | 33 |
| Uzbekistan | 1,376 | 1,675 | .. | .. | .. | .. | .. | .. | .. | .. | .. | .. |
| Venezuela, RB | 10,668 | 18,507 | .. | .. | .. | .. | .. | .. | .. | .. | .. | .. |
| Vietnam | 3,109 | 12,963 | .. | .. | .. | .. | .. | .. | .. | .. | .. | .. |
| West Bank and Gaza | .. | .. | .. | .. | .. | .. | .. | .. | .. | .. | .. | .. |
| Yemen, Rep. | 599 | .. | .. | 48 | .. | 7 | .. | 0 | .. | 1 | .. | 43 |
| Zambia | 344 | 1,112 | .. | .. | .. | .. | .. | .. | .. | .. | .. | .. |
| Zimbabwe | 1,370 | 324 | 30 | .. | 7 | .. | 29 | .. | 6 | .. | 29 | .. |
| **World** | **5,489,148 t** | **7,440,831 t** | | | | | | | | | | |
| **Low income** | 93,977 | 216,271 | | | | | | | | | | |
| **Middle income** | 935,581 | 1,874,533 | | | | | | | | | | |
| Lower middle income | 462,950 | 1,076,557 | | | | | | | | | | |
| Upper middle income | 481,141 | 909,966 | | | | | | | | | | |
| **Low & middle income** | 1,029,570 | 2,062,844 | | | | | | | | | | |
| East Asia & Pacific | 390,751 | 973,648 | | | | | | | | | | |
| Europe & Central Asia | .. | .. | | | | | | | | | | |
| Latin America & Carib. | 290,974 | 467,711 | | | | | | | | | | |
| Middle East & N. Africa | 40,026 | 77,125 | | | | | | | | | | |
| South Asia | 75,044 | 173,275 | | | | | | | | | | |
| Sub-Saharan Africa | 45,485 | 73,246 | | | | | | | | | | |
| **High income** | 4,480,402 | 5,382,611 | | | | | | | | | | |
| Euro area | 1,340,064 | 1,609,628 | | | | | | | | | | |

a. When data are shown as not available, they are included in other manufacturing. b. Includes unallocated data. c. Covers mainland Tanzania only.

# Structure of manufacturing | 4.3

## About the data

The data on the distribution of manufacturing value added by industry are provided by the United Nations Industrial Development Organization (UNIDO). UNIDO obtains the data from a variety of national and international sources, including the United Nations Statistics Division, the World Bank, the Organisation for Economic Co-operation and Development, and the International Monetary Fund. To improve comparability over time and across countries, UNIDO supplements these data with information from industrial censuses, statistics from national and international organizations, unpublished data that it collects in the field, and estimates by the UNIDO Secretariat. Nevertheless, coverage may be incomplete, particularly for the informal sector. When direct information on inputs and outputs is not available, estimates may be used, which may result in errors in industry totals. Moreover, countries use different reference periods (calendar or fiscal year) and valuation methods (basic or producer prices) to estimate value added. (See also *About the data* for table 4.2.)

The data on manufacturing value added in U.S. dollars are from the World Bank's national accounts files and may differ from those UNIDO uses to calculate shares of value added by industry, in part because of differences in exchange rates. Thus value added in a particular industry estimated by applying the shares to total manufacturing value added will not match those from UNIDO sources. Classification of manufacturing industries in the table accords with the United Nations International Standard Industrial Classification (ISIC) revision 3 for the first time. Previous editions of *World Development Indicators* used revision 2, first published in 1948. Revision 3 was completed in 1989, and many countries now use it. But revision 2 is still widely used for compiling cross-country data. UNIDO has converted these data to

accord with revision 3. Concordances matching ISIC categories to national classification systems and to related systems such as the Standard International Trade Classification are available.

In establishing classifications systems compilers must define both the types of activities to be described and the units whose activities are to be reported. There are many possibilities, and the choices affect how the statistics can be interpreted and how useful they are in analyzing economic behavior. The ISIC emphasizes commonalities in the production process and is explicitly not intended to measure outputs (for which there is a newly developed Central Product Classification). Nevertheless, the ISIC views an activity as defined by "a process resulting in a homogeneous set of products" (UN 1990 [ISIC, series M, no. 4, rev. 3], p. 9).

Firms typically use multiple processes to produce a product. For example, an automobile manufacturer engages in forging, welding, and painting as well as advertising, accounting, and other service activities. Collecting data at such a detailed level is not practical, nor is it useful to record production data at the highest level of a large, multiplant, multiproduct firm. The ISIC has therefore adopted as the definition of an establishment "an enterprise or part of an enterprise which independently engages in one, or predominantly one, kind of economic activity at or from one location . . . for which data are available . . ." (UN 1990, p. 25). By design, this definition matches the reporting unit required for the production accounts of the United Nations System of National Accounts. The ISIC system is described in the United Nations' International Standard Industrial Classification of All Economic Activities, Third Revision (1990). The discussion of the ISIC draws on Jacob Ryten's "Fifty Years of ISIC: Historical Origins and Future Perspectives" (1998).

## Definitions

• **Manufacturing value added** is the sum of gross output less the value of intermediate inputs used in production for industries classified in ISIC major division 3. • **Food, beverages, and tobacco** correspond to ISIC division 15 and 16. • **Textiles and clothing** correspond to ISIC division 17 to 19. • **Machinery and transport equipment** correspond to ISIC 29, 30, 32, 34, and 35. • **Chemicals** correspond to ISIC division 24. • **Other manufacturing,** a residual, covers wood and related products (ISIC division 20), paper and related products (ISIC division 21 and 22), petroleum and related products (ISIC division 23), basic metals and mineral products (ISIC divisions 27), fabricated metal products and professional goods (ISIC division 28), and other industries (ISIC divisions 25, 26, 31, 33, 36, and 37).

## Manufacturing continues to show strong growth in East Asia | 4.3a

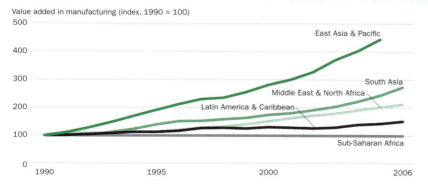

Value added in manufacturing (index, 1990 = 100)

Manufacturing continues to be the dominant sector in East Asia and Pacific, growing an average of about 10 percent a year between 1990 and 2006.

*Source: World Development Indicators data files.*

## Data sources

Data on manufacturing value added are from the World Bank's national accounts files. Data used to calculate shares of industry value added are provided to the World Bank in electronic files by UNIDO. The most recent published source is UNIDO's *International Yearbook of Industrial Statistics 2007.*

# 4.4 Structure of merchandise exports

| | Merchandise exports | | Food | | Agricultural raw materials | | Fuels | | Ores and metals | | Manufactures | |
|---|---|---|---|---|---|---|---|---|---|---|---|---|
| | $ millions | | % of total | | % of total | | % of total | | % of total | | % of total | |
| | 1995 | 2006 | 1995 | 2006 | 1995 | 2006 | 1995 | 2006 | 1995 | 2006 | 1995 | 2006 |
| Afghanistan | 156 | 430 | .. | .. | .. | .. | .. | .. | .. | .. | .. | .. |
| Albania | 202 | 793 | 11 | 8 | 9 | 13 | 3 | 14 | 12 | 38 | 65 | 27 |
| Algeria | 10,258 | 54,613 | 1 | 0 | 0 | 0 | 95 | 98 | 1 | 1 | 4 | 1 |
| Angola | 3,642 | 35,000 | .. | .. | .. | .. | .. | .. | .. | .. | .. | .. |
| Argentina | 20,967 | 46,569 | 50 | 45 | 4 | 1 | 10 | 15 | 2 | 5 | 34 | 32 |
| Armenia | 271 | 1,004 | 11 | 12 | 5 | 3 | 1 | 2 | 26 | 25 | 54 | 56 |
| Australia | 53,111 | 123,269 | 22 | 15 | 8 | 3 | 19 | 25 | 18 | 25 | 30 | 23 |
| Austria | 57,738 | 140,397 | 4 | 6 | 3 | 2 | 1 | 5 | 3 | 3 | 88 | 80 |
| Azerbaijan | 635 | 6,372 | 4 | 5 | 8 | 1 | 66 | 85 | 1 | 1 | 20 | 8 |
| Bangladesh | 3,501 | 11,802 | 10 | 6 | 3 | 1 | 0 | 0 | 0 | 0 | 85 | 92 |
| Belarus | 4,803 | 19,739 | .. | 7 | .. | 2 | .. | 38 | .. | 0 | .. | 50 |
| Belgium | 178,265[a] | 369,166 | .. | 8 | .. | 1 | .. | 8 | .. | 4 | .. | 77 |
| Benin | 420 | 560 | 14 | 26 | 75 | 64 | 5 | .. | 0 | 1 | 6 | 9 |
| Bolivia | 1,100 | 3,863 | 21 | 15 | 10 | 2 | 15 | 52 | 35 | 24 | 19 | 7 |
| Bosnia and Herzegovina | 152 | 3,312 | .. | 5 | .. | 8 | .. | 8 | .. | 17 | .. | 62 |
| Botswana | 2,142 | 4,670 | .. | .. | .. | .. | .. | .. | .. | .. | .. | .. |
| Brazil | 46,506 | 137,470 | 29 | 25 | 5 | 4 | 1 | 8 | 10 | 11 | 54 | 51 |
| Bulgaria | 5,355 | 15,064 | 18 | 9 | 3 | 2 | 7 | 13 | 10 | 20 | 60 | 53 |
| Burkina Faso | 276 | 440 | 25 | 16 | 69 | 72 | 0 | 3 | 0 | 1 | 6 | 8 |
| Burundi | 105 | 59 | 91 | 87 | 4 | 4 | 0 | 0 | 1 | 2 | 3 | 6 |
| Cambodia | 855 | 3,800 | .. | 1 | .. | 2 | .. | 0 | .. | 0 | .. | 97 |
| Cameroon | 1,651 | 3,573 | 27 | 12 | 28 | 16 | 29 | 62 | 8 | 5 | 8 | 3 |
| Canada | 192,197 | 389,538 | 8 | 7 | 9 | 4 | 9 | 20 | 7 | 7 | 63 | 56 |
| Central African Republic | 171 | 120 | 4 | 1 | 20 | 41 | 1 | 0 | 30 | 17 | 45 | 36 |
| Chad | 243 | 3,750 | .. | .. | .. | .. | .. | .. | .. | .. | .. | .. |
| Chile | 16,024 | 58,116 | 24 | 15 | 12 | 5 | 0 | 2 | 48 | 64 | 13 | 11 |
| China[†] | 148,780 | 968,936 | 8 | 3 | 2 | 0 | 4 | 2 | 2 | 2 | 84 | 92 |
|   Hong Kong, China[b] | 173,871 | 322,669 | 3 | 3 | 0 | 1 | 0 | 2 | 1 | 4 | 94 | 91 |
| Colombia | 10,056 | 24,388 | 31 | 16 | 5 | 5 | 28 | 40 | 1 | 2 | 35 | 37 |
| Congo, Dem. Rep. | 1,563 | 2,300 | .. | .. | .. | .. | .. | .. | .. | .. | .. | .. |
| Congo, Rep. | 1,172 | 6,400 | 1 | .. | 8 | .. | 88 | .. | 0 | .. | 3 | .. |
| Costa Rica | 3,453 | 8,216 | 63 | 30 | 5 | 3 | 1 | 1 | 1 | 2 | 25 | 65 |
| Côte d'Ivoire | 3,806 | 8,420 | 63 | 35 | 20 | 8 | 10 | 37 | 0 | 0 | 7 | 15 |
| Croatia | 4,633 | 10,376 | 11 | 11 | 5 | 3 | 9 | 15 | 2 | 4 | 74 | 66 |
| Cuba | 1,600 | 2,678 | .. | 30 | .. | 0 | .. | 1 | .. | 48 | .. | 22 |
| Czech Republic | 21,335 | 95,077 | 6 | 3 | 4 | 1 | 4 | 3 | 3 | 2 | 82 | 89 |
| Denmark | 50,906 | 92,752 | 24 | 18 | 3 | 3 | 3 | 10 | 1 | 2 | 60 | 65 |
| Dominican Republic | 3,780 | 6,440 | 19 | .. | 0 | .. | 0 | .. | 0 | .. | 78 | .. |
| Ecuador | 4,307 | 12,658 | 53 | 27 | 3 | 4 | 36 | 59 | 0 | 1 | 8 | 10 |
| Egypt, Arab Rep. | 3,450 | 13,702 | 10 | 7 | 6 | 2 | 37 | 56 | 6 | 2 | 40 | 21 |
| El Salvador | 1,652 | 3,513 | 57 | 36 | 1 | 1 | 0 | 3 | 3 | 4 | 39 | 55 |
| Eritrea | 86 | 10 | .. | .. | .. | .. | .. | .. | .. | .. | .. | .. |
| Estonia | 1,840 | 9,469 | 16 | 7 | 10 | 5 | 6 | 16 | 3 | 3 | 65 | 64 |
| Ethiopia | 422 | 1,014 | 73 | .. | 13 | .. | 3 | .. | 0 | .. | 11 | .. |
| Finland | 40,490 | 77,032 | 2 | 2 | 8 | 6 | 2 | 5 | 3 | 5 | 83 | 81 |
| France | 301,162 | 490,368 | 14 | 10 | 1 | 1 | 2 | 4 | 3 | 3 | 79 | 79 |
| Gabon | 2,713 | 5,600 | 0 | 1 | 13 | 7 | 83 | 86 | 2 | 3 | 2 | 4 |
| Gambia, The | 16 | 10 | 60 | 81 | 1 | 4 | 0 | .. | 1 | 1 | 36 | 14 |
| Georgia | 151 | 993 | 29 | 25 | 3 | 2 | 19 | 3 | 8 | 22 | 41 | 48 |
| Germany | 523,461 | 1,111,969 | 5 | 4 | 1 | 1 | 1 | 2 | 3 | 3 | 87 | 83 |
| Ghana | 1,724 | 3,703 | 58 | 61 | 15 | 4 | 5 | 1 | 9 | 3 | 13 | 31 |
| Greece | 11,054 | 20,898 | 30 | 20 | 4 | 2 | 7 | 13 | 7 | 10 | 50 | 52 |
| Guatemala | 2,155 | 6,025 | 65 | 50 | 4 | 5 | 2 | 9 | 0 | 1 | 28 | 35 |
| Guinea | 702 | 970 | 8 | .. | 1 | .. | 0 | .. | 67 | .. | 24 | .. |
| Guinea-Bissau | 24 | 75 | 89 | .. | 11 | .. | .. | .. | .. | .. | 0 | .. |
| Haiti | 110 | 507 | 37 | .. | 0 | .. | 0 | .. | 0 | .. | 62 | .. |
| [†]Data for Taiwan, China | 113,047 | 223,766 | 3 | 1 | 2 | 1 | 1 | 5 | 1 | 2 | 93 | 90 |

# Structure of merchandise exports | 4.4

| | Merchandise exports | | Food | | Agricultural raw materials | | Fuels | | Ores and metals | | Manufactures | |
|---|---|---|---|---|---|---|---|---|---|---|---|---|
| | $ millions | | % of total | | % of total | | % of total | | % of total | | % of total | |
| | 1995 | 2006 | 1995 | 2006 | 1995 | 2006 | 1995 | 2006 | 1995 | 2006 | 1995 | 2006 |
| Honduras | 1,220 | 1,929 | 87 | 64 | 3 | 3 | 0 | 3 | 0 | 9 | 9 | 21 |
| Hungary | 12,865 | 74,478 | 21 | 6 | 2 | 0 | 3 | 2 | 5 | 2 | 68 | 84 |
| India | 30,630 | 120,254 | 19 | 9 | 1 | 2 | 2 | 11 | 3 | 7 | 74 | 70 |
| Indonesia | 45,417 | 103,487 | 11 | 12 | 7 | 6 | 25 | 27 | 6 | 10 | 51 | 45 |
| Iran, Islamic Rep. | 18,360 | 73,700 | 4 | 4 | 1 | 0 | 86 | 83 | 1 | 2 | 9 | 10 |
| Iraq | 496 | 29,597 | .. | .. | .. | .. | .. | .. | .. | .. | .. | .. |
| Ireland | 44,705 | 111,066 | 19 | 10 | 1 | 0 | 0 | 1 | 1 | 1 | 72 | 85 |
| Israel | 19,046 | 46,449 | 5 | 2 | 2 | 1 | 0 | 0 | 1 | 1 | 89 | 82 |
| Italy | 233,766 | 410,572 | 7 | 6 | 1 | 1 | 1 | 4 | 1 | 2 | 89 | 85 |
| Jamaica | 1,427 | 1,980 | 22 | 17 | 0 | 0 | 1 | 14 | 6 | 11 | 71 | 58 |
| Japan | 443,116 | 649,931 | 0 | 0 | 1 | 1 | 1 | 1 | 1 | 2 | 95 | 91 |
| Jordan | 1,769 | 5,175 | 25 | 15 | 2 | 0 | 0 | 1 | 24 | 13 | 49 | 71 |
| Kazakhstan | 5,250 | 40,470 | 10 | 3 | 3 | 1 | 25 | 69 | 24 | 15 | 38 | 13 |
| Kenya | 1,878 | 3,437 | 56 | 52 | 7 | 16 | 6 | 1 | 3 | 6 | 28 | 26 |
| Korea, Dem. Rep. | 959 | 1,980 | .. | .. | .. | .. | .. | .. | .. | .. | .. | .. |
| Korea, Rep. | 125,058 | 325,465 | 2 | 1 | 1 | 1 | 2 | 6 | 1 | 3 | 93 | 89 |
| Kuwait | 12,785 | 55,673 | 0 | .. | 0 | .. | 95 | .. | 0 | .. | 5 | .. |
| Kyrgyz Republic | 409 | 796 | 23 | 19 | 13 | 10 | 11 | 18 | 13 | 6 | 40 | 46 |
| Lao PDR | 311 | 874 | .. | .. | .. | .. | .. | .. | .. | .. | .. | .. |
| Latvia | 1,305 | 6,153 | 14 | 12 | 23 | 14 | 2 | 5 | 1 | 4 | 58 | 60 |
| Lebanon | 816 | 2,814 | 20 | 16 | 2 | 1 | 0 | 0 | 8 | 12 | 70 | 70 |
| Lesotho | 160 | 694 | .. | .. | .. | .. | .. | .. | .. | .. | .. | .. |
| Liberia | 820 | 181 | .. | .. | .. | .. | .. | .. | .. | .. | .. | .. |
| Libya | 8,975 | 39,500 | 0 | .. | 0 | .. | 95 | .. | 0 | .. | 5 | .. |
| Lithuania | 2,705 | 14,113 | 18 | 14 | 8 | 3 | 11 | 24 | 5 | 2 | 58 | 58 |
| Macedonia, FYR | 1,204 | 2,401 | 18 | 16 | 5 | 1 | 0 | 9 | 18 | 4 | 58 | 69 |
| Madagascar | 507 | 953 | 69 | 35 | 6 | 4 | 1 | 6 | 7 | 4 | 14 | 41 |
| Malawi | 405 | 540 | 90 | 83 | 2 | 3 | 0 | 0 | 0 | 0 | 7 | 13 |
| Malaysia | 73,914 | 160,676 | 10 | 7 | 6 | 3 | 7 | 14 | 1 | 1 | 75 | 74 |
| Mali | 441 | 1,350 | 23 | 14 | 75 | 74 | 0 | 1 | 0 | 0 | 2 | 10 |
| Mauritania | 499 | 1,290 | 57 | 25 | 0 | 0 | 1 | .. | 42 | 69 | 0 | 0 |
| Mauritius | 1,538 | 2,173 | 29 | 29 | 1 | 1 | 0 | 0 | 0 | 1 | 70 | 69 |
| Mexico | 79,542 | 250,441 | 8 | 5 | 1 | 0 | 10 | 16 | 3 | 2 | 78 | 76 |
| Moldova | 745 | 1,052 | 72 | 63 | 2 | 1 | 1 | 0 | 3 | 5 | 23 | 31 |
| Mongolia | 473 | 1,543 | 2 | 2 | 28 | 13 | 0 | 6 | 60 | 66 | 10 | 13 |
| Morocco | 6,881 | 12,707 | 31 | 19 | 3 | 2 | 2 | 2 | 12 | 9 | 51 | 68 |
| Mozambique | 168 | 2,398 | 66 | 16 | 16 | 3 | 2 | 15 | 2 | 60 | 13 | 5 |
| Myanmar | 860 | 4,250 | .. | .. | .. | .. | .. | .. | .. | .. | .. | .. |
| Namibia | 1,409 | 2,648 | .. | 26 | .. | 1 | .. | 0 | .. | 26 | .. | 47 |
| Nepal | 345 | 760 | 8 | .. | 1 | .. | 0 | .. | 0 | .. | 84 | .. |
| Netherlands | 203,171 | 462,410 | 20 | 13 | 4 | 3 | 7 | 13 | 3 | 4 | 63 | 66 |
| New Zealand | 13,645 | 22,432 | 45 | 52 | 19 | 11 | 2 | 2 | 5 | 5 | 29 | 27 |
| Nicaragua | 466 | 1,027 | 75 | 86 | 3 | 2 | 1 | 1 | 1 | 2 | 21 | 9 |
| Niger | 288 | 540 | 17 | 24 | 1 | 4 | 0 | 2 | 80 | 54 | 1 | 14 |
| Nigeria | 12,342 | 52,000 | 2 | .. | 2 | .. | 96 | .. | 0 | .. | 1 | .. |
| Norway | 41,992 | 121,505 | 8 | 5 | 2 | 0 | 47 | 68 | 9 | 7 | 27 | 16 |
| Oman | 6,068 | 21,585 | 5 | 2 | 0 | 0 | 79 | 95 | 2 | 1 | 14 | 3 |
| Pakistan | 8,029 | 16,930 | 12 | 12 | 4 | 1 | 1 | 5 | 0 | 1 | 83 | 81 |
| Panama | 625 | 1,048 | 75 | 84 | 0 | 1 | 3 | 1 | 1 | 4 | 20 | 10 |
| Papua New Guinea | 2,654 | 4,122 | 13 | .. | 20 | .. | 38 | .. | 25 | .. | 4 | .. |
| Paraguay | 919 | 1,906 | 44 | 76 | 36 | 7 | 0 | 0 | 0 | 1 | 19 | 16 |
| Peru | 5,575 | 23,431 | 31 | 18 | 3 | 2 | 5 | 10 | 46 | 57 | 15 | 14 |
| Philippines | 17,502 | 47,037 | 13 | 5 | 1 | 1 | 2 | 2 | 4 | 4 | 42 | 87 |
| Poland | 22,895 | 110,303 | 10 | 9 | 3 | 1 | 8 | 4 | 7 | 5 | 71 | 79 |
| Portugal | 22,783 | 43,323 | 7 | 8 | 5 | 2 | 3 | 5 | 2 | 4 | 83 | 74 |
| Puerto Rico | .. | .. | .. | .. | .. | .. | .. | .. | .. | .. | .. | .. |

| | Merchandise exports $ millions | | Food % of total | | Agricultural raw materials % of total | | Fuels % of total | | Ores and metals % of total | | Manufactures % of total | |
|---|---|---|---|---|---|---|---|---|---|---|---|---|
| | 1995 | 2006 | 1995 | 2006 | 1995 | 2006 | 1995 | 2006 | 1995 | 2006 | 1995 | 2006 |
| Romania | 7,910 | 32,336 | 7 | 3 | 3 | 2 | 8 | 10 | 3 | 5 | 78 | 79 |
| Russian Federation | 81,095 | 304,520 | 2 | 2 | 3 | 3 | 43 | 63 | 10 | 8 | 26 | 17 |
| Rwanda | 54 | 138 | 57 | .. | 16 | .. | 0 | .. | 12 | .. | 14 | .. |
| Saudi Arabia | 50,040 | 209,483 | 1 | 1 | 0 | 0 | 88 | 91 | 1 | 0 | 10 | 8 |
| Senegal | 993 | 1,550 | 9 | 44 | 7 | 5 | 22 | 0 | 12 | 7 | 48 | 44 |
| Serbia | .. | 6,428 | .. | .. | .. | .. | .. | .. | .. | .. | .. | .. |
| Sierra Leone | 42 | 216 | .. | .. | .. | .. | .. | .. | .. | .. | .. | .. |
| Singapore[b] | 118,268 | 271,772 | 4 | 2 | 1 | 0 | 7 | 13 | 2 | 1 | 84 | 80 |
| Slovak Republic | 8,580 | 41,721 | 6 | 4 | 4 | 1 | 4 | 5 | 4 | 3 | 82 | 85 |
| Slovenia | 8,316 | 23,257 | 4 | 3 | 2 | 1 | 1 | 3 | 3 | 5 | 90 | 87 |
| Somalia | .. | .. | .. | .. | .. | .. | .. | .. | .. | .. | .. | .. |
| South Africa | 27,853[c] | 58,412 | 8[c] | 7 | 4[c] | 2 | 9[c] | 9 | 8[c] | 29 | 44[c] | 53 |
| Spain | 97,849 | 205,455 | 15 | 14 | 2 | 1 | 2 | 4 | 2 | 3 | 78 | 76 |
| Sri Lanka | 3,798 | 6,886 | 21 | 22 | 4 | 2 | 0 | 0 | 1 | 4 | 73 | 70 |
| Sudan | 555 | 5,657 | 44 | 7 | 47 | 5 | 0 | 87 | 0 | 0 | 6 | 0 |
| Swaziland | 866 | 2,060 | .. | 17 | .. | 8 | .. | 1 | .. | 0 | .. | 74 |
| Sweden | 80,440 | 147,377 | 2 | 4 | 6 | 4 | 2 | 5 | 3 | 4 | 79 | 78 |
| Switzerland | 81,641 | 147,457 | 3 | 3 | 1 | 0 | 0 | 3 | 3 | 4 | 94 | 91 |
| Syrian Arab Republic | 3,563 | 8,750 | 12 | 17 | 7 | 2 | 63 | 40 | 1 | 1 | 17 | 32 |
| Tajikistan | 750 | 1,399 | .. | .. | .. | .. | .. | .. | .. | .. | .. | .. |
| Tanzania | 682 | 1,690 | 65 | 53 | 23 | 11 | 0 | 0 | 0 | 17 | 10 | 18 |
| Thailand | 56,439 | 130,790 | 19 | 11 | 5 | 5 | 1 | 5 | 1 | 2 | 73 | 76 |
| Timor-Leste | .. | .. | .. | .. | .. | .. | .. | .. | .. | .. | .. | .. |
| Togo | 378 | 617 | 19 | 21 | 42 | 9 | 0 | 1 | 32 | 10 | 7 | 58 |
| Trinidad and Tobago | 2,455 | 14,147 | 8 | 2 | 0 | 0 | 48 | 76 | 0 | 0 | 43 | 21 |
| Tunisia | 5,475 | 11,513 | 10 | 10 | 1 | 1 | 8 | 13 | 2 | 1 | 79 | 75 |
| Turkey | 21,637 | 85,479 | 20 | 7 | 1 | 0 | 1 | 0 | 3 | 1 | 74 | 42 |
| Turkmenistan | 1,880 | 5,260 | 1 | .. | 13 | .. | 77 | .. | 1 | .. | 8 | .. |
| Uganda | 460 | 1,004 | 90 | 62 | 5 | 9 | 0 | 5 | 1 | 2 | 4 | 21 |
| Ukraine | 13,128 | 38,368 | 19 | 12 | 1 | 1 | 4 | 6 | 7 | 6 | 68 | 73 |
| United Arab Emirates | 28,364 | 139,353 | 8 | .. | 0 | .. | 9 | .. | 55 | .. | 28 | .. |
| United Kingdom | 237,953 | 448,291 | 8 | 5 | 1 | 1 | 6 | 10 | 3 | 3 | 81 | 77 |
| United States | 584,743 | 1,038,278 | 11 | 7 | 4 | 2 | 2 | 4 | 3 | 4 | 77 | 79 |
| Uruguay | 2,106 | 3,953 | 44 | 56 | 15 | 8 | 1 | 4 | 1 | 1 | 39 | 32 |
| Uzbekistan | 3,430 | 5,617 | .. | .. | .. | .. | .. | .. | .. | .. | .. | .. |
| Venezuela, RB | 18,457 | 65,210 | 3 | 0 | 0 | 0 | 77 | 93 | 6 | 2 | 14 | 5 |
| Vietnam | 5,449 | 39,605 | 30 | 20 | 3 | 3 | 18 | 26 | 0 | 1 | 44 | 50 |
| West Bank and Gaza | .. | .. | .. | .. | .. | .. | .. | .. | .. | .. | .. | .. |
| Yemen, Rep. | 1,945 | 7,285 | 3 | 4 | 1 | 0 | 95 | 94 | 1 | 0 | 1 | 1 |
| Zambia | 1,040 | 3,689 | 3 | 6 | 1 | 3 | 3 | 1 | 87 | 85 | 7 | 6 |
| Zimbabwe | 2,118 | 1,950 | 43 | 30 | 7 | 8 | 1 | 0 | 12 | 23 | 37 | 38 |
| **World** | **5,172,060 t** | **12,084,582 t** | **9 w** | **6 w** | **3 w** | **2 w** | **7 w** | **11 w** | **3 w** | **4 w** | **76 w** | **73 w** |
| **Low income** | 94,379 | 323,066 | 18 | 17 | 5 | 4 | 26 | 15 | 4 | 5 | 47 | 59 |
| **Middle income** | 880,315 | 3,312,091 | 14 | 8 | 3 | 2 | 12 | 21 | 5 | 6 | 63 | 60 |
| Lower middle income | 390,379 | 1,689,637 | 13 | 8 | 3 | 2 | 12 | 16 | 3 | 4 | 65 | 69 |
| Upper middle income | 490,027 | 1,621,751 | 15 | 9 | 4 | 2 | 12 | 25 | 6 | 7 | 62 | 53 |
| **Low & middle income** | 974,709 | 3,635,152 | 15 | 9 | 3 | 2 | 12 | 21 | 5 | 6 | 63 | 60 |
| East Asia & Pacific | 355,216 | 1,468,949 | 11 | 6 | 4 | 2 | 6 | 8 | 2 | 3 | 74 | 80 |
| Europe & Central Asia | 205,007 | 834,785 | 10 | 5 | 3 | 2 | 22 | 32 | 7 | 6 | 51 | 46 |
| Latin America & Carib. | 223,378 | 663,606 | 20 | 15 | 3 | 2 | 15 | 21 | 7 | 9 | 55 | 53 |
| Middle East & N. Africa | 68,070 | 280,990 | 6 | 5 | 1 | 0 | 73 | 76 | 2 | 2 | 17 | 15 |
| South Asia | 46,647 | 157,637 | 17 | 11 | 2 | 2 | 1 | 9 | 3 | 6 | 76 | 72 |
| Sub-Saharan Africa | 76,692 | 231,263 | 18 | .. | 7 | .. | 37 | .. | 8 | .. | 28 | .. |
| **High income** | 4,196,970 | 8,451,209 | 8 | 6 | 2 | 2 | 6 | 8 | 3 | 4 | 79 | 77 |
| Euro area | 1,733,625 | 3,492,756 | 11 | 8 | 2 | 1 | 2 | 5 | 2 | 3 | 81 | 79 |

**Note:** Components may not sum to 100 percent because of unclassified trade. Exports of gold are excluded.
a. Includes Luxembourg. b. Includes re-exports. c. Refers to the South African Customs Union (Botswana, Lesotho, Namibia, South Africa, and Swaziland).

## About the data

Data on merchandise trade are from customs reports of goods moving into or out of an economy or from reports of financial transactions related to merchandise trade recorded in the balance of payments. Because of differences in timing and definitions, estimates of trade flows from customs reports may differ from those based on the balance of payments. Moreover, several international agencies process trade data, each correcting unreported or misreported data, leading to other differences.

The most detailed source of data on international trade in goods is the Commodity Trade (Comtrade) database maintained by the United Nations Statistics Division. In addition, the International Monetary Fund (IMF) collects customs-based data on exports and imports of goods. The value of exports is recorded as the cost of the goods delivered to the frontier of the exporting country for shipment—the free on board (f.o.b.) value. Many countries report trade data in U.S. dollars. When countries report in local currency, the United Nations Statistics Division applies the average official exchange rate for the period shown.

Countries may report trade according to the general or special system of trade (see *Primary data documentation*). Under the general system exports comprise outward-moving goods that are (a) goods wholly or partly produced in the country; (b) foreign goods, neither transformed nor declared for domestic consumption in the country, that move outward from customs storage; and (c) goods previously included as imports for domestic consumption but subsequently exported without transformation. Under the special system exports comprise categories a and c. In some compilations categories b and c are classified as re-exports. Because of differences in reporting practices, data on exports may not be fully comparable across economies.

The data on total exports of goods (merchandise) are from the World Trade Organization (WTO), which uses two main sources: national statistical offices and the IMF's *International Financial Statistics*. It supplements these with the Comtrade database and publications or databases of regional organizations, specialized agencies, economic groups, and private sources (such as Eurostat, the Food and Agriculture Organization, and country reports of the Economist Intelligence Unit). Country websites and direct contact through email have improved collection of up-to-date statistics for many countries, reducing the proportion of estimated figures. The WTO database now covers most of the major traders in Africa, Asia, and Latin America, which together with high-income countries account for nearly 95 percent of world trade. The availability of reliable figures for countries in Europe and Central Asia has also improved.

The shares of exports by major commodity group are from Comtrade. The values of total exports reported here have not been fully reconciled with the estimates of exports of goods and services from the national accounts or from the balance of payments.

The classification of commodity groups is based on the Standard International Trade Classification (SITC) revision 1. Most countries now use later revisions of the SITC or the Harmonized System. Concordance tables are used to convert data reported in one system to another. This may introduce some classification errors, but conversions from later to earlier systems are generally reliable.

## Definitions

• **Merchandise exports** are the f.o.b. value of goods provided to the rest of the world, valued in U.S. dollars. • **Food** corresponds to the commodities in SITC sections 0 (food and live animals), 1 (beverages and tobacco), and 4 (animal and vegetable oils and fats) and SITC division 22 (oil seeds, oil nuts, and oil kernels). • **Agricultural raw materials** correspond to SITC section 2 (crude materials except fuels) excluding divisions 22, 27 (crude fertilizers and minerals excluding coal, petroleum, and precious stones), and 28 (metalliferous ores and scrap). • **Fuels** correspond to SITC section 3 (mineral fuels). • **Ores and metals** correspond to the commodities in SITC divisions 27, 28, and 68 (nonferrous metals). • **Manufactures** correspond to the commodities in SITC sections 5 (chemicals), 6 (basic manufactures), 7 (machinery and transport equipment), and 8 (miscellaneous manufactured goods), excluding division 68.

**Developing economies' share of world merchandise exports continues to expand**    **4.4a**

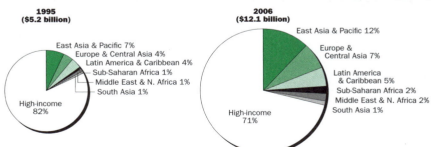

1995
($5.2 billion)

East Asia & Pacific 7%
Europe & Central Asia 4%
Latin America & Caribbean 4%
Sub-Saharan Africa 1%
Middle East & N. Africa 1%
South Asia 1%
High-income 82%

2006
($12.1 billion)

East Asia & Pacific 12%
Europe & Central Asia 7%
Latin America & Caribbean 5%
Sub-Saharan Africa 2%
Middle East & N. Africa 2%
South Asia 1%
High-income 71%

Developing economies' share of world merchandise exports increased 11 percentage points from 1995 to 2006. East Asia and Pacific was the biggest gainer, capturing an additional 5 percentage points. Except South Asia, every other region increased its share in world trade.

*Source: World Development Indicators data files and World Trade Organization.*

## Data sources

Data on merchandise exports are from the WTO. Data on shares of exports by major commodity group are from Comtrade. The WTO publishes data on world trade in its *Annual Report*. The IMF publishes estimates of total exports of goods in its *International Financial Statistics* and *Direction of Trade Statistics*, as does the United Nations Statistics Division in its *Monthly Bulletin of Statistics*. And the United Nations Conference on Trade and Development publishes data on the structure of exports in its *Handbook of International Trade and Development Statistics*. Tariff line records of exports are compiled in the United Nations Statistics Division's Comtrade database.

| | Merchandise imports | | Food | | Agricultural raw materials | | Fuels | | Ores and metals | | Manufactures | |
|---|---|---|---|---|---|---|---|---|---|---|---|---|
| | $ millions | | % of total | | % of total | | % of total | | % of total | | % of total | |
| | 1995 | 2006 | 1995 | 2006 | 1995 | 2006 | 1995 | 2006 | 1995 | 2006 | 1995 | 2006 |
| Afghanistan | 387 | 2,960 | .. | .. | .. | .. | .. | .. | .. | .. | .. | .. |
| Albania | 714 | 3,058 | 34 | 20 | 1 | 1 | 2 | 12 | 1 | 3 | 61 | 64 |
| Algeria | 10,100 | 21,456 | 29 | 19 | 3 | 2 | 1 | 1 | 2 | 2 | 65 | 76 |
| Angola | 1,468 | 11,600 | .. | .. | .. | .. | .. | .. | .. | .. | .. | .. |
| Argentina | 20,122 | 34,158 | 5 | 3 | 2 | 1 | 4 | 5 | 2 | 3 | 86 | 87 |
| Armenia | 674 | 2,194 | 31 | 16 | 0 | 1 | 27 | 17 | 0 | 2 | 39 | 60 |
| Australia | 61,283 | 139,252 | 5 | 5 | 2 | 1 | 5 | 14 | 1 | 1 | 86 | 79 |
| Austria | 66,237 | 140,258 | 6 | 6 | 3 | 2 | 4 | 14 | 4 | 5 | 82 | 73 |
| Azerbaijan | 668 | 5,268 | 39 | 10 | 1 | 1 | 4 | 12 | 2 | 2 | 53 | 74 |
| Bangladesh | 6,694 | 16,086 | 17 | 16 | 3 | 8 | 8 | 8 | 2 | 2 | 69 | 65 |
| Belarus | 5,564 | 22,323 | .. | 9 | .. | 2 | .. | 33 | .. | 4 | .. | 48 |
| Belgium | 164,934[a] | 353,720 | .. | 7 | .. | 1 | .. | 13 | .. | 5 | .. | 72 |
| Benin | 746 | 990 | 27 | 30 | 3 | 4 | 9 | 20 | 1 | 1 | 59 | 44 |
| Bolivia | 1,424 | 2,819 | 10 | 9 | 2 | 1 | 5 | 10 | 3 | 1 | 82 | 79 |
| Bosnia and Herzegovina | 1,082 | 7,305 | .. | 17 | .. | 1 | .. | 15 | .. | 3 | .. | 63 |
| Botswana | 1,911 | 3,160 | .. | .. | .. | .. | .. | .. | .. | .. | .. | .. |
| Brazil | 54,137 | 95,886 | 11 | 4 | 3 | 2 | 12 | 19 | 3 | 5 | 71 | 70 |
| Bulgaria | 5,660 | 23,136 | 8 | 5 | 3 | 1 | 34 | 5 | 4 | 9 | 48 | 62 |
| Burkina Faso | 455 | 1,450 | 21 | 12 | 2 | 1 | 14 | 24 | 1 | 1 | 62 | 62 |
| Burundi | 234 | 431 | 21 | 6 | 2 | 1 | 11 | 8 | 1 | 1 | 64 | 82 |
| Cambodia | 1,187 | 4,900 | .. | 8 | .. | 2 | .. | 10 | .. | 0 | .. | 79 |
| Cameroon | 1,199 | 2,990 | 17 | 18 | 3 | 2 | 3 | 31 | 2 | 1 | 76 | 48 |
| Canada | 168,426 | 357,652 | 6 | 6 | 2 | 1 | 4 | 9 | 3 | 3 | 83 | 79 |
| Central African Republic | 175 | 240 | 16 | 17 | 10 | 27 | 9 | 17 | 2 | 2 | 64 | 37 |
| Chad | 365 | 1,250 | 24 | .. | 1 | .. | 18 | .. | 1 | .. | 56 | .. |
| Chile | 15,900 | 38,409 | 7 | 7 | 2 | 1 | 9 | 24 | 2 | 3 | 79 | 65 |
| China[†] | 132,084 | 791,461 | 7 | 3 | 5 | 4 | 4 | 12 | 4 | 9 | 79 | 71 |
| Hong Kong, China | 196,072 | 335,754 | 5 | 3 | 2 | 1 | 2 | 3 | 2 | 3 | 88 | 91 |
| Colombia | 13,853 | 26,046 | 9 | 9 | 3 | 2 | 3 | 3 | 2 | 3 | 78 | 82 |
| Congo, Dem. Rep. | 871 | 2,800 | .. | .. | .. | .. | .. | .. | .. | .. | .. | .. |
| Congo, Rep. | 670 | 1,700 | 21 | .. | 1 | .. | 20 | .. | 1 | .. | 58 | .. |
| Costa Rica | 4,036 | 11,520 | 10 | 6 | 1 | 1 | 9 | 12 | 2 | 2 | 78 | 78 |
| Côte d'Ivoire | 2,931 | 5,310 | 21 | 17 | 1 | 1 | 19 | 32 | 1 | 1 | 57 | 43 |
| Croatia | 7,510 | 21,488 | 12 | 8 | 2 | 1 | 12 | 16 | 3 | 3 | 67 | 72 |
| Cuba | 2,825 | 9,410 | .. | 22 | .. | 1 | .. | 23 | .. | 1 | .. | 53 |
| Czech Republic | 25,085 | 93,217 | 7 | 5 | 3 | 1 | 8 | 9 | 4 | 4 | 77 | 79 |
| Denmark | 45,939 | 86,273 | 12 | 11 | 3 | 2 | 3 | 6 | 2 | 2 | 73 | 77 |
| Dominican Republic | 5,170 | 11,190 | .. | .. | .. | .. | .. | .. | .. | .. | .. | .. |
| Ecuador | 4,152 | 12,049 | 8 | 7 | 3 | 1 | 6 | 17 | 2 | 1 | 82 | 74 |
| Egypt, Arab Rep. | 11,760 | 20,595 | 28 | 19 | 7 | 4 | 1 | 16 | 3 | 3 | 61 | 43 |
| El Salvador | 3,329 | 7,628 | 15 | 13 | 2 | 2 | 9 | 18 | 2 | 1 | 72 | 66 |
| Eritrea | 454 | 540 | .. | .. | .. | .. | .. | .. | .. | .. | .. | .. |
| Estonia | 2,546 | 13,277 | 14 | 7 | 3 | 3 | 11 | 16 | 1 | 1 | 71 | 67 |
| Ethiopia | 1,145 | 4,594 | 14 | .. | 2 | .. | 11 | .. | 1 | .. | 72 | .. |
| Finland | 29,470 | 68,873 | 6 | 5 | 4 | 2 | 9 | 15 | 6 | 9 | 74 | 66 |
| France | 289,391 | 534,894 | 11 | 7 | 3 | 1 | 7 | 15 | 4 | 3 | 76 | 73 |
| Gabon | 882 | 1,728 | 19 | 17 | 1 | 0 | 4 | 4 | 1 | 1 | 75 | 77 |
| Gambia, The | 182 | 255 | 36 | 31 | 1 | 2 | 14 | 17 | 0 | 1 | 46 | 49 |
| Georgia | 392 | 3,678 | 36 | 16 | 0 | 0 | 39 | 19 | 0 | 1 | 24 | 61 |
| Germany | 463,872 | 908,630 | 10 | 6 | 3 | 1 | 6 | 12 | 4 | 5 | 73 | 66 |
| Ghana | 1,906 | 5,497 | 8 | 13 | 1 | 1 | 6 | 14 | 0 | 1 | 77 | 70 |
| Greece | 25,898 | 63,185 | 16 | 11 | 2 | 1 | 7 | 19 | 3 | 4 | 71 | 65 |
| Guatemala | 3,292 | 11,920 | 12 | 10 | 2 | 1 | 12 | 20 | 1 | 1 | 73 | 68 |
| Guinea | 819 | 930 | 31 | .. | 1 | .. | 19 | .. | 1 | .. | 47 | .. |
| Guinea-Bissau | 133 | 110 | 44 | .. | 0 | .. | 16 | .. | 0 | .. | 40 | .. |
| Haiti | 653 | 1,705 | .. | .. | .. | .. | .. | .. | .. | .. | .. | .. |
| [†]Data for Taiwan, China | 103,558 | 203,017 | 6 | 3 | 4 | 1 | 7 | 18 | 6 | 8 | 75 | 68 |

# Structure of merchandise imports | 4.5

| | Merchandise imports | | Food | | Agricultural raw materials | | Fuels | | Ores and metals | | Manufactures | |
|---|---|---|---|---|---|---|---|---|---|---|---|---|
| | $ millions | | % of total | | % of total | | % of total | | % of total | | % of total | |
| | 1995 | 2006 | 1995 | 2006 | 1995 | 2006 | 1995 | 2006 | 1995 | 2006 | 1995 | 2006 |
| Honduras | 1,642 | 5,418 | 13 | 16 | 1 | 1 | 12 | 20 | 1 | 1 | 74 | 62 |
| Hungary | 15,465 | 76,963 | 6 | 4 | 3 | 1 | 12 | 7 | 4 | 3 | 75 | 75 |
| India | 34,707 | 174,845 | 4 | 3 | 4 | 2 | 24 | 36 | 7 | 5 | 54 | 52 |
| Indonesia | 40,630 | 80,333 | 9 | 9 | 6 | 3 | 8 | 32 | 4 | 4 | 73 | 53 |
| Iran, Islamic Rep. | 13,882 | 51,100 | 21 | 2 | 2 | 1 | 2 | 4 | 3 | 0 | 71 | 16 |
| Iraq | 665 | 27,935 | .. | .. | .. | .. | .. | .. | .. | .. | .. | .. |
| Ireland | 32,340 | 72,806 | 8 | 8 | 1 | 1 | 3 | 8 | 2 | 2 | 76 | 76 |
| Israel | 29,578 | 49,985 | 7 | 6 | 2 | 1 | 6 | 16 | 2 | 2 | 82 | 75 |
| Italy | 205,990 | 437,386 | 12 | 8 | 6 | 3 | 7 | 12 | 5 | 6 | 68 | 64 |
| Jamaica | 2,818 | 5,648 | 14 | 14 | 2 | 2 | 13 | 25 | 1 | 1 | 68 | 57 |
| Japan | 335,882 | 579,574 | 16 | 9 | 6 | 2 | 16 | 28 | 7 | 8 | 54 | 52 |
| Jordan | 3,697 | 11,447 | 21 | 13 | 2 | 1 | 13 | 24 | 3 | 2 | 61 | 57 |
| Kazakhstan | 3,807 | 24,956 | 10 | 7 | 2 | 1 | 25 | 13 | 5 | 1 | 59 | 78 |
| Kenya | 2,991 | 7,311 | 10 | 10 | 2 | 2 | 15 | 24 | 2 | 2 | 71 | 61 |
| Korea, Dem. Rep. | 1,380 | 3,010 | .. | .. | .. | .. | .. | .. | .. | .. | .. | .. |
| Korea, Rep. | 135,119 | 309,383 | 6 | 4 | 6 | 2 | 14 | 28 | 6 | 8 | 68 | 58 |
| Kuwait | 7,790 | 15,991 | 16 | .. | 1 | .. | 1 | .. | 2 | .. | 81 | .. |
| Kyrgyz Republic | 522 | 1,718 | 18 | 14 | 3 | 1 | 36 | 29 | 3 | 2 | 40 | 53 |
| Lao PDR | 589 | 1,060 | .. | .. | .. | .. | .. | .. | .. | .. | .. | .. |
| Latvia | 1,815 | 11,510 | 10 | 10 | 2 | 2 | 21 | 13 | 1 | 2 | 66 | 70 |
| Lebanon | 7,278 | 9,647 | 21 | 16 | 2 | 1 | 9 | 22 | 2 | 2 | 66 | 58 |
| Lesotho | 1,107 | 1,465 | .. | .. | .. | .. | .. | .. | .. | .. | .. | .. |
| Liberia | 510 | 444 | .. | .. | .. | .. | .. | .. | .. | .. | .. | .. |
| Libya | 5,392 | 6,950 | 23 | 17 | 1 | 1 | 0 | 1 | 1 | 1 | 75 | 81 |
| Lithuania | 3,650 | 19,300 | 13 | 9 | 4 | 2 | 19 | 22 | 4 | 2 | 58 | 64 |
| Macedonia, FYR | 1,719 | 3,763 | 17 | 12 | 3 | 1 | 12 | 20 | 3 | 4 | 64 | 63 |
| Madagascar | 628 | 1,487 | 16 | 15 | 2 | 1 | 14 | 19 | 1 | 1 | 65 | 65 |
| Malawi | 475 | 1,209 | 14 | 15 | 1 | 1 | 11 | 11 | 1 | 1 | 73 | 71 |
| Malaysia | 77,691 | 131,152 | 5 | 5 | 1 | 1 | 2 | 9 | 3 | 5 | 86 | 78 |
| Mali | 772 | 1,860 | 20 | 14 | 1 | 1 | 16 | 21 | 1 | 1 | 62 | 64 |
| Mauritania | 494 | 974 | 24 | 25 | 1 | 1 | 22 | 27 | 0 | 0 | 53 | 47 |
| Mauritius | 1,976 | 3,630 | 17 | 17 | 3 | 2 | 7 | 17 | 1 | 1 | 72 | 64 |
| Mexico | 75,858 | 268,169 | 6 | 6 | 2 | 1 | 2 | 6 | 2 | 3 | 80 | 83 |
| Moldova | 840 | 2,693 | 8 | 11 | 3 | 2 | 46 | 24 | 2 | 1 | 42 | 62 |
| Mongolia | 415 | 1,486 | 14 | 12 | 1 | 0 | 19 | 29 | 1 | 0 | 65 | 58 |
| Morocco | 10,023 | 23,574 | 20 | 9 | 6 | 3 | 14 | 22 | 4 | 3 | 56 | 63 |
| Mozambique | 704 | 2,807 | 22 | 14 | 3 | 1 | 10 | 17 | 1 | 0 | 62 | 48 |
| Myanmar | 1,348 | 2,460 | .. | .. | .. | .. | .. | .. | .. | .. | .. | .. |
| Namibia | 1,616 | 2,920 | .. | 16 | .. | 1 | .. | 3 | .. | 1 | .. | 78 |
| Nepal | 1,333 | 2,100 | 12 | .. | 3 | .. | 12 | .. | 3 | .. | 46 | .. |
| Netherlands | 185,232 | 416,445 | 14 | 9 | 2 | 2 | 8 | 17 | 3 | 4 | 72 | 68 |
| New Zealand | 13,957 | 26,434 | 7 | 8 | 1 | 1 | 5 | 15 | 3 | 2 | 83 | 74 |
| Nicaragua | 975 | 2,988 | 18 | 12 | 1 | 0 | 18 | 25 | 1 | 0 | 63 | 61 |
| Niger | 374 | 950 | 32 | 34 | 1 | 4 | 13 | 15 | 3 | 1 | 51 | 46 |
| Nigeria | 8,222 | 21,809 | 18 | .. | 1 | .. | 1 | .. | 2 | .. | 77 | .. |
| Norway | 32,968 | 64,120 | 7 | 7 | 3 | 1 | 3 | 5 | 6 | 7 | 81 | 80 |
| Oman | 4,379 | 10,915 | 20 | 11 | 1 | 1 | 2 | 3 | 2 | 5 | 70 | 79 |
| Pakistan | 11,515 | 29,825 | 18 | 10 | 6 | 4 | 16 | 26 | 3 | 3 | 57 | 56 |
| Panama | 2,510 | 4,863 | 11 | 11 | 1 | 0 | 14 | 18 | 1 | 1 | 73 | 69 |
| Papua New Guinea | 1,452 | 2,252 | .. | .. | .. | .. | .. | .. | .. | .. | .. | .. |
| Paraguay | 3,144 | 5,879 | 19 | 6 | 0 | 1 | 7 | 13 | 1 | 1 | 74 | 80 |
| Peru | 7,584 | 15,327 | 14 | 10 | 2 | 2 | 9 | 19 | 1 | 1 | 75 | 68 |
| Philippines | 28,341 | 51,522 | 8 | 7 | 2 | 1 | 9 | 15 | 2 | 2 | 58 | 75 |
| Poland | 29,050 | 125,997 | 10 | 6 | 3 | 2 | 9 | 10 | 3 | 4 | 74 | 74 |
| Portugal | 32,610 | 66,618 | 14 | 11 | 4 | 1 | 8 | 15 | 2 | 3 | 72 | 64 |
| Puerto Rico | .. | .. | .. | .. | .. | .. | .. | .. | .. | .. | .. | .. |

# 4.5 | Structure of merchandise imports

| | Merchandise imports ($ millions) | | Food (% of total) | | Agricultural raw materials (% of total) | | Fuels (% of total) | | Ores and metals (% of total) | | Manufactures (% of total) | |
|---|---|---|---|---|---|---|---|---|---|---|---|---|
| | 1995 | 2006 | 1995 | 2006 | 1995 | 2006 | 1995 | 2006 | 1995 | 2006 | 1995 | 2006 |
| Romania | 10,278 | 51,106 | 8 | 6 | 2 | 1 | 21 | 14 | 4 | 3 | 63 | 77 |
| Russian Federation | 60,945 | 163,867 | 18 | 14 | 1 | 1 | 3 | 1 | 2 | 2 | 45 | 76 |
| Rwanda | 236 | 501 | 19 | .. | 3 | .. | 12 | .. | 3 | .. | 64 | .. |
| Saudi Arabia | 28,091 | 66,307 | 17 | 13 | 1 | 1 | 0 | 0 | 4 | 5 | 76 | 80 |
| Senegal | 1,412 | 3,434 | 25 | 23 | 2 | 2 | 30 | 26 | 1 | 1 | 42 | 48 |
| Serbia | .. | 13,172 | .. | .. | .. | .. | .. | .. | .. | .. | .. | .. |
| Sierra Leone | 133 | 389 | .. | .. | .. | .. | .. | .. | .. | .. | .. | .. |
| Singapore | 124,507 | 238,652 | 5 | 3 | 1 | 0 | 8 | 19 | 2 | 2 | 83 | 74 |
| Slovak Republic | 8,770 | 45,870 | 9 | 5 | 3 | 1 | 13 | 14 | 6 | 3 | 70 | 76 |
| Slovenia | 9,492 | 24,104 | 8 | 6 | 5 | 2 | 7 | 11 | 4 | 6 | 74 | 74 |
| Somalia | .. | .. | .. | .. | .. | .. | .. | .. | .. | .. | .. | .. |
| South Africa | 30,546[b] | 77,280 | 7[b] | 4 | 2[b] | 1 | 8[b] | 18 | 2[b] | 2 | 78[b] | 66 |
| Spain | 113,537 | 316,448 | 14 | 8 | 3 | 1 | 8 | 16 | 4 | 4 | 71 | 70 |
| Sri Lanka | 5,306 | 10,258 | 16 | 12 | 2 | 1 | 6 | 13 | 1 | 3 | 75 | 69 |
| Sudan | 1,218 | 8,074 | 24 | 13 | 2 | 1 | 14 | 1 | 0 | 1 | 59 | 83 |
| Swaziland | 1,008 | 2,200 | .. | 18 | .. | 1 | .. | 12 | .. | 1 | .. | 66 |
| Sweden | 65,036 | 126,738 | 7 | 7 | 2 | 1 | 6 | 12 | 4 | 4 | 80 | 72 |
| Switzerland | 80,152 | 141,374 | 6 | 5 | 2 | 1 | 3 | 8 | 3 | 6 | 85 | 80 |
| Syrian Arab Republic | 4,709 | 9,670 | 17 | 13 | 3 | 3 | 1 | 27 | 1 | 3 | 76 | 52 |
| Tajikistan | 810 | 1,723 | .. | .. | .. | .. | .. | .. | .. | .. | .. | .. |
| Tanzania | 1,675 | 4,253 | 10 | 12 | 1 | 1 | 1 | 24 | 4 | 1 | 84 | 61 |
| Thailand | 70,786 | 128,636 | 4 | 4 | 4 | 2 | 7 | 20 | 3 | 5 | 81 | 68 |
| Timor-Leste | .. | .. | .. | .. | .. | .. | .. | .. | .. | .. | .. | .. |
| Togo | 594 | 1,100 | 18 | 16 | 2 | 1 | 30 | 29 | 1 | 2 | 49 | 53 |
| Trinidad and Tobago | 1,714 | 6,485 | 16 | 8 | 1 | 1 | 1 | 35 | 6 | 5 | 77 | 52 |
| Tunisia | 7,902 | 14,865 | 13 | 8 | 4 | 3 | 7 | 14 | 3 | 3 | 73 | 72 |
| Turkey | 35,709 | 138,290 | 7 | 2 | 6 | 2 | 13 | 5 | 6 | 5 | 68 | 41 |
| Turkmenistan | 1,365 | 4,057 | 24 | .. | 0 | .. | 3 | .. | 2 | .. | 71 | .. |
| Uganda | 1,056 | 2,505 | 16 | 14 | 3 | 1 | 2 | 21 | 2 | 1 | 78 | 63 |
| Ukraine | 15,484 | 45,035 | 8 | 7 | 2 | 1 | 48 | 28 | 3 | 3 | 38 | 60 |
| United Arab Emirates | 23,778 | 97,754 | 15 | .. | 0 | .. | 4 | .. | 6 | .. | 75 | .. |
| United Kingdom | 267,250 | 619,385 | 10 | 8 | 2 | 1 | 4 | 9 | 3 | 3 | 80 | 67 |
| United States | 770,852 | 1,919,427 | 5 | 4 | 2 | 1 | 8 | 18 | 3 | 3 | 79 | 71 |
| Uruguay | 2,867 | 4,757 | 10 | 8 | 4 | 3 | 10 | 28 | 1 | 1 | 74 | 60 |
| Uzbekistan | 2,750 | 3,996 | .. | .. | .. | .. | .. | .. | .. | .. | .. | .. |
| Venezuela, RB | 12,649 | 33,616 | 14 | 8 | 4 | 1 | 1 | 1 | 4 | 1 | 77 | 69 |
| Vietnam | 8,155 | 44,410 | 5 | 6 | 2 | 4 | 10 | 15 | 2 | 3 | 76 | 71 |
| West Bank and Gaza | .. | .. | .. | .. | .. | .. | .. | .. | .. | .. | .. | .. |
| Yemen, Rep. | 1,582 | 4,935 | 29 | 21 | 2 | 1 | 8 | 22 | 1 | 1 | 59 | 55 |
| Zambia | 700 | 2,920 | 10 | 8 | 2 | 1 | 13 | 15 | 2 | 2 | 72 | 74 |
| Zimbabwe | 2,660 | 2,250 | 6 | 10 | 2 | 2 | 9 | 15 | 2 | 40 | 78 | 32 |
| **World** | **5,228,938 t** | **12,326,824 t** | **9 w** | **6 w** | **3 w** | **1 w** | **7 w** | **15 w** | **4 w** | **4 w** | **75 w** | **70 w** |
| **Low income** | 111,167 | 389,128 | 11 | 7 | 4 | 2 | 19 | 27 | 5 | 4 | 58 | 58 |
| **Middle income** | 940,577 | 2,958,062 | 8 | 6 | 3 | 2 | 7 | 12 | 3 | 4 | 76 | 70 |
| Lower middle income | 428,941 | 1,487,837 | 9 | 6 | 5 | 3 | 6 | 16 | 4 | 6 | 75 | 66 |
| Upper middle income | 511,391 | 1,466,978 | 8 | 6 | 3 | 1 | 7 | 9 | 3 | 4 | 77 | 74 |
| **Low & middle income** | 1,051,772 | 3,347,357 | 8 | 6 | 3 | 2 | 8 | 12 | 3 | 4 | 74 | 70 |
| East Asia & Pacific | 366,057 | 1,245,694 | 6 | 4 | 4 | 3 | 5 | 15 | 4 | 7 | 78 | 71 |
| Europe & Central Asia | 224,595 | 841,512 | 10 | 7 | 3 | 1 | 14 | 10 | 3 | 3 | 64 | 66 |
| Latin America & Carib. | 241,125 | 613,382 | 8 | 6 | 2 | 1 | 5 | 10 | 2 | 3 | 78 | 77 |
| Middle East & N. Africa | 81,546 | 213,435 | 22 | 12 | 3 | 2 | 6 | 13 | 2 | 2 | 66 | 50 |
| South Asia | 60,322 | 237,321 | 8 | 5 | 4 | 2 | 21 | 32 | 6 | 5 | 56 | 55 |
| Sub-Saharan Africa | 78,560 | 201,872 | 12 | 10 | 2 | 1 | 10 | 15 | 2 | 3 | 73 | 65 |
| **High income** | 4,176,841 | 8,984,577 | 9 | 6 | 3 | 1 | 7 | 15 | 4 | 4 | 76 | 70 |
| Euro area | 1,635,980 | 3,440,926 | 11 | 8 | 3 | 2 | 7 | 14 | 4 | 5 | 73 | 69 |

**Note:** Components may not sum to 100 percent because of unclassified trade.
a. Includes Luxembourg. b. Refers to the South African Customs Union (Botswana, Lesotho, Namibia, South Africa, and Swaziland).

## About the data

Data on imports of goods are derived from the same sources as data on exports. In principle, world exports and imports should be identical. Similarly, exports from an economy should equal the sum of imports by the rest of the world from that economy. But differences in timing and definitions result in discrepancies in reported values at all levels. For further discussion of indicators of merchandise trade, see *About the data* for tables 4.4 and 6.2.

The value of imports is generally recorded as the cost of the goods when purchased by the importer plus the cost of transport and insurance to the frontier of the importing country—the cost, insurance, and freight (c.i.f.) value, corresponding to the landed cost at the point of entry of foreign goods into the country. A few countries, including Australia, Canada, and the United States, collect import data on a free on board (f.o.b.) basis and adjust them for freight and insurance costs. Many countries collect and report trade data in U.S. dollars. When countries report in local currency, the United Nations Statistics Division applies the average official exchange rate for the period shown.

Countries may report trade according to the general or special system of trade (see *Primary data documentation*). Under the general system imports include goods imported for domestic consumption and imports into bonded warehouses and free trade zones. Under the special system imports comprise goods imported for domestic consumption (including transformation and repair) and withdrawals for domestic consumption from bonded warehouses and free trade zones. Goods transported through a country en route to another are excluded.

The data on total imports of goods (merchandise) in the table come from the World Trade Organization (WTO). For further discussion of the WTO's sources and methodology, see *About the data* for table 4.4. The shares of imports by major commodity group are from the United Nations Statistics Division's Commodity Trade (Comtrade) database. The values of total imports reported here have not been fully reconciled with the estimates of imports of goods and services from the national accounts (shown in table 4.8) or those from the balance of payments (table 4.15).

The classification of commodity groups is based on the Standard International Trade Classification (SITC) revision 1. Most countries now use later revisions of the SITC or the Harmonized System. Concordance tables convert data reported in one system to another. The conversion process may introduce some classification errors, but conversions from later to earlier systems are generally reliable.

## Definitions

• **Merchandise imports** are the c.i.f. value of goods purchased from the rest of the world valued in U.S. dollars. • **Food** corresponds to the commodities in SITC sections 0 (food and live animals), 1 (beverages and tobacco), and 4 (animal and vegetable oils and fats) and SITC division 22 (oil seeds, oil nuts, and oil kernels). • **Agricultural raw materials** correspond to SITC section 2 (crude materials except fuels) excluding divisions 22, 27 (crude fertilizers and minerals excluding coal, petroleum, and precious stones), and 28 (metalliferous ores and scrap). • **Fuels** correspond to SITC section 3 (mineral fuels). • **Ores and metals** correspond to the commodities in SITC divisions 27, 28, and 68 (nonferrous metals). • **Manufactures** correspond to the commodities in SITC sections 5 (chemicals), 6 (basic manufactures), 7 (machinery and transport equipment), and 8 (miscellaneous manufactured goods), excluding division 68.

**Top 10 developing country exporters of merchandise goods in 2006** — 4.5a

China continues to dominate merchandise exports among developing countries. Even when developed countries are included, China ranks as the third leading merchandise exporter.

*Source: World Development Indicators data files and World Trade Organization.*

## Data sources

Data on merchandise imports are from the WTO. Data on shares of imports by major commodity group are from Comtrade. The WTO publishes data on world trade in its *Annual Report*. The International Monetary Fund publishes estimates of total imports of goods in its *International Financial Statistics* and *Direction of Trade Statistics*, as does the United Nations Statistics Division in its *Monthly Bulletin of Statistics*. And the United Nations Conference on Trade and Development publishes data on the structure of imports in its *Handbook of International Trade and Development Statistics*. Tariff line records of imports are compiled in the United Nations Statistics Division's Comtrade database.

| | Commercial service exports | | Transport | | Travel | | Insurance and financial services | | Computer, information, communications, and other commercial services | |
|---|---|---|---|---|---|---|---|---|---|---|
| | $ millions | | % of total | | % of total | | % of total | | % of total | |
| | 1995 | 2006 | 1995 | 2006 | 1995 | 2006 | 1995 | 2006 | 1995 | 2006 |
| Afghanistan | .. | .. | .. | .. | .. | .. | .. | .. | .. | .. |
| Albania | 94 | 1,481 | 19.1 | 11.0 | 69.3 | 68.3 | 1.4 | 2.0 | 10.2 | 18.7 |
| Algeria | .. | .. | .. | .. | .. | .. | .. | .. | .. | .. |
| Angola | 113 | 1,484 | 31.8 | 1.4 | .. | 5.0 | 9.2 | .. | 59.0 | 93.6 |
| Argentina | 3,676 | 7,542 | 27.4 | 18.9 | 60.5 | 43.9 | 0.2 | 0.1 | 11.9 | 37.2 |
| Armenia | 27 | 475 | 53.4 | 21.5 | 5.2 | 57.0 | .. | 3.9 | 41.3 | 17.6 |
| Australia | 16,076 | 32,439 | 29.3 | 19.6 | 50.6 | 55.0 | 5.4 | 4.0 | 14.8 | 21.4 |
| Austria | 31,692 | 45,202 | 11.8 | 20.1 | 42.4 | 29.4 | 3.9 | 6.6 | 41.9 | 44.0 |
| Azerbaijan | 166 | 841 | 45.9 | 48.4 | 42.3 | 13.9 | 0.1 | 1.8 | 11.7 | 35.9 |
| Bangladesh | 469 | 603 | 15.0 | 14.7 | 5.3 | 13.3 | 0.1 | 5.7 | 79.6 | 66.3 |
| Belarus | 466 | 2,276 | 64.8 | 68.9 | 5.0 | 11.9 | 0.5 | 0.2 | 29.7 | 19.0 |
| Belgium | 33,619[a] | 57,285 | 29.4[a] | 27.3 | 17.4[a] | 17.9 | 14.8[a] | 7.9 | 38.4[a] | 46.9 |
| Benin | 159 | 179 | 25.8 | 18.3 | 53.2 | 57.7 | 6.9 | 2.3 | 14.1 | 21.7 |
| Bolivia | 174 | 419 | 44.8 | 26.6 | 31.5 | 48.0 | 9.8 | 12.2 | 13.9 | 13.2 |
| Bosnia and Herzegovina | 457 | 1,112 | 3.8 | 8.3 | 54.1 | 53.1 | 2.6 | 4.2 | 39.5 | 34.5 |
| Botswana | 236 | 771 | 16.2 | 10.5 | 68.5 | 69.7 | 7.8 | 2.9 | 7.5 | 16.9 |
| Brazil | 6,005 | 17,946 | 43.3 | 19.2 | 16.2 | 24.1 | 16.9 | 5.9 | 23.6 | 50.9 |
| Bulgaria | 1,431 | 5,041 | 34.5 | 27.3 | 33.0 | 51.8 | .. | 1.6 | 32.5 | 19.4 |
| Burkina Faso | 38 | .. | 17.3 | .. | 47.8 | .. | .. | .. | 34.8 | .. |
| Burundi | 4 | 6 | 46.2 | 14.7 | 32.4 | 23.5 | 0.5 | 0.9 | 21.0 | 60.9 |
| Cambodia | 103 | 1,244 | 30.5 | 13.4 | 51.7 | 77.5 | .. | 1.2 | 17.7 | 8.0 |
| Cameroon | 242 | 869 | 48.3 | 16.8 | 14.8 | 18.2 | 7.2 | 5.7 | 29.7 | 59.3 |
| Canada | 25,425 | 57,750 | 20.7 | 18.5 | 31.1 | 25.4 | 11.4 | 9.3 | 36.8 | 46.8 |
| Central African Republic | .. | .. | 34.1 | .. | 33.9 | .. | 19.6 | .. | 12.5 | .. |
| Chad | 23 | .. | 4.5 | .. | 49.8 | .. | 1.7 | .. | 43.9 | .. |
| Chile | 3,249 | 7,406 | 36.8 | 60.3 | 28.0 | 16.4 | 7.4 | 2.7 | 27.8 | 20.5 |
| China | 18,430 | 91,421 | 18.2 | 23.0 | 47.4 | 37.1 | 10.1 | 0.8 | 24.4 | 39.1 |
| Hong Kong, China | 33,790 | 72,283 | 32.5 | 31.9 | 16.8 | 16.2 | 9.2 | 10.6 | 41.5 | 41.4 |
| Colombia | 1,641 | 3,297 | 34.4 | 27.3 | 40.0 | 47.0 | 6.5 | 1.8 | 19.1 | 23.9 |
| Congo, Dem. Rep. | .. | .. | .. | .. | .. | .. | .. | .. | .. | .. |
| Congo, Rep. | 61 | 223 | 52.2 | 34.3 | 22.4 | 15.1 | 0.0 | .. | 25.4 | 50.6 |
| Costa Rica | 957 | 2,916 | 14.0 | 9.9 | 71.2 | 59.4 | -0.2 | 0.4 | 14.9 | 30.4 |
| Côte d'Ivoire | 426 | 680 | 28.9 | 26.2 | 20.9 | 12.4 | 12.3 | .. | 37.9 | 61.4 |
| Croatia | 2,223 | 10,808 | 31.8 | 11.5 | 60.7 | 73.9 | 1.3 | 0.7 | 6.2 | 13.9 |
| Cuba | .. | .. | .. | .. | .. | .. | .. | .. | .. | .. |
| Czech Republic | 6,638 | 13,296 | 22.0 | 28.1 | 43.4 | 37.8 | 1.1 | 3.0 | 33.5 | 31.1 |
| Denmark | 15,171 | 52,679 | 44.6 | 47.1 | 24.3 | 15.6 | .. | .. | 31.0 | 37.4 |
| Dominican Republic | 1,894 | 4,153 | 2.2 | 3.3 | 82.9 | 91.3 | .. | 0.7 | 14.9 | 4.7 |
| Ecuador | 687 | 939 | 46.8 | 37.5 | 37.1 | 52.2 | 0.0 | 0.0 | 16.0 | 10.3 |
| Egypt, Arab Rep. | 8,262 | 15,834 | 38.8 | 34.7 | 32.5 | 47.9 | 1.0 | 1.2 | 27.8 | 16.2 |
| El Salvador | 342 | 1,464 | 28.3 | 24.0 | 25.0 | 59.5 | 7.8 | 2.3 | 39.0 | 14.2 |
| Eritrea | 49 | .. | 70.4 | .. | 3.1 | .. | .. | .. | 26.5 | .. |
| Estonia | 868 | 3,451 | 43.0 | 41.5 | 41.1 | 30.0 | 0.4 | 2.4 | 15.5 | 26.1 |
| Ethiopia | 310 | 890 | 76.9 | 65.6 | 5.3 | 18.2 | 1.5 | 2.3 | 16.4 | 13.9 |
| Finland | 7,334 | 15,981 | 28.1 | 17.3 | 22.4 | 14.9 | 2.0 | 0.9 | 47.5 | 67.0 |
| France | 83,108 | 117,586 | 24.6 | 22.3 | 33.2 | 39.5 | 5.3 | 1.9 | 36.9 | 36.3 |
| Gabon | 191 | 136 | 46.4 | 59.8 | 9.0 | 7.2 | 3.3 | 17.1 | 41.3 | 15.9 |
| Gambia, The | 38 | 92 | 21.7 | 17.5 | 73.4 | 71.9 | 0.3 | 0.4 | 4.7 | 10.3 |
| Georgia | 188 | 817 | 48.2 | 52.2 | 25.0 | 38.3 | .. | 4.0 | 26.9 | 5.5 |
| Germany | 73,576 | 166,926 | 27.0 | 25.0 | 24.5 | 19.7 | 5.0 | 7.0 | 43.5 | 48.3 |
| Ghana | 139 | 1,301 | 58.7 | 15.8 | 7.9 | 66.2 | 3.0 | 0.8 | 30.3 | 17.3 |
| Greece | 9,528 | 35,671 | 3.9 | 50.4 | 43.4 | 40.4 | 0.3 | 1.0 | 52.4 | 8.2 |
| Guatemala | 628 | 1,292 | 8.6 | 9.5 | 33.9 | 75.0 | 4.0 | 7.7 | 53.6 | 7.8 |
| Guinea | 17 | 31 | 75.3 | 21.8 | 5.1 | .. | 1.4 | 0.4 | 18.2 | 77.8 |
| Guinea-Bissau | 2 | 6 | 18.2 | 22.9 | .. | 16.6 | .. | 19.5 | 81.8 | 41.0 |
| Haiti | 98 | 150 | 5.1 | .. | 91.9 | 90.5 | 0.6 | .. | 2.4 | 9.5 |

# Structure of service exports

| | Commercial service exports | | Transport | | Travel | | Insurance and financial services | | Computer, information, communications, and other commercial services | |
|---|---|---|---|---|---|---|---|---|---|---|
| | $ millions | | % of total | | % of total | | % of total | | % of total | |
| | 1995 | 2006 | 1995 | 2006 | 1995 | 2006 | 1995 | 2006 | 1995 | 2006 |
| Honduras | 221 | 709 | 25.6 | 8.5 | 36.3 | 68.9 | 2.0 | 2.3 | 36.1 | 20.3 |
| Hungary | 5,086 | 13,191 | 8.0 | 18.1 | 57.6 | 32.3 | 3.2 | 1.3 | 31.3 | 48.3 |
| India | 6,763 | 75,057 | 28.0 | 10.2 | 38.2 | 11.9 | 2.5 | 4.2 | 31.4 | 73.7 |
| Indonesia | 5,342 | 11,091 | .. | 19.0 | 97.9 | 40.1 | .. | 1.9 | 2.1 | 39.0 |
| Iran, Islamic Rep. | 533 | .. | 25.9 | .. | 12.6 | .. | 8.8 | .. | 52.7 | .. |
| Iraq | .. | .. | .. | .. | .. | .. | .. | .. | .. | .. |
| Ireland | 4,799 | 68,660 | 22.2 | 4.3 | 46.1 | 7.8 | .. | 27.4 | 31.7 | 60.5 |
| Israel | 7,741 | 19,229 | 26.0 | 19.3 | 38.7 | 14.4 | 0.2 | 0.1 | 35.1 | 66.1 |
| Italy | 61,173 | 97,151 | 17.7 | 16.2 | 47.0 | 39.4 | 6.6 | 3.9 | 28.8 | 40.5 |
| Jamaica | 1,568 | 2,613 | 16.0 | 17.6 | 68.2 | 71.6 | 1.1 | 2.1 | 14.7 | 8.8 |
| Japan | 63,966 | 115,140 | 35.2 | 32.7 | 5.0 | 7.4 | 0.9 | 6.7 | 58.8 | 53.2 |
| Jordan | 1,689 | 2,432 | 24.8 | 21.7 | 39.1 | 67.5 | .. | .. | 36.1 | 10.8 |
| Kazakhstan | 535 | 2,584 | 65.7 | 56.4 | 22.7 | 32.4 | 0.0 | 1.2 | 11.6 | 9.9 |
| Kenya | 851 | 2,011 | 33.2 | 50.8 | 57.1 | 34.2 | 2.3 | 0.4 | 7.4 | 14.6 |
| Korea, Dem. Rep. | .. | .. | .. | .. | .. | .. | .. | .. | .. | .. |
| Korea, Rep. | 22,133 | 50,385 | 41.9 | 51.3 | 23.3 | 10.6 | 0.4 | 5.8 | 34.5 | 32.3 |
| Kuwait | 1,124 | 6,024 | 83.6 | 38.6 | 10.7 | 3.4 | 5.7 | 1.6 | .. | 56.4 |
| Kyrgyz Republic | 39 | 351 | 39.6 | 16.1 | 11.9 | 47.5 | .. | 1.0 | 48.4 | 35.4 |
| Lao PDR | 68 | .. | 22.8 | .. | 76.0 | .. | 0.6 | .. | 0.6 | .. |
| Latvia | 718 | 2,613 | 91.9 | 54.1 | 2.8 | 18.4 | 2.4 | 7.3 | 3.0 | 20.3 |
| Lebanon | .. | 11,609 | .. | 4.1 | .. | 43.2 | .. | 2.2 | .. | 50.5 |
| Lesotho | 30 | 51 | 7.0 | 1.3 | 90.9 | 53.8 | 1.4 | -0.4 | 0.7 | 45.3 |
| Liberia | .. | .. | .. | .. | .. | .. | .. | .. | .. | .. |
| Libya | 20 | 385 | 62.7 | 33.2 | 12.0 | 49.4 | .. | 14.3 | 25.3 | 3.1 |
| Lithuania | 482 | 3,583 | 59.6 | 54.3 | 16.0 | 29.0 | 0.9 | 0.5 | 23.5 | 16.2 |
| Macedonia, FYR | 151 | 581 | 32.0 | 32.0 | 13.6 | 22.2 | 3.6 | 1.9 | 50.7 | 43.9 |
| Madagascar | 219 | 420 | 29.8 | 28.2 | 26.3 | 43.7 | 2.2 | 0.1 | 41.6 | 28.1 |
| Malawi | 24 | .. | 27.6 | .. | 72.4 | .. | .. | .. | .. | .. |
| Malaysia | 11,438 | 21,722 | 21.6 | 19.5 | 34.7 | 48.0 | .. | 1.7 | 43.7 | 30.9 |
| Mali | 68 | 253 | 32.5 | 13.8 | 37.3 | 58.5 | 5.1 | 2.9 | 25.2 | 24.7 |
| Mauritania | 19 | .. | 9.1 | .. | 57.9 | .. | .. | .. | 33.0 | .. |
| Mauritius | 773 | 1,663 | 25.8 | 21.8 | 55.6 | 60.5 | 0.0 | 1.7 | 18.5 | 16.1 |
| Mexico | 9,585 | 16,372 | 12.1 | 11.7 | 64.5 | 74.4 | 6.7 | 7.7 | 16.7 | 6.2 |
| Moldova | 143 | 471 | 29.5 | 47.5 | 39.8 | 23.7 | 11.6 | 1.0 | 19.1 | 27.7 |
| Mongolia | 47 | 483 | 31.7 | 44.4 | 43.6 | 46.6 | 5.3 | 2.0 | 19.5 | 7.0 |
| Morocco | 2,020 | 9,318 | 20.3 | 15.9 | 64.2 | 64.2 | 1.4 | 0.8 | 14.2 | 19.0 |
| Mozambique | 242 | 355 | 24.8 | 29.6 | .. | 39.4 | .. | 0.5 | 75.2 | 30.5 |
| Myanmar | 353 | 256 | 6.5 | 50.8 | 42.7 | 18.1 | 0.0 | .. | 50.9 | 31.2 |
| Namibia | 301 | 509 | .. | 20.6 | 92.4 | 75.0 | 1.5 | 0.3 | 6.2 | 4.1 |
| Nepal | 592 | 252 | 9.3 | 14.0 | 30.0 | 50.8 | .. | 0.6 | 60.7 | 34.6 |
| Netherlands | 44,646 | 80,180 | 40.4 | 25.7 | 14.7 | 14.2 | 1.2 | 1.9 | 43.7 | 58.2 |
| New Zealand | 4,401 | 7,776 | 34.7 | 21.3 | 52.7 | 58.7 | 0.1 | 1.4 | 12.6 | 18.7 |
| Nicaragua | 94 | 302 | 17.7 | 12.8 | 52.5 | 76.3 | 2.5 | 1.1 | 27.4 | 9.7 |
| Niger | 12 | 84 | 3.3 | 10.1 | 57.8 | 51.2 | 0.0 | 1.1 | 38.9 | 37.6 |
| Nigeria | 608 | 4,164 | 16.4 | 17.5 | 2.8 | 0.4 | 0.6 | 0.2 | 80.2 | 81.8 |
| Norway | 13,458 | 32,730 | 63.3 | 46.6 | 16.6 | 11.0 | 3.7 | 3.3 | 16.4 | 39.1 |
| Oman | 13 | 913 | 7.7 | 34.8 | 81.2 | 59.0 | 1.1 | 0.6 | 10.0 | 5.7 |
| Pakistan | 1,432 | 2,246 | 58.0 | 49.6 | 7.7 | 11.3 | 1.0 | 3.7 | 33.4 | 35.4 |
| Panama | 1,298 | 3,897 | 60.4 | 56.9 | 23.8 | 24.6 | 6.1 | 7.9 | 9.6 | 10.6 |
| Papua New Guinea | 321 | 285 | 10.8 | 10.9 | 7.8 | 1.3 | 1.2 | 5.4 | 80.2 | 82.4 |
| Paraguay | 566 | 735 | 13.3 | 13.2 | 24.3 | 12.3 | 5.0 | 4.2 | 57.4 | 70.3 |
| Peru | 1,042 | 2,323 | 32.5 | 22.6 | 41.1 | 59.4 | 7.2 | 4.7 | 19.3 | 13.3 |
| Philippines | 9,323 | 6,453 | 2.9 | 17.8 | 12.2 | 54.3 | 0.7 | 2.0 | 84.2 | 25.9 |
| Poland | 10,637 | 20,522 | 28.6 | 34.0 | 21.7 | 35.3 | 8.3 | 1.5 | 41.4 | 29.2 |
| Portugal | 8,161 | 17,624 | 18.6 | 22.7 | 59.2 | 47.6 | 4.5 | 2.1 | 17.7 | 27.6 |
| Puerto Rico | .. | .. | .. | .. | .. | .. | .. | .. | .. | .. |

2008 World Development Indicators

| | Commercial service exports | | Transport | | Travel | | Insurance and financial services | | Computer, information, communications, and other commercial services | |
|---|---|---|---|---|---|---|---|---|---|---|
| | $ millions | | % of total | | % of total | | % of total | | % of total | |
| | 1995 | 2006 | 1995 | 2006 | 1995 | 2006 | 1995 | 2006 | 1995 | 2006 |
| Romania | 1,476 | 7,005 | 31.9 | 26.9 | 40.0 | 18.7 | 5.4 | 2.0 | 22.7 | 52.5 |
| Russian Federation | 10,568 | 30,691 | 35.8 | 32.8 | 40.8 | 24.9 | 0.6 | 3.1 | 22.8 | 39.2 |
| Rwanda | 11 | 74 | 60.6 | 40.6 | 21.9 | 42.2 | .. | 3.8 | 17.6 | 13.4 |
| Saudi Arabia | 3,475 | 7,297 | .. | .. | .. | .. | .. | .. | .. | .. |
| Senegal | 364 | 598 | 15.4 | 16.1 | 46.1 | 35.3 | 0.6 | 1.6 | 37.9 | 47.0 |
| Serbia | .. | .. | .. | .. | .. | .. | .. | .. | .. | .. |
| Sierra Leone | 71 | 40 | 13.7 | 34.2 | 80.5 | 57.9 | 0.3 | 6.1 | 5.6 | 1.8 |
| Singapore | 25,404 | 58,957 | 32.7 | 35.6 | 30.0 | 12.0 | 8.5 | 9.4 | 28.9 | 43.1 |
| Slovak Republic | 2,378 | 3,270 | 25.9 | 43.2 | 26.2 | 26.4 | 4.9 | 2.3 | 43.0 | 28.0 |
| Slovenia | 2,016 | 4,337 | 25.1 | 30.7 | 53.8 | 41.4 | 0.6 | 1.2 | 20.6 | 26.7 |
| Somalia | .. | .. | .. | .. | .. | .. | .. | .. | .. | .. |
| South Africa | 4,414 | 11,712 | 24.2 | 12.7 | 48.2 | 67.2 | 9.9 | 7.3 | 17.7 | 12.7 |
| Spain | 40,019 | 105,483 | 15.8 | 17.2 | 63.4 | 48.6 | 3.9 | 4.4 | 16.9 | 29.7 |
| Sri Lanka | 800 | 1,604 | 41.9 | 46.8 | 28.2 | 25.6 | 3.4 | 3.6 | 26.5 | 24.0 |
| Sudan | 82 | 178 | 0.9 | 10.5 | 9.7 | 70.6 | 3.7 | 14.1 | 85.8 | 4.8 |
| Swaziland | 150 | 274 | 18.2 | 3.9 | 32.2 | 27.1 | 0.0 | 13.8 | 49.6 | 55.1 |
| Sweden | 15,336 | 49,921 | 32.2 | 18.5 | 22.6 | 18.3 | 2.4 | 5.7 | 42.7 | 57.5 |
| Switzerland | 25,179 | 50,729 | 15.1 | 9.3 | 37.6 | 21.0 | 27.8 | 33.4 | 19.5 | 36.4 |
| Syrian Arab Republic | 1,632 | 2,649 | 14.5 | 8.2 | 77.1 | 76.4 | .. | 2.4 | 8.4 | 12.9 |
| Tajikistan | .. | 110 | .. | 56.0 | .. | 1.9 | .. | 8.1 | .. | 34.0 |
| Tanzania | 566 | 1,422 | 0.3 | 24.0 | 88.6 | 64.3 | 0.0 | 1.1 | 11.1 | 10.7 |
| Thailand | 14,652 | 23,944 | 16.8 | 22.5 | 54.8 | 51.9 | 0.7 | 1.1 | 27.7 | 24.6 |
| Timor-Leste | .. | .. | .. | .. | .. | .. | .. | .. | .. | .. |
| Togo | 64 | 145 | 33.9 | 39.1 | 19.9 | 14.0 | 1.8 | 1.0 | 44.3 | 45.9 |
| Trinidad and Tobago | 331 | 883 | 58.6 | 24.4 | 23.4 | 51.3 | 9.2 | 15.3 | 8.8 | 9.0 |
| Tunisia | 2,401 | 4,162 | 24.9 | 29.9 | 63.7 | 54.7 | 1.5 | 2.7 | 9.8 | 12.7 |
| Turkey | 14,475 | 24,233 | 11.8 | 17.5 | 34.2 | 69.5 | 1.5 | 2.1 | 52.4 | 10.9 |
| Turkmenistan | 79 | .. | 79.9 | .. | 9.3 | .. | 0.9 | .. | 10.0 | .. |
| Uganda | 104 | 476 | 17.9 | 2.3 | 75.1 | 74.5 | .. | 5.2 | 7.0 | 18.0 |
| Ukraine | 2,846 | 10,822 | 75.6 | 49.4 | 6.7 | 32.2 | 2.7 | 1.4 | 15.0 | 17.0 |
| United Arab Emirates | .. | .. | .. | .. | .. | .. | .. | .. | .. | .. |
| United Kingdom | 77,549 | 225,868 | 20.7 | 13.6 | 26.4 | 15.0 | 17.5 | 26.0 | 35.4 | 45.4 |
| United States | 198,501 | 397,833 | 22.7 | 17.2 | 37.7 | 26.8 | 4.2 | 11.7 | 35.5 | 44.3 |
| Uruguay | 1,309 | 1,259 | 30.5 | 34.4 | 46.7 | 47.5 | 1.5 | 5.3 | 21.3 | 12.8 |
| Uzbekistan | .. | .. | .. | .. | .. | .. | .. | .. | .. | .. |
| Venezuela, RB | 1,529 | 1,469 | 38.2 | 27.8 | 55.5 | 52.3 | 0.1 | 0.1 | 6.1 | 19.7 |
| Vietnam | 2,243 | 4,176 | .. | .. | .. | .. | .. | .. | .. | .. |
| West Bank and Gaza | .. | .. | .. | .. | .. | .. | .. | .. | .. | .. |
| Yemen, Rep. | 141 | 468 | 21.9 | 6.7 | 35.3 | 38.6 | .. | .. | 42.8 | 54.7 |
| Zambia | 112 | 238 | 64.3 | 35.7 | 25.9 | 46.2 | .. | 7.4 | 9.8 | 10.7 |
| Zimbabwe | 353 | .. | 26.4 | .. | 50.6 | .. | 0.3 | .. | 22.7 | .. |
| **World** | **1,210,617 t** | **2,767,235 t** | **26.9 w** | **23.2 w** | **32.5 w** | **27.6 w** | **5.9 w** | **7.5 w** | **36.2 w** | **41.7 w** |
| **Low income** | 18,274 | 111,021 | 26.7 | 19.7 | 25.2 | 18.2 | 2.2 | 3.5 | 46.3 | 58.8 |
| **Middle income** | 183,341 | 459,244 | 25.0 | 22.9 | 45.6 | 45.8 | 6.0 | 2.9 | 26.4 | 28.4 |
| Lower middle income | 87,021 | 232,986 | 21.6 | 23.2 | 47.9 | 42.5 | 6.6 | 1.3 | 27.9 | 32.9 |
| Upper middle income | 96,501 | 227,532 | 27.4 | 22.7 | 43.7 | 48.3 | 5.5 | 4.1 | 25.1 | 25.0 |
| **Low & middle income** | 201,502 | 566,671 | 25.1 | 22.7 | 44.0 | 44.2 | 5.7 | 3.0 | 27.9 | 30.2 |
| East Asia & Pacific | 62,745 | 163,462 | 17.4 | 21.5 | 49.2 | 42.8 | 7.1 | 1.2 | 30.6 | 34.5 |
| Europe & Central Asia | 56,445 | 149,843 | 33.6 | 32.3 | 34.9 | 33.3 | 2.6 | 2.2 | 29.1 | 32.1 |
| Latin America & Carib. | 37,663 | 79,286 | 24.0 | 18.9 | 51.3 | 56.6 | 6.9 | 5.2 | 17.9 | 19.3 |
| Middle East & N. Africa | .. | .. | .. | .. | .. | .. | .. | .. | .. | .. |
| South Asia | 10,333 | 80,602 | 31.8 | 19.3 | 29.7 | 13.7 | 2.1 | 4.2 | 36.4 | 62.8 |
| Sub-Saharan Africa | 11,933 | 35,650 | 25.7 | 16.9 | 31.8 | 43.0 | 5.8 | 4.6 | 40.2 | 36.1 |
| **High income** | 1,006,903 | 2,200,476 | 27.4 | 23.4 | 29.1 | 22.7 | 6.0 | 8.8 | 38.7 | 45.1 |
| Euro area | 419,928 | 872,274 | 25.6 | 22.3 | 31.5 | 26.7 | 5.6 | 5.5 | 37.5 | 45.4 |

a. Includes Luxembourg.

# Structure of service exports | 4.6

## About the data

Balance of payments statistics, the main source of information on international trade in services, have many weaknesses. Some large economies—such as the former Soviet Union—did not report data on trade in services until recently. Disaggregation of important components may be limited and varies considerably across countries. There are inconsistencies in the methods used to report items. And the recording of major flows as net items is common (for example, insurance transactions are often recorded as premiums less claims). These factors contribute to a downward bias in the value of the service trade reported in the balance of payments.

Efforts are being made to improve the coverage, quality, and consistency of these data. Eurostat and the Organisation for Economic Co-operation and Development, for example, are working together to improve the collection of statistics on trade in services in member countries. In addition, the International Monetary Fund (IMF) has implemented the new classification of trade in services introduced in the fifth edition of its *Balance of Payments Manual* (1993).

Still, difficulties in capturing all the dimensions of international trade in services mean that the record is likely to remain incomplete. Cross-border intrafirm service transactions, which are usually not captured in the balance of payments, have increased in recent years. An example is transnational corporations' use of mainframe computers around the clock for data processing, exploiting time zone differences between their home country and the host countries of their affiliates. Another important dimension of service trade not captured by conventional balance of payments statistics is establishment trade—sales in the host country by foreign affiliates. By contrast, cross-border intrafirm transactions in merchandise may be reported as exports or imports in the balance of payments.

The data on exports of services in the table and on imports of services in table 4.7, unlike those in editions before 2000, include only commercial services and exclude the category "government services not included elsewhere." The data are compiled by the IMF based on returns from national sources. Data on total trade in goods and services from the IMF's Balance of Payments database are shown in table 4.15.

## Definitions

• **Commercial service exports** are total service exports minus exports of government services not included elsewhere. International transactions in services are defined by the IMF's *Balance of Payments Manual* (1993) as the economic output of intangible commodities that may be produced, transferred, and consumed at the same time. Definitions may vary among reporting economies. • **Transport** covers all transport services (sea, air, land, internal waterway, space, and pipeline) performed by residents of one economy for those of another and involving the carriage of passengers, movement of goods (freight), rental of carriers with crew, and related support and auxiliary services. Excluded are freight insurance, which is included in insurance services; goods procured in ports by nonresident carriers and repairs of transport equipment, which are included in goods; repairs of harbors, railway facilities, and airfield facilities, which are included in construction services; and rental of carriers without crew, which is included in other services. • **Travel** covers goods and services acquired from an economy by travelers in that economy for their own use during visits of less than one year for business or personal purposes. Travel services include the goods and services consumed by travelers, such as meals, lodging, and transport (within the economy visited), including car rental. • **Insurance and financial services** cover freight insurance on goods exported and other direct insurance such as life insurance; financial intermediation services such as commissions, foreign exchange transactions, and brokerage services; and auxiliary services such as financial market operational and regulatory services. • **Computer, information, communications, and other commercial services** include such activities as international telecommunications and postal and courier services; computer data; news-related service transactions between residents and nonresidents; construction services; royalties and license fees; miscellaneous business, professional, and technical services; and personal, cultural, and recreational services.

**Top 10 developing country exporters of commercial services in 2006**     **4.6a**

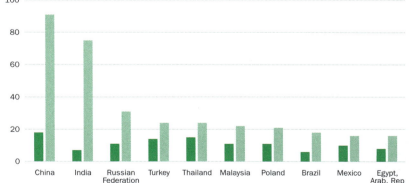

The top 10 developing country exporters of commercial services accounted for almost 60 percent of developing country commercial service exports and 12 percent of world commercial service exports.

*Source:* International Monetary Fund balance of payments data files.

### Data sources

Data on exports of commercial services are from the IMF, which publishes balance of payments data in its *International Financial Statistics* and *Balance of Payments Statistics Yearbook*.

| | Commercial service imports | | Transport | | Travel | | Insurance and financial services | | Computer, information, communications, and other commercial services | |
|---|---|---|---|---|---|---|---|---|---|---|
| | $ millions | | % of total | | % of total | | % of total | | % of total | |
| | 1995 | 2006 | 1995 | 2006 | 1995 | 2006 | 1995 | 2006 | 1995 | 2006 |
| Afghanistan | .. | .. | .. | .. | .. | .. | .. | .. | .. | .. |
| Albania | 98 | 1,552 | 61.4 | 16.1 | 6.7 | 62.1 | 22.1 | 3.6 | 9.8 | 18.1 |
| Algeria | .. | .. | .. | .. | .. | .. | .. | .. | .. | .. |
| Angola | 1,665 | 6,860 | 18.2 | 23.7 | 4.5 | 2.2 | 2.7 | 6.1 | 74.6 | 68.0 |
| Argentina | 6,992 | 8,222 | 30.1 | 27.8 | 46.9 | 38.1 | 7.1 | 4.4 | 15.9 | 29.7 |
| Armenia | 52 | 600 | 82.6 | 38.6 | 6.2 | 47.7 | 10.3 | 5.2 | 0.9 | 8.5 |
| Australia | 16,979 | 31,631 | 36.9 | 35.8 | 30.4 | 37.0 | 7.2 | 3.6 | 25.6 | 23.6 |
| Austria | 27,552 | 32,398 | 11.9 | 14.9 | 39.5 | 22.4 | 5.6 | 6.6 | 43.0 | 56.0 |
| Azerbaijan | 297 | 2,784 | 31.1 | 18.3 | 49.1 | 7.2 | 0.8 | 4.3 | 19.0 | 70.2 |
| Bangladesh | 1,192 | 2,111 | 65.0 | 76.1 | 19.6 | 6.6 | 5.6 | 9.3 | 9.7 | 8.0 |
| Belarus | 276 | 1,454 | 35.9 | 24.9 | 31.5 | 50.5 | 3.6 | 2.4 | 29.0 | 22.1 |
| Belgium | 32,511[a] | 52,285 | 24.1[a] | 24.9 | 27.7[a] | 29.6 | 10.2[a] | 7.7 | 38.0[a] | 37.8 |
| Benin | 235 | 267 | 59.2 | 65.2 | 14.7 | 10.1 | 10.4 | 11.2 | 15.7 | 13.5 |
| Bolivia | 321 | 787 | 65.9 | 38.0 | 15.0 | 28.7 | 9.3 | 15.5 | 9.9 | 17.8 |
| Bosnia and Herzegovina | 262 | 493 | 51.5 | 42.5 | 30.9 | 32.1 | 9.5 | 12.2 | 8.1 | 13.2 |
| Botswana | 440 | 834 | 42.6 | 38.6 | 33.0 | 33.2 | 8.1 | 3.5 | 16.3 | 24.7 |
| Brazil | 13,161 | 27,149 | 44.1 | 24.2 | 25.8 | 21.2 | 9.6 | 6.0 | 20.6 | 48.6 |
| Bulgaria | 1,278 | 4,103 | 41.5 | 32.6 | 15.3 | 35.9 | .. | 4.6 | 43.2 | 26.9 |
| Burkina Faso | 116 | .. | 56.0 | .. | 19.6 | .. | 4.8 | .. | 19.6 | .. |
| Burundi | 62 | 190 | 49.4 | 26.5 | 41.0 | 66.0 | 5.9 | 2.5 | 3.8 | 5.0 |
| Cambodia | 181 | 746 | 46.4 | 58.4 | 4.6 | 16.4 | 4.3 | 6.0 | 44.7 | 19.2 |
| Cameroon | 485 | 1,454 | 35.4 | 26.4 | 21.7 | 22.2 | 7.2 | 7.2 | 35.7 | 44.2 |
| Canada | 32,985 | 71,746 | 24.1 | 23.6 | 31.1 | 28.6 | 11.3 | 10.8 | 33.5 | 37.0 |
| Central African Republic | 114 | .. | 43.7 | .. | 38.0 | .. | 7.9 | .. | 10.4 | .. |
| Chad | 174 | .. | 55.0 | .. | 14.9 | .. | 1.5 | .. | 28.6 | .. |
| Chile | 3,524 | 8,289 | 54.0 | 54.9 | 19.9 | 15.1 | 4.1 | 9.7 | 21.9 | 20.3 |
| China | 24,635 | 100,327 | 38.7 | 34.3 | 15.0 | 24.2 | 17.3 | 9.7 | 29.0 | 31.8 |
| Hong Kong, China | 24,962 | 36,533 | 22.2 | 30.9 | 54.0 | 39.3 | 6.2 | 5.9 | 17.6 | 23.8 |
| Colombia | 2,813 | 5,425 | 42.4 | 41.5 | 31.2 | 24.5 | 11.9 | 8.8 | 14.5 | 25.1 |
| Congo, Dem. Rep. | .. | .. | .. | .. | .. | .. | .. | .. | .. | .. |
| Congo, Rep. | 690 | 1,550 | 18.6 | 19.9 | 7.5 | 6.6 | 7.3 | .. | 66.6 | 73.5 |
| Costa Rica | 895 | 1,608 | 41.4 | 38.9 | 36.1 | 30.2 | 4.6 | 7.1 | 17.9 | 23.8 |
| Côte d'Ivoire | 1,235 | 2,073 | 50.5 | 52.3 | 15.4 | 17.4 | 11.0 | .. | 23.2 | 30.3 |
| Croatia | 1,327 | 3,491 | 29.5 | 20.3 | 31.8 | 21.1 | 3.4 | 5.3 | 35.3 | 53.3 |
| Cuba | .. | .. | .. | .. | .. | .. | .. | .. | .. | .. |
| Czech Republic | 4,860 | 11,726 | 16.5 | 23.4 | 33.7 | 22.8 | 5.2 | 11.3 | 44.7 | 42.5 |
| Denmark | 13,945 | 46,137 | 45.1 | 43.4 | 30.8 | 21.8 | .. | .. | 24.1 | 34.8 |
| Dominican Republic | 957 | 1,486 | 61.1 | 62.5 | 18.1 | 22.4 | 10.2 | 8.2 | 10.6 | 6.9 |
| Ecuador | 1,141 | 2,265 | 42.4 | 51.7 | 20.6 | 20.6 | 5.9 | 6.3 | 31.1 | 21.4 |
| Egypt, Arab Rep. | 4,511 | 10,288 | 35.1 | 44.0 | 28.3 | 17.3 | 4.6 | 10.2 | 32.0 | 28.5 |
| El Salvador | 488 | 1,458 | 55.1 | 40.5 | 14.9 | 35.5 | 11.0 | 8.3 | 19.0 | 15.7 |
| Eritrea | 45 | .. | | | 6.9 | .. | .. | .. | 93.1 | .. |
| Estonia | 420 | 2,427 | 52.9 | 42.5 | 21.5 | 24.4 | 4.7 | 2.2 | 20.9 | 30.9 |
| Ethiopia | 337 | 1,154 | 63.4 | 54.9 | 7.5 | 8.4 | 7.4 | 5.7 | 21.7 | 31.0 |
| Finland | 9,418 | 15,571 | 22.8 | 28.5 | 24.2 | 22.0 | 5.0 | 1.3 | 48.0 | 48.2 |
| France | 64,523 | 106,949 | 32.9 | 27.5 | 25.4 | 29.2 | 6.1 | 5.7 | 35.6 | 37.5 |
| Gabon | 832 | 921 | 17.7 | 33.5 | 16.5 | 23.2 | 8.6 | 5.8 | 57.2 | 37.5 |
| Gambia, The | 47 | 94 | 59.6 | 36.1 | 30.4 | 6.8 | 5.8 | 5.4 | 4.2 | 51.7 |
| Georgia | 249 | 687 | 27.0 | 56.4 | 62.8 | 24.3 | 8.4 | 12.3 | 1.8 | 7.0 |
| Germany | 130,490 | 213,283 | 18.2 | 24.1 | 46.2 | 34.8 | 1.5 | 3.7 | 34.1 | 37.5 |
| Ghana | 331 | 1,442 | 61.3 | 51.3 | 6.2 | 23.9 | 6.5 | 4.8 | 26.0 | 20.0 |
| Greece | 4,003 | 15,899 | 29.9 | 55.2 | 33.1 | 18.9 | 4.5 | 6.8 | 32.5 | 19.2 |
| Guatemala | 672 | 1,628 | 41.4 | 52.0 | 21.0 | 30.4 | 8.7 | 12.6 | 28.9 | 5.1 |
| Guinea | 252 | 195 | 58.4 | 47.3 | 8.4 | 12.8 | 7.2 | 12.7 | 26.0 | 27.2 |
| Guinea-Bissau | 27 | 42 | 53.1 | 53.5 | 14.1 | 30.9 | 4.7 | 0.4 | 28.1 | 15.1 |
| Haiti | 236 | 370 | 77.6 | 79.5 | 14.7 | 15.1 | 1.7 | 1.7 | 5.9 | 3.7 |

# Structure of service imports | 4.7

| | Commercial service imports | | Transport | | Travel | | Insurance and financial services | | Computer, information, communications, and other commercial services | |
|---|---|---|---|---|---|---|---|---|---|---|
| | $ millions | | % of total | | % of total | | % of total | | % of total | |
| | 1995 | 2006 | 1995 | 2006 | 1995 | 2006 | 1995 | 2006 | 1995 | 2006 |
| Honduras | 326 | 994 | 60.4 | 48.7 | 17.5 | 28.5 | 2.5 | .. | 19.7 | 22.8 |
| Hungary | 3,765 | 11,485 | 12.8 | 21.0 | 39.8 | 18.5 | 4.9 | 4.0 | 42.5 | 56.5 |
| India | 10,062 | 63,053 | 56.7 | 40.0 | 9.9 | 11.7 | 5.6 | 6.3 | 27.9 | 42.1 |
| Indonesia | 13,230 | 21,406 | 36.7 | 38.2 | 16.4 | 16.8 | 3.4 | 3.5 | 43.4 | 41.5 |
| Iran, Islamic Rep. | 2,192 | .. | 43.0 | .. | 11.0 | .. | 9.9 | .. | 36.1 | .. |
| Iraq | .. | .. | .. | .. | .. | .. | .. | .. | .. | .. |
| Ireland | 11,252 | 78,460 | 15.9 | 3.2 | 18.1 | 8.7 | 1.4 | 17.5 | 64.6 | 70.5 |
| Israel | 8,134 | 14,704 | 44.9 | 32.5 | 26.1 | 20.3 | 3.0 | 2.8 | 26.0 | 44.4 |
| Italy | 54,613 | 98,005 | 24.5 | 23.1 | 27.2 | 23.6 | 9.7 | 4.0 | 38.6 | 49.3 |
| Jamaica | 1,073 | 1,969 | 46.3 | 45.0 | 13.8 | 13.9 | 9.2 | 10.7 | 30.8 | 30.5 |
| Japan | 121,547 | 133,899 | 29.6 | 32.0 | 30.2 | 20.1 | 2.4 | 5.6 | 37.8 | 42.3 |
| Jordan | 1,385 | 2,596 | 52.3 | 57.4 | 30.7 | 24.1 | 6.1 | 8.9 | 10.9 | 9.7 |
| Kazakhstan | 776 | 8,581 | 38.4 | 17.6 | 36.4 | 9.6 | .. | 5.0 | 25.2 | 67.8 |
| Kenya | 733 | 1,265 | 58.8 | 53.0 | 19.8 | 14.1 | 9.8 | 13.1 | 11.6 | 19.9 |
| Korea, Dem. Rep. | .. | .. | .. | .. | .. | .. | .. | .. | .. | .. |
| Korea, Rep. | 25,394 | 69,787 | 38.0 | 33.5 | 25.0 | 26.1 | 1.5 | 2.2 | 35.5 | 38.2 |
| Kuwait | 3,826 | 8,359 | 39.4 | 34.0 | 58.8 | 62.8 | 1.7 | 1.6 | 0.1 | 1.6 |
| Kyrgyz Republic | 193 | 456 | 27.1 | 39.0 | 3.4 | 20.1 | 4.3 | 4.8 | 65.3 | 36.1 |
| Lao PDR | 119 | .. | 43.3 | .. | 25.0 | .. | 4.0 | .. | 27.7 | .. |
| Latvia | 225 | 1,962 | 68.2 | 32.6 | 10.8 | 35.9 | 7.0 | 2.9 | 14.0 | 28.7 |
| Lebanon | .. | 8,692 | .. | 16.9 | .. | 34.6 | .. | 3.2 | .. | 45.3 |
| Lesotho | 58 | 75 | 74.9 | 72.9 | 22.6 | 25.1 | 0.2 | .. | 2.4 | 2.0 |
| Liberia | .. | .. | .. | .. | .. | .. | .. | .. | .. | .. |
| Libya | 510 | 2,324 | 60.4 | 50.9 | 15.0 | 28.7 | .. | 8.5 | 24.7 | 11.9 |
| Lithuania | 457 | 2,462 | 63.9 | 45.1 | 23.3 | 36.9 | 1.1 | 2.5 | 11.7 | 15.4 |
| Macedonia, FYR | 300 | 548 | 49.6 | 42.3 | 8.8 | 12.9 | 20.7 | 4.4 | 20.9 | 40.4 |
| Madagascar | 277 | 462 | 55.6 | 48.5 | 21.1 | 15.9 | 3.7 | 1.0 | 19.6 | 34.7 |
| Malawi | 151 | .. | 66.8 | .. | 26.0 | .. | 0.1 | .. | 7.2 | .. |
| Malaysia | 14,821 | 23,493 | 37.8 | 40.8 | 15.6 | 17.1 | .. | 3.1 | 46.5 | 39.0 |
| Mali | 412 | 583 | 59.6 | 61.9 | 11.9 | 13.2 | 1.4 | 6.8 | 27.1 | 18.0 |
| Mauritania | 197 | .. | 61.5 | .. | 11.6 | .. | 1.4 | .. | 25.4 | .. |
| Mauritius | 630 | 1,319 | 39.9 | 40.5 | 25.2 | 24.8 | 4.6 | 5.4 | 30.3 | 29.3 |
| Mexico | 9,021 | 22,329 | 38.0 | 12.0 | 35.1 | 36.3 | 12.5 | 43.2 | 14.4 | 8.4 |
| Moldova | 193 | 455 | 51.6 | 37.7 | 29.2 | 41.2 | 9.3 | 2.3 | 9.9 | 18.7 |
| Mongolia | 87 | 514 | 69.6 | 49.5 | 22.3 | 36.5 | .. | 3.9 | 8.1 | 10.1 |
| Morocco | 1,350 | 3,568 | 48.1 | 49.1 | 22.4 | 19.7 | 3.5 | 2.6 | 25.9 | 28.6 |
| Mozambique | 350 | 729 | 32.7 | 37.5 | .. | 24.6 | 2.2 | 2.0 | 65.1 | 35.9 |
| Myanmar | 233 | 547 | 11.0 | 46.5 | 7.7 | 6.8 | 0.5 | .. | 80.8 | 46.8 |
| Namibia | 538 | 421 | 36.5 | 35.6 | 16.7 | 28.1 | 9.5 | 5.5 | 37.3 | 30.8 |
| Nepal | 305 | 488 | 36.3 | 38.2 | 44.7 | 37.9 | 3.0 | 5.9 | 15.9 | 18.0 |
| Netherlands | 43,618 | 78,730 | 28.9 | 22.1 | 26.8 | 21.7 | 3.0 | 2.6 | 41.3 | 53.7 |
| New Zealand | 4,571 | 7,675 | 41.2 | 33.7 | 27.5 | 32.9 | 5.2 | 3.7 | 26.1 | 29.7 |
| Nicaragua | 207 | 457 | 39.1 | 56.0 | 19.3 | 21.2 | 3.3 | 9.6 | 38.3 | 13.2 |
| Niger | 120 | 277 | 74.4 | 77.1 | 11.1 | 11.0 | 2.6 | 2.2 | 12.0 | 9.7 |
| Nigeria | 4,398 | 7,321 | 22.4 | 20.7 | 20.6 | 15.1 | 2.5 | .. | 54.4 | 64.2 |
| Norway | 13,052 | 30,776 | 38.2 | 30.4 | 32.4 | 37.6 | 5.6 | 4.3 | 23.7 | 27.7 |
| Oman | 985 | 3,740 | 41.8 | 33.1 | 4.8 | 18.4 | 4.6 | 9.2 | 48.8 | 39.4 |
| Pakistan | 2,431 | 8,087 | 67.0 | 37.4 | 18.4 | 19.1 | 4.3 | 3.1 | 10.3 | 40.4 |
| Panama | 1,049 | 1,666 | 71.0 | 56.9 | 11.5 | 16.3 | 8.8 | 14.3 | 8.7 | 12.4 |
| Papua New Guinea | 642 | 1,151 | 25.2 | 24.2 | 9.1 | 4.8 | 2.8 | 10.3 | 63.0 | 60.7 |
| Paraguay | 676 | 405 | 66.4 | 61.9 | 19.7 | 22.5 | 12.4 | 12.3 | 1.4 | 3.3 |
| Peru | 1,781 | 3,269 | 50.8 | 44.7 | 16.7 | 23.3 | 10.2 | 8.8 | 22.3 | 23.3 |
| Philippines | 6,906 | 6,024 | 29.7 | 56.3 | 6.1 | 20.5 | 1.6 | 4.1 | 62.6 | 19.2 |
| Poland | 7,008 | 17,949 | 25.2 | 23.7 | 5.9 | 32.1 | 13.6 | 4.3 | 55.3 | 39.9 |
| Portugal | 6,339 | 11,314 | 26.8 | 31.5 | 33.1 | 29.2 | 8.9 | 4.4 | 31.1 | 35.0 |
| Puerto Rico | .. | .. | .. | .. | .. | .. | .. | .. | .. | .. |

| | Commercial service imports ($ millions) | | Transport (% of total) | | Travel (% of total) | | Insurance and financial services (% of total) | | Computer, information, communications, and other commercial services (% of total) | |
|---|---|---|---|---|---|---|---|---|---|---|
| | 1995 | 2006 | 1995 | 2006 | 1995 | 2006 | 1995 | 2006 | 1995 | 2006 |
| Romania | 1,801 | 6,901 | 33.5 | 34.8 | 38.7 | 19.0 | 5.3 | 5.4 | 22.4 | 40.8 |
| Russian Federation | 20,206 | 43,703 | 16.4 | 15.4 | 57.4 | 41.7 | 0.4 | 3.7 | 25.9 | 39.2 |
| Rwanda | 58 | 214 | 72.8 | 51.7 | 17.1 | 16.4 | .. | 6.9 | 10.1 | 25.0 |
| Saudi Arabia | 8,670 | 19,390 | 25.3 | 27.3 | .. | .. | 2.8 | 3.0 | 71.9 | 69.6 |
| Senegal | 405 | 681 | 57.1 | 55.8 | 17.7 | 8.4 | 7.0 | 10.2 | 18.2 | 25.6 |
| Serbia | .. | .. | .. | .. | .. | .. | .. | .. | .. | .. |
| Sierra Leone | 79 | 75 | 17.4 | 58.8 | 62.5 | 16.7 | 3.8 | 10.1 | 16.3 | 14.4 |
| Singapore | 20,728 | 61,745 | 44.8 | 37.2 | 22.5 | 16.8 | 10.1 | 6.6 | 22.6 | 39.5 |
| Slovak Republic | 1,800 | 3,012 | 17.0 | 29.8 | 17.8 | 19.0 | 4.9 | 8.7 | 60.2 | 42.4 |
| Slovenia | 1,429 | 3,222 | 30.6 | 23.5 | 40.2 | 30.2 | 1.8 | 2.5 | 27.4 | 43.8 |
| Somalia | .. | .. | .. | .. | .. | .. | .. | .. | .. | .. |
| South Africa | 5,756 | 13,949 | 39.9 | 47.5 | 32.1 | 24.3 | 14.1 | 5.5 | 13.8 | 22.7 |
| Spain | 22,354 | 77,902 | 31.1 | 26.4 | 20.3 | 21.4 | 7.4 | 7.8 | 41.2 | 44.4 |
| Sri Lanka | 1,169 | 2,359 | 58.1 | 62.0 | 15.9 | 15.8 | 5.4 | 5.9 | 20.5 | 16.2 |
| Sudan | 150 | 2,718 | 27.3 | 45.8 | 28.7 | 51.6 | 0.3 | 0.4 | 43.7 | 2.3 |
| Swaziland | 206 | 360 | 15.7 | 10.9 | 20.7 | 13.4 | 4.3 | 18.5 | 59.2 | 57.2 |
| Sweden | 17,112 | 39,638 | 28.4 | 16.3 | 31.8 | 29.1 | 1.4 | 3.7 | 38.4 | 50.9 |
| Switzerland | 14,899 | 28,616 | 35.2 | 21.3 | 49.8 | 34.7 | 1.1 | 6.1 | 13.9 | 37.9 |
| Syrian Arab Republic | 1,358 | 2,437 | 57.2 | 51.5 | 36.7 | 22.2 | .. | 15.2 | 6.1 | 11.2 |
| Tajikistan | .. | 393 | .. | 61.5 | .. | 1.5 | .. | 8.1 | .. | 28.9 |
| Tanzania | 729 | 1,212 | 29.8 | 34.5 | 49.4 | 44.1 | 2.7 | 4.6 | 18.0 | 16.8 |
| Thailand | 18,629 | 32,241 | 41.8 | 50.3 | 22.9 | 14.4 | 5.2 | 5.6 | 30.2 | 29.8 |
| Timor-Leste | .. | .. | .. | .. | .. | .. | .. | .. | .. | .. |
| Togo | 148 | 276 | 70.8 | 77.3 | 12.5 | 2.8 | 4.4 | 12.0 | 12.3 | 7.9 |
| Trinidad and Tobago | 223 | 471 | 42.2 | 40.7 | 31.0 | 38.2 | 7.9 | 6.5 | 18.8 | 14.6 |
| Tunisia | 1,245 | 2,338 | 45.3 | 52.8 | 20.1 | 17.5 | 6.5 | 8.9 | 28.1 | 20.8 |
| Turkey | 4,654 | 10,152 | 30.3 | 42.4 | 19.6 | 27.0 | 8.4 | 13.5 | 41.7 | 17.0 |
| Turkmenistan | 403 | .. | 40.4 | .. | 18.2 | .. | 6.9 | .. | 34.6 | .. |
| Uganda | 563 | 975 | 38.2 | 48.4 | 14.3 | 14.0 | 4.2 | 6.3 | 43.3 | 31.2 |
| Ukraine | 1,334 | 8,582 | 34.0 | 37.4 | 15.7 | 33.0 | 7.3 | 6.3 | 42.9 | 23.3 |
| United Arab Emirates | .. | .. | .. | .. | .. | .. | .. | .. | .. | .. |
| United Kingdom | 62,524 | 170,962 | 27.1 | 20.9 | 39.9 | 37.0 | 4.4 | 7.3 | 28.7 | 34.7 |
| United States | 129,227 | 308,349 | 32.3 | 30.1 | 35.8 | 24.9 | 5.9 | 13.6 | 26.0 | 31.4 |
| Uruguay | 814 | 863 | 46.2 | 49.1 | 29.0 | 24.7 | 4.5 | 4.6 | 20.2 | 21.6 |
| Uzbekistan | .. | .. | .. | .. | .. | .. | .. | .. | .. | .. |
| Venezuela, RB | 4,654 | 5,797 | 30.7 | 47.8 | 36.8 | 21.2 | 2.6 | 8.5 | 29.9 | 22.5 |
| Vietnam | 2,304 | 5,282 | .. | .. | .. | .. | .. | .. | .. | .. |
| West Bank and Gaza | .. | .. | .. | .. | .. | .. | .. | .. | .. | .. |
| Yemen, Rep. | 604 | 1,800 | 35.6 | 40.9 | 12.5 | 9.0 | 7.1 | 7.5 | 44.8 | 42.6 |
| Zambia | 282 | 560 | 78.9 | 57.6 | 9.2 | 9.4 | 0.0 | 10.1 | 11.9 | 23.0 |
| Zimbabwe | 645 | .. | 56.0 | .. | 18.7 | .. | 2.9 | .. | 22.5 | .. |
| **World** | **1,220,158 t** | **2,580,923 t** | **31.2 w** | **28.8 w** | **30.9 w** | **26.6 w** | **6.2 w** | **8.7 w** | **32.1 w** | **36.1 w** |
| **Low income** | 32,423 | 122,594 | 52.6 | 45.4 | 14.4 | 14.5 | 5.1 | 6.8 | 28.3 | 34.3 |
| **Middle income** | 210,450 | 497,838 | 37.0 | 33.4 | 23.8 | 25.8 | 9.8 | 12.6 | 30.1 | 28.3 |
| Lower middle income | 99,850 | 250,874 | 40.3 | 41.4 | 17.1 | 22.4 | 10.8 | 7.8 | 31.9 | 28.5 |
| Upper middle income | 110,799 | 247,787 | 34.6 | 27.3 | 28.9 | 28.4 | 9.0 | 16.1 | 28.8 | 28.1 |
| **Low & middle income** | 242,630 | 616,140 | 38.4 | 34.3 | 23.0 | 25.0 | 9.4 | 12.1 | 30.0 | 28.7 |
| East Asia & Pacific | 82,593 | 194,456 | 38.0 | 40.0 | 15.5 | 20.6 | 12.1 | 6.9 | 36.7 | 32.5 |
| Europe & Central Asia | 49,260 | 141,959 | 26.7 | 28.5 | 27.6 | 30.3 | 6.7 | 6.4 | 39.4 | 34.9 |
| Latin America & Carib. | 52,171 | 98,845 | 41.3 | 25.6 | 31.2 | 30.1 | 10.1 | 25.2 | 17.4 | 19.3 |
| Middle East & N. Africa | 20,192 | 49,265 | 44.6 | .. | 20.2 | .. | .. | .. | 29.7 | .. |
| South Asia | 15,377 | 77,047 | 58.6 | 45.4 | 13.4 | 13.1 | 5.3 | 6.1 | 22.6 | 35.3 |
| Sub-Saharan Africa | 24,433 | 58,709 | 40.2 | 45.5 | 24.1 | 22.8 | 8.8 | 6.0 | 27.7 | 26.1 |
| **High income** | 976,943 | 1,969,987 | 29.2 | 27.3 | 33.0 | 27.0 | 5.4 | 7.8 | 32.7 | 38.1 |
| Euro area | 421,365 | 818,771 | 24.9 | 24.9 | 31.8 | 27.6 | 5.4 | 5.2 | 38.0 | 42.4 |

a. Includes Luxembourg.

## About the data

Trade in services differs from trade in goods because services are produced and consumed at the same time. Thus services to a traveler may be consumed in the producing country (for example, use of a hotel room) but are classified as imports of the traveler's country. In other cases services may be supplied from a remote location; for example, insurance services may be supplied from one location and consumed in another. For further discussion of the problems of measuring trade in services, see *About the data* for table 4.6.

The data on imports of services in the table and on exports of services in table 4.6, unlike those in editions before 2000, include only commercial services and exclude the category "government services not included elsewhere." The data are compiled by the International Monetary Fund (IMF) based on returns from national sources.

## Definitions

• **Commercial service imports** are total service imports minus imports of government services not included elsewhere. International transactions in services are defined by the IMF's *Balance of Payments Manual* (1993) as the economic output of intangible commodities that may be produced, transferred, and consumed at the same time. Definitions may vary among reporting economies. • **Transport** covers all transport services (sea, air, land, internal waterway, space, and pipeline) performed by residents of one economy for those of another and involving the carriage of passengers, movement of goods (freight), rental of carriers with crew, and related support and auxiliary services. Excluded are freight insurance, which is included in insurance services; goods procured in ports by nonresident carriers and repairs of transport equipment, which are included in goods; repairs of harbors, railway facilities, and airfield facilities, which are included in construction services; and rental of carriers without crew, which is included in other services. • **Travel** covers goods and services acquired from an economy by travelers in that economy for their own use during visits of less than one year for business or personal purposes. Travel services include the goods and services consumed by travelers, such as meals, lodging, and transport (within the economy visited), including car rental. • **Insurance and financial services** cover freight insurance on goods imported and other direct insurance such as life insurance; financial intermediation services such as commissions, foreign exchange transactions, and brokerage services; and auxiliary services such as financial market operational and regulatory services. • **Computer, information, communications, and other commercial services** include such activities as international telecommunications, and postal and courier services; computer data; news-related service transactions between residents and nonresidents; construction services; royalties and license fees; miscellaneous business, professional, and technical services; and personal, cultural, and recreational services.

### The mix of commercial service imports by developing countries is changing
4.7a

1995
($1.2 billion)

Other 30%
Transport 38%
Insurance and financial 9%
Travel 23%

2006
($2.6 billion)

Other 29%
Transport 34%
Insurance and financial 12%
Travel 25%

Between 1995 and 2006 developing economies' commercial service imports more than doubled. Insurance and financial services and travel services are displacing transport and other services as the most important services imported.

*Source:* International Monetary Fund balance of payments data files.

## Data sources

Data on imports of commercial services are from the IMF, which publishes balance of payments data in its *International Financial Statistics* and *Balance of Payments Statistics Yearbook*.

# 4.8 | Structure of demand

| | Household final consumption expenditure | | General government final consumption expenditure | | Gross capital formation | | Exports of goods and services | | Imports of goods and services | | Gross savings | |
|---|---|---|---|---|---|---|---|---|---|---|---|---|
| | % of GDP | | % of GDP | | % of GDP | | % of GDP | | % of GDP | | % of GDP | |
| | 1990 | 2006 | 1990 | 2006 | 1990 | 2006 | 1990 | 2006 | 1990 | 2006 | 1990 | 2006 |
| Afghanistan | .. | 110 | .. | 9 | .. | 25 | .. | 12 | .. | 56 | .. | 24 |
| Albania | 87 | 90 | 14 | 9 | 21 | 25 | 12 | 25 | 35 | 49 | 21 | 17 |
| Algeria | 55 | 33 | 17 | 12 | 31 | 30 | 26 | 48 | 29 | 24 | 26 | 51 |
| Angola | 51 | 50 | ..a | ..a | 35 | 14 | 82 | 74 | 68 | 38 | 30 | 37 |
| Argentina | 69 | 59 | 13 | 12 | 18 | 24 | 10 | 25 | 10 | 19 | 16 | 26 |
| Armenia | 109 | 70 | 11 | 11 | 18 | 34 | 24 | 22 | 62 | 36 | −7 | 30 |
| Australia | 59 | 57 | 18 | 18 | 23 | 27 | 19 | 20 | 20 | 22 | 19 | 21 |
| Austria | 57 | 56 | 20 | 18 | 23 | 21 | 35 | 58 | 35 | 52 | 21 | 26 |
| Azerbaijan | 77 | 31 | 13 | 8 | 24 | 32 | 28 | 70 | 42 | 41 | 14 | 50 |
| Bangladesh | 83 | 76 | 5 | 6 | 19 | 25 | 11 | 19 | 17 | 25 | 21 | 34 |
| Belarus | 59 | 54 | 21 | 20 | 25 | 30 | 50 | 60 | 54 | 64 | 21 | 26 |
| Belgium | 54 | 53 | 22 | 23 | 20 | 22 | 68 | 88 | 63 | 85 | 25 | 24 |
| Benin | 82 | 78 | 11 | 15 | 20 | 20 | 20 | 13 | 33 | 26 | 8 | 11 |
| Bolivia | 76 | 63 | 14 | 15 | 15 | 12 | 23 | 42 | 27 | 33 | 11 | 26 |
| Bosnia and Herzegovina | 131 | 82 | ..a | 24 | 20 | 16 | 20 | 25 | 71 | 47 | 10 | 7 |
| Botswana | 34 | 28 | 29 | 20 | 25 | 26 | 51 | 55 | 38 | 29 | 36 | 52 |
| Brazil | 62 | 60 | 21 | 20 | 18 | 17 | 7 | 15 | 9 | 12 | 16 | 17 |
| Bulgaria | 71 | 70 | 15 | 17 | 16 | 32 | 45 | 64 | 46 | 83 | 12 | 16 |
| Burkina Faso | 63 | 77 | 25 | 21 | 24 | 17 | 14 | 11 | 27 | 25 | 18 | 6 |
| Burundi | 89 | 91 | 19 | 29 | 6 | 17 | 13 | 11 | 27 | 48 | 4 | 1 |
| Cambodia | 95 | 82 | 6 | 3 | 15 | 21 | 31 | 69 | 47 | 76 | 6 | 17 |
| Cameroon | 72 | 72 | 9 | 11 | 13 | 18 | 24 | 26 | 18 | 27 | 14 | 17 |
| Canada | 57 | 55 | 21 | 19 | 19 | 22 | 37 | 38 | 34 | 34 | 18 | 24 |
| Central African Republic | 79 | 88 | 15 | 10 | 14 | 9 | 20 | 14 | 28 | 22 | 6 | 6 |
| Chad | 91 | 52 | 7 | 6 | 13 | 22 | 22 | 59 | 34 | 38 | 5 | 23 |
| Chile | 61 | 55 | 10 | 10 | 26 | 20 | 29 | 45 | 27 | 31 | 25 | 24 |
| China | 42 | 33 | 14 | 14 | 42 | 45 | 23 | 40 | 21 | 32 | 43 | 54 |
| Hong Kong, China | 62 | 59 | 8 | 8 | 34 | 21 | 143 | 205 | 148 | 194 | 31 | 32 |
| Colombia | 65 | 61 | 15 | 18 | 26 | 24 | 15 | 22 | 21 | 25 | 18 | 20 |
| Congo, Dem. Rep. | 81 | 88 | 5 | 7 | 9 | 16 | 28 | 29 | 24 | 41 | 1 | 9 |
| Congo, Rep. | 49 | 17 | 13 | 14 | 37 | 24 | 65 | 91 | 64 | 46 | −3 | 20 |
| Costa Rica | 71 | 66 | 14 | 14 | 18 | 27 | 38 | 50 | 40 | 56 | 15 | 19 |
| Côte d'Ivoire | 66 | 72 | 11 | 8 | 16 | 10 | 42 | 51 | 34 | 41 | 12 | 14 |
| Croatia | 64 | 56 | 29 | 20 | 18 | 33 | 39 | 48 | 49 | 57 | 11 | 24 |
| Cuba | 71 | .. | 24 | .. | 7 | .. | 13 | .. | 16 | .. | .. | .. |
| Czech Republic | 51 | 48 | 21 | 21 | 33 | 27 | 51 | 76 | 55 | 73 | 29 | 24 |
| Denmark | 51 | 49 | 25 | 26 | 20 | 23 | 38 | 52 | 34 | 49 | 22 | 25 |
| Dominican Republic | 79 | 80 | 5 | 7 | 19 | 20 | 31 | 33 | 34 | 40 | 18 | 18 |
| Ecuador | 68 | 65 | 13 | 11 | 22 | 23 | 26 | 34 | 28 | 33 | 17 | 27 |
| Egypt, Arab Rep. | 74 | 71 | 11 | 12 | 20 | 19 | 23 | 30 | 28 | 32 | 22 | 22 |
| El Salvador | 87 | 94 | 9 | 10 | 20 | 16 | 22 | 27 | 38 | 47 | 15 | 12 |
| Eritrea | 94 | 81 | 44 | 42 | 23 | 19 | 22 | 8 | 83 | 50 | 4 | 9 |
| Estonia | 54 | 55 | 27 | 17 | 27 | 38 | 68 | 80 | 76 | 90 | 22 | 25 |
| Ethiopia | 80 | 94 | 8 | 12 | 18 | 20 | 10 | 16 | 16 | 42 | 21 | 9 |
| Finland | 52 | 51 | 23 | 21 | 18 | 21 | 36 | 44 | 29 | 38 | 21 | 27 |
| France | 57 | 57 | 24 | 24 | 19 | 21 | 23 | 27 | 22 | 28 | 19 | 19 |
| Gabon | 41 | 27 | 12 | 8 | 23 | 23 | 59 | 65 | 36 | 24 | 33 | 41 |
| Gambia, The | 90 | 96 | 14 | ..a | 20 | 25 | 49 | 45 | 73 | 65 | 6 | 10 |
| Georgia | 102 | 82 | 11 | 15 | 4 | 27 | 26 | 33 | 42 | 57 | −7 | 7 |
| Germany | 58 | 58 | 20 | 18 | 22 | 18 | 24 | 45 | 23 | 40 | 20 | 23 |
| Ghana | 76 | 79 | 12 | 13 | 20 | 32 | 24 | 39 | 33 | 64 | 18 | 27 |
| Greece | 74 | 68 | 14 | 14 | 20 | 26 | 15 | 19 | 23 | 27 | 20 | 16 |
| Guatemala | 86 | 90 | 6 | 6 | 15 | 19 | 19 | 16 | 25 | 31 | 11 | 14 |
| Guinea | 74 | 84 | 8 | 5 | 21 | 13 | 21 | 32 | 25 | 35 | 14 | 8 |
| Guinea-Bissau | 95 | 76 | 6 | 18 | 22 | 17 | 12 | 42 | 35 | 53 | 5 | 23 |
| Haiti | 87 | 91 | 7 | 9 | 24 | 29 | 9 | 14 | 27 | 43 | 10 | .. |

| | Household final consumption expenditure | | General government final consumption expenditure | | Gross capital formation | | Exports of goods and services | | Imports of goods and services | | Gross savings | |
|---|---|---|---|---|---|---|---|---|---|---|---|---|
| | % of GDP | | % of GDP | | % of GDP | | % of GDP | | % of GDP | | % of GDP | |
| | 1990 | 2006 | 1990 | 2006 | 1990 | 2006 | 1990 | 2006 | 1990 | 2006 | 1990 | 2006 |
| Honduras | 64 | 79 | 9 | 14 | 32 | 33 | 44 | 41 | 48 | 66 | 27 | 31 |
| Hungary | 66 | 64 | 11 | 10 | 23 | 25 | 45 | 78 | 45 | 77 | 19 | 19 |
| India | 64 | 58 | 11 | 11 | 27 | 34 | 11 | 23 | 12 | 26 | 27 | 34 |
| Indonesia | 62 | 62 | 8 | 9 | 32 | 25 | 26 | 31 | 28 | 26 | 28 | 26 |
| Iran, Islamic Rep. | 46 | 46 | 16 | 12 | 29 | 34 | 22 | 42 | 13 | 34 | 37 | 40 |
| Iraq | .. | .. | .. | .. | .. | .. | .. | .. | .. | .. | .. | .. |
| Ireland | 54 | *44* | 16 | *16* | 18 | *27* | 76 | *81* | 64 | 69 | 23 | *24* |
| Israel | 55 | 55 | 28 | 27 | 25 | 18 | 29 | 45 | 38 | 44 | 15 | .. |
| Italy | 58 | 59 | 18 | 20 | 20 | 21 | 26 | 28 | 22 | 29 | 22 | 19 |
| Jamaica | 70 | 66 | 11 | 18 | 29 | 33 | 51 | 46 | 61 | 63 | 24 | 26 |
| Japan | 55 | *57* | 15 | *18* | 28 | *23* | 9 | *14* | 8 | *13* | 30 | *27* |
| Jordan | 65 | 89 | 24 | 22 | 33 | 27 | 52 | 55 | 73 | 92 | 29 | 14 |
| Kazakhstan | 68 | 46 | 14 | 10 | 23 | 33 | 39 | 51 | 44 | 40 | 18 | 31 |
| Kenya | 70 | 74 | 15 | 16 | 22 | 19 | 33 | 26 | 39 | 36 | 16 | 13 |
| Korea, Dem. Rep. | .. | .. | .. | .. | .. | .. | .. | .. | .. | .. | .. | .. |
| Korea, Rep. | 52 | 54 | 11 | 15 | 38 | 30 | 29 | 43 | 30 | 42 | 36 | 30 |
| Kuwait | 43 | 28 | 32 | 15 | 15 | 20 | 52 | 68 | 42 | 30 | .. | .. |
| Kyrgyz Republic | 75 | 101 | 20 | 19 | 18 | 17 | 29 | 39 | 42 | 76 | 9 | 4 |
| Lao PDR | .. | 65 | .. | 9 | .. | 33 | 23 | 36 | 37 | 42 | 15 | 19 |
| Latvia | 63 | 65 | 24 | 17 | 14 | 38 | 43 | 44 | 45 | 64 | 14 | 17 |
| Lebanon | 101 | 89 | 15 | 15 | 36 | 12 | 11 | 24 | 62 | 40 | –3 | –4 |
| Lesotho | 120 | 97 | 18 | 18 | 61 | 33 | 21 | 51 | 120 | 99 | 26 | 27 |
| Liberia | .. | 86 | .. | *11* | .. | *16* | 9 | *38* | 72 | *52* | .. | *40* |
| Libya | 59 | .. | 22 | .. | 12 | .. | 29 | .. | 22 | .. | .. | .. |
| Lithuania | 67 | 65 | 22 | 18 | 22 | 27 | 49 | 60 | 60 | 70 | 12 | 13 |
| Macedonia, FYR | 70 | 79 | 19 | 19 | 21 | 21 | 33 | 50 | 43 | 68 | 14 | 22 |
| Madagascar | 90 | 78 | 7 | 9 | 11 | 25 | 24 | 30 | 32 | 41 | 1 | 16 |
| Malawi | 79 | 77 | 21 | 12 | 17 | 24 | 30 | 17 | 48 | 29 | –4 | 15 |
| Malaysia | 48 | 50 | 12 | 12 | 44 | 21 | 94 | 117 | 98 | 100 | 34 | 32 |
| Mali | 83 | 75 | 10 | 10 | 23 | 23 | 21 | 32 | 36 | 40 | 14 | 13 |
| Mauritania | 77 | 61 | 11 | 20 | 20 | 23 | 37 | 55 | 45 | 59 | 17 | 29 |
| Mauritius | 63 | 68 | 13 | 14 | 29 | 25 | 58 | 60 | 64 | 67 | 26 | 19 |
| Mexico | 67 | 68 | 10 | 12 | 20 | 22 | 30 | 32 | 28 | 33 | 19 | 22 |
| Moldova | 57 | 95 | 27 | 18 | 25 | 34 | 49 | 46 | 58 | 93 | 19 | 23 |
| Mongolia | 56 | 48 | 13 | 11 | 32 | 35 | 48 | 65 | 49 | 60 | 35 | 44 |
| Morocco | 68 | 55 | 17 | 18 | 21 | 32 | 27 | 33 | 34 | 38 | 17 | 34 |
| Mozambique | 90 | 76 | 8 | 11 | 27 | 19 | 16 | 41 | 41 | 47 | 1 | 3 |
| Myanmar | 87 | .. | ..[a] | .. | 14 | .. | 1 | .. | 2 | .. | 14 | .. |
| Namibia | 54 | 48 | 30 | 24 | 22 | 29 | 49 | 54 | 56 | 55 | 31 | 42 |
| Nepal | 75 | 83 | 9 | 9 | 25 | 26 | 25 | 14 | 35 | 32 | 23 | 28 |
| Netherlands | 49 | 47 | 24 | 25 | 21 | 20 | 59 | 74 | 54 | 66 | 27 | 30 |
| New Zealand | 58 | 60 | 17 | 18 | 23 | 25 | 29 | 28 | 28 | 30 | 18 | *15* |
| Nicaragua | 83 | 89 | 11 | 12 | 22 | 29 | 19 | 31 | 35 | 61 | –1 | 13 |
| Niger | 86 | 79 | 14 | *11* | 7 | *18* | 17 | *15* | 24 | *24* | –4 | *12* |
| Nigeria | 70 | 56 | 11 | ..[a] | 16 | 22 | 44 | 56 | 42 | 35 | 11 | 34 |
| Norway | 50 | 41 | 22 | 19 | 22 | 22 | 38 | 46 | 32 | 29 | 26 | *37* |
| Oman | 51 | *35* | 25 | *19* | 15 | *18* | 44 | *63* | 36 | 36 | .. | .. |
| Pakistan | 72 | 75 | 12 | 11 | 19 | 22 | 17 | 15 | 19 | 23 | 21 | 24 |
| Panama | 52 | 66 | 15 | 12 | 30 | 20 | 101 | 73 | 98 | 71 | 30 | 18 |
| Papua New Guinea | 42 | .. | 17 | .. | 22 | .. | 62 | .. | 43 | .. | 35 | .. |
| Paraguay | 76 | 86 | 10 | 10 | 26 | 21 | 59 | 49 | 71 | 66 | 18 | 7 |
| Peru | 71 | 61 | 10 | 10 | 25 | 20 | 13 | 29 | 18 | 20 | 25 | 23 |
| Philippines | 74 | 77 | 11 | 10 | 22 | 14 | 36 | 46 | 44 | 48 | 19 | 33 |
| Poland | 60 | 62 | 20 | 19 | 19 | 20 | 23 | 41 | 21 | 41 | 20 | 18 |
| Portugal | 65 | 65 | 18 | 21 | 23 | 22 | 29 | 31 | 35 | 39 | 23 | 12 |
| Puerto Rico | .. | .. | .. | .. | .. | .. | 72 | .. | 97 | .. | .. | .. |

| | Household final consumption expenditure | | General government final consumption expenditure | | Gross capital formation | | Exports of goods and services | | Imports of goods and services | | Gross savings | |
|---|---|---|---|---|---|---|---|---|---|---|---|---|
| | % of GDP | | % of GDP | | % of GDP | | % of GDP | | % of GDP | | % of GDP | |
| | 1990 | 2006 | 1990 | 2006 | 1990 | 2006 | 1990 | 2006 | 1990 | 2006 | 1990 | 2006 |
| Romania | 68 | 73 | 14 | 13 | 24 | 24 | 28 | 34 | 33 | 44 | 19 | 13 |
| Russian Federation | 52 | 50 | 19 | 18 | 25 | 20 | 29 | 34 | 26 | 21 | 28 | 30 |
| Rwanda | 97 | 85 | 10 | 13 | 13 | 21 | 5 | 12 | 26 | 32 | 12 | 14 |
| Saudi Arabia | 47 | 25 | 24 | 25 | 20 | 18 | 38 | 62 | 28 | 31 | 20 | .. |
| Senegal | 80 | 80 | 13 | 10 | 14 | 29 | 31 | 26 | 37 | 44 | 8 | 18 |
| Serbia | 73 | 78 | 23 | 21 | 12 | 21 | 17 | 27 | 24 | 47 | 6 | 10 |
| Sierra Leone | 88 | 85 | 14 | 13 | 6 | 15 | 19 | 23 | 26 | 36 | −3 | 9 |
| Singapore | 41 | 38 | 8 | 11 | 34 | 19 | .. | 253 | .. | 221 | 52 | .. |
| Slovak Republic | 52 | 57 | 22 | 19 | 24 | 29 | 57 | 86 | 55 | 90 | 27 | 20 |
| Slovenia | 60 | 54 | 19 | 19 | 23 | 27 | 51 | 69 | 53 | 70 | 23 | 25 |
| Somalia | .. | .. | .. | .. | .. | .. | .. | .. | .. | .. | .. | .. |
| South Africa | 63 | 63 | 18 | 19 | 18 | 20 | 23 | 30 | 22 | 33 | 17 | 14 |
| Spain | 60 | 58 | 18 | 18 | 22 | 31 | 22 | 26 | 22 | 32 | 22 | 22 |
| Sri Lanka | 73 | 74 | 11 | 9 | 26 | 29 | 36 | 32 | 46 | 43 | 20 | 25 |
| Sudan | 83 | 70 | 6 | 16 | 20 | 25 | 9 | 16 | 19 | 27 | −4 | 10 |
| Swaziland | 76 | 60 | 22 | 28 | 20 | 17 | 75 | 81 | 93 | 86 | 18 | 19 |
| Sweden | 50 | 47 | 27 | 27 | 17 | 18 | 39 | 51 | 33 | 43 | 20 | 25 |
| Switzerland | 60 | 60 | 12 | 11 | 23 | 22 | 35 | 48 | 30 | 41 | 30 | 36 |
| Syrian Arab Republic | 66 | 67 | 13 | 13 | 27 | 16 | 31 | 39 | 38 | 36 | 23 | 17 |
| Tajikistan | 62 | 109 | 16 | 10 | 29 | 15 | 66 | 23 | 72 | 58 | 22 | 12 |
| Tanzania[b] | 86 | 70 | 12 | 18 | 20 | 19 | 24 | 24 | 42 | 31 | 0 | 11 |
| Thailand | 55 | 57 | 10 | 12 | 42 | 28 | 42 | 74 | 49 | 70 | 34 | 31 |
| Timor-Leste | .. | 68 | .. | 50 | .. | 19 | .. | .. | .. | .. | .. | 249 |
| Togo | 77 | 85 | 12 | 10 | 16 | 18 | 32 | 35 | 37 | 49 | 11 | 11 |
| Trinidad and Tobago | 53 | 51 | 12 | 13 | 21 | 16 | 54 | 65 | 39 | 43 | 26 | 32 |
| Tunisia | 63 | 62 | 16 | 14 | 25 | 24 | 45 | 54 | 49 | 54 | 20 | 25 |
| Turkey | 68 | 71 | 11 | 13 | 25 | 24 | 20 | 28 | 24 | 36 | 25 | 17 |
| Turkmenistan | 44 | 46 | 8 | 13 | 49 | 23 | 75 | 72 | 75 | 54 | 50 | 34 |
| Uganda | 85 | 77 | 11 | 14 | 12 | 23 | 12 | 15 | 21 | 29 | 8 | 15 |
| Ukraine | 55 | 60 | 21 | 19 | 27 | 24 | 47 | 47 | 50 | 50 | 24 | 23 |
| United Arab Emirates | 48 | 46 | 16 | 11 | 30 | 24 | 69 | 94 | 63 | 76 | .. | .. |
| United Kingdom | 64 | 64 | 20 | 22 | 17 | 18 | 28 | 29 | 29 | 33 | 15 | 14 |
| United States | 68 | 71 | 15 | 16 | 18 | 19 | 11 | 11 | 12 | 16 | 16 | 13 |
| Uruguay | 73 | 73 | 12 | 11 | 15 | 16 | 19 | 30 | 19 | 30 | 14 | 14 |
| Uzbekistan | 51 | 51 | 22 | 15 | 27 | 22 | 28 | 38 | 28 | 26 | 27 | 36 |
| Venezuela, RB | 69 | 48 | 7 | 11 | 18 | 25 | 27 | 37 | 22 | 21 | 21 | 40 |
| Vietnam | 74 | 62 | 8 | 6 | 27 | 36 | 33 | 73 | 42 | 77 | 19 | 37 |
| West Bank and Gaza | 98 | 95 | 18 | 32 | 35 | 27 | 16 | 16 | 68 | 70 | 11 | 10 |
| Yemen, Rep. | 71 | .. | 14 | .. | 22 | .. | 51 | .. | 58 | .. | 20 | .. |
| Zambia | 72 | 57 | 15 | 10 | 16 | 24 | 36 | 38 | 40 | 30 | 5 | 23 |
| Zimbabwe | 65 | 72 | 18 | 27 | 20 | 17 | 38 | 57 | 41 | 73 | 17 | 0 |
| **World** | **61 w** | **61 w** | **17 w** | **17 w** | **22 w** | **22 w** | **21 w** | **27 w** | **21 w** | **27 w** | **22 w** | **21 w** |
| **Low income** | 68 | 64 | 11 | 11 | 24 | 30 | 17 | 27 | 19 | 30 | 22 | 30 |
| **Middle income** | 59 | 55 | 15 | 15 | 27 | 27 | 25 | 36 | 25 | 33 | 26 | 30 |
| Lower middle income | 53 | 48 | 13 | 13 | 35 | 35 | 26 | 40 | 27 | 36 | 34 | 41 |
| Upper middle income | 63 | 61 | 16 | 15 | 21 | 21 | 24 | 33 | 24 | 30 | 20 | 22 |
| **Low & middle income** | 60 | 56 | 14 | 14 | 26 | 27 | 24 | 35 | 25 | 33 | 25 | 30 |
| East Asia & Pacific | 47 | 41 | 13 | 13 | 40 | 39 | 29 | 47 | 29 | 40 | 38 | 47 |
| Europe & Central Asia | 61 | 61 | 17 | 16 | 23 | 23 | 29 | 40 | 31 | 40 | 23 | 22 |
| Latin America & Carib. | 66 | 63 | 15 | 15 | 20 | 21 | 18 | 26 | 19 | 23 | 18 | 22 |
| Middle East & N. Africa | 62 | 57 | 16 | 14 | 25 | 26 | 27 | 38 | 29 | 35 | 25 | 30 |
| South Asia | 67 | 62 | 10 | 11 | 25 | 32 | 12 | 22 | 15 | 26 | 25 | 32 |
| Sub-Saharan Africa | 69 | 67 | 15 | 17 | 18 | 21 | 28 | 35 | 30 | 36 | 14 | 18 |
| **High income** | 61 | 62 | 17 | 18 | 21 | 21 | 21 | 26 | 20 | 26 | 21 | 19 |
| Euro area | 57 | 57 | 20 | 20 | 21 | 21 | 29 | 40 | 28 | 38 | 21 | 22 |

a. Data for general government final consumption expenditure are not available separately; they are included in household final consumption expenditure. b. Covers mainland Tanzania only.

# Structure of demand

## About the data

Gross domestic product (GDP) from the expenditure side is made up of household final consumption expenditure, general government final consumption expenditure, gross capital formation (private and public investment in fixed assets, changes in inventories, and net acquisitions of valuables), and net exports (exports minus imports) of goods and services. Such expenditures are recorded in purchaser prices and include net taxes on products.

Because policymakers have tended to focus on fostering the growth of output, and because data on production are easier to collect than data on spending, many countries generate their primary estimate of GDP using the production approach. Moreover, many countries do not estimate all the components of national expenditures but instead derive some of the main aggregates indirectly using GDP (based on the production approach) as the control total. Household final consumption expenditure (private consumption in the 1968 System of National Accounts, or SNA) is often estimated as a residual, by subtracting all other known expenditures from GDP. The resulting aggregate may incorporate fairly large discrepancies. When household consumption is calculated separately, many of the estimates are based on household surveys, which tend to be one-year studies with limited coverage. Thus the estimates quickly become outdated and must be supplemented by estimates using price- and quantity-based statistical procedures. Complicating the issue, in many developing countries the distinction between cash outlays for personal business and those for household use may be blurred. *World Development Indicators* includes in household consumption the expenditures of nonprofit institutions serving households.

General government final consumption expenditure (general government consumption in the 1968 SNA) includes expenditures on goods and services for individual consumption as well as those on services for collective consumption. Defense expenditures, including those on capital outlays (with certain exceptions), are treated as current spending.

Gross capital formation (gross domestic investment in the 1968 SNA) consists of outlays on additions to the economy's fixed assets plus net changes in the level of inventories. It is generally obtained from reports by industry of acquisition and distinguishes only the broad categories of capital formation. The 1993 SNA recognizes a third category of capital formation: net acquisitions of valuables. Included in gross capital formation under the 1993 SNA

guidelines are capital outlays on defense establishments that may be used by the general public, such as schools, airfields, and hospitals, and intangibles such as computer software and mineral exploration outlays. Data on capital formation may be estimated from direct surveys of enterprises and administrative records or based on the commodity flow method using data from production, trade, and construction activities. The quality of data on government fixed capital formation depends on the quality of government accounting systems (which tend to be weak in developing countries). Measures of fixed capital formation by households and corporations—particularly capital outlays by small, unincorporated enterprises—are usually unreliable.

Estimates of changes in inventories are rarely complete but usually include the most important activities or commodities. In some countries these estimates are derived as a composite residual along with household final consumption expenditure. According to national accounts conventions, adjustments should be made for appreciation of the value of inventory holdings due to price changes, but this is not always done. In highly inflationary economies this element can be substantial.

Data on exports and imports are compiled from customs reports and balance of payments data. Although the data from the payments side provide reasonably reliable records of cross-border transactions, they may not adhere strictly to the appropriate definitions of valuation and timing used in the balance of payments or correspond to the change-of-ownership criterion. This issue has assumed greater significance with the increasing globalization of international business. Neither customs nor balance of payments data usually capture the illegal transactions that occur in many countries. Goods carried by travelers across borders in legal but unreported shuttle trade may further distort trade statistics.

Gross savings represent the difference between disposable income and consumption and replace gross domestic savings, a concept used by the World Bank and included in *World Development Indicators* editions before 2006. The change was made to conform to SNA concepts and definitions. For further discussion of the problems in compiling national accounts, see Srinivasan (1994), Heston (1994), and Ruggles (1994). For an analysis of the reliability of foreign trade and national income statistics, see Morgenstern (1963).

## Definitions

• **Household final consumption expenditure** is the market value of all goods and services, including durable products (such as cars and computers), purchased by households. It excludes purchases of dwellings but includes imputed rent for owner-occupied dwellings. It also includes government fees for permits and licenses. Expenditures of nonprofit institutions serving households are included, even when reported separately. Household consumption expenditure may include any statistical discrepancy in the use of resources relative to the supply of resources. • **General government final consumption expenditure** is all government current expenditures for purchases of goods and services (including compensation of employees). It also includes most expenditures on national defense and security but excludes military expenditures with potentially wider public use that are part of government capital formation. • **Gross capital formation** is outlays on additions to fixed assets of the economy, net changes in inventories, and net acquisitions of valuables. Fixed assets include land improvements (fences, ditches, drains); plant, machinery, and equipment purchases; and construction (roads, railways, schools, buildings, and so on). Inventories are goods held to meet temporary or unexpected fluctuations in production or sales, and "work in progress." • **Exports** and **imports of goods and services** are the value of all goods and other market services provided to or received from the rest of the world. They include the value of merchandise, freight, insurance, transport, travel, royalties, license fees, and other services (communication, construction, financial, information, business, personal, government services, and so on). They exclude compensation of employees and investment income (factor services in the 1968 SNA) and transfer payments. • **Gross savings** are gross national income less total consumption, plus net transfers.

## Data sources

Data on national accounts indicators for most developing countries are collected from national statistical organizations and central banks by visiting and resident World Bank missions. Data for high-income economies come from Organisation for Economic Co-operation and Development (OECD) data files (see *Annual National Accounts for OECD Member Countries: Data from 1970 Onwards*).

# 4.9 Growth of consumption and investment

| | Household final consumption expenditure | | | | General government final consumption expenditure | | Gross capital formation | | Goods and services | | | |
| | average annual % growth | | | | average annual % growth | | average annual % growth | | average annual % growth | | | |
| | Total | | Per capita | | | | | | Exports | | Imports | |
| | 1990–2000 | 2000–06 | 1990–2000 | 2000–06 | 1990–2000 | 2000–06 | 1990–2000 | 2000–06 | 1990–2000 | 2000–06 | 1990–2000 | 2000–06 |
|---|---|---|---|---|---|---|---|---|---|---|---|---|
| Afghanistan | .. | .. | .. | .. | .. | .. | .. | .. | .. | .. | .. | .. |
| Albania | 4.3 | 5.1 | 5.2 | 4.6 | 2.4 | 2.1 | 25.8 | 4.6 | 18.9 | 11.2 | 15.7 | 12.8 |
| Algeria | –0.1 | .. | –1.9 | .. | 3.6 | .. | –0.6 | .. | 3.2 | .. | –1.0 | .. |
| Angola | .. | .. | .. | .. | .. | .. | .. | .. | .. | .. | .. | .. |
| Argentina | 2.8 | 1.9 | 1.5 | 0.9 | 2.2 | 1.3 | 7.4 | 6.2 | 8.7 | 6.5 | 15.6 | 2.3 |
| Armenia | –0.5 | 8.1 | 1.1 | 8.5 | –1.5 | 10.9 | –1.9 | 20.7 | –18.4 | 15.3 | –12.7 | 10.8 |
| Australia | 3.6 | .. | 2.4 | .. | 3.0 | .. | 5.7 | .. | 7.4 | .. | 8.1 | .. |
| Austria | 1.9 | 1.3 | 1.5 | 0.8 | 2.5 | 1.0 | .. | .. | 5.5 | 6.2 | 5.0 | 5.0 |
| Azerbaijan | 1.5 | 11.3 | 0.4 | 10.5 | –1.7 | 10.0 | 42.9 | 32.0 | 6.8 | 16.4 | 15.5 | 20.3 |
| Bangladesh | 2.6 | 4.0 | 0.5 | 2.1 | 4.7 | 9.6 | 9.2 | 8.0 | 13.1 | 11.2 | 9.7 | 8.4 |
| Belarus | –0.5 | 10.9 | –0.3 | 11.4 | –1.9 | 2.0 | –7.5 | 12.5 | –4.8 | 8.0 | –8.7 | 10.1 |
| Belgium | 1.8 | 1.3 | 1.5 | 0.8 | 1.4 | 1.7 | 2.8 | 2.8 | 4.7 | 2.9 | 4.5 | 2.9 |
| Benin | 2.6 | .. | –0.8 | .. | 4.4 | .. | 12.2 | 7.6 | 1.8 | .. | 2.1 | .. |
| Bolivia | 3.6 | 2.4 | 1.3 | 0.5 | 3.6 | 3.2 | 8.5 | –1.8 | 4.5 | 9.8 | 6.0 | 5.3 |
| Bosnia and Herzegovina | .. | .. | .. | .. | .. | .. | .. | 5.8 | .. | 8.4 | .. | 0.7 |
| Botswana | 2.5 | 4.6 | 0.1 | 3.4 | 7.1 | 2.0 | 6.4 | –2.7 | 4.7 | 4.0 | 3.8 | 0.7 |
| Brazil[a] | 3.7 | 2.4 | 2.2 | 1.0 | 1.0 | 3.0 | 4.2 | 0.5 | 5.9 | 9.2 | 11.6 | 4.4 |
| Bulgaria | –3.7 | 5.2 | –3.0 | 6.0 | –8.4 | 3.5 | –5.0 | 13.6 | 3.9 | 9.4 | 2.7 | 12.3 |
| Burkina Faso | 5.7 | 4.4 | 2.7 | 1.2 | 2.9 | 8.8 | 3.1 | 7.5 | 4.4 | 9.6 | 1.9 | 6.0 |
| Burundi | –4.9 | .. | .. | .. | –2.6 | .. | –0.5 | .. | –1.2 | .. | –1.6 | .. |
| Cambodia[a] | 6.0 | 7.7 | 3.4 | 5.9 | 7.2 | 2.3 | 10.3 | 13.9 | 21.7 | 16.0 | 14.8 | 14.0 |
| Cameroon | 3.1 | 4.1 | 0.5 | 1.8 | 0.7 | 4.9 | 0.4 | 9.3 | 3.2 | 1.4 | 5.1 | 8.5 |
| Canada | 2.6 | .. | 1.6 | .. | 0.3 | .. | 4.5 | .. | 8.7 | .. | 7.1 | .. |
| Central African Republic[a] | .. | 0.3 | .. | –1.4 | .. | –4.9 | .. | –1.3 | .. | –2.6 | .. | –4.0 |
| Chad[a] | 1.5 | 3.2 | –1.8 | –0.3 | –8.3 | 6.5 | 4.0 | 10.4 | 2.3 | 32.5 | –1.8 | 13.4 |
| Chile | 7.3 | 5.1 | 5.6 | 4.0 | 3.7 | 3.8 | 9.3 | 7.5 | 9.4 | 5.6 | 11.7 | 9.4 |
| China | 8.9 | 7.2 | 7.8 | 6.6 | 9.7 | 8.8 | 11.5 | 12.4 | 12.9 | 21.1 | 14.3 | 16.9 |
| Hong Kong, China | 3.9 | 2.5 | 2.1 | 2.0 | 3.3 | 1.3 | 7.7 | 1.0 | 7.8 | 8.7 | 8.3 | 7.6 |
| Colombia | 2.2 | 4.2 | 0.4 | 2.7 | 10.5 | 1.3 | 2.0 | 13.4 | 5.3 | 4.4 | 9.0 | 11.3 |
| Congo, Dem. Rep.[a] | –4.5 | .. | –7.2 | .. | –17.4 | .. | –0.7 | .. | –0.5 | 6.5 | –2.4 | 18.3 |
| Congo, Rep.[a] | –1.8 | .. | .. | .. | –4.4 | .. | 10.4 | .. | 3.0 | .. | 2.0 | .. |
| Costa Rica[a] | 5.1 | 3.2 | 2.5 | 1.4 | 2.0 | 1.6 | 5.1 | 11.4 | 10.9 | 5.7 | 9.2 | 6.3 |
| Côte d'Ivoire | 4.1 | 0.0 | 1.2 | –1.7 | 0.8 | 2.9 | 8.1 | –0.9 | 1.9 | 7.2 | 8.2 | 3.4 |
| Croatia | 2.7 | 4.6 | 3.2 | 4.9 | 1.3 | 0.4 | 5.4 | 13.2 | 5.9 | 6.1 | 4.6 | 8.1 |
| Cuba | .. | .. | .. | .. | .. | .. | .. | .. | .. | .. | .. | .. |
| Czech Republic | 3.0 | 3.3 | 3.0 | 3.3 | –0.9 | 2.5 | 4.6 | 5.1 | 8.7 | 10.4 | 12.0 | 9.9 |
| Denmark | 2.2 | 2.4 | 1.8 | 2.1 | 2.4 | 1.5 | .. | .. | 5.1 | 4.1 | 6.1 | 6.2 |
| Dominican Republic[a] | 5.3 | 3.3 | 3.4 | 1.8 | 5.2 | 6.1 | 10.4 | 0.7 | 9.1 | 2.6 | 9.4 | 0.5 |
| Ecuador[a] | 2.1 | 5.8 | 0.3 | 4.7 | –1.5 | 2.5 | –0.6 | 10.7 | 5.3 | 6.5 | 2.8 | 11.0 |
| Egypt, Arab Rep. | 4.0 | 3.6 | 2.1 | 1.8 | 4.4 | 3.5 | 6.0 | 3.6 | 3.6 | 11.4 | 3.1 | 8.5 |
| El Salvador | 5.3 | 3.1 | 3.3 | 1.6 | 2.8 | 1.6 | 7.1 | 2.5 | 13.4 | 4.5 | 11.6 | 4.6 |
| Eritrea | –5.0 | .. | –6.7 | .. | 22.6 | .. | 19.1 | –3.9 | –2.5 | –3.2 | 7.5 | –3.3 |
| Estonia | 0.6 | 8.9 | 2.2 | 9.3 | 4.9 | 1.8 | 0.1 | 13.7 | 11.2 | 9.3 | 12.0 | 10.3 |
| Ethiopia | 3.5 | 7.3 | 1.1 | 4.7 | 9.5 | –2.2 | 2.3 | 4.6 | 7.1 | 11.1 | 5.8 | 12.5 |
| Finland | 1.7 | 3.2 | 1.4 | 2.9 | 0.6 | 1.6 | .. | .. | 10.3 | 4.7 | 6.4 | 5.1 |
| France | 1.6 | 2.2 | 1.2 | 1.6 | 1.4 | 1.6 | 1.8 | 2.0 | 6.9 | 2.5 | 5.7 | 3.9 |
| Gabon[a] | –0.3 | 2.7 | –2.8 | 1.0 | 3.7 | 4.2 | 3.0 | 3.3 | 2.1 | –2.9 | 0.1 | –0.5 |
| Gambia, The | 3.6 | .. | –0.1 | .. | –2.2 | .. | 1.9 | 8.2 | 0.1 | 4.3 | 0.1 | 0.8 |
| Georgia | 6.1 | 7.9 | 7.5 | 8.9 | 12.0 | 4.3 | –12.5 | 16.1 | 12.2 | 5.6 | 11.2 | 6.9 |
| Germany | 1.9 | 0.3 | 1.6 | 0.3 | 1.9 | 0.5 | .. | .. | 6.0 | 6.8 | 5.8 | 4.8 |
| Ghana | 4.1 | 4.5 | 1.4 | 2.3 | 4.8 | –0.8 | 4.3 | 17.2 | 10.1 | 3.5 | 10.4 | 6.8 |
| Greece | 2.1 | 4.0 | 1.4 | 3.6 | 2.1 | 1.9 | .. | .. | 7.6 | 1.5 | 7.4 | 2.1 |
| Guatemala[a] | 4.2 | 3.8 | 1.8 | 1.3 | 5.1 | –0.3 | 6.1 | 5.6 | 6.1 | 0.1 | 9.2 | 5.3 |
| Guinea | 5.2 | 4.3 | 2.0 | 2.5 | –0.5 | 0.0 | 0.1 | –9.1 | 0.3 | 1.3 | –1.1 | –1.4 |
| Guinea-Bissau | 2.6 | 6.8 | –0.4 | 3.8 | 1.9 | –2.9 | –6.5 | 0.8 | 15.4 | 4.1 | –0.4 | –0.6 |
| Haiti | .. | .. | .. | .. | .. | .. | .. | .. | .. | .. | .. | .. |

| | Household final consumption expenditure | | | | General government final consumption expenditure | | Gross capital formation | | Goods and services | | | |
|---|---|---|---|---|---|---|---|---|---|---|---|---|
| | average annual % growth | | | | average annual % growth | | average annual % growth | | average annual % growth | | | |
| | Total | | Per capita | | | | | | Exports | | Imports | |
| | 1990–2000 | 2000–06 | 1990–2000 | 2000–06 | 1990–2000 | 2000–06 | 1990–2000 | 2000–06 | 1990–2000 | 2000–06 | 1990–2000 | 2000–06 |
| Honduras[a] | 3.0 | 5.4 | 0.6 | 3.5 | 2.0 | 5.4 | 6.9 | 3.0 | 1.6 | 6.0 | 3.8 | 8.2 |
| Hungary | −0.1 | 4.9 | 0.1 | 5.1 | 0.9 | 2.9 | 9.6 | −0.6 | 9.9 | 10.1 | 11.4 | 8.9 |
| India | 4.7 | 5.3 | 2.9 | 3.8 | 6.4 | 5.2 | 6.9 | 11.8 | 12.3 | 11.6 | 14.4 | 10.2 |
| Indonesia | 6.6 | 3.8 | 5.0 | 2.5 | 0.1 | 8.1 | −0.6 | 5.0 | 5.9 | 7.0 | 5.7 | 8.0 |
| Iran, Islamic Rep. | 3.2 | 6.7 | 1.6 | 5.2 | 1.6 | 2.8 | −0.1 | 7.2 | 1.2 | 10.3 | −6.8 | 20.2 |
| Iraq | .. | .. | .. | .. | .. | .. | .. | .. | .. | .. | .. | .. |
| Ireland | 5.3 | .. | 4.5 | .. | 4.2 | .. | .. | .. | 15.7 | .. | 14.5 | .. |
| Israel | 4.6 | 2.9 | 2.0 | 1.0 | 2.9 | 1.6 | 1.7 | −1.8 | 10.9 | 3.3 | 7.5 | 1.6 |
| Italy | 1.5 | 0.8 | 1.5 | 0.2 | −0.3 | 1.7 | .. | .. | 5.1 | 0.3 | 3.8 | 1.2 |
| Jamaica | .. | .. | .. | .. | .. | .. | .. | .. | .. | .. | .. | .. |
| Japan | 1.5 | .. | 1.3 | .. | 2.9 | .. | −0.8 | .. | 4.1 | .. | 4.2 | .. |
| Jordan | 4.9 | 5.6 | 1.1 | 3.2 | 4.7 | 2.7 | 0.3 | 7.0 | 2.6 | 8.2 | 1.5 | 6.6 |
| Kazakhstan[a] | −8.1 | 9.8 | −7.0 | 9.3 | −7.1 | 7.4 | −18.3 | 20.1 | −2.6 | 6.5 | −11.2 | 5.1 |
| Kenya | 3.6 | 3.9 | 0.6 | 1.3 | 6.9 | 1.5 | 6.1 | 7.1 | 1.0 | 6.6 | 9.4 | 6.4 |
| Korea, Dem. Rep. | .. | .. | .. | .. | .. | .. | .. | .. | .. | .. | .. | .. |
| Korea, Rep. | 4.9 | 3.1 | 3.9 | 2.6 | 4.7 | 4.8 | 3.4 | 3.0 | 16.0 | 10.3 | 10.0 | 8.4 |
| Kuwait | 4.5 | .. | 0.6 | .. | −2.4 | .. | 1.0 | .. | −1.6 | .. | 0.8 | .. |
| Kyrgyz Republic | −6.5 | 10.6 | −7.4 | 9.7 | −8.8 | 0.3 | −3.9 | −1.4 | −1.6 | 1.6 | −8.2 | 11.0 |
| Lao PDR | .. | 1.6 | .. | 0.0 | .. | 9.4 | .. | 13.6 | .. | .. | .. | .. |
| Latvia | −3.9 | 10.0 | −2.7 | 10.6 | 1.8 | 2.6 | −3.7 | 16.1 | 4.3 | 8.4 | 7.6 | 12.6 |
| Lebanon | 1.3 | 3.0 | −0.5 | 1.8 | 10.5 | 2.7 | −7.7 | −3.8 | 15.1 | 11.6 | −2.8 | 3.3 |
| Lesotho | 0.5 | 4.0 | −1.2 | 3.0 | 6.2 | 2.3 | 1.5 | −1.9 | 11.1 | 9.0 | 0.9 | 3.7 |
| Liberia | .. | .. | .. | .. | .. | .. | .. | .. | .. | .. | .. | .. |
| Libya | .. | .. | .. | .. | .. | .. | .. | .. | .. | .. | .. | .. |
| Lithuania[a] | 5.3 | 8.9 | 6.0 | 9.4 | 1.9 | 4.1 | 11.1 | 12.1 | 4.9 | 12.6 | 7.5 | 14.2 |
| Macedonia, FYR | 2.2 | 2.6 | 1.7 | 2.3 | −0.4 | 1.0 | 3.6 | 0.9 | 4.2 | 1.5 | 7.5 | 1.9 |
| Madagascar | 2.2 | 2.5 | −0.8 | −0.3 | 0.0 | 6.9 | 3.3 | 12.1 | 3.8 | 0.1 | 4.1 | 6.1 |
| Malawi | 5.4 | 4.1 | 3.4 | 1.5 | −4.4 | 5.1 | −8.4 | 21.3 | 4.0 | −9.8 | −1.1 | 4.3 |
| Malaysia | 5.3 | 6.3 | 2.6 | 4.4 | 4.8 | 9.2 | 5.3 | 1.2 | 12.0 | 5.3 | 10.3 | 6.0 |
| Mali | 3.0 | 0.8 | 0.3 | −2.2 | 3.2 | 16.8 | 0.4 | 8.3 | 9.9 | 8.7 | 3.5 | 5.4 |
| Mauritania | .. | .. | .. | .. | .. | .. | .. | .. | −1.3 | 11.9 | 0.6 | .. |
| Mauritius | 5.1 | 4.9 | 3.9 | 4.0 | 4.8 | 4.7 | 4.7 | 3.5 | 5.4 | 3.7 | 5.2 | 2.9 |
| Mexico | 3.9 | 3.0 | 2.2 | 2.0 | 1.8 | 0.7 | 4.7 | 0.5 | 14.6 | 4.8 | 12.3 | 5.2 |
| Moldova[a] | 9.9 | 9.6 | 10.7 | 10.9 | −12.4 | 13.1 | −15.5 | 9.8 | 0.7 | 13.0 | 5.6 | 15.1 |
| Mongolia[a] | .. | .. | .. | .. | .. | .. | .. | .. | .. | .. | .. | .. |
| Morocco | 1.8 | 3.9 | 0.1 | 2.8 | 3.9 | 2.9 | 2.5 | 9.7 | 5.9 | 6.0 | 5.1 | 6.3 |
| Mozambique[a] | 3.9 | 4.5 | 0.8 | 2.1 | 4.2 | 8.5 | 10.0 | 1.5 | 13.1 | 18.9 | 5.0 | 5.2 |
| Myanmar | 3.9 | .. | .. | .. | .. | .. | 15.3 | .. | 10.0 | .. | 5.8 | .. |
| Namibia | 4.8 | 2.0 | 1.9 | 0.6 | 3.3 | 1.8 | 6.9 | 10.3 | 3.8 | 6.0 | 5.4 | 5.1 |
| Nepal | .. | .. | .. | .. | .. | .. | .. | .. | .. | .. | .. | .. |
| Netherlands | 3.1 | 0.4 | 2.4 | 0.0 | 2.0 | 3.2 | 4.4 | 0.2 | 7.3 | 4.1 | 7.6 | 3.9 |
| New Zealand | 3.2 | .. | 2.0 | .. | 2.5 | .. | 6.1 | .. | 5.2 | .. | 6.2 | .. |
| Nicaragua[a] | 6.1 | 3.3 | 3.9 | 2.0 | −1.5 | 1.2 | 11.3 | −0.3 | 9.3 | 7.9 | 12.2 | 4.0 |
| Niger | 1.8 | .. | .. | .. | 0.8 | .. | 4.0 | .. | 3.1 | .. | −2.1 | .. |
| Nigeria | 0.2 | .. | .. | .. | −1.8 | .. | 5.4 | .. | 5.0 | .. | 4.0 | .. |
| Norway | 3.5 | 3.5 | 2.9 | 2.9 | 2.7 | 2.4 | 6.1 | 5.1 | 5.5 | 1.2 | 5.8 | 4.9 |
| Oman | 5.4 | .. | 2.6 | .. | 2.4 | .. | 4.0 | .. | 6.2 | .. | 5.9 | .. |
| Pakistan | 4.9 | 4.4 | 2.3 | 2.1 | 0.7 | 9.6 | 1.8 | 5.3 | 1.7 | 10.5 | 2.5 | 9.7 |
| Panama[a] | 6.4 | 5.9 | 4.2 | 4.1 | 1.7 | 4.2 | 10.4 | 1.7 | −0.4 | 4.3 | 1.2 | 4.3 |
| Papua New Guinea | 5.6 | .. | .. | .. | 2.7 | .. | 0.5 | .. | 4.3 | .. | 2.8 | .. |
| Paraguay | 2.6 | 3.4 | 0.2 | 1.5 | 2.5 | −1.8 | 0.7 | 3.6 | 3.1 | 4.4 | 2.9 | 5.0 |
| Peru[a] | 4.0 | 4.0 | 2.3 | 2.7 | 5.2 | 4.0 | 7.4 | 6.0 | 8.5 | 8.1 | 9.0 | 6.7 |
| Philippines | 3.7 | 4.7 | 1.5 | 2.7 | 3.8 | 0.4 | 4.1 | −1.4 | 7.8 | 5.7 | 7.8 | 4.8 |
| Poland[a] | 5.2 | 3.1 | 5.1 | 3.3 | 3.7 | 3.3 | 10.6 | 1.6 | 11.3 | 9.2 | 16.7 | 6.6 |
| Portugal | 3.0 | 1.4 | 2.7 | 0.8 | 2.8 | 1.7 | .. | .. | 5.3 | 3.5 | 7.3 | 2.0 |
| Puerto Rico | .. | .. | .. | .. | .. | .. | .. | .. | 1.6 | .. | 4.5 | .. |

| | Household final consumption expenditure | | | | General government final consumption expenditure | | Gross capital formation | | Goods and services | | | |
|---|---|---|---|---|---|---|---|---|---|---|---|---|
| | average annual % growth | | | | average annual % growth | | average annual % growth | | average annual % growth | | | |
| | Total | | Per capita | | | | | | Exports | | Imports | |
| | 1990–2000 | 2000–06 | 1990–2000 | 2000–06 | 1990–2000 | 2000–06 | 1990–2000 | 2000–06 | 1990–2000 | 2000–06 | 1990–2000 | 2000–06 |
| Romania[a] | 1.3 | 6.1 | 1.7 | 6.8 | 0.8 | 5.1 | −5.1 | 9.7 | 8.1 | 10.3 | 6.0 | 11.5 |
| Russian Federation | −0.9 | 7.6 | −0.7 | 8.0 | −2.2 | 1.7 | −19.1 | 9.4 | 0.8 | 8.3 | −6.1 | 17.2 |
| Rwanda[a] | 1.1 | 3.5 | 0.1 | 1.0 | −1.7 | 9.3 | 1.4 | 6.0 | −3.8 | 15.7 | 5.0 | 6.6 |
| Saudi Arabia | .. | .. | .. | .. | .. | .. | .. | .. | .. | .. | .. | .. |
| Senegal | 2.6 | 4.3 | −0.2 | 1.8 | 0.9 | 3.8 | 3.5 | 10.0 | 4.1 | 0.8 | 2.0 | 4.3 |
| Serbia | .. | 4.7 | .. | 4.9 | .. | 4.2 | .. | 20.8 | .. | 9.1 | .. | 13.1 |
| Sierra Leone | −4.4 | .. | .. | .. | 10.4 | .. | −5.6 | .. | −11.2 | .. | −0.2 | .. |
| Singapore | .. | .. | .. | .. | .. | .. | .. | .. | .. | .. | .. | .. |
| Slovak Republic | 5.6 | 4.5 | 5.4 | 4.5 | 2.0 | 3.3 | 8.1 | 7.7 | 8.8 | 10.9 | 12.2 | 10.8 |
| Slovenia | 3.9 | 2.7 | 3.9 | 2.6 | 2.1 | 3.0 | 10.9 | 5.1 | 1.7 | 7.8 | 5.2 | 7.2 |
| Somalia | .. | .. | .. | .. | .. | .. | .. | .. | .. | .. | .. | .. |
| South Africa | 2.9 | 5.0 | 0.6 | 3.7 | 0.3 | 5.0 | 5.0 | 7.9 | 5.6 | 3.2 | 7.1 | 9.0 |
| Spain | 2.4 | 3.5 | 2.0 | 1.9 | 2.7 | 4.7 | .. | .. | 10.5 | 3.5 | 9.4 | 6.4 |
| Sri Lanka[a] | 5.7 | .. | .. | .. | 7.5 | .. | 6.9 | 5.9 | 7.5 | 3.9 | 8.6 | 5.0 |
| Sudan | 3.8 | 6.7 | 1.2 | 4.7 | 5.5 | 9.8 | 21.5 | 12.3 | 11.6 | 8.2 | 8.4 | 14.3 |
| Swaziland[a] | 3.8 | 1.6 | 0.6 | 0.4 | 5.5 | −0.5 | 2.7 | 3.7 | 3.8 | 4.0 | 4.5 | 3.0 |
| Sweden | 1.3 | 1.8 | 0.9 | 1.4 | 0.6 | 1.1 | 1.8 | 2.4 | 8.6 | 5.2 | 6.3 | 3.6 |
| Switzerland | 1.1 | .. | 0.5 | .. | 0.8 | .. | .. | .. | 4.0 | .. | 4.2 | .. |
| Syrian Arab Republic | 3.0 | 6.1 | 0.3 | 3.4 | 2.0 | 5.0 | 3.3 | 14.5 | 12.0 | 0.6 | 4.4 | 11.5 |
| Tajikistan | −4.2 | 10.6 | −5.6 | 9.4 | −19.1 | 0.9 | −17.6 | 5.8 | −1.3 | 7.8 | −3.9 | 8.3 |
| Tanzania[b] | 4.9 | 2.5 | 2.0 | −0.1 | −7.0 | 15.1 | −1.6 | 7.1 | 9.3 | 10.4 | 3.9 | 4.2 |
| Thailand | 3.7 | 4.8 | 2.5 | 4.1 | 5.1 | 4.5 | −4.0 | 6.2 | 9.5 | 5.9 | 4.5 | 6.4 |
| Timor-Leste | .. | −7.7 | .. | −12.2 | .. | 6.4 | .. | −4.5 | .. | .. | .. | .. |
| Togo | 5.0 | .. | 1.7 | .. | 0.0 | .. | −0.1 | .. | 1.2 | .. | 1.1 | .. |
| Trinidad and Tobago | 0.7 | .. | 0.1 | .. | 0.3 | .. | 12.5 | .. | 6.9 | .. | 9.9 | .. |
| Tunisia | 4.3 | 4.7 | 2.6 | 3.7 | 4.1 | 4.1 | 3.6 | 1.9 | 5.1 | 3.6 | 3.8 | 2.4 |
| Turkey | 3.6 | 3.7 | 1.7 | 2.3 | 4.9 | 1.0 | 5.0 | 5.7 | 11.6 | 10.1 | 11.0 | 8.3 |
| Turkmenistan | .. | .. | .. | .. | .. | .. | 1.9 | .. | −6.1 | .. | 0.6 | .. |
| Uganda | 6.7 | 4.8 | 3.3 | 1.6 | 7.1 | 5.9 | 8.9 | 8.5 | 14.7 | 7.7 | 10.0 | 6.6 |
| Ukraine | −6.9 | 11.8 | −6.4 | 12.7 | −4.1 | 3.2 | −18.5 | 8.3 | −3.6 | 3.5 | −6.6 | 5.3 |
| United Arab Emirates | 7.1 | .. | 0.7 | .. | 6.8 | .. | 5.5 | .. | 5.5 | .. | 6.4 | .. |
| United Kingdom | 2.9 | 2.7 | 2.6 | 2.4 | 1.0 | 2.9 | 5.0 | 3.6 | 6.6 | 4.8 | 6.8 | 5.9 |
| United States | 3.6 | .. | 2.4 | .. | 0.7 | .. | 7.4 | .. | 7.3 | .. | 9.8 | .. |
| Uruguay[a] | 5.0 | 0.6 | 4.3 | 0.5 | 2.3 | −1.9 | 6.3 | 3.1 | 6.0 | 5.4 | 9.9 | 2.3 |
| Uzbekistan | .. | .. | .. | .. | .. | .. | −2.5 | 5.1 | 2.4 | 4.4 | −1.2 | 4.6 |
| Venezuela, RB | 0.6 | 7.0 | −1.5 | 5.2 | 3.7 | 6.5 | 11.0 | 7.1 | 1.0 | −1.0 | 8.2 | 10.7 |
| Vietnam | 5.4 | 6.8 | 3.9 | 5.4 | 3.2 | 7.0 | 19.8 | 10.5 | 24.1 | 16.2 | 28.2 | 17.1 |
| West Bank and Gaza | 5.3 | −1.8 | 0.9 | −5.8 | 12.7 | 1.0 | 9.2 | −4.3 | 8.7 | −1.4 | 7.5 | −2.5 |
| Yemen, Rep. | 3.2 | .. | −0.7 | .. | 1.7 | .. | 11.4 | .. | 16.6 | .. | 8.3 | .. |
| Zambia | 2.4 | 0.3 | −0.2 | −1.6 | −8.1 | 21.1 | 13.3 | −5.2 | 6.7 | 20.5 | 15.5 | 15.0 |
| Zimbabwe | 0.0 | .. | −1.9 | .. | −2.2 | .. | −2.5 | .. | 10.5 | .. | 9.4 | .. |
| **World** | **3.0 w** | **.. w** | **1.5 w** | **.. w** | **1.7 w** | **.. w** | **3.5 w** | **.. w** | **6.9 w** | **6.2 w** | **7.0 w** | **.. w** |
| **Low income** | 4.2 | 5.0 | 2.1 | 3.1 | 4.2 | 5.9 | 6.4 | 10.6 | 8.7 | 10.2 | 9.4 | 10.5 |
| **Middle income** | 4.0 | 4.7 | 2.7 | 3.8 | 3.3 | 4.7 | 2.6 | 7.8 | 7.3 | 10.5 | 6.5 | 9.9 |
| Lower middle income | 5.5 | 6.0 | 4.2 | 5.0 | 6.5 | 6.9 | 5.6 | 10.6 | 7.3 | 14.1 | 5.8 | 12.1 |
| Upper middle income | 3.0 | 3.8 | 2.0 | 3.0 | 1.3 | 2.8 | −0.1 | 4.1 | 7.2 | 6.8 | 7.0 | 7.9 |
| **Low & middle income** | 4.0 | 4.7 | 2.4 | 3.4 | 3.3 | 4.8 | 3.0 | 8.2 | 7.4 | 10.5 | 6.7 | 9.9 |
| East Asia & Pacific | 7.5 | 6.4 | 6.1 | 5.6 | 8.1 | 8.3 | 8.1 | 11.0 | 11.0 | 14.9 | 10.3 | 12.5 |
| Europe & Central Asia | 1.0 | 5.6 | 0.9 | 5.6 | 0.1 | 2.5 | −7.8 | 7.3 | 3.1 | 8.9 | 1.2 | 10.6 |
| Latin America & Carib. | 3.6 | 3.1 | 2.0 | 1.7 | 2.1 | 2.4 | 5.4 | 3.1 | 8.5 | 5.4 | 10.8 | 5.7 |
| Middle East & N. Africa | 3.0 | 4.6 | 0.9 | 2.8 | 3.4 | 3.7 | 1.2 | 7.1 | 4.2 | .. | 0.2 | 10.7 |
| South Asia | 4.5 | 5.1 | 2.5 | 3.4 | 5.6 | 5.9 | 6.5 | 10.9 | 10.0 | 11.0 | 11.1 | 9.6 |
| Sub-Saharan Africa | 3.1 | 4.3 | 0.4 | 1.8 | 0.4 | 4.9 | 4.5 | 7.6 | 5.0 | 4.5 | 5.6 | 8.3 |
| **High income** | 2.8 | .. | 2.0 | .. | 1.5 | .. | 3.7 | .. | 6.8 | .. | 7.0 | .. |
| Euro area | 1.9 | 1.4 | 1.6 | 0.9 | 1.4 | 1.8 | .. | .. | 6.6 | 4.2 | 6.1 | 4.1 |

a. Household final consumption expenditure includes statistical discrepancy. b. Covers mainland Tanzania only.

# Growth of consumption and investment | 4.9

## About the data

Measures of growth in consumption and capital formation are subject to two kinds of inaccuracy. The first stems from the difficulty of measuring expenditures at current price levels, as described in *About the data* for table 4.8. The second arises in deflating current price data to measure volume growth, where results depend on the relevance and reliability of the price indexes and weights used. Measuring price changes is more difficult for investment goods than for consumption goods because of the one-time nature of many investments and because the rate of technological progress in capital goods makes capturing change in quality difficult. (An example is computers—prices have fallen as quality has improved.) Several countries estimate capital formation from the supply side, identifying capital goods entering an economy directly from detailed production and international trade statistics. This means that the price indexes used in deflating production and international trade, reflecting delivered or offered prices, will determine the deflator for capital formation expenditures on the demand side.

Growth rates of household final consumption expenditure, household final consumption expenditure per capita, general government final consumption expenditure, gross capital formation, and exports and imports of goods and services are estimated using constant price data. (Consumption, capital formation, and exports and imports of goods and services as shares of GDP are shown in table 4.8.)

To obtain government consumption in constant prices, countries may deflate current values by applying a wage (price) index or extrapolate from the change in government employment. Neither

technique captures improvements in productivity or changes in the quality of government services. Deflators for household consumption are usually calculated on the basis of the consumer price index. Many countries estimate household consumption as a residual that includes statistical discrepancies associated with the estimation of other expenditure items, including changes in inventories; thus these estimates lack detailed breakdowns of household consumption expenditures.

## Definitions

• **Household final consumption expenditure** is the market value of all goods and services, including durable products (such as cars and computers), purchased by households. It excludes purchases of dwellings but includes imputed rent for owner-occupied dwellings. It also includes government fees for permits and licenses. Expenditures of nonprofit institutions serving households are included, even when reported separately. Household consumption expenditure may include any statistical discrepancy in the use of resources relative to the supply of resources. • **Household final consumption expenditure per capita** is household final consumption expenditure divided by midyear population. • **General government final consumption expenditure** is all government current expenditures for goods and services (including compensation of employees). It also includes most expenditures on national defense and security but excludes military expenditures with potentially wider public use that are part of government capital formation. • **Gross capital formation** is outlays on additions to fixed assets of the economy, net changes in inventories, and net acquisitions of valuables. Fixed assets include land improvements (fences, ditches, drains); plant, machinery, and equipment purchases; and construction (roads, railways, schools, buildings, and so on). Inventories are goods held to meet temporary or unexpected fluctuations in production or sales, and "work in progress." • **Exports** and **imports of goods and services** are the value of all goods and other market services provided to or received from the rest of the world. They include the value of merchandise, freight, insurance, transport, travel, royalties, license fees, and other services (communication, construction, financial, information, business, personal, government services, and so on). They exclude compensation of employees and investment income (factor services in the 1968 SNA) and transfer payments.

## Data sources

Data on national accounts indicators for most developing countries are collected from national statistical organizations and central banks by visiting and resident World Bank missions. Data for high-income economies come from Organisation for Economic Co-operation and Development (OECD) data files (see *Annual National Accounts for OECD Member Countries: Data from 1970 Onwards*). ✻

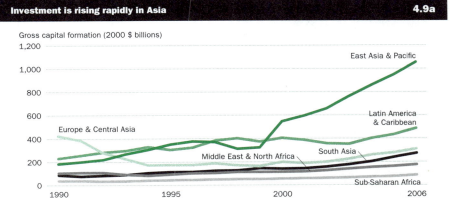

**Investment is rising rapidly in Asia** | 4.9a

Gross capital formation (2000 $ billions)

East Asia & Pacific

Latin America & Caribbean

Europe & Central Asia

Middle East & North Africa

South Asia

Sub-Saharan Africa

Between 1990 and 2006 investment increased nearly sixfold in East Asia and Pacific and threefold in South Asia.

*Source: World Development Indicators data files.*

# 4.10 Central government finances

| | Revenue[a] % of GDP | | Expense % of GDP | | Cash surplus or deficit % of GDP | | Net incurrence of liabilities % of GDP Domestic | | Foreign | | Debt and interest payments Total debt % of GDP | Interest % of revenue |
|---|---|---|---|---|---|---|---|---|---|---|---|---|
| | 1995 | 2006 | 1995 | 2006 | 1995 | 2006 | 1995 | 2006 | 1995 | 2006 | 2006 | 2006 |
| Afghanistan[b] | .. | 7.4 | .. | 17.1 | .. | −1.7 | .. | 0.3 | .. | 2.1 | 9.3 | 0.2 |
| Albania[b] | 21.2 | 23.6 | 25.6 | 21.9 | −8.9 | −3.0 | 7.4 | 1.9 | 2.1 | 1.0 | .. | 15.5 |
| Algeria[b] | 30.2 | 43.1 | 24.2 | 17.5 | −1.3 | 13.8 | −7.4 | 3.3 | 8.6 | −2.0 | .. | 1.9 |
| Angola | .. | .. | .. | .. | .. | .. | .. | .. | .. | .. | .. | .. |
| Argentina | .. | 18.1 | .. | 18.3 | .. | −0.5 | .. | 0.5 | .. | 1.5 | .. | 26.5 |
| Armenia[b] | .. | 18.8 | .. | 16.2 | .. | −0.3 | .. | 0.3 | .. | 1.0 | .. | 1.8 |
| Australia | .. | 26.0 | .. | 24.2 | .. | 1.7 | .. | .. | .. | .. | 20.5 | 3.6 |
| Austria | 38.4 | 39.8 | 44.2 | 42.0 | −5.4 | −1.6 | .. | .. | .. | .. | 63.4 | 6.9 |
| Azerbaijan[b] | 18.0 | .. | 19.8 | .. | −3.1 | .. | .. | .. | .. | .. | .. | .. |
| Bangladesh[b] | .. | 10.0 | .. | 8.8 | .. | −0.7 | .. | 2.3 | .. | 0.9 | 36.2 | 16.4 |
| Belarus[b] | 30.0 | 36.0 | 28.7 | 30.4 | −2.7 | 1.4 | 2.2 | 1.2 | 0.4 | 0.0 | .. | 0.9 |
| Belgium | 41.5 | 41.2 | 45.6 | 41.4 | −3.8 | 0.3 | .. | .. | .. | .. | 84.8 | 9.2 |
| Benin[b] | .. | 16.7 | .. | 13.4 | .. | 0.2 | .. | −2.6 | .. | 2.4 | .. | 1.3 |
| Bolivia | .. | 23.8 | .. | 24.6 | .. | 12.5 | .. | 0.7 | .. | −11.2 | .. | 7.9 |
| Bosnia and Herzegovina | .. | 39.8 | .. | 35.7 | .. | 2.9 | .. | −0.5 | .. | 0.1 | .. | 1.4 |
| Botswana[b] | 40.5 | .. | 30.4 | .. | 4.9 | .. | 0.2 | .. | −0.4 | .. | .. | .. |
| Brazil[b] | 26.9 | .. | 32.9 | .. | −2.7 | .. | .. | .. | .. | .. | .. | .. |
| Bulgaria[b] | 35.5 | 36.8 | 39.4 | 31.9 | −5.1 | 3.4 | 7.4 | −0.9 | −0.8 | −1.2 | .. | 3.4 |
| Burkina Faso | .. | 12.1 | .. | 12.0 | .. | −5.7 | .. | 0.1 | .. | 4.0 | .. | 3.1 |
| Burundi[b] | 19.3 | .. | 23.6 | .. | −4.7 | .. | 3.1 | .. | 4.0 | .. | .. | .. |
| Cambodia | .. | 9.8 | .. | 8.6 | .. | −1.7 | .. | −0.3 | .. | 2.1 | .. | 1.5 |
| Cameroon[b] | 11.8 | .. | 10.6 | .. | 0.2 | .. | −0.3 | .. | 0.3 | .. | .. | .. |
| Canada[b] | 20.3 | 19.5 | 24.2 | 17.9 | −4.3 | 1.5 | 4.9 | 0.1 | 0.0 | 0.3 | 48.6 | 6.9 |
| Central African Republic[b] | .. | 8.1 | .. | 9.4 | .. | −0.5 | .. | 1.2 | .. | 0.1 | .. | 8.0 |
| Chad | .. | .. | .. | .. | .. | .. | .. | .. | .. | .. | .. | .. |
| Chile | .. | 25.9 | .. | 17.1 | .. | 7.7 | .. | −1.9 | .. | −0.1 | .. | 2.7 |
| China[b] | 5.4 | 9.6 | .. | 10.8 | .. | −1.6 | 1.6 | 1.7 | .. | 0.0 | .. | 4.4 |
| Hong Kong, China | .. | .. | .. | .. | .. | .. | .. | .. | .. | .. | .. | .. |
| Colombia | .. | 26.0 | .. | 28.7 | .. | −3.9 | .. | 9.7 | .. | 1.5 | 68.0 | 35.5 |
| Congo, Dem. Rep.[b] | 5.3 | .. | 8.2 | .. | 0.0 | .. | 0.0 | .. | 0.2 | .. | .. | .. |
| Congo, Rep. | .. | 30.9 | .. | 19.9 | .. | 6.4 | .. | .. | .. | .. | 0.2 | 18.1 |
| Costa Rica[b] | .. | 24.1 | .. | 22.1 | .. | 1.2 | .. | .. | −0.8 | .. | .. | 15.9 |
| Côte d'Ivoire[b] | 20.1 | 17.4 | .. | 19.0 | .. | −1.4 | −1.2 | −0.1 | 3.8 | 1.2 | 107.9 | 8.2 |
| Croatia[b] | 43.1 | 40.0 | 42.5 | 39.4 | −1.3 | −1.8 | −2.7 | 2.1 | 0.8 | −1.4 | .. | 5.4 |
| Cuba | .. | .. | .. | .. | .. | .. | .. | .. | .. | .. | .. | .. |
| Czech Republic[b] | 33.2 | 30.6 | 32.6 | 35.5 | −0.9 | −4.3 | −0.5 | 2.4 | −0.4 | 1.0 | 24.6 | 3.1 |
| Denmark | 39.1 | 36.0 | 38.2 | 32.2 | 1.5 | 5.1 | .. | .. | .. | .. | 29.0 | 5.5 |
| Dominican Republic[b] | .. | 17.9 | .. | 16.5 | .. | −1.2 | .. | −1.0 | .. | 2.5 | .. | 8.5 |
| Ecuador[b] | 30.9 | .. | 26.3 | .. | 0.1 | .. | .. | .. | .. | .. | .. | .. |
| Egypt, Arab Rep.[b] | 25.9 | 24.1 | 23.8 | 26.8 | −1.1 | −5.8 | .. | .. | .. | .. | .. | .. |
| El Salvador | .. | 17.2 | .. | 19.3 | .. | −3.2 | .. | 1.5 | .. | 2.5 | 43.3 | 15.3 |
| Eritrea | .. | .. | .. | .. | .. | .. | .. | .. | .. | .. | .. | .. |
| Estonia | .. | 31.8 | .. | 26.6 | .. | 3.6 | .. | .. | .. | .. | 7.0 | 0.3 |
| Ethiopia[b] | .. | .. | .. | .. | .. | .. | .. | .. | .. | .. | .. | .. |
| Finland | 39.9 | 38.3 | 38.6 | 35.2 | 1.9 | 3.9 | 0.3 | −1.0 | −1.3 | 2.3 | 39.7 | 3.6 |
| France | 43.3 | 43.0 | 47.6 | 45.6 | −4.1 | −2.3 | .. | .. | .. | .. | 67.4 | 5.6 |
| Gabon | .. | .. | .. | .. | .. | .. | .. | .. | .. | .. | .. | .. |
| Gambia, The[b] | 23.7 | .. | .. | .. | .. | .. | .. | .. | .. | .. | .. | .. |
| Georgia[b] | 12.2 | 22.5 | 15.4 | 20.3 | −4.3 | 1.6 | 2.2 | −0.2 | 2.4 | −0.4 | 28.0 | 3.1 |
| Germany | 29.9 | 28.9 | 38.6 | 30.6 | −8.3 | −1.4 | .. | 1.6 | .. | −0.1 | 43.5 | 5.9 |
| Ghana[b] | 17.0 | 23.8 | .. | 20.9 | .. | −2.9 | .. | .. | .. | 3.3 | .. | 14.4 |
| Greece | 30.6 | 33.6 | 37.1 | 35.8 | −8.0 | −4.5 | .. | .. | .. | .. | 102.1 | 11.4 |
| Guatemala[b] | 8.4 | 10.7 | 7.6 | 11.6 | −0.5 | −1.7 | .. | 1.6 | 0.4 | 1.0 | 19.0 | 10.7 |
| Guinea[b] | 11.2 | .. | 12.1 | .. | −4.3 | .. | −0.1 | .. | 4.5 | .. | .. | .. |
| Guinea-Bissau | .. | .. | .. | .. | .. | .. | .. | .. | .. | .. | .. | .. |
| Haiti | .. | .. | .. | .. | .. | .. | .. | .. | .. | .. | .. | .. |

| | Revenue[a] (% of GDP) | | Expense (% of GDP) | | Cash surplus or deficit (% of GDP) | | Net incurrence of liabilities (% of GDP) | | | | Debt and interest payments | |
|---|---|---|---|---|---|---|---|---|---|---|---|---|
| | | | | | | | Domestic | | Foreign | | Total debt % of GDP | Interest % of revenue |
| | 1995 | 2006 | 1995 | 2006 | 1995 | 2006 | 1995 | 2006 | 1995 | 2006 | 2006 | 2006 |
| Honduras | .. | 19.4 | .. | 20.8 | .. | −1.3 | .. | 1.4 | .. | 1.0 | .. | 4.7 |
| Hungary | 42.6 | 35.8 | 49.6 | 44.1 | −4.7 | −8.6 | 3.9 | 2.0 | −0.7 | 4.4 | 70.2 | 10.7 |
| India[b] | 12.3 | 12.7 | 14.4 | 15.1 | −2.2 | −2.8 | 5.1 | 3.2 | 0.0 | 0.2 | 60.0 | 25.8 |
| Indonesia[b] | 17.7 | 18.4 | 9.7 | 16.9 | 3.0 | −1.1 | −0.6 | 0.0 | −0.4 | −0.4 | 28.8 | 14.8 |
| Iran, Islamic Rep.[b] | 24.2 | 36.2 | 15.8 | 24.8 | 1.1 | 3.3 | .. | 1.4 | 0.1 | 0.0 | .. | 0.8 |
| Iraq | .. | .. | .. | .. | .. | .. | .. | .. | .. | .. | .. | .. |
| Ireland | 33.6 | 34.2 | 37.5 | 30.9 | −2.2 | 2.7 | .. | .. | .. | .. | 28.2 | 2.9 |
| Israel | .. | 39.9 | .. | 44.0 | .. | −1.6 | .. | .. | .. | .. | .. | 10.7 |
| Italy | 40.4 | 37.2 | 48.0 | 40.8 | −7.5 | −3.3 | .. | .. | .. | .. | 109.8 | 11.9 |
| Jamaica[b] | .. | 39.2 | 33.3 | 38.7 | .. | 0.3 | .. | .. | .. | .. | 140.1 | 37.6 |
| Japan | 20.7 | .. | .. | .. | .. | .. | 1.5 | .. | .. | .. | .. | .. |
| Jordan[b] | 28.2 | 31.7 | 26.1 | 35.0 | 0.9 | −3.9 | −2.5 | 3.1 | 6.1 | −3.0 | 77.5 | 7.7 |
| Kazakhstan[b] | 14.0 | 16.8 | 18.7 | 14.6 | −1.8 | 1.6 | 0.8 | −0.5 | 2.8 | 0.0 | 7.1 | 1.5 |
| Kenya[b] | 21.6 | 19.8 | 25.9 | 17.8 | −5.1 | 1.5 | 3.9 | −0.5 | −1.3 | −3.8 | .. | 8.9 |
| Korea, Dem. Rep. | .. | .. | .. | .. | .. | .. | .. | .. | .. | .. | .. | .. |
| Korea, Rep.[b] | 17.8 | 23.3 | 14.3 | 21.3 | 2.4 | 0.7 | −0.3 | −0.1 | −0.1 | −0.3 | .. | 5.4 |
| Kuwait | 36.8 | 37.2 | 46.4 | 26.2 | −13.6 | 8.2 | .. | .. | .. | .. | .. | 0.1 |
| Kyrgyz Republic[b] | .. | 18.5 | .. | 17.5 | .. | −0.6 | .. | .. | .. | .. | .. | 4.4 |
| Lao PDR | .. | .. | .. | .. | .. | .. | .. | .. | .. | .. | .. | .. |
| Latvia[b] | 25.8 | 27.0 | 28.3 | 28.7 | −2.7 | −0.5 | 2.4 | 0.6 | 1.5 | 0.4 | .. | 1.6 |
| Lebanon | .. | 21.6 | .. | 26.5 | .. | −8.5 | .. | −1.3 | .. | 12.4 | .. | 56.0 |
| Lesotho[b] | 49.9 | 50.0 | 34.5 | 40.3 | 5.1 | 4.1 | 0.0 | .. | .. | 6.3 | .. | 4.8 |
| Liberia | .. | .. | .. | .. | .. | .. | .. | .. | .. | .. | .. | .. |
| Libya | .. | .. | .. | .. | .. | .. | .. | .. | .. | .. | .. | .. |
| Lithuania | .. | 29.0 | .. | 28.2 | .. | −0.2 | .. | −3.3 | .. | 4.1 | 20.0 | 2.4 |
| Macedonia, FYR | .. | .. | .. | .. | .. | .. | .. | .. | .. | .. | .. | .. |
| Madagascar | .. | 11.7 | .. | 11.6 | .. | 9.9 | .. | 0.8 | .. | 3.0 | .. | 11.2 |
| Malawi | .. | .. | .. | .. | .. | .. | .. | .. | .. | .. | .. | .. |
| Malaysia[b] | 24.4 | 23.7 | 17.2 | 20.1 | 2.4 | −4.3 | .. | .. | −0.8 | .. | .. | 10.5 |
| Mali | .. | 16.7 | .. | 15.7 | .. | 32.1 | .. | −1.0 | .. | −34.0 | .. | 0.9 |
| Mauritania | .. | .. | .. | .. | .. | .. | .. | .. | .. | .. | .. | .. |
| Mauritius[b] | 21.6 | 21.5 | 19.9 | 22.2 | −1.3 | −3.0 | 3.1 | 4.7 | −0.6 | −0.6 | 43.2 | 12.0 |
| Mexico[b] | 15.3 | .. | 15.0 | .. | −0.6 | .. | .. | .. | .. | 5.5 | .. | .. |
| Moldova[b] | 28.4 | 33.8 | 38.4 | 32.4 | −6.3 | 0.2 | 3.0 | 0.0 | 2.7 | −0.5 | 29.6 | 2.8 |
| Mongolia | .. | 33.3 | .. | 27.1 | .. | −0.4 | .. | 9.9 | .. | −6.0 | 105.5 | 3.1 |
| Morocco[b] | .. | 25.1 | .. | 25.9 | .. | −1.8 | .. | 1.0 | .. | −0.5 | 43.7 | 12.6 |
| Mozambique | .. | .. | .. | .. | .. | .. | .. | .. | .. | .. | .. | .. |
| Myanmar | 6.4 | 8.0 | .. | 3.4 | .. | −1.8 | .. | 1.8 | .. | 0.0 | .. | .. |
| Namibia[b] | 31.7 | 28.1 | 35.7 | 31.1 | −5.0 | −6.8 | .. | −20.0 | .. | −0.1 | .. | 9.1 |
| Nepal[b] | 10.5 | 10.9 | .. | 14.7 | .. | −1.6 | 0.6 | 0.7 | 2.5 | 0.2 | 50.3 | 7.3 |
| Netherlands | 41.5 | 42.2 | 50.8 | 41.5 | −9.2 | 0.5 | .. | .. | .. | .. | 49.0 | 4.4 |
| New Zealand | .. | 39.6 | .. | 33.8 | .. | 4.7 | .. | −1.7 | .. | 2.8 | 45.9 | 3.9 |
| Nicaragua[b] | 12.8 | 18.8 | 14.2 | 19.2 | 0.6 | 0.1 | .. | .. | 3.4 | .. | .. | 7.9 |
| Niger | .. | .. | .. | .. | .. | .. | .. | .. | .. | .. | .. | .. |
| Nigeria | .. | .. | .. | .. | .. | .. | .. | .. | .. | .. | .. | .. |
| Norway | .. | 50.4 | .. | 32.1 | .. | 17.9 | .. | 0.5 | .. | 15.1 | 48.4 | 2.3 |
| Oman[b] | 27.8 | .. | 32.4 | .. | −8.9 | .. | −0.1 | .. | 0.0 | .. | .. | .. |
| Pakistan[b] | 17.2 | 13.5 | 19.1 | 15.3 | −5.3 | −4.2 | .. | .. | .. | .. | .. | 33.9 |
| Panama[b] | 26.1 | .. | 22.0 | .. | 1.5 | .. | .. | .. | .. | .. | .. | .. |
| Papua New Guinea[b] | 23.9 | .. | 25.8 | .. | −0.5 | .. | 1.5 | .. | −0.7 | .. | .. | .. |
| Paraguay[b] | .. | 21.3 | .. | 16.7 | .. | 1.2 | .. | 1.0 | .. | −0.3 | .. | 4.6 |
| Peru[b] | 17.4 | 17.6 | 17.4 | 17.3 | −1.3 | −0.8 | .. | 1.9 | 3.9 | −1.2 | .. | 10.6 |
| Philippines[b] | 17.7 | 16.2 | 15.9 | 17.5 | −0.8 | −1.3 | −0.5 | −0.1 | −0.7 | 2.0 | 77.7 | 33.1 |
| Poland | .. | 32.2 | .. | 36.2 | .. | −3.6 | .. | 2.9 | .. | 2.2 | 47.9 | 7.1 |
| Portugal | 35.3 | 38.6 | 37.8 | 42.3 | −3.0 | −3.9 | −3.5 | 0.3 | 4.1 | 6.3 | 72.2 | 6.9 |
| Puerto Rico | .. | .. | .. | .. | .. | .. | .. | .. | .. | .. | .. | .. |

| | Revenue[a] | | Expense | | Cash surplus or deficit | | Net incurrence of liabilities | | | | Debt and interest payments | |
|---|---|---|---|---|---|---|---|---|---|---|---|---|
| | % of GDP | | % of GDP | | % of GDP | | Domestic | | Foreign | | Total debt % of GDP | Interest % of revenue |
| | | | | | | | | % of GDP | | | | |
| | 1995 | 2006 | 1995 | 2006 | 1995 | 2006 | 1995 | 2006 | 1995 | 2006 | 2006 | 2006 |
| Romania | .. | 24.5 | .. | 24.0 | .. | –1.0 | .. | –1.0 | .. | 0.1 | .. | 4.1 |
| Russian Federation | 21.3 | 28.8 | 11.6 | 19.6 | 9.3 | 8.1 | .. | 0.5 | .. | –2.8 | .. | 2.2 |
| Rwanda[b] | 10.6 | .. | 15.0 | .. | –5.6 | .. | 2.9 | .. | .. | .. | .. | .. |
| Saudi Arabia | .. | .. | .. | .. | .. | .. | .. | .. | .. | .. | .. | .. |
| Senegal[b] | 15.2 | .. | .. | .. | .. | .. | .. | .. | .. | .. | .. | .. |
| Serbia[b] | .. | .. | .. | .. | .. | .. | .. | .. | .. | .. | .. | .. |
| Sierra Leone[b] | 9.4 | 12.3 | .. | 23.8 | .. | –2.5 | 0.3 | .. | .. | .. | .. | 21.0 |
| Singapore[b] | 26.7 | 19.9 | 12.4 | 13.8 | 19.8 | 7.0 | 10.3 | 6.1 | 0.0 | .. | 104.0 | 0.5 |
| Slovak Republic | .. | 30.5 | .. | 33.6 | .. | –3.4 | .. | 4.5 | .. | 0.4 | 42.4 | 5.2 |
| Slovenia[b] | 36.7 | 40.2 | 35.2 | 40.3 | –0.2 | –0.8 | –0.4 | 1.5 | 0.3 | –0.4 | .. | 3.7 |
| Somalia | .. | .. | .. | .. | .. | .. | .. | .. | .. | .. | .. | .. |
| South Africa | .. | 31.8 | .. | 30.4 | .. | 1.2 | .. | 0.2 | .. | 0.1 | .. | 9.5 |
| Spain | 32.0 | 27.2 | 37.1 | 25.2 | –5.8 | 1.9 | .. | .. | .. | .. | 39.8 | 4.8 |
| Sri Lanka[b] | 20.4 | 17.0 | 26.0 | 22.2 | –7.6 | –7.2 | 5.2 | 6.1 | 3.2 | 1.5 | 93.0 | 29.7 |
| Sudan[b] | 7.2 | .. | 6.8 | .. | –0.4 | .. | 0.3 | .. | .. | .. | .. | .. |
| Swaziland[b] | .. | 26.6 | .. | 24.4 | .. | –2.6 | .. | .. | .. | .. | .. | 4.5 |
| Sweden | 40.4 | 37.9 | 39.0 | 35.4 | 2.2 | 1.9 | .. | .. | .. | .. | 48.5 | 4.3 |
| Switzerland[b] | 22.7 | 18.6 | 25.8 | 19.5 | –0.6 | –0.4 | –0.5 | 0.3 | .. | .. | 28.6 | 4.3 |
| Syrian Arab Republic[b] | 22.9 | .. | .. | .. | .. | .. | .. | .. | .. | .. | .. | .. |
| Tajikistan[b] | 9.3 | 13.5 | 11.4 | 13.7 | –3.3 | –6.6 | 0.1 | .. | 2.3 | .. | .. | 5.1 |
| Tanzania | .. | .. | .. | .. | .. | .. | .. | .. | .. | .. | .. | .. |
| Thailand | .. | 20.2 | .. | 16.2 | .. | 1.9 | .. | 3.0 | .. | –0.6 | 26.2 | 7.1 |
| Timor-Leste | .. | .. | .. | .. | .. | .. | .. | .. | .. | .. | .. | .. |
| Togo[b] | .. | 17.7 | .. | 17.8 | .. | –0.1 | .. | .. | .. | .. | .. | .. |
| Trinidad and Tobago[b] | 27.2 | 32.5 | 25.3 | 24.0 | –0.1 | 6.1 | 2.8 | .. | 2.6 | .. | .. | 8.2 |
| Tunisia[b] | 30.0 | 30.1 | 28.4 | 29.4 | –2.5 | –2.8 | 0.9 | 0.9 | 2.9 | –2.3 | 55.1 | 9.3 |
| Turkey[b] | .. | 32.9 | .. | 29.1 | .. | 2.5 | .. | 2.2 | .. | –0.1 | 67.8 | 25.4 |
| Turkmenistan | .. | .. | .. | .. | .. | .. | .. | .. | .. | .. | .. | .. |
| Uganda[b] | 10.6 | 13.5 | .. | 17.4 | .. | –2.0 | .. | 1.7 | .. | 1.6 | .. | 7.8 |
| Ukraine[b] | .. | 36.6 | .. | 37.2 | .. | –1.0 | .. | –0.4 | .. | 0.9 | .. | 1.7 |
| United Arab Emirates[b] | 10.1 | .. | 9.3 | .. | 0.5 | .. | .. | .. | .. | .. | .. | .. |
| United Kingdom | 37.2 | 38.8 | 37.1 | 41.2 | 0.3 | –2.8 | –0.3 | 3.5 | 0.0 | 0.0 | 49.9 | 5.3 |
| United States | .. | 19.3 | .. | 21.3 | .. | –2.0 | .. | 1.4 | .. | 0.6 | 46.9 | 10.9 |
| Uruguay[b] | 27.6 | 27.7 | 27.1 | 27.2 | –1.2 | –0.9 | 7.9 | 0.5 | 1.1 | –1.9 | 70.0 | 15.4 |
| Uzbekistan | .. | .. | .. | .. | .. | .. | .. | .. | .. | .. | .. | .. |
| Venezuela, RB[b] | 16.9 | 28.4 | 18.5 | 25.2 | –2.3 | 2.2 | 1.1 | 1.2 | 0.1 | 3.3 | .. | 10.4 |
| Vietnam | .. | .. | .. | .. | .. | .. | .. | .. | .. | .. | .. | .. |
| West Bank and Gaza | .. | .. | .. | .. | .. | .. | .. | .. | .. | .. | .. | .. |
| Yemen, Rep.[b] | 17.3 | .. | 19.1 | .. | –3.9 | .. | .. | .. | .. | .. | .. | .. |
| Zambia[b] | 20.0 | 17.7 | 21.4 | 20.0 | –3.1 | –2.8 | 28.0 | .. | 16.2 | .. | .. | 13.7 |
| Zimbabwe[b] | 26.7 | .. | 32.1 | .. | –5.4 | .. | –1.4 | .. | 1.6 | .. | .. | .. |
| **World** | .. w | 27.0 w | .. w | 28.0 w | .. w | –1.2 w | .. m | .. m | .. m | .. m | .. m | 5.8 m |
| **Low income** | 13.3 | 12.9 | 15.4 | 15.2 | –2.6 | –2.6 | .. | .. | .. | .. | .. | .. |
| **Middle income** | 17.2 | .. | .. | .. | .. | .. | .. | 1.3 | .. | 0.1 | .. | 7.1 |
| Lower middle income | 11.5 | 16.0 | .. | 15.8 | .. | –0.9 | .. | 1.4 | .. | 0.3 | .. | 7.7 |
| Upper middle income | .. | .. | .. | .. | .. | .. | .. | 0.6 | .. | 0.0 | .. | 5.4 |
| **Low & middle income** | 16.5 | .. | .. | .. | .. | .. | .. | .. | .. | .. | .. | 9.4 |
| East Asia & Pacific | 8.4 | 11.0 | .. | 11.7 | .. | –1.3 | .. | 2.1 | .. | 0.0 | .. | 7.6 |
| Europe & Central Asia | .. | 31.5 | .. | 28.9 | .. | 1.8 | .. | 0.4 | .. | 0.0 | .. | 2.8 |
| Latin America & Carib. | 21.2 | .. | 23.4 | .. | –1.5 | .. | .. | 1.5 | .. | 1.2 | .. | 9.6 |
| Middle East & N. Africa | 26.1 | 31.8 | .. | 25.0 | .. | 1.0 | .. | .. | .. | .. | .. | .. |
| South Asia | 13.1 | 12.9 | 15.3 | 15.4 | –2.7 | –3.1 | 3.8 | 1.9 | 1.1 | 0.8 | 55.1 | 25.8 |
| Sub-Saharan Africa | .. | .. | .. | .. | .. | .. | .. | .. | .. | .. | .. | .. |
| **High income** | .. | 27.2 | .. | 28.6 | .. | –1.3 | .. | .. | .. | .. | 47.6 | 5.1 |
| Euro area | 34.7 | 35.5 | 42.2 | 37.1 | –7.4 | –1.3 | .. | .. | .. | .. | 63.4 | 5.7 |

a. Excludes grants. b. Data were reported on a cash basis and have been adjusted to the accrual framework.

## About the data

Tables 4.10–4.12 present an overview of the size and role of central governments relative to national economies. The tables are based on the concepts and recommendations of the International Monetary Fund's (IMF) *Government Finance Statistics Manual 2001,* 2nd edition. Before 2005 *World Development Indicators* reported data derived on the basis of the 1986 manual. The 2001 manual, harmonized with the 1993 System of National Accounts, recommends an accrual accounting method over the cash-based method of the 1986 manual. The new manual focuses on all economic events affecting assets, liabilities, revenues, and expenses, not only those represented by cash transactions. It takes all stocks into account, so that stock data at the end of an accounting period are equal to stock data at the beginning of the period plus flows during the period. The 1986 manual considered only the debt stock data. Further, the new manual does not distinguish between current and capital revenue or expenditures, unlike the 1986 manual. The new manual also introduces the concepts of nonfinancial and financial assets. Most countries still follow the 1986 manual, however. The IMF has reclassified historical *Government Finance Statistics Yearbook* data to conform to the format of the 2001 manual. Because of differences in reporting, the reclassified data understate both revenue and expense.

The 2001 manual describes the economic functions of a government as the provision of goods and services to the community on a nonmarket basis for collective or individual consumption, and the redistribution of income and wealth through transfer payments. Government activities are financed mainly by taxation and other income transfers, though other forms of financing such as borrowing for temporary periods can also be used. The definition of government excludes public corporations and quasi corporations (such as the central bank).

Units of government meeting this definition exist at many levels, from local administrative units to the national government, but inadequate statistical coverage precludes the presentation of subnational data. Although data for general government are available for a few countries under the 2001 manual, only data for the central government are shown to minimize disparities. Still, different accounting concepts of central government make cross-country comparisons potentially misleading.

*Central government* can refer to consolidated or budgetary accounting concepts. For most countries central government finance data have been consolidated into one account, but for others only budgetary central government accounts are available. Countries reporting budgetary data are noted in *Primary data documentation.* Because budgetary accounts do not necessarily include all central government units (such as extrabudgetary accounts and social security funds), the picture they provide is usually incomplete.

Data on government revenue and expense are collected by the IMF through questionnaires to member countries and by the Organisation for Economic Co-operation and Development. Despite IMF efforts to standardize the collection of public finance data, statistics are often incomplete, untimely, and not comparable across countries.

Government finance statistics are reported in local currency. The indicators here are shown as percentages of GDP. Many countries report government finance data by fiscal year; see *Primary data documentation* for information on fiscal year end by country.

- **Revenue** is cash receipts from taxes, social contributions, and other revenues such as fines, fees, rent, and income from property or sales. Grants, usually considered revenue, are excluded. • **Expense** is cash payments for government operating activities in providing goods and services. It includes compensation of employees, interest and subsidies, grants, social benefits, and other expenses such as rent and dividends. • **Cash surplus or deficit** is revenue (including grants) minus expense, minus net acquisition of nonfinancial assets. In editions before 2005 nonfinancial assets were included under revenue and expenditure in gross terms. This cash surplus or deficit is close to the earlier overall budget balance (still missing is lending minus repayments, which are brought in below as a financing item under net acquisition of financial assets). • **Net incurrence of liabilities** is domestic financing (obtained from residents) and foreign financing (obtained from nonresidents), or the means by which a government provides financial resources to cover a budget deficit or allocates financial resources arising from a budget surplus. The net incurrence of liabilities should be offset by the net acquisition of financial assets (a third financing item). The difference between the cash surplus or deficit and the three financing items is the net change in the stock of cash. • **Total debt** is the entire stock of direct government fixed-term contractual obligations to others outstanding on a particular date. It includes domestic and foreign liabilities such as currency and money deposits, securities other than shares, and loans. It is the gross amount of government liabilities reduced by the amount of equity and financial derivatives held by the government. Because debt is a stock rather than a flow, it is measured as of a given date, usually the last day of the fiscal year. • **Interest payments** are interest payments on government debt—including long-term bonds, long-term loans, and other debt instruments—to domestic and foreign residents.

### Data sources

Data on central government finances are from the IMF's *Government Finance Statistics Yearbook 2007* and data files. Each country's accounts are reported using the system of common definitions and classifications in the IMF's *Government Finance Statistics Manual 2001.* See these sources for complete and authoritative explanations of concepts, definitions, and data sources.

**Fifteen developing economies had a total debt to GDP ratio of 50 percent or higher**     **4.10a**

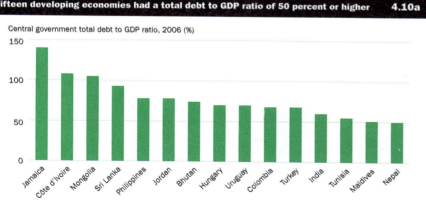

Central government total debt to GDP ratio, 2006 (%)

**Note:** Data are for the most recent year available for 2004–06.
*Source:* International Monetary Fund, *Government Finance Statistics* data files, and *World Development Indicators* data files.

| | Goods and services % of expense | | Compensation of employees % of expense | | Interest payments % of expense | | Subsidies and other transfers % of expense | | Other expense % of expense | |
|---|---|---|---|---|---|---|---|---|---|---|
| | 1995 | 2006 | 1995 | 2006 | 1995 | 2006 | 1995 | 2006 | 1995 | 2006 |
| Afghanistan[a] | .. | 57 | .. | 37 | .. | 0 | .. | 6 | .. | 0 |
| Albania[a] | 18 | 12 | 14 | 30 | 9 | 17 | 59 | 42 | 0 | 0 |
| Algeria[a] | 6 | 6 | 39 | 28 | 13 | 5 | 34 | 31 | 8 | 29 |
| Angola | .. | .. | .. | .. | .. | .. | .. | .. | .. | .. |
| Argentina | .. | 5 | .. | 12 | .. | 26 | .. | 50 | .. | 7 |
| Armenia[a] | .. | 37 | .. | 23 | .. | 2 | .. | 33 | .. | 5 |
| Australia | .. | 10 | .. | 10 | .. | 4 | .. | 70 | .. | 6 |
| Austria | 5 | 5 | 13 | 12 | 8 | 7 | 65 | 65 | 11 | 12 |
| Azerbaijan[a] | 49 | .. | 10 | .. | 0 | .. | 41 | .. | 0 | .. |
| Bangladesh[a] | .. | 17 | .. | 25 | .. | 20 | .. | 29 | .. | 9 |
| Belarus[a] | 39 | 12 | 5 | 12 | 1 | 1 | 55 | 69 | 0 | 5 |
| Belgium | 3 | 2 | 7 | 7 | 18 | 9 | 71 | 79 | 3 | 3 |
| Benin[a] | .. | 31 | .. | 40 | .. | 2 | .. | 8 | .. | 20 |
| Bolivia | .. | 14 | .. | 21 | .. | 13 | .. | 47 | .. | 5 |
| Bosnia and Herzegovina | .. | 25 | .. | 29 | .. | 2 | .. | 41 | .. | 4 |
| Botswana[a] | 32 | .. | 30 | .. | 2 | .. | 36 | .. | 2 | .. |
| Brazil[a] | 5 | .. | 8 | .. | 45 | .. | 45 | .. | 1 | .. |
| Bulgaria[a] | 18 | 14 | 7 | 18 | 37 | 4 | 38 | 61 | 2 | 3 |
| Burkina Faso | .. | 21 | .. | 39 | .. | 4 | .. | 35 | .. | 0 |
| Burundi[a] | 20 | .. | 30 | .. | 6 | .. | 14 | .. | 10 | .. |
| Cambodia | .. | 41 | .. | 33 | .. | 2 | .. | 19 | .. | 5 |
| Cameroon[a] | 17 | .. | 40 | .. | 26 | .. | 14 | .. | .. | .. |
| Canada[a] | 8 | 8 | 10 | 12 | 18 | 8 | 64 | 67 | .. | 6 |
| Central African Republic[a] | .. | 27 | .. | 53 | .. | 9 | .. | .. | .. | 11 |
| Chad | .. | .. | .. | .. | .. | .. | .. | .. | .. | .. |
| Chile | .. | 11 | .. | 21 | .. | 4 | .. | 57 | .. | 11 |
| China[a] | .. | 28 | .. | 1 | .. | 4 | .. | 62 | .. | 5 |
| Hong Kong, China | .. | .. | .. | .. | .. | .. | .. | .. | .. | .. |
| Colombia | .. | 5 | .. | 19 | .. | 32 | .. | 41 | .. | 3 |
| Congo, Dem. Rep.[a] | 37 | .. | 58 | .. | 1 | .. | 2 | .. | .. | .. |
| Congo, Rep. | .. | 29 | .. | 37 | .. | 29 | .. | 5 | .. | 0 |
| Costa Rica[a] | .. | 11 | .. | 42 | .. | 17 | .. | 16 | .. | 14 |
| Côte d'Ivoire[a] | .. | 22 | .. | 34 | .. | 8 | .. | 16 | .. | 20 |
| Croatia[a] | 35 | 9 | 27 | 26 | 3 | 5 | 32 | 53 | 3 | 6 |
| Cuba | .. | .. | .. | .. | .. | .. | .. | .. | .. | .. |
| Czech Republic[a] | 7 | 6 | 9 | 8 | 3 | 3 | 75 | 69 | 5 | 13 |
| Denmark | 8 | 10 | 13 | 14 | 13 | 6 | 64 | 68 | 4 | 4 |
| Dominican Republic[a] | .. | 16 | .. | 25 | .. | 9 | .. | 42 | .. | 7 |
| Ecuador[a] | 6 | .. | 49 | .. | 26 | .. | .. | .. | .. | .. |
| Egypt, Arab Rep.[a] | 21 | 9 | 26 | 28 | 31 | .. | 7 | 33 | .. | 12 |
| El Salvador | .. | 16 | .. | 37 | .. | 14 | .. | 25 | .. | 10 |
| Eritrea | .. | .. | .. | .. | .. | .. | .. | .. | .. | .. |
| Estonia | .. | 15 | .. | 21 | .. | 0 | .. | 46 | .. | 4 |
| Ethiopia[a] | .. | .. | .. | .. | .. | .. | .. | .. | .. | .. |
| Finland | 10 | 10 | 10 | 10 | 9 | 4 | 68 | 71 | 7 | 7 |
| France | 8 | 6 | 23 | 22 | 6 | 5 | 59 | 53 | 6 | 2 |
| Gabon | .. | .. | .. | .. | .. | .. | .. | .. | .. | .. |
| Gambia, The[a] | .. | .. | .. | .. | .. | .. | .. | .. | .. | .. |
| Georgia[a] | 52 | 24 | 11 | 16 | 10 | 4 | 26 | 49 | .. | 7 |
| Germany | 4 | 5 | 5 | 5 | 6 | 6 | 67 | 82 | 20 | 3 |
| Ghana[a] | .. | .. | .. | 45 | .. | 21 | .. | 5 | .. | .. |
| Greece | 10 | 10 | 22 | 25 | 27 | 11 | 36 | 43 | 5 | 3 |
| Guatemala[a] | 15 | 13 | 50 | 24 | 12 | 10 | 18 | 25 | 6 | 27 |
| Guinea[a] | 17 | .. | 34 | .. | 28 | .. | 9 | .. | 1 | .. |
| Guinea-Bissau | .. | .. | .. | .. | .. | .. | .. | .. | .. | .. |
| Haiti | .. | .. | .. | .. | .. | .. | .. | .. | .. | .. |

# Central government expenses

| | Goods and services | | Compensation of employees | | Interest payments | | Subsidies and other transfers | | Other expense | |
|---|---|---|---|---|---|---|---|---|---|---|
| | % of expense | | % of expense | | % of expense | | % of expense | | % of expense | |
| | 1995 | 2006 | 1995 | 2006 | 1995 | 2006 | 1995 | 2006 | 1995 | 2006 |
| Honduras | .. | 15 | .. | 46 | .. | 5 | .. | 22 | .. | 12 |
| Hungary | 8 | 9 | 10 | 13 | 20 | 9 | 57 | 62 | 13 | 10 |
| India[a] | 14 | 13 | 10 | 8 | 27 | 22 | 33 | 34 | 0 | 0 |
| Indonesia[a] | 21 | 8 | 20 | 13 | 16 | 16 | 41 | 63 | 2 | 0 |
| Iran, Islamic Rep.[a] | 21 | 11 | 56 | 40 | 0 | 1 | .. | 29 | .. | 19 |
| Iraq | .. | .. | .. | .. | .. | .. | .. | .. | .. | .. |
| Ireland | 5 | 12 | 15 | 26 | 14 | 3 | 33 | 36 | 1 | 1 |
| Israel | .. | 27 | .. | 24 | .. | 10 | .. | 32 | .. | 9 |
| Italy | 4 | 4 | 14 | 15 | 24 | 11 | 54 | 61 | 6 | 10 |
| Jamaica[a] | 22 | 19 | 24 | 32 | 32 | 38 | 1 | 3 | 21 | 8 |
| Japan | .. | .. | .. | .. | .. | .. | .. | .. | .. | .. |
| Jordan[a] | 7 | 7 | 67 | 40 | 11 | 8 | 12 | 31 | 4 | 16 |
| Kazakhstan[a] | .. | 20 | .. | 8 | 3 | 2 | 58 | 54 | .. | 15 |
| Kenya[a] | 15 | 23 | 28 | 60 | 46 | 10 | .. | 5 | 2 | 2 |
| Korea, Dem. Rep. | .. | .. | .. | .. | .. | .. | .. | .. | .. | .. |
| Korea, Rep.[a] | 16 | 10 | 15 | 11 | 3 | 6 | 63 | 52 | 3 | 21 |
| Kuwait | 33 | 21 | 31 | 32 | 5 | 0 | 24 | 26 | 7 | 21 |
| Kyrgyz Republic[a] | .. | 26 | .. | 26 | .. | 5 | .. | 35 | .. | 8 |
| Lao PDR | .. | .. | .. | .. | .. | .. | .. | .. | .. | .. |
| Latvia[a] | 20 | 13 | 20 | 16 | 3 | 2 | 56 | 40 | 0 | 30 |
| Lebanon | .. | 3 | .. | 33 | .. | 46 | .. | 16 | .. | 2 |
| Lesotho[a] | 32 | 28 | 45 | 37 | 5 | 6 | 8 | 29 | 3 | .. |
| Liberia | .. | .. | .. | .. | .. | .. | .. | .. | .. | .. |
| Libya | .. | .. | .. | .. | .. | .. | .. | .. | .. | .. |
| Lithuania | .. | 14 | .. | 20 | .. | 3 | .. | 60 | .. | 6 |
| Macedonia, FYR | .. | .. | .. | .. | .. | .. | .. | .. | .. | .. |
| Madagascar | .. | 14 | .. | 43 | .. | 21 | .. | 14 | .. | 8 |
| Malawi | .. | .. | .. | .. | .. | .. | .. | .. | .. | .. |
| Malaysia[a] | 23 | 26 | 34 | 30 | 17 | 12 | 27 | 31 | 1 | 1 |
| Mali | .. | 32 | .. | 33 | .. | 3 | .. | 19 | .. | 13 |
| Mauritania | .. | .. | .. | .. | .. | .. | .. | .. | .. | .. |
| Mauritius[a] | 12 | 13 | 45 | 36 | 12 | 12 | 28 | 35 | 2 | 4 |
| Mexico[a] | 9 | .. | 19 | .. | 19 | .. | .. | .. | .. | .. |
| Moldova[a] | 10 | 19 | 8 | 16 | 11 | 3 | 71 | 57 | 1 | 6 |
| Mongolia | .. | 36 | .. | 30 | .. | 4 | .. | 31 | .. | 0 |
| Morocco[a] | .. | 12 | .. | 43 | .. | 12 | .. | 27 | .. | 6 |
| Mozambique | .. | .. | .. | .. | .. | .. | .. | .. | .. | .. |
| Myanmar | .. | .. | .. | .. | .. | .. | .. | .. | .. | .. |
| Namibia[a] | 28 | 28 | 53 | 49 | 1 | 8 | .. | 14 | 4 | 2 |
| Nepal[a] | .. | .. | .. | .. | .. | 6 | .. | .. | .. | .. |
| Netherlands | 5 | 7 | 8 | 8 | 9 | 5 | 77 | 80 | 3 | 3 |
| New Zealand | .. | 30 | .. | 25 | .. | 5 | .. | 37 | .. | 6 |
| Nicaragua[a] | 14 | 15 | 25 | 34 | 17 | 9 | 29 | 35 | 14 | 7 |
| Niger | .. | .. | .. | .. | .. | .. | .. | .. | .. | .. |
| Nigeria | .. | .. | .. | .. | .. | .. | .. | .. | .. | .. |
| Norway | .. | 11 | .. | 16 | .. | 4 | .. | 67 | .. | 5 |
| Oman[a] | 55 | .. | 30 | .. | 7 | .. | 8 | .. | 0 | .. |
| Pakistan[a] | .. | 37 | .. | 4 | 28 | 31 | 2 | 28 | .. | .. |
| Panama[a] | 16 | .. | 45 | .. | 8 | .. | 30 | .. | 1 | .. |
| Papua New Guinea[a] | 19 | .. | 36 | .. | 20 | .. | 26 | .. | 1 | .. |
| Paraguay[a] | .. | 12 | .. | 53 | .. | 6 | .. | 24 | .. | 5 |
| Peru[a] | 20 | 20 | 19 | 20 | 19 | 11 | 33 | 45 | 8 | 4 |
| Philippines[a] | 15 | 19 | 34 | 31 | 33 | 31 | 15 | 18 | .. | 2 |
| Poland | .. | 7 | .. | 12 | .. | 7 | .. | 70 | .. | 7 |
| Portugal | 7 | 6 | 30 | 28 | 10 | 6 | 43 | 48 | 11 | 2 |
| Puerto Rico | .. | .. | .. | .. | .. | .. | .. | .. | .. | .. |

| | Goods and services | | Compensation of employees | | Interest payments | | Subsidies and other transfers | | Other expense | |
|---|---|---|---|---|---|---|---|---|---|---|
| | % of expense | | % of expense | | % of expense | | % of expense | | % of expense | |
| | 1995 | 2006 | 1995 | 2006 | 1995 | 2006 | 1995 | 2006 | 1995 | 2006 |
| Romania | .. | 21 | .. | 19 | .. | 4 | .. | 44 | .. | 12 |
| Russian Federation | 27 | 19 | .. | 20 | .. | 3 | .. | 55 | .. | 3 |
| Rwanda[a] | 52 | .. | 36 | .. | 12 | .. | 5 | .. | .. | .. |
| Saudi Arabia | .. | .. | .. | .. | .. | .. | .. | .. | .. | .. |
| Senegal[a] | .. | .. | .. | .. | .. | .. | .. | .. | .. | .. |
| Serbia | .. | .. | .. | .. | .. | .. | .. | .. | .. | .. |
| Sierra Leone[a] | .. | 28 | .. | 26 | .. | 19 | .. | 9 | .. | 18 |
| Singapore[a] | 38 | 40 | 39 | 34 | 8 | 1 | 15 | 26 | .. | .. |
| Slovak Republic | .. | 11 | .. | 14 | .. | 5 | .. | 63 | .. | 7 |
| Slovenia[a] | 19 | 12 | 21 | 19 | 3 | 4 | 55 | 62 | 3 | 3 |
| Somalia | .. | .. | .. | .. | .. | .. | .. | .. | .. | .. |
| South Africa | .. | 11 | .. | 14 | .. | 10 | .. | 58 | .. | 8 |
| Spain | 5 | 5 | 14 | 9 | 11 | 5 | 42 | 75 | 2 | 8 |
| Sri Lanka[a] | 23 | 13 | 20 | 28 | 22 | 24 | 24 | 26 | 10 | 9 |
| Sudan[a] | 44 | .. | 38 | .. | 8 | .. | 10 | .. | .. | .. |
| Swaziland[a] | .. | 29 | .. | 42 | .. | 5 | .. | 21 | .. | 2 |
| Sweden | 11 | 11 | 9 | 10 | 13 | 5 | 64 | 52 | 5 | 3 |
| Switzerland[a] | 24 | 8 | 6 | 7 | 4 | 4 | 66 | 75 | 0 | 5 |
| Syrian Arab Republic[a] | .. | .. | .. | .. | .. | .. | .. | .. | .. | .. |
| Tajikistan[a] | 47 | 29 | 8 | 9 | 12 | 5 | 33 | 27 | .. | 30 |
| Tanzania | .. | .. | .. | .. | .. | .. | .. | .. | .. | .. |
| Thailand | .. | 21 | .. | 40 | .. | 9 | .. | 29 | .. | 4 |
| Timor-Leste | .. | .. | .. | .. | .. | .. | .. | .. | .. | .. |
| Togo[a] | .. | .. | .. | .. | .. | .. | .. | .. | .. | .. |
| Trinidad and Tobago[a] | 20 | 19 | 36 | 31 | 20 | 11 | 24 | 37 | 1 | 1 |
| Tunisia[a] | 7 | 6 | 37 | 39 | 13 | 10 | 36 | 36 | 7 | 9 |
| Turkey[a] | .. | 9 | .. | 22 | .. | 29 | .. | 40 | .. | 1 |
| Turkmenistan | .. | .. | .. | .. | .. | .. | .. | .. | .. | .. |
| Uganda[a] | .. | 30 | .. | 12 | .. | 8 | .. | 49 | .. | 0 |
| Ukraine[a] | .. | 12 | .. | 13 | .. | 2 | .. | 69 | .. | 4 |
| United Arab Emirates[a] | 50 | .. | 37 | .. | .. | .. | .. | .. | .. | .. |
| United Kingdom | 22 | 18 | 7 | 15 | 9 | 5 | 54 | 30 | 9 | 1 |
| United States | .. | 15 | .. | 13 | .. | 10 | .. | 61 | .. | 2 |
| Uruguay[a] | 13 | 15 | 17 | 22 | 6 | 16 | 64 | 46 | 0 | .. |
| Uzbekistan | .. | .. | .. | .. | .. | .. | .. | .. | .. | .. |
| Venezuela, RB[a] | 6 | 6 | 22 | 16 | 27 | 12 | 61 | 64 | 2 | 3 |
| Vietnam | .. | .. | .. | .. | .. | .. | .. | .. | .. | .. |
| West Bank and Gaza | .. | .. | .. | .. | .. | .. | .. | .. | .. | .. |
| Yemen, Rep.[a] | 8 | .. | 67 | .. | 16 | .. | 8 | .. | 0 | .. |
| Zambia[a] | 32 | 28 | 35 | 37 | 16 | 15 | 19 | 15 | 0 | 5 |
| Zimbabwe[a] | 16 | .. | 34 | .. | 31 | .. | 19 | .. | .. | .. |
| **World** | .. m | 13 m | .. m | 21 m | .. m | 6 m | .. m | 45 m | .. m | 5 m |
| **Low income** | .. | .. | .. | .. | .. | .. | .. | .. | .. | .. |
| **Middle income** | .. | 13 | .. | 24 | .. | 7 | .. | 40 | .. | 7 |
| Lower middle income | .. | 14 | .. | 28 | .. | 9 | .. | 32 | .. | 7 |
| Upper middle income | .. | 11 | .. | 20 | .. | 5 | .. | 55 | .. | 7 |
| **Low & middle income** | .. | 16 | .. | 26 | .. | 10 | .. | 34 | .. | .. |
| East Asia & Pacific | .. | 27 | .. | 31 | .. | 7 | .. | 31 | .. | 0 |
| Europe & Central Asia | .. | 14 | .. | 16 | .. | 3 | .. | 55 | .. | 6 |
| Latin America & Carib. | .. | 14 | .. | 29 | .. | 11 | .. | 30 | .. | 8 |
| Middle East & N. Africa | 8 | 8 | 39 | 40 | 13 | .. | .. | 25 | .. | 11 |
| South Asia | .. | 25 | .. | 18 | 27 | 22 | 24 | 27 | .. | 0 |
| Sub-Saharan Africa | .. | .. | .. | .. | .. | .. | .. | .. | .. | .. |
| **High income** | 7 | 10 | 15 | 14 | 8 | 5 | 59 | 62 | 5 | 4 |
| Euro area | 5 | 6 | 14 | 12 | 11 | 5 | 55 | 65 | 3 | 3 |

**Note:** Components may not sum to 100 percent because of rounding or missing data.
a. Data were reported on a cash basis and have been adjusted to the accrual framework.

## About the data

The term *expense* has replaced *expenditure* in the table since the 2005 edition of *World Development Indicators* in accordance with use in the International Monetary Fund's (IMF) *Government Finance Statistics Manual 2001*. Government expenses include all nonrepayable payments, whether current or capital, requited or unrequited. Total central government expense as presented in the IMF's *Government Finance Statistics Yearbook* is comparable to the concept used in the 1993 System of National Accounts.

Expenses can be measured either by function (health, defense, education) or by economic type (interest payments, wages and salaries, purchases of goods and services). Functional data are often incomplete, and coverage varies by country because functional responsibilities stretch across levels of government for which no data are available. Defense expenses, usually the central government's responsibility, are shown in table 5.7. For more information on education expenses, see table 2.10; for more on health expenses, see table 2.15.

The classification of expenses by economic type in the table shows whether the government produces goods and services and distributes them, purchases the goods and services from a third party and distributes them, or transfers cash to households to make the purchases directly. When the government produces and provides goods and services, the cost is reflected in compensation of employees, use of goods and services, and consumption of fixed capital. Purchases from a third party and cash transfers to households are shown as subsidies and other transfers, and other expenses. The economic classification can be problematic. For example, the distinction between current and capital expense may be arbitrary, and subsidies to public corporations or banks may be disguised as capital financing. Subsidies may also be hidden in special contractual pricing for goods and services. For further discussion of government finance statistics, see *About the data* for tables 4.10 and 4.12.

## Definitions

• **Goods and services** are all government payments in exchange for goods and services used for the production of market and nonmarket goods and services. Own-account capital formation is excluded. • **Compensation of employees** is all payments in cash, as well as in kind (such as food and housing), to employees in return for services rendered, and government contributions to social insurance schemes such as social security and pensions that provide benefits to employees. • **Interest payments** are payments made to nonresidents, to residents, and to other general government units for the use of borrowed money. (Repayment of principal is shown as a financing item, and commission charges are shown as purchases of services.) • **Subsidies and other transfers** include all unrequited, nonrepayable transfers on current account to private and public enterprises; grants to foreign governments, international organizations, and other government units; and social security, social assistance benefits, and employer social benefits in cash and in kind. • **Other expense** is spending on dividends, rent, and other miscellaneous expenses, including provision for consumption of fixed capital.

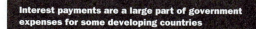

**Interest payments are a large part of government expenses for some developing countries**

4.11a

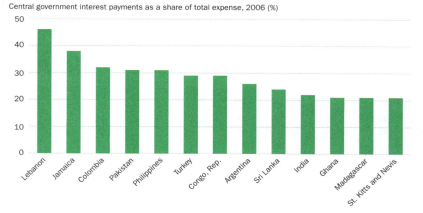

Central government interest payments as a share of total expense, 2006 (%)

Interest payments accounted for more than 20 percent of total expenses in 2006 for 13 countries.

**Note:** Data are for the most recent year for 2004–06.
*Source:* International Monetary Fund, *Government Finance Statistics* data files, and *World Development Indicators* data files.

## Data sources

Data on central government expenses are from the IMF's *Government Finance Statistics Yearbook 2007* and data files. Each country's accounts are reported using the system of common definitions and classifications in the IMF's *Government Finance Statistics Manual 2001*. See these sources for complete and authoritative explanations of concepts, definitions, and data sources.

| | Taxes on income, profits, and capital gains | | Taxes on goods and services | | Taxes on international trade | | Other taxes | | Social contributions | | Grants and other revenue | |
|---|---|---|---|---|---|---|---|---|---|---|---|---|
| | % of revenue | | % of revenue | | % of revenue | | % of revenue | | % of revenue | | % of revenue | |
| | 1995 | 2006 | 1995 | 2006 | 1995 | 2006 | 1995 | 2006 | 1995 | 2006 | 1995 | 2006 |
| Afghanistan[a] | .. | 4 | .. | 6 | .. | 11 | .. | 2 | .. | 0 | .. | 76 |
| Albania[a] | 8 | 15 | 39 | 49 | 14 | 8 | 1 | 1 | 15 | 18 | 22 | 10 |
| Algeria[a] | 65 | 6 | 10 | 64 | 18 | 3 | 1 | 1 | .. | .. | 5 | 26 |
| Angola | .. | .. | .. | .. | .. | .. | .. | .. | .. | .. | .. | .. |
| Argentina | .. | 19 | .. | 29 | .. | 16 | .. | 14 | .. | 17 | .. | 5 |
| Armenia[a] | .. | 20 | .. | 32 | .. | 3 | .. | 20 | .. | 12 | .. | 14 |
| Australia | .. | 65 | .. | 24 | .. | 2 | .. | 0 | .. | .. | .. | 9 |
| Austria | 20 | 24 | 21 | 22 | 0 | 0 | 5 | 4 | 41 | 38 | 14 | 12 |
| Azerbaijan[a] | 31 | .. | 34 | .. | 33 | .. | 2 | .. | 23 | .. | 0 | .. |
| Bangladesh[a] | .. | 12 | .. | 29 | .. | 33 | .. | 4 | .. | .. | .. | 22 |
| Belarus[a] | 16 | 7 | 33 | 40 | 6 | 7 | 11 | 8 | 31 | 33 | 3 | 6 |
| Belgium | 36 | 37 | 23 | 25 | .. | .. | 2 | 1 | 36 | 35 | 3 | 2 |
| Benin[a] | .. | 19 | .. | 36 | .. | 24 | .. | 6 | .. | .. | .. | 15 |
| Bolivia | .. | 7 | .. | 29 | .. | 2 | .. | 6 | .. | 5 | .. | 52 |
| Bosnia and Herzegovina | .. | 2 | .. | 42 | .. | 0 | .. | 11 | .. | 33 | .. | 11 |
| Botswana[a] | 21 | .. | 4 | .. | 15 | .. | 0 | .. | .. | .. | 59 | .. |
| Brazil[a] | 14 | .. | 24 | .. | 2 | .. | 4 | .. | 31 | .. | 26 | .. |
| Bulgaria[a] | 17 | 14 | 28 | 46 | 8 | 2 | 3 | 0 | 21 | 23 | 23 | 15 |
| Burkina Faso | .. | 15 | .. | 35 | .. | 13 | .. | 2 | .. | .. | .. | 35 |
| Burundi[a] | 14 | .. | 30 | .. | 20 | .. | 1 | .. | 5 | .. | 30 | .. |
| Cambodia | .. | 10 | .. | 40 | .. | 22 | .. | 0 | .. | .. | .. | 28 |
| Cameroon[a] | 17 | .. | 25 | .. | 28 | .. | 3 | .. | 2 | .. | 25 | .. |
| Canada[a] | 50 | 55 | 17 | 16 | 2 | 1 | .. | .. | 22 | 22 | 10 | 6 |
| Central African Republic[a] | .. | 14 | .. | 23 | .. | 19 | .. | 4 | .. | 6 | .. | 34 |
| Chad | .. | .. | .. | .. | .. | .. | .. | .. | .. | .. | .. | .. |
| Chile | .. | 41 | .. | 34 | .. | 2 | .. | 3 | .. | 5 | .. | 15 |
| China[a] | 9 | 24 | 61 | 79 | 7 | –16 | 0 | 0 | .. | .. | 22 | 12 |
| Hong Kong, China | .. | .. | .. | .. | .. | .. | .. | .. | .. | .. | .. | .. |
| Colombia | .. | 18 | .. | 23 | .. | 9 | .. | 4 | .. | 4 | .. | 42 |
| Congo, Dem. Rep.[a] | 21 | .. | 12 | .. | 21 | .. | 5 | .. | 1 | .. | 41 | .. |
| Congo, Rep. | .. | 4 | .. | 16 | .. | 7 | .. | 1 | .. | 4 | .. | 69 |
| Costa Rica[a] | .. | 14 | .. | 37 | .. | 5 | .. | 2 | .. | 31 | .. | 11 |
| Côte d'Ivoire[a] | 15 | 15 | 14 | 15 | 58 | 44 | 3 | 11 | 5 | 8 | 5 | 8 |
| Croatia[a] | 11 | 8 | 42 | 47 | 9 | 2 | 1 | 1 | 33 | 34 | 4 | 8 |
| Cuba | .. | .. | .. | .. | .. | .. | .. | .. | .. | .. | .. | .. |
| Czech Republic[a] | 15 | 18 | 32 | 27 | 4 | 0 | 1 | 1 | 40 | 46 | 8 | 8 |
| Denmark | 34 | 37 | 40 | 44 | .. | .. | 7 | 3 | 5 | 4 | 14 | 12 |
| Dominican Republic[a] | .. | 20 | .. | 54 | .. | 14 | .. | 4 | .. | 1 | .. | 8 |
| Ecuador[a] | 50 | .. | 26 | .. | 11 | .. | 1 | .. | .. | .. | 12 | .. |
| Egypt, Arab Rep.[a] | 22 | 32 | 17 | 23 | 13 | 6 | 13 | 3 | .. | .. | 35 | 35 |
| El Salvador | .. | 24 | .. | 44 | .. | 6 | .. | 1 | .. | 11 | .. | 14 |
| Eritrea | .. | .. | .. | .. | .. | .. | .. | .. | .. | .. | .. | .. |
| Estonia | .. | 11 | .. | 30 | .. | 0 | .. | 0 | .. | 33 | .. | .. |
| Ethiopia[a] | .. | .. | .. | .. | .. | .. | .. | .. | .. | .. | .. | .. |
| Finland | 21 | 20 | 34 | 34 | 0 | .. | 2 | 2 | 32 | 31 | 12 | 13 |
| France | 17 | 25 | 25 | 24 | 0 | 0 | 3 | 4 | 47 | 42 | 8 | 6 |
| Gabon | .. | .. | .. | .. | .. | .. | .. | .. | .. | .. | .. | .. |
| Gambia, The[a] | 14 | .. | 32 | .. | 42 | .. | 0 | .. | 0 | .. | 7 | .. |
| Georgia[a] | 7 | 10 | 48 | 51 | 10 | 4 | .. | 0 | 13 | 15 | 22 | 20 |
| Germany | 16 | 17 | 20 | 22 | .. | .. | 0 | .. | 58 | 57 | 6 | 4 |
| Ghana[a] | 15 | 22 | 31 | 22 | 24 | 29 | .. | 2 | .. | .. | 9 | 26 |
| Greece | 17 | 19 | 32 | 29 | 0 | 0 | 3 | 3 | 31 | 34 | 16 | 11 |
| Guatemala[a] | 19 | 28 | 46 | 55 | 23 | 9 | 3 | 1 | 2 | 2 | 6 | 4 |
| Guinea[a] | 8 | .. | 4 | .. | 62 | .. | 2 | .. | 1 | .. | 23 | .. |
| Guinea-Bissau | .. | .. | .. | .. | .. | .. | .. | .. | .. | .. | .. | .. |
| Haiti | .. | .. | .. | .. | .. | .. | .. | .. | .. | .. | .. | .. |

# Central government revenues | 4.12

| | Taxes on income, profits, and capital gains | | Taxes on goods and services | | Taxes on international trade | | Other taxes | | Social contributions | | Grants and other revenue | |
|---|---|---|---|---|---|---|---|---|---|---|---|---|
| | % of revenue | | % of revenue | | % of revenue | | % of revenue | | % of revenue | | % of revenue | |
| | 1995 | 2006 | 1995 | 2006 | 1995 | 2006 | 1995 | 2006 | 1995 | 2006 | 1995 | 2006 |
| Honduras | .. | 25 | .. | 52 | .. | 6 | .. | 1 | .. | .. | .. | 15 |
| Hungary | 18 | 20 | 28 | 34 | 8 | 0 | 1 | 2 | 33 | 35 | 12 | 10 |
| India[a] | 23 | 39 | 28 | 30 | 24 | 15 | 0 | 0 | 0 | 0 | 25 | 16 |
| Indonesia[a] | 46 | 28 | 33 | 32 | 4 | 3 | 1 | 4 | 6 | 3 | 9 | 30 |
| Iran, Islamic Rep.[a] | 12 | 13 | 5 | 2 | 9 | 6 | 1 | 1 | 6 | 11 | 66 | 68 |
| Iraq | .. | .. | .. | .. | .. | .. | .. | .. | .. | .. | .. | .. |
| Ireland | 37 | 38 | 35 | 35 | 0 | 0 | 2 | 6 | 17 | 17 | 9 | 4 |
| Israel | .. | 33 | .. | 28 | .. | 1 | .. | 5 | .. | 16 | .. | 17 |
| Italy | 32 | 34 | 21 | 22 | .. | .. | 5 | 5 | 35 | 35 | 6 | 4 |
| Jamaica[a] | .. | 14 | .. | 32 | .. | 8 | .. | 21 | .. | 9 | .. | 17 |
| Japan | 35 | .. | 14 | .. | 1 | .. | 5 | .. | 26 | .. | 18 | .. |
| Jordan[a] | 10 | 12 | 23 | 38 | 22 | 10 | 9 | 15 | .. | 0 | 36 | 24 |
| Kazakhstan[a] | 11 | 42 | 28 | 42 | 3 | 6 | 5 | 0 | 48 | .. | 6 | 9 |
| Kenya[a] | 35 | 33 | 40 | 44 | 14 | 10 | 1 | 0 | 0 | 0 | 10 | 12 |
| Korea, Dem. Rep. | .. | .. | .. | .. | .. | .. | .. | .. | .. | .. | .. | .. |
| Korea, Rep.[a] | 31 | 29 | 32 | 28 | 7 | 3 | 10 | 7 | 8 | 16 | 12 | 16 |
| Kuwait | 1 | 0 | 0 | .. | 2 | 1 | 0 | 0 | .. | .. | 97 | 98 |
| Kyrgyz Republic[a] | .. | 11 | .. | 52 | .. | 13 | .. | .. | .. | .. | .. | 24 |
| Lao PDR | .. | .. | .. | .. | .. | .. | .. | .. | .. | .. | .. | .. |
| Latvia[a] | 7 | 13 | 41 | 40 | 3 | 1 | 0 | 0 | 35 | 29 | 13 | 17 |
| Lebanon | .. | 11 | .. | 45 | .. | 8 | .. | 12 | .. | 1 | .. | 24 |
| Lesotho[a] | 15 | 19 | 12 | 16 | 49 | 49 | 1 | 0 | .. | .. | 24 | 15 |
| Liberia | .. | .. | .. | .. | .. | .. | .. | .. | .. | .. | .. | .. |
| Libya | .. | .. | .. | .. | .. | .. | .. | .. | .. | .. | .. | .. |
| Lithuania | .. | 24 | .. | 36 | .. | 0 | .. | 0 | .. | 31 | .. | 10 |
| Macedonia, FYR | .. | .. | .. | .. | .. | .. | .. | .. | .. | .. | .. | .. |
| Madagascar | .. | 9 | .. | 12 | .. | 25 | .. | 4 | .. | .. | .. | 50 |
| Malawi | .. | .. | .. | .. | .. | .. | .. | .. | .. | .. | .. | .. |
| Malaysia[a] | 37 | 47 | 26 | 21 | 12 | 6 | 5 | 0 | 1 | .. | 19 | 26 |
| Mali | .. | 5 | .. | 15 | .. | 4 | .. | 3 | .. | .. | .. | 73 |
| Mauritania | .. | .. | .. | .. | .. | .. | .. | .. | .. | .. | .. | .. |
| Mauritius[a] | 12 | 17 | 25 | 44 | 34 | 17 | 6 | 5 | 6 | 5 | 16 | 11 |
| Mexico[a] | 27 | .. | 54 | .. | 4 | .. | 2 | .. | 14 | .. | 16 | .. |
| Moldova[a] | 6 | 3 | 38 | 50 | 5 | 4 | 1 | 0 | 38 | 28 | 2 | 15 |
| Mongolia | .. | 16 | .. | 35 | .. | 6 | .. | 0 | .. | 16 | .. | 27 |
| Morocco[a] | .. | 33 | .. | 38 | .. | 9 | .. | 7 | .. | .. | .. | 12 |
| Mozambique | .. | .. | .. | .. | .. | .. | .. | .. | .. | .. | .. | .. |
| Myanmar | 20 | 25 | 26 | 31 | 12 | 2 | .. | .. | .. | .. | 42 | 42 |
| Namibia[a] | 27 | 38 | 32 | 20 | 28 | 32 | 2 | 2 | .. | 1 | 11 | 8 |
| Nepal[a] | 10 | 11 | 33 | 34 | 26 | 18 | 4 | 5 | .. | .. | 27 | 32 |
| Netherlands | 26 | 26 | 24 | 27 | .. | 1 | 2 | 3 | 40 | 35 | 8 | 9 |
| New Zealand | .. | 58 | .. | 26 | .. | 2 | .. | 0 | .. | 0 | .. | 14 |
| Nicaragua[a] | 9 | 23 | 52 | 49 | 7 | 5 | 0 | 0 | 11 | 19 | 31 | 23 |
| Niger | .. | .. | .. | .. | .. | .. | .. | .. | .. | .. | .. | .. |
| Nigeria | .. | .. | .. | .. | .. | .. | .. | .. | .. | .. | .. | .. |
| Norway | .. | 33 | .. | 23 | .. | 0 | .. | 1 | .. | 17 | .. | 25 |
| Oman[a] | 21 | .. | 1 | .. | 3 | .. | 2 | .. | .. | .. | 74 | .. |
| Pakistan[a] | 18 | 20 | 27 | 33 | 24 | 13 | 7 | 1 | .. | .. | 24 | 33 |
| Panama[a] | 20 | .. | 17 | .. | 11 | .. | 3 | .. | 16 | .. | 34 | .. |
| Papua New Guinea[a] | 40 | .. | 8 | .. | 27 | .. | 2 | .. | 0 | .. | 23 | .. |
| Paraguay[a] | .. | 9 | .. | 35 | .. | 8 | .. | 4 | .. | 15 | .. | 28 |
| Peru[a] | 15 | 24 | 46 | 40 | 10 | 6 | 8 | 6 | 10 | 9 | 11 | 15 |
| Philippines[a] | 33 | 39 | 26 | 25 | 29 | 20 | 4 | 4 | .. | .. | 8 | 12 |
| Poland | .. | 14 | .. | 38 | .. | 0 | .. | 1 | .. | 37 | .. | 10 |
| Portugal | 23 | 21 | 32 | 34 | 0 | 0 | 2 | 2 | 29 | 32 | 14 | 14 |
| Puerto Rico | .. | .. | .. | .. | .. | .. | .. | .. | .. | .. | .. | .. |

| | Taxes on income, profits, and capital gains | | Taxes on goods and services | | Taxes on international trade | | Other taxes | | Social contributions | | Grants and other revenue | |
|---|---|---|---|---|---|---|---|---|---|---|---|---|
| | % of revenue | | % of revenue | | % of revenue | | % of revenue | | % of revenue | | % of revenue | |
| | 1995 | 2006 | 1995 | 2006 | 1995 | 2006 | 1995 | 2006 | 1995 | 2006 | 1995 | 2006 |
| Romania | .. | 13 | .. | 33 | .. | 3 | .. | 0 | .. | 39 | .. | 13 |
| Russian Federation | .. | 7 | .. | 21 | .. | 29 | .. | 0 | .. | 19 | .. | 24 |
| Rwanda[a] | 11 | .. | 25 | .. | 23 | .. | 3 | .. | 2 | .. | 36 | .. |
| Saudi Arabia | .. | .. | .. | .. | .. | .. | .. | .. | .. | .. | .. | .. |
| Senegal[a] | 17 | .. | 19 | .. | 36 | .. | 2 | .. | .. | .. | 26 | .. |
| Serbia[a] | .. | .. | .. | .. | .. | .. | .. | .. | .. | .. | .. | .. |
| Sierra Leone[a] | 15 | 16 | 34 | 9 | 39 | 27 | 0 | .. | .. | .. | 12 | 48 |
| Singapore[a] | 26 | 30 | 20 | 23 | 1 | 0 | 15 | 10 | .. | .. | 38 | 36 |
| Slovak Republic | .. | 11 | .. | 35 | .. | 0 | .. | 0 | .. | 40 | .. | 15 |
| Slovenia[a] | 13 | 18 | 33 | 32 | 9 | 0 | 0 | 3 | 42 | 38 | 3 | 9 |
| Somalia | .. | .. | .. | .. | .. | .. | .. | .. | .. | .. | .. | .. |
| South Africa | .. | 51 | .. | 33 | .. | 4 | .. | 3 | .. | 2 | .. | 7 |
| Spain | 28 | 26 | 21 | 18 | 0 | 0 | 0 | 0 | 40 | 46 | .. | 7 |
| Sri Lanka[a] | 12 | 16 | 49 | 51 | 17 | 15 | 4 | 3 | 1 | 1 | 18 | 14 |
| Sudan[a] | 17 | .. | 41 | .. | 27 | .. | 1 | .. | .. | .. | 14 | .. |
| Swaziland[a] | .. | 28 | .. | 19 | .. | 48 | .. | 0 | .. | .. | .. | 5 |
| Sweden | 15 | 10 | 26 | 34 | .. | .. | 12 | 12 | 35 | 34 | 13 | 10 |
| Switzerland[a] | 11 | 19 | 21 | 33 | 1 | 1 | 2 | 2 | 49 | 37 | 17 | 8 |
| Syrian Arab Republic[a] | 23 | .. | 37 | .. | 13 | .. | 8 | .. | 0 | .. | 19 | .. |
| Tajikistan[a] | 6 | 3 | 63 | 54 | 12 | 11 | 0 | 1 | 13 | 12 | 5 | 18 |
| Tanzania | .. | .. | .. | .. | .. | .. | .. | .. | .. | .. | .. | .. |
| Thailand | .. | 36 | .. | 40 | .. | 6 | .. | 1 | .. | 5 | .. | 12 |
| Timor-Leste | .. | .. | .. | .. | .. | .. | .. | .. | .. | .. | .. | .. |
| Togo[a] | .. | .. | .. | .. | .. | .. | .. | .. | .. | .. | .. | .. |
| Trinidad and Tobago[a] | 50 | 52 | 26 | 15 | 6 | 5 | 1 | 15 | 2 | 4 | 15 | 10 |
| Tunisia[a] | 16 | 26 | 20 | 33 | 28 | 6 | 4 | 4 | 15 | 19 | 17 | 12 |
| Turkey[a] | .. | 22 | .. | 49 | .. | 1 | .. | 7 | .. | .. | .. | 21 |
| Turkmenistan | .. | .. | .. | .. | .. | .. | .. | .. | .. | .. | .. | .. |
| Uganda[a] | 10 | 19 | 45 | 30 | 7 | 21 | 2 | 0 | .. | .. | 37 | 30 |
| Ukraine[a] | .. | 13 | .. | 31 | .. | 4 | .. | 0 | .. | 35 | .. | 16 |
| United Arab Emirates[a] | .. | .. | 15 | .. | .. | .. | .. | .. | 1 | .. | 84 | .. |
| United Kingdom | 39 | 39 | 31 | 31 | .. | .. | 6 | 6 | 19 | 21 | 5 | 4 |
| United States | .. | 57 | .. | 3 | .. | 1 | .. | 1 | .. | 36 | .. | 3 |
| Uruguay[a] | 10 | 11 | 32 | 49 | 4 | 5 | 10 | 4 | 31 | 21 | 8 | 10 |
| Uzbekistan | .. | .. | .. | .. | .. | .. | .. | .. | .. | .. | .. | .. |
| Venezuela, RB[a] | 38 | 21 | 33 | 25 | 9 | 5 | 0 | 4 | 4 | 2 | 19 | 43 |
| Vietnam | .. | .. | .. | .. | .. | .. | .. | .. | .. | .. | .. | .. |
| West Bank and Gaza | .. | .. | .. | .. | .. | .. | .. | .. | .. | .. | .. | .. |
| Yemen, Rep.[a] | 17 | .. | 10 | .. | 18 | .. | 3 | .. | .. | .. | 51 | .. |
| Zambia[a] | 27 | 33 | 22 | 36 | 36 | 9 | 0 | 0 | 0 | .. | 15 | 21 |
| Zimbabwe[a] | 36 | .. | 22 | .. | 17 | .. | 3 | .. | 2 | .. | 19 | .. |
| **World** | .. m | 21 m | .. m | 34 m | .. m | 6 m | .. m | 2 m | .. m | .. m | .. m | 14 m |
| **Low income** | .. | .. | .. | .. | .. | .. | .. | .. | .. | .. | .. | .. |
| **Middle income** | .. | 16 | .. | 38 | .. | 5 | .. | 2 | .. | 15 | .. | 14 |
| Lower middle income | 19 | 17 | 34 | 39 | 14 | 6 | .. | 4 | .. | 13 | 16 | 15 |
| Upper middle income | .. | 14 | .. | 38 | .. | 6 | .. | 1 | .. | 27 | .. | 11 |
| **Low & middle income** | .. | 16 | .. | 36 | .. | 8 | .. | 2 | .. | .. | .. | 17 |
| East Asia & Pacific | 35 | 26 | 26 | 35 | 12 | 6 | .. | 1 | .. | .. | 20 | 22 |
| Europe & Central Asia | .. | 13 | .. | 40 | .. | 3 | .. | 0 | .. | 32 | .. | 15 |
| Latin America & Carib. | .. | 19 | .. | 41 | .. | 6 | .. | 3 | .. | 7 | .. | 15 |
| Middle East & N. Africa | 19 | 11 | 14 | 36 | 16 | 8 | 4 | 4 | .. | .. | 35 | 27 |
| South Asia | 15 | 16 | 31 | 33 | 24 | 15 | 4 | 2 | .. | 0 | 25 | 32 |
| Sub-Saharan Africa | .. | .. | .. | .. | .. | .. | .. | .. | .. | .. | .. | .. |
| **High income** | 24 | 26 | 24 | 27 | .. | 1 | 3 | 3 | 33 | 34 | 8 | 9 |
| Euro area | 26 | 24 | 23 | 26 | 0 | 0 | 2 | 3 | 40 | 35 | 7 | 7 |

**Note:** Components may not sum to 100 percent because of missing data or adjustment to tax revenue.
a. Data were reported on a cash basis and have been adjusted to the accrual framework.

The International Monetary Fund (IMF) classifies government revenues as taxes, grants, and property income. Taxes are classified by the base on which the tax is levied, grants by the source, and property income by type (for example, interest, dividends, or rent). The most important source of revenue is taxes. Grants are unrequited, nonrepayable, noncompulsory receipts from other government units and foreign governments or from international organizations. Transactions are generally recorded on an accrual basis.

The IMF's *Government Finance Statistics Manual 2001* describes taxes as compulsory, unrequited payments made to governments by individuals, businesses, or institutions. Taxes are classified in six major groups by the base on which the tax is levied: income, profits, and capital gains; payroll and workforce; property; goods and services; international trade and transactions; and other. However, the distinctions are not always clear. Taxes levied on the income and profits of individuals and corporations are classified as direct taxes, and taxes and duties levied on goods and services are classified as indirect taxes. This distinction may be a useful simplification, but it has no particular analytical significance except with respect to the capacity to fix tax rates.

Direct taxes tend to be progressive, whereas indirect taxes are proportional.

Social security taxes do not reflect compulsory payments made by employers to provident funds or other agencies with a like purpose. Similarly, expenditures from such funds are not reflected in government expenses (see table 4.11). For further discussion of taxes and tax policies, see *About the data* for table 5.6. For further discussion of government revenues and expenditures, see *About the data* for tables 4.10 and 4.11.

• **Taxes on income, profits, and capital gains** are levied on the actual or presumptive net income of individuals, on the profits of corporations and enterprises, and on capital gains, whether realized or not, on land, securities, and other assets. Intragovernmental payments are eliminated in consolidation. • **Taxes on goods and services** include general sales and turnover or value added taxes, selective excises on goods, selective taxes on services, taxes on the use of goods or property, taxes on extraction and production of minerals, and profits of fiscal monopolies. • **Taxes on international trade** include import duties, export duties, profits of export or import monopolies, exchange profits, and exchange taxes. • **Other taxes** include employer payroll or labor taxes, taxes on property, and taxes not allocable to other categories, such as penalties for late payment or nonpayment of taxes. • **Social contributions** include social security contributions by employees, employers, and self-employed individuals, and other contributions whose source cannot be determined. They also include actual or imputed contributions to social insurance schemes operated by governments. • **Grants and other revenue** include grants from other foreign governments, international organizations, and other government units; interest; dividends; rent; requited, nonrepayable receipts for public purposes (such as fines, administrative fees, and entrepreneurial income from government ownership of property); and voluntary, unrequited, nonrepayable receipts other than grants.

## Rich countries rely more on direct taxes | 4.12a

Taxes on income and capital gains as a share of central government revenue, 2006 (%)

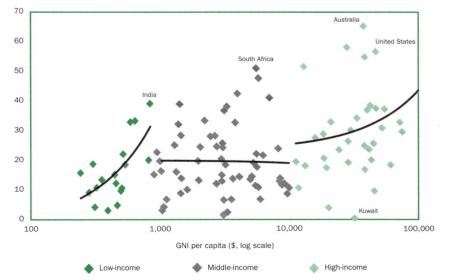

Low-income ◆    Middle-income ◆    High-income ◆

High-income economies tend to tax income and property, whereas low-income economies tend to rely on indirect taxes on international trade and goods and services. But there are exceptions in all groups.

**Note:** Data are for the most recent year for 2004–06.
*Source:* International Monetary Fund, *Government Finance Statistics* data files, and *World Development Indicators* data files.

# 4.13 | Monetary indicators

| | Money and quasi money | | Claims on private sector | | Claims on governments and other public entities | | Interest rate | | | | | |
|---|---|---|---|---|---|---|---|---|---|---|---|---|
| | annual % growth | | Annual growth % of M2 | | Annual growth % of M2 | | Deposit | | % Lending | | Real | |
| | 1995 | 2006 | 1995 | 2006 | 1995 | 2006 | 1995 | 2006 | 1995 | 2006 | 1995 | 2006 |
| Afghanistan | .. | .. | .. | .. | .. | .. | .. | .. | .. | .. | .. | .. |
| Albania | 51.8 | 16.0 | 1.8 | 12.4 | −8.3 | 1.9 | 15.3 | 5.2 | 19.7 | 12.9 | 8.9 | 10.8 |
| Algeria | 9.6 | 20.6 | 1.0 | 3.4 | −10.0 | −11.0 | 16.0 | 1.8 | 18.4 | 8.0 | −7.9 | −1.0 |
| Angola | 4,105.6 | 57.3 | 471.4 | 34.5 | 119.5 | −85.0 | 125.9 | 4.5 | 206.3 | 19.5 | −84.7 | 4.2 |
| Argentina | −2.8 | 20.3 | −1.1 | 13.1 | 7.8 | −15.0 | 11.9 | 6.4 | 17.9 | 8.6 | 14.2 | −4.3 |
| Armenia | 64.3 | 32.9 | 70.3 | 14.8 | 7.2 | −10.1 | 63.2 | 5.8 | 111.9 | 16.5 | −18.9 | 11.4 |
| Australia | 8.5 | 15.2 | 12.5 | 18.1 | 0.4 | −0.9 | 6.1 | 4.0 | 10.7 | 9.4 | 8.2 | 4.6 |
| Austria[a] | .. | .. | .. | .. | .. | .. | 2.2 | .. | 6.4 | .. | 6.1 | .. |
| Azerbaijan | 25.4 | 86.9 | 6.1 | 55.7 | −32.7 | 5.5 | .. | 10.6 | .. | 17.9 | .. | 10.1 |
| Bangladesh | 12.1 | 20.2 | 25.0 | 12.2 | 4.8 | 6.3 | 6.0 | 9.1 | 14.0 | 15.3 | 6.2 | 9.7 |
| Belarus | 158.4 | 39.9 | 61.4 | 45.5 | 44.7 | −4.3 | 100.8 | 7.7 | 175.0 | 8.8 | −63.9 | −1.7 |
| Belgium[a] | .. | .. | .. | .. | .. | .. | 4.0 | 1.6 | 8.4 | 7.5 | 7.1 | 5.4 |
| Benin | −1.8 | 14.5 | 2.2 | 6.4 | 6.0 | −13.3 | 3.5 | 3.5 | 16.8 | .. | 13.0 | .. |
| Bolivia | 7.7 | 24.0 | 13.7 | 4.3 | 1.1 | −11.5 | 18.9 | 4.0 | 51.0 | 11.9 | 35.5 | −0.3 |
| Bosnia and Herzegovina | 22.0 | 25.7 | 23.9 | 20.4 | −0.4 | −0.9 | 51.9 | 3.7 | 73.5 | 8.0 | 76.3 | 1.4 |
| Botswana | 12.3 | 67.4 | −1.7 | 14.2 | 10.0 | −55.0 | 9.8 | 8.9 | 14.4 | 16.5 | 5.2 | 2.6 |
| Brazil | 44.3 | 18.9 | 40.5 | 14.3 | 14.6 | 10.8 | 52.2 | 13.9 | 78.2 | 50.8 | 65.5 | 44.6 |
| Bulgaria | 40.5 | 27.6 | 22.1 | 17.8 | −7.2 | −7.0 | 35.9 | 3.2 | 79.4 | 8.9 | 10.1 | 0.7 |
| Burkina Faso | 22.3 | 11.0 | 2.9 | 12.1 | −7.3 | −7.5 | 3.5 | 3.5 | 16.8 | .. | 16.6 | .. |
| Burundi | −10.2 | 24.6 | −9.9 | 13.6 | −2.2 | 27.6 | .. | .. | 15.3 | 17.1 | −0.7 | 14.1 |
| Cambodia | 43.6 | 40.5 | 12.5 | 25.5 | 1.2 | −9.8 | 8.7 | 1.8 | 18.7 | 16.4 | 6.4 | 11.2 |
| Cameroon | −6.2 | 10.3 | 0.3 | 1.8 | −2.2 | −22.6 | 5.5 | 4.3 | 16.0 | 15.3 | −0.8 | 11.2 |
| Canada | 4.8 | 12.6 | 3.8 | 13.3 | 0.2 | 1.2 | 5.3 | 1.8 | 8.7 | 5.8 | 6.2 | 3.4 |
| Central African Republic | 4.3 | −4.2 | 3.9 | 2.2 | −7.9 | 5.7 | 5.5 | 4.3 | 16.0 | 15.3 | 5.2 | 11.0 |
| Chad | 48.8 | 52.3 | 6.4 | −1.3 | −18.6 | −25.1 | 5.5 | 4.3 | 16.0 | 15.3 | 6.6 | 5.2 |
| Chile | 24.3 | 16.1 | 34.9 | 20.4 | −2.0 | −4.5 | 13.7 | 5.1 | 18.2 | 8.0 | 7.0 | −3.3 |
| China | 29.5 | 16.0 | 21.1 | 10.1 | 0.7 | 0.1 | 11.0 | 2.5 | 12.1 | 6.1 | −1.5 | 2.4 |
| Hong Kong, China | 10.6 | 16.2 | 9.8 | 1.0 | −2.4 | −0.7 | 5.6 | 2.7 | 8.8 | 7.8 | 6.1 | 7.9 |
| Colombia | 28.2 | 20.2 | 34.3 | 43.9 | 2.9 | −10.6 | 32.3 | 6.3 | 42.7 | 12.9 | 20.1 | 7.1 |
| Congo, Dem. Rep. | 357.6 | 57.5 | 59.6 | 19.3 | −7.9 | 13.6 | 60.0 | .. | 293.9 | .. | −30.5 | .. |
| Congo, Rep. | −0.1 | 45.7 | 6.3 | 1.5 | 2.0 | −89.6 | 5.5 | 4.3 | 16.0 | 15.3 | 12.2 | 0.1 |
| Costa Rica | 4.8 | 26.3 | 0.0 | 21.7 | 5.7 | −2.2 | 23.9 | 9.8 | 36.7 | 22.2 | 11.9 | 11.0 |
| Côte d'Ivoire | 18.1 | 10.3 | 13.3 | 4.8 | 0.3 | −1.7 | 3.5 | 3.5 | 16.8 | .. | 16.8 | .. |
| Croatia | 40.4 | 18.0 | 30.5 | 20.6 | −2.4 | −1.5 | 5.5 | 1.7 | 20.2 | 9.9 | 14.2 | 6.3 |
| Cuba | .. | .. | .. | .. | .. | .. | .. | .. | .. | .. | .. | .. |
| Czech Republic | 29.3 | 9.9 | 15.8 | 10.5 | 2.1 | 2.3 | 7.0 | 1.2 | 12.8 | 5.6 | −3.6 | 3.5 |
| Denmark | 6.2 | 9.6 | 2.6 | 39.7 | −1.5 | −3.3 | 3.9 | 2.4 | 10.3 | .. | 9.0 | .. |
| Dominican Republic | 17.8 | 12.5 | 15.3 | 7.0 | −2.6 | 37.5 | 14.9 | 9.8 | 30.7 | 19.5 | 16.0 | 11.1 |
| Ecuador | 6.8 | 13.1 | 15.1 | 14.1 | −74.8 | −5.5 | 43.3 | 4.1 | 55.7 | 9.5 | 45.7 | 2.2 |
| Egypt, Arab Rep. | 9.9 | 15.0 | 12.1 | 5.5 | 0.6 | 6.8 | 10.9 | 6.0 | 16.5 | 12.6 | 4.5 | 4.9 |
| El Salvador | 13.5 | 11.9 | 22.6 | 9.9 | −0.9 | −2.5 | 14.4 | .. | 19.1 | .. | 7.8 | .. |
| Eritrea | 21.0 | 5.8 | 27.8 | 0.9 | 20.5 | 8.6 | .. | .. | .. | .. | .. | .. |
| Estonia | 27.5 | 28.2 | 22.0 | 74.3 | −5.5 | −1.2 | 8.7 | 2.8 | 19.0 | 5.0 | −9.4 | −1.0 |
| Ethiopia | 9.0 | 20.0 | 13.4 | 14.7 | −3.5 | 5.4 | 11.5 | 3.6 | 15.1 | 7.0 | 2.1 | −0.7 |
| Finland[a] | .. | .. | .. | .. | .. | .. | 3.2 | 1.0 | 7.8 | 3.7 | 2.9 | 3.0 |
| France[a] | .. | .. | .. | .. | .. | .. | 4.5 | 2.4 | 8.1 | 6.6 | 6.7 | 4.9 |
| Gabon | 10.1 | 16.4 | 11.9 | 10.1 | 5.8 | −13.7 | 5.5 | 4.3 | 16.0 | 15.3 | 14.5 | 6.9 |
| Gambia, The | 14.2 | 26.2 | −5.0 | 8.3 | 15.2 | 3.8 | 12.5 | 12.7 | 25.0 | 29.8 | 20.3 | 24.7 |
| Georgia | 40.2 | 39.7 | −11.1 | 50.5 | 73.8 | −11.2 | 31.0 | 11.4 | 58.2 | 18.8 | 10.6 | 9.5 |
| Germany[a] | .. | .. | .. | .. | .. | .. | 3.9 | .. | 10.9 | .. | 8.9 | .. |
| Ghana | 43.2 | 42.8 | 10.2 | 20.1 | 28.1 | 10.9 | 28.7 | 8.9 | .. | .. | .. | .. |
| Greece[a] | .. | .. | .. | .. | .. | .. | 15.8 | 2.2 | 23.1 | 6.8 | 12.1 | 3.1 |
| Guatemala | 15.6 | 13.4 | 36.1 | 12.0 | −7.1 | 0.8 | 7.9 | 4.5 | 21.2 | 12.8 | 11.5 | 6.1 |
| Guinea | 11.3 | 33.4 | 12.1 | 19.8 | 8.4 | 18.1 | 17.5 | 14.4 | 21.5 | .. | 14.7 | .. |
| Guinea-Bissau | 43.0 | 4.4 | −6.7 | 5.7 | −20.4 | −1.5 | 3.5 | 3.5 | 32.9 | .. | −8.2 | .. |
| Haiti | 27.1 | 4.6 | 15.7 | 3.1 | 0.1 | −5.4 | 10.7 | 6.2 | 24.8 | 43.3 | −2.4 | 27.2 |

| | Money and quasi money | | Claims on private sector | | Claims on governments and other public entities | | Interest rate | | | | | |
|---|---|---|---|---|---|---|---|---|---|---|---|---|
| | annual % growth | | Annual growth % of M2 | | Annual growth % of M2 | | Deposit | | % Lending | | Real | |
| | 1995 | 2006 | 1995 | 2006 | 1995 | 2006 | 1995 | 2006 | 1995 | 2006 | 1995 | 2006 |
| Honduras | 29.2 | 22.5 | 16.5 | 24.0 | −7.4 | −1.6 | 12.0 | 9.3 | 27.0 | 17.4 | 1.7 | 11.7 |
| Hungary | 20.9 | 14.3 | 4.9 | 17.1 | 20.2 | 5.5 | 24.4 | 7.4 | 32.6 | 8.1 | 4.6 | 4.2 |
| India | 11.0 | 21.6 | 6.0 | 16.8 | 3.4 | 2.4 | .. | .. | 15.5 | 11.2 | 5.9 | 5.0 |
| Indonesia | 27.5 | 14.9 | 25.9 | 7.4 | −2.3 | 0.8 | 16.7 | 11.4 | 18.9 | 16.0 | 8.3 | 2.1 |
| Iran, Islamic Rep. | 30.1 | 29.1 | 9.8 | 27.0 | 17.3 | −8.4 | .. | 11.8 | .. | 14.0 | .. | 2.7 |
| Iraq | .. | 30.8 | .. | 6.7 | .. | −29.9 | .. | .. | .. | 14.4 | .. | .. |
| Ireland[a] | .. | .. | .. | .. | .. | .. | 0.4 | 0.0 | 6.6 | 2.7 | 3.4 | −0.8 |
| Israel | 21.7 | 5.1 | 18.3 | 3.4 | −0.5 | −1.8 | 14.1 | 3.2 | 20.2 | 7.4 | 1.9 | 5.0 |
| Italy[a] | .. | .. | .. | .. | .. | .. | 6.4 | 0.9 | 13.2 | 5.6 | 7.9 | 3.8 |
| Jamaica | 28.0 | 15.8 | 18.0 | 11.5 | 6.1 | −3.5 | 23.2 | 7.0 | 43.6 | 17.6 | 17.5 | 10.7 |
| Japan | 4.1 | −0.7 | 1.3 | −0.1 | 2.5 | −0.3 | 0.9 | 0.7 | 3.5 | 1.7 | 4.0 | 2.5 |
| Jordan | 5.7 | 12.8 | 9.6 | 15.6 | −3.8 | −1.0 | 7.7 | 4.6 | 10.7 | 8.2 | 8.6 | 2.3 |
| Kazakhstan | 108.2 | 78.1 | −72.5 | 105.2 | 24.7 | −44.4 | .. | .. | .. | .. | .. | .. |
| Kenya | 29.0 | 18.0 | 26.7 | 10.2 | 6.6 | 3.1 | 13.6 | 5.1 | 28.8 | 13.6 | 15.8 | 14.1 |
| Korea, Dem. Rep. | .. | .. | .. | .. | .. | .. | .. | .. | .. | .. | .. | .. |
| Korea, Rep. | 15.6 | 4.4 | 21.6 | 19.5 | −1.2 | 1.2 | 8.8 | 4.5 | 9.0 | 6.0 | 1.5 | 6.4 |
| Kuwait | 9.4 | 21.7 | 10.9 | 23.7 | −0.2 | −5.7 | 6.5 | 4.9 | 8.4 | 8.6 | 3.4 | −13.6 |
| Kyrgyz Republic | 14.8 | 51.5 | 0.1 | 18.1 | 62.6 | −0.5 | 36.7 | 5.6 | 65.0 | 23.2 | 21.9 | 12.8 |
| Lao PDR | 16.4 | 26.7 | 18.1 | −1.5 | −7.2 | 1.8 | 14.0 | 5.0 | 25.7 | 30.0 | 5.0 | 24.2 |
| Latvia | −21.4 | 38.7 | −23.8 | 88.8 | 6.5 | −2.3 | 14.8 | 3.5 | 34.6 | 7.3 | 5.5 | −3.4 |
| Lebanon | 16.4 | 7.8 | 13.1 | 1.9 | 6.0 | 6.6 | 16.3 | 8.0 | 24.7 | 10.3 | 12.8 | 4.4 |
| Lesotho | 9.8 | 35.3 | −2.3 | 4.8 | −18.7 | −22.7 | 13.3 | 4.5 | 16.4 | 12.2 | 6.5 | 7.7 |
| Liberia | 29.5 | 34.6 | −6.0 | 15.9 | 37.2 | 76.6 | 6.4 | 3.4 | 15.6 | 15.5 | 8.5 | 2.7 |
| Libya | 9.6 | 14.1 | 3.1 | 1.0 | 3.6 | −112.6 | 5.5 | 2.5 | 7.0 | 6.3 | .. | −7.4 |
| Lithuania | 28.9 | 22.5 | 12.7 | 40.3 | −2.4 | −8.3 | 20.1 | 1.2 | 27.1 | 5.1 | −14.5 | −1.4 |
| Macedonia, FYR | 11.7 | 21.5 | −147.3 | 16.5 | −243.6 | −4.7 | 24.1 | 6.6 | 46.0 | 12.2 | 24.6 | 8.1 |
| Madagascar | 16.2 | 26.4 | 9.6 | 9.6 | −13.1 | −17.4 | 18.5 | 22.3 | 37.5 | 29.5 | −5.3 | 16.4 |
| Malawi | 56.2 | 16.4 | 2.8 | 19.0 | −10.4 | −9.8 | 37.3 | 11.0 | 47.3 | 32.3 | −16.9 | 11.6 |
| Malaysia | 18.5 | 11.5 | 29.2 | 6.2 | −0.7 | 1.6 | 5.9 | 3.1 | 8.7 | 6.5 | 4.9 | 2.3 |
| Mali | 7.3 | 6.0 | 18.9 | 1.4 | −11.6 | −9.9 | 3.5 | 3.5 | 16.8 | .. | 14.5 | .. |
| Mauritania | −5.1 | 10.5 | −42.5 | 18.7 | −28.9 | −15.8 | 9.0 | 8.0 | 20.3 | 23.1 | 17.0 | 4.3 |
| Mauritius | 18.6 | 10.1 | 8.7 | 7.2 | 3.0 | 0.5 | 12.2 | 9.6 | 20.8 | 21.1 | 16.1 | 16.3 |
| Mexico | 31.9 | 11.1 | −2.9 | 17.7 | 27.6 | 3.2 | 39.8 | 3.3 | 59.4 | 7.5 | 15.6 | 2.9 |
| Moldova | 65.3 | 23.5 | 34.6 | 21.5 | 19.1 | −0.7 | 25.4 | 11.9 | 36.7 | 18.1 | 7.7 | 4.9 |
| Mongolia | 32.6 | 30.8 | 14.4 | 31.8 | −31.8 | −37.3 | 74.6 | 13.0 | 134.4 | 21.4 | 46.9 | −1.4 |
| Morocco | 7.0 | 17.0 | 6.9 | 10.4 | 5.1 | 0.0 | 7.3 | 3.7 | 10.0 | 11.5 | 8.3 | 11.9 |
| Mozambique | 47.7 | 22.6 | 21.8 | 13.4 | −12.5 | −8.3 | 38.8 | 10.4 | 24.4 | 18.6 | 18.0 | 11.9 |
| Myanmar | 36.5 | 27.3 | 13.4 | 6.8 | 19.7 | 23.5 | 9.8 | 9.5 | 16.5 | 15.0 | −2.4 | −2.2 |
| Namibia | 22.6 | 29.6 | 30.5 | 20.3 | 1.7 | −7.2 | 10.8 | 6.3 | 18.5 | 11.2 | 12.1 | 1.9 |
| Nepal | 15.6 | 14.7 | 18.0 | 11.0 | 3.6 | 0.1 | 9.6 | 2.3 | 12.9 | 8.0 | 4.7 | 1.2 |
| Netherlands[a] | .. | .. | .. | .. | .. | .. | 4.4 | 3.0 | 7.2 | 3.5 | 5.0 | 2.0 |
| New Zealand | 9.3 | 16.0 | 15.8 | 16.6 | −3.9 | −1.0 | 8.5 | 6.9 | 12.1 | 12.3 | 9.9 | 10.8 |
| Nicaragua | 35.1 | 8.4 | 30.3 | 22.5 | −21.5 | −10.0 | 11.1 | 4.9 | 19.9 | 11.6 | 5.7 | 0.9 |
| Niger | 3.8 | 14.8 | −22.8 | 15.2 | 10.2 | −31.6 | 3.5 | 3.5 | 16.8 | .. | 15.5 | .. |
| Nigeria | 19.4 | −33.9 | 22.3 | 19.5 | −9.1 | −23.6 | 13.5 | 9.7 | 20.2 | 16.9 | −22.9 | 8.3 |
| Norway | 3.8 | 3.4 | 9.5 | 10.4 | −1.9 | −5.3 | 5.0 | 1.8 | 7.6 | 4.0 | 4.4 | −4.2 |
| Oman | 7.7 | 24.6 | 9.3 | 20.6 | −2.3 | −5.5 | 6.5 | 4.0 | 9.4 | 7.4 | 7.5 | −1.4 |
| Pakistan | 13.8 | 14.6 | 10.8 | 10.6 | 8.7 | 1.6 | .. | 4.2 | .. | 11.0 | .. | 1.6 |
| Panama | 8.4 | 22.3 | 14.5 | 13.8 | −4.3 | 0.1 | 7.2 | 3.8 | 11.1 | 8.4 | 10.6 | 6.1 |
| Papua New Guinea | 13.7 | 38.9 | 0.2 | 16.1 | 5.0 | −3.0 | 7.3 | 1.0 | 13.1 | 10.6 | 0.0 | 0.8 |
| Paraguay | 0.5 | 8.7 | 4.9 | 6.0 | 0.1 | −3.1 | 21.2 | 6.7 | 33.9 | 30.1 | 17.9 | 17.5 |
| Peru | 29.3 | 11.8 | 31.1 | 4.2 | −8.1 | −5.1 | 9.6 | 3.2 | 36.2 | 23.9 | 20.5 | 15.5 |
| Philippines | 23.9 | 19.6 | 27.9 | 3.7 | 3.0 | 1.2 | 8.4 | 5.3 | 14.7 | 9.8 | 6.6 | 4.3 |
| Poland | 35.6 | 14.8 | 19.1 | 15.7 | 3.1 | 2.1 | 26.8 | 2.8 | 33.5 | 5.5 | −5.2 | 4.5 |
| Portugal[a] | .. | .. | .. | .. | .. | .. | 8.4 | .. | 13.8 | .. | 10.0 | .. |
| Puerto Rico | .. | .. | .. | .. | .. | .. | .. | .. | .. | .. | .. | .. |

| | Money and quasi money | | Claims on private sector | | Claims on governments and other public entities | | Interest rate | | | | | |
|---|---|---|---|---|---|---|---|---|---|---|---|---|
| | annual % growth | | Annual growth % of M2 | | Annual growth % of M2 | | Deposit | | % Lending | | Real | |
| | 1995 | 2006 | 1995 | 2006 | 1995 | 2006 | 1995 | 2006 | 1995 | 2006 | 1995 | 2006 |
| Romania | 69.6 | 36.2 | 23.1 | 34.6 | 11.6 | −0.9 | .. | .. | .. | .. | .. | .. |
| Russian Federation | 112.6 | 40.5 | 46.2 | 37.2 | 73.6 | −21.8 | 102.0 | 4.1 | 320.3 | 10.4 | 72.3 | −4.9 |
| Rwanda | 69.5 | 18.0 | 32.7 | 14.5 | −41.0 | −13.8 | 10.9 | 7.9 | 18.5 | 16.1 | 6.9 | 6.4 |
| Saudi Arabia | 3.4 | 20.4 | 3.4 | 7.3 | 1.4 | −17.7 | 6.2 | 5.0 | .. | .. | .. | .. |
| Senegal | 7.4 | 12.5 | 1.2 | 4.8 | 1.0 | 2.7 | 3.5 | 3.5 | 16.8 | .. | 17.8 | .. |
| Serbia | 33.0 | 38.3 | 88.5 | 18.5 | 34.1 | −16.0 | 19.1 | 5.1 | 78.0 | 16.6 | .. | 0.8 |
| Sierra Leone | 19.6 | 21.4 | 1.6 | 4.1 | −101.6 | −62.0 | 7.0 | 10.4 | 28.8 | 24.0 | −3.6 | 8.6 |
| Singapore | 8.5 | 19.4 | 19.7 | 4.2 | −8.1 | 2.5 | 3.5 | 0.6 | 6.4 | 5.3 | 4.0 | 5.1 |
| Slovak Republic | 18.4 | 14.5 | 3.4 | 14.0 | −4.8 | −1.1 | 9.0 | 3.6 | 16.8 | 7.7 | 6.3 | 4.8 |
| Slovenia | 31.5 | 8.4 | 36.8 | 27.7 | 5.8 | −2.3 | 15.4 | 2.8 | 23.4 | 7.4 | −1.5 | 5.0 |
| Somalia | .. | .. | .. | .. | .. | .. | .. | .. | .. | .. | .. | .. |
| South Africa | 16.0 | 21.2 | 18.9 | 29.2 | −4.1 | −5.2 | 13.5 | 7.1 | 17.9 | 11.2 | 6.9 | 4.0 |
| Spain[a] | .. | .. | .. | .. | .. | .. | 7.7 | .. | 10.1 | .. | 4.9 | .. |
| Sri Lanka | 35.8 | 19.0 | 75.4 | 15.9 | 5.4 | 3.1 | 12.1 | 10.2 | 18.0 | 7.0 | 8.0 | −2.7 |
| Sudan | 72.7 | 29.7 | 10.6 | 26.3 | 389.1 | 17.7 | .. | .. | .. | .. | .. | .. |
| Swaziland | 3.9 | 25.1 | 1.3 | 22.5 | −14.8 | −24.6 | 9.4 | 4.9 | 17.1 | 11.2 | −0.2 | 5.2 |
| Sweden | 3.1 | 11.9 | −1.1 | 24.5 | −4.0 | 0.2 | 6.2 | 0.8 | 11.1 | 3.3 | 7.3 | 2.1 |
| Switzerland | 4.6 | 4.9 | 4.0 | 10.0 | 0.2 | 0.4 | 1.3 | 1.4 | 5.5 | 3.0 | 4.6 | 1.6 |
| Syrian Arab Republic | 9.2 | 7.3 | 3.9 | 2.9 | 6.1 | 0.9 | 4.0 | 1.0 | 9.0 | 8.0 | 2.2 | −4.4 |
| Tajikistan | .. | 59.7 | .. | 45.5 | .. | −13.8 | 23.9 | 9.1 | 75.5 | 24.4 | 6.2 | 3.4 |
| Tanzania | 33.0 | 18.3 | −3.9 | 13.2 | 16.3 | −16.2 | 24.6 | 6.6 | 42.8 | 15.4 | 12.6 | 8.6 |
| Thailand | 17.7 | 6.7 | 40.3 | 3.5 | −4.2 | −1.8 | 11.6 | 4.4 | 13.3 | 7.4 | 7.3 | 2.2 |
| Timor-Leste | .. | .. | .. | .. | .. | .. | .. | .. | .. | .. | .. | .. |
| Togo | 22.3 | 22.6 | 17.6 | 0.0 | 14.9 | 0.1 | 3.5 | 3.5 | 17.5 | .. | 13.8 | .. |
| Trinidad and Tobago | 4.0 | 21.7 | 9.0 | 16.0 | 0.6 | −18.3 | 6.9 | 4.8 | 15.2 | 10.9 | 10.7 | 3.1 |
| Tunisia | 6.6 | 11.6 | 10.4 | 8.0 | −1.2 | 3.4 | .. | .. | .. | .. | .. | .. |
| Turkey | 104.2 | 32.6 | 66.9 | 24.8 | 30.1 | 4.3 | 76.0 | 21.6 | .. | .. | .. | .. |
| Turkmenistan | 449.5 | .. | 76.3 | .. | −573.1 | .. | .. | .. | .. | .. | .. | .. |
| Uganda | 13.9 | 17.6 | 9.6 | 10.8 | −41.2 | −10.1 | 7.6 | 9.1 | 20.2 | 18.7 | 9.9 | 10.7 |
| Ukraine | 115.5 | 34.3 | 7.7 | 51.4 | 95.4 | −0.5 | 70.3 | 7.6 | 122.7 | 15.2 | −56.8 | 1.3 |
| United Arab Emirates | 10.2 | 23.2 | 10.7 | 29.5 | −4.3 | 1.1 | .. | .. | .. | .. | .. | .. |
| United Kingdom | 20.3 | 11.9 | 19.6 | 16.4 | 9.5 | −1.1 | 4.1 | .. | 6.7 | 4.7 | 3.9 | 2.2 |
| United States | 6.9 | 9.0 | 6.0 | 7.3 | 0.2 | 0.8 | .. | .. | 8.8 | 8.0 | 6.7 | 4.6 |
| Uruguay | 39.0 | 11.7 | 34.2 | 5.3 | 1.0 | −12.8 | 57.7 | 1.8 | 93.1 | 9.3 | 36.9 | 2.3 |
| Uzbekistan | .. | .. | .. | .. | .. | .. | .. | .. | .. | .. | .. | .. |
| Venezuela, RB | 36.6 | 75.4 | 15.3 | 38.1 | 32.8 | 11.2 | 24.7 | 10.3 | 39.7 | 15.5 | −7.9 | −1.2 |
| Vietnam | 25.7 | 29.7 | 12.7 | 21.8 | 0.8 | 0.9 | 8.5 | 7.6 | 20.1 | 11.2 | 10.5 | 3.6 |
| West Bank and Gaza | .. | 5.6 | .. | 2.9 | .. | 2.4 | .. | 3.0 | .. | 7.7 | .. | 8.0 |
| Yemen, Rep. | 50.7 | 26.1 | 6.0 | 3.6 | 13.3 | −5.2 | 23.8 | 13.0 | 31.5 | 18.0 | −3.2 | 4.1 |
| Zambia | 55.5 | 44.2 | 34.2 | 22.4 | 185.8 | −36.9 | 30.2 | 10.3 | 45.5 | 23.2 | 5.4 | 9.8 |
| Zimbabwe | 25.5 | 1,453.0 | 25.5 | 624.0 | −0.3 | 274.6 | 25.9 | 203.4 | 34.7 | 496.5 | 23.0 | −0.7 |

a. As members of the euro area, these countries share a single currency, the euro.

## About the data

Money and the financial accounts that record the supply of money lie at the heart of a country's financial system. There are several commonly used definitions of the money supply. The narrowest, M1, encompasses currency held by the public and demand deposits with banks. M2 includes M1 plus time and savings deposits with banks that require a prior notice for withdrawal. M3 includes M2 as well as various money market instruments, such as certificates of deposit issued by banks, bank deposits denominated in foreign currency, and deposits with financial institutions other than banks. However defined, money is a liability of the banking system, distinguished from other bank liabilities by the special role it plays as a medium of exchange, a unit of account, and a store of value.

The banking system's assets include its net foreign assets and net domestic credit. Net domestic credit includes credit extended to the private sector and general government and credit extended to the nonfinancial public sector in the form of investments in short- and long-term government securities and loans to state enterprises; liabilities to the public and private sectors in the form of deposits with the banking system are netted out. Net domestic credit also includes credit to banking and nonbank financial institutions.

Domestic credit is the main vehicle through which changes in the money supply are regulated, with central bank lending to the government often playing the most important role. The central bank can regulate lending to the private sector in several ways—for example, by adjusting the cost of the refinancing facilities it provides to banks, by changing market interest rates through open market operations, or by controlling the availability of credit through changes in the reserve requirements imposed on banks and ceilings on the credit provided by banks to the private sector.

Monetary accounts are derived from the balance sheets of financial institutions—the central bank, commercial banks, and nonbank financial intermediaries. Although these balance sheets are usually reliable, they are subject to errors of classification, valuation, and timing and to differences in accounting practices. For example, whether interest income is recorded on an accrual or a cash basis can make a substantial difference, as can the treatment of nonperforming assets. Valuation errors typically arise with respect to foreign exchange transactions, particularly in countries with flexible exchange rates or in those that have undergone currency devaluation during the reporting period. The valuation of financial derivatives and the net liabilities of the banking system can also be difficult. The quality of commercial bank reporting also may be adversely affected by delays in reports from bank branches, especially in countries where branch accounts are not computerized. Thus the data in the balance sheets of commercial banks may be based on preliminary estimates subject to constant revision. This problem is likely to be even more serious for nonbank financial intermediaries.

Many interest rates coexist in an economy, reflecting competitive conditions, the terms governing loans and deposits, and differences in the position and status of creditors and debtors. In some economies interest rates are set by regulation or administrative fiat. In economies with imperfect markets, or where reported nominal rates are not indicative of effective rates, it may be difficult to obtain data on interest rates that reflect actual market transactions. Deposit and lending rates are collected by the International Monetary Fund (IMF) as representative interest rates offered by banks to resident customers. The terms and conditions attached to these rates differ by country, however, limiting their comparability. Real interest rates are calculated by adjusting nominal rates by an estimate of the inflation rate in the economy. A negative real interest rate indicates a loss in the purchasing power of the principal. The real interest rates in the table are calculated as $(i - P) / (1 + P)$, where $i$ is the nominal lending interest rate and $P$ is the inflation rate (as measured by the GDP deflator).

## Definitions

• **Money and quasi money** are the sum of currency outside banks, demand deposits other than those of the central government, and the time, savings, and foreign currency deposits of resident sectors other than the central government. This definition of the money supply, often called M2, corresponds to lines 34 and 35 in the IMF's *International Financial Statistics* (IFS). The change in money supply is measured as the difference in end-of-year totals relative to M2 in the preceding year. • **Claims on private sector** (IFS line 32d) include gross credit from the financial system to individuals, enterprises, nonfinancial public entities not included under net domestic credit, and financial institutions not included elsewhere. • **Claims on governments and other public entities** (IFS line 32an + 32b + 32bx + 32c) usually comprise direct credit for specific purposes, such as financing the government budget deficit; loans to state enterprises; advances against future credit authorizations; and purchases of treasury bills and bonds, net of deposits by the public sector. Public sector deposits with the banking system also include sinking funds for the service of debt and temporary deposits of government revenues. • **Deposit interest rate** is the rate paid by commercial or similar banks for demand, time, or savings deposits. • **Lending interest rate** is the rate charged by banks on loans to prime customers. • **Real interest rate** is the lending interest rate adjusted for inflation as measured by the GDP deflator.

## Data sources

Data on monetary and financial statistics are published by the IMF in its monthly *International Financial Statistics* and annual *International Financial Statistics Yearbook*. The IMF collects data on the financial systems of its member countries. The World Bank receives data from the IMF in electronic files that may contain more recent revisions than the published sources. The discussion of monetary indicators draws from an IMF publication by Marcello Caiola, *A Manual for Country Economists* (1995). Also see the IMF's *Monetary and Financial Statistics Manual* (2000) for guidelines for the presentation of monetary and financial statistics. Data on real interest rates are derived from World Bank data on the GDP deflator.

# 4.14 Exchange rates and prices

| | Official exchange rate | | Purchasing power parity (PPP) conversion factor | | Ratio of PPP conversion factor to market exchange rate | Real effective exchange rate | GDP implicit deflator | | Consumer price index | | Wholesale price index | |
|---|---|---|---|---|---|---|---|---|---|---|---|---|
| | local currency units to $ | | local currency units to international $ | | | Index 2000 = 100 | average annual % growth | | average annual % growth | | average annual % growth | |
| | 2006 | 2007[a] | 1995 | 2006 | 2006 | 2006 | 1990–2000 | 2000–06 | 1990–2000 | 2000–06 | 1990–2000 | 2000–06 |
| Afghanistan | 49.50 | .. | .. | 17.5 | 0.4 | .. | .. | 11.8 | .. | .. | .. | .. |
| Albania | 98.10 | 83.02 | 27.1 | 48.0 | 0.5 | .. | 38.0 | 3.8 | 31.5 | 3.0 | .. | 5.1 |
| Algeria | 72.65 | 67.07 | 18.2 | 39.6 | 0.5 | 83.2 | 18.5 | 8.1 | 17.3 | 2.6 | 2.1 | 3.5 |
| Angola | 80.37 | 75.02 | 0.0 | 49.4 | 0.6 | .. | 739.4 | 67.2 | 711.0 | 65.1 | .. | .. |
| Argentina | 3.05 | 3.12 | 0.9 | 1.4 | 0.5 | .. | 5.2 | 12.2 | 8.9 | 10.9 | 0.3 | 19.8 |
| Armenia | 416.04 | 304.10 | 116.3 | 181.0 | 0.4 | 106.3 | 212.5 | 4.2 | 103.3 | 3.4 | 13.2 | 0.9 |
| Australia | 1.33 | 1.15 | 1.3 | 1.4 | 1.1 | 124.7 | 1.5 | 3.7 | 2.1 | 3.0 | 1.1 | 3.2 |
| Austria[b] | 0.80 | 0.69 | 1.0 | 0.9 | 1.1 | 105.4 | 1.7 | 1.6 | 2.2 | 1.9 | 0.3 | 2.2 |
| Azerbaijan | 0.89 | 0.85 | 0.2 | 0.3 | 0.4 | .. | 203.0 | 7.3 | 192.4 | 5.5 | .. | .. |
| Bangladesh | 68.93 | 68.59 | 19.2 | 23.1 | 0.3 | .. | 4.0 | 4.1 | 5.5 | 5.9 | .. | .. |
| Belarus | 2,144.56 | 2,153.40 | 3.5 | 836.5 | 0.4 | .. | 355.1 | 31.3 | 267.6 | 25.7 | 266.4 | 30.0 |
| Belgium[b] | 0.80 | 0.69 | 0.9 | 0.9 | 1.1 | 109.4 | 1.8 | 2.0 | 1.9 | 2.0 | 1.2 | 2.0 |
| Benin | 522.89 | 449.94 | 187.1 | 225.7 | 0.4 | .. | 8.7 | 3.3 | 8.3 | 2.7 | .. | .. |
| Bolivia | 8.01 | 7.65 | 1.6 | 2.4 | 0.3 | 79.5 | 8.6 | 6.0 | 8.7 | 3.4 | .. | .. |
| Bosnia and Herzegovina | 1.56 | 1.34 | 0.6 | 0.8 | 0.5 | .. | 3.3 | 3.4 | .. | .. | .. | .. |
| Botswana | 5.84 | 6.03 | 1.4 | 2.7 | 0.5 | .. | 9.7 | 6.1 | 10.4 | 8.4 | .. | .. |
| Brazil | 2.18 | 1.79 | 0.7 | 1.4 | 0.6 | .. | 211.9 | 9.2 | 199.5 | 8.4 | 204.9 | 13.2 |
| Bulgaria | 1.56 | 1.34 | 0.0 | 0.6 | 0.4 | 125.4 | 103.3 | 4.5 | 117.5 | 5.3 | 85.7 | 5.0 |
| Burkina Faso | 522.89 | 449.94 | 184.3 | 198.9 | 0.4 | .. | 3.7 | 3.1 | 5.5 | 2.6 | .. | .. |
| Burundi | 1,028.43 | 1,137.21 | 126.3 | 341.2 | 0.3 | 73.2 | 13.4 | 8.3 | 16.1 | 7.3 | .. | .. |
| Cambodia | 4,103.25 | 3,999.00 | 1,140.0 | 1,297.1 | 0.3 | 94.3 | 3.4 | 3.4 | 4.9 | 3.1 | .. | .. |
| Cameroon | 522.89 | 449.94 | 236.0 | 252.4 | 0.5 | 113.2 | 6.3 | 2.4 | 6.5 | 2.1 | .. | .. |
| Canada | 1.13 | 1.00 | 1.2 | 1.2 | 1.1 | 126.8 | 1.5 | 2.5 | 1.7 | 2.3 | 2.7 | 1.0 |
| Central African Republic | 522.89 | 449.94 | 267.5 | 265.2 | 0.5 | 129.3 | 4.5 | 2.1 | 5.3 | 2.1 | 6.3 | 4.4 |
| Chad | 522.89 | 449.94 | 134.9 | 221.1 | 0.4 | 126.7 | 7.1 | 8.8 | 6.9 | 2.8 | .. | .. |
| Chile | 530.29 | 499.28 | 261.8 | 361.2 | 0.7 | 96.6 | 7.9 | 6.8 | 8.9 | 2.6 | 7.0 | 5.7 |
| China | 7.97 | 7.37 | 3.3 | 3.5 | 0.4 | 94.4 | 7.9 | 3.5 | 8.6 | 1.5 | .. | .. |
|   Hong Kong, China | 7.77 | 7.80 | 8.2 | 5.5 | 0.7 | .. | 4.0 | –2.9 | 5.9 | –1.0 | 0.6 | 0.1 |
| Colombia | 2,361.14 | 2,016.70 | 484.1 | 1,104.8 | 0.5 | 103.6 | 21.7 | 6.7 | 20.3 | 6.1 | 16.4 | 6.0 |
| Congo, Dem. Rep. | 468.28 | .. | 0.0 | 234.8 | 0.5 | 32.8 | 964.9 | 35.7 | 932.8 | 41.1 | .. | .. |
| Congo, Rep. | 522.89 | 449.94 | 153.5 | 300.1 | 0.6 | .. | 9.0 | 4.7 | 9.6 | 2.7 | 0.6 | .. |
| Costa Rica | 511.30 | 498.69 | 106.3 | 270.2 | 0.5 | 92.7 | 15.9 | 9.8 | 15.6 | 11.2 | 14.1 | 11.8 |
| Côte d'Ivoire | 522.89 | 449.94 | 261.4 | 294.1 | 0.6 | 115.9 | 9.2 | 3.1 | 7.2 | 3.0 | .. | .. |
| Croatia | 5.84 | 5.02 | 3.1 | 3.9 | 0.7 | 111.8 | 86.0 | 3.7 | 86.2 | 2.5 | 83.7 | 2.3 |
| Cuba | .. | .. | .. | .. | .. | .. | 2.5 | 2.6 | .. | .. | .. | .. |
| Czech Republic | 22.60 | 18.04 | 11.2 | 14.2 | 0.6 | 132.3 | 12.8 | 2.3 | 6.9 | 2.0 | 8.2 | 2.0 |
| Denmark | 5.95 | 5.12 | 8.4 | 8.4 | 1.4 | 108.4 | 1.6 | 2.3 | 2.1 | 1.9 | 1.1 | 1.9 |
| Dominican Republic | 33.37 | 33.76 | 6.9 | 18.7 | 0.6 | 99.1 | 9.4 | 19.0 | 8.7 | 19.0 | .. | .. |
| Ecuador | 1.00 | 1.00 | 0.4 | 0.4 | 0.4 | 147.1 | 4.3 | 10.6 | 37.1 | 8.9 | .. | 8.5 |
| Egypt, Arab Rep. | 5.73 | 5.53 | 1.2 | 1.7 | 0.3 | .. | 8.7 | 6.4 | 8.8 | 5.8 | 6.1 | 9.5 |
| El Salvador | 1.00 | 1.00 | 0.4 | 0.5 | 0.5 | .. | 6.2 | 3.2 | 8.5 | 3.4 | .. | 3.9 |
| Eritrea | 15.38 | 15.38 | 1.8 | 5.2 | 0.3 | .. | 6.4 | 15.4 | .. | .. | .. | .. |
| Estonia | 12.47 | 10.74 | 4.6 | 8.0 | 0.6 | .. | 53.8 | 4.0 | 23.1 | 3.4 | 8.2 | 2.0 |
| Ethiopia | 8.70 | 9.12 | 2.2 | 2.4 | 0.3 | 100.0 | 5.8 | 4.6 | 5.5 | 7.1 | .. | .. |
| Finland[b] | 0.80 | 0.69 | 1.1 | 1.0 | 1.2 | 104.0 | 2.0 | 0.8 | 1.5 | 1.1 | 1.0 | 1.3 |
| France[b] | 0.80 | 0.69 | 1.0 | 0.9 | 1.1 | 107.6 | 1.3 | 1.9 | 1.6 | 1.9 | .. | 1.6 |
| Gabon | 522.89 | 449.94 | 187.6 | 268.0 | 0.5 | 102.1 | 7.0 | 4.3 | 4.6 | 1.2 | .. | .. |
| Gambia, The | 28.07 | 22.24 | 3.9 | 7.6 | 0.3 | 54.3 | 4.2 | 14.3 | 4.1 | 10.6 | .. | .. |
| Georgia | 1.78 | 1.60 | 0.4 | 0.8 | 0.4 | .. | 356.7 | 6.5 | 27.1 | 5.6 | .. | .. |
| Germany[b] | 0.80 | 0.69 | 1.0 | 0.9 | 1.1 | 106.7 | 1.7 | 0.9 | 2.1 | 1.6 | 0.4 | 2.4 |
| Ghana | 0.92 | 0.97 | 573.5 | 4,133.3 | 0.5 | 116.1 | 26.7 | 21.1 | 28.4 | 18.2 | .. | .. |
| Greece[b] | 0.80 | 0.69 | 0.6 | 0.7 | 0.9 | 114.6 | 9.2 | 3.4 | 9.0 | 3.4 | 3.0 | 3.8 |
| Guatemala | 7.60 | 7.63 | 2.3 | 4.0 | 0.5 | .. | 10.4 | 7.1 | 10.1 | 7.2 | .. | .. |
| Guinea | 3,644.33 | .. | 645.8 | 1,635.0 | 0.3 | .. | 5.5 | 17.2 | .. | .. | .. | .. |
| Guinea-Bissau | 522.89 | 449.94 | 116.0 | 202.6 | 0.4 | .. | 32.5 | 0.7 | 34.0 | 1.2 | .. | .. |
| Haiti | 40.41 | 36.22 | 5.4 | 17.4 | 0.4 | .. | 22.8 | 17.4 | 21.9 | 20.4 | .. | .. |

# Exchange rates and prices

| | Official exchange rate | | Purchasing power parity (PPP) conversion factor | | Ratio of PPP conversion factor to market exchange rate | Real effective exchange rate | GDP implicit deflator | | Consumer price index | | Wholesale price index | |
|---|---|---|---|---|---|---|---|---|---|---|---|---|
| | local currency units to $ | | local currency units to international $ | | | Index 2000 = 100 | average annual % growth | | average annual % growth | | average annual % growth | |
| | 2006 | 2007a | 1995 | 2006 | 2006 | 2006 | 1990–2000 | 2000–06 | 1990–2000 | 2000–06 | 1990–2000 | 2000–06 |
| Honduras | 18.90 | 18.90 | 2.8 | 7.1 | 0.4 | .. | 18.9 | 7.8 | 22.8 | 8.0 | .. | .. |
| Hungary | 210.39 | 173.86 | 60.2 | 129.1 | 0.6 | 127.0 | 19.6 | 5.3 | 20.3 | 5.4 | 16.8 | 2.9 |
| India | 45.31 | 39.44 | 11.2 | 15.1 | 0.3 | .. | 8.1 | 4.2 | 9.1 | 4.2 | 7.4 | 4.9 |
| Indonesia | 9,159.32 | 9,333.60 | 1,025.3 | 4,332.6 | 0.5 | .. | 15.8 | 9.6 | 13.7 | 9.3 | 15.4 | 8.6 |
| Iran, Islamic Rep. | 9,170.94 | 9,368.13 | 564.5 | 2,877.9 | 0.3 | 135.2 | 27.7 | 17.4 | 26.0 | 14.1 | 28.4 | 10.2 |
| Iraq | 1,467.42 | .. | .. | 558.7 | .. | .. | 13.9 | 0.3 | .. | .. | .. | .. |
| Irelandb | 0.80 | 0.69 | 0.8 | 1.0 | 1.3 | 125.9 | 3.5 | 3.3 | 2.3 | 3.4 | 1.6 | 0.1 |
| Israel | 4.46 | 3.90 | 3.1 | 3.7 | 0.8 | 78.0 | 10.8 | 1.3 | 9.7 | 1.6 | 8.1 | 4.5 |
| Italyb | 0.80 | 0.69 | 0.8 | 0.9 | 1.1 | 110.8 | 3.8 | 2.8 | 3.7 | 2.4 | 2.9 | 2.4 |
| Jamaica | 65.74 | 71.17 | 14.2 | 32.6 | 0.5 | .. | 23.0 | 10.0 | 23.5 | 10.8 | .. | .. |
| Japan | 116.30 | 112.25 | 174.9 | 124.5 | 1.1 | 72.0 | 0.1 | –1.3 | 0.8 | –0.3 | –0.9 | 0.0 |
| Jordan | 0.71 | 0.71 | 0.4 | 0.4 | 0.6 | .. | 3.2 | 2.6 | 3.5 | 2.9 | .. | 8.2 |
| Kazakhstan | 126.09 | 120.78 | 17.4 | 67.9 | 0.5 | .. | 204.7 | 13.5 | 86.7 | 7.1 | 12.6 | 11.5 |
| Kenya | 72.10 | 63.30 | 15.4 | 30.6 | 0.4 | .. | 16.6 | 5.3 | 15.6 | 8.9 | .. | .. |
| Korea, Dem. Rep. | .. | .. | .. | .. | .. | .. | .. | .. | .. | .. | .. | .. |
| Korea, Rep. | 954.79 | 930.76 | 735.8 | 761.8 | 0.8 | .. | 5.7 | 2.0 | 5.1 | 3.2 | 3.6 | 2.3 |
| Kuwait | 0.29 | 0.27 | 0.1 | 0.2 | 0.7 | .. | 0.8 | 8.3 | 2.0 | 1.8 | 1.4 | 2.3 |
| Kyrgyz Republic | 40.15 | 35.01 | 3.5 | 12.0 | 0.3 | .. | 110.6 | 5.3 | 18.1 | 4.0 | 36.0 | 7.2 |
| Lao PDR | 10,159.92 | 9,541.42 | 308.9 | 3,032.3 | 0.3 | .. | 27.0 | 10.3 | 28.2 | 10.3 | .. | .. |
| Latvia | 0.56 | 0.48 | 0.2 | 0.3 | 0.6 | .. | 48.0 | 6.1 | 33.8 | 4.5 | 15.2 | 5.3 |
| Lebanon | 1,507.50 | 1,507.50 | 841.3 | 867.1 | 0.6 | .. | 17.8 | 1.7 | 21.3 | .. | .. | .. |
| Lesotho | 6.77 | 6.81 | 2.1 | 3.5 | 0.5 | 129.4 | 9.8 | 5.5 | 9.9 | 8.1 | .. | .. |
| Liberia | 58.01 | 60.77 | 0.6 | 30.6 | 0.5 | .. | 51.8 | 10.1 | .. | .. | .. | .. |
| Libya | 1.31 | 1.22 | .. | 0.9 | 0.7 | .. | .. | 22.8 | 5.6 | –3.0 | .. | .. |
| Lithuania | 2.75 | 2.37 | 1.2 | 1.5 | 0.6 | .. | 75.1 | 2.0 | 40.5 | 1.1 | 32.6 | 3.5 |
| Macedonia, FYR | 48.80 | 42.02 | 17.1 | 19.0 | 0.4 | 100.0 | 79.3 | 2.3 | 14.4 | 1.8 | 10.9 | 0.7 |
| Madagascar | 2,142.30 | 1,792.15 | 286.8 | 700.4 | 0.3 | .. | 19.1 | 11.5 | 18.7 | 10.5 | .. | .. |
| Malawi | 136.01 | 140.17 | 3.9 | 45.3 | 0.3 | 73.3 | 33.6 | 23.6 | 33.8 | 13.8 | .. | .. |
| Malaysia | 3.67 | 3.33 | 1.4 | 1.7 | 0.5 | 99.0 | 3.9 | 4.9 | 3.6 | 1.9 | 3.4 | 4.3 |
| Mali | 522.89 | 449.94 | 226.3 | 242.2 | 0.5 | .. | 7.0 | 3.7 | 5.2 | 1.7 | .. | .. |
| Mauritania | 265.53 | .. | 62.2 | 124.3 | 0.5 | .. | 8.7 | 11.4 | 6.1 | 7.3 | .. | .. |
| Mauritius | 31.71 | 29.04 | 10.5 | 14.8 | 0.5 | .. | 6.4 | 5.4 | 6.9 | 5.4 | .. | .. |
| Mexico | 10.90 | 10.85 | 2.7 | 7.2 | 0.7 | .. | 19.0 | 6.7 | 19.4 | 4.7 | 18.4 | 6.5 |
| Moldova | 13.13 | 11.29 | 1.2 | 4.8 | 0.4 | 102.9 | 119.6 | 10.9 | 14.5 | 10.7 | .. | .. |
| Mongolia | 1,165.37 | 1,187.63 | 158.3 | 497.8 | 0.4 | .. | 57.8 | 13.3 | 39.8 | 6.5 | .. | .. |
| Morocco | 8.80 | 7.78 | 4.9 | 4.8 | 0.5 | 92.9 | 4.0 | 1.0 | 3.8 | 1.7 | 2.9 | –0.6 |
| Mozambique | 25.40 | 25.84 | 3,938.1 | 11,203.4 | 0.4 | .. | 34.7 | 8.0 | 31.8 | 12.2 | .. | .. |
| Myanmar | 5.78 | 5.45 | 40.9 | 254.4 | .. | .. | 25.5 | 21.1 | 25.9 | 23.7 | .. | .. |
| Namibia | 6.77 | 6.81 | 2.5 | 4.5 | 0.7 | .. | 10.4 | 5.2 | .. | 4.3 | .. | .. |
| Nepal | 72.76 | 63.63 | 15.5 | 23.4 | 0.3 | .. | 8.0 | 5.2 | 8.7 | 4.7 | .. | .. |
| Netherlandsb | 0.80 | 0.69 | 0.9 | 0.9 | 1.1 | 111.9 | 2.1 | 2.3 | 2.4 | 2.2 | 1.3 | 2.3 |
| New Zealand | 1.54 | 1.30 | 1.5 | 1.5 | 1.0 | 128.1 | 1.7 | 2.4 | 1.7 | 2.5 | 1.4 | 2.5 |
| Nicaragua | 17.57 | 18.87 | 3.0 | 6.0 | 0.3 | 88.2 | 42.4 | 7.2 | .. | 7.4 | .. | .. |
| Niger | 522.89 | 449.94 | 203.1 | 221.8 | 0.4 | .. | 6.0 | 2.3 | 6.1 | 2.0 | .. | .. |
| Nigeria | 128.65 | 118.21 | 17.3 | 63.0 | 0.5 | 133.1 | 29.5 | 15.8 | 32.5 | 14.6 | .. | .. |
| Norway | 6.41 | 5.50 | 7.0 | 9.2 | 1.4 | 111.3 | 2.7 | 3.9 | 2.2 | 1.7 | 1.6 | 5.8 |
| Oman | 0.39 | 0.39 | 0.2 | 0.2 | 0.6 | .. | 0.1 | 4.3 | .. | 0.7 | .. | .. |
| Pakistan | 60.27 | 61.22 | 10.1 | 20.2 | 0.3 | 97.0 | 11.1 | 6.1 | 9.7 | 5.6 | 10.4 | 6.7 |
| Panama | 1.00 | 1.00 | 0.5 | 0.6 | 0.6 | .. | 3.6 | 1.7 | 1.1 | 1.1 | 1.0 | 2.0 |
| Papua New Guinea | 3.06 | 2.83 | 0.8 | 1.5 | 0.5 | 101.3 | 7.0 | 7.9 | 9.3 | 7.1 | .. | .. |
| Paraguay | 5,635.46 | 4,731.70 | 966.4 | 2,153.9 | 0.4 | 88.1 | 11.5 | 10.9 | 13.1 | 8.8 | 5.8 | 13.1 |
| Peru | 3.27 | 2.98 | 1.2 | 1.5 | 0.5 | .. | 26.7 | 3.4 | 27.3 | 2.0 | 23.7 | 2.2 |
| Philippines | 51.31 | 41.74 | 14.1 | 22.2 | 0.4 | 102.5 | 8.3 | 5.3 | 7.7 | 5.3 | 5.0 | 9.0 |
| Poland | 3.10 | 2.48 | 1.2 | 1.9 | 0.6 | 109.8 | 24.7 | 2.3 | 25.3 | 2.3 | 19.8 | 2.8 |
| Portugalb | 0.80 | 0.69 | 0.6 | 0.7 | 0.9 | 111.5 | 5.2 | 3.1 | 4.5 | 3.0 | .. | 2.3 |
| Puerto Rico | 1.00 | 1.00 | .. | .. | .. | .. | 3.0 | .. | .. | .. | .. | .. |

| | Official exchange rate | | Purchasing power parity (PPP) conversion factor | | Ratio of PPP conversion factor to market exchange rate | Real effective exchange rate | GDP implicit deflator | | Consumer price index | | Wholesale price index | |
|---|---|---|---|---|---|---|---|---|---|---|---|---|
| | local currency units to $ | | local currency units to international $ | | | Index 2000 = 100 | average annual % growth | | average annual % growth | | average annual % growth | |
| | 2006 | 2007[a] | 1995 | 2006 | 2006 | 2006 | 1990–2000 | 2000–06 | 1990–2000 | 2000–06 | 1990–2000 | 2000–06 |
| Romania | 2.81 | 2.43 | 0.1 | 1.5 | 0.5 | 128.9 | 98.0 | 19.6 | 100.5 | 15.6 | 93.8 | 19.3 |
| Russian Federation | 27.19 | 24.57 | 1.5 | 14.3 | 0.5 | 163.4 | 161.5 | 17.0 | 108.0 | 13.6 | 110.8 | 17.2 |
| Rwanda | 551.71 | .. | 133.6 | 196.9 | 0.4 | .. | 14.6 | 6.6 | 15.8 | 7.4 | .. | .. |
| Saudi Arabia | 3.75 | 3.75 | 1.8 | 2.5 | 0.7 | 81.7 | 1.6 | 7.5 | 1.0 | 0.5 | 1.3 | 1.5 |
| Senegal | 522.89 | 449.94 | 252.4 | 250.9 | 0.5 | .. | 6.0 | 1.7 | 5.4 | 1.4 | .. | .. |
| Serbia | 67.15 | 54.68 | .. | 30.5 | 0.5 | .. | .. | 21.9 | 42.4 | 20.3 | .. | .. |
| Sierra Leone | 2,961.91 | 2,982.38 | 382.8 | 1,188.0 | 0.4 | 73.5 | 32.1 | 8.3 | 29.3 | 7.3 | .. | .. |
| Singapore | 1.59 | 1.45 | 1.3 | 1.0 | 0.7 | 94.3 | 1.3 | 0.2 | 1.7 | 0.7 | –1.0 | 3.3 |
| Slovak Republic | 29.70 | 22.64 | 12.6 | 17.1 | 0.6 | 142.7 | 11.2 | 4.4 | 7.4 | 5.8 | 9.5 | 5.3 |
| Slovenia | 191.03[c] | 0.69[d] | 96.0 | 145.8 | 0.8 | .. | 28.7 | 4.8 | 11.9 | 4.9 | 9.0 | 4.1 |
| Somalia | .. | .. | .. | .. | .. | .. | .. | .. | .. | .. | .. | .. |
| South Africa | 6.77 | 6.81 | 2.3 | 4.0 | 0.6 | 104.2 | 9.9 | 6.5 | 8.7 | 4.9 | 7.4 | 5.2 |
| Spain[b] | 0.80 | 0.69 | 0.7 | 0.8 | 1.0 | 114.9 | 3.9 | 4.1 | 3.8 | 3.2 | 2.4 | 2.8 |
| Sri Lanka | 103.91 | 109.13 | 18.9 | 37.6 | 0.4 | .. | 9.1 | 8.8 | 9.9 | 9.7 | 8.1 | 9.7 |
| Sudan | 217.15 | 2.03 | 15.3 | 111.6 | 0.5 | .. | 76.8 | 9.8 | 71.9 | 7.8 | .. | .. |
| Swaziland | 6.77 | 6.81 | 1.6 | 3.4 | 0.5 | .. | 12.5 | 8.4 | 9.4 | 6.5 | .. | .. |
| Sweden | 7.38 | 6.47 | 10.0 | 9.1 | 1.2 | 96.8 | 2.2 | 1.4 | 1.9 | 1.4 | 2.4 | 2.2 |
| Switzerland | 1.25 | 1.14 | 2.0 | 1.7 | 1.4 | 101.7 | 1.0 | 0.9 | 1.6 | 0.9 | –0.4 | 0.6 |
| Syrian Arab Republic | 11.23 | 11.23 | 12.7 | 20.8 | 0.4 | .. | 7.9 | 6.0 | 6.4 | 4.8 | 4.7 | 2.2 |
| Tajikistan | 3.30 | 3.46 | 0.0 | 0.9 | 0.3 | .. | 235.0 | 20.3 | .. | .. | .. | .. |
| Tanzania | 1,251.90 | 1,158.93 | 172.6 | 407.6 | 0.3 | .. | 21.6 | 7.3 | 20.9 | 3.7 | .. | .. |
| Thailand | 37.88 | 33.66 | 15.1 | 16.2 | 0.4 | .. | 4.2 | 2.7 | 4.9 | 2.6 | 3.8 | 5.2 |
| Timor-Leste | .. | .. | .. | 0.2 | .. | .. | .. | 1.5 | .. | .. | .. | .. |
| Togo | 522.89 | 449.94 | 238.0 | 232.0 | 0.4 | 112.4 | 7.0 | 0.7 | 8.5 | 2.3 | .. | .. |
| Trinidad and Tobago | 6.31 | 6.31 | 3.7 | 4.9 | 0.8 | 112.6 | 5.4 | 4.8 | 5.7 | 5.1 | 2.8 | 2.0 |
| Tunisia | 1.33 | 1.23 | 0.5 | 0.6 | 0.4 | 84.6 | 4.4 | 2.4 | 4.4 | 2.9 | 3.6 | 3.5 |
| Turkey | 1.43 | 1.18 | 0.0 | 0.9 | 0.7 | .. | 76.1 | 21.7 | 79.9 | 23.5 | .. | 9.5 |
| Turkmenistan | .. | .. | .. | 4,306.3 | 0.4 | .. | 408.0 | .. | .. | .. | .. | .. |
| Uganda | 1,831.45 | 1,747.17 | 483.6 | 644.1 | 0.4 | 87.8 | 11.8 | 5.5 | 10.5 | 4.7 | .. | .. |
| Ukraine | 5.05 | 5.05 | 0.3 | 1.9 | 0.4 | 110.7 | 271.0 | 12.6 | 190.4 | 7.8 | 198.5 | 11.4 |
| United Arab Emirates | 3.67 | 3.67 | 2.7 | 3.5 | 0.9 | .. | 2.2 | 4.9 | .. | .. | .. | .. |
| United Kingdom | 0.54 | 0.49 | 0.6 | 0.6 | 1.2 | 103.1 | 2.9 | 2.7 | 2.9 | 2.6 | 2.4 | 1.6 |
| United States | 1.00 | 1.00 | 1.0 | 1.0 | 1.0 | 92.4 | 2.0 | 2.5 | 2.7 | 2.6 | 1.2 | 3.9 |
| Uruguay | 24.07 | 21.69 | 5.7 | 13.7 | 0.6 | 78.1 | 31.1 | 10.0 | 33.9 | 10.5 | 27.2 | 17.1 |
| Uzbekistan | .. | .. | 11.1 | 356.9 | 0.3 | .. | 245.8 | 27.7 | .. | .. | .. | .. |
| Venezuela, RB | 2,147.00 | 2,147.00 | 72.7 | 1,306.5 | 0.6 | 73.4 | 45.3 | 28.2 | 49.0 | 20.8 | 44.1 | 29.6 |
| Vietnam | 15,994.25 | .. | 3,162.7 | 4,899.4 | 0.3 | .. | 15.2 | 6.3 | 3.3 | 5.2 | .. | .. |
| West Bank and Gaza | .. | .. | 1.1 | 1.3 | 0.3 | .. | 4.9 | 3.2 | 4.0 | 3.8 | .. | .. |
| Yemen, Rep. | 197.05 | 199.33 | 21.8 | 76.3 | 0.4 | .. | 22.4 | 13.0 | 26.3 | 12.8 | .. | .. |
| Zambia | 3,603.07 | 3,834.24 | 396.9 | 2,625.9 | 0.7 | 176.7 | 52.1 | 19.4 | 57.0 | 18.9 | 68.8 | .. |
| Zimbabwe | 22,364.00 | 255.00 | 25.7 | 33,068.2 | 1.5 | .. | 26.7 | 232.0 | 29.0 | 296.4 | 25.3 | .. |

**Note:** The differences in the growth rates of the GDP deflator and consumer and wholesale price indexes are due mainly to data availability of each of the indexes during the period.
a. December or latest monthly data available. b. As members of the euro area, these countries share a single currency, the euro. c. Tolars. d. Euros.

# Exchange rates and prices | 4.14

In a market-based economy household, producer, and government choices about resource allocation are influenced by relative prices, including the real exchange rate, real wages, real interest rates, and other prices in the economy. Relative prices also largely reflect these agents' choices. Thus relative prices convey vital information about the interaction of economic agents in an economy and with the rest of the world.

The exchange rate is the price of one currency in terms of another. Official exchange rates and exchange rate arrangements are established by governments. Other exchange rates recognized by governments include market rates, which are determined largely by legal market forces, and for countries with multiple exchange arrangements, principal rates, secondary rates, and tertiary rates. (Also see *Statistical methods* for alternative conversion factors in the *World Bank Atlas* method of calculating gross national income (GNI) per capita in U.S. dollars.)

Official or market exchange rates are often used to compare prices across currencies. Since rates reflect at best the relative prices of tradable goods, the volume of goods and services that a U.S. dollar buys in the United States may not correspond to what a U.S. dollar converted to another country's currency at the official exchange rate would buy in that country. Since identical volumes of goods and services in different countries correspond to different values (and vice versa) when official exchange rates are used, an alternative method to compare prices across countries converts national currency estimates of GNI to a common unit of account using conversion factors that reflect equivalent purchasing power. Based on price and expenditure surveys conducted by the International Comparison Program, purchasing power parity (PPP) conversion factors are applied to equalize price levels across countries. See *About the data* for table 1.1 for further discussion.

The ratio of the PPP conversion factor to the market exchange rate—or the national price level—allows comparison of the cost of the bundle of goods that make up gross domestic product (GDP) across countries. The market exchange rate (or alternative conversion factor) is the official exchange rate adjusted by World Bank staff for some countries to reflect actual price changes. National price levels vary systematically, rising with GNI per capita. The real effective exchange rate is a nominal effective exchange rate index adjusted for relative movements in national price or cost indicators of the home country, selected countries, and the euro area. A nominal effective exchange rate index is the ratio (expressed on the base 2000 = 100) of an index of a currency's period-average exchange rate to a weighted geometric average of exchange rates for currencies of selected

countries and the euro area. For most high-income countries weights are derived from industrial country trade in manufactured goods. Data are compiled from the nominal effective exchange rate index and a cost indicator of relative normalized unit labor costs in manufacturing. For selected other countries the nominal effective exchange rate index is based on manufactured goods and primary products trade with partner or competitor countries. For these countries the real effective exchange rate index is the nominal index adjusted for relative changes in consumer prices; an increase represents an appreciation of the local currency. Because of conceptual and data limitations, changes in real effective exchange rates should be interpreted with caution.

Inflation is measured by the rate of increase in a price index, but actual price change can be negative. The index used depends on the prices being examined. The GDP deflator reflects price changes for total GDP. The most general measure of the overall price level, it accounts for changes in government consumption, capital formation (including inventory appreciation), international trade, and the main component, household final consumption expenditure. The GDP deflator is usually derived implicitly as the ratio of current to constant price GDP—or a Paasche index. It is defective as a general measure of inflation for policy use because of long lags in deriving estimates and because it is often an annual measure.

Consumer price indexes are produced more frequently and so are more current. They are also constructed explicitly, based on surveys of the cost of a defined basket of consumer goods and services. Nevertheless, consumer price indexes should be interpreted with caution. The definition of a household, the basket of goods, and the geographic (urban or rural) and income group coverage of consumer price surveys can vary widely by country. In addition, weights are derived from household expenditure surveys, which, for budgetary reasons, tend to be conducted infrequently in developing countries, impairing comparability over time. Although useful for measuring consumer price inflation within a country, consumer price indexes are of less value in comparing countries.

Wholesale price indexes are based on the prices of commodities that are significant in a country's output or consumption at the first commercial transaction. Prices are farm-gate prices for agricultural commodities and ex-factory prices for industrial goods. Preference is given to indexes with the broadest coverage of the economy.

The least-squares method is used to calculate growth rates of the GDP implicit deflator, consumer price index, and wholesale price index.

• **Official exchange rate** is the exchange rate determined by national authorities or the rate determined in the legally sanctioned exchange market. It is calculated as an annual average based on monthly averages (local currency units relative to the U.S. dollar). • **Purchasing power parity (PPP) conversion factor** is the number of units of a country's currency required to buy the same amount of goods and services in the domestic market that a U.S. dollar would buy in the United States. • **Ratio of PPP conversion factor to market exchange rate** is the result obtained by dividing the PPP conversion factor by the market exchange rate. • **Real effective exchange rate** is the nominal effective exchange rate (a measure of the value of a currency against a weighted average of several foreign currencies) divided by a price deflator or index of costs. • **GDP implicit deflator** measures the average annual rate of price change in the economy as a whole for the periods shown. • **Consumer price index** reflects changes in the cost to the average consumer of acquiring a basket of goods and services that may be fixed or may change at specified intervals, such as yearly. The Laspeyres formula is generally used. • **Wholesale price index** refers to a mix of agricultural and industrial goods at various stages of production and distribution, including import duties. The Laspeyres formula is generally used.

**Data sources**

Data on official and real effective exchange rates and consumer and wholesale price indexes are from the International Monetary Fund's *International Financial Statistics*. PPP conversion factors and GDP deflators are from the World Bank's data files.

| | Goods and services | | | | Net income | | Net current transfers | | Current account balance | | Total reserves[a] | |
|---|---|---|---|---|---|---|---|---|---|---|---|---|
| | $ millions | | | | $ millions | | $ millions | | $ millions | | $ millions | |
| | Exports | | Imports | | | | | | | | | |
| | 1995 | 2006 | 1995 | 2006 | 1995 | 2006 | 1995 | 2006 | 1995 | 2006 | 1995 | 2006 |
| Afghanistan | .. | .. | .. | .. | .. | .. | .. | .. | .. | .. | .. | .. |
| Albania | 304 | 2,297 | 836 | 4,500 | 44 | 263 | 477 | 1,270 | –12 | –671 | 265 | 1,813 |
| Algeria | .. | .. | .. | .. | .. | .. | .. | .. | .. | .. | 4,164 | 81,463 |
| Angola | 3,836 | 33,346 | 3,519 | 16,289 | –767 | –6,178 | 156 | –190 | –295 | 10,690 | 213 | 8,599 |
| Argentina | 24,987 | 54,123 | 26,066 | 41,088 | –4,636 | –5,440 | 597 | 497 | –5,118 | 8,092 | 15,979 | 32,022 |
| Armenia | 300 | 1,510 | 726 | 2,536 | 40 | 215 | 168 | 694 | –218 | –117 | 111 | 1,072 |
| Australia | 69,710 | 158,002 | 74,841 | 166,759 | –14,036 | –32,076 | –109 | –213 | –19,277 | –41,046 | 14,952 | 55,079 |
| Austria | 89,906 | 179,503 | 92,055 | 166,059 | –1,597 | –1,830 | –1,702 | –1,355 | –5,448 | 10,259 | 23,369 | 12,911 |
| Azerbaijan | 785 | 13,955 | 1,290 | 8,133 | –6 | –2,681 | 111 | 566 | –401 | 3,708 | 121 | 2,500 |
| Bangladesh | 4,431 | 12,888 | 7,589 | 16,784 | 68 | –841 | 2,265 | 5,933 | –824 | 1,196 | 2,376 | 3,877 |
| Belarus | 5,269 | 22,137 | 5,752 | 23,723 | –51 | –107 | 76 | 182 | –458 | –1,512 | 377 | 1,417 |
| Belgium | 190,686[b] | 340,727 | 178,798[b] | 330,926 | 6,808[b] | 7,531 | –4,463[b] | –6,661 | 14,232[b] | 10,671 | 24,120 | 13,437 |
| Benin | 614 | 772 | 895 | 1,145 | –8 | –18 | 121 | 164 | –167 | –226 | 198 | 912 |
| Bolivia | 1,234 | 4,297 | 1,574 | 3,437 | –207 | –364 | 244 | 822 | –303 | 1,319 | 1,005 | 3,194 |
| Bosnia and Herzegovina | .. | 4,496 | .. | 8,187 | .. | 409 | .. | 2,049 | .. | –1,233 | 80 | 3,372 |
| Botswana | 2,421 | 5,292 | 2,050 | 3,451 | –32 | –772 | –39 | 871 | 300 | 1,940 | 4,695 | 7,992 |
| Brazil | 52,641 | 157,270 | 63,293 | 120,466 | –11,105 | –27,489 | 3,621 | 4,306 | –18,136 | 13,621 | 51,477 | 85,843 |
| Bulgaria | 6,776 | 20,108 | 6,502 | 25,985 | –432 | 47 | 132 | 821 | –26 | –5,010 | 1,635 | 11,756 |
| Burkina Faso | 272 | .. | 483 | .. | –29 | .. | 255 | .. | 15 | .. | 347 | 555 |
| Burundi | 129 | 93 | 259 | 448 | –13 | –9 | 153 | 229 | 10 | –135 | 216 | 131 |
| Cambodia | 969 | 4,989 | 1,375 | 5,539 | –57 | –290 | 277 | 503 | –186 | –337 | 192 | 1,411 |
| Cameroon | 2,040 | 3,630 | 1,608 | 3,970 | –412 | –443 | 69 | 176 | 90 | –608 | 15 | 1,735 |
| Canada | 219,501 | 461,118 | 200,991 | 429,289 | –22,721 | –10,416 | –117 | –616 | –4,328 | 20,797 | 16,369 | 35,063 |
| Central African Republic | 179 | .. | 244 | .. | –23 | .. | 63 | .. | –25 | .. | 238 | 132 |
| Chad | 190 | .. | 411 | .. | –7 | .. | 191 | .. | –38 | .. | 147 | 632 |
| Chile | 19,358 | 65,620 | 18,301 | 44,329 | –2,714 | –19,392 | 307 | 3,357 | –1,350 | 5,256 | 14,860 | 19,397 |
| China[†] | 147,240 | 1,061,682 | 135,282 | 852,769 | –11,774 | 11,755 | 1,435 | 29,199 | 1,618 | 249,866 | 80,288 | 1,080,756 |
| Hong Kong, China | .. | 389,883 | .. | 368,167 | .. | 657 | .. | –2,222 | .. | 20,151 | 55,424 | 133,211 |
| Colombia | 12,294 | 28,554 | 16,012 | 30,352 | –1,596 | –6,003 | 799 | 4,743 | –4,516 | –3,057 | 8,452 | 15,437 |
| Congo, Dem. Rep. | .. | .. | .. | .. | .. | .. | .. | .. | .. | .. | 157 | .. |
| Congo, Rep. | 1,374 | 4,964 | 1,346 | 2,917 | –695 | –1,122 | 42 | –22 | –625 | 903 | 64 | 1,848 |
| Costa Rica | 4,451 | 11,023 | 4,717 | 12,422 | –226 | –68 | 134 | 349 | –358 | –1,118 | 1,060 | 3,117 |
| Côte d'Ivoire | 4,337 | 9,010 | 3,806 | 7,256 | –787 | –728 | –237 | –496 | –492 | 529 | 529 | 1,798 |
| Croatia | 6,972 | 21,454 | 9,106 | 24,678 | –53 | –1,384 | 802 | 1,389 | –1,385 | –3,220 | 1,896 | 11,488 |
| Cuba | .. | .. | .. | .. | .. | .. | .. | .. | .. | .. | .. | .. |
| Czech Republic | 28,202 | 108,450 | 30,044 | 103,940 | –104 | –8,204 | 572 | –891 | –1,374 | –4,586 | 14,613 | 31,457 |
| Denmark | 65,655 | 143,295 | 57,860 | 134,061 | –4,549 | 2,611 | –1,391 | –4,506 | 1,855 | 7,339 | 11,652 | 31,084 |
| Dominican Republic | 5,731 | 10,664 | 6,137 | 12,748 | –769 | –1,735 | 992 | 3,033 | –183 | –786 | 373 | 2,127 |
| Ecuador | 5,196 | 14,141 | 5,708 | 13,737 | –930 | –1,950 | 442 | 3,049 | –1,000 | 1,503 | 1,788 | 2,027 |
| Egypt, Arab Rep. | 13,260 | 36,680 | 17,140 | 40,553 | –405 | 738 | 4,031 | 5,770 | –254 | 2,635 | 17,122 | 26,007 |
| El Salvador | 2,040 | 5,070 | 3,623 | 8,741 | –67 | –519 | 1,389 | 3,335 | –262 | –855 | 940 | 1,963 |
| Eritrea | 135 | .. | 498 | .. | 8 | .. | 324 | .. | –32 | .. | 40 | 25 |
| Estonia | 2,573 | 13,128 | 2,860 | 14,833 | 3 | –751 | 126 | 11 | –158 | –2,446 | 583 | 2,786 |
| Ethiopia | 768 | 2,199 | 1,446 | 5,276 | –19 | 18 | 736 | 1,274 | 39 | –1,786 | 815 | 833 |
| Finland | 47,973 | 93,630 | 37,705 | 81,955 | –4,440 | 885 | –597 | –1,682 | 5,231 | 10,878 | 10,657 | 7,499 |
| France | 362,717 | 601,590 | 333,746 | 628,801 | –8,964 | 26,452 | –9,167 | –27,555 | 10,840 | –28,315 | 58,510 | 98,239 |
| Gabon | 2,945 | 4,228 | 1,723 | 2,155 | –665 | –965 | –42 | –184 | 515 | 924 | 153 | 1,122 |
| Gambia, The | 177 | 201 | 232 | 316 | –5 | –38 | 52 | 87 | –8 | –66 | 106 | 121 |
| Georgia | 575 | 2,567 | 1,413 | 4,413 | 127 | 169 | 197 | 522 | –514 | –1,154 | 199 | 931 |
| Germany | 603,815 | 1,304,419 | 592,056 | 1,149,108 | –2,737 | 28,805 | –38,769 | –33,370 | –29,746 | 150,745 | 121,816 | 111,637 |
| Ghana | 1,582 | 5,125 | 2,120 | 8,286 | –129 | –127 | 523 | 2,248 | –144 | –1,040 | 804 | 2,269 |
| Greece | 15,523 | 56,063 | 24,711 | 80,952 | –1,684 | –8,958 | 8,008 | 4,282 | –2,864 | –29,565 | 16,119 | 2,850 |
| Guatemala | 2,823 | 7,420 | 3,728 | 12,750 | –159 | –379 | 491 | 4,117 | –572 | –1,592 | 783 | 4,055 |
| Guinea | 700 | 811 | 1,011 | 964 | –85 | –27 | 179 | 18 | –216 | –162 | 87 | 97 |
| Guinea-Bissau | 30 | 83 | 89 | 127 | –21 | –10 | 46 | 67 | –35 | 14 | 20 | 82 |
| Haiti | 192 | 698 | 802 | 2,086 | –31 | 7 | 553 | 1,382 | –87 | 1 | 199 | 254 |
| [†]Data for Taiwan, China | 128,369 | 253,061 | 124,171 | 234,046 | 4,188 | 9,581 | –2,912 | –3,935 | 5,474 | 24,661 | 95,559 | 274,800 |

# Balance of payments current account

| | Goods and services | | | | Net income | | Net current transfers | | Current account balance | | Total reserves[a] | |
|---|---|---|---|---|---|---|---|---|---|---|---|---|
| | $ millions | | | | $ millions | | $ millions | | $ millions | | $ millions | |
| | Exports | | Imports | | | | | | | | | |
| | 1995 | 2006 | 1995 | 2006 | 1995 | 2006 | 1995 | 2006 | 1995 | 2006 | 1995 | 2006 |
| Honduras | 1,635 | 3,796 | 1,852 | 6,055 | −226 | −287 | 243 | 2,352 | −201 | −195 | 270 | 2,642 |
| Hungary | 19,765 | 87,643 | 19,916 | 87,169 | −1,701 | −8,344 | 203 | 449 | −1,650 | −7,421 | 12,017 | 21,590 |
| India | 38,013 | 198,971 | 48,225 | 230,232 | −3,734 | −4,264 | 8,382 | 26,109 | −5,563 | −9,415 | 22,865 | 178,050 |
| Indonesia | 52,923 | 115,032 | 54,461 | 95,493 | −5,874 | −14,465 | 981 | 4,863 | −6,431 | 9,937 | 14,908 | 42,597 |
| Iran, Islamic Rep. | 18,953 | .. | 15,113 | .. | −478 | .. | −4 | .. | 3,358 | .. | .. | .. |
| Iraq | .. | .. | .. | .. | .. | .. | .. | .. | .. | .. | 8,347 | 19,655 |
| Ireland | 49,439 | 173,857 | 42,169 | 151,307 | −7,325 | −31,101 | 1,776 | −544 | 1,721 | −9,095 | 8,770 | 832 |
| Israel | 27,482 | 62,992 | 35,290 | 61,892 | −2,655 | −576 | 5,673 | 7,466 | −4,790 | 7,990 | 8,123 | 29,153 |
| Italy | 295,618 | 515,634 | 250,319 | 529,153 | −15,644 | −17,118 | −4,579 | −16,675 | 25,076 | −47,312 | 60,690 | 75,773 |
| Jamaica | 3,394 | 4,782 | 3,729 | 7,098 | −371 | −603 | 607 | 1,749 | −99 | −1,170 | 681 | 2,318 |
| Japan | 493,991 | 733,111 | 419,556 | 670,065 | 44,285 | 118,156 | −7,676 | −10,684 | 111,044 | 170,517 | 192,620 | 895,321 |
| Jordan | 3,479 | 7,693 | 4,903 | 12,972 | −279 | 581 | 1,444 | 2,790 | −259 | −1,909 | 2,279 | 6,982 |
| Kazakhstan | 5,975 | 41,570 | 6,102 | 32,840 | −146 | −9,317 | 59 | −1,207 | −213 | −1,795 | 1,660 | 19,127 |
| Kenya | 2,948 | 5,963 | 3,542 | 8,200 | −325 | −70 | 518 | 1,781 | −400 | −526 | 384 | 2,416 |
| Korea, Dem. Rep. | .. | .. | .. | .. | .. | .. | .. | .. | .. | .. | .. | .. |
| Korea, Rep. | 147,761 | 383,718 | 155,104 | 373,268 | −1,303 | −539 | −19 | −3,820 | −8,665 | 6,092 | 32,804 | 239,148 |
| Kuwait | 14,215 | 65,610 | 12,615 | 24,542 | 4,881 | 13,385 | −1,465 | −3,457 | 5,016 | 50,996 | 4,543 | 14,180 |
| Kyrgyz Republic | 448 | 1,185 | 726 | 2,253 | −35 | −34 | 79 | 716 | −235 | −386 | 134 | 817 |
| Lao PDR | 408 | .. | 748 | .. | −6 | .. | 110 | .. | −237 | .. | 99 | 460 |
| Latvia | 2,088 | 8,783 | 2,193 | 13,251 | 19 | −532 | 71 | 479 | −16 | −4,522 | 602 | 4,511 |
| Lebanon | .. | 14,417 | .. | 17,253 | .. | 210 | .. | 1,280 | .. | −1,347 | 8,100 | 19,239 |
| Lesotho | 199 | 754 | 1,046 | 1,456 | 314 | 379 | 210 | 390 | −323 | 67 | 457 | 658 |
| Liberia | .. | .. | .. | .. | .. | .. | .. | .. | .. | .. | 28 | 72 |
| Libya | 7,513 | 37,962 | 5,755 | 15,783 | 133 | −595 | −220 | 586 | 1,672 | 22,170 | 7,415 | 62,229 |
| Lithuania | 3,191 | 17,774 | 3,902 | 20,900 | −13 | −817 | 109 | 725 | −614 | −3,218 | 829 | 5,773 |
| Macedonia, FYR | 1,302 | 2,998 | 1,773 | 4,258 | −30 | −3 | 213 | 1,239 | −288 | −24 | 275 | 1,889 |
| Madagascar | 749 | 1,332 | 987 | 2,042 | −167 | −80 | 129 | 236 | −276 | −554 | 109 | 583 |
| Malawi | 470 | .. | 660 | .. | −44 | .. | 157 | .. | −78 | .. | 115 | 142 |
| Malaysia | 83,369 | 182,673 | 86,851 | 147,865 | −4,144 | −4,729 | −1,017 | −4,591 | −8,644 | 25,488 | 24,699 | 82,876 |
| Mali | 529 | 1,375 | 991 | 1,833 | −41 | −207 | 219 | 228 | −284 | −438 | 323 | 970 |
| Mauritania | 504 | .. | 510 | .. | −48 | .. | 76 | .. | 22 | .. | 90 | .. |
| Mauritius | 2,349 | 4,004 | 2,454 | 4,736 | −19 | 50 | 101 | 71 | −22 | −611 | 887 | 1,309 |
| Mexico | 89,321 | 266,390 | 82,168 | 278,963 | −12,689 | −13,544 | 3,960 | 24,124 | −1,576 | −1,993 | 17,046 | 76,329 |
| Moldova | 884 | 1,542 | 1,006 | 3,129 | −18 | 401 | 56 | 800 | −85 | −387 | 257 | 775 |
| Mongolia | 508 | 2,031 | 521 | 1,880 | −25 | −145 | 77 | 215 | 39 | 222 | 158 | 1,062 |
| Morocco | 9,044 | 21,751 | 11,243 | 25,811 | −1,318 | −421 | 2,330 | 6,333 | −1,186 | 1,851 | 3,874 | 20,791 |
| Mozambique | 411 | 2,767 | 1,055 | 3,407 | −140 | −496 | 339 | 501 | −445 | −634 | 195 | 1,216 |
| Myanmar | 1,307 | 4,834 | 2,020 | 2,906 | −110 | −1,248 | 562 | 122 | −261 | 802 | 651 | 1,383 |
| Namibia | 1,734 | 3,177 | 2,100 | 2,974 | 139 | −85 | 403 | 946 | 176 | 1,064 | 221 | 450 |
| Nepal | 1,029 | 1,234 | 1,624 | 2,934 | 9 | 62 | 230 | 1,787 | −356 | 150 | 646 | 1,565 |
| Netherlands | 241,517 | 469,195 | 216,558 | 421,267 | 7,247 | 20,371 | −6,434 | −12,504 | 25,773 | 55,795 | 47,162 | 23,902 |
| New Zealand | 17,882 | 30,364 | 17,248 | 32,376 | −3,957 | −7,878 | 255 | 509 | −3,068 | −9,381 | 4,410 | 14,068 |
| Nicaragua | 662 | 2,319 | 1,150 | 3,905 | −372 | −124 | 138 | 856 | −722 | −855 | 142 | 922 |
| Niger | 321 | 565 | 457 | 1,049 | −47 | −10 | 31 | 182 | −152 | −312 | 95 | 371 |
| Nigeria | 12,342 | 52,233 | 12,841 | 24,609 | −2,878 | −6,732 | 799 | 3,310 | −2,578 | 24,202 | 1,709 | 42,735 |
| Norway | 56,058 | 155,654 | 46,848 | 94,494 | −1,919 | −2,574 | −2,059 | −3,372 | 5,233 | 55,213 | 22,976 | 56,842 |
| Oman | 6,078 | 22,499 | 5,035 | 13,636 | −374 | −1,698 | −1,469 | −2,788 | −801 | 4,377 | 1,943 | 5,014 |
| Pakistan | 10,214 | 20,507 | 14,185 | 35,112 | −1,939 | −3,129 | 2,562 | 10,940 | −3,349 | −6,795 | 2,528 | 12,878 |
| Panama | 7,610 | 12,415 | 7,768 | 11,928 | −466 | −1,298 | 153 | 258 | −471 | −552 | 781 | 1,335 |
| Papua New Guinea | 2,992 | 3,580 | 1,905 | 2,692 | −488 | −538 | 75 | 291 | 674 | 640 | 267 | 1,441 |
| Paraguay | 4,802 | 5,645 | 5,200 | 6,197 | 110 | −51 | 195 | 386 | −92 | −217 | 1,106 | 1,702 |
| Peru | 6,622 | 26,251 | 9,597 | 18,266 | −2,482 | −7,581 | 832 | 2,185 | −4,625 | 2,589 | 8,653 | 17,442 |
| Philippines | 26,795 | 52,979 | 33,317 | 59,463 | 3,662 | −799 | 880 | 13,180 | −1,980 | 5,897 | 7,781 | 22,963 |
| Poland | 35,716 | 138,052 | 33,825 | 142,839 | −1,995 | −14,500 | 958 | 8,203 | 854 | −11,084 | 14,957 | 48,474 |
| Portugal | 32,260 | 61,387 | 39,545 | 76,063 | 21 | −6,753 | 7,132 | 3,147 | −132 | −18,281 | 22,063 | 9,883 |
| Puerto Rico | .. | .. | .. | .. | .. | .. | .. | .. | .. | .. | .. | .. |

# 4.15 | Balance of payments current account

| | Goods and services ($ millions) | | | | Net income ($ millions) | | Net current transfers ($ millions) | | Current account balance ($ millions) | | Total reserves[a] ($ millions) | |
| | Exports | | Imports | | | | | | | | | |
| | 1995 | 2006 | 1995 | 2006 | 1995 | 2006 | 1995 | 2006 | 1995 | 2006 | 1995 | 2006 |
|---|---|---|---|---|---|---|---|---|---|---|---|---|
| Romania | 9,404 | 39,368 | 11,306 | 54,199 | −241 | −4,079 | 369 | 6,125 | −1,774 | −12,785 | 2,624 | 30,206 |
| Russian Federation | 92,987 | 334,853 | 82,809 | 209,431 | −3,369 | −29,628 | 156 | −1,537 | 6,965 | 94,257 | 18,024 | 303,773 |
| Rwanda | 75 | 276 | 374 | 731 | 7 | −21 | 350 | 296 | 57 | −180 | 99 | 440 |
| Saudi Arabia | 53,450 | 218,602 | 44,874 | 104,466 | 2,800 | 641 | −16,694 | −15,711 | −5,318 | 99,066 | 10,399 | 30,445 |
| Senegal | 1,506 | 2,180 | 1,821 | 3,194 | −124 | −131 | 195 | 632 | −244 | −513 | 272 | 1,334 |
| Serbia | .. | .. | .. | .. | .. | .. | .. | .. | .. | .. | .. | 11,889 |
| Sierra Leone | 128 | 313 | 260 | 434 | −30 | −41 | 43 | 62 | −118 | −101 | 35 | 184 |
| Singapore | 157,658 | 334,055 | 144,520 | 292,161 | 2,130 | −4,185 | −894 | −1,383 | 14,373 | 36,326 | 68,816 | 136,259 |
| Slovak Republic | 10,969 | .. | 10,658 | .. | −14 | .. | 93 | .. | 390 | .. | 3,863 | 13,364 |
| Slovenia | 10,377 | 25,741 | 10,749 | 26,109 | 201 | −506 | 95 | −214 | −75 | −1,088 | 1,821 | 7,139 |
| Somalia | .. | .. | .. | .. | .. | .. | .. | .. | .. | .. | .. | .. |
| South Africa | 34,402 | 75,855 | 33,375 | 84,232 | −2,875 | −5,293 | −645 | −2,817 | −2,493 | −16,487 | 4,464 | 25,593 |
| Spain | 133,910 | 322,761 | 135,000 | 395,527 | −5,402 | −26,454 | 4,525 | −7,125 | −1,967 | −106,344 | 40,531 | 19,340 |
| Sri Lanka | 4,617 | 8,508 | 5,982 | 11,621 | −137 | −388 | 732 | 2,169 | −770 | −1,334 | 2,112 | 2,943 |
| Sudan | 681 | 5,862 | 1,238 | 9,894 | −3 | −2,014 | 60 | 1,324 | −500 | −4,722 | 2 | 1,660 |
| Swaziland | 1,020 | 2,259 | 1,274 | 2,329 | 81 | 1 | 144 | 168 | −30 | 98 | 298 | 373 |
| Sweden | 95,525 | 199,130 | 81,142 | 167,115 | −6,473 | 1,095 | −2,970 | −4,696 | 4,940 | 28,413 | 25,870 | 28,017 |
| Switzerland | 123,320 | 219,219 | 108,916 | 190,987 | 10,708 | 36,938 | −4,409 | −10,321 | 20,703 | 54,849 | 68,620 | 64,461 |
| Syrian Arab Republic | 5,757 | 13,169 | 5,541 | 11,879 | −560 | −935 | 607 | 565 | 263 | 920 | .. | .. |
| Tajikistan | .. | 1,646 | .. | 2,349 | .. | −64 | .. | 746 | .. | −21 | 39 | 204 |
| Tanzania | 1,265 | 3,206 | 2,139 | 5,113 | −110 | −85 | 395 | 550 | −590 | −1,442 | 270 | 2,259 |
| Thailand | 70,292 | 152,059 | 82,246 | 146,408 | −2,114 | −6,844 | 487 | 3,368 | −13,582 | 2,175 | 36,939 | 67,008 |
| Timor-Leste | .. | .. | .. | .. | .. | .. | .. | .. | .. | .. | .. | .. |
| Togo | 465 | 837 | 671 | 1,451 | −34 | −35 | 118 | 188 | −122 | −461 | 130 | 375 |
| Trinidad and Tobago | 2,799 | 10,569 | 2,110 | 6,265 | −390 | −760 | −4 | 50 | 294 | 3,594 | 379 | 6,608 |
| Tunisia | 7,979 | 15,802 | 8,811 | 16,489 | −716 | −1,586 | 774 | 1,639 | −774 | −634 | 1,689 | 6,912 |
| Turkey | 36,581 | 116,484 | 40,113 | 144,361 | −3,204 | −6,584 | 4,398 | 1,687 | −2,338 | −32,774 | 13,891 | 63,265 |
| Turkmenistan | 1,774 | .. | 1,796 | .. | 17 | .. | 5 | .. | 0 | .. | 1,168 | .. |
| Uganda | 664 | 1,494 | 1,490 | 3,229 | −96 | −225 | 639 | 1,720 | −281 | −240 | 459 | 1,811 |
| Ukraine | 17,090 | 50,239 | 18,280 | 53,307 | −434 | −1,722 | 472 | 3,173 | −1,152 | −1,617 | 1,069 | 22,360 |
| United Arab Emirates | .. | .. | .. | .. | .. | .. | .. | .. | .. | .. | 7,778 | 27,617 |
| United Kingdom | 322,114 | 679,164 | 327,000 | 768,279 | 3,393 | 33,509 | −11,943 | −21,943 | −13,436 | −77,548 | 49,144 | 47,039 |
| United States | 794,397 | 1,445,702 | 890,784 | 2,204,226 | 20,899 | 36,633 | −38,073 | −89,595 | −113,561 | −811,486 | 175,996 | 221,089 |
| Uruguay | 3,507 | 5,660 | 3,568 | 5,762 | −227 | −469 | 76 | 134 | −213 | −436 | 1,813 | 3,091 |
| Uzbekistan | .. | .. | .. | .. | .. | .. | .. | .. | .. | .. | .. | .. |
| Venezuela, RB | 20,753 | 66,782 | 16,905 | 38,503 | −1,943 | −1,092 | 109 | −38 | 2,014 | 27,149 | 10,715 | 36,715 |
| Vietnam | 9,498 | 36,618 | 12,334 | 38,562 | −384 | −1,219 | 1,200 | 3,380 | −2,020 | 217 | 1,324 | 13,384 |
| West Bank and Gaza | .. | .. | .. | .. | .. | .. | .. | .. | .. | .. | .. | .. |
| Yemen, Rep. | 2,160 | 7,865 | 2,471 | 7,781 | −561 | −1,234 | 1,056 | 1,356 | 184 | 206 | 638 | 7,543 |
| Zambia | 1,222 | 4,125 | 1,338 | 3,222 | −249 | −124 | 182 | 171 | −182 | 950 | 223 | 720 |
| Zimbabwe | 2,344 | .. | 2,515 | .. | −294 | .. | 40 | .. | −425 | .. | 888 | .. |
| **World** | **6,395,987 t** | **14,635,235 t** | **6,247,521 t** | **14,403,234 t** | | | | | | | | |
| **Low income** | 111,208 | 453,874 | 145,057 | 504,594 | | | | | | | | |
| **Middle income** | 1,085,148 | 3,830,081 | 1,112,568 | 3,340,141 | | | | | | | | |
| Lower middle income | 485,240 | 1,991,516 | 508,950 | 1,683,108 | | | | | | | | |
| Upper middle income | 598,809 | 1,861,137 | 604,464 | 1,666,426 | | | | | | | | |
| **Low & middle income** | 1,196,157 | 4,281,393 | 1,256,657 | 3,837,134 | | | | | | | | |
| East Asia & Pacific | 397,583 | 1,632,160 | 413,802 | 1,371,821 | | | | | | | | |
| Europe & Central Asia | 269,117 | 1,014,166 | 278,118 | 973,486 | | | | | | | | |
| Latin America & Carib. | 272,866 | 760,863 | 288,144 | 692,844 | | | | | | | | |
| Middle East & N. Africa | .. | .. | 108,418 | 257,095 | | | | | | | | |
| South Asia | 58,893 | 243,917 | 78,652 | 300,538 | | | | | | | | |
| Sub-Saharan Africa | 89,634 | 230,089 | 97,459 | 248,989 | | | | | | | | |
| **High income** | 5,194,902 | 10,422,094 | 4,989,710 | 10,616,832 | | | | | | | | |
| Euro area | 2,090,190 | 4,175,306 | 1,968,796 | 4,061,245 | | | | | | | | |

a. International reserves including gold valued at London gold price. b. Includes Luxembourg.

ECONOMY

## About the data

The balance of payments records an economy's transactions with the rest of the world. Balance of payments accounts are divided into two groups: the current account, which records transactions in goods, services, income, and current transfers, and the capital and financial account, which records capital transfers, acquisition or disposal of non-produced, nonfinancial assets, and transactions in financial assets and liabilities. The table presents data from the current account plus gross international reserves.

The balance of payments is a double-entry accounting system that shows all flows of goods and services into and out of an economy; all transfers that are the counterpart of real resources or financial claims provided to or by the rest of the world without a quid pro quo, such as donations and grants; and all changes in residents' claims on and liabilities to nonresidents that arise from economic transactions. All transactions are recorded twice—once as a credit and once as a debit. In principle the net balance should be zero, but in practice the accounts often do not balance, requiring inclusion of a balancing item, net errors and omissions.

Discrepancies may arise in the balance of payments because there is no single source for balance of payments data and therefore no way to ensure that the data are fully consistent. Sources include customs data, monetary accounts of the banking

system, external debt records, information provided by enterprises, surveys to estimate service transactions, and foreign exchange records. Differences in collection methods—such as in timing, definitions of residence and ownership, and the exchange rate used to value transactions—contribute to net errors and omissions. In addition, smuggling and other illegal or quasi-legal transactions may be unrecorded or misrecorded. For further discussion of issues relating to the recording of data on trade in goods and services, see *About the data* for tables 4.4–4.7.

The concepts and definitions underlying the data in the table are based on the fifth edition of the International Monetary Fund's (IMF) *Balance of Payments Manual* (1993). That edition redefined as capital transfers some transactions previously included in the current account, such as debt forgiveness, migrants' capital transfers, and foreign aid to acquire capital goods. Thus the current account balance now reflects more accurately net current transfer receipts in addition to transactions in goods, services (previously nonfactor services), and income (previously factor income). Many countries maintain their data collection systems according to the fourth edition of the *Balance of Payments Manual* (1977). Where necessary, the IMF converts such reported data to conform to the fifth edition (see *Primary data documentation*). Values are in U.S. dollars converted at market exchange rates.

## Definitions

• **Exports** and **imports of goods and services** are all transactions between residents of an economy and the rest of the world involving a change in ownership of general merchandise, goods sent for processing and repairs, nonmonetary gold, and services. • **Net income** is receipts and payments of employee compensation for nonresident workers, and investment income (receipts and payments on direct investment, portfolio investment, and other investments and receipts on reserve assets). Income derived from the use of intangible assets is recorded under business services. • **Net current transfers** are recorded in the balance of payments whenever an economy provides or receives goods, services, income, or financial items without a quid pro quo. All transfers not considered to be capital are current. • **Current account balance** is the sum of net exports of goods and services, net income, and net current transfers.

• **Total reserves** are holdings of monetary gold, special drawing rights, reserves of IMF members held by the IMF, and holdings of foreign exchange under the control of monetary authorities. The gold component of these reserves is valued at year-end (December 31) London prices ($386.75 an ounce in 1995 and $635.70 an ounce in 2006).

### Top 15 economies with the largest current account surplus—and top 15 economies with the largest current account deficit in 2006 — 4.15a

| Economy | Surplus ($ billions) | Share of GDP (%) | Economy | Deficit ($ billions) | Share of GDP (%) |
|---|---|---|---|---|---|
| China | 249.9 | 9.4 | United States | −811.5 | −6.2 |
| Japan | 170.5 | 3.9 | Spain | −106.3 | −8.7 |
| Germany | 150.7 | 5.2 | United Kingdom | −77.5 | −3.3 |
| Saudi Arabia | 99.1 | | Italy | −47.3 | −2.6 |
| Russian Federation | 94.3 | 9.6 | Australia | −41.0 | −5.3 |
| Netherlands | 55.8 | 8.4 | Turkey | −32.8 | −8.1 |
| Norway | 55.2 | 16.5 | Greece | −29.6 | −9.6 |
| Switzerland | 54.8 | 14.4 | France | −28.3 | −1.3 |
| Kuwait | 51.0 | | Portugal | −18.3 | −9.4 |
| Singapore | 36.3 | 27.5 | Congo, Dem. Rep | −16.5 | −6.5 |
| Sweden | 28.4 | 7.4 | Romania | −12.8 | −10.5 |
| Venezuela, RB | 27.1 | 14.9 | Poland | −11.1 | −3.3 |
| Malaysia | 25.5 | 16.9 | India | −9.4 | −1.0 |
| Taiwan, China | 24.7 | 6.7 | New Zealand | −9.4 | −9.0 |
| Libya | 22.2 | 44.1 | Ireland | −9.1 | −4.1 |

*Source:* International Monetary Fund balance of payments data files and *World Development Indicators* data files.

## Data sources

Data on the balance of payments are published in the IMF's *Balance of Payments Statistics Yearbook* and *International Financial Statistics*. The World Bank exchanges data with the IMF through electronic files that in most cases are more timely and cover a longer period than the published sources. More information about the design and compilation of the balance of payments can be found in the IMF's *Balance of Payments Manual,* fifth edition (1993), *Balance of Payments Textbook* (1996), and *Balance of Payments Compilation Guide* (1995). The IMF's International Financial Statistics and Balance of Payments databases are available on CD-ROM.

5

STATES AND MARKETS

# Measuring governance

The breakup of the Soviet Union and the emergence of democracies in many developing countries have increased interest in governance. Good governance, strong institutions, and control of corruption are important for development success. Failures of the state can negate development gains, particularly in low-income economies, many of them fragile states.

Improvements in data and econometric techniques have permitted large cross-country studies on the impact of governance and institutions on investment and growth. This research has produced strong evidence that the quality of governance has a big impact on economic growth, a relationship that is robust over time and across countries (figure 5a). It shows that corruption discourages private investment and distorts resource allocation in ways that hurt the poor. Research also finds that public spending to expand primary education and reduce child and infant mortality produces more benefits in countries with less corruption. And it finds that good governance in a country increases the likelihood of development projects succeeding.

The World Bank defines *governance* as the way public officials and institutions acquire and exercise authority to provide public goods and services, including education, health care, infrastructure, and a sound investment climate. Bad governance is often equated with corruption. But the concepts, while related, are different. Corruption, the abuse of public office for private gain, is an outcome of poor governance, reflecting the breakdown of accountability. Fighting corruption requires addressing underlying failures of governance.

As citizens, investors, policymakers, and donors become more aware of the importance of good governance to development, they increasingly demand information that better tracks progress and increases the transparency of public sector management and anticorruption programs (box 5b). The growing interest in the quality of governance has driven what a recent Organisation for Economic Co-operation and Development publication describes as "explosive growth in the use of quantitative indicators in developing countries" (OECD 2006, p. 13). At least 140 sets of governance indicators, with thousands of individual indicators, are now publicly available. Some look at rules, some at how the rules are implemented, some at outcomes, and some are aggregate measures, summarizing more specific indicators.

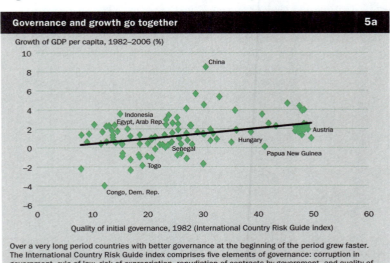

**Governance and growth go together** — 5a

Growth of GDP per capita, 1982–2006 (%)

Quality of initial governance, 1982 (International Country Risk Guide index)

Over a very long period countries with better governance at the beginning of the period grew faster. The International Country Risk Guide index comprises five elements of governance: corruption in government, rule of law, risk of expropriation, repudiation of contracts by government, and quality of the bureaucracy.
*Source:* World Bank staff estimates.

## Types of governance indicators

Rules indicators attempt to establish the presence or absence of rules and processes. Do countries have laws guaranteeing the right to information? Do they have independent anticorruption commissions? Are budget documents published?

Such indicators are used to measure specific institutional reforms. They require narrow and explicit definitions of what is being measured. Typically, these indicators are prepared by country experts and validated by outside experts.

Interpreting these indicators is not easy. There may be clarity about the existence of a specific rule, law, or legal body, but this does not make the resulting indicators more objective than perception-based indicators. Those who frame the questions have a concept of a "good system" and may impose their own prejudices and values. Nor do formal rules necessarily lead to desired outcomes. An anticorruption commission, for example, may not guarantee less corruption (figure 5c). And while the rules may have normative values of their own—access to budget documents, for instance, is desirable in itself—it is not clear how they influence governance outcomes or reforms. Most important, assessments of complicated rules are subject to errors of fact and judgment, particularly when the analyst has to determine the net effect of many conflicting rules and regulations.

The *Doing Business* indicators in table 5.3 are based on information collected by local experts. The methodology uses factual information about laws and regulations to assess the business climate of a country. The results at the two extremes are far from surprising. New Zealand, Singapore, and the United States are the easiest countries to do business in, while the fragile states of Democratic Republic of Congo, Central African Republic, and Guinea-Bissau are the most difficult. However, China and India, two of the fastest growing economies in the world, rank 83rd and 120th, suggesting either that their rules are not a serious impediment to growth or that the business environment is not as unfavorable as these rankings imply.

Part of the explanation may lie in what the data represent. For comparability, the data refer to businesses in each country's most populous city, which may not be representative. The reports cover only domestically owned, limited liability companies and a limited set of transactions. Indicators of the time it takes to start a business involve judgment by local experts. Businesses may get things done faster, if they deploy "speed money," or slower, if they are poorly informed about policies and procedures. For the serious analyst the indicators are only a starting point. Understanding what the data say opens doors to better understanding governance.

---

**Who uses governance indicators?**  Box 5b

- *Citizens* are more conscious of the need to hold their governments accountable, and governance indicators increase awareness of the quality of governance. The indicators can provide citizens with information to monitor service delivery and measure how their government—local, provincial, or national—is performing. Citizens can compare indicators with those of similar countries.
- *Investors, lenders,* and *businesses,* both domestic and foreign, know that the quality of governance influences the investment climate and the return on investments. They want to be better informed about the governance and corruption risks that they are likely to face. Many of the earliest efforts to provide governance indicators came from credit and investment risk evaluation agencies in response to these commercial needs.
- *Governments,* following the maxim that "what you cannot measure you cannot manage," need to monitor their own

performance to improve the effectiveness of their policies and institutions and to better understand how outcomes can be improved. Governance indicators can provide benchmarks against which governments can measure their progress.
- *Donors* are accountable to their citizens for the development assistance they provide. They are thus anxious to know that the resources that they provide will be used for the intended purposes and to compare performance across countries. In preparing their development assistance strategies, they rely on governance assessments that use a wide range of governance indicators. These governance assessments are used to inform country programming and assistance priorities, allocate aid money using transparent and consistent criteria, provide a basis for a dialogue with partner governments, and assess political and fiduciary risks, among other purposes.

Outcome indicators—some highly specific, others more general—attempt to measure the consequences of governance. Typically, they are perceptions-based indicators that capture the views of relevant stakeholders or interested observers, including experts, officials, researchers, decisionmakers, opinion makers, businesses, and citizens. The indicators provide information on how the rules operate in practice (figure 5d). But they have some problems. It is difficult to identify a connection between particular rules and particular outcomes. And outcome indicators are often measured on a cardinal scale—say, from 1 to 5 or 10. Unless the criteria for assigning specific scores are clear and independently verified, there is a risk of arbitrary scoring and confusion about the relative importance of scores.

Four frequently used sets of outcome indicators—covering civil and political rights, political risk, corruption, and overall governance (table 5e)—rely on expert assessments or a combination of expert assessments and surveys of firms, households, and opinion makers. Expert assessments are cheaper and with careful benchmarking may be used for cross-country comparisons. But experts often disagree, so it is best not to rely on any one set of experts.

Surveys of firms and households may be better grounded in country realities. The views of respondents matter,

because they are able to act on their beliefs. If they believe the courts are highly corrupt, they will avoid seeking legal recourse through the courts and instead choose arbitration or informal means of settling disputes. While governments may discount outsiders' views, citizens and firms' views matter.

There are few household surveys on governance, but many firm-level surveys. The World Bank's Enterprise Surveys provide an overview of the international investment climate, reporting on some governance outcomes, such as unofficial payments as a share of firms' sales, the time required to resolve disputes in court, the cost of providing security against crime, and the efficiency and client orientation of the tax system.

The distinction between rules and outcome indicators is not absolute. Some rules indicators also implicitly measure outcomes. As noted, the time required to register a business is the outcome of applicable regulations and not a measure of the time it actually takes.

Actionable indicators or second-generation indicators stem from the desire to identify specific policies, procedures, and institutional arrangements that contribute to the overall quality of governance. Actionable indicators have received greater attention as part of the World Bank's Governance and

---

**Not producing the desired results**     **5c**

Global Integrity Index Rating of the anticorruption agency

Global Corruption Barometer
Proportion of people who think government anticorruption efforts are "effective" (percent)

Anticorruption agencies should help reduce corruption, but even when agency rules and implementation are rated highly by experts, citizens are not convinced that their governments' efforts are effective. This appears to confirm other research findings that cast doubt on the effectiveness of such agencies. Citizens may also be using their survey responses to send a message to their governments about the need to do more.
Source: World Bank staff estimates.

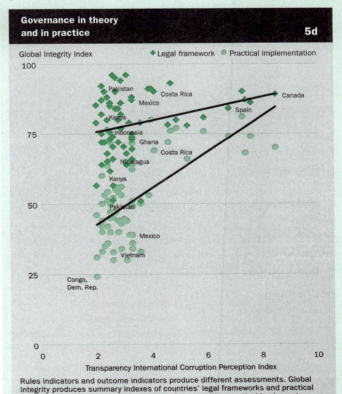

**Governance in theory and in practice**     **5d**

Global Integrity Index    ◆ Legal framework    ● Practical implementation

Transparency International Corruption Perception Index

Rules indicators and outcome indicators produce different assessments. Global Integrity produces summary indexes of countries' legal frameworks and practical implementation of controls on corruption. Scores on the practical implementation measure generally lie below the legal framework measure. And the practical measure is more strongly correlated with Transparency International's broad-based Corruption Perception Index, suggesting that the Transparency International sources put more weight on outcomes than on rules.
Source: World Bank staff estimates.

Anticorruption Strategy. These indicators look beyond the rules to how they are actually implemented (table 5f). Some examples of these indicators follow:

- The Public Expenditure and Financial Accountability program aims to provide governments and donors a shared pool of information on public financial management performance and a common platform for policy dialogue.
- The Global Integrity Index is based on six key aspects of global integrity: civil society; public information and media; elections; government accountability, administration. and civil service; oversight and regulation; and anticorruption and rule of law. These six aspects cover 23 subcategories and 290 indicators, all narrowly and explicitly defined.

Such indicators are called "actionable" for four reasons:

- They provide more clarity about the steps governments can take to improve their ratings.
- They shed light on the efficacy of certain public sector reforms in improving governance.
- They are replicable—that is, independent observers can arrive at roughly the same scores when the questions are explicit and precise.
- They allow meaningful discussion between the raters and those being rated and thus stimulate policy dialogue on these issues.

Efforts like those described in table 5f are planned or under way in other areas, including public accountability, human resources management, and provincial and local governance.

Despite these efforts, major gaps remain in topical coverage (such as legal and judicial reforms), country coverage, periodicity, and methods. Actionable indicators are subject to many of the same measurement errors as other governance indicators. Experts may disagree even over narrowly defined assessments. The coverage of countries and years, while expanding, is still limited. The Global Integrity Index provides two observations for only 25 countries and three observations for only 8. Much work remains to be done in understanding which of the profusion of "actionable" indicators are also "action worthy," in the sense of leading to desired governance and development outcomes. Progress is bound to be gradual, a long-term undertaking needing the support of key development institutions.

*Aggregate indicators* are composite measures combining the scores on many separate indicators. Among the most widely used and cited governance indicators are the World Bank's Worldwide Governance Indicators, which draw on 33 sources to produce indicators on six dimensions of governance for 212 countries and territories, and Transparency International's Corruption Perceptions Index, which draws on 12 sources and covers 180 countries.

| Examples of governance outcome indicators | | 5e |
|---|---|---|
| **Indicator or objective** | **Nature and number of indicators** | **Country coverage** |
| Since 1972 *Freedom House* has produced *Freedom in the World,* an annual survey that provides an "evaluation of the state of global freedom as experienced by individuals." http://www.freedomhouse.org | Countries are scored on political rights and civil liberties outcomes on a 1–7 scale and then rated not free, partly free, or free. The ratings are based on a checklist of 10 political rights and 15 civil liberties. | 193 countries and 15 related and disputed territories. |
| Since 1980 *Political Risk Services Group* has produced *International Country Risk Guide* (ICRG) to meet the needs of clients for an in-depth analysis of potential risks to international business. http://www.prsgroup.com | The political risk guide assigns points to 12 risk components relevant to governance. | 140 countries monthly and 21 annually. |
| Since 1995 *Transparency International* has ranked countries by the degree to which corruption is perceived to exist among public officials and politicians. The Corruption Perceptions Index (CPI) defines corruption as "the abuse of public office for private gain," encompassing both administrative and political corruption. http://www.transparency.org | The CPI is a composite, a poll of polls, that draws on corruption-related data from expert and business surveys by a variety of independent institutions. The CPI reflects views from around the world, including in-country experts. The 2007 CPI draws on 14 polls and surveys from 12 independent institutions. | 180 countries. |
| Since 1999 *Worldwide Governance Indicators* have provided aggregate governance outcomes from 1996 onward. http://www.govindicators.org | Governance is measured along six dimensions: voice and accountability, political stability and absence of violence, government effectiveness, regulatory quality, rule of law, and control of corruption. | 212 countries. |

Aggregation is not unique to governance indicators. Weighted averages or more complex statistical methods are used to produce broad indicators of social conditions. The United Nations Development Programme's Human Development Index is an example. Aggregation is also necessary to summarize the results of large sets of "actionable indicators." For example, the World Bank uses the aggregate Country Policy and Institutional Assessment (CPIA) rating, an average of 16 more detailed components, to allocate concessional lending across countries. Properly designed, aggregation can provide estimates of the variance of the underlying indicators. But it also loses some of the detail, reducing its usefulness as a policy tool. It is important, therefore, to provide access to the underlying indicators, as the Worldwide Governance Indicators now do in most cases (figure 5g).

Aggregate indicators, despite their limitations, have opened doors to much research and analysis on governance and corruption. They provide a starting point for drilling down deeper into country governance systems. And the increasing variety and richness of disaggregated indicators—covering more topics in more depth for more countries over longer periods, using a variety of methods—enables drilling down even further and increasing understanding of the factors driving aggregate success or failure.

## Drilling down: the Worldwide Governance Indicators 5g

| Worldwide Governance Indicators Indonesia 2006 | Sources | Year | Governance score | Standard error |
|---|---|---|---|---|
| Voice and accountability | 14 | 2006 | −0.25 | 0.14 |
| Political stability | 10 | 2006 | −1.17 | 0.22 |
| Government effectiveness | 14 | 2006 | −0.38 | 0.15 |
| Regulatory quality | 12 | 2006 | −0.26 | 0.17 |
| Rule of law | 19 | 2006 | −0.82 | 0.13 |
| Control of corruption | 17 | 2006 | −0.77 | 0.13 |

| WGI sources (partial list) | Type | Values |
|---|---|---|
| Bertelsmann Transformation Index | Experts | 0.61 |
| Institute for Management and Development World Competitiveness Yearbook | Survey | 0.38 |
| International Budget Project Open Budget Index | Experts | 0.41 |
| Political Risk Services International Country Risk Guide | Experts | 0.41 |

| Open Budget Index 2006 (partial list) | |
|---|---|
| Executive's budget proposal | Questions 1–55, 67, 68, 69 |
| Citizens budget | Question 61 |
| Pre-budget statement | Questions 72, 73, 74 |
| Auditors report | Questions 112–114, 116, 120–122 |

**61. Does the executive publish a "citizens budget" or some nontechnical presentation intended for a wide audience that describes the budget and its proposals?**

Starting from the Worldwide Governance Indicator of Voice and accountability, it is possible to drill down to the underlying indicators on which it is based. And for some it is possible to go farther, to the scoring of individual questions. Good documentation and access to the original data make aggregate indicators more useful.

## Selected actionable governance indicators 5f

| Indicator or objective | Nature and number of indicators | Country coverage |
|---|---|---|
| *Public Expenditure and Financial Accountability Assessment*, initiated in 2001, measures critical dimensions of open and orderly public financial management systems. www.pefa.org. | 28 high-level indicators that capture six dimensions of public financial management. | 67 completed, of which 26 are publicly available. |
| *OECD Assessment Methodology for Public Procurement Systems*, developed over 2003–04 through an Organisation for Economic Co-operation and Development Development Assistance Committee– and World Bank–led roundtable and now being piloted, measures compliance, performance, and transparency and integrity of public procurement systems. www.oecd.org/dac. | 12 indicators with 54 subindicators in four broad areas: legislative and regulatory framework, institutional framework and management capacity, procurement operations and market practice, and integrity and transparency. | 22 countries participating in pilot program; reports available online for 9. |
| *Open Budget Index*, launched in October 2006 by civil society organizations in 59 counties, provides comprehensive practical information to gauge a government's commitment to budget transparency and accountability. www.openbudgetindex.org | 122 items that assess public availability of key budget documents, quality of information, and timeliness of dissemination. | 59 in 2006; 88 targeted and 80 expected for 2008 |
| *Global Integrity Index*, launched in 2002 by the Washington, D.C.,–based Center for Public Integrity and a new independent nonprofit called Global Integrity formally started in 2005, assesses the existence and effectiveness of anticorruption mechanisms that promote public integrity. The index evaluates the existence of laws, regulations, and institutions; their implementation; and the access average citizens have to those mechanisms. www.globalintegrity.org | More than 290 discrete integrity indicators generate the index, which is organized into six broad categories. | 25 countries in 2004, 41 in 2006, 48 in 2007, 33 assessed at least twice. |

## Why governance is difficult to measure

Measuring governance is not easy. A broad concept, governance embraces many institutions and the formal and informal rules that guide their operation. Governance also involves a range of players—citizens, their elected leaders, public officials, and those delivering services—who respond to the incentives created by these rules. Formal rules are more readily observed. Informal rules, less easily measured, may have a greater influence on the quality of governance and require a much deeper understanding of the workings of society. That is why many governance measures rely on the views of experts or the managers of firms—because they understand the principles of governance or have practical experience of the formal and informal rules of the game (figure 5h). Demand for such measures comes from a variety of stakeholders (see box 5b).

Measuring governance can involve assessing how public institutions work as a whole or in their many parts, such as the effectiveness of the judiciary or the bureaucracy or the process for setting and monitoring the budget. Because the concepts are so broad, the same terms may be applied in many different ways. Thus, the *rule of law* may be interpreted narrowly—to mean whether the country's laws are clear and well understood, whether property rights and contracts are effectively enforced. Or they may be interpreted more broadly—to mean

the equality of all citizens in the eyes of the law so that no individual, however powerful, stands above the law. Reaching a consensus on such concepts is not easy (figure 5i). Because most definitions tend to be broad, the boundaries between different indicators risk being blurred.

That governance is difficult to measure does not imply that governance is not measurable. Nor should demonstrable errors of measurement deter the effort. All indicators are subject to error. The national accounts reported in *World Development Indicators* are estimated and later subject to revision, at times very large. Because it is difficult and costly to obtain reliable data through surveys and official records, maternal mortality is often estimated from models. Poverty estimates depend on surveys of household consumption patterns and the judgment of experts about an appropriate poverty line.

Still, measuring corruption is particularly problematic. Those with direct knowledge of corruption are likely to want to keep it secret. In some cases administrative corruption can be gauged through surveys of citizens and business or the judgments of informed experts. But often the state's capture by special interests is difficult to assess because that lies outside the direct experience of citizens and small businesses.

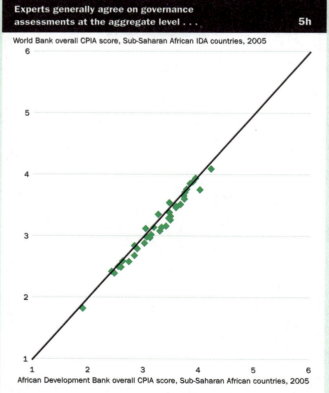

**Experts generally agree on governance assessments at the aggregate level . . .** 5h

World Bank overall CPIA score, Sub-Saharan African IDA countries, 2005

African Development Bank overall CPIA score, Sub-Saharan African countries, 2005

The World Bank and African Development Bank rate countries independently using similar Country Performance and Institutional Assessments (CPIA), an aggregation of 16 specific scores. Overall scores are normalized to a scale of 1 to 6.
Source: World Bank staff estimates.

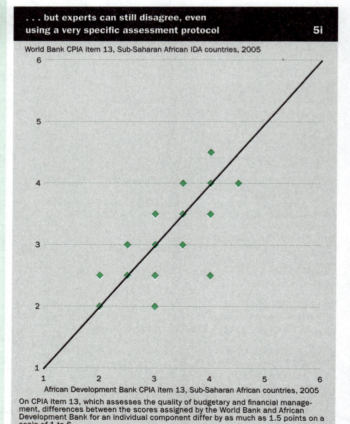

**. . . but experts can still disagree, even using a very specific assessment protocol** 5i

World Bank CPIA item 13, Sub-Saharan African IDA countries, 2005

African Development Bank CPIA item 13, Sub-Saharan African countries, 2005

On CPIA item 13, which assesses the quality of budgetary and financial management, differences between the scores assigned by the World Bank and African Development Bank for an individual component differ by as much as 1.5 points on a scale of 1 to 6.
Source: World Bank staff estimates.

## Measurement errors

All governance indicators are subject to significant measurement errors, but these errors are rarely reported. Measures based on sample surveys are subject to sampling error, and those based on expert assessments to informant error. Because any indicator is an imperfect measure of the broader concepts it pertains to, a third source of error might be called proxy error. High levels of overall corruption in the customs service, even if accurately measured, might not reflect corruption in the country. To increase the reliability of governance measures, measurement errors should be quantified and reported where possible.

In combining information from different sources, aggregate indicators can smooth the idiosyncrasies of their underlying components. The Worldwide Governance Indicators, for instance, draw on indicators from 33 sources to produce six aggregate indicators. The statistical model for combining the indicators assumes that the observed empirical indicators of governance provide noisy or imperfect signals of the fundamentally unobservable concept of governance. The model estimates the variance of the aggregate estimate for each country, conditional on the observed data, and provides estimates of the variance of the underlying indicators as well (Kaufmann and Kraay forthcoming). The more the individual indicators agree, the smaller is the measured error of the aggregate.

In explicitly measuring margins of error, the Worldwide Governance Indicators inform users of the uncertainty surrounding the estimates. For some countries with similar scores, overlapping confidence intervals make comparisons of differences meaningless. But statistically reliable statements can be made in many cases when scores differ by larger amounts. Figure 5j shows the World Governance Indicators government effectiveness scores and margins of error for 212 countries. The 81 countries at the lower end of the distribution of governance have scores that are almost certainly below the median, and the 85 countries at the upper end of the distribution are almost certainly above the median (with a probability of 90 percent or higher). But for the 46 countries in the middle of the distribution there is at least a 10 percent chance that a score below the median could be above it, or vice versa.

Recognition of measurement errors should discourage naïve ranking of countries on governance performance. Transparency International, which uses country rankings as a way of shaming countries into fighting corruption, nevertheless cautions users against comparing countries with close scores. Its country rankings also cannot be compared from year to year as country coverage keeps changing and expanding.

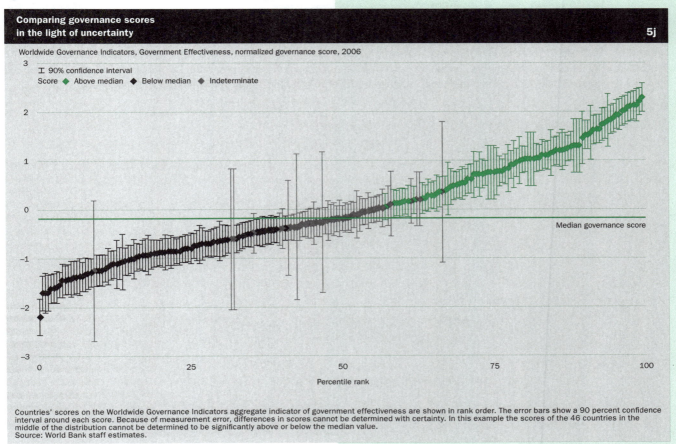

**Comparing governance scores in the light of uncertainty**　　5j

Worldwide Governance Indicators, Government Effectiveness, normalized governance score, 2006

⊥ 90% confidence interval
Score ◆ Above median ◆ Below median ◆ Indeterminate

Median governance score

Percentile rank

Countries' scores on the Worldwide Governance Indicators aggregate indicator of government effectiveness are shown in rank order. The error bars show a 90 percent confidence interval around each score. Because of measurement error, differences in scores cannot be determined with certainty. In this example the scores of the 46 countries in the middle of the distribution cannot be determined to be significantly above or below the median value.
Source: World Bank staff estimates.

## Looking ahead

The proliferation of governance indicators has led to several recent efforts to take stock of where this work stands and what the next areas of emphasis should be (see UNDP 2007a; Knack, Kugler, and Manning 2003; Arndt and Oman 2006; World Bank 2006g; Kaufmann and Kraay forthcoming; Levy 2007; Thomas 2006).

Four priorities stand out.

First, it is important to evaluate all governance indicators, exposing them to peer review and strengthening them to increase public confidence in their use. The methods and underlying assumptions used to produce them should be carefully reviewed. The quality of the underlying data should be evaluated, including the role of experts and surveys. And methods of better estimating the uncertainties associated with all measures of governance should be studied so that users of data are aware of the uncertainties they are dealing with.

Second, given the strong interest from policymakers in indicators of remediable policy or institutional failures, progress on action-worthy indicators is a high priority. To build on the promise of the initial round of Public Expenditure and Financial Accountability (PEFA) Assessments, formally launched two years ago, it will be important to extend them to more countries, to conduct regular periodic assessments, and to ensure that results are disseminated. The example of PEFA generating information on the quality of public financial systems also opens the door to similar approaches in other areas. The World Bank has already identified some key areas for undertaking similar assessments, including decentralization, public accountability, and human resources management.

Decentralization is particularly promising, because it enables central governments to monitor the performance of provincial and local governments, improving information on governance in the country as a whole.

Third, one difficulty with the proliferation of disaggregated, specific indicators is that they do not provide guidance to users on which of the many subindicators are most critical to particular governance outcomes. Research on this is a high priority, to identify a core set of the most important indicators that influence governance outcomes, allowing governments and donors to focus their reforms on those critical areas.

Fourth, given the growing recognition of how understanding a country's political economy can produce better development outcomes, the quality of current efforts to measure political trends and outcomes should be reviewed for their capacity to shed light on development prospects and outcomes.

These and other issues could be part of a program of work led by the World Bank, as a major user and producer of governance indicators (box 5k).

This section of *World Development Indicators* includes a broad range of indicators that shed light on the effectiveness and accountability of governments and their interaction with the private sector. Tables 5.2–5.6 provide an overview of the climate for investment and doing business and of the tax and regulatory roles of the state. Table 5.8 provides the World Bank's Country Policy and Institutional Assessment data for 77 International Development Association–eligible countries. Other tables show data on financial markets, public and private provision of infrastructure, and defense, all of which depend on effective government spending and oversight.

Governance indicators are now routinely collected and used by the World Bank for a number of purposes.

*Resource allocation.* The Bank's Country Policy and Institutional Assessment Indicators (CPIA) enter into the International Development Association (IDA) country performance rating (CPR) with an effective weight of 67 percent. The CPR is used as part of the IDA performance assessment, which is used to allocate IDA resources among eligible countries.

*Global monitoring.* The 2006 *Global Monitoring Report* included 13 governance indicators in its statistical appendix (see table).

## Governance indicators from *Global Monitoring Report*

| Category | Indicator |
|---|---|
| Overall governance performance | 1. Control of corruption (Worldwide Governance Indicators)<br>2. Corruption perceptions index (Transparency International)<br>3. Unofficial payments (Enterprise Surveys)<br>4. Policy outcome (CPIA cluster a–c average)<br>5. Aggregate public institutions (CPIA cluster d)<br>6. Licensing time (Doing Business)<br>7. Time spent on regulations (Enterprise Surveys) |
| Bureaucratic capability | 8. Budget/financial management (CPIA 13)<br>9. Public administration (CPIA 15) |
| Checks and balances institutions | 10. Voice and accountability (Worldwide Governance Indicators)<br>11. Rule of law (Worldwide Governance Indicators)<br>12. Property rights and rule-based governance (CPIA 12)<br>13. Executive constraints (Polity IV) |

*Country governance monitoring.* Diagnosing governance obstacles at the country level and designing and monitoring reforms, now a requirement under the World Bank's new Governance and Anticorruption Strategy, employ a range of aggregate and actionable indicators including the Worldwide Governance Indicators, the Transparency International indicator, Public Expenditure and Financial Accountability indicators, the Doing Business indicators, the investment climate assessments, public financial management studies, the World Bank Institute Governance and Anticorruption diagnostic surveys, and quantitative service delivery surveys and report cards. These feature in the Bank's analytical and advisory assistance, project documents, and country assistance strategies.

*Actionable indicators.* The Bank's new Governance and Anticorruption Strategy calls for the development and promotion of actionable indicators, including decentralization, public accountability, human resources management, and the Public Expenditure and Financial Accountability (PEFA). This work includes extending the coverage of PEFA and the Global Integrity Index to more countries and encouraging countries to permit the publication of PEFA data.

*Research.* In studies on governance outcomes World Bank research increasingly uses large cross-country governance databases including Polity IV, the database of political institutions; the Worldwide Governance Indicators; and Transparency International's Corruption Perceptions Index.

*Data.* Bank staff manage, produce, and analyze several databases on governance: the Investment Climate Assessments, the Doing Business database, the Database of Political Institutions, and the annual *Governance Matters* report (Kaufmann, Kraay, and Mastruzzi 2007, *Governance Matters VI*), which since 2003 has generated annual aggregate indicators on worldwide governance based on external data sources.

# 5.1 Private sector in the economy

| | Investment commitments in infrastructure projects with private participation[a] | | | | | | | | Domestic credit to private sector | Businesses registered | | Micro, small, and medium-size enterprises | |
|---|---|---|---|---|---|---|---|---|---|---|---|---|---|
| | | | | | | | | | | | | | per 1,000 |
| | Telecommunications | | Energy | | Transport | | Water and sanitation | | % of GDP | New | Total | Total | people |
| | 1995–99 | 2000–06 | 1995–99 | 2000–06 | 1995–99 | 2000–06 | 1995–99 | 2000–06 | 2006 | 2005 | 2005 | 2000–05[b] | 2000–05 |
| Afghanistan | .. | 747.5 | .. | 1.6 | .. | .. | .. | .. | 21.8 | 2,388 | 16,423 | 38,331 | 12.2 |
| Albania | .. | 569.2 | 0.0 | 789.0 | .. | 308.0 | .. | 8.0 | 12.5 | 12,164 | 103,482 | 580,000 | 18.7 |
| Algeria | .. | 4,124.5 | .. | 2,720.0 | .. | 120.9 | .. | 510.0 | 12.5 | 12,164 | 103,482 | 580,000 | 18.7 |
| Angola | .. | 528.7 | .. | 54.4 | .. | 55.0 | .. | .. | 7.5 | .. | .. | .. | .. |
| Argentina | 10,498.6 | 6,859.8 | 12,992.6 | 5,642.1 | 6,996.5 | 522.2 | 3,307.1 | 791.6 | 13.0 | 53,000 | 450,535 | .. | .. |
| Armenia | 112.5 | 317.1 | 0.0 | 67.0 | .. | 63.0 | .. | 0.0 | 8.8 | 9,667 | 123,951 | 99,805 | 33.1 |
| Australia | .. | .. | .. | .. | .. | .. | .. | .. | 109.6 | 81,079 | 935,047 | 1,269,000 | 63.0 |
| Austria | .. | .. | .. | .. | .. | .. | .. | .. | 114.9 | 14,669 | 172,602 | 252,399 | 30.9 |
| Azerbaijan | 122.0 | 769.2 | .. | 375.2 | .. | .. | .. | 0.0 | 12.2 | .. | .. | 49,527 | 6.0 |
| Bangladesh | 438.1 | 2,187.3 | 554.9 | 501.5 | 0.0 | 0.0 | .. | .. | 36.2 | 5,328 | 67,459 | 177,000 | 1.2 |
| Belarus | 20.0 | 955.8 | 500.0 | .. | .. | .. | .. | .. | 20.2 | .. | .. | 25,108 | 2.5 |
| Belgium | .. | .. | .. | .. | .. | .. | .. | .. | 83.3 | 25,492 | 343,761 | 686,533 | 66.2 |
| Benin | .. | 133.9 | .. | 590.0 | .. | .. | .. | .. | 16.7 | .. | .. | .. | .. |
| Bolivia | 528.0 | 594.3 | 2,777.3 | 934.3 | 168.7 | 16.6 | 682.0 | .. | 36.1 | 1,625 | 24,649 | .. | .. |
| Bosnia and Herzegovina | 0.0 | 860.5 | .. | 277.9 | .. | .. | .. | .. | 48.4 | 1,409 | 34,035 | 14,986 | 3.8 |
| Botswana | 97.0 | 122.0 | .. | .. | .. | .. | .. | .. | 19.6 | 7,301 | 79,543 | 13,137 | 7.2 |
| Brazil | 45,135.2 | 46,959.3 | 33,042.3 | 29,351.3 | 16,960.8 | 4,060.7 | 1,850.0 | 1,215.3 | 36.5 | .. | .. | 4,903,268 | 27.4 |
| Bulgaria | 202.5 | 2,641.1 | .. | 3,566.1 | .. | 533.7 | .. | 152.0 | 47.4 | .. | .. | 216,489 | 27.7 |
| Burkina Faso | .. | 331.9 | 5.6 | .. | 63.3 | .. | .. | .. | 16.7 | .. | .. | .. | .. |
| Burundi | .. | 53.6 | .. | .. | .. | .. | .. | .. | 21.0 | .. | .. | .. | .. |
| Cambodia | 102.4 | 198.1 | 143.0 | 88.1 | 120.0 | 325.3 | .. | .. | 9.1 | 1,551 | 10,349 | .. | .. |
| Cameroon | 12.7 | 457.4 | .. | 531.8 | 90.0 | 0.0 | .. | .. | 9.0 | .. | .. | .. | .. |
| Canada | .. | .. | .. | .. | .. | .. | .. | .. | 195.3 | 85,083 | 1,357,881 | 2,245,245 | 69.5 |
| Central African Republic | 1.1 | 0.0 | .. | .. | .. | .. | .. | .. | 6.6 | .. | .. | .. | .. |
| Chad | 2.0 | 37.4 | .. | 0.0 | .. | .. | .. | .. | 2.5 | .. | .. | .. | .. |
| Chile | 673.5 | 1,485.6 | 6,594.1 | 1,525.1 | 3,104.1 | 4,936.2 | 4,190.3 | 1,495.2 | 82.4 | 31,088 | 170,636 | 700,000 | 43.4 |
| China | 5,970.0 | 8,548.0 | 17,166.6 | 10,847.0 | 10,852.5 | 20,347.4 | 985.9 | 4,300.4 | 113.6 | .. | .. | 8,000,000 | 6.3 |
| Hong Kong, China | .. | .. | .. | .. | .. | .. | .. | .. | 139.5 | 74,122 | 557,002 | 263,959 | 38.9 |
| Colombia | 1,384.3 | 3,012.0 | 6,985.4 | 695.0 | 995.5 | 1,919.8 | 321.0 | 619.3 | 35.7 | 987 | 20,026 | 664,000 | 15.2 |
| Congo, Dem. Rep. | 48.0 | 547.4 | .. | .. | 0.0 | .. | .. | .. | 2.9 | .. | .. | .. | .. |
| Congo, Rep. | 54.7 | 71.8 | 325.0 | .. | .. | .. | .. | 0.0 | 2.2 | 2,160 | 34,514 | .. | .. |
| Costa Rica | .. | .. | 301.2 | 160.0 | .. | 508.2 | .. | .. | 39.1 | 44,301 | 392,726 | 40,921 | 9.6 |
| Côte d'Ivoire | 752.3 | 147.9 | 260.6 | 0.0 | 241.3 | 140.0 | .. | .. | 14.1 | .. | .. | .. | .. |
| Croatia | 978.0 | 1,602.1 | 368.5 | 7.1 | 672.2 | 451.0 | .. | 298.7 | 68.7 | 8,733 | 113,708 | 94,088 | 21.2 |
| Cuba | .. | 60.0 | 165.0 | .. | .. | 0.0 | .. | 600.0 | .. | .. | .. | .. | .. |
| Czech Republic | 6,178.5 | 8,996.0 | 944.1 | 3,865.3 | 283.7 | 106.7 | 135.5 | 263.7 | 40.9 | 30,945 | 273,688 | .. | .. |
| Denmark | .. | .. | .. | .. | .. | .. | .. | .. | 185.1 | 33,047 | 234,432 | 257,950 | 47.8 |
| Dominican Republic | 163.0 | 424.0 | 979.0 | 1,306.6 | .. | 1,148.9 | .. | .. | 25.8 | .. | .. | .. | .. |
| Ecuador | 696.4 | 588.6 | 30.0 | 431.0 | 686.8 | 1,651.0 | .. | 500.0 | 24.0 | .. | .. | 1,043,440 | 83.7 |
| Egypt, Arab Rep. | 1,914.5 | 7,222.9 | 634.0 | 678.0 | 123.9 | 821.5 | .. | .. | 55.3 | 9,595 | 367,559 | .. | .. |
| El Salvador | 720.2 | 1,282.1 | 900.2 | 85.0 | .. | .. | .. | .. | 42.9 | 2,617 | 40,739 | 461,642 | 73.3 |
| Eritrea | .. | 40.0 | .. | .. | .. | .. | .. | .. | 29.0 | .. | .. | .. | .. |
| Estonia | 628.2 | 467.1 | 26.5 | .. | 1.0 | 298.4 | .. | 115.0 | 78.4 | 9,945 | 73,999 | 65,194 | 48.4 |
| Ethiopia | .. | .. | .. | .. | .. | .. | .. | .. | 27.2 | .. | .. | .. | .. |
| Finland | .. | .. | .. | .. | .. | .. | .. | .. | 77.8 | 7,710 | 114,061 | 221,000 | 42.4 |
| France | .. | .. | .. | .. | .. | .. | .. | .. | 98.7 | 144,521 | 1,225,291 | 2,612,960 | 43.2 |
| Gabon | 8.4 | 26.6 | 294.0 | 0.0 | 46.7 | 177.4 | .. | .. | 9.3 | .. | .. | .. | .. |
| Gambia, The | .. | 6.6 | .. | 0.0 | .. | .. | .. | .. | 15.6 | .. | .. | .. | .. |
| Georgia | 61.0 | 493.8 | 159.0 | 134.5 | .. | 168.5 | .. | .. | 19.5 | 5,035 | 56,840 | 33,860 | 7.6 |
| Germany | .. | .. | .. | .. | .. | .. | .. | .. | 109.8 | 66,747 | 465,615 | 3,162,111 | 38.3 |
| Ghana | 491.1 | 371.5 | 110.0 | 590.0 | .. | 10.0 | .. | 0.0 | 18.0 | 6,189 | 100,272 | 25,679 | 1.2 |
| Greece | .. | .. | .. | .. | .. | .. | .. | .. | 72.3 | 2,381 | 33,839 | 771,000 | 69.9 |
| Guatemala | 1,366.3 | 836.1 | 1,223.2 | 110.0 | 33.8 | .. | .. | .. | 26.8 | 4,251 | 68,451 | .. | .. |
| Guinea | 120.3 | 98.6 | 36.4 | .. | .. | .. | .. | .. | 5.0 | .. | .. | .. | .. |
| Guinea-Bissau | .. | 6.9 | .. | .. | .. | .. | .. | .. | 4.0 | .. | .. | .. | .. |
| Haiti | 102.5 | 148.0 | 4.7 | 5.5 | .. | .. | .. | .. | 13.3 | 9 | 300 | .. | .. |

| | Investment commitments in infrastructure projects with private participation[a] | | | | | | | | Domestic credit to private sector | Businesses registered | | Micro, small, and medium-size enterprises | |
|---|---|---|---|---|---|---|---|---|---|---|---|---|---|
| | $ millions | | | | | | | | | | | | per 1,000 |
| | Telecommunications | | Energy | | Transport | | Water and sanitation | | % of GDP | New | Total | Total | people |
| | 1995–99 | 2000–06 | 1995–99 | 2000–06 | 1995–99 | 2000–06 | 1995–99 | 2000–06 | 2006 | 2005 | 2005 | 2000–05[b] | 2000–05[b] |
| Honduras | 51.3 | 224.2 | 112.1 | 358.8 | 10.5 | 120.0 | .. | 207.9 | 49.0 | .. | .. | 257,953 | 41.6 |
| Hungary | 6,430.2 | 5,798.1 | 3,812.1 | 2,090.6 | 135.0 | 3,297.5 | 205.8 | 0.0 | 55.4 | 22,251 | 240,556 | | |
| India | 7,456.8 | 27,912.6 | 7,096.7 | 11,572.2 | 1,349.1 | 11,365.7 | .. | 2.1 | 45.0 | 38,129 | 712,800 | | |
| Indonesia | 8,847.5 | 8,108.1 | 9,942.1 | 2,485.7 | 1,530.8 | 2,400.7 | 955.2 | 36.7 | 24.6 | 19,851 | 259,799 | 41,362,315 | 195.3 |
| Iran, Islamic Rep. | 28.0 | 695.0 | .. | 650.0 | .. | .. | .. | .. | 47.3 | .. | .. | | |
| Iraq | .. | 1,074.0 | .. | .. | .. | .. | .. | .. | | .. | .. | | |
| Ireland | .. | .. | .. | .. | .. | .. | .. | .. | 183.4 | 17,234 | 160,707 | 97,000 | 24.3 |
| Israel | .. | .. | .. | .. | .. | .. | .. | .. | 89.6 | 14,687 | 379,503 | 468,338 | 67.6 |
| Italy | .. | .. | .. | .. | .. | .. | .. | .. | 95.6 | 104,364 | 1,688,198 | 4,486,000 | 77.9 |
| Jamaica | .. | 701.0 | 43.0 | 279.0 | 0.0 | 565.0 | .. | .. | 27.9 | .. | .. | | |
| Japan | .. | .. | .. | .. | .. | .. | .. | .. | 182.0 | 114,013 | 2,572,088 | 5,712,191 | 44.7 |
| Jordan | 39.9 | 1,952.6 | .. | .. | 182.0 | 0.0 | 0.0 | 169.0 | 98.0 | 7,706 | 102,716 | 141,327 | 26.7 |
| Kazakhstan | 1,633.5 | 1,788.9 | 1,825.0 | 300.0 | .. | .. | .. | 100.0 | 47.8 | 3,302 | 32,150 | | |
| Kenya | 193.0 | 2,053.0 | 238.0 | 116.7 | 53.4 | 404.0 | 0.0 | .. | 27.7 | 7,371 | 125,102 | 2,800,000 | 85.1 |
| Korea, Dem. Rep. | .. | .. | .. | .. | .. | .. | .. | .. | .. | .. | .. | | |
| Korea, Rep. | .. | .. | .. | .. | .. | .. | .. | .. | 102.0 | .. | .. | 2,998,223 | 62.4 |
| Kuwait | .. | .. | .. | .. | .. | .. | .. | .. | 63.1 | .. | .. | | |
| Kyrgyz Republic | 100.8 | 47.4 | .. | .. | .. | .. | .. | .. | 10.5 | .. | .. | 142,475 | 28.3 |
| Lao PDR | 100.1 | 97.7 | 535.5 | 2,050.0 | 0.0 | 0.0 | .. | .. | 6.0 | .. | .. | | |
| Latvia | 600.9 | 817.4 | 106.0 | 71.1 | 75.0 | 135.0 | .. | .. | 86.8 | 10,856 | 193,893 | 32,571 | 13.8 |
| Lebanon | 485.7 | 138.1 | .. | .. | .. | 153.0 | .. | 0.0 | 77.9 | 3,127 | 63,423 | | |
| Lesotho | 15.7 | 93.9 | .. | 0.0 | .. | .. | .. | .. | 8.9 | .. | .. | | |
| Liberia | .. | 80.8 | .. | .. | .. | .. | .. | .. | 8.4 | .. | .. | | |
| Libya | .. | .. | .. | .. | .. | .. | .. | .. | 15.5 | .. | .. | | |
| Lithuania | 832.7 | 1,112.0 | 10.0 | 399.3 | .. | .. | .. | .. | 50.6 | 4,507 | 71,085 | 56,428 | 16.5 |
| Macedonia, FYR | .. | 808.6 | .. | 391.0 | .. | .. | .. | .. | 30.2 | 10,814 | 157,973 | 55,742 | 27.5 |
| Madagascar | 30.0 | 12.6 | .. | 0.0 | .. | 48.5 | .. | .. | 10.2 | 1,234 | 19,305 | | |
| Malawi | 23.1 | 66.8 | .. | 0.0 | 6.0 | .. | .. | .. | 8.7 | 420 | 5,595 | 747,396 | 64.3 |
| Malaysia | 3,188.6 | 3,770.8 | 1,610.2 | 6,840.6 | 8,135.6 | 4,992.4 | 10.0 | 6,502.2 | 108.1 | .. | .. | 518,996 | 20.2 |
| Mali | .. | 82.6 | .. | 365.9 | .. | 55.4 | .. | .. | 17.2 | .. | .. | | |
| Mauritania | .. | 92.1 | .. | .. | .. | .. | .. | .. | .. | .. | .. | | |
| Mauritius | .. | 393.0 | 109.3 | 0.0 | 42.6 | .. | .. | .. | 78.0 | .. | .. | 75,267 | 62.2 |
| Mexico | 10,757.5 | 20,763.4 | 2,120.8 | 6,795.3 | 4,706.1 | 5,388.4 | 305.0 | 548.7 | 22.1 | 306,400 | 4,290,000 | 2,891,300 | 28.3 |
| Moldova | 84.6 | 80.1 | 60.0 | 25.3 | 38.0 | 0.0 | .. | .. | 27.9 | 5,033 | 61,333 | 25,667 | 6.5 |
| Mongolia | 21.9 | 22.1 | .. | .. | .. | .. | .. | .. | 32.8 | .. | .. | | |
| Morocco | 1,240.0 | 6,715.1 | 5,978.0 | 1,049.0 | .. | 340.0 | .. | .. | 58.1 | 13,407 | 155,947 | 450,000 | 15.4 |
| Mozambique | 29.0 | 138.6 | .. | 1,205.8 | 441.0 | 334.6 | 25.5 | .. | 13.8 | .. | .. | | |
| Myanmar | .. | .. | 719.0 | .. | 50.0 | .. | .. | .. | 5.6 | .. | .. | | |
| Namibia | 55.0 | 35.0 | 4.0 | 1.0 | .. | .. | .. | 0.0 | 61.7 | .. | .. | | |
| Nepal | .. | 97.3 | 98.2 | 39.0 | .. | .. | .. | .. | 37.7 | .. | .. | 3,040 | 0.1 |
| Netherlands | .. | .. | .. | .. | .. | .. | .. | .. | 176.2 | 116,000 | 1,030,000 | 735,160 | 45.0 |
| New Zealand | .. | .. | .. | .. | .. | .. | .. | .. | 144.2 | 62,695 | 388,846 | 334,031 | 81.7 |
| Nicaragua | 24.5 | 294.3 | 232.4 | 126.3 | .. | 104.0 | .. | .. | 33.8 | .. | .. | | |
| Niger | .. | 85.5 | .. | .. | .. | .. | .. | 3.4 | 8.3 | .. | .. | | |
| Nigeria | 69.0 | 9,485.8 | .. | 1,920.0 | .. | 2,617.6 | .. | .. | 15.0 | .. | .. | | |
| Norway | .. | .. | .. | .. | .. | .. | .. | .. | .. | 47,436 | 298,360 | 316,243 | 68.4 |
| Oman | .. | 1,047.0 | 183.0 | 1,364.3 | 77.5 | 473.8 | .. | 0.0 | 34.9 | .. | .. | 7,373 | 3.0 |
| Pakistan | 75.5 | 9,068.0 | 4,298.3 | 800.7 | 421.3 | 322.0 | .. | .. | 29.0 | 4,227 | 44,897 | 2,956,704 | 19.0 |
| Panama | 1,429.2 | 307.9 | 669.2 | 455.5 | 994.6 | 51.4 | 25.0 | .. | 88.6 | .. | .. | | |
| Papua New Guinea | .. | .. | 65.0 | .. | .. | .. | 71.0 | .. | 17.1 | .. | .. | | |
| Paraguay | 259.3 | 365.5 | .. | .. | 58.0 | .. | .. | .. | 16.9 | .. | .. | 548,000 | 98.4 |
| Peru | 4,774.5 | 2,643.2 | 3,004.9 | 2,511.2 | 86.3 | 1,537.5 | .. | 152.0 | 17.8 | 33,349 | 554,135 | 658,837 | 24.4 |
| Philippines | 5,358.3 | 5,235.3 | 6,998.0 | 4,275.2 | 1,364.0 | 1,260.5 | 7,567.2 | 503.9 | 30.0 | 13,328 | .. | 808,634 | 10.0 |
| Poland | 4,913.2 | 18,179.1 | 628.1 | 2,352.7 | 169.4 | 1,672.0 | 6.1 | 64.3 | 33.6 | 23,864 | 509,894 | 1,654,822 | 43.3 |
| Portugal | .. | .. | .. | .. | .. | .. | .. | .. | 157.4 | 16,770 | 262,686 | 693,000 | 66.4 |
| Puerto Rico | .. | .. | .. | .. | .. | .. | .. | .. | .. | .. | .. | 2,069 | 0.5 |

| | Investment commitments in infrastructure projects with private participation[a] $ millions | | | | | | | | Domestic credit to private sector % of GDP 2006 | Businesses registered New 2005 | Total 2005 | Micro, small, and medium-size enterprises Total 2000–05[b] | per 1,000 people 2000–05 |
|---|---|---|---|---|---|---|---|---|---|---|---|---|---|
| | Telecommunications 1995–99 | 2000–06 | Energy 1995–99 | 2000–06 | Transport 1995–99 | 2000–06 | Water and sanitation 1995–99 | 2000–06 | | | | | |
| Romania | 2,072.8 | 4,179.9 | 100.0 | 2,065.6 | 23.4 | .. | .. | 1,116.0 | 26.3 | 91,386 | 851,562 | 392,544 | 18.1 |
| Russian Federation | 5,639.1 | 27,700.4 | 2,281.3 | 1,726.0 | 406.0 | 253.4 | 108.0 | 938.5 | 30.8 | 446,605 | 4,767,300 | 6,891,300 | 48.1 |
| Rwanda | 8.0 | 82.3 | .. | 1.6 | .. | .. | .. | .. | 13.5 | .. | .. | .. | .. |
| Saudi Arabia | .. | .. | .. | .. | .. | .. | .. | .. | 50.7 | .. | .. | .. | .. |
| Senegal | 273.9 | 805.1 | 124.0 | 93.3 | .. | 55.4 | 20.0 | 0.0 | 23.1 | 23 | 1,000 | .. | .. |
| Serbia | 1,590.0 | 3,197.0 | .. | .. | .. | .. | .. | 0.0 | 26.8 | 14,608 | 270,872 | 68,220 | 9.1 |
| Sierra Leone | 7.0 | 88.8 | .. | .. | .. | .. | .. | .. | 4.4 | .. | .. | .. | .. |
| Singapore | .. | .. | .. | .. | .. | .. | .. | .. | 98.6 | 19,501 | 102,662 | 136,363 | 32.2 |
| Slovak Republic | 488.5 | 2,993.9 | .. | 4,459.6 | .. | 42.0 | 0.0 | 13.6 | 39.2 | 7,507 | 81,775 | 70,553 | 13.1 |
| Slovenia | .. | .. | .. | .. | .. | .. | .. | .. | 68.8 | 3,237 | 40,560 | 91,066 | 45.6 |
| Somalia | 0.0 | 13.4 | .. | .. | .. | .. | .. | .. | .. | .. | .. | .. | .. |
| South Africa | 2,975.3 | 6,856.5 | 3.0 | 1,261.2 | 1,386.4 | 3,987.7 | 56.9 | 31.3 | 160.8 | 41,356 | 553,425 | .. | .. |
| Spain | .. | .. | .. | .. | .. | .. | .. | .. | 167.4 | 139,119 | 2,193,691 | 3,168,735 | 73.0 |
| Sri Lanka | 559.9 | 938.2 | 192.3 | 270.8 | 240.0 | .. | .. | .. | 32.8 | 4,754 | 58,518 | 121,426 | 6.3 |
| Sudan | 18.3 | 1,454.0 | .. | .. | .. | 30.0 | .. | .. | 0.1 | .. | .. | 22,460 | 0.7 |
| Swaziland | 21.2 | 27.7 | .. | .. | .. | .. | .. | .. | 23.7 | .. | .. | .. | .. |
| Sweden | .. | .. | .. | .. | .. | .. | .. | .. | 117.3 | 21,695 | 301,814 | 898,454 | 99.6 |
| Switzerland | .. | .. | .. | .. | .. | .. | .. | .. | 174.3 | 8,998 | 140,580 | 344,000 | 46.9 |
| Syrian Arab Republic | .. | 628.0 | .. | .. | .. | 37.0 | .. | .. | 14.9 | 216 | 2,268 | .. | .. |
| Tajikistan | 1.2 | 8.5 | .. | 16.0 | .. | .. | .. | .. | 16.0 | .. | .. | 92,964 | 14.7 |
| Tanzania | 100.2 | 585.3 | 127.0 | 376.4 | 16.5 | 27.7 | .. | 8.5 | 12.2 | 3,933 | 59,163 | 2,700,000 | 75.8 |
| Thailand | 2,735.2 | 6,732.7 | 6,875.4 | 4,693.3 | 1,941.1 | 939.0 | 289.0 | 306.5 | 88.0 | .. | .. | 842,360 | 13.7 |
| Timor-Leste | .. | 0.0 | .. | .. | .. | .. | .. | .. | .. | .. | .. | 4,138 | 4.5 |
| Togo | 5.0 | 0.0 | 0.0 | 657.7 | 0.0 | .. | .. | .. | 16.9 | .. | .. | .. | .. |
| Trinidad and Tobago | 0.0 | 190.0 | 207.0 | 39.0 | .. | .. | 0.0 | 120.0 | 34.3 | .. | .. | 19,150 | 14.5 |
| Tunisia | .. | 3,094.0 | 291.0 | 30.0 | .. | .. | .. | .. | 65.0 | 6,353 | 62,563 | .. | .. |
| Turkey | 3,269.7 | 14,780.3 | 2,992.2 | 6,084.5 | 610.0 | 4,160.6 | 942.0 | .. | 34.1 | 86,900 | 593,166 | 210,134 | 3.1 |
| Turkmenistan | .. | 36.3 | .. | .. | .. | .. | .. | .. | .. | .. | .. | .. | .. |
| Uganda | 119.3 | 387.6 | .. | 125.7 | .. | 404.0 | 0.0 | 0.0 | 7.9 | 8,096 | 89,503 | 160,453 | 6.1 |
| Ukraine | 1,094.6 | 4,028.1 | .. | 160.0 | .. | .. | .. | .. | 44.9 | 28,716 | 471,839 | 343,786 | 7.3 |
| United Arab Emirates | .. | .. | .. | .. | .. | .. | .. | .. | 60.9 | .. | .. | .. | .. |
| United Kingdom | .. | .. | .. | .. | .. | .. | .. | .. | 175.8 | 333,700 | 2,160,000 | 4,415,260 | 73.8 |
| United States | .. | .. | .. | .. | .. | .. | .. | .. | 201.1 | 676,830 | 5,156,000 | 5,868,737 | 20.0 |
| Uruguay | 63.7 | 144.2 | 86.0 | 330.0 | 20.0 | 251.1 | .. | 368.0 | 26.2 | .. | .. | 125,000 | 37.9 |
| Uzbekistan | 513.8 | 385.6 | .. | .. | .. | .. | .. | 0.0 | .. | .. | .. | 212,424 | 8.3 |
| Venezuela, RB | 4,877.9 | 4,428.0 | 103.0 | 39.5 | 268.0 | 34.0 | 25.0 | 15.0 | 17.1 | .. | .. | 11,314 | 0.5 |
| Vietnam | 256.0 | 690.0 | 435.5 | 2,279.0 | 85.0 | 20.0 | 38.8 | 174.0 | 71.3 | .. | .. | 90,935 | 1.1 |
| West Bank and Gaza | 265.0 | 279.8 | .. | 150.0 | .. | .. | 0.0 | .. | 8.0 | .. | .. | 97,194 | 27.7 |
| Yemen, Rep. | .. | 647.6 | .. | 15.8 | 190.0 | .. | .. | .. | 6.9 | 1,800 | 21,332 | 310,000 | 16.1 |
| Zambia | 64.2 | 446.3 | 274.0 | 3.0 | .. | 15.6 | .. | 0.0 | 9.7 | 3,389 | 65,155 | .. | .. |
| Zimbabwe | 46.0 | 92.0 | 600.0 | .. | 85.0 | .. | .. | .. | 26.6 | .. | .. | .. | .. |
| **World** | .. s | .. s | .. s | .. s | .. s | .. s | .. s | .. s | 136.7 w | 3,658,665 s | 38,885,427 s | | |
| **Low income** | 11,569.9 | 60,085.8 | 15,726.4 | 23,465.5 | 3,121.9 | 16,176.2 | 155.3 | 188.0 | 38.3 | 75,510 | 1,221,960 | | |
| **Middle income** | 147,572.8 | 255,063.3 | 136,018.9 | 114,473.2 | 63,231.9 | 70,618.4 | 21,831.5 | 21,613.6 | 60.1 | 1,389,189 | 16,463,270 | | |
| Lower middle income | 38,688.6 | 76,783.1 | 65,675.8 | 37,500.4 | 18,401.9 | 34,404.2 | 10,800.3 | 7,913.7 | 81.3 | 182,097 | 2,737,021 | | |
| Upper middle income | 108,884.2 | 178,280.2 | 70,343.1 | 76,972.8 | 44,829.9 | 36,214.2 | 11,031.2 | 13,699.9 | 41.4 | 1,207,092 | 13,726,249 | | |
| **Low & middle income** | 159,142.7 | 315,149.1 | 151,745.3 | 137,938.7 | 66,353.8 | 86,794.6 | 21,986.8 | 21,801.6 | 57.3 | 1,464,699 | 17,685,230 | | |
| East Asia & Pacific | 26,616.5 | 33,533.1 | 44,490.3 | 33,565.9 | 24,079.0 | 30,285.2 | 9,917.1 | 11,823.7 | 98.7 | 21,402 | 270,148 | | |
| Europe & Central Asia | 30,761.6 | 94,150.4 | 12,842.2 | 25,358.4 | 2,129.0 | 11,084.7 | 1,261.9 | 2,691.1 | 35.1 | 783,581 | 8,648,355 | | |
| Latin America & Carib. | 83,557.9 | 92,346.7 | 72,527.6 | 51,226.9 | 35,089.7 | 22,852.5 | 10,705.4 | 6,562.5 | 30.9 | 477,627 | 5,971,458 | | |
| Middle East & N. Africa | 3,973.1 | 27,618.6 | 7,086.0 | 6,657.1 | 573.4 | 2,426.2 | 0.0 | 679.0 | 41.3 | 54,368 | 879,290 | | |
| South Asia | 8,530.3 | 41,008.4 | 12,240.4 | 13,185.8 | 2,010.4 | 11,687.7 | .. | 2.1 | 42.6 | 52,438 | 883,674 | | |
| Sub-Saharan Africa | 5,703.3 | 26,491.9 | 2,558.8 | 7,944.5 | 2,472.2 | 8,458.3 | 102.4 | 43.2 | 78.4 | 75,283 | 1,032,305 | | |
| **High income** | .. | .. | .. | .. | .. | .. | .. | .. | 161.7 | 2,193,966 | 21,200,197 | | |
| Euro area | .. | .. | .. | .. | .. | .. | .. | .. | 115.7 | 658,331 | 7,178,119 | | |

a. Data refer to total for the period shown. Includes projects that became privatized during financial closure years 1990–2006. b. Data are for the most recent year available.

## About the data

Private sector development and investment—tapping private sector initiative and investment for socially useful purposes—are critical for poverty reduction. In parallel with public sector efforts, private investment, especially in competitive markets, has tremendous potential to contribute to growth. Private markets are the engine of productivity growth, creating productive jobs and higher incomes. And with government playing a complementary role of regulation, funding, and service provision, private initiative and investment can help provide the basic services and conditions that empower poor people—by improving health, education, and infrastructure.

Investment in infrastructure projects with private participation has made important contributions to easing fiscal constraints, improving the efficiency of infrastructure services, and extending delivery to poor people. Developing countries have been in the forefront, pioneering better approaches to infrastructure services and reaping the benefits of greater competition and customer focus. Between 1990 and 2006 more than 3,800 projects in more than 139 developing countries introduced private participation in at least one infrastructure sector.

The data on investment in infrastructure projects with private participation refer to all investment (public and private) in projects in which a private company assumes operating risk during the operating period or development and operating risk during the contract period. Investment refers to commitments not disbursements. Foreign state-owned companies are considered private entities for the purposes of this measure. The data are from the World Bank's Private Participation in Infrastructure (PPI) Project Database, which tracks more than 3,800 projects, newly owned or managed by private companies, that reached financial closure in developing economies in 1990–2006. Geographic and income aggregates are calculated by the World Bank's Development Data Group. For more information, see http://ppi.worldbank.org/.

Credit is an important link in money transmission; it finances production, consumption, and capital formation, which in turn affect economic activity. The data on domestic credit to the private sector are taken from the banking survey of the International Monetary Fund's (IMF) *International Financial Statistics* or, when unavailable, from its monetary survey. The monetary survey includes monetary authorities (the central bank), deposit money banks, and other banking institutions, such as finance companies, development banks, and savings and loan institutions. Credit to the private sector may sometimes include credit to state-owned or partially state-owned enterprises.

Entrepreneurship is essential to the dynamism of the modern market economy, and a greater entry rate of new businesses can foster competition and economic growth. The table includes data on business registrations from the 2007 World Bank Group Entrepreneurship Survey, which includes entrepreneurial activity in 84 countries for 2003–05. Survey data are used to analyze firm creation, its relationship to economic growth and poverty reduction, and the impact of regulatory and institutional reforms. The 2007 survey improves on the 2006 survey's methodology and country coverage for better cross-country comparability. Data on total and newly registered businesses were collected directly from national registrars of companies. For cross-country comparability, only limited liability corporations that operate in the formal sector are included. For additional information on sources, methodology, calculation of entrepreneurship rates, and data limitations see www.ifc.org/ifcext/sme.nsf/Content/Entrepreneurship+Database.

Formal and informal micro, small, and medium-size enterprises employ more than half the working population in many market economies and account for about 90 percent of firms. And they contribute significantly to innovation. If small businesses are allowed to compete on a level playing field, the good ones can become larger, workers can earn higher wages, and productivity will increase. A good investment climate—one that provides opportunities and incentives for firms, reduces legal and regulatory costs, lowers the costs of providing financial services, and facilitates the transfer of technology and knowledge and the upgrading of capabilities in small and medium-size firms—is important for economic progress, better jobs, and a more inclusive society.

Data on the business registration of micro, small, and medium-size enterprises are collected by governments, international organizations, foundations, and small business organizations. These data have been collated by the International Finance Corporation (IFC) and are available in two databases: Entrepreneurship Data, and Micro, Small, and Medium Enterprises: A Collection of Published Data. This IFC initiative is a work in progress, improved and updated as new data become available. Because the concepts and definitions of micro, small, and medium-size enterprises vary by source, using these data for precise country rankings may be inappropriate. See www. Ifc.org/ifcext/sme.nsf/Content/Resources for additional information on sources and precise firm size.

## Definitions

• **Investment commitments in infrastructure projects with private participation** refers to infrastructure projects in telecommunications, energy (electricity and natural gas transmission and distribution), transport, and water and sanitation that have reached financial closure and directly or indirectly serve the public. Incinerators, movable assets, standalone solid waste projects, and small projects such as windmills are excluded. Included are operation and management contracts, operation and management contracts with major capital expenditure, greenfield projects (new facilities built and operated by a private entity or a public-private joint venture), and divestitures. Investment commitments are the sum of investments in facilities and investments in government assets. Investments in facilities are resources the project company commits to invest during the contract period in new facilities or in expansion and modernization of existing facilities. Investments in government assets are the resources the project company spends on acquiring government assets such as state-owned enterprises, rights to provide services in a specific area, or use of specific radio spectrums. • **Domestic credit to private sector** is financial resources provided to the private sector—such as through loans, purchases of nonequity securities, and trade credits and other accounts receivable—that establish a claim for repayment. For some countries these claims include credit to public enterprises. • **New businesses registered** are the number of limited liability firms registered in the calendar year. • **Total businesses registered** are the year-end stock of total registered limited liability firms. • **Micro, small, and medium-size enterprises** are business that may be defined by the number of employees. There is no international standard definition of firm size; however, many institutions that collect information use the following size categories: micro enterprises, 0–9 employees; small enterprises, 10–49 employees; and medium-size enterprises, 50–249 employees.

## Data sources

Data on investment commitments in infrastructure projects with private participation are from the World Bank's PPI Project database (http://ppi.worldbank.org). Data on domestic credit are from the IMF's *International Financial Statistics.* Data on business registration and micro, small, and medium-size enterprises are from the IFC's Micro, Small, and Medium Enterprises database (www.ifc.org/ifcext/sme.nsf/Content/Resources).

| | Survey year | Regulations and tax | | Permits and licenses | Corruption | Crime | Informality | Gender | Finance | Infrastructure | Innovation | Trade | Workforce |
|---|---|---|---|---|---|---|---|---|---|---|---|---|---|
| | | Time dealing with officials % of management time | Average number of times management met with tax officials | Time required to obtain operating license days | Unofficial payments to public officials % of firms | Losses due to theft, robbery, vandalism, and arson % of sales | Firms that do not report all sales for tax purposes % of firms | Firms with female participation in ownership % of firms | Firms using banks to finance investment % of firms | Value lost due to electrical outages % of sales | ISO certification ownership % of firms | Average time to clear exports through customs days | Firms offering formal training % of firms |
| Afghanistan | | .. | .. | .. | .. | .. | .. | .. | .. | .. | .. | .. | .. |
| Albania[a] | 2005 | 10.4 | 6.6 | .. | 64.3 | 0.0 | 66.2 | 14.1 | 27.9 | 10.9 | 16.7 | 1.4 | 47.5 |
| Algeria | 2002 | .. | .. | .. | 75.2 | 0.5 | 70.4 | .. | 16.9 | 4.3 | .. | 8.6 | 31.8 |
| Angola[a] | 2006 | 7.1 | 5.2 | 24.1 | 46.3 | 2.4 | 67.8 | 23.4 | 2.1 | 3.7 | 5.1 | 16.5 | 19.4 |
| Argentina[a] | 2006 | 14.1 | 4.6 | 175.8 | 18.7 | 3.7 | 49.1 | 30.3 | 6.9 | 1.4 | 26.9 | 5.5 | 52.2 |
| Armenia[a] | 2005 | 3.0 | 2.9 | .. | 24.6 | 0.0 | 26.2 | 12.5 | 35.0 | 2.5 | 5.7 | 5.0 | 35.9 |
| Australia | | .. | .. | .. | .. | .. | .. | .. | .. | .. | .. | .. | .. |
| Austria | | .. | .. | .. | .. | .. | .. | .. | .. | .. | .. | .. | .. |
| Azerbaijan[a] | 2005 | 5.2 | 1.3 | .. | 37.8 | 0.2 | 38.7 | 14.4 | 0.6 | 5.9 | 10.3 | 1.6 | 16.3 |
| Bangladesh[a] | 2007 | 3.2 | 1.4 | 6.1 | 82.2 | 1.2 | .. | 16.1 | 11.6 | 10.6 | 7.8 | 8.4 | 16.2 |
| Belarus[a] | 2005 | 3.6 | 3.1 | .. | 26.2 | 0.2 | 20.0 | 23.8 | 10.5 | 3.8 | 8.9 | 3.0 | 49.7 |
| Belgium | | .. | .. | .. | .. | .. | .. | .. | .. | .. | .. | .. | .. |
| Benin | 2004 | 6.5 | 6.3 | 39.9 | 57.7 | 0.3 | 39.6 | .. | 20.8 | 6.5 | 2.7 | 6.3 | 35.3 |
| Bolivia[a] | 2006 | 13.5 | 3.5 | 30.0 | 32.0 | 3.3 | 51.4 | 41.1 | 21.1 | 4.4 | 13.8 | 15.3 | 53.9 |
| Bosnia and Herzegovina[a] | 2005 | 4.3 | 1.9 | .. | 24.1 | 0.4 | 29.2 | 25.2 | 17.5 | 2.4 | 14.5 | 2.0 | 47.2 |
| Botswana[a] | 2006 | 5.0 | 2.4 | 13.7 | 27.6 | 3.2 | 65.3 | 40.9 | 11.3 | 1.4 | 12.7 | 1.4 | 37.7 |
| Brazil | 2003 | 7.2 | .. | .. | .. | 0.4 | 82.8 | .. | 22.9 | 1.6 | 19.1 | 8.2 | 67.1 |
| Bulgaria[a] | 2005 | 2.8 | 4.7 | .. | 36.1 | 0.3 | 39.7 | 36.5 | 24.7 | 1.3 | 11.0 | 2.0 | 32.3 |
| Burkina Faso[a] | 2006 | 9.5 | 2.5 | .. | 87.0 | 1.8 | 58.8 | 23.3 | 22.3 | 3.9 | 7.4 | 2.8 | 43.1 |
| Burundi[a] | 2006 | 5.7 | 2.1 | 27.3 | 56.5 | 4.9 | 42.7 | 34.8 | 12.3 | 10.7 | 7.1 | .. | 22.1 |
| Cambodia | 2003 | 8.6 | 7.2 | .. | 82.4 | 1.6 | 91.0 | .. | 6.8 | 2.2 | 2.8 | .. | 22.5 |
| Cameroon[a] | 2006 | 12.8 | 6.4 | 15.6 | 77.4 | 3.8 | 38.7 | 35.3 | 18.0 | 3.9 | 16.4 | 4.3 | 42.4 |
| Canada | | .. | .. | .. | .. | .. | .. | .. | .. | .. | .. | .. | .. |
| Central African Republic | | .. | .. | .. | .. | .. | .. | .. | .. | .. | .. | .. | .. |
| Chad | | .. | .. | .. | .. | .. | .. | .. | .. | .. | .. | .. | .. |
| Chile[a] | 2006 | 9.0 | 5.4 | 67.7 | 8.2 | 1.3 | 27.9 | 27.8 | 29.0 | 1.8 | 22.0 | 5.8 | 46.9 |
| China | 2003 | 18.3 | 14.4 | 11.8 | 72.6 | 0.1 | 49.5 | .. | 9.8 | 1.3 | 35.9 | 6.7 | 84.8 |
| Hong Kong, China | | .. | .. | .. | .. | .. | .. | .. | .. | .. | .. | .. | .. |
| Colombia[a] | 2006 | 14.3 | 2.5 | 28.2 | 8.2 | 2.9 | 38.7 | 43.0 | 30.5 | 2.3 | 5.9 | 7.1 | 39.5 |
| Congo, Dem. Rep.[a] | 2006 | 6.3 | 10.0 | 17.8 | 83.8 | 6.5 | 65.4 | 21.2 | 3.3 | 5.6 | 4.3 | 3.6 | 11.4 |
| Congo, Rep. | | .. | .. | .. | .. | .. | .. | .. | .. | .. | .. | .. | .. |
| Costa Rica | 2005 | 9.6 | 0.7 | .. | 33.8 | 0.4 | 68.3 | 34.7 | 9.3 | 1.9 | 10.5 | 3.5 | 46.4 |
| Côte d'Ivoire | | .. | .. | .. | .. | .. | .. | .. | .. | .. | .. | .. | .. |
| Croatia[a] | 2005 | 2.7 | 2.3 | .. | 20.8 | 0.2 | 33.3 | 20.0 | 29.7 | 2.4 | 16.1 | 2.0 | 59.9 |
| Cuba | | .. | .. | .. | .. | .. | .. | .. | .. | .. | .. | .. | .. |
| Czech Republic[a] | 2005 | 2.1 | 1.7 | .. | 25.5 | 0.4 | 51.1 | 21.8 | 11.4 | 1.6 | 12.5 | 3.6 | 60.3 |
| Denmark | | .. | .. | .. | .. | .. | .. | .. | .. | .. | .. | .. | .. |
| Dominican Republic | 2005 | 8.8 | 2.7 | .. | 26.3 | 0.7 | 73.6 | .. | 3.6 | 15.2 | 9.6 | 11.4 | 53.3 |
| Ecuador[a] | 2006 | 17.3 | 2.6 | 19.9 | 20.7 | 3.0 | 37.6 | 32.7 | 23.8 | 2.7 | 18.2 | 7.0 | 61.6 |
| Egypt, Arab Rep. | 2004 | .. | 7.2 | 112.8 | 21.2 | .. | 33.0 | .. | 7.9 | 4.5 | 12.0 | 4.8 | 13.4 |
| El Salvador[a] | 2006 | 9.2 | 4.1 | 35.4 | 27.3 | 5.6 | 42.3 | 39.6 | 17.3 | 2.9 | 11.0 | 2.6 | 49.6 |
| Eritrea | 2002 | 3.8 | .. | .. | 6.8 | .. | 84.2 | 5.3 | 30.5 | .. | 6.6 | .. | 20.3 |
| Estonia[a] | 2005 | 2.3 | 2.2 | .. | 16.2 | 0.4 | 24.7 | 34.1 | 17.8 | 1.1 | 13.2 | 1.8 | 64.9 |
| Ethiopia[a] | 2006 | 3.8 | 1.8 | 11.4 | 12.4 | 1.4 | 51.6 | 30.9 | 11.0 | 0.9 | 4.2 | 4.3 | 38.2 |
| Finland | | .. | .. | .. | .. | .. | .. | .. | .. | .. | .. | .. | .. |
| France | | .. | .. | .. | .. | .. | .. | .. | .. | .. | .. | .. | .. |
| Gabon | | .. | .. | .. | .. | .. | .. | .. | .. | .. | .. | .. | .. |
| Gambia, The[a] | 2006 | 7.3 | 3.2 | 9.1 | 52.1 | 8.7 | 88.1 | 21.3 | 7.6 | 11.8 | 22.2 | 5.0 | 25.6 |
| Georgia[a] | 2005 | 3.1 | 7.9 | .. | 11.1 | 0.3 | 36.0 | 36.9 | 12.5 | 9.2 | 13.0 | 3.4 | 24.0 |
| Germany | | .. | .. | .. | .. | .. | .. | .. | .. | .. | .. | .. | .. |
| Ghana[a] | 2007 | 4.0 | 4.6 | 6.4 | 38.8 | 3.7 | 59.2 | 44.0 | 16.0 | 6.0 | 6.8 | 7.8 | 33.0 |
| Greece | | .. | .. | .. | .. | .. | .. | .. | .. | .. | .. | .. | .. |
| Guatemala[a] | 2006 | 9.2 | 3.9 | 75.4 | 13.0 | 5.2 | 44.2 | 28.4 | 12.8 | 4.5 | 8.0 | 4.5 | 28.1 |
| Guinea[a] | 2006 | 2.7 | 3.6 | 13.0 | 84.8 | 8.3 | 95.4 | 25.4 | 0.9 | 14.0 | 5.2 | 4.3 | 21.1 |
| Guinea-Bissau[a] | 2006 | 2.9 | 4.4 | 30.4 | 62.2 | 3.3 | 68.2 | 19.9 | 0.7 | 5.3 | 8.4 | 5.6 | 12.4 |
| Haiti | | .. | .. | .. | .. | .. | .. | .. | .. | .. | .. | .. | .. |

| | Survey year | Regulations and tax | | Permits and licenses | Corruption | Crime | Informality | Gender | Finance | Infrastructure | Innovation | Trade | Workforce |
|---|---|---|---|---|---|---|---|---|---|---|---|---|---|
| | | Time dealing with officials % of management time | Average number of times management met with tax officials | Time required to obtain operating license days | Unofficial payments to public officials % of firms | Losses due to theft, robbery, vandalism, and arson % of sales | Firms that do not report all sales for tax purposes % of firms | Firms with female participation in ownership % of firms | Firms using banks to finance investment % of firms | Value lost due to electrical outages % of sales | ISO certification ownership % of firms | Average time to clear exports through customs days | Firms offering formal training % of firms |
| Honduras[a] | 2006 | 4.6 | 2.4 | 31.6 | 12.7 | 6.1 | 36.0 | 39.9 | 8.5 | 3.8 | 16.5 | 6.0 | 33.3 |
| Hungary[a] | 2005 | 4.0 | 2.5 | .. | 32.1 | 0.1 | 40.0 | 40.1 | 22.3 | 1.4 | 23.1 | 4.5 | 39.9 |
| India | 2006 | 6.7 | 3.1 | .. | 47.5 | 0.1 | 59.2 | 9.1 | 19.4 | 6.6 | 22.5 | 15.6 | 15.9 |
| Indonesia | 2003 | 4.0 | 2.0 | 18.6 | 44.2 | 0.2 | 44.0 | .. | 13.9 | 3.3 | 22.1 | 4.1 | 23.8 |
| Iran, Islamic Rep. | | .. | .. | .. | .. | .. | .. | .. | .. | .. | .. | .. | .. |
| Iraq | | .. | .. | .. | .. | .. | .. | .. | .. | .. | .. | .. | .. |
| Ireland | | .. | .. | .. | .. | .. | .. | .. | .. | .. | .. | .. | .. |
| Israel | | .. | .. | .. | .. | .. | .. | .. | .. | .. | .. | .. | .. |
| Italy | | .. | .. | .. | .. | .. | .. | .. | .. | .. | .. | .. | .. |
| Jamaica | 2005 | 6.3 | 2.2 | .. | 17.7 | 1.1 | 28.8 | 32.2 | 10.6 | 11.8 | 16.4 | 4.3 | 53.5 |
| Japan | | .. | .. | .. | .. | .. | .. | .. | .. | .. | .. | .. | .. |
| Jordan | 2006 | 6.7 | 2.2 | 6.4 | 4.1 | 1.3 | 13.0 | 13.1 | 8.6 | 1.7 | 15.5 | 3.8 | 23.9 |
| Kazakhstan[a] | 2005 | 3.1 | 4.0 | .. | 45.1 | 0.3 | 23.2 | 36.1 | 15.4 | 2.2 | 9.9 | 6.8 | 30.7 |
| Kenya | 2003 | 11.7 | 5.5 | 11.6 | 63.0 | 0.8 | 45.9 | .. | 25.7 | 8.1 | .. | 4.7 | 48.5 |
| Korea, Dem. Rep. | 2005 | 3.2 | .. | .. | .. | .. | .. | .. | .. | .. | .. | .. | .. |
| Korea, Rep. | 2005 | 3.2 | 2.4 | .. | 14.1 | 0.0 | 43.7 | 19.1 | 11.5 | .. | 17.6 | 7.2 | 39.5 |
| Kuwait | | .. | .. | .. | .. | .. | .. | .. | .. | .. | .. | .. | .. |
| Kyrgyz Republic[a] | 2005 | 6.1 | 3.5 | 43.9 | 66.3 | 0.7 | 43.2 | 27.3 | 7.9 | 4.1 | 11.9 | 4.1 | 47.0 |
| Lao PDR | 2005 | 4.5 | 3.8 | .. | 31.2 | 1.5 | 14.9 | .. | 13.8 | 4.3 | 3.3 | 2.0 | 28.2 |
| Latvia[a] | 2005 | 2.9 | 2.2 | .. | 31.3 | 0.5 | 26.3 | 42.3 | 15.1 | 1.4 | 9.3 | 2.0 | 51.7 |
| Lebanon | 2006 | 12.0 | 4.7 | .. | 51.2 | 0.5 | 67.5 | 27.9 | 26.8 | 6.0 | 20.9 | 7.4 | 67.8 |
| Lesotho | 2003 | 19.8 | 14.3 | .. | 33.3 | 0.1 | 35.4 | .. | 6.7 | 8.5 | 8.6 | 2.3 | 24.6 |
| Liberia | | .. | .. | .. | .. | .. | .. | .. | .. | .. | .. | .. | .. |
| Libya | | .. | .. | .. | .. | .. | .. | .. | .. | .. | .. | .. | .. |
| Lithuania[a] | 2005 | 5.1 | 4.2 | 55.5 | 44.6 | 0.4 | 39.0 | 25.5 | 15.6 | 1.2 | 15.1 | 1.8 | 52.6 |
| Macedonia, FYR[a] | 2005 | 8.2 | 2.7 | .. | 26.0 | 0.3 | 52.2 | 17.5 | 9.0 | 1.8 | 11.0 | 2.4 | 37.4 |
| Madagascar | 2005 | 20.8 | 2.7 | .. | 24.5 | 1.9 | 21.0 | .. | 13.0 | 6.6 | 6.6 | 3.5 | 48.5 |
| Malawi[a] | 2006 | 5.8 | 8.9 | 17.4 | 35.7 | 2.3 | 55.3 | 15.8 | 20.6 | 22.6 | 17.2 | 3.5 | 51.6 |
| Malaysia | 2002 | 7.3 | 5.2 | .. | .. | 0.3 | .. | .. | 23.8 | 1.8 | 31.4 | 2.5 | 42.0 |
| Mali | 2003 | 7.5 | 6.9 | 8.1 | 59.6 | 0.5 | 55.1 | .. | 16.8 | 1.7 | 6.5 | 8.1 | 25.5 |
| Mauritania[a] | 2006 | 5.8 | 1.9 | 10.7 | 82.1 | 5.6 | 82.5 | 17.3 | 3.2 | 1.6 | 5.9 | 3.9 | 25.5 |
| Mauritius | 2005 | 9.6 | 2.1 | .. | 17.5 | 0.1 | 26.3 | .. | 36.3 | 2.9 | 28.4 | 4.4 | 62.1 |
| Mexico[a] | 2006 | 20.5 | 2.3 | 11.9 | 20.0 | 3.4 | 57.7 | 24.8 | 2.6 | 2.4 | 20.3 | 5.4 | 24.6 |
| Moldova[a] | 2005 | 3.6 | 2.7 | 44.7 | 36.0 | 0.1 | 40.2 | 27.5 | 17.7 | 2.7 | 6.9 | 2.6 | 32.5 |
| Mongolia | 2004 | 6.0 | 7.3 | .. | .. | 0.6 | 80.4 | .. | 32.8 | 1.5 | 20.5 | 3.5 | 46.2 |
| Morocco | 2004 | 9.2 | 0.8 | 4.9 | .. | 0.0 | 10.7 | .. | 24.7 | 0.7 | 22.3 | 2.2 | 33.5 |
| Mozambique | | .. | .. | .. | .. | .. | .. | .. | .. | .. | .. | .. | .. |
| Myanmar | | .. | .. | .. | .. | .. | .. | .. | .. | .. | .. | .. | .. |
| Namibia[a] | 2006 | 2.9 | 1.6 | 9.6 | 11.4 | 3.0 | 45.5 | 33.4 | 8.1 | 0.7 | 17.6 | 1.5 | 44.5 |
| Nepal | | .. | .. | .. | .. | .. | .. | .. | .. | .. | .. | .. | .. |
| Netherlands | | .. | .. | .. | .. | .. | .. | .. | .. | .. | .. | .. | .. |
| New Zealand | | .. | .. | .. | .. | .. | .. | .. | .. | .. | .. | .. | .. |
| Nicaragua[a] | 2006 | 9.3 | 2.5 | 19.7 | 16.8 | 3.8 | 60.4 | 41.4 | 13.0 | 8.7 | 18.7 | 5.0 | 28.9 |
| Niger[a] | 2006 | 11.5 | 4.3 | 10.9 | 69.7 | 6.1 | 29.7 | 10.0 | 14.4 | 2.5 | 4.8 | 7.4 | 34.4 |
| Nigeria | | .. | .. | .. | .. | .. | .. | .. | .. | .. | .. | .. | .. |
| Norway | | .. | .. | .. | .. | .. | .. | .. | .. | .. | .. | .. | .. |
| Oman | | .. | 5.2 | 11.8 | 33.2 | .. | 42.5 | .. | 6.5 | 4.2 | 10.8 | 4.2 | 20.9 |
| Pakistan | 2002 | 8.7 | 4.2 | 35.2 | 57.0 | 0.1 | .. | .. | 3.6 | 4.9 | 17.0 | 9.7 | 11.1 |
| Panama[a] | 2006 | 10.3 | 2.7 | 41.2 | 24.2 | 2.7 | 54.2 | 37.1 | 19.2 | 2.4 | 14.7 | 5.7 | 43.9 |
| Papua New Guinea | | .. | .. | .. | .. | .. | .. | .. | .. | .. | .. | .. | .. |
| Paraguay[a] | 2006 | 7.9 | 2.2 | 37.8 | 68.0 | 3.1 | 42.8 | 44.8 | 8.0 | 2.5 | 7.1 | 5.5 | 46.9 |
| Peru[a] | 2006 | 13.5 | 2.5 | 81.1 | 9.2 | 2.4 | 27.2 | 32.8 | 30.8 | 3.2 | 14.6 | 5.6 | 57.7 |
| Philippines | 2003 | 6.9 | 3.9 | 25.0 | 44.7 | 0.9 | 57.9 | .. | 5.5 | 5.9 | 15.8 | 6.6 | 21.7 |
| Poland[a] | 2005 | 3.0 | 2.7 | 16.5 | 23.7 | 0.4 | 43.9 | 33.6 | 20.7 | 1.6 | 13.9 | 3.3 | 48.4 |
| Portugal | | .. | .. | .. | .. | .. | .. | .. | .. | .. | .. | .. | .. |
| Puerto Rico | | .. | .. | .. | .. | .. | .. | .. | .. | .. | .. | .. | .. |

| | Survey year | Regulations and tax | | Permits and licenses | Corruption | Crime | Informality | Gender | Finance | Infrastructure | Innovation | Trade | Workforce |
|---|---|---|---|---|---|---|---|---|---|---|---|---|---|
| | | Time dealing with officials | Average number of times management met with tax officials | Time required to obtain operating license | Unofficial payments to public officials | Losses due to theft, robbery, vandalism, and arson | Firms that do not report all sales for tax purposes | Firms with female participation in ownership | Firms using banks to finance investment | Value lost due to electrical outages | ISO certification ownership | Average time to clear exports through customs | Firms offering formal training |
| | | % of management time | | days | % of firms | % of sales | % of firms | % of firms | % of firms | % of sales | % of firms | days | % of firms |
| Romania[a] | 2005 | 1.1 | 1.8 | .. | 33.1 | 0.2 | 26.9 | 27.7 | 23.2 | 2.1 | 16.8 | 2.4 | 32.7 |
| Russian Federation[a] | 2005 | 6.3 | 2.5 | .. | 59.9 | 0.5 | 40.3 | 28.6 | 10.2 | 2.0 | 9.3 | 8.2 | 37.3 |
| Rwanda[a] | 2006 | 5.9 | 4.0 | 6.5 | 20.0 | 7.1 | 28.9 | 41.0 | 15.9 | 8.7 | 10.8 | 6.7 | 27.6 |
| Saudi Arabia | | .. | .. | .. | .. | .. | .. | .. | .. | .. | .. | .. | .. |
| Senegal | 2003 | .. | 6.7 | 30.5 | 25.3 | 0.6 | .. | .. | 26.3 | 4.3 | 6.1 | 6.6 | 32.7 |
| Serbia[a] | 2005 | 8.1 | 4.1 | .. | 31.8 | 0.6 | 33.3 | 25.0 | 16.7 | 2.4 | 11.7 | 3.2 | 47.5 |
| Sierra Leone | | .. | .. | .. | .. | .. | .. | .. | .. | .. | .. | .. | .. |
| Singapore | | .. | .. | .. | .. | .. | .. | .. | .. | .. | .. | .. | .. |
| Slovak Republic[a] | 2005 | 3.0 | 1.8 | .. | 34.3 | 0.4 | 22.0 | 18.2 | 13.2 | 1.2 | 10.0 | 5.8 | 79.4 |
| Slovenia | 2005 | 3.7 | 1.4 | .. | 11.2 | 0.2 | 35.6 | 34.5 | 29.6 | 1.1 | 20.2 | 2.9 | 69.9 |
| Somalia | | .. | .. | .. | .. | .. | .. | .. | .. | .. | .. | .. | .. |
| South Africa | 2003 | 9.2 | 3.3 | 6.4 | 2.1 | 0.5 | 15.9 | .. | 24.2 | 0.4 | 42.4 | 4.5 | 64.0 |
| Spain | | .. | .. | .. | .. | .. | .. | .. | .. | .. | .. | .. | .. |
| Sri Lanka | 2004 | 3.5 | 5.1 | 49.5 | 16.3 | 0.5 | 42.0 | .. | 16.2 | .. | .. | 7.6 | 32.6 |
| Sudan | | .. | .. | .. | .. | .. | .. | .. | .. | .. | .. | .. | .. |
| Swaziland | 2006 | 4.4 | 1.9 | 24.0 | 40.6 | 3.4 | 74.6 | 28.6 | 7.7 | 2.5 | 22.1 | 4.0 | 51.0 |
| Sweden | | .. | .. | .. | .. | .. | .. | .. | .. | .. | .. | .. | .. |
| Switzerland | | .. | .. | .. | .. | .. | .. | .. | .. | .. | .. | .. | .. |
| Syrian Arab Republic | 2003 | 10.3 | 6.0 | .. | .. | .. | 79.9 | .. | 2.9 | 8.6 | 7.4 | 6.3 | 21.0 |
| Tajikistan | 2005 | 3.3 | 3.0 | 15.3 | 45.7 | 0.3 | 34.5 | 21.8 | 1.0 | 7.3 | 6.5 | 5.4 | 30.9 |
| Tanzania | 2006 | 4.0 | 3.3 | 15.9 | 49.1 | 3.9 | 71.0 | 30.9 | 6.8 | 9.6 | 14.7 | 5.7 | 36.5 |
| Thailand | 2004 | 1.3 | 1.7 | 37.1 | .. | 0.1 | .. | .. | 74.7 | 1.4 | 44.6 | 1.4 | 76.3 |
| Timor-Leste | | .. | .. | .. | .. | .. | .. | .. | .. | .. | .. | .. | .. |
| Togo | | .. | .. | .. | .. | .. | .. | .. | .. | .. | .. | .. | .. |
| Trinidad and Tobago | | .. | .. | .. | .. | .. | .. | .. | .. | .. | .. | .. | .. |
| Tunisia | | .. | .. | .. | .. | .. | .. | .. | .. | .. | .. | .. | .. |
| Turkey | 2005 | 10.8 | 2.2 | .. | 45.7 | 0.2 | 63.1 | 8.9 | 7.5 | 2.2 | 12.6 | 4.5 | 25.5 |
| Turkmenistan | | .. | .. | .. | .. | .. | .. | .. | .. | .. | .. | .. | .. |
| Uganda | 2006 | 5.2 | 2.9 | 9.3 | 50.6 | 4.1 | 74.5 | 34.7 | 7.7 | 10.2 | 15.5 | 4.7 | 35.0 |
| Ukraine | 2005 | 8.1 | 4.7 | .. | 48.0 | 0.4 | 24.4 | 34.9 | 14.7 | 2.7 | 10.8 | 4.7 | 44.0 |
| United Arab Emirates | | .. | .. | .. | .. | .. | .. | .. | .. | .. | .. | .. | .. |
| United Kingdom | | .. | .. | .. | .. | .. | .. | .. | .. | .. | .. | .. | .. |
| United States | | .. | .. | .. | .. | .. | .. | .. | .. | .. | .. | .. | .. |
| Uruguay | 2006 | 7.0 | 2.2 | 133.8 | 7.1 | 2.1 | 45.5 | 41.6 | 6.8 | 0.9 | 6.8 | 2.8 | 24.6 |
| Uzbekistan | 2005 | 2.5 | 3.5 | .. | 36.8 | 0.1 | 14.6 | 17.2 | 3.3 | 2.7 | 8.7 | 5.1 | 16.2 |
| Venezuela, RB | 2006 | 33.6 | 3.4 | 41.6 | .. | 6.8 | .. | .. | 35.7 | 4.4 | 12.5 | 14.1 | 42.3 |
| Vietnam | 2005 | 3.1 | 2.2 | .. | 67.2 | 0.1 | 70.3 | 27.4 | 29.2 | .. | 11.4 | 4.9 | 44.0 |
| West Bank and Gaza | 2006 | 5.7 | 5.2 | 21.3 | 5.2 | 7.5 | 25.7 | 18.0 | 4.2 | 4.6 | 18.2 | 6.0 | 26.5 |
| Yemen, Rep. | | .. | .. | .. | .. | .. | .. | .. | .. | .. | .. | .. | .. |
| Zambia | 2002 | 13.0 | 2.9 | .. | 44.4 | 2.8 | 53.5 | .. | 17.4 | 3.8 | 5.8 | 2.3 | 34.2 |
| Zimbabwe | | .. | .. | .. | .. | .. | .. | .. | .. | .. | .. | .. | .. |

a. Representative sample of the nonagricultural economy, excluding financial and public services.

The World Bank Group's Enterprise Surveys collect firm-level data on the business environment to analyze how it changes and affects firm performance and growth. Enterprise Surveys cover 11 dimensions of the business environment and are available for more than 70,000 firms in 104 countries.

Firms evaluating alternative investment options, governments interested in improving business conditions, and economists seeking to explain economic performance have all grappled with defining and measuring the business environment. The firm-level data from Enterprise Surveys provide a useful tool for benchmarking performance and monitoring progress.

Most countries can improve regulation and taxation without compromising broader social interests. Excessive regulation may harm business performance and growth. For example, time spent with tax officials is a burden firms may face in paying taxes. The business environment suffers when governments increase uncertainty and risks or impose unnecessary costs and unsound regulation and taxation. The time needed to obtain licenses and permits and the associated red tape constrains firm operations.

In some countries doing business requires unofficial payments or gifts to "get things done" in customs, taxes, licenses, regulations, services, and the like. Corruption such as this harms the business environment by distorting policymaking, undermining government credibility, and diverting public resources. Crime, theft, and disorder may also impose costs on businesses and society.

In many developing countries informal businesses operate without licenses, which constrains private sector growth because these firms have less access to financial and public services and can engage in fewer types of contracts and investments.

Equal opportunities for men and women contribute to development. The table shows female participation in firm ownership as a measure of women's integration as decisionmakers in business.

When financial markets work well, they connect firms to lenders and investors, allowing firms to seize opportunities and grow their businesses: creditworthy firms can obtain credit from financial intermediaries at competitive prices. But too often market imperfections and government-induced distortions limit a firm's access to credit and thus restrain private sector development and economic growth.

The reliability and availability of infrastructure benefit households and are crucial for development. Firms with access to modern and efficient infrastructure—telecommunications, reliable electricity, and transport—can be more productive. Firm-level innovation and use of modern technology may improve enterprises' ability to compete in the business environment.

Delays in clearing customs can be costly, deterring firms from engaging in foreign trade or making them uncompetitive in foreign markets. Ill-considered labor regulations discourage firms from creating jobs, and while employed workers may benefit, unemployed, low-skilled, and informally employed workers will not. A trained labor force enables firms to thrive, compete, innovate, and adopt new technology.

The table presents data for 27 countries in Europe and Central Asia and 2 comparator countries in Asia (Republic of Korea and Vietnam) that are based on the joint European Bank for Reconstruction and Development (EBRD)–World Bank Business Environment and Enterprise Performance Surveys (BEEPS). All other data are from the World Bank Financial and Private Sector Development Group's Enterprise Surveys. All BEEPS economies project plus the Latin American and Caribbean and Sub-Saharan African countries for 2006 (except Burkina Faso, Cameroon, and Cape Verde), Jordan, and the 2007 surveys for Bangladesh and Ghana draw a sample from the universe of registered nonagricultural businesses, excluding the financial and public sectors. Economies in the table with samples that are representative of the economy are footnoted. Samples for most of the remaining economies were drawn from the manufacturing sector.

Samples are selected by simple random sampling or stratified random sampling. Typical sample sizes range from 100 to 1,800, depending on the size of the economy. BEEPS use a simple random sample method based on GDP contributions, and therefore samples are self-weighted. Latin American and Caribbean and Sub-Saharan African countries (except Burkina Faso, Cameroon, and Cape Verde), Bangladesh, and Jordan use stratified random sampling, with three levels of stratification: sector, firm size, and geographic region. At the sector level the strata were defined by a few selected manufacturing industries, the retail industry (to represent the services sector), and a residual stratum for the rest of the economy. Firm size is stratified into small, medium, and large. Geographic stratification is defined by country. Stratified random sampling allows indicators to be computed by sector, size, and geographic region. Economywide indicators can also be computed with more precision than under simple random sampling when individual observations are properly weighted.

• **Survey year** is the year in which the underlying data were collected. • **Time dealing with officials** is the time senior management spends dealing with the requirements of government regulation. • **Average number of times management met with tax officials** is the average number of visits or required meetings with tax officials. • **Time required to obtain operating license** is the average wait to obtain an operating license from the day the establishment applied for it to the day it was granted. • **Unofficial payments to public officials** are the percentage of firms expected to make informal payments to public officials to "get things done" with regard to customs, taxes, licenses, regulations, services, and the like. • **Losses due to theft, robbery, vandalism, and arson** are the estimated losses from those causes that occurred on establishments' premises as a percentage of annual sales. • **Firms that do not report all sales for tax purposes** are the percentage of firms that expressed that a typical firm reports less than 100 percent of sales for tax purposes; such firms are termed "informal firms." • **Firms with female participation in ownership** are the percentage of firms with a woman among the principal owners. • **Firms using banks to finance investment** are the percentage of firms using banks to finance investments. • **Value lost due to electrical outages** is the percentage of sales lost due to power outages. • **ISO certification ownership** is the percentage of firms that have earned a quality certification recognized by the International Organization for Standardization (ISO). • **Average time to clear exports through customs** is the average number of days to clear direct exports through customs. • **Firms offering formal training** are the percentage of firms offering formal training programs for their permanent, full-time employees.

**Data sources**

Data on the business environment are from the World Bank Group's Enterprise Surveys website (www.enterprisesurveys.org).

# 5.3 Business environment: Doing Business indicators

| | Starting a business | | | Registering property | | Dealing with licenses | | Employing workers | Enforcing contracts | | Protecting investors | Closing a business |
|---|---|---|---|---|---|---|---|---|---|---|---|---|
| | Number of procedures | Time required days | Cost % of per capita income | Number of procedures | Time required days | Number of procedures to build a warehouse | Time required to build a warehouse days | Rigidity of employment index 0–100 (least to most rigid) | Number of procedures | Time required days | Disclosure index 0–10 (least to most disclosure) | Time to resolve insolvency years |
| | June 2007 | June 2007 | June 2007 | June 2007 | June 2007 | June 2007 | June 2007 | June 2007 | June 2007 | June 2007 | June 2007 | June 2007 |
| Afghanistan | 4 | 9 | 84.6 | 9 | 250 | 13 | 340 | 23 | 47 | 1,642 | 0 | .. |
| Albania | 10 | 36 | 20.9 | 7 | 47 | 24 | 331 | 35 | 39 | 390 | 0 | .. |
| Algeria | 14 | 24 | 13.2 | 14 | 51 | 22 | 240 | 48 | 47 | 630 | 6 | 2.5 |
| Angola | 12 | 119 | 343.7 | 7 | 334 | 14 | 337 | 69 | 46 | 1,011 | 5 | 6.2 |
| Argentina | 14 | 31 | 9.7 | 5 | 65 | 28 | 338 | 41 | 36 | 590 | 6 | 2.8 |
| Armenia | 9 | 18 | 4.8 | 3 | 4 | 19 | 116 | 31 | 50 | 285 | 5 | 1.9 |
| Australia | 2 | 2 | 0.8 | 5 | 5 | 16 | 221 | 3 | 28 | 262 | 8 | 1.0 |
| Austria | 8 | 28 | 5.4 | 3 | 32 | 13 | 194 | 37 | 26 | 397 | 3 | 1.1 |
| Azerbaijan | 13 | 30 | 6.9 | 7 | 61 | 31 | 207 | 38 | 39 | 267 | 4 | 2.7 |
| Bangladesh | 8 | 74 | 46.2 | 8 | 425 | 14 | 252 | 35 | 41 | 1,442 | 6 | 4.0 |
| Belarus | 10 | 48 | 8.8 | 7 | 231 | 17 | 350 | 27 | 28 | 225 | 5 | 5.8 |
| Belgium | 3 | 4 | 5.3 | 7 | 132 | 14 | 169 | 20 | 27 | 505 | 8 | 0.9 |
| Benin | 7 | 31 | 195.0 | 3 | 118 | 15 | 332 | 40 | 42 | 720 | 6 | 4.0 |
| Bolivia | 15 | 50 | 134.1 | 7 | 92 | 17 | 249 | 79 | 37 | 591 | 1 | 1.8 |
| Bosnia and Herzegovina | 12 | 54 | 30.1 | 7 | 331 | 16 | 467 | 46 | 38 | 595 | 3 | 3.3 |
| Botswana | 11 | 108 | 9.9 | 4 | 30 | 24 | 167 | 20 | 29 | 987 | 8 | 1.7 |
| Brazil | 18 | 152 | 10.4 | 14 | 45 | 18 | 411 | 46 | 45 | 616 | 6 | 4.0 |
| Bulgaria | 9 | 32 | 8.4 | 9 | 19 | 22 | 131 | 29 | 40 | 564 | 10 | 3.3 |
| Burkina Faso | 6 | 18 | 82.1 | 8 | 182 | 32 | 226 | 61 | 37 | 446 | 6 | 4.0 |
| Burundi | 11 | 43 | 251.0 | 5 | 94 | 20 | 384 | 41 | 44 | 558 | 4 | .. |
| Cambodia | 10 | 86 | 190.3 | 7 | 56 | 23 | 709 | 45 | 44 | 401 | 5 | .. |
| Cameroon | 13 | 37 | 129.2 | 5 | 93 | 15 | 426 | 46 | 43 | 800 | 6 | 3.2 |
| Canada | 2 | 3 | 0.9 | 6 | 17 | 14 | 75 | 4 | 36 | 570 | 8 | 0.8 |
| Central African Republic | 10 | 14 | 205.4 | 3 | 69 | 21 | 239 | 61 | 43 | 660 | 6 | 4.8 |
| Chad | 19 | 75 | 188.8 | 6 | 44 | 9 | 181 | 46 | 41 | 743 | 6 | .. |
| Chile | 9 | 27 | 8.6 | 6 | 31 | 18 | 155 | 24 | 36 | 480 | 7 | 4.5 |
| China | 13 | 35 | 8.4 | 4 | 29 | 37 | 336 | 24 | 35 | 406 | 10 | 1.7 |
| Hong Kong, China | 5 | 11 | 3.1 | 5 | 54 | 23 | 155 | 0 | 24 | 211 | 10 | 1.1 |
| Colombia | 11 | 42 | 19.3 | 9 | 23 | 14 | 146 | 27 | 34 | 1,346 | 8 | 3.0 |
| Congo, Dem. Rep. | 13 | 155 | 487.2 | 8 | 57 | 14 | 322 | 74 | 43 | 685 | 3 | 5.2 |
| Congo, Rep. | 10 | 37 | 150.1 | 7 | 137 | 14 | 169 | 69 | 44 | 560 | 6 | 3.0 |
| Costa Rica | 12 | 77 | 21.3 | 6 | 21 | 23 | 178 | 32 | 40 | 877 | 2 | 3.5 |
| Côte d'Ivoire | 10 | 40 | 135.8 | 7 | 62 | 21 | 628 | 38 | 33 | 770 | 6 | 2.2 |
| Croatia | 8 | 40 | 11.7 | 5 | 174 | 22 | 255 | 50 | 38 | 561 | 1 | 3.1 |
| Cuba | .. | .. | .. | .. | .. | .. | .. | .. | .. | .. | .. | .. |
| Czech Republic | 10 | 17 | 10.6 | 4 | 123 | 36 | 180 | 31 | 27 | 820 | 2 | 6.5 |
| Denmark | 4 | 6 | 0.0 | 6 | 42 | 6 | 69 | 10 | 34 | 380 | 7 | 1.1 |
| Dominican Republic | 9 | 22 | 31.1 | 7 | 60 | 17 | 214 | 32 | 34 | 460 | 5 | 3.5 |
| Ecuador | 14 | 65 | 29.2 | 10 | 17 | 19 | 148 | 51 | 39 | 498 | 1 | 5.3 |
| Egypt, Arab Rep. | 7 | 9 | 28.6 | 7 | 193 | 28 | 249 | 27 | 42 | 1,010 | 7 | 4.2 |
| El Salvador | 9 | 26 | 73.1 | 5 | 31 | 34 | 155 | 24 | 30 | 786 | 5 | 4.0 |
| Eritrea | 13 | 84 | 125.8 | 12 | 101 | .. | .. | 20 | 39 | 405 | 4 | .. |
| Estonia | 5 | 7 | 2.0 | 3 | 51 | 13 | 117 | 58 | 36 | 425 | 8 | 3.0 |
| Ethiopia | 7 | 16 | 41.3 | 13 | 43 | 12 | 128 | 34 | 39 | 690 | 4 | 3.0 |
| Finland | 3 | 14 | 1.0 | 3 | 14 | 18 | 38 | 48 | 33 | 235 | 6 | 0.9 |
| France | 5 | 7 | 1.1 | 9 | 123 | 13 | 137 | 56 | 30 | 331 | 10 | 1.9 |
| Gabon | 9 | 58 | 164.0 | 8 | 60 | 14 | 210 | 59 | 38 | 1,070 | 6 | 5.0 |
| Gambia, The | 9 | 32 | 279.0 | 5 | 371 | 17 | 146 | 23 | 32 | 434 | 2 | 3.0 |
| Georgia | 5 | 11 | 9.5 | 5 | 5 | 12 | 113 | 7 | 36 | 285 | 8 | 3.3 |
| Germany | 9 | 18 | 5.7 | 4 | 40 | 12 | 100 | 44 | 33 | 394 | 5 | 1.2 |
| Ghana | 11 | 42 | 41.4 | 5 | 34 | 18 | 220 | 37 | 36 | 487 | 7 | 1.9 |
| Greece | 15 | 38 | 23.3 | 12 | 23 | 15 | 169 | 55 | 39 | 819 | 1 | 2.0 |
| Guatemala | 11 | 26 | 47.3 | 5 | 30 | 22 | 235 | 28 | 28 | 1,459 | 3 | 3.0 |
| Guinea | 13 | 41 | 138.3 | 6 | 104 | 32 | 255 | 41 | 50 | 276 | 6 | 3.8 |
| Guinea-Bissau | 17 | 233 | 255.5 | 9 | 211 | 15 | 167 | 66 | 41 | 1,140 | 6 | .. |
| Haiti | 12 | 202 | 133.9 | 5 | 405 | 11 | 1,179 | 21 | 35 | 508 | 2 | 5.7 |

| | Starting a business | | | Registering property | | Dealing with licenses | | Employing workers | Enforcing contracts | | Protecting investors | Closing a business |
|---|---|---|---|---|---|---|---|---|---|---|---|---|
| | Number of procedures | Time required days | Cost % of per capita income | Number of procedures | Time required days | Number of procedures to build a warehouse | Time required to build a warehouse days | Rigidity of employment index 0–100 (least to most rigid) | Number of procedures | Time required days | Disclosure index 0–10 (least to most disclosure) | Time to resolve insolvency years |
| | June 2007 | June 2007 | June 2007 | June 2007 | June 2007 | June 2007 | June 2007 | June 2007 | June 2007 | June 2007 | June 2007 | June 2007 |
| Honduras | 13 | 21 | 59.9 | 7 | 24 | 17 | 125 | 43 | 45 | 480 | 1 | 3.8 |
| Hungary | 6 | 16 | 17.7 | 4 | 63 | 31 | 211 | 30 | 33 | 335 | 2 | 2.0 |
| India | 13 | 33 | 74.6 | 6 | 62 | 20 | 224 | 30 | 46 | 1,420 | 7 | 10.0 |
| Indonesia | 12 | 105 | 80.0 | 7 | 42 | 19 | 196 | 44 | 39 | 570 | 9 | 5.5 |
| Iran, Islamic Rep. | 8 | 47 | 5.3 | 9 | 36 | 19 | 670 | 40 | 39 | 520 | 5 | 4.5 |
| Iraq | 11 | 77 | 93.5 | 5 | 8 | 14 | 215 | 38 | 51 | 520 | 4 | .. |
| Ireland | 4 | 13 | 0.3 | 5 | 38 | 11 | 185 | 17 | 20 | 515 | 10 | 0.4 |
| Israel | 5 | 34 | 4.4 | 7 | 144 | 20 | 235 | 24 | 35 | 890 | 7 | 4.0 |
| Italy | 9 | 13 | 18.7 | 8 | 27 | 14 | 257 | 38 | 41 | 1,210 | 7 | 1.8 |
| Jamaica | 6 | 8 | 8.7 | 5 | 54 | 10 | 236 | 4 | 34 | 565 | 4 | 1.1 |
| Japan | 8 | 23 | 7.5 | 6 | 14 | 15 | 177 | 17 | 30 | 316 | 7 | 0.6 |
| Jordan | 10 | 14 | 66.2 | 8 | 22 | 18 | 122 | 30 | 39 | 689 | 5 | 4.3 |
| Kazakhstan | 8 | 21 | 7.6 | 8 | 52 | 38 | 231 | 20 | 38 | 230 | 7 | 3.3 |
| Kenya | 12 | 44 | 46.1 | 8 | 64 | 10 | 100 | 21 | 44 | 465 | 3 | 4.5 |
| Korea, Dem. Rep. | .. | .. | .. | .. | .. | .. | .. | .. | .. | .. | .. | .. |
| Korea, Rep. | 10 | 17 | 16.9 | 7 | 11 | 13 | 34 | 37 | 35 | 230 | 7 | 1.5 |
| Kuwait | 13 | 35 | 1.6 | 8 | 55 | 25 | 104 | 13 | 50 | 566 | 7 | 4.2 |
| Kyrgyz Republic | 8 | 21 | 8.8 | 4 | 4 | 20 | 291 | 38 | 39 | 177 | 8 | 4.0 |
| Lao PDR | 8 | 103 | 16.5 | 9 | 135 | 24 | 172 | 37 | 42 | 443 | 0 | .. |
| Latvia | 5 | 16 | 3.0 | 8 | 54 | 26 | 188 | 43 | 27 | 279 | 5 | 3.0 |
| Lebanon | 6 | 46 | 94.1 | 8 | 25 | 20 | 211 | 25 | 37 | 721 | 9 | 4.0 |
| Lesotho | 8 | 73 | 37.4 | 6 | 101 | 15 | 601 | 24 | 41 | 695 | 2 | 2.6 |
| Liberia | 12 | 99 | 493.3 | 13 | 50 | 25 | 398 | 31 | 41 | 1,280 | 4 | 3.0 |
| Libya | .. | .. | .. | .. | .. | .. | .. | .. | .. | .. | .. | .. |
| Lithuania | 7 | 26 | 3.0 | 3 | 3 | 17 | 156 | 48 | 30 | 210 | 5 | 1.7 |
| Macedonia, FYR | 9 | 15 | 6.6 | 6 | 98 | 19 | 192 | 50 | 39 | 385 | 5 | 3.7 |
| Madagascar | 5 | 7 | 22.7 | 8 | 134 | 16 | 268 | 63 | 38 | 871 | 5 | .. |
| Malawi | 10 | 37 | 188.7 | 6 | 88 | 21 | 213 | 25 | 42 | 432 | 4 | 2.6 |
| Malaysia | 9 | 24 | 18.1 | 5 | 144 | 25 | 285 | 10 | 30 | 600 | 10 | 2.3 |
| Mali | 11 | 26 | 132.1 | 5 | 29 | 14 | 208 | 38 | 39 | 860 | 6 | 3.6 |
| Mauritania | 11 | 65 | 56.2 | 4 | 49 | 25 | 201 | 45 | 46 | 400 | 5 | 8.0 |
| Mauritius | 6 | 7 | 5.3 | 6 | 210 | 18 | 107 | 23 | 37 | 750 | 6 | 1.7 |
| Mexico | 8 | 27 | 13.3 | 5 | 74 | 11 | 131 | 48 | 38 | 415 | 8 | 1.8 |
| Moldova | 9 | 23 | 11.5 | 6 | 48 | 30 | 292 | 38 | 31 | 365 | 7 | 2.8 |
| Mongolia | 8 | 20 | 4.3 | 5 | 11 | 21 | 126 | 34 | 32 | 314 | 5 | 4.0 |
| Morocco | 6 | 12 | 11.5 | 8 | 47 | 19 | 163 | 63 | 40 | 615 | 6 | 1.8 |
| Mozambique | 10 | 29 | 21.6 | 8 | 42 | 17 | 361 | 54 | 31 | 1,010 | 5 | 5.0 |
| Myanmar | .. | .. | .. | .. | .. | .. | .. | .. | .. | .. | .. | .. |
| Namibia | 10 | 99 | 22.3 | 9 | 23 | 12 | 139 | 20 | 33 | 270 | 5 | 1.5 |
| Nepal | 7 | 31 | 73.9 | 3 | 5 | 15 | 424 | 52 | 39 | 735 | 6 | 5.0 |
| Netherlands | 6 | 10 | 6.0 | 2 | 5 | 18 | 230 | 42 | 25 | 514 | 4 | 1.1 |
| New Zealand | 2 | 12 | 0.1 | 2 | 2 | 7 | 65 | 7 | 30 | 216 | 10 | 1.3 |
| Nicaragua | 6 | 39 | 119.1 | 8 | 124 | 17 | 219 | 27 | 35 | 540 | 4 | 2.2 |
| Niger | 11 | 23 | 174.8 | 5 | 32 | 16 | 293 | 70 | 39 | 545 | 6 | 5.0 |
| Nigeria | 9 | 34 | 56.6 | 14 | 82 | 18 | 350 | 7 | 39 | 457 | 5 | 2.0 |
| Norway | 6 | 10 | 2.3 | 1 | 3 | 14 | 252 | 47 | 33 | 310 | 7 | 0.9 |
| Oman | 9 | 34 | 4.3 | 2 | 16 | 16 | 242 | 24 | 51 | 598 | 8 | 4.0 |
| Pakistan | 11 | 24 | 14.0 | 6 | 50 | 12 | 223 | 43 | 47 | 880 | 6 | 2.8 |
| Panama | 7 | 19 | 22.0 | 7 | 44 | 25 | 149 | 69 | 31 | 686 | 1 | 2.5 |
| Papua New Guinea | 8 | 56 | 26.4 | 4 | 72 | 24 | 217 | 10 | 43 | 591 | 5 | 3.0 |
| Paraguay | 7 | 35 | 77.6 | 6 | 46 | 13 | 291 | 59 | 38 | 591 | 6 | 3.9 |
| Peru | 10 | 72 | 29.9 | 5 | 33 | 21 | 210 | 55 | 37 | 468 | 8 | 3.1 |
| Philippines | 15 | 58 | 26.8 | 8 | 33 | 21 | 177 | 35 | 37 | 842 | 1 | 5.7 |
| Poland | 10 | 31 | 21.2 | 6 | 197 | 30 | 308 | 37 | 38 | 830 | 7 | 3.0 |
| Portugal | 7 | 7 | 3.4 | 5 | 42 | 20 | 327 | 48 | 35 | 577 | 6 | 2.0 |
| Puerto Rico | 7 | 7 | 0.8 | 8 | 194 | 22 | 209 | 21 | 41 | 620 | 7 | 3.8 |

| | Starting a business | | | Registering property | | Dealing with licenses | | Employing workers | Enforcing contracts | | Protecting investors | Closing a business |
|---|---|---|---|---|---|---|---|---|---|---|---|---|
| | Number of procedures | Time required days | Cost % of per capita income | Number of procedures | Time required days | Number of procedures to build a warehouse | Time required to build a warehouse days | Rigidity of employment index 0–100 (least to most rigid) | Number of procedures | Time required days | Disclosure index 0–10 (least to most disclosure) | Time to resolve insolvency years |
| | June 2007 | June 2007 | June 2007 | June 2007 | June 2007 | June 2007 | June 2007 | June 2007 | June 2007 | June 2007 | June 2007 | June 2007 |
| Romania | 6 | 14 | 4.7 | 8 | 150 | 17 | 243 | 66 | 32 | 537 | 9 | 3.3 |
| Russian Federation | 8 | 29 | 3.7 | 6 | 52 | 54 | 704 | 44 | 37 | 281 | 6 | 3.8 |
| Rwanda | 9 | 16 | 171.5 | 5 | 371 | 16 | 227 | 42 | 24 | 310 | 2 | .. |
| Saudi Arabia | 7 | 15 | 32.3 | 4 | 4 | 18 | 125 | 13 | 44 | 635 | 7 | 2.8 |
| Senegal | 10 | 58 | 107.0 | 6 | 114 | 14 | 217 | 61 | 44 | 780 | 6 | 3.0 |
| Serbia | 11 | 23 | 8.9 | 6 | 111 | 20 | 204 | 46 | 36 | 635 | 7 | 2.7 |
| Sierra Leone | 9 | 26 | 1,075.2 | 8 | 235 | 47 | 235 | 51 | 40 | 515 | 3 | 2.6 |
| Singapore | 5 | 5 | 0.8 | 3 | 9 | 11 | 102 | 0 | 22 | 120 | 10 | 0.8 |
| Slovak Republic | 9 | 25 | 4.2 | 3 | 17 | 13 | 287 | 36 | 30 | 565 | 3 | 4.0 |
| Slovenia | 9 | 60 | 8.5 | 6 | 391 | 15 | 208 | 63 | 32 | 1,350 | 3 | 2.0 |
| Somalia | .. | .. | .. | .. | .. | .. | .. | .. | .. | .. | .. | .. |
| South Africa | 8 | 31 | 7.1 | 6 | 24 | 17 | 174 | 42 | 30 | 600 | 8 | 2.0 |
| Spain | 10 | 47 | 15.1 | 4 | 18 | 11 | 233 | 56 | 39 | 515 | 5 | 1.0 |
| Sri Lanka | 5 | 39 | 8.5 | 8 | 83 | 22 | 214 | 27 | 40 | 1,318 | 4 | 1.7 |
| Sudan | 10 | 39 | 57.9 | 6 | 9 | 19 | 271 | 36 | 53 | 810 | 0 | .. |
| Swaziland | 13 | 61 | 38.7 | 11 | 46 | 13 | 93 | 17 | 40 | 972 | 0 | 2.0 |
| Sweden | 3 | 15 | 0.6 | 1 | 2 | 8 | 116 | 39 | 30 | 508 | 6 | 2.0 |
| Switzerland | 6 | 20 | 2.1 | 4 | 16 | 14 | 154 | 17 | 32 | 417 | 0 | 3.0 |
| Syrian Arab Republic | 13 | 43 | 55.7 | 4 | 34 | 21 | 128 | 37 | 55 | 872 | 6 | 4.1 |
| Tajikistan | 13 | 49 | 39.6 | 6 | 37 | 32 | 191 | 51 | 34 | 295 | 0 | 3.0 |
| Tanzania | 12 | 29 | 47.1 | 10 | 119 | 21 | 308 | 63 | 38 | 462 | 3 | 3.0 |
| Thailand | 8 | 33 | 5.6 | 2 | 2 | 11 | 156 | 18 | 35 | 479 | 10 | 2.7 |
| Timor-Leste | 9 | 82 | 11.9 | .. | .. | 22 | 208 | 34 | 51 | 1,800 | 3 | .. |
| Togo | 13 | 53 | 245.7 | 5 | 295 | 15 | 277 | 54 | 41 | 588 | 6 | 3.0 |
| Trinidad and Tobago | 9 | 43 | 0.9 | 8 | 162 | 20 | 261 | 7 | 42 | 1,340 | 4 | .. |
| Tunisia | 10 | 11 | 8.3 | 5 | 49 | 20 | 93 | 49 | 39 | 565 | 0 | 1.3 |
| Turkey | 6 | 6 | 20.7 | 6 | 6 | 25 | 188 | 42 | 36 | 420 | 8 | 3.3 |
| Turkmenistan | .. | .. | .. | .. | .. | .. | .. | .. | .. | .. | .. | .. |
| Uganda | 18 | 28 | 92.0 | 13 | 227 | 16 | 143 | 3 | 38 | 535 | 2 | 2.2 |
| Ukraine | 10 | 27 | 7.8 | 10 | 93 | 29 | 429 | 45 | 30 | 354 | 1 | 2.9 |
| United Arab Emirates | 11 | 62 | 36.9 | 3 | 6 | 21 | 125 | 20 | 50 | 607 | 4 | 5.1 |
| United Kingdom | 6 | 13 | 0.8 | 2 | 21 | 19 | 144 | 7 | 30 | 404 | 10 | 1.0 |
| United States | 6 | 6 | 0.7 | 4 | 12 | 19 | 40 | 0 | 32 | 300 | 7 | 1.5 |
| Uruguay | 11 | 44 | 46.0 | 8 | 66 | 30 | 234 | 31 | 40 | 720 | 3 | 2.1 |
| Uzbekistan | 7 | 15 | 14.2 | 12 | 78 | 26 | 260 | 34 | 42 | 195 | 4 | 4.0 |
| Venezuela, RB | 16 | 141 | 28.2 | 8 | 47 | 11 | 395 | 79 | 29 | 510 | 3 | 4.0 |
| Vietnam | 11 | 50 | 20.0 | 4 | 67 | 13 | 194 | 27 | 34 | 295 | 6 | 5.0 |
| West Bank and Gaza | 12 | 92 | 280.4 | 10 | 72 | 21 | 199 | 31 | 44 | 700 | 6 | .. |
| Yemen, Rep. | 12 | 63 | 178.8 | 6 | 21 | 13 | 107 | 33 | 37 | 520 | 6 | 3.0 |
| Zambia | 6 | 33 | 30.5 | 6 | 70 | 17 | 254 | 34 | 35 | 471 | 3 | 2.7 |
| Zimbabwe | 10 | 96 | 21.3 | 4 | 30 | 19 | 952 | 33 | 38 | 410 | 8 | 3.3 |
| **World** | **9 u** | **44 u** | **61.1 u** | **6 u** | **81 u** | **18 u** | **223 u** | **34 u** | **38 u** | **605 u** | **5 u** | **3.0 u** |
| **Low income** | 10 | 54 | 134.9 | 7 | 114 | 19 | 288 | 40 | 40 | 645 | 5 | 3.8 |
| **Middle income** | 9 | 48 | 43.1 | 6 | 76 | 19 | 216 | 34 | 38 | 621 | 5 | 3.1 |
| Lower middle income | 10 | 53 | 56.5 | 6 | 86 | 18 | 218 | 33 | 39 | 635 | 4 | 3.3 |
| Upper middle income | 9 | 41 | 24.0 | 6 | 61 | 21 | 212 | 35 | 38 | 602 | 5 | 2.9 |
| **Low & middle income** | 10 | 50 | 75.9 | 7 | 89 | 19 | 241 | 36 | 39 | 630 | 5 | 3.3 |
| East Asia & Pacific | 9 | 47 | 40.8 | 5 | 112 | 19 | 179 | 21 | 37 | 591 | 5 | 3.1 |
| Europe & Central Asia | 9 | 26 | 11.6 | 6 | 81 | 24 | 261 | 39 | 36 | 392 | 5 | 3.2 |
| Latin America & Carib. | 10 | 73 | 47.8 | 7 | 67 | 17 | 242 | 34 | 39 | 692 | 4 | 3.2 |
| Middle East & N. Africa | 10 | 39 | 80.5 | 7 | 47 | 19 | 218 | 38 | 43 | 707 | 6 | 3.5 |
| South Asia | 8 | 33 | 40.7 | 6 | 134 | 16 | 247 | 27 | 44 | 1,047 | 4 | 5.0 |
| Sub-Saharan Africa | 11 | 56 | 148.1 | 7 | 105 | 18 | 262 | 43 | 39 | 643 | 5 | 3.4 |
| **High income** | 7 | 22 | 6.6 | 5 | 51 | 17 | 158 | 28 | 34 | 516 | 6 | 2.0 |
| Euro area | 7 | 22 | 7.4 | 6 | 70 | 14 | 190 | 45 | 31 | 591 | 6 | 1.4 |

## About the data

These indicators on the environment for doing business identify regulations that enhance or constrain business investment, productivity, and growth. The data are from the World Bank's Doing Business database, which includes data on 178 economies. The indicators in the table point to the administrative and regulatory reforms and institutions needed to create a favorable environment for doing business.

When entrepreneurs start a business, the first obstacles they face are the administrative and legal procedures required to register the new firm. Countries differ widely in how they regulate the entry of new businesses. In some countries the process is straightforward and affordable. In others the procedures are so burdensome that entrepreneurs may opt to run their business informally. The data on starting a business cover the number of start-up procedures, the time required, and the cost to complete them.

Property registries were developed to raise tax revenue, but they have benefited entrepreneurs as well. Securing rights to legally transfer land and buildings, a major source of wealth in most countries, strengthens incentives to invest and facilitates trade. More complex procedures to register property are associated with less perceived security of property rights, more informality, and more corruption. The data cover the number of procedures required and time required to legally transfer property.

Construction is a large sector in most economies, and the table includes data on the number of procedures and time required for a business in the construction industry to complete the legal procedures to build a standardized warehouse. These include obtaining all necessary licenses and permits, completing all required notifications and inspections, and submitting the relevant documents to the authorities.

Every economy has a complex system of laws and institutions to protect the interests of workers and guarantee a minimum standard of living for its population. The rigidity of employment index focuses on the regulation of employment. The index is the average of three subindexes: a difficulty of hiring index, a rigidity of working hours index, and a difficulty of firing index. All subindexes have several components and take values between 0 and 100, with higher values indicating more rigid regulation.

Contract enforcement is critical to enable businesses to engage with new borrowers or customers. The institution that enforces contracts between debtors and creditors, and suppliers and customers, is the court. The efficiency of contract enforcement is reflected in two indicators: the number of judicial procedures to resolve a commercial dispute and the time to enforce a commercial contract.

What companies disclose to the public has a large impact on investor protection. Both investors and entrepreneurs benefit greatly from such legal protection. The disclosure index is based on several measures that cover disclosure of ownership and interests in related party transactions to reduce expropriation of minority investors.

Unviable businesses prevent assets and human capital from being allocated to more productive uses in new companies or in viable companies that are financially distressed. The time to close a business (resolve insolvency) captures the average time to complete a procedure, as estimated by insolvency lawyers. Delays due to legal derailment tactics that parties to the insolvency may use, in particular extension of response periods or appeals, are taken into account.

To ensure cross-country comparability, several standard characteristics of a company are defined in all surveys, such as size, ownership, location, legal status, and type of activities undertaken. For example, for the starting a business data, standard characteristics include that the business is a limited liability company; operates in the country's most populous city; is 100 percent domestically owned and has five owners, none of them a legal entity; has start-up capital of 10 times income per capita; has paid-in cash; performs general industrial or commercial activities, such as production or sale of products or services to the public; does not perform foreign trade activities or handle products subject to a special tax regime; does not use heavily polluting production processes; leases the commercial plant and offices and is not a proprietor of real estate; does not qualify for investment incentives or any special benefits; has up to 50 employees within one month of commencement of operations, all of them nationals; has turnover at least 100 times income per capita; and has a company deed at least 10 pages long. The data were collected through a study of laws and regulations in each country, surveys of regulators or private sector professionals on each topic, and cooperative arrangements with private consulting firms and business and law associations. Note that some of these assumptions do not apply to all *Doing Business* indicators.

For more information on the methodology, see www.doingbusiness.org/.

## Definitions

• **Number of procedures for starting a business** is the number of procedures required to start a business, including interactions to obtain necessary permits and licenses and to complete all inscriptions, verifications, and notifications to start operations. Data are for businesses with specific characteristics of ownership, size, and type of production. • **Time required for starting a business** is the number of calendar days to complete the procedures for legally operating a business. If a procedure can be expedited at additional cost, the fastest procedure, independent of cost, is chosen. • **Cost for starting a business** is normalized as a percentage of gross national income (GNI) per capita. • **Number of procedures for registering property** is the number of procedures required for a business to legally transfer property. • **Time required for registering property** is the number of calendar days for a business to legally transfer property. • **Number of procedures for dealing with licenses to build a warehouse** is the number of interactions of a company's employees or managers with external parties, including government staff, public inspectors, notaries, land registry and cadastre staff, and technical experts apart from architects and engineers. • **Time required for dealing with licenses to build a warehouse** is the number of calendar days to complete the required procedures for building a warehouse. If a procedure can be expedited at additional cost, the fastest procedure, independent of cost, is chosen. • **Rigidity of employment index,** a measure of employment regulation, is the average of three subindexes: a difficulty of hiring index, a rigidity of hours index, and a difficulty of firing index. Higher values indicate more rigid regulations. • **Number of procedures for enforcing contracts** is the number of independent actions, mandated by law or court regulation, that demand interaction between the parties to a contract or between them and the judge or court officer. • **Time required for enforcing contracts** is the number of calendar days from the time of the filing of a lawsuit in court to the final determination and payment. • **Disclosure index** measures the degree to which investors are protected through disclosure of ownership and financial information. Higher values indicate more disclosure. • **Time to resolve insolvency** is the number of years from time of filing for insolvency in court until resolution of distressed assets and payment of creditors.

### Data sources

Data on the business environment are from the World Bank's Doing Business project (www.doingbusiness.org).

| | Market capitalization | | | | Market liquidity | | Turnover ratio | | Listed domestic companies | | S&P/EMDB indexes | |
|---|---|---|---|---|---|---|---|---|---|---|---|---|
| | $ millions | | % of GDP | | Value of shares traded % of GDP | | Value of shares traded % of market capitalization | | number | | % change | |
| | **2000** | **2007** | **2000** | **2006** | **2000** | **2006** | **2000** | **2007** | **2000** | **2007** | **2006** | **2007** |
| Afghanistan | .. | .. | .. | .. | .. | .. | .. | .. | .. | .. | .. | .. |
| Albania | .. | .. | .. | .. | .. | .. | .. | .. | .. | .. | .. | .. |
| Algeria | .. | .. | .. | .. | .. | .. | .. | .. | .. | .. | .. | .. |
| Angola | .. | .. | .. | .. | .. | .. | .. | .. | .. | .. | .. | .. |
| Argentina | 166,068 | 86,684 | 58.4 | 37.2 | 2.1 | 2.1 | 4.8 | 9.8 | 127 | 107 | 57.6 | 0.7[a] |
| Armenia | 2 | 60 | 0.1 | 0.9 | 0.0 | 0.1 | 4.6 | 9.4 | 105 | 35 | .. | .. |
| Australia | 372,794 | 1,095,858 | 93.3 | 140.4 | 56.6 | 105.9 | 56.5 | 87.0 | 1,330 | 1,751 | .. | .. |
| Austria | 29,935 | 191,300 | 15.4 | 59.4 | 4.8 | 24.7 | 29.8 | 50.4 | 97 | 96 | .. | .. |
| Azerbaijan | 4 | .. | 0.1 | .. | .. | .. | .. | .. | 2 | .. | .. | .. |
| Bangladesh | 1,186 | 6,793 | 2.5 | 5.8 | 1.6 | 1.5 | 74.4 | 95.5 | 221 | 278 | 12.9 | 126.4[b] |
| Belarus | .. | .. | .. | .. | .. | .. | .. | .. | .. | .. | .. | .. |
| Belgium | 182,481 | 396,220 | 78.7 | 100.6 | 16.4 | 42.1 | 20.7 | 48.5 | 174 | 153 | .. | .. |
| Benin | .. | .. | .. | .. | .. | .. | .. | .. | .. | .. | .. | .. |
| Bolivia | 1,742 | 2,223 | 20.7 | 19.9 | 0.8 | 0.0 | 0.1 | 0.0 | 26 | 35 | .. | .. |
| Bosnia and Herzegovina | .. | .. | .. | .. | .. | .. | .. | .. | .. | .. | .. | .. |
| Botswana | 978 | 5,887 | 15.8 | 37.2 | 0.8 | 0.7 | 4.8 | 2.1 | 16 | 18 | 53.0 | 37.2[b] |
| Brazil | 226,152 | 1,370,377 | 35.1 | 66.6 | 15.7 | 23.8 | 43.5 | 56.2 | 459 | 442 | 43.1 | 74.7[a] |
| Bulgaria | 617 | 21,793 | 4.9 | 32.8 | 0.5 | 4.8 | 9.2 | 34.1 | 503 | 369 | 31.4 | 39.0[b] |
| Burkina Faso | .. | .. | .. | .. | .. | .. | .. | .. | .. | .. | .. | .. |
| Burundi | .. | .. | .. | .. | .. | .. | .. | .. | .. | .. | .. | .. |
| Cambodia | .. | .. | .. | .. | .. | .. | .. | .. | .. | .. | .. | .. |
| Cameroon | .. | .. | .. | .. | .. | .. | .. | .. | .. | .. | .. | .. |
| Canada | 841,385 | 1,700,708 | 116.1 | 133.7 | 87.6 | 101.5 | 77.3 | 81.1 | 1,418 | 3,790 | .. | .. |
| Central African Republic | .. | .. | .. | .. | .. | .. | .. | .. | .. | .. | .. | .. |
| Chad | .. | .. | .. | .. | .. | .. | .. | .. | .. | .. | .. | .. |
| Chile | 60,401 | 212,910 | 79.7 | 119.7 | 8.0 | 19.7 | 9.4 | 21.8 | 258 | 238 | 28.6 | 22.6[a] |
| China | 580,991 | 6,226,305 | 48.5 | 91.7 | 60.2 | 61.8 | 158.3 | 197.5 | 1,086 | 1,530 | 80.7 | 66.6[a] |
| Hong Kong, China | 623,398 | 1,714,953 | 368.6 | 903.6 | 223.4 | 437.7 | 61.3 | 60.0 | 779 | 1,165 | .. | .. |
| Colombia | 9,560 | 101,956 | 11.4 | 36.6 | 0.5 | 7.4 | 3.8 | 15.4 | 126 | 96 | 12.7 | 12.7[b] |
| Congo, Dem. Rep. | .. | .. | .. | .. | .. | .. | .. | .. | .. | .. | .. | .. |
| Congo, Rep. | .. | .. | .. | .. | .. | .. | .. | .. | .. | .. | .. | .. |
| Costa Rica | 2,924 | 1,944 | 18.3 | 8.7 | 0.7 | 0.2 | 12.0 | 3.1 | 21 | 16 | .. | .. |
| Côte d'Ivoire | 1,185 | 8,353 | 11.4 | 23.7 | 0.3 | 0.6 | 2.6 | 2.3 | 41 | 38 | 35.6 | 115.6[b] |
| Croatia | 2,742 | 65,977 | 14.9 | 67.6 | 1.0 | 4.2 | 7.4 | 7.2 | 64 | 353 | 85.2 | 68.1[b] |
| Cuba | .. | .. | .. | .. | .. | .. | .. | .. | .. | .. | .. | .. |
| Czech Republic | 11,002 | 73,420 | 19.4 | 34.0 | 11.6 | 23.0 | 60.3 | 73.4 | 131 | 32 | 30.9 | 49.7[a] |
| Denmark | 107,666 | 231,015 | 67.3 | 83.9 | 57.2 | 64.2 | 86.0 | 86.4 | 225 | 201 | .. | .. |
| Dominican Republic | 141 | .. | 0.8 | .. | .. | .. | .. | .. | 6 | .. | .. | .. |
| Ecuador | 704 | 4,266 | 4.4 | 9.8 | 0.1 | 0.7 | 5.5 | 7.0 | 30 | 35 | 32.0 | 3.8[b] |
| Egypt, Arab Rep. | 28,741 | 139,289 | 28.8 | 87.0 | 11.1 | 44.2 | 34.7 | 48.3 | 1,076 | 435 | 10.2 | 52.2[a] |
| El Salvador | 2,041 | 5,465 | 15.5 | 29.3 | 0.2 | 0.9 | 1.3 | 3.7 | 40 | 48 | .. | .. |
| Eritrea | .. | .. | .. | .. | .. | .. | .. | .. | .. | .. | .. | .. |
| Estonia | 1,846 | 6,037 | 32.8 | 36.3 | 5.8 | 5.9 | 18.9 | 31.6 | 23 | 18 | 30.3 | −15.5[b] |
| Ethiopia | .. | .. | .. | .. | .. | .. | .. | .. | .. | .. | .. | .. |
| Finland | 293,635 | 265,477 | 241.0 | 126.0 | 169.6 | 169.4 | 64.3 | 150.2 | 154 | 134 | .. | .. |
| France | 1,446,634 | 2,428,572 | 108.9 | 108.0 | 81.6 | 111.4 | 74.1 | 119.6 | 808 | 717 | .. | .. |
| Gabon | .. | .. | .. | .. | .. | .. | .. | .. | .. | .. | .. | .. |
| Gambia, The | .. | .. | .. | .. | .. | .. | .. | .. | .. | .. | .. | .. |
| Georgia | 24 | 668 | 0.8 | 8.6 | 0.1 | 1.2 | .. | 18.6 | 269 | 231 | .. | .. |
| Germany | 1,270,243 | 1,637,826 | 66.8 | 56.5 | 56.3 | 85.8 | 79.1 | 173.9 | 1,022 | 656 | .. | .. |
| Ghana | 502 | 2,380 | 10.1 | 25.0 | 0.2 | 0.4 | 1.5 | 5.1 | 22 | 32 | 9.7 | 21.6[b] |
| Greece | 110,839 | 208,284 | 76.9 | 67.5 | 66.0 | 34.8 | 63.7 | 60.8 | 329 | 318 | .. | .. |
| Guatemala | 240 | .. | 1.2 | .. | 0.0 | .. | 0.0 | .. | 44 | .. | .. | .. |
| Guinea | .. | .. | .. | .. | .. | .. | .. | .. | .. | .. | .. | .. |
| Guinea-Bissau | .. | .. | .. | .. | .. | .. | .. | .. | .. | .. | .. | .. |
| Haiti | .. | .. | .. | .. | .. | .. | .. | .. | .. | .. | .. | .. |

| | Market capitalization | | | | Market liquidity | | Turnover ratio | | Listed domestic companies | | S&P/EMDB indexes | |
|---|---|---|---|---|---|---|---|---|---|---|---|---|
| | $ millions | | % of GDP | | Value of shares traded % of GDP | | Value of shares traded % of market capitalization | | number | | % change | |
| | **2000** | **2007** | **2000** | **2006** | **2000** | **2006** | **2000** | **2007** | **2000** | **2007** | **2006** | **2007** |
| Honduras | 458 | .. | 8.8 | .. | .. | .. | .. | .. | 46 | .. | .. | .. |
| Hungary | 12,021 | 47,651 | 25.1 | 37.1 | 25.3 | 27.6 | 90.7 | 102.6 | 60 | 41 | 31.4 | 13.1[a] |
| India | 148,064 | 1,819,101 | 32.2 | 89.8 | 110.8 | 70.0 | 133.6 | 95.9 | 5,937 | 4,887 | 46.7 | 78.6[a] |
| Indonesia | 26,834 | 211,693 | 16.3 | 38.1 | 8.7 | 13.4 | 32.9 | 66.7 | 290 | 383 | 67.9 | 49.3[a] |
| Iran, Islamic Rep. | 7,350 | 37,943 | 7.3 | 17.4 | 1.1 | 2.2 | 12.7 | 12.7 | 304 | 332 | .. | .. |
| Iraq | .. | .. | .. | .. | .. | .. | .. | .. | .. | .. | .. | .. |
| Ireland | 81,882 | 163,358 | 85.0 | 74.2 | 15.0 | 36.3 | 19.2 | 57.6 | 76 | 57 | .. | .. |
| Israel | 64,081 | 236,361 | 53.0 | 123.4 | 19.3 | 63.2 | 36.3 | 54.8 | 654 | 654 | –6.3 | 34.3[a] |
| Italy | 768,364 | 1,026,640 | 70.0 | 55.5 | 70.9 | 73.8 | 104.0 | 149.7 | 291 | 284 | .. | .. |
| Jamaica | 3,582 | 12,335 | 44.6 | 122.5 | 0.9 | 3.0 | 2.5 | 3.1 | 46 | 41 | –1.5 | 0.3[b] |
| Japan | 3,157,222 | 4,726,269 | 67.6 | 108.2 | 57.7 | 143.1 | 69.9 | 132.1 | 2,561 | 3,362 | 5.9 | –5.2[b] |
| Jordan | 4,943 | 41,216 | 58.4 | 210.8 | 4.9 | 142.2 | 7.7 | 52.2 | 163 | 245 | –36.0 | 32.6[b] |
| Kazakhstan | 1,342 | 43,688 | 7.3 | 53.9 | 0.5 | 4.9 | 25.1 | 14.7 | 23 | 67 | .. | ..[c] |
| Kenya | 1,283 | 13,387 | 10.1 | 49.9 | 0.4 | 5.7 | 3.6 | 11.6 | 57 | 51 | 60.3 | 11.8[b] |
| Korea, Dem. Rep. | .. | .. | .. | .. | .. | .. | .. | .. | .. | .. | .. | .. |
| Korea, Rep. | 171,587 | 1,123,633 | 33.5 | 94.1 | 208.7 | 150.9 | 233.2 | 191.6 | 1,308 | 1,767 | 13.3 | 27.7[a] |
| Kuwait | 20,772 | 188,046 | 55.1 | 161.0 | 11.2 | 116.4 | 21.3 | 74.0 | 77 | 181 | –4.6 | 39.9[b] |
| Kyrgyz Republic | 4 | 93 | 0.3 | 3.3 | 1.7 | 3.5 | .. | 148.2 | 80 | 8 | .. | .. |
| Lao PDR | .. | .. | .. | .. | .. | .. | .. | .. | .. | .. | .. | .. |
| Latvia | 563 | 3,111 | 7.2 | 13.4 | 2.9 | 0.6 | 48.6 | 4.7 | 64 | 41 | 1.5 | 1.9[b] |
| Lebanon | 1,583 | 10,858 | 9.4 | 36.4 | 0.7 | 9.0 | 6.7 | 10.9 | 12 | 11 | –9.2 | 40.5[b] |
| Lesotho | .. | .. | .. | .. | .. | .. | .. | .. | .. | .. | .. | .. |
| Liberia | .. | .. | .. | .. | .. | .. | .. | .. | .. | .. | .. | .. |
| Libya | .. | .. | .. | .. | .. | .. | .. | .. | .. | .. | .. | .. |
| Lithuania | 1,588 | 10,134 | 13.9 | 34.2 | 1.8 | 7.0 | 14.8 | 9.2 | 54 | 40 | 9.7 | 14.3[b] |
| Macedonia, FYR | 7 | 1,098 | 0.2 | 17.7 | 3.3 | 3.1 | 6.6 | 22.4 | 1 | 43 | .. | .. |
| Madagascar | .. | .. | .. | .. | .. | .. | .. | .. | .. | .. | .. | .. |
| Malawi | .. | 587 | .. | 18.6 | .. | 0.5 | 13.8 | 3.5 | .. | 10 | .. | .. |
| Malaysia | 116,935 | 325,663 | 129.5 | 156.2 | 64.8 | 44.4 | 44.6 | 51.6 | 795 | 1,036 | 34.6 | 44.6[a] |
| Mali | .. | .. | .. | .. | .. | .. | .. | .. | .. | .. | .. | .. |
| Mauritania | 1,090 | | 97.2 | | .. | .. | .. | .. | 40 | | .. | .. |
| Mauritius | 1,331 | 5,666 | 29.8 | 56.7 | 1.7 | 2.2 | 5.0 | 8.7 | 40 | 41 | 44.3 | 94.0[b] |
| Mexico | 125,204 | 397,725 | 21.5 | 41.5 | 7.8 | 9.5 | 32.3 | 29.5 | 179 | 125 | 41.1 | 12.8[a] |
| Moldova | 392 | .. | 30.4 | 22.1 | 1.9 | 0.8 | 5.8 | 5.9 | 36 | .. | .. | .. |
| Mongolia | 37 | 113 | 3.4 | 3.6 | 0.7 | 0.3 | 7.3 | 13.5 | 410 | 386 | .. | .. |
| Morocco | 10,899 | 75,495 | 29.4 | 75.5 | 3.0 | 20.6 | 9.2 | 39.6 | 53 | 74 | 78.5 | 45.3[a] |
| Mozambique | .. | .. | .. | .. | .. | .. | .. | .. | .. | .. | .. | .. |
| Myanmar | .. | .. | .. | .. | .. | .. | .. | .. | .. | .. | .. | .. |
| Namibia | 311 | 702 | 9.1 | 8.3 | 0.6 | 0.3 | 4.5 | 3.5 | 13 | 9 | 12.8 | 39.4[b] |
| Nepal | 790 | 1,805 | 14.4 | 20.2 | 0.6 | 0.8 | 6.9 | 4.4 | 110 | 135 | .. | .. |
| Netherlands | 640,456 | 779,645 | 166.3 | 117.7 | 175.9 | 165.5 | 101.4 | 159.7 | 234 | 226 | .. | .. |
| New Zealand | 18,866 | 44,940 | 35.8 | 43.0 | 20.5 | 18.9 | 45.9 | 44.7 | 142 | 154 | .. | .. |
| Nicaragua | .. | .. | .. | .. | .. | .. | .. | .. | .. | .. | .. | .. |
| Niger | .. | .. | .. | .. | .. | .. | .. | .. | .. | .. | .. | .. |
| Nigeria | 4,237 | 86,347 | 9.2 | 28.5 | 0.6 | 3.1 | 7.3 | 28.7 | 195 | 212 | 34.0 | 108.3[b] |
| Norway | 65,034 | 281,081 | 38.6 | 83.9 | 35.7 | 104.8 | 93.4 | 148.7 | 191 | 195 | .. | .. |
| Oman | 3,463 | 23,060 | 17.4 | 49.5 | 2.8 | 10.4 | 14.2 | 30.9 | 131 | 125 | 7.9 | 67.0[b] |
| Pakistan | 6,581 | 70,262 | 8.9 | 35.9 | 44.6 | 99.8 | 475.5 | 167.3 | 762 | 654 | 1.3 | 41.7[b] |
| Panama | 2,794 | 5,716 | 24.0 | 33.4 | 1.3 | 0.8 | 1.7 | 2.7 | 29 | 22 | .. | .. |
| Papua New Guinea | 1,520 | 6,632 | 49.6 | 117.3 | 0.0 | 0.4 | .. | 0.5 | 7 | 9 | .. | .. |
| Paraguay | 224 | 409 | 3.5 | 4.4 | 0.1 | 0.0 | 3.5 | 0.5 | 56 | 55 | .. | .. |
| Peru | 10,562 | 105,960 | 19.8 | 64.6 | 2.9 | 4.6 | 12.6 | 7.8 | 230 | 190 | 82.5 | 66.4[a] |
| Philippines | 25,957 | 103,224 | 34.2 | 58.2 | 10.8 | 9.6 | 15.8 | 33.1 | 228 | 242 | 50.3 | 36.0[a] |
| Poland | 31,279 | 207,322 | 18.3 | 44.0 | 8.5 | 16.2 | 49.9 | 44.1 | 225 | 328 | 38.1 | 23.2[a] |
| Portugal | 60,681 | 104,201 | 53.9 | 53.5 | 48.3 | 36.1 | 85.5 | 82.1 | 109 | 47 | .. | .. |
| Puerto Rico | .. | .. | .. | .. | .. | .. | .. | .. | .. | .. | .. | .. |

| | Market capitalization | | | | Market liquidity | | Turnover ratio | | Listed domestic companies | | S&P/EMDB indexes | |
|---|---|---|---|---|---|---|---|---|---|---|---|---|
| | $ millions | | % of GDP | | Value of shares traded % of GDP | | Value of shares traded % of market capitalization | | number | | % change | |
| | 2000 | 2007 | 2000 | 2006 | 2000 | 2006 | 2000 | 2007 | 2000 | 2007 | 2006 | 2007 |
| Romania | 1,069 | 44,925 | 2.9 | 27.0 | 0.6 | 3.5 | 23.1 | 19.2 | 5,555 | 2,096 | 54.2 | 32.8[b] |
| Russian Federation | 38,922 | 1,503,011 | 15.0 | 107.1 | 7.8 | 52.1 | 36.9 | 63.9 | 249 | 328 | 62.0 | 21.9[a] |
| Rwanda | .. | .. | .. | .. | .. | .. | .. | .. | .. | .. | .. | .. |
| Saudi Arabia | 67,171 | 515,111 | 35.6 | 93.6 | 9.2 | 401.9 | 27.1 | 199.2 | 75 | 111 | −48.9 | 35.6[b] |
| Senegal | .. | .. | .. | .. | .. | .. | .. | .. | .. | .. | .. | .. |
| Serbia | 734 | 10,985 | 4.6 | 34.3 | 0.1 | 4.2 | 0.0 | 16.3 | 6 | 1,111 | .. | .. |
| Sierra Leone | .. | .. | .. | .. | .. | .. | .. | .. | .. | .. | .. | .. |
| Singapore | 152,827 | 276,329 | 164.8 | 209.1 | 98.7 | 139.5 | 52.1 | 62.2 | 418 | 461 | .. | .. |
| Slovak Republic | 1,217 | 6,971 | 6.0 | 10.1 | 4.4 | 0.2 | 129.8 | 0.5 | 493 | 153 | 24.0 | 57.4[b] |
| Slovenia | 2,547 | 28,963 | 13.2 | 40.7 | 2.4 | 2.7 | 20.7 | 10.7 | 38 | 87 | 74.3 | 95.0[b] |
| Somalia | .. | .. | .. | .. | .. | .. | .. | .. | .. | .. | .. | .. |
| South Africa | 204,952 | 833,548 | 154.2 | 280.2 | 58.3 | 122.5 | 33.9 | 52.5 | 616 | 422 | 17.2 | 15.5[a] |
| Spain | 504,219 | 1,323,090 | 86.8 | 108.0 | 169.8 | 157.6 | 210.7 | 169.1 | 1,019 | 3,339 | .. | .. |
| Sri Lanka | 1,074 | 7,553 | 6.6 | 28.8 | 0.9 | 3.7 | 11.0 | 12.3 | 239 | 235 | 45.3 | −10.6[b] |
| Sudan | .. | .. | .. | .. | .. | .. | .. | .. | .. | .. | .. | .. |
| Swaziland | 73 | 200 | 5.3 | 7.5 | 0.0 | 0.0 | 9.8 | 0.0 | 6 | 6 | .. | .. |
| Sweden | 328,339 | 573,250 | 135.7 | 149.4 | 161.2 | 176.4 | 111.2 | 138.6 | 292 | 321 | .. | .. |
| Switzerland | 792,316 | 1,212,508 | 322.0 | 318.7 | 247.6 | 338.3 | 82.0 | 119.6 | 252 | 256 | .. | .. |
| Syrian Arab Republic | .. | .. | .. | .. | .. | .. | .. | .. | .. | .. | .. | .. |
| Tajikistan | .. | .. | .. | .. | .. | .. | .. | .. | .. | .. | .. | .. |
| Tanzania | 233 | 541 | 2.6 | 4.2 | 0.4 | 0.1 | 2.4 | 2.1 | 4 | 6 | .. | .. |
| Thailand | 29,489 | 196,046 | 24.0 | 68.4 | 19.0 | 48.9 | 53.2 | 62.0 | 381 | 475 | 6.2 | 39.4[a] |
| Timor-Leste | .. | .. | .. | .. | .. | .. | .. | .. | .. | .. | .. | .. |
| Togo | .. | .. | .. | .. | .. | .. | .. | .. | .. | .. | .. | .. |
| Trinidad and Tobago | 4,330 | 15,605 | 53.1 | 85.9 | 1.7 | 2.3 | 3.1 | 2.4 | 27 | 37 | −6.5 | −2.8[b] |
| Tunisia | 2,828 | 5,355 | 14.5 | 14.7 | 3.2 | 1.7 | 23.3 | 13.0 | 44 | 50 | 47.9 | 15.6[b] |
| Turkey | 69,659 | 286,572 | 34.9 | 40.3 | 89.7 | 56.5 | 206.2 | 134.2 | 315 | 319 | −4.0 | 74.8[a] |
| Turkmenistan | .. | .. | .. | .. | .. | .. | .. | .. | .. | .. | .. | .. |
| Uganda | 35 | 116 | 0.6 | 1.2 | 0.0 | 0.1 | .. | 5.2 | 2 | 5 | .. | .. |
| Ukraine | 1,881 | 111,757 | 6.0 | 40.3 | 0.9 | 1.1 | 19.6 | 2.7 | 139 | 276 | 48.6 | 112.2[b] |
| United Arab Emirates | 5,727 | 224,675 | 8.1 | 173.9 | 0.2 | 110.4 | 3.9 | 85.0 | 54 | 90 | −44.6 | 52.1[b] |
| United Kingdom | 2,576,992 | 3,794,310 | 178.7 | 159.6 | 127.2 | 178.5 | 66.6 | 123.8 | 1,904 | 2,913 | 26.2 | 5.6[d] |
| United States | 15,104,037 | 19,425,855 | 154.7 | 147.6 | 326.3 | 252.7 | 200.8 | 182.8 | 7,524 | 5,133 | 13.6 | 3.5[e] |
| Uruguay | 161 | 125 | 0.8 | 0.6 | 0.0 | 0.0 | 0.5 | 1.6 | 16 | 10 | .. | .. |
| Uzbekistan | 32 | 715 | 0.2 | 4.2 | 0.1 | 0.1 | .. | 5.9 | 5 | 114 | .. | .. |
| Venezuela, RB | 8,128 | 8,251 | 6.9 | 4.5 | 0.6 | 0.4 | 8.9 | 1.3 | 85 | 53 | 79.0 | .. |
| Vietnam | .. | 19,542 | .. | 14.9 | .. | 1.8 | .. | 85.6 | .. | 121 | .. | 10.7[b] |
| West Bank and Gaza | 765 | 2,729 | 18.6 | 67.2 | 4.6 | 26.3 | 10.0 | 29.7 | 24 | 33 | .. | .. |
| Yemen, Rep. | .. | .. | .. | .. | .. | .. | .. | .. | .. | .. | .. | .. |
| Zambia | 236 | 1,186 | 7.3 | 11.0 | 0.2 | 0.2 | 20.8 | 2.1 | 9 | 14 | .. | .. |
| Zimbabwe | 2,432 | 5,333 | 32.9 | 70.3 | 3.8 | 9.7 | 10.8 | 11.0 | 69 | 82 | 912.3 | −83.8[b] |
| **World** | **32,187,756 s** | **54,194,991 s** | **102.7 w** | **113.9 w** | **152.8 w** | **143.4 w** | **122.1 w** | **94.3 w** | **47,877 s** | **50,212 s** | | |
| **Low income** | 166,802 | 967,029 | 23.9 | 67.0 | 78.1 | 55.0 | 151.9 | 93.3 | 7,922 | 6,911 | | |
| **Middle income** | 1,833,330 | 7,056,701 | 37.2 | 74.2 | 26.8 | 36.8 | 71.5 | 94.5 | 15,335 | 13,195 | | |
| Lower middle income | 751,235 | 3,186,679 | 35.8 | 74.5 | 37.5 | 44.5 | 107.8 | 146.4 | 4,940 | 5,205 | | |
| Upper middle income | 1,082,095 | 3,870,022 | 38.3 | 74.0 | 18.7 | 30.6 | 46.0 | 50.8 | 10,395 | 7,990 | | |
| **Low & middle income** | 2,000,132 | 8,023,730 | 35.6 | 73.3 | 33.2 | 39.2 | 81.4 | 94.3 | 23,257 | 20,106 | | |
| East Asia & Pacific | 780,487 | 3,026,517 | 47.2 | 85.1 | 49.9 | 52.4 | 125.2 | 163.5 | 3,190 | 4,080 | | |
| Europe & Central Asia | 163,360 | 1,603,092 | 19.0 | 66.7 | 26.3 | 35.1 | 83.9 | 64.1 | 8,141 | 6,070 | | |
| Latin America & Carib. | 620,263 | 1,470,534 | 31.8 | 51.7 | 8.4 | 13.5 | 27.4 | 34.8 | 1,762 | 1,509 | | |
| Middle East & N. Africa | 60,573 | 242,122 | 19.7 | 48.9 | 5.0 | 19.4 | 12.6 | 28.3 | 1,807 | 1,443 | | |
| South Asia | 157,695 | 877,581 | 26.1 | 77.2 | 90.2 | 67.5 | 167.9 | 101.3 | 7,269 | 6,089 | | |
| Sub-Saharan Africa | 217,754 | 803,885 | 89.9 | 159.9 | 32.3 | 65.4 | 22.2 | 30.1 | 1,088 | 915 | | |
| **High income** | 30,187,624 | 46,171,261 | 117.3 | 126.1 | 178.8 | 174.6 | 130.7 | 150.2 | 24,620 | 30,106 | | |
| Euro area | 5,432,330 | 8,639,721 | 87.0 | 81.2 | 80.4 | 96.4 | 90.4 | 139.0 | 4,535 | 6,318 | | |

a. Data refer to the S&P/IFC investable index. b. Data refer to the S&P/IFC Global index. c. Data refer to the Nikkei 225 index. d. Data refer to the FT 100 index. e. Data refer to the S&P 500 index.

## About the data

The development of an economy's financial markets is closely related to its overall development. Well functioning financial systems provide good and easily accessible information. That lowers transaction costs, which in turn improves resource allocation and boosts economic growth. Both banking systems and stock markets enhance growth, the main factor in poverty reduction. At low levels of economic development commercial banks tend to dominate the financial system, while at higher levels domestic stock markets tend to become more active and efficient relative to domestic banks.

Open economies with sound macroeconomic policies, good legal systems, and shareholder protection attract capital and therefore have larger financial markets. Recent research on stock market development shows that modern communications technology and increased financial integration have resulted in more cross-border capital flows, a stronger presence of financial firms around the world, and the migration of stock exchange activities to international exchanges. Many firms in emerging markets now cross-list on international exchanges, which provides them with lower cost capital and more liquidity-traded shares. However, this also means that exchanges in emerging markets may not have enough financial activity to sustain them, putting pressure on them to rethink their operations.

The stock market indicators in the table include measures of size (market capitalization, number of listed domestic companies) and liquidity (value of shares traded as a percentage of gross domestic product, value of shares traded as a percentage of market capitalization). The comparability of such indicators between countries may be limited by conceptual and statistical weaknesses, such as inaccurate reporting and differences in accounting standards. The percentage change in stock market prices in U.S. dollars, from the Standard & Poor's Emerging Markets Data Base (S&P/EMDB) indexes, is an important measure of overall performance. Regulatory and institutional factors that can affect investor confidence, such as entry and exit restrictions, the existence of a securities and exchange commission, and the quality of laws to protect investors, may influence the functioning of stock markets but are not included in the table.

Stock market size can be measured in various ways, and each may produce a different ranking of countries. Market capitalization shows the overall size of the stock market in U.S. dollars and as a percentage of GDP. The number of listed domestic companies is another measure of market size. Market size is positively correlated with the ability to mobilize capital and diversify risk.

Market liquidity, the ability to easily buy and sell securities, is measured by dividing the total value of shares traded by GDP. The turnover ratio—the value of shares traded as a percentage of market capitalization—is also a measure of liquidity as well as of transaction costs. (High turnover indicates low transaction costs.) The turnover ratio complements the ratio of value traded to GDP, because the turnover ratio is related to the size of the market and the value traded ratio to the size of the economy. A small, liquid market will have a high turnover ratio but a low value of shares traded ratio. Liquidity is an important attribute of stock markets because, in theory, liquid markets improve the allocation of capital and enhance prospects for long-term economic growth. A more comprehensive measure of liquidity would include trading costs and the time and uncertainty in finding a counterpart in settling trades.

The S&P/EMDB, the source for all the data in the table, provides regular updates on 58 emerging stock markets encompassing more than 3,800 stocks. Standard & Poor's maintains a series of indexes for investors interested in investing in stock markets in developing countries. At the core of the S&P/EMDB indexes, the Global (S&P/IFCG) index is intended to represent the most active stocks in the markets it covers and to be the broadest possible indicator of market movements. The Investable (S&P/IFCI) index, which applies the same calculation methodology as the S&P/IFCG index, is designed to measure the returns that foreign portfolio investors might receive from investing in emerging market stocks that are legally and practically open to foreign portfolio investment. These indexes are widely used benchmarks for international portfolio management. See Standard & Poor's (2000) for further information on the indexes.

Because markets included in Standard & Poor's emerging markets category vary widely in level of development, it is best to look at the entire category to identify the most significant market trends. And it is useful to remember that stock market trends may be distorted by currency conversions, especially when a currency has registered a significant devaluation.

*About the data* is based on Demirgüç-Kunt and Levine (1996), Beck and Levine (2001), and Claessens, Klingebiel, and Schmukler (2002).

## Definitions

- **Market capitalization** (also known as market value) is the share price times the number of shares outstanding. • **Market liquidity** is the total value of shares traded during the period divided by gross domestic product (GDP). This indicator complements the market capitalization ratio by showing whether market size is matched by trading. • **Turnover ratio** is the total value of shares traded during the period divided by the average market capitalization for the period. Average market capitalization is calculated as the average of the end-of-period values for the current period and the previous period. • **Listed domestic companies** are the domestically incorporated companies listed on the country's stock exchanges at the end of the year. This indicator does not include investment companies, mutual funds, or other collective investment vehicles. • **S&P/EMDB indexes** measure the U.S. dollar price change in the stock markets covered by the S&P/IFCI country index and S&P/IFCG indexes.

## Data sources

Data on stock markets are from Standard & Poor's *Global Stock Markets Factbook 2007,* which draws on the Emerging Markets Data Base, supplemented by other data from Standard & Poor's. The firm collects data through an annual survey of the world's stock exchanges, supplemented by information provided by its network of correspondents and by Reuters. Data on GDP are from the World Bank's national accounts data files.

# 5.5

# Financial access, stability, and efficiency

| | Getting credit | | | | Bank capital to asset ratio | Ratio of bank nonperforming loans to total gross loans | Domestic credit provided by banking sector | Interest rate spread | Risk premium on lending |
|---|---|---|---|---|---|---|---|---|---|
| | Legal rights index 0–10 (weak to strong) | Credit information index 0–6 (low to high) | % of adult population Public credit registry coverage | Private credit bureau coverage | % | % | % of GDP | Lending rate minus deposit rate percentage points | Prime lending rate minus treasury bill rate percentage points |
| | June 2007 | June 2007 | June 2007 | June 2007 | 2006 | 2006 | 2006 | 2006 | 2006 |
| Afghanistan | 0 | 0 | 0.0 | 0.0 | .. | .. | .. | .. | .. |
| Albania | 9 | 0 | 0.0 | 0.0 | 6.2 | 3.1 | 54.5 | 7.7 | 7.5 |
| Algeria | 3 | 2 | 0.2 | 0.0 | .. | .. | 4.0 | 6.3 | 5.9 |
| Angola | 3 | 4 | 2.3 | 0.0 | 11.3 | 13.3 | −3.6 | 15.0 | .. |
| Argentina | 3 | 6 | 25.5 | 100.0 | 13.6 | 3.4 | 30.8 | 2.2 | .. |
| Armenia | 5 | 5 | 2.8 | 13.5 | 22.9 | 2.5 | 8.1 | 10.7 | 11.7 |
| Australia | 9 | 5 | 0.0 | 100.0 | 4.9 | 0.2 | 115.0 | 5.5 | .. |
| Austria | 5 | 6 | 1.3 | 40.6 | 5.2 | 2.6 | 128.4 | .. | .. |
| Azerbaijan | 7 | 4 | 1.4 | 0.0 | 14.2 | 7.2 | 13.6 | 7.3 | 7.8 |
| Bangladesh | 7 | 2 | 0.7 | 0.0 | 4.0 | 13.2 | 58.1 | 6.2 | .. |
| Belarus | 2 | 3 | 0.0 | 0.0 | 17.8 | 1.2 | 27.2 | 1.2 | .. |
| Belgium | 5 | 4 | 57.2 | 0.0 | 3.7 | 1.8 | 110.2 | .. | 4.8 |
| Benin | 4 | 1 | 7.8 | 0.0 | .. | .. | 10.2 | .. | .. |
| Bolivia | 1 | 5 | 12.1 | 22.6 | 10.0 | 8.7 | 39.4 | 7.9 | 7.3 |
| Bosnia and Herzegovina | 7 | 5 | 0.0 | 63.7 | 13.8 | 4.0 | 47.8 | 4.3 | .. |
| Botswana | 7 | 4 | 0.0 | 58.3 | 9.7 | 2.8 | −14.3 | 7.6 | .. |
| Brazil | 2 | 5 | 17.1 | 46.4 | 9.9 | 4.1 | 81.7 | 36.9 | 36.4 |
| Bulgaria | 6 | 6 | 25.4 | 3.0 | 10.4 | 2.2 | 43.0 | 5.7 | 6.3 |
| Burkina Faso | 4 | 1 | 2.1 | 0.0 | .. | .. | 14.4 | .. | .. |
| Burundi | 1 | 1 | 0.2 | 0.0 | .. | .. | 42.1 | .. | .. |
| Cambodia | 0 | 0 | 0.0 | 0.0 | .. | .. | 6.0 | 14.6 | .. |
| Cameroon | 3 | 2 | 1.0 | 0.0 | .. | .. | 8.2 | 11.0 | .. |
| Canada | 7 | 6 | 0.0 | 100.0 | 5.7 | 0.4 | 220.8 | 4.0 | 1.8 |
| Central African Republic | 3 | 2 | 1.4 | 0.0 | .. | .. | 17.5 | 11.0 | .. |
| Chad | 3 | 1 | 0.2 | 0.0 | .. | .. | 4.7 | 11.0 | .. |
| Chile | 4 | 5 | 26.2 | 33.5 | 6.8 | 0.8 | 83.5 | 2.9 | .. |
| China | 3 | 4 | 49.2 | 0.0 | 6.1 | 7.5 | 136.9 | 3.6 | .. |
| Hong Kong, China | 1 | 5 | 0.0 | 64.7 | 11.8 | 1.1 | 134.6 | 5.1 | 4.5 |
| Colombia | 2 | 5 | 0.0 | 39.9 | 10.8 | 2.6 | 48.0 | 6.6 | .. |
| Congo, Dem. Rep. | 3 | 0 | 0.0 | 0.0 | .. | .. | 4.6 | .. | .. |
| Congo, Rep. | 3 | 2 | 2.4 | 0.0 | .. | .. | −9.3 | 11.0 | .. |
| Costa Rica | 4 | 5 | 6.1 | 52.7 | 10.2 | 1.5 | 44.7 | 12.4 | .. |
| Côte d'Ivoire | 3 | 1 | 2.8 | 0.0 | .. | .. | 17.8 | .. | .. |
| Croatia | 6 | 3 | 0.0 | 72.4 | 10.3 | 5.2 | 80.6 | 8.2 | .. |
| Cuba | .. | .. | .. | .. | .. | .. | .. | .. | .. |
| Czech Republic | 6 | 5 | 4.2 | 53.0 | 6.2 | 4.1 | 48.4 | 4.4 | 3.1 |
| Denmark | 8 | 4 | 0.0 | 11.5 | 6.2 | 0.4 | 189.3 | .. | .. |
| Dominican Republic | 4 | 6 | 13.3 | 35.4 | 10.0 | 4.5 | 47.1 | 9.6 | .. |
| Ecuador | 1 | 5 | 37.9 | 44.1 | 13.7 | 3.3 | 17.5 | 5.4 | .. |
| Egypt, Arab Rep. | 1 | 4 | 1.6 | 0.0 | 5.5 | 24.7 | 99.3 | 6.6 | 3.1 |
| El Salvador | 3 | 6 | 17.2 | 74.6 | 11.8 | 1.9 | 45.7 | .. | .. |
| Eritrea | 3 | 0 | 0.0 | 0.0 | .. | .. | 139.0 | .. | .. |
| Estonia | 4 | 5 | 0.0 | 19.7 | 8.4 | 0.2 | 81.6 | 2.2 | .. |
| Ethiopia | 4 | 2 | 0.1 | 0.0 | .. | .. | 53.7 | 3.4 | 6.9 |
| Finland | 6 | 5 | 0.0 | 14.9 | 9.2 | 0.3 | 81.3 | 2.7 | .. |
| France | 6 | 4 | 24.8 | 0.0 | 5.8 | 3.2 | 115.5 | 4.3 | .. |
| Gabon | 3 | 2 | 2.4 | 0.0 | .. | 11.1 | 8.3 | 11.0 | .. |
| Gambia, The | 4 | 0 | 0.0 | 0.0 | .. | .. | 27.0 | 17.1 | .. |
| Georgia | 5 | 4 | 0.0 | 0.2 | 18.8 | 2.5 | 23.9 | 7.3 | 12.1 |
| Germany | 8 | 6 | 0.7 | 98.1 | 4.7 | 4.0 | 132.0 | .. | .. |
| Ghana | 5 | 0 | 0.0 | 0.0 | 12.4 | 7.9 | 32.4 | .. | .. |
| Greece | 3 | 4 | 0.0 | 38.7 | 5.2 | 5.5 | 90.5 | .. | .. |
| Guatemala | 3 | 5 | 20.7 | 13.1 | 8.2 | 4.6 | 32.8 | 8.3 | .. |
| Guinea | 4 | 0 | 0.0 | 0.0 | .. | .. | 15.7 | .. | .. |
| Guinea-Bissau | 3 | 1 | 0.9 | 0.0 | .. | .. | 10.5 | .. | .. |
| Haiti | 3 | 2 | 0.7 | 0.0 | .. | .. | 27.8 | 37.1 | 32.7 |

| | Getting credit | | | | Bank capital to asset ratio | Ratio of bank nonperforming loans to total gross loans | Domestic credit provided by banking sector | Interest rate spread | Risk premium on lending |
|---|---|---|---|---|---|---|---|---|---|
| | Legal rights index 0–10 (weak to strong) | Credit information index 0–6 (low to high) | % of adult population Public credit registry coverage | Private credit bureau coverage | % | % | % of GDP | Lending rate minus deposit rate percentage points | Prime lending rate minus treasury bill rate percentage points |
| | June 2007 | June 2007 | June 2007 | June 2007 | 2006 | 2006 | 2006 | 2006 | 2006 |
| Honduras | 6 | 6 | 12.7 | 58.0 | 8.4 | 6.6 | 40.6 | 8.1 | .. |
| Hungary | 6 | 5 | 0.0 | 6.9 | 8.7 | 2.5 | 68.1 | 0.6 | 1.2 |
| India | 6 | 4 | 0.0 | 10.8 | 6.6 | 3.5 | 63.4 | .. | .. |
| Indonesia | 5 | 3 | 20.5 | 0.2 | 10.7 | 13.1 | 41.7 | 4.6 | .. |
| Iran, Islamic Rep. | 5 | 3 | 22.2 | 0.0 | .. | .. | 49.2 | 4.2 | .. |
| Iraq | 4 | 0 | 0.0 | 0.0 | .. | .. | .. | .. | .. |
| Ireland | 8 | 5 | 0.0 | 100.0 | 4.3 | 0.7 | 182.0 | 2.6 | .. |
| Israel | 8 | 5 | 0.0 | 91.6 | 5.9 | 1.9 | 76.6 | 3.2 | 2.1 |
| Italy | 3 | 5 | 11.0 | 71.5 | 7.1 | 5.3 | 112.9 | .. | 2.4 |
| Jamaica | 5 | 0 | 0.0 | 0.0 | 8.7 | 2.6 | 63.9 | 10.6 | 4.9 |
| Japan | 6 | 6 | 0.0 | 68.3 | 5.3 | 2.5 | 307.7 | 1.0 | 1.2 |
| Jordan | 5 | 2 | 0.8 | 0.0 | 10.7 | 4.3 | 116.5 | 3.6 | .. |
| Kazakhstan | 5 | 4 | 0.0 | 13.7 | 8.9 | 4.8 | 32.5 | .. | .. |
| Kenya | 8 | 4 | 0.0 | 1.5 | .. | 5.2 | 40.3 | 8.5 | 6.9 |
| Korea, Dem. Rep. | .. | .. | .. | .. | .. | .. | .. | .. | .. |
| Korea, Rep. | 5 | 5 | 0.0 | 74.2 | 9.2 | 0.8 | 107.1 | 1.5 | .. |
| Kuwait | 4 | 4 | 0.0 | 14.5 | 12.0 | 3.9 | 71.7 | 3.7 | .. |
| Kyrgyz Republic | 5 | 3 | 0.0 | 1.6 | .. | .. | 11.7 | 17.6 | 18.4 |
| Lao PDR | 2 | 0 | 0.0 | 0.0 | .. | .. | 7.3 | 25.0 | 11.7 |
| Latvia | 8 | 4 | 2.6 | 0.0 | 7.6 | 0.4 | 89.0 | 3.8 | 3.2 |
| Lebanon | 4 | 5 | 4.7 | 0.0 | 8.4 | 13.5 | 196.2 | 2.3 | 5.0 |
| Lesotho | 5 | 0 | 0.0 | 0.0 | .. | 1.0 | −5.7 | 7.6 | 5.3 |
| Liberia | 4 | 0 | 0.0 | 0.0 | .. | .. | 177.8 | 13.6 | .. |
| Libya | .. | .. | .. | .. | .. | .. | −53.8 | 3.8 | 0.6 |
| Lithuania | 4 | 6 | 6.6 | 7.3 | 7.1 | 1.0 | 49.5 | 4.5 | 2.2 |
| Macedonia, FYR | 6 | 3 | 4.0 | 0.0 | .. | 11.2 | 23.7 | 5.5 | .. |
| Madagascar | 1 | 0 | 0.1 | 0.0 | 6.2 | 10.1 | 9.7 | 7.2 | 8.3 |
| Malawi | 7 | 0 | 0.0 | 0.0 | .. | .. | 13.9 | 21.3 | 13.0 |
| Malaysia | 8 | 6 | 44.5 | .. | 7.6 | 8.5 | 119.4 | 3.3 | 3.3 |
| Mali | 3 | 1 | 2.5 | 0.0 | .. | .. | 13.6 | .. | .. |
| Mauritania | 4 | 1 | 0.2 | 0.0 | .. | .. | .. | 15.1 | 11.2 |
| Mauritius | 5 | 1 | 38.6 | 0.0 | .. | .. | 111.1 | 11.5 | .. |
| Mexico | 3 | 6 | 0.0 | 61.2 | 13.2 | 2.1 | 39.3 | 4.2 | 0.3 |
| Moldova | 6 | 0 | 0.0 | 0.0 | 17.0 | 4.3 | 35.0 | 6.2 | 10.8 |
| Mongolia | 5 | 3 | 9.5 | 0.0 | .. | .. | 20.9 | 8.4 | .. |
| Morocco | 3 | 1 | 2.3 | 0.0 | 7.4 | 10.9 | 78.5 | 7.9 | .. |
| Mozambique | 3 | 3 | 0.9 | 0.0 | 6.4 | 3.7 | 10.0 | 8.2 | 3.5 |
| Myanmar | .. | .. | .. | .. | .. | .. | 28.1 | 5.5 | .. |
| Namibia | 5 | 5 | 0.0 | 59.9 | 8.3 | 2.9 | 63.9 | 4.9 | 3.9 |
| Nepal | 4 | 2 | 0.0 | 0.2 | .. | .. | 50.4 | 5.9 | 6.0 |
| Netherlands | 7 | 5 | 0.0 | 78.1 | 4.0 | 1.0 | 186.7 | 0.6 | .. |
| New Zealand | 9 | 5 | 0.0 | 100.0 | .. | .. | 142.3 | 5.3 | 5.2 |
| Nicaragua | 3 | 5 | 14.8 | 100.0 | 8.8 | 8.0 | 74.4 | 6.7 | .. |
| Niger | 3 | 1 | 1.0 | 0.0 | .. | .. | 7.9 | .. | .. |
| Nigeria | 7 | 0 | 0.0 | 0.0 | 14.7 | 21.9 | .. | 7.2 | 6.9 |
| Norway | 6 | 4 | 0.0 | 100.0 | 5.0 | 0.6 | .. | 2.2 | .. |
| Oman | 4 | 2 | 12.4 | 0.0 | 13.2 | 7.8 | 34.9 | 3.4 | .. |
| Pakistan | 4 | 4 | 4.6 | 1.4 | 8.8 | 7.7 | 43.0 | 6.8 | 2.4 |
| Panama | 6 | 6 | 0.0 | 41.6 | 11.3 | 1.5 | 90.8 | 4.6 | .. |
| Papua New Guinea | 5 | 0 | 0.0 | 0.0 | .. | .. | 23.2 | 9.6 | 6.6 |
| Paraguay | 3 | 6 | 11.0 | 48.7 | 12.5 | 3.3 | 18.0 | 23.4 | .. |
| Peru | 4 | 6 | 20.7 | 33.0 | 9.5 | 1.6 | 15.0 | 20.7 | .. |
| Philippines | 3 | 3 | 0.0 | 5.5 | 11.7 | 18.6 | 48.6 | 4.5 | 4.5 |
| Poland | 4 | 4 | 0.0 | 51.5 | 7.9 | 9.4 | 42.4 | 4.0 | 1.3 |
| Portugal | 4 | 4 | 67.1 | 11.3 | 6.4 | 1.3 | 160.9 | .. | .. |
| Puerto Rico | 6 | 5 | 0.0 | 62.0 | .. | .. | .. | .. | .. |

| | Getting credit | | | | Bank capital to asset ratio | Ratio of bank nonperforming loans to total gross loans | Domestic credit provided by banking sector | Interest rate spread | Risk premium on lending |
|---|---|---|---|---|---|---|---|---|---|
| | Legal rights index 0–10 (weak to strong) | Credit information index 0–6 (low to high) | % of adult population | | | | | Lending rate minus deposit rate percentage points | Prime lending rate minus treasury bill rate percentage points |
| | | | Public credit registry coverage | Private credit bureau coverage | % | % | % of GDP | | |
| | June 2007 | June 2007 | June 2007 | June 2007 | 2006 | 2006 | 2006 | 2006 | 2006 |
| Romania | 7 | 5 | 4.1 | 10.9 | 8.9 | 8.4 | 26.8 | .. | .. |
| Russian Federation | 3 | 4 | 0.0 | 4.4 | 12.5 | 2.6 | 21.4 | 6.4 | .. |
| Rwanda | 1 | 2 | 0.2 | 0.0 | 9.2 | 27.2 | 9.7 | 8.1 | 6.2 |
| Saudi Arabia | 3 | 6 | 0.0 | 23.5 | 9.3 | 2.0 | 37.3 | .. | .. |
| Senegal | 3 | 1 | 4.0 | 0.0 | 8.1 | 16.0 | 23.3 | .. | .. |
| Serbia | 7 | 5 | 0.1 | 51.3 | 15.6 | 21.4 | 23.6 | 11.5 | 6.3 |
| Sierra Leone | 5 | 0 | 0.0 | 0.0 | 19.0 | 20.9 | 10.6 | 13.6 | 6.3 |
| Singapore | 9 | 4 | 0.0 | 42.7 | 9.6 | 2.8 | 72.6 | 4.7 | 2.4 |
| Slovak Republic | 9 | 4 | 1.2 | 56.0 | 8.0 | 3.7 | 50.4 | 4.1 | .. |
| Slovenia | 6 | 2 | 2.5 | 0.0 | 7.4 | 4.9 | 76.3 | 4.6 | 4.1 |
| Somalia | .. | .. | .. | .. | .. | .. | .. | .. | .. |
| South Africa | 5 | 6 | 0.0 | 52.1 | 7.8 | 1.2 | 197.4 | 4.0 | 3.8 |
| Spain | 6 | 6 | 44.9 | 8.3 | 7.2 | 0.6 | 177.7 | .. | .. |
| Sri Lanka | 3 | 3 | 0.0 | 2.9 | 6.7 | 9.6 | 44.1 | -3.2 | -2.0 |
| Sudan | 4 | 0 | 0.0 | 0.0 | .. | .. | 0.2 | .. | .. |
| Swaziland | 5 | 5 | 0.0 | 37.6 | .. | 2.0 | 15.7 | 6.2 | 3.6 |
| Sweden | 6 | 4 | 0.0 | 100.0 | 4.9 | 0.5 | 125.8 | 2.5 | 1.6 |
| Switzerland | 6 | 5 | 0.0 | 24.0 | 4.9 | 0.3 | 187.4 | 1.6 | 1.7 |
| Syrian Arab Republic | 3 | 0 | 0.0 | 0.0 | .. | .. | 33.5 | 7.0 | .. |
| Tajikistan | 4 | 0 | 0.0 | 0.0 | .. | .. | 15.4 | 15.3 | .. |
| Tanzania | 5 | 0 | 0.0 | 0.0 | .. | .. | 11.2 | 8.8 | 3.8 |
| Thailand | 5 | 5 | 0.0 | 27.9 | 9.2 | 7.5 | 101.3 | 2.9 | .. |
| Timor-Leste | 2 | 0 | 0.0 | 0.0 | .. | .. | .. | .. | .. |
| Togo | 3 | 1 | 2.7 | 0.0 | .. | .. | 17.4 | .. | .. |
| Trinidad and Tobago | 5 | 4 | 0.0 | 34.4 | .. | .. | 21.0 | 6.1 | 4.8 |
| Tunisia | 2 | 4 | 13.7 | 0.0 | 7.7 | 19.2 | 72.4 | .. | .. |
| Turkey | 3 | 5 | 10.3 | 2.7 | 11.3 | 3.2 | 60.2 | .. | .. |
| Turkmenistan | .. | .. | .. | .. | .. | .. | .. | .. | .. |
| Uganda | 3 | 0 | 0.0 | 0.0 | 9.7 | 2.8 | 9.4 | 9.6 | 10.6 |
| Ukraine | 8 | 0 | 0.0 | 0.0 | 12.1 | 17.8 | 46.2 | 7.6 | .. |
| United Arab Emirates | 3 | 2 | 1.4 | 0.0 | 12.6 | 6.3 | 59.5 | .. | .. |
| United Kingdom | 10 | 6 | 0.0 | 84.6 | 8.9 | 0.9 | 176.9 | .. | 0.0 |
| United States | 7 | 6 | 0.0 | 100.0 | 10.5 | 0.8 | 230.8 | .. | 3.2 |
| Uruguay | 5 | 6 | 14.1 | 93.8 | 9.8 | 1.9 | 32.2 | 7.4 | 4.7 |
| Uzbekistan | 2 | 0 | 0.0 | 0.0 | .. | .. | .. | .. | .. |
| Venezuela, RB | 4 | 0 | 0.0 | 0.0 | 9.8 | 1.1 | 18.8 | 5.2 | .. |
| Vietnam | 6 | 3 | 9.2 | 0.0 | .. | .. | 75.0 | 3.5 | 6.4 |
| West Bank and Gaza | 5 | 3 | 1.8 | 0.0 | .. | .. | 9.2 | 4.8 | .. |
| Yemen, Rep. | 3 | 0 | 0.1 | 0.0 | .. | .. | 4.8 | 5.0 | 2.4 |
| Zambia | 6 | 0 | 0.0 | 0.0 | .. | 10.8 | 16.6 | 12.8 | 12.8 |
| Zimbabwe | 6 | 0 | 0.0 | 0.0 | 12.1 | 23.2 | 93.1 | 293.1 | 174.1 |
| **World** | **4.6 u** | **2.7 u** | **4.6 u** | **19.6 u** | **8.9 m** | **3.0 m** | **187.9 w** | **6.6 m** | |
| **Low income** | 3.8 | 0.9 | 1.0 | 0.3 | .. | .. | 53.2 | 11.3 | |
| **Middle income** | 4.4 | 2.9 | 6.2 | 17.5 | 10.0 | 3.4 | 76.7 | 6.6 | |
| Lower middle income | 4.0 | 2.7 | 5.9 | 13.9 | 10.7 | 4.0 | 99.1 | 7.2 | |
| Upper middle income | 5.0 | 3.3 | 6.6 | 22.8 | 9.8 | 3.2 | 63.4 | 5.9 | |
| **Low & middle income** | 4.2 | 2.2 | 4.3 | 11.3 | 9.4 | 5.3 | 76.7 | 7.3 | |
| East Asia & Pacific | 3.9 | 1.6 | 6.6 | 3.9 | .. | .. | 119.6 | 6.5 | |
| Europe & Central Asia | 5.6 | 3.3 | 2.4 | 14.4 | 10.3 | 3.2 | 37.6 | 6.8 | |
| Latin America & Carib. | 4.0 | 3.4 | 8.9 | 32.1 | 10.1 | 2.6 | 54.9 | 7.4 | |
| Middle East & N. Africa | 3.5 | 2.1 | 4.6 | 0.0 | .. | .. | 49.8 | 4.3 | |
| South Asia | 3.9 | 1.9 | 0.7 | 1.9 | 6.6 | 7.7 | 60.6 | 6.7 | |
| Sub-Saharan Africa | 4.0 | 1.3 | 2.1 | 4.6 | .. | .. | 94.4 | 9.6 | |
| **High income** | 5.8 | 4.4 | 5.7 | 49.9 | 6.2 | 1.1 | 194.3 | 4.4 | |
| Euro area | 5.6 | 4.3 | 16.1 | 35.5 | 5.2 | 1.6 | 132.2 | .. | |

# Financial access, stability, and efficiency

## About the data

Financial sector development has positive impacts on economic growth and poverty. The size of the sector determines the amount of resources mobilized for investment. Access to finance can expand opportunities for all—not just the rich and well connected—with higher levels of access and use of banking services associated with lower financing obstacles for people and businesses. A stable financial system that promotes efficient savings and investment is also crucial for a thriving democracy and market economy. The banking system is the largest sector in the financial system in most countries, so most indicators in the table cover the banking system.

There are several aspects of access to financial services: availability, cost, and quality of services. The development and growth of credit markets depend on access to timely, reliable, and accurate data on borrowers' credit experiences. For secured transactions, such as mortgages or vehicle loans, having rapid access to information in property registries is also vital, and for small business loans corporate registry data are needed. An effective way to improve access to credit is to increase information about potential borrowers' creditworthiness and make it easy to create and enforce collateral agreements. Lenders look at a borrower's credit history and collateral when extending loans. Where credit registries and effective collateral laws are absent—as in many developing countries—banks make fewer loans. Indicators that cover financial access, or getting credit, include the legal rights index (ranges from 0, weaker, to 10, stronger), credit information index (ranges from 0, less, to 6, more), public registry coverage, and private bureau coverage. The legal rights index is based on seven aspects related to legal rights in collateral law and three aspects in bankruptcy law. The depth of credit information index assesses six features of the public registry or the private credit bureau. For more information on these indexes, see www.doingbusiness.org/MethodologySurveys/.

The size and mobility of international capital flows have made it increasingly important to monitor the strength of financial systems. Robust financial systems can increase economic activity and welfare, but instability in the financial system can disrupt financial activity and impose huge and widespread costs on the economy. The ratio of bank capital to assets, a measure of bank solvency and resiliency, provides a measure of the extent to which banks can deal with unexpected losses. Capital includes tier 1 capital (paid-up shares and common stock), which is a common feature in all countries' banking systems,

and total regulatory capital, which includes several specified types of subordinated debt instruments that need not be repaid if the funds are required to maintain minimum capital levels (these comprise tier 2 and tier 3 capital). Total assets include all nonfinancial and financial assets. Data are from internally consistent financial statements, to enhance the quality and analytical usefulness of the indicator.

The ratio of bank nonperforming loans to total gross loans is a measure of bank health and efficiency. It helps to identify problems with asset quality in the loan portfolio. A high ratio may signal deterioration in the quality of the credit portfolio. International guidelines recommend that loans be classified as nonperforming when payments of principal and interest are past due by 90 days or more or when future payments are not expected to be received in full. See the International Monetary Fund's (IMF) *Global Financial Stability Report* for detailed information.

Domestic credit provided by the banking sector as a share of GDP is a measure of banking sector depth and financial sector development in terms of size. In a few countries governments may hold international reserves as deposits in the banking system rather than in the central bank. Since the claims on the central government are a net item (claims on the central government minus central government deposits), this net figure may be negative, resulting in a negative figure of domestic credit provided by the banking sector.

The interest rate spread—the margin between the cost of mobilizing liabilities and the earnings on assets—is a measure of the efficiency by which the financial sector intermediates funds. A narrow interest rate spread means low transaction costs, which lowers the overall cost of funds for investment, crucial to economic growth.

The risk premium on lending is the spread between the lending rate to the private sector and the "risk-free" government rate. A small spread indicates that the market considers its best corporate customers to be low risk. Interest rate spreads are expressed as annual averages. In some countries this spread may be negative, indicating that the market considers its best corporate clients to be lower risk than the government.

## Definitions

• **Legal rights index** measures the degree to which collateral and bankruptcy laws protect the rights of borrowers and lenders and thus facilitate lending. Higher values indicate that the laws are better designed to expand access to credit. • **Credit information index** measures rules affecting the scope, accessibility, and quality of information available through public or private credit registries. Higher values indicate the availability of more credit information. • **Public credit registry coverage** is the number of individuals and firms listed in a public credit registry with current information on repayment history, unpaid debts, or credit outstanding as a percentage of the adult population. • **Private credit bureau coverage** is the number of individuals or firms listed by a private credit bureau with current information on repayment history, unpaid debts, or credit outstanding as a percentage of the adult population. • **Bank capital to asset ratio** is the ratio of bank capital and reserves to total assets. Capital and reserves include funds contributed by owners, retained earnings, general and special reserves, provisions, and valuation adjustments. • **Ratio of bank nonperforming loans to total gross loans** is the value of nonperforming loans divided by the total value of the loan portfolio (including nonperforming loans before the deduction of loan loss provisions). The amount recorded as nonperforming should be the gross value of the loan as recorded on the balance sheet, not just the amount overdue. • **Domestic credit provided by banking sector** is all credit to various sectors on a gross basis, except to the central government, which is net. The banking sector includes monetary authorities, deposit money banks, and other banking institutions for which data are available. • **Interest rate spread** is the interest rate charged by banks on loans to prime customers minus the interest rate paid by commercial or similar banks for demand, time, or savings deposits. • **Risk premium on lending** is the interest rate charged by banks on loans to prime private sector customers minus the "risk-free" treasury bill interest rate at which short-term government securities are issued or traded in the market.

## Data sources

Data on getting credit are from the World Bank's Doing Business project (www.doingbusiness.org). Data on bank capital and nonperforming loans are from the IMF's *Global Financial Stability Report*. Data on credit and interest rates are from the IMF's *International Financial Statistics*.

# 5.6 Tax policies

| | Tax revenue collected by central government | | Taxes payable by businesses | | | Highest marginal tax rate[a] | | | |
|---|---|---|---|---|---|---|---|---|---|
| | % of GDP | | Number of payments | Time to prepare, file, and pay taxes hours | Total tax rate % of profit | Individual | | | Corporate % |
| | 2000 | 2006 | June 2007 | June 2007 | June 2007 | % 2006 | | On income over $ 2006 | 2006 |
| Afghanistan[b] | .. | 5.8 | 6 | 275 | 35.5 | .. | | .. | .. |
| Albania[b] | *16.1* | *17.3* | 44 | 240 | 46.8 | 20 | | 2,003 | 20 |
| Algeria[b] | 36.9 | 32.1 | 33 | 451 | 72.6 | .. | | .. | .. |
| Angola | .. | .. | 31 | 272 | 53.2 | .. | | .. | .. |
| Argentina | 9.8 | 14.2 | 19 | 615 | 112.9 | 35 | | 41,379 | 35 |
| Armenia[b] | .. | 14.4 | 50 | 1,120 | 36.6 | .. | | .. | .. |
| Australia | 22.1 | 23.7 | 12 | 107 | 50.6 | 47 | | 72,519 | 30 |
| Austria | 19.6 | 20.0 | 22 | 170 | 54.6 | 50 | | 63,750 | 25 |
| Azerbaijan[b] | 12.7 | .. | 38 | 952 | 40.9 | 35 | | 12,632 | 22 |
| Bangladesh[b] | 7.6 | 8.1 | 17 | 400 | 39.5 | .. | | .. | .. |
| Belarus[b] | 16.6 | 22.2 | 124 | 1,188 | 144.4 | .. | | .. | .. |
| Belgium | 27.4 | 26.1 | 11 | 156 | 64.3 | 50 | | 39,625 | 34 |
| Benin[b] | *15.5* | 15.8 | 55 | 270 | 73.3 | 35 | | .. | 38 |
| Bolivia | *13.2* | 17.3 | 41 | 1,080 | 78.1 | .. | | .. | 25 |
| Bosnia and Herzegovina | .. | 22.4 | 51 | 368 | 44.1 | 15 | | .. | 30 |
| Botswana[b] | .. | .. | 19 | 140 | 17.2 | 25 | | 19,569 | 15 |
| Brazil[b] | 11.3 | .. | 11 | 2,600 | 69.2 | 28 | | 11,486 | 15 |
| Bulgaria[b] | 18.3 | 23.7 | 17 | 616 | 36.7 | 24 | | 4,586 | 15 |
| Burkina Faso[b] | .. | 11.2 | 45 | 270 | 48.9 | .. | | .. | .. |
| Burundi[b] | 13.6 | .. | 32 | 140 | 278.7 | .. | | .. | .. |
| Cambodia | 8.2 | 8.2 | 27 | 137 | 22.6 | 20 | | 36,652 | 20 |
| Cameroon[b] | 11.2 | .. | 41 | 1,400 | 51.9 | .. | | .. | .. |
| Canada[b] | 15.0 | 14.1 | 9 | 119 | 45.9 | 29 | | 97,756 | 22 |
| Central African Republic[b] | .. | 6.0 | 54 | 504 | 203.8 | .. | | .. | .. |
| Chad | .. | .. | 54 | 122 | 63.7 | .. | | .. | .. |
| Chile | 16.7 | 20.7 | 10 | 316 | 25.9 | *40* | | *6,127* | *17* |
| China[b] | 6.8 | 8.7 | 35 | 872 | 73.9 | 45 | | 8,637 | .. |
|   Hong Kong, China | .. | .. | 4 | 80 | 24.4 | 20 | | 11,568 | 18 |
| Colombia | *13.3* | 14.1 | 69 | 268 | 82.4 | 22 | | 43,154 | 39 |
| Congo, Dem. Rep.[b] | 3.5 | .. | 32 | 308 | 229.8 | 50 | | 4,920 | 40 |
| Congo, Rep. | 9.2 | .. | 89 | 606 | 65.4 | .. | | .. | .. |
| Costa Rica[b] | .. | 14.1 | 43 | 402 | 55.7 | 25 | | 19,414 | 30 |
| Côte d'Ivoire[b] | 14.6 | 14.9 | 66 | 270 | 45.4 | 10 | | 4,550 | 35 |
| Croatia[b] | 26.2 | 23.3 | 28 | 196 | 32.5 | 45 | | 3,765 | *20* |
| Cuba | .. | .. | .. | .. | .. | .. | | .. | .. |
| Czech Republic[b] | 15.4 | 14.6 | 12 | 930 | 48.6 | 32 | | 13,823 | 24 |
| Denmark | 31.0 | 31.2 | 9 | 135 | 33.3 | 59 | | 53,117 | 28 |
| Dominican Republic[b] | .. | 16.8 | 74 | 286 | 40.2 | 30 | | 29,596 | 30 |
| Ecuador[b] | .. | .. | 8 | 600 | 35.3 | 25 | | 61,440 | 25 |
| Egypt, Arab Rep.[b] | 14.6 | 15.8 | 36 | 711 | 47.9 | 20 | | 6,920 | .. |
| El Salvador | *10.7* | 13.4 | 66 | 224 | 33.8 | .. | | .. | .. |
| Eritrea | .. | .. | 18 | 216 | 84.5 | .. | | .. | .. |
| Estonia | 15.9 | 16.6 | 10 | 81 | 49.2 | 23 | | 1,908 | 23 |
| Ethiopia[b] | *10.7* | .. | 20 | 198 | 31.1 | 35[c] | | .. | 30[c] |
| Finland | 24.6 | 21.9 | 20 | 269 | 47.8 | 28 | | 72,750 | 26 |
| France | 23.2 | 22.7 | 23 | 132 | 66.3 | *48* | | *60,673* | 33 |
| Gabon | .. | .. | 28 | 272 | 44.2 | .. | | .. | .. |
| Gambia, The[b] | .. | .. | 50 | 376 | 286.7 | .. | | .. | .. |
| Georgia[b] | 7.7 | 15.5 | 29 | 387 | 38.6 | 12 | | .. | 20 |
| Germany | 11.9 | 11.4 | 16 | 196 | 50.8 | 42 | | 65,190 | 25 |
| Ghana[b] | *17.2* | *22.4* | 32 | 304 | 32.9 | 25 | | 10,581 | 25 |
| Greece | 20.2 | 17.2 | 21 | 264 | 48.6 | 40 | | 28,750 | 29 |
| Guatemala[b] | 10.1 | 10.2 | 39 | 344 | 37.5 | 31 | | 38,663 | 31 |
| Guinea[b] | *11.1* | .. | 56 | 416 | 49.9 | .. | | .. | .. |
| Guinea-Bissau | .. | .. | 46 | 208 | 45.9 | .. | | .. | .. |
| Haiti | .. | .. | 53 | 160 | 40.0 | .. | | .. | .. |

| | Tax revenue collected by central government | | Taxes payable by businesses | | | Highest marginal tax rate[a] | | |
|---|---|---|---|---|---|---|---|---|
| | % of GDP | | Number of payments | Time to prepare, file, and pay taxes hours | Total tax rate % of profit | Individual | | Corporate % |
| | 2000 | 2006 | June 2007 | June 2007 | June 2007 | % 2006 | On income over $ 2006 | 2006 |
| Honduras | .. | 17.9 | 47 | 424 | 51.4 | 25 | 26,553 | 25 |
| Hungary[b] | 21.9 | 20.1 | 24 | 340 | 55.1 | 36 | 7,766 | 16 |
| India[b] | 9.0 | 10.7 | 60 | 271 | 70.6 | 30 | 5,669 | 34 |
| Indonesia[b] | 11.6 | 12.3 | 51 | 266 | 37.3 | 35 | 20,608 | 30 |
| Iran, Islamic Rep.[b] | 6.3 | 7.6 | 22 | 292 | 47.4 | 35 | 114,101 | 25 |
| Iraq | .. | .. | 13 | 312 | 24.7 | .. | .. | .. |
| Ireland | 26.1 | 26.7 | 9 | 76 | 28.9 | 42 | 40,000 | 13 |
| Israel | 29.6 | 28.6 | 33 | 230 | 36.0 | 49 | 94,530 | 31 |
| Italy | 23.2 | 22.9 | 15 | 360 | 76.2 | 43 | 125,000 | 33 |
| Jamaica[b] | 24.7 | 29.2 | 72 | 414 | 51.3 | 25 | 1,993 | 33 |
| Japan[b] | .. | .. | 13 | 350 | 52.0 | 37 | 163,310 | 30 |
| Jordan[b] | 19.0 | 26.2 | 26 | 101 | 31.1 | .. | .. | .. |
| Kazakhstan[b] | 10.2 | 16.3 | 9 | 271 | 36.7 | 20 | 55,810 | 30 |
| Kenya[b] | 16.8 | 18.3 | 41 | 432 | 50.9 | 30 | 5,841 | 30 |
| Korea, Dem. Rep.[b] | .. | .. | .. | .. | .. | .. | .. | .. |
| Korea, Rep.[b] | 16.1 | 15.7 | 48 | 290 | 34.9 | 35 | 78,116 | 25 |
| Kuwait | 1.3 | 1.0 | 14 | 118 | 14.4 | 0 | .. | 0 |
| Kyrgyz Republic[b] | .. | 14.3 | 75 | 202 | 61.4 | .. | .. | .. |
| Lao PDR | .. | .. | 34 | 672 | 35.5 | .. | .. | .. |
| Latvia | 14.2 | 15.7 | 7 | 219 | 32.6 | 25 | .. | 15 |
| Lebanon | 12.2 | 16.3 | 19 | 180 | 35.4 | .. | .. | .. |
| Lesotho | 32.7 | 44.3 | 22 | 342 | 20.8 | .. | .. | .. |
| Liberia | .. | .. | 37 | 158 | 81.6 | .. | .. | .. |
| Libya | .. | .. | .. | .. | .. | .. | .. | .. |
| Lithuania | 14.6 | 18.1 | 24 | 166 | 48.3 | 33 | .. | 15 |
| Macedonia, FYR[b] | .. | .. | 52 | 96 | 49.8 | 24 | 14,610 | 15 |
| Madagascar | 11.3 | 10.7 | 26 | 238 | 46.5 | .. | .. | .. |
| Malawi | .. | .. | 30 | 370 | 32.2 | .. | .. | .. |
| Malaysia[b] | 14.3 | .. | 35 | 166 | 36.0 | 28 | 65,963 | 28 |
| Mali | 13.2 | 15.7 | 58 | 270 | 51.4 | .. | .. | .. |
| Mauritania | .. | .. | 38 | 696 | 107.5 | .. | .. | .. |
| Mauritius[b] | 18.2 | 18.2 | 7 | 161 | 21.7 | 30 | 16,949 | 25 |
| Mexico[b] | 11.7 | .. | 27 | 552 | 51.2 | 29 | 9,470 | 29 |
| Moldova[b] | 14.7 | 19.9 | 49 | 218 | 44.0 | 20 | 1,667 | 15 |
| Mongolia | .. | .. | 42 | 204 | 38.4 | .. | .. | .. |
| Morocco | 19.9 | 22.5 | 28 | 358 | 53.1 | .. | .. | .. |
| Mozambique | .. | .. | 37 | 230 | 34.3 | 32 | 43,710 | 32 |
| Myanmar[b] | 3.0 | 4.7 | .. | .. | .. | .. | .. | .. |
| Namibia[b] | 30.0 | .. | 37 | .. | 26.5 | 35 | 31,447 | 35 |
| Nepal[b] | 8.7 | 8.9 | 33 | 408 | 32.5 | .. | .. | .. |
| Netherlands | 22.3 | 23.7 | 9 | 180 | 43.4 | 52 | 65,285 | 30 |
| New Zealand | 29.5 | 34.2 | 8 | 70 | 35.1 | 39 | 42,254 | 33 |
| Nicaragua[b] | 13.8 | 17.5 | 64 | 240 | 63.2 | 30 | 29,886 | 30 |
| Niger | .. | .. | 42 | 270 | 42.4 | .. | .. | .. |
| Nigeria | .. | .. | 35 | 1,120 | 29.9 | .. | .. | .. |
| Norway | 27.4 | 29.2 | 4 | 87 | 42.0 | .. | .. | 28 |
| Oman[b] | 7.2 | .. | 14 | 62 | 21.6 | 0 | .. | 12 |
| Pakistan[b] | 10.1 | 9.5 | 47 | 560 | 40.7 | 35 | 11,763 | 37 |
| Panama[b] | 10.2 | .. | 59 | 482 | 50.8 | 30 | 200,000 | 30 |
| Papua New Guinea[b] | 19.4 | .. | 33 | 206 | 41.7 | .. | .. | .. |
| Paraguay[b] | .. | 12.1 | 35 | 328 | 35.3 | 10 | .. | 0 |
| Peru[b] | 12.2 | 13.5 | 9 | 424 | 41.5 | 30 | 49,899 | 30 |
| Philippines[b] | 13.7 | 14.3 | 47 | 195 | 52.8 | 32 | 9,076 | 35 |
| Poland | 16.0 | 17.5 | 41 | 418 | 38.4 | 40 | 22,854 | 19 |
| Portugal | 21.5 | 22.0 | 8 | 328 | 44.8 | 42 | 75,000 | 25 |
| Puerto Rico | .. | .. | 16 | 140 | 44.3 | 33 | 50,000 | 20 |

| | Tax revenue collected by central government | | Taxes payable by businesses | | | Highest marginal tax rate[a] | | |
|---|---|---|---|---|---|---|---|---|
| | % of GDP | | Number of payments | Time to prepare, file, and pay taxes hours | Total tax rate % of profit | Individual | | Corporate % |
| | 2000 | 2006 | June 2007 | June 2007 | June 2007 | % 2006 | On income over $ 2006 | 2006 |
| Romania | 11.7 | 12.2 | 96 | 202 | 46.9 | 16 | 4,617 | 16 |
| Russian Federation | 13.7 | 16.7 | 22 | 448 | 51.4 | 13 | .. | 24 |
| Rwanda | .. | .. | 34 | 168 | 33.8 | .. | .. | .. |
| Saudi Arabia | .. | .. | 14 | 79 | 14.5 | 0 | .. | 0 |
| Senegal[b] | 16.1 | .. | 59 | 696 | 46.0 | 0 | .. | .. |
| Serbia[b] | .. | .. | 66 | 279 | 35.8 | .. | .. | .. |
| Sierra Leone[b] | 10.2 | 11.0 | 22 | 399 | 233.5 | .. | .. | .. |
| Singapore[b] | 15.4 | 12.7 | 5 | 49 | 23.2 | 21 | 192,771 | 20 |
| Slovak Republic | .. | 14.0 | 31 | 344 | 50.5 | 19 | 14,087 | 19 |
| Slovenia[b] | 21.2 | 21.9 | 22 | 260 | 39.2 | 50 | .. | 25 |
| Somalia | .. | .. | .. | .. | .. | .. | .. | .. |
| South Africa | 24.0 | 29.0 | 11 | 350 | 37.1 | 40 | 47,170 | 29 |
| Spain | 16.2 | 12.9 | 8 | 298 | 62.0 | 29 | 58,524 | 35 |
| Sri Lanka[b] | 14.5 | 15.3 | 62 | 256 | 63.7 | 35 | 4,975 | 35 |
| Sudan[b] | 6.4 | .. | 42 | 180 | 31.6 | .. | .. | .. |
| Swaziland[b] | .. | .. | 33 | 104 | 36.6 | 33 | 11,792 | 30 |
| Sweden | 19.7 | 21.3 | 2 | 122 | 54.5 | 25 | 61,673 | 28 |
| Switzerland[b] | 11.3 | 10.5 | 24 | 63 | 29.1 | .. | .. | 9 |
| Syrian Arab Republic[b] | 17.4 | .. | 21 | 336 | 46.7 | .. | .. | .. |
| Tajikistan | 7.7 | 9.8 | 54 | 224 | 82.2 | .. | .. | .. |
| Tanzania | .. | .. | 48 | 172 | 44.3 | 30 | 5,740 | 30 |
| Thailand | .. | 16.9 | 35 | 264 | 37.7 | 37 | 99,453 | 30 |
| Timor-Leste | .. | .. | 15 | 640 | 28.3 | .. | .. | .. |
| Togo[b] | .. | 13.9 | 53 | 270 | 48.2 | .. | .. | .. |
| Trinidad and Tobago[b] | 22.1 | 27.9 | 40 | 114 | 33.1 | 25 | 7,937 | 25 |
| Tunisia[b] | 21.3 | 21.0 | 46 | 268 | 61.0 | .. | .. | .. |
| Turkey[b] | .. | 25.9 | 15 | 223 | 45.1 | 35 | 100,298 | 30 |
| Turkmenistan | .. | .. | .. | .. | .. | .. | .. | .. |
| Uganda[b] | 10.9 | 13.0 | 33 | 237 | 32.3 | 30 | 2,763 | 30 |
| Ukraine[b] | 14.1 | 18.0 | 99 | 2,085 | 57.3 | 13 | .. | 25 |
| United Arab Emirates[b] | 1.7 | .. | 14 | 12 | 14.4 | 0 | .. | .. |
| United Kingdom | 29.0 | 28.8 | 8 | 105 | 35.7 | 40 | 60,545 | 30 |
| United States | 12.7 | 11.9 | 10 | 325 | 46.2 | 35 | 326,450 | 35 |
| Uruguay[b] | 16.7 | 19.3 | 53 | 304 | 40.7 | 0 | .. | 30 |
| Uzbekistan | .. | .. | 118 | 196 | 96.3 | 29 | 960 | 12 |
| Venezuela, RB[b] | 13.3 | 15.6 | 70 | 864 | 53.3 | 34 | 93,767 | 34 |
| Vietnam[b] | .. | .. | 32 | 1,050 | 41.1 | 40 | 5,044 | 28 |
| West Bank and Gaza | .. | .. | 27 | 154 | 17.1 | .. | .. | .. |
| Yemen, Rep.[b] | 9.4 | .. | 32 | 248 | 41.4 | .. | .. | .. |
| Zambia[b] | 18.6 | 17.2 | 37 | 132 | 16.1 | 30 | 368 | 35 |
| Zimbabwe[b] | .. | .. | 52 | 256 | 53.0 | 45 | 26,249 | 30 |
| **World** | **15.7 w** | **16.8 w** | **34 u** | **323 u** | **50.7 u** | | | |
| **Low income** | 9.5 | 10.7 | 41 | 327 | 67.4 | | | |
| **Middle income** | .. | .. | 37 | 377 | 45.3 | | | |
| Lower middle income | 9.4 | 11.4 | 40 | 401 | 45.8 | | | |
| Upper middle income | .. | .. | 32 | 344 | 44.5 | | | |
| **Low & middle income** | .. | .. | 38 | 359 | 53.2 | | | |
| East Asia & Pacific | 7.7 | 9.5 | 31 | 295 | 39.9 | | | |
| Europe & Central Asia | 16.1 | 18.9 | 50 | 455 | 51.4 | | | |
| Latin America & Carib. | 11.4 | .. | 40 | 435 | 48.7 | | | |
| Middle East & N. Africa | 15.7 | 17.3 | 27 | 276 | 41.4 | | | |
| South Asia | 9.3 | 10.6 | 31 | 306 | 41.4 | | | |
| Sub-Saharan Africa | .. | .. | 39 | 321 | 68.0 | | | |
| **High income** | 16.5 | 16.7 | 17 | 188 | 41.5 | | | |
| Euro area | 19.1 | 18.5 | 16 | 211 | 50.9 | | | |

a. Data are from PriceWaterhouseCoopers's *World Wide Tax Summaries Online.* b. Data on central government taxes were reported on a cash basis and have been adjusted to the accrual framework of the International Monetary Fund's *Government Finance Statistics Manual 2001.*

## About the data

Taxes are the main source of revenue for most governments. The sources of tax revenue and their relative contributions are determined by government policy choices about where and how to impose taxes and by changes in the structure of the economy. Tax policy may reflect concerns about distributional effects, economic efficiency (including corrections for externalities), and the practical problems of administering a tax system. There is no ideal level of taxation. But taxes influence incentives and thus the behavior of economic actors and the economy's competitiveness.

The level of taxation is typically measured by tax revenue as a share of gross domestic product (GDP). Comparing levels of taxation across countries provides a quick overview of the fiscal obligations and incentives facing the private sector. The table shows only central government data, which may significantly understate the total tax burden, particularly in countries where provincial and municipal governments are large or have considerable tax authority.

Low ratios of tax revenue to GDP may reflect weak administration and large-scale tax avoidance or evasion. Low ratios may also reflect a sizable parallel economy with unrecorded and undisclosed incomes. Tax revenue ratios tend to rise with income, with higher income countries relying on taxes to finance a much broader range of social services and social security than lower income countries are able to.

The indicators covering taxes payable by businesses measure all taxes and contributions that are government mandated (at any level—federal, state, or local), apply to standardized businesses, and have an impact in their income statements. The taxes covered go beyond the definition of a tax for government national accounts (compulsory, unrequited payments to general government) and also measure any imposts that affect business accounts. The main differences are in labor contributions and value-added taxes. The indicators account for government-mandated contributions paid by the employer to a requited private pension fund or workers insurance fund but exclude value-added taxes because they do not affect the accounting profits of the business—that is, they are not reflected in the income statement.

To make the data comparable across countries, several assumptions are made about businesses. The main assumptions are that they are limited liability companies, they operate in the country's most populous city, they are domestically owned, they perform general industrial or commercial activities, and

they have certain levels of start-up capital, employees, and turnover. For details about the assumptions, see *Doing Business 2008*.

A potentially important influence on both domestic and international investors is a tax system's progressivity, as reflected in the highest marginal tax rate levied at the national level on individual and corporate income. Data for individual marginal tax rates generally refer to employment income. In some countries the highest marginal tax rate is also the basic or flat rate, and other surtaxes, deductions, and the like may apply. And in many countries several different corporate tax rates may be levied, depending on the type of business (mining, banking, insurance, agriculture, manufacturing), ownership (domestic or foreign), volume of sales, and whether surtaxes or exemptions are included. The corporate tax rates in the table are mainly general rates applied to domestic companies. For more detailed information, see the country's laws, regulations, and tax treaties and PricewaterhouseCoopers's *Worldwide Tax Summaries Online* (www.pwc.com).

## Definitions

• **Tax revenue collected by central government** refers to compulsory transfers to the central government for public purposes. Certain compulsory transfers such as fines, penalties, and most social security contributions are excluded. Refunds and corrections of erroneously collected tax revenue are treated as negative revenue. The analytic framework of the International Monetary Fund's (IMF) *Government Finance Statistics Manual 2001* (GFSM 2001) is based on accrual accounting and balance sheets. For countries still reporting government finance data on a cash basis, the IMF adjusts reported data to the GFSM 2001 accrual framework. These countries are footnoted in the table. • **Number of tax payments by businesses** is the total number of taxes paid by businesses during one year. When electronic filing is available, the tax is counted as paid once a year even if payments are more frequent. • **Time to prepare, file, and pay taxes** is the time, in hours per year, it takes to prepare, file, and pay (or withhold) three major types of taxes: the corporate income tax, the value-added or sales tax, and labor taxes, including payroll taxes and social security contributions. • **Total tax rate** is the total amount of taxes payable by businesses (except for consumption taxes) after accounting for deductions and exemptions as a percentage of profit. For further details on the method used for assessing the total tax payable, see *Doing Business 2008*. • **Highest marginal tax rate** is the highest rate shown on the national schedule of tax rates applied to the annual taxable income of individuals and corporations. Also presented are the income levels for individuals above which the highest marginal tax rates levied at the national level apply.

## Data sources

Data on central government tax revenue are from print and electronic editions of the IMF's *Government Finance Statistics Yearbook*. Data on taxes payable by businesses are from *Doing Business 2008* (www.doingbusiness.org). Data on individual and corporate tax rates are from PricewaterhouseCoopers's *Worldwide Tax Summaries Online* (www.pwc.com).

| | Military expenditures | | | | Armed forces personnel | | | | Arms transfers | | | |
|---|---|---|---|---|---|---|---|---|---|---|---|---|
| | % of GDP | | % of central government expenditure | | thousands | | % of labor force | | $ millions 1990 prices | | | |
| | | | | | | | | | Exports | | Imports | |
| | 1995 | 2006 | 1995 | 2006 | 1995 | 2006 | 1995 | 2006 | 1995 | 2006 | 1995 | 2006 |
| Afghanistan | .. | 9.9 | .. | .. | 383 | 51 | 6.2 | 0.6 | 0 | .. | .. | 28 |
| Albania | 2.1 | 1.6 | 8.2 | 6.3 | 87 | 12 | 6.0 | 0.8 | .. | .. | 24 | 42 |
| Algeria | 3.0 | 2.7 | 12.2 | 15.3 | 163 | 334 | 1.8 | 2.4 | .. | .. | 365 | 173 |
| Angola | 8.1 | 5.4 | .. | .. | 122 | 110 | 2.3 | 1.5 | .. | .. | 1 | 22 |
| Argentina | 1.6 | 0.9 | .. | 5.9 | 99 | 107 | 0.7 | 0.6 | 3 | .. | 75 | 53 |
| Armenia | 4.1 | 2.8 | .. | 17.3 | 61 | 47 | 4.2 | 3.7 | .. | .. | 49 | 151 |
| Australia | 1.9 | 1.8 | .. | 7.5 | 57 | 51 | 0.6 | 0.5 | 28 | 4 | 149 | 777 |
| Austria | 1.1 | 0.8 | 2.4 | 2.0 | 56 | 40 | 1.4 | 1.0 | 11 | 61 | 24 | 21 |
| Azerbaijan | 2.7 | 3.3 | 13.8 | .. | 127 | 82 | 3.8 | 1.9 | .. | .. | 25 | 45 |
| Bangladesh | 1.4 | 1.1 | .. | 13.6 | 171 | 214 | 0.3 | 0.3 | .. | .. | 121 | 208 |
| Belarus | 1.6 | 1.7 | 5.7 | 5.5 | 106 | 183 | 2.1 | 3.8 | 8 | 24 | .. | 254 |
| Belgium | 1.6 | 1.1 | 3.4 | 2.7 | 47 | 40 | 1.1 | 0.9 | 299 | 50 | 16 | 4 |
| Benin | .. | .. | .. | .. | 7 | 8 | 0.3 | 0.2 | .. | .. | .. | .. |
| Bolivia | 1.8 | 1.5 | .. | 5.9 | 64 | 83 | 2.2 | 1.9 | .. | .. | 1 | 25 |
| Bosnia and Herzegovina | .. | 1.6 | .. | 4.8 | 92 | 9 | 5.3 | 0.4 | .. | .. | 52 | .. |
| Botswana | 3.5 | 3.0 | 11.5 | .. | 9 | 11 | 1.5 | 1.6 | .. | .. | 7 | 9 |
| Brazil | 1.9 | 1.5 | 4.8 | .. | 681 | 754 | 0.9 | 0.8 | 28 | 1 | 259 | 323 |
| Bulgaria | 2.6 | 2.3 | 6.6 | 7.1 | 136 | 75 | 3.5 | 2.5 | 2 | .. | 1 | 20 |
| Burkina Faso | 1.5 | 1.4 | .. | 11.5 | 10 | 11 | 0.2 | 0.2 | .. | .. | .. | 19 |
| Burundi | 4.2 | 5.5 | 17.8 | .. | 15 | 82 | 0.5 | 2.1 | .. | .. | .. | .. |
| Cambodia | 5.4 | 1.7 | .. | 19.4 | 309 | 191 | 6.2 | 2.8 | 0 | .. | 33 | .. |
| Cameroon | 1.3 | 1.4 | 11.8 | .. | 24 | 23 | 0.4 | 0.3 | .. | .. | 4 | 5 |
| Canada | 1.6 | 1.2 | 6.4 | 6.5 | 76 | 64 | 0.5 | 0.4 | 326 | 227 | 356 | 109 |
| Central African Republic | 1.2 | 1.1 | .. | 12.3 | 5 | 3 | 0.3 | 0.2 | .. | .. | .. | 9 |
| Chad | 1.7 | 0.9 | .. | .. | 35 | 35 | 1.2 | 0.9 | .. | .. | 1 | 2 |
| Chile | 3.1 | 3.6 | .. | 21.2 | 130 | 103 | 2.3 | 1.6 | 30 | .. | 459 | 1,125 |
| China | 1.7[a] | 1.9[a] | ..[a] | 18.2[a] | 4,130 | 3,605 | 0.6 | 0.5 | 1,017 | 564 | 641 | 3,261 |
| Hong Kong, China | .. | .. | .. | .. | .. | .. | .. | .. | .. | .. | .. | .. |
| Colombia | 2.6 | 3.5 | .. | 12.1 | 233 | 398 | 1.4 | 1.7 | .. | .. | 37 | 33 |
| Congo, Dem. Rep. | 1.5 | 0.0 | 13.5 | .. | 65 | 65 | 0.4 | 0.3 | .. | .. | 0 | 13 |
| Congo, Rep. | .. | 1.1 | .. | .. | 17 | 12 | 1.4 | 0.8 | .. | .. | 27 | 4 |
| Costa Rica | .. | .. | .. | .. | 16 | 10 | 1.2 | 0.5 | .. | .. | 3 | .. |
| Côte d'Ivoire | 0.8 | .. | .. | .. | 15 | 19 | 0.3 | 0.3 | .. | .. | 2 | 14 |
| Croatia | 9.4 | 1.6 | 22.2 | 4.1 | 150 | 21 | 7.2 | 1.1 | .. | .. | 22 | 8 |
| Cuba | .. | .. | .. | .. | 124 | 76 | 2.5 | 1.4 | .. | .. | .. | .. |
| Czech Republic | 1.9 | 1.7 | 5.9 | 4.9 | 92 | 26 | 1.8 | 0.5 | 122 | 56 | 0 | 65 |
| Denmark | 1.7 | 1.4 | .. | 4.4 | 33 | 30 | 1.2 | 1.1 | 8 | 3 | 130 | 133 |
| Dominican Republic | 0.6 | 0.5 | .. | 3.1 | 40 | 65 | 1.3 | 1.6 | .. | .. | 4 | 27 |
| Ecuador | 2.4 | 2.3 | 6.0 | .. | 57 | 57 | 1.3 | 0.9 | .. | .. | 11 | 33 |
| Egypt, Arab Rep. | 3.9 | 2.7 | 16.3 | 9.9 | 610 | 866 | 3.5 | 3.7 | 7 | .. | 1,698 | 538 |
| El Salvador | 1.0 | 0.6 | .. | 3.0 | 39 | 28 | 1.8 | 1.0 | 0 | .. | 3 | .. |
| Eritrea | 20.8 | .. | .. | .. | 55 | 202 | 4.4 | 10.6 | .. | .. | 3 | 70 |
| Estonia | 1.0 | 1.4 | .. | 5.4 | 6 | 7 | 0.8 | 1.1 | 8 | .. | 17 | 8 |
| Ethiopia | 1.6 | 2.6 | .. | .. | 120 | 183 | 0.5 | 0.5 | .. | .. | 70 | 162 |
| Finland | 1.5 | 1.4 | .. | 3.8 | 35 | 32 | 1.4 | 1.2 | 20 | 31 | 159 | 84 |
| France | 3.0 | 2.4 | 6.2 | 5.3 | 502 | 354 | 2.0 | 1.3 | 795 | 1,557 | 43 | 121 |
| Gabon | .. | 1.2 | .. | .. | 10 | 7 | 2.1 | 1.2 | .. | .. | .. | 63 |
| Gambia, The | 0.8 | 0.5 | .. | .. | 1 | 1 | 0.2 | 0.1 | .. | .. | .. | 7 |
| Georgia | 2.2 | 3.1 | 8.2 | 15.2 | 14 | 33 | 0.5 | 1.5 | .. | 7 | 8 | 70 |
| Germany | 1.6 | 1.3 | 4.2 | 4.3 | 365 | 246 | 0.9 | 0.6 | 1,430 | 1,855 | 252 | 216 |
| Ghana | 0.8 | 0.7 | .. | 3.8 | 13 | 7 | 0.2 | 0.1 | .. | .. | 7 | 27 |
| Greece | 3.3 | 3.2 | 9.0 | 9.1 | 202 | 161 | 4.5 | 3.1 | 18 | 23 | 870 | 1,452 |
| Guatemala | 1.0 | 0.4 | 13.1 | 3.6 | 57 | 35 | 1.8 | 0.8 | .. | .. | 3 | .. |
| Guinea | 1.4 | 2.0 | .. | .. | 19 | 13 | 0.6 | 0.3 | .. | .. | .. | .. |
| Guinea-Bissau | 0.9 | 4.0 | .. | .. | 9 | 9 | 1.9 | 1.4 | .. | .. | 4 | .. |
| Haiti | .. | .. | .. | .. | 7 | 5 | 0.2 | 0.1 | .. | .. | .. | .. |

| | Military expenditures | | | | Armed forces personnel | | | | Arms transfers | | | |
|---|---|---|---|---|---|---|---|---|---|---|---|---|
| | % of GDP | | % of central government expenditure | | thousands | | % of labor force | | $ millions 1990 prices Exports | | Imports | |
| | **1995** | **2006** | **1995** | **2006** | **1995** | **2006** | **1995** | **2006** | **1995** | **2006** | **1995** | **2006** |
| Honduras | .. | 0.6 | .. | 2.8 | 24 | 20 | 1.3 | 0.7 | .. | .. | .. | .. |
| Hungary | 1.6 | 1.2 | 3.0 | 2.7 | 73 | 44 | 1.7 | 1.0 | 6 | 68 | 24 | 337 |
| India | 2.7 | 2.7 | 18.4 | 17.7 | 2,150 | 2,589 | 0.6 | 0.6 | 2 | 11 | 968 | 1,710 |
| Indonesia | 1.6 | 1.2 | 16.2 | 8.3 | 461 | 582 | 0.5 | 0.5 | 25 | 8 | 319 | 54 |
| Iran, Islamic Rep. | 2.4 | 4.8 | 15.2 | 19.4 | 763 | 585 | 4.4 | 2.0 | 1 | 9 | 355 | 891 |
| Iraq | .. | .. | .. | .. | 407 | 495 | 7.0 | 6.0 | .. | .. | .. | 195 |
| Ireland | 1.0 | 0.5 | 2.7 | 1.7 | 13 | 10 | 0.9 | 0.5 | .. | .. | 43 | 11 |
| Israel | 8.6 | 8.4 | .. | 19.0 | 178 | 185 | 8.5 | 6.7 | 113 | 287 | 308 | 994 |
| Italy | 1.7 | 1.7 | 3.6 | 4.1 | 585 | 440 | 2.6 | 1.8 | 365 | 878 | 332 | 697 |
| Jamaica | 0.6 | 0.6 | 1.7 | 1.4 | 4 | 3 | 0.3 | 0.3 | .. | .. | .. | 25 |
| Japan | 1.0 | 0.9 | .. | .. | 252 | 252 | 0.4 | 0.4 | 158 | .. | 1,254 | 392 |
| Jordan | 5.8 | 4.9 | 22.3 | 14.1 | 129 | 111 | 10.3 | 5.9 | 77 | 13 | 19 | 117 |
| Kazakhstan | 1.1 | 0.9 | 5.7 | 6.2 | 75 | 81 | 1.0 | 1.0 | 25 | 5 | 99 | 53 |
| Kenya | 1.6 | 1.6 | 6.4 | 9.3 | 29 | 29 | 0.2 | 0.2 | .. | .. | 12 | 25 |
| Korea, Dem. Rep. | .. | .. | .. | .. | 1,243 | 1,295 | 12.0 | 11.4 | 52 | 13 | 82 | 5 |
| Korea, Rep. | 2.8 | 2.7 | 19.4 | 12.1 | 641 | 692 | 3.0 | 2.8 | 21 | 89 | 1,788 | 1,292 |
| Kuwait | 13.6 | 4.8 | 29.3 | 17.1 | 22 | 23 | 2.5 | 1.6 | .. | .. | 608 | 107 |
| Kyrgyz Republic | 3.5 | 3.1 | .. | 17.5 | 7 | 21 | 0.4 | 0.9 | 61 | .. | .. | 1 |
| Lao PDR | 2.9 | .. | .. | .. | 137 | 129 | 7.9 | 5.5 | .. | .. | 14 | 4 |
| Latvia | 0.9 | 1.6 | 3.1 | 5.7 | 11 | 17 | 0.9 | 1.5 | 8 | .. | 16 | 4 |
| Lebanon | 6.4 | 4.1 | .. | 16.8 | 63 | 76 | 5.0 | 4.7 | .. | .. | 34 | 1 |
| Lesotho | 3.7 | 2.4 | 10.7 | 5.9 | 2 | 2 | 0.3 | 0.3 | .. | .. | .. | 1 |
| Liberia | 31.2 | .. | .. | .. | 21 | 2 | 2.6 | 0.2 | .. | .. | .. | .. |
| Libya | 4.1 | 1.5 | .. | .. | 81 | 76 | 5.1 | 3.0 | 8 | 24 | .. | 5 |
| Lithuania | 0.4 | 1.2 | .. | 4.2 | 9 | 24 | 0.5 | 1.5 | .. | .. | 4 | 33 |
| Macedonia, FYR | 3.0 | 2.0 | .. | .. | 18 | 19 | 2.2 | 2.2 | 0 | 29 | 0 | .. |
| Madagascar | 0.9 | 1.0 | .. | 8.5 | 29 | 22 | 0.5 | 0.3 | .. | .. | 19 | .. |
| Malawi | 0.8 | .. | .. | .. | 10 | 7 | 0.2 | 0.1 | .. | .. | 2 | .. |
| Malaysia | 2.8 | 2.0 | 16.0 | .. | 140 | 134 | 1.7 | 1.2 | 0 | .. | 876 | 654 |
| Mali | 2.2 | 2.2 | .. | 14.3 | 15 | 12 | 0.4 | 0.2 | .. | .. | 7 | 13 |
| Mauritania | 2.0 | 2.5 | .. | .. | 21 | 21 | 2.4 | 1.7 | .. | .. | 2 | .. |
| Mauritius | 0.4 | 0.2 | 1.8 | 0.9 | 2 | 2 | 0.4 | 0.4 | .. | .. | 30 | .. |
| Mexico | 0.6 | 0.4 | 3.8 | .. | 189 | 280 | 0.5 | 0.6 | .. | .. | 42 | 68 |
| Moldova | 0.9 | 0.3 | 2.4 | 0.9 | 15 | 8 | 0.8 | 0.4 | 36 | 4 | 6 | .. |
| Mongolia | 1.7 | 1.3 | .. | .. | 31 | 16 | 3.3 | 1.3 | .. | .. | .. | .. |
| Morocco | 5.9 | 3.7 | .. | 14.2 | 238 | 246 | 2.7 | 2.2 | .. | .. | 30 | 49 |
| Mozambique | 1.5 | 0.9 | .. | .. | 12 | 11 | 0.2 | 0.1 | .. | .. | .. | .. |
| Myanmar | 3.7 | .. | .. | .. | 371 | 513 | 1.7 | 1.9 | .. | .. | 245 | 7 |
| Namibia | 2.0 | 2.9 | .. | .. | 8 | 15 | 1.5 | 2.2 | .. | .. | 4 | 13 |
| Nepal | 0.9 | 1.9 | .. | 12.8 | 63 | 131 | 0.8 | 1.2 | .. | .. | 1 | 4 |
| Netherlands | 1.9 | 1.5 | 3.8 | 3.6 | 78 | 46 | 1.0 | 0.5 | 421 | 1,481 | 47 | 171 |
| New Zealand | 1.4 | 1.0 | .. | 3.0 | 10 | 9 | 0.6 | 0.4 | 3 | 1 | 7 | 8 |
| Nicaragua | 1.1 | 0.7 | 7.8 | 3.4 | 12 | 14 | 0.8 | 0.7 | 5 | .. | .. | .. |
| Niger | 1.0 | 1.1 | .. | .. | 11 | 10 | 0.3 | 0.2 | .. | .. | 3 | .. |
| Nigeria | 0.7 | 0.7 | .. | .. | 89 | 162 | 0.2 | 0.3 | .. | .. | 2 | 72 |
| Norway | 2.4 | 1.5 | .. | 4.7 | 31 | 16 | 1.4 | 0.6 | 22 | 2 | 84 | 509 |
| Oman | 14.6 | 11.8 | 45.2 | .. | 48 | 47 | 6.2 | 4.9 | 1 | 1 | 182 | 406 |
| Pakistan | 6.0 | 3.8 | 31.4 | 24.9 | 846 | 923 | 2.2 | 1.5 | 1 | 17 | .. | .. |
| Panama | 1.2 | .. | 5.6 | .. | 12 | 12 | 1.1 | 0.8 | .. | .. | 0 | .. |
| Papua New Guinea | 1.0 | 0.5 | 3.9 | .. | 4 | 3 | 0.2 | 0.1 | .. | .. | 0 | .. |
| Paraguay | 1.4 | 0.8 | .. | 4.9 | 28 | 26 | 1.4 | 0.9 | .. | .. | 2 | 1 |
| Peru | 1.9 | 1.2 | 10.7 | 7.9 | 178 | 198 | 1.8 | 1.5 | .. | 5 | 32 | 365 |
| Philippines | 1.4 | 0.9 | 8.5 | 5.0 | 149 | 147 | 0.5 | 0.4 | .. | .. | 30 | 43 |
| Poland | 2.0 | 2.0 | .. | 5.4 | 302 | 148 | 1.7 | 0.9 | 176 | 169 | 195 | 224 |
| Portugal | 2.4 | 2.1 | 5.7 | 5.0 | 104 | 91 | 2.1 | 1.6 | 1 | .. | 24 | 431 |
| Puerto Rico | .. | .. | .. | .. | .. | .. | .. | .. | .. | .. | .. | .. |

| | Military expenditures | | | | Armed forces personnel | | | | Arms transfers | | | |
| | % of GDP | | % of central government expenditure | | thousands | | % of labor force | | $ millions 1990 prices Exports | | Imports | |
| | 1995 | 2006 | 1995 | 2006 | 1995 | 2006 | 1995 | 2006 | 1995 | 2006 | 1995 | 2006 |
|---|---|---|---|---|---|---|---|---|---|---|---|---|
| Romania | 2.8 | 1.9 | .. | 8.2 | 297 | 154 | 2.4 | 1.5 | 6 | .. | 3 | 131 |
| Russian Federation | 4.4 | 4.0 | 38.3 | 20.5 | 1,800 | 1,446 | 2.5 | 2.0 | 3,363 | 6,623 | 40 | 4 |
| Rwanda | 4.4 | 2.7 | .. | .. | 47 | 53 | 1.9 | 1.2 | .. | .. | 1 | .. |
| Saudi Arabia | 9.3 | 8.5 | .. | .. | 178 | 240 | 3.0 | 2.8 | 2 | 36 | 987 | 148 |
| Senegal | 1.7 | 1.6 | .. | .. | 17 | 19 | 0.5 | 0.4 | .. | .. | 2 | .. |
| Serbia | 4.3 | 2.1 | .. | .. | 165 | 24 | .. | .. | 2 | 5 | 20 | .. |
| Sierra Leone | 2.9 | 1.0 | .. | 5.1 | 7 | 11 | 0.4 | 0.4 | .. | .. | 15 | .. |
| Singapore | 4.4 | 4.7 | 35.1 | 34.0 | 66 | 167 | 3.7 | 7.3 | 0 | 3 | 269 | 54 |
| Slovak Republic | 3.2 | 1.7 | .. | 5.1 | 51 | 17 | 2.1 | 0.6 | 91 | 79 | 218 | 4 |
| Slovenia | 1.6 | 1.7 | 4.7 | 4.2 | 13 | 11 | 1.3 | 1.1 | .. | .. | 19 | 2 |
| Somalia | .. | .. | .. | .. | 225 | 0 | 8.4 | 0.0 | .. | .. | .. | .. |
| South Africa | 2.2 | 1.4 | .. | 4.5 | 277 | 103 | 1.7 | 0.5 | 15 | 115 | 38 | 862 |
| Spain | 1.4 | 1.0 | 3.9 | 4.2 | 282 | 222 | 1.7 | 1.1 | 82 | 803 | 363 | 378 |
| Sri Lanka | 5.3 | 2.4 | 20.3 | 11.0 | 236 | 213 | 3.3 | 2.5 | .. | .. | 49 | 20 |
| Sudan | 2.7 | .. | .. | .. | 134 | 123 | 1.6 | 1.2 | .. | .. | 3 | 48 |
| Swaziland | 2.4 | 1.9 | .. | .. | 3 | .. | 1.1 | .. | .. | .. | .. | .. |
| Sweden | 2.3 | 1.4 | .. | 4.0 | 100 | 25 | 2.2 | 0.5 | 222 | 472 | 96 | 122 |
| Switzerland | 1.3 | 0.9 | 5.2 | 4.9 | 31 | 23 | 0.8 | 0.5 | 36 | 144 | 93 | 72 |
| Syrian Arab Republic | 6.2 | 3.8 | .. | .. | 531 | 401 | 11.4 | 5.1 | 0 | 3 | 43 | 9 |
| Tajikistan | 1.0 | 2.2 | .. | 15.8 | 18 | 17 | 0.9 | 0.8 | .. | .. | 27 | 13 |
| Tanzania | 1.6 | 1.1 | .. | .. | 36 | 28 | 0.2 | 0.1 | .. | .. | 3 | .. |
| Thailand | 2.3 | 1.1 | .. | 6.8 | 421 | 420 | 1.3 | 1.2 | .. | 5 | 520 | 47 |
| Timor-Leste | .. | .. | .. | .. | .. | 1 | .. | 0.3 | .. | .. | .. | .. |
| Togo | 2.4 | 1.6 | .. | .. | 8 | 10 | 0.4 | 0.4 | .. | .. | 3 | .. |
| Trinidad and Tobago | .. | .. | .. | .. | 7 | 3 | 1.3 | 0.5 | .. | .. | .. | .. |
| Tunisia | 1.9 | 1.4 | 6.7 | 4.8 | 59 | 48 | 2.1 | 1.2 | .. | .. | 46 | 16 |
| Turkey | 3.9 | 2.9 | .. | 9.8 | 690 | 612 | 3.0 | 2.2 | 0 | 45 | 1,580 | 486 |
| Turkmenistan | 2.3 | .. | .. | .. | 11 | 22 | 0.7 | 1.0 | .. | .. | .. | 10 |
| Uganda | 2.2 | 2.1 | .. | 12.0 | 52 | 47 | 0.6 | 0.4 | .. | .. | 32 | 15 |
| Ukraine | 2.8 | 2.1 | .. | 5.7 | 519 | 215 | 2.0 | 1.0 | 215 | 133 | 0 | 29 |
| United Arab Emirates | 5.2 | 2.0 | 49.2 | .. | 71 | 51 | 5.5 | 1.9 | 27 | 7 | 427 | 2,439 |
| United Kingdom | 3.0 | 2.6 | .. | 6.3 | 233 | 181 | 0.8 | 0.6 | 1,402 | 1,063 | 659 | 463 |
| United States | 3.8 | 4.1 | .. | 19.5 | 1,636 | 1,498 | 1.2 | 1.0 | 11,288 | 7,938 | 767 | 443 |
| Uruguay | 2.1 | 1.2 | 7.9 | 4.3 | 27 | 25 | 1.8 | 1.5 | .. | .. | 8 | 7 |
| Uzbekistan | 1.1 | .. | .. | .. | 42 | 87 | 0.5 | 0.7 | .. | 4 | .. | .. |
| Venezuela, RB | 1.6 | 1.1 | 8.7 | 4.4 | 80 | 82 | 0.9 | 0.6 | .. | 5 | 5 | 388 |
| Vietnam | 2.6 | .. | .. | .. | 622 | 495 | 1.8 | 1.1 | .. | .. | 269 | 179 |
| West Bank and Gaza | .. | .. | .. | .. | .. | 56 | .. | 7.0 | .. | .. | 1 | 0 |
| Yemen, Rep. | 6.4 | 6.0 | 33.4 | .. | 70 | 138 | 1.7 | 2.2 | .. | .. | 175 | 308 |
| Zambia | 1.6 | 2.3 | .. | 11.3 | 23 | 16 | 0.6 | 0.3 | .. | .. | 5 | 15 |
| Zimbabwe | 19.1 | 2.3 | 0.1 | .. | 68 | 51 | 1.4 | 0.9 | .. | .. | 1 | 20 |
| **World** | **2.5 w** | **2.5 w** | **.. w** | **11.2 w** | **30,182 s** | **27,030 s** | **1.2 w** | **0.9 w** | **21,064 s** | **22,904 s** | **22,357 s** | **26,241 s** |
| **Low income** | 2.7 | 2.4 | 19.4 | 18.3 | 7,694 | 7,160 | 1.0 | 0.9 | 115 | 11 | 2,250 | 2,681 |
| **Middle income** | 2.3 | 2.0 | .. | .. | 16,027 | 14,271 | 1.2 | 0.9 | 4,996 | 7,717 | 8,509 | 11,361 |
| Lower middle income | 2.1 | 2.0 | .. | 15.7 | 10,405 | 9,878 | 1.0 | 0.8 | 1,304 | 730 | 4,302 | 6,115 |
| Upper middle income | 2.5 | 2.0 | .. | .. | 5,622 | 4,393 | 1.7 | 1.2 | 3,692 | 6,987 | 4,207 | 5,246 |
| **Low & middle income** | 2.4 | 2.1 | .. | .. | 23,721 | 21,431 | 1.1 | 0.9 | 5,111 | 7,728 | 10,759 | 14,042 |
| East Asia & Pacific | 1.8 | 1.8 | .. | 17.2 | 8,021 | 7,535 | 0.9 | 0.7 | 1,039 | 572 | 2,994 | 4,250 |
| Europe & Central Asia | 3.5 | 2.9 | .. | 13.0 | 4,874 | 3,434 | 2.3 | 1.6 | 4,011 | 6,975 | 2,301 | 1,560 |
| Latin America & Carib. | 1.7 | 1.3 | 5.1 | .. | 2,105 | 2,281 | 1.0 | 0.9 | 36 | 6 | 935 | 2,412 |
| Middle East & N. Africa | 4.2 | 3.5 | 17.6 | 16.2 | 3,172 | 3,479 | 4.2 | 3.1 | 8 | 49 | 2,951 | 2,399 |
| South Asia | 3.0 | 2.7 | 20.4 | 18.4 | 3,852 | 4,121 | 0.8 | 0.7 | 2 | 11 | 1,463 | 2,247 |
| Sub-Saharan Africa | 2.0 | 1.3 | .. | .. | 1,698 | 582 | 0.7 | 0.5 | 15 | 115 | 115 | 1,174 |
| **High income** | 2.5 | 2.6 | .. | 10.6 | 6,461 | 5,599 | 1.4 | 1.1 | 15,953 | 15,176 | 11,598 | 12,199 |
| Euro area | 2.0 | 1.6 | 4.0 | 4.3 | 2,298 | 1,707 | 1.7 | 1.1 | 3,235 | 4,884 | 2,149 | 3,351 |

**Note:** For some countries data are partial or uncertain or based on rough estimates; see SIPRI (2007).
a. Estimates differ from official statistics of the government of China, which has published the following estimates: military expenditure as 1.0 percent of GDP in 1995 and 1.4 percent in 2005 and 9.3 percent of central government expenditure in 1995 and 7.3 percent in 2005 (see National Bureau of Statistics of China, www.stats.gov.cn).

# Military expenditures and arms transfers | 5.7

## About the data

Although national defense is an important function of government and security from external threats that contributes to economic development, high levels of military expenditures for defense or civil conflicts burden the economy and may impede growth. Data on military expenditures as a share of gross domestic product (GDP) are a rough indicator of the portion of national resources used for military activities and of the burden on the national economy. As an "input" measure military expenditures are not directly related to the "output" of military activities, capabilities, or security. Comparisons of military spending between countries should take into account the many factors that influence perceptions of vulnerability and risk, including historical and cultural traditions, the length of borders that need defending, the quality of relations with neighbors, and the role of the armed forces in the body politic.

Data on military spending reported by governments are not compiled using standard definitions. They are often incomplete and unreliable. Even in countries where the parliament vigilantly reviews budgets and spending, military expenditures and arms transfers rarely receive close scrutiny or full, public disclosure (see Ball 1984 and Happe and Wakeman-Linn 1994). Therefore, SIPRI has adopted a definition of military expenditure derived from the North Atlantic Treaty Organization (NATO) definition (see *Definitions*). The data on military expenditures as a share of GDP and as a share of central government expenditure are estimated by the Stockholm International Peace Research Institute (SIPRI). Central government expenditures are from the International Monetary Fund (IMF). Therefore the data in the table may differ from comparable data published by national governments.

SIPRI's primary source of military expenditure data is official data provided by national governments. These data are derived from national budget documents, defense white papers, and other public documents from official government agencies, including governments' responses to questionnaires sent by SIPRI, the United Nations, or the Organization for Security and Co-operation in Europe. Secondary sources include international statistics, such as those of NATO and the IMF's *Government Finance Statistics Yearbook*. Other secondary sources include country reports of the Economist Intelligence Unit, country reports by IMF staff, and specialist journals and newspapers.

In the many cases where SIPRI cannot make independent estimates, it uses the national data provided. Because of the differences in definitions and the difficulty in verifying the accuracy and completeness of data, data on military expenditures are not strictly comparable across countries. More information on SIPRI's military expenditure project can be found at www.sipri.org/contents/milap/.

Data on armed forces refer to military personnel on active duty, including paramilitary forces. Because data exclude personnel not on active duty, they underestimate the share of the labor force working for the defense establishment. Governments rarely report the size of their armed forces, so such data typically come from intelligence sources.

SIPRI's Arms Transfers Project collects data on arms transfers from open sources. Since publicly available information is inadequate for tracking all weapons and other military equipment, SIPRI covers only what it terms *major conventional weapons*. Data cover the supply of weapons through sales, aid, gifts, and manufacturing licenses; therefore the term *arms transfers* rather than *arms trade* is used. SIPRI data also cover weapons supplied to or from rebel forces in an armed conflict as well as arms deliveries for which neither the supplier nor the recipient can be identified with acceptable certainty; these data are available in SIPRI's database.

SIPRI's estimates of arms transfers are designed as a trend-measuring device in which similar weapons have similar values, reflecting both the value and quality of weapons transferred. SIPRI cautions that the estimated values do not reflect financial value (payments for weapons transferred) because reliable data on the value of the transfer are not available, and even when values are known, the transfer usually includes more than the actual conventional weapons, such as spares, support systems, and training, and details of the financial arrangements (such as credit and loan conditions and discounts) are usually not known.

Given these measurement issues, SIPRI's method of estimating the transfer of military resources includes an evaluation of the technical parameters of the weapons. Weapons for which a price is not known are compared with the same weapons for which actual acquisition prices are available (core weapons) or for the closest match. These weapons are assigned a value in an index that reflects their military resource value in relation to the core weapons. These matches are based on such characteristics as size, performance, and type of electronics, and adjustments are made for secondhand weapons. More information on SIPRI's Arms Transfers Project is available at www.sipri.org/contents/armstrad/.

## Definitions

• **Military expenditures** are SIPRI data derived from the NATO definition, which includes all current and capital expenditures on the armed forces, including peacekeeping forces; defense ministries and other government agencies engaged in defense projects; paramilitary forces, if judged to be trained and equipped for military operations; and military space activities. Such expenditures include military and civil personnel, including retirement pensions and social services for military personnel; operation and maintenance; procurement; military research and development; and military aid (in the military expenditures of the donor country). Excluded are civil defense and current expenditures for previous military activities, such as for veterans benefits, demobilization, and weapons conversion and destruction. This definition cannot be applied for all countries, however, since that would require more detailed information than is available about military budgets and off-budget military expenditures (for example, whether military budgets cover civil defense, reserves and auxiliary forces, police and paramilitary forces, and military pensions). • **Armed forces personnel** are active duty military personnel, including paramilitary forces if the training, organization, equipment, and control suggest they may be used to support or replace regular military forces. Reserve forces, which are not fully staffed or operational in peace time, are not included. The data also exclude civilians in the defense establishment and so are not consistent with the data on military expenditures on personnel. • **Arms transfers** cover the supply of military weapons through sales, aid, gifts, and manufacturing licenses. Weapons must be transferred voluntarily by the supplier, have a military purpose, and be destined for the armed forces, paramilitary forces, or intelligence agencies of another country. The trends shown in the table are based on actual deliveries only. Data cover major conventional weapons such as aircraft, armored vehicles, artillery, radar systems, missiles, and ships designed for military use. Excluded are transfers of other military equipment such as small arms and light weapons, trucks, small artillery, ammunition, support equipment, technology transfers, and other services.

### Data sources

Data on military expenditures are from SIPRI's *Yearbook 2007: Armaments, Disarmament, and International Security*. Data on armed forces personnel are from the International Institute for Strategic Studies' *The Military Balance 2008*. Data on arms transfers are from SIPRI's Arms Transfer Project (www.sipri.org/contents/armstrad/).

| | IDA Resource Allocation Index 1–6 (low to high) | Economic management 1–6 (low to high) | | | | Structural policies 1–6 (low to high) | | | |
|---|---|---|---|---|---|---|---|---|---|
| | | Macroeconomic management | Fiscal policy | Debt policy | Average | Trade | Financial sector | Business regulatory environment | Average |
| | 2006 | 2006 | 2006 | 2006 | 2006 | 2006 | 2006 | 2006 | 2006 |
| Afghanistan | 2.6 | 4.0 | 3.0 | 3.0 | 3.3 | 3.0 | 2.0 | 2.5 | 2.5 |
| Albania | 3.7 | 4.5 | 3.5 | 4.0 | 4.0 | 5.0 | 4.0 | 3.5 | 4.2 |
| Angola | 2.7 | 3.0 | 3.0 | 2.0 | 2.7 | 4.0 | 2.5 | 2.0 | 2.8 |
| Armenia | 4.3 | 5.5 | 5.0 | 5.5 | 5.3 | 4.5 | 3.5 | 4.0 | 4.5 |
| Azerbaijan | 3.7 | 4.5 | 4.5 | 4.5 | 4.5 | 4.0 | 3.0 | 3.5 | 3.5 |
| Bangladesh | 3.4 | 4.0 | 3.5 | 4.5 | 4.0 | 3.5 | 3.0 | 3.5 | 3.3 |
| Benin | 3.6 | 4.5 | 4.0 | 3.5 | 4.0 | 4.5 | 3.5 | 3.5 | 3.8 |
| Bhutan | 3.8 | 4.5 | 4.0 | 4.0 | 4.2 | 3.0 | 3.0 | 3.5 | 3.2 |
| Bolivia | 3.7 | 4.0 | 4.0 | 4.5 | 4.2 | 5.0 | 3.5 | 2.5 | 3.7 |
| Bosnia and Herzegovina | 3.7 | 4.5 | 3.5 | 4.0 | 4.0 | 3.5 | 4.0 | 3.5 | 3.7 |
| Burkina Faso | 3.7 | 4.5 | 4.5 | 4.0 | 4.3 | 4.0 | 3.0 | 3.0 | 3.3 |
| Burundi | 3.0 | 3.5 | 3.5 | 2.5 | 3.2 | 3.5 | 3.0 | 2.5 | 3.0 |
| Cambodia | 3.2 | 4.0 | 3.0 | 3.5 | 3.5 | 3.5 | 2.5 | 3.5 | 3.2 |
| Cameroon | 3.2 | 4.0 | 4.0 | 2.5 | 3.5 | 3.5 | 3.0 | 3.0 | 3.2 |
| Cape Verde | 4.1 | 4.5 | 4.5 | 4.0 | 4.3 | 4.0 | 4.0 | 3.5 | 3.8 |
| Central African Republic | 2.4 | 3.0 | 3.0 | 1.5 | 2.5 | 3.5 | 2.5 | 2.0 | 2.7 |
| Chad | 2.8 | 3.5 | 3.0 | 2.5 | 3.0 | 3.0 | 3.0 | 3.0 | 3.0 |
| Comoros | 2.4 | 2.5 | 2.0 | 1.5 | 2.0 | 2.5 | 2.5 | 2.5 | 2.5 |
| Congo, Dem. Rep. | 2.8 | 3.5 | 3.5 | 2.5 | 3.2 | 4.0 | 2.0 | 3.0 | 3.0 |
| Congo, Rep. | 2.8 | 3.5 | 2.5 | 2.5 | 2.8 | 3.5 | 2.5 | 2.5 | 2.8 |
| Côte d'Ivoire | 2.5 | 2.5 | 2.0 | 1.0 | 1.8 | 3.5 | 3.0 | 3.0 | 3.2 |
| Djibouti | 3.1 | 3.5 | 2.5 | 2.5 | 2.8 | 4.0 | 3.5 | 3.0 | 3.5 |
| Dominica | 3.8 | 4.0 | 4.5 | 3.0 | 3.8 | 4.0 | 4.0 | 4.5 | 4.2 |
| Eritrea | 2.5 | 2.0 | 2.0 | 2.5 | 2.2 | 1.5 | 2.0 | 2.0 | 1.8 |
| Ethiopia | 3.4 | 3.0 | 4.0 | 3.5 | 3.5 | 3.0 | 3.0 | 3.5 | 3.2 |
| Gambia, The | 3.1 | 3.5 | 3.0 | 2.5 | 3.0 | 4.0 | 3.0 | 3.0 | 3.3 |
| Georgia | 4.1 | 4.5 | 4.5 | 4.5 | 4.5 | 4.5 | 3.5 | 4.5 | 4.2 |
| Ghana | 3.9 | 4.0 | 4.5 | 4.0 | 4.2 | 4.0 | 3.5 | 4.0 | 3.8 |
| Grenada | 3.8 | 4.0 | 3.0 | 3.0 | 3.3 | 4.0 | 3.5 | 4.5 | 4.0 |
| Guinea | 2.9 | 2.5 | 3.0 | 2.5 | 2.7 | 4.5 | 3.0 | 3.0 | 3.5 |
| Guinea-Bissau | 2.6 | 2.0 | 2.5 | 1.5 | 2.0 | 4.0 | 3.0 | 2.5 | 3.2 |
| Guyana | 3.4 | 3.5 | 3.5 | 4.0 | 3.7 | 4.0 | 3.5 | 3.0 | 3.5 |
| Haiti | 2.9 | 3.5 | 3.5 | 2.5 | 3.2 | 4.0 | 3.0 | 2.5 | 3.2 |
| Honduras | 3.9 | 4.5 | 4.0 | 4.0 | 4.2 | 5.0 | 3.5 | 4.0 | 4.2 |
| India | 3.8 | 4.5 | 3.5 | 4.5 | 4.2 | 3.5 | 4.0 | 3.5 | 3.7 |
| Indonesia | 3.7 | 4.5 | 4.0 | 4.5 | 4.3 | 4.5 | 3.5 | 3.0 | 3.7 |
| Kenya | 3.7 | 4.5 | 4.0 | 4.0 | 4.2 | 4.0 | 3.5 | 4.0 | 3.8 |
| Kiribati | 3.1 | 2.5 | 2.0 | 5.0 | 3.2 | 3.0 | 3.0 | 3.0 | 3.0 |

## About the data

The International Development Association (IDA) is the part of the World Bank Group that helps the poorest countries reduce poverty by providing concessional loans and grants for programs aimed at boosting economic growth and improving living conditions. IDA funding helps these countries deal with the complex challenges they face in striving to meet the Millennium Development Goals.

The World Bank's IDA Resource Allocation Index (IRAI), which is presented in the table, is based on the results of the annual Country Policy and Institutional Assessment (CPIA) exercise, which covers the IDA-eligible countries. The table does not include Liberia, Myanmar, and Somalia because they were not rated in the 2006 exercise even though they are

IDA eligible. Serbia and Montenegro as a unified country was IDA eligible in 2005, rated in that year's exercise, and included in last year's table, but neither Serbia nor Montenegro is IDA eligible as an independent country and thus neither is rated in the 2006 exercise nor included in this year's table. Afghanistan and Timor-Leste are included in this year's table. Country assessments have been carried out annually by World Bank staff since the mid-1970s. Over time the criteria have been revised from a largely macroeconomic focus to include governance aspects and a broader coverage of social and structural dimensions. Country performance is assessed against a set of 16 criteria grouped into four clusters: economic management, structural policies, policies for social

inclusion and equity, and public sector management and institutions. IDA resources are allocated to a country on per capita terms based on its IDA country performance rating and, to a limited extent, based on its per capita gross national income. This ensures that good performers receive a higher IDA allocation in per capita terms. The IRAI is a key element in the country performance rating.

The CPIA exercise is intended to capture the quality of a country's policies and institutional arrangements, focusing on key elements that are within the country's control, rather than on outcomes (such as economic growth rates) that are influenced by events beyond the country's control. More specifically, the CPIA measures the extent to which a country's policy

# Public policies and institutions | 5.8

| | IDA Resource Allocation Index 1–6 (low to high) | Economic management 1–6 (low to high) | | | | Structural policies 1–6 (low to high) | | | |
|---|---|---|---|---|---|---|---|---|---|
| | | Macroeconomic management | Fiscal policy | Debt policy | Average | Trade | Financial sector | Business regulatory environment | Average |
| | 2006 | 2006 | 2006 | 2006 | 2006 | 2006 | 2006 | 2006 | 2006 |
| Kyrgyz Republic | 3.6 | 4.5 | 3.5 | 4.0 | 4.0 | 5.0 | 3.5 | 3.5 | 4.0 |
| Lao PDR | 3.1 | 4.0 | 3.5 | 3.5 | 3.7 | 3.5 | 2.0 | 3.0 | 2.8 |
| Lesotho | 3.5 | 4.0 | 4.0 | 4.0 | 4.0 | 3.5 | 3.5 | 3.0 | 3.3 |
| Madagascar | 3.6 | 4.0 | 3.0 | 3.5 | 3.5 | 4.0 | 3.5 | 4.0 | 3.8 |
| Malawi | 3.4 | 3.5 | 3.0 | 3.0 | 3.2 | 4.0 | 3.0 | 3.5 | 3.5 |
| Maldives | 3.6 | 3.0 | 2.5 | 3.5 | 3.0 | 4.0 | 4.0 | 4.0 | 4.0 |
| Mali | 3.7 | 4.5 | 4.0 | 4.5 | 4.3 | 4.0 | 3.0 | 3.5 | 3.5 |
| Mauritania | 3.3 | 3.0 | 3.0 | 4.0 | 3.3 | 4.5 | 2.5 | 3.5 | 3.5 |
| Moldova | 3.7 | 4.0 | 4.0 | 4.0 | 4.0 | 3.5 | 3.5 | 3.5 | 3.5 |
| Mongolia | 3.4 | 4.0 | 3.0 | 3.0 | 3.3 | 4.5 | 3.0 | 3.5 | 3.7 |
| Mozambique | 3.5 | 4.0 | 4.0 | 4.5 | 4.2 | 4.5 | 3.0 | 3.0 | 3.5 |
| Nepal | 3.4 | 4.5 | 3.5 | 3.5 | 3.8 | 4.0 | 3.0 | 3.0 | 3.3 |
| Nicaragua | 3.8 | 4.0 | 4.0 | 4.5 | 4.2 | 4.5 | 3.5 | 3.5 | 3.8 |
| Niger | 3.3 | 4.0 | 3.5 | 3.5 | 3.7 | 4.0 | 3.0 | 3.0 | 3.3 |
| Nigeria | 3.2 | 4.0 | 4.0 | 4.0 | 4.0 | 3.0 | 3.0 | 3.0 | 3.0 |
| Pakistan | 3.6 | 4.0 | 3.5 | 4.5 | 4.0 | 4.0 | 4.5 | 4.0 | 4.2 |
| Papua New Guinea | 3.1 | 4.0 | 3.5 | 4.0 | 3.8 | 4.0 | 3.0 | 3.0 | 3.3 |
| Rwanda | 3.6 | 4.0 | 4.0 | 3.5 | 3.8 | 3.5 | 3.5 | 3.5 | 3.5 |
| Samoa | 3.9 | 4.0 | 3.5 | 4.0 | 3.8 | 4.5 | 4.0 | 3.5 | 4.0 |
| São Tomé and Principe | 3.0 | 3.0 | 3.0 | 2.5 | 2.8 | 4.0 | 2.5 | 3.0 | 3.2 |
| Senegal | 3.7 | 4.0 | 4.0 | 4.0 | 4.0 | 4.0 | 3.5 | 3.5 | 3.7 |
| Sierra Leone | 3.1 | 4.0 | 3.5 | 3.5 | 3.7 | 3.0 | 3.0 | 2.5 | 3.0 |
| Solomon Islands | 2.8 | 3.5 | 3.5 | 2.5 | 3.2 | 3.5 | 3.0 | 2.5 | 2.8 |
| Sri Lanka | 3.6 | 3.0 | 3.0 | 3.5 | 3.2 | 4.0 | 4.0 | 4.0 | 3.8 |
| St. Lucia | 3.9 | 4.5 | 3.5 | 4.0 | 4.0 | 4.0 | 4.0 | 4.5 | 4.2 |
| St. Vincent & Grenadines | 3.8 | 4.0 | 3.5 | 3.5 | 3.7 | 2.5 | 4.0 | 4.5 | 4.2 |
| Sudan | 2.5 | 3.5 | 3.0 | 1.5 | 2.7 | 4.0 | 3.0 | 3.0 | 2.8 |
| Tajikistan | 3.3 | 4.5 | 4.0 | 4.0 | 4.2 | 4.0 | 3.0 | 3.5 | 3.5 |
| Tanzania | 3.9 | 5.0 | 4.5 | 4.0 | 4.5 | 3.5 | 3.5 | 3.5 | 3.7 |
| Timor-Leste | 2.7 | 2.5 | 3.0 | 3.5 | 3.0 | 3.5 | 2.5 | 1.5 | 2.5 |
| Togo | 2.5 | 2.5 | 2.0 | 1.5 | 2.0 | 4.0 | 2.5 | 3.0 | 3.2 |
| Tonga | 2.9 | 3.0 | 2.0 | 3.0 | 2.7 | 3.0 | 3.0 | 3.0 | 3.0 |
| Uganda | 3.9 | 4.5 | 4.5 | 4.5 | 4.5 | 4.0 | 3.5 | 4.0 | 3.8 |
| Uzbekistan | 3.0 | 3.0 | 3.5 | 4.0 | 3.5 | 2.5 | 2.5 | 2.5 | 2.5 |
| Vanuatu | 3.1 | 3.5 | 3.0 | 4.0 | 3.5 | 3.5 | 3.0 | 3.0 | 3.2 |
| Vietnam | 3.9 | 5.5 | 4.5 | 4.0 | 4.7 | 3.5 | 3.0 | 3.5 | 3.3 |
| Yemen, Rep. | 3.3 | 3.5 | 3.0 | 4.5 | 3.7 | 4.5 | 2.5 | 3.0 | 3.3 |
| Zambia | 3.4 | 4.0 | 3.5 | 3.5 | 3.7 | 4.0 | 3.0 | 3.0 | 3.3 |
| Zimbabwe | 1.8 | 1.0 | 1.0 | 1.0 | 1.0 | 2.0 | 2.5 | 2.0 | 2.2 |

and institutional framework supports sustainable growth and poverty reduction and, consequently, the effective use of development assistance.

All criteria within each cluster receive equal weight, and each cluster has a 25 percent weight in the overall score, which is obtained by averaging the average scores of the four clusters. For each of the 16 criteria countries are rated on a scale of 1 (low) to 6 (high). The scores depend on the level of performance in a given year assessed against the criteria, rather than on changes in performance compared with the previous year. All 16 CPIA criteria contain a detailed description of each rating level. In assessing country performance, World Bank staff evaluate the country's actual performance on each of the criteria and assign a rating. The ratings reflect a variety of indicators, observations, and judgments based on country knowledge and on relevant publicly available indicators. In interpreting the assessment scores, it should be noted that the criteria are designed in a developmentally neutral manner. Accordingly, higher scores can be attained by a country that, given its stage of development, has a policy and institutional framework that more strongly fosters growth and poverty reduction.

The country teams that prepare the ratings are very familiar with the country, and their assessments are based on country diagnostic studies prepared by the World Bank or other development organizations and on their own professional judgment. An early consultation is conducted with country authorities to make sure that the assessments are informed by up-to-date information. To ensure that scores are consistent across countries, the process involves two key phases. In the benchmarking phase a small representative sample of countries drawn from all regions is rated. Country teams prepare proposals that are reviewed first at the regional level and then in a Bankwide review process. A similar process is followed to assess the performance of the remaining countries, using the benchmark countries' scores as guideposts. The final ratings are determined following a Bankwide review. The overall numerical IRAI score and the separate criteria scores were first publicly disclosed in June 2006.

See IDA's website at www.worldbank.org/ida for more information.

| | Policies for social inclusion and equity 1–6 (low to high) | | | | | | Public sector management and institutions 1–6 (low to high) | | | | | |
|---|---|---|---|---|---|---|---|---|---|---|---|---|
| | Gender equality 2006 | Equity of public resource use 2006 | Building human resources 2006 | Social protection and labor 2006 | Policies and institutions for environmental sustainability 2006 | Average 2006 | Property rights and rule-based governance 2006 | Quality of budgetary and financial management 2006 | Efficiency of revenue mobilization 2006 | Quality of public administration 2006 | Transparency, accountability, and corruption in the public sector 2006 | Average 2006 |
| Afghanistan | 2.0 | 2.5 | 3.0 | 2.0 | 2.0 | 2.3 | 1.5 | 3.0 | 2.5 | 2.0 | 2.5 | 2.3 |
| Albania | 4.0 | 3.5 | 3.5 | 3.5 | 3.0 | 3.5 | 3.0 | 4.0 | 4.0 | 3.0 | 2.5 | 3.3 |
| Angola | 3.0 | 2.5 | 2.5 | 2.5 | 3.0 | 2.7 | 2.0 | 2.5 | 2.5 | 2.5 | 2.5 | 2.4 |
| Armenia | 4.5 | 4.5 | 4.0 | 4.5 | 3.5 | 4.2 | 3.5 | 4.0 | 3.5 | 4.0 | 3.5 | 3.5 |
| Azerbaijan | 4.0 | 4.0 | 3.0 | 4.0 | 3.0 | 3.6 | 3.0 | 4.0 | 3.5 | 3.0 | 2.5 | 3.2 |
| Bangladesh | 4.0 | 3.5 | 4.0 | 3.5 | 3.0 | 3.6 | 2.5 | 3.0 | 3.0 | 3.0 | 2.5 | 2.8 |
| Benin | 3.0 | 3.0 | 3.5 | 3.0 | 3.5 | 3.2 | 3.0 | 3.5 | 3.5 | 3.0 | 3.5 | 3.3 |
| Bhutan | 4.0 | 4.0 | 4.5 | 3.5 | 4.5 | 4.1 | 3.5 | 3.5 | 4.0 | 4.0 | 4.0 | 3.8 |
| Bolivia | 4.0 | 4.0 | 4.5 | 3.0 | 3.5 | 3.8 | 2.5 | 3.5 | 4.0 | 3.0 | 3.5 | 3.3 |
| Bosnia and Herzegovina | 4.5 | 3.0 | 3.5 | 3.5 | 3.5 | 3.6 | 3.0 | 3.5 | 4.5 | 3.0 | 3.0 | 3.4 |
| Burkina Faso | 3.5 | 4.0 | 3.5 | 3.5 | 3.5 | 3.6 | 3.5 | 4.0 | 3.5 | 3.5 | 3.0 | 3.5 |
| Burundi | 3.5 | 3.0 | 3.0 | 3.0 | 3.0 | 3.1 | 2.5 | 3.0 | 3.0 | 2.5 | 2.5 | 2.7 |
| Cambodia | 4.0 | 3.0 | 3.5 | 3.0 | 3.0 | 3.3 | 2.5 | 3.0 | 3.0 | 2.5 | 2.5 | 2.7 |
| Cameroon | 3.5 | 3.0 | 3.5 | 3.0 | 3.0 | 3.2 | 2.5 | 3.5 | 3.5 | 3.0 | 2.5 | 3.0 |
| Cape Verde | 4.5 | 4.5 | 4.5 | 4.5 | 3.5 | 4.3 | 4.0 | 3.5 | 3.5 | 4.0 | 4.5 | 3.9 |
| Central African Republic | 2.5 | 2.0 | 2.0 | 2.0 | 2.5 | 2.2 | 2.0 | 2.0 | 2.5 | 2.0 | 2.5 | 2.2 |
| Chad | 2.5 | 3.0 | 2.5 | 2.5 | 2.5 | 2.6 | 2.0 | 2.5 | 2.5 | 3.0 | 2.0 | 2.4 |
| Comoros | 3.0 | 3.0 | 3.0 | 2.5 | 2.0 | 2.7 | 2.5 | 1.5 | 2.5 | 2.0 | 2.5 | 2.2 |
| Congo, Dem. Rep. | 3.0 | 3.0 | 3.0 | 3.0 | 2.5 | 2.9 | 2.0 | 2.5 | 2.5 | 2.5 | 2.0 | 2.3 |
| Congo, Rep. | 3.0 | 2.5 | 3.0 | 2.5 | 2.5 | 2.7 | 2.5 | 3.0 | 3.0 | 2.5 | 2.5 | 2.7 |
| Côte d'Ivoire | 2.5 | 1.5 | 2.0 | 2.5 | 3.0 | 2.3 | 2.0 | 2.5 | 4.0 | 2.0 | 2.0 | 2.5 |
| Djibouti | 3.0 | 3.0 | 3.5 | 3.0 | 3.0 | 3.1 | 2.5 | 3.0 | 3.5 | 2.5 | 2.5 | 2.8 |
| Dominica | 4.0 | 3.5 | 4.0 | 3.5 | 3.5 | 3.7 | 4.0 | 3.0 | 3.5 | 3.5 | 4.0 | 3.6 |
| Eritrea | 3.5 | 3.0 | 3.5 | 3.0 | 2.0 | 3.0 | 2.5 | 2.5 | 3.5 | 3.0 | 2.5 | 2.8 |
| Ethiopia | 3.0 | 4.5 | 3.5 | 3.5 | 3.5 | 3.6 | 3.0 | 4.0 | 4.0 | 3.0 | 2.5 | 3.3 |
| Gambia, The | 3.5 | 3.0 | 3.5 | 2.5 | 3.0 | 3.1 | 2.5 | 3.5 | 3.5 | 3.0 | 2.0 | 2.9 |
| Georgia | 4.5 | 4.5 | 4.0 | 4.0 | 3.5 | 4.1 | 3.5 | 4.0 | 4.0 | 3.5 | 3.5 | 3.7 |
| Ghana | 4.0 | 4.0 | 4.0 | 3.5 | 3.5 | 3.8 | 3.5 | 4.0 | 4.5 | 3.5 | 4.0 | 3.9 |
| Grenada | 5.0 | 3.5 | 4.0 | 3.5 | 4.0 | 4.0 | 3.5 | 4.0 | 3.5 | 3.5 | 4.0 | 3.7 |
| Guinea | 3.5 | 3.0 | 3.0 | 3.0 | 2.5 | 3.0 | 2.0 | 2.5 | 3.0 | 3.0 | 2.5 | 2.6 |
| Guinea-Bissau | 2.5 | 3.0 | 2.5 | 2.5 | 2.5 | 2.6 | 2.5 | 2.5 | 3.0 | 2.5 | 2.5 | 2.6 |
| Guyana | 4.0 | 3.5 | 3.5 | 3.0 | 3.0 | 3.4 | 3.0 | 3.5 | 3.5 | 2.5 | 3.0 | 3.1 |
| Haiti | 3.0 | 3.0 | 2.5 | 2.5 | 2.5 | 2.7 | 2.0 | 3.0 | 2.5 | 2.5 | 2.0 | 2.4 |
| Honduras | 4.0 | 4.0 | 4.0 | 3.5 | 3.0 | 3.7 | 3.5 | 4.0 | 4.0 | 3.0 | 3.0 | 3.5 |
| India | 3.5 | 4.0 | 4.0 | 3.5 | 3.5 | 3.7 | 3.5 | 4.0 | 4.0 | 3.5 | 3.5 | 3.7 |
| Indonesia | 3.5 | 4.0 | 3.5 | 3.5 | 3.0 | 3.5 | 2.5 | 3.5 | 3.5 | 3.5 | 3.0 | 3.2 |
| Kenya | 3.0 | 3.5 | 3.5 | 3.0 | 3.0 | 3.2 | 3.0 | 3.5 | 4.0 | 3.5 | 3.0 | 3.4 |
| Kiribati | 3.0 | 3.0 | 2.5 | 3.0 | 3.0 | 2.9 | 3.5 | 3.0 | 3.0 | 3.0 | 3.5 | 3.2 |

## Definitions

• **IDA Resource Allocation Index** is obtained by calculating the average score for each cluster and then by averaging those scores. For each of 16 criteria countries are rated on a scale of 1 (low) to 6 (high) • **Economic management** cluster: **Macroeconomic management** assesses the monetary, exchange rate, and aggregate demand policy framework. • **Fiscal policy** assesses the short- and medium-term sustainability of fiscal policy (taking into account monetary and exchange rate policy and the sustainability of the public debt) and its impact on growth. • **Debt policy** assesses whether the debt management strategy is conducive to minimizing budgetary risks and ensuring long-term debt

sustainability. • **Structural policies** cluster: **Trade** assesses how the policy framework fosters trade in goods. • **Financial sector** assesses the structure of the financial sector and the policies and regulations that affect it. • **Business regulatory environment** assesses the extent to which the legal, regulatory, and policy environments help or hinder private businesses in investing, creating jobs, and becoming more productive. • **Policies for social inclusion and equity** cluster: **Gender equality** assesses the extent to which the country has installed institutions and programs to enforce laws and policies that promote equal access for men and women in education, health, the economy, and protection under law.

• **Equity of public resource use** assesses the extent to which the pattern of public expenditures and revenue collection affects the poor and is consistent with national poverty reduction priorities. • **Building human resources** assesses the national policies and public and private sector service delivery that affect the access to and quality of health and education services, including prevention and treatment of HIV/AIDS, tuberculosis, and malaria. • **Social protection and labor** assess government policies in social protection and labor market regulations that reduce the risk of becoming poor, assist those who are poor to better manage further risks, and ensure a minimal level of welfare to all people. • **Policies**

| | Policies for social inclusion and equity 1–6 (low to high) | | | | | | Public sector management and institutions 1–6 (low to high) | | | | | |
|---|---|---|---|---|---|---|---|---|---|---|---|---|
| | Gender equality 2006 | Equity of public resource use 2006 | Building human resources 2006 | Social protection and labor 2006 | Policies and institutions for environmental sustainability 2006 | Average 2006 | Property rights and rule-based governance 2006 | Quality of budgetary and financial manage-ment 2006 | Efficiency of revenue mobilization 2006 | Quality of public administration 2006 | Transparency, accountability, and corruption in the public sector 2006 | Average 2006 |
| Kyrgyz Republic | 4.5 | 3.5 | 3.5 | 3.5 | 3.0 | 3.6 | 2.5 | 3.0 | 3.5 | 2.5 | 2.5 | 2.8 |
| Lao PDR | 3.5 | 3.5 | 3.0 | 2.0 | 3.5 | 3.1 | 3.0 | 3.0 | 2.5 | 3.0 | 2.0 | 2.7 |
| Lesotho | 4.0 | 3.0 | 3.5 | 3.0 | 3.5 | 3.4 | 3.5 | 3.0 | 4.0 | 3.0 | 3.5 | 3.4 |
| Madagascar | 3.5 | 3.5 | 3.5 | 3.5 | 4.0 | 3.6 | 3.5 | 3.0 | 3.5 | 3.5 | 3.5 | 3.4 |
| Malawi | 3.5 | 3.5 | 3.5 | 3.5 | 3.5 | 3.5 | 3.5 | 3.0 | 4.0 | 3.5 | 3.0 | 3.4 |
| Maldives | 4.0 | 4.0 | 4.0 | 3.5 | 4.0 | 3.9 | 4.0 | 3.0 | 4.0 | 4.0 | 2.5 | 3.5 |
| Mali | 3.5 | 3.5 | 3.5 | 3.5 | 3.0 | 3.4 | 3.5 | 3.5 | 4.0 | 3.0 | 3.5 | 3.5 |
| Mauritania | 3.5 | 3.5 | 3.5 | 3.0 | 3.5 | 3.4 | 3.0 | 2.5 | 3.5 | 3.0 | 2.5 | 2.9 |
| Moldova | 5.0 | 3.5 | 4.0 | 3.5 | 3.5 | 3.9 | 3.5 | 3.5 | 3.0 | 3.0 | 3.0 | 3.2 |
| Mongolia | 3.5 | 3.0 | 3.5 | 3.5 | 2.5 | 3.2 | 3.0 | 4.0 | 3.5 | 3.5 | 2.5 | 3.3 |
| Mozambique | 3.5 | 3.5 | 3.5 | 3.0 | 3.0 | 3.3 | 3.0 | 3.5 | 3.5 | 2.5 | 3.0 | 3.1 |
| Nepal | 3.5 | 3.5 | 3.5 | 3.0 | 3.0 | 3.3 | 3.0 | 3.5 | 3.5 | 3.0 | 3.0 | 3.2 |
| Nicaragua | 3.5 | 4.0 | 3.5 | 3.5 | 3.5 | 3.6 | 3.0 | 4.0 | 4.0 | 3.0 | 3.0 | 3.4 |
| Niger | 2.5 | 3.5 | 3.0 | 3.0 | 3.0 | 3.0 | 3.0 | 3.5 | 3.5 | 3.0 | 3.0 | 3.2 |
| Nigeria | 3.0 | 3.5 | 3.0 | 3.0 | 3.0 | 3.1 | 2.5 | 3.0 | 3.5 | 2.5 | 3.0 | 2.8 |
| Pakistan | 2.0 | 3.5 | 3.5 | 3.0 | 3.5 | 3.1 | 3.0 | 3.5 | 3.5 | 3.5 | 2.5 | 3.2 |
| Papua New Guinea | 2.5 | 3.0 | 2.5 | 3.0 | 1.5 | 2.5 | 2.0 | 3.5 | 3.5 | 2.5 | 3.0 | 2.9 |
| Rwanda | 3.5 | 4.5 | 4.5 | 3.5 | 3.0 | 3.8 | 3.0 | 4.0 | 3.5 | 3.5 | 3.0 | 3.4 |
| Samoa | 4.0 | 4.0 | 4.0 | 3.5 | 4.0 | 3.9 | 4.0 | 3.5 | 4.0 | 4.0 | 4.0 | 3.9 |
| São Tomé and Principe | 3.0 | 3.5 | 2.5 | 2.5 | 2.5 | 2.8 | 2.5 | 2.5 | 3.5 | 3.0 | 3.5 | 3.0 |
| Senegal | 3.5 | 3.5 | 3.5 | 3.0 | 3.5 | 3.4 | 3.5 | 3.5 | 4.5 | 3.5 | 3.0 | 3.6 |
| Sierra Leone | 3.0 | 3.0 | 3.0 | 2.5 | 2.0 | 2.8 | 2.5 | 3.5 | 2.5 | 3.0 | 2.5 | 2.9 |
| Solomon Islands | 3.0 | 2.5 | 3.0 | 3.5 | 2.0 | 2.6 | 2.5 | 2.5 | 3.5 | 2.0 | 3.0 | 2.5 |
| Sri Lanka | 4.0 | 3.5 | 4.0 | 4.0 | 3.5 | 3.7 | 3.5 | 4.0 | 3.5 | 3.0 | 3.5 | 3.5 |
| St. Lucia | 4.0 | 3.5 | 4.0 | 3.5 | 3.5 | 3.8 | 4.0 | 3.5 | 3.5 | 3.5 | 4.5 | 3.8 |
| St. Vincent & Grenadines | 4.5 | 3.5 | 4.0 | 2.0 | 3.5 | 3.8 | 4.0 | 3.5 | 3.0 | 3.5 | 4.0 | 3.7 |
| Sudan | 2.0 | 2.5 | 2.5 | 3.5 | 2.5 | 2.3 | 2.0 | 2.0 | 3.0 | 2.5 | 2.0 | 2.3 |
| Tajikistan | 3.5 | 3.0 | 3.0 | 3.5 | 2.5 | 3.1 | 2.5 | 3.0 | 4.0 | 2.5 | 2.0 | 2.6 |
| Tanzania | 4.0 | 4.0 | 4.0 | 2.5 | 3.5 | 3.8 | 3.5 | 4.5 | 3.0 | 3.5 | 3.5 | 3.8 |
| Timor-Leste | 3.0 | 3.0 | 2.5 | 2.5 | 2.0 | 2.6 | 1.5 | 3.0 | 3.0 | 2.5 | 3.0 | 2.6 |
| Togo | 3.0 | 2.0 | 3.0 | 2.5 | 2.5 | 2.6 | 2.5 | 2.0 | 2.5 | 2.0 | 2.0 | 2.2 |
| Tonga | 2.5 | 3.5 | 4.0 | 3.0 | 3.0 | 3.2 | 3.5 | 2.5 | 3.0 | 2.5 | 2.0 | 2.7 |
| Uganda | 3.5 | 4.5 | 4.0 | 3.5 | 4.0 | 3.9 | 3.5 | 4.0 | 3.0 | 3.0 | 3.0 | 3.3 |
| Uzbekistan | 3.5 | 3.5 | 4.0 | 3.5 | 3.5 | 3.6 | 2.0 | 3.0 | 3.0 | 2.5 | 1.5 | 2.4 |
| Vanuatu | 3.0 | 3.5 | 2.5 | 2.0 | 3.0 | 2.8 | 3.0 | 3.5 | 3.5 | 2.5 | 3.0 | 3.1 |
| Vietnam | 4.5 | 4.5 | 4.0 | 3.0 | 3.5 | 3.9 | 3.5 | 4.0 | 3.5 | 3.5 | 3.0 | 3.5 |
| Yemen, Rep. | 2.5 | 3.5 | 3.0 | 3.5 | 3.0 | 3.1 | 2.5 | 3.0 | 3.0 | 3.0 | 3.0 | 2.9 |
| Zambia | 3.5 | 3.5 | 3.5 | 3.0 | 3.5 | 3.4 | 3.0 | 3.5 | 3.5 | 3.0 | 3.0 | 3.2 |
| Zimbabwe | 2.5 | 1.5 | 2.0 | 1.5 | 2.5 | 2.0 | 1.0 | 2.0 | 3.5 | 2.0 | 1.0 | 1.9 |

and institutions for environmental sustainability assess the extent to which environmental policies foster the protection and sustainable use of natural resources and the management of pollution. • Public sector management and institutions cluster: Property rights and rule-based governance assess the extent to which private economic activity is facilitated by an effective legal system and rule-based governance structure in which property and contract rights are reliably respected and enforced. • Quality of budgetary and financial management assesses the extent to which there is a comprehensive and credible budget linked to policy priorities, effective financial management systems, and timely and

accurate accounting and fiscal reporting, including timely and audited public accounts. • Efficiency of revenue mobilization assesses the overall pattern of revenue mobilization—not only the de facto tax structure, but also revenue from all sources as actually collected. • Quality of public administration assesses the extent to which civilian central government staff is structured to design and implement government policy and deliver services effectively. • Transparency, accountability, and corruption in the public sector assess the extent to which the executive can be held accountable for its use of funds and for the results of its actions by the electorate, the legislature, and the judiciary and the extent

to which public employees within the executive are required to account for administrative decisions, use of resources, and results obtained. The three main dimensions assessed are the accountability of the executive to oversight institutions and of public employees for their performance, access of civil society to information on public affairs, and state capture by narrow vested interests.

## Data sources

Data on public policies and institutions are from the World Bank Group's CPIA database available at www.worldbank.org/ida.

| | Roads | | | | Railways | | | Ports | Air | | |
|---|---|---|---|---|---|---|---|---|---|---|---|
| | Total road network km 2000–05ª | Paved roads % 2000–05ª | Passengers carried million passenger-km 2000–05ª | Goods hauled million ton-km 2000–05ª | Rail lines total route-km 2000–06ª | Passengers carried million passenger-km 2000–06ª | Goods hauled million ton-km 2000–06ª | Port container traffic thousand TEU 2006 | Registered carrier departures worldwide thousands 2006 | Passengers carried thousands 2006 | Air freight million ton-km 2006 |
| Afghanistan | 34,782 | 23.7 | .. | .. | 447 | 73 | 26 | .. | 4 | 213 | 0 |
| Albania | 18,000 | 39.0 | 197 | 2,200 | 447 | 73 | 26 | .. | 4 | 213 | 0 |
| Algeria | 108,302 | 70.2 | .. | .. | 3,572 | 929 | 1,471 | .. | 45 | 2,900 | 24 |
| Angola | 51,429 | 10.4 | 166,045 | 4,709 | 2,761 | | .. | .. | 5 | 263 | 81 |
| Argentina | 231,374 | 30.0 | .. | .. | .. | .. | .. | 1,758 | 74 | 6,612 | 125 |
| Armenia | 7,515 | 90.0 | 2,131 | 231 | 711 | 27 | 654 | | 6 | 606 | 7 |
| Australia | 812,972 | .. | 290,280 | 168,630 | 9,528 | 1,290 | 46,164 | 5,689 | 353 | 46,952 | 2,570 |
| Austria | 133,928 | 100.0 | 69,000 | 26,411 | 5,690 | 8,470 | 17,036 | .. | 150 | 8,785 | 572 |
| Azerbaijan | 59,141 | 49.4 | 10,892 | 7,536 | 2,122 | 878 | 10,067 | .. | 13 | 1,253 | 16 |
| Bangladesh | 239,226 | 9.5 | .. | .. | 2,855 | 4,164 | 817 | 904 | 8 | 1,729 | 191 |
| Belarus | 94,797 | 88.6 | 9,231 | 15,055 | 5,498 | 13,568 | 43,559 | .. | 6 | 307 | 1 |
| Belgium | 150,567 | 78.0 | 126,680 | 54,856 | 3,542 | 9,150 | 8,130 | 8,672 | 158 | 3,641 | 740 |
| Benin | 19,000 | 9.5 | .. | .. | 578 | 66 | 86 | .. | .. | .. | .. |
| Bolivia | 62,479 | 7.0 | .. | .. | .. | .. | .. | .. | 22 | 1,443 | 11 |
| Bosnia and Herzegovina | 21,846 | 52.3 | .. | 300 | 1,000 | 53 | 1,173 | .. | .. | .. | .. |
| Botswana | 24,455 | 33.2 | .. | .. | 888 | 171 | 842 | .. | 7 | 214 | 0 |
| Brazil | 1,751,868 | 5.5 | .. | .. | .. | .. | .. | 6,305 | 561 | 40,945 | 1,412 |
| Bulgaria | 44,033 | 99.0 | 14,401 | 6,840 | 4,154 | 2,389 | 5,164 | .. | 12 | 808 | 3 |
| Burkina Faso | 92,495 | 4.2 | .. | .. | 622 | | | .. | 2 | 73 | 0 |
| Burundi | 12,322 | 10.4 | .. | .. | .. | .. | .. | .. | .. | .. | .. |
| Cambodia | 38,257 | 6.3 | 201 | 3 | 650 | 45 | 92 | .. | 4 | 256 | 1 |
| Cameroon | 50,000 | 10.0 | .. | .. | 1,016 | 357 | 1,076 | .. | 11 | 425 | 29 |
| Canada | 1,408,900 | 39.9 | 493,814 | 184,774 | 67,346 | 1,430 | 445,689 | 4,309 | 1,042 | 46,727 | 1,503 |
| Central African Republic | 24,307 | .. | .. | .. | .. | .. | .. | .. | .. | .. | .. |
| Chad | 33,400 | 0.8 | .. | .. | .. | .. | .. | .. | .. | .. | .. |
| Chile | 79,604 | 20.2 | .. | .. | 2,035 | 737 | 1,241 | 2,127 | 95 | 6,017 | 1,028 |
| China | 1,930,544 | 81.6 | 929,210 | 869,320 | 62,200 | 666,200 | 2,170,700 | 84,686 | 1,543 | 158,013 | 7,692 |
| Hong Kong, China | 1,955 | 100.0 | | | | | | 23,539 | 130 | 21,796 | 8,326 |
| Colombia | 164,257 | .. | 157 | 38,199 | 2,137 | .. | 7,751 | 1,511 | 175 | 10,616 | 1,051 |
| Congo, Dem. Rep. | 153,497 | 1.8 | .. | .. | 3,641 | 140 | 444 | .. | .. | .. | .. |
| Congo, Rep. | 17,289 | 5.0 | .. | .. | 795 | 135 | 231 | .. | .. | .. | .. |
| Costa Rica | 35,330 | 24.4 | .. | .. | .. | .. | .. | 834 | 36 | 943 | 10 |
| Côte d'Ivoire | 80,000 | 8.1 | .. | .. | 639 | 10 | 129 | 710 | .. | .. | .. |
| Croatia | 28,472 | 84.4 | 3,403 | 9,328 | 2,726 | 1,266 | 2,835 | .. | 22 | 1,389 | 2 |
| Cuba | 60,856 | 49.0 | .. | .. | .. | .. | .. | .. | 12 | 812 | 30 |
| Czech Republic | 127,781 | 100.0 | 90,055 | 46,600 | 9,513 | 6,631 | 14,385 | .. | 75 | 4,922 | 39 |
| Denmark | 72,257 | 100.0 | 70,635 | 11,058 | 2,212 | 5,459 | 2,030 | 669 | 14 | 582 | 1 |
| Dominican Republic | 12,600 | 49.4 | .. | .. | 1,743 | .. | .. | 537 | .. | .. | .. |
| Ecuador | 43,197 | 15.0 | 10,641 | 5,453 | 966 | .. | .. | 671 | 31 | 2,110 | 6 |
| Egypt, Arab Rep. | 92,370 | 81.0 | .. | .. | 5,150 | 40,837 | 3,917 | 4,916 | 47 | 4,988 | 309 |
| El Salvador | 10,029 | 19.8 | .. | .. | 283 | .. | .. | .. | 25 | 2,579 | 20 |
| Eritrea | 4,010 | 21.8 | | | 306 | | | .. | .. | .. | .. |
| Estonia | 57,016 | 22.7 | 3,190 | 7,641 | 959 | 248 | 10,311 | .. | 8 | 598 | 1 |
| Ethiopia | 37,018 | 13.4 | 219,113 | 2,456 | .. | .. | .. | .. | 34 | 1,720 | 157 |
| Finland | 78,821 | 65.0 | 70,300 | 27,800 | 5,732 | 3,478 | 9,706 | 1,401 | 115 | 7,597 | 409 |
| France | 950,985 | 100.0 | 771,000 | 193,000 | 29,286 | 76,159 | 41,898 | 4,005 | 806 | 59,538 | 6,135 |
| Gabon | 9,170 | 10.2 | .. | .. | 810 | 95 | 2,219 | .. | 9 | 508 | 78 |
| Gambia, The | 3,742 | 19.3 | 16 | .. | .. | .. | .. | .. | .. | .. | .. |
| Georgia | 20,247 | 39.4 | 5,200 | 570 | 1,515 | 720 | 6,127 | .. | 5 | 272 | 3 |
| Germany | .. | 100.0 | 1,062,700 | 237,609 | 34,218 | 72,554 | 88,022 | 15,053 | 1,085 | 99,647 | 8,134 |
| Ghana | 57,613 | 17.9 | .. | .. | 977 | 85 | 242 | .. | 1 | 96 | 7 |
| Greece | 117,533 | 91.8 | .. | 18,360 | 2,576 | 1,854 | 613 | 1,769 | 133 | 9,481 | 71 |
| Guatemala | 14,095 | 34.5 | .. | .. | 886 | .. | .. | 800 | .. | .. | .. |
| Guinea | 44,348 | 9.8 | .. | .. | 1,115 | .. | .. | .. | .. | .. | .. |
| Guinea-Bissau | 3,455 | 27.9 | | | | | | .. | .. | .. | .. |
| Haiti | 4,160 | 24.3 | | | | | | | | | |

| | **Roads** | | | | **Railways** | | | **Ports** | **Air** | | |
|---|---|---|---|---|---|---|---|---|---|---|---|
| | Total road network km | Paved roads % | Passengers carried million passenger-km | Goods hauled million ton-km | Rail lines total route-km | Passengers carried million passenger-km | Goods hauled million ton-km | Port container traffic thousand TEU | Registered carrier departures worldwide thousands | Passengers carried thousands | Air freight million ton-km |
| | 2000–05[a] | 2000–05[a] | 2000–05[a] | 2000–05[a] | 2000–06[a] | 2000–06[a] | 2000–06[a] | 2006 | 2006 | 2006 | 2006 |
| Honduras | 13,600 | 20.4 | .. | .. | 699 | .. | .. | 553 | .. | .. | .. |
| Hungary | 159,568 | 43.9 | 13,300 | 12,505 | 7,730 | 6,953 | 8,537 | .. | 46 | 2,592 | 20 |
| India | 3,383,344 | 47.4 | .. | .. | 63,465 | 575,702 | 407,398 | 6,190 | 454 | 40,289 | 843 |
| Indonesia | 372,929 | 55.3 | .. | .. | .. | 14,345 | 4,430 | 3,740 | 357 | 29,867 | 469 |
| Iran, Islamic Rep. | 179,388 | 67.4 | .. | .. | 7,131 | 11,149 | 19,127 | 1,529 | 136 | 13,623 | 92 |
| Iraq | 45,550 | 84.3 | .. | .. | 1,963 | 570 | 1,682 | .. | .. | .. | .. |
| Ireland | 96,602 | 100.0 | .. | 15,900 | 1,919 | 1,781 | 303 | 1,065 | 350 | 50,738 | 131 |
| Israel | 17,589 | 100.0 | .. | .. | 899 | 1,618 | 1,149 | 1,774 | 36 | 4,357 | 1,124 |
| Italy | 484,688 | 100.0 | 97,560 | 192,700 | 16,225 | 46,144 | 20,131 | 9,963 | 448 | 36,709 | 1,377 |
| Jamaica | 21,532 | 73.9 | .. | .. | 272 | .. | .. | 2,150 | 21 | 1,527 | 15 |
| Japan | 1,177,278 | 77.7 | 947,562 | 327,632 | 20,052 | 245,957 | 22,632 | 18,274 | 670 | 102,845 | 8,480 |
| Jordan | 7,601 | 100.0 | .. | .. | 293 | .. | 1,024 | .. | 27 | 2,046 | 259 |
| Kazakhstan | 90,800 | 83.0 | 91,651 | 47,100 | 14,205 | 12,129 | 191,200 | .. | 19 | 1,283 | 16 |
| Kenya | 63,265 | 14.1 | .. | 22 | 1,917 | 226 | 1,399 | .. | 29 | 2,685 | 301 |
| Korea, Dem. Rep. | 31,200 | 6.4 | .. | .. | 5,214 | .. | .. | .. | 2 | 105 | 2 |
| Korea, Rep. | 102,293 | 76.8 | 91,665 | 12,545 | 3,392 | 31,004 | 10,108 | 15,711 | 224 | 34,843 | 7,752 |
| Kuwait | 5,749 | 85.0 | .. | .. | .. | .. | .. | 750 | 21 | 2,628 | 239 |
| Kyrgyz Republic | 18,500 | 91.1 | 5,874 | 1,336 | 424 | 50 | 561 | .. | 5 | 219 | 1 |
| Lao PDR | 31,210 | 14.4 | .. | .. | .. | .. | .. | .. | 10 | 327 | 3 |
| Latvia | 69,829 | 100.0 | 2,869 | 2,767 | 2,375 | 894 | 17,921 | .. | 29 | 1,410 | 13 |
| Lebanon | 6,970 | .. | .. | .. | 401 | .. | .. | .. | 11 | 969 | 74 |
| Lesotho | 5,940 | 18.3 | .. | .. | .. | .. | .. | .. | .. | .. | .. |
| Liberia | 10,600 | 6.2 | .. | .. | 490 | .. | .. | .. | .. | .. | .. |
| Libya | 83,200 | 57.2 | .. | .. | 2,757 | .. | .. | .. | 13 | 1,152 | 0 |
| Lithuania | 79,497 | 78.2 | 38,484 | 15,908 | 1,772 | 428 | 12,457 | .. | 11 | 430 | 1 |
| Macedonia, FYR | 13,182 | .. | 842 | 4,100 | 699 | 94 | 441 | .. | 2 | 209 | 0 |
| Madagascar | 49,827 | 11.6 | .. | .. | 732 | 10 | 12 | .. | 14 | 573 | 19 |
| Malawi | 15,451 | 45.0 | .. | .. | 710 | 26 | 38 | .. | 6 | 146 | 2 |
| Malaysia | 98,721 | 81.3 | .. | .. | 1,667 | 1,181 | 1,178 | 13,419 | 164 | 17,833 | 2,597 |
| Mali | 18,709 | 18.0 | .. | .. | 733 | 196 | 189 | .. | .. | .. | .. |
| Mauritania | 7,660 | 11.3 | .. | .. | 717 | .. | .. | .. | 2 | 149 | 0 |
| Mauritius | 2,015 | 100.0 | .. | .. | .. | .. | .. | .. | 14 | 1,056 | 195 |
| Mexico | 355,796 | 37.0 | 422,915 | 204,217 | .. | .. | .. | 2,680 | 318 | 21,243 | 457 |
| Moldova | 12,737 | 86.3 | 1,640 | 1,577 | 1,075 | 355 | 2,980 | .. | 4 | 274 | 1 |
| Mongolia | 49,250 | 3.5 | 557 | 242 | 1,810 | 1,228 | 8,857 | .. | 6 | 348 | 6 |
| Morocco | 57,626 | 61.9 | .. | 1,256 | 1,907 | 2,987 | 5,919 | 561 | 55 | 4,109 | 51 |
| Mozambique | 30,400 | 18.7 | .. | .. | 3,070 | 172 | 768 | .. | 10 | 350 | 5 |
| Myanmar | 27,966 | 11.4 | .. | .. | .. | .. | .. | .. | 29 | 1,621 | 3 |
| Namibia | 42,237 | 12.8 | 47 | 591 | .. | .. | .. | .. | 7 | 401 | 0 |
| Nepal | 17,280 | 56.9 | .. | .. | 59 | .. | .. | .. | 7 | 510 | 7 |
| Netherlands | 126,100 | 90.0 | .. | 77,100 | 2,813 | 14,730 | 4,331 | 10,044 | 251 | 27,454 | 4,959 |
| New Zealand | 93,460 | 64.9 | .. | .. | .. | .. | 4,078 | 1,718 | 221 | 12,382 | 819 |
| Nicaragua | 18,669 | 11.4 | .. | .. | 6 | .. | .. | .. | .. | .. | .. |
| Niger | 18,423 | 20.6 | .. | .. | .. | .. | .. | .. | .. | .. | .. |
| Nigeria | 193,200 | 15.0 | .. | .. | 3,528 | 174 | 77 | 513 | 16 | 1,308 | 11 |
| Norway | 92,864 | 77.5 | 58,247 | 14,966 | 4,087 | 2,440 | 9,568 | .. | 254 | 12,277 | 177 |
| Oman | 34,965 | 27.7 | .. | .. | .. | .. | .. | 2,620 | 32 | 3,267 | 235 |
| Pakistan | 258,340 | 64.7 | 209,959 | .. | 7,791 | 24,237 | 5,013 | 1,699 | 51 | 5,715 | 427 |
| Panama | 11,643 | 34.6 | .. | .. | 355 | .. | .. | 3,383 | 33 | 2,029 | 36 |
| Papua New Guinea | 19,600 | 3.5 | .. | .. | .. | .. | .. | .. | 22 | 919 | 22 |
| Paraguay | 29,500 | 50.8 | .. | .. | 441 | .. | .. | .. | 10 | 433 | 0 |
| Peru | 78,829 | 14.4 | .. | .. | .. | .. | .. | 1,085 | 56 | 4,218 | 112 |
| Philippines | 200,037 | 9.9 | .. | .. | 491 | 144 | 1 | 3,596 | 62 | 8,305 | 319 |
| Poland | 423,997 | 69.7 | 29,314 | 119,740 | 19,507 | 16,742 | 45,438 | 428 | 83 | 3,626 | 80 |
| Portugal | 78,470 | 86.0 | .. | 23,187 | 2,839 | 3,412 | 2,422 | 1,012 | 120 | 9,441 | 294 |
| Puerto Rico | 25,645 | 95.0 | .. | 10 | 96 | .. | .. | 1,729 | .. | .. | .. |

| | Roads | | | | Railways | | | Ports | Air | | |
|---|---|---|---|---|---|---|---|---|---|---|---|
| | Total road network km | Paved roads % | Passengers carried million passenger-km | Goods hauled million ton-km | Rail lines total route-km | Passengers carried million passenger-km | Goods hauled million ton-km | Port container traffic thousand TEU | Registered carrier departures worldwide thousands | Passengers carried thousands | Air freight million ton-km |
| | 2000–05[a] | 2000–05[a] | 2000–05[a] | 2000–05[a] | 2000–06[a] | 2000–06[a] | 2000–06[a] | 2006 | 2006 | 2006 | 2006 |
| Romania | 198,817 | 30.2 | 9,438 | 37,220 | 10,844 | 7,960 | 16,032 | 1,018 | 43 | 2,047 | 5 |
| Russian Federation | 537,289 | .. | .. | 25,200 | 85,245 | 177,639 | 1,950,900 | 2,326 | 421 | 28,837 | 1,926 |
| Rwanda | 14,008 | 19.0 | .. | .. | .. | .. | .. | .. | .. | .. | .. |
| Saudi Arabia | 152,044 | 29.9 | .. | .. | 1,020 | 393 | 1,192 | 3,919 | 132 | 16,831 | 1,066 |
| Senegal | 13,576 | 29.3 | .. | .. | 906 | 88 | 265 | | 0 | 501 | 0 |
| Serbia | 45,290 | 62.4 | 3,865 | 3,100 | 3,809 | 852 | 3,482 | | 20 | 1,042 | 4 |
| Sierra Leone | 11,300 | 8.0 | .. | .. | .. | .. | .. | | 0 | 19 | 10 |
| Singapore | 3,234 | 100.0 | .. | .. | .. | .. | .. | 24,792 | 85 | 19,566 | 7,981 |
| Slovak Republic | 43,000 | 87.3 | 32,214 | 18,517 | 3,659 | 2,166 | 9,326 | .. | 15 | 780 | 0 |
| Slovenia | 38,485 | 100.0 | 848 | 11,033 | 1,228 | 777 | 3,245 | .. | 20 | 861 | 2 |
| Somalia | 22,100 | 11.8 | .. | .. | .. | .. | .. | .. | .. | .. | .. |
| South Africa | 364,131 | 17.3 | .. | 434 | 20,247 | 991 | 109,721 | 3,552 | 147 | 12,933 | 1,233 |
| Spain | 666,292 | 99.0 | 397,117 | 132,868 | 14,484 | 21,047 | 11,586 | 10,033 | 603 | 53,122 | 1,100 |
| Sri Lanka | 97,286 | 81.0 | 21,067 | .. | 1,200 | 4,358 | 135 | 3,079 | 21 | 3,101 | 325 |
| Sudan | 11,900 | 36.3 | .. | .. | 5,478 | 40 | 766 | .. | 9 | 563 | 51 |
| Swaziland | 3,594 | 30.0 | .. | .. | 301 | | 11,394 | .. | .. | .. | .. |
| Sweden | 425,383 | 31.5 | 112,010 | 39,373 | 9,867 | 5,673 | 13,120 | 1,281 | 190 | 11,624 | 257 |
| Switzerland | 71,296 | 100.0 | 97,996 | 15,753 | 3,011 | 13,830 | 8,571 | .. | 125 | 10,647 | 1,039 |
| Syrian Arab Republic | 94,890 | 20.1 | 589 | .. | 1,888 | 607 | 2,256 | .. | 17 | 1,252 | 16 |
| Tajikistan | 27,767 | .. | .. | .. | 616 | 50 | 1,117 | .. | 3 | 394 | 13 |
| Tanzania | 78,891 | 8.6 | .. | .. | 4,582[b] | 946[b] | 1,990[b] | .. | 5 | 190 | 2 |
| Thailand | 57,403 | 98.5 | .. | .. | 4,044 | 9,195 | 4,037 | 5,574 | 127 | 20,102 | 2,107 |
| Timor-Leste | .. | .. | .. | .. | .. | .. | .. | .. | .. | .. | .. |
| Togo | 7,520 | 31.6 | .. | .. | 568 | | | | .. | .. | .. |
| Trinidad and Tobago | 8,320 | 51.1 | .. | .. | .. | .. | .. | | 14 | 1,024 | 46 |
| Tunisia | 19,232 | 65.8 | .. | 16,611 | 1,909 | 1,319 | 2,067 | | 22 | 2,055 | 19 |
| Turkey | 426,914 | .. | 182,152 | 166,831 | 8,697 | 6,183 | 9,078 | 3,648 | 177 | 19,361 | 464 |
| Turkmenistan | 24,000 | 81.2 | .. | .. | 2,529 | 1,286 | 8,670 | .. | 16 | 1,843 | 10 |
| Uganda | 70,746 | 23.0 | .. | .. | 259 | | 218 | .. | 0 | 55 | 34 |
| Ukraine | 169,323 | 97.4 | 51,820 | 23,895 | 22,001 | 52,655 | 223,980 | 730 | 49 | 2,802 | 44 |
| United Arab Emirates | 4,030 | 100.0 | .. | .. | .. | .. | .. | 10,967 | 87 | 14,314 | 3,734 |
| United Kingdom | 388,008 | 100.0 | 736,000 | 163,000 | 15,810 | 43,200 | 22,110 | 8,226 | 1,037 | 97,545 | 6,215 |
| United States | 6,544,257 | 65.3 | 7,814,575 | 2,116,532 | 153,787 | 47,717 | 2,589,349[c] | 40,875 | 9,739[d] | 725,531[d] | 39,882[d] |
| Uruguay | 77,732 | 10.0 | .. | .. | 3,003 | 12 | 331 | .. | 9 | 569 | 4 |
| Uzbekistan | 81,600 | 87.3 | .. | 1,200 | 4,014 | 2,012 | 18,007 | .. | 22 | 1,665 | 68 |
| Venezuela, RB | 96,155 | 33.6 | .. | .. | 336 | .. | 54 | 1,218 | 140 | 5,226 | 2 |
| Vietnam | 222,179 | .. | .. | .. | 2,671 | 4,558 | 2,928 | 3,000 | 51 | 5,284 | 216 |
| West Bank and Gaza | 4,996 | 100.0 | .. | .. | .. | .. | .. | .. | .. | .. | .. |
| Yemen, Rep. | 71,300 | 8.7 | .. | .. | .. | .. | .. | .. | 19 | 1,162 | 66 |
| Zambia | 91,440 | 22.0 | .. | .. | 1,273 | 183 | .. | .. | 6 | 59 | 0 |
| Zimbabwe | 97,267 | 19.0 | .. | .. | .. | .. | .. | .. | 7 | 239 | 9 |
| **World** | **35.9 m** | .. m | .. m | .. s | **2,278 m** | **7,751 m** | **414,087 s** | **24,843 s** | **2,072,237 s** | **143,212 s** | |
| **Low income** | 12.1 | .. | .. | | | | | 9,772 | 846 | 69,322 | 2,469 |
| **Middle income** | 44.0 | .. | .. | | 1,286 | 5,542 | 158,956 | 5,580 | 467,938 | 23,065 | |
| Lower middle income | 65.8 | .. | .. | | 1,286 | 3,449 | 114,068 | 3,034 | 285,540 | 13,248 | |
| Upper middle income | 34.1 | .. | .. | | 1,716 | 9,202 | 44,888 | 2,546 | 182,398 | 9,817 | |
| **Low & middle income** | 26.8 | .. | .. | | | | 170,749 | 6,426 | 537,260 | 25,535 | |
| East Asia & Pacific | 11.4 | .. | .. | | 4,558 | 1,902 | 114,016 | 2,454 | 244,449 | 13,538 | |
| Europe & Central Asia | .. | 9,859 | 13,124 | 196,529 | 1,286 | 8,874 | 5,530 | 1,032 | 73,664 | 2,700 | |
| Latin America & Carib. | 24.3 | .. | .. | | | | 24,523 | 1,621 | 107,627 | 4,346 | |
| Middle East & N. Africa | 70.2 | .. | .. | | | 2,256 | | 392 | 34,257 | 909 | |
| South Asia | 56.9 | .. | .. | | 14,297 | 2,915 | 11,872 | 549 | 51,488 | 1,793 | |
| Sub-Saharan Africa | 11.9 | .. | .. | | | | | 378 | 25,776 | 2,249 | |
| **High income** | 90.9 | .. | 51,147 | | 6,152 | 10,311 | 243,338 | 18,417 | 1,534,977 | 117,678 | |
| Euro area | 100.0 | 126,680 | 51,147 | 120,827 | 8,810 | 9,706 | 64,550 | 4,314 | 371,383 | 29,254 | |

a. Data are for the latest year available in the period shown. b. Includes Tazara railway. c. Refers to Class 1 railways only. d. Covers only carriers designated by the U.S. Department of Transportation as major and national air carriers.

Transport infrastructure—highways, railways, ports and waterways, and airports and air traffic control systems—and the services that flow from it are crucial to the activities of households, producers, and governments. Because performance indicators vary widely by transport mode and focus (whether physical infrastructure or the services flowing from that infrastructure), highly specialized and carefully specified indicators are required. The table provides selected indicators of the size, extent, and productivity of roads, railways, and air transport systems and of the volume of traffic in these modes as well as in ports.

Data for transport sectors are not always internationally comparable. Unlike for demographic statistics, national income accounts, and international trade data, the collection of infrastructure data has not been "internationalized." But data on roads are collected by the International Road Federation (IRF), and data on air transport by the International Civil Aviation Organization (ICAO).

National road associations are the primary source of IRF data. In countries where a national road association is lacking or does not respond, other agencies are contacted, such as road directorates, ministries of transport or public works, or central statistical offices. As a result, definitions and data collection methods and quality differ, and the compiled data are of uneven quality. Moreover, the quality of transport service (reliability, transit time, and condition of goods delivered) is rarely measured, though it may be as important as quantity in assessing an economy's transport system. Several new initiatives are under way to improve data availability and consistency. The IRF is collaborating with national and international development agencies to improve the quality and coverage of road statistics. To improve measures of progress and performance, the World Bank is also working on better measures of access, affordability, efficiency, quality, and fiscal and institutional aspects of infrastructure.

Unlike the road sector, where numerous qualified motor vehicle operators can operate anywhere on the road network, railways are a restricted transport system with vehicles confined to a fixed guideway. Considering the cost and service characteristics, railways generally are best suited to carry—and can effectively compete for—bulk commodities and containerized freight for distances of 500–5,000 kilometers, and passengers for distances of 50–1,000 kilometers. Below these limits road transport tends to be more competitive, while above these limits

air transport for passengers and freight and sea transport for freight tend to be more competitive. The railways indicators in the table focus on scale and output measures: total route-kilometers, passenger-kilometers, and goods (freight) hauled in ton-kilometers.

Measures of port container traffic, much of it commodities of medium to high value added, give some indication of economic growth in a country. But when traffic is merely transshipment, much of the economic benefit goes to the terminal operator and ancillary services for ships and containers rather than to the country more broadly. In transshipment centers empty containers may account for as much as 40 percent of traffic.

The air transport data represent the total (international and domestic) scheduled traffic carried by the air carriers registered in a country. Countries submit air transport data to ICAO on the basis of standard instructions and definitions issued by ICAO. In many cases, however, the data include estimates by ICAO for nonreporting carriers. Where possible, these estimates are based on previous submissions supplemented by information published by the air carriers, such as flight schedules.

The data cover the air traffic carried on scheduled services, but changes in air transport regulations in Europe have made it more difficult to classify traffic as scheduled or nonscheduled. Thus recent increases shown for some European countries may be due to changes in the classification of air traffic rather than actual growth. For countries with few air carriers or only one, the addition or discontinuation of a home-based air carrier may cause significant changes in air traffic.

• **Total road network** covers motorways, highways, main or national roads, secondary or regional roads, and all other roads in a country. • **Paved roads** are roads surfaced with crushed stone (macadam) and hydrocarbon binder or bituminized agents, with concrete, or with cobblestones. • **Passengers carried by road** are the number of passengers transported by road times kilometers traveled. • **Goods hauled by road** are the volume of goods transported by road vehicles, measured in millions of metric tons times kilometers traveled. • **Rail lines** are the length of railway route available for train service, irrespective of the number of parallel tracks. • **Passengers carried by railway** are the number of passengers transported by rail times kilometers traveled. • **Goods hauled by railway** are the volume of goods transported by railway, measured in metric tons times kilometers traveled. • **Port container traffic** measures the flow of containers from land to sea transport modes and vice versa in twenty-foot-equivalent units (TEUs), a standard-size container. Data cover coastal shipping as well as international journeys. Transshipment traffic is counted as two lifts at the intermediate port (once to off-load and again as an outbound lift) and includes empty units. • **Registered carrier departures worldwide** are domestic takeoffs and takeoffs abroad of air carriers registered in the country. • **Passengers carried by air** include both domestic and international passengers of air carriers registered in the country. • **Air freight** is the volume of freight, express, and diplomatic bags carried on each flight stage (operation of an aircraft from takeoff to its next landing), measured in metric tons times kilometers traveled.

**Data sources**

Data on roads are from the IRF's *World Road Statistics*, supplemented by World Bank staff estimates. Data on railways are from a database maintained by the World Bank's Transport and Urban Development Department, Transport Division, based on data from the International Union of Railways. Data on port container traffic are from Containerisation International's *Containerisation International Yearbook*. Data on air transport are from the ICAO's *Civil Aviation Statistics of the World* and ICAO staff estimates.

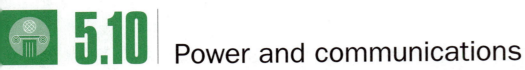

| | Electric power | | Telephones | | | | | | | | | |
|---|---|---|---|---|---|---|---|---|---|---|---|---|
| | | | Access | | | | Quality | Affordability and efficiency | | | | |
| | | Transmission and distribution losses % of output | per 100 people | | Population covered by mobile telephony[a] % | International voice traffic[a] minutes per person | Faults per 100 mainlines[a] | $ per month | | Cost of call to U.S.[a] $ per 3 minutes | Telecom-munications revenue[a] % of GDP | Subscrib-ers per employee[a] |
| | Consumption per capita kWh | | Fixed mainlines[a] | Mobile subscribers[a] | | | | Price basket for residential fixed line[b] | Price basket for mobile[a] | | | |
| | 2005 | 2005 | 2006 | 2006 | 2006 | 2006 | 2006 | 2006 | 2006 | 2005 | 2006 | 2006 |
| Afghanistan | .. | .. | 1 | 10 | .. | 1 | 25.0 | 0.1 | 10.8 | 0.39 | 5.1 | 60 |
| Albania | 1,167 | 39 | 11 | 49 | 97 | 160 | .. | 5.1 | 22.1 | 1.34 | .. | 623 |
| Algeria | 899 | 13 | 9 | 63 | 75 | 17 | 0.8 | 6.3 | 7.5 | 2.08 | 4.7 | 302 |
| Angola | 141 | 14 | 1 | 14 | .. | .. | .. | .. | 12.2 | 3.23 | 2.0 | 586 |
| Argentina | 2,418 | 15 | 24 | 81 | .. | 33 | .. | 6.8 | 7.8 | .. | 3.4 | 972 |
| Armenia | 1,503 | 16 | 20 | 11 | 88 | 128 | 64.4 | 2.4 | 8.7 | 2.42 | 3.0 | 173 |
| Australia | 11,481 | 7 | 48 | 95 | 98 | .. | 12.0 | 30.5 | 18.2 | .. | 3.6 | 317 |
| Austria | 7,889 | 5 | 43 | 112 | 99 | .. | 5.7 | 29.0 | 23.2 | 0.71 | 2.3 | 642 |
| Azerbaijan | 2,407 | 10 | 14 | 39 | 99 | 33 | 48.1 | 5.3 | 15.1 | 4.18 | 1.3 | 229 |
| Bangladesh | 136 | 8 | 1 | 12 | 90 | 6 | .. | 4.0 | 2.6 | 2.02 | 1.5 | .. |
| Belarus | 3,209 | 12 | 35 | 61 | 93 | 64 | 23.1 | 1.6 | 11.8 | 1.90 | 2.1 | 280 |
| Belgium | 8,510 | 5 | 45 | 92 | 99 | .. | 6.3 | 33.1 | 18.5 | 0.75 | 3.2 | 634 |
| Benin | 69 | .. | 1 | 12 | .. | 6 | 7.5 | 16.1 | 13.0 | 4.80 | 1.6 | 621 |
| Bolivia | 479 | 16 | 7 | 29 | .. | 49 | .. | 8.5 | 5.6 | .. | 5.7 | 810 |
| Bosnia and Herzegovina | 2,316 | 18 | 25 | 48 | 97 | 208 | .. | 6.3 | 6.6 | 3.62 | 5.5 | 366 |
| Botswana | 1,406 | 15 | 7 | 53 | 99 | 74 | .. | 10.2 | 8.7 | 2.88 | 2.6 | 1,101 |
| Brazil | 2,008 | 17 | 20 | 53 | 88 | .. | 1.6 | 15.6 | 26.2 | 0.71 | 3.4 | 1,545 |
| Bulgaria | 4,121 | 11 | 31 | 107 | 100 | 72 | 2.8 | 10.0 | 16.2 | 0.57 | 6.2 | 347 |
| Burkina Faso | .. | .. | 1 | 7 | 26 | 11 | 18.4 | 16.9 | 12.8 | 1.14 | 3.7 | 440 |
| Burundi | .. | .. | 0 | 2 | .. | .. | .. | 2.6 | 12.2 | 2.45 | .. | 234 |
| Cambodia | .. | .. | 0 | 8 | .. | 10 | .. | .. | 5.1 | 2.94 | .. | .. |
| Cameroon | 196 | 16 | 1 | 13 | 73 | 9 | .. | 9.3 | 16.3 | .. | 3.1 | 730 |
| Canada | 17,285 | 7 | 64 | 53 | 97 | .. | .. | .. | 6.9 | .. | 2.5 | 425 |
| Central African Republic | .. | .. | 0 | 2 | .. | .. | .. | .. | 12.4 | 1.99 | 1.1 | .. |
| Chad | .. | .. | 0 | 4 | .. | .. | .. | 16.9 | 13.2 | .. | .. | .. |
| Chile | 3,074 | 4 | 20 | 76 | 100 | 48 | .. | 9.7 | 11.8 | .. | .. | .. |
| China | 1,781 | 7 | 28 | 35 | .. | 7 | .. | .. | 2.9 | 2.90 | 3.1 | 1,043 |
| Hong Kong, China | 5,878 | 13 | 56 | 136 | 100 | 1,179 | 1.3 | 12.6 | 2.2 | 0.77 | 3.7 | 657 |
| Colombia | 890 | 19 | 17 | 65 | 80 | 68 | 27.9 | 8.0 | 10.4 | .. | 5.3 | .. |
| Congo, Dem. Rep. | 91 | 4 | 0 | 7 | 50 | 5 | .. | .. | 11.0 | .. | 6.4 | 1,428 |
| Congo, Rep. | 160 | 56 | 0 | 14 | 80 | .. | .. | .. | 11.0 | 5.39 | 2.9 | .. |
| Costa Rica | 1,719 | 10 | 31 | 33 | 86 | 127 | 3.8 | 6.0 | 1.9 | .. | 2.4 | 459 |
| Côte d'Ivoire | 170 | 18 | 1 | 21 | 55 | 17 | .. | 22.5 | 21.8 | 2.25 | 5.4 | 1,442 |
| Croatia | 3,475 | 17 | 41 | 101 | 100 | 231 | 12.0 | 13.1 | 14.5 | .. | 5.5 | 540 |
| Cuba | 1,152 | 15 | 9 | 1 | 71 | 31 | 9.2 | 13.1 | 22.6 | 7.49 | 2.6 | 58 |
| Czech Republic | 6,343 | 6 | 31 | 118 | 100 | 95 | 6.1 | 24.1 | 17.2 | 1.06 | 3.9 | 768 |
| Denmark | 6,663 | 4 | 57 | 107 | .. | 318 | .. | 30.7 | 6.0 | 0.89 | 2.6 | 474 |
| Dominican Republic | 1,000 | 27 | 9 | 48 | 90 | .. | .. | 18.2 | 8.6 | 0.22 | 0.5 | .. |
| Ecuador | 714 | 43 | 13 | 64 | 67 | 216 | 3.8 | 7.9 | 18.9 | .. | 3.8 | 660 |
| Egypt, Arab Rep. | 1,245 | 16 | 15 | 24 | 98 | 30 | 0.1 | 4.0 | 5.8 | 1.45 | 3.8 | 443 |
| El Salvador | 666 | 13 | 15 | 57 | 95 | 410 | 1.7 | 2.0 | 8.5 | 2.40 | 4.6 | 1,182 |
| Eritrea | .. | .. | 1 | 1 | .. | 9 | 73.7 | 6.2 | .. | 3.59 | 2.4 | 80 |
| Estonia | 5,567 | 11 | 40 | 124 | 99 | 109 | .. | 15.6 | 8.6 | 0.90 | 5.4 | 641 |
| Ethiopia | 34 | 10 | 1 | 1 | .. | 3 | .. | 2.2 | 3.1 | 4.01 | 2.4 | 142 |
| Finland | 16,120 | 4 | 36 | 108 | 99 | .. | .. | 28.7 | 6.7 | 1.80 | 2.7 | 451 |
| France | 7,938 | 6 | 55 | 84 | 99 | 183 | .. | 29.0 | 29.4 | 0.84 | 2.3 | 582 |
| Gabon | 999 | 18 | 3 | 58 | 78 | 74 | 13.4 | 32.4 | 14.9 | 2.77 | 1.5 | 244 |
| Gambia, The | .. | .. | 3 | 24 | .. | .. | .. | .. | .. | 1.81 | .. | .. |
| Georgia | 1,672 | 16 | 12 | 38 | 96 | .. | .. | 9.7 | 44.1 | .. | 7.3 | 197 |
| Germany | 7,111 | 5 | 66 | 102 | 99 | .. | .. | 26.5 | 17.0 | 0.43 | 2.9 | 559 |
| Ghana | 266 | 14 | 2 | 23 | 69 | 20 | 5.6 | 9.8 | 7.0 | 0.39 | .. | 563 |
| Greece | 5,242 | 9 | 55 | 100 | 100 | 182 | 12.8 | 21.1 | 23.1 | 1.09 | 3.4 | 632 |
| Guatemala | 522 | 8 | 10 | 55 | .. | 195 | .. | 9.8 | 6.1 | 1.21 | .. | .. |
| Guinea | .. | .. | 0 | 2 | .. | .. | .. | .. | 7.7 | .. | .. | .. |
| Guinea-Bissau | .. | .. | 1 | 6 | .. | .. | .. | .. | 21.9 | .. | .. | .. |
| Haiti | 37 | 38 | 2 | 5 | .. | .. | .. | .. | 4.5 | 2.15 | .. | .. |

# Power and communications

| | Electric power | | Telephones | | | | | | | | | |
|---|---|---|---|---|---|---|---|---|---|---|---|---|
| | | | Access | | | International | Quality | Affordability and efficiency | | | | |
| | Consumption per capita kWh | Transmission and distribution losses % of output | per 100 people Fixed mainlines[a] | per 100 people Mobile subscribers[a] | Population covered by mobile telephony[a] % | voice traffic[a] minutes per person | Faults per 100 mainlines[a] | $ per month Price basket for residential fixed line[b] | Price basket for mobile[a] | Cost of call to U.S.[a] $ per 3 minutes | Telecommunications revenue[a] % of GDP | Subscribers per employee[a] |
| | 2005 | 2005 | 2006 | 2006 | 2006 | 2006 | 2006 | 2006 | 2006 | 2005 | 2006 | 2006 |
| Honduras | 626 | 24 | 10 | 32 | .. | 96 | .. | 5.9 | 10.8 | 2.52 | 7.1 | 187 |
| Hungary | 3,771 | 11 | 33 | 99 | 99 | 105 | 8.2 | 23.6 | 12.1 | 1.01 | 4.4 | 780 |
| India | 480 | 25 | 4 | 15 | 61 | .. | .. | 3.3 | 2.5 | 1.19 | 2.0 | .. |
| Indonesia | 509 | 12 | 7 | 29 | 90 | 5 | .. | 5.8 | 4.3 | 2.79 | 2.2 | 1,084 |
| Iran, Islamic Rep. | 2,117 | 19 | 31 | 19 | 90 | 9 | .. | 2.1 | 2.7 | 0.55 | 1.4 | 856 |
| Iraq | 1,188 | 6 | 4 | 2 | 72 | .. | .. | 2.6 | .. | .. | .. | .. |
| Ireland | 6,234 | 8 | 49 | 110 | 99 | .. | 3.2 | 39.5 | 19.3 | 0.71 | 2.4 | 406 |
| Israel | 6,759 | 3 | 43 | 119 | 100 | 364 | .. | 10.5 | 9.3 | 0.59 | 4.2 | 692 |
| Italy | 5,669 | 7 | 43 | 122 | 100 | .. | .. | 24.9 | 14.1 | 0.79 | 3.0 | 1,116 |
| Jamaica | 2,474 | 12 | 12 | 106 | 95 | .. | .. | 9.1 | 7.5 | 0.87 | 4.9 | .. |
| Japan | 8,233 | 5 | 43 | 80 | 99 | 43 | 0.0 | 26.1 | 20.4 | 1.63 | 3.7 | 1,722 |
| Jordan | 1,676 | 14 | 11 | 78 | 99 | 139 | 7.9 | 10.0 | 6.9 | 1.44 | 7.8 | 707 |
| Kazakhstan | 3,206 | 10 | 19 | 51 | .. | .. | .. | .. | 11.4 | .. | 2.6 | 98 |
| Kenya | 138 | 18 | 1 | 18 | .. | 6 | 145.4 | 13.9 | 16.6 | 3.00 | 4.6 | 220 |
| Korea, Dem. Rep. | 817 | 16 | .. | .. | .. | .. | .. | .. | .. | .. | .. | .. |
| Korea, Rep. | 7,779 | 4 | 55 | 83 | 99 | 92 | .. | 8.3 | 14.2 | 0.76 | 4.9 | .. |
| Kuwait | 15,345 | 11 | 20 | 94 | 100 | .. | 4.0 | 10.5 | 75.0 | 1.51 | 3.4 | 387 |
| Kyrgyz Republic | 1,842 | 26 | 9 | 11 | 90 | 30 | .. | 4.7 | 6.4 | 5.40 | 4.5 | 134 |
| Lao PDR | .. | .. | 1 | 11 | 55 | 7 | .. | 3.8 | .. | 1.11 | 1.7 | 496 |
| Latvia | 2,702 | 17 | 29 | 95 | 98 | 67 | 1.1 | 13.3 | 9.3 | 1.63 | 3.9 | 731 |
| Lebanon | 2,242 | 16 | 17 | 27 | 100 | 279 | .. | 15.0 | 20.1 | 2.19 | 5.0 | .. |
| Lesotho | .. | .. | 2 | 13 | 29 | 18 | 60.0 | 18.4 | 14.8 | 3.28 | .. | 1,111 |
| Liberia | .. | .. | .. | 5 | .. | .. | .. | .. | .. | .. | .. | .. |
| Libya | 3,299 | 13 | 8 | 65 | 71 | 66 | .. | 1.9 | 6.1 | .. | .. | 1,566 |
| Lithuania | 3,104 | 8 | 23 | 139 | 100 | 49 | 9.3 | 17.7 | 8.9 | 1.55 | 3.3 | .. |
| Macedonia, FYR | 3,417 | 23 | 24 | 70 | 99 | 63 | 9.0 | 10.5 | 14.8 | .. | 7.1 | .. |
| Madagascar | .. | .. | 1 | 5 | .. | 1 | .. | 10.5 | 8.1 | 0.59 | 2.6 | .. |
| Malawi | .. | .. | 1 | 3 | .. | .. | .. | 5.8 | 10.2 | .. | 3.3 | .. |
| Malaysia | 3,262 | 4 | 17 | 75 | .. | .. | 22.5 | 8.7 | 5.0 | 0.71 | 4.6 | 770 |
| Mali | .. | .. | 1 | 13 | .. | .. | .. | 16.1 | 13.5 | .. | 5.2 | .. |
| Mauritania | .. | .. | 1 | 35 | .. | .. | 5.5 | 11.6 | .. | .. | 5.9 | 1,003 |
| Mauritius | .. | .. | 29 | 62 | 100 | 150 | 23.0 | 7.9 | 4.2 | 1.59 | 3.7 | 492 |
| Mexico | 1,899 | 16 | 19 | 55 | 100 | 174 | 1.4 | 16.1 | 13.9 | 0.83 | 3.0 | 691 |
| Moldova | 1,428 | 38 | 27 | 35 | 97 | 110 | 5.1 | 5.3 | 17.1 | 1.46 | 10.2 | 250 |
| Mongolia | .. | .. | 6 | 22 | .. | 5 | 18.5 | 1.6 | 5.4 | .. | 3.6 | 147 |
| Morocco | 644 | 18 | 4 | 52 | 98 | 65 | 25.0 | 23.0 | 15.9 | 1.69 | 4.5 | 821 |
| Mozambique | 450 | 12 | 0 | 11 | .. | 13 | 46.0 | 13.1 | 10.0 | 1.17 | 1.5 | 980 |
| Myanmar | 82 | 35 | 1 | 0 | .. | 3 | 125.0 | 1.3 | .. | 0.17 | 0.6 | 81 |
| Namibia | 1,428 | 18 | 7 | 25 | 88 | .. | 35.0 | 9.1 | 14.2 | .. | 4.8 | 470 |
| Nepal | 70 | 20 | 2 | 4 | 1 | 6 | 68.0 | 3.1 | 2.1 | 2.04 | 0.9 | 145 |
| Netherlands | 6,988 | 4 | 47 | 97 | 100 | .. | .. | .. | 22.9 | 0.32 | .. | .. |
| New Zealand | 9,656 | 7 | 42 | 85 | 98 | 361 | .. | 28.6 | 19.4 | 1.30 | .. | 962 |
| Nicaragua | 414 | 22 | 4 | 33 | 60 | 62 | 4.8 | 9.2 | 15.1 | 3.15 | .. | .. |
| Niger | .. | .. | 0 | 2 | 15 | .. | .. | 9.5 | 16.5 | .. | 2.2 | .. |
| Nigeria | 127 | 24 | 1 | 22 | 58 | .. | .. | 10.7 | .. | 1.49 | 3.5 | .. |
| Norway | 25,137 | 7 | 44 | 108 | .. | 193 | .. | 37.9 | 19.8 | .. | 1.4 | 445 |
| Oman | 3,757 | 26 | 11 | 71 | 92 | 189 | 89.7 | 12.1 | 5.5 | 1.87 | 2.4 | 583 |
| Pakistan | 456 | 24 | 3 | 22 | 36 | 10 | .. | 4.1 | 2.4 | 1.03 | 2.5 | 433 |
| Panama | 1,500 | 16 | 13 | 52 | 89 | .. | 12.2 | 10.3 | 16.7 | .. | 3.9 | 330 |
| Papua New Guinea | .. | .. | 1 | 1 | .. | .. | .. | .. | 14.6 | .. | .. | .. |
| Paraguay | 849 | 5 | 6 | 54 | .. | 31 | 8.2 | 6.4 | 3.4 | 0.90 | 4.4 | .. |
| Peru | 848 | 9 | 8 | 31 | .. | 99 | .. | 18.8 | 23.0 | 1.80 | 2.7 | 670 |
| Philippines | 588 | 12 | 4 | 50 | 99 | 28 | 4.5 | 11.6 | 5.3 | 1.20 | 4.4 | 1,555 |
| Poland | 3,437 | 9 | 30 | 96 | 99 | .. | 5.0 | .. | 7.6 | 1.35 | 3.8 | .. |
| Portugal | 4,663 | 9 | 40 | 115 | 99 | 178 | 10.4 | 31.8 | 23.1 | 1.04 | 4.9 | 1,126 |
| Puerto Rico | .. | .. | 27 | 86 | 100 | .. | .. | 33.5 | .. | .. | .. | .. |

# Power and communications

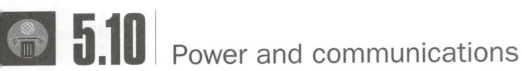

| | Electric power | | Telephones | | | | | | | | | |
| | Consumption per capita kWh | Transmission and distribution losses % of output | Access | | | | Quality | Affordability and efficiency | | | | |
| | | | per 100 people | | Population covered by mobile telephony[a] % | International voice traffic[a] minutes per person | Faults per 100 mainlines[a] | $ per month | | Cost of call to U.S.[a] $ per 3 minutes | Telecommunications revenue[a] % of GDP | Subscribers per employee[a] |
| | | | Fixed mainlines[a] | Mobile subscribers[a] | | | | Price basket for residential fixed line[b] | Price basket for mobile[a] | | | |
| | 2005 | 2005 | 2006 | 2006 | 2006 | 2006 | 2006 | 2006 | 2006 | 2005 | 2006 | 2006 |
|---|---|---|---|---|---|---|---|---|---|---|---|---|
| Romania | 2,342 | 10 | 19 | 81 | 98 | .. | 10.4 | 7.2 | 10.5 | 0.82 | 5.0 | .. |
| Russian Federation | 5,785 | 12 | 28 | 84 | .. | .. | 7.1 | .. | 5.9 | 2.03 | 2.9 | 439 |
| Rwanda | .. | .. | 0 | 3 | 75 | .. | .. | 6.6 | 12.3 | 2.43 | 3.3 | .. |
| Saudi Arabia | 6,813 | 11 | 17 | 83 | 96 | 216 | .. | 11.7 | 9.7 | .. | 3.1 | 927 |
| Senegal | 151 | 30 | 2 | 25 | 85 | 39 | 2.0 | 15.4 | 9.4 | 1.02 | 9.1 | 1,100 |
| Serbia | .. | .. | 36 | 70 | 99 | .. | .. | .. | 5.8 | .. | 0.0 | 605 |
| Sierra Leone | .. | .. | .. | .. | .. | .. | .. | .. | 70.9 | .. | .. | .. |
| Singapore | 8,358 | 5 | 41 | 107 | 100 | 1,045 | 0.3 | 6.3 | 6.1 | 0.69 | 3.1 | .. |
| Slovak Republic | 4,920 | 5 | 22 | 91 | 100 | 90 | 7.9 | 19.8 | 12.2 | 1.06 | 3.6 | 559 |
| Slovenia | 6,918 | 6 | 42 | 91 | 99 | .. | 13.4 | 17.6 | 10.1 | 0.65 | 3.5 | 1,225 |
| Somalia | .. | .. | 1 | 6 | .. | .. | .. | .. | 5.1 | .. | .. | .. |
| South Africa | 4,847 | 6 | 10 | 72 | 96 | .. | .. | 22.7 | 13.8 | 0.79 | 6.4 | 1,145 |
| Spain | 6,147 | 9 | 42 | 105 | 99 | 173 | .. | 25.8 | 21.7 | 0.60 | 4.3 | 656 |
| Sri Lanka | 378 | 15 | 9 | 27 | 85 | 28 | 8.6 | 8.2 | 1.2 | 2.11 | 2.6 | 619 |
| Sudan | 94 | 16 | 2 | 12 | .. | 12 | 95.5 | 6.3 | 4.0 | .. | 7.6 | 624 |
| Swaziland | .. | .. | 4 | 22 | .. | .. | 90.0 | 8.3 | 13.5 | 2.97 | 12.3 | .. |
| Sweden | 15,440 | 7 | 59 | 106 | 99 | .. | .. | 26.7 | 6.0 | 0.41 | 2.8 | 764 |
| Switzerland | 8,305 | 7 | 67 | 99 | 100 | .. | .. | 29.5 | 28.0 | 0.32 | 3.3 | 537 |
| Syrian Arab Republic | 1,411 | 24 | 17 | 24 | 99 | 44 | 50.0 | 2.7 | 10.0 | .. | 3.0 | 221 |
| Tajikistan | 2,267 | 15 | 4 | 4 | 4 | .. | .. | .. | 23.3 | 7.84 | 2.9 | 114 |
| Tanzania | 61 | 27 | 0 | 15 | .. | .. | 26.0 | 14.0 | 10.0 | 3.17 | .. | .. |
| Thailand | 1,988 | 8 | 11 | 64 | 31 | 14 | 2.7 | 8.3 | 4.3 | 0.67 | 3.2 | 1,850 |
| Timor-Leste | .. | .. | .. | .. | .. | .. | .. | .. | .. | .. | .. | .. |
| Togo | 94 | 46 | 1 | 11 | 85 | 21 | .. | 15.4 | 12.1 | 3.98 | 6.3 | 432 |
| Trinidad and Tobago | 5,038 | 6 | 25 | 125 | .. | 376 | .. | 7.0 | 6.7 | 2.19 | 2.4 | .. |
| Tunisia | 1,194 | 12 | 13 | 72 | 100 | 73 | 20.0 | 2.9 | 5.3 | .. | 4.4 | 915 |
| Turkey | 1,898 | 15 | 26 | 72 | 96 | 27 | 5.6 | 14.7 | 12.7 | 2.40 | 2.9 | 1,032 |
| Turkmenistan | 1,731 | 12 | 8 | 2 | 14 | .. | .. | .. | 17.2 | .. | 0.7 | 72 |
| Uganda | .. | .. | 0 | 7 | 80 | .. | .. | 13.8 | 9.4 | 3.21 | 3.4 | 255 |
| Ukraine | 3,246 | 13 | 26 | 105 | 96 | 57 | 41.3 | .. | 9.4 | 1.65 | 5.8 | 210 |
| United Arab Emirates | 13,708 | 7 | 31 | 130 | 100 | .. | 0.3 | 17.4 | 4.1 | 1.73 | 2.7 | 587 |
| United Kingdom | 6,253 | 8 | 55 | 115 | 99 | .. | .. | 28.2 | 13.7 | 0.77 | 3.7 | .. |
| United States | 13,648 | 6 | 57 | 78 | 99 | 279 | 13.8 | 25.0 | 5.2 | .. | 3.0 | 389 |
| Uruguay | 2,007 | 23 | 30 | 70 | 100 | 121 | .. | 10.7 | 16.1 | 0.52 | .. | .. |
| Uzbekistan | 1,659 | 9 | 7 | 3 | .. | 12 | 92.2 | 0.9 | 1.8 | .. | 2.5 | 117 |
| Venezuela, RB | 2,848 | 25 | 16 | 70 | .. | .. | .. | .. | 1.2 | 0.84 | 3.6 | 677 |
| Vietnam | 573 | 11 | 19 | 18 | .. | .. | .. | 2.7 | 6.3 | 1.95 | 4.7 | .. |
| West Bank and Gaza | .. | .. | 9 | 22 | 95 | 66 | 23.0 | 1.0 | 9.6 | 1.17 | 0.8 | 903 |
| Yemen, Rep. | 174 | 23 | 5 | 9 | 68 | .. | .. | 2.8 | 4.2 | 2.39 | 1.2 | .. |
| Zambia | 721 | 5 | 1 | 14 | 65 | .. | 108.0 | 7.7 | 14.2 | 1.41 | 2.5 | 175 |
| Zimbabwe | 953 | 7 | 3 | 6 | .. | 25 | 57.0 | 4.3 | 3.4 | .. | 4.3 | 375 |
| **World** | 2,678 w | 9 w | 20 w | 40 w | .. w | .. w | .. m | 10.0 m | 10.4 m | 1.42 m | 2.9 w | 572 m |
| **Low income** | 391 | 22 | 3 | 14 | 40 | .. | .. | 6.1 | 10.0 | 1.99 | 4.0 | .. |
| **Middle income** | 1,928 | 11 | 22 | 44 | .. | 31 | 8.2 | 9.2 | 10.2 | 1.65 | 2.1 | 586 |
| Lower middle income | 1,502 | 9 | 22 | 38 | .. | .. | 22.0 | 8.2 | 9.8 | 2.08 | 2.1 | 599 |
| Upper middle income | 3,131 | 13 | 22 | 66 | 95 | .. | 7.5 | 11.4 | 10.9 | 1.06 | 3.6 | 594 |
| **Low & middle income** | 1,290 | 12 | 13 | 31 | .. | .. | .. | 8.7 | 10.0 | 1.81 | 2.5 | 492 |
| East Asia & Pacific | 1,492 | 7 | 23 | 35 | .. | 8 | .. | 5.8 | 5.0 | 1.16 | 2.7 | 849 |
| Europe & Central Asia | 3,633 | 12 | 25 | 63 | .. | .. | 9.5 | 7.2 | 11.8 | 1.55 | 1.7 | 314 |
| Latin America & Carib. | 1,715 | 16 | 18 | 55 | 90 | .. | .. | 9.5 | 10.4 | 1.21 | 4.3 | 642 |
| Middle East & N. Africa | 1,358 | 17 | 17 | 36 | 84 | 36 | 23.5 | 5.2 | 6.5 | 1.66 | 1.5 | 466 |
| South Asia | 432 | 24 | 3 | 15 | 60 | .. | .. | 4.0 | 2.4 | 2.02 | 2.1 | 433 |
| Sub-Saharan Africa | 542 | 9 | 1 | 14 | .. | .. | .. | 11.6 | 12.3 | 2.43 | 3.2 | 586 |
| **High income** | 9,760 | 6 | 53 | 90 | 99 | 204 | .. | 26.6 | 17.0 | 0.77 | 4.4 | 641 |
| Euro area | 6,926 | 6 | 54 | 99 | 99 | .. | 8.3 | 28.8 | 20.5 | 0.73 | 3.3 | 638 |

a. Data are from the International Telecommunication Union's (ITU) World Telecommunication Development Report database. Please cite the ITU for third-party use of these data.
b. Calculated by the World Bank based on ITU data.

## About the data

The quality of an economy's infrastructure, including power and communications, is an important element in investment decisions for both domestic and foreign investors. Government effort alone is not enough to meet the need for investments in modern infrastructure; public-private partnerships, especially those involving local providers and financiers, are critical for lowering costs and delivering value for money. In telecommunications, competition in the marketplace, along with sound regulation, is lowering costs, improving quality, and easing access to services around the globe.

An economy's production and consumption of electricity are basic indicators of its size and level of development. Although a few countries export electric power, most production is for domestic consumption. Expanding the supply of electricity to meet the growing demand of increasingly urbanized and industrialized economies without incurring unacceptable social, economic, and environmental costs is one of the great challenges facing developing countries.

Data on electric power production and consumption are collected from national energy agencies by the International Energy Agency (IEA) and adjusted by the IEA to meet international definitions (for data on electricity production, see table 3.10). Electricity consumption is equivalent to production less power plants' own use and transmission, distribution, and transformation losses less exports plus imports. It includes consumption by auxiliary stations, losses in transformers that are considered integral parts of those stations, and electricity produced by pumping installations. Where data are available, it covers electricity generated by primary sources of energy—coal, oil, gas, nuclear, hydro, geothermal, wind, tide and wave, and combustible renewables. Neither production nor consumption data capture the reliability of supplies, including breakdowns, load factors, and frequency of outages.

Over the past decade new financing and technology, along with privatization and liberalization, have spurred dramatic growth in telecommunications in many countries. With the rapid development of mobile telephony and the global expansion of the Internet, information and communication technologies are increasingly recognized as essential tools of development, contributing to global integration and enhancing public sector effectiveness, efficiency, and transparency. The table presents telecommunications indicators covering access, quality, and affordability and efficiency.

Operators are the main source of telecommunications data, so information on subscribers is widely available for most countries. This gives a general idea of access, but a more precise measure is the penetration rate—the share of households with access to telecommunications. Also important are data on actual use of telecommunications equipment. Ideally, statistics on telecommunications (and other information and communications technologies) should be compiled for all three measures: subscription and possession, access, and use. The quality of data varies among reporting countries as a result of differences in regulations covering data provision.

Globally, there have been huge improvements in access to telecommunications, driven mainly by mobile telephony. By 2002 access to mobiles outpaced access to fixed-line telephones in developing countries, and rural areas are catching up with urban areas (although gaps are still large). By 2004 approximately 98 percent of the population in high-income countries and about 64 percent of the population in developing countries were covered by mobile telephony (within range of a mobile cellular signal). Indeed, in many developing countries, especially in Sub-Saharan Africa, the number of mobile phones has overtaken the number of fixed-line phones.

Telephone mainline faults are a measure of telecommunications quality. The definition varies among countries: some operators define faults as including malfunctioning customer equipment while others include only technical faults.

Although access is the key to delivering telecommunications services to people, if the service is not affordable to most people, then goals of universal usage will not be met. Three indicators of telecommunications affordability are presented in the table: price basket for fixed-line telephone service, price basket for mobile service, and the cost of an international call. Telecommunications efficiency is measured by total telecommunications revenue divided by GDP and by total telephone subscribers per employee.

## Definitions

• **Electric power consumption per capita** measures the production of power plants and combined heat and power plants less transmission, distribution, and transformation losses and own use by heat and power plants divided by midyear population. • **Electric power transmission and distribution losses** are losses in transmission between sources of supply and points of distribution and in distribution to consumers, including pilferage. • **Fixed telephone mainlines** are telephone lines connecting a subscriber to the telephone exchange equipment. • **Mobile telephone subscribers** are subscribers to a public mobile telephone service using cellular technology. • **Population covered by mobile telephony** is the percentage of people within range of a mobile cellular signal regardless of whether they are subscribers. • **International voice traffic** is the sum of international incoming and outgoing telephone traffic (in minutes) divided by total population. • **Telephone mainline faults** are the number of reported faults for the year per 100 telephone mainlines. • **Price basket for residential fixed line** is calculated as one-fifth of the installation charge, the monthly subscription charge, and the cost of local calls (15 peak and 15 off-peak calls of three minutes each). • **Price basket for mobile** is calculated as the prepaid price for 25 calls per month spread over the same mobile network, other mobile networks, and mobile to fixed calls and during peak, off-peak, and weekend times. It also includes 30 text messages per month. • **Cost of call to U.S.** is the cost of a three-minute, peak rate, fixed-line call from the country to the United States. • **Telecommunications revenue** is the revenue from the provision of telecommunications services such as fixed-line, mobile, and data divided by GDP. • **Subscribers per employee** are telephone subscribers (fixed-line plus mobile) divided by the total number of telecommunications employees.

## Data sources

Data on electricity consumption and losses are from the IEA's *Energy Statistics and Balances of Non-OECD Countries 2004–2005*, the IEA's *Energy Statistics of OECD Countries 2004–2005*, and the United Nations Statistics Division's *Energy Statistics Yearbook*. Data on telecommunications are from the International Telecommunication Union's World Telecommunication Development Report database and World Bank estimates.

# 5.11 The information age

| | Daily newspapers | Households with television[b] | Personal computers and the Internet | | | | | | Information and communications technology expenditures | |
| | | | Access | | Broadband subscribers[b] | Quality | Application | Affordability | | |
| | | | per 100 people | | per 100 people | International Internet bandwidth[b] | Secure Internet servers | Price basket for Internet[b] | | |
| | per 1,000 people | % | Personal computers[b] | Internet users[b] | | bits per capita | per million people | $ per month | % of GDP | Per capita $ |
| | 2000–06[a] | 2006 | 2006 | 2006 | 2006 | 2006 | December 2007 | 2006 | 2006 | 2006 |
|---|---|---|---|---|---|---|---|---|---|---|
| Afghanistan | .. | 6 | 0.4 | 2.1 | 0.00 | 0 | 0 | .. | .. | .. |
| Albania | 25 | 90 | 1.7 | 14.9 | 0.01 | 4 | 2 | 16.3 | .. | .. |
| Algeria | .. | 90 | 1.1 | 7.4 | 0.59 | 5 | 0 | 9.3 | 2.4 | 84 |
| Angola | 2 | 9 | 0.7 | 0.5 | 0.00 | 12 | 0 | 0.2 | .. | .. |
| Argentina | 36 | 97 | 9.0 | 20.9 | 4.01 | 690 | 12 | 5.4 | 6.9 | 379 |
| Armenia | 8 | 91 | 9.8 | 5.7 | 0.07 | 22 | 3 | 56.6 | .. | .. |
| Australia | 156 | 99 | 75.7 | 73.9 | 18.84 | 11,593 | 579 | 22.5 | 6.4 | 2,413 |
| Austria | 315 | 98 | 60.7 | 50.7 | 17.24 | 6,634 | 284 | 15.7 | 5.5 | 2,137 |
| Azerbaijan | 16 | 99 | 2.3 | 9.8 | 0.03 | 36 | 0 | 10.0 | .. | .. |
| Bangladesh | .. | 23 | 2.2 | 0.3 | 0.00 | 8 | 0 | 24.0 | 2.7 | 11 |
| Belarus | 82 | 97 | 0.8 | 56.3 | 0.12 | 192 | 1 | 10.5 | .. | .. |
| Belgium | 164 | 98 | 37.7 | 45.8 | 19.19 | 11,279 | 146 | 37.6 | 5.9 | 2,203 |
| Benin | 0 | 20 | 0.4 | 8.0 | 0.00 | 5 | 0 | 11.4 | .. | .. |
| Bolivia | .. | 50 | 2.4 | 6.2 | 0.12 | 43 | 3 | 12.1 | 4.9 | 58 |
| Bosnia and Herzegovina | .. | 87 | 5.4 | 24.2 | 1.02 | 40 | 4 | 7.6 | .. | .. |
| Botswana | 43 | 10 | 4.7 | 3.3 | 0.09 | 16 | 1 | 18.2 | .. | .. |
| Brazil | 36 | 91 | 16.1 | 22.5 | 3.13 | 150 | 16 | 10.1 | 6.4 | 363 |
| Bulgaria | 79 | 97 | 6.3 | 24.3 | 5.00 | 1,756 | 11 | 7.4 | 3.4 | 141 |
| Burkina Faso | .. | 8 | 0.2 | 0.6 | 0.01 | 15 | 0 | 33.9 | .. | .. |
| Burundi | .. | 14 | 0.7 | 0.7 | 0.00 | 1 | 0 | 40.0 | .. | .. |
| Cambodia | .. | 43 | 0.3 | 0.3 | 0.01 | 1 | 0 | 9.9 | .. | .. |
| Cameroon | .. | 26 | 1.1 | 2.0 | 0.00 | 9 | 0 | 17.6 | 5.1 | 52 |
| Canada | 175 | 99 | 87.6 | 68.1 | 23.51 | 6,732 | 644 | 9.5 | 5.7 | 2,201 |
| Central African Republic | .. | 5 | 0.3 | 0.3 | 0.00 | 0 | 0 | 100.1 | .. | .. |
| Chad | .. | 4 | 0.2 | 0.6 | 0.00 | 1 | .. | 86.3 | .. | .. |
| Chile | 51 | 90 | 14.1 | 25.3 | 5.95 | 780 | 22 | 26.7 | 5.2 | 465 |
| China | 74 | 89 | 4.3 | 10.4 | 3.88 | 196 | 0 | 10.0 | 5.4 | 108 |
|   Hong Kong, China | 223 | 99 | 61.2 | 55.0 | 26.20 | 13,439 | 194 | 3.9 | 8.8 | 2,428 |
| Colombia | 22 | 90 | 4.2 | 14.7 | 1.38 | 560 | 6 | 7.5 | 7.1 | 239 |
| Congo, Dem. Rep. | .. | 4 | 0.0 | 0.3 | 0.00 | 0 | 0 | 14.0 | .. | .. |
| Congo, Rep. | .. | 7 | 0.5 | 1.9 | 0.00 | 0 | 0 | 64.9 | .. | .. |
| Costa Rica | 65 | 89 | 23.1 | 27.6 | 1.34 | 176 | 67 | 18.3 | 7.3 | 368 |
| Côte d'Ivoire | .. | 35 | 1.7 | 1.6 | 0.01 | 3 | 0 | 67.7 | .. | .. |
| Croatia | .. | 98 | 19.9 | 35.5 | 5.67 | 1,074 | 48 | 16.5 | 0.0 | 0 |
| Cuba | 65 | 70 | 3.3 | 2.1 | 0.00 | 14 | 0 | 30.0 | .. | .. |
| Czech Republic | 182 | .. | 27.4 | 34.5 | 10.58 | 2,170 | 64 | 19.9 | 7.3 | 1,020 |
| Denmark | 352 | 97 | 69.6 | 58.3 | 31.79 | 34,796 | 614 | 23.4 | 6.0 | 3,036 |
| Dominican Republic | 42 | 76 | 2.2 | 20.8 | 0.69 | 6 | 6 | 12.3 | .. | .. |
| Ecuador | 99 | 80 | 6.6 | 11.7 | 0.21 | 227 | 5 | 20.2 | 3.0 | 93 |
| Egypt, Arab Rep. | .. | 88 | 3.7 | 8.1 | 0.28 | 126 | 1 | 5.0 | 1.4 | 20 |
| El Salvador | 37 | 83 | 5.2 | 9.6 | 0.63 | 23 | 6 | 22.6 | .. | .. |
| Eritrea | .. | 16 | 0.6 | 2.1 | 0.00 | 2 | .. | 13.0 | .. | .. |
| Estonia | 192 | .. | 48.3 | 56.6 | 17.00 | 11,175 | 163 | 10.9 | .. | .. |
| Ethiopia | 5 | 4 | 0.4 | 0.2 | 0.00 | 0 | 0 | 6.7 | .. | .. |
| Finland | 431 | 94 | 50.0 | 55.5 | 27.12 | 4,311 | 380 | 22.5 | 6.7 | 2,689 |
| France | 165 | 97 | 57.5 | 49.1 | 20.73 | 3,286 | 96 | 12.6 | 6.3 | 2,324 |
| Gabon | .. | 56 | 3.5 | 6.2 | 0.09 | 153 | 5 | 39.2 | .. | .. |
| Gambia, The | .. | 12 | 1.5 | 3.6 | 0.00 | 6 | 1 | 6.8 | .. | .. |
| Georgia | 4 | 89 | 4.7 | 7.5 | 0.61 | 7 | 5 | 9.9 | .. | .. |
| Germany | 267 | 98 | 60.6 | 46.9 | 17.10 | 6,864 | 349 | 7.5 | 6.2 | 2,174 |
| Ghana | .. | 26 | 0.6 | 2.7 | 0.06 | 9 | 0 | 11.9 | .. | .. |
| Greece | .. | 100 | 9.2 | 18.4 | 4.38 | 587 | 40 | 10.2 | 3.2 | 875 |
| Guatemala | .. | 50 | 2.1 | 10.1 | 0.21 | 56 | 6 | 54.3 | .. | .. |
| Guinea | .. | 11 | 0.5 | 0.5 | 0.00 | 0 | .. | 5.9 | .. | .. |
| Guinea-Bissau | .. | 31 | 0.2 | 2.2 | 0.00 | 1 | .. | 15.0 | .. | .. |
| Haiti | .. | 27 | 0.2 | 6.9 | 0.00 | 17 | 1 | 12.0 | .. | .. |

# The information age

| | Daily newspapers | Households with television[b] | Personal computers and the Internet | | | | | | Information and communications technology expenditures | |
|---|---|---|---|---|---|---|---|---|---|---|
| | | | Access | | Broadband subscribers[b] per 100 people | Quality | Application | Affordability | | |
| | | | per 100 people | | | International Internet bandwidth[b] bits per capita | Secure Internet servers per million people | Price basket for Internet[b] $ per month | | |
| | per 1,000 people | % | Personal computers[b] | Internet users[b] | | | | | % of GDP | Per capita $ |
| | 2000–06[a] | 2006 | 2006 | 2006 | 2006 | 2006 | December 2007 | 2006 | 2006 | 2006 |
| Honduras | .. | 58 | 1.8 | 4.8 | 0.00 | 6 | 5 | 12.0 | 4.6 | 60 |
| Hungary | 217 | 96 | 14.9 | 34.8 | 9.70 | 993 | 36 | 10.5 | 6.0 | 669 |
| India | 73 | 32 | 1.6 | 5.5 | 0.21 | 24 | 1 | 6.6 | 6.1 | 50 |
| Indonesia | .. | 65 | 1.5 | 7.3 | 0.05 | 7 | 1 | 6.6 | 3.1 | 51 |
| Iran, Islamic Rep. | .. | .. | 10.6 | 25.7 | 0.66 | 53 | 0 | 2.3 | 2.4 | 76 |
| Iraq | .. | .. | .. | 0.1 | 0.00 | .. | 0 | .. | .. | .. |
| Ireland | 182 | 98 | 52.8 | 33.7 | 12.12 | 5,912 | 415 | 31.4 | 4.3 | 2,207 |
| Israel | .. | 92 | 122.1 | 26.9 | 20.16 | 2,455 | 182 | 22.2 | 7.9 | 1,570 |
| Italy | 138 | 96 | 36.7 | 49.0 | 14.68 | 2,044 | 53 | 25.0 | 4.3 | 1,363 |
| Jamaica | .. | 70 | 6.7 | 46.4 | 1.70 | 15,822 | 18 | 26.5 | 10.2 | 383 |
| Japan | 551 | 99 | 67.6 | 68.5 | 20.16 | 1,038 | 331 | 13.1 | 7.9 | 2,688 |
| Jordan | .. | 96 | 6.6 | 14.4 | 0.88 | 57 | 4 | 10.9 | 8.0 | 204 |
| Kazakhstan | .. | .. | .. | 8.1 | 0.20 | 63 | 1 | 15.8 | .. | .. |
| Kenya | .. | 18 | 1.4 | 7.6 | 0.00 | 21 | 0 | 15.8 | 2.4 | 15 |
| Korea, Dem. Rep. | .. | .. | .. | .. | 0.00 | .. | .. | .. | .. | .. |
| Korea, Rep. | .. | .. | 53.2 | 70.5 | 29.00 | 1,028 | 60 | 34.6 | 6.6 | 1,214 |
| Kuwait | .. | 95 | 23.7 | 31.4 | 0.99 | 348 | 35 | 13.7 | 1.4 | 466 |
| Kyrgyz Republic | 1 | .. | 1.9 | 5.7 | 0.05 | 39 | 1 | 12.0 | .. | .. |
| Lao PDR | 3 | 30 | 1.8 | 0.4 | 0.00 | 4 | 0 | 25.0 | .. | .. |
| Latvia | 154 | 98 | 24.6 | 46.8 | 4.79 | 3,230 | 46 | 12.6 | .. | .. |
| Lebanon | 61 | 96 | 10.2 | 23.4 | 4.19 | 111 | 10 | 10.0 | .. | .. |
| Lesotho | .. | 2 | 0.1 | 2.6 | 0.00 | 2 | 0 | 38.6 | .. | .. |
| Liberia | .. | .. | .. | .. | 0.00 | .. | .. | .. | .. | .. |
| Libya | .. | 50 | 2.2 | 3.9 | 0.00 | 21 | 0 | 22.1 | .. | .. |
| Lithuania | 108 | 98 | 18.0 | 31.9 | 10.86 | 2,714 | 26 | 7.3 | .. | .. |
| Macedonia, FYR | 89 | 98 | 22.2 | 13.2 | 1.79 | 17 | 2 | 25.3 | .. | .. |
| Madagascar | .. | 10 | 0.5 | 0.6 | 0.00 | 2 | 0 | 2.8 | .. | .. |
| Malawi | .. | 3 | 0.2 | 0.4 | 0.00 | 1 | 0 | 22.5 | .. | .. |
| Malaysia | 111 | 95 | 21.8 | 43.2 | 3.44 | 124 | 17 | 2.7 | 6.7 | 388 |
| Mali | .. | 17 | 0.4 | 0.6 | 0.02 | 26 | 0 | 28.7 | .. | .. |
| Mauritania | .. | 25 | 2.6 | 3.3 | 0.02 | 30 | 1 | 16.0 | .. | .. |
| Mauritius | 77 | 93 | 16.9 | 14.5 | 1.75 | 153 | 18 | 16.2 | .. | .. |
| Mexico | 92 | 93 | 13.6 | 17.5 | 3.58 | 109 | 10 | 17.3 | 3.3 | 266 |
| Moldova | .. | 82 | 9.0 | 19.0 | 0.57 | 147 | 4 | 13.3 | .. | .. |
| Mongolia | 19 | 63 | 13.3 | 10.5 | 0.07 | 13 | 4 | 10.7 | .. | .. |
| Morocco | 11 | 78 | 2.5 | 20.0 | 1.28 | 377 | 1 | 26.8 | 5.6 | 119 |
| Mozambique | 3 | 6 | 1.4 | 0.9 | 0.00 | 1 | 0 | 32.9 | .. | .. |
| Myanmar | .. | 3 | 0.8 | 0.2 | 0.00 | 2 | 0 | 1.5 | .. | .. |
| Namibia | 28 | 39 | 12.3 | 4.0 | 0.00 | 18 | 8 | 48.7 | .. | .. |
| Nepal | .. | 13 | 0.5 | 0.9 | 0.00 | 5 | 1 | 8.0 | .. | .. |
| Netherlands | 308 | 99 | 85.4 | 89.0 | 31.78 | 20,501 | 413 | 8.8 | 6.2 | 2,531 |
| New Zealand | 185 | 98 | 50.2 | 76.5 | 13.77 | 1,107 | 588 | 11.0 | 10.6 | 2,635 |
| Nicaragua | .. | 60 | 4.0 | 2.8 | 0.34 | 1 | 3 | 10.0 | .. | .. |
| Niger | 0 | 7 | 0.1 | 0.3 | 0.00 | 2 | 0 | 101.8 | .. | .. |
| Nigeria | .. | 32 | 0.8 | 5.5 | 0.00 | 1 | 0 | 11.3 | 3.4 | 27 |
| Norway | 517 | 100 | 59.4 | 87.4 | 27.43 | 9,305 | 389 | 29.8 | 4.9 | 3,556 |
| Oman | .. | 79 | 5.2 | 12.5 | 0.60 | 174 | 4 | 5.2 | .. | .. |
| Pakistan | 51 | 46 | 0.5 | 7.5 | 0.04 | 5 | 0 | 9.5 | 6.9 | 55 |
| Panama | 65 | 79 | 4.6 | 6.7 | 0.54 | 287 | 57 | 38.5 | 8.2 | 425 |
| Papua New Guinea | 9 | 10 | 6.4 | 1.8 | 0.00 | 1 | 1 | 12.9 | .. | .. |
| Paraguay | .. | 82 | 7.8 | 4.3 | 0.27 | 83 | 1 | 0.2 | .. | .. |
| Peru | .. | 71 | 10.3 | 22.1 | 1.76 | 367 | 6 | 11.5 | 5.9 | 199 |
| Philippines | 80 | 63 | 5.3 | 5.5 | 0.15 | 38 | 3 | 2.0 | 6.7 | 91 |
| Poland | 113 | 91 | 24.2 | 28.8 | 6.92 | 560 | 38 | 11.7 | 4.2 | 369 |
| Portugal | .. | 99 | 13.3 | 30.3 | 13.79 | 829 | 65 | 28.7 | 4.3 | 797 |
| Puerto Rico | .. | 97 | 0.8 | 23.4 | 3.02 | 511 | 33 | .. | .. | .. |

# 5.11 | The information age

| | Daily newspapers | Households with television[b] | Personal computers and the Internet | | | | | | Information and communications technology expenditures | |
|---|---|---|---|---|---|---|---|---|---|---|
| | | | Access | | Quality | | Application | Affordability | | |
| | | | | | Broadband subscribers[b] per 100 people | International Internet bandwidth[b] bits per capita | Secure Internet servers per million people | Price basket for Internet[b] $ per month | | |
| | per 1,000 people | % | per 100 people Personal computers[b] | Internet users[b] | | | | | % of GDP | Per capita $ |
| | 2000–06[a] | 2006 | 2006 | 2006 | 2006 | 2006 | December 2007 | 2006 | 2006 | 2006 |
| Romania | 70 | 94 | 12.9 | 32.4 | 8.19 | 1,503 | 7 | 6.0 | 3.2 | 180 |
| Russian Federation | 92 | 98 | 12.2 | 18.0 | 2.04 | 100 | 3 | 12.7 | 3.2 | 222 |
| Rwanda | .. | 2 | 0.2 | 0.7 | 0.02 | 7 | .. | 30.1 | .. | .. |
| Saudi Arabia | .. | 99 | 13.6 | 19.8 | 0.92 | 126 | 5 | 5.3 | 2.1 | 308 |
| Senegal | 9 | 31 | 2.1 | 5.4 | 0.24 | 103 | 0 | 25.8 | 8.5 | 64 |
| Serbia | .. | .. | 5.2 | 20.3 | .. | 95 | 3 | 6.9 | .. | .. |
| Sierra Leone | .. | .. | .. | 0.2 | 0.00 | .. | 0 | 10.6 | .. | .. |
| Singapore | 361 | 98 | 68.2 | 38.3 | 17.76 | 7,052 | 291 | 13.2 | 9.3 | 2,743 |
| Slovak Republic | 125 | 98 | 35.8 | 41.8 | 5.88 | 2,913 | 28 | 19.8 | 5.5 | 557 |
| Slovenia | 175 | 96 | 40.4 | 62.3 | 13.14 | 1,255 | 95 | 18.8 | 3.1 | 575 |
| Somalia | .. | 8 | 0.9 | 1.1 | 0.00 | 0 | 0 | .. | .. | .. |
| South Africa | 30 | 59 | 8.5 | 10.9 | 0.35 | 19 | 23 | 11.6 | 10.0 | 537 |
| Spain | 145 | 99 | 27.7 | 42.1 | 15.08 | 2,776 | 100 | 32.0 | 3.6 | 1,004 |
| Sri Lanka | 24 | 32 | 3.7 | 2.2 | 0.15 | 25 | 2 | 4.4 | 5.4 | 73 |
| Sudan | .. | 16 | 11.2 | 9.3 | 0.01 | 5 | 0 | 52.5 | .. | .. |
| Swaziland | 26 | 18 | 3.7 | 3.7 | 0.00 | 1 | 4 | 15.1 | .. | .. |
| Sweden | 480 | 94 | 83.6 | 76.9 | 25.83 | 17,468 | 405 | 19.2 | 7.2 | 3,052 |
| Switzerland | 429 | 99 | 86.5 | 58.2 | 28.57 | 9,609 | 576 | 7.9 | 7.7 | 3,914 |
| Syrian Arab Republic | .. | 95 | 4.2 | 7.7 | 0.03 | 8 | 0 | 9.2 | .. | .. |
| Tajikistan | .. | 79 | 1.3 | 0.3 | 0.00 | 0 | .. | 12.3 | .. | .. |
| Tanzania | 2 | 14 | 0.9 | 1.0 | 0.00 | 0 | 0 | 36.0 | .. | .. |
| Thailand | .. | 92 | 7.0 | 13.3 | 0.17 | 156 | 6 | 5.8 | 4.0 | 129 |
| Timor-Leste | .. | .. | .. | .. | 0.00 | .. | 1 | 5.0 | .. | .. |
| Togo | 2 | 16 | 3.0 | 5.0 | 0.00 | 16 | 0 | 10.7 | .. | .. |
| Trinidad and Tobago | 151 | 88 | 9.7 | 12.3 | 1.55 | 370 | 27 | 12.6 | .. | .. |
| Tunisia | 23 | 92 | 6.3 | 12.8 | 0.18 | 126 | 2 | 3.1 | 6.0 | 180 |
| Turkey | .. | 92 | 5.7 | 16.8 | 3.80 | 631 | 25 | 6.7 | 8.2 | 452 |
| Turkmenistan | 9 | .. | 7.2 | 1.3 | 0.00 | 16 | .. | 23.1 | .. | .. |
| Uganda | .. | 10 | 1.7 | 2.5 | 0.00 | 4 | 0 | 99.6 | .. | .. |
| Ukraine | 132 | 97 | 4.5 | 11.9 | 0.00 | 17 | 2 | 2.1 | 7.8 | 177 |
| United Arab Emirates | .. | 86 | 25.6 | 40.2 | 5.66 | 2,371 | 59 | 5.4 | 3.6 | 1,201 |
| United Kingdom | 292 | 98 | 75.8 | 55.4 | 21.46 | 13,062 | 560 | 27.6 | 6.9 | 2,721 |
| United States | 194 | 99 | 76.2 | 69.5 | 19.42 | 3,307 | 868 | 15.0 | 8.7 | 3,846 |
| Uruguay | .. | 92 | 13.6 | 22.8 | 3.23 | 484 | 30 | 23.9 | 7.8 | 454 |
| Uzbekistan | .. | .. | 3.1 | 6.4 | 0.03 | 9 | 0 | 5.7 | .. | .. |
| Venezuela, RB | 93 | 90 | 9.3 | 15.3 | 1.99 | 50 | 5 | 12.5 | 3.7 | 248 |
| Vietnam | .. | 83 | 1.4 | 17.5 | 0.61 | 84 | 0 | 1.8 | 15.1 | 110 |
| West Bank and Gaza | 10 | 93 | 5.4 | 7.0 | 0.68 | 199 | 1 | 15.6 | .. | .. |
| Yemen, Rep. | 4 | 43 | 1.9 | 1.2 | 0.00 | 0 | 0 | 6.0 | .. | .. |
| Zambia | 5 | .. | 1.1 | 4.3 | 0.02 | 11 | 0 | 33.3 | .. | .. |
| Zimbabwe | .. | 34 | 6.5 | 9.2 | 0.08 | 4 | 0 | 1.3 | 12.7 | 17 |
| **World** | **105 w** | **83 m** | **10.6 w** | **21.4 w** | **5.46 w** | **529 w** | **74 w** | **12.1 m** | **6.7 w** | **564 w** |
| **Low income** | .. | 16 | 1.4 | 4.2 | 0.18 | 22 | 0 | 12.0 | 6.1 | 47 |
| **Middle income** | 71 | 89 | 6.6 | 14.1 | 3.33 | 144 | 5 | 11.2 | 5.1 | 166 |
| Lower middle income | 73 | 80 | 4.3 | 11.4 | 3.23 | 189 | 1 | 10.0 | 5.0 | 103 |
| Upper middle income | 68 | 93 | 13.3 | 22.2 | 3.57 | 242 | 15 | 11.7 | 5.2 | 339 |
| **Low & middle income** | 67 | 60 | 4.3 | 8.0 | 2.04 | 143 | 3 | 11.7 | 5.2 | 121 |
| East Asia & Pacific | 74 | 63 | 4.1 | 11.1 | 3.56 | 182 | 1 | 5.8 | 5.3 | 105 |
| Europe & Central Asia | 99 | 97 | 10.2 | 19.2 | 3.64 | 268 | 11 | 11.1 | 4.6 | 291 |
| Latin America & Carib. | 64 | 79 | 11.3 | 18.4 | 2.95 | 269 | 12 | 12.2 | 5.3 | 304 |
| Middle East & N. Africa | .. | 90 | 5.6 | 13.8 | 0.63 | 126 | 1 | 9.2 | 2.9 | 72 |
| South Asia | 70 | 32 | 1.4 | 4.9 | 0.18 | 22 | 1 | 6.6 | 6.0 | 47 |
| Sub-Saharan Africa | .. | 14 | 1.8 | 3.8 | 0.03 | 5 | 2 | 15.9 | .. | .. |
| **High income** | 263 | 98 | 56.7 | 59.3 | 19.20 | 4,346 | 441 | 13.7 | 7.2 | 2,555 |
| Euro area | 203 | 98 | 47.6 | 47.9 | 17.33 | 4,830 | 185 | 20.7 | 5.4 | 1,813 |

a. Data are for the most recent year available. b. Data are from the International Telecommunication Union's (ITU) World Telecommunication Development Report database. Please cite ITU for third-party use of these data.

**About the data**

The digital and information revolution has changed the way the world learns, communicates, does business, and treats illnesses. New information and communications technologies offer vast opportunities for progress in all walks of life in all countries—opportunities for economic growth, improved health, better service delivery, learning through distance education, and social and cultural advances.

The table presents indicators of the penetration of the information economy (newspapers, televisions, personal computers, and Internet use), quality (broadband subscribers, international Internet bandwidth, and secure Internet servers), and some of the economics of the information age (Internet access charges and spending on information and communications technologies).

Comparable statistics on access, use, quality, and affordability of information and communications technologies are needed to formulate growth-enabling policies for the sector and to monitor and evaluate the sector's impact on economic and social development. Although basic access data are available for many countries, in most developing countries little is known about who uses information and communications technologies (especially by age and gender); what they are used for (school, work, business, research, government, and the like); and how they affect people and businesses. To close this data gap, the global Partnership on Measuring ICT for Development is helping to set standards and harmonize information and communications technology statistics and to build capacity for compiling statistics in developing countries. For more information see www.itu.int/ITU-D/ict/partnership/.

Data on the number of daily newspapers in circulation are from surveys by the United Nations Educational, Scientific, and Cultural Organization (UNESCO) Institute for Statistics that cover such areas as newspaper circulation, online newspaper titles, journalists, community newspapers, and news agencies.

Estimates of households with television are derived from household surveys. Some countries report only the number of households with a color television set, and so the true number may be higher than reported.

Estimates of personal computers are from an annual International Telecommunication Union (ITU) questionnaire sent to member states, supplemented by other sources. Many governments lack the capacity to survey all places where personal computers are used—homes, schools, businesses, government offices, libraries, Internet cafes, and the like—so most estimates are derived from the number of personal computers sold each year in a country. Annual shipment data can also be multiplied by an estimated average useful lifespan before replacement to approximate the number of personal computers. There is no precise method for determining replacement rates, but in general personal computers are replaced every three to five years.

Data on Internet users and related Internet indicators are based on nationally reported data. Some countries derive these data from surveys, but since survey questions and definitions differ, the estimates may not be strictly comparable. For example, questions on the age of Internet users and frequency of use vary by country. Countries without surveys generally derive their estimates by multiplying subscriber counts reported by Internet service providers by a multiplier. This method may undercount the actual number of people using the Internet, particularly in developing countries, where many commercial subscribers rent out computers connected to the Internet or prepaid cards are used to access the Internet.

Broadband refers to technologies that provide Internet speeds of at least 256 kilobits per second of upstream and downstream capacity. These technologies—including digital subscriber lines, cable modems, satellite broadband Internet, fiber-to-home Internet access, ethernet local access networks, and wireless area networks—improve the online experience. Bandwidth, another measure of quality, refers to the range of frequencies available to be occupied by signals. The higher the bandwidth, the more information that can be transmitted at one time. Reporting countries may have different definitions of broadband, so data are not strictly comparable.

The number of secure Internet servers, from the Netcraft Secure Server Survey, gives an indication of how many companies are conducting encrypted transactions over the Internet. The Netcraft survey examines the use of encrypted transactions on the Internet through extensive automated exploration, tallying the number of Web sites using a secure socket layer (SSL). Some countries, such as the Republic of Korea, establish the encryption channel by using application layers, which are SSL equivalent.

According to the World Information Technology and Services Alliance's (WITSA) *Digital Planet 2006,* the global marketplace for information and communications technologies was expected to top $3 trillion in 2006 and to rise to almost $4 trillion by 2009. The data on information and communications technology expenditures cover the world's 75 largest buyers among countries and regions.

**Definitions**

• **Daily newspapers** are newspapers that report mainly on events occurring in the 24-hour period before going to press and that are issued at least four times a week. The indicator is average circulation (or copies printed) per 1,000 people. • **Households with television** are the percentage of households with a television set. • **Personal computers** are self-contained computers designed for use by a single individual, including laptops and notebooks and excluding terminals connected to mainframe and minicomputers intended primarily for shared use and devices such as smart phones and personal digital assistants. • **Internet users** are people with access to the worldwide network. • **Broadband subscribers** are the number of broadband subscribers with a digital subscriber line, cable modem, or other high-speed technologies. • **International Internet bandwidth** is the contracted capacity of international connections between countries for transmitting Internet traffic. • **Secure Internet servers** are servers using encryption technology in Internet transactions. • **Price basket for Internet** is based on the cheapest available tariff for accessing the Internet 20 hours a month (10 hours peak and 10 hours off-peak). The basket does not include telephone line rental but does include any telephone usage charges. • **Information and communications technology expenditures** include computer hardware (computers, storage devices, printers, and other peripherals); computer software (operating systems, programming tools, utilities, applications, and internal software development); computer services (information technology consulting, computer and network systems integration, Web hosting, data processing services, and other services); and communications services (voice and data communications services) and wired and wireless communications equipment.

**Data sources**

Data on newspapers are compiled by the UNESCO Institute for Statistics. Data on televisions, personal computers, Internet users, broadband subscribers, international Internet bandwidth, and price basket for Internet are from the ITU's World Telecommunication Development Report database. Data on secure Internet servers are from Netcraft (www.netcraft.com/) and official government sources. Data on information and communications technology expenditures are from WITSA's *Digital Planet 2006: The Global Information Economy* and from Global Insight, Inc.

# 5.12 Science and technology

| | Researchers in R&D per million people 2000–05[d] | Technicians in R&D per million people 2000–05[d] | Scientific and technical journal articles 2005 | Expenditures for R&D % of GDP 2000–05[d] | High-technology exports $ millions 2006 | High-technology exports % of manufactured exports 2006 | Royalty and license fees Receipts $ millions 2006 | Royalty and license fees Payments $ millions 2006 | Patent applications filed[a,b] Residents 2005 | Patent applications filed[a,b] Non-residents 2005 | Trademark applications filed[a,c] Residents 2005 | Trademark applications filed[a,c] Non-residents 2005 |
|---|---|---|---|---|---|---|---|---|---|---|---|---|
| Afghanistan | .. | .. | .. | .. | .. | .. | .. | .. | .. | .. | .. | .. |
| Albania | .. | .. | .. | .. | 8 | 13 | 1 | 7 | .. | .. | .. | .. |
| Algeria | 170 | 35 | 350 | 0.16 | 11 | 2 | .. | .. | 58 | 455 | 1,488 | 3,369 |
| Angola | .. | .. | .. | .. | .. | .. | 1,340 | 1 | .. | .. | .. | .. |
| Argentina | 768 | 338 | 3,058 | 0.44 | 994 | 7 | 71 | 807 | 206 | 2 | 61,953 | 19,139 |
| Armenia | .. | .. | 180 | 0.21 | 5 | 1 | .. | .. | 206 | 2 | 1,088 | 364 |
| Australia | 4,099 | .. | 15,957 | 1.77 | 3,371 | 12 | 621 | 2,221 | 8,630 | 22,562 | 38,728 | 17,053 |
| Austria | 3,444 | 1,477 | 4,566 | 2.35 | 14,037 | 13 | 177 | 1,334 | 1,904 | 601 | 7,565 | 1,018 |
| Azerbaijan | .. | .. | 116 | 0.23 | 8 | 2 | 0 | 1 | 281 | 6 | 774 | 823 |
| Bangladesh | .. | .. | 193 | .. | 21 | 0 | 0 | 5 | .. | .. | .. | .. |
| Belarus | .. | .. | 490 | 0.69 | 268 | 3 | 6 | 50 | 1,065 | 382 | 2,410 | 3,556 |
| Belgium | 3,067 | 1,473 | 6,841 | 1.82 | 22,644 | 8 | 1,544 | 1,075 | 533 | 175 | 20,831[e] | 30,665[e] |
| Benin | .. | .. | .. | .. | 0 | 0 | .. | 2 | .. | .. | .. | .. |
| Bolivia | 120 | 6 | .. | 0.28 | 13 | 4 | 2 | 14 | .. | .. | .. | .. |
| Bosnia and Herzegovina | .. | .. | .. | .. | 62 | 3 | .. | .. | 66 | 306 | 295 | 902 |
| Botswana | .. | .. | .. | 0.39 | .. | .. | 0 | 7 | .. | .. | .. | .. |
| Brazil | 462 | 395 | 9,889 | 0.91 | 8,426 | 12 | 150 | 1,664 | 3,821 | 2,560 | 83,117 | 15,981 |
| Bulgaria | 1,301 | 478 | 764 | 0.50 | 486 | 6 | 11 | 69 | 261 | 52 | 6,731 | 1,252 |
| Burkina Faso | 19 | 17 | .. | 0.18 | 3 | 10 | 0 | .. | .. | .. | .. | .. |
| Burundi | .. | .. | .. | .. | 0 | 4 | 0 | .. | .. | .. | .. | .. |
| Cambodia | 17 | 13 | .. | 0.05 | 4 | 0 | 0 | 7 | .. | .. | 409 | 1,638 |
| Cameroon | 28 | .. | 131 | .. | 3 | 3 | 0 | 2 | .. | .. | .. | .. |
| Canada | 3,922 | 1,467 | 25,836 | 2.01 | 32,740 | 15 | 3,245 | 7,320 | 3,942 | 35,946 | 17,719 | 22,169 |
| Central African Republic | .. | .. | .. | .. | 0 | 0 | .. | .. | .. | .. | .. | .. |
| Chad | .. | .. | .. | .. | .. | .. | .. | .. | .. | .. | .. | .. |
| Chile | 833 | 302 | 1,559 | 0.68 | 401 | 7 | 55 | 381 | 361 | 2,646 | .. | .. |
| China | 708 | .. | 41,596 | 1.34 | 271,170 | 30 | 205 | 6,634 | 93,172 | 80,155 | 593,382 | 63,902 |
|   Hong Kong, China | 2,096 | 417 | .. | 0.74 | 1,788 | 11 | 245 | 1,289 | 156 | 11,607 | 8,173 | 20,877 |
| Colombia | 125 | 95 | 400 | 0.17 | 349 | 4 | 11 | 127 | .. | .. | .. | .. |
| Congo, Dem. Rep. | .. | .. | .. | 0.48 | .. | .. | .. | .. | .. | .. | .. | .. |
| Congo, Rep. | 30 | 32 | .. | .. | .. | .. | .. | .. | .. | .. | .. | .. |
| Costa Rica | .. | .. | 105 | 0.37 | 2,088 | 45 | 0 | 87 | .. | .. | .. | .. |
| Côte d'Ivoire | .. | .. | .. | .. | 521 | 42 | 0 | 10 | .. | .. | .. | .. |
| Croatia | 1,573 | 567 | 953 | 1.22 | 691 | 10 | 47 | 175 | 355 | 657 | 1,180 | 831 |
| Cuba | .. | .. | 261 | 0.56 | 59 | 12 | .. | .. | 94 | 191 | 301 | 482 |
| Czech Republic | 2,365 | 1,348 | 3,169 | 1.42 | 11,897 | 14 | 31 | 526 | 586 | 244 | 9,279 | 973 |
| Denmark | 5,190 | .. | 5,040 | 2.45 | 11,455 | 20 | .. | .. | 1,655 | 168 | 4,585 | 1,289 |
| Dominican Republic | .. | .. | .. | .. | .. | .. | 0 | 32 | .. | .. | .. | .. |
| Ecuador | 50 | .. | .. | 0.06 | 96 | 8 | 0 | 44 | 11 | 580 | 5,907 | 2,148 |
| Egypt, Arab Rep. | .. | .. | 1,658 | 0.19 | 15 | 1 | 138 | 159 | 428 | 1,008 | .. | .. |
| El Salvador | 47 | .. | .. | .. | 22 | 3 | 1 | 27 | .. | .. | .. | .. |
| Eritrea | .. | .. | .. | .. | .. | .. | .. | .. | .. | .. | .. | .. |
| Estonia | 2,505 | 490 | 439 | 0.99 | 771 | 13 | 6 | 29 | 23 | 15 | 1,241 | 1,737 |
| Ethiopia | 21 | 10 | 88 | 0.20 | .. | .. | 0 | 1 | .. | .. | .. | .. |
| Finland | 7,541 | .. | 4,811 | 3.52 | 13,990 | 22 | 1,494 | 1,901 | 1,827 | 232 | 2,820 | 661 |
| France | 3,320 | .. | 30,309 | 2.13 | 80,525 | 21 | 6,230 | 3,298 | 14,230 | 3,060 | 62,330 | 3,224 |
| Gabon | .. | .. | .. | .. | 71 | 32 | .. | .. | .. | .. | .. | .. |
| Gambia, The | 30 | 18 | .. | .. | 0 | 1 | .. | .. | .. | .. | .. | .. |
| Georgia | .. | .. | 145 | 0.18 | 74 | 16 | 13 | 5 | 225 | 22 | 507 | 518 |
| Germany | 3,242 | 1,056 | 44,145 | 2.51 | 154,757 | 17 | 5,888 | 7,843 | 47,537 | 12,685 | 67,208 | 3,718 |
| Ghana | .. | .. | 81 | .. | 1 | 0 | 0 | .. | .. | .. | .. | .. |
| Greece | 1,531 | 831 | 4,291 | 0.61 | 1,139 | 11 | 67 | 406 | 487 | 50 | 5,872 | 893 |
| Guatemala | .. | .. | .. | .. | 35 | 3 | 0 | 0 | 10 | 267 | .. | .. |
| Guinea | .. | .. | .. | .. | .. | .. | .. | 0 | .. | .. | .. | .. |
| Guinea-Bissau | .. | .. | .. | .. | .. | .. | .. | 0 | .. | .. | .. | .. |
| Haiti | .. | .. | .. | .. | .. | .. | 4 | 1 | .. | .. | .. | .. |

| | Researchers in R&D | Technicians in R&D | Scientific and technical journal articles | Expenditures for R&D | High-technology exports | | Royalty and license fees | | Patent applications filed[a,b] | | Trademark applications filed[a,c] | |
|---|---|---|---|---|---|---|---|---|---|---|---|---|
| | per million people 2000–05[d] | per million people 2000–05[d] | 2005 | % of GDP 2000–05[d] | $ millions 2006 | % of manufactured exports 2006 | Receipts $ millions 2006 | Payments $ millions 2006 | Residents 2005 | Non-residents 2005 | Residents 2005 | Non-residents 2005 |
| Honduras | .. | .. | .. | 0.05 | 3 | 1 | 0 | 25 | .. | .. | 1,149 | 3,388 |
| Hungary | 1,572 | 466 | 2,614 | 0.95 | 14,915 | 24 | 627 | 1,056 | 697 | 505 | 3,515 | 659 |
| India | .. | .. | 14,608 | 0.61 | 3,511 | 5 | 112 | 949 | 6,795 | 10,671 | .. | .. |
| Indonesia | 202 | .. | 205 | 0.05 | 5,900 | 13 | 14 | 870 | 234 | 4,069 | .. | .. |
| Iran, Islamic Rep. | .. | .. | 2,635 | 0.59 | 375 | 6 | .. | .. | .. | .. | 17,607 | 1,356 |
| Iraq | .. | .. | .. | .. | .. | .. | .. | .. | .. | .. | .. | .. |
| Ireland | 2,688 | 654 | 2,120 | 1.24 | 31,840 | 34 | 1,028 | 20,815 | 789 | 75 | 1,285 | 2,677 |
| Israel | .. | .. | 6,309 | 4.95 | 5,565 | 14 | 596 | 679 | 1,329 | 5,124 | 2,816 | 6,159 |
| Italy | 1,241 | .. | 24,645 | 1.10 | 25,046 | 7 | 1,116 | 1,840 | .. | .. | .. | .. |
| Jamaica | .. | .. | .. | 0.07 | 1 | 0 | 12 | 11 | 10 | 59 | .. | .. |
| Japan | 5,294 | 528 | 55,471 | 3.18 | 126,618 | 22 | 20,096 | 15,500 | 359,382 | 67,696 | 114,015 | 11,792 |
| Jordan | .. | .. | 275 | 0.34 | 35 | 1 | .. | .. | .. | .. | .. | .. |
| Kazakhstan | 803 | 86 | 96 | 0.28 | 987 | 21 | 0 | 48 | 1,696 | 102 | 2,908 | 1,070 |
| Kenya | .. | .. | 226 | .. | 17 | 3 | 10 | 50 | .. | .. | .. | .. |
| Korea, Dem. Rep. | .. | .. | .. | .. | .. | .. | .. | .. | .. | .. | .. | .. |
| Korea, Rep. | 3,760 | 567 | 16,396 | 2.99 | 92,945 | 32 | 2,011 | 4,487 | 121,942 | 38,979 | 99,435 | 16,454 |
| Kuwait | 74 | 95 | 233 | 0.18 | .. | .. | 0 | 0 | .. | .. | .. | .. |
| Kyrgyz Republic | .. | .. | .. | 0.20 | 6 | 3 | 2 | 19 | 179 | 1 | 133 | 345 |
| Lao PDR | .. | .. | .. | .. | .. | .. | .. | .. | .. | .. | .. | .. |
| Latvia | 1,423 | 460 | 134 | 0.57 | 242 | 7 | 11 | 20 | 112 | 57 | 1,367 | 487 |
| Lebanon | .. | .. | 234 | .. | 26 | 2 | 0 | 0 | .. | .. | .. | .. |
| Lesotho | .. | .. | .. | 0.06 | .. | .. | 18 | .. | .. | .. | .. | .. |
| Liberia | .. | .. | .. | .. | .. | .. | .. | .. | .. | .. | .. | .. |
| Libya | 361 | 493 | .. | .. | .. | .. | .. | 0 | .. | .. | .. | .. |
| Lithuania | 2,226 | 419 | 406 | 0.76 | 653 | 8 | 1 | 24 | 68 | 47 | 1,839 | 411 |
| Macedonia, FYR | 547 | 83 | .. | 0.25 | 18 | 1 | 3 | 9 | 37 | 415 | 619 | 437 |
| Madagascar | 43 | 6 | .. | 0.16 | 4 | 1 | 2 | 9 | 16 | 22 | 439 | 419 |
| Malawi | .. | .. | .. | .. | 9 | 11 | .. | .. | .. | .. | .. | .. |
| Malaysia | 509 | 64 | 615 | 0.63 | 63,411 | 54 | 26 | 1,052 | .. | .. | 10,479 | 11,668 |
| Mali | .. | .. | .. | .. | 2 | 4 | 0 | 1 | .. | .. | .. | .. |
| Mauritania | .. | .. | .. | .. | .. | .. | .. | .. | .. | .. | .. | .. |
| Mauritius | .. | .. | .. | 0.38 | 360 | 24 | 0 | 4 | .. | .. | .. | .. |
| Mexico | 321 | 147 | 3,902 | 0.41 | 35,732 | 19 | 171 | 503 | 549 | 13,887 | 45,736 | 22,962 |
| Moldova | .. | .. | 89 | .. | 10 | 5 | 2 | 4 | 377 | 11 | 1,941 | 474 |
| Mongolia | .. | .. | .. | 0.32 | 3 | 2 | .. | .. | 100 | 87 | 369 | 1,854 |
| Morocco | .. | .. | 443 | 0.75 | 830 | 10 | 5 | 48 | 139 | 521 | .. | .. |
| Mozambique | .. | .. | .. | 0.52 | 3 | 2 | 1 | 2 | .. | .. | .. | .. |
| Myanmar | 17 | 133 | .. | 0.16 | .. | .. | .. | .. | .. | .. | .. | .. |
| Namibia | .. | .. | .. | .. | 102 | 7 | .. | 3 | .. | .. | .. | .. |
| Nepal | 59 | 137 | .. | .. | .. | .. | .. | .. | .. | .. | .. | .. |
| Netherlands | 2,309 | 1,765 | 13,885 | 1.79 | 69,210 | 28 | 4,126 | 3,865 | 2,217 | 633 | .. | .. |
| New Zealand | 3,945 | 833 | 2,983 | 1.14 | 587 | 11 | 123 | 487 | 1,856 | 5,149 | 8,269 | 8,564 |
| Nicaragua | .. | .. | .. | 0.05 | 5 | 7 | 0 | .. | .. | .. | .. | .. |
| Niger | 7 | 10 | .. | .. | 5 | 11 | 0 | 1 | .. | .. | .. | .. |
| Nigeria | .. | .. | 362 | .. | .. | .. | .. | 45 | .. | .. | .. | .. |
| Norway | 4,729 | .. | 3,644 | 1.51 | 3,577 | 19 | 760 | 553 | 1,143 | 4,843 | .. | 5,996 |
| Oman | .. | .. | 111 | .. | 4 | 1 | .. | .. | .. | .. | .. | .. |
| Pakistan | 80 | 41 | 492 | 0.43 | 197 | 1 | 53 | 106 | .. | 1,081 | 8,319 | 5,117 |
| Panama | 97 | 387 | .. | 0.24 | 0 | 0 | 0 | 50 | .. | .. | .. | .. |
| Papua New Guinea | .. | .. | .. | .. | .. | .. | .. | .. | .. | .. | .. | .. |
| Paraguay | 82 | 118 | .. | 0.08 | 25 | 8 | 236 | 2 | .. | .. | .. | .. |
| Peru | .. | .. | 133 | 0.15 | 57 | 2 | 3 | 86 | 27 | 993 | 10,468 | 8,353 |
| Philippines | .. | .. | 178 | 0.14 | 27,626 | 68 | 6 | 349 | 157 | 1,731 | 7,031 | 5,526 |
| Poland | 1,613 | 232 | 6,844 | 0.57 | 3,284 | 4 | 38 | 1,313 | 2,028 | 4,555 | 13,828 | 984 |
| Portugal | 2,001 | 307 | 2,910 | 0.81 | 2,971 | 9 | 82 | 349 | 158 | 47 | 8,589 | 1,134 |
| Puerto Rico | .. | .. | .. | .. | .. | .. | .. | .. | .. | .. | .. | .. |

| | Researchers in R&D | Technicians in R&D | Scientific and technical journal articles | Expenditures for R&D | High-technology exports | | Royalty and license fees | | Patent applications filed[a,b] | | Trademark applications filed[a,c] | |
|---|---|---|---|---|---|---|---|---|---|---|---|---|
| | | | | | | % of manufactured exports | Receipts $ millions | Payments $ millions | Residents | Non-residents | Residents | Non-residents |
| | per million people 2000–05[d] | per million people 2000–05[d] | 2005 | % of GDP 2000–05[d] | $ millions 2006 | 2006 | 2006 | 2006 | 2005 | 2005 | 2005 | 2005 |
| Romania | 976 | 254 | 887 | 0.39 | 1,129 | 4 | 35 | 236 | 916 | 68 | 11,121 | 2,090 |
| Russian Federation | 3,244 | 553 | 14,412 | 1.07 | 4,755 | 9 | 299 | 2,002 | 23,588 | 8,665 | 26,460 | 7,926 |
| Rwanda | .. | .. | .. | .. | .. | .. | 0 | 1 | .. | .. | .. | .. |
| Saudi Arabia | .. | .. | 575 | .. | 148 | 1 | 0 | 0 | .. | .. | .. | .. |
| Senegal | .. | .. | 83 | 0.09 | 17 | 6 | .. | 7 | .. | .. | .. | .. |
| Serbia | .. | .. | 849 | 1.41 | 176 | 4 | .. | .. | 381 | 658 | 1,089 | 736 |
| Sierra Leone | .. | .. | .. | .. | .. | .. | 1 | 1 | .. | .. | .. | .. |
| Singapore | 5,500 | 381 | 3,609 | 2.36 | 124,133 | 58 | 730 | 10,470 | 435 | 8,170 | 4,839 | 26,986 |
| Slovak Republic | 2,022 | 416 | 919 | 0.52 | 2,196 | 6 | .. | .. | 154 | 96 | 2,740 | 1,146 |
| Slovenia | 1,949 | 1,264 | 1,035 | 1.22 | 941 | 5 | 17 | 154 | 323 | 27 | 1,399 | 417 |
| Somalia | .. | .. | .. | .. | .. | .. | .. | .. | .. | .. | .. | .. |
| South Africa | 379 | 110 | 2,392 | 0.87 | 1,799 | 6 | 46 | 1,282 | .. | 5,554 | .. | 28,331 |
| Spain | 2,549 | 888 | 18,336 | 1.12 | 10,037 | 6 | 922 | 2,504 | 3,027 | 326 | 54,268 | 2,541 |
| Sri Lanka | 130 | 72 | 136 | 0.19 | 99 | 2 | .. | .. | 95 | 189 | 3,989 | 1,773 |
| Sudan | .. | .. | .. | 0.30 | 0 | 1 | .. | .. | .. | .. | .. | .. |
| Swaziland | .. | .. | .. | .. | 2 | 0 | 0 | 106 | .. | .. | .. | .. |
| Sweden | 5,977 | .. | 10,012 | 3.86 | 18,078 | 16 | 3,964 | 1,618 | 2,512 | 448 | .. | 9,864 |
| Switzerland | 3,508 | 2,366 | 8,749 | 2.94 | 29,261 | 22 | .. | .. | 1,643 | 455 | 9,393 | 4,479 |
| Syrian Arab Republic | .. | .. | 77 | .. | 29 | 1 | .. | 20 | .. | .. | .. | .. |
| Tajikistan | .. | .. | .. | 0.10 | .. | .. | 1 | 0 | 32 | 2 | 63 | 277 |
| Tanzania | .. | .. | 107 | .. | 1 | 0 | 0 | 1 | .. | .. | .. | .. |
| Thailand | 287 | 208 | 1,249 | 0.25 | 26,953 | 27 | 46 | 2,046 | 891 | 5,449 | 22,612 | 9,241 |
| Timor-Leste | .. | .. | .. | .. | .. | .. | .. | .. | .. | .. | .. | .. |
| Togo | .. | .. | .. | .. | 0 | 0 | 0 | 3 | .. | .. | .. | .. |
| Trinidad and Tobago | .. | .. | .. | 0.12 | 30 | 1 | .. | .. | .. | 205 | .. | .. |
| Tunisia | 1,450 | 41 | 571 | 1.03 | 344 | 4 | 14 | 11 | 56 | 282 | .. | .. |
| Turkey | 469 | 37 | 7,815 | 0.67 | 258 | .. | 0 | 531 | 465 | 383 | 48,981 | 3,096 |
| Turkmenistan | .. | .. | .. | .. | .. | .. | .. | .. | .. | .. | .. | .. |
| Uganda | .. | .. | 93 | 1.25 | 60 | 34 | 2 | 11 | .. | .. | .. | .. |
| Ukraine | .. | .. | 2,105 | 1.07 | 926 | 3 | 32 | 428 | 3,535 | 2,057 | 13,184 | 3,182 |
| United Arab Emirates | .. | .. | 229 | .. | 10 | .. | .. | .. | .. | .. | .. | .. |
| United Kingdom | .. | .. | 45,572 | 1.75 | 115,464 | 34 | 13,588 | 9,962 | 17,488 | 10,500 | 24,163 | 4,529 |
| United States | 4,605 | .. | 205,320 | 2.68 | 219,179 | 30 | 62,378 | 26,433 | 202,776 | 187,957 | 224,269 | 28,359 |
| Uruguay | 366 | 50 | 204 | 0.26 | 36 | 3 | 0 | 7 | 37 | 514 | 5,626 | 8,189 |
| Uzbekistan | .. | .. | 157 | .. | .. | .. | .. | .. | 264 | 180 | 349 | 611 |
| Venezuela, RB | .. | .. | 534 | 0.25 | 80 | 2 | 0 | 257 | .. | .. | .. | .. |
| Vietnam | 115 | .. | 221 | 0.19 | 869 | 5 | .. | .. | .. | .. | .. | .. |
| West Bank and Gaza | .. | .. | .. | .. | .. | .. | .. | .. | .. | .. | .. | .. |
| Yemen, Rep. | .. | .. | .. | .. | 3 | 5 | 149 | 9 | .. | .. | .. | .. |
| Zambia | .. | .. | .. | 0.03 | 4 | 2 | .. | 0 | .. | .. | .. | .. |
| Zimbabwe | .. | .. | .. | .. | 8 | 2 | .. | .. | .. | .. | .. | .. |
| **World** | .. w | .. w | 708,086 s | 2.10 w | 1,418,509 s | 21 w | 135,278 s | 148,518 s | 915,598 s | 553,167 s | 1,584,746 s | 420,729 s |
| **Low income** | .. | .. | 16,711 | 0.57 | .. | 6 | 334 | 1,163 | 364 | 267 | 1,157 | 2,884 |
| **Middle income** | 803 | .. | 112,719 | 0.85 | 478,215 | 20 | 3,743 | 22,719 | 132,662 | 137,246 | 898,687 | 200,348 |
| Lower middle income | 500 | .. | 53,423 | 1.03 | 272,746 | 24 | 2,154 | 11,140 | 99,752 | 97,897 | 634,878 | 93,599 |
| Upper middle income | 1,285 | 372 | 59,296 | 0.72 | 143,179 | 16 | 1,589 | 11,579 | 32,910 | 39,349 | 263,809 | 106,749 |
| **Low & middle income** | .. | .. | 129,430 | 0.83 | .. | 20 | 4,077 | 23,882 | 133,026 | 137,513 | 899,844 | 203,232 |
| East Asia & Pacific | 704 | .. | 44,064 | 1.34 | .. | 33 | 297 | 10,959 | 94,397 | 91,491 | 611,261 | 82,950 |
| Europe & Central Asia | 2,019 | 371 | 39,975 | 0.87 | 31,160 | 9 | 1,129 | 5,998 | 33,133 | 17,286 | 136,989 | 30,048 |
| Latin America & Carib. | 392 | 256 | 20,045 | 0.59 | 48,368 | 12 | 753 | 4,146 | 4,873 | 20,916 | 151,155 | 58,115 |
| Middle East & N. Africa | .. | .. | 6,354 | .. | 1,263 | 5 | 306 | 247 | 623 | 2,266 | 17,607 | 3,369 |
| South Asia | .. | .. | 15,429 | 0.59 | .. | 4 | 175 | 1,060 | 6,795 | 11,752 | 8,319 | 5,117 |
| Sub-Saharan Africa | .. | .. | 3,563 | .. | .. | .. | 1,417 | 1,471 | 16 | 5,554 | 439 | 28,750 |
| **High income** | 3,731 | .. | 578,656 | 2.38 | 1,322,714 | 21 | 131,201 | 124,636 | 782,572 | 415,654 | 684,902 | 217,497 |
| Euro area | 2,734 | .. | 158,066 | 2.02 | 428,463 | 16 | 23,049 | 44,309 | 58,359 | 14,865 | 148,179 | 43,724 |

a. Original information was provided by the World Intellectual Property Organization (WIPO). The International Bureau of WIPO assumes no responsibility with respect to the transformation of these data. b. Excludes applications filed under the auspices of the European Patent Office (33,410 by residents, 95,303 by nonresidents) and the Eurasian Patent Organization (1,940 by nonresidents). c. Excludes applications filed under the auspices of the EU Office for Harmonization in the Internal Market (64,798 by nonresidents). d. Data are for the most recent year available. e. Includes Luxembourg and the Netherlands.

## About the data

Technological innovation, often fueled by government-led research and development (R&D), has been the driving force for industrial growth. The best opportunities to improve living standards, including new ways of reducing poverty, will come from science and technology. Science is playing a growing economic role: countries able to access, generate, and apply scientific knowledge will have a competitive edge. And there is greater appreciation of the need for high-quality scientific input into public policy issues such as regional and global environmental concerns.

Science and technology cover a range of issues too broad and complex to be quantified by a single set of indicators, but those in the table shed light on countries' technology base.

The United Nations Educational, Scientific, and Cultural Organization (UNESCO) Institute for Statistics collects data on researchers, technicians, and expenditure on R&D from around the world, through questionnaires and surveys and from other international sources. Data on researchers and technicians are normally calculated as full-time equivalents.

Scientific and technical article counts are from a set of journals classified and covered by the Institute for Scientific Information's Science Citation Index (SCI) and Social Sciences Citation Index (SSCI). Counts are based on fractional assignments; for example, an article with two authors from different countries is counted as one-half of an article for each country (see *Definitions* for fields covered). The SCI and SSCI databases cover the core set of scientific journals but may exclude some of regional or local importance. They may also reflect some bias toward English-language journals.

R&D expenditures include all expenditures for R&D performed within a country, including capital expenditures and current costs (annual wages and salaries and all associated costs of researchers, technicians, and supporting staff and other current costs, including noncapital purchases of materials, supplies, and R&D equipment such as utilities, books, journals, reference materials, subscriptions to libraries and scientific societies, and materials for laboratories).

The method used for determining a country's high-technology exports was developed by the Organisation for Economic Co-operation and Development in collaboration with Eurostat. Termed the "product approach" to distinguish it from a "sectoral approach," the method is based on R&D intensity (R&D expenditure divided by total sales) for groups of products from six countries (Germany, Italy, Japan, the Netherlands, Sweden, and the United States). Because industrial sectors specializing in a few high-technology products may also produce many low-technology products, the product approach is more appropriate than the sectoral approach for analyzing international trade. This method takes only R&D intensity into account, but other characteristics of high technology are also important, such as know-how, scientific and technical personnel, and technology embodied in patents. Considering these characteristics would yield a different list. (See Hatzichronoglou 1997 for further details.) Moreover, the R&D for high-technology exports may not have occurred in the reporting country.

A patent is an exclusive right granted for an invention (a product or process that provides a new way of doing something or a new technical solution to a problem). It must be of practical use and display a characteristic unknown in the body of existing knowledge in its technical field. A patent grants protection for the invention to the owner of the patent for a specified period, generally 20 years.

Most countries have systems to protect patentable inventions. The Patent Cooperation Treaty provides a system for filing patent applications. It consists of an international phase followed by a national or regional phase. An applicant files an international application and designates the countries in which patent protection is sought (since 2004 all eligible countries are automatically designated in every application under the treaty). The application is searched, published, and, optionally, an international preliminary examination is conducted. In the national (or regional) phase the applicant requests national processing of the application, pays additional fees, and initiates the national search and granting procedure. International applications under the treaty provide for a national patent grant only—there is no international patent. The national phase filing represents the applicant's seeking of patent protection for a given territory, whereas international filings, while they represent a legal right, do not accurately reflect where patent protection is eventually sought. Resident filings are those from residents of the country or region concerned. Nonresident filings are from applicants outside the country or region. For regional offices such as the European Patent Office, applications from residents of any member state of the regional patent convention are considered a resident filing. Some offices (notably the U.S. Patent and Trademark Office) use the residence of the inventor rather than the applicant to classify resident and nonresident filings. A trademark protects its owner by ensuring exclusive right to use it to identify goods or services or to authorize another to use it in return for payment. The period of protection varies, but a trademark can be renewed indefinitely for a fee. Trademarks help consumers identify a product or service whose nature and quality, indicated by its unique trademark, meet their needs.

• **Researchers in R&D** are professionals engaged in conceiving of or creating new knowledge, products, processes, methods, and systems and in managing the projects concerned. Postgraduate students at the doctoral level (ISCED97 level 6) engaged in R&D are considered researchers. • **Technicians in R&D** and equivalent staff are people whose main tasks require technical knowledge and experience in engineering, physical and life sciences (technicians), and social sciences and humanities (equivalent staff). They engage in R&D by performing scientific and technical tasks involving the application of concepts and operational methods, normally under the supervision of researchers. • **Scientific and technical journal articles** are published articles in physics, biology, chemistry, mathematics, clinical medicine, biomedical research, engineering and technology, and earth and space sciences. • **Expenditures for R&D** are current and capital expenditures on creative work undertaken systematically to increase the stock of knowledge, including knowledge of humanity, culture, and society, and the use of knowledge to devise new applications. R&D covers basic research, applied research, and experimental development. • **High-technology exports** are products with high R&D intensity, such as in aerospace, computers, pharmaceuticals, scientific instruments, and electrical machinery. • **Royalty and license fees** are payments and receipts between residents and nonresidents for authorized use of intangible, nonproduced, nonfinancial assets and proprietary rights (such as patents, copyrights, trademarks, franchises, and industrial processes) and for the use, through licensing agreements, of produced originals of prototypes (such as films and manuscripts). • **Patent applications filed** are worldwide patent applications filed through the Patent Cooperation Treaty procedure or with a national patent office. • **Trademark applications filed** are applications to register a trademark with a national or regional trademark office.

## Data sources

Data on R&D are provided by the UNESCO Institute for Statistics. Data on scientific and technical journal articles are from the U.S. National Science Foundation's *Science and Engineering Indicators 2008*. Data on high-technology exports are from the United Nations Statistics Division's Commodity Trade (Comtrade) database. Data on royalty and license fees are from the International Monetary Fund's *Balance of Payments Statistics Yearbook*. Data on patents and trademarks are from the World Intellectual Property Organization's *WIPO Patent Report: Statistics on Worldwide Patent Activity* (2007 edition) and www.wipo.int.

6

GLOBAL LINKS

# The world economy expands and economies grow closer

Economic integration is the widening and deepening of the ties that link national economies. Trade, finance, movement of people, and transportation and communication infrastructure are the mechanisms. But integration is not a simple or certain process. Political and cultural connections underpin economic alliances. Geography may pose obstacles to integration, while technology can overcome them.

The past two decades have seen an enormous increase in the size of the global economy and of the economic ties between countries. Between 1990 and 2006 East Asia and Pacific's trade increased from 47 percent of its gross domestic product (GDP) to 87 percent, and gross private capital flows from international sources increased from 7 percent of GDP to 11 percent. In Sub-Saharan Africa trade within the region and with the rest of the world increased from 52 percent of GDP to 72 percent, and gross private capital flows rose from 12 percent to 14 percent. Evidence of integration? Yes, but the two regions have had much different experiences. Each had about 3.5 percent of global exports in 1980, but by 2006 East Asia and Pacific's share had grown to 10.8 percent while Sub-Saharan Africa's had fallen to 1.9 percent.

As global integration proceeds, developing countries are likely to expand their share of the global economy, especially regional centers with large populations and a significant economic base, such as Brazil, China, India, the Russian Federation, and South Africa. But even small and remote economies can take part. Better air and ocean transport gets products to markets faster and with more precise timing. Better transportation has been complemented by improvements in technology and favorable regulatory environments, reducing the costs of global communication, information dissemination, and management of economic activities. But as Dollar (2005, p. 148) notes, "As in previous waves of integration . . . change is driven partly by technological advances in transport and communications and partly by deliberate policy choices." Integration does not happen automatically.

All developing countries have the potential to gain from an integrated global environment. Like all economic forces, global integration may produce winners and losers. To realize the benefits of integration, countries need the capacity to absorb new technologies, use capital productively, and increase their labor force's knowledge and skills. Countries do not start with the same endowments—and wars, political divisions, and plain bad luck may blight their opportunities. The challenge is to ensure sustainable and widely shared growth.

Monitoring the development of global links provides the underpinning for policies aimed at managing challenges and aiding integration that is inclusive for all. The data in this section provide a snapshot of the world's integration and and a framework for measuring it.

## Developing countries' growing world trade

International trade is a critical channel for integration. It increases economic efficiency and brings producers and consumers together. Developing countries' share in world trade has been rising from 16 percent in 1990 to 30 percent in 2006, led by China, whose exports now rival those of the United States, and with Brazil and India not far behind (figure 6a). Projections of further increases in developing countries' share, to 45 percent by 2030 (*Global Economic Prospects 2007*), reflect increasing integration.

Developing country trade integration, measured by the share of imports plus exports in GDP, has been rising rapidly, increasing from 40 percent of GDP in 1990 to almost 67 percent in 2006, surpassing the share in high-income economies. Developing country exports are changing as well. The share of manufactured goods in exports is large and rising while that of food and commodities (excluding fuels) is small and falling (figure 6b). And despite the attention given to the spread of offshore services, trade in goods remains many times greater than trade in services. India is a notable exception: its service sector now produces almost 40 percent of its exports.

## Financial integration: resilient and unabated

More access to international capital markets and foreign direct investment (FDI) has helped developing countries surmount their less developed capital markets. Developing countries have decreased their vulnerability to financial crises by reducing their external debt burden from 39 percent of gross national income in 1995 to 26 percent in 2006 and increasing foreign exchange reserves to 92 percent of long-term debt and 423 percent of more volatile, short-term debt in 2006 (figure 6c).

Private capital flows to developing countries increased more than 10-fold between 1990 and 2006. In 2006 developing countries received almost one-third of global FDI, though just over one-tenth of that went to low-income economies. Sub-Saharan Africa's 34 low-income economies received only 1 percent. The main source of external financing for low-income countries remains official development assistance (ODA). ODA, however, includes debt relief, technical assistance, and emergency relief, which do not provide the long-term investment needed to raise productive capacity. In constant prices ODA has risen more than 50 percent since 2000, but excluding debt, technical assistance, and emergency relief, it has risen only 25 percent (figure 6d).

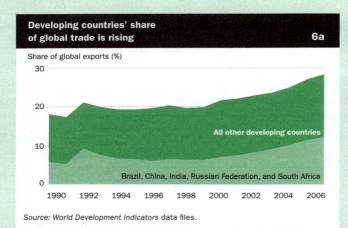

**Developing countries' share of global trade is rising** — 6a

Share of global exports (%)

All other developing countries

Brazil, China, India, Russian Federation, and South Africa

*Source: World Development Indicators data files.*

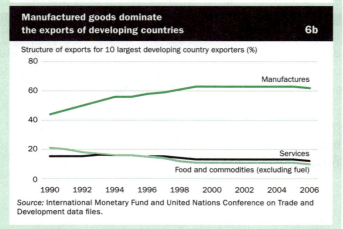

**Manufactured goods dominate the exports of developing countries** — 6b

Structure of exports for 10 largest developing country exporters (%)

Manufactures

Services

Food and commodities (excluding fuel)

*Source: International Monetary Fund and United Nations Conference on Trade and Development data files.*

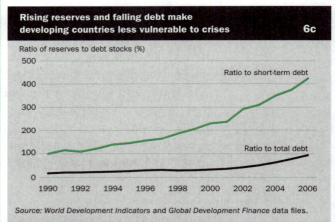

**Rising reserves and falling debt make developing countries less vulnerable to crises** — 6c

Ratio of reserves to debt stocks (%)

Ratio to short-term debt

Ratio to total debt

*Source: World Development Indicators and Global Development Finance data files.*

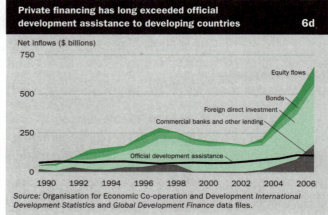

**Private financing has long exceeded official development assistance to developing countries** — 6d

Net inflows ($ billions)

Equity flows

Bonds

Foreign direct investment

Commercial banks and other lending

Official development assistance

*Source: Organisation for Economic Co-operation and Development International Development Statistics and Global Development Finance data files.*

## Movement of people facilitates common economic and social goals

Movement of people as tourists, migrants, or business travelers raises awareness and spreads knowledge, important elements of globalization. These movements link diverse populations with common economic and social goals. Global tourism increased 5.6 percent in 2006, a pace well above its long-term average. Tourist departures from developing economies have risen 43 percent since 2000, and 7 of the top 15 tourist destinations are in developing economies.

Migration increased sharply over the past two decades. Like other elements of globalization, migration patterns are shaped by market forces and official policies. Opportunities in high-income economies are a strong lure (figure 6e), and a need for workers has led many countries to relax entry barriers. Successful migration requires resources, skills, and adaptation to a new culture. So, the largest net flows of migrants are from middle-income economies.

Migration facilitates cross-border remittances, a major source of foreign earnings for many developing countries. Remittances to developing countries almost quadrupled between 1995 and 2006, to more than $220 billion (figure 6f), rivaling other forms of private financing.

## The role of information and communication technologies is expanding

Communication and information networks are crucial for overcoming geographic barriers, bringing people and markets closer. These networks enable effective management of enterprises across borders and participation in global production and service supply chains. Deregulation and competition have reduced communication costs. The average cost of a three-minute call to the United States fell from $4.00 in 1999 to $1.40 in 2004.

Over that period the share of people with access to the Internet tripled. The Internet promises to be an even greater force for globalization and development. But diffusion of technology around the world and within countries is unequal (figures 6g and 6h). Average contracted capacity for international Internet connections in developing economies grew from 3 bits per second per person in 2000 to 140 in 2006, still far short of the estimated 5,000 high-income average. Low-income economies' Internet capacity was still less than 20 bits per second per person in 2006, and international voice traffic less than 5 percent of the high-income average. Capital, policies, and infrastructure are needed to develop, adapt, and diffuse communication networks to accelerate development.

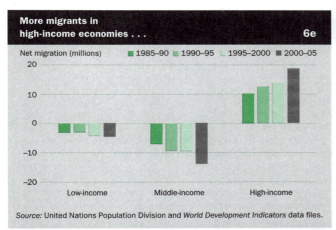

**More migrants in high-income economies . . .**     **6e**

Net migration (millions)    ■ 1985–90   ■ 1990–95   ■ 1995–2000   ■ 2000–05

*Source:* United Nations Population Division and *World Development Indicators* data files.

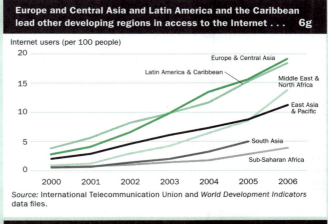

**Europe and Central Asia and Latin America and the Caribbean lead other developing regions in access to the Internet . . .**     **6g**

Internet users (per 100 people)

*Source:* International Telecommunication Union and *World Development Indicators* data files.

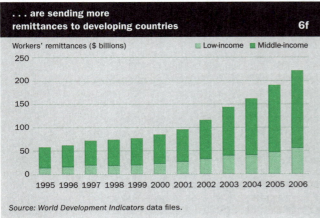

**. . . are sending more remittances to developing countries**     **6f**

Workers' remittances ($ billions)    ■ Low-income   ■ Middle-income

*Source: World Development Indicators* data files.

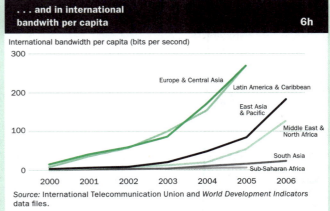

**. . . and in international bandwith per capita**     **6h**

International bandwidth per capita (bits per second)

*Source:* International Telecommunication Union and *World Development Indicators* data files.

| | Trade % of GDP | | International finance — % of GDP | | | | Movement of people | | | International communication | | |
|---|---|---|---|---|---|---|---|---|---|---|---|---|
| | Merchandise | Services | Financing through international capital markets Gross inflows | Foreign direct investment Net inflows | Net outflows | Workers' remittances and compensation of employees received | Net migration | International tourists Inbound | Outbound | Cost of call to U.S.[a] $ per 3 minutes | Voice traffic[a] minutes per person | Internet bandwidth[a] bits per capita |
| | 2006 | 2006 | 2006 | 2006 | 2006 | 2006 | 2000–05 | 2006 | 2006 | 2005 | 2006 | 2006 |
| Afghanistan | 40.4 | .. | 0.0 | .. | .. | .. | 1,112 | .. | .. | 0.4 | 1 | 0 |
| Albania | 42.3 | 34.0 | 0.2 | 3.6 | 0.1 | 14.9 | −110 | 60[b] | 2,616 | 1.3 | 160 | 4 |
| Algeria | 66.3 | .. | 0.9 | 1.6 | .. | 2.2[c] | −140 | 1,443[d,e] | 1,513 | 2.1 | 17 | 5 |
| Angola | 103.2 | 19.9 | 3.6 | −0.1 | 0.4 | .. | 175 | 121 | .. | 3.2 | .. | 12 |
| Argentina | 37.7 | 7.5 | 1.5 | 2.3 | 1.0 | 0.3 | −100 | 4,156 | 4,009 | .. | 33 | 690 |
| Armenia | 50.1 | 17.2 | 0.4 | 5.4 | 0.0 | 18.4[c] | −100 | 381 | 329 | 2.4 | 128 | 22 |
| Australia | 33.6 | 8.4 | .. | 3.4 | 3.0 | 0.4 | 593 | 5,064[f] | 4,941 | .. | .. | 11,593 |
| Austria | 87.2 | 24.1 | .. | 0.0 | 1.2 | 0.6 | 180 | 20,261[g] | 10,042 | 0.7 | .. | 6,634 |
| Azerbaijan | 58.6 | 19.2 | 28.2 | −2.9 | 3.6 | 4.1 | −100 | 1,194 | 1,836 | 4.2 | 33 | 36 |
| Bangladesh | 45.1 | 5.9 | 0.2 | 1.1 | 0.0 | 8.8 | −500 | 200 | 1,819 | 2.0 | 6 | 8 |
| Belarus | 113.8 | 10.2 | 0.9 | 1.0 | 0.0 | 0.9 | 0 | 89 | 525 | 1.9 | 64 | 192 |
| Belgium | 183.5 | 28.6 | .. | 15.7 | 14.0 | 1.9 | 180 | 6,995[g] | 7,852 | 0.8 | .. | 11,279 |
| Benin | 32.5 | 11.0 | 2.1 | 1.3 | 0.0 | 3.6[c] | 99 | 180 | .. | 4.8 | 6 | 5 |
| Bolivia | 59.9 | 11.1 | 0.0 | 2.2 | 0.0 | 5.5 | −100 | 515 | 466 | .. | 49 | 43 |
| Bosnia and Herzegovina | 86.6 | 13.2 | 0.8 | 3.5 | 0.0 | 16.9 | 115 | 256[g] | .. | 3.6 | 208 | 40 |
| Botswana | 73.9 | 15.2 | 0.0 | 4.6 | −0.5 | 1.1 | 20 | 1,675 | .. | 2.9 | 74 | 16 |
| Brazil | 21.9 | 4.6 | 6.0 | 1.8 | 2.6 | 0.4 | −229 | 5,019 | 4,825 | 0.7 | .. | 150 |
| Bulgaria | 121.3 | 29.1 | 9.0 | 16.4 | 0.5 | 5.4 | −43 | 5,158 | 4,180 | 0.6 | 72 | 1,756 |
| Burkina Faso | 30.6 | .. | 0.6 | 0.4 | .. | 0.8[c] | 100 | 264[h] | .. | 1.1 | 11 | 15 |
| Burundi | 54.2 | 25.8 | 0.0 | 0.0 | .. | 0.0 | 192 | 201[e] | .. | 2.5 | .. | 1 |
| Cambodia | 119.9 | 28.7 | 1.5 | 6.7 | 0.1 | 4.1 | 10 | 1,700 | 427 | 2.9 | 10 | 1 |
| Cameroon | 35.8 | 15.3 | 0.0 | 1.7 | 0.0 | 0.6[c] | 6 | 176[h] | .. | .. | 9 | 9 |
| Canada | 58.8 | 10.4 | .. | 5.4 | 3.6 | .. | 1,041 | 18,265 | 22,732 | .. | .. | 6,732 |
| Central African Republic | 24.1 | .. | 0.0 | 1.6 | .. | .. | −45 | 12[f] | 7 | 2.0 | .. | 0 |
| Chad | 76.4 | .. | 0.0 | 10.7 | .. | .. | 219 | 29[h] | .. | .. | .. | 1 |
| Chile | 66.2 | 10.9 | 6.2 | 5.5 | 2.0 | 0.0 | 30 | 2,027 | 2,651 | .. | 48 | 780 |
| China | 66.6 | 7.3 | 2.6 | 3.0 | 0.7 | 0.9[c] | −1,900 | 49,913 | 34,524 | 2.9 | 7 | 196 |
| Hong Kong, China | 346.9 | 57.3 | .. | 22.6 | 22.9 | 0.2 | 300 | 15,821 | 75,812 | 0.8 | 1,179 | 13,439 |
| Colombia | 32.9 | 5.8 | 3.4 | 4.2 | 0.7 | 2.6 | −120 | 1,053[d] | 1,553 | .. | 68 | 560 |
| Congo, Dem. Rep. | 59.7 | .. | 0.0 | 2.1 | .. | .. | −237 | 61[f] | .. | .. | 5 | 0 |
| Congo, Rep. | 109.7 | 30.1 | 0.0 | 4.7 | 0.1 | 0.2[c] | −10 | .. | .. | 5.4 | .. | 0 |
| Costa Rica | 88.8 | 20.5 | 1.1 | 6.6 | 0.4 | 2.3 | 84 | 1,725 | 485 | .. | 127 | 176 |
| Côte d'Ivoire | 78.2 | 17.3 | 0.0 | 1.8 | .. | 0.9 | −339 | .. | .. | 2.2 | 17 | 3 |
| Croatia | 74.2 | 33.4 | 6.1 | 7.9 | 0.5 | 2.9 | 100 | 8,659[g] | .. | .. | 231 | 1,074 |
| Cuba | .. | .. | .. | .. | .. | .. | −129 | 2,150[f] | 199 | 7.5 | 31 | 14 |
| Czech Republic | 131.7 | 17.6 | .. | 4.2 | 0.9 | 0.8 | 67 | 6,435[g] | .. | 1.1 | 95 | 2,170 |
| Denmark | 65.0 | 35.9 | .. | 1.2 | 3.0 | 0.3 | 46 | 4,699[g] | 5,469 | 0.9 | 318 | 34,796 |
| Dominican Republic | 55.4 | 18.2 | 4.3 | 3.7 | 0.0 | 9.6 | −148 | 3,965[e,f] | 420 | 0.2 | .. | 6 |
| Ecuador | 59.7 | 8.1 | 0.2 | 0.7 | 0.0 | 7.1 | −400 | 841[d,i] | 733 | .. | 216 | 227 |
| Egypt, Arab Rep. | 31.9 | 25.8 | 5.3 | 9.3 | 0.1 | 5.0 | −525 | 8,646 | 4,531 | 1.5 | 30 | 126 |
| El Salvador | 59.7 | 16.0 | 7.7 | 1.1 | −0.3 | 17.8 | −143 | 1,138 | 1,382 | 2.4 | 410 | 23 |
| Eritrea | 50.7 | .. | 0.0 | 0.3 | .. | .. | 229 | 78[d,e] | .. | 3.6 | 9 | 2 |
| Estonia | 138.6 | 36.3 | 3.6 | 9.7 | 6.3 | 2.4 | 1 | 1,940 | .. | 0.9 | 109 | 11,175 |
| Ethiopia | 42.1 | 17.6 | 0.0 | 2.7 | 0.0 | 1.3 | −140 | 290[e] | .. | 4.0 | 3 | 0 |
| Finland | 69.3 | 15.1 | .. | 2.5 | 0.8 | 0.3 | 33 | 3,375 | 5,756 | 1.8 | .. | 4,311 |
| France | 45.6 | 10.1 | .. | 3.6 | 5.2 | 0.6 | 722 | 79,083 | 22,466 | 0.8 | 183 | 3,286 |
| Gabon | 76.8 | 15.3 | 0.6 | 2.8 | −0.3 | 0.1[c] | 10 | .. | .. | 2.8 | 74 | 153 |
| Gambia, The | 51.9 | 36.4 | 0.0 | 16.1 | .. | 12.5 | 31 | 125 | .. | 1.8 | .. | 6 |
| Georgia | 60.3 | 21.0 | 2.1 | 13.7 | −0.2 | 6.3 | −248 | 983[d] | .. | .. | .. | 7 |
| Germany | 69.8 | 13.4 | .. | 1.5 | 2.7 | 0.2 | 1,000 | 23,569[g] | 71,200 | 0.4 | .. | 6,864 |
| Ghana | 71.3 | 22.7 | 7.1 | 3.4 | 0.0 | 0.8 | 12 | 429[e] | .. | 0.4 | 20 | 9 |
| Greece | 27.3 | 16.9 | .. | 1.8 | 1.4 | 0.5 | 154 | 16,039 | .. | 1.1 | 182 | 587 |
| Guatemala | 50.8 | 8.7 | 0.0 | 1.0 | 0.0 | 10.3 | −300 | 1,502 | 1,055 | 1.2 | 195 | 56 |
| Guinea | 57.3 | 9.1 | 0.0 | 3.3 | .. | 1.3[c] | −425 | 46[f] | .. | .. | .. | 0 |
| Guinea-Bissau | 60.8 | 19.3 | 0.0 | 13.8 | −2.8 | 9.2[c] | 1 | 12[f] | .. | .. | .. | 1 |
| Haiti | 44.5 | 14.9 | 2.7 | 3.2 | .. | 21.5 | −140 | 112 | .. | 2.2 | .. | 17 |

# Integration with the global economy

| | Trade | | International finance % of GDP | | | | Movement of people | | | International communication | | |
|---|---|---|---|---|---|---|---|---|---|---|---|---|
| | % of GDP | | Financing through international capital markets Gross inflows | Foreign direct investment Net inflows | Net outflows | Workers' remittances and compensation of employees received | Net migration | International tourists Inbound | Outbound | Cost of call to U.S.[a] $ per 3 minutes | Voice traffic[a] minutes per person | Internet bandwidth[a] bits per capita |
| | Merchandise | Services | | | | | | | | | | |
| | 2006 | 2006 | 2006 | 2006 | 2006 | 2006 | 2000–05 | 2006 | 2006 | 2005 | 2006 | 2006 |
| Honduras | 79.6 | 19.2 | 0.0 | 4.2 | 0.0 | 25.6 | −150 | 739 | 308 | 2.5 | 96 | 6 |
| Hungary | 134.1 | 22.1 | 10.3 | 5.4 | 14.5 | 0.3 | 65 | 9,259 | 17,612 | 1.0 | 105 | 993 |
| India | 32.4 | 15.2 | 4.2 | 1.9 | 1.1 | 2.8 | −1,350 | 4,447[i] | 8,340 | 1.2 | .. | 24 |
| Indonesia | 50.4 | 9.1 | 3.7 | 1.5 | 0.7 | 1.6 | −1,000 | 4,871 | 4,106 | 2.8 | 5 | 7 |
| Iran, Islamic Rep. | 57.3 | .. | 0.5 | 0.4 | .. | 0.5[c] | −1,250 | 1,659 | | 0.5 | 9 | 53 |
| Iraq | .. | .. | .. | .. | .. | .. | −375 | .. | .. | .. | .. | .. |
| Ireland | 83.5 | 67.1 | .. | −0.4 | 6.7 | 0.2 | 188 | 8,001 | 6,848 | 0.7 | .. | 5,912 |
| Israel | 68.7 | 24.3 | .. | 10.2 | 10.3 | 0.8 | 115 | 1,825[i] | 3,713 | 0.6 | 364 | 2,455 |
| Italy | 45.8 | 10.8 | .. | 2.1 | 2.3 | 0.1 | 1,125 | 41,058 | 25,697 | 0.8 | .. | 2,044 |
| Jamaica | 76.1 | 46.6 | 11.0 | 8.8 | 0.9 | 19.4 | −100 | 1,679[e,f] | .. | 0.9 | .. | 15,822 |
| Japan | 28.1 | 5.8 | .. | −0.2 | 1.1 | 0.0 | 270 | 7,334[d,i] | 17,535 | 1.6 | 43 | 1,038 |
| Jordan | 117.9 | 36.9 | 0.4 | 22.8 | −1.0 | 20.4 | 130 | 3,225[e] | 1,628 | 1.4 | 139 | 57 |
| Kazakhstan | 80.8 | 14.2 | 25.3 | 7.6 | −0.5 | 0.2 | −200 | 3,143 | 3,004 | .. | .. | 63 |
| Kenya | 47.2 | 17.1 | 1.4 | 0.2 | 0.1 | 5.0[c] | 25 | 1,536 | .. | 3.0 | 6 | 21 |
| Korea, Dem. Rep. | .. | .. | .. | .. | .. | .. | 0 | .. | .. | .. | .. | .. |
| Korea, Rep. | 71.5 | 13.8 | .. | 0.4 | 0.8 | 0.1 | −80 | 6,155[d,e] | 11,610 | 0.8 | 92 | 1,028 |
| Kuwait | 75.1 | 16.5 | .. | 0.3 | 6.4 | .. | 264 | 91[h] | 1,928 | 1.5 | .. | 348 |
| Kyrgyz Republic | 89.2 | 29.6 | 0.0 | 6.5 | 2.0 | 17.1 | −75 | 766 | 454 | 5.4 | 30 | 39 |
| Lao PDR | 56.3 | .. | 0.0 | 5.5 | .. | 0.0[c] | −115 | 842 | .. | 1.1 | 7 | 4 |
| Latvia | 87.8 | 23.0 | 7.5 | 8.3 | 0.9 | 2.4 | −20 | 1,535 | 3,151 | 1.6 | 67 | 3,230 |
| Lebanon | 54.8 | 89.5 | 18.3 | 12.3 | 0.3 | 22.9 | 0 | 1,063 | .. | 2.2 | 279 | 111 |
| Lesotho | 144.5 | 10.4 | 0.0 | 5.2 | 0.0 | 24.2 | −36 | 347 | .. | 3.3 | 18 | 2 |
| Liberia | 99.0 | .. | 246.8 | −13.0 | .. | .. | −119 | .. | .. | .. | .. | .. |
| Libya | 92.3 | 6.1 | 0.0 | .. | 0.9 | 0.0 | 10 | 149 | .. | .. | 66 | 21 |
| Lithuania | 112.3 | 20.7 | 4.3 | 6.1 | 1.0 | 3.3 | −30 | 2,000 | .. | 1.6 | 49 | 2,714 |
| Macedonia, FYR | 99.1 | 18.9 | 1.1 | 5.6 | 0.0 | 4.3 | −10 | 202[g] | .. | .. | 63 | 17 |
| Madagascar | 44.4 | 22.1 | 0.0 | 4.2 | .. | 0.2[c] | −5 | 312[f] | .. | 0.6 | 1 | 2 |
| Malawi | 55.3 | .. | 0.0 | 0.9 | .. | 0.0[c] | −30 | 438 | .. | .. | .. | 1 |
| Malaysia | 193.7 | 30.2 | 7.0 | 4.0 | 4.0 | 1.0 | 150 | 17,547 | 30,761 | 0.7 | .. | 124 |
| Mali | 54.7 | 16.3 | 0.0 | 3.2 | 0.0 | 3.0[c] | −134 | 153[f,h] | .. | .. | .. | 26 |
| Mauritania | 85.0 | .. | 0.0 | −0.1 | .. | 0.1[c] | 30 | .. | .. | .. | .. | 30 |
| Mauritius | 91.4 | 47.2 | 2.8 | 1.7 | 0.2 | 3.4[c] | 0 | 788 | 186 | 1.6 | 150 | 153 |
| Mexico | 61.8 | 4.7 | 4.6 | 2.3 | 0.7 | 3.0 | −3,983 | 21,353[e] | 14,002 | 0.8 | 174 | 109 |
| Moldova | 111.6 | 29.0 | 0.0 | 7.2 | 0.0 | 35.2 | −250 | 13 | 68 | 1.5 | 110 | 147 |
| Mongolia | 96.7 | 32.2 | 0.0 | 11.0 | 0.0 | 5.8 | −50 | 386 | .. | .. | 5 | 13 |
| Morocco | 55.5 | 21.9 | 1.4 | 4.1 | 0.7 | 8.3 | −550 | 6,558[e] | 2,247 | 1.7 | 65 | 377 |
| Mozambique | 76.2 | 16.7 | 0.6 | 2.2 | 0.0 | 1.2 | −20 | 578 | .. | 1.2 | 13 | 1 |
| Myanmar | .. | .. | .. | .. | .. | .. | −99 | 264 | .. | 0.2 | 3 | 2 |
| Namibia | 84.8 | 14.6 | 0.0 | .. | −0.2 | 0.3 | −1 | 833 | .. | .. | .. | 18 |
| Nepal | 32.0 | 9.8 | 0.0 | −0.1 | .. | 16.3 | −100 | 375 | 373 | 2.0 | 6 | 5 |
| Netherlands | 132.7 | 24.4 | .. | 1.1 | 7.0 | 0.4 | 110 | 10,739[g] | 16,695 | 0.3 | .. | 20,501 |
| New Zealand | 46.8 | 15.0 | .. | 7.6 | 0.7 | 0.6 | 102 | 2,409[d] | 1,861 | 1.3 | 361 | 1,107 |
| Nicaragua | 75.8 | 15.6 | 1.6 | 5.3 | 0.0 | 12.4 | −210 | 773[e] | 788 | 3.2 | 62 | 1 |
| Niger | 40.7 | 10.7 | 0.0 | 0.6 | 0.3 | 1.8[c] | −28 | 60 | .. | .. | .. | 2 |
| Nigeria | 64.0 | 11.7 | 1.0 | 4.7 | .. | 2.9[c] | −170 | 1,010 | .. | 1.5 | .. | 1 |
| Norway | 55.4 | 19.2 | .. | 1.4 | 4.6 | 0.2 | 84 | 3,945 | 3,193 | .. | 193 | 9,305 |
| Oman | 89.2 | 12.3 | 22.8 | 2.9 | 0.4 | 0.1 | −150 | 1,306[h] | .. | 1.9 | 189 | 174 |
| Pakistan | 36.9 | 9.4 | 3.0 | 3.4 | 0.1 | 4.0 | −1,239 | 898 | .. | 1.0 | 10 | 5 |
| Panama | 34.6 | 33.1 | 7.6 | 15.1 | 0.0 | 0.9 | 8 | 843 | 284 | .. | .. | 287 |
| Papua New Guinea | 112.7 | 29.7 | 1.4 | 0.6 | 0.1 | 0.2[c] | 0 | 78 | .. | .. | .. | 1 |
| Paraguay | 83.9 | 13.3 | 0.0 | 2.0 | 0.0 | 4.7 | −45 | 388[i] | 210 | 0.9 | 31 | 83 |
| Peru | 41.9 | 6.3 | 3.6 | 3.8 | .. | 2.0 | −510 | 1,635 | 1,857 | 1.8 | 99 | 367 |
| Philippines | 83.8 | 10.7 | 8.6 | 2.0 | 0.1 | 13.0 | −900 | 2,843[e] | 2,144 | 1.2 | 28 | 38 |
| Poland | 69.8 | 11.5 | 3.6 | 5.7 | 2.7 | 1.3 | −200 | 15,670 | 44,696 | 1.4 | .. | 560 |
| Portugal | 56.5 | 15.1 | .. | 3.8 | 1.8 | 1.7 | 276 | 11,282[e] | 18,378 | 1.0 | 178 | 829 |
| Puerto Rico | .. | .. | .. | .. | .. | .. | −10 | 3,722[f] | 1,468 | .. | .. | 511 |

| | Trade — % of GDP | | International finance — % of GDP | | | | Movement of people | | | International communication | | |
|---|---|---|---|---|---|---|---|---|---|---|---|---|
| | Merchandise | Services | Financing through international capital markets Gross inflows | Foreign direct investment Net inflows | Net outflows | Workers' remittances and compensation of employees received | Net migration | International tourists Inbound | Outbound | Cost of call to U.S.[a] $ per 3 minutes | Voice traffic[a] minutes per person | Internet bandwidth[a] bits per capita |
| | 2006 | 2006 | 2006 | 2006 | 2006 | 2006 | 2000–05 | 2006 | 2006 | 2005 | 2006 | 2006 |
| Romania | 68.6 | 11.6 | 1.2 | 9.4 | 0.3 | 5.5 | –270 | 6,037[d] | 8,906 | 0.8 | .. | 1,503 |
| Russian Federation | 47.5 | 7.7 | 7.9 | 3.1 | 2.3 | 0.3 | 917 | 22,486 | 29,107 | 2.0 | .. | 100 |
| Rwanda | 25.6 | 15.0 | 0.0 | 0.5 | –0.6 | 0.8 | 43 | .. | .. | 2.4 | .. | 7 |
| Saudi Arabia | 79.0 | 13.7 | .. | 0.2 | 0.0 | .. | 285 | 8,620 | 2,000 | .. | 216 | 126 |
| Senegal | 54.3 | 17.2 | 1.0 | 0.6 | 0.2 | 6.9[c] | –100 | 769 | .. | 1.0 | 39 | 103 |
| Serbia | 61.3 | .. | 0.0 | 16.0 | .. | 14.7[c,j] | –339 | 469[g] | 67 | .. | .. | 95 |
| Sierra Leone | 41.7 | 8.5 | 0.0 | 4.1 | 0.0 | 2.3 | 472 | 34[f] | .. | 0.7 | 1,045 | 7,052 |
| Singapore | 386.2 | 91.6 | .. | 18.3 | 6.5 | .. | 200 | 7,588 | 5,533 | 0.7 | 1,045 | 7,052 |
| Slovak Republic | 159.1 | .. | 2.4 | 7.6 | .. | 0.8[c] | 3 | 1,612[g] | 22,688 | 1.1 | 90 | 2,913 |
| Slovenia | 127.0 | 20.4 | 1.7 | 2.4 | 0.8 | | 22 | 1,617[g] | 2,680 | 0.7 | .. | 1,255 |
| Somalia | .. | .. | .. | .. | .. | .. | 100 | .. | .. | .. | .. | 0 |
| South Africa | 53.2 | 10.3 | 10.3 | 0.0 | 2.6 | 0.3 | 75 | 8,396 | .. | 0.8 | .. | 19 |
| Spain | 42.6 | 15.1 | .. | 1.6 | 7.2 | 0.7 | 2,846 | 58,451 | 10,676 | 0.6 | 173 | 2,776 |
| Sri Lanka | 63.6 | 14.9 | 0.1 | 1.8 | 0.1 | 8.7 | –442 | 560[i] | 757 | 2.1 | 28 | 25 |
| Sudan | 36.7 | 8.0 | 0.2 | 9.4 | 0.0 | 3.1 | –532 | 328[e] | .. | .. | 12 | 5 |
| Swaziland | 160.9 | 24.6 | 0.0 | 1.4 | 0.1 | 3.7 | –6 | 873[h] | 1,072 | 3.0 | .. | 1 |
| Sweden | 71.4 | 23.5 | .. | 7.1 | 6.2 | 0.1 | 152 | 3,270[g] | 12,591 | 0.4 | .. | 17,468 |
| Switzerland | 75.9 | 21.2 | .. | 7.1 | 18.6 | 0.5 | 100 | 7,863[h] | .. | 0.3 | .. | 9,609 |
| Syrian Arab Republic | 55.1 | 16.3 | 0.0 | 1.8 | 0.0 | 2.4 | 200 | 4,422 | 4,042 | .. | 44 | 8 |
| Tajikistan | 111.0 | 18.8 | 0.0 | 12.0 | .. | 36.2 | –345 | .. | .. | 7.8 | .. | 0 |
| Tanzania | 46.5 | 21.4 | 0.0 | 3.7 | 0.0 | 0.1 | –345 | 622 | .. | 3.2 | .. | 0 |
| Thailand | 125.7 | 27.4 | 3.2 | 4.4 | 0.5 | 0.6 | 231 | 13,822[i] | 3,382 | 0.7 | 14 | 156 |
| Timor-Leste | .. | .. | 0.0 | .. | .. | .. | 100 | .. | .. | .. | .. | .. |
| Togo | 77.8 | 21.6 | 0.0 | 2.6 | –0.6 | 8.7[c] | –4 | 81[h] | .. | 4.0 | 21 | 16 |
| Trinidad and Tobago | 113.8 | 9.5 | 13.5 | 6.2 | –2.3 | 0.5[c] | –20 | 463[f] | .. | 2.2 | 376 | 370 |
| Tunisia | 87.1 | 22.3 | 1.6 | 10.8 | 0.1 | 5.0 | –29 | 6,549[i] | 2,241 | .. | 73 | 126 |
| Turkey | 55.6 | 8.9 | 9.1 | 5.0 | 0.2 | 0.3 | –30 | 18,916 | 8,275 | 2.4 | 27 | 631 |
| Turkmenistan | 88.8 | .. | 0.0 | 7.0 | .. | .. | –10 | 12 | 33 | .. | .. | 16 |
| Uganda | 37.2 | 15.7 | 0.0 | 4.2 | 0.0 | 8.6 | –5 | 539 | 254 | 3.2 | .. | 4 |
| Ukraine | 78.3 | 19.2 | 5.3 | 5.3 | –0.1 | 0.8 | –173 | 18,900 | 16,875 | 1.6 | 57 | 17 |
| United Arab Emirates | 155.7 | .. | .. | .. | .. | .. | 577 | 7,126[b,e] | .. | 1.7 | .. | 2,371 |
| United Kingdom | 44.9 | 17.1 | .. | 5.9 | 5.4 | 0.3 | 948 | 30,654 | 69,536 | 0.8 | .. | 13,062 |
| United States | 22.5 | 5.8 | .. | 1.4 | 1.8 | 0.0 | 6,493 | 50,978 | 63,662 | .. | 279 | 3,307 |
| Uruguay | 45.1 | 11.3 | 13.0 | 7.0 | 0.0 | 0.5 | –104 | 1,749 | 666 | 0.5 | 121 | 484 |
| Uzbekistan | 56.0 | .. | 0.2 | 1.0 | .. | .. | –300 | 262 | 455 | .. | 12 | 9 |
| Venezuela, RB | 54.3 | 4.2 | 0.3 | –0.3 | 1.1 | 0.1 | 40 | 748 | 1,095 | 0.8 | .. | 50 |
| Vietnam | 137.7 | 17.8 | 2.7 | 3.8 | 0.1 | 7.9[c] | –200 | 3,583[d] | .. | 1.9 | .. | 84 |
| West Bank and Gaza | .. | .. | 0.0 | .. | .. | 14.7[c] | 11 | 123[h] | .. | 1.2 | 66 | 199 |
| Yemen, Rep. | 64.1 | 12.6 | 0.3 | 5.9 | .. | 6.7 | –100 | 382[h] | .. | 2.4 | .. | 0 |
| Zambia | 61.6 | 8.3 | 8.5 | 5.4 | .. | 0.5 | –82 | 669 | .. | 1.4 | .. | 11 |
| Zimbabwe | 121.4 | .. | 0.0 | 3.0 | .. | .. | –75 | 2,287[d] | .. | .. | 25 | 4 |
| **World** | **49.9 w** | **11.3 w** | **.. w** | **2.8 w** | **3.0 w** | **0.6 w** | **..[k] s** | **850,778 t** | **1,030,976 t** | **1.4 m** | **.. w** | **529 w** |
| **Low income** | 44.1 | 14.3 | 3.1 | 2.6 | 0.9 | 3.6 | –4,690 | 27,246 | .. | 2.0 | .. | 22 |
| **Middle income** | 61.8 | 9.8 | 4.7 | 3.3 | 1.4 | 1.7 | –14,021 | 301,883 | 344,318 | 1.6 | 31 | 144 |
| Lower middle income | 66.5 | 10.5 | 2.9 | 3.0 | 0.6 | 2.2 | –9,750 | 148,352 | 107,329 | 2.1 | 21 | 189 |
| Upper middle income | 57.6 | 9.2 | 6.3 | 3.5 | 2.0 | 1.2 | –4,271 | 155,980 | 222,638 | 1.1 | .. | 242 |
| **Low & middle income** | 59.4 | 10.3 | 4.5 | 3.2 | 1.3 | 1.9 | –18,711 | 332,275 | 419,006 | 1.8 | .. | 143 |
| East Asia & Pacific | 75.7 | 9.9 | 3.1 | 2.9 | 0.8 | 1.5 | –3,847 | 98,476 | 81,142 | 1.2 | 8 | 182 |
| Europe & Central Asia | 66.2 | 11.5 | 7.3 | 5.0 | 2.1 | 1.4 | –1,730 | 108,942 | 176,948 | 1.6 | .. | 268 |
| Latin America & Carib. | 43.1 | 6.2 | 4.5 | 2.4 | 1.6 | 1.9 | –6,811 | 55,387 | 38,100 | 1.2 | .. | 269 |
| Middle East & N. Africa | 59.8 | .. | 2.0 | 4.2 | .. | 3.9 | –2,768 | 36,214 | 26,968 | 1.7 | 36 | 126 |
| South Asia | 34.4 | 14.1 | 3.7 | 2.0 | 0.9 | 3.5 | –2,484 | 7,296 | 12,998 | 2.0 | .. | 22 |
| Sub-Saharan Africa | 60.8 | 13.7 | 4.8 | 2.4 | 0.4 | 1.6 | –1,070 | 27,486 | .. | 2.4 | .. | 5 |
| **High income** | 46.9 | 11.6 | .. | 2.7 | 3.5 | 0.2 | 18,604 | 510,271 | 533,390 | 0.8 | 204 | 4,346 |
| Euro area | 65.2 | 16.1 | .. | 3.8 | 5.3 | 0.5 | 6,887 | 284,903 | 194,611 | 0.7 | .. | 4,830 |

a. Data are from the International Telecommunication Union's (ITU) World Telecommunication Development Report database. Please cite the ITU for third-party use of these data.
b. Arrivals in hotels only. c. World Bank estimates. d. Refers to arrivals of nonresident visitors at national borders. e. Includes nationals residing abroad. f. Arrivals by air only. g. Arrivals in all types of accommodation establishments. h. Arrivals in hotels and similar establishments. i. Excludes nationals residing abroad. j. Includes Montenegro. k. World totals computed by the United Nations sum to zero, but because the aggregates shown here refer to World Bank definitions, regional and income group totals do not equal zero.

## About the data

Globalization—the integration of the world economy—has been a persistent theme of the past quarter century. Growth of cross-border economic activity has changed the structure of economies and the political and social organization of countries. Not all effects of globalization can be measured directly. But the scope and pace of change can be monitored along four key dimensions: trade in goods and services, financial flows, movement of people, and communication. Globalization has created opportunities and challenges for developing countries, but many poor people and countries have been unable to take full advantage of globalization's opportunities and benefits.

Trade data are based on gross flows that capture the two-way flow of goods and services. In conventional balance of payments accounting exports are recorded as a credit and imports as a debit. See tables 4.4 and 4.5 for data on the main trade components of merchandise trade and tables 4.6 and 4.7 for data on the main trade components of services trade.

Financing through international capital markets includes gross bond issuance, bank lending, and new equity placement as reported by Dealogic, a company specializing in the investment banking industry. In financial accounting inward investment is a credit and outward investment a debit. Gross flow is a better measure of integration than net flow because gross flow shows the total value of financial transactions over a given period, while net flow is the sum of credits and debits and represents a balance in which many transactions are canceled out.

Components of financing through international capital markets are reported in U.S. dollars by market sources.

Foreign direct investment (FDI) has three components: equity investment, reinvested earnings, and short-and long-term loans between parent firms and foreign affiliates. Distinguished from other kinds of international investment, FDI is made to establish a lasting interest in or effective management control over an enterprise in another country. FDI may be understated in many developing countries because some countries fail to report reinvested earnings and because the definition of long-term loans differs across countries. However, the quality and coverage of the data are improving as a result of continuous efforts by international and national statistics agencies. See *About the data* for table 6.10 for more information.

Workers' remittances comprise workers' remittances, compensation of employees, and migrants' transfers. Migration and tourism have increased in importance over time, now accounting for a substantial part of global integration. See *About the data* and *Definitions* for tables 6.16 and 6.17 for information on migration and tourism.

Well developed communications infrastructure attracts investments and allows investors to capitalize on benefits offered by the digital age. See *About the data* for tables 5.10 and 5.11 for more information.

## Definitions

- **Trade in merchandise** is the sum of merchandise exports and imports. • **Trade in services** is the sum of services exports and imports. • **Financing through international capital markets** is the sum of the absolute values of new bond issuance, syndicated bank lending, and new equity placements. • **Foreign direct investment net inflows** are net inflows of investment in the reporting economy. FDI is the sum of equity capital, reinvestment of earnings, and other short- and long-term capital. • **Foreign direct investment net outflows** are net outflows of investment from the reporting economy to the rest of the world. • **Workers' remittances and compensation of employees**

**received** are current transfers by migrant workers and wages and salaries earned by nonresident workers. Workers' remittances are current private transfers from migrant workers resident in the host country for more than a year, irrespective of their immigration status, to recipients in their country of origin. Compensation of employees is the income of migrants who have lived in the host country for less than a year. • **Net migration** is the total number of immigrants minus the total number of emigrants, including citizens and noncitizens, for the five-year period. • **International inbound tourists** (overnight visitors) are the number of tourists who travel to a country other than that in which they have their usual residence, but outside their usual environment, for less than 12 months whose main purpose in visiting is not for paid work. When data on the number of tourists are not available, the number of day visitors, which includes tourists, cruise passengers, and crew members, is shown instead. • **International outbound tourists** are the number of departures that people make from their country of usual residence to any other country for any purpose other than paid work. • **Cost of call to U.S.** is the cost of a three-minute, peak rate, fixed-line call from the country to the United States. • **International voice traffic** is the sum of international incoming and outgoing telephone traffic (in minutes) divided by total population. • **International Internet bandwidth** is the contracted capacity of international connections between countries for transmitting Internet traffic.

## Data sources

Data on merchandise trade are from the World Trade Organization's (WTO) *Annual Report.* Data on trade in services are from the International Monetary Fund's (IMF) Balance of Payments database. Data on international capital market financing are based on data reported by Dealogic. Data on FDI are based on balance of payments data reported by the IMF, supplemented by staff estimates using data reported by the United Nations Conference on Trade and Development and official national sources. Data on workers' remittances are World Bank staff estimates based on IMF balance of payments data. Data on net migration are from the United Nations Population Division's *World Population Prospects: The 2006 Revision.* Data on international tourism are from the WTO's *Yearbook of Tourism Statistics and Compendium of Tourism Statistics 2008* and electronic updates. Data on cost of call to U.S., international voice traffic, and international Internet bandwidth are from the International Telecommunication Union's *International Development Report* database.

### Trade and international finance are leading globalization | 6.1a

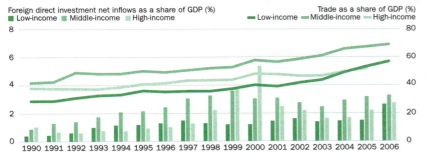

Foreign direct investment net inflows as a share of GDP (%)
■ Low-income ■ Middle-income ■ High-income

Trade as a share of GDP (%)
— Low-income — Middle-income — High-income

Trade in low- and middle-income economies has grown faster than trade in high-income economies since 2000. FDI net inflows in low-income economies soared in 2006.

*Source: World Development Indicators data files.*

| | Export volume | | Import volume | | Export value | | Import value | | Net barter terms of trade index | |
|---|---|---|---|---|---|---|---|---|---|---|
| | average annual % growth | | average annual % growth | | average annual % growth | | average annual % growth | | 2000 = 100 | |
| | 1985–95 | 1995–2006 | 1985–95 | 1995–2006 | 1985–95 | 1995–2006 | 1985–95 | 1995–2006 | 1995 | 2006 |
| Afghanistan | .. | .. | .. | .. | .. | .. | .. | .. | .. | .. |
| Albania | .. | .. | .. | .. | .. | .. | .. | .. | .. | .. |
| Algeria | 2.5 | 2.6 | 1.4 | 5.8 | 1.3 | 14.2 | 4.4 | 6.1 | 57.9 | 178.9 |
| Angola | 8.1 | 7.7 | −1.4 | 15.7 | 6.9 | 19.8 | 2.3 | 17.5 | 80.8 | 196.6 |
| Argentina | 6.9 | 5.4 | 17.8 | 0.4 | 10.4 | 5.9 | 20.3 | −0.7 | 91.6 | 112.9 |
| Armenia | .. | .. | .. | .. | .. | .. | .. | .. | .. | .. |
| Australia[a] | 6.9 | 4.9 | 6.9 | 6.9 | 9.1 | 7.9 | 10.0 | 7.0 | 99.4 | 145.5 |
| Austria[a] | 5.1 | 6.1 | 3.6 | 4.8 | .. | .. | .. | .. | .. | .. |
| Azerbaijan | .. | .. | .. | .. | .. | .. | .. | .. | .. | .. |
| Bangladesh | 13.4 | 8.3 | 4.9 | 2.9 | 14.1 | 9.3 | 8.1 | 7.9 | 111.8 | 73.2 |
| Belarus | .. | .. | .. | .. | .. | .. | .. | .. | .. | .. |
| Belgium[a] | 2.9 | 5.6 | 2.4 | 5.4 | 3.4 | 7.7 | 3.3 | 8.1 | 104.3 | 99.1 |
| Benin | 13.0 | 3.8 | 3.5 | 1.9 | 17.4 | 2.7 | 6.8 | 2.6 | 106.6 | 80.8 |
| Bolivia | 8.9 | 8.1 | 4.4 | 2.8 | 5.5 | 10.9 | 8.5 | 3.4 | 89.4 | 134.6 |
| Bosnia and Herzegovina | .. | .. | .. | .. | .. | .. | .. | .. | .. | .. |
| Botswana | 0.1 | 4.9 | 3.0 | 4.1 | 6.3 | 5.4 | 9.3 | 4.5 | 89.3 | 94.5 |
| Brazil | 4.5 | 9.8 | 15.0 | 1.6 | 6.4 | 9.8 | 11.9 | 2.8 | 110.4 | 103.8 |
| Bulgaria | .. | .. | .. | .. | .. | .. | .. | .. | .. | .. |
| Burkina Faso | 0.6 | 10.0 | 1.6 | 8.4 | 3.7 | 7.3 | 1.7 | 9.7 | 131.0 | 89.8 |
| Burundi | 4.2 | 6.2 | 2.4 | 13.5 | −3.1 | −4.1 | 1.7 | 5.2 | 163.6 | 125.5 |
| Cambodia | .. | 16.4 | .. | 11.9 | 50.3 | 17.0 | 25.4 | 14.9 | .. | 88.7 |
| Cameroon | 9.7 | −0.4 | −4.5 | 8.9 | 10.4 | 4.8 | −3.4 | 9.4 | 90.4 | 136.1 |
| Canada[a] | 6.3 | 4.3 | 6.5 | 5.7 | 7.9 | 5.5 | 8.2 | 6.0 | 103.2 | 115.8 |
| Central African Republic | 9.2 | 4.9 | 1.9 | 0.5 | 5.1 | −1.7 | −0.4 | 0.4 | 193.0 | 90.2 |
| Chad | .. | .. | .. | .. | .. | .. | .. | .. | .. | .. |
| Chile | 11.0 | 7.7 | 9.4 | 5.2 | 13.3 | 10.5 | 17.1 | 5.7 | 135.6 | 183.7 |
| China[†] | 15.1 | 19.5 | 11.8 | 17.6 | 17.7 | 18.8 | 12.7 | 19.3 | 101.9 | 82.1 |
| Hong Kong, China | 16.1 | 6.9 | 17.1 | 6.0 | 19.1 | 5.4 | 20.2 | 4.7 | 99.1 | 96.8 |
| Colombia | 8.7 | 4.2 | 9.5 | 4.0 | 8.9 | 7.0 | 13.1 | 4.2 | 86.8 | 115.2 |
| Congo, Dem. Rep. | −9.9 | 10.6 | −13.4 | 28.3 | −4.7 | 2.8 | −7.1 | 12.7 | 79.8 | 125.9 |
| Congo, Rep. | 1.5 | 3.3 | −7.6 | 9.9 | 1.6 | 15.0 | −2.8 | 9.3 | 52.0 | 184.4 |
| Costa Rica | 11.3 | 8.4 | 13.3 | 8.9 | 13.0 | 6.3 | 15.0 | 8.7 | 104.6 | 85.8 |
| Côte d'Ivoire | 1.7 | 2.6 | −5.0 | 1.0 | −0.2 | 6.4 | 2.2 | 3.2 | 122.0 | 135.4 |
| Croatia | .. | .. | .. | .. | .. | .. | .. | .. | .. | .. |
| Cuba | .. | −3.0 | .. | 5.5 | −18.9 | 2.8 | −15.0 | 8.7 | .. | 148.8 |
| Czech Republic | .. | .. | .. | .. | .. | .. | .. | .. | .. | .. |
| Denmark[a] | 5.0 | 4.3 | 3.3 | 4.3 | 4.8 | 5.9 | 2.4 | 5.7 | 102.1 | 105.0 |
| Dominican Republic | 0.3 | 1.1 | 7.7 | 4.9 | −1.6 | 1.2 | 11.9 | 5.3 | 98.1 | 94.9 |
| Ecuador | 9.0 | 5.6 | 5.4 | 9.1 | 5.9 | 8.5 | 7.9 | 10.1 | 80.6 | 109.9 |
| Egypt, Arab Rep. | −5.7 | 7.9 | −9.3 | −1.6 | −3.1 | 12.6 | −4.6 | 1.9 | 116.3 | 127.0 |
| El Salvador | 1.0 | 4.4 | 11.0 | 5.6 | 2.9 | 3.7 | 11.7 | 7.2 | 121.1 | 95.5 |
| Eritrea | .. | .. | .. | .. | .. | .. | .. | .. | .. | .. |
| Estonia | .. | .. | .. | .. | .. | .. | .. | .. | .. | .. |
| Ethiopia | 9.8 | 8.6 | 6.7 | 10.9 | 17.5 | 6.3 | 8.0 | 12.9 | 151.0 | 98.9 |
| Finland | .. | .. | .. | .. | .. | .. | .. | .. | .. | .. |
| France[a] | 5.1 | 7.5 | 5.0 | 8.6 | 2.9 | 5.8 | 1.8 | 7.1 | 106.4 | 102.2 |
| Gabon | 7.4 | 4.7 | −3.1 | 3.4 | 6.9 | 5.9 | −0.1 | 3.7 | 125.4 | 179.1 |
| Gambia, The | −8.5 | −6.9 | 4.1 | −1.3 | −3.4 | −7.6 | 9.0 | −0.6 | 100.0 | 80.5 |
| Georgia | .. | .. | .. | .. | .. | .. | .. | .. | .. | .. |
| Germany[a] | .. | .. | .. | .. | .. | .. | .. | .. | 107.5 | 96.6 |
| Ghana | 6.8 | 3.6 | 7.8 | 8.4 | 6.6 | 6.8 | 11.5 | 9.8 | 106.7 | 132.0 |
| Greece[a] | 6.4 | .. | 9.6 | .. | 15.1 | .. | 17.2 | .. | 112.1 | .. |
| Guatemala | 4.6 | 5.6 | 9.3 | 8.6 | 6.1 | 4.3 | 11.8 | 9.9 | 117.9 | 89.6 |
| Guinea | 5.6 | −2.3 | 5.3 | 4.8 | 3.8 | 1.7 | 8.2 | 1.9 | 89.6 | 204.0 |
| Guinea-Bissau | .. | .. | .. | .. | .. | .. | .. | .. | .. | .. |
| Haiti | −3.4 | 12.3 | −2.3 | 6.8 | −8.6 | 13.0 | 0.1 | 9.4 | 113.2 | 88.9 |
| [†]Data for Taiwan, China | 17.0 | 3.7 | 21.3 | 2.9 | 11.5 | 5.9 | 16.2 | 5.8 | 89.9 | 84.4 |

| | Export volume | | Import volume | | Export value | | Import value | | Net barter terms of trade index | |
|---|---|---|---|---|---|---|---|---|---|---|
| | average annual % growth | | average annual % growth | | average annual % growth | | average annual % growth | | 2000 = 100 | |
| | 1985–95 | 1995–2006 | 1985–95 | 1995–2006 | 1985–95 | 1995–2006 | 1985–95 | 1995–2006 | 1995 | 2006 |
| Honduras | 3.7 | 4.9 | 4.3 | 10.4 | 1.9 | 2.6 | 4.6 | 10.0 | 96.3 | 83.2 |
| Hungary[a] | −0.1 | 14.5 | 2.6 | 13.0 | 2.7 | 15.4 | 6.0 | 14.6 | 104.3 | 95.5 |
| India[a] | .. | .. | .. | .. | .. | .. | .. | .. | 107.7 | *105.2* |
| Indonesia | 10.4 | 1.8 | 10.1 | 1.1 | 11.7 | 5.6 | 15.3 | 3.2 | 90.4 | 100.9 |
| Iran, Islamic Rep. | 7.4 | 2.3 | .. | 14.3 | 7.7 | 12.7 | 4.3 | 13.1 | .. | 155.3 |
| Iraq | .. | .. | .. | .. | .. | .. | .. | .. | .. | .. |
| Ireland[a] | 10.5 | 8.9 | 6.9 | 6.6 | 10.8 | 9.0 | 8.2 | 7.0 | 98.9 | 94.4 |
| Israel[a] | 6.2 | 7.1 | 8.6 | 3.7 | 21.6 | 12.3 | 22.8 | 8.7 | 92.1 | 93.8 |
| Italy[a] | 5.6 | 0.7 | 4.8 | 2.8 | 9.7 | 4.5 | 7.1 | 6.7 | 95.9 | 97.5 |
| Jamaica | 7.2 | −5.5 | .. | 0.6 | 8.7 | 1.0 | 9.4 | 4.8 | .. | 192.0 |
| Japan[a] | 2.4 | 3.5 | 7.3 | 3.9 | 1.5 | 4.2 | 2.1 | 4.9 | 105.5 | 91.8 |
| Jordan | 5.1 | 10.8 | 3.8 | 7.6 | 7.5 | 10.7 | 3.8 | 10.4 | 115.6 | 84.3 |
| Kazakhstan | .. | .. | .. | .. | .. | .. | .. | .. | .. | .. |
| Kenya | 7.7 | 4.6 | 9.0 | 4.8 | 5.8 | 5.1 | 4.2 | 7.2 | 103.9 | 91.3 |
| Korea, Dem. Rep. | .. | .. | .. | .. | .. | .. | .. | .. | .. | .. |
| Korea, Rep. | 10.6 | 14.2 | 13.3 | 6.9 | 13.0 | 8.8 | 15.0 | 7.6 | 138.5 | 73.2 |
| Kuwait | 9.7 | 5.5 | .. | 13.7 | 0.6 | 13.3 | 2.5 | 7.0 | .. | 195.2 |
| Kyrgyz Republic | .. | .. | .. | .. | .. | .. | .. | .. | .. | .. |
| Lao PDR | .. | 9.0 | .. | 7.7 | 21.7 | 5.7 | 12.7 | 2.6 | .. | 117.6 |
| Latvia[a] | −6.8 | 8.9 | .. | .. | *−1.7* | 9.9 | .. | .. | .. | .. |
| Lebanon | .. | 17.8 | .. | 2.1 | 1.7 | 15.9 | 13.9 | 2.7 | .. | 101.1 |
| Lesotho | 12.1 | 19.2 | 5.3 | 4.3 | 21.0 | 17.1 | 12.1 | 4.2 | 100.0 | 81.1 |
| Liberia | .. | .. | .. | .. | .. | .. | .. | .. | .. | .. |
| Libya | .. | 4.7 | 1.6 | 5.3 | −0.2 | 12.8 | 1.7 | 7.9 | .. | 171.7 |
| Lithuania | .. | .. | .. | .. | .. | .. | .. | .. | .. | .. |
| Macedonia, FYR | .. | .. | .. | .. | .. | .. | .. | .. | .. | .. |
| Madagascar | 2.5 | 11.0 | 1.6 | 9.2 | 4.6 | 12.4 | 7.3 | 11.4 | 79.6 | 76.5 |
| Malawi | 2.6 | 3.3 | 0.8 | 5.4 | 5.1 | 1.8 | 7.8 | 7.1 | 105.7 | 84.4 |
| Malaysia | 10.3 | 8.7 | 18.8 | 5.6 | 18.0 | 6.8 | 22.3 | 4.8 | 108.5 | 98.7 |
| Mali | 10.5 | 10.5 | 4.8 | 8.1 | 11.8 | 11.1 | 7.7 | 8.5 | 109.6 | 107.2 |
| Mauritania | −0.9 | −0.7 | 7.3 | 7.6 | 2.9 | 0.9 | 9.2 | 5.5 | 102.2 | 169.7 |
| Mauritius | 5.6 | 0.7 | 7.9 | 5.6 | 10.4 | 1.2 | 12.5 | 3.5 | 88.5 | 115.2 |
| Mexico | 12.2 | 7.7 | 14.7 | 9.6 | 12.0 | 9.4 | 18.6 | 10.4 | 92.5 | 104.0 |
| Moldova | .. | .. | .. | .. | .. | .. | .. | .. | .. | .. |
| Mongolia | .. | 4.1 | .. | 9.1 | −7.7 | 10.1 | −14.9 | 11.7 | .. | 162.4 |
| Morocco | 6.7 | 4.4 | 7.9 | 7.9 | 9.3 | 3.9 | 9.9 | 8.0 | 89.1 | 86.2 |
| Mozambique | 10.0 | 28.6 | 3.2 | 11.7 | 8.1 | 29.1 | 6.2 | 14.1 | 151.1 | 130.6 |
| Myanmar | 14.3 | 18.6 | 11.8 | −1.1 | 14.8 | 18.0 | 18.3 | 2.6 | 214.3 | 111.1 |
| Namibia | 5.9 | 3.4 | 4.2 | 5.8 | 3.5 | 4.3 | 3.8 | 4.2 | 82.6 | 127.3 |
| Nepal | .. | −1.9 | .. | −1.8 | 11.7 | 7.8 | 10.4 | 3.5 | .. | 79.0 |
| Netherlands[a] | 5.8 | 5.3 | 5.1 | 4.5 | 4.0 | 6.4 | 3.4 | 6.0 | 103.2 | 100.5 |
| New Zealand[a] | 4.1 | 3.5 | 5.4 | 6.1 | 8.2 | 4.8 | 7.7 | 6.3 | 101.8 | 111.5 |
| Nicaragua | 2.6 | 7.8 | −1.4 | 5.8 | 2.9 | 5.9 | 0.1 | 8.6 | 128.9 | 79.4 |
| Niger | 1.7 | −0.5 | −3.9 | 5.6 | −0.5 | 4.9 | 0.5 | 8.5 | 121.4 | 163.7 |
| Nigeria | −2.0 | −1.6 | −9.1 | 10.5 | 5.3 | 10.2 | 3.3 | 13.2 | 55.6 | 160.6 |
| Norway[a] | 6.8 | 2.6 | 2.5 | 5.8 | 5.4 | 9.4 | 3.6 | 5.1 | 60.3 | 139.2 |
| Oman | 12.4 | −0.4 | .. | 8.9 | 10.2 | 11.6 | 6.9 | 8.0 | .. | 182.3 |
| Pakistan | 9.8 | 7.5 | 4.1 | 4.4 | 10.7 | 6.5 | 7.2 | 8.0 | 119.2 | 76.2 |
| Panama | 3.2 | 3.4 | 6.6 | 2.4 | 7.1 | 4.0 | 9.2 | 3.9 | 100.0 | 90.9 |
| Papua New Guinea | 6.3 | −6.4 | .. | 5.2 | 11.4 | 3.2 | 3.6 | 1.8 | .. | 160.4 |
| Paraguay | 5.5 | 6.7 | 19.4 | 0.7 | 12.4 | 6.2 | 19.9 | 2.2 | 118.3 | 95.5 |
| Peru | 4.4 | 10.5 | 8.5 | 1.1 | 6.1 | 12.1 | 13.2 | 2.3 | 123.4 | 151.1 |
| Philippines | 12.8 | 7.2 | 16.0 | 4.7 | 13.1 | 7.7 | 18.0 | 4.3 | 80.2 | 84.1 |
| Poland[a] | 4.8 | 13.0 | 7.9 | 10.5 | 4.6 | 15.3 | 7.1 | 12.1 | 101.7 | 107.1 |
| Portugal[a] | 6.8 | −0.5 | 8.8 | −1.0 | 11.0 | −4.7 | 10.2 | −5.1 | 104.7 | *101.6* |
| Puerto Rico | .. | .. | .. | .. | .. | .. | .. | .. | .. | .. |

| | Export volume | | Import volume | | Export value | | Import value | | Net barter terms of trade index | |
|---|---|---|---|---|---|---|---|---|---|---|
| | average annual % growth | | average annual % growth | | average annual % growth | | average annual % growth | | 2000 = 100 | |
| | 1985–95 | 1995–2006 | 1985–95 | 1995–2006 | 1985–95 | 1995–2006 | 1985–95 | 1995–2006 | 1995 | 2006 |
| Romania | .. | .. | .. | .. | .. | .. | .. | .. | .. | .. |
| Russian Federation | .. | .. | .. | .. | .. | .. | .. | .. | .. | .. |
| Rwanda | –13.2 | 3.8 | 0.1 | 2.2 | –12.6 | 6.3 | –5.4 | 4.5 | 110.1 | 128.7 |
| Saudi Arabia | 12.7 | 0.2 | .. | 11.5 | 9.3 | 13.5 | 3.6 | 7.6 | .. | 205.1 |
| Senegal | 2.0 | 6.9 | –0.5 | 6.9 | 4.2 | 4.8 | 2.7 | 9.7 | 156.3 | 101.8 |
| Serbia | .. | .. | .. | .. | .. | .. | .. | .. | .. | .. |
| Sierra Leone | .. | .. | .. | .. | .. | .. | .. | .. | .. | .. |
| Singapore | 16.0 | 9.1 | 13.5 | 4.7 | 17.9 | 7.0 | 17.3 | 4.8 | 104.3 | 86.1 |
| Slovak Republic | .. | .. | .. | .. | .. | .. | .. | .. | .. | .. |
| Slovenia | .. | .. | .. | .. | .. | .. | .. | .. | .. | .. |
| Somalia | .. | .. | .. | .. | .. | .. | .. | .. | .. | .. |
| South Africa | 2.2 | 4.6 | 5.2 | 7.1 | 4.2 | 6.5 | 7.7 | 8.0 | 106.0 | 125.3 |
| Spain[a] | 8.7 | 6.7 | 12.1 | 8.5 | 11.0 | 8.0 | 12.0 | 10.2 | 104.3 | 103.5 |
| Sri Lanka | 6.3 | 4.5 | 6.8 | 3.2 | 12.1 | 4.4 | 11.6 | 5.3 | 99.0 | 80.0 |
| Sudan | 14.9 | 19.2 | 16.7 | 15.4 | 1.2 | 26.3 | 3.1 | 17.0 | 100.0 | 189.5 |
| Swaziland | 7.9 | 9.3 | 5.9 | 6.6 | 13.9 | 9.3 | 11.8 | 7.4 | 100.0 | 93.3 |
| Sweden[a] | 3.8 | 6.3 | 3.1 | 4.8 | 8.0 | 3.9 | 6.4 | 4.5 | 109.5 | 88.1 |
| Switzerland[a] | 2.3 | 4.5 | 1.2 | 4.1 | .. | .. | .. | .. | .. | .. |
| Syrian Arab Republic | 24.4 | 1.2 | .. | 10.1 | 11.1 | 7.2 | 5.9 | 6.1 | .. | 133.0 |
| Tajikistan | .. | .. | .. | .. | .. | .. | .. | .. | .. | .. |
| Tanzania | 6.0 | 7.6 | –0.4 | 8.0 | 8.2 | 10.0 | 7.9 | 9.2 | 98.0 | 115.7 |
| Thailand | 17.3 | 7.1 | 17.3 | 3.3 | 22.2 | 7.8 | 23.1 | 6.3 | 116.0 | 92.3 |
| Timor-Leste | .. | .. | .. | .. | .. | .. | .. | .. | .. | .. |
| Togo | 4.0 | 4.6 | –4.2 | 3.9 | 3.6 | 4.5 | –0.7 | 5.9 | 99.1 | 78.0 |
| Trinidad and Tobago | 1.4 | 8.7 | –5.8 | 3.1 | 2.6 | 16.2 | 0.6 | 10.3 | .. | 122.7 |
| Tunisia | 9.5 | 7.4 | 6.2 | 6.2 | 12.1 | 7.3 | 11.5 | 6.1 | 95.8 | 94.3 |
| Turkey | 11.6 | 12.6 | 14.0 | 9.2 | 9.9 | 12.8 | 11.6 | 10.6 | 105.7 | 96.2 |
| Turkmenistan | .. | .. | .. | .. | .. | .. | .. | .. | .. | .. |
| Uganda | 7.2 | 9.7 | 8.7 | 3.7 | –2.5 | 4.8 | 6.7 | 5.6 | 197.2 | 102.0 |
| Ukraine | .. | .. | .. | .. | .. | .. | .. | .. | .. | .. |
| United Arab Emirates | 8.2 | 7.9 | .. | 17.6 | 10.5 | 15.1 | 14.7 | 15.1 | .. | 152.7 |
| United Kingdom[a] | 4.6 | 4.0 | 4.5 | 6.7 | 8.8 | 4.7 | 8.3 | 7.1 | 100.1 | 104.3 |
| United States[a] | 8.2 | 3.6 | 5.0 | 7.1 | 10.3 | 4.0 | 7.3 | 8.1 | 103.3 | 96.0 |
| Uruguay | 5.9 | 4.6 | 12.9 | –0.4 | 7.4 | 3.1 | 14.9 | 0.4 | 116.2 | 88.7 |
| Uzbekistan | .. | .. | .. | .. | .. | .. | .. | .. | .. | .. |
| Venezuela, RB | 6.7 | 0.1 | –0.2 | 5.9 | 5.1 | 9.9 | 3.6 | 6.2 | 63.4 | 184.4 |
| Vietnam | .. | 13.2 | .. | 13.9 | 22.7 | 18.1 | 12.1 | 15.8 | .. | 96.8 |
| West Bank and Gaza | .. | .. | .. | .. | .. | .. | .. | .. | .. | .. |
| Yemen, Rep. | .. | –3.2 | 2.3 | 13.3 | 8.1 | 12.1 | 4.3 | 11.4 | .. | 150.3 |
| Zambia | –3.1 | 9.1 | –9.7 | 12.5 | 2.3 | 8.1 | –0.1 | 13.5 | 189.7 | 187.0 |
| Zimbabwe | 6.5 | 0.1 | 13.8 | –1.4 | 4.4 | –1.3 | 11.5 | –2.8 | 96.8 | 93.4 |

a. Data are from the International Monetary Fund's International Financial Statistics database.

## About the data

Data on international trade in goods are available from each country's balance of payments and customs records. While the balance of payments focuses on the financial transactions that accompany trade, customs data record the direction of trade and the physical quantities and value of goods entering or leaving the customs area. Customs data may differ from data recorded in the balance of payments because of differences in valuation and time of recording. The 1993 System of National Accounts and the fifth edition of the International Monetary Fund's (IMF) *Balance of Payments Manual* (1993) attempted to reconcile definitions and reporting standards for international trade statistics, but differences in sources, timing, and national practices limit comparability. Real growth rates derived from trade volume indexes and terms of trade based on unit price indexes may therefore differ from those derived from national accounts aggregates.

Trade in goods, or merchandise trade, includes all goods that add to or subtract from an economy's material resources. Trade data are collected on the basis of a country's customs area, which in most cases is the same as its geographic area. Goods provided as part of foreign aid are included, but goods destined for extraterritorial agencies (such as embassies) are not.

Collecting and tabulating trade statistics are difficult. Some developing countries lack the capacity to report timely data, especially landlocked countries and countries whose territorial boundaries are porous. Their trade has to be estimated from the data reported by their partners. (For further discussion of the use of partner country reports, see *About the data* for table 6.3.) Countries that belong to common customs unions may need to collect data through direct inquiry of companies. Economic or political concerns may lead some national authorities to suppress or misrepresent data on certain trade flows, such as oil, military equipment, or the exports of a dominant producer. In other cases reported trade data may be distorted by deliberate under- or over-invoicing to affect capital transfers or avoid taxes. And in some regions smuggling and black market trading result in unreported trade flows.

By international agreement customs data are reported to the United Nations Statistics Division, which maintains the Commodity Trade (Comtrade) and Monthly Bulletin of Statistics databases. The United Nations Conference on Trade and Development (UNCTAD) compiles international trade statistics, including price, value, and volume indexes,

from national and international sources such as the IMF's International Financial Statistics database, the United Nations Economic Commission for Latin America and the Caribbean, the United Nations Statistics Division's Monthly Bulletin of Statistics database, the World Bank Africa Database, the U.S. Bureau of Labor Statistics, Japan Customs, and UNCTAD's Commodity Price Statistics. The IMF also compiles data on trade prices and volumes in its International Financial Statistics (IFS) database.

Unless otherwise noted, the growth rates and terms of trade in the table were calculated from index numbers compiled by UNCTAD. The growth rates and terms of trade for selected economies were calculated from index numbers compiled in the IMF's *International Financial Statistics.* In some cases price and volume indexes from different sources vary significantly as a result of differences in estimation procedures. Because the IMF does not publish trade value indexes, for selected economies the trade value indexes were derived from the volume and price indexes. All indexes are rescaled to a 2000 base year.

The terms of trade measures the relative prices of a country's exports and imports. There are several ways to calculate it. The most common is the net barter (or commodity) terms of trade index, or the ratio of the export price index to the import price index. When a country's net barter terms of trade index increases, its exports become more valuable or its imports cheaper.

## Definitions

• **Export** and **import volumes** are indexes of the quantity of goods traded. They are derived from UNCTAD's quantum index series and are the ratio of the export or import value indexes to the corresponding unit value indexes. Unit value indexes are based on data reported by countries that demonstrate consistency under UNCTAD quality controls, supplemented by UNCTAD's estimates using the previous year's trade values at the Standard International Trade Classification three-digit level as weights. For economies for which UNCTAD does not publish data, the export and import volume indexes (lines 72 and 73) in the IMF's *International Financial Statistics* are used to calculate the average annual growth rates. • **Export** and **import values** are the current value of exports (f.o.b.) or imports (c.i.f.), converted to U.S. dollars and expressed as a percentage of the average for the base period (2000). UNCTAD's export or import value indexes are reported for most economies. For selected economies for which UNCTAD does not publish data, the value indexes are derived from export or import volume indexes (lines 72 and 73) and corresponding unit value indexes of exports or imports (lines 74 and 75) in the IMF's *International Financial Statistics.* • **Net barter terms of trade index** is calculated as the percentage ratio of the export unit value indexes to the import unit value indexes, measured relative to the base year 2000.

## Data sources

Data on trade indexes are from UNCTAD's annual *Handbook of Statistics* for most economies and from the IMF's *International Financial Statistics* for selected economies.

### High-income importers

% of world trade, 2006

| Source of exports | European Union | Japan | United States | Other high-income | Total |
|---|---|---|---|---|---|
| High-income economies | 29.1 | 2.6 | 8.7 | 10.3 | 50.8 |
| European Union | 22.8 | 0.5 | 2.8 | 2.5 | 28.6 |
| Japan | 0.8 | .. | 1.2 | 1.6 | 3.6 |
| United States | 1.9 | 0.5 | .. | 3.3 | 5.7 |
| Other high-income economies | 3.6 | 1.7 | 4.7 | 2.9 | 12.9 |
| Low- and middle-income economies | 8.2 | 1.8 | 6.3 | 5.1 | 21.4 |
| East Asia & Pacific | 2.0 | 1.3 | 2.4 | 3.7 | 9.5 |
| China | 1.5 | 0.8 | 1.7 | 2.5 | 6.4 |
| Europe & Central Asia | 3.7 | 0.1 | 0.2 | 0.2 | 4.2 |
| Russian Federation | 1.3 | 0.0 | 0.1 | 0.1 | 1.5 |
| Latin America & Caribbean | 0.8 | 0.1 | 2.7 | 0.4 | 4.1 |
| Brazil | 0.3 | 0.0 | 0.2 | 0.1 | 0.6 |
| Middle East & N. Africa | 0.9 | 0.1 | 0.3 | 0.3 | 1.6 |
| Algeria | 0.2 | 0.0 | 0.1 | 0.0 | 0.4 |
| South Asia | 0.3 | 0.0 | 0.2 | 0.3 | 0.9 |
| India | 0.2 | 0.0 | 0.2 | 0.3 | 0.7 |
| Sub-Saharan Africa | 0.5 | 0.1 | 0.5 | 0.1 | 1.2 |
| South Africa | 0.2 | 0.1 | 0.1 | 0.0 | 0.3 |
| World | 37.3 | 4.4 | 15.1 | 15.4 | 72.2 |

### Low- and middle-income importers

% of world trade, 2006

| Source of exports | East Asia & Pacific | Europe & Central Asia | Latin America & Caribbean | Middle East & N. Africa | South Asia | Sub-Saharan Africa | Total |
|---|---|---|---|---|---|---|---|
| High-income economies | 7.3 | 4.0 | 3.1 | 1.1 | 1.0 | 0.9 | 17.4 |
| European Union | 1.0 | 3.4 | 0.7 | 0.7 | 0.3 | 0.5 | 6.5 |
| Japan | 1.3 | 0.1 | 0.2 | 0.0 | 0.1 | 0.1 | 1.8 |
| United States | 0.7 | 0.2 | 1.8 | 0.1 | 0.1 | 0.1 | 3.0 |
| Other high-income economies | 4.4 | 0.4 | 0.5 | 0.3 | 0.5 | 0.3 | 6.2 |
| Low- and middle-income economies | 2.3 | 2.6 | 1.5 | 0.7 | 0.6 | 0.6 | 8.3 |
| East Asia & Pacific | 1.2 | 0.5 | 0.4 | 0.2 | 0.3 | 0.2 | 2.8 |
| China | 0.4 | 0.4 | 0.3 | 0.1 | 0.2 | 0.2 | 1.6 |
| Europe & Central Asia | 0.2 | 1.8 | 0.0 | 0.2 | 0.1 | 0.0 | 2.4 |
| Russian Federation | 0.1 | 0.7 | 0.0 | 0.0 | 0.0 | 0.0 | 0.9 |
| Latin America & Caribbean | 0.3 | 0.1 | 1.0 | 0.1 | 0.0 | 0.1 | 1.5 |
| Brazil | 0.1 | 0.0 | 0.3 | 0.0 | 0.0 | 0.0 | 0.5 |
| Middle East & N. Africa | 0.2 | 0.1 | 0.0 | 0.2 | 0.0 | 0.1 | 0.6 |
| Algeria | 0.0 | 0.0 | 0.0 | 0.0 | 0.0 | 0.0 | 0.0 |
| South Asia | 0.1 | 0.0 | 0.0 | 0.0 | 0.1 | 0.1 | 0.4 |
| India | 0.1 | 0.0 | 0.0 | 0.0 | 0.1 | 0.1 | 0.3 |
| Sub-Saharan Africa | 0.2 | 0.0 | 0.1 | 0.0 | 0.0 | 0.2 | 0.5 |
| South Africa | 0.0 | 0.0 | 0.0 | 0.0 | 0.0 | 0.1 | 0.1 |
| World | 9.7 | 6.6 | 4.7 | 1.7 | 1.6 | 1.5 | 25.7 |

**Nominal growth of trade**

## High-income importers

| Source of exports | European Union | Japan | United States | Other high-income | Total |
|---|---|---|---|---|---|
| | annual % growth, 1996–2006 | | | | |
| High-income economies | 6.8 | 3.7 | 6.2 | 5.7 | 6.3 |
| European Union | 7.0 | 2.1 | 8.6 | 5.7 | 6.9 |
| Japan | 3.5 | .. | 2.7 | 4.4 | 3.6 |
| United States | 5.0 | −1.2 | .. | 4.8 | 4.2 |
| Other high-income economies | 7.4 | 6.6 | 6.0 | 7.4 | 6.8 |
| Low- and middle-income economies | 14.1 | 8.5 | 13.1 | 13.6 | 13.1 |
| East Asia & Pacific | 16.2 | 8.5 | 15.9 | 13.8 | 13.8 |
| China | 23.8 | 11.5 | 22.5 | 18.8 | 19.3 |
| Europe & Central Asia | 16.3 | 6.3 | 9.2 | 13.4 | 15.4 |
| Russian Federation | 16.3 | 4.9 | 3.3 | 7.5 | 14.1 |
| Latin America & Caribbean | 9.1 | 5.2 | 10.6 | 11.8 | 10.2 |
| Brazil | 8.7 | 2.5 | 10.2 | 14.0 | 9.5 |
| Middle East & N. Africa | 11.8 | 8.5 | 28.5 | 13.4 | 13.4 |
| Algeria | 15.2 | 6.9 | 24.0 | 25.4 | 18.1 |
| South Asia | 9.9 | 3.4 | 11.3 | 13.9 | 11.1 |
| India | 11.3 | 6.1 | 13.0 | 16.2 | 13.0 |
| Sub-Saharan Africa | 10.7 | 25.3 | 15.9 | 15.4 | 13.7 |
| South Africa | 6.9 | 7.1 | 4.7 | 1.3 | 5.6 |
| World | 7.9 | 5.3 | 8.5 | 7.6 | 7.8 |

## Low- and middle-income importers

| Source of exports | East Asia & Pacific | Europe & Central Asia | Latin America & Caribbean | Middle East & N. Africa | South Asia | Sub-Saharan Africa | Total |
|---|---|---|---|---|---|---|---|
| | annual % growth, 1996–2006 | | | | | | |
| High-income economies | 10.0 | 11.9 | 6.8 | 7.9 | 9.3 | 7.5 | 9.4 |
| European Union | 7.8 | 12.3 | 5.8 | 7.0 | 8.5 | 6.6 | 9.4 |
| Japan | 7.2 | 16.7 | 5.5 | 5.5 | 5.0 | 4.9 | 7.2 |
| United States | 8.6 | 6.5 | 7.3 | 6.0 | 10.0 | 7.0 | 7.6 |
| Other high-income economies | 11.8 | 10.5 | 6.7 | 12.1 | 10.6 | 10.5 | 11.1 |
| Low- and middle-income economies | 17.8 | 14.1 | 12.2 | 16.1 | 17.0 | 17.9 | 15.2 |
| East Asia & Pacific | 17.1 | 27.5 | 22.8 | 20.1 | 20.1 | 22.2 | 20.0 |
| China | 21.5 | 31.6 | 27.7 | 26.8 | 26.5 | 26.0 | 26.2 |
| Europe & Central Asia | 11.1 | 12.4 | 10.7 | 15.0 | 15.7 | 14.8 | 12.6 |
| Russian Federation | 11.3 | 11.8 | 9.5 | 17.7 | 15.1 | 15.0 | 12.0 |
| Latin America & Caribbean | 19.0 | 13.1 | 9.3 | 9.9 | 18.7 | 15.6 | 11.2 |
| Brazil | 16.3 | 16.3 | 11.4 | 16.2 | 14.4 | 18.6 | 13.4 |
| Middle East & N. Africa | 22.8 | 11.1 | 13.9 | 18.7 | 12.2 | 23.2 | 17.5 |
| Algeria | 43.3 | 4.3 | 13.2 | 18.1 | 8.0 | 23.1 | 11.3 |
| South Asia | 19.0 | 11.2 | 21.9 | 15.6 | 17.0 | 16.3 | 17.0 |
| India | 20.5 | 12.1 | 25.9 | 19.0 | 14.9 | 17.0 | 18.0 |
| Sub-Saharan Africa | 30.1 | 17.2 | 22.7 | 8.8 | 2.9 | 15.3 | 18.6 |
| South Africa | 6.7 | 8.1 | 10.5 | 11.7 | 7.1 | 4.1 | 5.7 |
| World | 11.4 | 12.8 | 8.2 | 10.3 | 11.6 | 10.1 | 10.9 |

## About the data

The table provides estimates of the flow of trade in goods between groups of economies. The data are from the International Monetary Fund's (IMF) Direction of Trade database. All developed and 23 developing countries report trade on a timely basis, covering about 80 percent of trade for recent years. Trade by less timely reporters and by countries that do not report is estimated using reports of trading partner countries. Because the largest exporting and importing countries are reliable reporters, a large portion of the missing trade flows can be estimated from partner reports. Partner country data may introduce discrepancies due to smuggling, confidentiality, different exchange rates, overreporting of transit trade, inclusion or exclusion of freight rates, and different points of valuation and times of recording.

In addition, estimates of trade within the European Union (EU) have been significantly affected by changes in reporting methods following the creation of a customs union. The current system for collecting data on trade between EU members—Intrastat, introduced in 1993—has less exhaustive coverage than the previous customs-based system and has resulted in some problems of asymmetry (estimated imports are about 5 percent less than exports). Despite these issues, only a small portion of world trade is estimated to be omitted from the IMF's *Direction of Trade Statistics Yearbook* and Direction of Trade database.

Most countries report their trade data in national currencies, which are converted into U.S. dollars using the IMF's published period average exchange rate (series rf or rh, monthly averages of the market or official rates) for the reporting country or, if unavailable, monthly average rates in New York. Because imports are reported at cost, insurance, and freight (c.i.f.) valuations, and exports at free on board (f.o.b.) valuations, the IMF adjusts country reports of import values by dividing them by 1.10 to estimate equivalent export values. The accuracy of this approximation depends on the set of partners and the items traded. Other factors affecting the accuracy of trade data include lags in reporting, recording differences across countries, and whether the country reports trade according to the general or special system of trade. (For further discussion of the measurement of exports and imports, see *About the data* for tables 4.4 and 4.5.)

The regional trade flows in the table are calculated from current price values. The growth rates are in nominal terms; that is, they include the effects of changes in both volumes and prices.

## Definitions

• **Merchandise trade** includes all trade in goods; trade in services is excluded. • **High-income economies** are those classified as such by the World Bank (see inside front cover). • **European Union** is defined as all high-income EU members: Austria, Belgium, Cyprus, Czech Republic, Denmark, Estonia, Finland, France, Germany, Greece, Ireland, Italy, Luxembourg, Malta, the Netherlands, Portugal, Slovenia, Spain, Sweden, and the United Kingdom. • **Other high-income economies** include all high-income economies (both Organisation for Economic Co-operation and Development members and others) except the high-income European Union, Japan, and the United States. • **Low- and middle-income regional groupings** are based on World Bank classifications and may differ from those used by other organizations.

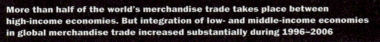

More than half of the world's merchandise trade takes place between high-income economies. But integration of low- and middle-income economies in global merchandise trade increased substantially during 1996–2006          6.3a

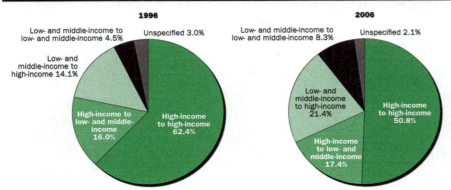

Trade between low- and middle-income economies accounted for about 8.3 percent of world merchandise trade in 2006, compared with 4.5 percent in 1996. The share of trade from low- and middle-income economies to high-income economies increased 7.3 percentage points between 1996 and 2006.

*Source:* International Monetary Fund's Direction of Trade database.

## Data sources

Data on the direction and growth of merchandise trade were calculated using the IMF's Direction of Trade database.

# High-income economy trade with low- and middle-income economies

## Exports to low-income economies

| | High-income economies | | European Union[a] | | Japan | | United States | |
|---|---|---|---|---|---|---|---|---|
| | 1996 | 2006 | 1996 | 2006 | 1996 | 2006 | 1996 | 2006 |
| **Total ($ billions)** | **73.8** | **165.0** | **34.5** | **68.7** | **8.3** | **14.5** | **8.9** | **18.8** |
| **% of total exports** | | | | | | | | |
| Food | 8.3 | 5.7 | 8.8 | 6.3 | 0.5 | 0.4 | 16.5 | 10.6 |
| Cereals | 3.2 | 1.8 | 3.0 | 1.7 | 0.2 | 0.1 | 12.8 | 6.1 |
| Agricultural raw materials | 2.1 | 1.9 | 1.2 | 1.4 | 1.5 | 1.4 | 3.9 | 4.1 |
| Ores and nonferrous metals | 2.2 | 3.3 | 1.6 | 2.2 | 0.8 | 1.5 | 1.8 | 2.5 |
| Fuels | 5.2 | 9.5 | 3.3 | 5.5 | 1.2 | 0.9 | 1.4 | 2.9 |
| Crude petroleum | 0.0 | 1.0 | 0.0 | 0.0 | 0.0 | 0.0 | 0.0 | 0.0 |
| Petroleum products | 3.9 | 6.7 | 3.2 | 5.3 | 1.1 | 0.5 | 1.3 | 2.3 |
| Manufactured goods | 80.4 | 75.9 | 83.2 | 81.6 | 94.8 | 92.6 | 72.7 | 72.1 |
| Chemical products | 12.0 | 11.9 | 12.1 | 11.0 | 7.2 | 7.2 | 11.7 | 10.7 |
| Iron and steel | 3.8 | 3.3 | 4.3 | 3.0 | 6.7 | 9.4 | 1.6 | 1.4 |
| Machinery and transport equipment | 43.9 | 42.1 | 43.3 | 44.4 | 66.6 | 61.8 | 49.7 | 47.6 |
| Furniture | 0.2 | 0.2 | 0.3 | 0.4 | 0.1 | 0.2 | 0.1 | 0.2 |
| Textiles | 4.3 | 3.1 | 1.7 | 1.3 | 3.7 | 3.3 | 1.5 | 1.6 |
| Footwear | 0.1 | 0.1 | 0.2 | 0.1 | 0.0 | 0.0 | 0.1 | 0.1 |
| Other | 16.0 | 15.2 | 21.2 | 21.6 | 10.5 | 10.6 | 7.9 | 10.6 |
| Miscellaneous goods | 1.8 | 3.7 | 1.9 | 3.1 | 1.1 | 3.2 | 3.7 | 7.8 |

## Imports from low-income economies

| | High-income economies | | European Union | | Japan | | United States | |
|---|---|---|---|---|---|---|---|---|
| | 1996 | 2006 | 1996 | 2006 | 1996 | 2006 | 1996 | 2006 |
| **Total ($ billions)** | **81.4** | **217.1** | **38.1** | **81.2** | **8.5** | **15.7** | **18.3** | **77.2** |
| **% of total imports** | | | | | | | | |
| Food | 18.9 | 9.7 | 23.6 | 13.8 | 25.9 | 14.1 | 8.9 | 4.6 |
| Cereals | 0.9 | 0.5 | 0.4 | 0.4 | 0.1 | 0.3 | 0.2 | 0.2 |
| Agricultural raw materials | 6.2 | 1.9 | 6.9 | 3.1 | 8.0 | 1.6 | 2.6 | 0.9 |
| Ores and nonferrous metals | 4.7 | 4.8 | 4.1 | 6.3 | 13.6 | 9.0 | 1.8 | 0.7 |
| Fuels | 21.1 | 31.7 | 15.5 | 18.6 | 16.5 | 39.8 | 36.0 | 43.2 |
| Crude petroleum | 19.6 | 25.0 | 15.0 | 13.0 | 13.4 | 29.3 | 33.5 | 39.6 |
| Petroleum products | 1.3 | 4.8 | 0.4 | 2.3 | 2.1 | 8.4 | 2.4 | 2.4 |
| Manufactured goods | 48.7 | 51.4 | 49.6 | 57.8 | 35.8 | 35.0 | 50.2 | 50.0 |
| Chemical products | 2.7 | 3.9 | 2.3 | 4.1 | 1.3 | 2.8 | 2.3 | 3.0 |
| Iron and steel | 1.1 | 2.0 | 0.7 | 2.3 | 2.0 | 1.0 | 1.1 | 1.7 |
| Machinery and transport equipment | 3.6 | 5.9 | 3.7 | 6.0 | 1.4 | 10.7 | 2.2 | 4.4 |
| Furniture | 0.4 | 1.5 | 0.3 | 1.5 | 0.8 | 1.6 | 0.2 | 1.9 |
| Textiles | 24.1 | 22.2 | 25.0 | 27.2 | 17.7 | 8.6 | 27.4 | 25.5 |
| Footwear | 1.7 | 2.9 | 2.8 | 5.2 | 0.6 | 2.1 | 0.7 | 1.6 |
| Other | 15.2 | 13.0 | 14.7 | 11.6 | 12.0 | 8.2 | 16.2 | 12.0 |
| Miscellaneous goods | 0.3 | 0.6 | 0.3 | 0.4 | 0.2 | 0.5 | 0.5 | 0.7 |

### Simple applied tariff rates on imports from low-income economies (%)[b]

| | High-income economies | | European Union | | Japan | | United States | |
|---|---|---|---|---|---|---|---|---|
| Food | 9.2 | 5.9 | 9.7 | 6.5 | 13.0 | 5.6 | 4.6 | 3.1 |
| Cereals | 14.9 | 7.4 | 42.7 | 20.6 | 14.4 | 13.4 | 6.5 | 1.3 |
| Agricultural raw materials | 2.4 | 1.8 | 0.3 | 0.3 | 1.1 | 0.5 | 1.1 | 0.3 |
| Ores and nonferrous metals | 1.8 | 1.6 | 0.6 | 0.5 | 2.7 | 0.0 | 0.3 | 0.3 |
| Fuels | 3.8 | 1.8 | 0.0 | 0.1 | 1.3 | 0.3 | 2.5 | 1.4 |
| Crude petroleum | 7.8 | 1.0 | 0.0 | 0.0 | 0.0 | 0.0 | 0.0 | 0.0 |
| Petroleum products | 3.7 | 2.1 | 0.0 | 0.2 | 1.7 | 0.6 | 2.5 | 2.1 |
| Manufactured goods | 5.0 | 3.7 | 1.6 | 1.1 | 4.2 | 2.2 | 6.9 | 4.1 |
| Chemical products | 3.1 | 2.5 | 1.4 | 1.8 | 1.1 | 0.1 | 2.4 | 0.9 |
| Iron and steel | 3.2 | 2.2 | 0.4 | 0.3 | 0.3 | 0.2 | 3.6 | 0.2 |
| Machinery and transport equipment | 2.4 | 2.0 | 0.4 | 0.4 | 0.0 | 0.0 | 1.6 | 0.4 |
| Furniture | 3.7 | 3.4 | 0.2 | 0.0 | 0.2 | 0.0 | 4.6 | 0.8 |
| Textiles | 8.8 | 6.4 | 4.2 | 2.6 | 6.9 | 4.9 | 13.7 | 9.5 |
| Footwear | 11.9 | 6.7 | 4.1 | 2.5 | 11.0 | 9.1 | 19.6 | 9.9 |
| Other | 3.0 | 2.5 | 0.6 | 0.4 | 1.4 | 0.9 | 3.2 | 0.9 |
| Miscellaneous goods | 5.3 | 1.3 | 0.9 | 0.4 | 0.0 | 0.0 | 3.5 | 0.1 |
| **Average** | **5.4** | **3.9** | **2.5** | **1.7** | **5.3** | **2.4** | **6.2** | **3.8** |

## Exports to middle-income economies

| | High-income economies | | European Union[a] | | Japan | | United States | |
|---|---|---|---|---|---|---|---|---|
| | 1996 | 2006 | 1996 | 2006 | 1996 | 2006 | 1996 | 2006 |
| **Total ($ billions)** | **693.4** | **1,698.0** | **292.9** | **760.2** | **98.3** | **199.6** | **157.2** | **305.0** |
| **% of total exports** | | | | | | | | |
| Food | 7.9 | 4.8 | 8.4 | 5.0 | 0.3 | 0.4 | 11.9 | 8.6 |
| Cereals | 2.2 | 0.9 | 1.5 | 0.6 | 0.0 | 0.0 | 5.0 | 2.5 |
| Agricultural raw materials | 2.0 | 1.9 | 1.4 | 1.4 | 1.1 | 0.9 | 3.1 | 3.8 |
| Ores and nonferrous metals | 1.9 | 3.8 | 1.6 | 2.7 | 1.4 | 3.4 | 1.7 | 4.3 |
| Fuels | 2.5 | 4.4 | 1.8 | 2.6 | 0.7 | 0.9 | 2.6 | 4.9 |
| Crude petroleum | 0.1 | 0.3 | 0.2 | 0.1 | 0.0 | 0.0 | 0.0 | 0.0 |
| Petroleum products | 1.8 | 3.5 | 1.4 | 2.2 | 0.6 | 0.9 | 1.8 | 4.4 |
| Manufactured goods | 83.4 | 82.2 | 84.4 | 85.3 | 95.1 | 90.7 | 76.9 | 74.5 |
| Chemical products | 10.8 | 12.8 | 12.2 | 13.0 | 6.6 | 9.0 | 11.0 | 12.7 |
| Iron and steel | 2.8 | 3.4 | 3.0 | 3.7 | 5.7 | 6.1 | 1.1 | 1.2 |
| Machinery and transport equipment | 48.5 | 48.1 | 46.0 | 47.9 | 67.7 | 61.7 | 45.8 | 45.0 |
| Furniture | 0.6 | 0.5 | 1.0 | 0.8 | 0.1 | 0.2 | 0.6 | 0.4 |
| Textiles | 5.7 | 3.5 | 5.8 | 4.2 | 3.0 | 1.9 | 4.8 | 3.0 |
| Footwear | 0.3 | 0.2 | 0.5 | 0.4 | 0.0 | 0.0 | 0.1 | 0.0 |
| Other | 14.6 | 13.7 | 16.1 | 15.3 | 11.9 | 11.8 | 13.7 | 12.3 |
| Miscellaneous goods | 2.3 | 3.0 | 2.4 | 3.1 | 1.5 | 3.8 | 3.8 | 3.8 |

## Imports from middle-income economies

| | High-income economies | | European Union[a] | | Japan | | United States | |
|---|---|---|---|---|---|---|---|---|
| | 1996 | 2006 | 1996 | 2006 | 1996 | 2006 | 1996 | 2006 |
| **Total ($ billions)** | **848.3** | **2,679.3** | **281.6** | **1,006.7** | **107.2** | **234.9** | **247.2** | **826.2** |
| **% of total imports** | | | | | | | | |
| Food | 10.9 | 5.9 | 14.0 | 7.1 | 15.4 | 8.3 | 7.8 | 4.6 |
| Cereals | 0.3 | 0.3 | 0.3 | 0.3 | 0.4 | 0.3 | 0.2 | 0.1 |
| Agricultural raw materials | 3.1 | 1.4 | 3.9 | 1.8 | 5.1 | 2.3 | 1.7 | 1.0 |
| Ores and nonferrous metals | 5.2 | 5.4 | 6.5 | 5.9 | 8.7 | 11.0 | 2.9 | 2.9 |
| Fuels | 14.6 | 18.8 | 18.8 | 22.8 | 18.1 | 16.4 | 13.4 | 18.9 |
| Crude petroleum | 9.4 | 12.7 | 12.2 | 15.3 | 9.5 | 7.9 | 10.1 | 15.1 |
| Petroleum products | 2.5 | 3.4 | 3.4 | 4.4 | 1.4 | 1.5 | 3.0 | 3.2 |
| Manufactured goods | 64.3 | 67.0 | 54.1 | 60.8 | 51.5 | 60.8 | 72.1 | 70.6 |
| Chemical products | 3.6 | 3.4 | 4.7 | 3.4 | 2.8 | 3.8 | 2.3 | 2.5 |
| Iron and steel | 2.7 | 2.8 | 2.7 | 3.4 | 1.7 | 1.4 | 2.1 | 2.3 |
| Machinery and transport equipment | 24.1 | 33.2 | 16.0 | 28.3 | 15.1 | 26.8 | 32.9 | 35.7 |
| Furniture | 1.5 | 2.1 | 1.7 | 2.0 | 1.5 | 1.6 | 1.7 | 3.1 |
| Textiles | 13.2 | 8.5 | 13.5 | 8.5 | 14.9 | 10.5 | 11.9 | 8.1 |
| Footwear | 2.8 | 1.5 | 1.6 | 1.3 | 1.7 | 1.1 | 4.0 | 2.0 |
| Other | 16.5 | 15.4 | 13.9 | 14.0 | 13.9 | 15.6 | 17.2 | 16.8 |
| Miscellaneous goods | 1.8 | 1.4 | 2.8 | 1.5 | 1.2 | 1.3 | 2.0 | 2.0 |

## Simple applied tariff rates on imports from middle-income economies[b] (%)

| | High-income economies | | European Union[a] | | Japan | | United States | |
|---|---|---|---|---|---|---|---|---|
| | 1996 | 2006 | 1996 | 2006 | 1996 | 2006 | 1996 | 2006 |
| Food | 12.5 | 7.3 | 20.3 | 11.9 | 14.4 | 7.7 | 2.9 | 2.4 |
| Cereals | 16.9 | 10.2 | 42.2 | 28.5 | 22.8 | 12.0 | 1.6 | 0.8 |
| Agricultural raw materials | 2.4 | 1.9 | 1.1 | 0.4 | 0.6 | 0.6 | 0.5 | 0.4 |
| Ores and nonferrous metals | 1.4 | 1.1 | 1.1 | 0.7 | 0.5 | 0.1 | 0.5 | 0.5 |
| Fuels | 3.5 | 1.7 | 0.1 | 0.1 | 0.6 | 0.3 | 0.9 | 1.4 |
| Crude petroleum | 13.4 | 1.2 | 0.0 | 0.0 | 0.0 | 0.0 | 0.0 | 0.0 |
| Petroleum products | 3.6 | 2.2 | 0.1 | 0.2 | 1.1 | 0.6 | 1.2 | 2.1 |
| Manufactured goods | 4.6 | 3.5 | 2.3 | 1.1 | 1.9 | 2.2 | 3.7 | 2.8 |
| Chemical products | 3.1 | 2.4 | 1.7 | 1.8 | 1.4 | 0.3 | 1.4 | 1.0 |
| Iron and steel | 2.7 | 1.5 | 0.8 | 0.2 | 0.6 | 0.2 | 3.2 | 0.2 |
| Machinery and transport equipment | 2.7 | 2.1 | 0.8 | 0.4 | 0.0 | 0.0 | 0.6 | 0.3 |
| Furniture | 4.5 | 3.9 | 0.4 | 0.4 | 0.0 | 0.0 | 0.5 | 0.3 |
| Textiles | 9.0 | 6.9 | 6.2 | 3.0 | 4.9 | 6.8 | 10.6 | 8.5 |
| Footwear | 10.4 | 7.0 | 6.1 | 3.0 | 15.4 | 17.9 | 13.0 | 8.3 |
| Other | 3.2 | 2.7 | 1.1 | 0.4 | 0.5 | 0.7 | 1.0 | 0.7 |
| Miscellaneous goods | 4.0 | 1.2 | 2.2 | 0.4 | 0.0 | 0.0 | 0.7 | 0.3 |
| **Average** | **5.3** | **3.8** | **3.9** | **2.1** | **3.2** | **2.6** | **3.4** | **2.6** |

a. Tariff data are from the Trade Analysis and Information System (TRAINS) database and may have a different country coverage than that for the 20 EU members whose trade values are reported. b. Includes ad valorem equivalents of specific rates.

## About the data

Developing countries are becoming increasingly important in the global trading system. Since the early 1990s trade between high-income economies and low- and middle-income economies has grown faster than trade among high-income economies. The increased trade benefits consumers and producers. But as was apparent at the World Trade Organization's (WTO) Ministerial Conferences in Doha, Qatar, in October 2001, Cancun, Mexico, in September 2003, and Hong Kong, China, in December 2005, achieving a more pro-development outcome from trade remains a challenge. Meeting it will require strengthening international consultation. After the Doha meetings negotiations were launched on services, agriculture, manufactures, WTO rules, the environment, dispute settlement, intellectual property rights protection, and disciplines on regional integration. At the most recent negotiations in Hong Kong, China, trade ministers agreed to eliminate subsidies of agricultural exports by 2013; to abolish cotton export subsidies and grant unlimited export access to selected cotton-growing countries in Sub-Saharan Africa; to cut more domestic farm supports in the European Union, Japan, and the United States; and to offer more aid to developing countries to help them compete in global trade.

Trade flows between high-income and low- and middle-income economies reflect the changing mix of exports to and imports from developing economies. While food and primary commodities have continued to fall as a share of high-income economies' imports, manufactures as a share of goods imports from both low- and middle-income economies have grown. And trade between developing economies has grown substantially over the past decade, a result of their increasing share of world output and liberalization of trade, among other influences.

Yet trade barriers remain high. The table includes information about tariff rates by selected product groups. Applied tariff rates are the tariffs in effect for partners in preferential trade agreements such as the North American Free Trade Agreement. When these rates are unavailable, most favored nation rates are used. The difference between most favored nation and applied rates can be substantial. Simple averages of applied rates are shown because they are generally a better indicator of tariff protection than weighted average rates are.

The data are from the United Nations Conference on Trade and Development (UNCTAD). Partner country reports by high-income economies were used for both exports and imports. Because of differences in sources of data, timing, and treatment of missing data, the numbers in the table may not be fully comparable with those used to calculate the direction of trade statistics in table 6.3 or the aggregate flows in tables 4.4, 4.5, and 6.2. Tariff line data were matched to Standard International Trade Classification (SITC) revision 1 codes to define commodity groups. For further discussion of merchandise trade statistics, see *About the data* for tables 4.4, 4.5, 6.2, and 6.3, and for information about tariff barriers, see table 6.7.

## Definitions

The product groups in the table are defined in accordance with the SITC revision 1: **food** (0, 1, 22, and 4) and **cereals** (04); **agricultural raw materials** (2 excluding 22, 27, and 28); **ores and nonferrous metals** (27, 28, and 68); **fuels** (3), **crude petroleum** (331), and **petroleum products** (332); **manufactured goods** (5–8 excluding 68), **chemical products** (5), **iron and steel** (67), **machinery and transport equipment** (7), **furniture** (82), **textiles** (65 and 84), **footwear** (85), and **other manufactured goods** (6 and 8 excluding 65, 67, 68, 82, 84, and 85); and **miscellaneous goods** (9). • **Exports** are all merchandise exports by high-income economies to low-income and middle-income economies as recorded in the United Nations Statistics Division's Comtrade database. Exports are recorded free on board (f.o.b.). • **Imports** are all merchandise imports by high-income economies from low-income and middle-income economies as recorded in the United Nations Statistics Division's Commodity Trade (Comtrade) database. Imports include insurance and freight charges (c.i.f.). • **High-, middle-, and low-income economies** are those classified as such by the World Bank (see inside front cover). • **European Union** is defined as all high-income EU members: Austria, Belgium, Cyprus, Czech Republic, Denmark, Estonia, Finland, France, Germany, Greece, Ireland, Italy, Luxembourg, Malta, the Netherlands, Portugal, Slovenia, Spain, Sweden, and the United Kingdom.

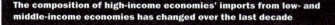

**The composition of high-income economies' imports from low- and middle-income economies has changed over the last decade**   **6.4a**

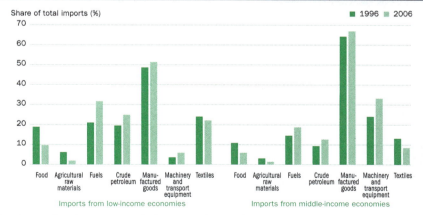

The shares of high-income economies' imports of food, agricultural raw materials, and textiles from low- and middle-income economies dropped noticeably between 1996 and 2006, while the shares of fuels (especially crude petroleum) and machinery and transport equipment have increased considerably.

*Source:* United Nations Statistics Division's Comtrade database.

## Data sources

Data on trade values are from United Nations Statistics Division's Comtrade database. Data on tariffs are from UNCTAD's Trade Analysis and Information System database and are calculated by World Bank staff using the World Integrated Trade Solution system.

| | 1970 | 1980 | 1990 | 1995 | 2000 | 2001 | 2002 | 2003 | 2004 | 2005 | 2006 | 2007 |
|---|---|---|---|---|---|---|---|---|---|---|---|---|
| **World Bank commodity price index (1990 = 100)** | | | | | | | | | | | | |
| Nonenergy commodities | 156 | 159 | 100 | 104 | 89 | 84 | 89 | 91 | 100 | 114 | 140 | 158 |
| Agriculture | 163 | 175 | 100 | 112 | 90 | 84 | 93 | 95 | 98 | 106 | 116 | 131 |
| Beverages | 203 | 230 | 100 | 129 | 91 | 76 | 91 | 87 | 88 | 109 | 113 | 125 |
| Food | 166 | 177 | 100 | 100 | 87 | 91 | 97 | 96 | 103 | 103 | 111 | 131 |
| Raw materials | 130 | 133 | 100 | 116 | 93 | 81 | 89 | 98 | 99 | 107 | 126 | 134 |
| Fertilizers | 108 | 164 | 100 | 88 | 109 | 105 | 108 | 106 | 118 | 126 | 126 | 204 |
| Metals and minerals | 144 | 120 | 100 | 87 | 85 | 80 | 78 | 82 | 105 | 133 | 198 | 220 |
| Petroleum | 19 | 204 | 100 | 64 | 127 | 113 | 117 | 126 | 154 | 218 | 258 | 279 |
| Steel products[a] | 111 | 100 | 100 | 91 | 79 | 71 | 73 | 79 | 114 | 129 | 124 | 121 |
| MUV G-5 index | 28 | 79 | 100 | 117 | 97 | 94 | 93 | 100 | 107 | 107 | 109 | 111 |
| **Commodity prices (1990 prices)** | | | | | | | | | | | | |
| **Agricultural raw materials** | | | | | | | | | | | | |
| Cotton (cents/kg) | 225 | 260 | 182 | 182 | 134 | 112 | 109 | 140 | 128 | 114 | 116 | 125 |
| Logs, Cameroon ($/cu. m)[a] | 153 | 319 | 344 | 290 | 283 | 282 | 253 | 279 | 310 | 312 | 293 | 343 |
| Logs, Malaysian ($/cu. m) | 154 | 248 | 177 | 218 | 195 | 169 | 175 | 187 | 184 | 190 | 220 | 241 |
| Rubber (cents/kg) | 145 | 181 | 86 | 135 | 69 | 61 | 82 | 108 | 122 | 140 | 194 | 206 |
| Sawnwood, Malaysian ($/cu. m) | 625 | 503 | 533 | 632 | 612 | 510 | 565 | 550 | 543 | 616 | 689 | 725 |
| Tobacco ($/mt) | 3,836 | 2,887 | 3,392 | 2,258 | 3,063 | 3,185 | 2,947 | 2,643 | 2,560 | 2,606 | 2,730 | 2,966 |
| **Beverages (cents/kg)** | | | | | | | | | | | | |
| Cocoa | 240 | 330 | 127 | 122 | 93 | 113 | 191 | 175 | 145 | 144 | 146 | 176 |
| Coffee, robustas | 330 | 411 | 118 | 237 | 94 | 64 | 71 | 81 | 74 | 104 | 137 | 172 |
| Coffee, Arabica | 409 | 440 | 197 | 285 | 198 | 146 | 146 | 141 | 166 | 237 | 232 | 245 |
| Tea, avg., 3 auctions | 298 | 211 | 206 | 127 | 193 | 169 | 162 | 151 | 157 | 154 | 172 | 183 |
| **Energy** | | | | | | | | | | | | |
| Coal, Australian ($/mt) | 0 | 51 | 40 | 34 | 27 | 34 | 27 | 26 | 49 | 44 | 45 | 59 |
| Coal, U.S. ($/mt) | 0 | 55 | 42 | 33 | 34 | 48 | 43 | .. | .. | .. | .. | .. |
| Natural gas, Europe ($/mmbtu) | 0 | 4 | 3 | 2 | 4 | 4 | 3 | 4 | 4 | 6 | 8 | 8 |
| Natural gas, U.S. ($/mmbtu) | 1 | 2 | 2 | 1 | 4 | 4 | 4 | 5 | 6 | 8 | 6 | 6 |
| Petroleum ($/bbl) | 4 | 47 | 23 | 15 | 29 | 26 | 27 | 29 | 35 | 50 | 59 | 64 |

## About the data

Primary commodities—raw or partially processed materials that will be transformed into finished goods—are often the most significant exports of developing countries, and revenues obtained from them have an important effect on living standards. Price data for primary commodities are collected from a variety of sources, including trade journals, international study groups, government market surveys, newspaper and wire service reports, and commodity exchange spot and near-term forward prices.

The table is based on frequently updated price reports. When available, the prices received by exporters are used; otherwise, the prices paid by importers are used. Annual price series are generally simple averages based on higher frequency data. The constant price series in the table is deflated using the manufactures unit value (MUV) index for the Group of Five (G-5) countries (see below).

The commodity price indexes are calculated as Laspeyres index numbers, in which the fixed weights are the 1987–89 export values for low- and middle-income economies rebased to 1990. Each index represents a fixed basket of primary commodity exports. The nonenergy commodity price index contains 37 price series for 31 nonenergy commodities.

Separate indexes are compiled for petroleum and steel products, which are not included in the nonenergy commodity price index.

The MUV index is a composite index of prices for manufactured exports from the five major (G-5) industrial economies (France, Germany, Japan, the United Kingdom, and the United States) to low- and middle-income economies, valued in U.S. dollars. The index covers products in groups 5–8 of the Standard International Trade Classification revision 1. To construct the MUV G-5 index, unit value indexes for each country are combined using weights determined by each country's export share.

| | 1970 | 1980 | 1990 | 1995 | 2000 | 2001 | 2002 | 2003 | 2004 | 2005 | 2006 | 2007 |
|---|---|---|---|---|---|---|---|---|---|---|---|---|
| **Commodity prices (continued)** | | | | | | | | | | | | |
| **(1990 prices)** | | | | | | | | | | | | |
| **Fertilizers ($/mt)** | | | | | | | | | | | | |
| Phosphate rock | 39 | 59 | 41 | 30 | 45 | 44 | 43 | 38 | 38 | 39 | 41 | 64 |
| Triple superphosphate | 152 | 229 | 132 | 128 | 142 | 135 | 143 | 149 | 174 | 188 | 185 | 305 |
| **Food** | | | | | | | | | | | | |
| Fats and oils ($/mt) | | | | | | | | | | | | |
| Coconut oil | 1,417 | 855 | 337 | 572 | 463 | 337 | 452 | 467 | 617 | 576 | 558 | 826 |
| Groundnut oil | 1,350 | 1,090 | 964 | 846 | 734 | 721 | 738 | 1,242 | 1,085 | 991 | 892 | 1,216 |
| Palm oil | 927 | 740 | 290 | 536 | 319 | 303 | 419 | 443 | 440 | 394 | 440 | 701 |
| Soybeans | 417 | 376 | 247 | 221 | 218 | 208 | 228 | 264 | 286 | 257 | 247 | 345 |
| Soybean meal | 367 | 332 | 200 | 168 | 195 | 192 | 188 | 211 | 225 | 200 | 192 | 276 |
| Soybean oil | 1,021 | 758 | 447 | 534 | 348 | 375 | 488 | 553 | 576 | 509 | 550 | 792 |
| Grains ($/mt) | | | | | | | | | | | | |
| Sorghum | 185 | 164 | 104 | 102 | 91 | 101 | 109 | 106 | 103 | 90 | 113 | 146 |
| Maize | 208 | 159 | 109 | 105 | 91 | 95 | 107 | 105 | 104 | 92 | 112 | 147 |
| Rice | 450 | 521 | 271 | 274 | 208 | 183 | 206 | 197 | 222 | 267 | 280 | 293 |
| Wheat | 196 | 219 | 136 | 151 | 117 | 134 | 159 | 146 | 147 | 142 | 177 | 229 |
| Other food | | | | | | | | | | | | |
| Bananas ($/mt) | 590 | 481 | 541 | 380 | 436 | 618 | 568 | 374 | 490 | 563 | 623 | 608 |
| Beef (cents/kg) | 465 | 350 | 256 | 163 | 199 | 226 | 226 | 198 | 235 | 245 | 234 | 234 |
| Oranges ($/mt) | 599 | 496 | 531 | 454 | 374 | 631 | 606 | 680 | 803 | 817 | 763 | 860 |
| Sugar, EU domestic (cents/kg) | 40 | 62 | 58 | 59 | 57 | 56 | 59 | 60 | 63 | 62 | 59 | 61 |
| Sugar, U.S. domestic (cents/kg) | 59 | 84 | 51 | 43 | 44 | 50 | 50 | 47 | 42 | 44 | 45 | 41 |
| Sugar, world (cents/kg) | 29 | 80 | 28 | 25 | 19 | 20 | 16 | 16 | 15 | 20 | 30 | 20 |
| **Metals and minerals** | | | | | | | | | | | | |
| Aluminum ($/mt) | 1,982 | 1,847 | 1,639 | 1,542 | 1,594 | 1,531 | 1,449 | 1,430 | 1,603 | 1,774 | 2,363 | 2,372 |
| Copper ($/mt) | 5,038 | 2,768 | 2,662 | 2,508 | 1,866 | 1,673 | 1,674 | 1,777 | 2,678 | 3,437 | 6,182 | 6,399 |
| Iron ore (cents/dmtu) | 35 | 36 | 33 | 24 | 30 | 32 | 31 | 32 | 35 | 61 | 71 | 76 |
| Lead (cents/kg) | 108 | 115 | 81 | 54 | 47 | 50 | 49 | 51 | 83 | 91 | 119 | 232 |
| Nickel ($/mt) | 10,148 | 8,270 | 8,864 | 7,028 | 8,888 | 6,303 | 7,271 | 9,617 | 12,915 | 13,776 | 22,305 | 33,462 |
| Tin (cents/kg) | 1,310 | 2,128 | 609 | 531 | 559 | 475 | 436 | 489 | 795 | 690 | 807 | 1,307 |
| Zinc (cents/kg) | 105 | 97 | 151 | 88 | 116 | 94 | 84 | 83 | 98 | 129 | 301 | 291 |

a. Series not included in the nonenergy index.

## Definitions

• **Nonenergy commodity price index** covers the 31 nonenergy primary commodities that make up the agriculture, fertilizer, and metals and minerals indexes. • **Agriculture** includes beverages, food, and agricultural raw materials. • **Beverages** include cocoa, coffee, and tea. • **Food** includes rice, wheat, maize, sorghum, soybeans, soybean oil, soybean meal, palm oil, coconut oil, groundnut oil, bananas, beef, oranges, and sugar. • **Agricultural raw materials** include cotton, timber (logs and sawnwood), natural rubber, and tobacco. • **Fertilizers** include phosphate rock and triple superphosphate. • **Metals and minerals** include aluminum, copper, iron ore, lead, nickel, tin, and zinc. • **Petroleum price index** refers to the average spot price of Brent, Dubai, and West Texas Intermediate crude oils, equally weighted. • **Steel products price index** is the composite price index for eight steel products based on quotations free on board (f.o.b.) Japan excluding shipments to China and the United States, weighted by product shares of apparent combined consumption (volume of deliveries) for Germany, Japan, and the United States. • **MUV G-5 index** is the manufactures unit value index for G-5 country exports to low- and middle-income economies. • **Commodity prices**— for definitions and sources, see "Commodity price data" (also known as the "Pink Sheet") at the Global Prospects Web site (www.worldbank.org/prospects, click on Products).

### Data sources

Data on commodity prices and the MUV G-5 index are compiled by the World Bank's Development Prospects Group. Monthly updates of commodity prices are available on the Web at www.worldbank.org/prospects.

**Merchandise exports within bloc**

| | Year of creation | Year of entry into force of the most recent agreement | Type of the most recent agreement[a] | \$ millions | | | | | | |
|---|---|---|---|---|---|---|---|---|---|---|
| | | | | 1990 | 1995 | 2000 | 2003 | 2004 | 2005 | 2006 |
| **High-income and low- and middle-income economies** | | | | | | | | | | |
| APEC[b] | 1989 | | None | 901,560 | 1,688,708 | 2,261,791 | 2,436,516 | 2,924,291 | 3,309,117 | 3,763,569 |
| CEFTA[c] | 1992 | 1994 | FTA | 322 | 2,886 | 2,136 | 3,147 | 3,915 | 5,382 | 6,474 |
| CIS | 1991 | 1994 | FTA | .. | 31,529 | 28,753 | 38,576 | 43,446 | 59,423 | 66,583 |
| EEA | 1994 | 1994 | EIA | 1,070,201 | 1,444,732 | 1,680,468 | 2,175,403 | 2,589,764 | 2,780,586 | 3,142,002 |
| EFTA | 1960 | 2002 | EIA | 782 | 925 | 831 | 967 | 1,128 | 1,252 | 1,524 |
| European Union[c] | 1957 | 1958 | EIA, CU | 1,022,933 | 1,385,805 | 1,608,174 | 2,087,311 | 2,482,418 | 2,649,078 | 2,987,188 |
| NAFTA | 1994 | 1994 | FTA | 226,273 | 394,472 | 676,141 | 651,060 | 737,591 | 824,550 | 902,085 |
| SPARTECA | 1981 | 1981 | PS | 4,737 | 8,535 | 8,139 | 10,864 | 13,047 | 14,413 | 14,531 |
| Trans-Pacific SEP | 2006 | 2006 | EIA, FTA | 1,110 | 2,614 | 1,438 | 1,621 | 2,096 | 2,345 | 2,927 |
| **Latin America and the Caribbean** | | | | | | | | | | |
| Andean Community | 1969 | 1988 | CU | 1,312 | 4,812 | 5,293 | 5,064 | 7,619 | 8,676 | 11,300 |
| CACM | 1961 | 1961 | CU | 667 | 1,594 | 2,586 | 3,156 | 3,574 | 4,064 | 5,022 |
| CARICOM | 1973 | 1997 | EIA | 456 | 877 | 1,078 | 1,419 | 1,746 | 2,090 | 2,429 |
| LAIA (ALADI) | 1980 | 1981 | PS | 13,350 | 35,986 | 44,252 | 40,425 | 57,732 | 71,711 | 91,651 |
| MERCOSUR | 1991 | 2005 | EIA | 4,909 | 16,811 | 20,082 | 13,765 | 19,675 | 24,211 | 30,902 |
| OECS | 1981[d] | 1981[d] | NNA | 29 | 39 | 38 | 48 | 60 | 68 | 84 |
| **Middle East and Asia** | | | | | | | | | | |
| ASEAN | 1967 | 1992 | FTA | 27,365 | 79,544 | 98,060 | 116,831 | 141,934 | 165,169 | 194,321 |
| Bangkok Agreement | 1975 | 1976 | PS | 2,429 | 21,728 | 37,895 | 70,845 | 99,369 | 127,277 | 150,545 |
| EAEC | 1997 | 1997 | CU | .. | 13,556 | 15,467 | 19,933 | 17,291 | 27,297 | 27,930 |
| ECO | 1985 | 2003[d] | PS | 1,243 | 4,746 | 4,518 | 7,468 | 9,989 | 13,936 | 19,053 |
| GCC | 1981 | 2003 | CU | 6,906 | 6,832 | 7,954 | 9,915 | 12,532 | 16,507 | 20,050 |
| PAFTA (GAFTA) | 1997 | 1998 | FTA | 13,204 | 12,948 | 16,140 | 21,918 | 35,328 | 44,468 | 54,862 |
| SAARC[e] | 1985 | 1995 | PS | 863 | 2,024 | 2,680 | 4,954 | 5,830 | 7,266 | 9,109 |
| UMA | 1989 | 1994[d] | NNA | 958 | 1,109 | 1,094 | 1,338 | 1,375 | 1,926 | 2,400 |
| **Sub-Saharan Africa** | | | | | | | | | | |
| CEMAC | 1994 | 1999 | CU | 139 | 120 | 96 | 146 | 174 | 198 | 245 |
| COMESA | 1994 | 1994 | FTA | 1,164 | 1,390 | 1,448 | 2,041 | 2,427 | 2,869 | 3,546 |
| EAC | 1996 | 2000 | CU | 230 | 530 | 595 | 706 | 750 | 857 | 1,059 |
| ECCAS | 1983 | 2004[d] | NNA | 163 | 163 | 191 | 198 | 240 | 271 | 334 |
| ECOWAS | 1975 | 1993 | PS | 1,532 | 1,875 | 2,715 | 3,037 | 4,366 | 5,497 | 5,957 |
| Indian Ocean Commission | 1984 | 2005[d] | NNA | 73 | 127 | 106 | 179 | 155 | 159 | 172 |
| SADC | 1992 | 2000 | FTA | 677 | 1,015 | 4,383 | 5,609 | 6,590 | 7,668 | 8,571 |
| UEMOA | 1994 | 2000 | CU | 621 | 560 | 741 | 1,076 | 1,233 | 1,390 | 1,545 |

**Note:** Regional bloc memberships are as follows: **Andean Community,** Bolivia, Colombia, Ecuador, Peru, and Bolivarian Republic of Venezuela; **Arab Maghreb Union (UMA),** Algeria, Libyan Arab Republic, Mauritania, Morocco, and Tunisia; **Asia Pacific Economic Cooperation (APEC),** Australia, Brunei Darussalam, Canada, Chile, China, Hong Kong (China), Indonesia, Japan, the Republic of Korea, Malaysia, Mexico, New Zealand, Papua New Guinea, Peru, the Philippines, the Russian Federation, Singapore, Taiwan (China), Thailand, the United States, and Vietnam; **Association of South East Asian Nations (ASEAN),** Brunei Darussalam, Cambodia, Indonesia, the Lao People's Democratic Republic, Malaysia, Myanmar, the Philippines, Singapore, Thailand, and Vietnam; **Bangkok Agreement,** Bangladesh, China, India, the Republic of Korea, the Lao People's Democratic Republic, and Sri Lanka; **Caribbean Community and Common Market (CARICOM),** Antigua and Barbuda, the Bahamas, Barbados, Belize, Dominica, Grenada, Guyana, Haiti, Jamaica, Montserrat, St. Kitts and Nevis, St. Lucia, St. Vincent and the Grenadines, Suriname, and Trinidad and Tobago; **Central American Common Market (CACM),** Costa Rica, El Salvador, Guatemala, Honduras, and Nicaragua; **Central European Free Trade Area (CEFTA),** Bulgaria, Croatia, Macedonia, Romania, and Slovenia; **Common Market for Eastern and Southern Africa (COMESA),** Angola, Burundi, Comoros, the Democratic Republic of Congo, Djibouti, the Arab Republic of Egypt, Eritrea, Ethiopia, Kenya, Libyan Arab Republic, Madagascar, Malawi, Mauritius, Rwanda, Seychelles, Sudan, Swaziland, Uganda, Zambia, and Zimbabwe; **Commonwealth of Independent States (CIS),** Armenia, Azerbaijan, Belarus, Georgia, Kazakhstan, Kyrgyz Republic, Moldova, Russian Federation, Tajikistan, Turkmenistan, Ukraine, and Uzbekistan; **East African Community (EAC),** Kenya, Tanzania, and Uganda; **Economic and Monetary Community of Central Africa (CEMAC; formerly Union Douanière et Economique de l'Afrique Centrale [UDEAC]),** Cameroon, the Central African Republic, Chad, the Republic of Congo, Equatorial Guinea, and Gabon; **Economic Community of Central African States (ECCAS),** Angola, Burundi, Cameroon, the Central African Republic, Chad, the Democratic Republic of Congo, the Republic of Congo, Equatorial Guinea, Gabon, Rwanda, and São Tomé and Principe; **Economic Community of West African States (ECOWAS),** Benin, Burkina Faso, Cape Verde, Côte d'Ivoire, the Gambia, Ghana, Guinea, Guinea-Bissau, Liberia, Mali, Niger, Nigeria, Senegal, Sierra Leone, and Togo; **Economic Cooperation Organization (ECO),** Afghanistan, Azerbaijan, the Islamic Republic of Iran, Kazakhstan, the

## Merchandise exports within bloc

| | Year of creation | Year of entry into force of the most recent agreement | Type of agreement[a] | % of total bloc exports | | | | | | |
|---|---|---|---|---|---|---|---|---|---|---|
| | | | | 1990 | 1995 | 2000 | 2003 | 2004 | 2005 | 2006 |
| **High-income and low- and middle-income economies** | | | | | | | | | | |
| APEC[b] | 1989 | | None | 68.3 | 71.7 | 73.1 | 72.7 | 72.2 | 70.8 | 69.4 |
| CEFTA[c] | 1992 | 1994 | FTA | 4.1 | 10.5 | 7.3 | 7.0 | 6.8 | 7.8 | 7.9 |
| CIS | 1991 | 1994 | FTA | .. | 28.6 | 20.0 | 20.3 | 17.6 | 18.0 | 16.5 |
| EEA | 1994 | 1994 | EIA | 68.6 | 67.5 | 68.1 | 68.4 | 68.1 | 67.5 | 67.7 |
| EFTA | 1960 | 2002 | EIA | 0.8 | 0.7 | 0.6 | 0.6 | 0.5 | 0.5 | 0.6 |
| European Union[c] | 1957 | 1958 | EIA, CU | 67.1 | 66.1 | 66.8 | 67.2 | 66.8 | 66.0 | 66.2 |
| NAFTA | 1994 | 1994 | FTA | 41.4 | 46.2 | 55.7 | 56.1 | 55.9 | 55.8 | 53.8 |
| SPARTECA | 1981 | 1981 | PS | 9.4 | 12.1 | 10.2 | 11.8 | 11.6 | 10.8 | 9.6 |
| Trans-Pacific SEP | 2006 | 2006 | EIA, FTA | 1.5 | 1.7 | 0.8 | 0.8 | 0.8 | 0.8 | 0.8 |
| **Latin America and the Caribbean** | | | | | | | | | | |
| Andean Community | 1969 | 1988 | CU | 4.1 | 12.0 | 8.9 | 8.9 | 9.7 | 8.2 | 8.1 |
| CACM | 1961 | 1961 | CU | 15.3 | 21.8 | 19.1 | 20.2 | 20.9 | 18.9 | 16.2 |
| CARICOM | 1973 | 1997 | EIA | 8.0 | 12.1 | 14.4 | 12.0 | 12.2 | 11.5 | 11.1 |
| LAIA (ALADI) | 1980 | 1981 | PS | 11.6 | 17.3 | 13.2 | 11.5 | 13.2 | 13.6 | 14.3 |
| MERCOSUR | 1991 | 2005 | EIA | 7.6 | 18.9 | 16.4 | 10.3 | 11.1 | 11.0 | 11.6 |
| OECS | 1981[a] | 1981 | NNA | 8.1 | 12.6 | 10.0 | 7.6 | 11.7 | 11.4 | 8.0 |
| **Middle East and Asia** | | | | | | | | | | |
| ASEAN | 1967 | 1992 | FTA | 18.9 | 24.5 | 23.0 | 24.7 | 24.9 | 25.3 | 24.9 |
| Bangkok Agreement | 1975 | 1976 | NNA | 1.6 | 6.8 | 8.0 | 10.0 | 10.6 | 11.0 | 10.7 |
| EAEC | 1997 | 1997 | CU | .. | 14.8 | 12.5 | 12.6 | 8.5 | 9.6 | 8.0 |
| ECO | 1985 | 2003[d] | PS | 3.2 | 7.9 | 5.6 | 6.6 | 6.7 | 7.6 | 8.5 |
| GCC | 1981 | 2003 | CU | 8.0 | 6.8 | 4.8 | 5.2 | 5.0 | 4.8 | 4.8 |
| PAFTA (GAFTA) | 1997 | 1998 | FTA | 10.2 | 9.8 | 7.2 | 8.7 | 10.0 | 9.8 | 9.7 |
| SAARC[e] | 1985 | 1995 | PS | 3.2 | 4.4 | 4.2 | 5.8 | 5.7 | 5.6 | 5.6 |
| UMA | 1989 | 1994[d] | NNA | 2.9 | 3.8 | 2.3 | 2.4 | 1.9 | 2.0 | 2.0 |
| **Sub-Saharan Africa** | | | | | | | | | | |
| CEMAC | 1994 | 1999 | CU | 2.3 | 2.1 | 1.0 | 1.4 | 1.2 | 0.9 | 0.9 |
| COMESA | 1994 | 1994 | FTA | 4.2 | 5.4 | 3.7 | 4.4 | 4.1 | 3.4 | 3.2 |
| EAC | 1996 | 2000 | CU | 13.4 | 17.4 | 20.5 | 18.3 | 16.7 | 15.1 | 16.5 |
| ECCAS | 1983 | 2004[d] | NNA | 1.4 | 1.5 | 1.1 | 1.0 | 0.9 | 0.6 | 0.6 |
| ECOWAS | 1975 | 1993 | PS | 8.0 | 9.0 | 7.6 | 8.5 | 9.3 | 9.3 | 8.3 |
| Indian Ocean Commission | 1984 | 2005[d] | NNA | 4.1 | 6.0 | 4.4 | 6.2 | 4.3 | 4.6 | 4.7 |
| SADC | 1992 | 2000 | FTA | 6.8 | 9.2 | 9.4 | 10.1 | 9.7 | 9.2 | 9.1 |
| UEMOA | 1994 | 2000 | CU | 13.0 | 10.3 | 13.1 | 13.3 | 12.9 | 13.4 | 13.1 |

Kyrgyz Republic, Pakistan, Tajikistan, Turkey, Turkmenistan, and Uzbekistan; **Eurasian Economic Community (EAEC)**, Belarus, Kazakhstan, Kyrgyz Republic, Russian Federation, Tajikistan, and Uzbekistan; **European Economic Area (EEA)**, European Union plus Iceland, Liechtenstein, and Norway; **European Free Trade Association (EFTA)**, Iceland, Liechtenstein, Norway, and Switzerland; **European Union (EU; formerly European Economic Community and European Community)**, Austria, Belgium, Cyprus, Czech Republic, Denmark, Estonia, Finland, France, Germany, Greece, Hungary, Ireland, Italy, Latvia, Lithuania, Luxembourg, the Netherlands, Malta, Poland, Portugal, Slovak Republic, Slovenia, Spain, Sweden, and the United Kingdom; **Gulf Cooperation Council (GCC)**, Bahrain, Kuwait, Oman, Qatar, Saudi Arabia, and the United Arab Emirates; **Indian Ocean Commission**, Comoros, Madagascar, Mauritius, Réunion, and Seychelles; **Latin American Integration Association (LAIA; formerly Latin American Free Trade Area)**, Argentina, Bolivia, Brazil, Chile, Colombia, Cuba, Ecuador, Mexico, Paraguay, Peru, Uruguay, and Bolivarian Republic of Venezuela; **North American Free Trade Agreement (NAFTA)**, Canada, Mexico, and the United States; **Organization of Eastern Caribbean States (OECS)**, Anguilla, Antigua and Barbuda, British Virgin Islands, Dominica, Grenada, Montserrat, St. Kitts and Nevis, St. Lucia, and St. Vincent and the Grenadines; **Pan-Arab Free Trade Area (PAFTA; also known as Greater Arab Trade Area [GAFTA])**, Bahrain, Egypt, Iraq, Jordan, Kuwait, Lebanon, Libya, Morocco, Oman, Qatar, Saudi Arabia, Sudan, Syrian Arab Republic, Tunisia, the United Arab Emirates, and Yemen; **South Asian Association for Regional Cooperation (SAARC)**, Bangladesh, Bhutan, India, Maldives, Nepal, Pakistan, and Sri Lanka; **South Pacific Regional Trade and Economic Cooperation Agreement (SPARTECA)**, Australia, Cook Islands, Fiji, Kiribati, Marshall Islands, Micronesia (Federated States of), Nauru, New Zealand, Niue, Papua New Guinea, Solomon Islands, Tonga, Tuvalu, Vanuatu, and Western Samoa; **Southern African Development Community (SADC)**, Angola, Botswana, the Democratic Republic of Congo, Lesotho, Malawi, Madagascar, Mauritius, Mozambique, Namibia, South Africa, Swaziland, Tanzania, Zambia, and Zimbabwe; **Southern Common Market (MERCOSUR)**, Argentina, Brazil, Paraguay, Uruguay, and Bolivarian Republic of Venezuela; **Trans-Pacific Strategic Economic Partnership (Trans-Pacific SEP)**, Brunei Darussalam, Chile, New Zealand, and Singapore; **West African Economic and Monetary Union (UEMOA)**, Benin, Burkina Faso, Côte d'Ivoire, Guinea-Bissau, Mali, Niger, Senegal, and Togo.

# 6.6 | Regional trade blocs

## Merchandise exports by bloc

| | Year of creation | Year of entry into force of the most recent agreement | Type of agreement[a] | % of world exports | | | | | | |
|---|---|---|---|---|---|---|---|---|---|---|
| | | | | 1990 | 1995 | 2000 | 2003 | 2004 | 2005 | 2006 |
| **High-income and low- and middle-income economies** | | | | | | | | | | |
| APEC[b] | 1989 | | None | 39.0 | 46.3 | 48.5 | 44.6 | 44.4 | 45.1 | 45.3 |
| CEFTA[c] | 1992 | 1994 | FTA | 0.2 | 0.5 | 0.5 | 0.6 | 0.6 | 0.7 | 0.7 |
| CIS | 1991 | 1994 | FTA | 0.0 | 2.2 | 2.2 | 2.5 | 2.7 | 3.2 | 3.4 |
| EEA | 1994 | 1994 | EIA | 46.1 | 42.1 | 38.7 | 42.3 | 41.6 | 39.7 | 38.8 |
| EFTA | 1960 | 2002 | EIA | 2.9 | 2.4 | 2.2 | 2.3 | 2.3 | 2.3 | 2.3 |
| European Union[c] | 1957 | 1958 | EIA, CU | 45.1 | 41.3 | 37.7 | 41.4 | 40.7 | 38.7 | 37.7 |
| NAFTA | 1994 | 1994 | FTA | 16.2 | 16.8 | 19.0 | 15.4 | 14.5 | 14.3 | 14.0 |
| SPARTECA | 1981 | 1981 | PS | 1.5 | 1.4 | 1.3 | 1.2 | 1.2 | 1.3 | 1.3 |
| Trans-Pacific SEP | 2006 | 2006 | EIA, FTA | 2.2 | 3.0 | 2.7 | 2.7 | 2.8 | 2.9 | 3.0 |
| **Latin America and the Caribbean** | | | | | | | | | | |
| Andean Community | 1969 | 1988 | CU | 0.9 | 0.8 | 0.9 | 0.8 | 0.9 | 1.0 | 1.2 |
| CACM | 1961 | 1961 | CU | 0.1 | 0.1 | 0.2 | 0.2 | 0.2 | 0.2 | 0.3 |
| CARICOM | 1973 | 1997 | EIA | 0.2 | 0.1 | 0.1 | 0.2 | 0.2 | 0.2 | 0.2 |
| LAIA (ALADI) | 1980 | 1981 | PS | 3.4 | 4.1 | 5.3 | 4.7 | 4.8 | 5.1 | 5.4 |
| MERCOSUR | 1991 | 2005 | EIA | 1.9 | 1.8 | 1.9 | 1.8 | 1.9 | 2.1 | 2.2 |
| OECS | 1981 | 1981[d] | NNA | 0.0 | 0.0 | 0.0 | 0.0 | 0.0 | 0.0 | 0.0 |
| **Middle East and Asia** | | | | | | | | | | |
| ASEAN | 1967 | 1992 | FTA | 4.3 | 6.4 | 6.7 | 6.3 | 6.2 | 6.3 | 6.5 |
| Bangkok Agreement | 1975 | 1976 | NNA | 4.5 | 6.3 | 7.4 | 9.4 | 10.3 | 11.2 | 11.8 |
| EAEC | 1997 | 1997 | CU | 0.0 | 1.8 | 1.9 | 2.1 | 2.2 | 2.7 | 2.9 |
| ECO | 1985 | 2003[d] | PS | 1.1 | 1.2 | 1.3 | 1.5 | 1.6 | 1.8 | 1.9 |
| GCC | 1981 | 2003 | CU | 2.6 | 2.0 | 2.6 | 2.5 | 2.7 | 3.3 | 3.5 |
| PAFTA (GAFTA) | 1997 | 1998 | FTA | 3.8 | 2.6 | 3.5 | 3.4 | 3.9 | 4.4 | 4.7 |
| SAARC[e] | 1985 | 1995 | PS | 0.8 | 0.9 | 1.0 | 1.1 | 1.1 | 1.3 | 1.3 |
| UMA | 1989 | 1994[d] | NNA | 1.0 | 0.6 | 0.8 | 0.7 | 0.8 | 0.9 | 1.0 |
| **Sub-Saharan Africa** | | | | | | | | | | |
| CEMAC | 1994 | 1999 | CU | 0.2 | 0.1 | 0.1 | 0.1 | 0.2 | 0.2 | 0.2 |
| COMESA | 1994 | 1994 | FTA | 0.8 | 0.5 | 0.6 | 0.6 | 0.7 | 0.8 | 0.9 |
| EAC | 1996 | 2000 | CU | 0.1 | 0.1 | 0.0 | 0.1 | 0.0 | 0.1 | 0.1 |
| ECCAS | 1983 | 2004[d] | NNA | 0.3 | 0.2 | 0.3 | 0.3 | 0.3 | 0.4 | 0.5 |
| ECOWAS | 1975 | 1993 | PS | 0.6 | 0.4 | 0.6 | 0.5 | 0.5 | 0.6 | 0.6 |
| Indian Ocean Commission | 1984 | 2005[d] | NNA | 0.1 | 0.0 | 0.0 | 0.0 | 0.0 | 0.0 | 0.0 |
| SADC | 1992 | 2000 | FTA | 0.3 | 0.2 | 0.7 | 0.7 | 0.7 | 0.8 | 0.8 |
| UEMOA | 1994 | 2000 | CU | 0.1 | 0.1 | 0.1 | 0.1 | 0.1 | 0.1 | 0.1 |

a. FTA is free trade agreement, CU is customs union, EIA is economic integration agreement, PS is partial scope agreement, and NNA is not notified agreement, which refers to preferential trade arrangements established among member countries that are not notified to the World Trade Organization (these agreements may be functionally equivalent to any of the other agreements). b. No preferential trade agreement c. Members changed and new agreements entered into force in 2007, but are not reflected in the data shown. d. Years of the most recent agreement are collected from official trade bloc website. e. Free trade agreement was signed in 2006 but has not entered into force yet.

## About the data

Trade blocs are groups of countries that have established special preferential arrangements governing trade between members. Although in some cases the preferences—such as lower tariff duties or exemptions from quantitative restrictions—may be no greater than those available to other trading partners, such arrangements are intended to encourage exports by bloc members to one another—sometimes called intratrade.

Most countries are members of a regional trade bloc, and more than a third of the world's trade takes place within such arrangements. While trade blocs vary in structure, they all have the same objective: to reduce trade barriers between member countries. But effective integration requires more than reducing tariffs and quotas. Economic gains from competition and scale may not be achieved unless other barriers that divide markets and impede the free flow of goods, services, and investments are lifted. For example, many regional trade blocs retain contingent protections on intrabloc trade, including antidumping, countervailing duties, and "emergency protection" to address balance of payments problems or protect an industry from import surges. Other barriers include differing product standards, discrimination in public procurement, and cumbersome border formalities.

Membership in a regional trade bloc may reduce the frictional costs of trade, increase the credibility of reform initiatives, and strengthen security among partners. But making it work effectively is challenging. All economic sectors may be affected, and some may expand while others contract, so it is important to weigh the potential costs and benefits of membership.

The table shows the value of merchandise intratrade (service exports are excluded) for important regional trade blocs and the size of intratrade relative to each bloc's exports of goods and the share of the bloc's exports in world exports. Although the Asia Pacific Economic Cooperation (APEC) has no preferential arrangements, it is included because of the volume of trade between its members.

The data on country exports are from the International Monetary Fund's (IMF) Direction of Trade database and should be broadly consistent with those from sources such as the United Nations Statistics Division's Commodity Trade (Comtrade) database. However, trade flows between many developing countries, particularly in Sub-Saharan Africa, are not well recorded, so the value of intratrade for certain groups may be understated. Data on trade between developing and high-income countries are generally complete.

Membership in the trade blocs shown is based on the most recent information available (see *Data sources*). The table includes the date of each bloc's creation, the date of entry into force of the most recent preferential trade agreement, and the type of the agreement. Other types of preferential trade agreements may have entered into force earlier than those shown in the table and are still effective.

Under a free trade agreement members substantially eliminate all tariff and nontariff barriers but set tariffs on imports from nonmembers. Under a customs union members substantially eliminate all tariff and nontariff barriers among themselves and establish a common external tariff for nonmembers.

An economic integration agreement liberalizes trade in services among members and covers a substantial number of sectors, affects a sufficient volume of trade, includes substantial modes of supply, and is nondiscriminatory (in the sense that similarly situated service suppliers are treated the same). Partial scope agreements are preferential trade agreements notified to the World Trade Organization (WTO) that are not a free trade agreement, a customs union, or an economic integration agreement. Unless otherwise indicated in the footnotes, information on the type of agreement and date of enforcement are based on the WTO's list of regional trade agreements.

Although bloc exports have been calculated back to 1990 on the basis of current membership, several blocs came into existence after that and membership may have changed over time. For this reason, and because systems of preferences also change over time, intratrade in earlier years may not have been affected by the same preferences as in recent years. In addition, some countries belong to more than one trade bloc, so shares of world exports exceed 100 percent. Exports of blocs include all commodity trade, which may include items not specified in trade bloc agreements. Differences from previously published estimates may be due to changes in membership or revisions in underlying data.

• **Merchandise exports within bloc** are the sum of merchandise exports by members of a trade bloc to other members of the bloc. They are shown both in U.S. dollars and as a percentage of total merchandise exports by the bloc. • **Merchandise exports by bloc** as a share of world exports are the bloc's total merchandise exports (within the bloc and to the rest of the world) as a share of total merchandise exports by all economies in the world.

**The number of trade agreements has increased rapidly since 1990, especially free trade agreements** 6.6a

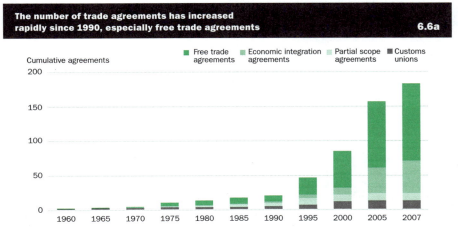

Cumulative agreements

■ Free trade agreements  ■ Economic integration agreements  ■ Partial scope agreements  ■ Customs unions

**Note:** Data are the cumulative number of bilateral and multilateral trade agreements notified to the General Agreement on Tariffs and Trade/World Trade Organization at the time they entered into force. Agreements on accessions of new members to existing agreement are not included. Movements from one kind of agreement to another are taken into account.
*Source:* World Bank staff calculations based on World Trade Organization's Web portal on regional trade agreements.

### Data sources

Data on merchandise trade flows are published in the IMF's *Direction of Trade Statistics Yearbook* and *Direction of Trade Statistics Quarterly;* the data in the table were calculated using the IMF's Direction of Trade database. Data on trade bloc membership are from the World Bank Policy Research Report *Trade Blocs* (2000a), UNCTAD's *Trade and Development Report 2007,* WTO's Web portal on regional trade agreements, and the World Bank's International Trade Unit.

# 6.7 Tariff barriers

| | Most recent year | Binding coverage | Simple mean bound rate | All products %<br>Simple mean tariff | All products %<br>Weighted mean tariff | All products %<br>Share of tariff lines with international peaks | All products %<br>Share of tariff lines with specific rates | Primary products %<br>Simple mean tariff | Primary products %<br>Weighted mean tariff | Manufactured products %<br>Simple mean tariff | Manufactured products %<br>Weighted mean tariff |
|---|---|---|---|---|---|---|---|---|---|---|---|
| Afghanistan | | .. | .. | .. | .. | .. | .. | .. | .. | .. | .. |
| Albania | 2005 | 100.0 | 7.0 | 6.3 | 7.1 | 0.0 | 6.0 | 7.3 | 6.5 | 6.1 | 7.3 |
| Algeria | 2006 | .. | .. | 15.8 | 10.7 | 38.7 | 0.0 | 15.5 | 9.3 | 15.8 | 11.1 |
| Angola | 2006[a] | 100.0 | 59.2 | 7.6 | 6.5 | 10.4 | 0.8 | 11.5 | 13.1 | 6.9 | 5.0 |
| Antigua and Barbuda | 2006 | 97.9 | 58.7 | 11.6 | 12.5 | 39.7 | 0.0 | 13.6 | 12.0 | 11.1 | 12.7 |
| Argentina | 2006 | 100.0 | 31.9 | 10.1 | 5.0 | 22.1 | 0.0 | 7.4 | 1.4 | 10.4 | 5.6 |
| Armenia | 2006 | 100.0 | 8.5 | 3.6 | 1.8 | 0.0 | 0.5 | 5.1 | 1.5 | 3.4 | 2.0 |
| Australia | 2006 | 97.1 | 10.0 | 3.9 | 2.6 | 5.6 | 0.3 | 1.3 | 0.4 | 4.3 | 3.0 |
| Azerbaijan | 2005[a] | .. | .. | 10.4 | 5.8 | 0.0 | 2.8 | 12.0 | 5.4 | 10.2 | 6.0 |
| Bahamas, The | 2006[a] | .. | .. | 28.5 | 17.0 | 77.1 | 1.4 | 22.2 | 20.1 | 29.8 | 15.0 |
| Bahrain | 2006 | 72.5 | 35.8 | 4.4 | 5.0 | 0.2 | 0.6 | 5.2 | 5.5 | 4.2 | 4.0 |
| Bangladesh | 2006 | 15.1 | 161.7 | 15.5 | 19.9 | 41.5 | 0.1 | 15.6 | 8.8 | 15.5 | 26.1 |
| Barbados | 2006 | 97.8 | 78.2 | 15.0 | 12.7 | 45.3 | 1.0 | 23.6 | 10.0 | 13.8 | 14.2 |
| Belarus | 2002[a] | .. | .. | 11.3 | 8.9 | 16.4 | 2.2 | 11.1 | 7.1 | 11.3 | 10.3 |
| Belize | 2006 | 97.9 | 58.2 | 11.9 | 10.2 | 36.0 | 1.4 | 15.7 | 6.7 | 11.4 | 12.4 |
| Benin | 2006 | 39.1 | 28.6 | 13.4 | 11.3 | 53.4 | 0.0 | 13.2 | 10.9 | 13.4 | 11.7 |
| Bermuda | 2005[a] | .. | .. | 17.3 | 27.0 | 61.5 | 2.2 | 9.0 | 14.0 | 18.8 | 28.2 |
| Bhutan | 2005 | .. | .. | 22.2 | 21.5 | 61.6 | 0.0 | 42.6 | 37.7 | 17.5 | 14.5 |
| Bolivia | 2006 | 100.0 | 40.0 | 6.5 | 4.1 | 0.0 | 0.0 | 6.4 | 3.4 | 6.5 | 4.3 |
| Bosnia and Herzegovina | 2006[a] | .. | .. | 7.7 | 6.4 | 0.0 | 5.4 | 4.0 | 4.0 | 8.1 | 7.5 |
| Botswana | 2006 | 96.3 | 19.0 | 8.7 | 10.5 | 20.9 | 1.3 | 3.6 | 0.8 | 9.2 | 12.4 |
| Brazil | 2006 | 100.0 | 31.4 | 12.1 | 6.7 | 25.6 | 0.0 | 7.7 | 1.2 | 12.6 | 9.0 |
| Brunei | 2006 | 95.3 | 24.3 | 2.9 | 4.0 | 23.2 | 1.5 | 0.1 | 0.0 | 3.5 | 5.0 |
| Bulgaria | 2006 | 100.0 | 24.7 | 4.0 | 1.9 | 11.6 | 2.4 | 8.6 | 4.2 | 3.5 | 1.3 |
| Burkina Faso | 2006 | 38.9 | 42.2 | 12.2 | 9.8 | 43.5 | 0.0 | 11.3 | 7.8 | 12.4 | 11.0 |
| Burundi | 2006[a] | 21.2 | 66.7 | 14.7 | 13.5 | 27.9 | 0.0 | 15.1 | 11.7 | 14.6 | 13.8 |
| Cambodia | 2005 | 100.0 | 19.1 | 14.1 | 10.8 | 20.8 | 0.0 | 16.2 | 11.2 | 13.8 | 10.6 |
| Cameroon | 2005[a] | 12.6 | 79.9 | 19.2 | 14.5 | 55.9 | 0.0 | 23.0 | 14.0 | 18.7 | 14.8 |
| Canada | 2006 | 99.7 | 5.1 | 3.7 | 0.9 | 6.5 | 3.5 | 1.8 | 0.3 | 4.0 | 1.0 |
| Central African Republic | 2005[a] | 62.2 | 36.2 | 18.8 | 17.3 | 58.3 | 0.0 | 23.1 | 20.2 | 18.2 | 15.2 |
| Chad | 2005[a] | 12.7 | 79.9 | 17.9 | 13.3 | 52.5 | 0.0 | 23.0 | 21.7 | 17.3 | 11.4 |
| Chile | 2006 | 100.0 | 25.1 | 2.3 | 2.1 | 0.0 | 0.0 | 2.1 | 1.8 | 2.3 | 2.3 |
| China[†] | 2006 | 100.0 | 10.0 | 8.9 | 4.3 | 12.2 | 0.2 | 8.9 | 3.5 | 8.9 | 4.5 |
|   Hong Kong, China | 2006[a] | 45.7 | 0.0 | 0.0 | 0.0 | 0.0 | 0.0 | 0.0 | 0.0 | 0.0 | 0.0 |
| Colombia | 2006 | 100.0 | 42.8 | 11.2 | 8.8 | 19.2 | 0.0 | 10.0 | 7.9 | 11.3 | 8.9 |
| Congo, Dem. Rep. | 2006[a] | 100.0 | 96.2 | 13.1 | 11.4 | 43.3 | 0.2 | 14.2 | 11.3 | 12.8 | 11.5 |
| Congo, Rep. | 2005[a] | 15.2 | 27.5 | 19.3 | 17.3 | 57.1 | 0.0 | 23.3 | 21.4 | 18.7 | 15.9 |
| Costa Rica | 2005[a] | 100.0 | 42.9 | 7.0 | 4.1 | 0.5 | 0.0 | 10.4 | 6.1 | 6.6 | 3.7 |
| Côte d'Ivoire | 2006 | 33.0 | 11.1 | 13.5 | 7.3 | 49.9 | 0.0 | 15.4 | 4.2 | 13.1 | 9.5 |
| Croatia | 2006 | 100.0 | 5.9 | 2.4 | 1.2 | 3.1 | 4.0 | 4.8 | 2.2 | 2.1 | 0.8 |
| Cuba | 2006 | 31.0 | 21.3 | 11.3 | 7.8 | 11.9 | 0.0 | 11.2 | 5.2 | 11.3 | 10.1 |
| Cyprus | 2002[a] | 86.2 | 40.4 | 9.0 | 10.4 | 12.2 | 4.5 | 40.4 | 27.2 | 5.1 | 5.1 |
| Czech Republic | 2003[a] | 100.0 | 5.0 | 5.0 | 4.4 | 4.8 | 0.0 | 5.6 | 4.1 | 5.0 | 4.4 |
| Djibouti | 2006 | 100.0 | 41.0 | 30.2 | 29.1 | 87.9 | 6.3 | 23.1 | 23.2 | 31.3 | 31.0 |
| Dominica | 2006 | 94.7 | 58.7 | 12.3 | 7.8 | 38.9 | 0.0 | 19.3 | 5.6 | 10.9 | 9.1 |
| Dominican Republic | 2006 | 100.0 | 34.9 | 9.3 | 8.5 | 28.6 | 0.2 | 12.7 | 7.3 | 8.8 | 9.0 |
| Ecuador | 2006 | 99.9 | 21.8 | 9.8 | 6.2 | 17.7 | 0.0 | 9.1 | 4.4 | 9.9 | 6.8 |
| Egypt, Arab Rep. | 2005 | 99.1 | 36.5 | 19.1 | 13.3 | 23.0 | 0.1 | 84.8 | 17.8 | 12.0 | 11.9 |
| El Salvador | 2006 | 99.9 | 36.6 | 5.0 | 4.1 | 6.6 | 0.8 | 5.7 | 2.5 | 4.9 | 5.2 |
| Equatorial Guinea | 2005[a] | .. | .. | 19.0 | 15.3 | 56.1 | 0.0 | 23.4 | 18.5 | 18.3 | 14.3 |
| Estonia | 2003[a] | 100.0 | 8.6 | 1.0 | 0.9 | 5.4 | 0.0 | 8.1 | 4.0 | 0.0 | 0.0 |
| Ethiopia[b] | 2006[a] | .. | .. | 16.4 | 10.7 | 49.2 | 0.1 | 18.1 | 12.6 | 16.3 | 10.4 |
| European Union[c] | 2005 | 100.0 | 4.2 | 2.8 | 2.1 | 6.8 | 9.0 | 8.2 | 2.5 | 1.7 | 1.8 |
| Gabon | 2005[a] | 100.0 | 21.4 | 20.1 | 16.5 | 61.3 | 0.0 | 23.2 | 19.4 | 19.6 | 15.6 |
| Gambia | 2003 | 13.0 | 101.8 | .. | .. | .. | .. | .. | .. | .. | .. |
| Georgia | 2006 | 100.0 | 7.2 | 5.6 | 4.7 | 3.3 | 0.0 | 8.6 | 4.4 | 5.3 | 4.8 |
| Ghana | 2004[a] | 13.5 | 92.1 | 13.2 | 11.0 | 45.3 | 0.3 | 17.4 | 17.1 | 12.4 | 8.8 |
| Grenada | 2006 | 100.0 | 56.8 | 10.7 | 9.5 | 35.3 | 0.0 | 13.9 | 9.7 | 10.2 | 9.4 |
| Guatemala | 2005[a] | 100.0 | 42.2 | 6.7 | 5.8 | 1.0 | 0.0 | 8.8 | 5.5 | 6.5 | 6.0 |
| [†]Data for Taiwan, China | 2006 | 100.0 | 5.9 | 5.4 | 2.4 | 7.7 | 1.5 | 8.3 | 2.2 | 5.0 | 2.4 |

| | Most recent year | Binding coverage | Simple mean bound rate | All products % | | | | Primary products % | | Manufactured products % | |
|---|---|---|---|---|---|---|---|---|---|---|---|
| | | | | Simple mean tariff | Weighted mean tariff | Share of tariff lines with international peaks | Share of tariff lines with specific rates | Simple mean tariff | Weighted mean tariff | Simple mean tariff | Weighted mean tariff |
| Guinea | 2005[a] | 38.6 | 20.3 | 14.2 | 12.7 | 58.6 | 0.7 | 16.3 | 14.3 | 13.9 | 11.2 |
| Guinea-Bissau | 2006 | 97.7 | 48.7 | 12.7 | 9.1 | 50.1 | 0.0 | 14.3 | 9.0 | 12.4 | 9.2 |
| Guyana | 2006 | 100.0 | 56.6 | 11.4 | 6.2 | 34.5 | 0.0 | 17.8 | 4.1 | 10.6 | 7.9 |
| Honduras | 2005[a] | 100.0 | 32.5 | 6.7 | 6.0 | 0.2 | 0.0 | 9.7 | 7.2 | 6.4 | 5.3 |
| Hungary | 2002[a] | 96.2 | 9.8 | 8.9 | 7.9 | 10.9 | 0.0 | 17.9 | 6.7 | 7.8 | 8.1 |
| Iceland | 2006 | 95.0 | 13.5 | 2.6 | 1.0 | 2.0 | 2.9 | 2.9 | 1.4 | 2.5 | 0.9 |
| India | 2005 | 73.8 | 49.6 | 16.8 | 14.5 | 15.7 | 0.0 | 24.4 | 16.5 | 15.7 | 12.7 |
| Indonesia | 2006 | 96.6 | 37.1 | 6.0 | 4.3 | 7.9 | 0.3 | 6.6 | 3.3 | 5.9 | 4.6 |
| Iran, Islamic Rep. | 2004[a] | .. | .. | 18.7 | 13.8 | 43.4 | 0.5 | 14.9 | 11.2 | 19.1 | 14.6 |
| Israel | 2006 | 76.3 | 20.9 | 4.5 | 2.0 | 1.0 | 3.5 | 5.1 | 1.8 | 4.4 | 2.1 |
| Jamaica | 2006 | 100.0 | 49.6 | 9.2 | 9.7 | 36.1 | 0.2 | 16.0 | 10.1 | 8.5 | 9.2 |
| Japan | 2006 | 99.7 | 3.0 | 2.7 | 1.5 | 7.0 | 5.8 | 5.0 | 1.6 | 2.3 | 1.5 |
| Jordan | 2006 | 100.0 | 16.3 | 10.9 | 5.6 | 31.8 | 0.1 | 14.3 | 3.4 | 10.4 | 7.1 |
| Kazakhstan | 2004[a] | .. | .. | 2.4 | 1.9 | 0.0 | 1.5 | 3.4 | 3.4 | 2.3 | 1.5 |
| Kenya | 2006 | 14.0 | 95.1 | 11.9 | 6.6 | 36.2 | 0.4 | 14.8 | 6.4 | 11.6 | 6.6 |
| Korea, Rep. | 2006 | 94.5 | 15.7 | 9.1 | 7.4 | 5.5 | 0.0 | 21.2 | 11.4 | 7.3 | 4.5 |
| Kuwait | 2006 | 99.9 | 100.0 | 4.6 | 4.5 | 0.0 | 0.7 | 3.7 | 3.2 | 4.7 | 4.7 |
| Kyrgyz Republic | 2006 | 99.9 | 7.4 | 3.0 | 1.2 | 0.1 | 1.2 | 4.5 | 0.9 | 2.8 | 1.4 |
| Lao PDR | 2006 | .. | .. | 6.5 | 9.3 | 16.4 | 0.0 | 10.7 | 11.7 | 5.9 | 8.0 |
| Latvia | 2001[a] | 100.0 | 12.7 | 3.3 | 2.6 | 3.0 | 0.0 | 8.1 | 5.4 | 2.5 | 1.6 |
| Lebanon | 2006 | .. | .. | 6.1 | 4.6 | 10.0 | 0.3 | 10.5 | 3.6 | 5.5 | 5.4 |
| Lesotho | 2006 | 100.0 | 78.4 | 9.9 | 16.5 | 24.2 | 1.9 | 7.5 | 3.2 | 10.0 | 17.3 |
| Libya | 2006[a] | .. | .. | 0.0 | 0.0 | 0.0 | 0.0 | 0.0 | 15.1 | 0.0 | 0.0 |
| Lithuania | 2003 | 100.0 | 9.2 | 1.3 | 0.7 | 3.3 | 0.0 | 3.6 | 1.3 | 1.0 | 0.4 |
| Macedonia, FYR | 2006 | 100.0 | 6.9 | 5.5 | 4.2 | 11.7 | 2.5 | 8.8 | 5.6 | 5.1 | 3.4 |
| Madagascar | 2006 | 29.7 | 27.4 | 13.3 | 8.7 | 43.5 | 0.0 | 14.2 | 3.0 | 13.2 | 12.2 |
| Malawi | 2006 | 30.2 | 74.9 | 12.9 | 8.1 | 40.3 | 0.0 | 12.8 | 6.1 | 12.9 | 8.9 |
| Malaysia | 2006 | 84.2 | 14.6 | 6.2 | 3.4 | 22.9 | 0.8 | 3.0 | 2.4 | 6.8 | 3.7 |
| Maldives | 2006 | 97.1 | 37.0 | 21.3 | 20.5 | 72.3 | 0.0 | 17.8 | 18.0 | 22.2 | 22.0 |
| Mali | 2006 | 40.7 | 29.3 | 12.6 | 8.5 | 46.3 | 0.0 | 11.5 | 8.6 | 12.7 | 8.5 |
| Malta | 2003[a] | 97.1 | 48.3 | 6.7 | 5.7 | 7.5 | 0.0 | 5.8 | 4.6 | 6.9 | 6.0 |
| Mauritania | 2006[a] | 39.4 | 19.6 | 11.6 | 7.2 | 44.3 | 3.9 | 11.5 | 9.3 | 11.6 | 6.6 |
| Mauritius | 2006 | 18.0 | 94.0 | 4.2 | 1.6 | 8.5 | 8.1 | 6.1 | 1.5 | 3.9 | 1.7 |
| Mexico | 2006 | 100.0 | 35.0 | 8.0 | 2.4 | 10.7 | 0.3 | 6.8 | 1.7 | 8.1 | 2.5 |
| Moldova | 2006 | 99.9 | 6.7 | 4.4 | 1.7 | 16.0 | 2.1 | 7.3 | 1.4 | 4.0 | 1.9 |
| Mongolia | 2006[a] | 100.0 | 17.5 | 4.2 | 4.4 | 0.0 | 0.0 | 5.0 | 5.1 | 4.1 | 3.9 |
| Montserrat | 1999[a] | .. | .. | 18.2 | 13.3 | 41.2 | 31.0 | 22.3 | 15.5 | 16.4 | 12.2 |
| Morocco | 2006 | 100.0 | 41.3 | 15.5 | 11.0 | 45.3 | 2.0 | 21.9 | 11.7 | 14.9 | 10.6 |
| Mozambique | 2006 | 12.9 | 97.4 | 12.7 | 8.3 | 38.2 | 0.0 | 15.4 | 8.9 | 12.3 | 8.0 |
| Myanmar | 2006 | 16.8 | 83.4 | 4.4 | 3.9 | 4.0 | 0.0 | 6.5 | 4.2 | 4.1 | 3.7 |
| Namibia | 2006 | 96.3 | 19.4 | 5.8 | 0.8 | 15.7 | 2.6 | 3.5 | 0.6 | 6.2 | 0.9 |
| Nepal | 2006 | 99.4 | 26.0 | 12.5 | 13.4 | 16.8 | 0.6 | 12.5 | 9.9 | 12.5 | 15.2 |
| New Zealand | 2006 | 99.9 | 10.3 | 3.7 | 2.7 | 8.0 | 2.4 | 1.8 | 0.5 | 4.0 | 3.3 |
| Nicaragua | 2005[a] | 100.0 | 41.7 | 6.8 | 5.4 | 0.5 | 0.0 | 10.6 | 5.4 | 6.4 | 5.4 |
| Niger | 2006 | 96.8 | 44.6 | 13.1 | 9.8 | 50.3 | 0.0 | 13.1 | 10.0 | 13.1 | 9.7 |
| Nigeria | 2006[a] | 18.1 | 118.5 | 11.7 | 11.6 | 41.5 | 0.0 | 14.8 | 15.1 | 11.4 | 10.2 |
| Norway | 2006 | 100.0 | 3.0 | 0.5 | 0.4 | 0.6 | 5.8 | 1.9 | 1.3 | 0.3 | 0.2 |
| Oman | 2006 | 100.0 | 13.7 | 3.8 | 3.2 | 0.1 | 0.6 | 4.1 | 2.9 | 3.8 | 3.3 |
| Pakistan | 2006 | 44.8 | 52.2 | 14.8 | 12.2 | 43.2 | 0.5 | 14.1 | 8.8 | 14.9 | 14.6 |
| Panama | 2006 | 99.9 | 23.4 | 7.4 | 6.9 | 1.8 | 0.0 | 11.2 | 7.9 | 7.0 | 6.5 |
| Papua New Guinea | 2006 | 100.0 | 31.7 | 4.8 | 1.7 | 14.1 | 0.7 | 12.1 | 2.6 | 3.9 | 1.3 |
| Paraguay | 2006 | 100.0 | 33.6 | 7.2 | 3.2 | 15.7 | 0.0 | 5.4 | 1.1 | 7.3 | 3.8 |
| Peru | 2006 | 100.0 | 30.1 | 8.6 | 5.3 | 10.0 | 0.0 | 9.2 | 2.5 | 8.5 | 6.6 |
| Philippines | 2006 | 67.0 | 25.6 | 5.4 | 3.2 | 4.8 | 0.0 | 6.9 | 5.3 | 5.2 | 2.8 |
| Poland | 2003 | 96.2 | 11.9 | 7.6 | 4.4 | 10.2 | 3.5 | 45.7 | 18.2 | 2.5 | 1.2 |
| Qatar | 2006 | 100.0 | 15.9 | 4.0 | 4.2 | 0.1 | 0.8 | 3.7 | 3.7 | 4.1 | 4.3 |
| Romania | 2005 | 100.0 | 39.8 | 6.6 | 3.1 | 21.0 | 0.0 | 13.3 | 7.2 | 5.7 | 1.8 |
| Russian Federation | 2005[a] | .. | .. | 11.4 | 9.6 | 17.9 | 2.6 | 10.7 | 12.2 | 11.5 | 8.9 |
| Rwanda | 2006 | 100.0 | 89.4 | 19.7 | 14.4 | 52.2 | 0.1 | 17.4 | 14.0 | 20.0 | 14.5 |

| | Most recent year | Binding coverage | Simple mean bound rate | All products % | | | | Primary products | | Manufactured products | |
|---|---|---|---|---|---|---|---|---|---|---|---|
| | | | | Simple mean tariff | Weighted mean tariff | Share of tariff lines with international peaks | Share of tariff lines with specific rates | Simple mean tariff % | Weighted mean tariff | Simple mean tariff % | Weighted mean tariff |
| Saudi Arabia | 2006 | .. | .. | 4.1 | 4.1 | 0.0 | 0.5 | 3.2 | 2.7 | 4.3 | 4.4 |
| Senegal | 2006 | 100.0 | 30.0 | 13.5 | 9.4 | 51.3 | 0.0 | 14.4 | 8.5 | 13.4 | 10.3 |
| Serbia[d] | 2005[a] | .. | .. | 8.1 | 6.0 | 17.8 | 0.0 | 10.9 | 4.5 | 7.8 | 6.8 |
| Seychelles | 2006[a] | .. | .. | 6.3 | 30.7 | 12.2 | 1.6 | 12.8 | 49.6 | 4.9 | 6.7 |
| Sierra Leone | 2004 | 100.0 | 47.4 | .. | .. | .. | .. | .. | .. | .. | .. |
| Singapore | 2006 | 69.8 | 7.0 | 0.0 | 0.0 | 0.0 | 0.1 | 0.0 | 0.0 | 0.0 | 0.0 |
| Slovak Republic | 2002[a] | 100.0 | 5.0 | 5.0 | 4.6 | 4.3 | 0.0 | 5.5 | 3.7 | 4.9 | 4.9 |
| Slovenia | 2003 | 100.0 | 23.7 | 4.4 | 1.8 | 11.4 | 1.5 | 7.0 | 4.0 | 4.0 | 1.2 |
| Solomon Islands | 2006 | 100.0 | 78.7 | 14.6 | 11.7 | 53.1 | 1.6 | 16.8 | 10.4 | 14.2 | 12.8 |
| South Africa | 2006 | 96.3 | 19.4 | 8.3 | 5.1 | 19.3 | 2.1 | 5.5 | 1.7 | 8.6 | 6.4 |
| Sri Lanka | 2006 | 36.8 | 29.6 | 11.0 | 7.0 | 23.1 | 1.5 | 15.2 | 9.5 | 10.5 | 5.9 |
| St. Kitts and Nevis | 2006 | 97.9 | 75.9 | 12.8 | 12.4 | 39.0 | 0.8 | 14.1 | 11.6 | 12.5 | 12.7 |
| St. Lucia | 2006 | 99.6 | 62.0 | 10.5 | 9.9 | 37.2 | 0.0 | 12.9 | 6.0 | 10.1 | 12.3 |
| St. Vincent & Grenadines | 2006 | 99.7 | 62.5 | 3.8 | 3.8 | 14.3 | 0.0 | 13.6 | 6.4 | 1.9 | 2.7 |
| Sudan | 2006 | .. | .. | 17.1 | 15.3 | 38.1 | 0.0 | 22.9 | 19.7 | 16.6 | 14.6 |
| Suriname | 2000[a] | 25.0 | 18.5 | 14.8 | 12.9 | 6.6 | 70.5 | 23.8 | 13.7 | 11.7 | 11.6 |
| Swaziland | 2006 | 96.3 | 19.4 | 10.3 | 9.2 | 25.0 | 2.4 | 8.0 | 3.8 | 10.5 | 9.6 |
| Switzerland | 2005 | 99.8 | 0.0 | 4.7 | 2.3 | 13.3 | 35.1 | 23.1 | 12.7 | 1.4 | 0.2 |
| Syrian Arab Republic | 2002[a] | .. | .. | 14.7 | 15.5 | 23.3 | 0.1 | 14.4 | 11.7 | 14.7 | 17.1 |
| Tajikistan | 2006 | .. | .. | 4.7 | 3.7 | 0.0 | 1.4 | 5.1 | 2.5 | 4.7 | 4.3 |
| Tanzania | 2006 | 13.4 | 120.0 | 12.5 | 7.2 | 37.6 | 0.4 | 16.9 | 7.7 | 12.0 | 7.0 |
| Thailand | 2006 | 75.1 | 25.7 | 10.8 | 4.7 | 22.8 | 1.1 | 13.5 | 2.3 | 10.4 | 5.8 |
| Timor-Leste | | .. | .. | .. | .. | .. | .. | .. | .. | .. | .. |
| Togo | 2006 | 13.2 | 80.0 | 14.0 | 9.7 | 52.3 | 0.0 | 13.9 | 8.7 | 14.0 | 10.7 |
| Trinidad and Tobago | 2006 | 100.0 | 55.8 | 9.4 | 5.1 | 35.2 | 0.6 | 13.1 | 3.5 | 8.9 | 6.7 |
| Tunisia | 2006 | 57.9 | 57.7 | 22.9 | 18.5 | 55.5 | 0.0 | 33.1 | 14.7 | 22.0 | 20.0 |
| Turkey | 2006 | 47.7 | 29.6 | 1.8 | 1.7 | 2.6 | 0.6 | 11.3 | 3.4 | 1.1 | 1.1 |
| Turkmenistan | 2002[a] | .. | .. | 5.4 | 2.9 | 14.8 | 0.3 | 14.8 | 12.6 | 3.8 | 1.1 |
| Uganda | 2006 | 14.9 | 73.5 | 12.0 | 7.4 | 37.1 | 0.5 | 14.6 | 7.0 | 11.7 | 7.6 |
| Ukraine | 2006 | .. | .. | 4.8 | 3.0 | 4.5 | 3.9 | 4.7 | 0.7 | 4.8 | 4.5 |
| United Arab Emirates | 2006 | 100.0 | 14.7 | 4.7 | 4.6 | 0.2 | 0.8 | 4.8 | 4.7 | 4.7 | 4.6 |
| United States | 2006 | 100.0 | 3.6 | 3.0 | 1.6 | 3.7 | 6.4 | 2.4 | 1.0 | 3.1 | 1.8 |
| Uruguay | 2006 | 100.0 | 31.6 | 9.6 | 3.3 | 26.0 | 0.0 | 5.6 | 1.2 | 10.0 | 4.7 |
| Uzbekistan | 2006 | .. | .. | 11.3 | 7.3 | 20.9 | 5.7 | 10.8 | 4.8 | 11.3 | 7.8 |
| Vanuatu | 2006 | .. | .. | 16.7 | 8.2 | 45.0 | 5.0 | 19.9 | 18.0 | 16.1 | 7.0 |
| Venezuela, RB | 2006 | 99.9 | 36.8 | 11.1 | 10.2 | 16.8 | 0.0 | 10.5 | 8.9 | 11.2 | 10.5 |
| Vietnam | 2006 | .. | .. | 13.1 | 13.3 | 33.5 | 0.0 | 17.8 | 14.6 | 12.4 | 12.8 |
| Yemen | 2006[a] | .. | .. | 6.7 | 6.9 | 1.8 | 0.5 | 9.6 | 8.6 | 6.3 | 5.6 |
| Zambia | 2005 | 16.0 | 105.8 | 14.6 | 9.4 | 34.5 | 0.0 | 14.9 | 9.3 | 14.6 | 9.4 |
| Zimbabwe | 2003[a] | 20.8 | 90.7 | 16.7 | 17.3 | 38.8 | 6.5 | 19.5 | 19.8 | 16.3 | 15.3 |
| **World** | | **77.3** | **31.5** | **7.5** | **3.1** | **13.7** | **0.5** | **9.3** | **3.1** | **7.3** | **3.2** |
| **Low income** | | 48.2 | 47.1 | 12.7 | 12.4 | 29.5 | 0.6 | 15.0 | 13.0 | 12.3 | 12.1 |
| **Middle income** | | 86.6 | 30.9 | 8.5 | 4.9 | 16.2 | 0.7 | 11.3 | 4.4 | 8.1 | 5.0 |
| Lower middle-income | | 83.8 | 31.6 | 10.1 | 5.3 | 19.6 | 0.0 | 13.2 | 4.4 | 9.7 | 5.6 |
| Upper middle income | | 90.2 | 30.0 | 6.9 | 4.3 | 13.2 | 1.3 | 9.5 | 4.4 | 6.6 | 4.2 |
| **Low & middle income** | | 74.4 | 34.9 | 9.2 | 5.6 | 17.9 | 0.6 | 11.8 | 5.6 | 8.9 | 5.5 |
| East Asia & Pacific | | 79.0 | 32.4 | 8.4 | 4.4 | 16.7 | 0.0 | 9.4 | 3.7 | 8.2 | 4.7 |
| Europe & Central Asia | | 74.8 | 10.9 | 6.0 | 4.6 | 8.9 | 2.0 | 8.3 | 5.3 | 5.7 | 4.4 |
| Latin America & Carib. | | 97.0 | 41.5 | 8.6 | 4.5 | 15.1 | 0.0 | 9.7 | 2.9 | 8.5 | 4.9 |
| Middle East & N. Africa | | 93.4 | 34.8 | 11.3 | 8.9 | 28.4 | 0.0 | 16.3 | 8.4 | 10.7 | 9.2 |
| South Asia | | 61.1 | 42.7 | 14.9 | 13.9 | 32.0 | 1.5 | 17.8 | 14.2 | 14.5 | 13.7 |
| Sub-Saharan Africa | | 47.6 | 42.8 | 12.1 | 7.9 | 34.8 | 0.0 | 13.5 | 7.5 | 11.9 | 8.0 |
| **High-income** | | 87.7 | 22.6 | 3.8 | 1.9 | 5.3 | 0.2 | 5.3 | 2.0 | 3.6 | 1.8 |
| OECD | | 98.6 | 7.4 | 3.8 | 2.1 | 4.8 | 0.0 | 3.8 | 2.0 | 3.8 | 2.1 |
| Non-OECD | | 78.1 | 34.1 | 4.6 | 1.2 | 7.3 | 0.6 | 7.2 | 1.8 | 4.1 | 1.1 |

**Note:** Tariff rates include ad valorem equivalents of specific rates whenever available.
a. Rates are most favored nation rates. b. Excludes Eritrea. c. Refers to all member states of the European Union except Bulgaria and Romania. d. Includes Montenegro.

Poor people in developing countries work primarily in agriculture and labor-intensive manufactures, sectors that confront the greatest trade barriers. Removing barriers to merchandise trade could increase growth in these countries—even more if trade in services (retailing, business, financial, and telecommunications services) were also liberalized.

In general, tariffs in high-income countries on imports from developing countries, though low, are twice those collected from other high-income countries. But protection is also an issue for developing countries, which maintain high tariffs on agricultural commodities, labor-intensive manufactures, and other products and services. In some developing regions new trade policies could make the difference between achieving important Millennium Development Goals—reducing poverty, lowering maternal and child mortality rates, improving educational attainment—and falling far short.

Countries use a combination of tariff and nontariff measures to regulate imports. The most common form of tariff is an ad valorem duty, based on the value of the import, but tariffs may also be levied on a specific, or per unit, basis or may combine ad valorem and specific rates. Tariffs may be used to raise fiscal revenues or to protect domestic industries from foreign competition—or both. Nontariff barriers, which limit the quantity of imports of a particular good, include quotas, prohibitions, licensing schemes, export restraint arrangements, and health and quarantine measures. Because of the difficulty of combining nontariff barriers into an aggregate indicator, they are not included in the table.

Unless specified as most favored nation rates, the tariff rates used in calculating the indicators in the table are effectively applied rates. Effectively applied rates are those in effect for partners in preferential trade arrangements such as the North American Free Trade Agreement. The difference between most favored nation and applied rates can be substantial. As more countries report their free trade agreements, suspensions of tariffs, or other special preferences, *World Development Indicators* will include their effectively applied rates. All estimates are calculated using the most recent information, which is not necessarily revised every year. As a result, data for the same year may differ from data in last year's edition.

Three measures of average tariffs are shown: simple bound rates and the simple and the weighted tariffs. Bound rates are based on all products in a country's tariff schedule, while the most favored nation or applied rates are calculated using all traded items. Weighted mean tariffs are weighted by the value of the country's trade with each trading partner. Simple averages are often a better indicator of tariff protection than weighted averages, which are biased downward because higher tariffs discourage trade and reduce the weights applied to these tariffs. Bound rates result from trade negotiations incorporated into a country's schedule of concessions and are thus enforceable.

Some countries set fairly uniform tariff rates across all imports. Others are selective, setting high tariffs to protect favored domestic industries. The share of tariff lines with international peaks provides an indication of how selectively tariffs are applied. The effective rate of protection—the degree to which the value added in an industry is protected—may exceed the nominal rate if the tariff system systematically differentiates among imports of raw materials, intermediate products, and finished goods.

The share of tariff lines with specific rates shows the extent to which countries use tariffs based on physical quantities or other, non–ad valorem measures. Some countries such as Switzerland apply mainly specific duties. To the extent possible, these specific rates have been converted to their ad valorem equivalent rates and have been included in the calculation of simple and weighted tariffs.

Data are classified using the Harmonized System of trade at the six- or eight-digit level. Tariff line data were matched to Standard International Trade Classification (SITC) revision 1 codes to define commodity groups and import weights. Import weights were calculated using the United Nations Statistics Division's Commodity Trade (Comtrade) database. Data are shown only for the last year for which complete data are available.

• **Binding coverage** is the percentage of product lines with an agreed bound rate. • **Simple mean bound rate** is the unweighted average of all the lines in the tariff schedule in which bound rates have been set. • **Simple mean tariff** is the unweighted average of effectively applied rates or most favored nation rates for all products subject to tariffs calculated for all traded goods. • **Weighted mean tariff** is the average of effectively applied rates or most favored nation rates weighted by the product import shares corresponding to each partner country. • **Share of tariff lines with international peaks** is the share of lines in the tariff schedule with tariff rates that exceed 15 percent. • **Share of tariff lines with specific rates** is the share of lines in the tariff schedule that are set on a per unit basis or that combine ad valorem and per unit rates. • **Primary products** are commodities classified in SITC revision 2 sections 0–4 plus division 68 (nonferrous metals). • **Manufactured products** are commodities classified in SITC revision 2 sections 5–8 excluding division 68.

All indicators in the table were calculated by World Bank staff using the World Integrated Trade Solution system. Data on tariffs were provided by the United Nations Conference on Trade and Development and the World Trade Organization. Data on global imports are from the United Nations Statistics Division's Comtrade database.

# 6.8 External debt

| | Total external debt | | Long-term debt | | | | | | Short-term debt | | Use of IMF credit | |
|---|---|---|---|---|---|---|---|---|---|---|---|---|
| | | | | | $ millions Public and publicly guaranteed | | | | | | | |
| | | | Total | | IBRD loans and IDA credits | | Private nonguaranteed | | | | | |
| | $ millions | | | | | | | | $ millions | | $ millions | |
| | 1995 | 2006 | 1995 | 2006 | 1995 | 2006 | 1995 | 2006 | 1995 | 2006 | 1995 | 2006 |
| Afghanistan | .. | 1,771 | .. | 1,761 | .. | 358 | .. | 0 | .. | 11 | .. | 0 |
| Albania | 456 | 2,340 | 330 | 1,588 | 109 | 729 | 0 | 84 | 62 | 575 | 65 | 93 |
| Algeria | 33,042 | 5,583 | 31,303 | 3,738 | 2,049 | 119 | 0 | 1,304 | 261 | 541 | 1,478 | 0 |
| Angola | 11,500 | 9,563 | 9,543 | 7,398 | 81 | 347 | 0 | 0 | 1,958 | 2,165 | 0 | 0 |
| Argentina | 98,465 | 122,190 | 54,913 | 64,711 | 4,913 | 6,206 | 16,066 | 22,441 | 21,355 | 35,039 | 6,131 | 0 |
| Armenia | 371 | 2,073 | 298 | 1,037 | 96 | 847 | 0 | 574 | 2 | 298 | 70 | 164 |
| Australia | .. | .. | .. | .. | .. | .. | .. | .. | .. | .. | .. | .. |
| Austria | .. | .. | .. | .. | .. | .. | .. | .. | .. | .. | .. | .. |
| Azerbaijan | 321 | 1,900 | 206 | 1,359 | 30 | 588 | 0 | 104 | 14 | 302 | 101 | 134 |
| Bangladesh | 15,927 | 20,521 | 15,106 | 18,866 | 5,692 | 9,297 | 0 | 0 | 199 | 1,178 | 622 | 476 |
| Belarus | 1,694 | 6,124 | 1,301 | 846 | 116 | 50 | 0 | 855 | 110 | 4,423 | 283 | 0 |
| Belgium | .. | .. | .. | .. | .. | .. | .. | .. | .. | .. | .. | .. |
| Benin | 1,614 | 824 | 1,483 | 782 | 498 | 126 | 0 | 0 | 47 | 39 | 84 | 3 |
| Bolivia | 5,272 | 5,292 | 4,459 | 3,203 | 865 | 233 | 239 | 1,855 | 307 | 220 | 268 | 15 |
| Bosnia and Herzegovina | .. | 5,669 | .. | 2,830 | 472 | 1,449 | .. | 1,675 | .. | 1,144 | 48 | 20 |
| Botswana | 717 | 408 | 707 | 384 | 108 | 7 | 0 | 0 | 10 | 24 | 0 | 0 |
| Brazil | 160,469 | 194,150 | 98,260 | 84,936 | 6,038 | 9,694 | 30,830 | 88,889 | 31,238 | 20,325 | 142 | 0 |
| Bulgaria | 10,379 | 20,925 | 8,808 | 5,001 | 444 | 1,331 | 342 | 7,543 | 512 | 8,040 | 717 | 341 |
| Burkina Faso | 1,271 | 1,142 | 1,140 | 1,022 | 608 | 361 | 0 | 0 | 56 | 85 | 75 | 35 |
| Burundi | 1,162 | 1,411 | 1,099 | 1,291 | 591 | 797 | 0 | 0 | 15 | 38 | 48 | 83 |
| Cambodia | 2,284 | 3,527 | 2,110 | 3,318 | 65 | 500 | 0 | 0 | 102 | 209 | 72 | 0 |
| Cameroon | 10,632 | 3,171 | 9,301 | 2,078 | 1,067 | 216 | 288 | 489 | 991 | 596 | 51 | 8 |
| Canada | .. | .. | .. | .. | .. | .. | .. | .. | .. | .. | .. | .. |
| Central African Republic | 946 | 1,020 | 854 | 863 | 414 | 395 | 0 | 0 | 57 | 115 | 35 | 42 |
| Chad | 912 | 1,772 | 843 | 1,686 | 379 | 956 | 0 | 0 | 20 | 18 | 49 | 68 |
| Chile | 22,038 | 47,977 | 7,178 | 9,454 | 1,383 | 349 | 11,429 | 29,112 | 3,431 | 9,411 | 0 | 0 |
| China | 118,090 | 322,845 | 94,674 | 85,802 | 14,248 | 21,412 | 1,090 | 63,666 | 22,325 | 173,377 | 0 | 0 |
| Hong Kong, China | .. | .. | .. | .. | .. | .. | .. | .. | .. | .. | .. | .. |
| Colombia | 25,044 | 39,698 | 13,946 | 25,764 | 2,559 | 4,566 | 5,553 | 9,112 | 5,545 | 4,822 | 0 | 0 |
| Congo, Dem. Rep. | 13,239 | 11,201 | 9,636 | 9,848 | 1,413 | 2,251 | 0 | 0 | 3,118 | 520 | 485 | 833 |
| Congo, Rep. | 5,982 | 6,130 | 4,942 | 5,328 | 279 | 295 | 0 | 0 | 1,022 | 767 | 19 | 35 |
| Costa Rica | 3,802 | 6,832 | 3,133 | 3,669 | 303 | 54 | 214 | 837 | 430 | 2,326 | 24 | 0 |
| Côte d'Ivoire | 18,899 | 13,840 | 11,902 | 10,830 | 2,386 | 2,303 | 2,660 | 847 | 3,910 | 2,013 | 427 | 150 |
| Croatia | 3,830 | 37,480 | 1,860 | 10,235 | 117 | 1,028 | 1,257 | 21,674 | 492 | 5,571 | 221 | 0 |
| Cuba | .. | .. | .. | .. | .. | .. | .. | .. | .. | .. | .. | .. |
| Czech Republic | .. | .. | .. | .. | .. | .. | .. | .. | .. | .. | .. | .. |
| Denmark | .. | .. | .. | .. | .. | .. | .. | .. | .. | .. | .. | .. |
| Dominican Republic | 4,447 | 8,905 | 3,653 | 6,571 | 300 | 448 | 19 | 414 | 616 | 1,461 | 160 | 459 |
| Ecuador | 13,994 | 16,536 | 12,068 | 10,108 | 1,108 | 760 | 440 | 4,981 | 1,312 | 1,424 | 173 | 23 |
| Egypt, Arab Rep. | 33,499 | 29,339 | 30,710 | 26,072 | 2,356 | 2,024 | 313 | 1,633 | 2,372 | 1,635 | 103 | 0 |
| El Salvador | 2,509 | 9,136 | 1,979 | 5,504 | 327 | 428 | 5 | 2,401 | 525 | 1,230 | 0 | 0 |
| Eritrea | 37 | 800 | 37 | 781 | 24 | 419 | 0 | 0 | 0 | 19 | 0 | 0 |
| Estonia | .. | .. | .. | .. | .. | .. | .. | .. | .. | .. | .. | .. |
| Ethiopia | 10,308 | 2,326 | 9,774 | 2,212 | 1,470 | 553 | 0 | 0 | 460 | 114 | 73 | 0 |
| Finland | .. | .. | .. | .. | .. | .. | .. | .. | .. | .. | .. | .. |
| France | .. | .. | .. | .. | .. | .. | .. | .. | .. | .. | .. | .. |
| Gabon | 4,360 | 4,350 | 3,976 | 3,860 | 110 | 19 | 0 | 0 | 287 | 434 | 97 | 57 |
| Gambia, The | 426 | 725 | 385 | 689 | 162 | 263 | 0 | 0 | 15 | 18 | 26 | 18 |
| Georgia | 1,240 | 1,964 | 1,039 | 1,457 | 84 | 785 | 0 | 159 | 85 | 111 | 116 | 236 |
| Germany | .. | .. | .. | .. | .. | .. | .. | .. | .. | .. | .. | .. |
| Ghana | 5,495 | 3,192 | 4,200 | 1,891 | 2,434 | 810 | 27 | 0 | 620 | 1,143 | 648 | 159 |
| Greece | .. | .. | .. | .. | .. | .. | .. | .. | .. | .. | .. | .. |
| Guatemala | 3,282 | 5,496 | 2,328 | 3,921 | 158 | 642 | 142 | 91 | 812 | 1,484 | 0 | 0 |
| Guinea | 3,242 | 3,281 | 2,987 | 2,980 | 847 | 1,259 | 0 | 0 | 161 | 229 | 94 | 72 |
| Guinea-Bissau | 898 | 711 | 798 | 695 | 210 | 297 | 0 | 0 | 95 | 8 | 6 | 8 |
| Haiti | 738 | 1,189 | 683 | 1,034 | 307 | 238 | 0 | 0 | 27 | 123 | 29 | 32 |

| | Total external debt | | Long-term debt | | | | | | Short-term debt | | Use of IMF credit | |
|---|---|---|---|---|---|---|---|---|---|---|---|---|
| | | | | | $ millions Public and publicly guaranteed | | | | | | | |
| | | | | Total | IBRD loans and IDA credits | | Private nonguaranteed | | | | | |
| | $ millions | | | | | | | | $ millions | | $ millions | |
| | 1995 | 2006 | 1995 | 2006 | 1995 | 2006 | 1995 | 2006 | 1995 | 2006 | 1995 | 2006 |
| Honduras | 4,797 | 4,076 | 4,193 | 2,986 | 828 | 349 | 123 | 527 | 382 | 533 | 99 | 31 |
| Hungary | 31,650 | 107,677 | 23,974 | 28,017 | 2,218 | 137 | 4,089 | 64,681 | 3,203 | 14,979 | 385 | 0 |
| India | 94,464 | 153,075 | 80,422 | 59,570 | 27,348 | 30,236 | 6,618 | 81,535 | 5,049 | 11,971 | 2,374 | 0 |
| Indonesia | 124,398 | 130,956 | 65,309 | 67,273 | 13,259 | 8,741 | 33,123 | 30,683 | 25,966 | 33,000 | 0 | 0 |
| Iran, Islamic Rep. | 21,879 | 20,113 | 15,116 | 11,090 | 316 | 559 | 314 | 59 | 6,449 | 8,964 | 0 | 0 |
| Iraq | .. | .. | .. | .. | .. | .. | .. | .. | .. | .. | .. | .. |
| Ireland | .. | .. | .. | .. | .. | .. | .. | .. | .. | .. | .. | .. |
| Israel | .. | .. | .. | .. | .. | .. | .. | .. | .. | .. | .. | .. |
| Italy | .. | .. | .. | .. | .. | .. | .. | .. | .. | .. | .. | .. |
| Jamaica | 4,577 | 7,994 | 3,716 | 6,010 | 595 | 387 | 128 | 811 | 492 | 1,173 | 240 | 0 |
| Japan | .. | .. | .. | .. | .. | .. | .. | .. | .. | .. | .. | .. |
| Jordan | 7,661 | 8,000 | 6,624 | 7,143 | 806 | 939 | 0 | 0 | 785 | 699 | 251 | 158 |
| Kazakhstan | 3,750 | 74,148 | 2,834 | 2,136 | 295 | 502 | 103 | 59,433 | 381 | 12,579 | 432 | 0 |
| Kenya | 7,309 | 6,534 | 5,857 | 5,807 | 2,412 | 2,764 | 445 | 0 | 634 | 574 | 374 | 153 |
| Korea, Dem. Rep. | .. | .. | .. | .. | .. | .. | .. | .. | .. | .. | .. | .. |
| Korea, Rep. | .. | .. | .. | .. | .. | .. | .. | .. | .. | .. | .. | .. |
| Kuwait | .. | .. | .. | .. | .. | .. | .. | .. | .. | .. | .. | .. |
| Kyrgyz Republic | 609 | 2,382 | 472 | 1,860 | 141 | 612 | 0 | 251 | 13 | 108 | 124 | 163 |
| Lao PDR | 2,165 | 2,985 | 2,091 | 2,191 | 285 | 643 | 0 | 762 | 10 | 5 | 64 | 27 |
| Latvia | 463 | 22,795 | 271 | 1,555 | 55 | 100 | 0 | 10,764 | 31 | 10,476 | 160 | 0 |
| Lebanon | 2,966 | 23,963 | 1,550 | 18,958 | 113 | 314 | 50 | 805 | 1,365 | 4,200 | 0 | 0 |
| Lesotho | 684 | 670 | 642 | 633 | 207 | 284 | 0 | 0 | 4 | 0 | 38 | 36 |
| Liberia | 2,154 | 2,674 | 1,161 | 1,115 | 269 | 256 | 0 | 0 | 657 | 1,223 | 336 | 336 |
| Libya | .. | .. | .. | .. | .. | .. | .. | .. | .. | .. | .. | .. |
| Lithuania | 769 | 18,955 | 430 | 3,244 | 62 | 81 | 29 | 8,011 | 49 | 7,700 | 262 | 0 |
| Macedonia, FYR | 1,277 | 2,661 | 788 | 1,498 | 181 | 642 | 289 | 805 | 143 | 303 | 57 | 56 |
| Madagascar | 4,302 | 1,453 | 3,687 | 1,236 | 1,121 | 636 | 0 | 0 | 542 | 189 | 73 | 29 |
| Malawi | 2,239 | 850 | 2,079 | 767 | 1,306 | 157 | 0 | 0 | 44 | 64 | 116 | 19 |
| Malaysia | 34,343 | 52,526 | 16,023 | 21,899 | 1,059 | 437 | 11,046 | 18,824 | 7,274 | 11,803 | 0 | 0 |
| Mali | 2,958 | 1,436 | 2,739 | 1,411 | 863 | 282 | 0 | 0 | 72 | 17 | 147 | 8 |
| Mauritania | 2,396 | 1,630 | 2,127 | 1,401 | 347 | 130 | 0 | 0 | 169 | 229 | 100 | 0 |
| Mauritius | 1,757 | 1,997 | 1,148 | 585 | 157 | 71 | 267 | 49 | 342 | 1,363 | 0 | 0 |
| Mexico | 165,379 | 160,700 | 93,902 | 96,304 | 13,823 | 4,418 | 18,348 | 57,050 | 37,300 | 7,346 | 15,828 | 0 |
| Moldova | 695 | 2,416 | 450 | 735 | 152 | 393 | 9 | 718 | 6 | 822 | 230 | 141 |
| Mongolia | 531 | 1,444 | 472 | 1,361 | 59 | 301 | 0 | 3 | 12 | 50 | 47 | 31 |
| Morocco | 23,771 | 18,493 | 23,190 | 14,108 | 3,999 | 2,285 | 331 | 2,588 | 198 | 1,797 | 52 | 0 |
| Mozambique | 7,458 | 3,265 | 5,209 | 2,511 | 890 | 655 | 1,769 | 0 | 279 | 744 | 202 | 10 |
| Myanmar | 5,771 | 6,828 | 5,378 | 5,234 | 777 | 776 | 0 | 0 | 393 | 1,595 | 0 | 0 |
| Namibia | .. | .. | .. | .. | .. | .. | .. | .. | .. | .. | .. | .. |
| Nepal | 2,410 | 3,409 | 2,339 | 3,285 | 1,023 | 1,468 | 0 | 0 | 23 | 81 | 48 | 43 |
| Netherlands | .. | .. | .. | .. | .. | .. | .. | .. | .. | .. | .. | .. |
| New Zealand | .. | .. | .. | .. | .. | .. | .. | .. | .. | .. | .. | .. |
| Nicaragua | 10,390 | 4,391 | 8,566 | 3,425 | 341 | 256 | 0 | 288 | 1,785 | 615 | 39 | 63 |
| Niger | 1,572 | 805 | 1,315 | 703 | 598 | 189 | 133 | 26 | 72 | 49 | 52 | 27 |
| Nigeria | 34,092 | 7,693 | 28,140 | 3,800 | 3,489 | 2,074 | 301 | 0 | 5,651 | 3,893 | 0 | 0 |
| Norway | .. | .. | .. | .. | .. | .. | .. | .. | .. | .. | .. | .. |
| Oman | 5,776 | 4,819 | 2,637 | 819 | 25 | 0 | 2,598 | 2,047 | 541 | 1,953 | 0 | 0 |
| Pakistan | 30,229 | 35,909 | 23,788 | 32,309 | 6,403 | 10,015 | 1,593 | 907 | 3,235 | 1,230 | 1,613 | 1,462 |
| Panama | 6,099 | 9,989 | 3,782 | 7,774 | 175 | 185 | 0 | 1,694 | 2,207 | 505 | 111 | 15 |
| Papua New Guinea | 2,506 | 1,675 | 1,668 | 1,225 | 407 | 322 | 711 | 283 | 78 | 167 | 50 | 0 |
| Paraguay | 2,574 | 3,426 | 1,453 | 2,235 | 189 | 254 | 338 | 480 | 784 | 711 | 0 | 0 |
| Peru | 30,833 | 28,174 | 18,931 | 21,825 | 1,729 | 2,633 | 1,288 | 3,318 | 9,659 | 3,011 | 955 | 20 |
| Philippines | 39,379 | 60,324 | 28,525 | 36,793 | 5,185 | 2,886 | 4,847 | 18,522 | 5,279 | 5,009 | 728 | 0 |
| Poland | 44,080 | 125,831 | 40,890 | 39,248 | 2,067 | 1,961 | 1,012 | 65,228 | 2,178 | 21,355 | 0 | 0 |
| Portugal | .. | .. | .. | .. | .. | .. | .. | .. | .. | .. | .. | .. |
| Puerto Rico | .. | .. | .. | .. | .. | .. | .. | .. | .. | .. | .. | .. |

| | Total external debt | | Long-term debt | | | | | | Short-term debt | | Use of IMF credit | |
|---|---|---|---|---|---|---|---|---|---|---|---|---|
| | | | | | Public and publicly guaranteed ($ millions) | | | | | | | |
| | | | Total | | IBRD loans and IDA credits | | Private nonguaranteed | | | | | |
| | $ millions | | | | | | | | $ millions | | $ millions | |
| | 1995 | 2006 | 1995 | 2006 | 1995 | 2006 | 1995 | 2006 | 1995 | 2006 | 1995 | 2006 |
| Romania | 6,832 | 55,114 | 3,957 | 14,204 | 844 | 2,481 | 534 | 23,081 | 1,303 | 17,725 | 1,038 | 104 |
| Russian Federation | 121,401 | 251,067 | 101,582 | 50,254 | 1,524 | 4,759 | 0 | 160,364 | 10,201 | 40,448 | 9,617 | 0 |
| Rwanda | 1,029 | 419 | 971 | 390 | 512 | 169 | 0 | 0 | 32 | 25 | 26 | 4 |
| Saudi Arabia | .. | .. | .. | .. | .. | .. | .. | .. | .. | .. | .. | .. |
| Senegal | 3,906 | 1,984 | 3,256 | 1,712 | 1,160 | 495 | 44 | 151 | 260 | 95 | 347 | 26 |
| Serbia | 10,785[a] | 13,831 | 6,788[a] | 7,686 | 1,252[a] | 3,072 | 1,773[a] | 4,105 | 2,139[a] | 1,796 | 84[a] | 244 |
| Sierra Leone | 1,250 | 1,428 | 1,058 | 1,323 | 234 | 533 | 0 | 0 | 27 | 70 | 165 | 35 |
| Singapore | .. | .. | .. | .. | .. | .. | .. | .. | .. | .. | .. | .. |
| Slovak Republic | 5,744 | 27,085 | 3,488 | 4,508 | 263 | 298 | 85 | 6,994 | 1,714 | 15,584 | 457 | 0 |
| Slovenia | .. | .. | .. | .. | .. | .. | .. | .. | .. | .. | .. | .. |
| Somalia | 2,678 | 2,836 | 1,961 | 1,923 | 432 | 435 | 0 | 0 | 551 | 745 | 166 | 168 |
| South Africa | 25,358 | 35,549 | 9,837 | 13,940 | 0 | 29 | 4,935 | 6,349 | 9,673 | 15,260 | 913 | 0 |
| Spain | .. | .. | .. | .. | .. | .. | .. | .. | .. | .. | .. | .. |
| Sri Lanka | 8,395 | 11,446 | 7,175 | 10,140 | 1,512 | 2,245 | 90 | 206 | 535 | 855 | 595 | 244 |
| Sudan | 17,603 | 19,158 | 9,779 | 11,609 | 1,279 | 1,271 | 496 | 496 | 6,368 | 6,535 | 960 | 518 |
| Swaziland | 291 | 544 | 279 | 494 | 25 | 26 | 0 | 0 | 11 | 51 | 0 | 0 |
| Sweden | .. | .. | .. | .. | .. | .. | .. | .. | .. | .. | .. | .. |
| Switzerland | .. | .. | .. | .. | .. | .. | .. | .. | .. | .. | .. | .. |
| Syrian Arab Republic | 21,415 | 6,502 | 16,853 | 5,576 | 471 | 21 | 0 | 0 | 4,562 | 925 | 0 | 0 |
| Tajikistan | 634 | 1,154 | 590 | 982 | 0 | 339 | 0 | 33 | 43 | 95 | 0 | 44 |
| Tanzania | 7,421 | 4,240 | 6,217 | 2,929 | 2,269 | 1,056 | 44 | 6 | 963 | 1,293 | 197 | 13 |
| Thailand | 100,039 | 55,233 | 16,826 | 11,914 | 1,906 | 405 | 39,117 | 25,507 | 44,095 | 17,812 | 0 | 0 |
| Timor-Leste | .. | .. | .. | .. | .. | .. | .. | .. | .. | .. | .. | .. |
| Togo | 1,476 | 1,806 | 1,286 | 1,565 | 541 | 696 | 0 | 0 | 85 | 233 | 105 | 8 |
| Trinidad and Tobago | .. | .. | .. | .. | .. | .. | .. | .. | .. | .. | .. | .. |
| Tunisia | 10,818 | 18,480 | 9,215 | 15,144 | 1,766 | 1,470 | 0 | 0 | 1,310 | 3,336 | 293 | 0 |
| Turkey | 73,781 | 207,854 | 50,317 | 67,214 | 5,069 | 6,919 | 7,079 | 87,563 | 15,701 | 42,315 | 685 | 10,762 |
| Turkmenistan | 402 | 881 | 385 | 725 | 1 | 21 | 0 | 4 | 17 | 152 | 0 | 0 |
| Uganda | 3,609 | 1,264 | 3,089 | 1,107 | 1,792 | 436 | 0 | 0 | 103 | 148 | 417 | 9 |
| Ukraine | 8,429 | 49,887 | 6,581 | 9,538 | 491 | 2,362 | 84 | 24,158 | 223 | 15,361 | 1,542 | 830 |
| United Arab Emirates | .. | .. | .. | .. | .. | .. | .. | .. | .. | .. | .. | .. |
| United Kingdom | .. | .. | .. | .. | .. | .. | .. | .. | .. | .. | .. | .. |
| United States | .. | .. | .. | .. | .. | .. | .. | .. | .. | .. | .. | .. |
| Uruguay | 5,318 | 9,804 | 3,833 | 7,211 | 513 | 653 | 127 | 385 | 1,336 | 2,208 | 21 | 0 |
| Uzbekistan | 1,799 | 3,892 | 1,415 | 3,322 | 157 | 342 | 15 | 403 | 212 | 166 | 157 | 0 |
| Venezuela, RB | 35,538 | 44,635 | 28,223 | 27,180 | 1,639 | 51 | 2,013 | 5,606 | 3,063 | 11,848 | 2,239 | 0 |
| Vietnam | 25,428 | 20,202 | 21,778 | 17,518 | 231 | 3,663 | 0 | 0 | 3,272 | 2,504 | 377 | 181 |
| West Bank and Gaza | .. | .. | .. | .. | .. | .. | .. | .. | .. | .. | .. | .. |
| Yemen, Rep. | 6,217 | 5,563 | 5,528 | 5,000 | 827 | 1,894 | 0 | 0 | 689 | 318 | 0 | 246 |
| Zambia | 6,958 | 2,325 | 5,291 | 1,003 | 1,434 | 260 | 13 | 826 | 415 | 455 | 1,239 | 41 |
| Zimbabwe | 4,989 | 4,677 | 3,462 | 3,452 | 896 | 946 | 381 | 19 | 685 | 1,093 | 461 | 113 |
| **World** | .. s | .. s | .. s | .. s | .. s | .. s | .. s | .. s | .. s | .. s | .. s | .. s |
| **Low income** | 366,231 | 375,060 | 298,243 | 240,914 | 77,144 | 85,474 | 15,299 | 86,554 | 39,576 | 41,895 | 13,113 | 5,697 |
| **Middle income** | 1,585,166 | 2,608,599 | 1,035,719 | 1,026,218 | 105,438 | 109,106 | 202,465 | 951,635 | 299,174 | 616,340 | 47,809 | 14,406 |
| Lower middle income | 698,032 | 921,093 | 460,313 | 427,332 | 60,740 | 63,722 | 88,238 | 198,074 | 141,256 | 292,828 | 8,226 | 2,860 |
| Upper middle income | 887,133 | 1,687,506 | 575,406 | 598,886 | 44,697 | 45,384 | 114,226 | 753,561 | 157,918 | 323,512 | 39,583 | 11,547 |
| **Low & middle income** | 1,951,397 | 2,983,659 | 1,333,962 | 1,267,133 | 182,582 | 194,579 | 217,764 | 1,038,189 | 338,750 | 658,235 | 60,922 | 20,103 |
| East Asia & Pacific | 455,619 | 659,985 | 255,393 | 255,163 | 37,604 | 40,233 | 90,050 | 158,260 | 108,839 | 246,324 | 1,337 | 239 |
| Europe & Central Asia | 331,945 | 1,047,027 | 259,527 | 261,993 | 16,242 | 31,826 | 16,699 | 549,276 | 38,868 | 222,425 | 16,851 | 13,333 |
| Latin America & Carib. | 608,475 | 734,499 | 371,682 | 397,231 | 38,402 | 32,992 | 87,303 | 230,312 | 122,859 | 106,219 | 26,632 | 737 |
| Middle East & N. Africa | 167,325 | 141,318 | 142,996 | 108,074 | 12,776 | 9,759 | 3,606 | 8,435 | 18,546 | 24,386 | 2,177 | 423 |
| South Asia | 151,740 | 227,303 | 129,135 | 126,989 | 42,036 | 53,764 | 8,301 | 82,647 | 9,051 | 15,435 | 5,252 | 2,232 |
| Sub-Saharan Africa | 236,293 | 173,526 | 175,229 | 117,683 | 35,521 | 26,005 | 11,804 | 9,258 | 40,587 | 43,445 | 8,673 | 3,140 |
| **High income** | | | | | | | | | | | | |
| Euro area | | | | | | | | | | | | |

a. Includes Montenegro.

# External debt | 6.8

A country's external indebtedness plays an important role in its creditworthiness and in perceptions by investors. Data on the external debt of developing countries are gathered by the World Bank through its Debtor Reporting System. Indebtedness is calculated using loan-by-loan reports submitted by countries on long-term public and publicly guaranteed borrowing, along with information on short-term debt collected by the countries or collected from creditors through the reporting systems of the Bank for International Settlements and the Organisation for Economic Co-operation and Development. These data are supplemented by information from major multilateral banks and official lending agencies in major creditor countries as well as estimates by World Bank and International Monetary Fund (IMF) staff. In addition, the table includes data on long-term private nonguaranteed debt that is either reported to the World Bank or estimated by its staff.

The coverage, quality, and timeliness of data vary across countries. Coverage varies for both debt instruments and borrowers. The widening spectrum of debt instruments and investors alongside the expansion of private nonguaranteed borrowing makes comprehensive coverage of external debt more complex. Reporting countries differ in their capacity to monitor debt, especially private nonguaranteed debt. Even data on public and publicly guaranteed debt are affected by coverage and accuracy in reporting—again because of monitoring capacity and sometimes because of an unwillingness to provide information. A key part often underreported is military debt.

Because debt data are normally reported in the currency of repayment, they have to be converted into a single currency (U.S. dollars) to produce summary tables. Stock figures (amount of debt outstanding) are converted using end-of-period exchange rates, as published in the IMF's *International Financial Statistics* (line ae). Flow figures are converted at annual average exchange rates (line rf). Projected debt service is converted using end-of-period exchange rates. Debt repayable in multiple currencies, goods, or services and debt with a provision for maintenance of the value of the currency of repayment are shown at book value.

Because flow data are converted at annual average exchange rates and stock data at end-of-period exchange rates, year-to-year changes in debt outstanding and disbursed are sometimes not equal to net flows (disbursements less principal repayments); similarly, changes in debt outstanding, including undisbursed debt, differ from commitments less repayments. Discrepancies are particularly notable when exchange rates have moved sharply during the year. Cancellations and reschedulings of other liabilities into long-term public debt also contribute to the differences.

Variations in reporting rescheduled debt also affect cross-country comparability. For example, rescheduling under the auspices of the Paris Club of official creditors may be subject to lags between the completion of the general rescheduling agreement and the completion of the specific bilateral agreements that define the terms of the rescheduled debt. Other areas of inconsistency include country treatment of arrears and of nonresident national deposits denominated in foreign currency.

• **Total external debt** is debt owed to nonresidents repayable in foreign currency, goods, or services. It is the sum of public, publicly guaranteed, and private nonguaranteed long-term debt, short-term debt, and use of IMF credit. • **Long-term debt** is debt that has an original or extended maturity of more than one year. It has three components: public, publicly guaranteed, and private nonguaranteed debt. • **Public and publicly guaranteed debt** comprises the long-term external obligations of public debtors, including the national government and political subdivisions (or an agency of either) and autonomous public bodies, and the external obligations of private debtors that are guaranteed for repayment by a public entity. • **IBRD loans and IDA credits** are extended by the World Bank. The International Bank for Reconstruction and Development (IBRD) lends at market rates. The International Development Association (IDA) provides credits at concessional rates. • **Private nonguaranteed debt** consists of the long-term external obligations of private debtors that are not guaranteed for repayment by a public entity. • **Short-term debt** is debt owed to nonresidents having an original maturity of one year or less and interest in arrears on long-term debt. • **Use of IMF credit** denotes repurchase obligations to the IMF for all uses of IMF resources (excluding those resulting from drawings on the reserve tranche). These obligations, shown for the end of the year specified, comprise purchases outstanding under the credit tranches (including enlarged access resources) and all special facilities (the Buffer Stock, Compensatory and Contingency Financing, Extended Fund, Supplemental Reserve, Oil, Supplementary Financing, Policy on Enlarged Access, and Systemic Transformation), trust fund loans, and operations under the structural adjustment and poverty reduction and growth facilities.

## Data sources

Data on external debt are mainly reports to the World Bank through its Debtor Reporting System from member countries that have received IBRD loans or IDA credits, with additional information from the files of the World Bank, the IMF, the African Development Bank and African Development Fund, the Asian Development Bank and Asian Development Fund, and the Inter-American Development Bank. Summary tables of the external debt of developing countries are published annually in the World Bank's *Global Development Finance* and on its *Global Development Finance* CD-ROM.

## Financial integration has complemented growth — 6.8a

Total external debt ($ trillions) — External debt as a share of GNI (%)

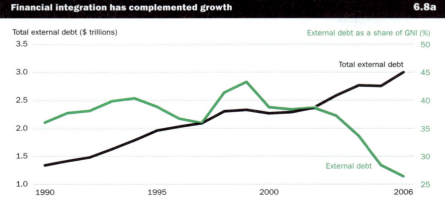

For developing countries economic growth has exceeded debt accumulation since 1999.

*Source: World Development Indicators data files.*

# 6.9 | Ratios for external debt

| | Total external debt | | Total debt service | | Multilateral debt service | | Short-term debt | | | | Present value of debt | |
|---|---|---|---|---|---|---|---|---|---|---|---|---|
| | % of GNI | | % of exports of goods and services and income[a] | | % of public and publicly guaranteed debt service | | % of total debt | | % of total reserves | | % of GNI | % of exports of goods and services and income[a] |
| | 1995 | 2006 | 1995 | 2006 | 1995 | 2006 | 1995 | 2006 | 1995 | 2006 | 2006[b] | 2006[b] |
| Afghanistan | .. | 21.1 | .. | .. | .. | 100.0 | .. | 0.6 | .. | .. | 5[c] | 22[c] |
| Albania | 18.4 | 25.2 | 1.4 | 3.5 | 11.4 | 44.6 | 13.7 | 24.6 | 23.5 | 31.7 | 21 | 55 |
| Algeria | 83.5 | 5.2 | .. | .. | 17.7 | 18.7 | 0.8 | 9.7 | 6.3 | 0.7 | 5 | 10 |
| Angola | 311.9 | 24.1 | 12.0 | 12.8 | 0.6 | 0.5 | 17.0 | 22.6 | 919.7 | 25.2 | 33 | 39 |
| Argentina | 38.9 | 58.6 | 30.1 | 31.6 | 21.6 | 80.5 | 21.7 | 28.7 | 133.6 | 109.4 | 68 | 230 |
| Armenia | 25.3 | 32.0 | 3.1 | 7.6 | 69.8 | 87.5 | 0.6 | 14.4 | 1.9 | 27.8 | 29 | 78 |
| Australia | .. | .. | .. | .. | .. | .. | .. | .. | .. | .. | .. | .. |
| Austria | .. | .. | .. | .. | .. | .. | .. | .. | .. | .. | .. | .. |
| Azerbaijan | 10.6 | 11.1 | 1.3 | 1.6 | 21.8 | 39.2 | 4.4 | 15.9 | 11.6 | 12.1 | 12 | 15 |
| Bangladesh | 40.7 | 31.1 | 13.2 | 3.7 | 27.1 | 74.7 | 1.3 | 5.7 | 8.4 | 30.4 | 22 | 91 |
| Belarus | 12.2 | 16.6 | 3.4 | 3.3 | 55.4 | 12.8 | 6.5 | 72.2 | 29.2 | 312.2 | 17 | 28 |
| Belgium | .. | .. | .. | .. | .. | .. | .. | .. | .. | .. | .. | .. |
| Benin | 82.1 | 17.5 | 6.8 | .. | 54.8 | 47.9 | 2.9 | 4.8 | 23.7 | 4.3 | 14[c] | 70[c] |
| Bolivia | 81.2 | 49.0 | 29.4 | 8.5 | 75.5 | 91.1 | 5.8 | 4.2 | 30.5 | 6.9 | 51[c] | 123[c] |
| Bosnia and Herzegovina | .. | 44.2 | .. | 8.7 | .. | 52.4 | .. | 20.2 | .. | 33.9 | 43 | 84 |
| Botswana | 15.1 | 4.1 | 3.1 | 0.9 | 76.0 | 70.7 | 1.4 | 5.9 | 0.2 | 0.3 | 4 | 6 |
| Brazil | 21.2 | 18.7 | 36.6 | 37.3 | 18.5 | 7.8 | 19.5 | 10.5 | 60.7 | 23.7 | 26 | 158 |
| Bulgaria | 81.8 | 66.5 | 16.5 | 12.4 | 10.5 | 59.3 | 4.9 | 38.4 | 31.3 | 68.4 | 74 | 110 |
| Burkina Faso | 53.6 | 18.5 | .. | .. | 76.7 | 77.6 | 4.4 | 7.5 | 16.1 | 15.4 | 13[c] | 110[c] |
| Burundi | 117.6 | 162.2 | 27.6 | 40.4 | 70.6 | 88.3 | 1.3 | 2.7 | 6.9 | 28.7 | 119[c] | 1,061[c] |
| Cambodia | 67.5 | 50.6 | 0.7 | 0.6 | 11.9 | 67.7 | 4.5 | 5.9 | 53.1 | 14.8 | 48 | 66 |
| Cameroon | 129.6 | 17.5 | 20.8 | .. | 60.8 | 39.3 | 9.3 | 18.8 | 6,444.5 | 34.3 | 18[c] | 70[c] |
| Canada | .. | .. | .. | .. | .. | .. | .. | .. | .. | .. | .. | .. |
| Central African Republic | 85.9 | 68.4 | .. | .. | 100.0 | 100.0 | 6.0 | 11.2 | 24.0 | 86.6 | 57[c] | 597[c] |
| Chad | 63.3 | 34.2 | .. | .. | 87.1 | 76.9 | 2.2 | 1.0 | 13.7 | 2.9 | 24[c] | 36[c] |
| Chile | 32.1 | 37.9 | 24.5 | 20.0 | 76.2 | 5.0 | 15.6 | 19.6 | 23.1 | 48.5 | 42 | 86 |
| China | 16.5 | 12.2 | 9.9 | 2.5 | 7.6 | 26.0 | 18.9 | 53.7 | 27.8 | 16.0 | 14 | 35 |
| Hong Kong, China | .. | .. | .. | .. | .. | .. | .. | .. | .. | .. | .. | .. |
| Colombia | 27.5 | 26.9 | 31.5 | 31.3 | 32.7 | 27.0 | 22.1 | 12.1 | 65.6 | 31.2 | 32 | 143 |
| Congo, Dem. Rep. | 271.4 | 137.5 | .. | .. | .. | 38.1 | 23.6 | 4.6 | 1,980.9 | .. | 130[c] | 388[c] |
| Congo, Rep. | 487.1 | .. | 13.1 | .. | 21.0 | 60.6 | 17.1 | 12.5 | 1,606.5 | 41.5 | 104[c] | 104[c] |
| Costa Rica | 33.1 | 31.9 | 13.8 | 5.0 | 50.7 | 66.0 | 11.3 | 34.0 | 40.6 | 74.6 | 35 | 66 |
| Côte d'Ivoire | 188.7 | 82.6 | 23.1 | 1.4 | 59.3 | 71.8 | 20.7 | 14.5 | 739.1 | 112.0 | 82[c] | 150[c] |
| Croatia | 20.4 | 90.2 | 4.8 | 33.1 | 73.1 | 10.9 | 12.8 | 14.9 | 25.9 | 48.5 | 93 | 168 |
| Cuba | .. | .. | .. | .. | .. | .. | .. | .. | .. | .. | .. | .. |
| Czech Republic | .. | .. | .. | .. | .. | .. | .. | .. | .. | .. | .. | .. |
| Denmark | .. | .. | .. | .. | .. | .. | .. | .. | .. | .. | .. | .. |
| Dominican Republic | 37.8 | 29.6 | 6.1 | 9.6 | 39.8 | 17.1 | 13.8 | 16.4 | 165.3 | 68.7 | 35 | 66 |
| Ecuador | 72.6 | 41.9 | 24.9 | 24.1 | 31.7 | 30.7 | 9.4 | 8.6 | 73.4 | 70.3 | 52 | 129 |
| Egypt, Arab Rep. | 55.8 | 27.4 | 13.2 | 4.9 | 26.3 | 17.2 | 7.1 | 5.6 | 13.9 | 6.3 | 28 | 69 |
| El Salvador | 26.7 | 50.4 | 8.9 | 13.1 | 55.1 | 50.8 | 20.9 | 13.5 | 55.9 | 62.7 | 55 | 119 |
| Eritrea | 6.3 | 74.1 | 0.1 | .. | 100.0 | 75.8 | 0.0 | 2.3 | 0.0 | 73.2 | 52[c] | 742[c] |
| Estonia | .. | .. | .. | .. | .. | .. | .. | .. | .. | .. | .. | .. |
| Ethiopia | 136.6 | 17.5 | 18.4 | 6.8 | 41.7 | 55.0 | 4.5 | 4.9 | 56.5 | 13.7 | 16[c] | 84[c] |
| Finland | .. | .. | .. | .. | .. | .. | .. | .. | .. | .. | .. | .. |
| France | .. | .. | .. | .. | .. | .. | .. | .. | .. | .. | .. | .. |
| Gabon | 101.6 | 57.9 | 15.3 | .. | 17.9 | 100.0 | 6.6 | 10.0 | 187.8 | 38.7 | 64 | 79 |
| Gambia, The | 113.0 | 145.2 | 15.5 | 12.4 | 49.1 | 59.2 | 3.5 | 2.5 | 14.0 | 15.3 | 108[c] | 191[c] |
| Georgia | 48.2 | 26.2 | .. | 8.8 | 0.4 | 30.2 | 6.9 | 5.7 | 43.0 | 12.0 | 22 | 57 |
| Germany | .. | .. | .. | .. | .. | .. | .. | .. | .. | .. | .. | .. |
| Ghana | 86.9 | 24.9 | 24.0 | 4.9 | 48.4 | 44.6 | 11.3 | 35.8 | 77.1 | 50.4 | 24[c] | 59[c] |
| Greece | .. | .. | .. | .. | .. | .. | .. | .. | .. | .. | .. | .. |
| Guatemala | 22.6 | 15.7 | 11.1 | 4.8 | 47.7 | 58.6 | 24.7 | 27.0 | 103.7 | 36.6 | 18 | 59 |
| Guinea | 89.8 | 100.2 | 25.0 | .. | 30.4 | 55.8 | 5.0 | 7.0 | 185.6 | .. | 71[c] | 261[c] |
| Guinea-Bissau | 380.7 | 241.2 | 51.9 | .. | 88.3 | 45.2 | 10.5 | 1.1 | 467.0 | 9.9 | 169[c] | 360[c] |
| Haiti | 25.3 | 27.5 | 50.4 | 3.2 | 92.0 | 83.0 | 3.6 | 10.4 | 13.4 | 48.5 | 24[c] | 64[c] |

| | Total external debt | | Total debt service | | Multilateral debt service | | Short-term debt | | | | Present value of debt | |
|---|---|---|---|---|---|---|---|---|---|---|---|---|
| | % of GNI | | % of exports of goods and services and income[a] | | % of public and publicly guaranteed debt service | | % of total debt | | % of total reserves | | % of GNI | % of exports of goods and services and income[a] |
| | 1995 | 2006 | 1995 | 2006 | 1995 | 2006 | 1995 | 2006 | 1995 | 2006 | 2006[b] | 2006[b] |
| Honduras | 131.5 | 45.7 | 34.0 | 5.1 | 52.6 | 63.9 | 8.0 | 13.1 | 141.7 | 20.2 | 41[c] | 61[c] |
| Hungary | 73.7 | 102.7 | 33.8 | 33.1 | 20.1 | 8.8 | 10.1 | 13.9 | 26.7 | 69.4 | 100 | 127 |
| India | 26.8 | 16.9 | 29.7 | 7.7 | 24.3 | 24.6 | 5.3 | 8.9 | 22.1 | 6.7 | 15 | 63 |
| Indonesia | 63.4 | 37.5 | 29.9 | 16.6 | 28.4 | 48.3 | 20.9 | 25.2 | 174.2 | 77.5 | 45 | 122 |
| Iran, Islamic Rep. | 24.3 | 9.3 | 30.2 | .. | 1.3 | 4.5 | 29.5 | 44.6 | .. | .. | 10 | 27 |
| Iraq | .. | .. | .. | .. | .. | .. | .. | .. | .. | .. | .. | .. |
| Ireland | .. | .. | .. | .. | .. | .. | .. | .. | .. | .. | .. | .. |
| Israel | .. | .. | .. | .. | .. | .. | .. | .. | .. | .. | .. | .. |
| Italy | .. | .. | .. | .. | .. | .. | .. | .. | .. | .. | .. | .. |
| Jamaica | 82.2 | 85.6 | 16.2 | 11.9 | 40.6 | 28.2 | 10.7 | 14.7 | 72.2 | 50.6 | 99 | 144 |
| Japan | .. | .. | .. | .. | .. | .. | .. | .. | .. | .. | .. | .. |
| Jordan | 118.8 | 54.5 | 12.4 | 6.1 | 33.5 | 47.0 | 10.2 | 8.7 | 34.4 | 10.0 | 58 | 77 |
| Kazakhstan | 18.6 | 103.4 | 3.9 | 33.7 | 7.8 | 60.8 | 10.2 | 17.0 | 23.0 | 65.8 | 132 | 222 |
| Kenya | 83.8 | 28.6 | 30.4 | 6.5 | 32.5 | 64.5 | 8.7 | 8.8 | 164.9 | 23.7 | 26 | 87 |
| Korea, Dem. Rep. | .. | .. | .. | .. | .. | .. | .. | .. | .. | .. | .. | .. |
| Korea, Rep. | .. | .. | .. | .. | .. | .. | .. | .. | .. | .. | .. | .. |
| Kuwait | .. | .. | .. | .. | .. | .. | .. | .. | .. | .. | .. | .. |
| Kyrgyz Republic | 37.5 | 85.6 | 13.2 | 5.7 | 59.0 | 93.5 | 2.1 | 4.5 | 9.7 | 13.2 | 71[c] | 126[c] |
| Lao PDR | 123.2 | 98.6 | 6.3 | .. | 37.4 | 65.7 | 0.5 | 0.2 | 10.2 | 1.1 | 87 | 245 |
| Latvia | 8.8 | 117.2 | 1.6 | 33.3 | 60.3 | 45.0 | 6.7 | 46.0 | 5.2 | 232.2 | 135 | 266 |
| Lebanon | 24.3 | 107.0 | .. | 21.0 | 13.2 | 3.8 | 46.0 | 17.5 | 16.9 | 21.8 | 116 | 128 |
| Lesotho | 51.9 | 35.8 | 6.1 | 4.0 | 60.3 | 54.7 | 0.6 | 0.0 | 0.9 | 0.0 | 25 | 38 |
| Liberia | .. | 541.3 | .. | .. | .. | 100.0 | 30.5 | 45.7 | 2,340.6 | 1,699.1 | 674[c] | 2,030[c] |
| Libya | .. | .. | .. | .. | .. | .. | .. | .. | .. | .. | .. | .. |
| Lithuania | 10.2 | 68.9 | 1.3 | 22.1 | 31.8 | 14.5 | 6.4 | 40.6 | 6.0 | 133.4 | 79 | 121 |
| Macedonia, FYR | 29.0 | 42.8 | .. | 15.7 | 99.9 | 16.5 | 11.2 | 11.4 | 51.9 | 16.0 | 50 | 102 |
| Madagascar | 143.3 | 26.8 | 7.6 | .. | 74.3 | 66.4 | 12.6 | 13.0 | 497.1 | 32.4 | 20[c] | 65[c] |
| Malawi | 165.8 | 27.2 | 24.9 | .. | 51.4 | 89.6 | 1.9 | 7.5 | 37.8 | 45.1 | 21[c] | 79[c] |
| Malaysia | 40.6 | 36.0 | 7.0 | 4.0 | 15.5 | 5.7 | 21.2 | 22.5 | 29.5 | 14.2 | 39 | 31[*] |
| Mali | 122.3 | 26.0 | 13.4 | .. | 45.5 | 76.4 | 2.4 | 1.2 | 22.2 | 1.8 | 20[c] | 63[c] |
| Mauritania | 175.3 | 58.9 | 22.9 | .. | 49.6 | 88.1 | 7.1 | 14.0 | 187.9 | .. | 60[c] | 121[c] |
| Mauritius | 46.2 | 31.2 | 9.4 | 7.1 | 34.5 | 25.6 | 19.5 | 68.2 | 38.5 | 104.1 | 31 | 50 |
| Mexico | 60.5 | 19.5 | 27.0 | 18.9 | 19.5 | 29.6 | 22.6 | 4.6 | 218.8 | 9.6 | 21 | 62 |
| Moldova | 40.3 | 64.3 | 7.9 | 12.2 | 79.1 | 48.7 | 0.9 | 34.0 | 2.3 | 105.9 | 65 | 90 |
| Mongolia | 44.2 | 47.4 | 10.2 | 2.2 | 2.8 | 38.6 | 2.2 | 3.5 | 7.4 | 4.7 | 43 | 57 |
| Morocco | 75.1 | 28.7 | 33.4 | 12.2 | 30.3 | 40.6 | 0.8 | 9.7 | 5.1 | 8.6 | 30 | 72 |
| Mozambique | 360.6 | 53.2 | 34.5 | 1.9 | 17.4 | 69.6 | 3.7 | 22.8 | 142.8 | 61.1 | 45[c] | 115[c] |
| Myanmar | .. | .. | 17.8 | 1.7 | 15.0 | 3.4 | 6.8 | 23.4 | 60.4 | 115.3 | 70 | 202 |
| Namibia | .. | .. | .. | .. | .. | .. | .. | .. | .. | .. | .. | .. |
| Nepal | 54.7 | 37.8 | 7.5 | 5.1 | 54.2 | 68.8 | 0.9 | 2.4 | 3.5 | .. | 28[c] | 93[c] |
| Netherlands | .. | .. | .. | .. | .. | .. | .. | .. | .. | .. | .. | .. |
| New Zealand | .. | .. | .. | .. | .. | .. | .. | .. | .. | .. | .. | .. |
| Nicaragua | 368.3 | 84.8 | 38.7 | 4.1 | 30.3 | 59.5 | 17.2 | 14.0 | 1,256.8 | 66.7 | 72[c] | 131[c] |
| Niger | 85.9 | 22.1 | 16.7 | .. | 95.5 | 76.0 | 4.6 | 6.1 | 75.6 | 13.3 | 17[c] | 93[c] |
| Nigeria | 131.7 | 7.6 | 13.8 | .. | 45.4 | 6.9 | 16.6 | 50.6 | 330.7 | 9.1 | 9 | 13 |
| Norway | .. | .. | .. | .. | .. | .. | .. | .. | .. | .. | .. | .. |
| Oman | 43.1 | .. | 14.8 | 1.3 | 7.3 | 58.6 | 9.4 | 40.5 | 27.9 | 38.9 | 16 | 25 |
| Pakistan | 49.5 | 27.8 | 26.5 | 8.6 | 43.2 | 60.5 | 10.7 | 3.4 | 128.0 | 9.6 | 26 | 123 |
| Panama | 80.9 | 62.2 | 3.4 | 24.7 | 52.7 | 7.0 | 36.2 | 5.1 | 282.4 | 37.9 | 77 | 94 |
| Papua New Guinea | 56.5 | 33.0 | 20.8 | .. | 31.7 | 68.7 | 3.1 | 10.0 | 29.1 | 11.6 | 35 | 42 |
| Paraguay | 31.5 | 36.9 | 5.6 | 6.8 | 48.0 | 47.5 | 30.4 | 20.8 | 70.8 | 41.8 | 43 | 69 |
| Peru | 60.3 | 33.3 | 15.9 | 12.9 | 49.9 | 41.3 | 31.3 | 10.7 | 111.6 | 17.3 | 42 | 140 |
| Philippines | 51.7 | 47.1 | 16.1 | 19.6 | 29.2 | 12.6 | 13.4 | 8.3 | 67.8 | 21.8 | 57 | 101 |
| Poland | 32.2 | 38.7 | 11.0 | 24.7 | 13.5 | 4.8 | 4.9 | 17.0 | 14.6 | 44.1 | 41 | 97 |
| Portugal | .. | .. | .. | .. | .. | .. | .. | .. | .. | .. | .. | .. |
| Puerto Rico | .. | .. | .. | .. | .. | .. | .. | .. | .. | .. | .. | .. |

# 6.9 | Ratios for external debt

| | Total external debt | | Total debt service | | Multilateral debt service | | Short-term debt | | | | Present value of debt | |
|---|---|---|---|---|---|---|---|---|---|---|---|---|
| | | | % of exports of goods and services and income[a] | | % of public and publicly guaranteed debt service | | % of total debt | | % of total reserves | | % of GNI | % of exports of goods and services and income[a] |
| | % of GNI | | | | | | | | | | | |
| | 1995 | 2006 | 1995 | 2006 | 1995 | 2006 | 1995 | 2006 | 1995 | 2006 | 2006[b] | 2006[b] |
| Romania | 19.4 | 46.6 | 10.5 | 18.4 | 21.3 | 32.4 | 19.1 | 32.2 | 49.7 | 58.7 | 58 | 148 |
| Russian Federation | 31.0 | 26.2 | 6.3 | 13.8 | 9.7 | 3.0 | 8.4 | 16.1 | 56.6 | 13.3 | 34 | 88 |
| Rwanda | 79.2 | 16.9 | 20.5 | 9.6 | 99.0 | 86.1 | 3.1 | 6.0 | 32.3 | 5.7 | 13[c] | 100[c] |
| Saudi Arabia | .. | .. | .. | .. | .. | .. | .. | .. | .. | .. | .. | .. |
| Senegal | 82.7 | 22.0 | 16.8 | .. | 62.2 | 64.2 | 6.7 | 4.8 | 95.6 | 7.1 | 17[c] | 46[c] |
| Serbia | .. | 43.8 | .. | .. | 100.0[d] | 76.0 | 19.8[d] | 13.0 | .. | 15.1 | 52 | 127 |
| Sierra Leone | 152.7 | 100.9 | 54.3 | 9.6 | 8.3 | 84.0 | 2.2 | 4.9 | 77.8 | 37.8 | 83[c] | 349[c] |
| Singapore | .. | .. | .. | .. | .. | .. | .. | .. | .. | .. | .. | .. |
| Slovak Republic | 29.2 | 51.1 | 11.3 | .. | 7.5 | 17.1 | 29.8 | 57.5 | 44.4 | 116.6 | 58 | 67 |
| Slovenia | .. | .. | .. | .. | .. | .. | .. | .. | .. | .. | .. | .. |
| Somalia | .. | .. | .. | .. | .. | .. | 20.6 | 26.3 | .. | .. | .. | .. |
| South Africa | 17.1 | 14.2 | 9.5 | 6.7 | 0.0 | 1.6 | 38.1 | 42.9 | 216.7 | 59.6 | 15 | 51 |
| Spain | .. | .. | .. | .. | .. | .. | .. | .. | .. | .. | .. | .. |
| Sri Lanka | 65.3 | 42.6 | 8.0 | 8.6 | 14.0 | 22.6 | 6.4 | 7.5 | 25.3 | 29.1 | 40 | 92 |
| Sudan | 276.2 | 55.5 | 6.7 | 4.1 | 100.0 | 10.2 | 36.2 | 34.1 | .. | 393.7 | 69[c] | 304[c] |
| Swaziland | 20.1 | 20.4 | 1.8 | 1.8 | 55.0 | 62.1 | 3.9 | 9.3 | 3.8 | 13.6 | 21 | 23 |
| Sweden | .. | .. | .. | .. | .. | .. | .. | .. | .. | .. | .. | .. |
| Switzerland | .. | .. | .. | .. | .. | .. | .. | .. | .. | .. | .. | .. |
| Syrian Arab Republic | 184.8 | 20.0 | 4.3 | 1.3 | 66.6 | 30.1 | 21.3 | 14.2 | .. | .. | 23 | 51 |
| Tajikistan | 53.6 | 42.5 | .. | 5.1 | .. | 18.1 | 6.8 | 8.2 | .. | 46.4 | 36 | 42 |
| Tanzania | 144.6 | 33.6 | 17.9 | 3.4 | 66.7 | 79.2 | 13.0 | 30.5 | 356.6 | 57.2 | 29[c] | 116[c] |
| Thailand | 60.6 | 27.3 | 11.6 | 9.4 | 20.9 | 8.0 | 44.1 | 32.2 | 119.4 | 26.6 | 30 | 40 |
| Timor-Leste | .. | .. | .. | .. | .. | .. | .. | .. | .. | .. | .. | .. |
| Togo | 116.7 | 82.8 | 6.0 | .. | 75.5 | 60.5 | 5.8 | 12.9 | 65.1 | 62.2 | 74[c] | 154[c] |
| Trinidad and Tobago | .. | .. | .. | .. | .. | .. | .. | .. | .. | .. | .. | .. |
| Tunisia | 63.0 | 64.5 | 16.9 | 14.4 | 43.8 | 48.1 | 12.1 | 18.1 | 77.6 | 48.3 | 66 | 112 |
| Turkey | 43.0 | 51.7 | 27.7 | 33.2 | 20.7 | 13.3 | 21.3 | 20.4 | 113.0 | 66.9 | 61 | 200 |
| Turkmenistan | 16.1 | 8.9 | .. | .. | 1.9 | 6.0 | 4.3 | 17.2 | 1.5 | .. | 11 | 15 |
| Uganda | 63.3 | 13.6 | 19.8 | 4.8 | 69.7 | 68.6 | 2.8 | 11.7 | 22.4 | 8.2 | 11[c] | 46[c] |
| Ukraine | 17.6 | 47.6 | 6.6 | 18.1 | 13.6 | 22.2 | 2.6 | 30.8 | 20.9 | 68.7 | 58 | 106 |
| United Arab Emirates | .. | .. | .. | .. | .. | .. | .. | .. | .. | .. | .. | .. |
| United Kingdom | .. | .. | .. | .. | .. | .. | .. | .. | .. | .. | .. | .. |
| United States | .. | .. | .. | .. | .. | .. | .. | .. | .. | .. | .. | .. |
| Uruguay | 29.4 | 52.1 | 22.1 | 87.8 | 27.3 | 31.7 | 25.1 | 22.5 | 73.7 | 71.4 | 66 | 185 |
| Uzbekistan | 13.5 | 22.7 | .. | .. | 1.9 | 17.1 | 11.8 | 4.3 | .. | .. | 26 | 67 |
| Venezuela, RB | 48.7 | 24.7 | 22.9 | 13.3 | 11.5 | 9.2 | 8.6 | 26.5 | 28.6 | 32.3 | 34 | 83 |
| Vietnam | 124.0 | 33.9 | .. | .. | 2.9 | 12.9 | 12.9 | 12.4 | 247.2 | 18.7 | 33 | 45 |
| West Bank and Gaza | .. | .. | .. | .. | .. | .. | .. | .. | .. | .. | .. | .. |
| Yemen, Rep. | 169.0 | 31.6 | 3.1 | 2.4 | 78.3 | 56.1 | 11.1 | 5.7 | 107.9 | 4.2 | 25 | 46 |
| Zambia | 215.1 | 23.9 | .. | 3.6 | 50.6 | 69.0 | 6.0 | 19.6 | 186.2 | 63.2 | 29[c] | 70[c] |
| Zimbabwe | 73.5 | .. | .. | .. | 33.6 | 0.0 | 13.7 | 23.4 | 77.2 | .. | 110 | 248 |
| **World** | .. w | .. w | .. w | .. w | .. w | .. w | .. w | .. w | .. w | .. w | .. w | .. w |
| **Low income** | 56.3 | 23.7 | 22.9 | 6.6 | 32.9 | 28.4 | 10.8 | 11.2 | 78.5 | 13.5 | | |
| **Middle income** | 36.3 | 26.8 | 16.7 | 13.4 | 21.0 | 18.5 | 18.9 | 23.6 | 66.2 | 25.1 | | |
| Lower middle income | 39.9 | 19.9 | 15.3 | 7.0 | 22.0 | 24.7 | 20.2 | 31.8 | 64.7 | 19.3 | | |
| Upper middle income | 33.9 | 33.0 | 17.8 | 20.1 | 20.2 | 15.7 | 17.8 | 19.2 | 67.5 | 34.0 | | |
| **Low & middle income** | 38.9 | 26.4 | 17.3 | 12.6 | 22.7 | 19.4 | 17.4 | 22.1 | 67.2 | 23.9 | | |
| East Asia & Pacific | 35.5 | 18.4 | 12.7 | 5.0 | 18.2 | 22.3 | 23.9 | 37.3 | 64.9 | 18.7 | | |
| Europe & Central Asia | 33.9 | 43.2 | 12.2 | 20.0 | 16.9 | 9.8 | 11.7 | 21.2 | 48.0 | 38.1 | | |
| Latin America & Carib. | 35.9 | 25.8 | 26.2 | 23.0 | 26.2 | 23.2 | 20.2 | 14.5 | 88.6 | 34.0 | | |
| Middle East & N. Africa | 58.4 | 21.9 | 19.0 | 10.4 | 19.4 | 20.5 | 11.1 | 17.3 | 18.9 | 8.3 | | |
| South Asia | 32.0 | 19.8 | 25.5 | 7.5 | 27.4 | 33.9 | 6.0 | 6.8 | 29.5 | 7.7 | | |
| Sub-Saharan Africa | 77.9 | 26.2 | 15.9 | .. | 35.0 | 15.1 | 17.2 | 25.0 | 164.3 | 34.6 | | |
| **High income** | | | | | | | | | | | | |
| Euro area | | | | | | | | | | | | |

a. Includes workers' remittances. b. The numerator refers to 2006, whereas the denominator is a three-year average of 2004–06 data. c. Data are from debt sustainability analyses undertaken as part of the Heavily Indebted Poor Countries Initiative. Present value estimates for these countries are for public and publicly guaranteed debt only. d. Includes Montenegro.

# 6.9

GLOBAL LINKS

A country's external debt burden, both debt outstanding and debt service, affects a country's creditworthiness and vulnerability. The table shows total external debt relative to a country's size—gross national income (GNI). Total debt service is contrasted with countries' ability to obtain foreign exchange through exports of goods, services, income, and workers' remittances. The ratios shown here may differ from those published elsewhere because estimates of exports and GNI have been revised to incorporate data available as of February 15, 2008.

Multilateral debt service (shown as a share of the country's total public and publicly guaranteed debt service) are obligations to international financial institutions, such as the World Bank, the International Monetary Fund (IMF), and regional development banks. Multilateral debt service takes priority over private and bilateral debt service, and borrowers must stay current with multilateral debts to remain creditworthy. While bilateral and private creditors often write off debts, international financial institution bylaws prohibit granting debt relief or canceling debts directly. However, the recent decrease in multilateral debt service ratios for some countries reflects debt relief from special programs, such as the Heavily Indebted Poor Countries (HIPC) Debt Initiative and the Multilateral Debt Relief Initiative (MDRI) (see table 1.4.) Other countries have accelerated repayment of debt outstanding. Indebted countries may also apply to the Paris and London Clubs to renegotiate obligations to public and private creditors.

Because short-term debt poses an immediate burden and is particularly important for monitoring vulnerability, it is compared with the total debt and foreign exchange reserves that are instrumental in providing coverage for such obligations. The present value of external debt provides a measure of future debt service obligations.

The present value of external debt is calculated by discounting the debt service (interest plus amortization) due on long-term external debt over the life of existing loans. Short-term debt is included at face value. The data on debt are in U.S. dollars converted at official exchange rates (see *About the data* for table 6.8). The discount rate on long-term debt depends on the currency of repayment and is based on commercial interest reference rates established by the Organisation for Economic Co-operation and Development. Loans from the International Bank for Reconstruction and Development (IBRD), credits from the International Development Association (IDA), and obligations to the IMF are discounted using a special drawing rights reference rate. When the discount rate is greater than the loan interest rate, the present value is less than the nominal sum of future debt service obligations.

Debt ratios are used to assess the sustainability of a country's debt service obligations, but no absolute rules determine what values are too high. Empirical analysis of developing countries' experience and debt service performance shows that debt service difficulties become increasingly likely when the present value of debt reaches 200 percent of exports. Still, what constitutes a sustainable debt burden varies by country. Countries with fast-growing economies and exports are likely to be able to sustain higher debt levels.

• **Total external debt** is debt owed to nonresidents and comprises public, publicly guaranteed, and private nonguaranteed long-term debt, short-term debt, and use of IMF credit. It is presented as a share of gross national income (GNI). • **Total debt service** is the sum of principal repayments and interest actually paid on total long-term debt (public and publicly guaranteed and private nonguaranteed), use of IMF credit, and interest on short-term debt. • **Exports of goods, services, and income** refer to international transactions involving a change in ownership of general merchandise, goods sent for processing and repairs, nonmonetary gold, services, receipts of employee compensation for nonresident workers, investment income, and workers' remittances. • **Multilateral debt service** is the repayment of principal and interest to the World Bank, regional development banks, and other multilateral and intergovernmental agencies. • **Short-term debt** includes all debt having an original maturity of one year or less and interest in arrears on long-term debt. • **Total reserves** comprise holdings of monetary gold, special drawing rights, reserves of IMF members held by the IMF, and holdings of foreign exchange under the control of monetary authorities. • **Present value of debt** is the sum of short-term external debt plus the discounted sum of total debt service payments due on public, publicly guaranteed, and private nonguaranteed long-term external debt over the life of existing loans.

Data on external debt are mainly from reports to the World Bank through its Debtor Reporting System from member countries that have received IBRD loans or IDA credits, with additional information from the files of the World Bank, the IMF, the African Development Bank and African Development Fund, the Asian Development Bank and Asian Development Fund, and the Inter American Development Bank. Data on GNI, exports of goods and services, and total reserves are from the World Bank's national accounts files and the IMF's Balance of Payments and International Financial Statistics databases. Summary tables of the external debt of developing countries are published annually in the World Bank's *Global Development Finance* and on its *Global Development Finance* CD-ROM.

---

**Developing countries have reduced financial vulnerability** | 6.9a

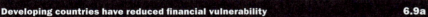

Foreign reserves (% of short-term debt)      Total debt service (% of exports of goods, services, and income)

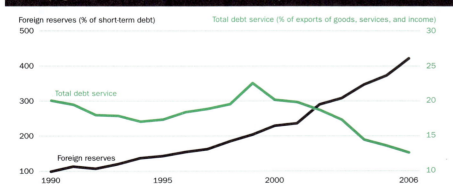

Since 1990 developing countries have increased their buffer for external debt and its service. Total debt services have decreased significantly since 1999, due largely to debt relief initiatives by multilateral and bilateral donors.

*Source:* World Bank's *Global Development Finance.*

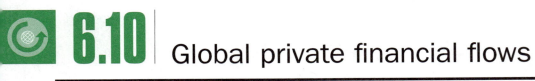

| | Equity flows | | | | Debt flows | | | |
|---|---|---|---|---|---|---|---|---|
| | $ millions | | | | $ millions | | | |
| | Foreign direct investment | | Portfolio equity | | Bonds | | Commercial bank and other lending | |
| | 1995 | 2006 | 1995 | 2006 | 1995 | 2006 | 1995 | 2006 |
| Afghanistan | .. | .. | .. | 0 | .. | 0 | .. | 0 |
| Albania | 70 | 325 | 0 | 0 | 0 | 0 | 0 | −11 |
| Algeria | 0 | 1,795 | 0 | 0 | −278 | 0 | 788 | −1,348 |
| Angola | 472 | −38 | 0 | 0 | 0 | 0 | 123 | −1,517 |
| Argentina | 5,609 | 4,840 | 1,552 | 662 | 3,705 | 1,690 | 754 | 825 |
| Armenia | 25 | 343 | 0 | −1 | 0 | 0 | 0 | 108 |
| Australia | 12,026 | 26,599 | .. | .. | .. | .. | .. | .. |
| Austria | 1,901 | 157 | .. | .. | .. | .. | .. | .. |
| Azerbaijan | 330 | −584 | 0 | 1 | 0 | 0 | 0 | −100 |
| Bangladesh | 2 | 697 | −15 | 31 | 0 | 0 | −21 | −24 |
| Belarus | 15 | 354 | 0 | −1 | 0 | 0 | 103 | 264 |
| Belgium | 10,689[a] | 61,990 | .. | .. | .. | .. | .. | .. |
| Benin | 13 | 63 | 0 | 2 | 0 | 0 | 0 | 0 |
| Bolivia | 393 | 240 | 0 | 0 | 0 | 0 | 41 | 93 |
| Bosnia and Herzegovina | 0 | 423 | 0 | 0 | .. | 0 | .. | −185 |
| Botswana | 70 | 486 | 6 | 36 | 0 | 0 | −6 | −2 |
| Brazil | 4,859 | 18,782 | 2,775 | 7,716 | 2,636 | −7,136 | 8,283 | 13,333 |
| Bulgaria | 90 | 5,172 | 0 | 95 | −6 | 166 | −93 | 2,062 |
| Burkina Faso | 10 | 26 | 0 | 0 | 0 | 0 | 0 | 0 |
| Burundi | 2 | 0 | 0 | 0 | 0 | 0 | −1 | −2 |
| Cambodia | 151 | 483 | 0 | 0 | 0 | 0 | 13 | 0 |
| Cameroon | 7 | 309 | 0 | 0 | 0 | 0 | −65 | −122 |
| Canada | 9,319 | 69,068 | .. | .. | .. | .. | .. | .. |
| Central African Republic | 6 | 24 | 0 | 0 | 0 | 0 | 0 | 0 |
| Chad | 33 | 700 | 0 | 0 | 0 | 0 | 0 | −1 |
| Chile | 2,957 | 7,952 | −249 | 63 | 489 | 580 | 1,773 | −278 |
| China | 35,849 | 78,095 | 0 | 42,861 | 317 | 1,705 | 4,696 | 5,795 |
| Hong Kong, China | .. | 42,891 | .. | .. | .. | .. | .. | .. |
| Colombia | 968 | 6,463 | 165 | −30 | 1,008 | 642 | 1,250 | −789 |
| Congo, Dem. Rep. | 122 | 180 | 0 | 0 | 0 | 0 | 0 | −6 |
| Congo, Rep. | 125 | 344 | 0 | 0 | 0 | 0 | −50 | 0 |
| Costa Rica | 337 | 1,469 | 0 | 0 | −4 | −25 | −9 | 251 |
| Côte d'Ivoire | 211 | 315 | 1 | 48 | 0 | 0 | 14 | 0 |
| Croatia | 114 | 3,376 | 4 | 411 | 0 | −280 | 265 | 3,745 |
| Cuba | .. | .. | .. | .. | .. | .. | .. | .. |
| Czech Republic | 2,568 | 6,021 | .. | .. | .. | .. | .. | .. |
| Denmark | 4,139 | 3,343 | .. | .. | .. | .. | .. | .. |
| Dominican Republic | 414 | 1,183 | 0 | 0 | 0 | 716 | −31 | −429 |
| Ecuador | 452 | 271 | 13 | 0 | 0 | −740 | 63 | 434 |
| Egypt, Arab Rep. | 598 | 10,043 | 0 | 502 | 0 | 0 | −311 | −250 |
| El Salvador | 38 | 204 | 0 | 0 | 0 | 504 | −31 | 290 |
| Eritrea | 37 | 4 | 0 | 0 | 0 | 0 | 0 | 0 |
| Estonia | 201 | 1,600 | .. | .. | .. | .. | .. | .. |
| Ethiopia | 14 | 364 | 0 | 0 | 0 | 0 | −48 | −45 |
| Finland | 1,044 | 5,311 | .. | .. | .. | .. | .. | .. |
| France | 23,736 | 81,045 | .. | .. | .. | .. | .. | .. |
| Gabon | −315 | 268 | 0 | 0 | 0 | 0 | −75 | 21 |
| Gambia, The | 8 | 82 | 0 | 0 | 0 | 0 | 0 | 0 |
| Georgia | 6 | 1,060 | 0 | 118 | 0 | 0 | 0 | 37 |
| Germany | 11,985 | 43,410 | .. | .. | .. | .. | .. | .. |
| Ghana | 107 | 435 | 0 | 0 | 0 | 0 | 38 | 9 |
| Greece | 1,053 | 5,401 | .. | .. | .. | .. | .. | .. |
| Guatemala | 75 | 354 | 0 | 0 | 44 | 0 | −32 | −25 |
| Guinea | 1 | 108 | 0 | 0 | 0 | 0 | −15 | 0 |
| Guinea-Bissau | 0 | 42 | 0 | 0 | 0 | 0 | 0 | 0 |
| Haiti | 7 | 160 | 0 | 0 | 0 | 0 | 0 | 0 |

# Global private financial flows

| | Equity flows | | | | Debt flows | | | |
|---|---|---|---|---|---|---|---|---|
| | $ millions | | | | $ millions | | | |
| | Foreign direct investment | | Portfolio equity | | Bonds | | Commercial bank and other lending | |
| | 1995 | 2006 | 1995 | 2006 | 1995 | 2006 | 1995 | 2006 |
| Honduras | 50 | 385 | 0 | 0 | −13 | 0 | 38 | 17 |
| Hungary | 4,804 | 6,098 | −62 | 917 | 2,120 | 6,315 | 781 | 30,327 |
| India | 2,144 | 17,453 | 1,591 | 9,549 | 286 | 3,206 | 967 | 12,892 |
| Indonesia | 4,346 | 5,580 | 1,493 | 1,898 | 2,248 | 3,784 | 55 | 992 |
| Iran, Islamic Rep. | 17 | 901 | 0 | 0 | 0 | 0 | −115 | −158 |
| Iraq | .. | .. | .. | .. | .. | .. | .. | .. |
| Ireland | 1,447 | −882 | .. | .. | .. | .. | .. | .. |
| Israel | 1,351 | 14,302 | .. | .. | .. | .. | .. | .. |
| Italy | 4,842 | 38,884 | .. | .. | .. | .. | .. | .. |
| Jamaica | 147 | 882 | 0 | 0 | 13 | 880 | 15 | 27 |
| Japan | 39 | −6,784 | .. | .. | .. | .. | .. | .. |
| Jordan | 13 | 3,219 | 0 | 144 | 0 | −1 | −201 | −11 |
| Kazakhstan | 964 | 6,143 | 0 | 2,797 | 0 | 6,219 | 240 | 19,549 |
| Kenya | 32 | 51 | 6 | 2 | 0 | 0 | −163 | −69 |
| Korea, Dem. Rep. | .. | .. | .. | .. | .. | .. | .. | .. |
| Korea, Rep. | 1,776 | 3,645 | .. | .. | .. | .. | .. | .. |
| Kuwait | 7 | 110 | .. | .. | .. | .. | .. | .. |
| Kyrgyz Republic | 96 | 182 | 0 | 0 | 0 | 0 | 0 | 82 |
| Lao PDR | 95 | 187 | 0 | 0 | 0 | 0 | 0 | 15 |
| Latvia | 180 | 1,664 | 0 | 22 | 43 | 240 | 3 | 3,987 |
| Lebanon | 35 | 2,794 | 0 | 551 | 350 | 834 | 333 | −36 |
| Lesotho | 275 | 78 | 0 | 0 | 0 | 0 | 12 | −8 |
| Liberia | 5 | −82 | 0 | 0 | 0 | 0 | 0 | 0 |
| Libya | .. | .. | .. | .. | .. | .. | .. | .. |
| Lithuania | 73 | 1,812 | 6 | 72 | 0 | 1,256 | 55 | 3,222 |
| Macedonia, FYR | 9 | 351 | 0 | 77 | 0 | 0 | 0 | −61 |
| Madagascar | 10 | 230 | 0 | 0 | 0 | 0 | −4 | −3 |
| Malawi | 6 | 30 | 0 | 0 | 0 | 0 | −23 | −2 |
| Malaysia | 4,178 | 6,064 | 0 | 2,392 | 2,440 | 363 | 1,231 | 1,822 |
| Mali | 111 | 185 | 0 | 6 | 0 | 0 | 0 | 1 |
| Mauritania | 7 | −3 | 0 | 0 | 0 | 0 | 0 | −2 |
| Mauritius | 19 | 107 | 22 | 32 | 150 | 0 | 126 | −102 |
| Mexico | 9,526 | 19,222 | 519 | 2,805 | 3,758 | −9,727 | 1,401 | 5,747 |
| Moldova | 26 | 242 | −1 | 2 | 0 | −6 | 24 | 137 |
| Mongolia | 10 | 344 | 0 | 0 | 0 | 0 | −14 | 15 |
| Morocco | 92 | 2,699 | 20 | −309 | 0 | 0 | 158 | −825 |
| Mozambique | 45 | 154 | 0 | 0 | 0 | 0 | 24 | 0 |
| Myanmar | 280 | 279 | 0 | 0 | 0 | 0 | 36 | −8 |
| Namibia | .. | .. | .. | .. | .. | .. | .. | .. |
| Nepal | 19 | −7 | 0 | 0 | 0 | 0 | −5 | 0 |
| Netherlands | 12,206 | 7,197 | .. | .. | .. | .. | .. | .. |
| New Zealand | 3,316 | 7,941 | .. | .. | .. | .. | .. | .. |
| Nicaragua | 89 | 282 | 0 | 0 | 0 | 0 | −81 | −9 |
| Niger | 7 | 20 | 0 | 1 | 0 | 0 | −24 | −7 |
| Nigeria | 1,079 | 5,445 | 0 | 0 | 0 | −1,442 | −448 | −60 |
| Norway | 2,393 | 4,653 | .. | .. | .. | .. | .. | .. |
| Oman | 46 | 952 | 0 | 1,020 | 0 | 25 | −15 | 505 |
| Pakistan | 723 | 4,273 | 10 | 1,152 | 0 | 1,050 | 317 | −233 |
| Panama | 223 | 2,574 | 0 | 0 | 0 | 186 | −12 | −10 |
| Papua New Guinea | 455 | 32 | 0 | 0 | −32 | 0 | −311 | −110 |
| Paraguay | 103 | 189 | 0 | 0 | 0 | 0 | −16 | −18 |
| Peru | 2,557 | 3,467 | 171 | 182 | 0 | −90 | 43 | 151 |
| Philippines | 1,478 | 2,345 | 0 | 2,388 | 1,110 | 1,734 | −215 | −2,725 |
| Poland | 3,659 | 19,198 | 219 | −2,134 | 250 | 3,036 | 228 | 13,987 |
| Portugal | 685 | 7,366 | .. | .. | .. | .. | .. | .. |
| Puerto Rico | .. | .. | .. | .. | .. | .. | .. | .. |

# 6.10 | Global private financial flows

| | Equity flows | | | | Debt flows | | | |
|---|---|---|---|---|---|---|---|---|
| | $ millions | | | | $ millions | | | |
| | Foreign direct investment | | Portfolio equity | | Bonds | | Commercial bank and other lending | |
| | **1995** | **2006** | **1995** | **2006** | **1995** | **2006** | **1995** | **2006** |
| Romania | 419 | 11,394 | 0 | 301 | 0 | 0 | 413 | 4,800 |
| Russian Federation | 2,065 | 30,827 | 46 | 6,149 | −810 | 12,175 | 444 | 14,591 |
| Rwanda | 2 | 11 | 0 | 0 | 0 | 0 | 0 | 0 |
| Saudi Arabia | −1,875 | 660 | .. | .. | .. | .. | .. | .. |
| Senegal | 32 | 58 | 4 | 0 | 0 | 0 | −25 | 18 |
| Serbia | 45[b] | 5,128 | 0[b] | 0 | 0[b] | 0 | 0[b] | 3,786 |
| Sierra Leone | 7 | 59 | 0 | 0 | 0 | 0 | −28 | 0 |
| Singapore | 11,566 | 24,191 | .. | .. | .. | .. | .. | .. |
| Slovak Republic | 236 | 4,165 | −16 | 0 | 0 | −351 | 245 | 2,271 |
| Slovenia | 150 | 649 | .. | .. | .. | .. | .. | .. |
| Somalia | 1 | 96 | 0 | 0 | 0 | 0 | 0 | 0 |
| South Africa | 1,248 | −120 | 2,914 | 14,959 | 731 | 1,576 | 748 | −553 |
| Spain | 8,086 | 20,167 | .. | .. | .. | .. | .. | .. |
| Sri Lanka | 56 | 480 | 0 | −304 | 0 | 0 | 103 | −83 |
| Sudan | 12 | 3,534 | 0 | −35 | 0 | 0 | 0 | 0 |
| Swaziland | 52 | 36 | 1 | 0 | 0 | 0 | 0 | 6 |
| Sweden | 14,939 | 27,299 | .. | .. | .. | .. | .. | .. |
| Switzerland | 4,158 | 27,185 | .. | .. | .. | .. | .. | .. |
| Syrian Arab Republic | 100 | 600 | 0 | 0 | 0 | 0 | −5 | −1 |
| Tajikistan | 10 | 339 | 0 | 0 | 0 | 0 | 0 | 3 |
| Tanzania | 120 | 474 | 0 | 3 | 0 | 0 | 15 | 1 |
| Thailand | 2,068 | 9,010 | 2,123 | 5,300 | 2,123 | −2,036 | 3,702 | 3,729 |
| Timor-Leste | .. | .. | .. | .. | .. | .. | .. | .. |
| Togo | 26 | 57 | 0 | 14 | 0 | 0 | 0 | 0 |
| Trinidad and Tobago | 299 | 940 | .. | .. | .. | .. | .. | .. |
| Tunisia | 264 | 3,270 | 12 | 65 | 588 | −301 | −96 | 36 |
| Turkey | 885 | 20,070 | 195 | 1,939 | 627 | 4,773 | 174 | 28,627 |
| Turkmenistan | 233 | 731 | 0 | 0 | 0 | 0 | 20 | −76 |
| Uganda | 121 | 392 | 0 | 19 | 0 | 0 | −9 | −1 |
| Ukraine | 267 | 5,604 | 0 | 322 | −200 | 360 | −19 | 9,118 |
| United Arab Emirates | .. | .. | .. | .. | .. | .. | .. | .. |
| United Kingdom | 21,731 | 139,745 | .. | .. | .. | .. | .. | .. |
| United States | 57,800 | 180,580 | .. | .. | .. | .. | .. | .. |
| Uruguay | 157 | 1,346 | 0 | −2 | 144 | 320 | 39 | −233 |
| Uzbekistan | −24 | 164 | 0 | 0 | 0 | 0 | 201 | −460 |
| Venezuela, RB | 985 | −543 | 270 | 41 | −468 | −4,738 | −247 | −355 |
| Vietnam | 1,780 | 2,315 | 0 | 0 | 0 | −26 | 356 | −41 |
| West Bank and Gaza | .. | .. | .. | .. | .. | .. | .. | .. |
| Yemen, Rep. | −218 | 1,121 | 0 | 0 | 0 | 0 | −2 | 7 |
| Zambia | 97 | 575 | 0 | 2 | 0 | 0 | −37 | 221 |
| Zimbabwe | 118 | 40 | 0 | 0 | −30 | 0 | 140 | −10 |
| **World** | **328,368 s** | **1,352,442 s** | **.. s** | **.. s** | **.. s** | **.. s** | **.. s** | **.. s** |
| **Low income** | 7,878 | 41,711 | 1,597 | 10,793 | 224 | 2,788 | 944 | 12,182 |
| **Middle income** | 96,122 | 325,781 | 12,198 | 94,056 | 23,114 | 24,633 | 27,003 | 164,242 |
| Lower middle income | 52,300 | 142,109 | 3,997 | 53,211 | 6,959 | 7,151 | 9,938 | 12,478 |
| Upper middle income | 43,822 | 183,673 | 8,201 | 40,845 | 16,155 | 17,482 | 17,066 | 151,765 |
| **Low & middle income** | 104,001 | 367,492 | 13,794 | 104,849 | 23,338 | 27,421 | 27,947 | 176,424 |
| East Asia & Pacific | 50,798 | 104,972 | 3,616 | 54,837 | 8,206 | 5,525 | 9,529 | 9,482 |
| Europe & Central Asia | 14,598 | 124,581 | 392 | 11,085 | 1,958 | 33,902 | 3,084 | 139,815 |
| Latin America & Carib. | 30,202 | 70,457 | 5,216 | 11,440 | 11,311 | −16,952 | 13,225 | 18,969 |
| Middle East & N. Africa | 952 | 27,503 | 32 | 1,971 | 660 | 557 | 534 | −2,080 |
| South Asia | 2,931 | 22,916 | 1,585 | 10,428 | 286 | 4,256 | 1,362 | 12,556 |
| Sub-Saharan Africa | 4,520 | 17,063 | 2,954 | 15,088 | 851 | 5,802 | 213 | −2,316 |
| **High income** | 224,367 | 984,950 | .. | .. | .. | .. | .. | .. |
| Euro area | 78,196 | 400,472 | .. | .. | .. | .. | .. | .. |

a. Includes Luxembourg. b. Includes Montenegro.

## About the data

Private financial flows account for the bulk of development finance and are split into two broad categories—equity and debt. Equity flows comprise foreign direct investment (FDI) and portfolio equity. Debt flows are financing raised through bond issuance, bank lending, and supplier credits.

The data on FDI and portfolio equity are based on balance of payments data reported by the International Monetary Fund (IMF). These data are supplemented by staff estimates using data from the United Nations Conference on Trade and Development and official national sources for FDI data and from market sources for portfolio equity data.

Under the internationally accepted definition of FDI, provided in the fifth edition of the IMF's *Balance of Payments Manual* (1993), FDI has three components: equity investment, reinvested earnings, and short- and long-term loans between parent firms and foreign affiliates. Distinguished from other kinds of international investment, FDI is made to establish a lasting interest in or effective management control over an enterprise in another country. As a guideline the IMF suggests that investments should account for at least 10 percent of voting stock to be counted as FDI. In practice many countries set a higher threshold. Also, many countries fail to report reinvested earnings, and the definition of long-term loans differs among countries.

FDI data do not give a complete picture of international investment in an economy. Balance of payments data on FDI do not include capital raised locally, which has become an important source of financing for investment projects in some developing countries. In addition, FDI data capture only cross-border investment flows involving equity participation and thus omit nonequity crossborder transactions such as intrafirm flows of goods and services. For a detailed discussion of the data issues, see the World Bank's *World Debt Tables 1993–94* (vol. 1, chap. 3).

Statistics on bonds, bank lending, and supplier credits are produced by aggregating individual transactions of public and publicly guaranteed debt and private nonguaranteed debt. Data on public and publicly guaranteed debt are reported through the Debtor Reporting System by World Bank member economies that have received either loans from the International Bank for Reconstruction and Development or credits from the International Development Association. These reports are cross-checked with data reported from market sources that also provide transactional data. Information on private nonguaranteed bonds and bank lending is collected from market sources, because official national sources reporting to the Debtor Reporting System are not asked to report the breakdown between private nonguaranteed bonds and private nonguaranteed loans.

The volume of global private financial flows reported by the World Bank generally differs from that reported by other sources because of differences in sources, classification of economies, and method used to adjust and disaggregate reported information. In addition, particularly for debt financing, differences may also result based on whether particular installments of the transactions are included and how certain offshore issuances are treated.

## Definitions

• **Foreign direct investment** is net inflows of investment to acquire a lasting interest in or management control over an enterprise operating in an economy other than that of the investor. It is the sum of equity capital, reinvestment of earnings, other long-term capital, and short-term capital, as shown in the balance of payments. • **Portfolio equity** includes net inflows from equity securities other than those recorded as direct investment and including shares, stocks, depository receipts and direct purchases of shares in local stock markets by foreign investors • **Bonds** are securities issued with a fixed rate of interest for a period of more than one year. They include net flows through cross-border public and publicly guaranteed and private nonguaranteed bond issues. • **Commercial bank and other lending** includes net commercial bank lending (public and publicly guaranteed and private nonguaranteed) and other private credits.

### Financial integration of low-income economies remains marginal     6.10a

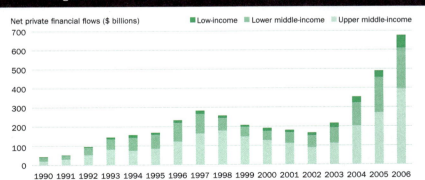

Net private financial flows ($ billions)   ■ Low-income  ■ Lower middle-income  ■ Upper middle-income

Since 2002 net private financial flows to developing countries have risen sharply, driven by increased foreign direct investment. However, financial integration of low-income economies remains marginal.

**Note:** Net private financial flows are the sum of net flows of foreign direct investment, portfolio equity, bonds, and commercial bank and other lending.
*Source:* World Bank Debtor Reporting System.

## Data sources

Data on equity and debt flows are compiled from a variety of public and private sources, including the World Bank's Debtor Reporting System, the IMF's *International Financial Statistics* and Balance of Payments databases, and Dealogic. These data are also published in the World Bank's *Global Development Finance 2008*.

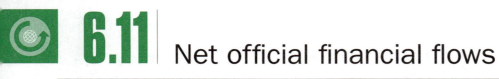
| | Total | | International financial institutions | | | | | | | United Nations[a] | | | |
|---|---|---|---|---|---|---|---|---|---|---|---|---|---|
| | $ millions | | | | | | | | | $ millions | | | |
| | | | World Bank | | IMF | | Regional development banks[a] | | Other institutions | | | | |
| | From bilateral sources[a,b] | From multilateral sources[a,b] | IDA | IBRD | Conces-sional | Non-concessional | Conces-sional | Non-concessional | | UNICEF | UNRWA | WFP | Others |
| | 2006 | 2006 | 2006 | 2006 | 2006 | 2006 | 2006 | 2006 | 2006 | 2006 | 2006 | 2006 | 2006 |
| Afghanistan | 39.7 | 163.1 | 37.0 | 0.0 | 0.0 | 0.0 | 66.2 | 0.0 | 0.1 | 18.5 | 0.0 | 1.5 | 39.8 |
| Albania | 25.6 | 97.3 | 40.9 | 0.0 | −7.6 | 3.6 | 0.0 | 17.2 | 37.5 | 1.1 | 0.0 | 0.0 | 4.6 |
| Algeria | −8,452.4 | −2,262.6 | 0.0 | −661.0 | 0.0 | 0.0 | 0.0 | −234.1 | −1,377.7 | 1.3 | 0.0 | 2.2 | 6.7 |
| Angola | −685.3 | 42.1 | 12.4 | 0.0 | 0.0 | 0.0 | 1.7 | −1.6 | −6.0 | 10.2 | 0.0 | 1.8 | 23.6 |
| Argentina | −1.2 | −10,548.3 | 0.0 | −674.6 | 0.0 | −9,793.3 | 0.0 | −85.0 | 0.0 | 0.6 | 0.0 | 0.0 | 4.0 |
| Armenia | 9.1 | 49.1 | 57.7 | −0.7 | −21.5 | 0.0 | 0.0 | −7.9 | 7.6 | 0.8 | 0.0 | 1.2 | 11.9 |
| Australia | | | | | | | | | | | | | |
| Austria | | | | | | | | | | | | | |
| Azerbaijan | −18.6 | 48.2 | 56.3 | 5.4 | −24.1 | −13.1 | 4.0 | 7.2 | −1.3 | 1.5 | 0.0 | 1.7 | 10.6 |
| Bangladesh | 115.6 | 639.9 | 225.7 | 0.0 | 150.0 | 0.0 | 106.1 | 81.8 | 23.9 | 11.8 | 0.0 | 5.1 | 35.5 |
| Belarus | 19.3 | −14.1 | 0.0 | −10.3 | 0.0 | 0.0 | 0.0 | −7.9 | 0.0 | 0.6 | 0.0 | 0.0 | 3.5 |
| Belgium | | | | | | | | | | | | | |
| Benin | −16.5 | 52.2 | 24.2 | 0.0 | 1.3 | 0.0 | 17.5 | −0.2 | −9.2 | 4.3 | 0.0 | 2.5 | 11.8 |
| Bolivia | 57.4 | 9.1 | 22.4 | 0.0 | 0.0 | 0.0 | 42.0 | −54.7 | −11.0 | 1.5 | 0.0 | 2.9 | 6.0 |
| Bosnia and Herzegovina | −26.4 | 11.1 | 22.9 | −23.6 | 0.0 | −43.9 | 0.0 | 2.5 | 38.7 | 1.1 | 0.0 | 0.0 | 13.4 |
| Botswana | −7.4 | −23.8 | −0.5 | −1.1 | 0.0 | 0.0 | −2.2 | −8.9 | −17.2 | 1.0 | 0.0 | 0.0 | 5.1 |
| Brazil | −2,658.8 | 2,255.6 | 0.0 | 1,460.1 | 0.0 | 0.0 | 0.0 | 794.0 | −9.7 | 2.2 | 0.0 | 0.0 | 9.0 |
| Bulgaria | 20.0 | −686.1 | 0.0 | −237.3 | 0.0 | −346.1 | 0.0 | −7.1 | −95.6 | .. | .. | .. | 0.0 |
| Burkina Faso | 29.1 | 170.4 | 28.1 | 0.0 | 19.0 | 0.0 | 48.2 | 0.0 | 43.6 | 7.3 | 0.0 | 2.4 | 21.8 |
| Burundi | 0.0 | 69.1 | 12.5 | 0.0 | 21.0 | 0.0 | 9.3 | 0.0 | 1.2 | 8.0 | 0.0 | 1.5 | 15.6 |
| Cambodia | 67.6 | 94.9 | 15.1 | 0.0 | 0.0 | 0.0 | 51.0 | 0.0 | 4.3 | 5.0 | 0.0 | 2.7 | 16.8 |
| Cameroon | −84.6 | 1.2 | 20.7 | −38.7 | −17.3 | 0.0 | 19.5 | −15.4 | 10.5 | 3.6 | 0.0 | 1.8 | 16.5 |
| Canada | | | | | | | | | | | | | |
| Central African Republic | 0.0 | −24.8 | −46.7 | 0.0 | −6.0 | 10.2 | 0.0 | 0.0 | 0.0 | 2.7 | 0.0 | 3.7 | 11.3 |
| Chad | 23.6 | 65.7 | 20.5 | −4.7 | −15.6 | 0.0 | 27.7 | 0.0 | 16.3 | 5.8 | 0.0 | 3.4 | 12.3 |
| Chile | −19.6 | 70.8 | −0.7 | 56.8 | 0.0 | 0.0 | −1.0 | 13.7 | 0.0 | 0.4 | 0.0 | 0.0 | 1.6 |
| China | 81.0 | 868.6 | −208.2 | 233.2 | 0.0 | 0.0 | 0.0 | 800.5 | −5.3 | 11.1 | 0.0 | 0.0 | 37.3 |
| Hong Kong, China | .. | .. | | | | | | | | | | | |
| Colombia | −101.2 | 1,224.1 | −0.7 | 683.9 | 0.0 | 0.0 | −14.3 | 698.2 | −151.9 | 1.1 | 0.0 | 1.7 | 6.1 |
| Congo, Dem. Rep. | −114.6 | 163.1 | 106.4 | 0.0 | 0.0 | 0.0 | 3.1 | 0.0 | −13.8 | 26.1 | 0.0 | 2.0 | 39.3 |
| Congo, Rep. | −18.3 | 1.5 | 3.1 | 0.0 | 7.5 | 0.0 | −0.9 | −17.2 | −2.3 | 1.7 | 0.0 | 0.6 | 9.0 |
| Costa Rica | 0.1 | −114.9 | −0.2 | −5.7 | 0.0 | 0.0 | −11.6 | −44.2 | −57.5 | 0.6 | 0.0 | 0.0 | 3.7 |
| Côte d'Ivoire | 12.5 | −12.6 | 0.0 | 0.0 | −57.5 | 0.0 | 0.0 | −1.4 | 19.1 | 6.4 | 0.0 | 3.3 | 17.5 |
| Croatia | −134.4 | 454.2 | 0.0 | 169.5 | 0.0 | 0.0 | 0.0 | 94.5 | 185.1 | 0.3 | 0.0 | 0.0 | 4.8 |
| Cuba | .. | 8.3 | .. | .. | .. | .. | .. | .. | .. | 0.7 | 0.0 | 3.4 | 4.2 |
| Czech Republic | .. | .. | .. | .. | .. | .. | .. | .. | .. | .. | .. | .. | .. |
| Denmark | | | | | | | | | | | | | |
| Dominican Republic | 244.3 | 111.6 | −0.7 | 32.7 | 0.0 | 37.0 | −21.0 | 59.1 | −0.6 | 1.0 | 0.0 | 0.0 | 4.1 |
| Ecuador | −247.0 | 284.1 | −1.1 | −53.5 | 0.0 | −58.3 | −26.5 | 26.4 | 391.3 | 1.0 | 0.0 | 1.0 | 3.8 |
| Egypt, Arab Rep. | −954.3 | −62.9 | 14.4 | 42.0 | 0.0 | 0.0 | 1.5 | −34.2 | −109.5 | 3.0 | 0.0 | 1.1 | 18.8 |
| El Salvador | −37.7 | 50.7 | −0.8 | −19.1 | 0.0 | 0.0 | −23.1 | 24.5 | 61.5 | 0.8 | 0.0 | 1.0 | 5.9 |
| Eritrea | 2.4 | 48.6 | 19.5 | 0.0 | 0.0 | 0.0 | 5.1 | 0.0 | 4.3 | 3.9 | 0.0 | 0.7 | 15.1 |
| Estonia | .. | .. | .. | .. | .. | .. | .. | .. | .. | .. | .. | .. | .. |
| Ethiopia | 74.1 | 327.6 | 156.5 | 0.0 | 0.0 | 0.0 | 35.2 | −18.5 | 59.0 | 25.8 | 0.0 | 16.0 | 53.6 |
| Finland | | | | | | | | | | | | | |
| France | | | | | | | | | | | | | |
| Gabon | 14.4 | −0.8 | 0.0 | −11.8 | 0.0 | −14.4 | −0.2 | −1.1 | 20.9 | 0.6 | 0.0 | 0.0 | 5.2 |
| Gambia, The | 0.8 | 43.9 | 7.7 | 0.0 | −4.0 | 0.0 | 6.7 | 0.0 | 24.9 | 1.2 | 0.0 | 1.4 | 6.0 |
| Georgia | −66.0 | 42.4 | 72.3 | 0.0 | −8.0 | 0.0 | 0.0 | 3.1 | −35.0 | 1.0 | 0.0 | 1.2 | 7.8 |
| Germany | | | | | | | | | | | | | |
| Ghana | −66.2 | 413.9 | 231.6 | 0.0 | 116.4 | 0.0 | 47.8 | −16.7 | 6.4 | 4.5 | 0.0 | 2.4 | 21.5 |
| Greece | | | | | | | | | | | | | |
| Guatemala | −62.1 | 427.8 | 0.0 | 162.6 | 0.0 | 0.0 | −18.6 | 83.9 | 181.6 | 1.0 | 0.0 | 4.9 | 12.4 |
| Guinea | −40.6 | −15.7 | −1.8 | 0.0 | −19.4 | 0.0 | 9.5 | −7.3 | −24.2 | 4.4 | 0.0 | 4.3 | 18.8 |
| Guinea-Bissau | −10.5 | 9.1 | −0.3 | 0.0 | −3.8 | 0.0 | 0.8 | 0.0 | 1.9 | 2.0 | 0.0 | 1.7 | 6.8 |
| Haiti | −4.3 | 65.8 | −9.1 | 0.0 | −4.4 | 14.9 | 43.5 | 0.0 | −1.3 | 2.8 | 0.0 | 2.8 | 16.6 |

| | Total ($ millions) | | International financial institutions ($ millions) | | | | | | | United Nations[a] ($ millions) | | | |
|---|---|---|---|---|---|---|---|---|---|---|---|---|---|
| | | | World Bank | | IMF | | Regional development banks[a] | | | | | | |
| | From bilateral sources | From multilateral sources[a,b] | IDA | IBRD | Conces-sional | Non-concessional | Conces-sional | Non-concessional | Other institutions | UNICEF | UNRWA | WFP | Others |
| | 2006 | 2006 | 2006 | 2006 | 2006 | 2006 | 2006 | 2006 | 2006 | 2006 | 2006 | 2006 | 2006 |
| Honduras | −13.4 | 156.3 | 49.9 | 0.0 | 15.0 | 0.0 | 76.5 | −19.0 | 24.1 | 1.0 | 0.0 | 0.6 | 8.2 |
| Hungary | −33.2 | 134.2 | 0.0 | −39.0 | 0.0 | 0.0 | 0.0 | 162.4 | 10.8 | .. | .. | .. | 0.0 |
| India | 703.1 | 1,553.5 | 239.2 | 606.2 | 0.0 | 0.0 | 0.0 | 564.0 | 31.1 | 38.0 | 0.0 | 9.6 | 65.4 |
| Indonesia | 154.3 | −8,026.3 | 288.3 | −706.4 | 0.0 | −8,037.1 | 75.8 | 242.0 | 0.0 | 7.7 | 0.0 | 67.1 | 36.3 |
| Iran, Islamic Rep. | −36.4 | 190.0 | 0.0 | 181.2 | 0.0 | 0.0 | 0.0 | 0.0 | −9.0 | 2.1 | 0.0 | 0.2 | 15.5 |
| Iraq | .. | 12.6 | .. | .. | .. | .. | .. | .. | .. | 2.2 | 0.0 | 0.6 | 9.8 |
| Ireland | | | | | | | | | | | | | |
| Israel | .. | .. | .. | .. | .. | .. | .. | .. | .. | .. | .. | .. | .. |
| Italy | | | | | | | | | | | | | |
| Jamaica | −87.4 | −52.9 | 0.0 | −25.3 | 0.0 | 0.0 | −5.3 | −34.7 | 10.1 | 0.8 | 0.0 | 0.0 | 1.5 |
| Japan | | | | | | | | | | | | | |
| Jordan | −89.1 | 42.9 | −2.6 | −35.1 | 0.0 | −88.4 | 0.0 | 0.0 | 63.5 | 0.8 | 100.8 | 0.4 | 3.5 |
| Kazakhstan | 30.6 | −47.9 | 0.0 | −101.1 | 0.0 | 0.0 | −0.9 | −3.6 | 51.8 | 1.1 | 0.0 | 0.0 | 4.8 |
| Kenya | 12.0 | −102.4 | −18.4 | 0.0 | −13.6 | 0.0 | 9.8 | −8.4 | −126.4 | 6.9 | 0.0 | 14.0 | 33.7 |
| Korea, Dem. Rep. | .. | 13.9 | .. | .. | .. | .. | .. | .. | .. | 1.7 | 0.0 | 1.8 | 10.4 |
| Korea, Rep. | .. | .. | .. | .. | .. | .. | .. | .. | .. | .. | .. | .. | .. |
| Kuwait | .. | .. | .. | .. | .. | .. | .. | .. | .. | .. | .. | .. | .. |
| Kyrgyz Republic | 8.8 | 35.6 | 19.4 | 0.0 | −23.7 | 0.0 | 40.5 | −8.8 | −0.2 | 1.1 | 0.0 | 0.0 | 7.3 |
| Lao PDR | −20.4 | 92.5 | 16.9 | 0.0 | −3.3 | 0.0 | 57.9 | 5.0 | −2.7 | 2.0 | 0.0 | 3.0 | 13.7 |
| Latvia | −0.5 | 95.2 | 0.0 | −19.0 | 0.0 | 0.0 | 0.0 | −0.8 | 115.0 | .. | .. | .. | 0.0 |
| Lebanon | −54.1 | 0.5 | 0.0 | −52.5 | 0.0 | 0.0 | 0.0 | 0.0 | −15.6 | 2.0 | 62.0 | 0.0 | 4.6 |
| Lesotho | −8.6 | 16.8 | 5.6 | −3.6 | −0.5 | 0.0 | 8.2 | −1.0 | −1.2 | 1.1 | 0.0 | 2.5 | 5.7 |
| Liberia | 0.0 | 27.2 | 0.0 | 0.0 | 0.0 | −0.7 | 0.0 | 0.0 | 0.0 | 4.1 | 0.0 | 3.1 | 20.7 |
| Libya | .. | 2.0 | | | | | | | | 0.0 | 0.0 | 0.4 | 1.6 |
| Lithuania | −158.4 | −26.0 | 0.0 | −8.6 | 0.0 | 0.0 | 0.0 | −2.8 | −14.6 | .. | .. | .. | 0.0 |
| Macedonia, FYR | −30.0 | 28.7 | 1.8 | −0.3 | −8.5 | −1.0 | 0.0 | 12.7 | 16.5 | 0.6 | 0.0 | 0.0 | 6.9 |
| Madagascar | 8.4 | 266.1 | 162.2 | 0.0 | 11.6 | 0.0 | 60.1 | 0.0 | 4.2 | 6.0 | 0.0 | 2.9 | 19.1 |
| Malawi | −0.9 | 64.0 | 20.3 | 0.0 | 3.7 | −6.4 | 16.9 | −1.8 | −0.7 | 7.8 | 0.0 | 4.4 | 19.8 |
| Malaysia | −278.3 | −131.3 | 0.0 | −96.3 | 0.0 | 0.0 | 0.0 | −54.6 | 14.1 | 0.6 | 0.0 | 0.0 | 4.9 |
| Mali | 20.6 | 155.4 | 93.4 | 0.0 | 5.9 | 0.0 | 22.6 | 0.0 | 4.0 | 9.5 | 0.0 | 2.5 | 17.5 |
| Mauritania | 3.6 | 118.7 | 42.0 | 0.0 | −23.0 | 0.0 | 6.9 | −7.6 | 82.9 | 1.8 | 0.0 | 4.7 | 11.0 |
| Mauritius | −50.3 | −35.3 | −0.6 | −7.3 | 0.0 | 0.0 | −0.1 | −29.1 | −1.0 | 0.0 | 0.0 | 0.0 | 2.8 |
| Mexico | −272.7 | −8,302.2 | 0.0 | −4,671.1 | 0.0 | 0.0 | 0.0 | −3,641.6 | 0.0 | 0.8 | 0.0 | 0.0 | 9.7 |
| Moldova | −19.4 | 53.2 | 22.6 | −13.9 | 59.8 | −20.1 | 0.0 | −5.4 | 1.2 | 0.8 | 0.0 | 0.0 | 8.2 |
| Mongolia | 10.5 | 45.8 | 10.4 | 0.0 | −6.0 | 0.0 | 23.3 | 0.0 | 7.3 | 0.9 | 0.0 | 0.0 | 9.9 |
| Morocco | 23.2 | 448.7 | −1.4 | −154.0 | 0.0 | 0.0 | −0.8 | 364.0 | 231.0 | 1.6 | 0.0 | 0.0 | 8.3 |
| Mozambique | −5.7 | 411.3 | 215.3 | 0.0 | 4.8 | 0.0 | 102.4 | 20.0 | 11.0 | 9.5 | 0.0 | 8.5 | 39.8 |
| Myanmar | −51.1 | 33.9 | 0.0 | 0.0 | 0.0 | 0.0 | 0.0 | 0.0 | −2.2 | 9.9 | 0.0 | 1.1 | 25.1 |
| Namibia | .. | 8.4 | .. | .. | .. | .. | .. | .. | .. | 1.5 | 0.0 | 1.0 | 5.9 |
| Nepal | −31.2 | 150.8 | 12.4 | 0.0 | 21.2 | 0.0 | 75.2 | 0.0 | 1.2 | 6.3 | 0.0 | 7.5 | 27.0 |
| Netherlands | | | | | | | | | | | | | |
| New Zealand | | | | | | | | | | | | | |
| Nicaragua | 8.4 | 295.3 | 56.3 | 0.0 | 61.5 | 0.0 | 111.9 | −8.8 | 61.0 | 1.3 | 0.0 | 0.6 | 11.5 |
| Niger | −10.4 | 3.1 | 46.6 | 0.0 | −105.5 | 0.0 | 21.6 | −2.5 | 6.1 | 12.2 | 0.0 | 7.3 | 17.3 |
| Nigeria | −4,336.1 | 133.8 | 342.7 | −210.8 | 0.0 | 0.0 | 7.3 | −78.8 | 0.0 | 31.1 | 0.0 | 0.0 | 42.3 |
| Norway | | | | | | | | | | | | | |
| Oman | 14.6 | −39.6 | 0.0 | 0.0 | 0.0 | 0.0 | 0.0 | 0.0 | −41.3 | 0.1 | 0.0 | 0.0 | 1.6 |
| Pakistan | −49.7 | 1,274.8 | 688.3 | −128.6 | −78.9 | −28.2 | 105.8 | 448.3 | 172.8 | 14.9 | 0.0 | 10.9 | 69.5 |
| Panama | −11.2 | 44.0 | 0.0 | −26.2 | 0.0 | −9.8 | −7.9 | 70.0 | 13.4 | 0.4 | 0.0 | 0.3 | 3.8 |
| Papua New Guinea | −15.8 | −27.2 | −3.6 | −5.6 | 0.0 | 0.0 | 6.1 | −29.3 | −2.6 | 1.9 | 0.0 | 0.0 | 5.9 |
| Paraguay | −20.8 | 14.5 | −1.5 | 5.8 | 0.0 | 0.0 | −15.1 | 21.2 | −0.4 | 1.0 | 0.0 | 0.0 | 3.5 |
| Peru | −305.5 | −144.1 | 0.0 | −182.5 | 0.0 | −39.4 | −8.2 | 202.3 | −144.7 | 1.5 | 0.0 | 0.6 | 26.3 |
| Philippines | −213.0 | −192.4 | −6.8 | −250.8 | 0.0 | −400.3 | −25.0 | 468.3 | −2.4 | 3.3 | 0.0 | 1.7 | 19.6 |
| Poland | −1,991.5 | 15.3 | 0.0 | 15.3 | 0.0 | 0.0 | 0.0 | 0.0 | 0.0 | .. | .. | .. | 0.0 |
| Portugal | | | | | | | | | | | | | |
| Puerto Rico | | | | | | | | | | | | | |

# 6.11 | Net official financial flows

| | Total | | International financial institutions | | | | | | | United Nations[a] | | | |
|---|---|---|---|---|---|---|---|---|---|---|---|---|---|
| | $ millions | | | | | | | | | $ millions | | | |
| | | | World Bank | | IMF | | Regional development banks[a] | | | | | | | |
| | From bilateral sources | From multilateral sources[a,b] | IDA | IBRD | Concessional | Non-concessional | Concessional | Non-concessional | Other institutions | UNICEF | UNRWA | WFP | Others |
| | 2006 | 2006 | 2006 | 2006 | 2006 | 2006 | 2006 | 2006 | 2006 | 2006 | 2006 | 2006 | 2006 |
| Romania | 17.9 | −44.6 | 0.0 | −54.3 | 0.0 | −167.3 | 6.8 | −32.9 | 203.1 | .. | .. | .. | 0.0 |
| Russian Federation | −25,232.5 | −221.1 | 0.0 | −369.6 | 0.0 | 0.0 | 0.0 | 119.9 | 28.6 | .. | .. | .. | 0.0 |
| Rwanda | −3.9 | 85.5 | 28.6 | 0.0 | 2.5 | 0.0 | 24.3 | 0.0 | −3.3 | 6.1 | 0.0 | 5.4 | 21.9 |
| Saudi Arabia | .. | 2.8 | .. | .. | .. | .. | .. | .. | .. | 0.0 | 0.0 | 0.0 | 2.8 |
| Senegal | −19.5 | 183.9 | 115.8 | 0.0 | 20.4 | 0.0 | 21.3 | −12.5 | 9.6 | 4.0 | 0.0 | 3.9 | 21.4 |
| Serbia | 7.5 | −651.5 | 56.5 | −250.2 | 0.0 | −652.9 | 0.0 | 53.9 | 118.2 | 1.0 | 0.0 | 0.0 | 22.0 |
| Sierra Leone | 0.0 | 69.3 | 7.2 | 0.0 | 8.9 | 0.0 | 16.7 | 0.0 | 6.4 | 5.3 | 0.0 | 4.8 | 20.0 |
| Singapore | .. | .. | .. | .. | .. | .. | .. | .. | .. | .. | .. | .. | .. |
| Slovak Republic | −63.9 | −42.8 | 0.0 | −32.9 | 0.0 | 0.0 | 0.0 | −3.9 | −6.0 | .. | .. | .. | 0.0 |
| Slovenia | .. | .. | .. | .. | .. | .. | .. | .. | .. | .. | .. | .. | .. |
| Somalia | 0.0 | 24.6 | 0.0 | 0.0 | 0.0 | 0.0 | 0.0 | 0.0 | 0.0 | 7.4 | 0.0 | 4.4 | 12.8 |
| South Africa | 0.0 | 31.7 | 0.0 | −1.8 | 0.0 | 0.0 | 0.0 | 24.5 | 0.0 | 1.2 | 0.0 | 0.0 | 7.8 |
| Spain | | | | | | | | | | | | | |
| Sri Lanka | 86.8 | 70.3 | 57.1 | 0.0 | 0.0 | −153.6 | 88.4 | 39.1 | 14.4 | 0.9 | 0.0 | 0.8 | 23.2 |
| Sudan | −41.7 | 229.5 | −2.0 | 0.0 | 0.0 | −27.0 | 0.0 | 0.0 | 136.9 | 17.4 | 0.0 | 55.9 | 48.3 |
| Swaziland | −5.4 | 45.6 | −0.3 | −1.2 | 0.0 | 0.0 | −1.0 | 11.5 | 30.6 | 1.0 | 0.0 | 0.0 | 5.0 |
| Sweden | | | | | | | | | | | | | |
| Switzerland | | | | | | | | | | | | | |
| Syrian Arab Republic | −92.5 | 6.1 | −1.5 | 0.0 | 0.0 | 0.0 | 0.0 | 0.0 | −34.8 | 1.6 | 35.2 | 0.9 | 4.7 |
| Tajikistan | 46.8 | 97.1 | 16.2 | 0.0 | 14.4 | 0.0 | 35.2 | −1.4 | 20.6 | 2.6 | 0.0 | 1.2 | 8.3 |
| Tanzania | 54.1 | 522.4 | 384.9 | 0.0 | 4.1 | 0.0 | 44.4 | −0.9 | 42.0 | 12.9 | 0.0 | 5.5 | 29.5 |
| Thailand | −512.6 | −171.2 | −3.4 | −50.2 | 0.0 | 0.0 | −2.9 | −117.1 | −14.0 | 1.8 | 0.0 | 0.0 | 14.6 |
| Timor-Leste | .. | 9.1 | .. | .. | .. | .. | .. | .. | .. | 1.6 | 0.0 | 0.2 | 7.3 |
| Togo | −1.8 | 13.0 | 0.0 | 0.0 | −6.4 | 0.0 | 0.1 | −1.4 | 9.8 | 2.2 | 0.0 | 0.4 | 8.3 |
| Trinidad and Tobago | .. | 0.7 | .. | .. | .. | .. | .. | .. | .. | 0.0 | 0.0 | 0.0 | 0.7 |
| Tunisia | −29.4 | −174.0 | −2.1 | −254.6 | 0.0 | 0.0 | 0.0 | −124.9 | 203.2 | 1.0 | 0.0 | 0.0 | 3.4 |
| Turkey | −323.1 | −3,496.3 | −5.9 | 989.1 | 0.0 | −4,552.0 | 0.0 | 0.0 | 60.0 | 2.0 | 0.0 | 0.0 | 10.5 |
| Turkmenistan | −125.5 | −6.3 | 0.0 | −8.2 | 0.0 | 0.0 | 0.0 | 0.0 | −2.8 | 1.1 | 0.0 | 0.0 | 3.6 |
| Uganda | −32.5 | 266.8 | 131.4 | 0.0 | 2.9 | 0.0 | 50.6 | −2.4 | 29.3 | 11.7 | 0.0 | 9.7 | 33.6 |
| Ukraine | −279.8 | −546.7 | 0.0 | −85.8 | 0.0 | −410.5 | 0.0 | −48.2 | −13.0 | 1.4 | 0.0 | 0.0 | 9.4 |
| United Arab Emirates | .. | .. | .. | .. | .. | .. | .. | .. | .. | .. | .. | .. | .. |
| United Kingdom | | | | | | | | | | | | | |
| United States | | | | | | | | | | | | | |
| Uruguay | −9.8 | −2,934.8 | 0.0 | −162.8 | 0.0 | −2,372.1 | −2.4 | −401.7 | 0.5 | 0.5 | 0.0 | 0.0 | 3.2 |
| Uzbekistan | −106.4 | 71.1 | 13.4 | 11.2 | 0.0 | 0.0 | 0.2 | 22.8 | 13.3 | 2.5 | 0.0 | 0.0 | 7.7 |
| Venezuela, RB | 226.0 | 179.5 | 0.0 | −149.7 | 0.0 | 0.0 | 0.0 | −164.3 | 484.1 | 0.8 | 0.0 | 0.0 | 8.6 |
| Vietnam | 357.4 | 500.1 | 317.4 | 0.0 | −32.8 | 0.0 | 159.0 | 10.1 | 19.0 | 3.9 | 0.0 | 0.0 | 23.5 |
| West Bank and Gaza | .. | 408.0 | .. | .. | .. | .. | .. | .. | .. | 5.0 | 402.0 | 0.9 | 0.1 |
| Yemen, Rep. | 45.1 | 172.8 | 129.2 | 0.0 | −47.1 | −13.0 | 0.0 | 0.0 | 71.1 | 5.2 | 0.0 | 6.6 | 20.8 |
| Zambia | −24.6 | 120.2 | 23.1 | 0.0 | 24.3 | 0.0 | 27.9 | −14.8 | 11.6 | 5.8 | 0.0 | 16.4 | 25.9 |
| Zimbabwe | 12.4 | 22.8 | 0.0 | 0.0 | −0.4 | −3.1 | 0.0 | 0.0 | 1.6 | 2.5 | 0.0 | 8.3 | 13.9 |
| **World** | .. s | .. s | .. s | .. s | .. s | .. s | .. s | .. s | .. s | 740.1 s | 599.9 s | 473.5 s | 2,099.4 s |
| **Low income** | −3,358.6 | 8,923.0 | 3,879.8 | 267.8 | −18.0 | −53.1 | 1,415.6 | 937.2 | 708.1 | 398.4 | 0.0 | 261.8 | 1,125.4 |
| **Middle income** | −42,730.3 | −30,303.7 | 679.4 | −5,522.5 | 87.5 | −27,136.2 | 287.0 | −798.2 | 643.9 | 114.5 | 599.9 | 108.3 | 632.7 |
| Lower middle income | −11,843.3 | −6,312.8 | 616.3 | −1,234.0 | 81.8 | −9,225.0 | 314.2 | 2,362.3 | −441.3 | 91.8 | 538.0 | 107.6 | 475.5 |
| Upper middle income | −30,887.0 | −24,025.7 | 63.1 | −4,288.4 | 5.7 | −17,911.2 | −27.2 | −3,160.4 | 1,085.1 | 17.7 | 62.0 | 0.7 | 127.2 |
| **Low & middle income** | −46,088.9 | −20,714.6 | 4,559.2 | −5,254.7 | 69.5 | −27,189.3 | 1,702.6 | 139.0 | 1,352.0 | 738.2 | 599.9 | 473.3 | 2,095.7 |
| East Asia & Pacific | −421.0 | −6,844.8 | 430.3 | −878.3 | −42.0 | −8,437.4 | 345.4 | 1,330.9 | 34.7 | 54.7 | 0.0 | 77.5 | 239.4 |
| Europe & Central Asia | −28,383.9 | −4,526.2 | 374.0 | −64.4 | −19.2 | −6,203.2 | 85.7 | 367.1 | 758.1 | 24.2 | 0.0 | 5.3 | 146.2 |
| Latin America & Carib. | −3,235.8 | −16,719.7 | 127.3 | −3,572.8 | 105.0 | −12,224.2 | 161.0 | −2,454.8 | 896.7 | 23.7 | 0.0 | 20.2 | 198.2 |
| Middle East & N. Africa | −9,625.6 | −1,168.0 | 143.8 | −934.0 | −48.7 | −101.4 | 1.0 | −21.4 | −997.7 | 27.4 | 599.9 | 14.4 | 148.7 |
| South Asia | 893.5 | 3,917.0 | 1,271.4 | 477.7 | 92.3 | −181.7 | 449.3 | 1,133.1 | 271.3 | 92.6 | 0.0 | 36.7 | 274.3 |
| Sub-Saharan Africa | −5,316.0 | 4,063.2 | 2,212.3 | −282.9 | −17.9 | −41.3 | 660.2 | −216.0 | 389.0 | 293.3 | 0.0 | 217.4 | 849.1 |
| **High income** | .. | 5.7 | .. | .. | .. | .. | .. | .. | .. | 1.8 | 0.0 | 0.2 | 3.7 |
| Euro area | | | | | | | | | | | | | |

a. Aggregates include amounts for economies not specified elsewhere. b. World and income group aggregates include flows not allocated by country or region.

## About the data

The table shows financing from official bilateral and multilateral sources. It shows concessional and nonconcessional financial flows from the major multilateral institutions—the World Bank, the International Monetary Fund (IMF), regional development banks, other international financial institutions, and UN agencies.

The multilateral development banks fund their nonconcessional lending operations primarily by selling low-interest, highly rated bonds backed by prudent lending and financial policies and the strong financial support of their members. Funds are then on-lent at slightly higher interest rates with 15- to 20-year maturities to developing countries. Lending terms vary with market conditions and bank policies.

Concessional flows from multilateral development banks are credits provided through their concessional lending facilities. The cost of these loans is reduced through subsidies from donors or other resources. Grants from multilateral agencies are not included in the net flows. Concessional flows from bilateral donors are defined by the Organisation for Economic Co-operation and Development's (OECD) Development Assistance Committee (DAC) as financial flows with a grant element of at least 25 percent. The grant element is evaluated assuming a 10 percent nominal discount rate. The grant element is nil for a loan with a 10 percent interest rate and 100 percent for a grant, which requires no repayment.

All World Bank concessional lending is carried out by the International Development Association (IDA). Eligibility for IDA resources is based on gross national income (GNI) per capita and performance standards assessed by World Bank staff. The cutoff for IDA eligibility is set at the beginning of the World Bank's fiscal year. Since July 1, 2007, the GNI per capita cutoff has been $1,065, measured in 2006 U.S. dollars using the *World Bank Atlas* method (see *Users guide*). In exceptional circumstances IDA extends temporary eligibility to countries above the cutoff and that are undertaking major adjustment efforts but are not creditworthy for International Bank for Reconstruction and Development (IBRD) lending. Exceptions are also made for small island economies. The IBRD lends to creditworthy countries at an initial interest rate that consists of a variable base rate of six-month LIBOR, and a spread, either variable or fixed, for the life of the loan. The lending rate is reset every six months on the interest payment dates for the loan and applies to the interest period beginning on that date. Although some outstanding IBRD loans have a low enough interest rate to be classified as concessional under the DAC definition, all IBRD loans in the table are classified as nonconcessional. Lending by the International Finance Corporation is not included in the table.

The IMF makes concessional funds available through its Poverty Reduction and Growth Facility and the IMF Trust Fund. Eligibility is based principally on a country's per capita income and eligibility under IDA.

Regional development banks also maintain concessional windows. Loans from the major regional development banks are recorded in the table according to each institution's classification and not according to the DAC definition.

## Definitions

• **Total net official financial flows** are disbursements of public or publicly guaranteed loans and credits, less repayments of principal. • **IDA** is the International Development Association, the concessional loan window of the World Bank Group. • **IBRD** is the International Bank for Reconstruction and Development, the founding and largest member of the World Bank Group. • **IMF** is the International Monetary Fund, which provides concessional lending through the Poverty Reduction and Growth Facility and the IMF Trust Fund and nonconcessional lending through the credit it provides to its members, mainly to meet balance of payments needs. • **Regional development banks** are the African Development Bank, in Tunis, Tunisia, which serves all of Africa, including North Africa; the Asian Development Bank, in Manila, Philippines, which serves South and Central Asia and East Asia and Pacific; the European Bank for Reconstruction and Development, in London, United Kingdom, which serves Europe and Central Asia; and the Inter-American Development Bank, in Washington, D.C., which serves the Americas. • **Concessional** financial flows are disbursements made through concessional lending facilities. • **Nonconcessional** financial flows are all disbursements that are not concessional. • **Other institutions** is a residual category in the World Bank's Debtor Reporting System that includes other multilateral institutions such as the Caribbean Development Fund, Council of Europe, European Development Fund, Islamic Development Bank, Nordic Development Fund, and the like. • **United Nations** includes the United Nations Children's Fund (UNICEF), United Nations Relief and Works Agency for Palestine Refugees in the Near East (UNRWA), World Food Programme (WFP), and other UN agencies, such as the International Fund for Agricultural Development, United Nations Development Programme, United Nations Population Fund, United Nations Refugee Agency, and United Nations Regular Programme for Technical Assistance.

## Data sources

Data on net financial flows from international financial institutions are from the World Bank's Debtor Reporting System and published in the World Bank's *Global Development Finance 2008* and electronically as *GDF Online*. Data on aid from UN agencies are from the DAC annual *Development Cooperation Report* and are available electronically on the OECD's *International Development Statistics* CD-ROM and at www.oecd.org/dac/stats/idsonline.

---

**While net financial flows to middle-income economies are falling, low-income economies are still borrowing from international financial institutions** 6.11a

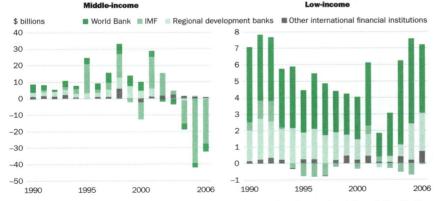

In recent years, as many middle-income economies paid off loans from international financial institutions, net disbursement fell sharply. But international financial institutions still maintain a positive flow of net disbursement to low-income economies.

*Source:* World Bank Debtor Reporting System.

## Net disbursements

| $ millions | Total net flows[a] 2006 | Official development assistance[a] Total 2006 | Bilateral grants 2006 | Bilateral loans 2006 | Contributions to multilateral institutions 2006 | Other official flows[a] 2006 | Private flows[a] Total 2006 | Foreign direct investment 2006 | Bilateral portfolio investment 2006 | Multilateral portfolio investment 2006 | Private export credits 2006 | Net grants by NGOs[a] 2006 |
|---|---|---|---|---|---|---|---|---|---|---|---|---|
| Australia | 9,120 | 2,123 | 1,773 | 23 | 327 | 308 | 6,074 | 4,968 | 978 | .. | 129 | 615 |
| Austria | 3,215 | 1,498 | 1,101 | −9 | 407 | −448 | 2,045 | 1,613 | 0 | .. | 433 | 119 |
| Belgium | 5,309 | 1,978 | 1,365 | −7 | 620 | −434 | 3,514 | 3,533 | 0 | .. | −19 | 251 |
| Canada | 14,234 | 3,684 | 2,573 | −42 | 1,153 | 356 | 9,093 | 7,717 | 427 | .. | 950 | 1,100 |
| Denmark | 2,686 | 2,236 | 1,525 | −61 | 772 | −77 | 454 | 454 | 0 | .. | .. | 73 |
| Finland | 1,413 | 834 | 442 | 13 | 380 | .. | 553 | 402 | 137 | .. | 14 | 25 |
| France | 22,329 | 10,601 | 8,422 | −503 | 2,681 | −1,388 | 13,116 | 10,589 | 3,983 | .. | −1,456 | .. |
| Germany | 27,203 | 10,435 | 7,576 | −542 | 3,401 | −5,728 | 21,149 | 12,401 | 7,672 | 1,057 | 19 | 1,348 |
| Greece | 2,896 | 424 | 189 | .. | 235 | 8 | 2,454 | 2,454 | 0 | .. | .. | 10 |
| Ireland | 5,237 | 1,022 | 632 | .. | 389 | .. | 3,877 | .. | 3,877 | .. | .. | 339 |
| Italy | 5,512 | 3,641 | 2,147 | −146 | 1,640 | −957 | 2,705 | 1,151 | −1,049 | .. | 2,602 | 123 |
| Japan | 26,230 | 11,187 | 7,660 | −347 | 3,874 | 2,438 | 12,290 | 14,144 | −1,201 | −928 | 275 | 315 |
| Luxembourg | 299 | 291 | 205 | .. | 86 | .. | .. | .. | .. | .. | .. | 8 |
| Netherlands | 28,616 | 5,452 | 4,415 | −133 | 1,169 | 343 | 22,544 | 6,351 | 10,728 | −248 | 5,713 | 277 |
| New Zealand | 338 | 259 | 203 | .. | 56 | 7 | 24 | 24 | 0 | .. | .. | 48 |
| Norway | 4,304 | 2,954 | 2,119 | 79 | 756 | 5 | 1,345 | 1,351 | 0 | .. | −6 | .. |
| Portugal | 666 | 396 | 198 | 14 | 185 | −20 | 286 | 44 | 0 | .. | 243 | 4 |
| Spain | 11,146 | 3,814 | 2,012 | 80 | 1,722 | .. | 7,333 | 7,608 | 0 | .. | −275 | .. |
| Sweden | 4,175 | 3,955 | 2,838 | 14 | 1,103 | −2 | 210 | 333 | 0 | .. | −123 | 12 |
| Switzerland | 11,306 | 1,646 | 1,241 | 13 | 392 | 17 | 9,241 | 10,001 | 0 | −239 | −521 | 402 |
| United Kingdom | 26,941 | 12,459 | 8,809 | −92 | 3,741 | −187 | 14,127 | 7,530 | 11,292 | .. | −4,696 | 543 |
| United States | 90,897 | 23,532 | 22,005 | −843 | 2,370 | −4,017 | 62,345 | 36,624 | 23,662 | 3,156 | −1,097 | 9,037 |
| **Total** | **304,074** | **104,421** | **79,450** | **−2,490** | **27,461** | **−9,774** | **194,779** | **129,291** | **60,507** | **2,798** | **2,183** | **14,648** |

## Official development assistance

| | Commitments[b] ($ millions) 2000 | 2006 | Gross disbursements[b] ($ millions) 2000 | 2006 | Net disbursements ($ millions)[b] 2000 | 2006 | per capita[b] $ 2000 | 2006 | % of GNI[a] 2000 | 2006 | % of general government disbursements[a] 2000 | 2006 |
|---|---|---|---|---|---|---|---|---|---|---|---|---|
| Australia | 1,793 | 2,058 | 1,545 | 2,058 | 1,545 | 2,058 | 80 | 100 | 0.27 | 0.30 | 0.72 | 0.82 |
| Austria | 841 | 1,485 | 649 | 1,476 | 645 | 1,465 | 80 | 177 | 0.23 | 0.47 | 0.44 | 0.94 |
| Belgium | 1,253 | 2,343 | 1,253 | 1,988 | 1,219 | 1,921 | 119 | 182 | 0.36 | 0.50 | 0.72 | 1.03 |
| Canada | 2,746 | 3,520 | 2,434 | 3,426 | 2,400 | 3,385 | 78 | 103 | 0.25 | 0.29 | 0.59 | 0.74 |
| Denmark | 2,390 | 2,051 | 2,549 | 2,249 | 2,523 | 2,173 | 472 | 399 | 1.06 | 0.80 | 1.93 | 1.58 |
| Finland | 502 | 947 | 537 | 824 | 527 | 820 | 102 | 156 | 0.31 | 0.40 | 0.63 | 0.81 |
| France | 6,960 | 14,617 | 7,422 | 12,417 | 6,094 | 10,313 | 103 | 163 | 0.30 | 0.47 | 0.60 | 0.88 |
| Germany | 8,119 | 13,005 | 8,241 | 11,844 | 7,140 | 10,257 | 87 | 124 | 0.27 | 0.36 | 0.59 | 0.79 |
| Greece | 354 | 407 | 354 | 407 | 354 | 407 | 32 | 37 | 0.20 | 0.17 | 0.39 | 0.37 |
| Ireland | 378 | 984 | 378 | 984 | 378 | 984 | 100 | 232 | 0.29 | 0.54 | 0.77 | 1.36 |
| Italy | 2,512 | 4,015 | 2,485 | 3,884 | 2,139 | 3,533 | 37 | 60 | 0.13 | 0.20 | 0.27 | 0.39 |
| Japan | 15,627 | 18,520 | 14,885 | 18,276 | 12,335 | 11,946 | 97 | 94 | 0.28 | 0.25 | 0.74 | 0.70 |
| Luxembourg | 191 | 269 | 191 | 269 | 191 | 269 | 433 | 584 | 0.71 | 0.89 | 1.61 | 1.75 |
| Netherlands | 5,305 | 12,343 | 4,975 | 5,757 | 4,833 | 5,329 | 303 | 326 | 0.84 | 0.81 | 1.84 | 1.76 |
| New Zealand | 212 | 378 | 200 | 275 | 200 | 275 | 52 | 66 | 0.25 | 0.27 | 0.55 | 0.60 |
| Norway | 1,798 | 3,148 | 2,029 | 2,732 | 2,020 | 2,732 | 450 | 584 | 0.76 | 0.89 | 1.77 | 2.16 |
| Portugal | 655 | 390 | 655 | 390 | 426 | 385 | 42 | 37 | 0.26 | 0.21 | 0.56 | 0.44 |
| Spain | 2,293 | 3,974 | 2,293 | 3,974 | 1,974 | 3,643 | 49 | 81 | 0.22 | 0.32 | 0.53 | 0.80 |
| Sweden | 1,907 | 4,141 | 2,386 | 3,854 | 2,386 | 3,854 | 269 | 423 | 0.80 | 1.02 | 1.30 | 1.85 |
| Switzerland | 1,276 | 1,874 | 1,257 | 1,652 | 1,254 | 1,641 | 175 | 219 | 0.34 | 0.39 | 1.07 | 1.24 |
| United Kingdom | 6,225 | 12,630 | 6,225 | 12,630 | 6,156 | 12,034 | 105 | 200 | 0.32 | 0.51 | 0.84 | 1.16 |
| United States | 14,215 | 25,920 | 12,246 | 23,834 | 11,223 | 22,863 | 41 | 76 | 0.10 | 0.18 | 0.30 | 0.49 |
| **Total** | **77,553** | **129,018** | **75,187** | **115,201** | **67,961** | **102,287** | **81** | **115** | **0.22** | **0.31** | **0.57** | **0.75** |

**Note:** Components may not sum to totals because of gaps in reporting.
a. At current prices and exchange rates. b. At 2005 prices and exchange rates.

The flows of official and private financial resources from the members of the Development Assistance Committee (DAC) of the Organisation for Economic Co-operation and Development (OECD) to developing economies are compiled by DAC, based principally on reporting by DAC members using standard questionnaires issued by the DAC Secretariat.

The table shows data reported by DAC member economies and does not include aid provided by the Commission of the European Communities—a multilateral member of DAC.

DAC exists to help its members coordinate their development assistance and to encourage the expansion and improve the effectiveness of the aggregate resources flowing to recipient economies. In this capacity DAC monitors the flow of all financial resources, but its main concern is official development assistance (ODA). Grants or loans to countries and territories on the DAC list of aid recipients have to meet three criteria to be counted as ODA. They are undertaken by the official sector. They promote economic development and welfare as the main objective. And they are provided at concessional financial terms (loans must have a grant element of at least 25 percent, calculated at a discount rate of 10 percent). The DAC Statistical Reporting Directives provide the most detailed explanation of this definition and all ODA-related rules.

This definition excludes nonconcessional flows from official creditors, which are classified as "other official flows," and aid for military purposes. Transfer payments to private individuals, such as pensions, reparations, and insurance payouts, are in general not counted. In addition to financial flows, technical cooperation is included in ODA. Most expenditures for peacekeeping under UN mandates and assistance to refugees are counted in ODA. Also included are contributions to multilateral institutions, such as the United Nations and its specialized agencies, and concessional funding to multilateral development banks.

DAC has revised the list of countries and territories that are counted as aid recipients. These revisions will govern aid reporting for three years, starting with 2005 flows. In the past DAC distinguished aid going to Part I and Part II countries. Part I countries, the recipients of ODA, comprised many of the countries classified by the World Bank as low- and middle-income economies. Part II countries, whose assistance was designated official aid, included the more advanced countries of Central and Eastern Europe, countries of the former Soviet Union, and certain advanced developing countries and territories. This distinction has been dropped. ODA recipients now comprise all low- and middle-income countries except those that are members of the Group of Eight or the European Union (including countries with a firm date for EU accession). The content and structure of tables 6.12 through 6.15 have been revised to reflect this change. Because official aid flows are quite small relative to ODA, the net effect of these changes is believed to be minor.

Flows are transfers of resources, either in cash or in the form of commodities or services measured on a cash basis. Short-term capital transactions (with one year or less maturity) are not counted. Repayments of the principal (but not interest) of ODA loans are recorded as negative flows. Proceeds from official equity investments in a developing country are reported as ODA, while proceeds from their later sale are recorded as negative flows.

Because the table is based on donor country reports, it does not provide a complete picture of the resources received by developing economies for two reasons. First, flows from DAC members are only part of the aggregate resource flows to these economies. Second, the data that record contributions to multilateral institutions measure the flow of resources made available to those institutions by DAC members, not the flow of resources from those institutions to developing and transition economies.

Aid as a share of gross national income (GNI), aid per capita, and ODA as a share of the general government disbursements of the donor are calculated by the OECD. The denominators used in calculating these ratios may differ from corresponding values elsewhere in this book because of differences in timing or definitions.

are concessional funding received by multilateral institutions from DAC members as grants or capital subscriptions. • **Other official flows** are transactions by the official sector whose main objective is other than development or whose grant element is less than 25 percent. • **Private flows** are flows at market terms financed from private sector resources in donor countries. They include changes in holdings of private long-term assets by reporting country residents. • **Foreign direct investment** is investment by residents of DAC member countries to acquire a lasting management interest (at least 10 percent of voting stock) in an enterprise operating in the recipient country. The data reflect changes in the net worth of subsidiaries in recipient countries whose parent company is in the DAC source country. • **Bilateral portfolio investment** covers bank lending and the purchase of bonds, shares, and real estate by residents of DAC member countries in recipient countries. • **Multilateral portfolio investment** are transactions of private banks and nonbanks in DAC member countries in the securities issued by multilateral institutions. • **Private export credits** are loans extended to recipient countries by the private sector in DAC member countries to promote trade; they may be supported by an official guarantee. • **Net grants by nongovernmental organizations (NGOs)** are private grants by NGOs, net of subsidies from the official sector. • **Commitments** are obligations, expressed in writing and backed by funds, undertaken by an official donor to provide specified assistance to a recipient country or multilateral organization. • **Gross disbursements** are the international transfer of financial resources and goods and services, valued at the cost to the donor.

• **Net disbursements** are gross disbursements of grants and loans minus repayments of principal on earlier loans. • **Total net flows** comprise ODA or official aid flows, other official flows, private flows, and net grants by nongovernmental organizations. • **Official development assistance** comprises flows that meet the DAC definition of ODA and are made to countries and territories on the DAC list of aid recipients. • **Bilateral grants** are transfers of money or in kind for which no repayment is required. • **Bilateral loans** are loans extended by governments or official agencies that have a grant element of at least 25 percent (calculated at a 10 percent discount rate). • **Contributions to multilateral institutions**

**Data sources**

Data on financial flows are compiled by OECD-DAC and published in its annual statistical report, *Geographical Distribution of Financial Flows to Aid Recipients*, and its annual *Development Cooperation Report*. Data are available electronically on the OECD's *International Development Statistics* CD-ROM and at www.oecd.org/dac/stats/idsonline.

# 6.13 Allocation of bilateral aid from Development Assistance Committee members

| | Net disbursements | | Share of bilateral ODA net disbursements | | | | | | | | | |
| | | | % | | | | | | | | | |
| | | | Development projects, programs, and other resource provisions | | Technical cooperation[b] | | Debt-related aid | | Humanitarian assistance | | Administrative costs | |
| | $ millions[a] | | | | | | | | | | | |
| | 2000 | 2006 | 2000 | 2006 | 2000 | 2006 | 2000 | 2006 | 2000 | 2006 | 2000 | 2006 |
|---|---|---|---|---|---|---|---|---|---|---|---|---|
| Australia | 758 | 1,796 | 27.8 | 21.6 | 55.1 | 48.0 | 1.1 | 15.4 | 9.7 | 10.6 | 6.2 | 4.3 |
| Austria | 273 | 1,092 | 28.7 | 6.8 | 41.8 | 19.4 | 20.4 | 69.3 | 2.7 | 1.5 | 6.4 | 2.9 |
| Belgium | 477 | 1,357 | 33.6 | 10.0 | 46.9 | 50.3 | 6.6 | 29.3 | 5.4 | 6.4 | 7.5 | 4.0 |
| Canada | 1,160 | 2,531 | 39.6 | 44.2 | 43.0 | 27.3 | 1.1 | 10.3 | 5.0 | 9.1 | 11.4 | 9.0 |
| Denmark | 1,024 | 1,464 | 65.8 | 63.3 | 25.3 | 11.1 | 1.0 | 7.7 | 0.0 | 10.3 | 8.0 | 7.6 |
| Finland | 217 | 455 | 40.8 | 54.6 | 41.4 | 22.6 | 0.0 | 0.0 | 10.5 | 15.5 | 7.2 | 7.4 |
| France | 2,829 | 7,919 | 25.4 | 9.5 | 50.6 | 41.4 | 17.0 | 44.2 | 0.4 | 0.6 | 6.7 | 4.3 |
| Germany | 2,687 | 7,034 | 16.8 | 8.9 | 63.8 | 44.9 | 6.6 | 37.8 | 4.1 | 5.1 | 8.7 | 3.2 |
| Greece | 99 | 189 | 69.6 | 29.8 | 23.8 | 49.9 | 0.0 | 0.0 | 6.4 | 10.2 | 0.2 | 10.1 |
| Ireland | 154 | 632 | 79.1 | 75.8 | 0.4 | 4.9 | 0.0 | 0.0 | 15.5 | 13.8 | 5.1 | 5.4 |
| Italy | 377 | 2,001 | 10.2 | 4.8 | 8.1 | 8.6 | 57.5 | 80.2 | 18.3 | 3.7 | 5.9 | 2.8 |
| Japan | 9,768 | 7,313 | 60.4 | 19.2 | 24.9 | 25.4 | 4.2 | 43.8 | 0.9 | 2.5 | 9.5 | 9.1 |
| Luxembourg | 99 | 205 | 84.4 | 71.9 | 3.2 | 3.6 | 0.8 | 0.0 | 10.4 | 18.1 | 1.2 | 6.4 |
| Netherlands | 2,243 | 4,282 | 41.1 | 62.8 | 33.7 | 14.7 | 6.8 | 7.3 | 9.1 | 9.3 | 9.4 | 5.9 |
| New Zealand | 85 | 203 | 39.7 | 51.7 | 48.1 | 29.7 | 0.0 | 0.0 | 3.4 | 10.6 | 8.8 | 8.0 |
| Norway | 934 | 2,198 | 57.9 | 57.1 | 23.0 | 20.4 | 1.0 | 1.0 | 11.3 | 14.1 | 6.9 | 7.5 |
| Portugal | 179 | 211 | 30.4 | 34.5 | 50.4 | 55.9 | 14.6 | 0.2 | 1.9 | 3.3 | 2.7 | 6.1 |
| Spain | 720 | 2,092 | 69.3 | 39.7 | 17.9 | 24.3 | 2.3 | 24.6 | 3.7 | 6.6 | 6.8 | 4.8 |
| Sweden | 1,242 | 2,852 | 60.9 | 61.6 | 13.6 | 11.0 | 3.1 | 10.3 | 14.6 | 10.3 | 7.7 | 6.8 |
| Switzerland | 627 | 1,254 | 58.6 | 49.8 | 19.4 | 24.2 | 0.9 | 7.8 | 20.2 | 14.0 | 0.9 | 4.1 |
| United Kingdom | 2,710 | 8,718 | 47.7 | 34.7 | 25.5 | 10.0 | 5.7 | 40.2 | 12.7 | 9.6 | 8.4 | 5.5 |
| United States | 7,405 | 21,162 | 14.6 | 26.5 | 64.4 | 46.2 | 1.7 | 8.0 | 9.6 | 14.3 | 9.7 | 5.1 |
| **Total** | **36,064** | **76,960** | **40.5** | **29.1** | **39.4** | **31.6** | **5.4** | **25.0** | **6.1** | **8.8** | **8.6** | **5.5** |

a. At current exchange rates and prices. b. Includes aid for promoting development awareness and aid provided to refugees in donor economies.

## About the data

Aid can be used in many ways. The sector to which aid goes, the form it takes, and the procurement restrictions attached to it are important influences on aid effectiveness. The data on allocation of official development assistance (ODA) in the table are based principally on reporting by members of the Organisation for Economic Co-operation and Development (OECD) Development Assistance Committee (DAC). For more detailed explanation of ODA, see *About the data* for table 6.12.

The form in which an ODA contribution reaches the benefiting sector or the economy is important. A distinction is made between resource provision and technical cooperation. Resource provision involves mainly cash or in-kind transfers and financing of capital projects, with the deliverables being financial support and the provision of commodities and supplies. Technical cooperation includes grants to nationals of aid-recipient countries receiving education or training at home or abroad, and payments to consultants, advisers, and similar personnel and to teachers and administrators serving in recipient countries. Technical cooperation is spent mostly in the donor economy.

Two other types of aid are presented because they serve distinctive purposes. Debt-related aid aims to

provide debt relief on liabilities that recipient countries have difficulty servicing. Thus, this type of aid may not provide a full value of new resource flows for development, in particular for heavily indebted poor countries. Humanitarian assistance provides relief following sudden disasters and supports food programs in emergency situations. This type of aid does not generally contribute to financing long-term development.

## Definitions

• **Net disbursements** are gross disbursements of grants and loans minus repayments of principal on earlier loans • **Development projects, programs, and other resource provisions** are aid provided as cash transfers, aid in kind, development food aid, and the financing of capital projects, intended to increase or improve the recipient's stock of physical capital and to support recipient's development plans and other activities with finance and commodity supply. • **Technical cooperation** is the provision of resources whose main aim is to augment the stock of human intellectual capital, such as the level of knowledge, skills, and technical know-how in the recipient country (including the cost of associated equipment). Contributions take the form mainly of the supply of

human resources from donors or action directed to human resources (such as training or advice). Also included are aid for promoting development awareness and aid provided to refugees in the donor economy. Assistance specifically to facilitate a capital project is not included. • **Debt-related aid** groups all actions relating to debt, including forgiveness, swaps, buybacks, rescheduling, and refinancing. • **Humanitarian assistance** is emergency and distress relief (including aid to refugees and assistance for disaster preparedness). • **Administrative costs** are the total current budget outlays of institutions responsible for the formulation and implementation of donor's aid programs and other administrative costs incurred by donors in aid delivery.

## Data sources

Data on aid flows are published by OECD-DAC in its annual statistical report, *Geographical Distribution of Financial Flows to Aid Recipients*, and its annual *Development Cooperation Report*. Data are available electronically on the OECD's *International Development Statistics* CD-ROM and at www.oecd.org/dac/stats/idsonline.

## 6.13b  Aid by sector

| Share of bilateral ODA commitment (%) | Total sector-allocable aid 2006 | Social infrastructure and services | | | | | | Economic infrastructure, services, and production sector | | | Multi-sector or cross-cutting 2006 | Untied aid[a] 2006 |
|---|---|---|---|---|---|---|---|---|---|---|---|---|
| | | Total 2006 | Education 2006 | Health 2006 | Population 2006 | Water supply and sanitation 2006 | Government and civil society 2006 | Total 2006 | Transport and communication 2006 | Agriculture 2006 | | |
| Australia | 68.7 | 53.2 | 8.6 | 11.5 | 2.5 | 0.4 | 24.8 | 8.0 | 1.8 | 4.1 | 7.5 | .. |
| Austria | 24.8 | 19.8 | 9.8 | 1.7 | 0.4 | 1.9 | 5.3 | 3.0 | 0.2 | 0.9 | 2.0 | 89.5 |
| Belgium | 53.6 | 39.0 | 11.0 | 6.7 | 1.7 | 4.0 | 10.4 | 11.4 | 2.1 | 4.5 | 3.1 | 90.7 |
| Canada | 61.5 | 44.6 | 11.9 | 8.0 | 1.9 | 0.7 | 18.3 | 9.6 | 1.0 | 5.5 | 7.3 | 62.9 |
| Denmark | 55.2 | 32.4 | 1.2 | 7.8 | 2.2 | 10.8 | 9.0 | 17.6 | 4.5 | 5.3 | 5.2 | 95.3 |
| Finland | 67.7 | 39.5 | 5.7 | 8.3 | 1.4 | 7.6 | 14.8 | 14.2 | 1.6 | 4.1 | 14.0 | 86.5 |
| France | 47.4 | 29.5 | 18.0 | 2.7 | 0.0 | 2.4 | 1.4 | 8.4 | 4.3 | 1.7 | 9.5 | 95.6 |
| Germany | 60.1 | 34.5 | 14.5 | 2.6 | 2.4 | 5.3 | 7.2 | 19.9 | 3.2 | 3.8 | 5.7 | 93.3 |
| Greece | 75.0 | 59.1 | 12.5 | 12.7 | 4.2 | 0.5 | 24.7 | 10.1 | 7.6 | 1.2 | 5.7 | 39.1 |
| Ireland | 67.2 | 56.2 | 10.1 | 12.1 | 12.6 | 2.7 | 13.2 | 5.9 | 0.6 | 4.3 | 5.0 | 100.0 |
| Italy | 29.0 | 12.1 | 1.7 | 3.8 | 0.2 | 2.2 | 1.6 | 12.2 | 5.9 | 1.2 | 4.7 | 77.0 |
| Japan | 61.1 | 22.6 | 6.8 | 2.3 | 0.1 | 9.4 | 2.8 | 34.5 | 16.4 | 4.5 | 4.0 | 95.6 |
| Luxembourg | 67.4 | 50.2 | 16.0 | 15.9 | 6.3 | 5.4 | 3.1 | 8.0 | 1.2 | 2.9 | 9.2 | 100.0 |
| Netherlands | 47.1 | 35.7 | 17.5 | 5.3 | 1.8 | 4.3 | 6.0 | 8.1 | 0.2 | 1.2 | 3.3 | 100.0 |
| New Zealand | 59.6 | 45.1 | 20.5 | 5.5 | 3.3 | 1.4 | 12.8 | 10.8 | 2.8 | 3.0 | 3.7 | 90.2 |
| Norway | 69.6 | 45.6 | 9.2 | 8.6 | 2.5 | 1.3 | 20.1 | 13.8 | 1.2 | 4.0 | 10.3 | 99.8 |
| Portugal | 85.5 | 65.1 | 30.3 | 4.8 | 0.0 | 0.3 | 20.6 | 13.7 | 11.8 | 0.7 | 6.7 | 61.3 |
| Spain | 61.1 | 33.2 | 9.6 | 4.6 | 1.8 | 3.0 | 8.1 | 20.2 | 8.4 | 3.2 | 7.6 | 82.8 |
| Sweden | 54.1 | 35.2 | 4.6 | 5.8 | 3.5 | 2.4 | 15.5 | 11.2 | 1.6 | 3.8 | 7.8 | 100.0 |
| Switzerland | 52.3 | 22.1 | 3.8 | 3.3 | 0.2 | 2.5 | 11.4 | 15.5 | 1.0 | 4.7 | 14.7 | 96.3 |
| United Kingdom | 37.5 | 30.5 | 4.9 | 4.6 | 3.3 | 0.6 | 15.8 | 5.3 | 0.8 | 1.6 | 1.7 | 100.0 |
| United States | 69.4 | 44.1 | 2.0 | 5.6 | 11.7 | 3.4 | 11.1 | 18.6 | 3.8 | 2.6 | 6.7 | .. |
| **Total** | **56.9** | **34.9** | **8.7** | **4.7** | **4.1** | **4.0** | **8.9** | **16.2** | **4.7** | **2.9** | **5.8** | **94.5** |

a. Excludes technical cooperation and administrative costs.

### About the data

The Development Assistance Committee (DAC) records the sector classification of aid using a three-level hierarchy. The top level is grouped by themes, such as social infrastructure and services; economic infrastructure, services, and production; and multisector or cross-cutting areas. The second level is more specific. Education and health and transport and storage are examples. The third level comprises subsectors such as basic education and basic health. Some contributions are reported as non-sector-allocable aid.

Reporting on the sectoral destination and the form of aid by donors may not be complete. Also, measures of aid allocation may differ from the perspectives of donors and recipients because of difference in classification, available information, and recording time.

The proportion of untied aid is reported because tying arrangements may prevent recipients from obtaining the best value for their money. Tying requires recipients to purchase goods and services from the donor country or from a specified group of countries. Such arrangements prevent a recipient from misappropriating or mismanaging aid receipts, but they may also be motivated by a desire to benefit donor country suppliers.

### Definitions

• **Bilateral official development assistance (ODA) commitments** are firm obligations, expressed in writing and backed by the necessary funds, undertaken by official bilateral donors to provide specified assistance to a recipient country or a multilateral organization. Bilateral commitments are recorded in the full amount of expected transfer, irrespective of the time required for completing disbursements. • **Total sector-allocable aid** is the sum of aid that can be assigned to specific sectors or multisector activities. • **Social infrastructure and services** refer to efforts to develop the human resources potential of aid recipients. • **Education** includes general teaching and instruction at all levels, as well as construction to improve or adapt educational establishments. Training in a particular field is reported for the sector concerned. • **Health** covers assistance to hospitals, clinics, other medical and dental services, public health administration, and medical insurance programs. • **Population** covers all activities related to family planning and research into population problems. • **Water supply and sanitation** cover assistance for water supply and use, sanitation, and water resources development (including rivers). • **Government and civil society** include assistance to strengthen government administrative apparatus and planning and activities promoting good governance and civil society. • **Economic infrastructure, services, and production sector** group assistance for networks, utilities, services that facilitate economic activity, and contributions to all directly productive sectors. • **Transport and communication** cover road, rail, water, and air transport; post and telecommunications; and radio, television, and print media. • **Agriculture** includes sector policy, development, and inputs; crop and livestock production; and agricultural credit, cooperatives, and research. • **Multisector or cross-cutting** includes support for projects that straddle several sectors. • **Untied aid** is ODA not subject to restrictions by donors on procurement sources.

### Data sources

Data on aid flows are published annually by the Organisation for Economic Co-operation and Development (OECD) DAC in *Geographical Distribution of Financial Flows to Aid Recipients* and *Development Cooperation Report*. Data are available electronically on the OECD's *International Development Statistics* CD-ROM and at www.oecd.org/dac/stats/idsonline.

| | Net official development assistance[a] | | Aid per capita | | Aid dependency ratios | | | | | | | |
| | $ millions | | $ | | Aid as % of GNI | | Aid as % of gross capital formation | | Aid as % of imports of goods, services, and income | | Aid as % of central government expense | |
| | 2000 | 2006 | 2000 | 2006 | 2000 | 2006 | 2000 | 2006 | 2000 | 2006 | 2000 | 2006 |
|---|---|---|---|---|---|---|---|---|---|---|---|---|
| Afghanistan | 136 | 3,000 | .. | .. | .. | 35.7 | .. | .. | .. | .. | .. | .. |
| Albania | 317 | 321 | 103 | 101 | 8.4 | 3.5 | 34.8 | 14.1 | 21.0 | 7.0 | .. | .. |
| Algeria | 201 | 209 | 7 | 6 | 0.4 | 0.2 | 1.5 | .. | .. | .. | 1.8 | 1.0 |
| Angola | 302 | 171 | 22 | 10 | 4.1 | 0.4 | 22.0 | 2.8 | 4.1 | 0.8 | .. | .. |
| Argentina | 53 | 114 | 1 | 3 | 0.0 | 0.1 | 0.1 | 0.2 | 0.1 | 0.2 | .. | .. |
| Armenia | 216 | 213 | 70 | 71 | 11.0 | 3.3 | 60.6 | 9.9 | 21.2 | 7.2 | .. | 20.7 |
| Australia | | | | | | | | | | | | |
| Austria | | | | | | | | | | | | |
| Azerbaijan | 139 | 206 | 17 | 24 | 2.8 | 1.2 | 12.8 | 3.3 | 5.8 | 1.9 | .. | .. |
| Bangladesh | 1,168 | 1,223 | 8 | 8 | 2.4 | 1.9 | 10.8 | 8.0 | 11.7 | 6.9 | .. | .. |
| Belarus | 40 | 73 | 4 | 7 | 0.3 | 0.2 | 1.2 | 0.6 | 0.5 | 0.3 | 1.5 | 0.6 |
| Belgium | | | | | | | | | | | | |
| Benin | 238 | 375 | 33 | 43 | 10.6 | 8.0 | 55.9 | .. | 32.1 | .. | .. | 58.4 |
| Bolivia | 472 | 581 | 57 | 62 | 5.8 | 5.4 | 31.0 | 43.1 | 19.3 | 14.5 | .. | 21.2 |
| Bosnia and Herzegovina | 737 | 494 | 195 | 126 | 12.4 | 3.9 | 65.1 | 24.9 | 17.4 | 5.8 | .. | 11.3 |
| Botswana | 31 | 65 | 18 | 35 | 0.5 | 0.7 | 1.4 | 2.4 | 1.0 | 1.4 | .. | .. |
| Brazil | 232 | 82 | 1 | 0 | 0.0 | 0.0 | 0.2 | 0.0 | 0.2 | 0.1 | .. | .. |
| Bulgaria[b] | 311 | .. | 39 | .. | 2.5 | .. | 13.5 | .. | 3.7 | .. | 7.6 | .. |
| Burkina Faso | 335 | 871 | 28 | 61 | 12.9 | 14.1 | 76.6 | 83.3 | 48.5 | .. | .. | 117.5 |
| Burundi | 93 | 415 | 14 | 51 | 12.8 | 47.7 | 212.6 | 275.7 | 56.1 | 89.9 | .. | .. |
| Cambodia | 396 | 529 | 31 | 37 | 11.2 | 7.6 | 61.8 | 33.9 | 16.1 | 8.9 | .. | 84.7 |
| Cameroon | 379 | 1,684 | 24 | 93 | 4.0 | 9.3 | 22.5 | 51.0 | 12.8 | .. | .. | .. |
| Canada | | | | | | | | | | | | |
| Central African Republic | 75 | 134 | 19 | 31 | 8.0 | 9.0 | 82.4 | 101.3 | .. | .. | .. | .. |
| Chad | 130 | 284 | 15 | 27 | 9.5 | 5.5 | 40.4 | 20.2 | .. | .. | .. | .. |
| Chile | 49 | 83 | 3 | 5 | 0.1 | 0.1 | 0.3 | 0.3 | 0.2 | 0.1 | 0.3 | 0.3 |
| China | 1,728 | 1,245 | 1 | 1 | 0.1 | 0.0 | 0.4 | 0.1 | 0.6 | 0.1 | .. | .. |
| Hong Kong, China[b] | 4 | .. | 1 | .. | 0.0 | .. | 0.0 | .. | 0.0 | .. | .. | .. |
| Colombia | 187 | 988 | 4 | 22 | 0.2 | 0.7 | 1.6 | 2.7 | 1.1 | 2.6 | .. | 2.5 |
| Congo, Dem. Rep. | 177 | 2,056 | 3 | 34 | 4.5 | 25.2 | 119.1 | 148.8 | .. | .. | 15.2 | .. |
| Congo, Rep. | 33 | 254 | 10 | 69 | 1.5 | .. | 4.6 | 14.4 | 1.6 | .. | .. | .. |
| Costa Rica | 11 | 24 | 3 | 5 | 0.1 | 0.1 | 0.4 | 0.4 | 0.1 | 0.2 | .. | 0.5 |
| Côte d'Ivoire | 351 | 251 | 21 | 13 | 3.6 | 1.5 | 31.2 | 14.7 | 7.9 | 3.1 | .. | 7.5 |
| Croatia | 66 | 200 | 15 | 45 | 0.4 | 0.5 | 1.8 | 1.4 | 0.6 | 0.7 | 0.8 | 1.2 |
| Cuba | 44 | 78 | 4 | 7 | .. | .. | .. | .. | .. | .. | .. | .. |
| Czech Republic[b] | 438 | .. | 43 | .. | 0.8 | .. | 2.6 | .. | 1.1 | .. | 2.3 | .. |
| Denmark | | | | | | | | | | | | |
| Dominican Republic | 56 | 53 | 6 | 6 | 0.3 | 0.2 | 1.2 | 0.8 | 0.5 | 0.4 | .. | 1.0 |
| Ecuador | 146 | 189 | 12 | 14 | 1.0 | 0.5 | 4.6 | 2.0 | 2.3 | 1.2 | .. | .. |
| Egypt, Arab Rep. | 1,328 | 873 | 20 | 12 | 1.3 | 0.8 | 6.8 | 4.3 | 5.6 | 2.1 | 6.6 | 3.0 |
| El Salvador | 180 | 157 | 29 | 23 | 1.4 | 0.9 | 8.1 | 5.2 | 3.0 | 1.7 | .. | 38.2 |
| Eritrea | 176 | 129 | 48 | 28 | 27.7 | 12.0 | 86.9 | 63.6 | 34.5 | .. | .. | .. |
| Estonia[b] | 64 | .. | 47 | .. | 1.2 | .. | 4.0 | .. | 1.2 | .. | 3.8 | .. |
| Ethiopia | 686 | 1,947 | 10 | 25 | 8.7 | 14.7 | 45.3 | 74.0 | 41.0 | 36.6 | .. | .. |
| Finland | | | | | | | | | | | | |
| France | | | | | | | | | | | | |
| Gabon | 12 | 31 | 10 | 24 | 0.3 | 0.4 | 1.1 | 1.4 | 0.5 | .. | .. | .. |
| Gambia, The | 49 | 74 | 35 | 45 | 12.2 | 14.8 | 66.9 | 59.7 | .. | 20.7 | .. | .. |
| Georgia | 169 | 361 | 36 | 81 | 5.3 | 4.8 | 20.8 | 17.4 | 13.6 | 7.9 | 47.9 | 22.9 |
| Germany | | | | | | | | | | | | |
| Ghana | 600 | 1,176 | 30 | 51 | 12.4 | 9.2 | 50.2 | 28.1 | 17.3 | 13.9 | .. | .. |
| Greece | | | | | | | | | | | | |
| Guatemala | 263 | 487 | 23 | 37 | 1.4 | 1.4 | 7.7 | 7.4 | 4.4 | 3.6 | 12.5 | 11.9 |
| Guinea | 153 | 164 | 19 | 18 | 5.0 | 5.0 | 24.9 | 38.3 | 15.7 | .. | .. | .. |
| Guinea-Bissau | 80 | 82 | 59 | 50 | 39.5 | 27.9 | 329.8 | 157.2 | .. | .. | .. | .. |
| Haiti | 208 | 581 | 24 | 62 | 5.4 | 13.4 | 20.8 | 40.6 | 15.1 | 27.7 | .. | .. |

| | Net official development assistance[a] | | Aid per capita | | Aid dependency ratios | | | | | | | |
| | $ millions | | $ | | Aid as % of GNI | | Aid as % of gross capital formation | | Aid as % of imports of goods, services, and income | | Aid as % of central government expense | |
| | 2000 | 2006 | 2000 | 2006 | 2000 | 2006 | 2000 | 2006 | 2000 | 2006 | 2000 | 2006 |
|---|---|---|---|---|---|---|---|---|---|---|---|---|
| Honduras | 449 | 587 | 72 | 84 | 7.7 | 6.6 | 24.5 | 19.3 | 12.7 | 9.0 | .. | 30.3 |
| Hungary[b] | 252 | .. | 25 | .. | 0.6 | .. | 1.7 | .. | 0.6 | .. | 1.3 | .. |
| India | 1,463 | 1,379 | 1 | 1 | 0.3 | 0.2 | 1.3 | 0.4 | 1.8 | 0.6 | 2.0 | 1.0 |
| Indonesia | 1,654 | 1,405 | 8 | 6 | 1.1 | 0.4 | 4.5 | 1.6 | 2.5 | 1.2 | .. | .. |
| Iran, Islamic Rep. | 130 | 121 | 2 | 2 | 0.1 | 0.1 | 0.4 | 0.2 | 0.7 | .. | 0.2 | 0.2 |
| Iraq | 100 | 8,661 | .. | .. | .. | .. | .. | .. | .. | .. | .. | .. |
| Ireland | | | | | | | | | | | | |
| Israel[b] | 800 | .. | 127 | .. | 0.7 | .. | 3.2 | .. | 1.4 | .. | 1.5 | .. |
| Italy | | | | | | | | | | | | |
| Jamaica | 10 | 37 | 4 | 14 | 0.1 | 0.4 | 0.5 | 1.1 | 0.2 | 0.5 | 0.4 | 0.9 |
| Japan | .. | .. | | | | | | | | | | |
| Jordan | 552 | 580 | 115 | 105 | 6.4 | 3.9 | 29.2 | 15.4 | 8.7 | 4.3 | 24.1 | 11.8 |
| Kazakhstan | 189 | 172 | 13 | 11 | 1.1 | 0.2 | 5.7 | 0.6 | 1.8 | 0.4 | 7.5 | 1.4 |
| Kenya | 510 | 943 | 16 | 26 | 4.1 | 4.1 | 23.0 | 21.4 | 12.9 | 11.3 | 23.9 | .. |
| Korea, Dem. Rep. | 73 | 55 | 3 | 2 | .. | .. | .. | .. | .. | .. | .. | .. |
| Korea, Rep.[b] | −198 | .. | −4 | .. | 0.0 | .. | −0.1 | .. | −0.1 | .. | −0.2 | .. |
| Kuwait | 3 | .. | 1 | .. | 0.0 | .. | 0.1 | .. | 0.0 | .. | .. | .. |
| Kyrgyz Republic | 215 | 311 | 44 | 60 | 16.7 | 11.2 | 78.3 | 63.4 | 28.5 | 13.4 | .. | 62.9 |
| Lao PDR | 282 | 364 | 54 | 63 | 16.9 | 12.0 | 77.7 | 32.6 | 44.1 | .. | .. | .. |
| Latvia[b] | 91 | .. | 38 | .. | 1.2 | .. | 4.9 | .. | 2.3 | .. | 4.1 | .. |
| Lebanon | 199 | 707 | 53 | 174 | 1.2 | 3.2 | 5.9 | 25.5 | .. | 3.7 | 3.8 | .. |
| Lesotho | 37 | 72 | 19 | 36 | 3.4 | 3.8 | 10.1 | 14.5 | 4.4 | 4.8 | .. | .. |
| Liberia | 67 | 269 | 22 | 75 | 17.4 | 54.4 | .. | .. | .. | .. | .. | .. |
| Libya | 14 | 37 | 3 | 6 | .. | 0.1 | 0.3 | .. | 0.2 | 0.2 | .. | .. |
| Lithuania[b] | 99 | .. | 28 | .. | 0.9 | .. | 4.4 | .. | 1.6 | .. | 3.2 | .. |
| Macedonia, FYR | 251 | 200 | 125 | 98 | 7.1 | 3.2 | 31.5 | 15.4 | 10.6 | 4.5 | .. | .. |
| Madagascar | 322 | 754 | 20 | 39 | 8.4 | 13.9 | 55.1 | 55.3 | 20.3 | .. | 78.1 | 117.9 |
| Malawi | 446 | 669 | 38 | 49 | 26.1 | 21.4 | 188.7 | 89.1 | 65.7 | .. | .. | .. |
| Malaysia | 45 | 240 | 2 | 9 | 0.1 | 0.2 | 0.2 | 0.8 | 0.0 | 0.1 | 0.3 | .. |
| Mali | 359 | 825 | 36 | 69 | 15.0 | 14.9 | 60.4 | 61.5 | 34.4 | .. | 127.7 | 89.7 |
| Mauritania | 211 | 188 | 82 | 62 | 19.4 | 6.8 | 101.0 | 30.3 | .. | .. | .. | .. |
| Mauritius | 20 | 19 | 17 | 15 | 0.5 | 0.3 | 1.8 | 1.2 | 0.7 | 0.4 | 2.2 | 1.4 |
| Mexico | −56 | 247 | −1 | 2 | 0.0 | 0.0 | 0.0 | 0.1 | 0.0 | 0.1 | −0.1 | .. |
| Moldova | 123 | 228 | 30 | 60 | 9.4 | 6.1 | 39.7 | 19.8 | 11.3 | 6.8 | 32.9 | 21.0 |
| Mongolia | 217 | 203 | 91 | 78 | 20.1 | 6.7 | 68.8 | 18.4 | 27.5 | 9.9 | .. | .. |
| Morocco | 419 | 1,046 | 15 | 34 | 1.2 | 1.6 | 4.4 | 5.1 | 3.1 | 3.9 | .. | 6.2 |
| Mozambique | 876 | 1,611 | 48 | 77 | 21.8 | 26.2 | 66.6 | 122.0 | 49.7 | 39.7 | .. | .. |
| Myanmar | 106 | 147 | 2 | 3 | .. | .. | .. | .. | 4.0 | 3.4 | .. | .. |
| Namibia | 152 | 145 | 81 | 71 | 4.4 | 2.2 | 22.8 | 7.5 | 8.2 | 4.4 | 14.1 | .. |
| Nepal | 387 | 514 | 16 | 19 | 7.0 | 5.7 | 29.0 | 22.1 | 21.2 | 17.0 | .. | 39.4 |
| Netherlands | | | | | | | | | | | | |
| New Zealand | | | | | | | | | | | | |
| Nicaragua | 561 | 733 | 110 | 132 | 15.0 | 14.2 | 47.2 | 47.0 | 23.5 | 18.0 | 86.5 | 71.8 |
| Niger | 208 | 401 | 19 | 29 | 11.7 | 11.0 | 101.4 | .. | 43.0 | .. | .. | .. |
| Nigeria | 174 | 11,434 | 1 | 79 | 0.4 | 11.3 | 1.9 | 45.1 | 1.1 | .. | .. | .. |
| Norway | | | | | | | | | | | | |
| Oman | 45 | 35 | 19 | 14 | 0.2 | .. | 1.9 | .. | 0.6 | 0.2 | 0.9 | .. |
| Pakistan | 692 | 2,147 | 5 | 14 | 0.9 | 1.7 | 5.4 | 7.8 | 4.8 | 5.5 | 5.6 | 11.1 |
| Panama | 16 | 30 | 5 | 9 | 0.1 | 0.2 | 0.6 | 0.9 | 0.2 | 0.2 | 0.6 | .. |
| Papua New Guinea | 275 | 279 | 51 | 45 | 8.4 | 5.5 | .. | .. | 13.7 | .. | 26.2 | .. |
| Paraguay | 82 | 56 | 15 | 9 | 1.1 | 0.6 | 6.1 | 2.9 | 2.3 | 0.9 | .. | 3.6 |
| Peru | 398 | 468 | 15 | 17 | 0.8 | 0.6 | 3.7 | 2.5 | 3.4 | 1.7 | 4.2 | .. |
| Philippines | 575 | 562 | 8 | 7 | 0.7 | 0.4 | 3.6 | 3.3 | 1.1 | 0.9 | 4.3 | 2.7 |
| Poland[b] | 1,396 | .. | 36 | .. | 0.8 | .. | 3.3 | .. | 2.3 | .. | .. | .. |
| Portugal | | | | | | | | | | | | |
| Puerto Rico | | | | | | | | | | | | |

# 6.14 | Aid dependency

| | Net official development assistance[a] | | Aid per capita | | Aid dependency ratios | | | | | | | |
|---|---|---|---|---|---|---|---|---|---|---|---|---|
| | | | | | Aid as % of GNI | | Aid as % of gross capital formation | | Aid as % of imports of goods, services, and income | | Aid as % of central government expense | |
| | $ millions | | $ | | | | | | | | | |
| | 2000 | 2006 | 2000 | 2006 | 2000 | 2006 | 2000 | 2006 | 2000 | 2006 | 2000 | 2006 |
| Romania[b] | 432 | .. | 19 | .. | 1.2 | .. | 6.0 | .. | 2.9 | .. | .. | .. |
| Russian Federation[b] | 1,561 | .. | 11 | .. | 0.6 | .. | 3.2 | .. | 2.2 | .. | 2.8 | .. |
| Rwanda | 321 | 585 | 39 | 62 | 17.9 | 23.6 | 101.3 | 109.4 | 71.2 | 75.1 | .. | .. |
| Saudi Arabia | 22 | 25 | 1 | 1 | 0.0 | 0.0 | 0.1 | 0.0 | 0.0 | 0.0 | .. | .. |
| Senegal | 423 | 825 | 41 | 68 | 9.2 | 9.1 | 44.1 | 30.8 | 21.9 | .. | 70.9 | .. |
| Serbia | 1,134[c] | 1,586 | 151[c] | 213 | 12.6[c] | 5.0 | 150.1[c] | 23.4 | .. | .. | .. | .. |
| Sierra Leone | 181 | 364 | 40 | 63 | 29.4 | 25.7 | 356.3 | 163.6 | 68.8 | 74.8 | 98.8 | .. |
| Singapore[b] | 1 | .. | 0 | .. | 0.0 | .. | 0.0 | .. | 0.0 | .. | 0.0 | .. |
| Slovak Republic[b] | 113 | .. | 21 | .. | 0.6 | .. | 2.1 | .. | 0.7 | .. | .. | .. |
| Slovenia[b] | 61 | .. | 31 | .. | 0.3 | .. | 1.2 | .. | 0.5 | .. | 0.8 | .. |
| Somalia | 101 | 392 | 14 | 46 | .. | .. | .. | .. | .. | .. | .. | .. |
| South Africa | 487 | 718 | 11 | 15 | 0.4 | 0.3 | 2.3 | 1.4 | 1.3 | 0.8 | 1.3 | 0.9 |
| Spain | | | | | | | | | | | | |
| Sri Lanka | 276 | 796 | 14 | 40 | 1.7 | 3.0 | 6.0 | 10.3 | 3.2 | 6.5 | 7.3 | 13.3 |
| Sudan | 220 | 2,058 | 7 | 55 | 2.1 | 6.0 | 9.7 | 22.3 | 8.5 | 17.2 | .. | .. |
| Swaziland | 13 | 35 | 13 | 30 | 0.9 | 1.3 | 5.1 | 7.6 | 0.9 | 1.4 | .. | .. |
| Sweden | | | | | | | | | | | | |
| Switzerland | | | | | | | | | | | | |
| Syrian Arab Republic | 158 | 27 | 10 | 1 | 0.9 | 0.1 | 4.7 | 0.5 | 2.4 | 0.2 | .. | .. |
| Tajikistan | 124 | 240 | 20 | 36 | 13.7 | 8.8 | 109.9 | 58.8 | .. | 9.9 | 160.3 | .. |
| Tanzania | 1,019 | 1,825 | 30 | 46 | 11.4 | 14.5 | 63.7 | 77.0 | 45.7 | 34.6 | .. | .. |
| Thailand | 698 | −216 | 12 | −3 | 0.6 | −0.1 | 2.5 | −0.4 | 0.9 | −0.1 | .. | −0.6 |
| Timor-Leste | 231 | 210 | 295 | 204 | 71.6 | 24.7 | 285.9 | 310.3 | .. | .. | .. | .. |
| Togo | 70 | 79 | 13 | 12 | 5.4 | 3.6 | 29.4 | .. | 10.5 | .. | .. | 20.1 |
| Trinidad and Tobago | −2 | 13 | −1 | 10 | 0.0 | 0.1 | −0.1 | .. | 0.0 | .. | .. | .. |
| Tunisia | 222 | 432 | 23 | 43 | 1.2 | 1.5 | 4.2 | 5.9 | 2.1 | 2.4 | 4.1 | 4.8 |
| Turkey | 327 | 570 | 5 | 8 | 0.2 | 0.1 | 0.7 | 0.6 | 0.5 | 0.4 | .. | 0.5 |
| Turkmenistan | 31 | 26 | 7 | 5 | 1.2 | 0.3 | 3.1 | .. | .. | .. | .. | .. |
| Uganda | 817 | 1,551 | 33 | 52 | 14.0 | 16.7 | 69.1 | 70.3 | 51.9 | 44.0 | 92.4 | 95.0 |
| Ukraine | 541 | 484 | 11 | 10 | 1.8 | 0.5 | 8.8 | 1.9 | 2.8 | 0.9 | 6.4 | 1.2 |
| United Arab Emirates[b] | 3 | .. | 1 | .. | 0.0 | .. | 0.0 | .. | .. | .. | .. | .. |
| United Kingdom | | | | | | | | | | | | |
| United States | | | | | | | | | | | | |
| Uruguay | 17 | 21 | 5 | 6 | 0.1 | 0.1 | 0.6 | 0.7 | 0.3 | 0.3 | 0.3 | 0.4 |
| Uzbekistan | 186 | 149 | 8 | 6 | 1.4 | 0.9 | 8.3 | 3.9 | .. | .. | .. | .. |
| Venezuela, RB | 76 | 58 | 3 | 2 | 0.1 | 0.0 | 0.3 | 0.1 | 0.3 | 0.1 | 0.3 | .. |
| Vietnam | 1,681 | 1,846 | 22 | 22 | 5.5 | 3.1 | 18.2 | 8.5 | 9.3 | .. | .. | .. |
| West Bank and Gaza | 637 | 1,449 | 215 | 384 | 13.3 | 34.6 | 47.4 | 132.6 | .. | .. | .. | .. |
| Yemen, Rep. | 263 | 284 | 14 | 13 | 3.0 | 1.6 | 14.3 | .. | 6.2 | 3.0 | .. | .. |
| Zambia | 795 | 1,425 | 76 | 122 | 25.8 | 14.6 | 140.8 | 55.4 | 53.1 | 42.0 | .. | 66.5 |
| Zimbabwe | 176 | 280 | 14 | 21 | 2.5 | .. | 17.5 | .. | .. | .. | .. | .. |
| **World** | 57,760 s | 105,292 s | 10 w | 16 w | 0.2 w | 0.2 w | 0.8 w | .. w | 0.6 w | 0.6 w | .. w | .. w |
| **Low income** | 18,665 | 48,150 | 9 | 20 | 2.3 | 3.0 | 9.8 | 10.1 | 9.2 | 8.8 | .. | .. |
| **Middle income** | 24,441 | 34,522 | 8 | 11 | 0.5 | 0.3 | 1.9 | 1.2 | 1.5 | 0.9 | .. | .. |
| Lower middle income | 15,763 | 27,649 | 7 | 12 | 0.7 | 0.6 | 2.3 | 1.6 | 2.1 | 1.5 | .. | .. |
| Upper middle income | 7,518 | 5,722 | 10 | 7 | 0.3 | 0.1 | 1.3 | 0.5 | 0.8 | 0.3 | .. | .. |
| **Low & middle income** | 55,463 | 105,252 | 11 | 19 | 0.9 | 0.9 | 3.8 | 3.2 | 3.0 | 2.5 | .. | .. |
| East Asia & Pacific | 8,589 | 7,888 | 5 | 4 | 0.5 | 0.2 | 1.6 | 0.6 | 1.4 | 0.5 | .. | .. |
| Europe & Central Asia | 10,327 | 6,224 | 22 | 14 | 1.2 | 0.3 | 5.2 | 1.1 | 2.8 | 0.6 | .. | .. |
| Latin America & Carib. | 4,835 | 6,923 | 9 | 12 | 0.2 | 0.2 | 1.2 | 1.2 | 0.9 | 0.8 | .. | .. |
| Middle East & N. Africa | 4,534 | 16,778 | 16 | 54 | 1.0 | 2.1 | 4.0 | 7.9 | 3.3 | 6.1 | .. | .. |
| South Asia | 4,194 | 9,277 | 3 | 6 | 0.7 | 0.8 | 2.9 | 2.5 | 3.6 | 2.9 | .. | .. |
| Sub-Saharan Africa | 13,194 | 40,516 | 20 | 52 | 4.1 | 6.0 | 21.5 | 27.1 | 10.9 | 13.9 | .. | .. |
| **High income** | 2,297 | 40 | 2 | 0 | 0.0 | .. | 0.0 | .. | 0.0 | 0.0 | .. | .. |
| Euro area | | | | | | | | | | | | |

**Note:** Regional aggregates include data for economies not listed in the table. World and income group totals include aid not allocated by country or region—including administrative costs, research on development issues, and aid to nongovernmental organizations. Thus regional and income group totals do not sum to the world total.

a. The distinction between official aid, for countries on the Part II list of the Organisation for Economic Co-operation and Development Development Assistance Committee (DAC), and official development assistance was dropped in 2005. b. No longer on the DAC list of eligible official development assistance recipients. Data for 2000 are official aid. c. Includes Montenegro.

## About the data

Unless otherwise noted, aid includes official development assistance (ODA; see *About the data* for table 6.12). The data cover loans and grants from Development Assistance Committee (DAC) member countries, multilateral organizations, and non-DAC donors. They do not reflect aid given by recipient countries to other developing countries. As a result, some countries that are net donors (such as Saudi Arabia) are shown in the table as aid recipients (see table 6.14a). Data before 2005 for countries that were Part II recipients (see *About the data* for table 6.12 for more information) are defined as official aid.

The table does not distinguish types of aid (program, project, or food aid; emergency assistance; postconflict peacekeeping assistance; or technical cooperation), which may have different effects on the economy. Expenditures on technical cooperation do not always directly benefit the economy to the extent that they defray costs incurred outside the country on salaries and benefits of technical experts and overhead costs of firms supplying technical services.

Ratios of aid to gross national income (GNI), gross capital formation, imports, and government spending provide measures of recipient country dependency on aid. But care must be taken in drawing policy conclusions. For foreign policy reasons some countries have traditionally received large amounts of aid. Thus aid dependency ratios may reveal as much about a donor's interest as about a recipient's needs. Ratios are generally much higher in Sub-Saharan Africa than in other regions, and they increased in the 1980s. High ratios are due only in part to aid flows. Many African countries saw severe erosion in their terms of trade in the 1980s, which, along with weak policies, contributed to falling incomes, imports, and investment. Thus the increase in aid dependency ratios reflects events affecting both the numerator (aid) and the denominator (GNI).

Because the table relies on information from donors, it is not necessarily consistent with information recorded by recipients in the balance of payments, which often excludes all or some technical assistance—particularly payments to expatriates made directly by the donor. Similarly, grant commodity aid may not always be recorded in trade data or in the balance of payments. Moreover, DAC statistics exclude purely military aid.

The nominal values used here may overstate the real value of aid to recipients. Changes in international prices and exchange rates can reduce the purchasing power of aid. Tying aid, still prevalent though declining in importance, also tends to reduce its purchasing power (see *About the data* for table 6.13).

The aggregates refer to World Bank definitions. Therefore the ratios shown may differ from those of the Organisation for Economic Co-operation and Development (OECD).

### Definitions

• **Net official development assistance** is flows (net of repayment of principal) that meet the DAC definition of ODA and are made to countries and territories on the DAC list of aid recipients. See *About the data* for table 6.12. • **Aid per capita** is ODA divided by midyear population. • **Aid dependency ratios** are calculated using values in U.S. dollars converted at official exchange rates. Imports of goods, services, and income refer to international transactions involving a change in ownership of general merchandise, goods sent for processing and repairs, nonmonetary gold, services, receipts of employee compensation for nonresident workers, and investment income. For definitions of GNI, gross capital formation, and central government expense, see *Definitions* for tables 1.1, 4.8, and 4.10.

### Official development assistance from non-DAC donors, 2002–06 — 6.14a

Net disbursements ($ millions)

| | 2002 | 2003 | 2004 | 2005 | 2006 |
|---|---|---|---|---|---|
| **OECD members (non-DAC)** | | | | | |
| Czech Republic | 45 | 91 | 108 | 135 | 161 |
| Hungary | .. | 21 | 70 | 100 | 149 |
| Iceland | 13 | 18 | 21 | 27 | 41 |
| Korea, Rep. | 279 | 366 | 423 | 752 | 455 |
| Poland | 14 | 27 | 118 | 205 | 297 |
| Slovak Republic | 7 | 15 | 28 | 56 | 55 |
| Turkey | 73 | 67 | 339 | 601 | 714 |
| **Arab countries** | | | | | |
| Kuwait | 20 | 138 | 161 | 218 | 158 |
| Saudi Arabia | 2,478 | 2,391 | 1,734 | 1,005 | 2,095 |
| United Arab Emirates | 156 | 188 | 181 | 141 | 249 |
| **Other donors** | | | | | |
| Israel[a] | 131 | 112 | 84 | 95 | 90 |
| Taiwan, China | .. | .. | 421 | 483 | 513 |
| Thailand | .. | .. | .. | .. | 74 |
| Other donors | 3 | 4 | 22 | 86 | 121 |
| **Total** | 3,218 | 3,436 | 3,712 | 3,905 | 5,172 |

**Note:** The table does not reflect aid provided by several major emerging non–Organisation for Economic Co-operation and Development donors because information on their aid has not been disclosed.
a. Includes $87.8 million in 2002, $68.8 million in 2003, $47.9 million in 2004, $49.2 million in 2005, and $45.5 million in 2006 for first-year sustenance expenses for people arriving from developing countries (many of which are experiencing civil war or severe unrest) or people who have left their country for humanitarian or political reasons.
*Source:* Organisation for Economic Co-operation and Development.

### Data sources

Data on financial flows are compiled by DAC and published in its annual statistical report, *Geographical Distribution of Financial Flows to Aid Recipients,* and in its annual *Development Cooperation Report.* Data are available electronically on the OECD's *International Development Statistics* CD-ROM and at www.oecd.org/dac/stats/idsonline. Data on population, GNI, gross capital formation, imports of goods and services, and central government expense used in computing the ratios are from World Bank and International Monetary Fund databases.

# Distribution of net aid by Development Assistance Committee members

|  | Total $ millions 2006 | United States 2006 | European Commission 2006 | United Kingdom 2006 | France 2006 | Japan 2006 | Germany 2006 | Netherlands 2006 | Sweden 2006 | Canada 2006 | Norway 2006 | Other DAC donors $ millions 2006 |
|---|---|---|---|---|---|---|---|---|---|---|---|---|
|  |  |  | **Ten major DAC donors** |  |  | $ millions |  |  |  |  |  |  |
| Afghanistan | 2,625.5 | 1,403.7 | 220.9 | 246.5 | 14.6 | 107.4 | 118.0 | 87.3 | 46.4 | 140.3 | 69.7 | 167.3 |
| Albania | 248.3 | 40.6 | 71.4 | 3.6 | 4.5 | 1.9 | 29.6 | 5.3 | 12.5 | 0.6 | 5.7 | 72.5 |
| Algeria | 190.8 | 0.8 | −13.8 | 0.0 | 173.4 | −11.7 | −25.5 | 0.1 | 0.5 | −3.5 | 1.0 | 69.4 |
| Angola | −6.6 | 32.9 | 48.6 | 12.6 | −97.1 | 12.4 | 11.4 | 2.1 | 7.2 | 1.4 | 23.4 | −61.5 |
| Argentina | 105.6 | 2.0 | 24.6 | 0.0 | 15.9 | 8.0 | 10.9 | 0.1 | 0.4 | 1.5 | 0.0 | 42.1 |
| Armenia | 156.1 | 64.9 | 21.1 | 8.4 | 14.1 | 7.7 | 16.7 | 8.5 | 2.3 | 0.1 | 5.2 | 7.2 |
| Australia |  |  |  |  |  |  |  |  |  |  |  |  |
| Austria |  |  |  |  |  |  |  |  |  |  |  |  |
| Azerbaijan | 113.9 | 56.5 | 18.7 | 0.0 | 10.7 | 4.1 | 12.0 | 0.1 | 0.6 | 0.1 | 5.6 | 5.6 |
| Bangladesh | 557.3 | 41.8 | 100.9 | 139.1 | −2.2 | −7.3 | 29.1 | 67.5 | 38.4 | 56.7 | 21.4 | 71.3 |
| Belarus | 53.6 | 4.4 | 15.5 | 0.0 | 5.1 | 0.2 | 16.0 | 0.0 | 7.8 | 0.1 | 0.2 | 4.4 |
| Belgium |  |  |  |  |  |  |  |  |  |  |  |  |
| Benin | 263.5 | 20.3 | 35.1 | 2.3 | 73.8 | 10.1 | 26.5 | 24.5 | 0.2 | 6.0 | 0.0 | 64.9 |
| Bolivia | 621.7 | 193.1 | 52.0 | 8.7 | 39.8 | 100.4 | 47.0 | 34.4 | 17.9 | 17.0 | 3.6 | 107.7 |
| Bosnia and Herzegovina | 409.5 | 66.0 | 89.3 | 5.9 | 2.9 | 16.1 | 26.7 | 18.9 | 40.2 | 7.6 | 19.0 | 116.8 |
| Botswana | 63.8 | 24.8 | 27.5 | 0.1 | 1.5 | 0.3 | 2.7 | 0.6 | 1.6 | 1.7 | 2.0 | 1.1 |
| Brazil | 83.4 | −67.9 | 8.6 | 1.6 | 30.9 | −13.0 | 65.6 | 2.0 | 3.2 | 7.1 | 2.8 | 42.3 |
| Bulgaria |  |  |  |  |  |  |  |  |  |  |  |  |
| Burkina Faso | 519.5 | 21.9 | 133.7 | 2.8 | 131.4 | 18.5 | 29.5 | 55.1 | 15.0 | 17.1 | 0.4 | 94.1 |
| Burundi | 269.5 | 46.6 | 47.1 | 26.9 | 13.9 | 15.4 | 14.5 | 17.0 | 8.2 | 4.5 | 13.1 | 62.3 |
| Cambodia | 376.3 | 57.9 | 28.8 | 22.3 | 29.8 | 106.3 | 27.6 | 2.0 | 17.1 | 8.1 | 3.1 | 70.0 |
| Cameroon | 1,549.0 | 13.6 | 43.7 | 169.6 | 243.6 | 18.8 | 228.1 | 19.0 | 12.9 | 206.9 | 0.7 | 592.2 |
| Canada |  |  |  |  |  |  |  |  |  |  |  |  |
| Central African Republic | 79.2 | 21.0 | 13.9 | 0.9 | 26.8 | 0.1 | 4.9 | 0.0 | 1.8 | 0.6 | 5.6 | 3.6 |
| Chad | 210.2 | 37.2 | 57.7 | 2.4 | 42.1 | 8.7 | 26.7 | 6.1 | 3.6 | 2.2 | 1.6 | 21.9 |
| Chile | 76.6 | −0.3 | 12.3 | 0.9 | 9.9 | 8.1 | 36.3 | 0.1 | 0.3 | 2.5 | 0.0 | 6.3 |
| China | 1,215.8 | 18.9 | 42.1 | 52.3 | 142.8 | 569.4 | 244.9 | 30.5 | 11.9 | 29.6 | 14.4 | 57.4 |
| Hong Kong, China |  |  |  |  |  |  |  |  |  |  |  |  |
| Colombia | 986.9 | 719.8 | 69.8 | 0.6 | 24.4 | −5.8 | 22.4 | 33.5 | 18.3 | 10.6 | 9.9 | 83.3 |
| Congo, Dem. Rep. | 1,722.6 | 838.5 | 222.2 | 139.9 | 57.2 | 23.2 | 35.7 | 29.9 | 40.0 | 28.1 | 20.7 | 287.2 |
| Congo, Rep. | 225.0 | 9.0 | 55.9 | 0.6 | 123.4 | 0.4 | 3.8 | 0.1 | 3.2 | 3.7 | 1.0 | 23.9 |
| Costa Rica | 27.4 | −9.6 | 7.3 | −0.5 | 5.4 | 6.1 | 7.4 | 1.0 | 0.9 | 2.8 | 0.1 | 6.5 |
| Côte d'Ivoire | 275.4 | 30.9 | 76.5 | 1.9 | 106.8 | 13.0 | 12.5 | 1.0 | 7.8 | 3.4 | 3.8 | 17.8 |
| Croatia | 189.9 | 30.9 | 121.7 | 0.3 | 3.4 | −0.1 | 6.9 | 0.0 | 5.1 | 0.4 | 14.9 | 6.2 |
| Cuba | 59.7 | 14.0 | 2.8 | −2.9 | 3.2 | 3.4 | 3.8 | 0.4 | 0.9 | 7.6 | 1.0 | 25.5 |
| Czech Republic |  |  |  |  |  |  |  |  |  |  |  |  |
| Denmark |  |  |  |  |  |  |  |  |  |  |  |  |
| Dominican Republic | 61.9 | 30.3 | 48.9 | −71.9 | 7.3 | 6.2 | 23.2 | 0.1 | 0.0 | 1.7 | 0.8 | 15.4 |
| Ecuador | 199.0 | 70.1 | 28.5 | −2.0 | 1.8 | 4.5 | 16.5 | 1.9 | 0.6 | 2.2 | 1.9 | 72.8 |
| Egypt, Arab Rep. | 765.2 | 195.6 | 228.5 | 18.8 | 62.7 | −5.2 | 140.6 | 13.1 | 2.0 | 15.9 | 0.5 | 92.8 |
| El Salvador | 167.6 | 24.5 | 17.0 | 11.3 | 3.3 | 29.8 | 9.2 | 0.9 | 4.3 | 3.0 | 0.5 | 63.8 |
| Eritrea | 78.1 | 6.6 | 14.9 | 5.5 | 0.9 | 9.9 | 4.8 | 3.3 | 2.1 | 0.8 | 17.9 | 11.5 |
| Estonia |  |  |  |  |  |  |  |  |  |  |  |  |
| Ethiopia | 1,218.5 | 315.8 | 194.4 | 164.6 | 17.4 | 57.9 | 56.8 | 49.8 | 41.5 | 62.5 | 41.8 | 216.0 |
| Finland |  |  |  |  |  |  |  |  |  |  |  |  |
| France |  |  |  |  |  |  |  |  |  |  |  |  |
| Gabon | 34.6 | 1.1 | 2.7 | 0.0 | 30.1 | −0.3 | −0.2 | 0.0 | 0.0 | 1.3 | 0.0 | −0.2 |
| Gambia, The | 26.5 | 4.7 | 1.5 | 4.1 | 0.6 | 11.0 | 1.3 | 0.1 | 0.8 | 1.2 | 0.3 | 1.1 |
| Georgia | 265.5 | 103.2 | 55.1 | 4.9 | 4.4 | 11.6 | 46.4 | 11.1 | 9.4 | 0.8 | 7.4 | 11.1 |
| Germany |  |  |  |  |  |  |  |  |  |  |  |  |
| Ghana | 656.5 | 68.4 | 61.9 | 167.2 | 23.2 | 43.7 | 59.8 | 97.0 | 0.8 | 53.9 | 1.0 | 79.7 |
| Greece |  |  |  |  |  |  |  |  |  |  |  |  |
| Guatemala | 476.8 | 67.3 | 31.7 | −4.7 | 3.6 | 38.9 | 17.9 | 20.0 | 32.6 | 10.2 | 14.9 | 243.6 |
| Guinea | 124.2 | 34.9 | 21.3 | 1.0 | 20.6 | 17.1 | 14.0 | 0.1 | 1.5 | 7.2 | 0.6 | 6.1 |
| Guinea-Bissau | 72.6 | 5.5 | 33.3 | 0.0 | 9.9 | 0.0 | 0.3 | 0.0 | 0.0 | 0.7 | 0.4 | 22.5 |
| Haiti | 445.7 | 190.7 | 82.4 | 2.0 | 26.9 | 5.5 | 3.3 | 0.2 | 2.9 | 97.5 | 8.0 | 26.3 |

**Ten major DAC donors**

| | Total $ millions 2006 | United States 2006 | European Commission 2006 | United Kingdom 2006 | France 2006 | Japan 2006 | Germany 2006 | Netherlands 2006 | Sweden 2006 | Canada 2006 | Norway 2006 | Other DAC donors $ millions 2006 |
|---|---|---|---|---|---|---|---|---|---|---|---|---|
| Honduras | 417.0 | 84.1 | 32.3 | 1.1 | 34.8 | 138.0 | 13.7 | 1.1 | 18.7 | 15.1 | 1.6 | 76.4 |
| Hungary | | | | | | | | | | | | |
| India | 862.8 | 96.8 | 209.7 | 349.3 | 4.3 | 29.6 | 55.7 | 13.1 | 17.1 | 25.5 | 18.3 | 42.6 |
| Indonesia | 825.7 | 190.1 | 137.2 | 101.6 | −55.7 | −73.9 | 50.4 | 75.6 | 23.9 | 37.3 | 10.3 | 320.2 |
| Iran, Islamic Rep. | 90.9 | 2.3 | 20.1 | 0.0 | 15.4 | −7.3 | 38.4 | 1.0 | 0.0 | 0.0 | 2.6 | 18.3 |
| Iraq | 8,495.8 | 4,781.8 | 8.0 | 203.0 | 790.7 | 780.8 | 388.2 | 3.2 | 278.3 | 17.7 | 22.6 | 1,219.0 |
| Ireland | | | | | | | | | | | | |
| Israel | | | | | | | | | | | | |
| Italy | | | | | | | | | | | | |
| Jamaica | 32.2 | 9.4 | 32.9 | 14.5 | −1.3 | −16.2 | −7.6 | −3.0 | 0.1 | 3.3 | 0.4 | −0.2 |
| Japan | | | | | | | | | | | | |
| Jordan | 412.1 | 329.5 | 50.2 | 0.9 | −3.5 | −15.6 | 17.2 | 0.3 | 0.4 | 5.5 | 3.8 | 23.4 |
| Kazakhstan | 108.4 | 51.5 | 12.4 | 0.2 | 3.0 | 24.9 | 11.3 | 0.3 | 0.9 | 0.1 | 2.6 | 1.4 |
| Kenya | 818.6 | 282.4 | 57.4 | 107.8 | 20.1 | 106.2 | 45.4 | 26.3 | 51.9 | 24.2 | 12.3 | 83.3 |
| Korea, Dem. Rep. | 40.9 | 0.4 | 12.1 | 0.0 | 0.6 | 0.0 | 2.9 | 0.6 | 5.1 | 0.3 | 3.8 | 14.9 |
| Korea, Rep. | | | | | | | | | | | | |
| Kuwait | | | | | | | | | | | | |
| Kyrgyz Republic | 135.5 | 50.3 | 12.0 | 11.2 | 1.1 | 17.2 | 17.9 | 0.1 | 5.0 | 0.1 | 2.3 | 18.2 |
| Lao PDR | 196.4 | 4.3 | 8.8 | 0.3 | 22.9 | 64.1 | 18.3 | 0.1 | 23.7 | 2.9 | 11.4 | 37.1 |
| Latvia | | | | | | | | | | | | |
| Lebanon | 600.0 | 91.4 | 211.4 | 6.9 | 74.3 | 5.3 | 28.9 | 13.4 | 9.7 | 16.4 | 27.8 | 113.8 |
| Lesotho | 42.5 | 3.2 | 4.0 | 7.6 | −1.2 | 4.8 | 6.6 | 0.1 | 0.0 | 0.9 | 1.3 | 15.2 |
| Liberia | 231.7 | 88.4 | 44.2 | 15.3 | 2.1 | 17.4 | 9.0 | 6.5 | 15.2 | 1.6 | 8.9 | 23.1 |
| Libya | 34.2 | 25.1 | 0.8 | 0.0 | 2.4 | 0.1 | 3.9 | 0.0 | 0.0 | 0.0 | 0.1 | 1.9 |
| Lithuania | | | | | | | | | | | | |
| Macedonia, FYR | 189.7 | 39.2 | 58.7 | 0.6 | 3.3 | 9.5 | 17.2 | 11.4 | 13.4 | 0.1 | 12.4 | 24.0 |
| Madagascar | 428.0 | 61.1 | 162.4 | 5.1 | 103.8 | 43.8 | 11.2 | 0.2 | 13.1 | 1.7 | 16.1 | 9.6 |
| Malawi | 476.6 | 64.0 | 78.7 | 170.9 | 0.6 | 23.4 | 23.8 | 10.4 | 17.4 | 12.5 | 50.3 | 24.3 |
| Malaysia | 231.6 | 3.2 | 1.4 | 9.9 | −3.0 | 201.9 | 8.0 | 0.2 | 0.5 | 0.2 | 2.0 | 7.3 |
| Mali | 525.1 | 65.0 | 126.7 | 4.1 | 81.6 | 26.7 | 40.2 | 66.1 | 25.4 | 27.3 | 17.0 | 44.9 |
| Mauritania | 119.9 | 12.2 | 26.2 | 1.0 | 31.6 | 12.1 | 13.8 | 0.4 | 1.1 | 2.3 | 0.5 | 18.8 |
| Mauritius | 23.1 | 0.4 | 14.6 | −0.1 | 2.7 | 4.0 | −0.1 | 0.0 | 0.0 | 0.4 | 0.0 | 1.2 |
| Mexico | 226.2 | 153.5 | 17.3 | 0.0 | 22.2 | 21.4 | 25.8 | −0.2 | 0.1 | 6.8 | 0.0 | −21.0 |
| Moldova | 109.7 | 23.9 | 26.2 | 3.4 | 6.6 | 6.1 | 9.4 | 7.0 | 11.9 | 0.2 | 2.7 | 12.2 |
| Mongolia | 129.8 | 12.4 | 3.1 | 0.4 | 1.4 | 47.0 | 29.7 | 8.0 | 2.6 | 1.3 | 1.1 | 22.3 |
| Morocco | 905.4 | −6.5 | 338.7 | 0.0 | 301.4 | 61.1 | 104.5 | 0.4 | 1.5 | 7.2 | 0.1 | 97.0 |
| Mozambique | 1,112.9 | 108.9 | 174.6 | 99.4 | 9.0 | 106.8 | 64.9 | 59.7 | 91.8 | 49.4 | 64.3 | 284.2 |
| Myanmar | 103.1 | 10.9 | 11.1 | 13.5 | 1.5 | 30.9 | 5.5 | 0.7 | 3.8 | 0.1 | 8.1 | 16.5 |
| Namibia | 110.5 | 50.6 | 4.8 | 1.5 | 2.0 | 1.0 | 13.9 | 0.9 | 9.0 | 1.4 | 1.7 | 23.8 |
| Nepal | 341.9 | 61.5 | 24.4 | 74.8 | −2.4 | 41.7 | 33.0 | 4.2 | 2.1 | 11.1 | 25.0 | 65.2 |
| Netherlands | | | | | | | | | | | | |
| New Zealand | | | | | | | | | | | | |
| Nicaragua | 472.1 | 67.5 | 86.6 | 9.3 | 1.9 | 35.9 | 22.8 | 34.6 | 40.2 | 11.2 | 25.2 | 136.3 |
| Niger | 322.4 | 30.6 | 87.2 | 6.1 | 88.8 | 12.1 | 21.3 | 0.0 | 0.1 | 6.8 | 2.5 | 67.0 |
| Nigeria | 10,969.6 | 787.2 | 150.0 | 3,185.7 | 2,027.2 | 1,631.6 | 1,710.4 | 228.8 | 1.0 | 15.7 | 2.9 | 1,229.0 |
| Norway | | | | | | | | | | | | |
| Oman | −14.5 | −17.1 | 0.0 | 0.0 | 0.8 | 1.5 | 0.3 | 0.0 | 0.0 | 0.0 | 0.0 | 0.0 |
| Pakistan | 1,202.8 | 477.7 | 57.9 | 203.2 | 15.8 | 225.0 | 59.5 | 20.8 | 11.8 | 43.4 | 18.7 | 68.4 |
| Panama | 32.0 | 18.7 | 12.8 | −10.7 | 0.3 | 2.1 | 1.1 | 0.1 | 0.0 | 0.9 | 0.0 | 6.8 |
| Papua New Guinea | 264.9 | 0.2 | 16.7 | −0.4 | 0.1 | −9.0 | −0.9 | 0.3 | 0.0 | 0.5 | 0.6 | 243.3 |
| Paraguay | 64.3 | 17.6 | 2.2 | −0.4 | 0.8 | 25.9 | 4.2 | 0.0 | 1.6 | 0.9 | 0.8 | 10.7 |
| Peru | 428.9 | 187.3 | 54.1 | 22.1 | 11.4 | −0.5 | 25.1 | −0.3 | 4.0 | 14.5 | 1.4 | 108.6 |
| Philippines | 540.0 | 97.8 | 20.5 | 0.9 | −9.3 | 263.6 | 47.2 | 16.6 | 5.9 | 19.9 | 4.7 | 67.7 |
| Poland | | | | | | | | | | | | |
| Portugal | | | | | | | | | | | | |
| Puerto Rico | | | | | | | | | | | | |

|  | Total $ millions 2006 | United States 2006 | European Commission 2006 | United Kingdom 2006 | France 2006 | Japan 2006 | Germany 2006 | Netherlands 2006 | Sweden 2006 | Canada 2006 | Norway 2006 | Other DAC donors $ millions 2006 |
|---|---|---|---|---|---|---|---|---|---|---|---|---|
| | | | | | | | Ten major DAC donors | | | | | |
| | | | | | | | $ millions | | | | | |
| Romania | | | | | | | | | | | | |
| Russian Federation | | | | | | | | | | | | |
| Rwanda | 386.1 | 77.6 | 65.0 | 95.4 | 10.6 | 12.7 | 19.4 | 24.7 | 17.5 | 6.2 | 4.0 | 53.0 |
| Saudi Arabia | 11.2 | 0.7 | 0.0 | 0.0 | 4.5 | 4.6 | 1.1 | 0.0 | 0.0 | 0.0 | 0.0 | 0.3 |
| Senegal | 542.8 | 37.7 | 33.7 | 10.1 | 287.5 | 34.5 | 34.8 | 19.5 | 0.6 | 17.1 | 0.6 | 66.7 |
| Serbia | 1,503.7 | 147.0 | 334.5 | 180.5 | 109.8 | 8.4 | 202.5 | 21.3 | 44.3 | 49.9 | 32.6 | 373.0 |
| Sierra Leone | 258.4 | 21.0 | 59.3 | 65.6 | 1.9 | 62.7 | 10.8 | 5.8 | 3.9 | 5.2 | 2.7 | 19.5 |
| Singapore | | | | | | | | | | | | |
| Slovak Republic | | | | | | | | | | | | |
| Slovenia | | | | | | | | | | | | |
| Somalia | 351.7 | 95.2 | 88.5 | 53.2 | 1.7 | 0.2 | 7.0 | 14.1 | 13.3 | 7.1 | 33.8 | 37.4 |
| South Africa | 697.3 | 140.5 | 136.7 | 1.5 | 158.8 | 15.9 | 40.5 | 53.2 | 22.1 | 11.1 | 14.1 | 101.5 |
| Spain | | | | | | | | | | | | |
| Sri Lanka | 509.8 | 29.2 | 24.5 | 6.9 | −0.7 | 202.7 | 63.9 | 15.0 | 20.6 | 15.4 | 37.3 | 93.6 |
| Sudan | 1,817.6 | 738.8 | 299.4 | 215.6 | 14.7 | 42.7 | 50.7 | 96.1 | 47.5 | 79.3 | 106.9 | 123.9 |
| Swaziland | 22.7 | 1.9 | 10.4 | 0.2 | 0.2 | 11.6 | −3.0 | 0.0 | 0.0 | 1.0 | 0.4 | 0.0 |
| Sweden | | | | | | | | | | | | |
| Switzerland | | | | | | | | | | | | |
| Syrian Arab Republic | 17.2 | 0.6 | 28.6 | 0.0 | 27.4 | −41.5 | −9.4 | 0.1 | 0.8 | 0.1 | 0.9 | 9.6 |
| Tajikistan | 125.3 | 43.6 | 33.5 | 7.0 | 0.6 | 8.0 | 8.7 | 0.0 | 8.9 | 0.4 | 1.7 | 13.0 |
| Tanzania | 1,180.5 | 121.6 | 188.8 | 218.9 | 2.0 | 39.4 | 49.3 | 114.6 | 111.7 | 41.7 | 75.4 | 215.6 |
| Thailand | −262.2 | 25.0 | 30.6 | −2.3 | 64.9 | −453.3 | 26.8 | 9.3 | 7.9 | 2.6 | 6.4 | 19.9 |
| Timor-Leste | 199.3 | 20.6 | 25.6 | 4.2 | 0.1 | 21.8 | 5.4 | 0.2 | 1.6 | 1.8 | 14.5 | 98.2 |
| Togo | 65.1 | 2.0 | 10.4 | 0.7 | 33.3 | 0.4 | 8.0 | 0.0 | 0.7 | 2.0 | 0.1 | 7.5 |
| Trinidad and Tobago | 11.4 | 0.2 | 7.3 | 0.1 | 1.2 | 1.3 | 0.3 | 0.0 | 0.0 | 0.7 | 0.0 | 0.2 |
| Tunisia | 436.3 | −12.8 | 149.3 | 16.5 | 176.3 | 18.6 | 39.6 | −2.1 | 0.7 | 0.7 | 0.0 | 49.4 |
| Turkey | 530.5 | −20.1 | 383.3 | −1.4 | 32.9 | 62.3 | −52.8 | 5.0 | 3.2 | −2.3 | 1.8 | 118.5 |
| Turkmenistan | 7.2 | 3.1 | 1.8 | 0.0 | 0.8 | 0.6 | 0.8 | 0.0 | 0.0 | 0.0 | 0.0 | 0.0 |
| Uganda | 1,093.7 | 246.2 | 155.5 | 214.4 | 5.4 | 21.8 | 54.6 | 82.4 | 62.6 | 14.1 | 50.5 | 186.1 |
| Ukraine | 414.0 | 130.2 | 133.4 | 12.0 | 14.3 | 6.6 | 58.7 | 0.3 | 18.4 | 15.8 | 0.5 | 23.7 |
| United Arab Emirates | | | | | | | | | | | | |
| United Kingdom | | | | | | | | | | | | |
| United States | | | | | | | | | | | | |
| Uruguay | 17.6 | 0.4 | 6.8 | 0.0 | 6.3 | 2.3 | 0.3 | 0.0 | 0.4 | 1.1 | 0.0 | 0.1 |
| Uzbekistan | 105.1 | 49.2 | 12.6 | 0.1 | 2.7 | 18.6 | 15.8 | 0.0 | 1.4 | 0.0 | 0.5 | 4.2 |
| Venezuela, RB | 48.5 | 9.8 | 15.6 | 0.0 | 6.1 | 2.8 | 6.0 | 0.1 | 0.0 | 0.6 | 0.2 | 7.4 |
| Vietnam | 1,348.3 | 45.2 | 41.8 | 82.2 | 159.4 | 562.9 | 86.8 | 61.1 | 42.8 | 34.4 | 15.2 | 213.9 |
| West Bank and Gaza | 1,012.3 | 205.5 | 257.9 | 35.1 | 40.0 | 78.2 | 67.7 | 32.2 | 51.0 | 34.6 | 87.8 | 121.8 |
| Yemen, Rep. | 157.6 | 31.8 | 22.7 | 15.0 | 6.1 | 5.6 | 41.4 | 28.7 | 0.6 | 1.5 | 0.3 | 4.0 |
| Zambia | 1,213.5 | 309.9 | 98.3 | 86.8 | 63.7 | 31.5 | 287.5 | 55.7 | 48.3 | 10.6 | 66.2 | 154.2 |
| Zimbabwe | 254.5 | 36.4 | 54.7 | 69.9 | 3.6 | 6.5 | 9.9 | 7.4 | 17.8 | 6.8 | 11.2 | 29.5 |
| **World** | 86,449.2 s | 21,162.1 s | 9,489.1 s | 8,717.6 s | 7,919.4 s | 7,313.1 s | 7,034.0 s | 4,282.2 s | 2,851.9 s | 2,531.0 s | 2,197.6 s | 12,748.4 s |
| **Low income** | 37,148.5 | 7,237.9 | 3,827.2 | 6,316.1 | 3,619.5 | 3,751.0 | 3,319.1 | 1,397.0 | 895.2 | 946.0 | 856.8 | 4,921.8 |
| **Middle income** | 30,193.8 | 9,045.4 | 4,136.1 | 903.3 | 3,381.0 | 2,325.8 | 2,462.0 | 559.2 | 801.0 | 676.5 | 483.6 | 5,310.3 |
| Lower middle income | 23,889.9 | 8,184.8 | 2,515.9 | 680.7 | 2,383.5 | 1,939.1 | 1,889.8 | 454.4 | 693.6 | 533.2 | 344.6 | 4,216.7 |
| Upper middle income | 5,237.0 | 636.7 | 1,415.6 | 215.6 | 861.9 | 383.8 | 405.3 | 97.1 | 95.0 | 104.0 | 101.1 | 898.0 |
| **Low & middle income** | 86,425.0 | 21,159.1 | 9,485.2 | 8,717.4 | 7,913.5 | 7,305.0 | 7,032.6 | 4,282.2 | 2,851.9 | 2,530.1 | 2,197.6 | 12,747.7 |
| East Asia & Pacific | 6,195.1 | 725.1 | 459.8 | 289.0 | 473.5 | 1,420.4 | 580.8 | 207.6 | 161.9 | 140.4 | 99.6 | 1,490.1 |
| Europe & Central Asia | 5,017.7 | 1,034.8 | 1,465.5 | 236.6 | 224.7 | 204.1 | 471.8 | 90.5 | 190.1 | 83.3 | 131.8 | 884.5 |
| Latin America & Carib. | 6,076.9 | 1,952.9 | 827.3 | 58.7 | 303.8 | 428.1 | 446.7 | 167.8 | 187.4 | 368.7 | 94.5 | 1,236.0 |
| Middle East & N. Africa | 13,614.2 | 5,740.8 | 1,486.2 | 304.5 | 1,759.5 | 878.6 | 860.4 | 91.2 | 354.8 | 102.3 | 151.4 | 1,880.5 |
| South Asia | 6,264.8 | 2,165.9 | 650.9 | 1,019.7 | 32.2 | 624.8 | 377.4 | 212.5 | 143.7 | 297.3 | 192.6 | 539.0 |
| Sub-Saharan Africa | 33,091.4 | 5,592.7 | 3,370.5 | 5,404.0 | 4,362.1 | 2,553.6 | 3,191.7 | 1,330.3 | 881.6 | 1,041.6 | 773.8 | 4,579.5 |
| **High income** | 24.2 | 3.1 | 3.9 | 0.2 | 5.9 | 8.1 | 1.4 | 0.0 | 0.0 | 1.0 | 0.0 | 0.7 |
| Euro area | | | | | | | | | | | | |

**Note:** Regional aggregates include data for economies not specified elsewhere. World and income group totals include aid not allocated by country or region.

## About the data

The table shows net bilateral aid to low- and middle-income economies from members of the Development Assistance Committee (DAC) of the Organisation for Economic Co-operation and Development (OECD). The data include aid to some countries and territories not shown in the table and aid to unspecified economies recorded only at the regional or global level. Aid to countries and territories not shown in the table has been assigned to regional totals based on the World Bank's regional classification system. Aid to unspecified economies is included in regional totals and, when possible, income group totals. Aid not allocated by country or region—including administrative costs, research on development, and aid to nongovernmental organizations—is included in the world total. Thus regional and income group totals do not sum to the world total.

The table is based on donor country reports of bilateral programs, which may differ from reports by recipient countries. Recipients may lack access to information on such aid expenditures as development-oriented research, stipends and tuition costs for aid-financed students in donor countries, and payment of experts hired by donor countries. Moreover, a full accounting would include donor country contributions to multilateral institutions, the flow of resources from multilateral institutions to recipient countries, and flows from countries that are not members of DAC. Previous editions of the table included only DAC member economies. This year's edition includes net aid from the European Commission—a multilateral member of DAC.

The expenditures that countries report as official development assistance (ODA) have changed. For example, some DAC members have reported as ODA the aid provided to refugees during the first 12 months of their stay within the donor's borders.

Some of the aid recipients shown in the table are also aid donors. See table 6.14a for a summary of ODA from non-DAC countries.

## Definitions

• **Net aid** comprises net bilateral official development assistance that meets the DAC definition of official development assistance and are made to countries and territories on the DAC list of aid recipients. See *About the data* for table 6.12 • **Other DAC donors** are Australia, Austria, Belgium, Denmark, Finland, Greece, Ireland, Italy, Luxembourg, New Zealand, Portugal, Spain, and Switzerland.

## Debt relief and political interests have shaped the allocation of official development assistance

6.15a

Share of official development assistance (ODA) net disbursements received

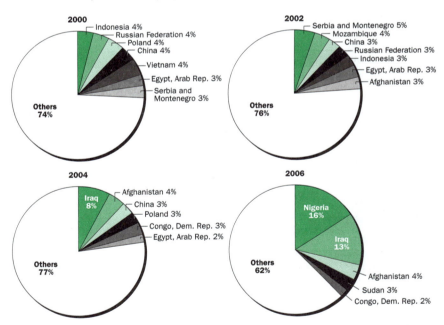

One-time disbursements of debt relief to Iraq and Nigeria increased their share of ODA in 2006. Large aid flows also went to fragile states and international hot spots. Some changes reflect administrative decisions: since 2005 aid to the Russian Federation and the new member states of the European Union are no longer counted as ODA.

**Note:** Only ODA allocated to specific economies are included in the denominators.
*Source:* Organisation for Economic Co-operation and Development Development Assistance Committee.

## Data sources

Data on financial flows are compiled by DAC and published in its annual statistical report, *Geographical Distribution of Financial Flows to Aid Recipients*, and its annual *Development Cooperation Report*. Data are available electronically on the OECD's *International Development Statistics* CD-ROM and at www.oecd.org/dac/stats/idsonline.

| | Net migration | | International migrant stock | | Refugees | | | | Workers' remittances and compensation of employees | | | |
|---|---|---|---|---|---|---|---|---|---|---|---|---|
| | | | | | | | | | | $ millions | | |
| | | | | | | thousands | | | | | | |
| | | | | | By country of origin | | By country of asylum | | Received | | Paid | |
| | thousands | | thousands | | | | | | | | | |
| | 1990–95 | 2000–05 | 1995 | 2005 | 1995 | 2006 | 1995 | 2006 | 1995 | 2006 | 1995 | 2006 |
| Afghanistan | 3,313 | 1,112 | 35 | 43 | 2,679.1 | 2,107.5 | 19.6 | .. | .. | .. | .. | .. |
| Albania | –409 | –110 | 71 | 83 | 5.8 | 14.1 | 4.7 | 0.1 | 427 | 1,359 | .. | 27 |
| Algeria | –50 | –140 | 299 | 242 | 1.5 | 8.4 | 192.5 | 94.2 | 1,120[a] | 2,527[a] | .. | .. |
| Angola | 143 | 175 | 38 | 56 | 246.7 | 206.5 | 10.9 | 13.1 | 5 | .. | 210 | 413 |
| Argentina | 50 | –100 | 1,590 | 1,500 | 0.3 | 0.9 | 10.3 | 3.2 | 56 | 541 | 190 | 366 |
| Armenia | –500 | –100 | 455 | 235 | 201.4 | 14.9 | 219.0 | 113.7 | 65[a] | 1,175[a] | 17 | 154 |
| Australia | 519 | 593 | 4,068 | 4,097 | .. | .. | 62.2 | 68.9 | 1,651 | 3,133 | 700 | 2,815 |
| Austria | 262 | 180 | 717 | 1,234 | .. | .. | 34.4 | 25.5 | 1,012 | 1,989 | 346 | 1,533 |
| Azerbaijan | –116 | –100 | 292 | 182 | 200.5 | 126.1 | 233.7 | 2.6 | 3 | 813 | 9 | 301 |
| Bangladesh | –260 | –500 | 1,006 | 1,032 | .. | .. | 51.1 | 26.3 | 1,202 | 5,428 | 1 | 3 |
| Belarus | 0 | 0 | 1,269 | 1,191 | 0.1 | 9.4 | 29.0 | 0.7 | 29 | 334 | 12 | 93 |
| Belgium | 85 | 180 | 909 | 719 | .. | 0.1 | 31.7 | 16.8 | 4,937 | 7,476 | 3,252 | 2,669 |
| Benin | 105 | 99 | 146 | 175 | .. | .. | 23.8 | 10.8 | 100[a] | 173[a] | 26[a] | 40[a] |
| Bolivia | –100 | –100 | 70 | 116 | 0.2 | 0.4 | 0.7 | 0.6 | 7 | 612 | 9 | 73 |
| Bosnia and Herzegovina | –1,000 | 115 | 73 | 41 | .. | .. | .. | 10.3 | .. | 2,068 | .. | 55 |
| Botswana | 14 | 20 | 39 | 80 | .. | .. | 0.3 | 3.2 | 59 | 117 | 200 | 118 |
| Brazil | –184 | –229 | 730 | 641 | 0.1 | 0.7 | 2.1 | 3.5 | 3,315 | 4,253 | 347 | 691 |
| Bulgaria | –349 | –43 | 47 | 104 | 4.2 | 3.4 | 1.3 | 4.5 | 42 | 1,695 | 34 | 47 |
| Burkina Faso | –128 | 100 | 464 | 773 | 0.1 | 0.4 | 29.8 | 0.5 | 80[a] | 50[a] | 51[a] | 44[a] |
| Burundi | –250 | 192 | 295 | 100 | 350.6 | 396.5 | 173.0 | 13.2 | .. | 0 | 5 | 0 |
| Cambodia | 150 | 10 | 116 | 304 | 61.2 | 18.0 | .. | 0.1 | 12 | 297 | 52 | 158 |
| Cameroon | –5 | 6 | 159 | 137 | 2.0 | 10.4 | 45.8 | 35.1 | 11[a] | 103[a] | 22[a] | 42[a] |
| Canada | 643 | 1,041 | 5,003 | 6,106 | .. | 0.1 | 152.1 | 151.8 | .. | .. | .. | .. |
| Central African Republic | 37 | –45 | 67 | 76 | 57.0 | 7.8 | 33.9 | 12.4 | 0 | .. | 27 | .. |
| Chad | –10 | 219 | 78 | 437 | 59.7 | 36.3 | 0.1 | 286.7 | 1 | .. | 15 | .. |
| Chile | 90 | 30 | 136 | 231 | 14.3 | 0.8 | 0.3 | 1.1 | .. | 3 | 7 | 6 |
| China | –1,281 | –1,900 | 441 | 596 | 104.7 | 140.6 | 288.3 | 301.0 | 1,053[a] | 23,319[a] | 19 | 3,025 |
| Hong Kong, China | 300 | 300 | 2,432 | 2,999 | 0.2 | .. | 1.5 | 1.9 | .. | 297 | .. | 365 |
| Colombia | –250 | –120 | 108 | 123 | .. | .. | 0.2 | 0.1 | 815 | 3,928 | 150 | 66 |
| Congo, Dem. Rep. | 1,208 | –237 | 2,049 | 539 | .. | .. | 1,433.8 | 208.4 | .. | .. | .. | .. |
| Congo, Rep. | 14 | –10 | 169 | 288 | 0.1 | 0.2 | 19.4 | 55.8 | 4[a] | 11[a] | 27[a] | 45[a] |
| Costa Rica | 62 | 84 | 228 | 441 | 0.2 | 0.3 | 24.2 | 11.5 | 123 | 513 | 36 | 246 |
| Côte d'Ivoire | 214 | –339 | 2,314 | 2,371 | .. | .. | 297.9 | 27.3 | 151 | 164 | 457 | 17 |
| Croatia | 153 | 100 | 721 | 661 | .. | .. | 198.7 | 2.4 | 544 | 1,234 | 17 | 274 |
| Cuba | –98 | –129 | 90 | 74 | 24.9 | 33.6 | 1.8 | 0.7 | .. | .. | .. | .. |
| Czech Republic | 8 | 67 | 454 | 453 | 769.8 | 199.9 | 2.7 | 1.9 | 191 | 1,186 | 101 | 2,831 |
| Denmark | 58 | 46 | 250 | 389 | .. | .. | 64.8 | 36.7 | 523 | 869 | 209 | 1,763 |
| Dominican Republic | –129 | –148 | 118 | 156 | .. | 0.2 | 1.0 | .. | 839 | 3,044 | 7 | 27 |
| Ecuador | –50 | –400 | 88 | 114 | 0.2 | 0.9 | 0.2 | 11.8 | 386 | 2,922 | 4 | 62 |
| Egypt, Arab Rep. | –600 | –525 | 172 | 166 | .. | .. | 5.4 | 88.0 | 3,226 | 5,330 | 223 | 135 |
| El Salvador | –90 | –143 | 26 | 24 | .. | .. | 0.2 | .. | 1,064 | 3,329 | 1 | 29 |
| Eritrea | –359 | 229 | 12 | 15 | 286.7 | 193.7 | 1.1 | 4.6 | .. | .. | .. | .. |
| Estonia | –108 | 1 | 309 | 202 | 0.4 | 0.6 | .. | .. | 1 | 402 | 3 | 75 |
| Ethiopia | 868 | –140 | 795 | 555 | 101.0 | 74.0 | 393.5 | 97.0 | 27 | 172 | 1 | 14 |
| Finland | 43 | 33 | 103 | 156 | .. | .. | 10.2 | 11.8 | 74 | 698 | 54 | 251 |
| France | 424 | 722 | 6,089 | 6,471 | .. | 0.1 | 155.3 | 146.0 | 4,640 | 12,479 | 4,935 | 4,330 |
| Gabon | 20 | 10 | 164 | 245 | .. | 0.1 | 0.8 | 8.4 | 4[a] | 7[a] | 99[a] | 110[a] |
| Gambia, The | 45 | 31 | 148 | 232 | 0.2 | 1.3 | 6.6 | 13.8 | 19 | 64 | .. | 1 |
| Georgia | –560 | –248 | 250 | 191 | 0.3 | 6.3 | 0.1 | 1.4 | 284 | 485 | 12 | 24 |
| Germany | 2,688 | 1,000 | 9,092 | 10,144 | 0.4 | 0.1 | 1,267.9 | 605.4 | 4,523 | 6,667 | 11,270 | 12,344 |
| Ghana | 40 | 12 | 1,038 | 1,669 | 13.6 | 10.0 | 83.2 | 44.9 | 17 | 105 | 5[a] | 6[a] |
| Greece | 470 | 154 | 549 | 974 | .. | .. | 4.4 | 2.3 | 3,286 | 1,543 | 300 | 982 |
| Guatemala | –360 | –300 | 45 | 53 | .. | .. | 1.5 | 0.4 | 358 | 3,626 | 8 | 35 |
| Guinea | 350 | –425 | 870 | 406 | 0.4 | 6.8 | 672.3 | 31.5 | 1[a] | 42[a] | 10[a] | 48[a] |
| Guinea-Bissau | 20 | 1 | 32 | 19 | 0.8 | 1.0 | 15.4 | 7.8 | 2[a] | 28[a] | 3[a] | 5[a] |
| Haiti | –133 | –140 | 22 | 30 | 13.9 | 20.8 | .. | .. | 109 | 1,070 | .. | 68 |

# Movement of people

| | Net migration | | International migrant stock | | Refugees | | | | Workers' remittances and compensation of employees | | | |
|---|---|---|---|---|---|---|---|---|---|---|---|---|
| | | | | | | | | | $ millions | | | |
| | | | | | | thousands | | | Received | | Paid | |
| | thousands | | thousands | | By country of origin | | By country of asylum | | | | | |
| | 1990–95 | 2000–05 | 1995 | 2005 | 1995 | 2006 | 1995 | 2006 | 1995 | 2006 | 1995 | 2006 |
| Honduras | −120 | −150 | 31 | 26 | 1.2 | 1.0 | 0.1 | .. | 124 | 2,367 | 8 | 1 |
| Hungary | 101 | 65 | 293 | 316 | .. | .. | 11.4 | 8.1 | 152 | 363 | 146 | 190 |
| India | −960 | −1,350 | 6,951 | 5,700 | 5.0 | 17.8 | 227.5 | 158.4 | 6,223 | 25,426 | 419 | 1,580 |
| Indonesia | −725 | −1,000 | 219 | 160 | 9.8 | 34.7 | .. | 0.3 | 651 | 5,722 | .. | 1,359 |
| Iran, Islamic Rep. | −1,587 | −1,250 | 2,478 | 1,959 | .. | 0.1 | 2,072.0 | 968.4 | 1,600[a] | 1,032[a] | .. | .. |
| Iraq | 170 | −375 | 134 | 28 | 1.9 | 72.8 | 116.7 | 44.4 | .. | .. | .. | .. |
| Ireland | −1 | 188 | 264 | 585 | .. | .. | 0.4 | 7.9 | 347 | 532 | 173 | 1,947 |
| Israel | 484 | 115 | 1,919 | 2,661 | 0.9 | 0.9 | .. | 0.8 | 702 | 1,063 | 1,408 | 2,428 |
| Italy | 573 | 1,125 | 1,483 | 2,519 | 0.1 | 0.1 | 74.3 | 26.9 | 2,364 | 2,626 | 1,824 | 8,216 |
| Jamaica | −100 | −100 | 20 | 18 | .. | 0.7 | .. | .. | 653 | 1,946 | 74 | 385 |
| Japan | 248 | 270 | 1,261 | 2,048 | .. | 0.2 | 5.4 | 1.8 | 1,151 | 1,380 | 1,820 | 3,476 |
| Jordan | 509 | 130 | 1,618 | 2,225 | 0.5 | 1.6 | 1,288.9[b] | 2,358.6[b] | 1,441 | 2,883 | 107 | 402 |
| Kazakhstan | −1,509 | −200 | 3,295 | 2,502 | 0.1 | 7.4 | 15.6 | 4.4 | 116 | 187 | 503 | 3,036 |
| Kenya | 222 | 25 | 366 | 345 | 9.3 | 5.4 | 234.7 | 272.5 | 298[a] | 1,128[a] | 4 | 25 |
| Korea, Dem. Rep. | 0 | 0 | 35 | 37 | .. | 0.4 | .. | .. | .. | .. | .. | .. |
| Korea, Rep. | −115 | −80 | 584 | 551 | .. | 1.3 | .. | 0.1 | 1,080 | 917 | 634 | 4,245 |
| Kuwait | −598 | 264 | 996 | 1,669 | 0.8 | 0.6 | 3.3 | 0.1 | .. | .. | 1,354 | 3,021 |
| Kyrgyz Republic | −273 | −75 | 482 | 288 | 0.2 | 26.3 | 13.4 | 0.4 | 1 | 481 | 41 | 145 |
| Lao PDR | −30 | −115 | 23 | 25 | 245.6 | 93.8 | .. | .. | 22[a] | 1[a] | 9[a] | 1[a] |
| Latvia | −134 | −20 | 713 | 449 | 0.2 | 1.4 | .. | .. | 41 | 482 | 1 | 30 |
| Lebanon | 230 | 0 | 594 | 657 | 13.5 | 12.3 | 348.1[b] | 428.6[b] | 1,225 | 5,202 | .. | 4,134 |
| Lesotho | −84 | −36 | 5 | 6 | .. | .. | .. | .. | 411 | 361 | 75 | 11 |
| Liberia | −283 | −119 | 199 | 50 | 744.6 | 160.5 | 120.1 | 16.2 | .. | .. | .. | .. |
| Libya | 10 | 10 | 506 | 618 | 0.6 | 1.6 | 4.0 | 2.8 | .. | 16 | 222 | 945 |
| Lithuania | −99 | −30 | 272 | 165 | 0.1 | 0.9 | .. | 0.5 | 1 | 994 | 1 | 426 |
| Macedonia, FYR | −27 | −10 | 114 | 121 | 42.9 | 6.5 | 9.1 | 1.2 | 68 | 267 | 1 | 18 |
| Madagascar | −7 | −5 | 60 | 63 | 0.1 | 0.3 | .. | .. | 14[a] | 11[a] | 11[a] | 21[a] |
| Malawi | −920 | −30 | 325 | 279 | .. | 0.1 | 1.0 | 3.9 | 1[a] | 1[a] | 1[a] | 1[a] |
| Malaysia | 287 | 150 | 1,135 | 1,639 | 0.1 | 0.6 | 5.3 | 37.2 | 716 | 1,535 | 1,329 | 5,560 |
| Mali | −260 | −134 | 63 | 46 | 77.2 | 0.6 | 17.9 | 10.6 | 112[a] | 177[a] | 42[a] | 69[a] |
| Mauritania | −15 | 30 | 118 | 66 | 84.3 | 33.4 | 34.4 | 0.8 | 5[a] | 2[a] | 14 | .. |
| Mauritius | −7 | 0 | 12 | 21 | .. | 0.1 | .. | .. | 132[a] | 215[a] | 1 | 13 |
| Mexico | −1,792 | −3,983 | 467 | 644 | 0.4 | 3.3 | 38.7 | 3.3 | 4,368 | 25,052 | .. | .. |
| Moldova | −121 | −250 | 473 | 440 | 0.5 | 11.7 | .. | 0.2 | 1 | 1,182 | 1 | 86 |
| Mongolia | −59 | −50 | 7 | 9 | .. | 0.9 | .. | .. | .. | 181 | .. | 77 |
| Morocco | −450 | −550 | 103 | 132 | 0.3 | 4.7 | 0.1 | 0.5 | 1,970 | 5,454 | 20 | 41 |
| Mozambique | 650 | −20 | 246 | 406 | 125.6 | 0.2 | 0.1 | 2.6 | 59 | 80 | 21 | 26 |
| Myanmar | −126 | −99 | 112 | 117 | 152.3 | 202.8 | .. | .. | 81 | 116 | .. | 32 |
| Namibia | 3 | −1 | 124 | 143 | .. | 1.2 | 1.7 | 5.5 | 16 | 17 | 11 | 20 |
| Nepal | −101 | −100 | 625 | 819 | .. | 2.6 | 124.8 | 128.2 | 57 | 1,453 | 9 | 79 |
| Netherlands | 190 | 110 | 1,387 | 1,638 | 0.1 | .. | 80.0 | 100.6 | 1,359 | 2,412 | 2,802[a] | 6,802[a] |
| New Zealand | 94 | 102 | 732 | 642 | .. | .. | 3.8 | 4.9 | 1,858 | 650 | 584 | 865 |
| Nicaragua | −115 | −210 | 27 | 28 | 23.9 | 1.8 | 0.6 | 0.2 | 75 | 656 | .. | .. |
| Niger | −3 | −28 | 139 | 124 | 10.3 | 0.8 | 27.6 | 0.3 | 8[a] | 66[a] | 29[a] | 29[a] |
| Nigeria | −96 | −170 | 582 | 971 | 1.9 | 13.3 | 8.1 | 8.8 | 804[a] | 3,329[a] | 5[a] | 18[a] |
| Norway | 42 | 84 | 231 | 344 | .. | .. | 47.6 | 43.3 | 239 | 524 | 603 | 2,620 |
| Oman | 23 | −150 | 573 | 628 | .. | .. | .. | .. | 39 | 39 | 1,537 | 2,788 |
| Pakistan | −2,611 | −1,239 | 4,077 | 3,254 | 5.3 | 25.6 | 1,202.5 | 1,044.5 | 1,712 | 5,121 | 4 | 2 |
| Panama | 8 | 8 | 73 | 102 | 0.2 | 0.1 | 0.9 | 1.8 | 112 | 149 | 20 | 121 |
| Papua New Guinea | 0 | 0 | 32 | 25 | 2.0 | .. | 9.6 | 10.2 | 16[a] | 13[a] | 16[a] | 135[a] |
| Paraguay | −30 | −45 | 183 | 168 | 0.1 | 0.1 | 0.1 | 0.1 | 287 | 432 | .. | .. |
| Peru | −441 | −510 | 51 | 42 | 5.9 | 7.0 | 0.6 | 0.9 | 599 | 1,837 | 34 | 133 |
| Philippines | −900 | −900 | 214 | 374 | 0.5 | 0.9 | 0.8 | 0.1 | 5,360 | 15,251 | 151 | 20 |
| Poland | −77 | −200 | 963 | 703 | 19.7 | 13.5 | 0.6 | 6.8 | 724 | 4,370 | 262 | 800 |
| Portugal | −7 | 276 | 528 | 764 | .. | .. | 0.3 | 0.3 | 3,953 | 3,328 | 527 | 1,386 |
| Puerto Rico | −4 | −10 | 351 | 418 | .. | .. | .. | .. | .. | .. | .. | .. |

| | Net migration | | International migrant stock | | Refugees | | | | Workers' remittances and compensation of employees | | | |
|---|---|---|---|---|---|---|---|---|---|---|---|---|
| | | | | | | | thousands | | | | $ millions | |
| | | | | | By country of origin | | By country of asylum | | Received | | Paid | |
| | thousands | | thousands | | | | | | | | | |
| | 1990–95 | 2000–05 | 1995 | 2005 | 1995 | 2006 | 1995 | 2006 | 1995 | 2006 | 1995 | 2006 |
| Romania | −529 | −270 | 135 | 133 | 17.0 | 7.2 | 0.2 | 1.7 | 9 | 6,718 | 2 | 57 |
| Russian Federation | 2,263 | 917 | 11,707 | 12,080 | 207.0 | 159.4 | .. | 1.4 | 2,503 | 3,091 | 3,939 | 11,438 |
| Rwanda | −1,714 | 43 | 60 | 121 | 1,819.4 | 93.0 | 7.8 | 49.2 | 21 | 21 | 1 | 47 |
| Saudi Arabia | −500 | 285 | 4,611 | 6,361 | 0.3 | 0.6 | 13.2 | 240.8 | .. | .. | 16,594 | 15,611 |
| Senegal | −100 | −100 | 320 | 326 | 17.6 | 15.2 | 66.8 | 20.6 | 146[a] | 633[a] | 76[a] | 77[a] |
| Serbia | 451 | −339 | .. | .. | 86.1[c] | 174.0 | 650.7[c] | 99.0 | 1,295[a,c] | 4,703[a,c] | .. | .. |
| Sierra Leone | −380 | 472 | 55 | 119 | 379.5 | 42.9 | 4.7 | 27.4 | 24 | 33 | .. | 35 |
| Singapore | 250 | 200 | 992 | 1,843 | .. | 0.1 | 0.1 | .. | .. | .. | .. | .. |
| Slovak Republic | 9 | 3 | 114 | 124 | .. | 0.7 | 2.3 | 0.2 | 26[a] | 424[a] | 3[a] | 16[a] |
| Slovenia | 38 | 22 | 200 | 167 | 12.9 | 1.8 | 22.3 | 0.3 | 272 | 282 | 31 | 129 |
| Somalia | −1,193 | 100 | 18 | 282 | 638.7 | 464.0 | 0.6 | 0.7 | .. | .. | .. | .. |
| South Africa | 1,125 | 75 | 1,098 | 1,106 | 0.5 | 0.5 | 101.4 | 35.1 | 105 | 734 | 629 | 1,068 |
| Spain | 292 | 2,846 | 1,009 | 4,790 | .. | 2.4 | 5.9 | 5.3 | 3,235 | 8,863 | 868 | 11,005 |
| Sri Lanka | −256 | −442 | 428 | 368 | 107.6 | 117.0 | .. | 0.2 | 809 | 2,349 | 16 | 283 |
| Sudan | −168 | −532 | 1,111 | 639 | 445.3 | 686.3 | 674.1 | 196.2 | 346 | 1,156 | 1 | 2 |
| Swaziland | −38 | −6 | 38 | 45 | .. | .. | 0.7 | 0.8 | 83 | 99 | 4 | 17 |
| Sweden | 151 | 152 | 906 | 1,117 | .. | .. | 199.2 | 79.9 | 288 | 336 | 336 | 589 |
| Switzerland | 200 | 100 | 1,471 | 1,660 | .. | .. | 82.9 | 48.5 | 1,473 | 1,859 | 10,114 | 13,805 |
| Syrian Arab Republic | −70 | 200 | 801 | 985 | 0.2 | 0.1 | 373.5[b] | 1,144.6[b] | 339 | 795 | 15 | 235 |
| Tajikistan | −313 | −345 | 305 | 306 | 59.0 | 0.6 | 0.6 | 0.9 | .. | 1,019 | .. | 395 |
| Tanzania | 591 | −345 | 1,130 | 792 | 0.1 | 1.7 | 829.7 | 485.3 | 1 | 15 | 1 | 30 |
| Thailand | 172 | 231 | 568 | 1,050 | 0.2 | 3.3 | 106.6 | 133.1 | 1,695 | 1,333 | .. | .. |
| Timor-Leste | 0 | 100 | 6 | 6 | .. | 0.3 | .. | .. | .. | .. | .. | .. |
| Togo | −122 | −4 | 169 | 183 | 93.2 | 27.3 | 10.9 | 6.3 | 15[a] | 193[a] | 5[a] | 35[a] |
| Trinidad and Tobago | −24 | −20 | 46 | 38 | .. | 0.2 | .. | .. | 32[a] | 92[a] | 14 | .. |
| Tunisia | −22 | −29 | 38 | 38 | 0.3 | 2.8 | 0.2 | 0.1 | 680 | 1,510 | 36 | 16 |
| Turkey | 109 | −30 | 1,210 | 1,328 | 44.9 | 227.2 | 12.8 | 2.6 | 3,327 | 1,111 | .. | 107 |
| Turkmenistan | 50 | −10 | 260 | 224 | .. | 0.7 | 23.3 | 0.8 | 4 | .. | 7 | .. |
| Uganda | 120 | −5 | 610 | 518 | 24.2 | 21.8 | 229.4 | 272.0 | .. | 814 | .. | 322 |
| Ukraine | 100 | −173 | 7,063 | 6,833 | 1.7 | 63.7 | 5.2 | 2.3 | 6 | 829 | 1 | 30 |
| United Arab Emirates | 340 | 577 | 1,716 | 3,212 | .. | 0.3 | 0.4 | 0.2 | .. | .. | .. | .. |
| United Kingdom | 167 | 948 | 4,198 | 5,408 | 0.1 | 0.2 | 90.9 | 301.6 | 2,469 | 6,954 | 2,581 | 4,525 |
| United States | 5,200 | 6,493 | 28,522 | 38,355 | 0.2 | 1.4 | 623.3 | 843.5 | 2,179 | 2,880 | 22,181 | 42,222 |
| Uruguay | −20 | −104 | 93 | 84 | 0.3 | 0.2 | 0.1 | 0.1 | .. | 89 | .. | 3 |
| Uzbekistan | −340 | −300 | 1,474 | 1,268 | 0.1 | 9.1 | 2.6 | 1.4 | .. | .. | .. | .. |
| Venezuela, RB | 40 | 40 | 1,019 | 1,010 | 0.5 | 3.8 | 1.6 | 0.7 | 2 | 165 | 203 | 253 |
| Vietnam | −256 | −200 | 27 | 21 | 2.3 | 3.1 | 34.4 | 2.4 | .. | 4,800[a] | .. | .. |
| West Bank and Gaza | 1 | 11 | 1,201 | 1,680 | 23.5 | 6.4 | 1,201.0[b] | 1,739.3[b] | 626[a] | 598[a] | .. | 16[a] |
| Yemen, Rep. | 650 | −100 | 228 | 265 | 0.4 | 1.4 | 53.5 | 95.8 | 1,080 | 1,283 | 61 | 120 |
| Zambia | −11 | −82 | 271 | 275 | .. | 0.2 | 130.0 | 120.3 | .. | 58 | 59 | 115 |
| Zimbabwe | −192 | −75 | 638 | 511 | .. | 12.8 | 0.5 | 3.5 | 44 | .. | 7 | .. |
| **World** | ..[d] s | ..[d] s | 164,017 s | 189,693 s | 18,068.7[b,e] s | 14,326.1[b,e] s | 18,068.7[b,f] s | 14,326.1[b,f] s | 101,562 s | 296,757 s | 98,648 s | 207,865 s |
| **Low income** | −3,098 | −4,690 | 30,412 | 27,110 | 8,567.8 | 4,838.6 | 7,304.4 | 3,724.7 | 12,776 | 55,239 | 1,342 | 3,828 |
| **Middle income** | −9,432 | −14,021 | 48,539 | 49,582 | 1,544.3 | 1,643.6 | 7,723.3 | 7,819.9 | 44,744 | 166,674 | 11,029 | 40,774 |
| Lower middle income | −9,775 | −9,750 | 20,522 | 21,249 | 1,133.4 | 1,021.7 | 6,282.9 | 7,140.4 | 27,044 | 102,551 | 1,341 | 7,884 |
| Upper middle income | 344 | −4,271 | 28,017 | 28,333 | 410.9 | 621.9 | 1,440.5 | 679.5 | 17,700 | 64,123 | 9,688 | 32,890 |
| **Low & middle income** | −12,529 | −18,711 | 78,951 | 76,692 | 10,112.1 | 6,482.2 | 15,027.7 | 11,544.6 | 57,520 | 221,912 | 12,371 | 44,602 |
| East Asia & Pacific | −2,828 | −3,847 | 3,001 | 4,432 | 578.9 | 501.1 | 447.0 | 484.4 | 9,701 | 52,847 | 1,618 | 10,431 |
| Europe & Central Asia | −3,106 | −1,730 | 32,049 | 29,970 | 891.8 | 884.6 | 1,434.3 | 274.5 | 7,928 | 35,385 | 4,920 | 17,747 |
| Latin America & Carib. | −3,847 | −6,811 | 5,280 | 5,713 | 87.5 | 78.0 | 94.0 | 40.5 | 13,335 | 56,860 | 1,114 | 2,646 |
| Middle East & N. Africa | −1,201 | −2,768 | 8,780 | 9,642 | 60.8 | 112.7 | 5,683.1 | 6,974.5 | 13,358 | 26,697 | 2,239 | 8,837 |
| South Asia | −976 | −2,484 | 13,133 | 11,229 | 2,901.8 | 2,378.6 | 1,625.5 | 1,357.6 | 10,005 | 39,779 | 475 | 2,031 |
| Sub-Saharan Africa | −572 | −1,070 | 16,707 | 15,706 | 5,591.3 | 2,527.2 | 5,743.8 | 2,413.1 | 3,193 | 10,344 | 2,005 | 2,911 |
| **High income** | 12,513 | 18,604 | 85,065 | 113,001 | 786.3 | 211.2 | 3,041.9 | 2,781.9 | 44,042 | 74,844 | 86,277 | 163,263 |
| Euro area | 5,078 | 6,849 | 22,466 | 30,335 | 13.5 | 4.6 | 1,688.3 | 954.6 | 30,071 | 50,391 | 26,443 | 59,452 |

a. World Bank estimates. b. Includes Palestinian refugees under the mandate of the United Nations Relief and Works Agency for Palestine Refugees in the Near East, who are not included in data from the UN Refugee Agency (UNHCR). c. Includes Montenegro. d. World totals computed by the United Nations sum to zero, but because the aggregates refer to World Bank definitions, regional and income group totals do not. e. Includes refugees without specified country of origin. f. Regional and income group totals do not sum to the world total because of rounding.

## About the data

Movement of people, most often through migration, is a significant part of global integration. Migrants contribute to the economies of both their host country and their country of origin. Yet reliable statistics on migration are difficult to collect and are often incomplete, making international comparisons a challenge.

The United Nations Population Division provides data on net migration and migration stock. To derive estimates of net migration, the organization takes into account the past migration history of a country or area, the migration policy of a country, and the influx of refugees in recent periods. The data to calculate these official estimates come from a variety of sources, including border statistics, administrative records, surveys, and censuses. When no official estimates can be made because of insufficient data, net migration is derived through the balance equation, which is the difference between overall population growth and the natural increase during the 1990–2000 intercensal period.

The data used to estimate the international migrant stock at a particular time are obtained mainly from population censuses. The estimates are derived from the data on foreign-born population—people who have residence in one country but were born in another country. When data on the foreign-born population are not available, data on foreign population—that is, people who are citizens of a country other than the country in which they reside—are used as estimates.

After the breakup of the Soviet Union in 1991 people living in one of the newly independent countries who were born in another were classified as international migrants. Estimates of migration stock in the newly independent states from 1990 on are based on the 1989 census of the Soviet Union.

For countries with information on the international migrant stock for at least two points in time, interpolation or extrapolation was used to estimate the international migrant stock on July 1 of the reference years. For countries with only one observation, estimates for the reference years were derived using rates of change in the migrant stock in the years preceding or following the single observation available. A model was used to estimate migration for countries that had no data.

Registrations, together with other sources—including estimates and surveys—are the main sources of refugee data. But there are difficulties in collecting accurate statistics. Although refugees are often registered individually, the accuracy of

registrations varies greatly. Many refugees may not be aware of the need to register or may choose not to do so. And administrative records tend to overestimate the number of refugees because it is easier to register than to de-register. The UN Refugee Agency (UNHCR) collects and maintains data on refugees, except for Palestinian refugees residing in areas under the mandate of the United Nations Relief and Works Agency for Palestine Refugees in the Near East (UNRWA). The UNRWA provides services to Palestinian refugees who live in certain areas and who register with the agency. Registration is voluntary, and estimates by the UNRWA are not an accurate count of the Palestinian refugee population. The table shows estimates of refugees collected by the UNHCR, complemented by estimates of Palestinian refugees under the UNRWA mandate. Thus, the aggregates differ from those published by the UNHCR.

Workers' remittances and compensation of employees are World Bank staff estimates based on data from the International Monetary Fund's (IMF) *Balance of Payments Yearbook*. The IMF data are supplemented by World Bank staff estimates for missing data for countries where workers' remittances are important. The data reported here are the sum of three items defined in the IMF's *Balance of Payments Manual* (fifth edition): workers' remittances, compensation of employees, and migrants' transfers.

The distinction between these three items is not always consistent in the data reported by countries to the IMF. In some cases countries compile data on the basis of the citizenship of migrant workers rather than their residency status. Some countries also report remittances entirely as workers' remittances or compensation of employees. Following the fifth edition of the *Balance of Payments Manual* in 1993, migrants' transfers are considered a capital transaction, but previous editions regarded them as current transfers. For these reasons the figures presented in the table take all three items into account.

## Definitions

• **Net migration** is the net total of migrants during the period. It is the total number of immigrants less the total number of emigrants, including both citizens and noncitizens. Data are five-year estimates. • **International migrant stock** is the number of people born in a country other than that in which they live. It includes refugees. • **Refugees** are people who are recognized as refugees under the 1951 Convention Relating to the Status of Refugees or its 1967 Protocol, the 1969 Organization of African Unity Convention Governing the Specific Aspects of Refugee Problems in Africa, people recognized as refugees in accordance with the UNHCR statute, people granted refugee-like humanitarian status, and people provided temporary protection. Asylum seekers are people who have applied for asylum or refugee status and who have not yet received a decision or who are registered as asylum seekers. Palestinian refugees are people (and their descendants) whose residence was Palestine between June 1946 and May 1948 and who lost their homes and means of livelihood as a result of the 1948 Arab-Israeli conflict. • **Country of origin** refers to the nationality or country of citizenship of a claimant. • **Country of asylum** is the country where an asylum claim was filed. • **Workers' remittances and compensation of employees** received and paid comprise current transfers by migrant workers and wages and salaries earned by nonresident workers. Remittances are classified as current private transfers from migrant workers resident in the host country for more than a year, irrespective of their immigration status, to recipients in their country of origin. Migrants' transfers are defined as the net worth of migrants who are expected to remain in the host country for more than one year that is transferred to another country at the time of migration. Compensation of employees is the income of migrants who have lived in the host country for less than a year.

## Data sources

Data on net migration are from the United Nations Population Division's *World Population Prospects: The 2006 Revision*. Data on migration stock come from the United Nations Population Division's *Trends in Total Migrant Stock: The 2005 Revision*. Data on refugees are from the UNHCR's *Statistical Yearbook 2006*, complemented by statistics on Palestinian refugees under the mandate of the UNRWA as published on its website. Data on remittances are World Bank staff estimates based on IMF balance of payments data.

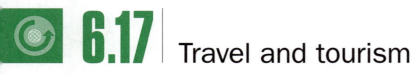

| | International tourists | | | | Inbound tourism expenditure | | | | Outbound tourism expenditure | | | |
|---|---|---|---|---|---|---|---|---|---|---|---|---|
| | thousands | | | | $ millions | | % of exports | | $ millions | | % of imports | |
| | Inbound | | Outbound | | | | | | | | | |
| | 1995 | 2006 | 1995 | 2006 | 1995 | 2006 | 1995 | 2006 | 1995 | 2006 | 1995 | 2006 |
| Afghanistan | .. | .. | .. | .. | .. | .. | .. | .. | 1 | .. | .. | .. |
| Albania | 40ᵃ | 60ᵃ | 12 | 2,616 | 70 | 1,057 | 23.2 | 46.0 | 19 | 989 | 2.3 | 22.0 |
| Algeria | 520ᵇ,ᶜ | 1,443ᵇ,ᶜ | 1,090 | 1,513 | 32ᵈ | 184ᵈ | .. | .. | 186ᵈ | 370ᵈ | .. | .. |
| Angola | 9 | 121 | 3 | .. | 27 | 91 | 0.7 | 0.3 | 113 | 393 | 3.2 | 2.4 |
| Argentina | 2,289 | 4,156 | 3,815 | 4,009 | 2,550 | 3,914 | 10.2 | 7.2 | 4,013 | 4,143 | 15.4 | 10.1 |
| Armenia | 12 | 381 | .. | 329 | 14 | 193 | 4.7 | 12.8 | 12 | 133 | 1.7 | 5.2 |
| Australia | 3,726ᵉ | 5,064ᵉ | 2,519 | 4,941 | 11,915 | 23,732 | 17.1 | 15.0 | 7,260 | 16,382 | 9.7 | 9.8 |
| Austria | 17,173ᶠ | 20,261ᶠ | 3,713 | 10,042 | 14,529 | 19,310 | 16.2 | 11.3 | 11,686 | 12,755 | 12.7 | 7.8 |
| Azerbaijan | 93 | 1,194 | 432 | 1,836 | 88 | 201 | 11.2 | 1.4 | 165 | 256 | 12.8 | 3.1 |
| Bangladesh | 156 | 200 | 830 | 1,819 | 25 | 80 | 0.6 | 0.6 | 234 | 444 | 3.1 | 2.6 |
| Belarus | 161 | 89 | 626 | 525 | 28 | 386 | 0.5 | 1.7 | 101 | 823 | 1.8 | 3.5 |
| Belgium | 5,560ᶠ | 6,995ᶠ | 5,645 | 7,852 | 4,548 | 12,680 | 2.4 | 3.7 | 8,115 | 19,557 | 4.5 | 5.9 |
| Benin | 138 | 180 | .. | .. | 85 | 108 | 13.8 | 14.0 | 48 | 58 | 5.4 | 5.1 |
| Bolivia | 284 | 515 | 249 | 466 | 92 | 287 | 7.5 | 6.7 | 72 | 328 | 4.6 | 9.5 |
| Bosnia and Herzegovina | 115ᶠ | 256ᶠ | .. | .. | .. | 643 | .. | 14.3 | .. | 198 | .. | 2.4 |
| Botswana | 521 | 1,675 | .. | .. | 176 | 539 | 7.3 | 10.2 | 153 | 285 | 7.5 | 8.3 |
| Brazil | 1,991 | 5,019 | 2,600 | 4,825 | 1,085 | 4,577 | 2.1 | 2.9 | 3,982 | 7,501 | 6.3 | 6.2 |
| Bulgaria | 3,466 | 5,158 | 3,524 | 4,180 | 662 | 3,315 | 9.8 | 16.5 | 312 | 2,092 | 4.8 | 8.1 |
| Burkina Faso | 124ᵍ | 264ᵍ | .. | .. | .. | .. | .. | .. | .. | .. | .. | .. |
| Burundi | 34ᶜ | 201ᶜ | 36 | .. | 2 | 2 | 1.9 | 1.7 | 25 | 126 | 9.7 | 28.1 |
| Cambodia | 220ᵉ | 1,700 | 31 | 427 | 71 | 1,080 | 7.3 | 21.6 | 22 | 176 | 1.6 | 3.2 |
| Cameroon | 100ᵍ | 176ᵍ | .. | .. | 75 | 212 | 3.7 | 5.8 | 140 | 394 | 8.7 | 9.9 |
| Canada | 16,932 | 18,265 | 18,206 | 22,732 | 9,176 | 16,976 | 4.2 | 3.7 | 12,658 | 25,994 | 6.3 | 6.1 |
| Central African Republic | 26ᵉ | 12ᵉ | .. | 7 | 4ᵈ | 4ᵈ | .. | .. | 43ᵈ | 32ᵈ | .. | .. |
| Chad | 19ᵍ | 29ᵍ | .. | .. | 43ᵈ | .. | .. | .. | 38ᵈ | .. | .. | .. |
| Chile | 1,540 | 2,027 | 1,070 | 2,651 | 1,186 | 1,816 | 6.1 | 2.8 | 934 | 1,581 | 5.1 | 3.6 |
| China | 20,034 | 49,913 | 4,520 | 34,524 | 8,730 | 37,132 | 5.9 | 3.5 | 3,688 | 28,242 | 2.7 | 3.3 |
| Hong Kong, China | 10,200 | 15,821 | 3,023 | 75,812 | 9,604ᵈ | 15,311ᵈ | .. | 3.9ᵈ | 10,497ᵈ,ʰ | 13,974ᵈ,ʰ | .. | 3.8ᵈ,ʰ |
| Colombia | 1,433ᵇ | 1,053ᵇ | 1,057 | 1,553 | 887 | 2,005 | 7.2 | 7.0 | 1,162 | 1,796 | 7.3 | 5.9 |
| Congo, Dem. Rep. | 35ᵉ | 61ᵉ | .. | .. | .. | .. | .. | .. | .. | .. | .. | .. |
| Congo, Rep. | 37ᵍ | .. | .. | .. | 15 | 34 | 1.1 | 0.7 | 69 | 103 | 5.1 | 3.5 |
| Costa Rica | 785 | 1,725 | 273 | 485 | 763 | 1,890 | 17.1 | 17.1 | 336 | 577 | 7.1 | 4.6 |
| Côte d'Ivoire | 188 | .. | .. | .. | 103 | 84 | 2.4 | 0.9 | 312 | 361 | 8.2 | 5.0 |
| Croatia | 1,485ᶠ | 8,659ᶠ | .. | .. | 1,349 | 8,296 | 19.3 | 38.7 | 422 | 770 | 4.6 | 3.1 |
| Cuba | 742ᵉ | 2,150ᵉ | 72 | 199 | 1,100ᵈ | 2,404ᵈ | .. | .. | .. | .. | .. | .. |
| Czech Republic | 3,381ᶠ | 6,435ᶠ | .. | .. | 2,880 | 5,869 | 10.2 | 5.4 | 1,635 | 2,781 | 5.4 | 2.7 |
| Denmark | 2,124ᶠ | 4,699ᶠ | 5,035 | 5,469 | 3,691ʰ | 4,493ʰ | 5.6ʰ | 3.5ʰ | 4,288ʰ | 5,690ʰ | 7.4ʰ | 5.0ʰ |
| Dominican Republic | 1,776ᶜ,ᵉ | 3,965ᶜ,ᵉ | 168 | 420 | 1,571ʰ | 3,792ʰ | 27.4ʰ | 35.6ʰ | 267 | 499 | 4.4 | 3.9 |
| Ecuador | 440ᵇ,ⁱ | 841ᵇ,ⁱ | 271 | 733 | 315 | 492 | 6.1 | 3.5 | 331 | 706 | 5.8 | 5.1 |
| Egypt, Arab Rep. | 2,871 | 8,646 | 2,683 | 4,531 | 2,954 | 8,133 | 22.3 | 22.2 | 1,371 | 2,156 | 8.0 | 5.3 |
| El Salvador | 235 | 1,138 | 348 | 1,382 | 152 | 1,175 | 7.5 | 23.2 | 99 | 601 | 2.7 | 6.9 |
| Eritrea | 315ᵇ,ᶜ | 78ᵇ,ᶜ | .. | .. | 58ᵈ | 60ᵈ | 43.1ᵈ | .. | .. | .. | .. | .. |
| Estonia | 530 | 1,940 | 1,764 | .. | 452 | 1,372 | 17.6 | 10.5 | 121 | 705 | 4.2 | 4.8 |
| Ethiopia | 103ᵉ | 290ᶜ | 120 | .. | 177 | 639 | 23.1 | 29.1 | 30 | 97 | 2.1 | 1.8 |
| Finland | .. | 3,375 | 5,147 | 5,756 | 2,384 | 3,326 | 5.0 | 3.6 | 2,853 | 3,988 | 7.6 | 4.9 |
| France | 60,033 | 79,083 | 18,686 | 22,466 | 31,295 | 54,033 | 8.6 | 9.0 | 20,699 | 37,793 | 6.2 | 6.0 |
| Gabon | 125ᵉ | .. | .. | .. | 94 | 74 | 3.2 | 1.8 | 183 | 275 | 10.6 | 12.8 |
| Gambia, The | 45 | 125 | .. | .. | 28 | 69 | 15.8 | 34.4 | 16 | 8 | 6.9 | 2.5 |
| Georgia | 85ᵇ | 983ᵇ | 228 | .. | 75 | 361 | 13.1 | 14.1 | 171 | 257 | 12.1 | 5.8 |
| Germany | 14,847ᶠ | 23,569ᶠ | 55,800 | 71,200 | 24,052 | 42,792 | 4.0 | 3.3 | 66,527 | 84,205 | 11.2 | 7.3 |
| Ghana | 286ᶜ | 429ᶜ | .. | .. | 30 | 910 | 1.9 | 17.8 | 74 | 575 | 3.5 | 6.9 |
| Greece | 10,130 | 16,039 | .. | .. | 4,182 | 14,495 | 26.9 | 25.9 | 1,495 | 3,004 | 6.0 | 3.7 |
| Guatemala | 563 | 1,502 | 333 | 1,055 | 216 | 1,008 | 7.7 | 13.6 | 167 | 572 | 4.5 | 4.5 |
| Guinea | 12ᵉ | 46ᵉ | .. | .. | 1 | 70 | 0.1 | 3.7 | 29 | 41 | 2.9 | 3.0 |
| Guinea-Bissau | .. | 12ᵉ | .. | .. | 3 | 2 | 5.3 | 2.6 | 6 | 18 | 6.7 | 17.3 |
| Haiti | 145 | 112 | .. | .. | 90ʰ | 135ʰ | 46.8ʰ | 19.3ʰ | 35 | 233 | 4.4 | 11.2 |

| | International tourists | | | | Inbound tourism expenditure | | | | Outbound tourism expenditure | | | |
|---|---|---|---|---|---|---|---|---|---|---|---|---|
| | thousands | | | | $ millions | | % of exports | | $ millions | | % of imports | |
| | Inbound | | Outbound | | | | | | | | | |
| | 1995 | 2006 | 1995 | 2006 | 1995 | 2006 | 1995 | 2006 | 1995 | 2006 | 1995 | 2006 |
| Honduras | 271 | 739 | 149 | 308 | 85 | 490 | 5.2 | 12.9 | 99 | 353 | 5.3 | 5.8 |
| Hungary | .. | 9,259 | 13,083 | 17,612 | 2,938 | 5,223 | 14.9 | 6.0 | 1,501 | 3,076 | 7.5 | 3.5 |
| India | 2,124[i] | 4,447[i] | 3,056 | 8,340 | 2,582 | 9,227 | 6.8 | 4.6 | 996 | 9,296 | 2.1 | 4.0 |
| Indonesia | 4,324 | 4,871 | 1,782 | 4,106 | 5,229 | 4,890 | 9.9 | 4.3 | 2,172 | 5,028 | 4.0 | 5.3 |
| Iran, Islamic Rep. | 489 | 1,659 | 1,000 | .. | 205 | 1,513 | 1.1 | .. | 247 | 5,004 | 1.6 | .. |
| Iraq | 61[b] | .. | .. | .. | 18[d,h] | .. | .. | .. | 117[d,h] | .. | .. | .. |
| Ireland | 4,818 | 8,001 | 2,547 | 6,848 | 2,698 | 7,664 | 5.5 | 4.4 | 2,034 | 6,978 | 4.8 | 4.6 |
| Israel | 2,215[i] | 1,825[i] | 2,259 | 3,713 | 3,491 | 3,319 | 12.7 | 5.3 | 2,626 | 3,870 | 7.4 | 6.3 |
| Italy | 31,052 | 41,058 | 18,173 | 25,697 | 30,426 | 41,644 | 10.3 | 8.1 | 17,219 | 27,437 | 6.9 | 5.2 |
| Jamaica | 1,147[c,e] | 1,679[c,e] | .. | .. | 1,199 | 2,094 | 35.3 | 43.8 | 173 | 315 | 4.6 | 4.4 |
| Japan | 3,345[b,i] | 7,334[b,i] | 15,298 | 17,535 | 4,894 | 11,490 | 1.0 | 1.6 | 46,966 | 37,659 | 11.2 | 5.6 |
| Jordan | 1,075 | 3,225[c] | 1,128 | 1,628 | 973 | 2,008 | 28.0 | 26.1 | 719 | 698 | 14.7 | 5.4 |
| Kazakhstan | .. | 3,143 | 523 | 3,004 | 155 | 973 | 2.6 | 2.3 | 296 | 1,060 | 4.9 | 3.2 |
| Kenya | 896 | 1,536 | .. | .. | 590 | 1,182 | 20.0 | 19.8 | 183 | 178 | 5.2 | 2.2 |
| Korea, Dem. Rep. | .. | .. | .. | .. | .. | .. | .. | .. | .. | .. | .. | .. |
| Korea, Rep. | 3,753[b,c] | 6,155[b,c] | 3,819 | 11,610 | 6,670 | 8,069 | 4.5 | 2.1 | 6,947 | 20,386 | 4.5 | 5.5 |
| Kuwait | 72[g] | 91[g] | 878 | 1,928 | 307 | 470 | 2.2 | 0.7 | 2,514 | 5,753 | 19.9 | 23.4 |
| Kyrgyz Republic | 36 | 766 | 42 | 454 | 5 | 176 | 1.1 | 14.8 | 7 | 115 | 1.0 | 5.1 |
| Lao PDR | 60 | 842 | .. | .. | 52 | 173 | 12.8 | .. | 34 | .. | 4.5 | .. |
| Latvia | 539 | 1,535 | 1,812 | 3,151 | 37 | 622 | 1.8 | 7.1 | 62 | 788 | 2.8 | 5.9 |
| Lebanon | 450 | 1,063 | .. | .. | 710 | 5,491 | .. | 38.1 | .. | 3,783 | .. | 21.9 |
| Lesotho | 87 | 347 | .. | .. | 29 | 28 | 14.6 | 3.7 | 17 | 22 | 1.6 | 1.5 |
| Liberia | .. | .. | .. | .. | .. | .. | .. | .. | .. | .. | .. | .. |
| Libya | 56 | 149 | 484 | .. | 4 | 244 | 0.1 | 0.6 | 98 | 915 | 1.7 | 5.8 |
| Lithuania | 650 | 2,000 | 1,925 | .. | 102 | 1,077 | 3.2 | 6.1 | 107 | 931 | 2.7 | 4.5 |
| Macedonia, FYR | 147[f] | 202[f] | .. | .. | 19 | 156 | 2.7 | 5.2 | 27 | 110 | 1.7 | 2.6 |
| Madagascar | 75[e] | 312[e] | 39 | .. | 106 | 386 | 14.2 | 21.8 | 79 | 86 | 8.0 | 3.9 |
| Malawi | 192 | 438 | .. | .. | 22 | 43 | 4.7 | .. | 53 | 75 | 8.0 | .. |
| Malaysia | 7,469 | 17,547 | 20,642 | 30,761 | 5,044 | 12,355 | 6.1 | 6.8 | 2,722 | 4,847 | 3.1 | 3.3 |
| Mali | 42[e,g] | 153[e,g] | .. | .. | 26 | 167 | 4.9 | 10.8 | 74 | 133 | 7.5 | 7.3 |
| Mauritania | .. | .. | .. | .. | 11[h] | .. | 2.2[h] | .. | 30 | .. | 5.9 | .. |
| Mauritius | 422 | 788 | 107 | 186 | 616 | 1,302 | 26.2 | 32.5 | 184 | 347 | 7.5 | 7.3 |
| Mexico | 20,241[c] | 21,353[c] | 8,450 | 14,002 | 6,847 | 13,341 | 7.7 | 5.0 | 3,587 | 9,399 | 4.4 | 3.4 |
| Moldova | 32 | 13 | 71 | 68 | 71 | 145 | 8.0 | 9.4 | 73 | 220 | 7.3 | 7.0 |
| Mongolia | 108 | 386 | .. | .. | 33 | 261 | 6.5 | 12.9 | 22 | 212 | 4.2 | 11.3 |
| Morocco | 2,602[c] | 6,558[c] | 1,317 | 2,247 | 1,469 | 6,899 | 16.2 | 31.7 | 356 | 1,123 | 3.2 | 4.4 |
| Mozambique | .. | 578 | .. | .. | 49 | 145 | 10.2 | 5.2 | 68 | 205 | 6.6 | 6.0 |
| Myanmar | 117 | 264 | .. | .. | 169 | 59 | 12.9 | 1.2 | 18 | 40 | 0.9 | 1.4 |
| Namibia | 272 | 833 | .. | .. | 278 | 473 | 16.0 | 14.9 | 90[h] | 118[h] | 4.3[h] | 4.0[h] |
| Nepal | 363 | 375 | 100 | 373 | 232 | 157 | 22.5 | 12.7 | 167 | 261 | 10.3 | 8.9 |
| Netherlands | 6,574[f] | 10,739[f] | 12,313 | 16,695 | 10,611 | 11,548 | 4.4 | 2.5 | 13,151 | 17,125 | 6.1 | 4.1 |
| New Zealand | 1,409[b] | 2,409[b] | 920 | 1,861 | 2,318[h] | 4,563[h] | 13.0[h] | 15.0[h] | 1,289[h] | 2,526[h] | 7.5[h] | 7.8[h] |
| Nicaragua | 281 | 773[c] | 255 | 788 | 51 | 237 | 7.7 | 10.2 | 56 | 177 | 4.9 | 4.5 |
| Niger | 35 | 60 | 10 | .. | 7 | 35 | 2.2 | 7.8 | 26 | 54 | 5.7 | 4.0 |
| Nigeria | 656 | 1,010 | .. | .. | 47 | 46 | 0.4 | 0.1 | 939 | 1,385 | 7.3 | 5.6 |
| Norway | 2,880[a] | 3,945 | 590 | 3,193 | 2,730 | 4,224 | 4.9 | 2.7 | 4,481 | 11,400 | 9.6 | 12.1 |
| Oman | 279[g] | 1,306[g] | .. | .. | 193 | 743 | 2.5 | 3.3 | 47 | 868 | 0.9 | 6.4 |
| Pakistan | 378 | 898 | .. | .. | 582 | 919 | 5.7 | 4.5 | 654 | 2,029 | 4.6 | 5.8 |
| Panama | 345 | 843 | 185 | 284 | 372 | 1,446 | 4.9 | 11.6 | 181 | 401 | 2.3 | 3.4 |
| Papua New Guinea | 42 | 78 | 51 | .. | 25 | 4 | 0.8 | 0.1 | 58 | 56 | 3.0 | 2.1 |
| Paraguay | 438[i] | 388[i] | 427 | 210 | 162 | 111 | 3.4 | 2.0 | 173 | 143 | 3.3 | 2.3 |
| Peru | 479 | 1,635 | 508 | 1,857 | 521 | 1,586 | 7.9 | 6.0 | 428 | 1,005 | 4.5 | 5.5 |
| Philippines | 1,760[c] | 2,843[c] | 1,615 | 2,144 | 1,141 | 3,063 | 4.3 | 5.8 | 551 | 1,550 | 1.7 | 2.6 |
| Poland | 19,215 | 15,670 | 36,387 | 44,696 | 6,927 | 8,121 | 19.4 | 5.9 | 5,865 | 6,151 | 17.3 | 4.3 |
| Portugal | 9,511[i] | 11,282[c] | .. | 18,378 | 5,646 | 10,036 | 17.5 | 16.3 | 2,540 | 4,050 | 6.4 | 5.3 |
| Puerto Rico | 3,131[e] | 3,722[e] | 1,237 | 1,468 | 1,828[d] | 3,369[d] | .. | .. | 1,155[d] | 1,752[d] | .. | .. |

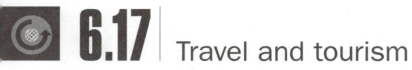

| | International tourists (thousands) | | | | Inbound tourism expenditure | | | | Outbound tourism expenditure | | | |
|---|---|---|---|---|---|---|---|---|---|---|---|---|
| | Inbound | | Outbound | | $ millions | | % of exports | | $ millions | | % of imports | |
| | 1995 | 2006 | 1995 | 2006 | 1995 | 2006 | 1995 | 2006 | 1995 | 2006 | 1995 | 2006 |
| Romania | 5,445[b] | 6,037[b] | 5,737 | 8,906 | 689 | 1,650 | 7.3 | 4.2 | 749 | 1,457 | 6.6 | 2.7 |
| Russian Federation | 10,290 | 22,486 | 21,329 | 29,107 | 4,312 | 9,720 | 4.6 | 2.9 | 11,599 | 19,601 | 14.0 | 9.4 |
| Rwanda | .. | .. | .. | .. | 4 | 31 | 5.4 | 11.2 | 13 | 35 | 3.5 | 4.8 |
| Saudi Arabia | 3,325 | 8,620 | .. | 2,000 | .. | 4,961[d] | .. | 2.3[d] | .. | 1,806[d] | .. | 1.7[d] |
| Senegal | .. | 769 | .. | .. | 168 | 334 | 11.2 | 13.2 | 154 | 144 | 8.5 | 4.3 |
| Serbia | .. | 469[f] | .. | .. | .. | 398[d] | .. | .. | .. | 322[d] | .. | .. |
| Sierra Leone | 38[e] | 34[e] | 6 | 67 | 57[h] | 23[h] | 44.4[h] | 7.4[h] | 51 | 15 | 19.4 | 3.5 |
| Singapore | 6,070 | 7,588 | 2,867 | 5,533 | 7,611[h] | 7,069[h] | 4.8[h] | 2.1[h] | 4,663[h] | 10,384[h] | 3.2[h] | 3.6[h] |
| Slovak Republic | 903[f] | 1,612[f] | 218 | 22,688 | 630 | 1,513 | 5.7 | .. | 338 | 1,055 | 3.2 | .. |
| Slovenia | 732[f] | 1,617[f] | .. | 2,680 | 1,128 | 1,911 | 10.9 | 7.4 | 606 | 1,058 | 5.6 | 4.1 |
| Somalia | .. | .. | .. | .. | .. | .. | .. | .. | .. | .. | .. | .. |
| South Africa | 4,488 | 8,396 | 2,520 | .. | 2,655 | 8,967 | 7.7 | 11.8 | 2,414 | 5,230 | 7.2 | 6.2 |
| Spain | 34,920 | 58,451 | 3,648 | 10,676 | 27,369 | 57,537 | 20.4 | 17.8 | 5,826 | 20,348 | 4.3 | 5.1 |
| Sri Lanka | 403[i] | 560[i] | 504 | 757 | 367 | 733 | 7.9 | 8.6 | 279 | 666 | 4.7 | 5.7 |
| Sudan | 29[i] | 328[c] | 195 | .. | 8[h] | 126[h] | 1.2[h] | 2.1[h] | 43[h] | 1,403[h] | 3.5[h] | 14.2[h] |
| Swaziland | 300[a] | 873[g] | .. | 1,072 | 54 | 74 | 5.3 | 3.3 | 45 | 53 | 3.5 | 2.3 |
| Sweden | 2,310[f] | 3,270[f] | 10,127 | 12,591 | 4,390 | 10,437 | 4.6 | 5.2 | 6,816 | 12,844 | 8.4 | 7.7 |
| Switzerland | 6,946[g] | 7,863[g] | 11,148 | .. | 11,354 | 12,755 | 9.2 | 5.8 | 9,478 | 11,866 | 8.7 | 6.2 |
| Syrian Arab Republic | .. | 4,422 | 1,746 | 4,042 | 1,258 | 2,113 | 21.9 | 16.0 | 498 | 585 | 9.0 | 4.9 |
| Tajikistan | .. | .. | .. | .. | .. | 11 | .. | 0.7 | .. | 6[h] | .. | 0.3[h] |
| Tanzania | 285 | 622 | 157 | .. | 502 | 950 | 39.7 | 29.6 | 360 | 571 | 16.8 | 11.2 |
| Thailand | 6,952[c] | 13,822[i] | 1,820 | 3,382 | 9,257 | 15,559 | 13.2 | 10.2 | 4,791 | 6,140 | 5.8 | 4.2 |
| Timor-Leste | .. | .. | .. | .. | .. | .. | .. | .. | .. | .. | .. | .. |
| Togo | 53[g] | 81[g] | .. | .. | 13 | 27 | 2.8 | 3.2 | 40 | 42 | 6.0 | 2.9 |
| Trinidad and Tobago | 260[e] | 463[e] | 261 | .. | 232 | 593 | 8.3 | 5.6 | 91 | 234 | 4.3 | 3.7 |
| Tunisia | 4,120[i] | 6,549[i] | 1,778 | 2,241 | 1,838 | 2,999 | 23.0 | 19.0 | 294 | 498 | 3.3 | 3.0 |
| Turkey | 7,083 | 18,916 | 3,981 | 8,275 | 4,957 | 18,441 | 13.6 | 15.8 | 911 | 3,154 | 2.3 | 2.2 |
| Turkmenistan | 218 | 12 | 21 | 33 | 13 | .. | 0.7 | .. | 74 | .. | 4.1 | .. |
| Uganda | 160 | 539 | 148 | 254 | 78 | 356 | 11.7 | 23.8 | 80 | 210 | 5.4 | 6.5 |
| Ukraine | 3,716 | 18,900 | 6,552 | 16,875 | 191 | 4,018 | 1.1 | 8.0 | 210 | 3,202 | 1.1 | 6.0 |
| United Arab Emirates | 2,315[a,c] | 7,126[a,c] | .. | .. | 632[d] | 4,972[d] | .. | .. | .. | 8,827[d] | .. | .. |
| United Kingdom | 21,719 | 30,654 | 41,345 | 69,536 | 27,577 | 43,041 | 8.6 | 6.3 | 30,749 | 78,325 | 9.4 | 10.2 |
| United States | 43,490 | 50,978 | 51,285 | 63,662 | 93,700 | 128,922 | 11.8 | 8.9 | 60,924 | 104,310 | 6.8 | 4.7 |
| Uruguay | 2,022 | 1,749 | 562 | 666 | 725 | 706 | 20.7 | 12.5 | 332 | 306 | 9.3 | 5.3 |
| Uzbekistan | 92 | 262 | 246 | 455 | 15[d] | 57[d] | .. | .. | .. | .. | .. | .. |
| Venezuela, RB | 700 | 748 | 534 | 1,095 | 995 | 745 | 4.8 | 1.1 | 1,852 | 1,807 | 11.0 | 4.7 |
| Vietnam | 1,351[b] | 3,583[b] | .. | .. | .. | 3,200[d] | .. | 5.1[d] | .. | .. | .. | .. |
| West Bank and Gaza | 220[g] | 123[g] | .. | .. | 255[h] | 121[h] | .. | .. | 162[h] | 265[h] | .. | .. |
| Yemen, Rep. | 61[g] | 382[g] | .. | .. | 50[h] | 181[h] | 2.3[h] | 2.3[h] | 76 | 225 | 3.1 | 2.9 |
| Zambia | 163 | 669 | .. | .. | 29[h] | 110[h] | 2.4[h] | 2.7[h] | 83 | 96 | 6.2 | 3.0 |
| Zimbabwe | 1,416[b] | 2,287[b] | 256 | .. | 145[d] | 338[d] | .. | .. | 106[d] | .. | .. | .. |
| **World** | 538,992 t | 850,778 t | 579,267 t | 1,030,976 t | 486,150 t | 887,743 t | 7.6 w | 6.0 w | 458,239 t | 803,866 t | 7.5 w | 5.6 w |
| **Low income** | 11,056 | 27,246 | .. | .. | 7,285 | 22,549 | 6.5 | 5.7 | 6,477 | 24,213 | 4.2 | 4.4 |
| **Middle income** | 156,970 | 301,883 | 179,154 | 344,318 | 90,126 | 231,020 | 8.4 | 6.3 | 64,580 | 148,415 | 6.0 | 4.6 |
| Lower middle income | 60,125 | 148,352 | 35,370 | 107,329 | 42,277 | 111,524 | 9.1 | 6.1 | 20,190 | 67,636 | 3.9 | 3.8 |
| Upper middle income | 97,893 | 155,980 | 134,188 | 222,638 | 47,852 | 119,501 | 7.9 | 6.4 | 44,492 | 80,578 | 7.5 | 5.4 |
| **Low & middle income** | 170,318 | 332,275 | 212,104 | 419,006 | 97,598 | 253,983 | 8.3 | 6.2 | 71,208 | 171,125 | 5.8 | 4.6 |
| East Asia & Pacific | 44,243 | 98,476 | 36,056 | 81,142 | 31,197 | 78,567 | 7.8 | 4.8 | 14,769 | 48,335 | 3.5 | 3.5 |
| Europe & Central Asia | 56,887 | 108,942 | 101,318 | 176,948 | 24,108 | 68,438 | 9.1 | 7.0 | 24,473 | 49,564 | 9.4 | 5.8 |
| Latin America & Carib. | 38,965 | 55,387 | 21,780 | 38,100 | 21,591 | 45,333 | 7.5 | 5.6 | 18,751 | 33,091 | 6.5 | 4.9 |
| Middle East & N. Africa | 13,617 | 36,214 | 13,353 | 26,968 | 9,947 | 30,744 | 12.8 | 16.2 | 4,459 | 13,835 | 4.3 | 6.4 |
| South Asia | 3,819 | 7,296 | 5,151 | 12,998 | 4,016 | 11,608 | 6.8 | 4.8 | 2,393 | 12,923 | 3.0 | 4.2 |
| Sub-Saharan Africa | 12,878 | 27,486 | .. | .. | 6,729 | 19,170 | 7.6 | 10.0 | 6,766 | 15,177 | 7.0 | 5.5 |
| **High income** | 361,206 | 510,271 | 320,789 | 533,390 | 388,504 | 633,422 | 7.5 | 5.9 | 386,329 | 632,672 | 7.9 | 6.0 |
| Euro area | 201,613 | 284,903 | 139,868 | 194,611 | 163,394 | 285,919 | 7.8 | 6.5 | 154,655 | 243,434 | 7.8 | 5.9 |

a. Arrivals in hotels only. b. Arrivals of nonresident visitors at national borders. c. Includes nationals residing abroad. d. Country estimates. e. Arrivals by air only. f. Arrivals in all types of accommodation establishments. g. Arrivals in hotels and similar establishments. h. Expenditure on travel-related items only; excludes passenger transport items. i. Excludes nationals residing abroad.

## About the data

Tourism is defined as the activities of people traveling to and staying in places outside their usual environment for no more than one year for leisure, business, and other purposes not related to an activity remunerated from within the place visited. The social and economic phenomenon of tourism has grown substantially over the past quarter century.

Statistical information on tourism is based mainly on data on arrivals and overnight stays along with balance of payments information. But these data do not completely capture the economic phenomenon of tourism or give governments, businesses, and citizens the information needed for effective public policies and efficient business operations. Credible data are needed on the scale and significance of tourism. Information on the role of tourism in national economies is particularly deficient. Although the World Tourism Organization reports that progress has been made in harmonizing definitions and measurement, differences in national practices still prevent full international comparability.

The data in the table are from the World Tourism Organization, an agency of the United Nations. The data on international inbound and outbound tourists refer to the number of arrivals and departures of visitors, not to the number of people traveling. Thus a person who makes several trips to a country during a given period is counted each time as a new arrival. Unless otherwise indicated in the footnotes, the data on inbound tourism show the arrivals of nonresident tourists (overnight visitors) at national borders. When data on international tourists are unavailable or incomplete, the table shows the arrivals of international visitors, which include tourists, same-day visitors, cruise passengers, and crew members.

Sources and collection methods for data on arrivals differ across countries. In some cases data are obtained from border statistics (police, immigration, and the like) and supplemented by border surveys. In other cases data are obtained from tourism accommodation establishments. For some countries number of arrivals is limited to arrivals by air and for others to arrivals staying in hotels. Some countries include arrivals of nationals residing abroad while others do not. Comparison of arrivals across countries should thus be treated with caution.

The World Tourism Organization is improving its coverage of tourism expenditure data. It is now using balance of payments data from the International Monetary Fund (IMF), supplemented by data received from individual countries. The new data, shown in the table, include travel and passenger transport items as defined in the IMF's *Balance of Payments Manual.* When the IMF does not report data on passenger transport items, expenditure data for travel items are shown instead.

Aggregates are based on the World Bank's classification of countries and differ from those of the World Tourism Organization. Countries not shown in the table but for which data are available are included in the regional and income group totals. The aggregates are calculated using the World Bank's weighted aggregation methodology (see *Statistical methods*) and differ from the World Tourism Organization's aggregates.

## Definitions

- **International inbound tourists** (overnight visitors) are the number of tourists who travel to a country other than that in which they have their usual residence, but outside their usual environment, for a period not exceeding 12 months and whose main purpose in visiting is other than an activity remunerated from within the country visited. When data on number of tourists are not available, the number of visitors, which includes tourists, same-day visitors, cruise passengers, and crew members, is shown instead. • **International outbound tourists** are the number of departures that people make from their country of usual residence to any other country for any purpose other than a remunerated activity in the country visited. • **Inbound tourism expenditure** is expenditures by international inbound visitors, including payments to national carriers for international transport. These receipts include any other prepayment made for goods or services received in the destination country. They also may include receipts from same-day visitors, except when these are important enough to justify separate classification. For some countries they do not include receipts for passenger transport items. Their share in exports is calculated as a ratio to exports of goods and services, which comprise all transactions between residents of a country and the rest of the world involving a change of ownership from residents to nonresidents of general merchandise, goods sent for processing and repairs, nonmonetary gold, and services. • **Outbound tourism expenditure** is expenditures of international outbound visitors in other countries, including payments to foreign carriers for international transport. These expenditures may include those by residents traveling abroad as same-day visitors, except in cases where these are important enough to justify separate classification. For some countries they do not include expenditures for passenger transport items. Their share in imports is calculated as a ratio to imports of goods and services, which comprise all transactions between residents of a country and the rest of the world involving a change of ownership from nonresidents to residents of general merchandise, goods sent for processing and repairs, nonmonetary gold, and services.

### Data sources

Data on visitors and tourism expenditure are from the World Tourism Organization's *Yearbook of Tourism Statistics* and *Compendium of Tourism Statistics 2008.* Data in the table are updated from electronic files provided by the World Tourism Organization. Data on exports and imports are from the IMF's *Balance of Payments Statistics Yearbook* and data files.

---

### Developing countries are spending more on tourism in other countries
**6.17a**

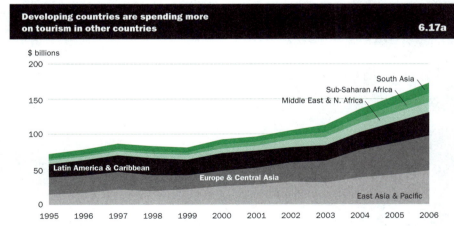

Although almost 80 percent of the world's expenditure on tourism in other countries originated in high-income countries in 2006, developing countries' share has been gradually rising. Developing countries' expenditures on tourism in other countries nearly doubled between 2000 and 2006.

*Source:* World Bank staff calculations based on World Tourism Organization data.

# PRIMARY DATA DOCUMENTATION

The World Bank is not a primary data collection agency for most areas other than business and investment climate surveys, living standards surveys, and external debt. As a major user of socioeconomic data, however, the World Bank recognizes the importance of data documentation to inform users of differences in the methods and conventions used by primary data collectors—usually national statistical agencies, central banks, and customs services—and by international organizations, which compile the statistics that appear in the World Development Indicators database. These differences may give rise to significant discrepancies over time both within countries and across them. Delays in reporting data and the use of old surveys as the base for current estimates may further compromise the quality of data reported here.

The tables in this section provide information on sources, methods, and reporting standards of the principal demographic, economic, and environmental indicators in World Development Indicators. Additional documentation is available from the World Bank's Country Statistical Information Database at www.worldbank.org/data.

The demand for good quality statistical data is increasing. Timely and reliable statistics are key to the broad development strategy often referred to as "managing for results." Monitoring and reporting on publicly agreed indicators are central to implementing poverty reduction strategies and lie at the heart of the Millennium Development Goals and the new Results Measurement System adopted for the 14th replenishment of the International Development Association.

A global action plan to improve national and international statistics was agreed on during the Second Roundtable on Managing for Development Results in February 2004 in Marrakech, Morocco. The plan, now referred to as the Marrakech Action Plan for Statistics, or MAPS, has been widely endorsed and forms the overarching framework for statistical capacity building. The third roundtable conference, held in February 2007 in Hanoi, Vietnam, reaffirmed MAPS as the guiding strategy for improving the capacity of the national and international statistical systems. See www.mfdr.org/RT3 for reports from the conference.

| | Currency | Base year | Reference year | System of National Accounts | SNA price valuation | Alternative conversion factor | PPP survey year | Balance of Payments Manual in use | External debt | System of trade | Accounting concept | IMF data dissemination standard |
|---|---|---|---|---|---|---|---|---|---|---|---|---|
| Afghanistan | Afghan afghani | 2002/03 | | | VAB | | | | Preliminary | | C | G |
| Albania | Albanian lek | [a] | 1996 | b | VAB | | 2005 | BPM5 | Actual | G | C | G |
| Algeria | Algerian dinar | 1980 | | | VAB | | | BPM5 | Actual | S | B | |
| Angola | Angolan kwanza | 1997 | | | VAP | 1991–96 | 2005 | BPM5 | Actual | S | | G |
| Argentina | Argentine peso | 1993 | | b | VAB | 1971–84 | 2005 | BPM5 | Actual | S | C | S |
| Armenia | Armenian dram | [a] | 1996 | b | VAB | 1990–95 | 2005 | BPM5 | Actual | S | C | S |
| Australia | Australian dollar | [a] | 2000 | b | VAB | | 2005 | BPM5 | | G | C | S |
| Austria | Euro | 2000 | | b | VAB | | 2005 | BPM5 | | S | C | S |
| Azerbaijan | New Azeri manat | [a] | 2003 | b | VAB | 1992–95 | 2005 | BPM5 | Actual | G | C | G |
| Bangladesh | Bangladesh taka | 1995/96 | | b | VAB | | 2005 | BPM5 | Actual | G | C | G |
| Belarus | Belarusian rubel | [a] | 2000 | b | VAB | 1990–95 | 2005 | BPM5 | Actual | G | C | S |
| Belgium | Euro | 2000 | | b | VAB | | 2005 | BPM5 | | S | C | S |
| Benin | CFA franc | 1985 | | | VAP | 1992 | 2005 | BPM5 | Preliminary | S | B | G |
| Bolivia | Boliviano | 1990 | | b | VAB | 1960–85 | 2005 | BPM5 | Actual | S | C | G |
| Bosnia and Herzegovina | Konvertible mark | [a] | 1996 | b | VAB | | 2005 | BPM5 | Actual | | C | |
| Botswana | Botswana pula | 1993/94 | | b | VAB | | 2005 | BPM5 | Actual | G | B | G |
| Brazil | Brazilian real | [a] | 2000 | b | VAB | | 2005 | BPM5 | Actual | S | C | S |
| Bulgaria | Bulgarian lev | [a] | 2002 | b | VAB | 1978–89, 1991–92 | 2005 | BPM5 | Actual | G | C | S |
| Burkina Faso | CFA franc | 1999 | | | VAB | 1992–93 | 2005 | BPM4 | Actual | G | B | G |
| Burundi | Burundi franc | 1980 | | | VAB | | 2005 | BPM5 | Actual | S | C | |
| Cambodia | Cambodian riel | 2000 | | | VAB | | 2005 | BPM5 | Actual | G | C | G |
| Cameroon | CFA franc | 2000 | | b | VAB | | 2005 | BPM5 | Preliminary | S | B | S |
| Canada | Canadian dollar | 2000 | | b | VAB | | 2005 | BPM5 | | G | C | S |
| Central African Republic | CFA franc | 2000 | | | VAB | | 2005 | BPM4 | Estimate | S | B | G |
| Chad | CFA franc | 1995 | | | VAB | | 2005 | BPM5 | Preliminary | S | C | G |
| Chile | Chilean peso | 1996 | | b | VAB | | 2005 | BPM5 | Actual | S | C | S |
| China | Chinese yuan | 2000 | | b | VAP | 1978–93 | 2005 | BPM5 | Preliminary | S | B | G |
| Hong Kong, China | Hong Kong dollar | 2000 | | b | VAB | | 2005 | BPM5 | | G | C | S |
| Colombia | Colombian peso | 1994 | | b | VAB | 1992–94 | 2005 | BPM5 | Actual | S | B | S |
| Congo, Dem. Rep. | Congo franc | 1987 | | | VAB | 1999–2001 | 2005 | BPM5 | Estimate | S | C | G |
| Congo, Rep. | CFA Franc | 1978 | | | VAP | | 2005 | BPM5 | Estimate | S | C | G |
| Costa Rica | Costa Rican colon | 1991 | | b | VAB | | | BPM5 | Actual | S | C | S |
| Côte d'Ivoire | CFA franc | 1996 | | | VAP | | 2005 | BPM5 | Actual | S | C | S |
| Croatia | Croatian kuna | [a] | 1997 | b | VAB | | 2005 | BPM5 | Actual | G | C | S |
| Cuba | Cuban peso | 1984 | | | VAP | | | | | G | | |
| Czech Republic | Czech koruna | 2000 | 1995 | b | VAB | | 2005 | BPM5 | | G | C | S |
| Denmark | Danish krone | 2000 | | b | VAB | | 2005 | BPM5 | | G | C | S |
| Dominican Republic | Dominican peso | 1990 | | | VAP | | | BPM5 | Actual | G | C | G |
| Ecuador | U.S. dollar | 2000 | | b | VAB | | 2005 | BPM5 | Actual | S | B | S |
| Egypt, Arab Rep. | Egyptian pound | 1991/92 | | | VAB | | 2005 | BPM5 | Actual | S | B | S |
| El Salvador | U.S. dollar | 1990 | | | VAB | 1982–90 | | BPM5 | Actual | S | C | S |
| Eritrea | Eritrean nakfa | 1992 | | | VAB | | | BPM4 | Actual | | | |
| Estonia | Estonian kroon | 2000 | | b | VAB | 1991–95 | 2005 | BPM5 | | G | C | G |
| Ethiopia | Ethiopian birr | 1999/2000 | | b | VAB | | 2005 | BPM5 | Actual | G | C | G |
| Finland | Euro | 2000 | | b | VAB | | 2005 | BPM5 | | G | C | S |
| France | Euro | [a] | 2000 | b | VAB | | 2005 | BPM5 | | S | C | S |
| Gabon | CFA franc | 1991 | | | VAP | 1993 | 2005 | BPM5 | Estimate | S | B | G |
| Gambia, The | Gambian dalasi | 1987 | | | VAB | | 2005 | BPM5 | Actual | G | B | G |
| Georgia | Georgian lari | [a] | 1994 | b | VAB | 1990–95 | 2005 | BPM5 | Actual | G | C | G |
| Germany | Euro | 2000 | | b | VAB | | 2005 | BPM5 | | S | C | S |
| Ghana | Ghanaian cedi | 1975 | | | VAP | 1973–87 | 2005 | BPM5 | Actual | G | B | G |
| Greece | Euro | [a] | 2000 | | VAB | | 2005 | BPM5 | | S | C | S |
| Guatemala | Guatemalan quetzal | 1958 | | | VAP | | | BPM5 | Actual | S | B | G |
| Guinea | Guinean franc | 1996 | 1994 | | VAB | | 2005 | BPM5 | Preliminary | S | B | G |
| Guinea-Bissau | CFA franc | 1986 | | | VAB | | 2005 | BPM5 | Estimate | G | | G |

# PRIMARY DATA DOCUMENTATION

| | Latest population census | Latest demographic, education, or health household survey | Source of most recent income and expenditure data | Vital registration complete | Latest agricultural census | Latest industrial data | Latest trade data | Latest water withdrawal data |
|---|---|---|---|---|---|---|---|---|
| Afghanistan | 1979 | MICS, 2003 | | | | | 1977 | 1987 |
| Albania | 2001 | RHS, 2002 | LSMS, 2004 | Yes | 1998 | 2004 | 2006 | 1995 |
| Algeria | 1998 | MICS, 2000 | HLSS, 1995 | | 2001 | | 2006 | 1995 |
| Angola | 1970 | MICS, 2001 | | | 1964–65 | | 1991 | 1987 |
| Argentina | 2001 | | EPH, 2003 | Yes | 2002 | 2002 | 2006 | 1995 |
| Armenia | 2001 | DHS, 2005 | ILCS, 2003 | Yes | | | 2006 | 1994 |
| Australia | 2006 | | SIHC, 1994 | Yes | 2001 | 2003 | 2006 | 1985 |
| Austria | 2001 | | Microcensus, 2000 | Yes | 1999–2000 | 2003 | 2006 | 1991 |
| Azerbaijan | 1999 | RHS, 2001 | HBS, 2003 | Yes | | | 2006 | 1995 |
| Bangladesh | 2001 | DHS, 2004; MICS 2006 | HES, 2005 | | 2005 | 1998 | 2004 | 1990 |
| Belarus | 1999 | MICS, 2005 | IES, 2005 | Yes | 1994 | | 2006 | 1990 |
| Belgium | 2001 | | ECHP, 2000 | Yes | 1999–2000c | 2001 | 2006 | |
| Benin | 2002 | DHS, 2001 | CWIQ, 2003 | | 1992 | | 2005 | 1994 |
| Bolivia | 2001 | DHS, 2003 | MECOVI, 2002 | | 1984–88 | 2001 | 2006 | 1987 |
| Bosnia and Herzegovina | 1991 | MICS, 2006 | LSMS, 2005 | Yes | | | 2006 | 1995 |
| Botswana | 2001 | MICS, 2000 | HIES, 1993/94 | | 1993 | 2004 | 2006 | 1992 |
| Brazil | 2000 | DHS, 1996 | PNAD, 2005 | | 1996 | 2004 | 2006 | 1992 |
| Bulgaria | 2001 | | HBS, 2003 | Yes | | | 2006 | 1988 |
| | | | | | | | | |
| Burkina Faso | 2006 | DHS, 2003 | EVCBM, 2003 | | 1993 | | 2004 | 1992 |
| Burundi | 1990 | MICS, 2000 | Priority survey, 1998 | | | | 2005 | 1987 |
| Cambodia | 1998 | DHS, 2005 | SES, 2004 | | | | 2004 | 1987 |
| Cameroon | 1987 | DHS, 2004 | Priority survey, 2001 | | 1984 | | 2006 | 1987 |
| Canada | 2006 | | SLID, 2000 | Yes | 1996/2001 | 2002 | 2006 | 1991 |
| Central African Republic | 2003 | MICS, 2006 | EPI, 1993 | | 1985 | | 2005 | 1987 |
| Chad | 1993 | DHS, 2004 | ECOSIT, 1995 | | | | 1995 | 1987 |
| Chile | 2002 | | CASEN, 2003 | Yes | 1996–97 | | 2006 | 1987 |
| China | 2000 | Intercensal survey, 1995 | HHS (Rural/Urban), 2004 | | 1997 | | 2006 | 1993 |
| Hong Kong, China | 2006 | | | Yes | | | 2006 | |
| Colombia | 2005–06 | DHS, 2005 | ECV, 2004 | | 2001 | 2000 | 2006 | 1996 |
| Congo, Dem. Rep. | 1984 | MICS, 2001 | | | 1990 | | 1986 | 1990 |
| Congo, Rep. | 1996 | DHS, 2005 | | | 1985–86 | | 1995 | 1987 |
| Costa Rica | 2000 | RHS, 1993 | EHPM, 2004 | Yes | 1973 | | 2006 | 1997 |
| Côte d'Ivoire | 1998 | MICS, 2006; AIS, 2005 | LSMS, 2002 | | 2001 | | 2006 | 1987 |
| Croatia | 2001 | | HBS, 2005 | Yes | 2003 | | 2006 | 1996 |
| Cuba | 2002 | MICS, 2006 | | Yes | | | 2004 | 1995 |
| Czech Republic | 2001 | RHS, 1993 | Microcensus, 1996/97 | Yes | 2000 | | 2006 | 1991 |
| Denmark | 2001 | | Income Tax Register, 1997 | Yes | 1999–2000 | 2003 | 2006 | 1990 |
| Dominican Republic | 2002 | DHS, 2002; ENHOGAR, 2006 | ENFT, 2005 | | 1971 | | 2001 | 1994 |
| Ecuador | 2001 | RHS, 2004 | LSMS, 1998 | | 1999–2000 | 2004 | 2006 | 1997 |
| Egypt, Arab Rep. | 2006 | DHS, 2005; SPA 2004 | HECS, 2004/05 | Yes | 1999–2000 | 2002 | 2006 | 1996 |
| El Salvador | 1992 | RHS, 2002/03 | EHPM, 2002 | Yes | 1970–71 | | 2006 | 1992 |
| Eritrea | 1984 | DHS, 2002 | | | | | 2003 | |
| Estonia | 2000 | | HBS, 2004 | Yes | 2001 | | 2006 | 1995 |
| Ethiopia | 1994 | DHS, 2005 | ICES, 2000 | | 2001–02 | | 2006 | 1987 |
| Finland | 2000 | | IDS, 2000 | Yes | 1990–2000 | 2002 | 2006 | 1991 |
| France | 2004 | | HBS, 1994/95 | Yes | 1999–2000 | 2003 | 2006 | 1999 |
| Gabon | 2003 | DHS, 2000 | | | 1974–75 | | 2006 | 1987 |
| Gambia, The | 2003 | MICS, 2005/06 | HHS, 2003/04 | | 2001–02 | 1995 | 2006 | 1982 |
| Georgia | 2002 | MICS, 1999; RHS, 1999 | SGH, 2005 | Yes | | | 2006 | 1990 |
| Germany | 2004 | | GSOEP, 2000 | Yes | 1999–2000 | 2003 | 2006 | 1991 |
| Ghana | 2000 | DHS, 2003; MICS, 2006 | LSMS, 1998/99 | | 1984 | 2003 | 2006 | 1997 |
| Greece | 2001 | | ECHP, 2000 | Yes | 1999–2000 | 1998 | 2006 | 1980 |
| Guatemala | 2002 | RHS, 2002 | ENEI-2, 2004 | Yes | 2003 | | 2006 | 1992 |
| Guinea | 1996 | DHS, 2005 | LSMS, 2003 | | 2000–01 | | 2002 | 1987 |
| Guinea-Bissau | 1991 | MICS, 2000 | IES, 1993 | | 1988 | | 1995 | 1991 |

# PRIMARY DATA DOCUMENTATION

| | Currency | National accounts | | | | | | Balance of payments and trade | | | Government finance | IMF data dissem-ination standard |
|---|---|---|---|---|---|---|---|---|---|---|---|---|
| | | Base year | Reference year | System of National Accounts | SNA price valuation | Alternative conversion factor | PPP survey year | Balance of Payments Manual in use | External debt | System of trade | Accounting concept | |
| Haiti | Haitian gourde | 1975/76 | | | VAB | 1991 | | BPM5 | Preliminary | G | | |
| Honduras | Honduran lempira | 1978 | | | VAB | 1988–89 | | BPM5 | Actual | S | B | G |
| Hungary | Hungarian forint | | [a] 2000 | [b] | VAB | | 2005 | BPM5 | Actual | G | C | S |
| India | Indian rupee | 1999/2000 | | [b] | VAB | | 2005 | BPM5 | Actual | G | C | S |
| Indonesia | Indonesian rupiah | 2000 | | | VAP | | 2005 | BPM5 | Actual | S | C | S |
| Iran, Islamic Rep. | Iranian rial | 1997/98 | | | VAB | 1980–90 | 2005 | BPM5 | Actual | G | C | |
| Iraq | Iraqi dinar | 1997 | | | VAB | | 2005 | | | S | | |
| Ireland | Euro | 2000 | | [b] | VAB | | 2005 | BPM5 | | S | C | G |
| Israel | Israeli new shekel | 2005 | | [b] | VAP | | 2005 | BPM5 | | S | C | S |
| Italy | Euro | 2000 | | [b] | VAB | | 2005 | BPM5 | | G | C | G |
| Jamaica | Jamaica dollar | 1996 | | | VAB | | 1996 | BPM5 | | G | C | S |
| Japan | Japanese yen | 2000 | | | VAB | | 2005 | BPM5 | | G | C | S |
| Jordan | Jordan dinar | 1994 | | | VAB | | 2005 | BPM5 | Actual | G | B | G |
| Kazakhstan | Kazakh tenge | | [a] 1995 | [b] | VAB | 1987–95 | 2005 | BPM5 | Actual | G | C | S |
| Kenya | Kenya shilling | 2001 | | [b] | VAB | | 2005 | BPM5 | Actual | G | B | G |
| Korea, Dem. Rep. | Democratic Republic of Korea won | | | | | | | BPM5 | | | | |
| Korea, Rep. | Korean won | 2000 | | [b] | VAB | | 2005 | BPM5 | | S | C | S |
| Kuwait | Kuwaiti dinar | 1995 | | | VAP | | 2005 | BPM5 | | S | C | S |
| Kyrgyz Republic | Kyrgyz som | | [a] 1995 | [b] | VAB | 1990–95 | 2005 | BPM5 | Actual | G | C | S |
| Lao PDR | Lao kip | 1990 | | | VAB | | 2005 | BPM5 | Preliminary | G | | |
| Latvia | Latvian lat | 2000 | | [b] | VAB | 1991–95 | 2005 | BPM5 | Actual | G | C | S |
| Lebanon | Lebanese pound | 2004 | | | VAB | | 2005 | BPM5 | Actual | G | B | G |
| Lesotho | Lesotho loti | 1995 | | [b] | VAB | | 2005 | BPM5 | Actual | G | C | G |
| Liberia | Liberian dollar | 1992 | | | VAB | | 2005 | | Estimate | | | G |
| Libya | Libyan dinar | 1975 | | | VAB | 1986 | | BPM5 | | G | | |
| Lithuania | Lithuanian litas | 2000 | | [b] | VAB | 1990–95 | 2005 | BPM5 | Actual | G | C | S |
| Macedonia, FYR | Macedonian denar | 1997 | 1995 | [b] | VAB | | 2005 | BPM5 | Actual | G | | G |
| Madagascar | Malagasy ariary | 1984 | | | VAB | | 2005 | BPM5 | Actual | S | C | G |
| Malawi | Malawi kwacha | 1994 | | | VAB | | 2005 | BPM5 | Estimate | G | B | G |
| Malaysia | Malaysian ringgit | 1987 | | | VAP | | 2005 | BPM5 | Estimate | G | C | S |
| Mali | CFA franc | 1987 | | | VAB | | 2005 | BPM4 | Actual | G | B | G |
| Mauritania | Mauritanian ouguiya | 1985 | | | VAB | | 2005 | BPM4 | Actual | G | | G |
| Mauritius | Mauritian rupee | 1997/98 | | | VAB | | 2005 | BPM5 | Actual | G | C | G |
| Mexico | Mexican new peso | 1993 | | [b] | VAB | | 2005 | BPM5 | Actual | G | C | S |
| Moldova | Moldovan leu | | [a] 1996 | [b] | VAB | 1987–95 | 2005 | BPM5 | Actual | G | C | S |
| Mongolia | Mongolian tugrik | 2005 | | [b] | VAB | | 2005 | BPM5 | Actual | S | C | G |
| Morocco | Moroccan dirham | 1998 | | | VAB | | 2005 | BPM5 | Actual | S | C | S |
| Mozambique | Mozambican metical | 1995 | | | VAB | 1992–95 | 2005 | BPM5 | Preliminary | S | | G |
| Myanmar | Myanmar kyat | 1985/86 | | | VAP | | | BPM5 | Estimate | G | C | |
| Namibia | Namibia dollar | 1995/96 | | [b] | VAB | | 2005 | BPM5 | | | B | G |
| Nepal | Nepalese rupee | 1994/95 | | | VAB | | 2005 | BPM5 | Actual | S | C | G |
| Netherlands | Euro | | [a] 2000 | [b] | VAB | | 2005 | BPM5 | | S | C | S |
| New Zealand | New Zealand dollar | 2000/01 | | | VAB | | 2005 | BPM5 | | G | C | |
| Nicaragua | Nicaraguan gold cordoba | 1994 | | [b] | VAB | 1965–93 | | BPM5 | Actual | S | B | G |
| Niger | CFA franc | 1987 | | | VAP | 1993 | 2005 | BPM5 | Preliminary | S | | G |
| Nigeria | Nigerian naira | 1987 | | | VAB | 1971–98 | 2005 | BPM5 | Preliminary | G | | G |
| Norway | Norwegian krone | | [a] 2000 | [b] | VAB | | 2005 | BPM5 | | S | C | S |
| Oman | Rial Omani | 1988 | | | VAP | | 2005 | BPM5 | Actual | G | B | G |
| Pakistan | Pakistan rupee | 1999/2000 | | [b] | VAB | | 2005 | BPM5 | Actual | G | C | G |
| Panama | Panamanian balboa | 1996 | | [b] | VAB | | 1996 | BPM5 | Actual | S | C | G |
| Papua New Guinea | Papua New Guinea kina | 1983 | | | VAB | 1989 | | BPM5 | Actual | G | B | |
| Paraguay | Paraguayan guarani | 1994 | | [b] | VAP | 1982–88 | 2005 | BPM5 | Actual | S | C | G |
| Peru | Peruvian new sol | 1994 | | | VAB | 1985–91 | 2005 | BPM5 | Actual | S | C | S |
| Philippines | Philippine peso | 1985 | | | VAP | | 2005 | BPM5 | Actual | G | B | S |
| Poland | Polish zloty | | [a] 2002 | [b] | VAB | | 2005 | BPM5 | Actual | S | C | S |

| | Latest population census | Latest demographic, education, or health household survey | Source of most recent income and expenditure data | Vital registration complete | Latest agricultural census | Latest industrial data | Latest trade data | Latest water withdrawal data |
|---|---|---|---|---|---|---|---|---|
| Haiti | 2003 | DHS, 2005 | ECVH, 2001 | | 1971 | | 1997 | 1991 |
| Honduras | 2001 | DHS, 2005 | EPHPM, 2003 | | 1993 | | 2006 | 1992 |
| Hungary | 2001 | | FBS, 2004 | Yes | 2000 | 2002 | 2006 | 1991 |
| India | 2001 | DHS, 2005/06 | NSS, 2004/05 | | 1995–1996/2000–2001 | 2003 | 2006 | 1990 |
| Indonesia | 2000 | DHS, 2002/03 | SUSENAS, 2005 | | 2003 | 2003 | 2006 | 1990 |
| Iran, Islamic Rep. | 2006 | DHS, 2000 | SECH, 2005 | Yes | 2003 | 2003 | 2006 | 1993 |
| Iraq | 1997 | MICS, 2006 | | | 1981 | | 1976 | 1990 |
| Ireland | 2006 | | ECHP, 2000 | Yes | 2000 | | 2006 | 1980 |
| Israel | 1995 | | HES, 2001 | Yes | 1981 | | 2006 | 1997 |
| Italy | 2001 | | SHIW, 2000 | Yes | 2000 | 2003 | 2006 | 1998 |
| Jamaica | 2001 | RHS, 2002/03; MICS 2005 | LSMS, 2004 | | 1978–79 | | 2006 | 1993 |
| Japan | 2005 | | | Yes | 2000 | 2002 | 2006 | 1992 |
| Jordan | 2004 | DHS, 2002 | HIES, 2002/03 | | 1997 | 2004 | 2006 | 1993 |
| Kazakhstan | 1999 | DHS, 1999; MICS, 2006 | HBS, 2003 | Yes | | | 2006 | 1993 |
| Kenya | 1999 | DHS, 2003; SPA, 2004 | WMS II, 1997 | | 1977–79 | 2004 | 2004 | 1990 |
| Korea, Dem. Rep. | 1993 | MICS, 2000 | | | | | | 1987 |
| Korea, Rep. | 2005 | | NSFIE, 1998/99 | Yes | 2000 | 2002 | 2006 | 1994 |
| Kuwait | 2005 | FHS, 1996 | | Yes | 1970 | | 2001 | 1994 |
| Kyrgyz Republic | 1999 | DHS, 1997; MICS 2005/06 | HBS, 2003 | Yes | 2002 | 2001 | 2006 | 1994 |
| Lao PDR | 2005 | MICS, 2000 | ECS I, 2002 | | 1998–99 | | 1975 | 1987 |
| Latvia | 2000 | | HBS, 2005 | Yes | 2001 | | 2006 | 1994 |
| Lebanon | 1970 | MICS, 2000 | | | 1998–99 | | 2004 | 1996 |
| Lesotho | 2006 | DHS, 2004 | HBS, 1995 | | 1999–2000 | | 2002 | 1987 |
| Liberia | 1984 | MICS, 1995 | | | | | 1984 | 1987 |
| Libya | 1995 | MICS, 2000 | | | 2001 | | 2004 | 1999 |
| Lithuania | 2001 | | HBS, 2004 | Yes | 1994 | 2004 | 2006 | 1995 |
| Macedonia, FYR | 2002 | | HBS, 2003 | Yes | 1994 | 2001 | 2006 | 1996 |
| Madagascar | 1993 | DHS, 2003/04 | Priority survey, 2001 | | 1984–85 | 2004 | 2006 | 1984 |
| Malawi | 1998 | DHS, 2004; MICS 2006 | HHS, 2004/05 | | 1993 | 2001 | 2006 | 1994 |
| Malaysia | 2000 | | HIBAS, 1997 | Yes | | 2003 | 2006 | 1995 |
| Mali | 1998 | DHS, 2001 | EMCES, 2001 | | 1984 | | 2004 | 1987 |
| Mauritania | 2000 | DHS, 2000/01 | LSMS, 2000 | | 1984–85 | | 2006 | 1985 |
| Mauritius | 2000 | | | Yes | | 2002 | 2006 | |
| Mexico | 2005 | ENPF, 1995 | ENIGH, 2004 | | 1991 | 2000 | 2006 | 1998 |
| Moldova | 2004 | DHS, 2005 | HBS, 2003 | Yes | | | 2006 | 1992 |
| Mongolia | 2000 | MICS, 2005 | LSMS/Integrated Survey, 2002 | Yes | | 2000 | 2006 | 1993 |
| Morocco | 2004 | DHS, 2003/04 | LSMS, 1998/99 | | 1996 | 2004 | 2006 | 1998 |
| Mozambique | 2007 | DHS, 2003 | NHS, 2002/03 | | 1999–2000 | | 2006 | 1992 |
| Myanmar | 1983 | MICS, 2000 | | | 2003 | | 1992 | 1987 |
| Namibia | 2001 | DHS, 2000 | NHIES, 1993 | | 1996–97 | | 2006 | 1991 |
| Nepal | 2001 | DHS, 2006 | LSMS, 2003/04 | | 2002 | 2002 | 2003 | 1994 |
| Netherlands | 2001 | | ECHP, 1999 | Yes | 1999–2000c | 2003 | 2006 | 1991 |
| New Zealand | 2006 | | | Yes | 2002 | 2002 | 2006 | 1991 |
| Nicaragua | 2005 | DHS, 2001 | LSMS, 2001 | Yes | 2001 | | 2006 | 1998 |
| Niger | 2001 | DHS/MICS, 2006 | | | 1980 | | 2005 | 1988 |
| Nigeria | 2006 | DHS, 2003 | LSMS, 2003 | | 1960 | | 2003 | 1987 |
| Norway | 2001 | | IF 2000 | Yes | 1999 | 2001 | 2006 | 1985 |
| Oman | 2003 | FHS, 1995 | | | 1978–79 | | 2006 | 1991 |
| Pakistan | 1998 | RHS, 2000/01 | PIHS, 2005 | | 2000 | | 2006 | 1991 |
| Panama | 2000 | LSMS, 2003 | EH, 2003 | | 2001 | 2001 | 2006 | 1990 |
| Papua New Guinea | 2000 | DHS, 1996 | HHS, 1996 | | | | 2004 | 1987 |
| Paraguay | 2002 | RHS, 2004 | EIH, 2003 | | 1991 | | 2006 | 1987 |
| Peru | 2005 | DHS, 2004 | ENAHO, 2003 | | 1994 | 1996 | 2006 | 1992 |
| Philippines | 2000 | DHS, 2003 | FIES, 2003 | Yes | 2002 | 2003 | 2006 | 1995 |
| Poland | 2002 | | HBS, 2005 | Yes | 1996/2002 | | 2006 | 1991 |

| | Currency | National accounts | | | | | | Balance of payments and trade | | | Government finance | IMF data dissemination standard |
|---|---|---|---|---|---|---|---|---|---|---|---|---|
| | | Base year | Reference year | System of National Accounts | SNA price valuation | Alternative conversion factor | PPP survey year | Balance of Payments Manual in use | External debt | System of trade | Accounting concept | |
| Portugal | Euro | 2000 | | b | VAB | | 2005 | BPM5 | | S | C | S |
| Puerto Rico | U.S. dollar | 1954 | | | VAP | | | | | G | | |
| Romania | New Romanian leu | a | 1999 | b | VAB | 1987–89, 1992 | 2005 | BPM5 | Preliminary | S | C | S |
| Russian Federation | Russian ruble | 2003 | 2000 | b | VAB | 1987–95 | 2005 | BPM5 | Preliminary | G | C | S |
| Rwanda | Rwanda franc | 1995 | | | VAP | | 2005 | BPM5 | Preliminary | G | C | G |
| Saudi Arabia | Saudi Arabian riyal | 1999 | | | VAP | | 2005 | BPM4 | | G | | |
| Senegal | CFA franc | 1999 | | b | VAB | | 2005 | BPM5 | Actual | S | B | G |
| Serbia | Serbian dinar | 2002 | | | VAB | | 2005 | | Actual | | | |
| Sierra Leone | Sierra Leonean leone | 2001 | 1990 | b | VAB | | 2005 | BPM5 | Preliminary | G | B | G |
| Singapore | Singapore dollar | 2000 | | b | VAB | | 2005 | BPM5 | | G | C | S |
| Slovak Republic | Slovak koruna | 2000 | 1995 | b | VAP | | 2005 | BPM5 | Actual | G | C | S |
| Slovenia | Euro | a | 2000 | b | VAB | | 2005 | BPM5 | | S | C | S |
| Somalia | Somali shilling | 1985 | | | VAB | 1977–90 | | | Estimate | | | |
| South Africa | South African rand | 2000 | | b | VAB | | 2005 | BPM5 | Preliminary | S | C | S |
| Spain | Euro | 2000 | | b | VAB | | 2005 | BPM5 | | S | C | S |
| Sri Lanka | Sri Lankan rupee | 1996 | | | VAB | | 2005 | BPM5 | Actual | G | B | G |
| Sudan | Sudanese dinar | 1981/82d | 1982 | | VAB | | 2005 | BPM5 | Actual | G | B | G |
| Swaziland | Lilangeni | 1985 | | | VAB | | 2005 | | Actual | | C | G |
| Sweden | Swedish krona | a | 2000 | | VAB | | 2005 | BPM5 | | G | C | S |
| Switzerland | Swiss franc | 2000 | | | VAB | | 2005 | BPM5 | | S | C | S |
| Syrian Arab Republic | Syrian pound | 2000 | | | VAB | 1970–2006 | 2005 | BPM5 | Estimate | S | C | G |
| Tajikistan | Tajik somoni | a | 1997 | b | VAB | 1990–95 | 2005 | BPM5 | Preliminary | S | C | G |
| Tanzania | Tanzania shilling | 1992 | | | VAB | | 2005 | BPM5 | Estimate | S | | G |
| Thailand | Thai baht | 1988 | | | VAP | | 2005 | BPM5 | Actual | G | C | S |
| Timor-Leste | U.S. dollar | 2000 | | | VAP | | | | | | | |
| Togo | CFA franc | 1978 | | | VAP | | 2005 | BPM5 | Actual | S | B | G |
| Trinidad and Tobago | Trinidad and Tobago dollar | 2000 | | b | VAB | | 1996 | BPM5 | | S | C | G |
| Tunisia | Tunisian dinar | 1990 | | | VAP | | 2005 | BPM5 | Actual | G | C | S |
| Turkey | New Turkish lira | 1987 | | | VAB | | 2005 | BPM5 | Actual | S | B | S |
| Turkmenistan | Turkmen manat | a | 1987 | b | VAB | 1987–95, 1997–2006 | 2000 | BPM5 | Actual | G | | |
| Uganda | Uganda shilling | 1997/98 | | | VAB | | 2005 | BPM5 | Actual | G | B | G |
| Ukraine | Ukrainian hryvnia | a | 2003 | b | VAB | 1990–95 | 2005 | BPM5 | Actual | G | C | S |
| United Arab Emirates | U.A.E. dirham | 1995 | | | VAB | | | BPM4 | | G | C | |
| United Kingdom | Pound sterling | 2000 | | b | VAB | | 2005 | BPM5 | | G | C | S |
| United States | U.S. dollar | a | 2000 | | VAB | | 2005 | BPM5 | | G | C | S |
| Uruguay | Uruguayan peso | 1983 | | | VAB | | 2005 | BPM5 | Actual | S | C | S |
| Uzbekistan | Uzbek sum | a | 1997 | b | VAB | 1990–95 | 2000 | BPM5 | Actual | G | | |
| Venezuela, RB | Venezuelan bolivar | 1997 | | | VAB | | 2005 | BPM5 | Actual | G | C | G |
| Vietnam | Vietnamese dong | 1994 | | b | VAP | 1991 | 2005 | BPM4 | Actual | G | C | G |
| West Bank and Gaza | Israeli new shekel | 1997 | | | VAB | | | | | | B | G |
| Yemen, Rep. | Yemen rial | 1990 | | | VAP | 1991–96 | 2005 | BPM5 | Actual | G | B | G |
| Zambia | Zambian kwacha | 1994 | | | VAB | 1990–92 | 2005 | BPM5 | Actual | G | B | G |
| Zimbabwe | Zimbabwe dollar | 1990 | | | VAB | 1991, 1998 | 2005 | BPM5 | Actual | G | C | G |

# PRIMARY DATA DOCUMENTATION

| | Latest population census | Latest demographic, education, or health household survey | Source of most recent income and expenditure data | Vital registration complete | Latest agricultural census | Latest industrial data | Latest trade data | Latest water withdrawal data |
|---|---|---|---|---|---|---|---|---|
| Portugal | 2001 | | | Yes | 1999 | 2003 | 2006 | 1990 |
| Puerto Rico | 2000 | RHS, 1995/96 | | Yes | 1997/2002 | | | |
| Romania | 2002 | RHS, 1999 | LSMS, 2005 | Yes | 2002 | 2004 | 2006 | 1994 |
| Russian Federation | 2002 | RHS, 1996 | LMS, Round 9, 2002 | Yes | 1994–95 | 2004 | 2006 | 1994 |
| Rwanda | 2002 | DHS, 2005 | LSMS, 1999/2000 | | 1984 | | 2003 | 1993 |
| Saudi Arabia | 2004 | Demographic survey, 1999 | | | 1999 | | 2006 | 1992 |
| Senegal | 2002 | DHS, 2005 | ESASM, 1995 | | 1998–99 | 2002 | 2006 | 1987 |
| Serbia | 2002 | MICS, 2000 | | Yes | | | 2006 | |
| Sierra Leone | 2004 | MICS, 2005 | SLIHS, 2003 | | 1984–85 | | 2002 | 1987 |
| Singapore | 2000 | General household, 2005 | | Yes | | 2003 | 2006 | 1975 |
| Slovak Republic | 2001 | | Microcensus, 1996 | Yes | 2001 | 2003 | 2006 | 1991 |
| Slovenia | 2002 | | HBS, 2004 | Yes | 2000 | | 2006 | 1996 |
| Somalia | 1987 | MICS, 1999 | | | | | 1982 | 1987 |
| South Africa | 2001 | DHS, 1998 | IES, 2000 | | 2002 | 2004 | 2006 | 1990 |
| Spain | 2001 | | ECHP, 2000 | Yes | 1999 | 2003 | 2006 | 1997 |
| Sri Lanka | 2001 | DHS, 1987 | HIES, 2002 | Yes | 2002 | | 2005 | 1990 |
| Sudan | 1993 | MICS, 2000 | | | | | 2006 | 1995 |
| Swaziland | 2007 | MICS, 2000 | SHIES, 2000/01 | | 2000 | | 2005 | .. |
| Sweden | 2005 | | HINK, 2000 | Yes | 1999–2000 | 2002 | 2006 | 1991 |
| Switzerland | 2000 | | EVE, 2000 | Yes | 2000 | | 2006 | 1991 |
| Syrian Arab Republic | 1994 | MICS, 2006 | | | 1981 | | 2006 | 1995 |
| Tajikistan | 2000 | MICS, 2005 | LSMS, 2004 | Yes | 1994 | | 2000 | 1994 |
| Tanzania | 2002 | DHS, 2004; AIS 2003 | HIES, 2000/01 | | 2002–03 | | 2006 | 1994 |
| Thailand | 2000 | DHS, 1987; MICS 2005/06 | SES, 2002 | | 2003 | 2000 | 2006 | 1990 |
| Timor-Leste | 2004 | | | | | | | |
| Togo | 1981 | MICS, 2006 | | | 1996 | | 2005 | 1987 |
| Trinidad and Tobago | 2000 | MICS, 2000 | LSMS, 1992 | Yes | 2004 | 2002 | 2006 | 1997 |
| Tunisia | 2004 | MICS, 2000 | LSMS, 2000 | | 2004 | | 2005 | 1996 |
| Turkey | 2000 | DHS, 2003 | LSMS, 2003 | | 2001 | 2001 | 2006 | 1997 |
| Turkmenistan | 1995 | DHS, 2000 | LSMS, 1998 | Yes | | | 2000 | 1994 |
| Uganda | 2002 | DHS, 2006; AIS, 2004 | NIHS III, 2002 | | 1991 | | 2006 | 1970 |
| Ukraine | 2001 | MICS, 2000 | HBS, 2003 | Yes | | 2004 | 2006 | 1992 |
| United Arab Emirates | 2005 | | | | 1998 | | 2005 | 1995 |
| United Kingdom | 2001 | | FRS, 1999 | Yes | 1999–2000c | 2002 | 2006 | 1991 |
| United States | 2000 | CPS (monthly) | CPS, 2000 | Yes | 1997/2002 | 2001 | 2006 | 1990 |
| Uruguay | 2004 | | ECH, 2003 | Yes | 2000 | 2003 | 2006 | 1965 |
| Uzbekistan | 1989 | MICS, 2006; DHS special, 2002 | FBS, 2003 | Yes | | | | 1994 |
| Venezuela, RB | 2001 | MICS, 2000 | EHM, 2003 | Yes | 1997 | | 2006 | 1970 |
| Vietnam | 1999 | DHS 2002; AIS 2005 | LSMS, 2004 | | 2001 | | 2005 | 1990 |
| West Bank and Gaza | 1997 | PAPFAM, 2006 | | | 1971 | | | |
| Yemen, Rep. | 2004 | DHS, 1997 | HBS, 2005 | | 2002 | 2003 | 2006 | 1990 |
| Zambia | 2000 | DHS, 2001/02, SPA, 2005 | LCMS II, 2004 | | 1990 | | 2006 | 1994 |
| Zimbabwe | 2002 | DHS, 2005/06 | LCMS III, 1995 | | 1960 | 1996 | 2005 | 1987 |

**Note:** For explanation of the abbreviations used in the table see notes following the table.
a. Original chained constant price data are rescaled. b. Country uses the 1993 System of National Accounts methodology. c. Conducted annually. d. Reporting period switch from fiscal year to calendar year from 1996. Pre-1996 data converted to calendar year.

• **Base year** is the base or pricing period used for constant price calculations in the country's national accounts. Price indexes derived from national accounts aggregates, such as the implicit deflator for gross domestic product (GDP), express the price level relative to base year prices. • **Reference year** is the year in which the local currency, constant price series of a country is valued. The reference year is usually the same as the base year used to report the constant price series. However, when the constant price data are chain linked, the base year is changed annually, so the data are rescaled to a specific reference year to provide a consistent time series. When the country has not rescaled following a change in base year, World Bank staff rescale the data to maintain a longer historical series. To allow for cross-country comparison and data aggregation, constant price data reported in *World Development Indicators* are rescaled to a common reference year (2000) and currency (U.S. dollars). • **System of National Accounts** identifies countries that use the 1993 System of National Accounts (1993 SNA), the terminology applied in *World Development Indicators* since 2001, to compile national accounts. Although more countries are adopting the 1993 SNA, many still follow the 1968 SNA, and some low-income countries use concepts from the 1953 SNA. • **SNA price valuation** shows whether value added in the national accounts is reported at basic prices (VAB) or producer prices (VAP). Producer prices include taxes paid by producers and thus tend to overstate the actual value added in production. However, VAB can be higher than VAP in countries with high agricultural subsidies. See *About the data* for tables 4.1 and 4.2 for further discussion of national accounts valuation. • **Alternative conversion factor** identifies the countries and years for which a World Bank–estimated conversion factor has been used in place of the official exchange rate (line rf in the International Monetary Fund's [IMF] *International Financial Statistics*). See *Statistical methods* for further discussion of alternative conversion factors. • **Purchasing power parity (PPP) survey year** is the latest available survey year for the International Comparison Program's estimates of PPPs. See *About the data* for table 1.1 for a more detailed description of PPPs. • **Balance of Payments Manual in use** refers to the classification system used to compile and report data on balance of payments items in table 4.15. BPM4 refers to the 4th edition of the IMF's *Balance of Payments Manual* (1977), and BPM5 to the 5th edition (1993). • **External debt** shows debt reporting status for 2006 data. *Actual* indicates that data are as reported, *preliminary* that data are preliminary and include an element of staff estimation, and *estimate* that data are World Bank staff estimates. • **System of trade** refers to the United Nations general trade system (G) or special trade system (S). Under the general trade system goods entering directly for domestic consumption and

goods entered into customs storage are recorded as imports at arrival. Under the special trade system goods are recorded as imports when declared for domestic consumption whether at time of entry or on withdrawal from customs storage. Exports under the general system comprise outward-moving goods: (a) national goods wholly or partly produced in the country; (b) foreign goods, neither transformed nor declared for domestic consumption in the country, that move outward from customs storage; and (c) nationalized goods that have been declared for domestic consumption and move outward without being transformed. Under the special system of trade, exports are categories a and c. In some compilations categories b and c are classified as re-exports. Direct transit trade—goods entering or leaving for transport only—is excluded from both import and export statistics. See *About the data* for tables 4.4, 4.5, and 6.2 for further discussion. • **Government finance accounting concept** is the accounting basis for reporting central government financial data. For most countries government finance data have been consolidated (C) into one set of accounts capturing all central government fiscal activities. Budgetary central government accounts (B) exclude some central government units. See *About the data* for tables 4.10, 4.11, and 4.12 for further details. • **IMF data dissemination standard** shows the countries that subscribe to the IMF's Special Data Dissemination Standard (SDDS) or General Data Dissemination System (GDDS). S refers to countries that subscribe to the SDDS and have posted data on the Dissemination Standards Bulletin Board at http://dsbb.imf.org. G refers to countries that subscribe to the GDDS. The SDDS was established for member countries that have or might seek access to international capital markets to guide them in providing their economic and financial data to the public. The GDDS helps countries disseminate comprehensive, timely, accessible, and reliable economic, financial, and sociodemographic statistics. IMF member countries elect to participate in either the SDDS or the GDDS. Both standards enhance the availability of timely and comprehensive data and therefore contribute to the pursuit of sound macroeconomic policies. The SDDS is also expected to improve the functioning of financial markets. • **Latest population census** shows the most recent year in which a census was conducted and in which at least preliminary results were released. It includes registration-based censuses. Some countries with complete population registration systems produce similar tables every 5 or 10 years instead of conducting regular censuses. • **Latest demographic, education, or health household survey** indicates the household surveys used to compile the demographic, education, and health data in section 2. AIS is AIDS Indicator Survey, CPS is Current Population Survey, DHS is Demographic and Health Survey, ENHOGAR is National Multiple Indicator

Cluster Survey (Encuesta Nacional de Hogares de Propósitos Múltiples), ENPF is National Family Planning Survey (Encuesta Nacional de Planificacion Familiar), FHS is Family Health Survey, LSMS is Living Standards Measurement Survey, MICS is Multiple Indicator Cluster Survey, PAPFAM is Pan Arab Project for Family Health, RHS is Reproductive Health Survey, and SPA is Service Provision Assessments. Detailed information for AIS, DHS, and SPA are available at www.measuredhs.com/aboutsurveys; for MICS at www.childinfo.org; and for RHS at www.cdc. gov/reproductivehealth/surveys. • **Source of most recent income and expenditure data** shows household surveys that collect income and expenditure data. CASEN is Caracterizacion Socioeconomica Nacional, CPS is Current Population Survey, CWIQ is Core Welfare Indicators Questionnaire, ECH is Encuesta Continua de Hogares, ECHP is European Community Household Panel, ECOSIT is Enquête sur la Consommation des Ménages et le Secteur Informel au Tchad, ECS is Expenditure and Consumption Survey, ECV is Encuesta Nacional de Calidad de Vida, ECVH is Enquête sur les Conditions de Vie en Haïti, EH is Encuesta de Hogares, EHM is Encuesta de Hogares por Muestreo, EHPM is Encuesta de Hogares de Propositos Multiples, EIH is Encuesta Integrada de Hogares, EMCES is Enquête Malienne de Conjoncture Economique et Sociale, ENAHO is Enquesta Nacional de Hogares, ENEI is Encuesta Nacional de Empleo e Ingresos, ENFT is Encuesta Nacional de Fuerza de Trabajo, ENIGH is Encuesta Nacional de Ingreso-Gasto de los Hogares, EPH is Encuesta Permanente de Hogares, EPHPM is Encuesta Permanente de Hogares de Propositos Multiples, EPI is Enquête Prioritaire sur les Conditions de Vie des Ménages, ESASM is Enquête Sénégalaise Auprès des Ménages, EVCBM is Enquête Burkinabé sur les Conditions de Die des Ménages, EVE is Einkommens- und Verbraucherserhebung, FBS and HBS are Household Budget Survey, FIES is Family Income and Expenditure Survey, FRS is Family Resources Survey, GSOEP is German Socio-Economic Panel, HECS is Household Expenditure and Consumption Survey, HES is Household Expenditure Survey, HHS is Household Survey, HIBAS is Household Income and Basic Amenities Survey, HIES is Household Income and Expenditure Survey, HINK is Household Income Survey, HLSS is Household Living Standards Survey, ICES is Income, Consumption, and Expenditure Survey, IDS is Income Distribution Survey, IES is Income and Expenditure Survey, IF is Inntekts- og formuesundersøkelsen for husholdninger, ILCS is Integrated Survey of Living Standards, LCMS is Living Conditions Monitoring Survey, LMS is Longitudinal Measurement Survey, LSMS is Living Standards Measurement Study, MECOVI is Measurement of Living Conditions in Latin America and the Caribbean, NHS is National Household Survey, NIHS is National Integrated Household Survey, NSFIE is National Survey of Family Income and

Expenditures, NSS is National Sample Survey of Households, PIHS is Pakistan Integrated Household Survey, PNAD is Pesquisa Nacional por Amostra de Domicilios, SECH is Socioeconomic Characteristics of Households, SES is Socioeconomic Survey, SGH is Survey of Georgian Households, SHIW is Survey of Household Income and Wealth, SIHC is Survey of Income and Housing Costs, SLID is Survey of Labour and Income Dynamics, SLIHS is Sierra Leone Integrated Household Survey, SUSENAS is Socioeconomic Survey, and WMS is Welfare Monitoring Survey. Detailed information on household surveys for developing countries can be found on the website of the International Household Survey Network (www.survey-network.org). • **Vital registration complete** identifies countries judged to have at least 90 percent complete registries of vital (birth and death) statistics by the United Nations Statistics Division and reported in Population and Vital Statistics Reports. Countries with complete vital statistics registries may have more accurate and more timely demographic indicators than other countries. • **Latest agricultural census** shows the most recent year in which an agricultural census was conducted and reported to the Food and Agriculture Organization of the United Nations. • **Latest industrial data** show the most recent year for which manufacturing value added data at the three-digit level of the International Standard Industrial Classification (ISIC, revision 2 or 3) are available in the United Nations Industrial Development Organization database. • **Latest trade data** show the most recent year for which structure of merchandise trade data from the United Nations Statistics Division's Commodity Trade (Comtrade) database are available. • **Latest water withdrawal data** show the most recent year for which data on freshwater withdrawals have been compiled from a variety of sources. See *About the data* for table 3.5 for more information.

### Exceptional reporting periods

In most economies the **fiscal year** is concurrent with the calendar year. Exceptions are shown in this table. The ending date reported here is for the fiscal year of the central government. Fiscal years for other levels of government and reporting years for statistical surveys may differ. And some countries that follow a fiscal year report their national accounts data on a calendar year basis as shown in the *reporting period* column.

The **reporting period for national accounts data** is designated as either calendar year basis (CY) or fiscal year basis (FY). Most economies report their national accounts and balance of payments data using calendar years, but some use fiscal years. In *World Development Indicators* fiscal year data are assigned to the calendar year that contains the larger share of the fiscal year. If a country's fiscal year ends before June 30, data are shown in the first year of the fiscal period; if the fiscal year ends on or after June 30, data

are shown in the second year of the period. Balance of payments data are reported in *World Development Indicators* by calendar year and so are not comparable to the national accounts data of the countries that report their national accounts on a fiscal year basis.

### Economies with exceptional reporting periods

| Economy | Fiscal year end | Reporting period for national accounts data |
|---|---|---|
| Afghanistan | Mar. 20 | FY |
| Australia | Jun. 30 | FY |
| Bangladesh | Jun. 30 | FY |
| Botswana | Jun. 30 | FY |
| Canada | Mar. 31 | CY |
| Egypt, Arab Rep. | Jun. 30 | FY |
| Ethiopia | Jul. 7 | FY |
| Gambia, The | Jun. 30 | CY |
| Haiti | Sep. 30 | FY |
| India | Mar. 31 | FY |
| Indonesia | Mar. 31 | CY |
| Iran, Islamic Rep. | Mar. 20 | FY |
| Japan | Mar. 31 | CY |
| Kenya | Jun. 30 | CY |
| Kuwait | Jun. 30 | CY |
| Lesotho | Mar. 31 | CY |
| Malawi | Mar. 31 | CY |
| Mauritius | Jun. 30 | FY |
| Myanmar | Mar. 31 | FY |
| Namibia | Mar. 31 | CY |
| Nepal | Jul. 14 | FY |
| New Zealand | Mar. 31 | FY |
| Pakistan | Jun. 30 | FY |
| Puerto Rico | Jun. 30 | FY |
| Sierra Leone | Jun. 30 | CY |
| Singapore | Mar. 31 | CY |
| South Africa | Mar. 31 | CY |
| Swaziland | Mar. 31 | CY |
| Sweden | Jun. 30 | CY |
| Thailand | Sep. 30 | CY |
| Uganda | Jun. 30 | FY |
| United States | Sep. 30 | CY |
| Zimbabwe | Jun. 30 | CY |

### Revisions to national accounts data

National accounts data are revised by national statistical offices when methodologies change or data sources improve. National accounts data in *World Development Indicators* are also revised when data sources change. The following notes, while not comprehensive, provide information on revisions from previous data.

• **Bhutan.** Data revisions reflect changes in sources. Current and constant price value added data from 1980 to 2006 are from the government of Bhutan. Current price expenditure data for 1989–2005 and constant price expenditure data for 2000–05 are from the Asian Development Bank's *Key Indicators 2007.* • **Botswana.** Large changes in constant price consumption indicators from 1998–2006 are due to

statistical discrepancy. The Central Statistical Office published large-scale revisions of constant price discrepancy in GDP for 1996/97–2004/05 in April 2006 and May 2007. • **Brazil.** The Institute of Geography and Statistics revised its national accounts data. Among the changes are new sources and a change in base year to 2000. • **Burkina Faso.** National accounts value added and expenditure data have been revised from 1985–2006 according to recently released data from the Ministry of Economy and Finance. Constant price series have been linked back since 1984. Valuation is value added at basic prices, and the new base year is 1999. • **Chile.** Data from 2003 onward reflect the Central Bank's new series using 2003 as the base year. • **China.** The base year for constant price data changed from 1990 to 2000. • **Côte d'Ivoire.** Data for 1999–2006 were revised using data from the IMF, national authorities, and World Bank staff estimates. • **Egypt.** Constant price data are updated from official published national accounts. Constant price imports and exports data have been revised based on data from the Central Bank website (www.cbe.org.eg), which lists the constant price expenditure components of GDP. • **Fiji.** Data revisions reflect changes in sources. Data for 1996–2005 were revised using data from the Asian Development Bank's *Key Indicators 2007.* • **India.** In May 2007 the Central Statistical Organization published revised national accounts data for 1951–99 consistent with the new series of national accounts statistics released on January 31, 2006. • **Jordan.** Data have been revised by the Central Bank and the Department of Statistics. • **Lebanon.** Data have been revised by the Central Bank. • **Malawi.** The central statistics office, with assistance from Norway, revised its national accounts data. The initial outcome is that GDP will increase by approximately 37 percent. • **Morocco.** The government revised national accounts data from 1998 onward. National accounts value added data switched from producer prices to basic prices. The new base year is 1998. • **São Tomé and Príncipe.** Data have been revised by the National Statistics Institute. Revised GDP estimates are much higher (47.5 percent for the new base year 2001) than those of the previous series and reflect improvements in coverage. • **Senegal.** National accounts data have been revised to conform to 1993 SNA methodology, and the base year has changed to 1999. Value added data are now in basic prices. Agricultural sector data are entered in the year of production (N) in the 1999 base year of the SNA as opposed to the year following the year of production (N+1) in base year 1987. • **Sudan.** Expenditure items in both current and constant prices for 1988–95 were revised using recent United Nations Statistics Division and IMF *World Economic Outlook* estimates. • **Tanzania.** National accounts expenditure data in current and constant prices have been revised from 1995 onward. Data are from IMF and World Bank staff estimates and Tanzanian authorities.

# STATISTICAL METHODS

This section describes some of the statistical procedures used in preparing the World Development Indicators. It covers the methods employed for calculating regional and income group aggregates and for calculating growth rates, and it describes the *World Bank Atlas* method for deriving the conversion factor used to estimate gross national income (GNI) and GNI per capita in U.S. dollars. Other statistical procedures and calculations are described in the *About the data* sections following each table.

## Aggregation rules

Aggregates based on the World Bank's regional and income classifications of economies appear at the end of most tables. The countries included in these classifications are shown on the flaps on the front and back covers of the book. Most tables also include the aggregate euro area. This aggregate includes the member states of the Economic and Monetary Union (EMU) of the European Union that have adopted the euro as their currency: Austria, Belgium, Cyprus, Finland, France, Germany, Greece, Ireland, Italy, Luxembourg, Malta, Netherlands, Portugal, Slovenia, and Spain. Other classifications, such as the European Union and regional trade blocs, are documented in *About the data* for the tables in which they appear.

Because of missing data, aggregates for groups of economies should be treated as approximations of unknown totals or average values. Regional and income group aggregates are based on the largest available set of data, including values for the 153 economies shown in the main tables, other economies shown in table 1.6, and Taiwan, China. The aggregation rules are intended to yield estimates for a consistent set of economies from one period to the next and for all indicators. Small differences between sums of subgroup aggregates and overall totals and averages may occur because of the approximations used. In addition, compilation errors and data reporting practices may cause discrepancies in theoretically identical aggregates such as world exports and world imports.

Five methods of aggregation are used in *World Development Indicators*:

- For group and world totals denoted in the tables by a *t,* missing data are imputed based on the relationship of the sum of available data to the total in the year of the previous estimate. The imputation process works forward and backward from 2000. Missing values in 2000 are imputed using one of several proxy variables for which complete data are available in that year. The imputed value is calculated so that it (or its proxy) bears the same relationship to the total of available data. Imputed values are usually not calculated if missing data account for more than a third of the total in the benchmark year. The variables used as proxies are GNI in U.S. dollars, total population, exports and imports of goods and services in U.S. dollars, and value added in agriculture, industry, manufacturing, and services in U.S. dollars.
- Aggregates marked by an s are sums of available data. Missing values are not imputed. Sums are not computed if more than a third of the observations in the series or a proxy for the series are missing in a given year.
- Aggregates of ratios are denoted by a w when calculated as weighted averages of the ratios (using the value of the denominator or, in some cases, another indicator as a weight) and denoted by a u when calculated as unweighted averages. The aggregate ratios are based on available data, including data for economies not shown in the main tables. Missing values are assumed to have the same average value as the available data. No aggregate is calculated if missing data account for more than a third of the value of weights in the benchmark year. In a few cases the aggregate ratio may be computed as the ratio of group totals after imputing values for missing data according to the above rules for computing totals.
- Aggregate growth rates are denoted by a w when calculated as a weighted average of growth rates. In a few cases growth rates may be computed from time series of group totals. Growth rates are not calculated if more than half the observations in a period are missing. For further discussion of methods of computing growth rates see below.
- Aggregates denoted by an m are medians of the values shown in the table. No value is shown if more than half the observations for countries with a population of more than 1 million are missing.

Exceptions to the rules occur throughout the book. Depending on the judgment of World Bank analysts, the aggregates may be based on as little as 50 percent of the available data. In other cases, where missing or excluded values are judged to be small or irrelevant, aggregates are based only on the data shown in the tables.

## Growth rates

Growth rates are calculated as annual averages and represented as percentages. Except where noted, growth rates of values are computed from constant price series. Three principal methods are used to calculate growth rates: least squares, exponential endpoint, and geometric endpoint. Rates of change from one period to the next are calculated as proportional changes from the earlier period.

**Least-squares growth rate**. Least-squares growth rates are used wherever there is a sufficiently long time series to permit a reliable calculation. No growth rate is calculated if more than half the observations in a period are missing. The least-squares growth rate, r, is estimated by fitting a linear regression trend line to the logarithmic annual values of the variable in the relevant period. The regression equation takes the form

$$\ln X_t = a + bt$$

which is equivalent to the logarithmic transformation of the compound growth equation,

$$X_t = X_o (1 + r)^t.$$

In this equation $X$ is the variable, $t$ is time, and $a = \ln X_o$ and $b = \ln (1 + r)$ are parameters to be estimated. If $b*$ is the least-squares estimate of $b$, then the average annual growth rate, $r$, is obtained as $[\exp(b*) - 1]$ and is multiplied by 100 for expression as a percentage. The calculated growth rate is an average rate that is representative of the available observations over the entire period. It does not necessarily match the actual growth rate between any two periods.

**Exponential growth rate.** The growth rate between two points in time for certain demographic indicators, notably labor force and population, is calculated from the equation

$$r = \ln(p_n/p_0)/n$$

where $p_n$ and $p_0$ are the last and first observations in the period, $n$ is the number of years in the period, and ln is the natural logarithm operator. This growth rate is based on a model of continuous, exponential growth between two points in time. It does not take into account the intermediate values of the series. Nor does it correspond to the annual rate of change measured at a one-year interval, which is given by $(p_n - p_{n-1})/p_{n-1}$.

**Geometric growth rate.** The geometric growth rate is applicable to compound growth over discrete periods, such as the payment and reinvestment of interest or dividends. Although continuous growth, as modeled by the exponential growth rate, may be more realistic, most economic phenomena are measured only at intervals, in which case the compound growth model is appropriate. The average growth rate over $n$ periods is calculated as

$$r = \exp[\ln(p_n/p_0)/n] - 1.$$

Like the exponential growth rate, it does not take into account intermediate values of the series.

### World Bank *Atlas* method

In calculating GNI and GNI per capita in U.S. dollars for certain operational purposes, the World Bank uses the *Atlas* conversion factor. The purpose of the *Atlas* conversion factor is to reduce the impact of exchange rate fluctuations in the cross-country comparison of national incomes.

The *Atlas* conversion factor for any year is the average of a country's exchange rate (or alternative conversion factor) for that year and its exchange rates for the two preceding years, adjusted for the difference between the rate of inflation in the country and that in Japan, the United Kingdom, the United States, and the euro area. A country's inflation rate is measured by the change in its GDP deflator.

The inflation rate for Japan, the United Kingdom, the United States, and the euro area, representing international inflation, is measured by the change in the "SDR deflator". (Special drawing rights, or SDRs, are the International Monetary Fund's unit of account.) The SDR deflator is calculated as a weighted average of these countries' GDP deflators in SDR terms, the weights being the amount of each country's currency in one SDR unit. Weights vary over time because both the composition of the SDR and the relative exchange rates for each currency change. The SDR deflator is calculated in SDR terms first and then converted to U.S. dollars using the SDR to dollar *Atlas* conversion factor. The *Atlas* conversion factor is then applied to a country's GNI. The resulting GNI in U.S. dollars is divided by the midyear population to derive GNI per capita.

When official exchange rates are deemed to be unreliable or unrepresentative of the effective exchange rate during a period, an alternative estimate of the exchange rate is used in the *Atlas* formula (see below).

The following formulas describe the calculation of the *Atlas* conversion factor for year $t$:

$$e_t^* = \frac{1}{3}\left[ e_{t-2}\left( \frac{p_t}{p_{t-2}} \Big/ \frac{p_t^{S\$}}{p_{t-2}^{S\$}} \right) + e_{t-1}\left( \frac{p_t}{p_{t-1}} \Big/ \frac{p_t^{S\$}}{p_{t-1}^{S\$}} \right) + e_t \right]$$

and the calculation of GNI per capita in U.S. dollars for year $t$:

$$Y_t^{\$} = (Y_t/N_t)/e_t^*$$

where $e_t^*$ is the *Atlas* conversion factor (national currency to the U.S. dollar) for year $t$, $e_t$ is the average annual exchange rate (national currency to the U.S. dollar) for year $t$, $p_t$ is the GDP deflator for year $t$, $p_t^{S\$}$ is the SDR deflator in U.S. dollar terms for year $t$, $Y_t^{\$}$ is the *Atlas* GNI per capita in U.S. dollars in year $t$, $Y_t$ is current GNI (local currency) for year $t$, and $N_t$ is the midyear population for year $t$.

### Alternative conversion factors

The World Bank systematically assesses the appropriateness of official exchange rates as conversion factors. An alternative conversion factor is used when the official exchange rate is judged to diverge by an exceptionally large margin from the rate effectively applied to domestic transactions of foreign currencies and traded products. This applies to only a small number of countries, as shown in *Primary data documentation*. Alternative conversion factors are used in the *Atlas* methodology and elsewhere in *World Development Indicators* as single-year conversion factors.

# CREDITS

*World Development Indicators* draws on a wide range of World Bank reports and numerous external sources, listed in the bibliography following this section. Many people inside and outside the World Bank helped in writing and producing the book. The team would like to particularly acknowledge the help and encouragement of Alan Gelb, Acting Senior Vice President and Chief Economist of the World Bank, and Shaida Badiee, Director, Development Data Group. The team is also grateful to the people who provided valuable comments on the entire book. This note identifies many of those who made specific contributions. Numerous others, too many to acknowledge here, helped in many ways for which the team is extremely grateful.

## 1. World view

The introduction to section 1 was prepared by Sebastien Dessus and Eric Swanson. Sarwar Lateef provided valuable suggestions. Rafael de Hoyos and Maurizio Bussolo of the Development Economics Prospects Group helped in computing the inequality estimates. Yuri Dikhanov and the International Comparison Program team provided the new estimates of purchasing power parities (PPP) and Sup Lee prepared the special PPP table. Changqing Sun prepared the estimates of gross national income in PPP terms. K.M. Vijayalakshmi prepared tables 1.1 and 1.6. Uranbileg Batjargal prepared table 1.4, with valuable assistance from Azita Amjadi. Tables 1.2, 1.3, and 1.5 were prepared by Masako Hiraga. Dominic Patrick Mellor of the World Bank's Economic Policy and Debt Department provided the estimates of debt relief for the Heavily Indebted Poor Countries Debt Initiative and Multilateral Debt Relief Initiative. The team is grateful to Yasmin Ahmad and Aimee Nichols at the Organisation for Economic Co-operation and Development for data and advice on official development assistance flows and agricultural support estimates.

## 2. People

Section 2 was prepared by Masako Hiraga and Sulekha Patel in partnership with the World Bank's Human Development Network and the Development Research Group in the Development Economics Vice Presidency. Kyoko Okamoto and William Prince provided invaluable assistance in data and table preparation, and Kiyomi Horiuchi prepared the demographic estimates and projections. Masako Hiraga and Sulekha Patel wrote the introduction with valuable inputs and comments from Sadia Chowdhury, Sarwar Lateef, and Eric Swanson. The poverty estimates were prepared by Shaohua Chen and and Prem Sangraula of the World Bank's Poverty Monitoring Group and Changquin Sun. The data for table 2.6 on children at work were prepared by Lorenzo Guarcello and Furio Rosati from the Understanding Children's Work project. The data on health gaps by income and gender were based on data prepared by Darcy Gallucio and Davidson Gwatkin of the Human Development Network. Other contributions were provided by Eduard Bos and Emi Suzuki (population, health, and nutrition); Montserrat Pallares-Miralles (vulnerability and security); Lawrence Jeffrey Johnson of the International Labour Organization (labor force); Juan Cruz Perusia and Jose Pessoae of the United Nations Educational, Scientific, and Cultural Organization Institute for Statistics (education and literacy); the World Health Organization's Chandika

Indikadahena (health expenditure), Monika Bloessner and Mercedes de Onis (malnutrition and overweight), Neeru Gupta (health workers), Mie Inoue (hospital beds), and Seyed Mehran Hosseini (tuberculosis); and Khin Wityee Oo of the United Nations Children's Fund (health).

## 3. Environment

Section 3 was prepared by Mehdi Akhlaghi and M. H. Saeed Ordoubadi in partnership with the World Bank's Sustainable Development Network. Important contributions were made by Carola Fabi and Edward Gillin of the Food and Agriculture Organization of the United Nations; Ricardo Quercioli of the International Energy Agency; Amay Cassara, Christian Layke, Daniel Prager, and Robin White of the World Resources Institute; Laura Battlebury of the World Conservation Monitoring Centre; and Gerhard Metchies of German Technical Cooperation (GTZ). The World Bank's Environment Department devoted substantial staff resources to the book, for which the team is very grateful. M.H. Saeed Ordoubadi wrote the introduction with valuable comments from Sarwar Lateef, Jeffrey Lewis, Bruce Ross-Larson, and Eric Swanson. Other contributions were made by Susmita Dasgupta, Kirk Hamilton, Craig Meisner, Kiran Pandey, Giovanni Ruta, and Jana Stover.

## 4. Economy

Section 4 was prepared by K.M. Vijayalakshmi in close collaboration with the Sustainable Development and Economic Data Team of the World Bank's Development Data Group, led by Soong Sup Lee. Eric Swanson and K.M. Vijayalakshmi wrote the introduction with valuable suggestions from Sarwar Lateef and Soong Sup Lee. Contributions to the section were provided by Azita Amjadi (trade). The national accounts data for low- and middle-income economies were gathered by the World Bank's regional staff through the annual Unified Survey. Maja Bresslauer, Mahyar Eshragh-Tabary, Victor Gabor, and Soong Sup Lee worked on updating, estimating, and validating the databases for national accounts. The team is grateful to the International Monetary Fund, Organisation for Economic Co-operation and Development, United Nations Industrial Development Organization, and World Trade Organization for access to the databases.

## 5. States and markets

Section 5 was prepared by David Cieslikowski and Raymond Muhula, in partnership with the World Bank's Financial and Private Sector Development Network, Poverty Reduction and Economic Management Network, Sustainable Development Network, the International Finance Corporation, and external partners. Sarwar Lateef wrote the introduction to the section with input from David Cieslikowski, Alan Gelb, Steve Knack, Aart Kraay, Brian Levy, and Eric Swanson. Other contributors include Ada Karina Izaguirre (privatization and infrastructure projects); Shokraneh Minovi and Leora Klapper (micro, small, and medium-size enterprises); Jorge Luis Rodriguez Meza and Federica Saliola (Enterprise Surveys); Svetlana Bagaudinova (Doing Business); Alka Banerjee and Isilay Cabuk (Standard & Poor's global stock market indexes); Himmat Kalsi (financial); Rui Coutinho (public policies and institutions); Nigel Adderley of the International Institute for Strategic Studies (military personnel); Bjorn Hagelin and Petter Stålenheim of the Stockholm International Peace Research Institute (military expenditures and arms transfers); Henrich Bofinger, Tsukasa Hattori, and Helene Stephan (transport); Jane Degerlund of Containerisation International (ports); Vanessa Grey and Esperanza Magpantay of the International Telecommunication Union and Mark Williams (communications and information); Ernesto Fernandez Polcuch of the United Nations Educational, Scientific, and Cultural Organization Institute for Statistics (research and development, researchers, and technicians); and Anders Halvorsen of the World Information Technology and Services Alliance (information and communication technology expenditures).

### 6. Global links

Section 6 was prepared by Uranbileg Batjargal and Azita Amjadi in partnership with the World Bank's Development Research Group (trade), Prospects Group (commodity prices), and external partners. Eric Swanson and Himmat Kalsi wrote the introduction, with assistance from Uranbileg Batjargal, David Cieslikowski, Ibrahim Levent, and K.M. Vijayalakshmi and comments from Sarwar Lateef and Changqing Sun. Substantial input for the data came from Azita Amjadi (trade), Jerzy Rozanski (tariffs), and Ibrahim Levent and Gloria Moreno (external debt and financial data). Other contributors include David Cristallo and Henri Laurencin of the United Nations Conference on Trade and Development, Rohini Acharya and Hubert Escaith of the World Trade Organization, and Francis Ng (trade); Betty Dow (commodity prices); Dilek Aykut (foreign direct investment flows); Eung Ju Kim (financing through capital markets); Yasmin Ahmad, Elena Bernaldo, and Aimee Nichols of the Organisation for Economic Co-operation and Development and Malvina Pollock (aid); Nanasamudd Chhim, Nevin Fahmy, and Nino Kostova (debt); Henrik Pilgaard of the United Nations Refugee Agency (refugees); Bela Hovy of the United Nations Population Division (migration); K.M. Vijayalakshmi (remittances); David Cieslikowski (table 6.1); and Teresa Ciller of the World Tourism Organization (tourism). Quality assurance of tables was provided by the Social Indicators team, led by Sulekha Patel, and the Financial Data team, lead by Ibrahim Levent. Mehdi Akhlaghi, Joseph Judkins, Gytis Kanchas, William Prince, and Atsushi Shimo provided valuable technical assistance.

### Other parts of the book

Jeff Lecksell of the World Bank's Map Design Unit coordinated preparation of the maps on the inside covers. David Cieslikowski prepared the *Users guide*. Eric Swanson wrote *Statistical methods*. K.M. Vijayalakshmi coordinated preparation of *Primary data documentation*, and Uranbileg Batjargal assisted in updating the *Primary data documentation* table. Richard Fix and Beatriz Prieto-Oramas prepared *Partners* and *Index of indicators*.

### Database management

Mehdi Akhlaghi coordinated management of the integrated World Development Indicators database with assistance from William Prince. Operation of the database management system was made possible by the Data and Information Systems Team under the leadership of Reza Farivari.

### Design, production, and editing

Richard Fix and Beatriz Prieto-Oramas coordinated all stages of production with Communications Development Incorporated, which provided overall design direction, editing, and layout, led by Meta de Coquereaumont, Bruce Ross-Larson, and Christopher Trott. Elaine Wilson created the graphics and typeset the book. Joseph Caponio and Amye Kenall provided proofreading and production assistance. Communications Development's London partner, Peter Grundy of Peter Grundy Art & Design, provided art direction and design. Staff from External Affairs oversaw printing and dissemination of the book.

### Client services

The Development Data Group's Client Services and Communications Team (Azita Amjadi, Richard Fix, Buyant Erdene Khaltarkhuu, William Prince, and Beatriz Prieto-Oramas) contributed to the design and planning of *World Development Indicators 2008* and helped coordinate work with the Office of the Publisher.

### Administrative assistance and office technology support

Awatif Abuzeid and Estela Zamora provided administrative assistance. Jean-Pierre Djomalieu, Gytis Kanchas, Nacer Megherbi, and Shahin Outadi provided information technology support.

### Publishing and dissemination

The Office of the Publisher, under the direction of Carlos Rossel, provided valuable assistance throughout the production process. Stephen McGroarty, Randi Park, and Nora Ridolfi coordinated printing and supervised marketing and distribution. Merrell Tuck-Primdahl of the Development Economics Vice President's Office managed the communications strategy.

### *World Development Indicators* CD-ROM

Programming and testing were carried out by Reza Farivari and his team: Azita Amjadi, Ying Chi, Ramgopal Erabelly, Nacer Megherbi, Shahin Outadi, and William Prince. Masako Hiraga produced the social indicators tables. William Prince coordinated user interface design and overall production and provided quality assurance. Photo credits belong to the World Bank photo library. The interactive text was produced by Dohatec.

### *WDI Online*

Design, programming, and testing were carried out by Reza Farivari and his team: Mehdi Akhlaghi, Azita Amjadi, and Shahin Outadi. William Prince coordinated production and provided quality assurance. Valentina Kalk and Triinu Tombak of the Office of the Publisher were responsible for implementation of *WDI Online* and management of the subscription service.

### Client feedback

The team is grateful to the many people who have taken the time to provide assistance on its publications. Their feedback and suggestions have helped improve this year's edition.

# BIBLIOGRAPHY

**Abbott, Alison.** 2004. "Saving Venice." *Nature*. January 10. [www.nature.com/news/2004/040112/full/040112-8.html;jsessionid=26CC93DEBA2BEDF87 62546E0413759D5]. January 2007.

**AbouZahr, Carla, and Tessa Wardlaw.** 2003. *Maternal Mortality in 2000: Estimates Developed by WHO, UNICEF, and UNFPA*. Geneva: World Health Organization.

**Ahmad, Sultan.** 1992. "Regression Estimates of Per Capita GDP Based on Purchasing Power Parities." Policy Research Working Paper 956. World Bank, International Economics Department, Washington, D.C.

———. 1994. "Improving Inter-Spatial and Inter-Temporal Comparability of National Accounts." *Journal of Development Economics* 44 (1): 53–75.

**An, F., and A. Sauer.** 2004. "Comparison of Passenger Vehicle Fuel Economy and Greenhouse Gas Emission Standards around the World." Pew Center on Global Climate Change, Arlington, Va.

**Anthoff, David, Robert J. Nichols, Richard S. J. Tol, and Athanasios T. Vafeidis.** 2006. "Global and Regional Exposure to Large Rises in Sea-level: A Sensitivity Analysis." Working Paper 96. Tyndall Centre for Climate Change Research, University of East Anglia, Norwich, U.K.

**Arndt, Christiane, and Charles Oman.** 2006. *Uses and Abuses of Governance Indicators*. Paris: Organisation for Economic Co-operation and Development. .

**Ashford, Lori S., Davidson R. Gwatkin, and Abdo S. Yazbeck.** 2006. *Designing Health and Population Programs to Reach the Poor*. Washington, D.C.: Population Reference Bureau.

**Baeza, Cristian C., and Truman G. Packard.** 2006. *Beyond Survival: Protecting Households from Health Shocks in Latin America*. Washington, D.C.: World Bank.

**Ball, Nicole.** 1984. "Measuring Third World Security Expenditure: A Research Note." *World Development* 12 (2): 157–64.

**Barro, Robert J.** 1991. "Economic Growth in a Cross-Section of Countries." *Quarterly Journal of Economics* 106 (2): 407–43.

**Beck, Thorsten, and Ross Levine.** 2001. "Stock Markets, Banks, and Growth: Correlation or Causality?" Policy Research Working Paper 2670. World Bank, Development Research Group, Washington, D.C.

**Bhalla, Surjit.** 2002. *Imagine There Is No Country: Poverty, Inequality, and Growth in the Era of Globalization*. Washington, D.C.: Institute for International Economics.

**Bilsborrow, R. E., Graeme Hugo, A. S. Oberai, and Hania Zlotnik.** 1997. *International Migration Statistics*. Geneva: International Labour Office.

**Bloom, David E., and Jeffrey G. Williamson.** 1998. "Demographic Transitions and Economic Miracles in Emerging Asia." *World Bank Economic Review* 12 (3): 419–55.

**Brown, Lester R., Michael Renner, and Brian Halweil.** 1999. *Vital Signs 1999: The Environmental Trends that Are Shaping Our Future*. New York: W.W. Norton.

**Brown, Lester R., Michael Renner, and Christopher Flavin.** 1998. *Vital Signs 1998: The Environmental Trends that Are Shaping Our Future*. New York: W.W. Norton.

**Brown, Lester R., Christopher Flavin, Hilary F. French, and others.** 1998. *State of the World 1998: A Worldwatch Institute Report on Progress toward a Sustainable Society*. New York: W.W. Norton.

**Bulatao, Rodolfo.** 1998. *The Value of Family Planning Programs in Developing Countries*. RAND Monograph Report. Santa Monica, Calif.: RAND Corporation.

**Burton, Ian, Elliot Diringer, and Joel Smith.** 2006. "Climate Change: International Policy Options." Pew Center on Global Climate Change, Arlington, Va.

**Caiola, Marcello.** 1995. *A Manual for Country Economists*. Training Series 1. Vol. 1. Washington, D.C.: International Monetary Fund.

**CAWMA (Comprehensive Assessment of Water Management in Agriculture).** 2007. *Water for Food, Water for Life*. London: Earthscan.

**Carr, Dara.** 2004. "Improving the Health of the World's Poorest People." Health Bulletin 1. Population Reference Bureau, Washington, D.C.

**Centro Latinoamericano de Demografía.** Various issues. *Boletín Demografico*.

**Chen, Shaohua, and Martin Ravallion.** 2004. "How Have the World's Poorest Fared since the 1980s?" *World Bank Research Observer* 19 (2): 141–69.

**Chomitz, Kenneth M., Piet Buys, and Timothy S. Thomas.** 2005. "Quantifying the Rural-Urban Gradient in Latin America and the Caribbean." Policy Research Working Paper 3634. World Bank, Development Research Group, Washington, D.C.

**CIESIN (Center for International Earth Science Information Network).** 2005. Gridded Population of the World. Columbia University and Centro Internacional de Agricultura Tropical. [http://sedac.ciesin.columbia.edu/gpw/].

**Claessens, Stijn, Daniela Klingebiel, and Sergio L. Schmukler.** 2002. "Explaining the Migration of Stocks from Exchanges in Emerging Economies to International Centers." Policy Research Working Paper 2816. World Bank, Development Research Group, Washington, D.C.

**Cleland J., S. Bernstein, A. Ezeh, A. Faundes, A. Glasier, and J. Innis.** 2006. "Family Planning: The Unfinished Agenda." *Lancet* 368 (9549): 1810–27

**Cline, William.** 2007. *Global Warming and Agriculture: Impact Estimate by Country*. Washington, D.C.: Center for Global Development, Peterson Institute for International Economics.

**Commission of the European Communities, IMF (International Monetary Fund), OECD (Organisation for Economic Co-operation and Development), United Nations, and World Bank.** 2002. *System of Environmental and Economic Accounts: SEEA 2000*. New York.

**Containerisation International.** 2008. *Containerisation International Yearbook 2008*. London: Informa Maritime and Transport.

**Corrao, Mario Ann, G. Emmanuel Guindon, Namita Sharma, and Donna Fakhrabadi Shokoohi, eds.** 2000. *Tobacco Control Country Profiles*. Atlanta, Ga.: American Cancer Society.

**CSD (Commission on Sustainable Development).** 1997. *Comprehensive Assessment of the Freshwater Resources of the World*. Report of the Secretary-General. New York.

**Dasgupta, Susmita, Benoît Laplante, Craig Meisner, David Wheeler, and Jianping Yan.** 2007. "The Impact of Sea Level Rise on Developing Countries: A

Comparative Analysis." Policy Research Working Paper 4136. World Bank, Development Research Group, Washington, D.C.

Deaton, Angus. 2002. "Counting the World's Poor: Problems and Possible Solutions." *World Bank Research Observer* 16 (2): 125–47.

DEFRA (Department for Environment, Food and Rural Affairs). 2007. "New Bill and Strategy Lay Foundations for Tackling Climate Change–Miliband." News Release. March 13. London. [www.defra.gov.uk/news/2007/070313a.htm].

Demirgüç-Kunt, Asli, and Ross Levine. 1996. "Stock Market Development and Financial Intermediaries: Stylized Facts." *World Bank Economic Review* 10 (2): 291–321.

De Onis, Mercedes, and Monika Blössner. 2000. "The WHO Global Database on Child Growth and Malnutrition: Methodology and Applications." *International Journal of Epidemiology* 32: 518–26.

De Onis, Mercedes, Adelheid W. Onyango, Elaine Borghi, Cutberto Garza, and Hong Yang. 2006. "Comparison of the World Health Organization (WHO) Child Growth Standards and the National Center for Health Statistics/WHO International Growth Reference: Implications for Child Health Programmes." *Public Health Nutrition* 9 (7): 942–47.

Development Committee. 2003. "Supporting Sound Policies with Adequate and Appropriate Financing: Implementing the Monterrey Consensus at the Country Level." SecM2003-0370. World Bank and International Monetary Fund, Washington, D.C.

Disease Control Priorities Project. 2006. *Global Burden of Disease and Risk Factors.* Washington, D.C.: Oxford University Press and World Bank.

Dollar, David. 2005. "Globalization, Poverty, and Inequality since 1980." *World Bank Research Observer* 20 (2): 145–75.

Doyle, John J., and Gabrielle J. Persley, eds. 1996. *Enabling the Safe Use of Biotechnology: Principles and Practice.* Environmentally Sustainable Development Studies and Monographs Series 10. Washington, D.C.: World Bank.

Easterly, William. 2000. "Growth Implosions, Debt Explosions, and My Aunt Marilyn: Do Growth Slowdowns Cause Public Debt Crises?" Policy Research Working Paper 2531. World Bank, Development Research Group, Washington, D.C.

Eastwood, Robert, and Michael Lipton. 1999. "The Impact of Changes in Human Fertility on Poverty." *Journal of Development Studies* 36 (1): 1–30.

EIA (Energy Information Administration). 2006. "Emission of Greenhouse Gases in the United States 2005." Washington, DC.

Eurostat (Statistical Office of the European Communities). Various years. *Demographic Statistics.* Luxembourg.

———. Various years. *Statistical Yearbook.* Luxembourg.

Faiz, Asif, Christopher S. Weaver, and Michael P. Walsh. 1996. *Air Pollution from Motor Vehicles: Standards and Technologies for Controlling Emissions.* Washington, D.C.: World Bank.

Fankhauser, Samuel. 1995. *Valuing Climate Change: The Economics of the Greenhouse.* London: Earthscan.

FAO (Food and Agriculture Organization). 1995. *Programme for the World Census of Agriculture 2000.* FAO Statistical Development Series 5. Rome.

———. 1996. *Food Aid in Figures 1994.* Vol. 12. Rome.

———. 2001. *Agriculture: Towards 2015/30.* Rome.

———. 2003. *State of the World's Forests 2003.* Rome.

———. 2005. *Global Forest Resources Assessment 2005.* Rome.

———. Various years. *Fertilizer Yearbook.* FAO Statistics Series. Rome.

———. Various years. *Production Yearbook.* FAO Statistics Series. Rome.

———. Various years. *State of Food Insecurity in the World.* Rome.

———. Various years. *Trade Yearbook.* FAO Statistics Series. Rome

Frankhauser, Pierre. 1994. "Fractales, tissus urbains et reseaux de transport." *Revue d'economie politique* 104: 435–55.

Fredricksen, Birger. 1993. *Statistics of Education in Developing Countries: An Introduction to Their Collection and Analysis.* Paris: United Nations Educational, Scientific, and Cultural Organization.

Gallup, John L., and Jeffrey D. Sachs. 1998. "The Economic Burden of Malaria." Harvard Institute for International Development, Cambridge, Mass.

Gannon, Colin, and Zmarak Shalizi. 1995. "The Use of Sectoral and Project Performance Indicators in Bank-Financed Transport Operations." TWU Discussion Paper 21. World Bank, Transportation, Water, and Urban Development Department, Washington, D.C.

Gardner-Outlaw, Tom, and Robert Engelman. 1997. "Sustaining Water, Easing Scarcity: A Second Update." Population Action International, Washington, D.C.

GEF (Global Environmental Facility). 2007. "Pledging Meeting for Climate Change Funds." 15 June. GEF Secretariat, Washington, D.C.

Glasier A., A. M. Gulmezoglu, G. Schmid, C. Garcia Moreno, and P. F. A. van Look. 2006. "Sexual and Reproductive Health: A Matter of Life and Death." *Lancet* 368 (9547): 1595–1607.

Goldfinger, Charles. 1994. *L'utile et le futile: L'économie de l'immatériel.* Paris: Editions Odile Jacob.

Grimes, D.A., J. Bensen, S. Singh, M. Romero, B. Ganatra, F. E. Okonofua, and I. H. Shah. 2006. "Unsafe abortion: the preventable pandemic." *Lancet* 368 (9550): 1908–19.

GTZ (German Agency for Technical Cooperation). 2004. *Fuel Prices and Taxation.* Eschborn, Germany.

Gupta, Sanjeev, Brian Hammond, and Eric Swanson. 2000. "Setting the Goals." *OECD Observer* 223: 15–17.

Gwatkin, Davidson R., Shea Rutstein, Kiersten Johnson, Eldaw Suliman, Adam Wagstaff, and Agbessi Amouzou. 2007. *Socio Economic Differences in Health, Nutrition, and Population.* Washington, D.C.: World Bank.

Habyarimana, James, Jishnu Das, Stefan Dercon, and Pramila Krishnan. 2003. "Sense and Absence: Absenteeism and Learning in Zambian Schools." World Bank, Washington, D.C.

Hamilton, Kirk, and Michael Clemens. 1999. "Genuine Savings Rates in Developing Countries." *World Bank Economic Review* 13 (2): 333–56.

# BIBLIOGRAPHY

**Hanushek, Eric.** 2002. *The Long-Run Importance of School Quality*. NBER Working Paper 9071. Cambridge, Mass.: National Bureau of Economic Research.

**Happe, Nancy, and John Wakeman-Linn.** 1994. "Military Expenditures and Arms Trade: Alternative Data Sources." IMF Working Paper 94/69. International Monetary Fund, Policy Development and Review Department, Washington, D.C.

**Hatzichronoglou, Thomas.** 1997. "Revision of the High-Technology Sector and Product Classification." STI Working Paper 1997/2. Organisation for Economic Co-operation and Development, Directorate for Science, Technology, and Industry, Paris.

**Heston, Alan.** 1994. "A Brief Review of Some Problems in Using National Accounts Data in Level of Output Comparisons and Growth Studies." *Journal of Development Economics* 44 (1): 29–52.

**Hettige, Hemamala, Muthukumara Mani, and David Wheeler.** 1998. "Industrial Pollution in Economic Development: Kuznets Revisited." Policy Research Working Paper 1876. World Bank, Development Research Group, Washington, D.C.

**IEA (International Energy Agency).** 2002. *World Energy Outlook: Energy and Poverty*. Paris.

————. 2006. *World Energy Outlook*. OECD (Organisation for Economic Co-operation and Development)/IEA, Paris.

————. Various years. *Energy Balances of OECD Countries*. Paris.

————. Various years. *Energy Statistics and Balances of Non-OECD Countries*. Paris.

————. Various years. *Energy Statistics of OECD Countries*. Paris.

**ILO (International Labour Organization).** Various years. *Key Indicators of the Labour Market*. Geneva: International Labour Office.

————. Various years. *Yearbook of Labour Statistics*. Geneva: International Labour Office.

————. 2006. *The End of Child Labour within Reach*. Geneva.

**IMF (International Monetary Fund).** 1977. *Balance of Payments Manual*. 4th ed. Washington, D.C.

————. 1993. *Balance of Payments Manual*. 5th ed. Washington, D.C.

————. 1995. *Balance of Payments Compilation Guide*. Washington, D.C.

————. 1996. *Balance of Payments Textbook*. Washington, D.C.

————. 2000. *Monetary and Financial Statistics Manual*. Washington, D.C.

————. 2001. *Government Finance Statistics Manual*. Washington, D.C.

————. 2004a. *Compilation Guide on Financial Soundness Indicators*. Washington, D.C.

————. 2004b. *World Economic Outlook*. Chapter 3. Washington, DC.

————. 2007. *Global Financial Stability Report*. Washington, D.C.

————. Various issues. *Direction of Trade Statistics*.

————. Various issues. *International Financial Statistics*.

————. Various years. *Balance of Payments Statistics Yearbook*. Parts 1 and 2. Washington, D.C.

————. Various years. *Direction of Trade Statistics Yearbook*. Washington, D.C.

————. Various years. *Government Finance Statistics Yearbook*. Washington, D.C.

————. Various years. *International Financial Statistics Yearbook*. Washington, D.C.

**International Budget Project.** 2006. "Open Budget Initiative" website. [www.openbudgetindex.org].

**International Civil Aviation Organization.** 2007. *Civil Aviation Statistics of the World*. Montreal.

**International Diabetes Federation.** Various years. *Diabetes Atlas*. Brussels.

**International Institute for Strategic Studies.** 2008. *The Military Balance 2008*. London: Oxford University Press.

**International Road Federation.** 2007. *World Road Statistics 2007*. Geneva.

**International Trade Center, UNCTAD (United Nations Conference on Trade and Development), and WTO (World Trade Organization). The Millennium Development Goals. Online database. [www.mdg-trade.org/]**

**International Working Group of External Debt Compilers (Bank for International Settlements, International Monetary Fund, Organisation for Economic Co-operation and Development, and World Bank).** 1987. *External Debt Definitions*. Washington, D.C.

**Inter-Secretariat Working Group on National Accounts (Commission of the European Communities, International Monetary Fund, Organisation for Economic Co-operation and Development, United Nations, and World Bank).** 1993. *System of National Accounts*. Brussels, Luxembourg, New York, and Washington, D.C.

**IPCC (Intergovernmental Panel on Climate Change).** 2001a. *Climate Change 2001*. Cambridge, U.K.: Cambridge University Press.

————. 2001b. *Climate Change 2001: The Scientific Basis; Contribution of Working Group I to the Third Assessment Report of the Intergovernmental Panel on Climate Change*. Cambridge, U.K.: Cambridge University Press.

————. 2001c. *Climate Change 2001: Impacts, Adaptation, and Vulnerability; Contribution of Working Group II to the Third Assessment Report of the Intergovernmental Panel on Climate Change*. Cambridge, U.K.: Cambridge University Press.

————. 2001d. *Climate Change 2001: Mitigation; Contribution of Working Group II to the Third Assessment Report of the Intergovernmental Panel on Climate Change*. Cambridge, U.K.: Cambridge University Press.

————. 2007a. *Climate Change 2007: The Physical Science Basis. Contribution of Working Group I to the Fourth Assessment Report of the Intergovernmental Panel on Climate Change*. Cambridge, U.K.: Cambridge University Press.

————. 2007b. "Summary for Policymakers." In *Climate Change 2007: The Physical Science Basis. Contribution of Working Group I to the Fourth Assessment Report of the Intergovernmental Panel on Climate Change*. Cambridge, U.K.: Cambridge University Press.

————. 2007c. "Summary for Policymakers." In S. Solomon, D. Qin, M. Manning, Z. Chen, M. Marquis, K. B. Averyt, M. Tignor, and H. L. Miller, eds., *Climate Change 2007: Climate Change Impacts, Adaptation and Vulnerability. Working Group II Contribution to the Fourth Assessment Report of the Intergovernmental Panel on Climate Change*. Cambridge, U.K.: Cambridge University Press.

————. 2007d. "Summary for Policymakers." In S. Solomon, D. Qin, M. Manning, Z. Chen, M. Marquis, K. B. Averyt, M. Tignor and H.L. Miller, eds., *Climate*

*Change 2007: Mitigation of Climate Change. Working Group III Contribution to the Fourth Assessment Report of the Intergovernmental Panel on Climate Change.* Cambridge, U.K.: Cambridge University Press.

———. 2007e. "Technical Summary." In S. Solomon, D. Qin, M. Manning, Z. Chen, M. Marquis, K.B. Averyt, M. Tignor and H. L. Miller, eds., *Climate Change 2007: Climate Change Impacts, Adaptation and Vulnerability. WorkingGroup II Contribution to the Fourth Assessment Report of the Intergovernmental Panel on Climate Change.* Cambridge, U.K.: Cambridge University Press.

**ITU (International Telecommunication Union).** 2007. World Telecommunication Indicators database. Geneva.

**IUCN (World Conservation Union).** 2007. *2007 IUCN Red List of Threatened Species.* Gland, Switzerland.

**Jamison, Dean T., Joel G. Breman, Anthony R. Measham, and others, eds.** 2006. *Priorities in Health.* Washington, D.C.: World Bank.

**Johnson, Simon.** Forthcoming. "Worldwide Governance Indicators: A Comment." *World Bank Research Observer.*

**Johnston, Michael.** 2001. "Measuring Corruption: Numbers versus Knowledge versus Understanding." In Arvind K. Jain, ed., *The Political Economy of Corruption.* London and New York: Routledge.

**Joint Learning Initiative.** 2004. *Human Resources for Health: Overcoming the Crisis.* Boston, Mass.

**Kaufmann, Daniel.** 2005. "Click Refresh Button: Investment Climate Reconsidered." *Development Outreach*, March.

**Kaufmann, Daniel, and Aart Kraay.** 2007a. "The Worldwide Governance Indicators Project: Answering the Critics." Policy Research Working Paper 4370. World Bank, Washington, D.C.

———. 2007b. "Governance Matters VI, Aggregate and Individual Governance Indicators 1996–2006." Policy Research Working Paper 4280. World Bank, Washington, D.C.

———. Forthcoming. "Governance Indicators: Where Are We, Where Should We Be Going?" *World Bank Research Observer.*

**Kaufmann, Daniel, Aart Kraay, and Massimo Mastruzzi.** 2005. "Governance Matters IV: Governance Indicators for 1996–2004." Policy Research Working Paper 3630. World Bank, Washington, D.C.

**Knack, Stephen.** 2007. "Measuring Corruption: A Critique of Indicators in Eastern Europe and Central Asia." *Journal of Public Policy* 27 (3): 255–91.

**Knack, Stephen, M. Kugler, and N. Manning.** 2003. "Second Generation Governance Indicators." *International Review of Administrative Sciences* 69 (3): 345–64.

**Kozak, Marta.** 2005. "Micro, Small, and Medium Enterprises: A Collection of Published Data." International Finance Corporation, Washington, D.C.

**Kunte, Arundhati, Kirk Hamilton, John Dixon, and Michael Clemens.** 1998. "Estimating National Wealth: Methodology and Results." Environmental Economics Series 57. World Bank, Environment Department, Washington, D.C.

**Lanjouw, Jean O., and Peter Lanjouw.** 2001. "The Rural Non-Farm Sector: Issues and Evidence from Developing Countries." *Agricultural Economics* 26 (1): 1–23.

**Lanjouw, Peter, and Gershon Feder.** 2001. "Rural Nonfarm Activities and Rural Development: From Experience toward Strategy." Rural Strategy Discussion Paper 4. World Bank, Washington, D.C.

**Levy, Brian.** 2007. *Governance Reform, Bridging, Monitoring and Action.* Washington, D.C.: World Bank.

**Lopez, Alan D., Colin D. Mathers, Majad Ezzati, Dean T. Jamison, and Christopher J. L. Murray.** 2006. *Global Burden of Disease and Risk Factors.* Washington, D.C.: World Bank.

**Lovei, Magdolna.** 1997. "Toward Effective Pollution Management." *Environment Matters* (Fall): 52–53.

**Lule, Elizabbeth, G. N. V. Ramana, Nandini Ooman, Joanne Epp, Dale Huntington, and James E. Rosen.** 2005. *Achieving the Millennium Development Goals of Improving Maternal Health: Determinants, Interventions and Challenges.* Washington, D.C.: World Bank.

**Mani, Muthukumara, and David Wheeler.** 1997. "In Search of Pollution Havens? Dirty Industry in the World Economy, 1960–95." World Bank, Policy Research Department, Washington, D.C.

**Mankiw, G., D. Romer, and D. Weil.** 1992. "A Contribution to the Empirics of Economic Growth." *The Quarterly Journal of Economics* 107 (2): 407–37.

**McCarthy, F. Desmond, and Holger Wolf.** 2001. "Comparative Life Expectancy in Africa." Policy Research Working Paper 2668. World Bank, Development Research Group, Washington, D.C.

**McCay, J., M. Erkson, and O. Shafey.** 2006. *Tobacco Atlas.* 2nd ed. Atlanta, Ga.: American Cancer Society.

**Morgenstern, Oskar.** 1963. *On the Accuracy of Economic Observations.* Princeton, N.J.: Princeton University Press.

**Morisset, Jacques.** 2000. "Foreign Direct Investment in Africa: Policies Also Matter." Policy Research Working Paper 2481. World Bank, Washington, D.C.

**Nanda, Geeta, Kimberly Switlick, and Elizabeth Lule.** 2005. "Accelerating Progress towards Achieving the MDG to Improve Maternal Health: A Collection of Promising Approaches." HNP Discussion Paper. World Bank, Washington D.C.

**National Science Board.** 2008. *Science and Engineering Indicators 2008.* Arlington, Va.: National Science Foundation.

**Netcraft.** 2007. "Netcraft Secure Server Survey." [www.netcraft.com/].

**Newfarmer, Richard, ed.** 2006. *Trade, Doha, and Development: A Window into the Issues.* Washington, D.C.: World Bank.

**NRI (National Research Institute) and World Bank.** 2003. "Public Expenditure and Service Delivery in Papua New Guinea: Draft." Washington, D.C.

**NREL (National Renewable Energy Laboratory) Energy Analysis Office.** 2005. Renewable Energy Cost Trends. Presentation. [www.nrel.gov/analysis/docs/cost_curves_2005.ppt].

**OECD (Organisation for Economic Co-operation and Development).** 1996. *Trade, Employment, and Labour Standards: A Study of Core Workers' Rights and International Trade.* Paris.

———. 1997. *Employment Outlook.* Paris.

# BIBLIOGRAPHY

——. 2006. *OECD Health Data 2006*. Paris.

——. 2007. Agricultural Policies in OECD Countries: Monitoring and Evaluation 2007, Paris

——. Various issues. *Main Economic Indicators*. Paris.

——. Various years. *National Accounts*. Vol. 1, Main Aggregates. Paris

——. Various years. *National Accounts*. Vol. 2, Detailed Tables. Paris.

——. Various years. *Producer and Consumer Support Estimates*. Paris.

——. Various years. *Trends in International Migration: Continuous Reporting System on Migration*. Paris

**OECD (Organisation for Economic Co-operation and Development) DAC (Development Assistance Committee).** Various years. International Development Statistics. CD-ROM.

——. Various years. International Development Statistics Online. Database. [www.oecd.org/dac/stats/idsonline].

——. Various years. *Development Cooperation Report*. Paris

——. Various years. *Geographical Distribution of Financial Flows to Aid Recipients* Paris

**OFDA (Office of U.S. Foreign Disaster Assistance) and CRED (Centre for Research on the Epidemiology of Disasters).** 2007. Emergency Events Database (EM-DAT). Database. [www.em-dat.net/who.htm].

**Özden, Çaglar, and Maurice Schiff, eds.** 2005. *International Migration, Remittances, and the Brain Drain*. New York: Palgrave Macmillan.

**Palacios, Robert, and Montserrat Pallares-Miralles.** 2000. "International Patterns of Pension Provision." Social Protection Discussion Paper 0009. World Bank, Human Development Network, Washington, D.C.

**Pandey, Kiran D., Piet Buys, Kenneth Chomitz, and David Wheeler.** 2006a. "Biodiversity Conservation Indicators: New Tools for Priority Setting at the Global Environmental Facility." World Bank, Development Economics Research Group and Environment Department, Washington, D.C.

**Pandey, Kiran D., Bart Ostro, David Wheeler, Uwe Deichmann, Kirk Hamilton, and Katie Bolt.** 2006b. "Ambient Particulate Matter Concentrations in Residential and Pollution Hotspots of World Cities: New Estimates Based on the Global Model of Ambient Particulates (GMAPS)." World Bank, Development Economics Research Group and Environment Department, Washington, D.C.

**Pandey, Kiran Dev, Katharine Bolt, Uwe Deichmann, Kirk Hamilton, Bart Ostro, and David Wheeler.** 2003. "The Human Cost of Air Pollution: New Estimates for Developing Countries." World Bank, Development Research Group and Environment Department, Washington, D.C.

**Pew Center on Global Climate Change.** 2007. A Look at Emission Targets. [www.pewclimate.org/what_s_being_done/targets].

**Pricewaterhouse Coopers.** 2006. *Worldwide Summaries Online*. New York. [www.pwc.com/extweb/pwcpublications.nsf/docid/9B2B76032544964C8525717E00606CBD].

**Rama, Martin, and Raquel Artecona.** 2002. "A Database of Labor Market Indicators across Countries." World Bank, Development Research Group, Washington, D.C.

**Ratha, Dilip, and William Shaw.** 2007. "South-South Migration and Remittances." World Bank, Development Prospects Group, Washington, D.C.

**Ravallion, Martin, and Shaohua Chen.** 1996. "What Can New Survey Data Tell Us about the Recent Changes in Living Standards in Developing and Transitional Economies?" World Bank, Policy Research Department, Washington, D.C.

**Ravallion, Martin, Gaurav Datt, and Dominique van de Walle.** 1991. "Quantifying Absolute Poverty in the Developing World." *Review of Income & Wealth* 37 (4): 345–61.

**Ronsman, Carine S., and Wendy J. Graham.** 2006. "Maternal Mortality: Who, When, Where and Why." *Lancet* 368: 1189–1200.

**Rosengrant, M. W. and P. B. R. Hazel.** 2000. *Transforming the Rural Asia Economy: The Unfinished Revolution*. Hong Kong, China: Oxford University Press.

**Rouen, Ren, and Kai Chen.** 1995. "China's GDP in U.S. Dollars, Based on Purchasing Power Parity." Policy Research Working Paper 1415. Washington, D.C.

**Ruggles, Robert.** 1994. "Issues Relating to the UN System of National Accounts and Developing Countries." *Journal of Development Economics* 44 (1): 77–85.

**Ryten, Jacob.** 1998. "Fifty Years of ISIC: Historical Origins and Future Perspectives." ECA/STAT.AC. 63/22. United Nations Statistics Division, New York.

**Saghir, Jamal.** 2005. "Energy and Poverty: Myths, Links, and Policy Issues. Energy Working Notes 4. World Bank, Washington, D.C.

**Sala-i-Martin, Xavier.** 2002. *The Disturbing "Rise" in Global Income Inequality*. NBER Working Paper 8904. Cambridge, Mass.: National Bureau of Economic Research.

**Salomon, Joshua A., Daniel R. Hogan, John Stover, Karen A. Stanecki, Neff Walker, Peter D. Ghys, and Bernhard Schwartländer.** 2005. "Integrating HIV Prevention and Treatment: From Slogans to Impact." *PLoS Medicine* 2 (1): e16.

**Scherr, Sara J.** 1999. "Soil Degradation: A Threat to Developing-Country Food Security by 2020." 2020 Vision for Food, Agriculture, and Environment Discussion Paper 27. International Food Policy Research Institute, Washington, D.C.

**Sedgh G, S. Henshaw, S. Singh, E. Ahman, and I. Shah.** 2007a. "Induced Abortion: Estimated Rates and Trends Worldwide." *Lancet* 370: 1338–45.

**Sedgh, G., Rubina Hussain, Akinrinola Bankole, and Susheela Singh.** 2007b. "Women with an Unmet Need for Contraception in Developing Countries and Their Reasons for Not Using a Method." New York: Guttmacher Institute.

**SIPRI (Stockholm International Peace Research Institute).** 2007. *SIPRI Yearbook 2007: Armaments, Disarmament, and International Security*. Oxford, U.K.: Oxford University Press.

**Smith, Lisa, and Laurence Haddad.** 2000. "Overcoming Child Malnutrition in Developing Countries: Past Achievements and Future Choices." 2020 Brief 64. International Food Policy Research Institute, Washington, D.C.

**Srinivasan, T. N.** 1994. "Database for Development Analysis: An Overview." *Journal of Development Economics* 44 (1): 3–28.

**Standard & Poor's.** 2000. *The S&P Emerging Market Indices: Methodology, Definitions, and Practices*. New York.

——. 2007. *Global Stock Markets Factbook 2007*. New York.

**Stern, Nicholas.** 2006. *The Economics of Climate Change: The Stern Review.* London: Cambridge University Press.

**Tarmann, Allison.** 2002. Response to Hunger Tests New Priorities. *Population Today,* November/December 2001.

**Thomas, M. A.** 2006. "What Do the Worldwide Governance Indicators Measure?" Draft. John Hopkins University. [http://siteresources.worldbank.org/INTWBIGOVANTCOR/Resources/1740479-1149112210081/2604389-1167941884942/what_do_wgi_measure.pdf].

**Transparency International.** 2007. "Corruption Perceptions Index." [www.transparency.org].

**UN (United Nations).** 1947. *Measurement of National Income and the Construction of Social Accounts.* New York.

———. 1968. "A System of National Accounts: Studies and Methods." Series F, no. 2, rev. 3. New York.

———. 1990. *International Standard Industrial Classification of All Economic Activities, Third Revision.* Statistical Papers Series M, no. 4, rev. 3. New York.

———. 1992. "Handbook of the International Comparison Programme." Studies in Methods Series F, no. 62. New York.

———. 1993. "SNA Handbook on Integrated Environmental and Economic Accounting." Series F, no. 61. Statistical Office, New York.

———. 1999. "Integrated Environmental and Economic Accounting: An Operational Manual." Studies in Methods Series F, no. 78. New York.

———. 2000. *We the Peoples: The Role of the United Nations in the 21st Century.* New York.

———. 2004. "Trends in Total Migrant Stock: The 2003 Revision." POP/DB/MIG/Rev.2003. Department of Economic and Social Affairs, New York.

———. 2005a. "The Energy Challenge for Achieving the Millennium Development Goals." New York.

———. 2005b. *The Millennium Development Goals Report.* New York.

———. 2007. *The Millennium Development Goals Report.* New York.

**UNACC/SCN (United Nations Administrative Committee on Coordination, Subcommittee on Nutrition).** Various years. *Update on the Nutrition Situation.* Geneva.

**UNAIDS (Joint United Nations Programme on HIV/AIDS) and WHO (World Health Organization).** 2005. *AIDS Epidemic Update: December 2005.* Geneva.

———. Various years. *Report on the Global AIDS Epidemic.* Geneva.

**UNCTAD (United Nations Conference on Trade and Development).** 2003. *The Least Developed Countries Report.* Geneva

———. Various years. *Handbook of Statistics.* Geneva.

——— 2007a. *Trade and Development Report, 2007.* New York and Geneva.

——— 2007b. *World Investment Report, 2007.* New York and Geneva.

**Understanding Children's Work (UCW).** n.d. Online database. [www.ucw-project.org].

**UNDP (United Nations Development Programme).** 2006. *Human Development Report 2006: Beyond Scarcity: Power, Poverty and Global Water Crisis.* New York.

———. 2007a. *Governance Indicators, A User's Guide.* 2nd ed. [www.undp.org/oslocentre].

———. 2007b. *Human Development Report 2007/2008: Fighting Climate Change: Human Solidarity in a Divided World.* New York.

**UNEP (United Nations Environment Programme).** 2002. *Global Environment Outlook 3.* London: Earthscan.

**UNESCO (United Nations Educational, Scientific, and Cultural Organization).** 1997. *International Standard Classification of Education.* Paris

———. 2005. *Literacy for Life.* Paris.

———. 2006. *EFA Global Monitoring Report.* Paris.

**UNESCO (United Nations Educational, Scientific, and Cultural Organization) Institute for Statistics.** Various years. *Global Education Digest.* Paris.

———. Online database. [www.uis.unesco.org/].

**UNESCWA (United Nations Economic and Social Commission for Western Asia).** 1997. "Purchasing Power Parities: Volume and Price Level Comparisons for the Middle East, 1993." E/ESCWA/STAT/1997/2. Amman, Jordan.

**UNFCCC (United Nations Framework Convention on Climate Change).** 2005. "Kyoto Protocol to the United Nations Framework Convention on Climate Change." Bonn, Germany.

**UNFPA (United Nations Population Fund).** 2005. *State of World Population.* New York.

**UN-HABITAT (United Nations Human Settlements Programme).** 2003. *Global Report on Human Settlements.* Nairobi.

**UNHCR (United Nations High Commissioner for Refugees).** Various years. *Statistical Yearbook.* Geneva.

**UNICEF (United Nations Children's Fund).** Various years. *State of the World's Children.* New York: Oxford University Press.

———. n.d. Childinfo. [www.childinfo.org].

**UNICEF (United Nations Children's Fund), WHO (World Health Organization), World Bank, and United Nations Population Division.** 2007. "Levels and Trends of Child Mortality in 2006: Estimates Developed by the Inter-agency Group for Child Mortality Estimation." Working Paper. New York.

**UNIDO (United Nations Industrial Development Organization).** Various years. *International Yearbook of Industrial Statistics.* Vienna.

**UNIFEM (United Nations Development Fund for Women).** 2005. *Progress of the World's Women.* New York.

**United Nations Population Division.** 2002. *International Migration Report 2002.* New York.

———. 2007. *World Population Prospects: The 2006 Revision Highlights.* New York.

———. Various years. *Levels and Trends of Contraceptive Use.* New York.

———. Various years. *Trends in Total Migrant Stock.* New York.

———. Various years. *World Population Prospects.* Department of Economic and Social Affairs, New York.

———. Various years. *World Urbanization Prospects.* New York.

# BIBLIOGRAPHY

**United Nations Statistics Division.** 1985. *National Accounts Statistics: Compendium of Income Distribution Statistics.* New York.

————. Various issues. *Monthly Bulletin of Statistics.* New York.

————. Various years. *Energy Statistics Yearbook.* New York.

————. Various years. *International Trade Statistics Yearbook.* New York

————. Various years. *National Accounts Statistics: Main Aggregates and Detailed Tables.* Parts 1 and 2. New York.

————. Various years. *National Income Accounts.* New York.

————. Various years. *Population and Vital Statistics Report.* New York.

————. Various years. *Statistical Yearbook.* New York

**University of California, Berkeley, and Max Planck Institute for Demographic Research.** n.d. Human Mortality Database. [www.mortality.org or www.human-mortality.de] (accessed December 9, 2007).

**UN Millennium Project.** 2005a. *Investing in Development: A Practical Plan to Achieve the Millennium Development Goals.* New York.

————. 2005b. *Taking Action: Achieving Gender Equality and Empowering Women.* Task Force on Education and Gender Equality. London: Earthscan.

**U.S. Census Bureau.** International Data Base (IDB). [www.census.gov/ipc/www/idb/].

**U.S. Centers for Disease Control and Prevention.** Various years. *International Reproductive Health Surveys.* [www.cdc.gov/reproductivehealth/surveys].

**U.S. Environmental Protection Agency.** 1995. *National Air Quality and Emissions Trends Report 1995.* Washington, D.C.

**Walsh, Michael P.** 1994. "Motor Vehicle Pollution Control: An Increasingly Critical Issue for Developing Countries." World Bank, Washington, D.C.

**Watson, Jim, Gordon MacKerron, David Ockwell, and Tao Wang.** 2007. "Technology and Carbon Mitigation in Developing Countries: Are Cleaner Coal Technologies a Viable Option?" Background paper for United Nations Development Programme, 2007, *Human Development Report 2007.* [http://hdr.undp.org/en/reports/global/hdr2007-2008/papers/watson_mackerron_ockwell_wang.pdf].

**Watson, Robert, John A. Dixon, Steven P. Hamburg, Anthony C. Janetos, and Richard H. Moss.** 1998. *Protecting Our Planet, Securing Our Future: Linkages among Global Environmental Issues and Human Needs.* Nairobi and Washington, D.C.: United Nations Environment Programme, U.S. National Aeronautics and Space Administration, and World Bank.

**Whitehouse, Edward.** 2007. *Pensions Panorama: Retirement-Income Systems in 53 Countries.* Washington, D.C.: World Bank.

**WHO (World Health Organization).** 1983. *International Classification of Diseases.* 10th rev. Geneva.

————. 2003. "Poverty and Health: Report by the Director-General." Geneva. [www.who.int/gb/EB_WHA/PDF/EB105/ee5.pdf].

————. 2006. *Reproductive Health Indicators: Guidelines for their Generation, Interpretation and Analysis for Global Monitoring.* Geneva.

————. 2007. *Unsafe Abortion: Global and Regional Incidence of Unsafe Abortion and Associated Mortality in 2003.* 5th ed. Geneva.

————. Various years. *Global Tuberculosis Control Report.* Geneva.

————. Various years. *World Health Report.* Geneva.

————. Various years. *World Health Statistics.* Geneva.

**WHO (World Health Organization) and UNICEF (United Nations Children's Fund).** 2003. *The Africa Malaria Report 2003.* Geneva.

————. 2004. *Beyond the Numbers: Reviewing Maternal Deaths and Complications to Make Pregnancy Safer.* Geneva.

————. 2006. *Meeting the MDG Drinking Water and Sanitation Target.* Geneva.

————. n.d. "Immunization, Surveillance, Assessment, and Monitoring." Online database. [www.who.int/immunization_monitoring].

**WHO (World Health Organization), UNICEF (United Nations Children's Fund), UNFPA (United Nations Population Fund), and World Bank.** 2007. *Maternal Mortality in 2005: Estimates Developed by WHO, UNICEF, UNFPA, and the World Bank.* Geneva.

**WHO (World Health Organization) and World Bank.** 2004. *World Report on Road Traffic Injury Prevention.* Geneva.

**WIPO (World Intellectual Property Organization).** 2007. *WIPO Patent Report: Statistics on Worldwide Patent Activity.* Geneva.

**WITSA (World Information Technology and Services Alliance).** 2006. *Digital Planet 2006: The Global Information Economy.* Vienna, Va.

**WMO (World Meteorological Organization).** 2006. *Statement on the Status of the Global Climate in 2005.* Geneva.

————. 2007. "Observing Stations." Publication No. 9, Volume A, (9 July 2007). [www.wmo.int/pages/prog/www/ois/volumea/vola-home.htm].

**Wolf, Holger C.** 1997. *Patterns of Intra- and Inter-State Trade.* NBER Working Paper 5939. Cambridge, Mass.: National Bureau of Economic Research.

**World Bank.** 1990. *World Development Report 1990: Poverty.* New York: Oxford University Pres

————. 1991. *Managing Development: The Governance Dimension.* Discussion Paper 34899. World Bank, Task Force from Operations; Policy, Research and External Affairs; Legal; Corporate Planning and Budget; and Finance Complexes, Washington, D.C.

————. 1992. *World Development Report 1992: Development and the Environment.* New York: Oxford University Press.

————. 1996a. *Environment Matters* (summer). Environment Department, Washington, D.C.

————. 1996b. "Livable Cities for the 21st Century: A Directions in Development book." Washington, D.C.

————. 1996c. "National Environmental Strategies: Learning from Experience." Environment Department, Washington, D.C.

————. 1997a. *Can the Environment Wait? Priorities for East Asia.* Washington, D.C.

————. 1997b. "Expanding the Measure of Wealth: Indicators of Environmentally Sustainable Development." Environmentally Sustainable Development Studies and Monographs Series, no. 17. Washington, D.C.

———. 1997c. "Rural Development: From Vision to Action." Environmentally Sustainable Development Studies and Monographs Series, no. 12. Washington, D.C.

———. 1997d. *World Development Report 1997: The State in a Changing World.*

———. 1999a. "Fuel for Thought: Environmental Strategy for the Energy Sector." Environment Department, Energy, Mining, and Telecommunications Department and International Finance Corporation, Washington, D.C.

———. 1999b. *Greening Industry: New Roles for Communities, Markets, and Governments.* New York: Oxford University Press.

———. 2000a. *Trade Blocs.* New York: Oxford University Press.

———. 2000b. *World Development Report 2000/2001: Attacking Poverty.* New York: Oxford University Press.

———. 2001. *World Development Report 2002: Building Institutions for Markets.* New York: Oxford University Press.

———. 2002a. *A Case for Aid: Building a Consensus for Development Assistance.* Washington, D.C.

———. 2002b. "The Environment and the Millennium Development Goals." Washington, D.C.

———. 2002c. "Financial Impact of the HIPC Initiative: First 24 Country Cases." Washington, D.C.

———. 2002d. *Globalization, Growth, and Poverty: Building an Inclusive World Economy.* New York: Oxford University Press.

———. 2002e. *World Development Report 2003: Sustainable Development in a Dynamic World.* New York: Oxford University Press.

———. 2003a. "The Millennium Development Goals for Health: Rising to the Challenges." Washington, D.C.

———. 2003b. *World Bank Atlas.* Washington, D.C.

———. 2003c. *World Development Report 2004: Making Services Work for the Poor.* New York: Oxford University Press.

———. 2004a. "Measuring Results: Improving National Statistics in IDA Countries." International Development Association, Washington, D.C. [http://siteresources.worldbank.org/IDA/Resources/MeasuringResultsStatistics.pdf].

———. 2004b. *Partnerships in Development: Progress in the Fight against Poverty.* Washington, D.C.

———. 2004c. *World Bank Atlas.* Washington, D.C.

———. 2005a. "Country Policy and Institutional Assessments, 2005 Assessment Questionnaire." Operational Policy and Country Services, Washington, D.C.

———. 2005b. "Meeting the Challenge of Africa's Development: A World Bank Group Action Plan." Africa Region, World Bank, Washington, D.C.

———. 2005c. *Rolling Back Malaria: The World Bank Global Strategy and Booster Program.* Washington, D.C.

———. 2005d. *World Development Report 2006: Equity and Development.* New York: Oxford University Press.

———. 2006a. "Anticorruption Diagnostic Surveys." World Bank Institute's Governance Diagnostic Capacity Building Program website. [www.worldbank. org/wbi/governance].

———. 2006b. "Debt Relief for the Poorest: An Evaluation Update of the HIPC Initiative." Intependent Evaluation Group, Washington, D.C.

———. 2006c. *Doing Business 2007: How to Reform.* Washington, D.C.

———. 2006d. *Private Participation in Infrastructure Project Database.* [http://ppi.worldbank.org/].

———. 2006e. *Where is the Wealth of Nations? Measuring Capital for the 21st Century.* Washington, D.C.

———. 2006f. *Health Financing Revisited.*

———. 2006g. *Global Monitoring Report 2006: Millennium Development Goals, Strengthening Mutual Accountability, Aid, Trade and Governance.* Washington D.C.: World Bank.

———. 2007a. "Enterprise Surveys Online" [www.enterprisesurveys.org]."

———. 2007b. "Performance Assessments and Allocation of IDA Resources". Online database. [www.worldbank.org/ida]. Washington, D.C.

———. 2007c. *Global Monitoring Report.* Washington, D.C.

———. 2007d. "An Investment Framework for Clean Energy and Development. A Platform for Convergence of Public and Private Investments." Washington, D.C.

———. 2007e. *Doing Business 2008.* Washington, D.C.

———. 2008. *Global Purchasing Parities and Real Expenditures: 2005 International Comparison Program.* Washington, D.C.

———. Forthcoming. *Progress Report of Pension Indicators.* Washington, D.C. [www.worldbank.org/pensions].

———. Various issues. *Global Commodity Markets.*

———. Various years. *Global Development Finance.* Washington, D.C.

———. Various years. *Global Economic Prospects and the Developing Countries.* Washington, D.C.

———. Various years. *World Debt Tables.* Washington, D.C.

———. Various years. *World Development Indicators.* Washington, D.C.

**World Bank and IMF (International Monetary Fund).** 2005a. *Global Monitoring Report 2005: Millennium Development Goals; From Consensus to Momentum.* Washington, D.C.

———. 2005b. "HIPC (Heavily Indebted Poor Countries) Public Expenditure Management Assessment and Action Plans." Washington, D.C. [www.worldbank.org/hipc].

———. 2007. "Heavily Indebted Poor Countries (HIPC) Initiative and Multilateral Debt Relief Initiative (MDRI)—Status of Implementation." Washington, D.C.

**World Bank and European Bank for Reconstruction and Development.** 2006. Business Environment and Enterprise Performance Survey (BEEPS), BEEPS Interactive Dataset. [http://info.worldbank.org/governance/beeps/].

**World Energy Council.** 1995. *Global Energy Perspectives to 2050 and Beyond.* London.

**World Tourism Organization.** Various years. *Compendium of Tourism Statistics.* Madrid.

———. Various years. *Yearbook of Tourism Statistics.* Vols. 1 and 2. Madrid.

# BIBLIOGRAPHY

**WRI (World Resources Institute).** 2005. "Navigating the Numbers." Washington, D.C.

———. 2007a. Climate Analysis Indicators Tool (CAIT). Online database. [www.wri. org/climate/project_description2.cfm?pid=93].

———. 2007b. Earth Trends, the Environmental Information Portal. Online database. (accessed July 2007).

**WRI (World Resources Institute), UNEP (United Nations Environment Programme), UNDP (United Nations Development Programme), and World Bank.** Various years. *World Resources: A Guide to the Global Environment*. New York: Oxford University Press.

**WTO (World Trade Organization).** Various years. *Annual Report*. Geneva.

———. n.d. "Regional Trade Agreements Gateway." Geneva. [www.wto.org/english/ tratop_e/region_e/region_e.htm].

# INDEX OF INDICATORS

References are to table numbers.

# INDEX OF INDICATORS

# INDEX OF INDICATORS

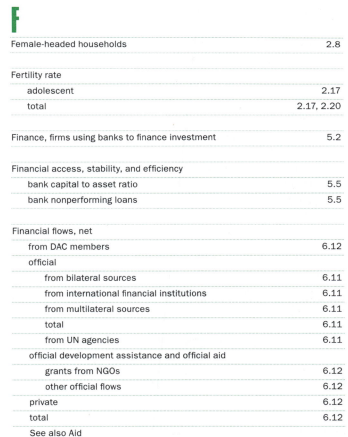

# F

# INDEX OF INDICATORS

# INDEX OF INDICATORS

# INDEX OF INDICATORS

# INDEX OF INDICATORS

# INDEX OF INDICATORS

# INDEX OF INDICATORS